AMERICAN DECADES
PRIMARY SOURCES

1950-1959

AMERICAN DECADES
PRIMARY SOURCES
1950-1959

CYNTHIA ROSE, PROJECT EDITOR

GALE®

THOMSON
™
GALE

Detroit • New York • San Diego • San Francisco • Cleveland • New Haven, Conn. • Waterville, Maine • London • Munich

THOMSON

GALE

American Decades Primary Sources, 1950–1959

Project Editor
Cynthia Rose

Editorial
Jason M. Everett, Rachel J. Kain, Pamela A. Dear, Andrew C. Claps, Thomas Carson, Kathleen Droste, Christy Justice, Lynn U. Koch, Michael D. Lesniak, Nancy Matuszak, John F. McCoy, Michael Reade, Mark Springer, Rebecca Parks, Mark Mikula, Polly A. Rapp.

Data Capture
Civie A. Green, Beverly Jendrowski, Gwendolyn S. Tucker

Permissions
Margaret Abendroth, Margaret A. Chamberlain, Lori Hines, Jacqueline Key, Mari Masalin-Cooper, William Sampson, Shalice Shah-Caldwell, Kim Smilay, Sheila Spencer, Ann Taylor

Indexing Services
Lynne Maday

Imaging and Multimedia
Randy Bassett, Dean Dauphinais, Leitha Etheridge-Sims, Mary K. Grimes, Lezlie Light, Daniel W. Newell, David G. Oblender, Christine O'Bryan, Kelly A. Quin, Luke A. Rademacher, Denay Wilding, Robyn V. Young

Product Design
Michelle DiMercurio

Composition and Electronic Prepress
Evi Seoud

Manufacturing
Rita Wimberley

For permission to use material from this product, submit your request via Web at http://gale-edit.com/permissions, or you may download our Permissions Request form and submit your request by fax or mail to:

Permissions Department
The Gale Group, Inc.
27500 Drake Rd.
Farmington Hills, MI 48331-3535
Permissions Hotline:
248-699-8006 or 800-877-4253, ext. 8006
Fax: 248-699-8074 or 800-762-4058

Cover photographs reproduced by permission of AP/Wide World Photos (Highway under construction in California, background; Dr. Jonas Salk administers the polio vaccine, spine; Senator Joseph McCarthy with lawyer Roy Cohn, left), Bettmann/Corbis (Dr. Martin Luther King, Jr. with other activists, right), and The Library of Congress (Drive-in movie theater marquee, center).

LIBRARY OF CONGRESS CATALOGING-IN-PUBLICATION DATA

American decades primary sources / edited by Cynthia Rose.
    v. cm.
Includes bibliographical references and index.
Contents: [1] 1900-1909 — [2] 1910-1919 — [3] 1920-1929 — [4] 1930-1939 — [5] 1940-1949 — [6] 1950-1959 — [7] 1960-1969 — [8] 1970-1979 — [9] 1980-1989 — [10] 1990-1999.
    ISBN 0-7876-6587-8 (set : hardcover : alk. paper) — ISBN 0-7876-6588-6 (v. 1 : hardcover : alk. paper) — ISBN 0-7876-6589-4 (v. 2 : hardcover : alk. paper) — ISBN 0-7876-6590-8 (v. 3 : hardcover : alk. paper) — ISBN 0-7876-6591-6 (v. 4 : hardcover : alk. paper) — ISBN 0-7876-6592-4 (v. 5 : hardcover : alk. paper) — ISBN 0-7876-6593-2 (v. 6 : hardcover : alk. paper) — ISBN 0-7876-6594-0 (v. 7 : hardcover : alk. paper) — ISBN 0-7876-6595-9 (v. 8 : hardcover : alk. paper) — ISBN 0-7876-6596-7 (v. 9 : hardcover : alk. paper) — ISBN 0-7876-6597-5 (v. 10 : hardcover : alk. paper)
    1. United States—Civilization—20th century—Sources. I. Rose, Cynthia.
E169.1.A471977 2004
973.91—dc21

2002008155

Printed in the United States of America
10 9 8 7 6 5 4 3 2 1

Contents

Entries are arranged in chronological order by date of primary source. For entries with one primary source, the entry title is the primary source title. Entries with more than one primary source have an overall entry title, followed by the titles of the primary sources.

Contents

Fashion and Design

Government and Politics

Law and Justice

Contents

Science and Technology

Sports

Advisors and Contributors

Advisors

CARL A. ANTONUCCI JR. has spent the past ten years as a reference librarian at various colleges and universities. Currently director of library services at Capital Community College, he holds two master's degrees and is a doctoral candidate at Providence College. He particularly enjoys researching Rhode Island political history during the 1960s and 1970s.

KATHY ARSENAULT is the dean of library at the University of South Florida, St. Petersburg's Poynter Library. She holds a master's degree in Library Science. She has written numerous book reviews for *Library Journal*, and has published articles in such publications as the *Journal of the Florida Medical Association* and *Collection Management*.

JAMES RETTIG holds two master's degrees. He has written numerous articles and has edited *Distinguished Classics of Reference Publishing* (1992). University librarian at the University of Richmond, he is the recipient of three American Library Association awards: the Isadore Gibert Mudge Citation (1988), the G.K. Hall Award for Library Literature (1993), and the Louis Shores-Oryx Press Award (1995).

HILDA K. WEISBURG is the head library media specialist at Morristown High School Library and specializes in building school library media programs. She has several publications to her credit, including *The School Librarians Workshop*, *Puzzles, Patterns, and Problem Solving: Creative Connections to Critical Thinking*, and *Learning, Linking & Critical Thinking: Information Strategies for the K-12 Library Media Curriculum*.

Contributors

PETER J. CAPRIOGLIO is professor emeritus at Middlesex Community College, where he taught social sciences for thirty years prior to his retirement. He has a master's in sociology, and is currently at work on a book entitled *The Glory of God's Religions: A Beginner's Guide to Exploring the Beauty of the World's Faiths*.

Chapter: Religion.

PAUL G. CONNORS has a strong interest in Great Lakes maritime history, and has contributed the article "Beaver Island Ice Walkers" to *Michigan History*. He earned a doctorate in American History from Loyola University in Chicago. He has worked for the Michigan Legislative Service Bureau as a research analyst since 1996.

Essay: Using Primary Sources. *Chronologies:* Selected World Events Outside the United States; Government and Politics, Sports Chapters. *General Resources:* General, Government and Politics, Sports.

CHRISTOPHER CUMO is a staff writer for *The Adjunct Advocate Magazine*. Formerly an adjunct professor of history at Walsh University, he has written two books, *A History of the Ohio Agricultural Experiment Station, 1882–1997* and *Seeds of Change*, and has contributed to numerous scholarly journals. He holds a doctorate in history from the University of Akron.

Chapters: Medicine and Health, Science and Technology.*Chapter Chronologies, General Resources:* Business and the Economy, Education, Medicine and Health, Science and Technology.

JENNIFER HELLER holds bachelor's degrees in Religious Studies and English Education, as well as a master's in Curriculum and Instruction, all from the University of Kansas. She has been an adjunct associate professor at Johnson County Community College in Kansas since 1998. She is currently at work on a dissertation on contemporary women's religious literature.

Chapter Chronology, General Resources: Religion.

DAVID M. HOLFORD has worked as an adjunct instructor at Ohio University, Park College, and Columbus State Community College; education curator for the Ohio Historical Society; and held editorial positions at Glencoe/McGraw Hill and Holt, Rinehard, and Winston. He also holds a doctorate degree in history from Ohio State University. A freelance writer/editor since 1996, he has published *Herbert Hoover* (1999) and *Abraham Lincoln and the Emancipation Proclamation* (2002).

Chapter Chronologies, General Resources: Lifestyles and Social Trends, The Media.

JONATHAN KOLKEY is the author of *The New Right, 1960–1968,* and *Germany on the March: A Reinterpretation of War and Domestic Politics Over the Past Two Centuries.* He earned a Ph.D. in history from UCLA. Currently an instructor at West Los Angeles College, he is at work on *The Decision for War,* a comprehensive historical study of the politics and decision-making process behind war. Dr. Kolkey lives in Playa Del Rey, California.

Chapter: Business and the Economy.

SCOTT A. MERRIMAN currently works as a part-time instructor at the University of Kentucky and is finishing his doctoral dissertation on Espionage and Sedition Acts in the Sixth Court of Appeals. He has contributed to *The History Highway* and *History.edu,* among others. Scott is a resident of Lexington, Kentucky.

Chapters: Law and Justice, Lifestyles and Social Trends, The Media.

KRISTINA PETERSON earned her bachelor's degree in Psychology from Northland College. She also holds a M.A.Ed. from the College of William and Mary, as well as a Ph.D. in History and Philosophy of Education from the University of Minnesota.

Chapter: Education.

JESSIE BISHOP POWELL is a librarian assistant at the Lexington Public Library and a cataloger at Book Wholesaler's Inc. She resides in Lexington, Kentucky.

Chapter: Fashion and Design.

DAN PROSTERMAN is an adjunct professor of history at St. Francis College, as well as an adjunct lecturer at Pace University. He holds an M.A. in history at New York University and is working on his doctoral dissertation on the subject of anti-Communism in New York City during the Great Depression and World War II.

Chapter: Government and Politics.

LORNA BIDDLE RINEAR is the editor and co-author of *The Complete Idiot's Guide to Women's History.* A PhD candidate at Rutger's University, she holds a B.A. from Wellesley College and a master's degree from Boston College. She resides in Bellingham, MA.

Chapter Chronologies, General Resources: The Arts, Fashion and Design.

MARY HERTZ SCARBROUGH earned both her B.A. in English and German and her J.D. from the Univeristy of South Dakota. Prior to becoming a freelance writer in 1996, she worked as a law clerk in the Federal District Court for the District of South Dakota and as legal counsel for the Immigration and Naturalization Service. She lives in Storm Lake, Iowa.

Chapter Chronology, General Resources: Law and Justice.

COREY SEEMAN is the assistant dean for library systems at the University of Toledo, University Libraries. The author of numerous articles, book reviews, and encyclopedia entries, he is currently at work on a history of the Midwest League (a baseball minor league) and a history of autism.

Chapter: Sports.

ALICE WU holds a B.A. in English from Wellesley College, as well as an M.F.A. in Sculpture from Yale University. An artist and fashion designer, she lives in New York City.

Chapter: Art

Acknowledgments

Following is a list of the copyright holders who have granted us permission to reproduce material in this volume of American Decades Primary Sources. *Every effort has been made to trace copyright, but if omissions have been made, please let us know.*

Copyrighted material in *Amercian Decades Primary Sources, 1950–1959*, was reproduced from the following periodicals: *Atlantic Monthly*, v. 204, July 1959 for "The Executives Man: Success by Imitation" by Alan Harrington. Copyright (c) 1959, renewed 1987. Reproduced by permission of the author. —*Esquire*, v. 51, June 1959 for "The Future of Twenty Cities" by Martin Mayer. Copyright (c) 1959, renewed 1987, Esquire Associates. Reproduced by permission of the author. —*Fortune*, July 1958. Copyright (c) 1958. Renewed 1986, by Time, Inc. Reproduced by permission. —*Harper's Magazine*, v. 200, May 1950 for "Battle Over Television: Hollywood Faces the Fifties, Part II," by John Houseman. Copyright 1950 by Harper's Magazine. Renewed 1978. All rights reserved. Reproduced by permission of John Michael Houseman/December 1951. Copyright 1951 by Harper's Magazine. Renewed 1979 by Minneapolis Star and Tribune Co., Inc. All rights reserved. Reproduced by special permission. —*High Fidelity Magazine*, v. 16, April 1966 for "The Prospects of Recording" by Glenn Gould. Reproduced by permission of the Estate of Glenn Gould. —Interview with Harry Ashmore adapted from the public radio series *Insight & Outlook*, hosted by Scott London. Copyright (c) 1999 by Scott London. All rights reserved. Reproduced by permission. —*Life*, November 27, 1950; March 18, 1957; v. 43, October 21, 1957, Copyright 1950, renewed 1978 by Time, Inc.; Copyright 1941, renewed 1985 by Time, Inc.; Copyright (c) 1957, renewed 1985 by Time, Inc. Reproduced by permission. —*The Nation*, v. 180, February 26, 1955. Copyright (c) 1955 The Nation magazine/The Nation Company, Inc. Renewed 1983. Reproduced by permission. —*National Review*, v. 6, March 28, 1959. Copyright (c) 1959, renewed 1987 by National Review, Inc, 215 Lexington Avenue. New York, NY 10016. Reproduced by permission. —*The New York Times*, April 24, 1950; December 13, 1950; January 18, 1951; April 6, 1952; May 25, 1952; September 8, 1953; October 4, 1953; November 18, 1953; September 19, 1954; May 30, 1955; July 6, 1955; October 1, 1955; October 9, 1955; December 4, 1955; July 7, 1957; November 17, 1957; December 8, 1957; December 29, 1957; April 7, 1958; May 6, 1958; June 20, 1958; June 22, 1958; September 10, 1958; December 29, 1958; February 4, 1959; February 23, 1959; September 27, 1959; November 22, 1959; November 29, 1959; December 6, 1959; October 30, 1960; April 16, 1967. Copyright 1950, renewed 1978; Copyright 1951, renewed 1978; Copyright 1952, renewed 1970; Copyright 1952, renewed 1980; Copyright 1953, renewed 1971; Copyright 1953, renewed 1981; Copyright 1954, renewed 1982; Copyright (c) 1955, renewed 1983; Copyright (c) 1955, renewed 1985; Copyright (c) 1955, renewed 1983; Copyright (c) 1955, renewed 1983; Copyright (c) 1957, renewed 1985; Copyright (c) 1958, renewed 1986; Copyright (c) 1959, renewed 1987; Copyright (c) 1960, renewed 1988; Copyright (c) 1967 by The New York Times Company. Reproduced by permission. —*The New Yorker*, v. 72, October 21–28, 1996 for "Why I Wrote 'The Crucible': An Artist's Answer to Politics" by Arthur Miller. Repro-

Women Artists. Charles Scribner's Sons, 1975. Copyright (c) 1975 by Cindy Nemser. All rights reserved. Reproduced by permission of the author. —Nabokov, Vladimir. From *Lolita*. Vintage International, 1989. Copyright (c) 1955 by Vladimir Nabokov. All rights reserved. Reproduced by permission. —Noguchi, Isamu. From *A Sculptor's World*. Harper Row, Publishers, 1968. Copyright (c) 1968 by Harper Row, Publishers. All rights reserved. Reproduced in the US by permission of HarperCollins Publishers. Reproduced in the UK by permission of Thames & Hudson Ltd., London. —O'Hara, Frank. From *Meditations in an Emergency*. Grove Press, 1957. Copyright (c) 1957 Frank O'Hara. All rights reserved. Reproduced by permission. —Peale, Norman Vincent. From *The Power of Positive Thinking*. Foundation for Christian Living, 1978. Copyright (c) 1952, 1978 by Prentice-Hall, Inc. All rights reserved. Reproduced by permission. —Pincus, Gregory. From *The Control of Fertility*. Academic Press, 1965. Copyright (c) 1965 by Academic Press, Inc. All rights reserved. —Remmers, H.H. and D.H. Radler. From *The American Teenager*. Charter Books, 1957. Copyright (c) 1957 by H.H. Remmers. Renewed 1985, by Edna F. Stalnakes and Jean D. Radler. All rights reserved. —Tallchief, Maria with Larry Kaplan. From *Maria Tallchief: America's Prima Ballerina*. Henry Holt and Company, 1997. Copyright (c) 1997 by Maria Tallchief and Larry Kaplan. All rights reserved. Reprinted by permission of Henry Holt and Company, LLC and Sanford Greenburger Associates. —Tillich, Paul. From *The Courage to Be*. Yale University Press, 1952. Copyright 1952, renewed 1980 by Hanna Tillich. All rights reserved. Reproduced by permission. —Urey, Harold C. From *The H Bomb*. Didier, 1950. Copyright (c) 1950 by Didier, Publishers. All rights reserved. —von Braun, Wernher, Fred L. Whipple, and Willy Ley. From Introduction to *Conquest of the Moon*. The Viking Press, 1953. Copyright (c) 1952, 1953 by the Crowell-Collier Publishing Company. Renewed 1981, by Chesley Bonestell & Kathryn Morgan Ryan. All rights reserved. —von Neumann, John. From *The Computer and the Brain*. Yale University Press, 1958. Copyright (c) 1958 by Yale University Press. Renewed 1986, by Marina U.N. Whitman. All rights reserved. Reproduced by permission. —Wertham, Fredric. From *Seduction of the Innocent*. Rinehart, 1954. Copyright (c) 1953, 1954, renewed 1982 by Fredric Wertham. All rights reserved. Reprinted by permission of Henry Holt and Company, LLC. —Wilson, Sloan. From *The Man in the Gray Flannel Suit*. Simon and Schuster, Inc., 1955. Copyright (c) 1955, renewed 1983 by Sloan Wilson. All rights reserved. Reproduced by permission of Four Walls Eight Windows.

Copyrighted material in *American Decades Primary Sources, 1950–1959*, was reproduced from the following web sites: "Ethel Rosenberg's Brother Admits Lying Under Oath." Online at: http://www.beloitdailynews.com/1201/rose5.htm (December 5, 2001). Published by BDN Connection. Reproduced by permission. —Moffat, Ivan, "Ivan Moffat: The Making of Giant." Online at: http://americanlegends.com/Interviews/dean_moffat.htm (September 11, 2000). Published by American Legends, Inc.. Reproduced by permission. —Martin Luther King, Jr., Speech delivered on November 17, 1957, "Loving Your Enemies." Online at: http://www.mlkonline.com—MLK Online. Reprinted by arrangement with the Estate of Martin Luther King Jr., c/o Writers House as agent for the proprietor New York, NY. Copyright 1957 Dr. Martin Luther King Jr., copyright renewed 1986 Coretta Scott King. Reproduced by arrangement with The Heirs to the Estate of Martin Luther King, Jr., c/o Writers House Inc. as agent for the proprietor.

ABOUT THE SET

American Decades Primary Sources is a ten-volume collection of more than two thousand primary sources on twentieth-century American history and culture. Each volume comprises about two hundred primary sources in 160–170 entries. Primary sources are enhanced by informative context, with illustrative images and sidebars—many of which are primary sources in their own right—adding perspective and a deeper understanding of both the primary sources and the milieu from which they originated.

Designed for students and teachers at the high school and undergraduate levels, as well as researchers and history buffs, *American Decades Primary Sources* meets the growing demand for primary source material.

Conceived as both a stand-alone reference and a companion to the popular *American Decades* set, *American Decades Primary Sources* is organized in the same subject-specific chapters for compatibility and ease of use.

Primary Sources

To provide fresh insights into the key events and figures of the century, thirty historians and four advisors selected unique primary sources far beyond the typical speeches, government documents, and literary works. Screenplays, scrapbooks, sports box scores, patent applications, college course outlines, military codes of conduct, environmental sculptures, and CD liner notes are but a sampling of the more than seventy-five types of primary sources included.

Diversity is shown not only in the wide range of primary source types, but in the range of subjects and opin-

ions, and the frequent combination of primary sources in entries. Multiple perspectives in religious, political, artistic, and scientific thought demonstrate the commitment of *American Decades Primary Sources* to diversity, in addition to the inclusion of considerable content displaying ethnic, racial, and gender diversity. *American Decades Primary Sources* presents a variety of perspectives on issues and events, encouraging the reader to consider subjects more fully and critically.

American Decades Primary Sources' innovative approach often presents related primary sources in an entry. The primary sources act as contextual material for each other—creating a unique opportunity to understand each and its place in history, as well as their relation to one another. These may be point-counterpoint arguments, a variety of diverse opinions, or direct responses to another primary source. One example is President Franklin Delano Roosevelt's letter to clergy at the height of the Great Depression, with responses by a diverse group of religious leaders from across the country.

Multiple primary sources created by particularly significant individuals—Dr. Martin Luther King, Jr., for example—reside in *American Decades Primary Sources*. Multiple primary sources on particularly significant subjects are often presented in more than one chapter of a volume, or in more than one decade, providing opportunities to see the significance and impact of an event or figure from many angles and historical perspectives. For example, seven primary sources on the controversial Scopes "monkey" trial are found in five chapters of the

1920s volume. Primary sources on evolutionary theory may be found in earlier and later volumes, allowing the reader to see and analyze the development of thought across time.

Entry Organization

Contextual material uses standardized rubrics that will soon become familiar to the reader, making the entries more accessible and allowing for easy comparison. Introduction and Significance essays—brief and focused— cover the historical background, contributing factors, importance, and impact of the primary source, encouraging the reader to think critically—not only about the primary source, but also about the way history is constructed. Key Facts and a Synopsis provide quick access and recognition of the primary sources, and the Further Resources are a stepping-stone to additional study.

Additional Features

Subject chronologies and thorough tables of contents (listing titles, authors, and dates) begin each chapter. The main table of contents assembles this information conveniently at the front of the book. An essay on using primary sources, a chronology of selected events outside the United States during the twentieth century, substantial general and subject resources, and primary source-type and general indexes enrich *American Decades Primary Sources*.

The ten volumes of *American Decades Primary Sources* provide a vast array of primary sources integrated with supporting content and user-friendly features.

This value-laden set gives the reader an unparalleled opportunity to travel into the past, to relive important events, to encounter key figures, and to gain a deep and full understanding of America in the twentieth century.

Acknowledgments

A number of people contributed to the successful completion of this project. The editor wishes to acknowledge them with thanks: Eugenia Bradley, Luann Brennan, Neva Carter, Katrina Coach, Pamela S. Dear, Nikita L. Greene, Madeline Harris, Alesia James, Cynthia Jones, Pamela M. Kalte, Arlene Ann Kevonian, Frances L. Monroe, Charles B. Montney, Katherine H. Nemeh, James E. Person, Tyra Y. Phillips, Elizabeth Pilette, Noah Schusterbauer, Andrew Specht, Susan Strickland, Karissa Walker, Tracey Watson, and Jennifer M. York.

Contact Us

The editors of *American Decades Primary Sources* welcome your comments, suggestions, and questions. Please direct all correspondence to:

Editor, *American Decades Primary Sources*
The Gale Group, Inc.
27500 Drake Road
Farmington Hills, MI 48331-3535
(800) 877-4253

For email inquiries, please visit the Gale website at www.gale.com, and click on the Contact Us tab.

ABOUT THE VOLUME

The Red Scare, the Rosenbergs, and Rosa Parks all made their mark on the United States of the 1950s. Senator Joseph McCarthy waged a domestic war against communists with his hearings and had everyone looking suspiciously for communists in their communities. At the same time, Julius and Ethel Rosenberg were tried and convicted of espionage, under evidence that they had passed secrets from the U.S. nuclear facility in Los Alamos to the Soviet Union; they were subsequently executed. Segregation was ruled by the Supreme Court to be illegal, and while African American children began integrating schools, Rosa Parks refused to give up her seat on a bus to a white passenger. The civil rights movement had begun. Culturally, color television was introduced, Disneyland opened, and hula hoops hit it big. The following documents are just a sampling of the offerings available in this volume.

Highlights of Primary Sources, 1950–1959

- *Brown v. Board of Education* landmark Supreme Court Decision
- "Situations Wanted" employment classifieds from *The New York Times*
- "Overtime at the Stadium," Arthur Daley's column covering December 12, 1958, game between the Baltimore Colts and the New York Giants.
- "Loving Your Enemies," sermon by Dr. Martin Luther King, Jr.
- Isamu Noguchi and his Akari light sculptures

- "Why the Edsel Laid an Egg," journal article discussing Ford's "flop"
- *The Long Shadow of Little Rock: A Memoir*, memoir of the experience of one of the "Little Rock Nine"
- Still of Marlon Brando from *A Streetcar Named Desire*
- "The Kitchen Debate," between Richard Nixon and Nikita Khrushchev
- Final letter from Julius and Ethel Rosenberg to their sons
- Chesterfield cigarette ad featuring Ronald Reagan
- *Peanuts* comic strip with Lucy pulling the football away from Charlie Brown for the very first time
- Autobiography of John Nash, the subject of the film *A Beautiful Mind*
- *Sexual Behavior in the Human Female*, study by Alfred Kinsey

Volume Structure and Content

Front matter

- Table of Contents—lists primary sources, authors, and dates of origin, by chapter and chronologically within chapters.
- About the Set, About the Volume, About the Entry essays—guide the reader through the set and promote ease of use.

- Highlights of Primary Sources—a quick look at a dozen or so primary sources gives the reader a feel for the decade and the volume's contents.

- Using Primary Sources—provides a crash course in reading and interpreting primary sources.

- Chronology of Selected World Events Outside the United States—lends additional context in which to place the decade's primary sources.

Chapters:

- The Arts

- Business and the Economy

- Education

- Fashion and Design

- Government and Politics

- Law and Justice

- Lifestyles and Social Trends

- The Media

- Medicine and Health

- Religion

- Science and Technology

- Sports

Chapter structure

- Chapter table of contents—lists primary sources, authors, and dates of origin chronologically, showing each source's place in the decade.

- Chapter chronology—highlights the decade's important events in the chapter's subject.

- Primary sources—displays sources surrounded by contextual material.

Back matter

- General Resources—promotes further inquiry with books, periodicals, websites, and audio and visual media, all organized into general and subject-specific sections.

- General Index—provides comprehensive access to primary sources, people, events, and subjects, and cross-referencing to enhance comparison and analysis.

- Primary Source Type Index—locates primary sources by category, giving readers an opportunity to easily analyze sources across genres.

ABOUT THE ENTRY

The primary source is the centerpiece and main focus of each entry in *American Decades Primary Sources.* In keeping with the philosophy that much of the benefit from using primary sources derives from the reader's own process of inquiry, the contextual material surrounding each entry provides access and ease of use, as well as giving the reader a springboard for delving into the primary source. Rubrics identify each section and enable the reader to navigate entries with ease.

Entry structure

- Key Facts—essential information pertaining to the primary source, including full title, author, source type, source citation, and notes about the author.

- Introduction—historical background and contributing factors for the primary source.

- Significance—importance and impact of the primary source, at the time and since.

- Primary Source—in text, text facsimile, or image format; full or excerpted.

- Synopsis—encapsulated introduction to the primary source.

- Further Resources—books, periodicals, websites, and audio and visual material.

Navigating an Entry

Entry elements are numbered and reproduced here, with an explanation of the data contained in these elements explained immediately thereafter according to the corresponding numeral.

Primary Source/Entry Title, Primary Source Type

•1• "Ego"
•2• Magazine article

•1• PRIMARY SOURCE/ENTRY TITLE The entry title is the primary source title for entries with one primary source. Entry titles appear as catchwords at the top outer margin of each page.

•2• PRIMARY SOURCE TYPE The type of primary source is listed just below the title. When assigning source types, great weight was given to how the author of the primary source categorized it. If a primary source comprised more than one type—for example, an article about art in the United States that included paintings, or a scientific essay that included graphs and photographs—each primary source type included in the entry appears below the title.

Composite Entry Title

•3• Debate Over *The Birth of a Nation*

•1• "Capitalizing Race Hatred"
•2• Editorial

•1• **"Reply to the *New York Globe*"**

•2• Letter

•3• **COMPOSITE ENTRY TITLE** An overarching entry title is used for entries with more than one primary source, with the primary source titles and types below.

Key Facts

•4• **By:** Norman Mailer

•5• **Date:** March 19, 1971

•6• **Source:** Mailer, Norman. "Ego." *Life* 70, March 19, 1971, 30, 32–36.

•7• **About the Author:** Norman Mailer (1923–) was born in Long Branch, New Jersey. After graduating from Harvard and military service in World War II (1939–1945), Mailer began writing, publishing his first book, the best-selling novel *The Naked and the Dead,* in 1948. Mailer has written over thirty books, including novels, plays, political commentary, and essay collections, as well as numerous magazine articles. He won the Pulitzer Prize in 1969 and 1979. ■

•4• **AUTHOR OR ORIGINATOR** The name of the author or originator of the primary source begins the Key Facts section.

•5• **DATE OF ORIGIN** The date of origin of the primary source appears in this field, and may differ from the date of publication in the source citation below it; for example, speeches are often given before they are published.

•6• **SOURCE CITATION** The source citation is a full bibliographic citation, giving original publication data as well as reprint and/or online availability (usually both the deep-link and home-page URLs).

•7• **ABOUT THE AUTHOR** A brief bio of the author or originator of the primary source gives birth and death dates and a quick overview of the person's life. This rubric has been customized in some cases. If the primary source is the autobiography of an artist, the term "author" appears; however, if the primary source is a work of art, the term "artist" is used, showing the person's direct relationship to the primary source. Terms like "inventor" and "designer" are used similarly. For primary sources created by a group, "organization" may have been used instead of "author." If an author is anonymous or unknown, a brief "About the Publication" sketch may appear.

Introduction and Significance Essays

•8• **Introduction**

. . . As images from the Vietnam War (1964–1975) flashed onto television screens across the United States in the late 1960s, however, some reporters took a more active role in questioning the pronouncements of public officials. The broad cul-

tural changes of the 1960s, including a sweeping suspicion of authority figures by younger people, also encouraged a more restive spirit in the reporting corps. By the end of the decade, the phrase "Gonzo Journalism" was coined to describe the new breed of reporter: young, rebellious, and unafraid to get personally involved in the story at hand. . . .

•8• **INTRODUCTION** The introduction is a brief essay on the contributing factors and historical context of the primary source. Intended to promote understanding and jump-start the reader's curiosity, this section may also describe an artist's approach, the nature of a scientific problem, or the struggles of a sports figure. If more than one primary source is included in the entry, the introduction and significance address each one, and often the relationship between them.

•9• **Significance**

Critics of the new style of journalism maintained that the emphasis on personalities and celebrity did not necessarily lead to better reporting. As political reporting seemed to focus more on personalities and images and less on substantive issues, some observers feared that the American public was ill-served by the new style of journalism. Others argued that the media had also encouraged political apathy among the public by superficial reporting. . . .

•9• **SIGNIFICANCE** The significance discusses the importance and impact of the primary source. This section may touch on how it was regarded at the time and since, its place in history, any awards given, related developments, and so on.

Primary Source Header, Synopsis, Primary Source

•10• **Primary Source**

The Boys on the Bus [excerpt]

•11• **SYNOPSIS:** A boisterous account of Senator George McGovern's ultimately unsuccessful 1972 presidential bid, Crouse's work popularized the term "pack journalism," describing the herd mentality that gripped reporters focusing endlessly on the same topic. In later years, political advisors would become more adept at "spinning" news stories to their candidates' advantage, but the essential dynamics of pack journalism remain in place.

•12• The feverish atmosphere was halfway between a high school bus trip to Washington and a gambler's jet junket to Las Vegas, where small-time Mafiosi were lured into betting away their restaurants. There was giddy camaraderie mixed with fear and low-grade hysteria. To file a story late, or to make one glaring factual error, was to chance losing everything—one's job, one's expense account, one's drinking buddies, one's mad-dash existence, and the methedrine buzz that comes from knowing stories that the public would not know for hours and secrets that the public would never know. Therefore reporters channeled their gambling instincts into late-night poker games and private bets on the outcome of the elections. When it came to writing a story, they were as cautious as diamond-cutters. . . .

•10• **PRIMARY SOURCE HEADER** The primary source header signals the beginning of the primary source, and "[excerpt]" is attached if the source does not appear in full.

•11• **SYNOPSIS** The synopsis gives a brief overview of the primary source.

•12• **PRIMARY SOURCE** The primary source may appear excerpted or in full, and may appear as text, text facsimile (photographic reproduction of the original text), image, or graphic display (such as a table, chart, or graph).

Text Primary Sources

The majority of primary sources are reproduced as plain text. The font and leading of the primary sources are distinct from that of the context—to provide a visual clue to the change, as well as to facilitate ease of reading. Often, the original formatting of the text was preserved in order to more accurately represent the original (screenplays, for example). In order to respect the integrity of the primary sources, content some readers may consider sensitive was retained where it was deemed to be integral to the source. Text facsimile formatting was used sparingly and where the original provided additional value (for example, Aaron Copland's typing and handwritten notes on "Notes for a Cowboy Ballet").

Narrative Break

•13•   I told him I'd rest and then fix him something to eat when he got home. I could hear someone enter his office then, and Medgar laughed at something that was said. "I've got to go, honey. See you tonight. I love you." "All right," I said. "Take care." Those were our last words to each other.

■ ■ ■

Medgar had told me that President Kennedy was speaking on civil rights that night, and I made a mental note of the time. We ate alone, the children and I. It had become a habit now to set only four places for supper. Medgar's chair stared at us, and the children, who had heard

about the President's address to the nation, planned to watch it with me. There was something on later that they all wanted to see, and they begged to be allowed to wait up for Medgar to return home. School was out, and I knew that Van would fall asleep anyway, so I agreed.

•13• **NARRATIVE BREAK** A narrative break appears where there is a significant amount of elided material, beyond what ellipses would indicate (for example, excerpts from a nonfiction work's introduction and second chapter, or sections of dialogue from two acts of a play).

Image Primary Sources

Primary source images (whether photographs, text facsimiles, or graphic displays) are bordered with a distinctive double rule. The Primary Source header and Synopsis appear under the image, with the image reduced in size to accommodate the synopsis. For multipart images, the synopsis appears only under the first part of the image; subsequent parts have brief captions.

•14• "Art: U.S. Scene": *The Tornado* by John Steuart Curry (2 OF 4)

•14• **PRIMARY SOURCE IMAGE HEADER** The primary source image header assists the reader in tracking the images in a series. Also, the primary source header listed here indicates a primary source with both text and image components. The text of the *Time* magazine article "Art: U.S. Scene," appears with four of the paintings from the article. Under each painting, the title of the article appears first, followed by a colon, then the title of the painting. The header for the text component has a similar structure, with the term "magazine article" after the colon. Inclusion of images or graphic elements from primary sources, and their designation in the entry as main primary sources, is discretionary.

Further Resources

•15• **Further Resources**

BOOKS
Dixon, Phil. *The Negro Baseball Leagues, 1867–1955: A Photographic History.* Mattituck, N.Y.: Amereon House, 1992.

PERIODICALS
"Steven Spielberg: The Director Says It's Good-Bye to Spaceships and Hello to Relationships." *American Film* 13, no. 8, June 1988, 12–16.

WEBSITES
Architecture and Interior Design for 20th Century America, 1935–1955. American Memory digital primary source collection, Library of Congress. Available online at http://memory.loc.gov/ammem/gschtml/gotthome

.html; website home page: http://memory.loc.gov /ammem/ammemhome.html (accessed March 27, 2003).

AUDIO AND VISUAL MEDIA

E.T.: The Extra-Terrestrial. Original release, 1982, Universal. Directed by Steven Spielberg. Widescreen Collector's Edition DVD, 2002, Universal Studios.

•**15**• **FURTHER RESOURCES** A brief list of resources provides a stepping stone to further study. If it's known that a resource contains additional primary source material specifically related to the entry, a brief note in italics appears at the end of the citation. For websites, both the deep link and home page usually appear.

USING PRIMARY SOURCES

The philosopher R.G. Collingwood once said, "Every new generation must rewrite history in its own way." What Collingwood meant is that new events alter our perceptions of the past and necessitate that each generation interpret the past in a different light. For example, since September 11, 2001, and the "War on Terrorism," the collapse of the Soviet Union seemingly is no longer as historically important as the rise of Islamic fundamentalism, which was once only a minor concern. Seen from this viewpoint, history is not a rigid set of boring facts, but a fascinating, ever-changing field of study. Much of this fascination rests on the fact that historical interpretation is based on the reading of primary sources. To historians and students alike, primary sources are ambiguous objects because their underlying meanings are often not crystal clear. To learn a primary document's meaning(s), students must identify its main subject and recreate the historical context in which the document was created. In addition, students must compare the document with other primary sources from the same historical time and place. Further, students must cross-examine the primary source by asking of it a series of probing investigative questions.

To properly analyze a primary source, it is important that students become "active" rather than "casual" readers. As in reading a chemistry or algebra textbook, historical documents require students to analyze them carefully and extract specific information. In other words, history requires students to read "beyond the text" and focus on what the primary source tells us about the person or group and the era in which they lived. Unlike chemistry and algebra, however, historical primary sources have the additional benefit of being part of a larger, interesting story full of drama, suspense, and hidden agendas. In order to detect and identify key historical themes, students need to keep in mind a set of questions. For example, Who created the primary source? Why did the person create it? What is the subject? What problem is being addressed? Who was the intended audience? How was the primary source received and how was it used? What are the most important characteristics of this person or group for understanding the primary source? For example, what were the authors' biases? What was their social class? Their race? Their gender? Their occupation? Once these questions have been answered reasonably, the primary source can be used as a piece of historical evidence to interpret history.

In each *American Decades Primary Sources* volume, students will study examples of the following categories of primary sources:

- Firsthand accounts of historic events by witnesses and participants. This category includes diary entries, letters, newspaper articles, oral-history interviews, memoirs, and legal testimony.

- Documents representing the official views of the nation's leaders or of their political opponents. These include court decisions, policy statements, political speeches, party platforms, petitions, legislative debates, press releases, and federal and state laws.

- Government statistics and reports on such topics as birth, employment, marriage, death, and taxation.

- Advertisers' images and jingles. Although designed to persuade consumers to purchase commodities or to adopt specific attitudes, advertisements can also be valuable sources of information about popular beliefs and concerns.

- Works of art, including paintings, symphonies, play scripts, photographs, murals, novels, and poems.

- The products of mass culture: cartoons, comic books, movies, radio scripts, and popular songs.

- Material artifacts. These are everyday objects that survived from the period in question. Examples include household appliances and furnishings, recipes, and clothing.

- Secondary sources. In some cases, secondary sources may be treated as primary sources. For example, from 1836 to 1920, public schools across America purchased 122 million copies of a series of textbooks called the McGuffey Reader. Although current textbooks have more instructional value, the Reader is an invaluable primary source. It provides important insights into the unifying morals and cultural values that shaped the worldview of several generations of Americans, who differed in ethnicity, race, class, and religion.

Each of the above-mentioned categories of primary sources reveals different types of historical information. A politician's diary, memoirs, or collection of letters, for example, often provide students with the politicians' unguarded, private thoughts and emotions concerning daily life and public events. Though these documents may be a truer reflection of the person's character and aspirations, students must keep in mind that when people write about themselves, they tend to put themselves at the center of the historical event or cast themselves in the best possible light. On the other hand, the politician's public speeches may be more cautious, less controversial, and limited to advancing his or her political party's goals or platform.

Like personal diaries, advertisements reveal other types of historical information. What information does the WAVES poster on this page reveal?

John Phillip Faller, a prolific commercial artist known for his *Saturday Evening Post* covers, designed this recruitment poster in 1944. It was one of over three hundred posters he produced for the U.S. Navy while enrolled in that service during World War II. The purpose of the poster was to encourage women to enlist in the WAVES (Women Accepted for Volunteer Emergency Service), a women's auxiliary to the Navy established in

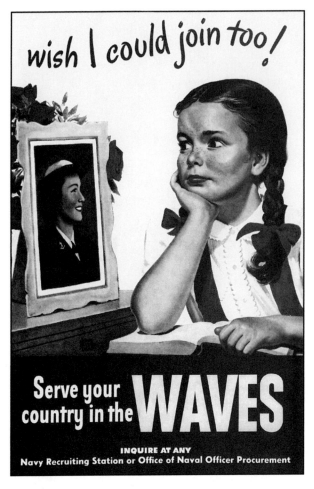

1942. It depicts a schoolgirl gazing admiringly at a photograph of a proud, happy WAVE (perhaps an older sister), thus portraying the military service as an appropriate and admirable aspiration for women during wartime. However, what type of military service? Does the poster encourage women to enlist in military combat like World War II male recruitment posters? Does it reflect gender bias? What does this poster reveal about how the military and society in general feel about women in the military? Does the poster reflect current military and societal attitudes toward women in the military? How many women joined the WAVES? What type of duties did they perform?

Like personal diaries, photographs reveal other types of historical information. What information does the next photograph reveal?

Today, we take electricity for granted. However, in 1935, although 90 percent of city dwellers in America had electricity, only 10 percent of rural Americans did. Private utility companies refused to string electric lines

THE LIBRARY OF CONGRESS.

to isolated farms, arguing that the endeavor was too expensive and that most farmers were too poor to afford it anyway. As part of the Second New Deal, President Franklin Delano Roosevelt issued an executive order creating the Rural Electrification Administration (REA). The REA lent money at low interest rates to utility companies to bring electricity to rural America. By 1950, 90 percent of rural America had electricity. This photograph depicts a 1930s tenant farmer's house in Greene County, Georgia. Specifically, it shows a brand-new electric meter on the wall. The picture presents a host of questions: What was rural life like without electricity? How did electricity impact the lives of rural Americans, particularly rural Georgians? How many rural Georgians did not have electricity in the 1930s? Did Georgia have more electricity-connected farms than other Southern states? What was the poverty rate in rural Georgia, particularly among rural African Americans? Did rural electricity help lift farmers out of poverty?

Like personal diaries, official documents reveal other types of historical information. What information does the next document, a memo, reveal?

From the perspective of the early twenty-first century, in a democratic society, integration of the armed services seems to have been inevitable. For much of American history, however, African Americans were prevented from joining the military, and when they did enlist they were segregated into black units. In 1940, of the nearly 170,000-man Navy, only 4,007, or 2.3 percent, were African American personnel. The vast majority of these men worked in the mess halls as stewards—or, as labeled by the black press, "seagoing bellhops." In this official document, the chairman of the General Board refers to compliance with a directive that would enlist African Americans into positions of "unlimited general service." Who issued the directive? What was the motivation behind the new directive? Who were the members of the General Board? How much authority did they wield? Why did the Navy restrict African Americans to the "messman branch"? Notice the use of the term "colored race." Why was this term used and what did it imply? What did the board conclude? When did the Navy become integrated? Who was primarily responsible for integrating the Navy?

CONFIDENTIAL

DoD Dir. 5200.10, June 29, 1960
NND by *PB* ___ date *Oct. 5, 1961*

DOWNGRADED AT 3 YEAR INTERVALS
DECLASSIFIED AFTER 12 YEARS
DOD DIR 5200.10 NARS-NT

SECRET

G.B. No. 421
(Serial No. 201)
SECRET

Feb 3, 1942

From: Chairman General Board.
To: Secretary of the Navy.

Subject: Enlistment of men of colored race to other than
               Messman branch.

Ref: (a) SecNav let. (SC)P14-4/MM (03200A)/Gen of
               Jan 16, 1942.

1.   The General Board, complying with the directive
contained in reference (a), has given careful attention to the
problem of enlisting in the Navy, men of the colored race
in other than the messman branch.

2.   The General Board has endeavored to examine the
problem placed before it in a realistic manner.

A.   Should negroes be enlisted for unlimited general service?

(a) Enlistment for general service implies that the
individual may be sent anywhere, - to any ship or station where
he is needed. Men on board ship live in particularly close
association; in their messes, one man sits beside another; their
hammocks or bunks are close together; in their common tasks they
work side by side; and in particular tasks such as those of a
gun's crew, they form a closely knit, highly coordinated team.
How many white men would choose, of their own accord, that their
closest associates in sleeping quarters, at mess, and in a gun's
crew should be of another race? How many would accept such
conditions, if required to do so, without resentment and just
as a matter of course? The General Board believes that the
answer is "Few, if any," and further believes that if the issue were
forced, there would be a lowering of contentment, teamwork
and discipline in the service.

(b) One of the tennets of the recruiting service
is that each recruit for general service is potentially a leading
petty officer. It is true that some men never do become petty
officers, and that when recruiting white men, it is not possible
to establish which will be found worthy of and secure promotion
and which will not. If negroes are recruited for general service,
it can be said at once that few will obtain advancement to petty
officers. With every desire to be fair, officers and leading
petty officers in general will not recommend negroes for promotion
to positions of authority over white men.

DOWNGRADED AND
DECLASSIFIED   - 1 -   CONFIDENTIAL

The General Board is convinced that the enlistment of negroes for unlimited general service is unadvisable.

B.   Should negroes be enlisted in general service but detailed in special ratings or for special ships or units?

(a) The ratings now in use in the naval service cover every phase of naval activity, and no new ratings are deemed necessary merely to promote the enlistment of negroes.

(b) At first thought, it might appear that assignment of negroes to certain vessels, and in particular to small vessels of the patrol type, would be feasible. In this connection, the following table is of interest:

Type of Ship	Total Crew	Men in Pay Grades 1 to 4	Men in Pay Grades 5 to 7 (Non-rated)
Battleship	1892	666	1226
Light Cruiser (10,000 ton)	988	365	623
Destroyer (1630 ton)	206	109	97
Submarine	54	47	7
Patrol Boat (180 foot)	55	36	19
Patrol Boat (110 foot)	20	15	5

NOTE: Pay grades 1 to 4 include Chief Petty Officers and Petty Officers, 1st, 2nd and 3rd Class; also Firemen, 1st Class and a few other ratings requiring length of service and experience equal to that required for qualification of Petty Officers, 3rd class. Pay grades 5 to 7 include all other non-rated men and recruits.

There are no negro officers and so few negro petty officers in the Navy at present that any vessels to which negroes might be assigned must have white officers and white petty officers. Examination of the table shows the small number of men in other than petty officer ratings that might be assigned to patrol vessels and in-dicates to the General Board that such assignments would not be happy ones. The assignment of negroes to the larger ships, where well over one-half of the crews are non-rated men, with mixture of whites and negroes, would inevitably lead to discontent on the part of one or the other, resulting in clashes and lowering of the efficiency of the vessels and of the Navy.

- 2 -

The material collected in these volumes of *American Decades Primary Sources* are significant because they will introduce students to a wide variety of historical sources that were created by those who participated in or witnessed the historical event. These primary sources not only vividly describe historical events, but also reveal the subjective perceptions and biases of their authors. Students should read these documents "actively," and with the contextual assistance of the introductory material, history will become relevant and entertaining.

—Paul G. Connors

CHRONOLOGY OF SELECTED WORLD EVENTS OUTSIDE THE UNITED STATES, 1950–1959

1950

- Norwegian anthropologist Thor Heyerdahl publishes *Kon-Tiki,* an account of his 1947 voyage from Peru to Raroia Atoll, a Polynesian island, in a wooden boat he had made.

- Russian painter Marc Chagall exhibits his painting *King David.*

- Italian sculptor Alberto Giacometti exhibits his sculpture *Seven Figures and a Head.*

- On January 18, Christopher Fry's play *Venus Observed* opens at Saint James Theatre in London.

- On January 21, British poet and dramatist T.S. Eliot's play *The Cocktail Party* opens at New York's Henry Miller Theater.

- On January 29, the Vatican recognizes the sacramental nature of baptism in the Presbyterian, Congregational, Baptist, Methodist, and Disciples of Christ faiths.

- On February 7, Great Britain and the United States recognize the Vietnamese government of Bao Dai.

- On February 24, the executive committee of the World Council of Churches in Bossey, Switzerland, appeals for world peace.

- On March 1, Chiang Kai-shek assumes the presidency of Nationalist China on the island of Formosa (Taiwan).

- On May 8, President Harry S. Truman sends the first U.S. military advisors to Vietnam.

- On May 11, Eugène Ionesco's play *The Bald Soprano* opens at Paris's Théâtre des Noctamules.

- On June 25, North Korea invades South Korea, upsetting U.S. calculations that Europe was the focus of communist aggression.

- On June 30, U.S. combat troops enter the Korean War under the command of General Douglas McArthur and under the authority of President Harry Truman and the United Nations (UN).

- In July, orchestras throughout the world sponsor Bach festivals to commemorate the bicentennial of Johann Sebastian Bach's death.

- On July 22, Leopold III, exiled king of Belgium, returns to his country.

- In August, Australia retains the Davis Cup in tennis, beating the United States in the finals.

- On August 1, Leopold III reluctantly abdicates Belgium's throne in favor of his son Baudouin.

- On August 3, Pope Pius XII declares abstract art and "art for art's sake" immoral.

- On October 25, Jean Anouilh's play *The Rehearsal* opens at Paris's Théâtre Marigny.

- On November 1, Pope Pius XII proclaims as doctrine the bodily assumption of the Virgin Mary into heaven.

- On November 5, the London *Sunday Times* awards £1000 to T.S. Eliot, naming his play *The Cocktail Party* the year's outstanding contribution to English literature.

- On November 30, the Soviet Union vetoes a UN demand that Chinese Communists withdraw from North Korea.

- On December 11, British philosopher and mathematician Bertrand Russell receives the Nobel Prize in literature.

- On December 19, the North Atlantic Treaty Organization (NATO) names General Dwight D. Eisenhower, who had commanded U.S. forces in Europe during World War II, supreme commander of Allied forces in Europe.

- On December 23, the Vatican confirms the discovery of Saint Peter's tomb beneath Saint Peter's Basilica.
- On December 28, *Time* magazine names the "U.S. Fighting Man, Man of the Year," the first time the magazine selected a symbol rather than an individual.

1951

- The Izod Company exports the Chemise Lacoste shirt to the United States for the first time.
- French writer Albert Camus publishes *L'Homme révolté* (The Rebel), which identifies the danger, and necessity, that humans follow their convictions in seeking to undermine totalitarian governments.
- Spanish painter Salvador Dali exhibits the painting *Christ of St. John of the Cross.*
- Spanish painter Pablo Picasso exhibits the painting *Massacre in Korea.*
- On January 11, the Vatican newspaper publishes a decree prohibiting Roman Catholic priests from membership in Rotary clubs, which, the church says, are connected with the Masons and are therefore anti-Catholic.
- On January 12, the UN Convention on Prevention and Punishment of Genocide takes effect.
- On February 14, Moscow's Communist youth newspaper *Komosomolskaya Pravda* reports a heart and lung transplant from one dog to another.
- On March 19, France, West Germany, Italy, Belgium, Holland, and Luxembourg form the European Coal and Steel Community to compete against U.S. steel manufacturers.
- On April 11, three unidentifed men return the stolen Stone of Scone to Westminster Abbey.
- On April 20, *Miracle in Milan* and *Julie* win the Cannes Film Festival's Grand Prize.
- On April 21, the Iranian Parliament nationalizes the country's oil industry.
- On June 13, the Roman Catholic church beatifies Pope Pius XII after a church investigation declares his recovery from two tumors miraculous.
- In August, Australia retains the Davis Cup in tennis, again beating the United States in the finals.
- On August 5, five hundred thousand youths participate in the communist-sponsored World Youth Festival in East Berlin.
- In September, Great Britain's first supermarket chain opens.
- On September 8, Japan signs a treaty with forty-eight non-communist countries, formally ending World War II.
- On October 25, Winston Churchill wins election as Great Britain's prime minister, his second tenure as prime minister.
- On November 26, Pope Pius XII, in response to criticism, retracts an earlier statement against abortion when the mother's life is in danger.
- On November 27, UN and North Korean negotiators agree on a cease-fire line and begin discussing truce enforcement proposals.

- On December 10, Swedish novelist Pär Lagerkvist receives the Nobel Prize in literature.
- On December 27, negotiators fail to agree on an armistice by midnight, voiding the November 27 cease-fire in Korea.

1952

- Irish dramatist Samuel Beckett premieres the play *Waiting for Godot.*
- Marc Chagall exhibits the painting *The Green Night.*
- The United States wins forty-three gold medals to the Soviet Union's twenty-two and Hungary's twenty-two at the Olympic Games in Helsinki, Finland.
- On February 6, Princess Elizabeth becomes queen of England upon the death of her father, King George VI. She is Queen Elizabeth II.
- On February 12, the Civil Aeronautics Board limits transatlantic air service to regularly scheduled lines.
- On March 10, former Cuban president Fulgencia Batista y Zaldívar becomes dictator after overthrowing President Prio Soccaras in a military coup.
- On March 14, the UN's Economic and Social Council's Subcommittee on Freedom of Information issues a draft of an international code of ethics for journalists.
- On March 16, Roman Catholic bishop auxilliary Fulton J. Sheen declares that American Catholics do not want an established church and will obey a government that "comes from God."
- On March 22, Pope Pius XII reaffirms the right of the Catholic Church to interpret divine law.
- On April 5, at the International Economic Conference, the Soviet Union offers to buy $7.5–$10 billion worth of goods from the West in the next two to three years.
- On April 29, New York's Lever House opens, an example of energy-wasting architecture throughout the world.
- On April 30, President Josip Tito announces that Yugoslavia will not join NATO.
- On May 6, King Farouk I of Egypt claims direct descent from Prophet Mohammed, assuming the title of El Sayed.
- On May 10, the Cannes International Film Festival names Orson Welles's *Othello* best film and Marlon Brando best actor for his role in *Viva Zapata.*
- On May 12, the International Press Institute says that an increasing number of governments are imposing restrictions on news organizations, limiting freedom of the press.
- On May 26, the Church of England refuses to ease divorce laws and recommends outlawing artificial insemination.
- On June 3, France replaces Tran Van Huu as premier with Nguyen Van Tam.
- On July 26, King Farouk I of Egypt abdicates when General Mohammed Naguik leads an anticorruption coup.
- On August 22, West German movie theaters show the movie *The Desert Fox,* an homage to German World War II general Erwin Rommel, after U.S. objections delayed its release ten months.

- On August 27, South Africa removes blacks from electoral rolls, prohibiting them from voting.
- On August 28, the Third World Conference on Faith and Order in Lund, Sweden, closes without agreeing to unite Christian religions.
- On September 18, the Soviet Union vetoes UN admission for Japan.
- On September 22, Sears, Roebuck and Company forms a partnership with the Toronto mail-order house Simpson, Ltd.
- On October 22, the American Biblical Encyclopedia Society publishes the Torah in English for the first time.
- On December 15, Communist China rejects the UN's Korean truce plan.

1953

- Christian Dior creates an uproar when he announces his 1953 fall hemlines will measure sixteen inches from the ground.
- Australian Ken Rosewall wins the French and Australian tennis singles titles.
- Maureen Connally wins tennis "Grand Slam" by winning the Australian, French, English, and U.S. women's singles titles.
- Marc Chagall exhibits the painting *Eiffel Tower.*
- Henri Matisse exhibits the painting *The Snail.*
- On January 1, Ernest Bloch's musical *Suite Hebraique* opens in Chicago.
- On February 1, Japan's first television station begins broadcasting.
- On February 14, Hollywood's Foreign Press Association announces that a 1952 poll of fans in fifty countries names Susan Hayward and John Wayne the most popular stars.
- In March, German chemist Karl Ziegler uses atmospheric pressure instead of a more difficult pressure method in a new catalytic process for producing polyethylene.
- On March 4, Iranian premier Mohammad Mossadegh retains power after four days of fighting by nationalists, royalists, communists, and religious groups.
- On March 6, Georgy Malenkov becomes Soviet premier after Joseph Stalin's death the previous day.
- On March 26, Jean Anouilh's play *Medea* opens at Paris's Théâtre de l'Atelier.
- On April 25, American chemist James Watson and British colleague Francis Crick publish the structure of deoxyribonucleic acid (DNA).
- On May 2, French anatomist Le Gross Clark exposes Piltdown Man as a hoax.
- On June 2, Queen Elizabeth II is coronated. The coronation influences fashion, making jeweled tiaras the year's most popular accessory for evening gowns.
- On June 6, radio broadcasts French composer Darius Milhaud's *Fifth Symphony* from Turin, Italy.

- On June 7, Vietnamese premier Nguyen Van Tam demands that France give his government independence in foreign affairs.
- In July, golfer Ben Hogan wins the British Open.
- On July 27, the Korean War ends in a stalemate.
- In August, Australia defeats the U.S. for the third consecutive year to retain the Davis Cup in tennis.
- On August 22, Shah Mohammad Reza Pahlevi replaces Mossadegh as Iran's prime minister.
- On September 13, Nikita Khrushchev becomes first secretary of the Soviet Communist Party's Central Committee.
- On September 26, Pope Pius XII proclaims 1954 a Marian Year to celebrate the centennial of the definition of Immaculate Conception as Catholic dogma.
- In October, researchers in Basel, Switzerland, synthesize carotene, the precursor of vitamin A, from acetone and acetylene.
- On October 12, six thousand sugar workers strike in British Guiana (Guyana).
- On November 5, Terrence Rattigan's play *The Sleeping Prince* opens at London's Phoenix Theater, with Laurence Olivier and Vivien Leigh.
- On November 6, Masao Oki's *Atomic Bomb* symphonic fantasy is performed in Tokyo.
- On November 20, U.S. Roman Catholics issue a statement condemning communist efforts to suppress religion as "the bitterest, the bloodiest persecution in all history."
- On December 1, AT&T announces it will lay the first telephone cable across the Atlantic.
- On December 10, Winston Churchill receives the Nobel Prize in literature.
- On December 17, Dmitry Shostakovich conducts his *Tenth Symphony* in Leningrad.
- On December 22, Friedrich Dürrenmatt's play *Ein Engel Kommt nach Babylon* (An Angel Comes to Babylon) opens at Munich's Kammerspiele.

1954

- Salvador Dali exhibits the painting *Crucifixion.*
- Pablo Picasso exhibits the painting *Sylvette.*
- Marc Chagall exhibits the painting *The Red Roofs.*
- Gabrielle "Coco" Chanel brings her famed "Chanel Look" back into haute couture after a fifteen-year absence.
- Britain permits antibiotic feed supplements for livestock.
- Mercedes introduces the first fuel-injection system for automobiles on its Mercedes 300SL.
- On January 19, United Fruit Company rejects Costa Rica's demand for 50 percent of company profits.
- On February 12, *The Legend of the Stone Flower,* a ballet, opens at Moscow's Bolshoi Theater, with music by the late Russian composer Sergey Prokofiev.
- On March 12, *Moses and Aaron,* an opera by the late Austrian composer Arnold Schoenberg, opens at Hamburg's Musikhalle.

- On March 13, Vietminh troops, loyal to Vietnamese nationalist and communist Ho Chi Minh, attack French fortress Dien Bien Phu in northern Vietnam.
- In April, Montreal physicians Heinz Lehmann and G.E. Hanrahan report success in treating psychotic patients with the French drug chlorpromazine.
- On April 5, President Dwight D. Eisenhower announces that the United States will not use the hydrogen bomb in a preemptive strike on any nation.
- On April 23, the United States lends $100 million to the European Coal and Steel Community to revive the European capital market.
- On April 30, Darius Milhaud's *Fourth Piano Concerto* premieres in Haifa, Israel.
- On May 6, Roger Bannister of Great Britain runs a mile in 3 minutes, 59.4 seconds at Oxford University, becoming the first runner to break the four-minute barrier.
- On May 7, French troops surrender Dienbienphu to the Viet Minh, ending seventy years of French colonialism.
- On May 29, Pope Pius XII proclaims the late Pope Pius X a saint of the Roman Catholic church.
- In July, West Germany defeats Hungary for the World Cup Soccer championship, 3-2, at Bern's Wanddorf Stadium.
- On July 6, American evangelist Billy Graham returns from a five-month tour, during which he preached at three hundred meetings in Great Britain and Western Europe.
- On July 21, the Geneva Accords divide Vietnam into North and South Vietnam at the seventeenth parallel.
- On August 1, Egypt ends its blockade of the Suez Canal Zone under U.S. pressure to restore trade through the canal.
- On August 17, the Vatican permits Roman Catholic clergy to use English in administering the sacraments of baptism, matrimony, and extreme unction.
- On August 30, the World Council of Churches calls for abolition of all weapons of mass destruction and reduction of conventional arms as steps to ending war.
- On September 8, the Manila Pact establishes the Southeast Treaty Organization (SEATO).
- On September 12, Jews celebrate the three hundredth anniversary of their first settlement in North America.
- On September 14, Benjamin Britten premieres the opera *Turn of the Screw,* with libretto adapted from Henry James's short story.
- On September 22, Terence Rattigan's plays *Separate Tables* and *Table Number Seven* open at London's Saint James's Theatre with Eric Portman.
- On September 27, Mao Tse-tung is reelected chairman of the People's Republic of China.
- On October 1, Yugoslavia and the Soviet Union settle their first trade agreement since 1948, involving the exchange of nonstrategic goods.
- On October 22, NATO admits West Germany.
- On November 4, French physician Albert Schweitzer delivers his Nobel lecture in Stockholm, Sweden.
- On November 6, the General Agreement on Trade and Tariffs members approve a Danish resolution censuring the United States for restricting dairy imports.

1955

- Ross and Norris McWhirter publish *The Guinness Book of World Records,* which sells twenty-four million copies.
- Oxford University medievalist J.R.R. Tolkien publishes the novel *The Lord of the Rings.*
- Pablo Picasso exhibits the painting *The Women of Algiers.*
- Salvador Dali exhibits the painting *The Lord's Supper.*
- Le Corbusier completes France's Notre Dame du Haut at Ronchamp.
- On January 5, the World Bank expels Czechoslovakia for nonpayment of dues and for not furnishing required economic information.
- On February 13, Israel buys four Dead Sea Scrolls from the Syrian archbishop Metropolitan, the leader of the Syrian Orthodox Church.
- In March, British biochemist Dorothy Hodgkins discovers vitamin B-12 (cyanocobalamin).
- On April 6, Anthony Eden becomes Great Britain's prime minister upon Winston Churchill's retirement.
- On April 12, Albert Einstein dies in Princeton, New Jersey. His study reveals a series of equations that Einstein had hoped to unite into the Unified Field.
- On May 14, the Soviet Union, Albania, Bulgaria, Czechoslovakia, East Germany, Hungary, Poland, and Romania form a unified military command under the Warsaw Pact.
- On May 30, fifteen South American coffee producers establish an International Coffee Bureau to control coffee prices, just as the Organization of Petroleum Exporting Countries (OPEC) controls oil prices.
- On June 5, evangelist Billy Graham opens a crusade in Paris, his first visit to a non-English-speaking and predominantly Catholic city.
- On July 25, Yugoslavian president Tito says Yugoslavia is willing to resume diplomatic relations with the Soviet Communist Party.
- On August 28, Israel and Egypt skirmish along the Gaza Strip.
- In September, the Vienna State Opera House reopens after bombing had destroyed it in World War II.
- On September 13, West Germany and the Soviet Union establish diplomatic relations.
- On October 26, Ngo Dinh Diem proclaims South Vietnam a republic and names himself premier.
- On November 16, Israel requests U.S. military aid to counteract Soviet aid to Egypt.
- On December 29, West Germany passes Great Britain as the major European steel producer.

1956

- German born psychologist Erich Fromm publishes *The Art of Loving.*
- French writer Albert Camus publishes the novel *La Chute* (The Fall).

- Swedish director Ingmar Bergman premieres the film *The Seventh Seal.* Christian symbolism suffuses the film.

- On January 29, Friederich Dürrenmatt premieres the play *Der Besuch der alten Dame* (The Visit of the Old Lady) at Zurich's Schauspielhaus.

- On February 25, Soviet First Secretary Nikita Khrushchev denounces former leader Joseph Stalin as a tyrant.

- In March, Brazilian soccer player Edson Arantes "Pele" do Nacimento signs with Brazil's Santos team, beginning an eighteen-year career of 1,253 games in which he will score 1,216 goals.

- On April 2, British actor and dramatist Peter Ustinov's play *Romanoff and Juliet* opens at England's Manchester Opera House.

- On April 4, Enid Bagnold premieres the play *The Chalk Garden* at London's Theatre Royal.

- On April 5, the Vatican announces the discovery of a catacomb containing fourth-century murals of Christian scenes, at a construction site in Rome.

- On April 11, North Korean troops attack UN forces on the cease-fire line, in violation of the Korean armistice.

- On May 8, John Osborne premieres the play *Look Back in Anger* at London's Royal Court Theatre, with Kenneth Haigh, Mary Ure, and Alan Bates.

- On May 14, Pope Pius XII approves, on moral grounds, the transplanting of corneas from a dead person to restore sight to the living, but disapproves the transplantation of organs from a living person.

- On May 24, Israel and Egypt agree on the establishment of UN truce-observation posts on the Gaza Strip border.

- On May 24, Brendan Behan premieres the play *The Quare Fellow* at Stratford's London Theatre Royale.

- From June to July, 3,539 athletes from sixty-seven nations compete in the Olympic Games in Melbourne, Australia.

- On June 17, Israeli labor minister Goldie Myerson (Golda Meir) becomes foreign minister.

- On June 19, archaeologists find biblical scrolls containing portions of the books of Genesis, Exodus, Leviticus, Numbers, and Deuteronomy (the Pentateuch) in a cave near the site of the Dead Sea Scrolls.

- On June 25, one hundred thousand members of Peru's Private Employees Central Union strike the International Petroleum Company for higher wages.

- In July, Parliament passes the Clean Air Act, banning the burning of soft coal and other smoky fuels.

- On July 16, Federico Fellini premieres the film *La Strada,* starring Anthony Quinn, in New York City.

- On August 4, the World Council of Churches central committee approves efforts to bring the Moscow Patriarchate of the Russian Orthodox Church into the organization.

- On August 30, Egyptian president Gamal Abdel Nasser nationalizes the Suez Canal, infuriating U.S. and European merchants, who consider it a route of free passage.

- On September 15, an Aeroflot Tupolev-104 airliner makes the first scheduled passenger flight from Moscow to Irkutsk.

- On October 14, in what may be the largest mass conversion in history, 250,000 untouchables convert to Buddhism in India.

- On October 17, England's Calder Hall becomes the first commercial nuclear power plant.

- On October 23, Hungary revolts against the Soviet Union in a bid for independence.

- On November 1, Hungary leaves the Warsaw Pact in another demonstration of its desire for independence.

- On November 4, Soviets forces attack Hungary to keep it in the Soviet bloc.

- On November 4, Hungarian Communist Party first secretary János Kádár replaces Imre Nagy as premier after the Soviet invasion.

1957

- Russian poet and novelist Boris Pasternak publishes the novel *Doctor Zhivago.*

- Swedish director Ingmar Bergman premieres the film *Wild Strawberries.*

- In January, Italian scientists develop rifampian, an antibiotic effective against tuberculosis.

- On January 16, the U.S. State Department supports a free-trade zone and European common market.

- On February 15, Andrei Gromyko becomes Soviet foreign minister.

- On February 24, *The New York Times* reports that rebel leader Fidel Castro's forces clash with government troops in Cuba.

- On March 22, Pope Pius XII decrees that Catholics reduce the amount of fasting before receiving Holy Communion to three hours.

- From April to June, an international team of physical anthropologists unearth the remains of eleven Neanderthal skeletons in Iraq.

- On April 10, John Osborne premieres his play *The Entertainer,* with music by John Addison, at London's Royal Court Theatre.

- On April 14, the U.S. Trade Fair, with exhibits from fifty-nine nations, opens in New York City.

- On May 10, pianist Maxim Shostakovich solos in Dmitry Shostakovich's *Piano Concerto* in Moscow.

- On June 25, the Congregational Christian General Council and the Evangelical and Reformed Church merge to form the United Church of Christ.

- On July 3, Soviet First Secretary Nikita Khrushchev removes several members of the Central Committee after they fail to remove him from power.

- On August 11, *Die Harmonie der Welt* (The Harmony of the World) opens in Munich, with music by German composer Paul Hindemith.

- In September, the chemise is introduced at the Paris and Rome couturière showings.

- On October 6, French conductor and composer Pierre Boulez conducts his *Polyphonie X for Seventeen Solo Instruments* at the Donaueschippu Festival of Contemporary Music.

- On October 19, Gian Carlo Menotti premieres the symphonic poem *Apocalypse* in Pittsburgh, Pennsylvania.

- On October 30, Dmitry Shostakovich premieres his *Eleventh Symphony* in Moscow.

- On November 7, Heitor Villa-Lobos's symphonic poem *Erosion, or the Origin of the Amazon River* is performed in Louisville, Kentucky.

- On December 10, French writer Albert Camus receives the Nobel Prize in literature.

- On December 23, NATO reports that U.S. delivery of missiles to Western Europe will not begin for two years.

1958

- Pablo Picasso exhibits the painting *Peace*.

- Gian Carlo Menotti founds the Spoleto Festival, which has its first season ninety miles north of Rome, Italy.

- The first parking meters appear in London.

- The last debutantes are presented at the British court.

- On January 1, Prime Minister David Ben-Gurion agrees to establish a new Israeli government.

- In February, Yves St. Laurent, a young designer and protégé of Christian Dior, debuts his Trapeze line.

- On February 11, John Osborne and Anthony Creighton premiere their play *Epitaph for George Dillon* at London's Royal Court Theatre.

- On March 27, Nikita Khrushchev becomes premier of the Soviet Union, consolidating Soviet party and state leadership.

- On March 29, Max Frisch premieres the play *Biedermann und die Brandstifter* (Biedermann and the Fire-bugs) at Zurich's Schauspielhaus.

- In April, Pan Am and BOAC (British Overseas Airways) begin transatlantic jet passenger flights.

- On April 4, French dramatist Eugène Ionesco premieres the play *Tueur sans gages* (The Killer) at Darmstadt's Landestheater.

- On April 24, Jews in Jerusalem celebrate the tenth anniversary of the founding of Israel.

- On April 28, British dramatist Harold Pinter premieres the play *The Birthday Party* at the Arts Theatre in Cambridge, England.

- On May 8, Terence Rattigan premieres the play *Variations on a Theme* at London's Globe Theatre.

- On May 10, Dmitry Shostakovich premieres his *Second Piano Concerto* in Moscow.

- On May 31, General Charles de Gaulle, the leader of the French Resistance during World War II, becomes premier of France.

- On June 18, the opera *Noye's Fludde* (Noah's Flood) premieres at Oxford Church, Suffolk, with music by British composer Benjamin Britten and the libretto from the fourteenth-century *Chester Miracle Play*.

- On June 24, Premier Charles de Gaulle demands a greater French role in NATO.

- In July, Brazil wins its first World Cup soccer championship, defeating Sweden, 5-2.

- On July 7, the Soviet Union and East Germany agree to coordinate industrial production.

- On July 17, Peter Shaffer premieres the play *Five Finger Exercise* at London's Comedy Theatre.

- On September 28, French voters approve by an 80 percent margin Premier Charles de Gaulle's constitution establishing a strong presidency.

- In October, the Swedish Royal Academy announces Russian novelist Boris Pasternak winner of the Nobel Prize in literature. Pasternak, however, refuses the award.

- On October 14, Brendan Behan premieres the play *The Hostage* at London's Theatre Royale in Stratford, England.

- On October 16, British composer Benjamin Britten premieres the *Nocturne* song cycle for tenor and small orchestra in Leeds, England.

- On October 26, Pan American World Airways begins daily New York–Paris service.

- On November 10, German dramatist Bertolt Brecht premieres the play *Der Aufhaltsame Aufstieg des Arturo Ui* (The Resistable Rise of Arturo Ui) in Stuttgart, Germany.

- On December 17, Mao Tse-tung retires as leader of Communist China.

- On December 21, voters elect Charles de Gaulle president of France's Fifth Republic.

1959

- British writer Ian Fleming publishes the novel *Goldfinger*.

- Marc Chagall exhibits the painting *Le Champ de Mars*.

- On January 2, Fidel Castro assumes control of Cuba.

- On January 5, *Time* magazine names French premier Charles de Gaulle Man of the Year.

- On February 10, Shelagh Delaney premieres the play *A Taste of Honey* at London's Wyndham Theatre.

- On February 16, Fidel Castro is sworn in as premier of Cuba.

- On March 5, Indonesia nationalizes 270 Dutch-owned enterprises.

- On March 27, Pope John XXIII withdraws references to Jews as "perfidious" from Good Friday services.

- On April 23, the first Arab Petroleum Congress ends with nine countries calling for an increase in Arab control of oil production, refinement, and distribution.

- On June 26, Swedish boxer Ingemar Johansson knocks out Floyd Patterson in the third round of the world heavyweight boxing championship in New York City.

- On July 5, Prime Minister Ben-Gurion of Israel resigns after his cabinet opposes the sale of arms to West Germany.

- On July 17, Cuban president Lleo resigns after he disagrees with Premier Fidel Castro on land reform and the death penalty for counterrevolutionaries.

• On August 8, President Nasser of Egypt bars Israel from using the Suez Canal.

• On September 3, Vatican radio reports that representatives of the Roman Catholic and Eastern Orthodox Churches will meet to discuss reunification.

• On September 5, Mary Leakey, the wife of British anthropologist Louis S.B. Leakey, discovers the skull of an early man in the rift valley of east Africa.

• On September 15, Soviet premier Nikita Khrushchev begins a two-week visit to the United States.

• On September 29, Premier Nikita Khrushchev leaves for Peking, China, to celebrate Communist China's tenth anniversary.

• In October, Russian archaeologist Tatiana Proskeuriakov announces a pattern of dates in the lives of Mayan rulers in the Yucatán.

• On October 4, Russian cellist Mstislau Rostropovich solos in Dmitry Shostakovich's *Concerto in E-flat for Violoncello and Orchestra* in Leningrad.

• On October 22, John Arden premieres the play *Sergeant Musgrave's Dance* at London's Royal Court Theatre.

• On October 26, Fidel Castro accuses the United States of dropping anticommunist propoganda from airplanes flying over Cuba.

• On November 3, President Charles de Gaulle announces his desire to withdraw France from NATO.

• On November 10, a Soviet-U.S. film exchange begins with simultaneous premieres of the Soviet film *The Cranes Are Flying* in Washington, D.C., and the U.S. film *Marty* in Moscow.

• On November 19, U.S. Roman Catholic bishops oppose the use of tax money to promote "artificial birth prevention for economically underdeveloped countries."

1

THE ARTS

ALICE WU

Entries are arranged in chronological order by date of primary source. For entries with one primary source, the entry title is the same as the primary source title. Entries with more than one primary source have an overall entry title, followed by the titles of the primary sources.

Important Events in the Arts, 1950–1959

1950

- *The Cardinal,* by Henry Morton Robinson, is the year's best seller.

- Musical festivals in the United States and abroad commemorate the bicentenary death of Johann Sebastian Bach. Notable among them are the yearlong Bach series at the University of California School of Music and the augmented program in the annual Bach series at the Berkshire Music Festival.

- *Basquet-Banquet,* by Karl Knaths, wins the $3,500 first prize in the New York Metropolitan Museum of Art exhibit "American Painting Today—1950."

- Abstract expressionist painter Jackson Pollack completes *Autumn Rhythm,* in which the paint is dribbled and flung all over the surface of the canvas.

- *South Pacific* by Richard Rodgers, Oscar Hammerstein II, and Joshua Logan wins the Pulitzer Prize.

- Photographer Margaret Bourke-White makes a photographic essay of South Africa.

- Marilyn Monroe, twenty-four, makes her debut in John Huston's film *The Asphalt Jungle.*

- In January, alto saxophonist Charlie "Yardbird" Parker and his quintet end a month-long series of performances. They began on December 15, 1949, at Birdland, opening the jazz nightclub named for Parker located at 52nd St. and Broadway in Manhattan.

- On January 5, Carson McCullers's dramatization of her novel *The Member of the Wedding* opens at New York's Empire Theatre, beginning a run of 501 performances.

- In March, Roberta Peters, a twenty-year-old opera singer from the Bronx, debuts with the Metropolitan Opera as a stand-in for Nadine O'Connor in Wolfgang Amadeus Mozart's *Don Giovanni.*

- In March, the Boston Institute of Contemporary Art in conjunction with the New York Metropolitan Museum and the Whitney Museum issue a joint Statement on Modern Art opposing "any attempt to make art or opinion about art conform to a single point of view."

- On May 31, Edward Johnson retires after fifteen years as manager of the Metropolitan Opera. His successor is Rudolph Bing.

- On November 14, the fiftieth birthday of composer Aaron Copland is celebrated by the League of Composers with a concert of his works.

- On November 24, *Guys and Dolls,* with music and lyrics by Frank Loesser, opens at the 46th Street Theater. It is one of the longest-running and most popular Broadway musicals ever staged.

- On December 10, the novelist William Faulkner receives the 1949 Nobel Prize in literature; no literature prize had been given in 1949, so both the 1949 and 1950 prizes are awarded in 1950. He is the fourth American to win the prize.

MOVIES: *Sunset Boulevard,* starring Gloria Swanson and William Holden; *All About Eve,* starring Bette Davis and Anne Baxter; *Adam's Rib,* starring Spencer Tracy and Katharine Hepburn; *The Asphalt Jungle,* starring Sterling Hayden, Louis Calhern, and Sam Jaffe; *Born Yesterday,* starring Judy Holliday and Broderick Crawford; *Broken Arrow,* starring Delmar Daves and James Stewart; *Cinderella,* animation by the Disney Studio; *Cyrano de Bergerac,* starring Jose Ferrer; *D.O.A.,* starring Neville Brand, Pamela Britton, and Edmond O'Brien; *Father of the Bride,* starring Elizabeth Taylor and Spencer Tracy; *The Gunfighter,* starring Gregory Peck, Karl Malden and Helen Westcott; *Harvey,* starring James Stewart; *In a Lonely Place,* starring Humphrey Bogart; *King Solomon's Mines,* starring Richard Carlson, Stewart Granger, Andrew Marton, and Deborah Kerr; *The Men,* starring Marlon Brando; *Panic in the Streets,* starring Richard Widmark, Jack Palance, Paul Douglas, and Barbara Bel Geddes; *Rio Grande,* starring John Wayne and Maureen O'Hara; *Wabash Avenue,* starring Betty Grable and Victor Mature; *Winchester '73,* starring James Stewart.

FICTION: Isaac Asimov, *I, Robot;* Ray Bradbury, *The Martian Chronicles;* Budd Schulberg, *The Disenchanted;* Ernest Hemingway, *Across the River and Into the Trees;* Henry Morton Robinson, *The Cardinal;* Jack Kerouac, *The Town and the City;* Francis Parkinson Keyes, *Joy Street;* John Hersey, *The Wall;* Kathleen Winsor, *Star Money;* Frank Yerby, *Floodtide;* Gwen Bristow, *Jubilee Trail;* William Styron, *Lie Down In Darkness.*

POPULAR SONGS: Bing Crosby, "Dear Hearts and Gentle People"; Red Foley, "Chattanoogie Shoe Shine Boy"; Eileen Barton, "If I Knew You Were Comin' I'd've Baked a Cake"; Billy Eckstine, "My Foolish Heart"; Bill Snyder and His Orchestra, "Bewitched, Bothered, and Bewildered"; Nat "King" Cole, "Mona Lisa"; Sammy Kaye and His Orchestra, "Harbor Lights"; Betty Hutton and Perry Como, "A Bushel and a Peck."

1951

- *The Sea Around Us,* by Rachel Carson, *The Caine Mutiny,* by Herman Wouk, *From Here to Eternity,* by James Jones, and *Look Younger, Live Longer,* by Gayelord Hauser are the year's best sellers.

- There are 691 orchestras in America, of which 32 are professional. The rest are college and community orchestras.

- United Artists, a leading film studio in the silent-film era, now losing one hundred thousand dollars a week, is taken over from surviving partners Charlie Chaplin and Mary

Pickford by two New York lawyers under the condition that they make it profitable by 1954.

- Hank Williams's "Cold, Cold Heart" is number one on the country-music charts; as sung by Tony Bennett, it is also number one on the pop-music charts.

- In January, President Harry S. Truman requests that the congressional Commission of Fine Arts begin a survey of the "activities of the federal government in the field of art."

- In the summer, NBC televises a series of concerts from the National Gallery of Art in Washington. During intermissions, artworks are discussed.

- From October 25 to December 16, the sixtieth annual American Exhibition at the Art Institute of Chicago takes place. Willem de Kooning's *Excavation* wins the one thousand dollar first prize.

- In November, the twenty-fifth anniversary issue of *Art Digest* is published; *Art News* celebrates its fiftieth anniversary.

- From November 1 to November 15, orchestras and operas "receiving substantial support from voluntary contributions" are exempted from the 20 percent federal admissions tax.

MOVIES: *The African Queen,* starring Humphrey Bogart and Katharine Hepburn; *An American in Paris,* starring Gene Kelly and Leslie Caron; *A Christmas Carol,* starring Alastair Sim; *The Day the Earth Stood Still,* starring Michael Rennie, Patricia Neal, and Hugh Marlowe; *Death of a Salesman,* starring Frederick March, Mildred Dunnock, and Kevin McCarthy; *A Place in the Sun,* starring Montgomery Clift and Shelley Winters; *Strangers on a Train,* starring Robert Walker; *A Streetcar Named Desire,* starring Karl Malden, Vivien Leigh, Kim Hunter, and Marlon Brando; *The Thing (From Another World),* starring Kenneth Tobey, Margaret Sheridan, and James Arness; *Alice in Wonderland,* Walt Disney animation.

FICTION: William Faulkner, *Requiem for a Nun;* James Jones, *From Here to Eternity;* Carson McCullers, *The Ballad of the Sad Cafe;* William Styron, *Lie Down in Darkness;* Herman Wouk, *The Caine Mutiny;* J.D. Salinger, *The Catcher in The Rye;* Sholem Asch, *Moses;* Frank Yerby, *A Woman Called Fancy;* Nicholas Monsarrat, *The Cruel Sea;* John P. Marquand, *Melville Goodwin, U.S.A;* James A. Michener, *Return to Paradise;* Cardinal Spellman, *The Foundling.*

POPULAR SONGS: Patti Page, "Tennessee Waltz"; Perry Como, "If"; The Weavers with Terry Gilkyson's Choir and Vic Schoen's Orchestra, "On Top of Old Smoky"; Nat "King" Cole, "Too Young"; Tony Bennett, "Because of You"; The Four Aces, "Sin."

1952

- Thomas B. Costain's *The Silver Chalice* and *The Holy Bible: New Revised Standard Version* are the year's bestsellers.

- In January, "American Bandstand," a popular-music show hosted by Dick Clark, debuts on ABC television.

- On January 15, Joseph Kramm's play *The Shrike* opens at the Cort Theater in New York; it wins the Pulitzer Prize in 1952.

- In July, the House Judiciary Committee recommends amending the U.S. copyright law to provide for payment of royalties to the copyright owner for jukebox play of music.

- In September, Ernest Hemingway's short novel *The Old Man and the Sea* is first printed in *Life* magazine (September 1, five million copies), as September co-main selection by the Book-of-the-Month Club (153,000 copies), and then for the trade by Scribner's (fifty thousand copies).

- In November, *Bwana Devil,* the first 3-D movie, is released.

- In December, the art critic Harold Rosenberg coins the term *action painting* to describe the work of the abstract expressionists.

MOVIES: *High Noon,* starring Gary Cooper and Grace Kelly; *The Greatest Show on Earth,* starring Betty Hutton and Charlton Heston; *Viva Zapata!,* starring Anthony Quinn, Marlon Brando, and Jean Peters; *The Quiet Man,* starring John Wayne and Maureen O'Hara; *Come Back, Little Sheba,* starring Shirley Booth and Burt Lancaster; *The Bad and the Beautiful,* starring Lana Turner, Kirk Douglas, Walter Pidgeon, and Dick Powell; *The Crimson Pirate,* starring Burt Lancaster; *Five Fingers,* starring James Mason and Danielle Darrieux; *The Man in the White Suit,* starring Alec Guinness and Joan Greenwood; *Moulin Rouge,* starring Jose Ferrer and Zsa Zsa Gabor; *Pat and Mike,* starring Spencer Tracy and Katharine Hepburn; *Singin' in the Rain,* starring Gene Kelly, Donald O'Connor, and Debbie Reynolds; *The Snows of Kilimanjaro,* starring Gregory Peck, Susan Hayward, and Ava Gardner; *My Cousin Rachel,* starring Richard Burton and Olivia de Haviland; *Peter Pan,* animation by Disney Studio.

FICTION: Thomas B. Costain, *The Silver Chalice;* Ralph Ellison, *The Invisible Man;* Edna Ferber, *Giant;* Shelby Foote, *Shiloh;* Bernard Malamud, *The Natural;* Frances Parkinson Keyes, *Steamboat Gothic;* Flannery O'Connor, *Wise Blood;* Howard Spring, *The Houses in Between;* John Steinbeck, *East of Eden;* Ernest Hemingway, *The Old Man and the Sea;* Agnes Sligh Turnbull, *The Gown of Glory;* Kurt Vonnegut, *Player Piano;* E. B. White, *Charlotte's Web;* Frank Yerby, *The Saracen Blade.*

POPULAR SONGS: Pee Wee King with Redd Stewart, "Slow Poke"; Johnnie Ray, "Cry"; Kay Starr, "Wheel of Fortune"; Georgia Gibbs, "Kiss of Fire"; Johnnie Ray, "Walkin' My Baby Back Home"; Vera Lynn, "Auf Wiederseh'n, Sweetheart"; The Mills Brothers, "The Glow Worm"; Joni James, "Why Don't You Believe Me?"

1953

- *A Man Called Peter* by Catherine Marshall, and *The Robe (reissue)* by Lloyd C. Douglas are the year's bestsellers.

- The National Music Council reports that of 1,834 performances by major symphony orchestras in the United States only 7.5 percent were of works by American composers.

- Doubleday Anchor Books, a new line of quality paperbacks, is introduced.

- Henry Koster's *The Robe,* starring Richard Burton, was the first film in CinemaScope, which used wider screens and stereophonic sound; the technique was designed to counter the popularity of television by attracting viewers to the big screen once again.

- Former Harvard *Lampoon* editor George Plimpton begins publication of the *Paris Review.*

- On February 19, William Inge's play *Picnic,* starring Paul Newman, opens a run of 477 performances at the Music Box Theatre in New York. It wins the 1953 Pulitzer Prize.

- From March 16 to April 11, Willem de Kooning's *Paintings on the Theme of Woman* is exhibited at the Sidney Janis Gallery in New York City.

- In August, the Commission of Fine Arts recommends that a music center be established in Washington, D.C., and that federal funds be appropriated for an auditorium to stage productions of operas, symphonies, and ballets.

- In October, a survey by the Metropolitan Opera Guild indicates that 744 performances of seventy-three contemporary operas, about half of which were by professional companies, were produced in the United States between October 1951 and October 1952.

- On October 15, John Patrick's *Teahouse of the August Moon* opens at the Martin Beck Theater in New York City. It wins the 1954 Pulitzer Prize.

- The Broadway production of Arthur Miller's *The Crucible,* dramatizing the 1692 Salem witch trials, serves as a parallel to the persecution of alleged Communist sympathizers in the United States.

MOVIES: *The Band Wagon,* starring Fred Astaire and Cyd Charisse; *The Big Heat,* starring Glenn Ford and Gloria Grahame; *From Here to Eternity,* starring Burt Lancaster, Deborah Kerr, and Frank Sinatra; *How to Marry a Millionaire,* starring Marilyn Monroe, Lauren Bacall, and William Powell; *House of Wax,* starring Vincent Price; *Julius Caesar,* starring Marlon Brando, James Mason, John Gielgud, Greer Garson, and Deborah Kerr; *The Naked Jungle,* starring Charleton Heston; *The Naked Spur,* starring James Stewart, Robert Ryan, and Janet Leigh; *Niagara,* starring Marilyn Monroe and Joseph Cotton; *The Robe,* starring Richard Burton, Michael Rennie, Victor Mature, and Jean Simmons; *Shane,* starring Alan Ladd, Jean Arthur, and Van Heflin; *Stalag 17,* starring William Holden; *Titanic,* starring Clifton Webb, Barbara Stanwyck, and Robert Wagner; *Roman Holiday,* starring Audrey Hepburn and Gregory Peck; *War of the Worlds,* starring Gene Barry and Ann Robinson; *The Wild One,* starring Marlon Brando.

FICTION: James Baldwin, *Go Tell It on the Mountain;* Saul Bellow, *The Adventures of Augie March;* Raymond Chandler, *The Long Goodbye;* A.J. Cronin, *Beyond This Place;* Lloyd C. Douglas, *The Robe;* Ernest K. Gann, *The High and the Mighty;* James Hilton, *Time and Time Again;* Louis L'Amour, *Hondo;* J.D. Salinger, *Nine Stories;* Annemarie Selinko, *Desiree;* Samuel Shellabarger, *Lord Vanity;* Leon Uris, *Battle Cry;* Ben Ames Williams, *The Unconquered;* William S. Burroughs, *Junky.*

POPULAR SONGS: Perry Como with Mitchell Ayres's Orchestra, "Don't Let the Stars Get in Your Eyes"; Teresa Brewer with Jack Pleis's Orchestra, "Till I Waltz Again With You"; Frankie Laine, "I Believe"; Pattie Page, "The Doggie in the Window"; Nat "King" Cole with the Nelson Riddle Orchestra, "Pretend"; Percy Faith and His Orchestra, "The Song From *Moulin Rouge* (Where Is Your Heart?)"; Les Paul and Mary Ford, "Vaya Con Dios (May God Be With You)"; the Ames Brothers with Hugo Winhalter and His Orchestra, "You, You, You"; Frank Chacksfield and His Orchestra, "Ebb Tide."

1954

- Norman Vincent Peale's *The Power of Positive Thinking* is the year's best-seller.

- Mark Rothko paints *Orange and Tan* in which a red-orange colorfield is above a pale yellow one.

- The Whitney Museum in New York is moved from quarters in Greenwich Village to a building adjoining the Museum of Modern Art.

- The International Congress of Art Historians and Museologists estimates that there are ten million amateur artists in the United States.

- Alfred Hitchcock's *Dial M for Murder* is the first serious film to be released in 3-D; when it fails to reach as many viewers as Hitchcock is used to, he re-releases the movie in a standard version.

- On March 31, Howard Hughes, criticized for capricious business practices in running RKO film studios, in which he has held controlling interest since 1948, buys the outstanding RKO stock for $23.5 million.

- On April 4, Arturo Toscanini conducts the last broadcast concert of the NBC Orchestra at Carnegie Hall.

- In July, the first Newport Jazz Festival is held in Newport, Rhode Island.

- On July 19, nineteen-year-old Elvis Presley's first professional record, "That's All Right, Mama" and "Blue Moon of Kentucky," is released on Sun Records (#219).

- On October 28, Ernest Hemingway is awarded the Nobel Prize in literature.

MOVIES: *The Caine Mutiny,* starring Humphrey Bogart, Jose Ferrer, Van Johnson, and Fred McMurray; *Desiree,* starring Marlon Brando, Jean Simmons, Merle Oberon, and Michael Rennie; *Dial M for Murder,* starring Ray Milland, Grace Kelly, and Robert Cummings; *Executive Suite,* starring William Holden, June Allyson, and Barbara Stanwyck; *Johnny Guitar,* starring Joan Crawford and Sterling Hayden; *On the Waterfront,* starring Marlon Brando and Karl Malden; *Rear Window,* starring James Stewart and Grace Kelly; *The Country Girl,* starring Bing Crosby, Grace Kelly, and William Holden; *A Star is Born,* starring Judy Garland; *Sabrina,* starring Humphrey Bogart, Audrey Hepburn, and William Holden; *Seven Brides for Seven Brothers,* starring Jane Powell and Howard Keel; *Them!,* starring James Whitmore, Edmund Gwenn, and James Arness.

FICTION: Hamilton Basso, *The View from Pompey's Head;* Taylor Caldwell, *Never Victorious, Never Defeated;* William Faulkner, *A Fable;* Evan Hunter, *The Blackboard Jungle;* Eudora Welty, *The Ponder Heart;* Morton Thompson, *Not as a Stranger;* Irving Stone, *Love is Eternal;* Frances Parkington Keyes, *The Royal Box;* Mac Hyman, *No Time for Sergeants;* John Steinbeck, *Sweet Thursday;* Frank Yerby, *Benton's Row.*

POPULAR SONGS: Roy Hamilton, "Ebb Tide"; Tony Bennett with the Percy Faith Orchestra, "Stranger in Paradise"; Frank Sinatra with the Nelson Riddle Orchestra, "Young at Heart"; Perry Como with the Hugo Winterhalter Orchestra, "Wanted"; Kitty Kallen with the Jack Pleis Orchestra, "Little Things Mean a Lot"; Archie Bleyer and His Orchestra, "Hernando's Hideaway"; Rosemary Clooney, "Hey, There"; Doris Day, "If I Give My Heart to You"; The Chordettes with Archie Bleyer's Orchestra, "Mister Sandman."

1955

- *Marjorie Morningstar* by Herman Wouk and *Gift from the Sea* by Anne Morrow Lindbergh are the year's best-sellers.

- The American Shakespeare Theatre has its first season at Stratford, Connecticut, which was founded in 1623 by settlers from Stratford-upon-Avon.

- In January, the contralto Marian Anderson is the first African American singer to appear at the Metropolitan Opera; the performance is Giuseppe Verdi's *Un Ballo in Maschera,* conducted by Dimitri Mitropoulos.

- On March 24, Tennessee Williams's *Cat on a Hot Tin Roof,* starring Barbara Bel Geddes and Burl Ives, opens a 694-performance run at New York's Morosco Theater. It wins the 1955 Pulitzer Prize.

- In July, Howard Hughes sells RKO Corporation, the motion-picture subsidiary of RKO Pictures, to General Tire and Rubber Company for $25 million.

- On August 20, Chuck Berry gains immediate success with his first release, "Maybelline," which he follows with many other hits including "Roll Over Beethoven" (1956), "School Day" (1957), and "Johnny B. Goode" (1958).

- On September 30, actor James Dean, twenty-four, is killed when he crashes his Porsche roadster.

- In October, Leopold Stopowski begins a three-year engagement as conductor of the Houston Symphony Orchestra.

- On October 5, *The Diary of Anne Frank* opens at the Cort Theater in New York City; it wins the Pulitzer Prize in 1956.

- On October 13, poet Allen Ginsberg gives the first reading of his controversial poem-in-progress, "Howl."

- On November 16, the option owned by Sam Phillips of Sun Records on Elvis Presley's recording contract is purchased by the RCA Record Company for thirty-five thousand dollars.

- On December 5, Thornton Wilder's *The Matchmaker,* a revision of *The Merchant of Yonkers* (1938), opens a 486-performance run at the Royal Theatre in New York. The play is the basis for the 1965 hit musical *Hello, Dolly.*

MOVIES: *Bad Day at Black Rock,* starring Spencer Tracy and Robert Ryan; *The Blackboard Jungle,* starring Glenn Ford, Anne Francis, and Sidney Poitier; *Kiss Me Deadly,* starring Ralph Meeker; *Lady and the Tramp,* animation by Disney Studio; *Love is a Many-Spendored Thing,* starring William Holden and Jennifer Jones; *Marty,* starring Ernest Borgnine; *The Night of the Hunter,* starring Robert Mitchum and Shelley Winters; *Picnic,* starring William Holden and Kim Novak; *Rebel Without a Cause,* starring James Dean; *The Seven Year Itch,* starring Marilyn Monroe and Tom Ewell; *Summertime,* starring Katharine Hepburn and Rossano Brazzi; *To Catch a Thief,* starring Cary Grant and Grace Kelly; *Mister Roberts,* starring Henry Fonda, James Cagney, William Powell, and Jack Lemmon; *The Rose Tattoo,* starring Anna Magnani and Burt Lancaster; *East of Eden,* starring James Dean, Julie Harris, Raymond Massey, Burl Ives, and Jo van Fleet.

FICTION: Herman Wouk, *Marjorie Morningstar;* Sloan Wilson, *The Man in the Gray Flannel Suit;* MacKinley Kantor, *Andersonville;* Norman Mailer, *The Deer Park;* Flannery O'Connor, *A Good Man is Hard to Find;* John O'Hara, *Ten North Frederick;* Wright Morris, *Field of Vision;* Patrick Dennis, *Auntie Mame;* Robert Ruark, *Something of Value;* Kay Thompson, *Eloise;* Thomas B. Costain, *The Tontine.*

POPULAR SONGS: Joan Weber, "Let Me Go Lover"; Fontaine Sisters, "Hearts of Stone"; McGuire Sisters, "Sincerely"; Bill Hayes, "The Ballad of Davy Crockett"; Perez Prado, "Cherry Pink and Apple Blossom White"; Bill Haley and His Comets, "Rock Around the Clock"; Tennessee Ernie Ford, "Sixteen Tons."

1956

- "I Could Have Danced All Night," words by Alan Jay Lerner and music by Frederick Loewe, is the song hit of 1956.

- *The Last Hurrah* by Edwin O'Connor, *Peyton Place* by Grace Metalious, and *The Search for Bridey Murphy* by Morey Bernstein are the year's best-sellers.

- Rock 'n' roll disc jockey Alan Freed stars in three movies: *Rock Around the Clock; Rock, Rock, Rock;* and *Don't Knock the Rock.*

- The North Carolina Museum of Art in Raleigh opens; it is the first museum in the United States to use state-voted public funds to purchase artwork.

- Construction begins on the Solomon R. Guggenheim Museum in Manhattan, designed by Frank Lloyd Wright.

- The Joffrey Ballet Company is founded by dancer-choreographer Robert Joffrey.

- Elvis Presley makes his film debut in *Love Me Tender.*

- Alan J. Lerner and Frederick Loewe's *My Fair Lady,* a musical based on George Bernard Shaw's *Pygmalion,* debuts at the Mark Hellinger Theatre in New York. running for 2,717 shows.

- On April 20, T.S. Eliot attracts an audience of fourteen thousand to a baseball stadium at the University of Minnesota to hear him speak on "The Frontiers of Criticism," a lecture on literary criticism.

- On August 10, painter Jackson Pollock and one of his passengers die when he crashes his Oldsmobile convertible while drunk.

- On October 20, at age twenty-four, country singer Johnny Cash releases "I Walk the Line," which makes the Billboard Top 40. As a result, he begins appearing on "Grand Ole Opry" and comes to be ranked as one of the top three male vocalists of the country charts.

- On October 29, soprano Maria Callas makes her New York debut at the Metropolitan Opera in *Norma.*

• On November 7, *A Long Day's Journey Into Night,* an autobiographical play by the late playwright Eugene O'Neill, opens at New York's Helen Hayes Theater. It wins the 1957 Pulitzer Prize.

MOVIES: *The King And I,* starring Yul Brynner and Deborah Kerr; *Lust for Life,* starring Anthony Quinn and Kirk Douglas; *Anastasia,* starring Ingrid Bergman and Yul Brynner; *Giant,* starring Elizabeth Taylor, Rock Hudson, and James Dean; *Around the World in Eighty Days,* starring David Niven and Shirley MacLaine; *Baby Doll,* starring Karl Malden, Carroll Baker, and Eli Wallach; *Bus Stop,* starring Marilyn Monroe; *Carousel,* starring Gordon MacRae and Shirley Jones; *Forbidden Planet,* starring Walter Pidgeon, Anne Francis, and Leslie Nielsen; *Friendly Persuasion,* starring Gary Cooper, Dorothy McGuire, and Anthony Perkins; *Invasion of the Body Snatchers,* starring Kevin McCarthy and Dana Wynter; *The Man Who Knew Too Much,* starring James Stewart and Doris Day; *Moby Dick,* starring Gregory Peck; *The Searchers,* starring John Wayne; *The Ten Commandments,* starring Charlton Heston and Yul Brynner; *Written on the Wind,* starring Rock Hudson, Lauren Bacall, and Robert Stack.

FICTION: Nelson Algren, *A Walk on the Wild Side;* John Barth, *The Floating Opera;* Saul Bellow, *Seize the Day;* Edwin O'Connor, *The Last Hurrah;* Grace Metalious, *Peyton Place;* William Brinkley, *Don't Go Near the Water;* Nicholas Monsarrat, *The Tribe That Lost Its Head.*

POPULAR SONGS: Chuck Berry, "Roll Over, Beethoven"; Dean Martin, "Memories Are made of This"; Platters, "The Great Pretender"; Kay Starr, "Rock and Roll Waltz"; Elvis Presley, "Heartbreak Hotel"; Perry Como, "Hot Diggity"; Morris Stoloff, "Moonglow" and the "Theme from *Picnic.*"

1957

• *By Love Possessed* by James G. Cozzens, *Compulsion* by Meyer Levin, and *The Hidden Persuaders* by Vance Packard are the year's best-sellers.

• *The Cat in the Hat,* by Dr. Seuss, is wildly popular with children learning to read, and becomes the first in a series of rhyming, entertainingly fanciful beginners' readers. The book is translated into many foreign languages and sells eight to nine million copies over the next twenty years.

• Motown Corporation is founded by thirty-year-old entrepreneur Berry Gordy, Jr., who invests seven hundred dollars to start the recording company that helps define African American popular music over the next two decades.

• On May 21, City Lights Bookshop owner and publisher Lawrence Ferlinghetti is charged with selling lewd and indecent materials when San Francisco undercover police buy a copy of Allen Ginsberg's *Howl.* Later in the year Ferlinghetti is found innocent.

• On September 26, *West Side Story,* a modern-day adaptation of William Shakespeare's *Romeo and Juliet,* premieres at the Winter Garden Theater with music by Leonard Bernstein.

• On November 28, *Look Homeward, Angel,* by Ketti Frings opens at the Ethel Barrymore Theater in New York City. It wins the 1958 Pulitzer Prize.

MOVIES: *The Bridge on the River Kwai,* starring William Holden and Alec Guinness; *A Face in the Crowd,* starring Andy Griffith, Patricia Neal, Anthony Franciosa, and Walter Matthau; *Funny Face,* starring Audrey Hepburn and Fred Astaire; *Gunfight at the O.K. Corral,* starring Kirk Douglas and Burt Lancaster; *The Incredible Shrinking Man,* starring Grant Williams; *Jailhouse Rock,* starring Elvis Presley; *The Pajama Game,* starring Doris Day; *Paths of Glory,* starring Kirk Douglas; *Peyton Place,* starring Lana Turner, Lee Philips, and Lloyd Nolan; *The Spirit of St. Louis,* starring James Stewart; *Sweet Smell of Success,* starring Burt Lancaster and Tony Curtis; *Twelve Angry Men,* starring Henry Fonda and Lee J. Cobb; *Love in the Afternoon,* starring Gary Cooper, Audrey Hepburn, and Maurice Chevalier; *Sayonara,* starring Marlon Brando, Miyoshi Umeki, and Red Buttons; *The Sun Also Rises,* starring Tyrone Power, Ava Gardner, Mel Ferrer, and Errol Flynn; *The Three Faces of Eve,* starring Joanne Woodward and Lee J. Cobb; *Witness for the Prosecution,* starring Charles Laughton, Tyrone Power, and Marlene Dietrich.

FICTION: James Agee, *A Death in the Family;* John Cheever, *The Wapshot Chronicles;* James Gould Cozzens, *By Love Possessed;* William Faulkner, *The Town;* Jack Kerouac, *On the Road;* Bernard Malamud, *The Assistant;* Ayn Rand, *Atlas Shrugged;* Kay Thompson, *Eloise in Paris.*

POPULAR SONGS: Pat Boone, "Don't Forbid Me" and "April Love"; Elvis Presley, "Too Much," "All Shook Up," "Let Me Be Your Teddy Bear," and "Jailhouse Rock"; Sonny James, "Young Love"; Buddy Knox, "Party Doll"; Debbie Reynolds, "Tammy"; Johnny Mathis, "Chances Are"; and Sam Cooke, "You Send Me."

1958

• *Anatomy of a Murder* by Robert Traver and *Some Came Running* by James Jones are the year's bestsellers.

• Seventy percent of all records sold are bought by teenagers.

• Choreographer Alvin Ailey's first critical and financial success *Blues Suite* marks the beginning of the Alvin Ailey Dance Company.

• Jasper Johns paints *Three Flags,* a fresh vision of the American flag that reveals a movement away from Abstract Expressionism toward Pop Art.

• Alan Freed is arrested in Boston for inciting a riot at a rock and roll show he had staged.

• Robert Rauschenberg pioneers "pop art" by creating a "semiabstraction" with a hole into which he has inserted four Coca-Cola bottles.

• Artist Louise Nevelson creates *Sky Cathedral,* an assemblage of found wooden objects painted black.

• The first Grammy Award is presented by the National Academy of Recording Arts and Sciences to the song "Volare" by Italian composer Dominic Modugno, with English lyrics by Mitchell Paris; the award is widely criticized for favoring older, more conservative white artists over youth-oriented pop artists.

• On April 13, American pianist Van Cliburn wins the Tchaikovsky International Competition in Moscow.

• On July 29, fifteen-year-old Paul Anka becomes an instant success with his first release, "Diana"; he has three more hits within a year and is a millionaire by the time he is seventeen.

• On October 2, Leonard Bernstein begins his first season as director of the New York Philharmonic Orchestra by introducing "previews," in which he comments on works being played.

MOVIES: *Auntie Mame,* starring Rosalind Russell; *The Big Country,* starring Gregory Peck, Jean Simmons, Charlton Heston, and Carroll Baker; *The Defiant Ones,* starring Tony Curtis and Sidney Poitier; *Gigi,* starring Leslie Caron and Maurice Chevalier; *Cat on a Hot Tin Roof,* starring Elizabeth Taylor, Paul Newman, and Burl Ives; *Man of the West,* starring Gary Cooper; *Marjorie Morningstar,* starring Gene Kelly and Natalie Wood; *A Night to Remember,* starring Kenneth Moore; *Run Silent Run Deep,* starring Clark Gable and Burt Lancaster; *Separate Tables,* starring Burt Lancaster, Rita Hayworth, David Niven, and Wendy Hiller; *I Want to Live!,* starring Susan Hayward; *South Pacific,* starring Rossano Brazzi and Mitzi Gaynor; *Touch of Evil,* starring Charlton Heston, Janet Leigh, and Orson Welles; *Vertigo,* starring James Stewart and Kim Novak.

FICTION: Truman Capote, *Breakfast at Tiffany's;* Patrick Dennis, *Around the World with Auntie Mame;* Edna Ferber, *Ice Palace;* Paul Gallico, *Mrs. 'Arris Goes to Paris;* Frances Parkington Keyes, *Victorine;* William J. Lederer and Eugene Burdick, *The Ugly American;* John O'Hara, *From the Terrace;* Bernard Malamud, *The Magic Barrel;* Anya Seton, *The Winthrop Woman;* Kay Thompson, *Eloise at Christmastime;* Robert Traver, *Anatomy of a Murder;* Vladimir Nabokov, *Lolita;* Leon Uris, *Exodus.*

• **Popular Songs** Danny and the Juniors, "At the Hop"; Elvis Presley, "Don't" and "Hard-Headed Woman"; McGuire Sisters, "Sugartime"; Silhouettes, "Get a Job"; Champs, "Tequila"; Everly Brothers, "All I Have to Do Is Dream" and "Bird Dog"; Platters, "Twilight Time"; Perry Como, "Catch a Falling Star"; and Laurie London, "He's Got the Whole World in His Hands."

1959

• *Exodus* by Leon Uris, *Act One* by Moss Hart, *Only in America* by Harry Golden, and *Folk Medicine* by D.C. Jarvis are the year's best-sellers.

• E.B. White's revision of *The Elements of Style,* by his Cornell professor, the late William Strunk, Jr., is published.

• On February 3, Buddy Holly, Richie Valens, and J.P. Richardson "The Big Bopper" are killed in a plane crash near Clear Lake, Iowa. They are the first rock 'n' roll stars to die.

• On March 11, Lorraine Hansberry's play *Raisin in the Sun,* starring Sidney Poitier, opens a 530-performance run at the Ethel Barrymore Theatre in New York.

• On July 21, the U.S. Post Office ban on distributing the 1928 novel *Lady Chatterley's Lover,* by D.H. Lawrence, is lifted by a federal district court. Judge Frederick van Pelt Bryan rules that the postmaster general is not qualified to judge obscenity of material to be sent through the mail.

• On October 7, 108 musicians in the Philadelphia Orchestra accept a contract after a strike that caused cancellation of the first three concerts of the season; the new contract stipulates a minimum wage of $170 per week for instumentalists.

• On October 21, New York's Solomon R. Guggenheim Museum, designed by architect Frank Lloyd Wright, opens to mixed reviews.

• On November 16, the long-running Rodgers and Hammerstein musical *The Sound of Music* opens at New York's Lunt-Fontanne Theater.

• On November 23, *Fiorello!* opens at New York's Broadhurst Theater. It wins the 1959 Pulitzer Prize.

MOVIES: *Anatomy of a Murder,* starring James Stewart and Lee Remick; *Ben Hur,* starring Charlton Heston; *Compulsion,* starring Orson Welles and Dean Stockwell; *The Diary of Anne Frank,* starring Millie Perkins and Joseph Schildkraut; *Imitation of Life,* starring Lana Turner, John Gavin, Robert Alda, and Sandra Dee; *North By Northwest,* starring Cary Grant, James Mason and Eva Marie Saint; *The Nun's Story,* starring Audrey Hepburn; *Pillow Talk,* starring Rock Hudson and Doris Day; *Rio Bravo,* starring John Wayne, Dean Martin and Ricky Nelson; *Room at the Top,* starring Simone Signoret and Laurence Harvey; *Sleeping Beauty,* animation by Disney Studio; *Some Like It Hot,* starring Marilyn Monroe, Tony Curtis, and Jack Lemmon; *Suddenly, Last Summer,* starring Elizabeth Taylor, Katharine Hepburn, and Montgomery Clift.

FICTION: Saul Bellow, *Henderson the Rain King;* William S. Burroughs, *Naked Lunch;* Taylor Caldwell, *Dear and Glorious Physician;* Allen Drury, *Advise and Consent;* William Faulkner, *The Mansion;* Shirley Jackson, *The Haunting of Hill House;* Paule Marshall, *Brown Girl, Brownstone;* James Michener, *Hawaii;* Philip Roth, *Goodbye, Columbus;* Robert Ruark, *Poor No More;* Kay Thompson, *Eloise in Moscow.*

POPULAR SONGS: Platters, "Smoke Gets in Your Eyes"; Lloyd Price, "Stagger Lee"; Frankie Avalon, "Venus"; Fleetwoods, "Come Softly to Me"; Dave "Baby" Cortez, "The Happy Organ"; Wilbert Harrison, "Kansas City"; Bobby Darin, "Mack the Knife."

Isamu Noguchi's Sculpture

Isamu Noguchi, with Akari Light Sculptures

Sculpture

By: Isamu Noguchi

Date: c. 1950

Source: The Isamu Noguchi Foundation, Inc., Long Island, New York.

A Sculptor's World

Memoir

By: Isamu Noguchi

Date: 1968

Source: Noguchi, Isamu. *A Sculptor's World*. New York: Harper & Row, 1968, 33, 159.

About the Artist: Isamu Noguchi (1904–1988) was born in Los Angeles of Japanese and Irish-American heritage. From the age of two to fourteen he was raised in Japan, returning to the United States for high school. Noguchi intended to study medicine, but after night classes in New York he realized he wanted to be a sculptor. Working with natural materials such as granite, marble, and wood, Noguchi's organic forms were featured in diverse contexts from public gardens to theater sets. ■

Introduction

Noguchi's first return trip to Japan after his long absence was in 1950, made possible by a Bollingen Foundation travel fellowship. His arrival there was met with fanfare, since at this time he already had an international reputation as one of the modernist vanguards. Noguchi had been making abstract sculpture from carved stone slab, along with a series of illuminated sculptures that he called "Lunars." Since the late 1940s, he created furniture designs that were distributed worldwide by prestigious design companies like Herman Miller and Knoll. Noguchi was also celebrated in the theater world for his stage designs, which he would continue to create until the mid-1960s. Even so, Noguchi was restless and ready for a change.

In Japan he began to experiment with traditional lighting systems, creating lantern-style lamps that he called *Akari,* after the Japanese word for light. Traditional lanterns were made from a structure of thin, coiled bamboo strip and covered with handmade mulberry paper. They were lit with candles, and the quality of the paper gave the cast light a soft glow. Noguchi, constantly trying out different crafting techniques, was able to make Akari in a wide variety of shapes. Many were asymmetrical and organic-looking. With their variety and handworked individuality, these Akari had the character of sculpture. They could be used singly or in a group; and some could be hung suspended from the ceiling, while others rested on a thin wire armature that made the structure seem to float. The lamps were handmade by traditional craftsmen in Gifu City, a Japanese city famous for its lanterns. Noguchi's interest in the lantern form gave locals hope for a revival of their traditional industry. Encouraged by Gifu's mayor, Noguchi produced the lamps for export to American and European markets. In the United States, Akari lamps were first sold at Bonniers, at the time an expensive New York department store specializing in modern furnishings.

Significance

When Noguchi tried to show his Akari in art galleries, he was refused. Noguchi had completely rejected the current sculptural trend for welded sculpture. In the earlier days of his artistic career, Noguchi's work was regarded in the United States as too "Oriental" or even "pseudo-Oriental," while in Japan his work was "too Western." The controversy arose from the nature of the Akari: they were lamps, and galleries did not consider this fine art. Even other artists placed a hierarchy on the various aspects of Noguchi's output—to them, a painting or sculpture was somehow better than "design."

Though frustrated by such attitudes, Noguchi had always thrived on exploring such diametric relationships: Early on he was interested in the idea of the ephemeral versus permanence and explored it through his proposals for public gardens. He also explored modern industrial processes at odds with traditional materials. Noguchi had called himself part of a "not exactly belonging people." Later in life, he finally considered himself less isolated.

Akari symbolized Noguchi's psychic journey to his past. To Noguchi the handmade paper of the lanterns held a distinct memory. He recalled the annual gifts of washi (paper) in his childhood—an item it seemed no Japanese household could do without. Washi was necessary for re-papering or mending shoji (sliding screens). It could be used for giftwrapping, or for serving fancy desserts. As a mature artist, Noguchi was fascinated by the particular kind of light and shadow cast by washi,

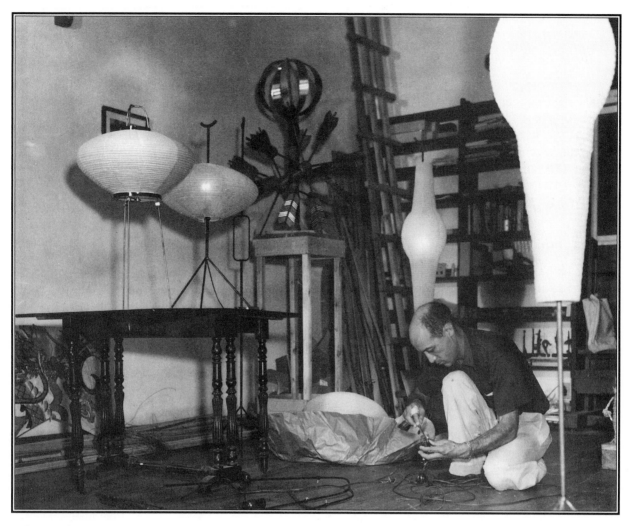

Primary Source

Isamu Noguchi, with Akari Light Sculptures

SYNOPSIS: Isamu Noguchi works on his Akari light sculptures in his shop in the 1950s. Noguchi pursued design as a more direct means of engaging with the public than by art alone. PHOTOGRAPH COURTESY OF THE ISAMU NOGUCHI FOUNDATION, INC. REPRODUCED BY PERMISSION.

and believed it could be appropriated for mid-twentieth century needs.

As he emphasized in his autobiography, Noguchi pursued design as a more direct means of engaging with the public than by art alone. His chosen medium of sculpture had a definite philosophical purpose. It was a way, through solid forms, to communicate humankind's relation to the earth and its environment. Introducing functionality to art could broaden the horizons of art itself, making it an accessible and more meaningful experience.

According to the ideals behind mid-century Modernist furniture, good design should be within the reach of the masses. Noguchi's Akari lamps have become a design classic, featured in museum collections. Reproductions of his designs are highly sought after and extremely expensive. However, in the late 1990s, the Isamu Noguchi Foundation, in Long Island City, New York, set out to revive this long-forgotten ideal. Noguchi's Akari light sculptures were introduced with lower, more affordable prices, placing them within reach of a greater number of people.

Primary Source

A Sculptor's World [excerpt]

SYNOPSIS: In his autobiography, *A Sculptor's World,* Noguchi describes his artistic journey from figurative to abstract sculptor and the inspirations behind his creations that have become icons of modern design. At the time of the publication of *A Sculptor's World* in 1968, Noguchi had a career retrospective exhibition at the Whitney Museum of American Art. Throughout his life, Noguchi constantly redefined the idea of sculpture, both for his own artistic sensibilities and for the public.

My other preoccupation at this time [1952] was the development of *akari,* the new use of lanterns that I had conceived on my previous trip. It was a logical convergence of my long interest in light sculptures, *lunars,* and my being in Japan. Paper and bamboo fitted in with my feeling for the quality and sensibility of light. Its very lightness questions materiality, and is consonant with our appreciation today of the less thingness of things, the less encumbered perceptions.

The name *akari* which I coined, means in Japanese light as illumination. It also suggests lightness as opposed to weight. The ideograph combines that of the sun and moon. The ideal of *akari* is exemplified with lightness (as essence) and light (for awareness). The quality is poetic, ephemeral, and tentative. Looking more fragile than they are *akari* seem to float, casting their light as in passing. They do not encumber our space as mass or as a possession; if they hardly exist in use, when not in use they fold away in an envelope. They perch light as a feather, some pinned to the wall, others clipped to a cord, and all may be moved with the thought.

Intrinsic to such other qualities are handmade papers and the skills that go with lantern-making. I believe *akari* to be a true development of an old tradition. The qualities that have been sought are those that were inherent to it, not as something oriental but as something we need. The superficial shapes or functions may be imitated but not these qualities. . . .

It is clear that I often craved to bring sculpture into a more direct involvement with the common experience of living. At such times I felt there must be a more direct way of contact than the rather remote one of art. Initially this may have been no more than an attempt to move beyond the narrowing horizons of artistic sensibility. It bothered me that art so soon became a style with little creation added to its production. Why should the artistic imagination be so contained, or be unequal to the broadening scope of our world awareness? I thought of function as a determinator of form, and invention of function as a possible opening to an art beyond the accepted categories. Not art? Invention is equally creation to me.

In the throw of chance, the free association and automatism of invention, the limits are those of the possible, not those of taste but of physical economy. Art might be an engineering, sculpture a structuring, functional in its purpose as art—or use, the lack of which I did not recognize as necessary to art.

I have described my very tentative attempts to design for industry, and my troubled efforts to find work through competitions or commissions, or to make work through invention as with light sculptures *(lunars)* which culminated in *akari.*

But beyond the reach of industrially realizable design or architecturally applied sculpture was, I felt, a larger, more fundamentally sculptural purpose for sculpture, a more direct expression of Man's relation to the earth and his environment.

Further Resources

BOOKS

Apostolos-Cappadona, Diane, and Bruce Altshuler, eds. *Isamu Noguchi: Essays and Conversations.* New York: H. N. Abrams in association with the Isamu Noguchi Foundation, 1994.

Ashton, Dore. *Noguchi East and West.* New York: Knopf, 1992.

Noguchi, Isamu. *Isamu Noguchi, Space of Akari and Stone.* San Francisco: Chronicle Books, 1986.

PERIODICALS

Davidsen, Judith. "Quiet Flows the Gleam of Light in Traveling Noguchi Exhibit." *Architectural Record* 182, no. 11, November 1994, 7–8.

Muschamp, Herbert. "How Noguchi Shed Light on Light Itself." *The New York Times,* July 21, 1994, C1.

Urbach, Henry. "Bodies of Light." *Interior Design* 66, no. 10, August 1995, 106–109.

WEBSITES

"Isamu Noguchi." Available online at http://isamunoguchi.com/ (accessed February 20, 2003).

"The Isamu Noguchi Garden Museum." Isamu Noguchi Foundation, Inc. Available online at http://www.noguchi.org; website home page: http://www.noguchi.org/foundation.html (accessed February 20, 2003).

Larry Rivers and Frank O'Hara

Washington Crossing the Delaware
Painting

By: Larry Rivers
Date: 1953

Source: Rivers, Larry. *Washington Crossing the Delaware.* Available online at http://www.emory.edu/ENGLISH

/Paintings&Poems/Washington.jpg; website home page: http://www.emory.edu (accessed January 31, 2003).

About the Author: Larry Rivers (1924–2002) was an artist, writer, and teacher who first made a reputation for himself as a jazz saxophonist. He came to prominence for his figurative paintings, which combined highbrow and low culture; throughout his varied career his artwork consistently defied easy categorization.

"On Seeing Larry Rivers' *Washington Crossing the Delaware* at the Museum of Modern Art"

Poem

By: Frank O'Hara

Date: 1957

Source: O'Hara, Frank. "On Seeing Larry Rivers' *Washington Crossing the Delaware* at the Museum of Modern Art." *Meditations in an Emergency.* New York: Grove, 1957, 47.

About the Author: Frank O'Hara (1926–1966) was a poet and playwright associated with the New York School. O'Hara wrote deceptively simple poems that often celebrated his artist and writer friends or the simple pleasures of everyday living. ∎

Introduction

Frank O'Hara took creative writing classes at Harvard, and moved to New York to write poetry and explore the city. He worked at the Museum of Modern Art (MoMA), selling postcards, publications, and tickets. It was an ideal situation that allowed him time to write poetry and meet fellow art enthusiasts while on the job. O'Hara met Larry Rivers at a cocktail party, and became his friend, supporter, occasional lover, and collaborator. O'Hara later was an editorial associate of *ArtNews,* a leading art magazine to which he frequently contributed. He eventually became a curator at the MoMA.

Larry Rivers, a New York native, studied at the Juilliard School of Music. He first encountered fine art when a friend showed him a Cubist painting by Georges Braque. In his memoirs *What Did I Do?: The Unauthorized Autobiography,* Rivers wrote, "I wanted to say, 'What's Cubism?' But suddenly I knew what Cubism was. Cubism told a young man from the Bronx he didn't know very much. Cubism didn't know about him or his nights walking all over Greenwich Village with his big horn slung over his shoulder, looking for a joint where he could sit and blow with a lot of other desperados. Cubism certainly didn't smoke pot or get high, Cubism was history in which he played no part. Where could I catch up?"

Around 1945, Rivers discovered he had a natural gift for painting, which he came to believe was on a "higher level" than jazz. While studying painting, Rivers met such artists as Hans Hofmann, William Baziotes, Willem

Painter Larry Rivers created *Washington Crossing the Delaware,* which inspired Frank O'Hara to write his poem. **HULTON ARCHIVE/GETTY IMAGES. REPRODUCED BY PERMISSION.**

de Kooning, and Jackson Pollock. In 1951, Rivers went to Paris to study the old masters, Courbet, and Manet. Upon his return he was struck by Leutze's *Washington Crossing the Delaware,* (1851) on view at the Metropolitan Museum of Art. Although initially disparaging of the painting for dealing with a subject that he felt was a cliche, Rivers decided to take on the same subject himself. His version of *Washington Crossing the Delaware* was seen as undermining the patriotism of Leutze's work. At the time, the Cold War and McCarthyism were at their height, and Leutze's painting had reemerged during the celebrations for the 175th anniversary of the river crossing. But Rivers' painting made Washington one of many individuals scattered about their business. He is depicted as an isolated figure, and much less heroic than in Leutze's portrayal.

Significance

Rivers was revolutionary for eschewing the meaty buildup of paint and the lush brushwork characteristic

Primary Source

Washington Crossing the Delaware

SYNOPSIS: Larry Rivers' paintings were characterized by a refusal to choose between abstraction and figuration, as evident in *Washington Crossing the Delaware*. Rivers' updated version of Emanuel Gottlieb Leutze's famous painting was a direct challenge to the prevailing style of Abstract Expressionism. © ESTATE OF LARRY RIVERS/LICENSED BY VAGA, NEW YORK, NY. © DIGITAL IMAGE. © THE MUSEUM OF MODERN ART/LICENSED BY SCALA/ART RESOURCE, NY.

of artists like de Kooning and Pollock, the decade's two most prominent Abstract Expressionist painters. Instead, Rivers used a thin wash to cover the surface of the canvas. His technique of charcoal drawing and rag wiping contributed to the deliberately unfinished look of his paintings, in which figures are simultaneously ambiguously and clearly defined. This time, it was the painters, not the public, who were outraged by the avant-garde. At Cedar Tavern, a favorite artist hangout, Rivers was sneered at by abstract painters. Siding with the painters against Rivers was Clement Greenberg, the art critic famous for his unflagging support for abstraction as the representative current of the modernist era. For Rivers, however, the painting was a personal breakthrough in finding his own language amidst the abstract expressionists.

Rivers' audacious work reintroduced to American painting a comic tone that the Abstract Expressionists severely lacked. In 1955, the MoMA purchased the painting. To Alfred H. Barr, Jr., the founding director of MoMA, *Washington Crossing the Delaware* signified a major shift in American art, a move away from abstraction and a return to figuration. O'Hara voiced his support via his poem "On Seeing Larry Rivers' *Washington Crossing the Delaware* at the Museum of Modern Art." O'Hara's verse was frequently inspired by visual art, but could be read independently of seeing the works with which they were concerned. His poetic response to Rivers' painting, for instance, can be read as a commentary on the major event in American history itself. O'Hara's poem characterizes Washington as cowardly, trigger-happy, and deceptive.

Primary Source

"On Seeing Larry Rivers' *Washington Crossing the Delaware* at the Museum of Modern Art"

> **SYNOPSIS:** Frank O'Hara, Larry Rivers' friend, was highly skeptical of the work at first but was won over and wrote a poem in response to the painting displayed at the Museum of Modern Art.

Now that our hero has come back to us
in his white pants and we know his nose
trembling like a flag under fire,
we see the calm cold river is supporting
our forces, the beautiful history.

To be more revolutionary than a nun
is our desire, to be secular and intimate
as, when sighting a redcoat, you smile
and pull the trigger. Anxieties
and animosities, flaming and feeding

on theoretical considerations and
the jealous spiritualities of the abstract
the robot? they're smoke, billows above
the physical event. They have burned up.
See how free we are! as a nation of persons.

Dear father of our country, so alive
you must have lied incessantly to be
immediate, here are your bones crossed
on my breast like a rusty flintlock,
a pirate's flag, bravely specific

and ever so light in the misty glare
of a crossing by water in winter to a shore
other than that the bridge reaches for.
Don't shoot until, the white of freedom glinting
on your gun barrel, you see the general fear.

Further Resources

BOOKS

Hunter, Sam. *Rivers.* New York: Harry N. Abrams, 1972.

O'Hara, Frank. *The Collected Poems of Frank O'Hara.* Donald M. Allen, ed. Berkeley: University of California Press, 1995.

Rivers, Larry, and Arnold Weinstein. *What Did I Do?: The Unauthorized Autobiography.* New York: HarperCollins, 1992.

PERIODICALS

Goldsmith, Barbara. "When Park Ave. Met Pop Art." *Vanity Fair,* January 2003, 98–107.

Kimmelman, Michael. "Larry Rivers, Artist with an Edge, Dies at 78." *The New York Times,* August 16, 2002, 1, B11.

Kramer, Hilton. "Does Abstract Art Have a Future?" *The New Criterion* 21, no. 4, December 2002, 9–12.

MacAdam, Barbara A. "Still Raging Rivers." *Art News* 93, no. 9, November 1994, 148–151.

WEBSITES

"Frank O'Hara 1926–1966." Prepared and compiled by Cary Nelson. Modern American Poetry. Available online at http://www.english.uiuc.edu/maps/poets/m_r/ohara/ohara .htm; website home page:http://www.english.uiuc.edu/maps /index.htm (accessed February 20, 2003).

AUDIO AND VISUAL MEDIA

Frank, Robert, and Alfred A. Leslie. *Pull My Daisy.* G String Enterprises. Videocassette, 1997.

Correspondence of Hannah Arendt and Mary McCarthy

Mary McCarthy to Hannah Arendt, August 10, 1954; Hannah Arendt to Mary McCarthy, August 20, 1954

Letters

By: Mary McCarthy and Hannah Arendt

Date: August 10 and August 20, 1954

Source: McCarthy, Mary, and Hannah Arendt. *Between Friends: The Correspondence of Hannah Arendt and Mary McCarthy, 1949–1975.* New York: Harcourt: 1996, 18–27.

About the Authors: Mary McCarthy (1912–1989) was an essayist, critic, novelist, and short story writer who developed her literary reputation writing book reviews for *The New Republic, The Nation,* and *Partisan Review.* In addition to her autobiographical novel *Memories of a Catholic Girlhood* (1957), McCarthy wrote on a wide range of topics from art history to politics.

Hannah Arendt (1906–1975), a Jewish German-American philosopher and political theorist, was one of the most important intellectual figures of her time. ∎

Introduction

Mary McCarthy and Hannah Arendt first met in 1944, at the Murray Hill Bar in Manhattan. At the time, Arendt began to extend her reputation beyond the German-Jewish émigré intellectual community, as her writing began to appear in periodicals such as *Commentary* and *Partisan Review.* Upon their meeting, McCarthy was instantly struck by Arendt's brand of "skeptical wit," but their friendship would not be sealed until they reconciled after a misunderstanding early in their relationship.

What transpired, as related by Claudia Roth Pierpont, was this: In 1945, at a New York party, in response to a conversation about the hostility of French citizens to the Germans who occupied Paris at the time, McCarthy said she felt sorry for Hitler who was so ridiculous as to expect the love of his victims. Arendt was offended, exclaiming, "How can you say such a thing in front of me—a victim of Hitler, a person who has been in a concentration camp!" Even though they often appeared at the same intellectual gatherings, they did not speak for three

Hannah Arendt, pictured, maintained a long correspondence with Mary McCarthy. THE LIBRARY OF CONGRESS.

concentration camps, Auschwitz, revolution, and school integration, among other topics.

The letters of McCarthy and Arendt are written in a conversational style that conveys news of their personal matters as well as "intellectual thought" in an almost theatrical manner. McCarthy's letters reveal her true gifts as a writer. In her essays and letters she demonstrates remarkable style and a witty voice. To some literary critics, fiction was not one of McCarthy's literary strengths, which lay instead in her keen intelligence and her powers of observation. In her reportage, essays, and letters to Arendt, McCarthy was an exciting writer with a unique style that is considered absent from her fiction.

In her political essays as well as the collected correspondence, Arendt attempted to bring philosophy "down to earth." She believed philosophy could be applied to examine not only intellectual thought, but politics and the social world. Typical of this attitude is Arendt's response to McCarthy's letter of August 20, in which McCarthy asks her friend what she makes of the "feebleminded thoughtfulness or thoughtful feeblemindedness of intellectuals." To McCarthy, modern intellectuals have a lust for argument that is mistaken for real, inner thought, the kind that comes from dialogue with oneself. To Arendt, the phenomenon gives some insight into the whys of modern alienation. She believes that this modern mode of being—this doubt—has come from a "distrust of the senses" that began with Enlightenment thinking in which reason or science could supposedly fix everything. The topic of "the senses" was a longstanding theme in the correspondence between the two women, with examples ranging from accounts of McCarthy's romantic affairs to Arendt's opinions on members of their social circle.

years, until one evening they found themselves next to each other on a subway platform. Arendt said to McCarthy: "Let's end this nonsense. We two think so much alike." McCarthy apologized for her Hitler remark, and Arendt confessed she had never been in a concentration camp, only an internment camp in France. They embarked on a friendship that lasted more than twenty-five years, until Arendt's death.

Of the two women, McCarthy was the more frequent correspondent. Her letter-writing style was more confessional and playful, while Arendt's letters are more reserved. Arendt was a philosopher whose favorite activity, as she wrote to McCarthy, was "this thinking business." In her letters she is elusive and affectionate, but objective. McCarthy always viewed her relationship with Arendt as transformative. She consulted Arendt in both moral and intellectual matters, but never hesitated to disagree with Arendt's thoughts, or point out when she felt her friend was being too obscure.

Significance

Mary McCarthy and Hannah Arendt were politically engaged and socially powerful in a circle that included W.H. Auden, Saul Bellow, Elizabeth Bishop, and dozens of other literary luminaries of the time. McCarthy and Arendt were of a moment in American intellectual history when New York dominated the intellectual life of the nation. It was a time to discuss advanced warfare,

Primary Source

Mary McCarthy to Hannah Arendt, August 10, 1954 [excerpt]

SYNOPSIS: These letters were compiled under the auspices of Mary McCarthy shortly before her death in 1989. The letters in the volume appear mostly intact, with cuts to eliminate obscure or unimportant references, to reduce repetition, and to remove material sensitive to those still living. The excerpted letters here were written in the summer of 1954, with McCarthy in Wellfleet in Cape Cod, Massachusetts, and Arendt in Palenville in the Catskills, New York.

August 10, 1954

Dear Hannah:

This is the second letter I've written you; the first I discarded as too boring. Are you and Heinrich coming up, the first part of September? I hope so,

I'm awfully eager to talk to you. At the moment, I'm dead beat with the social chatter of the Cape midsummer, gasping for air. Our defenses have somehow been breached and we've yielded to the relentless give-and-take of invitations. The early part of the summer was wonderful, but for the last three weeks we've been responding like invertebrates to the mysterious call of social duty. There are huge parties for a hundred people, outdoors. One can hear the noise and, literally, smell the fumes of alcohol half a mile off. One decides not to go, and then somehow, at the last minute, one finds oneself there, for fear of missing something. They're not even especially dissipated, they exhale a noxious boredom. . . .

. . . I've been working on my novel [*A Charmed Life*], fairly well, up till three weeks ago, when I began having visitors whom I felt I had to entertain. One thing I'm anxious to talk to you about is a problem connected with the novel, which is about bohemianized people and the dogmatization of ignorance. . . . This pseudoquesting or stupid "thoughtfulness" is getting more and more general in modern society, I think; the average man, mistrustful and cunning, is an intellectual, of sorts. He doubts, like a burlesque of a philosopher, and has a craving for information that's like the craving for sugar. I see this and am trying to describe it, but what I don't know—and would like to talk to you about—is how and when it happened, historically. I feel I have got hold of a subject that I'm not equipped to deal with. When did this ritualistic doubting begin to permeate, first, philosophy and then popular thinking? I presume that in its modern form it goes back to Kant. Or would you say Hume? My own ignorance and incapacity appall me when I consider trying to trace this thread back through the labyrinth. I want to begin reading but I don't know where to start. . . .

Philip Rahv was here and left me your manuscript which I've been reading and which I find not only very alive, like all your articles, but curiously pertinent to this topic that's oppressing me. I've also been thinking about your piece about Ideology and Terror—the section about logic, particularly. The use of logic as the prime tool of understanding is also characteristic of the "thoughtfulness" I've mentioned above. . . . There's nobody else I know who seems to be concerned with this matter, which appears to me crucial. Rahv's Marxist assurance strikes me as antediluvian; it's like talking with some fossilized mammoth. . . .

Mary McCarthy, pictured, often wrote to Hannah Arendt to discuss problems and themes with her novels. **THE LIBRARY OF CONGRESS**.

. . . Arthur Schlesinger was here, working mornings in our studio, writing a piece on the Oppenheimer case. He had the transcript and I read it. What do you think about the case? For my part, I can't see him as a security risk at all, though I don't precisely admire him. He is queer, eerie in a way, and it's that he's being punished for, plainly. People talk resentfully about his "arrogance" as if that were treasonable in a democracy. I myself wished he had been a little more arrogant during the proceedings, he was too serviable and deferential, too conformist to current opinion. He lacked political courage. And yet it makes my blood boil to hear beefy, middle-aged sultans like Herbert Solow and Allen Strook of the AJC [American Jewish Committee] condemn him for political "immaturity," like sententious pigs. I wish you would write something about it. I thought of it and laid the idea aside, my ideas were not clear enough. Rahv, as an old Marxist, opined that the case proved that intellectuals should not work for the government, it will first corrupt you and then degrade you. I rather agree with this. . . .

Well, I must stop. Please do come if you can. You don't know how I long to see you. . . .

Much love to you both,
Mary

Primary Source

Hannah Arendt to Mary McCarthy, August 20, 1954 [excerpt]

August 20, 1954

Dearest Mary—

Your letter was a real joy. Only when I got it, did I notice that I had been expecting it. Let me go into the midst of it, and leave the ends and odds for later. . . .

I am in complete agreement with you that all these people behave like burlesque philosophers because they have been put into a situation into which only philosophers throughout our history ever dared to risk themselves. The Socratic answer never worked really because this life by oneself, on which it is based, is the life of the thinker par excellence: in the activity of thought, I am together with myself—and neither with other people nor with the world as such, as the artist is. Our friends, craving for philosophic "information" (something which does not exist) are by no means "thinkers" or willing to enter the dialogue of thought with themselves. The Socratic answer would not help either. Help means here only: Cut short the argument.

As to the kind of argument that is being put up, it depends more than this general attitude on different national traditions, upbringings and so forth. . . . What both the French and the English tradition have in common and what I think is the root of modernity is the distrust in the senses which probably was the immediate result of the great discoveries of the natural sciences which demonstrated that human senses do not reveal the world as it is, but on the contrary lead men only into error. . . .

Now historically: The ritual of doubt started with Descartes and only in him will you find the original motives: the real anxiety that not God but an evil spirit is behind the whole spectacle of Being. . . .

If I may add a word of my own, independent of historical situations: The chief fallacy is to believe that Truth is a result which comes at the end of a thought-process. Truth, on the contrary, is always the beginning of thought; thinking is always result-less. That is the difference between "philosophy" and science: Science has results, philosophy never. Thinking starts after an experience of truth has struck home, so to speak. The difference between philosophers and other people is that the former refuse to let go, but not that they are the only receptacles of truth. This notion that truth is the re-

sult of thought is very old and goes back to ancient classical philosophy, possibly to Socrates himself. If I am right and it is a fallacy, then it probably is the oldest fallacy of Western philosophy. . . .

Enough of all this—which I feel is strictly not permitted me at this moment. Palenville is wonderful as ever and I was very much amused about your report on Wellfleet's society. . . .

Oppenheimer: I dislike him thoroughly, but of course he is not a security risk and the whole thing is a shame, though rather serious. In 10 years, America will have fallen behind in science and that can be a catastrophe in our age. Rahv on this point is not so wrong; one should really not work for the government. But if natural scientists wise up to this wisdom, it will be a catastrophe, and not a minor one.

I am glad you liked the essay on History. All this are odds and ends and I publish them maybe for no good reason. . . . Heinrich has a wonderful advice to give to his students when they talk about studying philosophy: he tells them you can do it only if you know that the most important thing in your life would be to succeed in this and the second most important thing, almost as important, to fail in precisely this.

I am very eagerly looking forward to seeing whatever you have of your novel [A Charmed Life] and would care to show. Needless to say, I think the sub-

---

Some Notes to The Letters of Mary McCarthy and Hannah Arendt

The manuscript McCarthy refers to may have been Arendt's essay "The Concept of History, Ancient and Modern," which later appeared as "History and Immortality" in *Partisan Review*, January 1957. Philip Rahv was a co-founder and editor of *Partisan Review*, a leading literary magazine to this day. Arthur Schlesinger was an American historian. In the summer of 1954, J. Robert Oppenheimer appeared in a number of highly publicized hearings and was eventually dismissed from the Atomic Energy Commission (AEC) and had his security clearances revoked. Oppenheimer, director of the AEC from 1947–1952, was the physicist often referred to as the "father" of the atomic bomb. After its use against Japan he was morally against developing the hydrogen bomb. Oppenheimer was considered a security risk because of this opposition as well as his early associations with left-wing groups.

ject fascinating. And let's get together soon, one way or another.

Love to both of you. Yours,
Hannah

Further Resources

BOOKS

Brightman, Carol. *Writing Dangerously: Mary McCarthy and Her World.* San Diego, Calif.: Harcourt Brace, 1994.

McCarthy, Mary. *Memories of a Catholic Girlhood.* New York: Harcourt Brace Jovanovich, 1957.

Pierpont, Claudia Roth. *Passionate Minds: Women Rewriting the World.* New York: Knopf, 2000.

PERIODICALS

Benhabib, Seyla. "A Public Life." *The Nation* 260, no. 12, March 27, 1995, 423–426.

Decter, Midge. "The Company They Kept." *Commentary* 99, no. 2, February 1995, 60–64.

WEBSITES

"The Hannah Arendt Papers: About the Collection." American Memory from the Library of Congress. Available online at http://memory.loc.gov/ammem/arendthtml/about.html; website home page: http://lcweb2.loc.gov/ammem/ (accessed February 20, 2003).

"The Mary McCarthy Papers Register Contents." Vassar College Libraries. Available online at http://library.vassar.edu/information/special-collections/mccarthy/mm_contents.html; website home page: http://library.vassar.edu/ (accessed February 20, 2003).

Pianist Glenn Gould

"Glenn Gould, Canadian Pianist"

Flyer

By: Walter Homburger
Date: January 1955
Source: Homburger, Walter. "Glenn Gould, Canadian Pianist" advertising flyer. January 1955. National Library of Canada. Available online at http://www.gould.nlc-bnc.ca/exhi/images/iii15.jpg; website home page: http://www.gould.nlc-bnc.ca (accessed June 27, 2003).

"The Prospects of Recording"

Magazine article

By: Glenn Gould
Date: 1966
Source: Gould, Glenn. "The Prospects of Recording." *High Fidelity* 16, no. 4, April 1966, 46–63.

About the Artist: Glenn Gould (1932–1982), one of the most fascinating classical music performers of the twentieth century, was born in Toronto, Canada. He entered the Royal Conservatory of music at the age of ten, graduating three years later, and made his United States debut in 1955. Though Gould's concerts were highly praised, he retired from the stage at age 32 to dedicate himself to the recording studio, as well as writing, broadcasting, composing, conducting, and experimenting with recording technology. ■

Introduction

Glenn Gould was one of the twentieth century's most unconventional classical musicians. He began playing the piano at age three, demonstrating perfect pitch and an excellent memory for music at such a young age. In 1952, he became the first pianist to be televised by a Canadian network station. He made his first American concert appearance on January 2, 1955, in Washington, DC. This was followed by his historic performance at New York City's Town Hall on January 11. The next day, Columbia Records signed Gould to an exclusive recording contract.

Gould's first recording on Columbia Records was a performance of J.S. Bach's *Goldberg Variations.* One of the most formidable monuments of keyboard literature, the *Goldberg Variations* were written in 1742 at the request of an insomniac patron who hoped Bach's music would help him fall asleep. Gould's recording of the work—which comprises 32 somber, formalistic variations on an eighteenth century song form called a sarabande—was perceived as a bold, modern interpretation. Instead of using an authentic period instrument, he performed the *Goldberg Variations* on a concert grand piano, using extreme tempos ranging from very slow to lightning fast, displaying an incredible technique. The recording has been a classical bestseller ever since its original release in June 1956, and was inducted into the National Academy of Recording Arts and Sciences Hall of Fame in 1983.

The critical praise Gould received from his two U.S. concerts and his first album instantly confirmed Gould's stature as a world-class performer. For the next nine years, he toured the world as a virtuosic concert pianist. He sometimes made controversial interpretations of classical repertoire; for instance, he performed the first movement of Beethoven's "Moonlight" Sonata much faster than other pianists did, in a way that made it sound more like a wistful dance than its typical melancholic despair.

Gould was an outstanding and eccentric musician. He was a hypochondriac—he wore gloves and an overcoat even in the summer, and always carried medication with him. He customized his Steinway grand piano to achieve a particular kind of resonance. Throughout his career, he performed hunched at the keyboard on a low chair his father had built, which Gould refused to have

Primary Source

"Glenn Gould, Canadian Pianist"

SYNOPSIS: This flyer advertises Glenn Gould's performance at the New York City Town Hall on January 11, 1955. This was Gould's first-ever performance in New York City, coming little more than a week after his American debut. Gould's brilliant performance here firmly established him as a star in the American, and world, classical music scene. **COURTESY OF THE ESTATE OF GLENN GOULD; WALTER HOMBURGER; AND THE NATIONAL LIBRARY OF CANADA.**

re-upholstered even after the original padding wore down to the bare wooden frame. When he played, Gould appeared to be lost in rapture, oblivious to the outside world. He swayed and waved a free hand as if to conduct himself. He would mouth, sing, or hum notes while performing, a habit audible in his vast body of recordings. He was reclusive, but to friends and family Gould was wonderfully charming and a brilliant conversationalist, an individual so dedicated to his music that he seemed to exist quite apart from everyday reality.

Significance

In 1964, Gould abruptly retired from public performance after a final concert in Los Angeles. He had never liked performing; it was too "vaudevillian" for his taste. Shortly thereafter, Gould prepared the written version of "The Prospects for Recording" for a special anniversary issue of *High Fidelity,* a magazine containing record reviews and articles on classical music. Gould's essay reveals his vast appetite for intellectual knowledge. To accompany his writing, Gould included commentary from notable contemporary figures in the fields of music, mass communications, and recording, such as Milton Babbitt, Leopold Stokowski, Aaron Copland, B.H. Haggin, and Marshall McLuhan. These quotations appeared in the margins of the article at appropriate points in the article, giving Gould's essay the effect of a multi-voiced conversation. He included quotations both for and against the recording of musical performance. Since he had been such a prominent figure as a concert pianist, his support of recording was especially inflammatory. Gould was an ardent supporter of splicing, a recording technique some music experts thought of as immoral and inauthentic. Gould includes a quote from Haggin, one of the skeptics and an influential music critic:

> As for the morality of splicing, I suppose there should be no objection to Toscanini's not liking what an oboe did on the first take and not liking what a flute did in the second and then taking the best parts of each take to make a whole. It's still essentially Toscanini. Whatever moral uneasiness I have about such things is just a holdover from the past and perhaps I should adapt myself to the possibilities of the present.

He also includes commentary from Richard Mohr, a musical director at RCA Victor: "Tape splicing borders on immorality because there are many artists today on the concert stage or in the opera house who cannot give you the performance in life that they can give you on records." Gould makes the case in favor of splicing by citing his own experience of recording an enormously difficult Bach fugue. For Gould, the advent of technology did not mean the extinction of the live performance, but instead, it was a way to both provide the performer with more editorial control and enhance the musical experience for the listener.

Primary Source

"The Prospects of Recording" [excerpt]

SYNOPSIS: Glenn Gould's 1965 radio script for a special 90-minute report on CBC (Canadian Broadcasting Corporation) called "The Prospects of Recording" provided the basis for this lengthy essay printed in *High Fidelity.* Drawing examples and comparisons from wide-ranging subjects, Gould's essay examines the profound effects of electronic technology on music, for the performer, composer, and listener.

I can think of few areas of contemporary endeavor that better display the confusion with which technological man evaluates the implications of his own achievements than the great debate about music and its recorded future. As is true for most of those areas in which the effect of a new technology has yet to be evaluated, an examination of the influence of recording must pertain not only to speculations about the future but to an accommodation of the past as well. . . .

As concerns its relations to the immediate past, the recording debate centers upon whether or not electronic media can present music in so viable a way as to threaten the survival of the public concert . . . I herewith reaffirm my prediction that the habit of concert-going and concert-giving, both as a social institution and as chief symbol of musical mercantilism, will be as dormant in the twenty-first century as, with luck, will Tristan da Cunha's Volcano; and that, because of its extinction, music will be able to provide a more cogent experience than is now possible. . . .

It cannot be overemphasized, however, that the fate of the public event is incidental to the future of music—a future deserving of far greater concern than is the fiscal stability of the concert hall. The influence of recordings upon that future will affect not only the performer and concert impresario but composer and technical engineer, critic and historian, as well. Most important, it will affect the listener to whom all of this activity is ultimately directed.

Change of Acoustic

If we were to take an inventory of those musical predilections most characteristic of our generation, we would discover that almost every item on such a list could be attributed directly to the influence [of] the recording. First of all, today's listeners

Glenn Gould plays the piano. © **BETTMANN/CORBIS. REPRODUCED BY PERMISSION.**

have come to associate musical performance with sounds possessed of characteristics which generations ago were neither available to the profession nor wanted by the public—characteristics such as analytic clarity, immediacy, and indeed almost tactile proximity. Within the last few decades the performance of music has ceased to be an occasion, requiring an excuse and tuxedo, and accorded, when encountered, an almost religious devotion; music has become a pervasive influence in our lives, and as our dependence upon it has increased, our reverence for it has, in a certain sense, declined. Two generations ago, concert-goers preferred that their occasional experience of music be fitted with an acoustic splendor, cavernously reverberant if possible, and pioneer recording ventures attempted to simulate the cathedral-like sound which the architects of that day tried to capture for the concert hall—the cathedral of the symphony. The more intimate terms of our experience with recordings have since suggested to us an acoustic with a direct and impartial presence, one with which we can live in our homes on rather casual terms. . . .

An Untapped Repertoire

Another item to be added to our catalogue of contemporary enthusiasms is the astonishing revival in recent years of music from preclassical times. . . .

The performer is inevitably challenged by the stimulus of this unexplored repertoire. . . . In the course of a lifetime spent in the recording studio he will necessarily encounter a wider range of repertoire than could possibly be his lot in the concert hall. The current archival approach of many recording companies demands a complete survey of the works of a given composer, and performers are expected to undertake productions of enormous scope which they would be inclined to avoid in the concert hall, and in many cases to investigate repertoire economically or acoustically unsuitable for public audition. . . .

But most important, this archival responsibility enables the performer to establish a contact with a work which is very much like that of the composer's own relation to it. It permits him to encounter a particular piece of music and to analyze and dissect it in a most thorough way, to make it a vital part of his life for a relatively brief period, and then to pass on to some other challenge and to the satisfaction of some other curiosity. . . .

The Splendid Splice

Of all the techniques peculiar to the studio recording, none has been the subject of such controversy as the tape splice. With due regard to the not so unusual phenomenon of a recording comprised of single-take sonata or symphony movements, the great majority of present-day recordings consist of a collection of tape segments varying in duration upwards from one twentieth of a second. . . . The anti-record lobby proclaims splicing a dishonest and dehumanizing technique . . . The lobbyists also claim that the common splice sabotages some unified architectural conception which they assume the performer possesses.

It seems to me that two facts challenge these objections. The first is that many of the supposed virtues of the performer's "unified conception" relate to nothing more inherently musical than the "running scared" and "go-for-broke" psychology built up through decades of exposure to the loggione of Parma and their like. . . . The second fact is that one cannot ever splice style—one can only splice segments which relate to a conviction about style. . . .

A recent personal experience will perhaps illustrate an interpretative conviction obtained post-taping. A year or so ago, while recording the concluding fugues from Volume I of the *Well-Tempered Clavier,* I arrived at one of Bach's celebrated contrapuntal obstacle courses, the Fugue in A minor. . . . In the process of recording this fugue we attempted eight takes. Two of these at the time were regarded, according to the producer's notes, as satisfactory. . . . Some weeks later, however, when the results of this session were surveyed in an editing cubicle and when Takes 6 and 8 were played several times in rapid alternation, it became apparent that both had a defect of which we had been quite unaware in the studio: both were monotonous. . . .

[S]omeone noted that, despite the vast differences in character between the two takes, they were performed at an almost identical tempo . . . and it was decided to turn this to advantage by creating one performance to consist alternately of Takes 6 and 8.

Once this decision had been made, it was a simple matter to expedite it. . . . And so two rudimentary splices were made, one which jumps from Take 6 to Take 8 in bar 14 and another which at the return to A minor . . . returns as well to Take 6. What had been achieved was a performance of this particular fugue far superior to anything that we could at the time have done in the studio. . . .

When the performer makes use of this post-performance editorial decision, his role is no longer compartmentalized. In a quest for perfection, he sets aside the hazards and compromises of his trade. As an interpreter, as a go-between serving both audience and composer, the performer has always been, after all, someone with a specialist's knowledge about the realization or actualization of notated sound symbols. It is, then, perfectly consistent with such experience that he should assume something of an editorial role. . . .

The "Live" Performance on Records

For a long time to come some portion of the industry's activity will be devoted to merchandising the celebrated masterworks which form our musical tradition. . . .

Among such occasions, none has proved more useful than the recent spate of recorded "live" performances—events which straddle two worlds and are at home in neither. These events affirm the humanistic ideal of performance; they eschew (so we are told!) splices and other mechanical adventures, and hence are decidedly "moral." . . .

Though a few companies solemnly inscribe the date of the studio sessions with each recorded package, and though the material released by most large companies can, except perhaps in the case of reissues, be related to a release number that will suggest an approximate date to the *aficionado,* it is possible that the music heard on that recording will have been obtained from sessions held weeks, months, or indeed years apart. Those sessions may easily have been held in different cities, different countries taped with different equipment and different technical personnel, and they may feature performers whose attitudes to the repertoire under consideration has metamorphosed dramatically between the taping of the first note and the last. Such a recording might currently pose insuperable contractual problems but its complicated gestation would be entirely consistent with the nature of the recording process.

It would also be consistent with that evolution of the performing musician which recording necessitates. As the performer's once sacrosanct privileges are merged with the responsibilities of the tape editor and the composer, the Van Meegeren syndrome can no longer be cited as an indictment but becomes rather an entirely appropriate description of the aesthetic condition in our time. The role of the forger, of the unknown maker of unauthenticated goods, is emblematic of electronic culture. And when the forger is done honor for his craft and no longer reviled for his acquisitiveness, the arts will have become a truly integral part of our civilization.

Further Resources

BOOKS

Gould, Glenn. *The Glenn Gould Reader.* New York: Vintage Books, 1990.

Payzant, Geoffrey. *Glenn Gould: Music & Mind.* Toronto: Key Porter, 1992.

Sachs, Harvey. *Virtuoso: The Life and Art of Niccolo Paganini, Franz Liszt, Anton Rubinstein, Ignace Jan Paderewski, Fritz Kreisler, Pablo Casals, Wanda Landowska, Vladimir Horowitz, Glenn Gould.* London: Thames and Hudson, 1982.

PERIODICALS

Clinch, Dermot. "Pure Gould." *New Statesman,* 128, no. 4467, December 20, 1999, 105–107.

Rothstein, Edward. "Glenn Gould's Legacy: A Persistent State of Awe." *The New York Times,* September 28, 2002, B9.

WEBSITES

F minor: A Mailing List Devoted to the Discussion of Glenn Gould. Available online at http://www.rci.rutgers.edu /~mwatts/glenn/fminor.html; website home page: http://www .rci.rutgers.edu/ (accessed February 22, 2003).

"Glenn Gould.com." Available online at http://www.glenngould .com (accessed February 22, 2003).

AUDIO AND VISUAL MEDIA

"The Goldberg Variations." *Glenn Gould Plays Bach.* Sony Classical 64226. CD, 1999.

Art and Life of Lee Krasner

Prophecy

Painting

By: Lee Krasner

Date: 1956

Source: Krasner, Lee. *Prophecy.* 1956. In the collection of Robert Miller Gallery, New York. Available online at http:// naples.cc.sunysb.edu/CAS/pkhouse.nsf/prophecy.jpg ?OpenImageResource; website home page: http://naples .cc.sunysb.edu/CAS/PKHouse.nsf/pages/krasner (accessed June 6, 2003).

"A Conversation with Lee Krasner"

Interview

By: Lee Krasner

Date: 1973

Source: Nemser, Cindy. "A Conversation with Lee Krasner." *Feminist Art Journal,* 1973. Reprinted in *Art Talk: Conversations with Twelve Women Artists.* New York: Charles Scriber's Sons, 1975, 91–97.

About the Artist: Lee Krasner (1908–1984) was born in Brooklyn, New York. Her parents were Russian Orthodox Jews who had emigrated to the United States and ran a grocery store. Krasner studied art in the New York area and by the 1930s her painting career was beginning to take off. Krasner was known for her keen intelligence and acerbic wit in New York's artistic circles. By the 1940s and 1950s, Krasner's mature works came to be largely associated with Abstract Expressionism. ■

Introduction

Lee Krasner studied art at Cooper Union, National Academy of Design, and with painter Hans Hofmann, who introduced her to abstraction. Krasner's earliest works were self-portraits done in a figurative or illustrative style. She was inspired by early modernist painters such as Henri Matisse, Pablo Picasso, Joan Miro, and Piet Mondrian. Krasner developed her own visual language by combining these influences with the innovations of Abstract Expressionism, which had begun to take root in American painting in the 1940s and became the dominant painting mode of the 1950s.

Abstract Expressionist paintings were characterized by an all-over intensity, unlike previous painting that limited pictorial energy to specific focal points. Abstract Expressionist painters attacked the canvas to create mostly non-representational works in which the emotional impact came from the marks made by the artist. Krasner noted that she wanted the struggle of painting to be visible in her pictures.

Krasner met painter Jackson Pollock in 1941 and they were married until his death in a car accident in 1956. Pollock was the most famous Abstract Expressionist artist, known as much for his flamboyant personality as his brash drip-paintings. He was difficult, unfaithful, and alcoholic. Krasner's intense relationship with Pollock made her personal artistic success much harder. She was aware of this, stating to newspaper reporter Rebecca Gratz, "I was not the average woman married to the average painter . . . I was married to Jackson Pollock. The context is bigger and even if I was not personally dominated by Pollock, the whole world was." To Louise Rago, Krasner said, "Unfortunately, it was most fortunate to know Jackson Pollock."

Significance

After Pollock's death, Krasner's work changed. Her painting reached a new level of maturity in the 1950s.

also continued to explore abstraction even as Abstract Expressionism began to fall out of favor in the 1960s and beyond. Krasner thrived on challenge, making raw, riotous paintings in the midst of Minimalism and Pop. Since then her work has been reassessed and awarded major retrospectives that were rare for women artists in the 1950s. Her first major recognition as a key participant in Abstract Expressionism came in 1978, when she was included in the Whitney Museum of American Art's exhibition *Expressionism: The Formative Years.* In 2000, the Brooklyn Museum mounted a traveling retrospective of Lee Krasner.

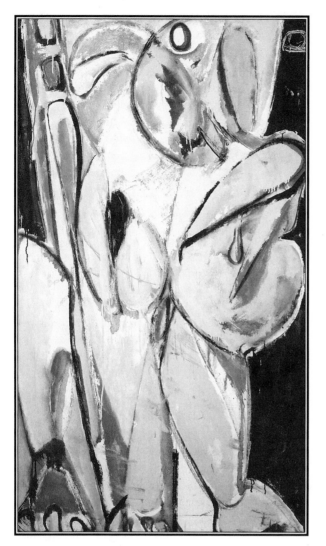

Primary Source

Prophecy

SYNOPSIS: Lee Krasner's *Prophecy.* In 1956 Krasner went to Europe and left the painting on her easel unfinished. While she was abroad Jackson Pollock was killed in a car crash. Krasner returned after the tragedy and completed the work. © 2003 THE POLLOCK-KRASNER FOUNDATION/ARTISTS RIGHTS SOCIETY (ARS), NEW YORK. COURTESY ROBERT MILLER GALLERY, NEW YORK.

She began to make collages made from cutups of her old paintings and drawings, works that she made in the 1930s. The canvases were larger and bolder than ever. Shapes that she had experimented with earlier returned with a greater ferocity. She used thick black strokes to outline the split-moon shapes and leaf-like forms that appeared throughout her pictures. In a sense, these abstract paintings were even more biographical than the self-portraits Krasner began with.

Lee Krasner's work matured in a time when women artists were largely ignored by the art establishment. She

Primary Source

"A Conversation with Lee Krasner" [excerpt]

SYNOPSIS: Lee Krasner was interviewed by journalist Cindy Nemser in 1973. The interview, "A Conversation with Lee Krasner," was first published in *The Feminist Art Journal,* a periodical edited by Cindy Nemser. This interview was included in *Art Talk: Conservations with Twelve Women Artists* along with contemporaries such as Grace Hartigan, Marisol, Alice Neel, and Eleanor Antin. Krasner's answers were carefully scripted and edited for approval before publication.

C.N.: It must have been hard for you to have been married to an artist like Pollock who was getting so much attention and then to have people seeing you, a serious painter in your own right, as the wife who was supposed to stay in the background. You must have been torn between wanting him to succeed and reaching out to discover your own identity.

L.K.: If you remember my family background, I didn't get much encouragement. This was another tough nut to crack. It was self-imposed and I'm aware of that. Since no one asked me to live with Pollock, and since I wanted my independence as well, I damn well have to deal with it.

C.N.: Many people have told me that you gave Pollock a great deal of your time and attention.

L.K.: Of course and continue to. Right up until today Pollock takes a lot of my time.

C.N.: How much did it take out of you?

L.K.: I wouldn't know. And while you ask, "How much did it take out of me as a creative artist?" I ask simultaneously, "What did it give?" It is a two-way affair at all times. I would give anything to have someone giving me what I was able to give Pollock.

Artist Lee Krasner, right, poses with her husband Jackson Pollock. © BURCKHARDT RUDOLPH/CORBIS SYGMA. REPRODUCED BY PERMISSION.

C.N.: Since you didn't have an exhibition of your paintings, was there a response to them?

L.K.: There was response. I didn't feel as though I were isolated. John B. Meyers admired my "Little Image" paintings and I can remember Clement Greenberg saying about an early one, "That's hot. It's cooking." I considered it a compliment. John Little, John Brooks, Linda Lindeberg, and Tomlin were others who saw the works and admired them. There wasn't time to do anything about the fact that I wasn't getting public recognition and showing. I was painting, Pollock was breaking through. We had our hands full. I couldn't take time off and say, "Look here. Why am I not being seen?" I didn't function that way.

C.N.: You also didn't have the support you needed. At that time there was no women's liberation movement.

L.K.: That's right. I couldn't run out and do a one-woman job on the sexist aspects of the art world, continue my painting, and stay in the role I was in as Mrs. Pollock. I just couldn't do that much. What I considered important was that I was able to work and other things would have to take their turn. You have to brush a lot of stuff out of the way or you get lost in the jungle. Now rightly or wrongly I made my decisions.

C.N.: Do you think it was easier for women like Frankenthaler, Mitchell, and Hartigan?

L.K.: They are the next generation and it is another scene—another story. You forget that in my generation Paris was still the leading school of painting and this situation was being changed by a tiny handful of artists to a scene called New York, America, which never before had a leading role in the art world. That didn't happen just by reading a newspaper. Now the next generation comes in and they may think it is rough for them but it is pie compared to what we went through. We broke the ground.

C.N.: It was still rough for women but *you* had to fight for everything—being an American artist and a woman artist at the same time.

L.K.: And as Mrs. Pollock it intensified that problem. Let's put it this way: Pollock being the figure he was in the art world it was a rough role seen from any view.

C.N.: How about the running of your household? Was that all on your shoulders?

L.K.: No. Jackson shared a lot of it. Certainly I took the bulk of it but I did not have a husband who had to be waited on at all times. He perhaps favored the outdoor work and I had to do the indoor. But I think we shared. And if I needed special assistance, I asked for it, and as a rule, I got it.

C.N.: How did Pollock react when you asked him to come up and look at your work? Did he act as if he were doing you a favor?

L.K.: No. It wasn't like that. It was like, "Not now, later." But he is the one who would pull me out of a state when I would say, "the work has changed and I can't stand it. It's just like so and so's work." Then he would come and look and say, "You're crazy. It is nothing like so and so's work. Just continue painting and stop hanging yourself up." We had that kind of support.

C.N.: Then Jackson wasn't afraid of your being successful? He didn't see you as a competitor?

L.K.: On the contrary, he asked Betty Parsons to come and see my work and she gave me my first New York solo show in 1951.

C.N.: But you never did get to show the "Little Image" paintings in New York.

L.K.: Not in New York, though some of them were shown in a bookshop in East Hampton. By the time Betty scheduled my New York show, the work had broken into a totally different image and I showed what I was doing then. . . .

L.K.: In July '56 there was another break in the work. There is a painting called *Prophecy* which I did just before I left for Europe. Every time the work broke it sent me into a tailspin because I couldn't tell what was happening. I asked Jackson to come and look at this painting and he did and said I needn't be nervous about it. He thought it was a good painting and the only thing he objected to was this image in the upper right hand which I had scratched in with the back of a brush. It made a kind of an eye form. He advised me to take it out. I said that I didn't agree with him and left it in, as you can see.

C.N.: You reacted to your own painting as if it came from some unknown place.

L.K.: It's not the source that shocked me, it's the change that I had to get used to and accept. It frightened me.

C.N.: I remember reading that after Henri Rousseau painted his jungle scenes he became so frightened he had to run out of the house.

L.K.: I didn't run out of the house but it frightened me, particularly because it happened just before I left for Europe. Jackson looked at it, said what he said, and I went off to Europe. Jackson was killed in the automobile accident while I was there and when I came back I had to confront myself with this painting before I was able to start again. I went through a rough period in that confrontation.

C.N.: It's a very powerful painting with rather monstrous forms. It's primeval. It drags up something from the unconscious.

L.K.: I felt that at the time and it frightened me. It took me quite some time to adjust to it.

C.N.: Were you involved with Jungian concepts or Jungian imagery at all at that time?

L.K.: No, in that sense, no. I hadn't had Jungian analysis, but I had read material by Jung and I knew Jackson had worked with Jungian analysis. I was somewhat sympathetic, but it was a fringe interest. I had had one year of analysis at the time I painted *Prophecy*. It was a splinter group from the Sullivan school and if one must separate Jung and Freud, this would be in the direction of Freud. So when you say I was dragging something up, and obviously I

was, very much so, it frightened me. It was coming through a source, but I didn't know what that source was.

C.N.: Then comes a series of paintings in the spirit of *Prophecy*.

L.K.: *Prophecy* was painted before Jackson died and these were the first to appear afterwards. As you can see the eye is really coming through now. That's why I wanted to mention it in relation to *Prophecy*.

C.N.: There seems in these paintings to be a representation of the essential male-female confrontation, even in the titles, *Three in Two, Embrace, Birth*.

L.K.: Remember what happened to me in my personal life at this point. There are certain factual things that cannot be denied—the date of the painting, the kind of paintings that preceded it, the kind of paintings that happen later. But again I don't see how you can separate these things out.

C.N.: Now recognizable images appear again. Did you do many of these paintings?

L.K.: Just a handful and they are all murky and dense grays.

C.N.: Some critics have said that this series is the beginning of Lee Krasner as an independent painter. They feel that only after Pollock's death were you able to be yourself.

L.K.: Where have I not been Lee Krasner prior to that? I don't understand that point of view. It is an outside point of view and I am not in touch with it.

C.N.: It implies that you couldn't be free or yourself until you moved out from the orbit of Pollock's influence.

L.K.: Hogwash is my answer to that kind of thinking. Esthetically I am very much Lee Krasner. I am undergoing emotional, psychological, and artistic changes but I hold Lee Krasner right through.

Further Resources

BOOKS

Friedman, B.H. "Introduction." In *Lee Krasner Paintings, Drawings and Collages*. London: Whitechapel Gallery, 1965.

Landau, Ellen G. *Lee Krasner: A Catalogue Raisonné*. New York: Abrams, 1995.

Lippard, Lucy. *From the Center: Feminist Essays on Women's Art*. New York: Dutton, 1976.

Wagner, Anne M. "Fictions: Krasner's Presence, Pollock's Absence." In *Significant Others: Creativity & Intimate Partnership*. Edited by Whitney Chadwick and Isabelle de Courtivron. London: Thames and Hudson, 1993.

PERIODICALS

Baker, Kenneth. "More than Mrs. Pollock: Considering the Many Sides of Lee Krasner." *Art News* 98, no. 8, September 1999, 132–134.

Brach, Paul. "Lee Krasner: Front and Center." *Art in America* 89, no. 2, 90–100.

Chave, Anna C. "Pollock and Krasner: Script and Postscript." *Res* 24, Autumn 1993, 95–111.

Gratz, Rebecca Brandes. "Daily Close-up: After Pollock." *The New York Post,* December 6, 1973.

Rago, Louise. "We Interview Lee Krasner." *School Arts,* September 1960, 32.

WEBSITES

"Lee Krasner." Pollock-Krasner House and Study Center. Stony Brook University. Available online at http://naples.cc.sunysb .edu/CAS/pkhouse.nsf/pages/krasner; website home page: http://www.stonybrook.edu/ (accessed February 24, 2003).

"Lee Krasner." Robert Miller Gallery. http://www.robertmiller gallery.com/Krasner_Main.htm; website home page: http:// www.robertmillergallery.com/(accessed February 24, 2003).

"On a Book Entitled *Lolita*"

Essay

By: Vladimir Nabokov

Date: June 1957

Source: Nabokov, Vladimir. "On a Book Entitled *Lolita.*" *The Anchor Review,* June 1957. Reprinted in *Lolita.* New York: Vintage Books, 1989, 311–315.

About the Author: Vladimir Nabokov (1899–1977) was born in St. Petersburg, Russia, and was educated in Western Europe. He wrote his early poetry, short stories, and novels in Russian. Emigrating to the United States in 1940, Nabokov published his first book in English, *The Real Life of Sebastian Knight,* the following year. His best-known novel, *Lolita,* created much controversy and is considered a twentieth-century classic. Nabokov taught literature at Wellesley, Stanford, and Cornell between 1941 and 1959. He was also an eminent lepidopterist (one who studies butterflies). He died in Montreux, Switzerland. ∎

Introduction

Nabokov's story of the affair between a middle-aged male and a twelve-year-old girl has secured *Lolita* a place in pop mythology. In the novel, the protagonist and perpetrator Humbert Humbert, a European man in his late thirties, arrives in a quiet New England town. He takes a room in the house of a Mrs. Haze and her daughter, Dolores Haze. The narrator perceives her as "Lolita," the sexually

precocious adolescent whom he adores. After an accident eliminates Mrs. Haze, Humbert becomes Lolita's legal guardian. The two begin an affair, mostly consisting of a series of car trips across the country. The novel's climax occurs when Lolita escapes with a playwright who has been shadowing them all along, and culminates with Humbert's eventual revenge on this rival lover.

In his concluding essay "On a Book Entitled *Lolita,*" Nabokov warns that readers merely seeking an erotic thrill in *Lolita* will be severely disappointed. He points out that there is not a single obscene term in the book. Its sexual content is often shrouded in Nabokov's fancy prose style, or explicated in a comic tone. By turns a love story, a comedy, and a tragedy, *Lolita* is a work of fiction in which its "place"—the American landscape—is everything to the narrative.

Nabokov wrote *Lolita* while butterfly hunting throughout the United States in the early 1950s. Like each of his works, he wrote out the manuscript longhand on thousands of index cards, which his wife and partner Vera carefully typed. The book was completed in Ithaca, New York, in 1954, but rejected by American publishers afraid of censorship.

Significance

Olympia Press, based in Paris, agreed to publish *Lolita* in 1955. The catalog of Olympia Press ran the gamut from English-language paperback "dirty books" to milestones in postwar literature such as William S. Burroughs's *Naked Lunch,* Pauline Réage's *Story of O,* and works by Samuel Beckett, Henry Miller, and Jean Genet. Ironically, *Lolita* was banned in France but met with no objections from U.S. Customs.

In addition to its literary merits, *Lolita* holds a significant place in publishing history, appearing in what is considered the golden age of literary paperback publishing. Olympia Press stayed afloat financially thanks to its erotic titles, which were distributed worldwide through an audience of American servicemen and tourists. The "legitimate" works of literature, often too controversial for other publishers, thus also found a means of distribution. This was the case with *Lolita,* celebrated by readers on both sides of the Atlantic.

Lolita is Nabokov's most "American" novel. It is an example of travel literature like its contemporary *On the Road* by Jack Kerouac (published in 1957). In Nabokov's story, the two fugitives make multiple cross-country road trips, mapped out in detail. Along the way, Humbert indulges all of Lolita's adolescent desires, from comic books to records and magazines. His description of everything she holds dear is like a catalog of fifties popular culture.

The success of *Lolita* secured Nabokov's international literary reputation, but *Lolita*'s 1956 publication in

The Anchor Review was the book's first opportunity for widespread distribution among American readers. Jason Epstein, the magazine's editor, prepared the excerpts of *Lolita* with Nabokov's approval. Nabokov contributed his essay "On a Book Entitled *Lolita*," describing his efforts to find a publisher. He also asserts that *Lolita* is simply a story that had long been burning in his imagination that he needed to get off his chest. Like the novel, the concluding essay brims with dense allusions to other texts and other subjects.

Primary Source

"On a Book Entitled *Lolita*," [excerpt]

SYNOPSIS: After much controversy, *Lolita* was finally published in the United States by *The Anchor Review,* a literary magazine under the imprint of Doubleday, which refused to print the book itself. Accompanying *The Anchor Review* excerpt was an essay "On a Book Entitled *Lolita*" that Nabokov had written especially for the magazine. The essay describes *Lolita*'s origins and the book's "invented" America. It was not until 1958 that the entirety of *Lolita* was finally printed by an American publisher, Putnam. Nabokov's essay has been included in many editions of *Lolita* since then.

Vladimir Nabokov authored the book *Lolita.* © BETTMANN/CORBIS. REPRODUCED BY PERMISSION.

The first little throb of *Lolita* went through me in late 1939 or early in 1940, in Paris, at a time when I was laid up with a severe attack of intercostal neuralgia. As far as I can recall, the initial shiver of inspiration was somehow prompted by a newspaper story about an ape in the Jardin des Plantes, who, after months of coaxing by a scientist, produced the first drawing ever charcoaled by an animal: this sketch showed the bars of the poor creature's cage. The impulse I record had no textual connection with the ensuing train of thought, which resulted, however, in a prototype of my present novel, a short story some thirty pages long. I wrote it in Russian . . . The man was a Central European, the anonymous nymphet was French, and the loci were Paris and Provence. I had him marry the little girl's sick mother who soon died, and after a thwarted attempt to take advantage of the orphan in a hotel room, Arthur (for that was his name) threw himself under the wheels of a truck . . . but I was not pleased with the thing and destroyed it sometime after moving to America in 1940.

Around 1949, in Ithaca, upstate New York, the throbbing, which had never quite ceased, began to plague me again. Combination joined inspiration with fresh zest and involved me in a new treatment of the theme, this time in English . . . The nymphet, now with a dash of Irish blood, was really much the same lass, and the basic marrying-her-mother idea also subsisted; but otherwise the thing was new and had grown in secret the claws and wings of a novel.

The book developed slowly, with many interruptions and asides. It had taken me some forty years to invent Russia and Western Europe, and now I was faced by the task of inventing America. . . . Once or twice I was on the point of burning the unfinished draft and had carried my Juanita Dark as far as the shadow of the leaning incinerator on the innocent lawn, when I was stopped by the thought that the ghost of the destroyed book would haunt my files for the rest of my life.

Every summer my wife and I go butterfly hunting. . . . It was at such of our headquarters in Telluride, Colorado; Afton, Wyoming; Portal, Arizona; and Ashland, Oregon, that *Lolita* was energetically resumed in the evenings or on cloudy days. I finished copying the thing out in longhand in the spring of 1954, and at once began casting around for a publisher.

At first, on the advice of a wary old friend, I was meek enough to stipulate that the book be brought out anonymously. I doubt that I shall ever regret that soon afterwards, realizing how likely a mask was to betray my own cause, I decided to sign *Lolita*. The four American publishers, W, X, Y, Z, who in turn were offered the typescript and had their readers glance at it, were shocked by *Lolita* to a degree that even my wary old friend F. P. had not expected. . . .

Certain techniques at the beginning of *Lolita* (Humbert's Journal, for example), misled some of my first readers into assuming that this was going to be a lewd book. They expected the rising succession of erotic scenes; when these stopped, the readers stopped too, and felt bored and let down. This, I suspect, is one of the reasons why not all the four firms read the typescript to the end. Whether they found it pornographic or not did not interest me. Their refusal to buy the book was based not on my treatment of the theme but on the theme itself, for there are at least three themes which are utterly taboo as far as most American publishers are concerned. The two others are: a Negro-White marriage which is a complete and glorious success resulting in lots of children and grandchildren; and the total atheist who lives a happy and useful life, and dies in his sleep at the age of 106.

Some of the reactions were very amusing: one reader suggested that his firm might consider publication if I turned my Lolita into a twelve-year-old lad and had him seduced by Humbert, a farmer, in a barn, amidst gaunt and arid surroundings, all this set forth in short, strong, "realistic" sentences ("He acts crazy. We all act crazy, I guess. I guess God acts crazy." Etc.). . . . Publisher X, whose advisers got so bored with Humbert that they never got beyond page 188, had the naïveté to write me that Part Two was too long. Publisher Y, on the other hand, regretted there were no good people in the book. Publisher Z said if he printed *Lolita,* he and I would go to jail. . . .

There are gentle souls who would pronounce *Lolita* meaningless because it does not teach them anything. I am neither a reader nor a writer of didactic fiction, and, despite John Ray's assertion, *Lolita* has no moral in tow. For me a work of fiction exists only insofar as it affords me what I shall bluntly call aesthetic bliss, that is a sense of being somehow, somewhere, connected with other states of being where art (curiosity, tenderness, kindness, ecstasy) is the norm. There are not many such books. . . .

Another charge which some readers have made is that *Lolita* is anti-American. This is something that

---

An Excerpt from *Lolita*

Mentally, I found her to be a disgustingly conventional little girl. Sweet hot jazz, square dancing, gooey fudge sundaes, musicals, movie magazines, and so forth—these were the obvious items in her list of beloved things. The Lord knows how many nickels I fed to the gorgeous music boxes that came with every meal we had! I still hear the nasal voices of those invisibles serenading her, people with names like Samy and Jo and Eddy and Tony and Peggy and Guy and Patty and Rex, and sentimental song hits, all of them as similar to my ear as her various candies were to my palate . . . She it was to whom ads were dedicated: the ideal consumer, the subject and object of every foul poster.

---

pains me considerably more than the idiotic accusation of immorality. Considerations of depth and perspective (a suburban lawn, a mountain meadow) led me to build a number of North American sets. I needed a certain exhilarating milieu. Nothing is more exhilarating than philistine vulgarity. But in regard to philistine vulgarity there is no intrinsic difference between Palearctic manners and Nearctic manners. Any proletarian from Chicago can be as bourgeois (in the Flaubertian sense) as a duke. I chose American motels instead of Swiss motels or English inns only because I am trying to be an American writer and claim only the same rights that other American writers enjoy. On the other hand, my creature Humbert is a foreigner and an anarchist, and there are many things, besides nymphets, in which I disagree with him. And all my Russian readers know that my old worlds—Russian, British, German, French—are just as fantastic and personal as my new one is.

Further Resources

BOOKS

Boyd, Brian. *Vladimir Nabokov: The American Years.* Princeton, NJ: Princeton University Press, 1991.

Johnson, Donald B. *Worlds in Regression: Some Novels of Vladimir Nabokov.* Ann Arbor, MI: Ardis, 1985.

Pifer, Ellen, ed. *Vladimir Nabokov's "Lolita": A Casebook.* New York: Oxford University Press, 2003.

PERIODICALS

Angell, Roger. "Lo Love, High Romance." *The New Yorker,* August 25, 1997, 156–159.

Castronovo, David. "Humbert's America." *New England Review* 23, no. 2, Spring 2002, 33–42.

Rolo, Charles. "*Lolita,* by Vladimir Nobokov." *The Atlantic Monthly* 202, no. 3, September 1958, 78.

WEBSITES

"Beyond *Lolita*: Discovering Nabokov on His Centennial." CNN. Available online at http://www.cnn.com/SPECIALS /books/1999/nabokov/; website home page: http://www.cnn .com (accessed Feburary 21, 2003).

Lombreglia, Ralph. "The Believer." Atlantic Unbound, January 18, 2001. Available online at http://www.theatlantic .com/unbound/digitalreader/dr2001-01-18.htm; website home page: http://www.theatlantic.com (accessed February 21, 2003).

"The Vladimir Nabokov Appreciation Site." Waxwing. Available online at http://www.fulmerford.com/waxwing/nabokov .html; website home page, http://www.fulmerford.com (accessed February 21, 2003).

"Zembla." International Vladimir Nabokov Society. Available online at http://www.libraries.psu.edu/iasweb/nabokov/zembla .htm; website home page: http://www.libraries.psu.edu (accessed February 21, 2003).

"Choreography and the Dance"

Interview

By: Merce Cunningham

Date: 1970

Source: Cunningham, Merce. "Choreography and the Dance." *The Creative Experience*. Edited by Stanley Rossner and Lawrence E. Abt. New York: Grossman, 1970. Reprinted in Celant Germano, ed. *Merce Cunningham*. Milan, Italy: Edizioni Charta, 1999, 42–49.

About the Artist: Merce Cunningham (1919–) has been directing and choreographing for more than fifty years. He began his dance education in Seattle, Washington, and was a solo dancer in Martha Graham's company when he first arrived in New York City in 1939. Eventually he left Graham's company to pursue his own ideas of dance. He began to choreograph his dances, and formed the Merce Cunningham Dance Company at Black Mountain College in the summer of 1953. Since then Cunningham has created nearly two hundred works for his company as well as for the New York City Ballet, American Ballet Theatre, and others. ∎

Introduction

Merce Cunningham left Martha Graham's company around 1945. Graham was part of the dance vanguard of the fifties that also included Doris Humphrey, Charles Weidman, and José Limón. Cunningham turned away from "modern" dance of the kind pioneered by Graham. Beginning in the 1920s, Graham had revolutionized modern dance by introducing literary or narrative content. She often used dance to illustrate a political or social commentary. In contrast, Cunningham emphasized a return to the idea of dance as pure movement. Rather than mak-

ing dances derived from ideas or images, Cunningham developed a movement vocabulary that expressed the human body's triumphs and limitations. His dancers were known for their agility and physical strength. His dances appear to consist of free-form movements, with an element of chaos.

In 1953 Merce Cunningham formed his own company, the Merce Cunningham Dance Company (MCDC), when he brought a group of dancers who had been working with him in New York to Black Mountain College, near Asheville, North Carolina. Black Mountain was a progressive liberal arts school renowned as a hotbed of artistic activity. For instance, it was at Black Mountain just the year before that legendary avant-garde composer John Cage presented a theatrical event described as the first "Happening." His *Theatre Piece No. 1* consisted of simultaneous performances of piano music by David Tudor, improvised dance by Cunningham, a poetry reading by M.C. Richards perched from a ladder, and a lecture given by Cage, all set in an environment of slide projections and films with paintings by Robert Rauschenberg hanging from the ceiling. This activity happened not on a stage, but with the audience interspersed throughout, thereby eliminating the traditional division between performers and audience members. John Cage was MCDC's music director from its inception until his death in 1992.

Significance

In this 1970 interview, Cunningham outlines the key points of his dance philosophy that took root in the earliest days of his independent career. To Cunningham, improvisation and experimental collaboration are key parts of his artistic process. He has worked with creative figureheads throughout the decades, from John Cage to cutting-edge fashion designer Rei Kawakubo. Robert Rauschenberg was the company's resident visual designer from 1954 to 1964. Other visual artists he has worked with include Jasper Johns, Frank Stella, Andy Warhol, and Robert Morris. Cunningham has always embraced the latest technologies and applied them to dance works. In the 1970s, for instance, he began to experiment with video, and in the late 1990s he created dances incorporating the newest Internet technologies.

Merce Cunningham's earliest dance innovations were a direct result of his relationship with John Cage. Cunningham and Cage introduced numerous radical ideas about the relationship between musical and choreographic composition. In this interview, Cunningham discusses how a dancer should not have to synchronize her or his movements to the rhythm or the nuances of the music. In fact, Cunningham's dancers are famous for often rehearsing a work in silence, and hearing its music for the first time only at the dress rehearsal or even the first performance. Cunningham emphasizes that despite this independence of dance and music, his dances are still highly structured.

Cunningham has also abandoned other conventions of dance structure such as conflict and resolution, cause and effect, or telling stories through dance. Instead, he achieves drama in his dances through a combination of the kinetic movements of his dancers and a theatrical experience for the viewer. In the past this has included bright lights directed to shine on the audience, microphones attached to potted plants on the stage that would produce sounds when touched by the dancers, or pieces of canvas placed on the floor for the dancers to "fall" on. Importantly, Cunningham's dancers are only portraying themselves on stage. They are not actors dancing in the guise of a fictional character. To Cunningham, regarding the dancer on stage, "you are not necessarily at your best, but at your most human."

Primary Source

"Choreography and the Dance"

SYNOPSIS: By the time of this interview, Merce Cunningham had been at the forefront of avant-garde dance in America for more than twenty years. Here, he outlines his approach to dance-making that has consistently centered around movement, the use of chance elements in choreography, and collaboration with other artists.

Mr. Cunningham, could you describe your approach to dance?

In my choreographic work, the basis for the dances is movement, that is, the human body moving in time-space. The scale for this movement ranges from being quiescent to the maximum amount of movement (physical activity) a person can produce at any given moment. The ideas of the dance come both from the movement, and are in the movement. It has no reference outside of that. A given dance does not have its origin in some thought I might have about a story, a mood, or an expression; rather, the proportions of the dance come from the activity itself. Any idea as to mood, story, or expression entertained by the spectator is a product of his mind, of his feelings; and he is free to act with it. So in starting to choreograph, I begin with movements, steps, if you like, in working by myself or with the members of my company, and from that, the dance continues.

This is a simplified statement, describing something that can take many work-hours daily for weeks and months, but it is essentially a process of watching and working with people who use movement as a force of life, not as something to be explained by reference, or used as illustration, but as something, if not necessarily grave, certainly constant in life. What is fascinating and interesting in movement, is, though we are all two-legged creatures, we all move differently, in accordance with our physical proportions as well as our temperaments. It is this that interests me. Not the sameness of one person to another, but the difference, not a corps de ballets, but a group of individuals acting together.

This non-reference of the movement is extended into a relationship with music. It is essentially a non-relationship. The dance is not performed to the music. For the dances that we present, the music is composed and performed as a separate identity of itself. It happens to take place at the same time as the dance. The two co-exist, as sight and sound do in our daily lives. And with that, the dance is not dependent upon the music. This does not mean I would prefer to dance in silence (although we have done that, on one notable occasion an entire program owing to a union dispute) because it would strike me as daily life without sound. I accept sound as one of the sensory areas along with sight, the visual sense.

What are the origins of the shapes and movements you find for your dancers?

. . . As you see, I am interested in experimenting with movements. Oh, I may see something out of the corner of my eye—the slight way a person climbs a curb, the special attack of a dancer to a familiar step in class, an unfamiliar stride in a sportsman, something I don't know about, and then I try it. Children do amazing kinds of motions, and one wonders how they got into that particular shape. . . .

In training, my concern has been to make the body as flexible, strong, and resilient as possible, and in as many directions as I could find. The human body is the instrument that dancing deals with. The human body moves in limited ways, very few actually. There are certain physical things it can't do that another animal might be able to do. But within the body's limitations, I wanted to be able to accept all the possibilities. I also felt that dancing concerned with states of mind involved one with one's own personal problems and feelings, which often had little or nothing to do with the possibilities in dancing; and I became more interested in opening that out to society and relating it to the contemporary scene, rather than hedging it in.

That was surely one of the reasons I began to use random methods in choreography, to break out

Merce Cunningham, center, a pioneer in modern dance, rehearses a routine with his dance group. © **CHARLES E. ROTKIN/CORBIS. REPRODUCED BY PERMISSION.**

the patterns of personal remembered physical co-ordinations. Other ways were then seen as possible. When I talk about these ideas of chance to students, they ask if something comes up you don't like, do you discard it? No, rather than using a principle of likes and dislikes, I prefer to try whatever comes up, to be flexible about it rather than fixed. If I can't handle it, perhaps another dancer can, and further there's always the possibility of extending things by the use of movies or visual electronics. I did not want the work turned in, preferably turned out, like dancers. . . .

It would be erroneous to think that my work is not structured. It's clearly structured, but in a different way. The structure is in time, rather than themes or through an idea. It's not dissimilar to the way continuity in television acts. Television shows fit the time between the commercials, which are spaced so many within the allotted half or hour period. TV has trouble with movies and commercials, as the movies were made another way. Composers now write for the length of recordings. They gear the composition to be within the time of a record. The expression fits the time.

In my work a dance may be forty-nine minutes long, and the structure twenty-one, ten, and eighteen. This is the case in *Walkaround Time*. The first part is twenty-one minutes, the entr'acte ten, and the second half is eighteen. The total, forty-nine, is a seven by seven structure. In the past when Mr. Cage and I worked together, he would have written music that would be as long as the dance. At present, he would more likely make a sound situation which could be of any length, and then for the purpose of the dance, it would end when the dance ended.

Would it be correct to say that every time your company performs a dance, that at a certain time when a certain note is played in the music, that the dancers would be performing a certain movement?

In answer to your question, no. The dance movement and the musical sound would not coincide the same from performance to performance. I can illustrate this again by one of the dances. The piece is called *How to Pass, Kick, Fall, and Run*. It's twenty-four minutes long. For this I asked Mr. Cage if he would do something. I explained the length and the structure points. After seeing the dance, Mr. Cage decided to make a sound accompaniment of stories. Each story in its telling would take a minute. He tells on an average of fifteen stories in the course of the twenty-four minutes, so there are lengths of silence as the dance continues. Using a stopwatch, he governs the speed of each telling, a story with few words being spaced out over the minute, a story with many having a faster rhythm. Since from one playing to another playing of the dance he never tells the same story at the same point in time, we cannot count on it to relate to us. Often audiences, having made a relationship for themselves, will say, it is funny when he told the story about my mother and a policeman, and I was doing a solo. But the next time, if he told the story again I might not be on the stage at all.

One of the better things to do on plane trips across the country is to watch Joe Namath on the professional football reruns, and plug the sound into the music channel. It makes an absorbing dance. Probably that's something new for the spectator. He has choices to make now. Of course, he always did. He could get up and leave, and often did.

Further Resources

BOOKS

Denby, Edwin. *Dance Writings*. New York: Knopf, 1986.

Harris, Mary Emma. *The Arts at Black Mountain*. Cambridge, Mass.: MIT Press, 1987.

Kostelanetz, Richard, ed. *Merce Cunningham: Dancing in Space and Time*. Chicago: Chicago Review Press, 1992.

Vaughan, David. *Merce Cunningham: Fifty Years*. New York: Aperture, 1997.

PERIODICALS

Garafola, Lynn. "Merce Gaining Momentum." *Dance Magazine* 76, no. 11, November 2002, 81–83.

Guillermoprieto, Alma. "Dancing in the City." *The New Yorker*, February 10, 2003, 70–79.

WEBSITES

"Merce Cunningham Dance." Available online at http://www.merce.org (accessed February 23, 2003).

"Merce Cunningham: A Lifetime of Dance." PBS American Masters. Available online at http://www.pbs.org/wnet/americanmasters/database/cunningham_m_homepage.html; website home page: http://www.pbs.org/ (accessed February 23, 2003).

AUDIO AND VISUAL MEDIA

Merce by Merce by Paik. Nam June Paik, in collaboration with Charles Atlas, Merce Cunningham, and Shigeko Kubota. WNET. Videocassette, 1978.

Merce Cunningham: A Lifetime of Dance. Directed by Charles Atlas. Winstar Home Entertainment. DVD, Videocassette, 2000.

Everything and Nothing: The Dorothy Dandridge Tragedy

Memoir

By: Dorothy Dandridge

Date: 1970

Source: Dandridge, Dorothy, and Earl Conrad. *Everything and Nothing: The Dorothy Dandridge Tragedy*. New York: Abelard-Schuman, 1970. Reprint. New York: Harper Collins, 2000, 179–183, 202–204.

About the Artist: Dorothy Jean Dandridge (1922–1965), singer and actress, was the first African American to receive a nomination for best actress. She was born in Cleveland, Ohio, the daughter of Cyril Dandridge, a laborer, and Ruby Butler. She was black-African and white-English on her father's side and Jamaican and Mexican on her mother's side. As a child, she and her older sister Vivian toured the United States as a song-and-dance act called The Wonder Kids, performing for Baptist churches. As a young woman in Los Angeles, Dandridge got her start as a popular cabaret singer before rising to fame for her screen performances in *Carmen Jones* (1954), *An Island in the Sun* (1956), and *Porgy and Bess* (1959). Actress Halle Berry's award-winning portrayal of Dandridge in a 1999 biographical film helped to bring Dandridge's tragic life story to a contemporary public that previously had little awareness of her. ∎

Introduction

Everything and Nothing tells of Dandridge's enormous pain as a beautiful and talented actress in a time when her race severely limited her opportunities in Hollywood. She begins her memoirs from her years as The Wonder Kids, later called The Dandridge Sisters. Dorothy sang at the famous Cotton Club in Harlem when she was just sixteen. Her dream was to star in films, though, and she left to pursue a solo career in film. Dandridge made her first screen appearance in 1937, with a minor part in the Marx Brothers' *A Day at the Races.* No directors then cast with a color-blind eye. Dandridge refused to play stereotypical roles given to African American women at the time, such as the maid character. Some roles she accepted reluctantly, such as the "African jungle queen" in *Tarzan's Peril* (1951). In *Bright Road* (1953), Dandridge had the opportunity to play a complex character. It was an all-black cast, but told a universal story involving Dandridge's schoolteacher character. Dandridge took on this role enthusiastically, and her performance was especially well reviewed.

Dandridge's screen appearances did not make getting Hollywood roles any easier, but advanced her career as a nightclub singer. Performing in nightclubs, however, brought unwelcome memories of her vaudeville days, and she did not enjoy live singing. Moreover, even while she sang in the finest hotels, Dandridge was not permitted to talk to any of the other hotel guests, and was forced to stay elsewhere.

Just a few years after her phenomenal rise to stardom, Dandridge declared bankruptcy in 1962. A series of bad investments and a growing problem with alcoholism accelerated her demise. In 1965, Dandridge overdosed on alcohol and barbiturates. Her autobiography, *Everything and Nothing,* was completed just prior to her death. According to co-author Earl Conrad, when Dandridge informed certain friends that she was writing her memoirs to tell of her friendships and romances crossing the color line, they criticized her and told her that she would be setting back "the march of black womanhood."

Significance

Shortly after completing *Bright Road,* Dandridge heard about a new film production of *Carmen Jones,* which had been a hit Broadway show in 1943. Otto Preminger, a famous director, would lead the project. Dandridge was determined to secure the lead role of Carmen, a seductress. The story was an updated version of Bizet's classic opera, taking place at an all-black army camp in which Carmen, a civilian parachute-maker, chases after Joe, a young pilot in training. The musical featured songs from the Bizet opera, with modernized lyrics. Dandridge won the role and was nominated for an Oscar for best actress, but lost to Grace Kelly, who received the award for her role in *A Country Girl.*

Primary Source

Everything and Nothing: The Dorothy Dandridge Tragedy [excerpt]

SYNOPSIS: Dorothy Dandridge's autobiography was co-written with Earl Conrad, her longtime agent and friend, and completed shortly before Dandridge's tragic death in 1965. Dandridge briefly enjoyed international acclaim for her screen performances, but by the end of her life she was in financial ruin, and an alcoholic. Her autobiography was titled *Everything and Nothing* posthumously, and first published five years after her death.

When *Carmen Jones* was previewed in Los Angeles, a group of my friends returned with me to my Sunset Strip apartment. Not one commented on my performance. No one said that I was any good or that I was bad. They carped about the choreography; they said there weren't enough Negroes in the fighting scene. I still had no idea whether I was good or bad in the role, except Otto assured me that I was fine and that it would show up in the reviews.

A few days later a preliminary report came in from San Francisco where the San Francisco-Oakland Critics Circle voted me the best actress of 1954, before the national release of the picture.

Otto and I went to New York for the premiere. For the event I had a special white lace sheath dress with a matching greatcoat designed for me by Robert Carlton.

When the reviews came in *Time,* remarking on my previous gentle schoolteacher role, said "The range between the two parts suggests that she is one of the outstanding dramatic actresses of the screen." When I read that I felt that all that I had ever believed about myself and my creative potential was vindicated. I was human enough to say to myself, This'll show 'em. But it was only the beginning.

A few days later my picture was on the cover of *Life,* billed as "Hollywood's Fiery Carmen Jones," and its story remarked that I was the most decorative Carmen in the history of that opera, and it predicted that no one would reach nationwide fame so quickly as I. In these accolades I was to reach a high and also the beginnings of a decline inevitable for a Negro actress for whom there was no place else to go, no higher or better role to play, no new story available, no chance to play roles meant for white only.

For weeks I was on the road helping to publicize the picture. This I combined with night club engagements, and one night in December, when I was singing in Denver, my maid rushed into my dressing room to tell me that I had received the nomination of *The Film Daily* as one of the Famous Fives of 1954. What that meant was that one of the five, perhaps even myself, might win an award as best actress for that year.

Other accolades trailed afterward, that of the Academy of Motion Picture Arts and Sciences, the Council of Motion Picture Organization Audience Award, the Hollywood Foreign Press Association—all nominating me as the best actress of 1954 or as the most promising new female personality.

. . . Otto knew something that I didn't know. Being mentioned as one of five candidates for best actress of the year was realization of much, for as *Life* put it, "She is the first Negro ever nominated for an Academy award for acting in a major role."

"You will not get the Oscar," Otto said.

"Why not?"

"The time is not ripe."

He spoke the truth.

The time would be ten years later, during the so-called Revolution when Sidney Poitier would secure it for a wonderful performance.

■ ■ ■

Prejudice can show itself in many subtle ways in American movie-making. I remember an instance during the shooting of the film *Malaga*. The scene was this: I was lying on the banks of a river in Spain; the sun was shining; a shade tree threw shadows over me. The camera ground out shots of the rapidly running stream. The sun and the Shadow played over my face. The camera panned from a river view to me; the light and dark of my features showed. Now there were close-ups, and audiences would see a unique love scene. Above me was a white man, passionate, trembling—Trevor Howard, my co-star. His face, truly an Englishman's face, was close to mine. My features might look Spanish, or Anglo-Saxon, but the viewer would know that this was an American Negro, Dorothy Dandridge.

Close by the camera eye pointed. Trevor bent over me, his lips only a few inches from mine. I folded my arms around him, drew him close. The camera would show my fingers clutching into his back. Another instant and there would have been a bit of motion picture history—a white man kissing

Talented actress Dorothy Dandridge, renowned for her performance in *Carmen Jones* and other works, blazed a trail for African American performers to follow. **THE LIBRARY OF CONGRESS.**

the lips of a Negro woman, on the screen, for the first time.

Suddenly the director's voice rang out. "Cut!"

Trevor started. I started. We looked at each other, still holding that pose, wanting to play out the business of lovemaking by the river edge.

I realized instantly what happened.

The kiss could not take place.

"That's all for today," the director said.

I was furious. Trevor and I discussed it, but the day's work was over.

The next morning we resumed shooting, Trevor and I in the same position, his lips close to mine. This time the director said, "Now break."

Trevor rose; I got up. The camera shot us as we stood, without that love scene being completed. Motion picture protocol had ruled again.

Very much the same thing had occurred to me a year earlier in making *Island in the Sun* in Jamaica. In that Darryl Zanuck picture a Negro-white relationship was suggested, and minimized. But a beginning was made by portraying an honest love relationship between a British attaché and a Jamaican girl of color.

These situations were very similar to the events in my private life—my social relations with white men were also barred by protocol and law at a certain point.

Malaga was a difficult film to make, owing to constant script changes. It was a Twentieth Century Fox picture with Douglas Fairbanks Jr. as the producer. There was confusion among the makers of the film about the love relationship itself, whether it should be wholesome or suggestive, and these indecisions characterized the entire production and created tensions on all sides. These problems underlined why there never could be for me a true motion picture career. The limitations of life reached into art—at least, the screen art.

I returned to America in some disgust, not alone with that incident, but the complications of the entire picture. I wanted surcease from stardom, moviemaking, singing.

Further Resources

BOOKS

Bogle, Donald. *Dorothy Dandridge: A Biography.* New York: St. Martin's Press, 1997.

Mills, Earl. *Dorothy Dandridge.* Los Angeles: Holloway House, 1999.

Null, Gary. *Black Hollywood: The Negro in Motion Pictures.* Secaucus, N.J.: Citadel, 1975.

PERIODICALS

Buckley, Gail Lumet. "Dorothy's Surrender." *Premiere,* September 13, 1993, 84–92.

Leavy, Walter. "Who Was The Real Dorothy Dandridge?" *Ebony* 54, no. 10, August 1999, 100–104.

WEBSITES

Oliver, Phillip. "Dorothy Dandridge: A Life Unfulfilled." Available online at http://home.hiwaay.net/~oliver/dandridge.html (accessed February 26, 2003).

"Presenting Dorothy Dandridge." Available online at http://members.aol.com/valsadie/dandridge.htm; website home page: http://www.valsadie.com/ (accessed February 26, 2003).

AUDIO AND VISUAL MEDIA

Biography: Dorothy Dandridge: Little Girl Lost. A&E Home Video. Videocassette, 1999.

Introducing Dorothy Dandridge. Directed by Martha Coolidge. HBO Home Video. Videocassette, 1999.

"Why I Wrote *The Crucible*"

Essay

By: Arthur Miller

Date: 1996

Source: Miller, Arthur. "Why I Wrote *The Crucible*." *The New Yorker,* October 21 and 28, 1996, 158–164.

About the Author: Playwright Arthur Miller (1915–) was born in New York. He worked numerous odd jobs from truck driving to singing for a radio show before he studied journalism and playwriting. During the 1940s he produced a series of popular radio plays. His Pulitzer Prize-winning *Death of a Salesman* (1949) is one of America's best known dramatic works. He was married to Marilyn Monroe from 1956 to 1961. In 1957, Miller was convicted for contempt of Congress because he refused to divulge names of associates who were suspected Communists to the House Un-American Activities Committee (HUAC), and he was blacklisted from Hollywood. The conviction was eventually reversed. Miller has also written screenplays, essays, and short stories. His only novel, *Focus,* was published in 1945. ∎

Introduction

The Crucible is both a tragedy and an allegory based on actual events and persons. The play opens with a scene of teenaged girls dancing naked around a bonfire in the woods. The girls are discovered by an adult, Reverend Parris, who suspects them of wrongdoing. Urged to confess their sins, the girls place blame on the witches living among them. Abigail Williams, the group's ringleader, points to Elizabeth, wife of John Proctor and her rival for his affections. Proctor has long regretted his adulterous affair with Abigail, but she continues to pursue him. Tension and anxiety overwhelm the citizens of the town, as false confessions and finger pointing lead to deaths of the innocent. The play is written in authentic seventeenth-century English for which Miller enlisted the assistance of his former classmate, poet and scholar Kimon Friar.

In developing his script, when Miller visited Salem in 1952 he immediately realized the parallels between Salem in 1692 and the then-current United States. Salem citizens were replaced by actors; witches were replaced by Communists; McCarthy and the HUAC were the so-called pillars of the community condemning those suspected of leftist activity.

The play debuted on Broadway in 1953. Some derided the play as a flawed parable of the Communist witch hunts. Famously, Elia Kazan's wife said to Arthur Miller that there were never any witches but there certainly were Communists. Elia Kazan had directed award-winning productions of Miller's *All My Sons* and *Death of a Salesman,* but their differences regarding the legitimacy of the HUAC ruptured their friendship. Kazan appeared before HUAC in the spring of 1952, after which Miller refused to speak to Kazan, considering him an informer. Kazan was conspicuously not invited to direct *The Crucible* for its Broadway debut in 1953.

Significance

The Crucible remains widely read in the early twenty-first century, and is considered one of Miller's most powerful works. The play is especially riveting because of the intense personal relationships among its central characters. It was an 1867 study by Charles W. Upham (Salem's then-mayor) that moved Miller to create a drama exploring such emotions as hysteria, anguish, remorse and courage. Other historical accounts of what had happened during the Salem witch hunts might be rich in facts and analysis, but Miller's fictional account of the lives at stake brought home to a contemporary public what it must have been like then—as well as the terror felt by the targets of the Communist witch hunts.

Miller's writing has often been celebrated for his unflinching examinations of human character in moments of both moral weakness and moral strength. Miller's essay of reflections on his work is a valuable contribution to the study of the political in art. Miller reiterates his affinity for the John Proctor character, who would rather die than give false testimony. Miller was willing to testify before the HUAC about his own leftist activities, but would not name others involved. The playwriting of *The Crucible* was also an artistic processing of the personal as well as political. Miller hints at his own marital infidelities and subsequent regret that are again paralleled in John Proctor.

More than five decades after its composition, *The Crucible* remains as powerful as when the specter of McCarthyism colored its every analysis. The play's artistic impact lies in its complex development of characters and the sheer drama of Miller's brilliant storytelling. Miller's fascination with legal language—he followed Senate hearings very closely—also inspired the style of the dialogue in *The Crucible*. Although contemporary audiences may experience Miller's play as period drama, he is ever astute in bringing to the audience's awareness that at any time, somewhere in the world, there are ongoing witch hunts of some kind. In the instance of *The Crucible,* the artistic is inherently political, but at its root is an unshakeable social concern.

Primary Source

"Why I Wrote *The Crucible*." [excerpt]

SYNOPSIS: Arthur Miller wrote *The Crucible* in 1952 largely in response to McCarthyism. *The Crucible* is set in Salem, Massachusetts, in 1692. Rumors of witchcraft throughout the town lead to accusations, roundups, and forced confessions. Eventually the innocent were sent to the gallows. Miller compared the hysteria of the Salem witch hunts centuries earlier to the outing of alleged Communists during his own lifetime. Miller's essay "Why I Wrote *The Crucible*" was written on the occasion of the play's first Hollywood adaptation, a little more than forty years after *The Crucible* and ironically, Miller's blacklisting by Hollywood.

As I watched "The Crucible" taking shape as a movie over much of the past year, the sheer depth of time that it represents for me kept returning to my mind. As those powerful actors blossomed on the screen, and the children and the horses, the crowds and the wagons, I thought again about how I came to cook all this up nearly fifty years ago, in an America nobody I know seems to remember clearly. In a way, there is a biting irony in this film's having been made by a Hollywood studio, something unimaginable in the fifties. . . .

"The Crucible" was an act of desperation. Much of my desperation branched out, I suppose, from a typical Depression-era trauma—the blow struck on the mind by the rise of European Fascism and the brutal anti-Semitism it had brought to power. But by 1950, when I began to think of writing about the hunt for Reds in America, I was motivated in some great part by the paralysis that had set in among many liberals who, despite their discomfort with the inquisitors' violations of civil rights, were fearful, and with good reason, of being identified as covert Communists if they should protest too strongly.

Nobody but a fanatic, it seemed, could really say all that he believed.

. . . The Red hunt, led by the House Committee on Un-American Activities and by McCarthy, was becoming the dominating fixation of the American psyche. It reached Hollywood when the studios, after first resisting, agreed to submit artists' names to the House Committee for "clearing" before employing them. This unleashed a veritable holy terror among actors, directors, and others, from Party members to those who had had the merest brush with a front organization.

. . . Harry Cohn, the head of Columbia Pictures, did something that would once have been considered unthinkable: he showed my script to the F.B.I. Cohn then asked me to take the gangsters in my script, who were threatening and murdering their opponents, and simply change them to Communists. When I declined to commit this idiocy (Joe Ryan, the head of the longshoremen's union, was soon to go to Sing Sing for racketeering), I got a wire from Cohn saying "The minute we try to make the script pro-American you pull out." By then—it was 1951—I had come to accept this terribly serious insanity as routine, but there was an element of the marvellous in it which I longed to put on the stage.

In those years, our thought processes were becoming so magical, so paranoid, that to imagine writing a play about this environment was like trying to pick one's teeth with a ball of wool: I lacked the tools to illuminate miasma. Yet I kept being drawn back to it.

I had read about the witchcraft trials in college, but it was not until I read a book published in 1867—a two-volume, thousand-page study by Charles W. Upham, who was then the mayor of Salem—that I knew I had to write about the period. Upham had not only written a broad and thorough investigation of what was even then an almost lost chapter of Salem's past but opened up to me the details of personal relationships among many participants in the tragedy. . . .

All this I understood. I had not approached the witchcraft out of nowhere, or from purely social and political considerations. My own marriage of twelve years was teetering and I knew more than I wished to know about where the blame lay. That John Proctor the sinner might overturn his paralyzing personal guilt and become the most forthright voice against the madness around him was a reassurance to me, and, I suppose, an inspiration: it demonstrated that a clear moral outcry could still spring even from an ambiguously unblemished soul. Moving crabwise across the profusion of evidence, I sensed that I had at last found something of myself in it, and a play began to accumulate around this man.

But as the dramatic form became visible, one problem remained unyielding: so many practices of the Salem trials were similar to those employed by the congressional committees that I could easily be accused of skewing history for a mere partisan purpose. Inevitably, it was no sooner known that my new play was about Salem than I had to confront the charge that such an analogy was specious—that there never were any witches but there certainly were Communists. . . .

The more I read into the Salem panic, the more it touched off corresponding images of common ex-

Playwright Arthur Miller wrote successful plays such as *Death of a Salesman* and *The Crucible*. © BETTMANN/CORBIS. REPRODUCED BY PERMISSION.

periences in the fifties: the old friend of a black-listed person crossing the street to avoid being seen talking to him; the overnight conversions of former leftists into born-again patriots; and so on. Apparently, certain processes are universal. When Gentiles in Hitler's Germany, for example, saw their Jewish neighbors being trucked off, or farmers in Soviet Ukraine saw the Kulaks vanishing before their eyes, the common reaction, even among those unsympathetic to Nazism or Communism, was quite naturally to turn away in fear of being identified and condemned. As I learned from non-Jewish refugees, however, there was often a despairing pity mixed with "Well, they must have done *something*." Few of us can easily surrender our belief that society must somehow make sense. The thought that the state has lost its mind and is punishing so many innocent people is intolerable. And so the evidence has to be internally denied.

I was also drawn into writing "The Crucible" by the chance it gave me to use a new language—that of the seventeenth-century New England. That plain, craggy English was liberating in a strangely sensuous way, with its swings from an almost legalistic precision to a wonder metaphoric richness. "The Lord doth terrible things amongst us, by lengthening the chain of the roaring lion in an extraordinary manner, so that the Devil is come down in great wrath," De-odat Lawson, one of the great witch-hunting preachers, said in a sermon. Lawson rallied his congregation for what was to be nothing less than a religious war against the Evil One—"Arm, arm, arm!"—and his concealed anti-Christian accomplices. . . .

I am not sure what "The Crucible" is telling people now, but I know that its paranoid center is still pumping out the same darkly attractive warning that it did in the fifties. For some, the play seems to be about the dilemma of relying on the testimony of small children accusing adults of sexual abuse, something I'd not dreamed of forty years ago. For others, it may simply be a fascination with the outbreak of paranoia that suffuses the play—the blind panic that, in our age, often seems to sit at the dim edges of consciousness. Certainly its political implications are the central issue for many people; the Salem interrogations turn out to be eerily exact models of those yet to come in Stalin's Russia, Pinochet's Chile, Mao's China, and other regimes. (Nien Cheng, the author of "Life and Death in Shanghai," has told me that she could hardly believe that a non-Chinese—someone who had not experienced the Cultural Revolution—had written the play.) But below its concerns with justice the play evokes a lethal brew of illicit sexuality, fear of the supernatural, and political manipulation, a combination not unfamiliar these days. The film, by reaching the broad American audiences as no play ever can, may well unearth still other connections to those buried public terrors that Salem first announced on this continent.

One thing more—something wonderful in the old sense of the word. I recall the weeks I spent reading testimony by the tome, commentaries, broadsides, confessions, and accusations. And always the crucial damning event was the signing of one's name in "the Devil's book." This Faustian agreement to hand over one's soul to the dreaded Lord of Darkness was the ultimate insult to God. But what were these new inductees supposed to have *done* once they'd signed on? Nobody seems even to have thought to ask. But, of course, actions are as irrelevant during cultural and religious wars are they are in nightmares. The thing at issue is buried intentions—the secret allegiances of the alienated heart, always the main threat to the theocratic mind, as well as its immemorial quarry.

Further Resources

BOOKS

Miller, Arthur. *The Crucible in History and Other Essays.* London: Methuen, 2000.

Moss, Leonard. *Arthur Miller.* Boston: G. K. Hall, 1980.

Siebold, Thomas, ed. *Readings on The Crucible.* San Diego, Calif.: Greenhaven, 1999.

PERIODICALS

Brustein, Robert. "Robert Brustein on Theater: Arthur Miller at 87." *New Republic* 227, no. 16, October 14, 2002, 26–29.

Decter, Midge. "The Crucible" [movie review]. *Commentary* 103, no. 3, March 1997, 54–57.

Midgette, Anne. "Responding to Crisis, Art Must Look Beyond It." *The New York Times,* March 3, 2002, AR1.

WEBSITES

The Arthur Miller Society Official Web Site. Available online at http://www.ibiblio.org/miller/ (accessed February 25, 2003).

Burns, Margo. "Arthur Miller's *The Crucible*: Fact & Fiction." 17th Century Colonial England. Available online at http://www.ogram.org/17thc/fact-fiction.shtml; website home page: http://www.ogram.org/ (accessed February 25, 2003).

"*The Crucible* on Broadway." Available online at http://www.thecrucibleonbroadway.com (accessed February 25, 2003).

AUDIO AND VISUAL MEDIA

The Crucible CD-ROM. Norfolk Technology Unit, The Arthur Miller Centre at the University of East Anglia, and Penguin Books USA Inc. CD-ROM, 1994.

Maria Tallchief: America's Prima Ballerina

Autobiography

By: Maria Tallchief

Date: 1997

Source: Tallchief, Maria, and Larry Kaplan. *Maria Tallchief: America's Prima Ballerina.* New York: Henry Holt and Company, 1997, 185–190.

About the Artist: Maria Tallchief (1925–), ballerina and dance teacher, was a major force in bringing international fame and prestige to American ballet. Tallchief was born in Fairfax, Oklahoma, the daughter of an Osage chief. Her grandfather is credited with negotiating the Osage Treaty, which created the Osage Reservation in Oklahoma and resulted in oil revenues for some Osage people. Tallchief began dancing at age four. She studied with and was briefly married to legendary choreographer George Balanchine (1904–1983) of the New York City Ballet. She was its prima ballerina for eighteen years. Tallchief retired from dancing in 1965. ∎

Introduction

Based on a story by German writer E.T.A. Hoffmann, *The Nutcracker* begins at a bourgeois Christmas

Eve party of children and parents. Marie, a young girl, has just received a nutcracker, her favorite new toy. Her brother Fritz breaks the nutcracker. Marie then has a dream, which begins as a nightmare in which the family Christmas tree grows to an enormous size and huge mice surround her menacingly. The mice are vanquished by the newly risen nutcracker, who is then transformed into a handsome prince. The prince takes Marie to the Kingdom of the Sweets, where dancing chocolates and candies led by the Sugar Plum Fairy perform in Marie's honor. In the end, Marie and the Nutcracker Prince ascend to the heavens in a reindeer-drawn sleigh.

The original *Nutcracker,* with music by Peter Ilych Tchaikovsky, debuted in 1892. There have been many versions since, but Balanchine's 1954 version is the modern standard. While some versions of *The Nutcracker* featured only adult dancers, Balanchine's production utilized nearly forty children, some as young as eight. He based some of the choreography on the version he danced as a child in Russia. Balanchine created the pivotal role of the Sugar Plum Fairy with Maria Tallchief in mind.

Tallchief starred in the very first dances that Balanchine created for the newly formed New York City Ballet. Her title role in Balanchine's *Firebird* was a daring venture, because ballet audiences were very familiar with the work, with its modernist score by Igor Stravinsky. The legacy of *Firebird*'s first performance in 1910 and a subsequent well-received production in 1945 were well remembered. Balanchine designed a lavish set for his version, along with opulent costumes. The new *Firebird* opened in 1949 and received rave reviews from critics. Tallchief amazed audiences with her strength, quickness, and technical brilliance. She also made star turns in *Orpheus* and *Swan Lake.*

Significance

Tallchief's ballet technique and artistry were unparalleled. She had an international reputation from dancing on tour and with several ballet companies abroad. With the formation of a ballet company in her home country, she became a central figure in making American ballet a major force in a tradition that had previously recognized only European and Russian dancers. Even when she retired from performing on stage, Tallchief continued to promote American ballet by teaching and directing dance companies. Since 1975 she has been artistic director for the Lyric Opera Ballet in Chicago. In 1980 she and her sister founded the Chicago City Ballet.

Tallchief's memoirs are an eyewitness account of the birth of American ballet. As "Prima Ballerina," she refers not only to her experiences as the principal dancer in the ballet corps, but also as the figurehead of ballet in Amer-

ica. Tallchief describes in detail what it was like to work with various ballet companies and particularly her collaboration with Balanchine, who masterfully balanced his own ideas with his dancers' artistic independence. Tallchief never loses her enthusiasm for dance. Her generous descriptions of her relationships with dance personalities, rehearsals, backstage preparations, and actual performances provide rare insight into the world of modern ballet.

Primary Source

Maria Tallchief: America's Prima Ballerina [excerpt]

SYNOPSIS: In this passage from Maria Tallchief's memoirs, she recalls the magic of the first production of Balanchine's holiday spectacular *The Nutcracker.* To this day, *The Nutcracker* is performed annually at New York City's Lincoln Center. Balanchine's ballet is a classic and a favorite of audiences. For aspiring dancers, appearing in the production is a rite of passage. Its performers graduate to greater roles each year, such as from angel to snowflake to Mouse King and Nutcracker.

For the first time, George had decided to choreograph his own full-length, two-act version of *The Nutcracker.* He planned it as a lavish spectacular in which I would dance the leading role of the Sugar Plum Fairy opposite André as my Cavalier. George threw himself—and all of us—into preparations for what was going to be his most ambitious project to date.

The production was far and away the most expensive that the New York City Ballet had ever mounted. In addition to an adult cast, there would be roles for close to forty children, opulent, costly sets designed by Horace Armistead, and costumes by Karinska. *The Nutcracker,* part of the great troika of scores that Tchaikovsky wrote for ballet, was music George cherished. The ballet, first created by Ivanov in 1892 from a libretto based on a story by E. T. A. Hoffmann, was a favorite of his from childhood. He danced in it when he was a little boy at the Maryinsky and when he was fifteen he appeared as the Nutcracker Prince.

George understood the magical qualities associated with the ballet as well as the grandeur and beauty contained in the music. He wanted to re-create the story in all its splendor. From the beginning, I could see that it was going to be a major undertaking. Perhaps George knew all along that the ballet would become a perennial favorite and solve most of New York City Ballet's financial problems. Who knows? He never said so.

Maria Tallchief was the prima ballerina of the United States during the 1950s. REPRINTED BY PERMISSION OF THE ESTATE OF GEORGE PLATT LYNES.

But at the time he was choreographing it, everyone else thought it was a foolhardy, extravagant enterprise that would put us in the poorhouse. The original budget of forty thousand dollars rose to eighty thousand dollars before the ballet was completed, a phenomenal sum for the time. But I wasn't concerned. I was confident of only one thing: When it came to ballet George knew exactly what he was doing. Why should people doubt him now? And anyone could see he genuinely loved the piece and was immersed in its background.

"I know all about *Nutcracker*," he told an interviewer. "In Russia, Christmas is German invention. Our Christmas is German. We had German postcards with snow, little deer. Very pretty. Children are told beautiful stories about it. Everything is on the tree, *pfefferkuchen, lebkuchen,* everything like that. Our tree was full of food—chocolate, oranges, apples. You just pick up from the tree and eat."

Two aspects were of primary importance to him in mounting the production: the real children he was using, young SAB [School of American Ballet] students, and the big Christmas tree in Act One. The

tree, which grows magically in size, was of the deepest significance. I believe he wouldn't have presented the ballet without it. And he seemed like a child himself when he was choreographing. I'd never seen him quite like that.

As ususal, he created the pas de deux for André and me with a minimum of fuss and simply demonstrated what he wanted. He was creating traditional choreography and wanted the dancing to reflect the formal, almost static grandeur of the original Ivanov production. But it still had to be a Balanchine pas de deux; he wanted it grand, but he wanted it to flow.

I could tell it was going to be marvelous. The movements were spacious, majestic, inventive. In one section, he had André and me cross the stage by moving around each other, leading with our shoulders. The pattern we made, intersecting lines, was like a flower opening up. It was inspired, I think, by the way André used his upper body. More and more I saw that his beautiful port de bras was a prime influence on George.

As we worked, it became clear that the pas de deux was going to be very difficult. For example, the opening moments of the music were very quiet; even so, every step required strong technique and precise timing. And as difficult as the opening moments were, what followed was even more complicated. George choreographed a step for me that was one of the most precarious I'd ever done. It was an off-center double turn, after which André would catch me by my wrist and place me in position to do it again. I don't think such an effect had ever been seen before. Split-second timing was required. If either one of us was off by a hair, we'd wind up on the floor. It was a harrowing passage that terrified me.

There were other intimidating passages. The one in which I had to take a running leap into André's shoulder and repeat it immediately from the opposite direction was especially nerve-wracking. These jumps required strength, timing, technical precision, practice, and luck.

In all, George really didn't spend much time with us. He was content to let us work on our own. After all these years he knew that he could count on André and me to perfect what he wanted. He had confidence in us. I never expected him to stand over me and hold my hand. I never bothered him if it wasn't absolutely necessary. I understood he had a million other details to take care of, especially in this production.

Major sequences like the "Waltz of the Flowers" had yet to be staged. Then there was everything else he had to oversee—the scenery, lighting, makeup, costumes, advertisements, the program, press interviews, and so on. Most important of all, it was he who rehearsed the children. At the time, there was no assistant ballet master to take charge. Instructing the children was up to George.

One afternoon, as the day of the premiere approached, he arrived unannounced in the studio where André and I were rehearsing. He wanted to see the progress we were making, and we showed him the pas de deux. He watched carefully with a smile on his face and never said a word. Finally, when we finished and he was getting ready to leave, he said, "You know, pas de deux must be like ballroom dancing. Very simple. Ballroom dancing."

"Ballroom dancing?" I rolled my eyes to André. "George, ballroom dancing is a lot easier than this."

"Yes, but should be like that."

"Ballroom dancing, indeed," I uttered aloud. How were we to execute steps that were technically impossible and pretend we were merely ballroom dancing? But just as he was walking out the door, what he meant suddenly hit me in a flash. Above all, he wanted us to be serene and joyful, as if we were having a good time.

"Oh, and by the way, you know, Maria," he said, stopping for a moment. "We have opening scene to do in second act when you greet children. Will be mime and a little dancing. We will do tomorrow."

"Tomorrow?"

"Yes, tomorrow. Plenty of time."

And he swept out the door. But he kept his word. The next morning he staged the opening of the second act in which the Sugar Plum Fairy is discovered in the Kingdom of the Sweets. He had me center stage at curtain rise, a dual vision standing there in my domain: a prima ballerina in all her glory in a beautiful tutu and crown, who is also a commanding, sparkling, bejeweled representation of the tsarina of all of the Russias surrounded by little angels.

By now, we were rehearsing *The Nutcracker* nonstop. Everything was going well until an accident occurred. André, so strong, so solid, and reliable, sprained his ankle during rehearsal. He'd never be able to dance the premiere. The worst of it was that he had no understudy. Nicky stepped in, and we had to teach him the difficult pas de deux in one afternoon.

George Balanchine

George Balanchine (1904–1983), a Russian born choreographer and ballet dancer, came to the United States in 1933. Balanchine and Lincoln Kirstein (1907–1996) founded the New York City Ballet (NYCB) in 1946, the same year that Balanchine and Tallchief married. Balanchine became the NYCB's artistic director and principal choreographer, and was involved with the company up until his death. Kirstein was an arts advocate and writer who led the NYCB as its administrative head. Under Balanchine's artistic direction, the company developed a distinctly American style of dancing, drawing upon Italian, Russian, and French ballet traditions, but with a new emphasis on movement patterns instead of plot. Balanchine created more than 200 dance works and also choreographed for films, operas, and musicals. His experimentation with new forms and movements helped free ballet from many nineteenth-century conventions

The following day, the day of the opening, the company rehearsed until the last minute, and everyone was distraught because our costumes hadn't arrived in time for the final dress. We'd be wearing them for the first time at the premiere that night! Only George remained calm.

I couldn't get too upset though. I was so tired that all I wanted was to lie down and rest on the City Center's dirty backstage floor in the middle of all the children in the ballet. They seemed to chatter away twenty-four hours a day. Noise and all, I would have relaxed, but there wasn't time. Before I knew it, I had to warm up, put on my makeup, and try on my costume, which had just been unpacked. Instead of sitting in my dressing room and being nervous, I decided to go down to the stage and watch Act One from the wings.

Even from that cramped vantage point, George's *Nutcracker* carried me away. What a magnificent spectacle! Midway through the first act, the antiquated City Center stage machinery started to crank and the great old Christmas tree began bouncing around and growing through the floor, hitting its full height precisely on the swelling chord of the music. Emotions welled up inside of me that threatened to burst.

The choreography for the Snowflakes resembled the swirling snowstorms inside the snow paperweights that decorated our home in Fairfax at Christ-

Kirstein, Lincoln. *Thirty Years: Lincoln Kirstein's The New York City Ballet.* New York: Knopf, 1978.

Livingston, Lili Cockerille. *American Indian Ballerinas.* Norman: University of Oklahoma Press, 1997.

Maynard, Olga. *Bird of Fire: The Story of Maria Tallchief.* New York: Dodd, Mead, 1961.

Meyerowitz, Joel. *George Balanchine's "The Nutcracker."* Boston: Little, Brown and Company, 1993.

PERIODICALS

Acocella, Joan. "Wise Child." *New Yorker* 78, no. 40, December 23, 2002, 114–116.

Austin, Beth. "Death of a Ballet Company." *Chicago* 45, no. 2, February 1989,104–117.

Hardy, Camille. "Oklahoma Salutes its Five Native American Ballerinas." *Dance Magazine* 72, no. 2, February 1998, 36–38.

WEBSITES

Lacy, Mark D. "Firebird from Oklahoma." Cultural Crossroads, Houston Institute for Culture. Available online at http://www.houstonculture.org/cr/maria.html; website home page: http://www.houstonculture.org/ (accessed February 25, 2003).

The George Balanchine Foundation. Available online at http://www.balanchine.org (accessed February 25, 2003).

The New York City Ballet. Available online at http://www.nycballet.com (accessed February 25, 2003).

AUDIO AND VISUAL MEDIA

Maria Tallchief: Her Complete Bell Telephone Hour Appearances, 1959–1966. Henry Jaffe Enterprises, Inc. Videocassette, 2001.

Maria Tallchief on her Native American Heritage

Above all, I wanted to be appreciated as a prima ballerina who happened to be a Native American, never as someone who was an American Indian ballerina. Perhaps I was being sensitive because of the way Marjorie and I had been exploited when we were young girls, performing novelty dances as some kind of gimmick.

Those days were long over. Marjorie and I had serious careers and were celebrated all over the world. That I was an Osage was less and less a factor in my career, but no matter how much I was being honored I was still sensitive to the issue and my feelings about it never went away.

SOURCE: Tallchief, Maria, with Larry Kaplan. *Maria Tallchief: America's Prima Ballerina.* New York: Henry Holt and Company, Inc., 1997, 183–184.

---

mas time, reminding me of my childhood. When the chorus started to sing, tears came to my eyes and I had to be sure my makeup didn't run.

After the intermission, dressed now in my beautiful tutu, I adjusted my tiara and made my entrance. I stood in the wings for most of the second act, preparing for the pas de deux. I was worried. To calm down I watched Tanny lead the "Waltz of the Flowers." What a performance! Watching her you could see all of George's training in the precision of her feet and legs, her beautiful port de bras, her response to the music. She was a dazzling dancer, and every time she left the stage I could hear the applause. By the end the audience was screaming "Bravo!" It took a while for the cheering to die down.

Then, suddenly, Nicky and I were on, and we began dancing to this quiet, but very grand music. The entree went well, and the adagio finished as I jumped into his arms. The audience started to shout and scream. The reaction was deafening, a true ovation. George had made magic again. He had created a monument to the joy of childhood and family life, and to the beauty of music and dancing. I wondered if, among all the treasures he had given me, this wasn't the greatest yet.

Further Resources

BOOKS

Guzzetti, Paula. *Prima Ballerina, Maria Tallchief.* New York: Benchmark, 1998.

As Though I Had Wings: The Lost Memoir

Autobiography

By: Chet Baker

Date: 1997

Source: Baker, Chet. *As Though I Had Wings: The Lost Memoir.* New York: St. Martin's Press, 1997, 6–9, 13–15, 56.

About the Artist: Chesney Henry ("Chet") Baker (1929–1988) was a musician whose playing came to epitomize the West Coast "cool jazz" style. He was born in Yale, Oklahoma, and began playing the trumpet at age 13. In the 1950s he performed with other jazz greats such as Charlie Parker and Sonny Rollins. He became popular as a vocalist, singing love ballads that, combined with his youthful good looks, made him enormously appealing to fans of both sexes. Baker's music career nearly ended in the 1960s when he had his front teeth knocked out after a botched drug deal. He died in Amsterdam, and in the early twenty-first century is considered a cult jazz figure. ∎

Introduction

Baker's father, Chesney Henry Baker, Sr., was a professional guitarist who was forced to turn to other work during the Depression. He bought his son a trombone and exchanged it for a trumpet when the larger instrument proved too cumbersome. Chet Baker played trumpet in his junior high school band, but had a hard time reading music and played largely by ear, a skill he developed and would rely on his entire life. His mother encouraged Chet to sing since he was a young boy, even entering him in singing contests. In 1946, at age 16, he dropped out of school and enlisted in the army. He was sent to Berlin, Germany, where he played in the 298th Army Band and heard jazz records for the first time.

Two years later, he was discharged and returned to Los Angeles, enrolling in El Camino College where he studied theory and harmony while playing in jazz clubs. In 1950 he quit college to re-enlist, and became a member of the Sixth Army Band at the Presidio in San Francisco. He continued to perform in jazz clubs, and when he obtained another discharge, he devoted himself to a professional jazz career.

Baker began playing in the Gerry Mulligan Quartet, a group that quickly scored a recording session on the newly formed Pacific Jazz Records label. This first LP by the Gerry Mulligan Quartet featured Baker's famous rendition of "My Funny Valentine." Alternating between singing and melancholy trumpet playing, the song became Baker's favorite encore. He liked singing, and was encouraged to do so by record producers because his soft, intimate voice was a big hit, particularly with female fans. When his lips got too tired to play the trumpet, Baker could always count on his singing. At the same time that he was developing his career as a trumpeter, Baker recorded the songs of Gershwin, Rodgers & Hart, Kern, and Cahn, among others. Baker became known as the James Dean of jazz. Like Dean, he was mysterious, with something unspoken and maybe ominous behind his ultra cool, handsome face.

Significance

Chet Baker left behind an enormous discography, but very little personal information. His "memoirs" were discovered by his widow Carol and first published in 1997. The autobiography, which includes facsimiles of the manuscript in Baker's handwriting, is titled *As Though I Had Wings,* after a lyric from the ballad "Like Someone in Love." Baker's vocal rendition of this Johnny Burke and Jimmy Van Heusen tune was one of his most requested. In 1945, Bing Crosby had taken the song to number 15, but like many of the songs in Chet's repertoire, it was a less well-known song by the most popular songwriters of the time. Once he began singing, Baker

was a vocalist in demand, but he shied away from simply covering "standards."

This particular passage from *As Though I Had Wings* is Chet before he developed his drug habit. The romantic memory of an early love was immortalized by Chet in his 1953 recording of "My Ideal," a Chase, Whiting and Robin tune that originally appeared in a 1930 film called *Playboy of Paris,* starring Maurice Chevalier. Just as in the lyrics of "My Ideal," in which Chet wonders if he will ever meet the "idol of my heart," the anecdote he relates here describes young Chet's own fantasy coming true.

Baker had some potential as a Hollywood star in the 1950s, playing some minor roles. He resumed acting in Europe in the 1960s, but his constant involvement in drugs eventually ended his acting aspirations. Ultimately, Baker left behind a mixed legacy. He produced many great records, he was careless with his family and finances, yet his music continues to gain fans years after his death.

Primary Source

As Though I Had Wings: The Lost Memoir
[excerpt]

> **SYNOPSIS:** *As Though I Had Wings* is an unfinished biography that covers Chet's early years in the military to the beginning of the 1960s, incidentally the beginning of his downward spiral. He kept his playing simple, a philosophy also reflected in his writing style. He writes, "It seems to me that most people are just interested with just three things: how fast you can play, how high you can play, and how loud you can play. I find this a little exasperating. . . ."

After billet assignment and the stowing of my gear, I was free to walk around the compound; naturally, I walked toward the sound of band music coming from somewhere nearby. I came to a door, the sign above it reading 298TH ARMY BAND. I walked into an orderly room where a master sergeant with an unsmiling, leathery face—he was about forty-five or fifty years old—sat at a desk in a corner with a four-foot brass-ended red, white, and blue-tasseled baton propped up behind him. He looked up and I started talking. I didn't stop speaking until I heard "Come around in the morning and you can talk to our first trumpet player." I left, thanking him profusely and eager to return.

The first trumpet player turned out to be a very nice guy named Martin who, after hearing me play a few minutes, said "That's enough, Chet, I'll have

Chet Baker and Charlie Parker

[Chet Baker's memoirs reminisce about people, places, and performances. His friendship with Charlie Parker is a unique insight into Parker as well as Baker, who never revealed very much of himself outside of his music. In *As Though I Had Wings*, Baker writes of Charlie Parker ("Bird"), who he first met in California. Baker reports Bird as a very strong musical influence. Charlie Parker was also very protective, urging Chet to stay away from drugs.]

During the breaks I'd drive him over to a taco stand a few blocks away and he'd eat a dozen *tacitos* with green sauce; he loved 'em. Sometimes, in the afternoon, we would drive down to the beach or around the Palos Verdes-San Pedro coastline. Bird would get out along the cliffs and stare out to sea, or watch the waves breaking on the rocks below for half an hour. I'm sure he liked California very much, for he enjoyed the open spaces, the beach, and the chicks. We played a few gigs for Billy Berg, and the old 54 Ballroom on 54th and Central was packed for Bird. There were hundreds of smiling black people giving him the respect and admiration that he so richly deserved. He made them happy, he made them dance, and he entertained them with his ideas and his heart. They loved him.

the sarge make out a transfer request." They must have been hard up for trumpet players.

I spent the next year falling out—sometimes two to three times a week—in honor guard uniform, being loaded into a truck and driven off to Tempelhoff Airport to pile out and wait for some congressman, senator, or four-star general to exit his plane. It wasn't so bad in the spring, summer, or fall, but the long German winter was a bitch, and it was rough standing out on the runway for up to three hours, often in four or five inches of snow, just to honor the arrival of these guys, most of whom really could not have cared less about the music that awaited them. They would inspect the band and the honor guard, with their chromed helmets and polished rifles flashing through the standard manual of arms—with some variations, of course. I remember thinking at the time, I wonder why those guys are all black and there are no black dudes in the band?

It was so cold in the winter you had to keep your mouthpiece in your mouth the whole time you stood there or else when you finally did touch your lips to the mouthpiece, it would freeze your lips to the metal. Sometimes the valves would freeze, too, so when it

was time to play Martin, the bandleader, would tell the commanding officer, Hawk, "No music this time." Hawk never complained when this happened. He'd just nod his head, understanding that we had gone through all of this bullshit for nothing.

When spring came, the band began to have more time off, including several afternoons during the week, and Saturday and Sunday. I did a lot of bowling, played cards and Ping-Pong, and went to see Dick at his post in the big theater. It wasn't a public theater; only servicemen, officers, and their dependents could attend. It was one of the biggest movie houses I'd ever seen, even bigger than the Palladium in New York City. Dick had a staff of Germans working for him, his own office, a private room in the basement fixed up with a parachute that draped from the ceiling, colored lights, a bar, and his own 16mm projector—need I say more? Dick was a hell of a smart guy at nineteen. The Army wanted to send him to officers training school, but he didn't want any part of it. He had enlisted to keep from being drafted. If you enlisted, you pulled down your eighteen months and you were finished, but if you were drafted, you had to serve two years, and had no choice regarding your assignment. Dick did well. He was doing a tremendous black-market business, selling cameras, soap, chocolate, cigarettes, and the like. These items were what people used for money on the base, and if you had coffee, forget about it. It was one of the most valuable forms of currency going. Any soldier could flag down a VW with a German driver (as long as the driver was alone) and he'd take you anywhere for five to six cigarettes.

As the weather got warmer that spring, I started spending more and more time at Lake Wansee, a spot on the edge of Berlin, bordering the Russian zone. It was a beautiful place. I started renting the sailboats, usually reserved for officers, and would sail for hours around the lake, with a portable radio blaring out Stan Kenton and Dizzy Gillespie. It was the first modern music I'd heard, and I couldn't believe it. This was the year that Stan Kenton came out with "Intermission Riff," "Artistry in Percussion," etc. And since we had a dance band made up of musicians from the Army Band that played almost every weekend at the NOO club, we were all interested in what was happening on the music scene.

I was pretty much a loner during that summer on the lake, and like most guys, I had a fantasy about a woman. A woman that I dreamed I would meet somewhere on the lake, perhaps wading in the shallows along the shore, holding her dress up out of the water to keep it dry. She would be older than me, maybe twenty-two—blond, slender, and beautiful. I daydreamed of her often and never gave up on our eventual meeting. I knew it would happen.

At that time, I didn't smoke, so I saved all my cigarette rations to trade for different things. I had fourteen cameras, all different kinds. For ten cartons I had an oil painting made of my mom and dad from a color photo. I eventually got a beautiful gold ring with a two-carat aquamarine and two sapphires, which I later traded for a little one-cylinder motorboat that I used to get from shore out to the sailboat, which was tied to a buoy fifty yards off-shore. She was thirty-eight feet overall with a steel hull and a rigged sloop that could sleep four. One day in midsummer I made my usual trip to the lake, and not caring about the poor weather, I jumped in my putt-putt and headed along the shore. All of a sudden, there she was, the very girl I'd pictured in my mind so many times. I headed toward her.

She was wading in a foot and a half of water, holding her cotton dress with one hand. She smiled as I pulled up beside her, and when I asked if she would like to go for a ride, she said "I'd love to" in perfect English. She sat on the edge of the boat, lifted her legs and swiveled right on in next to me. She was really cute, even perfect you might say. For four months, I hadn't thought much about chicks. I'd say to myself, Why should I go out of my way to look for women when I'm sure that if I wait, it will be so much better?

As soon as she was next to me in the boat, it began to sprinkle, so I turned and headed for the sloop and anchored two hundred yards away. We made it just in time, scampering into the dim cabin just as the big drops began to fall. The pounding of the rain on the deck helped to hide my own pounding heart. I had had a couple of experiences with girls, but they were just girls, if you know what I mean. Anyway, her name was Cisella, she was twenty-two, and for the next two hours I did my best to live up to the traditional American serviceman's standards.

I found out later that she and her sister were both being sent out by their mother and father in the hopes that they would meet a soldier—preferably an officer. The plan was for them to get married if possible—but not necessarily—and at the very least be taken care of with food from the PX, clothing, and money. Eventually, they hoped, this officer would arrange for the whole family to be shipped back to America and out of the living hell that it was for most Germans, especially in Berlin. They

Chet Baker plays the trumpet while on the road with his wife in 1955. **AP/WIDE WORLD PHOTOS. REPRODUCED BY PERMISSION.**

were both attractive girls. I heard later that Cisella's parents' plan worked, and she married a Russian officer. I'll never forget her and how she made my fantasy come true.

Further Resources

BOOKS

De Valk, Joren. *Chet Baker: His Life and Music.* Berkeley, Calif.: Berkeley Hills Books, 1989.

Gavin, James. *Deep in a Dream: The Long Night of Chet Baker.* New York: Knopf, 1992.

PERIODICALS

Koransky, Jason. "Chet Baker: Romantic Horror Show." *Down Beat* 69, no.8, August 2002, 16–17.

Santoro, Gene. "The Thrill Is Gone." *Nation* 275, no. 3, July 15, 2002, 38.

WEBSITES

Bloomfield, Harvey. "Chet Baker Lost and Found." Available online at http://www.chetbaker.net/ (accessed February 25, 2003).

Svarre, Jesper. "Chet Baker." Available online at http://hotel .prosa.dk/~jes//chet/; website home page: http://hotel.prosa .dk (accessed February 25, 2003).

AUDIO AND VISUAL MEDIA

Let's Get Lost. Directed by Bruce Weber. Zeitgeist Films. Videocassette, 1988.

"Ivan Moffat: The Making of *Giant*"

Interview

By: Ivan Moffat

Date: 2000

Source: "Ivan Moffat: The Making of *Giant*." Interview by Martin Pitts. American Legends. September 11, 2000. Available online at http://americanlegends.com/Interviews/dean_moffat.htm; website home page: http://americanlegends.com/ (accessed February 26, 2003).

About the Author: Ivan Moffat (1918–2002) was born in Cuba. He studied at the London College of Economics and served in the Army during World War II. He was also part of the documentary film unit that covered the Allies' efforts in Europe. Moffat was nominated for an Academy Award with Fred Guiol for the screen adaptation of Edna Ferber's novel *Giant* (1956). His other screenwriting credits included: *Black Sunday, The Wayward Bus,* and *Tender is the Night.* He also served as associate producer on the films *Shane* (1953) and *A Place in the Sun* (1951). ■

Introduction

George Stevens (1904–1975) had a distinguished reputation as filmmaker who had mastered multiple genres. He began as a cameraman shooting Laurel and Hardy comedies, and would be remembered for his own comic masterpiece *The More the Merrier* (1943). With *Giant,* he showed his maturity as a director of epic films. *Giant*'s tagline was "the legendary epic that's as big as Texas." With a running time of 201 minutes, *Giant* was Steven's grandest production yet.

Giant unfolds in Maryland, where Texan rancher Bick Benedict (Rock Hudson) has come to buy a prize horse. There he meets the rancher's daughter Leslie (Elizabeth Taylor). They marry and Leslie finds that her independence has been curtailed by Bick's old-fashioned sexism. Bick's ranch hand Jett Rink (James Dean) falls in love with Leslie but must keep his affections at a distance. The story of the Benedict family spans two generations. In the course of the film, Taylor's character ages from an eighteen-year-old belle to a grandmother of two, while Dean's portrayal of a lonely outsider becomes an oil tycoon, embittered and alcoholic. Bick, at odds with Jett Rink, watches his fortunes decline as Texan wealth shifts from cattle ranching to oiling. In *Giant,* Stevens attempted to capture numerous themes with varying degrees of success: the struggle between oilmen and cattlemen, old money and new, and racial bigotry and early feminism. With its star-studded cast (a young Dennis Hopper portrays Bick's sensitive son) and the instant mythologizing from James Dean's fatal crash just months before the film was completed, Stevens' film shot to the top of box office charts.

Significance

James Dean's third and final film, *Giant* was filmed in the summer and early fall of 1955 and released in 1956, a year after his death. Elizabeth Taylor, who had appeared in *A Place in the Sun,* was selected as the female lead in *Giant.* Stevens enlisted the efforts of his other previous collaborators, Fred Guiol (1898–1964) and Ivan Moffat. Guiol had been Stevens' screenwriter for his 1939 classic *Gunga Din.* He also worked with Stevens as associate producer of Stevens' *The More the Merrier* and had been associate director of *A Place in the Sun* and *Shane.* Moffat had previously worked with Stevens on *A Place in the Sun* and *Shane.*

Giant was filmed in Marfa, Texas, sixty miles from the Mexican border. Marfa produces no oil, so the film company erected wells to gush over with (ersatz) oil. A gigantic wind machine was constructed to simulate a dust storm for one scene. A three-story Victorian mansion, built in Hollywood studios, was shipped to Marfa and reassembled on a nearby ranch. The building was used only for exterior shots and left behind after filming. Stevens also imported a fleet of expensive cars to illustrate the lifestyle of the wealthy Texans.

Stevens took great care to preserve the good will of Marfans throughout filming. Visitors came from all over the state to watch the production. A former rodeo queen from the University of Texas appeared in a cameo. Among the sixty-five extras in a barbecue scene, ten were authentic Texas millionaires. Epic films, as typified in *Giant,* emerged at a time when cinema began to compete with the rise of television. Stevens was well prepared for the grand spectacle that only the big screen could give; he was known as a perfectionist who tried to control every aspect of his filmmaking. Texans had considered Ferber's book an unflattering portrait of their state, but were won over by Stevens' good will. In 1956, Guiol and Moffat shared an Academy Award nomination for Best Screen Adaptation for *Giant.*

Primary Source

Ivan Moffat: The Making of *Giant* [excerpt]

SYNOPSIS: *Giant* is the last of the three films comprising what Stevens called his American trilogy; the first two were *A Place in the Sun* and *Shane. Giant* was based on Edna Ferber's epic novel about a Texas cattle-raising family. Ferber (1887–1968) was the author of popular novels depicting the American experience. Her novel *So Big* garnered her a Pulitzer prize in 1924, and *Show Boat* (1926) was made into a musical. In Texas, however, Ferber's *Giant* was unpopular: Texans protested it as unflattering. Aware of the controversy, Stevens was careful to maintain good relations with Texans as he shot the film on location. In this interview with Martin Pitts

James Dean and Elizabeth Taylor in the film *Giant*, directed by George Stevens, 1956. © BETTMANN/CORBIS. REPRODUCED BY PERMISSION.

of American Legends (A.L.), screenwriter Ivan Moffat recalls some aspects of the production of *Giant.*

A.L.: Did George Stevens actively collaborate on the script?

I.M.: Yes. Stevens attended every story conference. He paid more attention than any director I worked with. And most of the writing was done at George's house on Riverside Drive. We spent a lot of time making tea in the morning to avoid getting down to work. We took our time. We started the script in March 1954 and did not finish until December.

A.L.: In filming *Giant* was Stevens faithful to your script?

I.M.: Almost without exception, the script was shot as written. And that was not George Stevens's usual habit. His normal routine was to spend a lot of time changing the script—working at night after a scene was shot—and then reshooting it the next morning. After, George wrote me a short letter, saying, "Thank God we worked as thoroughly . . . as we did because I wouldn't have had the energy down in Marfa, Texas to go through what we normally did. . . ."

A.L.: In filming *East of Eden,* Elia Kazan used only the latter part of John Steinbeck's novel. How much did you rely on Edna Ferber's story line?

I.M.: There are scenes that weren't in the book. For instance, the scene where Rock Hudson fights in a bar while the jukebox plays *The Yellow Rose of Texas* was our invention. Also, that wake scene at the ranch that gets out of hand and turns into a Texas "whoop-de-do." Edna Ferber didn't like that: She said to me, "You are a lot of necrophiliacs."

A.L.: The novel wasn't very popular among Texans to begin with. One Dallas paper claimed that if

James Dean in a scene from the 1956 film *Giant*. AP/WIDE WORLD PHOTOS. REPRODUCED BY PERMISSION.

the film was shown in Texas, the screen might be shot full of holes.

I.M.: Ferber had been a guest of the Kleberg family at their vast spread: The King Ranch. Then, she wrote the novel which appeared critical of them. After the book came out, she tried to avoid the family. Once, she hid her face behind a menu when one of them came into a Beverly Hills restaurant.

A.L.: Did Warner Bros. ask for changes to avoid controversy?

I.M.: George Stevens was very independent. He wouldn't take any orders from the studio. Several times Jack Warner tried to have certain scenes modified. Namely, the (derogatory) reference Elizabeth Taylor makes to the oil depletion allowance which favored oil companies. Something like, "How about an appreciation for first class brains?" The oil interests put pressure on the studio, and Jack Warner begged Stevens to take the line out. George said, "No dice."

A.L.: You observed James Dean on the set. What was he like?

I.M.: He was rather quiet and somewhat kept to himself. He was practicing this rope trick for a scene. And he fiddled with these ropes like a ranch hand might. He had this funny laugh—a slightly goat-like laugh and a nice, sort of cheeky sense of humor. I know that he and George had some run-ins.

A.L.: Once, supposedly Dean kept the whole cast waiting for him to show up to do a scene with Mercedes McCambridge.

I.M.: I was not there, but I heard about it. George told him, "Who do you think you are?" That kind of talk. Stevens thought it was bad manners and unprofessional. It was both. But Dean was extraordinary in that Jett Rink role. I remember looking at some of the dailies. There was a scene where Jett Rink is there with his lawyers discussing the future of this small property he is left in a will. Dean wasn't speaking much in the scene. But George said—I remember exactly, word for word: "He's like a magnet. You watch him: Even when he's not doing anything, you watch him and not the others."

A.L.: As a product of the Actors Studio, James Dean liked to improvise in creating a role. There are stories that Stevens, and some of the other actors in *Giant,* didn't appreciate Dean's technique.

I.M.: Well, Stevens was extremely thorough. He handled everything indirectly. He approached things almost ponderously. He didn't rush it. He would suggest to an actor: Shall we see how we can do this? Or, he might say, We will put a cushion over here. Try this. In that way, he would guide them. In *Giant,* there was this scene between Dean and Carroll Baker. There is this awkwardness between them. He has a few drinks. He suggests marriage. She plays it coy. It was written that way, indecisive, partly improvised. Dean improvised it even more. He threw in more hesitation and pauses and laughs. . . .

A.L.: Until it was displaced by *Superman* in the 1970s, *Giant* was Warner's top grossing film.

I.M.: The studio reissued it in a new color format a few years ago. They had this big opening in Dallas. In re-seeing the film, I thought it had become a bit dated. For example, the way Texans treated Mexicans was dealt with rather heavy handed. Today, there are different social issues. . . . And Carroll Baker played a 1950s teenager beautifully. But the '50s were rather priggish in terms of morals compared to the 1960s or now. Back then, teenagers still pretended to learn something in school.

Further Resources

BOOKS

Petri, Bruce Humleker. *A Theory of American Film: The Films and Techniques of George Stevens.* New York: Garland, 1987.

Richie, Donald. *George Stevens: An American Romantic.* New York: Museum of Modern Art, 1970.

PERIODICALS

Daly, Steve. "A Place of His Own." *Entertainment Weekly,* February 2, 2002, 101–107.

"Lives in Brief: Ivan Moffat." *The Times,* July 26, 2002, 32.

WEBSITES

"Flashback: October 27, 1956: What Boxoffice Said About *Giant.*" Boxoffice Online. Available online at http://www.boxoffice.com/scripts/fiw.dll?GetReview?&where=ID&terms=3792; website home page: http://www.boxoffice.com/ (accessed February 26, 2003).

Martinetti, Ronald. "A Myth-Shattering Biography of an Icon: The James Dean Story." *The Blacklisted Journalist,* December 1, 2002, Column 80. Available online at http://www.bigmagic.com/pages/blackj/column80h.html; website home page: http://www.bigmagic.com (accessed February 26, 2003).

AUDIO AND VISUAL MEDIA

George Stevens: A Filmmaker's Journey. Directed by George Stevens, Jr. Warner Studios. Videocassette, 1985.

Hidden Values: The Movies of the Fifties. Turner Classic Movies [television documentary], 2001.

2

BUSINESS AND THE ECONOMY

WENDY KAGAN, PAUL KOBEL, JONATHAN KOLKEY, PATRICK D. REAGAN

Entries are arranged in chronological order by date of primary source. For entries with one primary source, the entry title is the same as the primary source title. Entries with more than one primary source have an overall entry title, followed by the titles of the primary sources.

Important Events in Business and the Economy, 1950–1959

1950

- The gross national product (GNP) reaches $284.6 billion, up from $100.6 billion in 1940.
- Television advertisers spend $171 million.
- DuPont introduces Orlon and approves plans to spend $50 million on construction of research and development facilities.
- The first Xerox copy machine is produced.
- On January 1, some 31 percent of U.S. women work outside the home.
- From January 11 to March 5, the U.S. coal industry suffers from massive strikes.
- On January 22, auto inventor Preston Tucker is cleared of securities and fraud charges related to the failure of his attempt to build an innovative automobile.
- From February 8 to February 9, federal courts uphold U.S. Justice Department suits against U.S. film companies, ordering them to separate production and distribution.
- On March 1, Congress allocates $429 million for highway construction. Congress will increase this amount in 1956 and 1958.
- On March 29, RCA demonstrates the first single electronic color-television tube.
- On June 2, Congress passes the Celler-Kefauver Amendment, strengthening the Clayton Antitrust Act by prohibiting corporate acquisitions that reduce competition.
- On June 20, the housing industry reports housing starts rose 52 percent over the same period in 1949.
- From June to September, the Korean War tumbles stock prices and raises commodities prices as investors fear shortages at home.
- On August 25, President Harry S. Truman orders the U.S. Army to seize and operate the nation's railroads to avert a strike threatened by railroad unions.

1951

- On January 12, President Truman asks Congress to increase taxes to fund the Korean War.
- On March 26, Congress caps prices on food and oil, and on steel, iron, glass and other durables to counteract an in-

crease in prices that had followed the onset of the Korean War in June 1950.
- On April 9, the Federal Communications Commission (FCC) approves an agreement by American Telephone & Telegraph (AT&T) and Western Union not to compete in the other's market.
- On May 15, AT&T becomes the first American corporation with one million stockholders.
- On June 23, a Newport News shipbuilding company launches the SS *United States,* the biggest and fastest ocean liner ever built in the United States.
- On June 25, CBS debuts color television in a one-hour broadcast.
- In October, DuPont introduces Dacron and licenses nylon to other companies under pressure from the U.S. Justice Department that to do otherwise would risk an antitrust suit.

1952

- The U.S. GNP reaches a record $346.1 billion, up from the 1951 total of $328.2 billion.
- On March 4, the U.S. Justice Department charges 186 members of the DuPont family with restricting competition, and thus violating antitrust laws, through their ownership of controlling interest in General Motors, U.S. Rubber, and E.I. DuPont de Nemours & Company.
- On March 27, the Federal Reserve Board dissolves the A. P. Giannini banking empire, headed by Transamerica Corporation, which controls the nation's largest bank, Bank of America.
- On April 8, President Truman orders Commerce Secretary Charles Sawyer to seize the nation's $7 billion steel industry to avert a walkout of 650,000 steelworkers.
- From May to July 25, the steel strike ends, but when the U.S. Supreme Court rules Truman's seizure of the U.S. steel industry unconstitutional, workers walk out again.
- On July 23, movie industry box-office totals for 1951 reach $1.6 billion; professional football franchises earn $9 million.
- On September 23, Howard Hughes sells his controlling stock in RKO Radio Pictures.
- In November, General Dynamics Corporation is founded.

1953

- The annual income of an average American family reaches $4,011.
- IBM introduces its first computer, the 701.
- U.S. businesses spend $25 million on computers.
- On March 12, Congress removes the last price caps from the Korean War, on coffee, beer, and home-heating oil.
- In March, General Motors reports earnings of $558 million for 1952; General Electric tops $151 million; Standard Oil of New Jersey, $518 million.
- On May 17, Congress creates the Small Business Administration to offer guidance and loans to small business owners.

- From September 3 to September 28, the fortunes of the aerospace industry fluctuate as Air Force Secretary Harold E. Talbott announces a cut of 147 Boeing bombers then reverses course to order Boeing to build 80 new B-52s, the long-range bombers that have flown in every U.S. war since the Korean War.

- On November 26, the U.S. Commerce Department reports that the Gross National Product (GNP) has grown 5 percent ($368 billion) above 1952 levels.

1954

- Federal spending, much of it on Social Security payments and military research, reaches 12 percent of GNP.

- Swanson Foods introduces the first frozen "TV Dinners."

- On February 2, Congress raises the tax on incomes of one hundred thousand dollars to 67 percent, up from 16 percent on the same incomes in 1929.

- In March, Bell Laboratories physicist William B. Shockley and two colleagues announce their development of the silicon transistor, a component of computers.

- On March 9, General Motors leads all U.S. companies in income, reporting sales of $10.2 billion.

- On June 22, the Studebaker and Packard auto manufacturers announce their merger.

- On August 8, Hilton Hotels purchases 49 percent of Statler Hotels Corporation's stock.

- From September to October, the recession (two consecutive quarters of economic contraction) ends as consumer credit rises for six straight months; personal income also rises.

- On November 23, General Motors produces its fifty millionth motor vehicle since its formation in 1916

- On December 21, Eastman-Kodak settles its government antitrust suits, agreeing to sell color film to photographers without requiring advance charges for processing the negatives.

1955

- Consumer credit reaches an all-time high of $32.5 billion.

- The number of families owning their own homes increases by 6.5 million since 1948.

- Small corporations earn $1.233 billion before taxes, a $290 million increase over 1954 earnings.

- IBM introduces the first business computer, the 752.

- On January 4, the Federal Reserve Board raises the required down payment for purchasing stock to 60 percent of that stock's value to dampen speculation.

- On January 9, the U.S. Atomic Energy Commission invites private companies to submit proposals for construction of nuclear power plants.

- On January 13, directors of the Chase National Bank and the Bank of the Manhattan Company announce their merger into the second-largest U.S. bank.

- On February 2, the American Federation of Labor (AFL) and the Congress of Industrial Organizations (CIO) merge to form the AFL-CIO.

- On March 1, National City Bank and First National City Bank announce their merger into the nation's third-largest bank.

- From May 2 to May 6, U.S. steel companies set a one-week record by producing 2.32 million tons of ingots and casting.

- From June 6 to June 13, Ford and General Motors agree to provide unemployment benefits for laid-off workers for up to twenty-six weeks.

- On July 1, the Civil Aeronautics Board revokes the license of North American Airlines, the largest nonscheduled airline in the United States.

- On July 17, Disneyland opens in Orlando, Florida.

- On July 30, Congress raises the minimum wage to one dollar an hour. Business leaders protest the wage as excessive.

- From July to September, the U.S. GNP reaches what would be a record $392 billion if the economy could sustain that productivity for twelve months rather than merely three.

- On October 14, the U.S. Commerce Department reports that the U.S. GNP rose to a record equivalent to $321 billion from April to June if productivity would hold constant for twelve months.

1956

- Retail sales total $191 billion, a 3 percent increase over 1955.

- On March 4, Congress passes the Highway Act, pledging to spend $31 billion over the next thirteen years to build a forty-one-thousand-mile interstate highway system, the largest public-works project to date.

- On March 20, the AFL-CIO and Westinghouse settle their labor dispute, ending a 156-day strike at the electric plants.

- In May, Treasury Secretary George M. Humphrey predicts a U.S. budget surplus of $230 million. The actual surplus is larger: $1.7 billion.

- From May 4 to June 28, the Atomic Energy Commission issues permits to Consolidated Edison to begin construction in Illinois of the nation's first private nuclear power plant.

- In June, the U.S. Labor Department reported that white-collar workers outnumbered blue-collar workers for the first time in U.S. history.

- From June 30 to July 27, the 650,000 members of the United Steelworkers of America strike one hundred companies. The strike ends July 27.

- On November 4, personal income reaches a record $330.5 billion.

1957

- The wealthiest one-fifth of U.S. families take home 45.3 percent of U.S. income after taxes.

- In April, Ford introduces the Edsel, which attracts few consumers.

- On May 20, the AFL-CIO expels Dave Beck, the president of the International Brotherhood of Teamsters, for misuse of union funds.

- On July 25, William Zeckendorf of Webb & Knapp announces the biggest deal in New York real-estate history, selling 75 percent control of the Chrysler Building and its annex for $66 million.

- On October 7, farm real-estate value rises 8 percent to a record $112 million over the previous year.

- On October 20, *New York Times Magazine* lists Dallas, Texas oilman H. Lamar Hunt the richest American, with a fortune of $400–700 million.

- On December 2, the first civilian nuclear power plant, built by Westinghouse at a cost of $110 million, goes into operation in Shippingport, Pennsylvania.

1958

- Harvard University economist John Kenneth Galbraith publishes *The Affluent Society.*

- DuPont employs about 30 percent as many chemists as are employed in U.S. colleges and universities.

- The United States enters the sharpest recession since the 1930s.

- In January, fringe benefits for American employees rise from an average of $819 in 1955 to $981.

- On January 23, President Dwight D. Eisenhower recommends legislation to end labor racketeering.

- On March 16, Ford produces its fifty millionth vehicle.

- On April 16, President Dwight D. Eisenhower signs the Federal Aid Highway Act of 1958, adding $1.8 billion to the $31 billion Congress had pledged in 1956 for the construction of interstate highways.

- On June 30, International Ladies Garment Workers Union leader David Dubinsky claims that racketeers control 10 percent of New York's dress industry—down from 25 percent in the 1930s.

- On July 16, Congress creates the National Aeronautics and Space Administration (NASA), which will employ engineers, scientists, and mathematicians who might otherwise have taken jobs at colleges and universities.

- On November 25, Lloyd's Register of Shipping ranks the U.S. merchant fleet the world's largest at 25.5 million tons.

- On December 27, department stores report a $10 million increase in sales over 1957. Fewer businesses fail over the same period.

1959

- The federal government reports a surplus of $70 million.

- Unemployment dips below 5 percent for the first time since 1957, signaling an end to the recession.

- Personal income is a record $376 billion.

- Military expenditures fall to 10 percent of GNP compared to 34 percent in 1945.

- Private pension funds top $44 million compared to $11 million in 1950.

- On January 19, President Dwight D. Eisenhower recommends continuation of a 52 percent tax rate on corporate profits.

- In February, the United Auto Workers begin a 119-day strike against U.S. automakers to protest their attempt to increase the pace of work.

- In May, monthly steel output rises to a record 11.6 million tons. For the first half of 1959 steel output is a record 64.2 million tons.

- From July 15 to December 31, the United Steelworkers of America strike twenty-eight companies that produce 90 percent of American steel.

- On July 22, the consumer price index peaks at 124 percent of the 1947–1949 average.

- On September 29, the tobacco industry thrives as 47 percent of Americans over age fourteen smoke.

- On October 1, consumer credit rises to a record $47.2 billion.

- On November 19, Ford announces the end of Edsel production, which has lost the automaker $350 million.

"Battle Over Television: Hollywood Faces the Fifties: Part II"

Magazine article

By: John Houseman

Date: May 1950

Source: Houseman, John. "Battle Over Television: Hollywood Faces the Fifties: Part II." *Harper's Magazine,* 200, no. 1200, May 1950, 51–55.

About the Author: John Houseman (1902–1988), a native of Romania, was one of Hollywood's great twentieth century writers, directors, and producers, as well as an active spokesperson for the entire creative community. As an actor, he is best known to modern audiences for his performance as the crusty Professor Charles Kingsfield in the 1973 film *The Paper Chase,* and the subsequent television series of the same name. ∎

Introduction

Although the motion picture was introduced to the American public around 1890, it was not until the 1915 that movies came of age. In that year, director D.W. Griffith electrified audiences with *Birth of a Nation.* Up until that point, the motion picture was hardly a serious rival of the venerable live theater. Indeed, the American middle class largely eschewed movies, as they were deemed to be the entertainment staple of minorities and immigrants. But by 1915, the cinema as an art form was starting to compete with the stage.

Thirty-five years later, the motion picture, now the dominant form of entertainment in the United States, itself faced a vigorous challenge from a new upstart: television. Although the technology for television had been around for decades, it first captured the American public's attention at the 1939 New York World's Fair. It came of age by 1950. The advent of television, more than any other lifestyle or fashion trend, serves to differentiate the 1940s from the 1950s.

Naturally, the cinematic world looked with alarm at the arrival of television. First, Americans had developed extensive movie-going habits—millions of Americans went to their neighborhood cinema several times a week. The local movie house was a venue for both entertainment and information. The prospect of the at-home television set draining away patrons was alarming. Second, the early black-and-white television broadcasts were hardly a high quality product. Nothing matched the enveloping widescreen experience of a movie theater. And third, early television was a work in progress. By 1950, however, its technological progress could be expected to upgrade the product in much the same way that movies themselves had gradually evolved into a more complete entertainment vehicle over the first half of the twentieth century.

Significance

In an economic sense, the advent of television would prove a decidedly mixed bag for the movie industry. Clearly, the new medium required untold thousands of hours of programming, and Hollywood was in the best position to provide the talent to fill this need. Many movie makers made the seamless transition in search of work. Indeed, the silent motion picture industry earlier in the century had borrowed freely from the talent of the stage world. Numerous actors, writers, and directors had been theater people until making the switch to motion pictures.

But the real economic problem stemmed from the fact that television was doubtless going to be a free medium—at least at the outset. And once addicted to free viewing, many doubted that patrons would ever pay for home television even if it meant receiving superior entertainment. Radio had long established a tradition of free at-home entertainment, and television was more akin to radio than to the stage. Of course, some early executives did look into the idea of pay television, but early efforts to interest the public fizzled. Paying was reserved solely for movies and stage plays.

In the end, both mediums (television and motion pictures) survived and prospered. It goes without mention that television triumphed on a day-to-day basis. But films held on by various, cultivated niche markets, such as big budget spectaculars. The video revolution of the 1980s managed to bridge the gap between the motion picture and television even further.

Primary Source

"Battle Over Television: Hollywood Faces the Fifties: Part II"

> **SYNOPSIS:** Houseman examines the probable economic and financial impact of television on the established motion picture industry. The upstart medium, although still in its infancy, had become a serious rival to films by 1950. An alarmed Houseman foresees much trouble ahead for Hollywood as it seeks to fend off television.

A 1951 advertisement for Motorola televisions. The motion picture industry was concerned that at-home television viewing would drain patrons from movie theaters. **MOTOROLA, INC. AND HARTMAN CENTER FOR SALES, ADVERTISING, AND MARKETING HISTORY, DUKE UNIVERSITY. REPRODUCED BY PERMISSION.**

It is said of television that every household goes through two stages: first, wanting it; then, complaining about it. This year the Eastern seaboard finds itself predominantly in the latter stage: "Out of the wizardry of the television tube has come such an assault against the human mind, such a mobilized attack on the imagination, such an invasion against good taste as no other communications medium has known." Thus the *Saturday Review of Literature,* from the eminence of its editorial page, inveighs against the current vices of television programing, most of which, as it happens, were directly inherited from radio.

It is TV's misfortune to have been delivered, at birth, into the hands of those same powers—the advertisers and their harassed and nervous agents—whose "grinding lack of imagination and originality" long ago reduced radio to its present melancholy state. But, just as this lack of quality and poverty of content do not seem, until the arrival of television, seriously to have reduced the number of radio listeners, so TV's ultimate supremacy among the mass media will be due not at all to the virtues of its programing but almost entirely to its incontestible technical superiority over all other existing means of communication.

Television is not just the latest and most miraculous of these media. It is a synthesis of them all. It is radio with eyes; it is the press without the travail of printing; it is movies without the physical limitations of mechanical reproduction and projection. . . .

As between TV and movies, "studies by various agencies including Audience Research have shown that the frequency of television set owners' motion-picture attendance is anywhere from 20 to 30 per cent below what it was before they acquired a set. . . . Unless the industry can win many of these television owners back to greater frequencies of movie attendance by the excellence of the entertainment offered, the effect will be a serious one." . . .

One big theater-owner allowed that TV could be developed into a superb medium for advertising and publicizing the Hollywood product. "Television hasn't hurt the box office," declared another. "Good pictures do business as always." A prominent distributor expressed the opinion that TV was just "another way of selling soap, cigarettes, or Mad Man Muntz."

In contrast to these gay expressions of wishful thinking, here is another point of view—also out of Hollywood.

Motion pictures are entering their third major era. First there was the silent period. Then the sound era. Now we are on the threshold of the television age. . . . I predict that within just a few years a great many Hollywood producers, directors, writers, and actors who are still coasting on reputations built up in the past are going to wonder what hit them. . . . This will be hard on a great many people who have been enjoying a free ride on the Hollywood carrousel, but it will be a fine thing for motion pictures as a whole. . . .

This Magic Box that is now setting the communications world afire has been available, in roughly its present form, since the middle thirties. It has been held back for more than a dozen years, for the excellent reason that no one stood to profit by it and, therefore, nobody wanted it. The movie industry didn't, and still doesn't. Radio didn't. Why should it? Networks, advertising agencies, line-lessors, patent controllers, equipment manufacturers—why should any of these willingly disrupt the happy status quo which was capable of yielding an annual two billion dollars in radio billings and the profits from the sale of seventeen million radio sets a year?

It was not until the saturation point for equipment finally seemed to have been reached, and business as a whole began to show definite signs of sagging, that the radio industry and the financial interests that control it, at long last, gave the go-ahead to the new medium, and opened the floodgates of a public enthusiasm that now threatens to modify the entire structure of the entertainment business.

With faith in our still expanding economy and in the miraculous powers of applied science, we may assume that, within a decade, TV will be a technically perfect instrument with almost universal coverage. This will make it, automatically, the dominant medium of mass communication in the world. As such, what will be its relationship to those other, older forms of communication and entertainment which it is destined to supplement or replace? . . .

The *theater* has nothing to fear from the new competition—movies and radio having already done all the harm there is to be done in that department. Artistically, because home-viewed television is a more intimate and probably more articulate dramatic form than the full-screen movie, TV, whether it is produced "live" or "canned," is likely to have a closer and more constructive association with the living theater than any of the other mass media have had to date.

Radio was never more than a transitional stage, a step towards television. It is likely to continue fulfilling a useful, though minor, function as a carrier of music and a disseminator of cultural items not appreciably enhanced by the addition of sight. In the major fields of entertainment, including news and drama, radio is almost certainly a dead duck.

Motion pictures and television are the great and bitter rivals of the future, according to general belief. Actually, they are not competitors at all but variants of the same medium. (In both, an action or the imitation of an action is electrically projected upon a luminous screen—directly, in one case; in the

John Houseman foresaw trouble for the movie industry due to advent of television. **THE KOBAL COLLECTION. REPRODUCED BY PERMISSION.**

other, remotely.) The coming struggle for power is not between movies and TV as forms of entertainment and communication, but between the rival systems already set up for their exploitation.

In this struggle, two great empires stand opposed. On the one side is picture business, with its $2,500,000,000 investment in theaters, its tributary production industry, and its seventy million weekly patrons. On the other is radio—a $4,500,000,000 structure of four major networks, two thousand stations, seventy-five million receiving-sets and an estimated 150 million listening hours a day.

These are the giants locked in combat for the favor of the public. They are fighting to retain, and if possible increase, the huge profits they have been making for so many years by such radically different methods: movies, by direct levy, at the box-office; radio, through commercial advertising, by indirect levy upon the American people.

Further Resources

BOOKS

Balio, Tino, ed. *Hollywood in the Age of Television.* Boston: Unwin Hyman, 1990.

Schlossheimer, Michael. *The Films You Don't See on Television.* New York: Vantage, 1979.

Stokes, Jane C. *On Screen Rivals: Cinema and Television in the United States and Britain.* New York: St. Martin's, 2000.

Inflation

"U.S. Feels First Pinch of the New Credit Curbs: Auto Dealers Are Casualties in Anti-inflation War"

Magazine article

By: *Life Magazine*

Date: November 27, 1950

Source: "U.S. Feels First Pinch of the New Credit Curbs: Auto Dealers Are Casualties in Anti-inflation War." *Life Magazine,* November 25, 1950, 29.

About the Publication: Following the development of the portable 35 millimeter camera, Henry R. Luce founded *Life Magazine* in November 1936. What made this publication different from all the others was that its photographs, rather than its text, served as the skeleton of this weekly publication—something unheard of prior to its inception. After being a weekly for thirty-seven years, in December 1972 it was published in semiannual special reports, and then in 1978 it shifted yet again to being published monthly.

"Life With Tom and Helen Garland"

Magazine article

By: Abraham H. Raskin

Date: April 6, 1952

Source: Raskin, Abraham H. "Life With Tom and Helen Garland." *New York Times Magazine,* April 6, 1952, 12, 61, 63.

About the Author: Abraham H. Raskin (1911–1993) served as a reporter and editorial writer for *The New York Times* for four decades. A prize-winning labor journalist, Raskin fought fiercely against the forces of corruption that all too frequently infiltrated the American labor movement. He also wrote extensively about economics and the plight of working class families. ∎

Introduction

To understand concerns about inflation in 1950s America, it is important to know the difference between two kinds of inflation. *Price inflation* refers to an increase in prices in the consumer marketplace. *Monetary inflation* refers to an increase in the supply of money and credit, and is a primary cause of price inflation. *Life* magazine's 1950 article "U.S. Feels First Pinch of the New Credit Curbs" describes the decade's concern with monetary inflation, while the *New York Times Magazine*'s

1952 "Life with Tom and Helen Garland" touches on the subject of price inflation and its effect on the average middle class family.

During and after wartime, both kinds of inflation can become a problem, since wars lead to increased demand in the marketplace—a key trigger of inflation. After World War II (1939–1945), anxiety about inflation surfaced, as did worries about taxation. The requirements of waging war on a pair of fronts against both Germany and Japan placed a heavy tax burden on the wealthy, and for the first time, average citizens were called upon to pay federal income taxes. Up until 1942, most Americans had paid little or no income tax, but the need for money forced the federal government's hand.

Also in the 1950s, buying on credit became more prevalent than ever before. To purchase big-ticket items like automobiles or appliances, the average citizen had to buy on credit or make payments in an installment plan. Once considered wrong and something to be avoided at all costs, private debt became a common, accepted condition among Americans. Yet an increase in the supply of credit and money threatened to create price inflation—rising prices that would take a toll primarily on the middle and lower classes.

Significance

Compared with other decades, the 1950s was not burdened with steep inflation rates. Although inflation spiked briefly during the Korean War (1950–1953), these effects were short-lived, and inflation rates quickly returned to prewar levels. In fact, between 1952 and 1960 price inflation was kept under control, rising an average of less than 2 percent annually. The big economic picture in 1950s America was good: The economy expanded at an average annual rate of 2.9 percent, and unemployment remained low at an average of 4.7 percent.

So why did inflation remain a concern in prosperous 1950s America? The attitude of the country's economic policymakers might have had something to do with it. These policymakers, who operated within the Federal Reserve Open Market Committee (FOMC), kept a close watch on inflation rates, taking preventive measures to keep them low. One such measure was to impose credit restrictions, and to require larger down payments and higher monthly installments on cars and appliances. By attempting to lower the average household debt, and by decreasing the amount of money and credit available, policymakers effectively curtailed inflation.

Said one FOMC policymaker in 1958: "Inflation is a thief in the night and if we don't act promptly and decisively we will always be a little behind" (National Bureau of Economic Research). Yet the policymakers of succeeding decades would not be as successful in controlling inflation. In the 1960s and 1970s, FOMC poli-

cymakers did not take aggressive preventive measures, and inflation rates soared. The Vietnam War (1964–1973) contributed to rising inflation rates, compounded by dollar depreciation and a debilitating oil crisis. Indeed, Americans of the 1970s and early 1980s had to contend with some of the highest inflation rates in the nation's history.

Primary Source

"U.S. Feels First Pinch of the New Credit Curbs: Auto Dealers Are Casualties in Anti-inflation War"

SYNOPSIS: The economic impact of the Korean War on the home front is related in the following selection. High interest rates play havoc with consumer credit—in particular, the financing of new automobile sales.

The trouble with fighting inflation is that, as in fighting a war, somebody always gets hurt. In August, when the Korean war sent prices sky-rocketing, easy instalment credit and cheap mortgages fed the inflation. When the nation's private debt reached a peak, the Federal Reserve Board stepped in with credit restrictions. It clamped down on mortgages, raising down payments on new houses, in some cases, to as high as 50%. This took some of the steam out of the housing boom; in September alone new house building fell off 20% and, in the Northwest, lumber prices crashed 50%. The board also cracked down generally on instalment selling with the now-famous Regulation W, which in the case of autos required down payments of one third with the balance to be paid in 21 months. This slowed down sales of TV sets, appliances and automobiles a little but not enough to suit the board. So on Oct. 16 the Federal Reserve governors tightened the vise again by requiring all instalment sales to be completed within 15 months. So far as furniture and appliances were concerned, the effect was spotty. But it was a terrific blow to the automobile dealer.

With the average Ford and Chevy buyer now called upon to ante up about $100 a month, buyers vanished almost at once. One dealer who left happily on his vacation Oct. 1 with 40 unfilled orders returned two weeks later to find he had no orders at all and 25 unsold cars parked in his back lot. Even when they cut new-car prices by as much as $500, as did Ernest Alexander of Dallas, auto men complained it was hard to move enough cars to meet everyday expenses.

What hurt the dealers even more was the certainty that the cars they were selling today at cut-rate

Inflation caused by the Korean War meant that many Americans could not afford to purchase automobiles. © JACK MOEBES/CORBIS. REPRODUCED BY PERMISSION

prices would be worth more a year from now. Then automobile production will be curtailed to make way for defense orders. "If I could save stocks till then," one dealer said, "I would be all right. But we've got overhead. We've got to move." They had to move because in Detroit production was still roaring on toward a record year. With few customers and limited storage space some dealers were forced to park brand-new cars in open fields. In San Francisco, as in other cities, some big companies were offering to lease cars at reasonable monthly rates to responsible customers. But this required more capital than the average dealer could raise. Most of them felt like Elmer Grider, who said, "Maybe those fellows in Washington are smarter than I am, but it sure puts the dealer in an awful spot." These complaints did not move the governors of the Federal Reserve. "Of course it hurts," said their spokesman. "If the medicine weren't effective there would be no use in applying it."

Primary Source

"Life With Tom and Helen Garland

SYNOPSIS: The trials and tribulations of a typical working class family, Tom and Helen Garland, are exam-

ined in order to assess how well the family copes with wartime conditions during the Korean War.

This "average" couple has money troubles, but they don't feel sorry for themselves.

Tom Garland thinks it's time someone blew the whistle on prices. What Tom thinks is important. Not because there is anything exceptional about Tom, but because there is nothing exceptional about him. Tom comes as close to being Mr. Average Worker as it is possible to find among New York's army of wage-earners. The State Labor Department picked Tom out as a man notable for his averageness—the holder of an average sort of job, in an average sort of company, with an average sort of pay envelope, and an average sort of family to feed and clothe. Nobody is exploiting Tom. He is not one of the ground-down wage slaves Moscow is always weeping over. The factory he works for prides itself on keeping its wages well ahead of its competitors, and it stays on cordial terms with the strong union to which Tom belongs. . . .

He fell in love with Helen Dippolito, a slim, brunette timekeeper, and they were married on St. Valentine's Day 1948. Their first son, Thomas Joseph, is 3 years old; their second son, Gregory

Robert, was born last October. Helen has to carry the baby up three flights of poorly lit stairs to the dingy six-room flat they share with her father and mother at 1244 Woodycrest Avenue in the Highbridge section of the Bronx. Helen's father used to be an iceman, but a spinal injury has kept him from working for the past fifteen years. Her mother makes umbrella straps and the Dippolitos pay the $43.55 monthly rent for the jointly occupied apartment. The Garlands pick up the bulk of the food bill by way of evening things.

They spend $8 a week for canned goods, coffee, sugar, cereals and other groceries. Butter is so high that Helen has switched to oleomargarine for her baking. The baking is an economy measure, too. Tom, a 200-pounder, has an insistent sweet tooth, and Helen has decided she can keep it satisfied herself for a good deal less money than the neighborhood baker charges. "Tom's favorite dessert is chocolate cream pie," Helen confides, "and a small one costs 85 cents at the bakery. I can make one twice as big for 50 or 60 cents."

Helen's hot oven doesn't shut the bakery shop out altogether. Tom still has to plank down $1 a week for bread and rolls. The butcher is a bigger problem. He puts a $6 dent in the family fortune. On weekends the Garlands splurge with round steak, roast fresh ham or chicken. Monday is leftover day. Tuesday they have pork chops, Wednesday chopped meat and Thursday spaghetti and meat balls. None of the family cares much for fish, so soup or eggs usually make up the main dish on Friday. Fruit and vegetables take another $6. The only reason it is not more, Tom explains, is that a brother-in-law runs the fruit store and gives them a break on prices. The milkman leaves five quarts of milk every two days. That nicks the budget for $4 a week and $2.50 more goes into strained foods, evaporated milk and dextrimaltose for the baby.

Ever since their marriage four years ago the Garlands have been trying to get enough ahead of their food bills to buy an electric mixing machine to help Helen with her baking. They are still trying. Tom keeps a coin can at the factory and tosses some change into it every day or so toward the mixer. The total has got up close to $20 several times now, but some domestic emergency always comes along to empty the can before there is money enough for the machine.

The Garlands do have a washing machine, in which Helen does all the family laundry—including the baby's diapers and Tom's work clothes. Tom invested his $157 bonus check in the washing ma-

chine two years ago and the family would be lost without it. The other main prop of the Garland household is a $309 television set. Tom bought it on the installment plan in 1950. He made the last payment a few weeks ago.

Television is pretty much the beginning and end of the Garland entertainment program. They live half an hour by subway from Times Square, but they see less of the Great White Way than the average farmer from Pumpkin Corners. It has been so long since they went to a movie that Helen says she wouldn't know how to buy a ticket any more. Drama, musical comedy, opera and night clubs are part of a world they know only through TV. . . .

But, tough as life may get, the Garlands are glad they are Americans. "We're a lot better off than we would be anywhere else in the world." Tom says. "We may not get everything we want, but at least we can choose what to do with our money. In other countries they don't even have a choice. No matter how bad things are, we're better off than they are."

Tom and Helen are happy about reports from Washington that the cost of living is coming down, but they would be happier if they saw the drop reflected in what they pay at the meat market and the grocery. Falling prices are still something they read about in the newspapers, and every optimistic report is counterbalanced by warnings of more inflation on the way.

Tom's idea is that the Government ought to put a stop sign somewhere along the road to higher living costs. "They should set a date six months from now," is the way Tom has it figured out, "and say on prices, that's it, and on wages, that's it. There's got to be a stopping point somewhere, or else we're all finished."

Helen has an even simpler idea. "I only wish the prices would come down," she says.

Further Resources

BOOKS

Heller, Francis H., ed. *Economics and the Truman Administration.* Lawrence: Regents Press of Kansas, 1981.

Whitney, Simon Newcomb. *Inflation Since 1945: Fact and Theories.* New York: Praeger, 1982.

WEBSITES

"A Rehabilitation of Monetary Policy in the 1950s." National Bureau of Economic Research. Available online at http://www.nber.org/digest/jun02/w8800.html; website home page: http://www.nber.org (accessed June 19, 2003).

"War and Inflation." Massachusetts Institute of Technology. Available online at http://web.mit.edu/rudi/www/media/PDFs/WARANDINFLATION.pdf; website home page: http://web.mit.edu (accessed June 19,2003).

"Television's Big Boom: Still to Come"

Magazine article

By: *U.S. News and World Report*

Date: April 6, 1951

Source: "Television's Big Boom: Still to Come." *U.S. News and World Report,* April 6, 1951.

About the Publication: In 1933, David Lawrence founded the weekly newspaper *United States News.* Six years later, he established the magazine *World Report.* He merged these two publications in 1948 to create the *U.S. News and World Report.* Beginning the in the 1980s, it started its annual rankings of U.S. colleges in universities. Besides reporting on current news events around the world, it also publishes the annuals *America's Best Colleges* and *America's Best Graduate Schools.* ∎

Introduction

Herbert Hoover, the secretary of commerce under Republican presidents Warren Harding (served 1921–1923) and Calvin Coolidge (served 1923–1929), left his indelible stamp on the broadcast history of the United States. It was Hoover who brought the then-infant commercial radio industry under federal supervision. For instance, Hoover instituted the nationwide system of individual call letters that featured the well-known "W" east of the Mississippi River and "K" to the west, so as to avoid competing stations from utilizing the same frequencies. Hoover relied not on unfettered competition, but on industrywide competition. Hence, the early government regulation of the broadcast industry reflected Hoover's philosophy.

In 1934, Franklin Roosevelt's (served 1933–1945) administration completed Hoover's work. Hoover's ideas are embedded in the Federal Communications Commission (FCC) that was created that year—especially in its system of station licensing. Equally important, the FCC reflected Roosevelt's approach to economics—to purge the U.S. economy of excessive competition and to foster a system based on scarcity, which limited broadcasting in the same fashion that Roosevelt placed competitive limits on trucking, commercial aviation, and telephone service.

First adopted during the Progressive era as an alternative to outright government ownership, government regulation of private business was supposed to set up a system of regulation in the public interest. The appointees to regulatory boards and commissions, however, were invariably staffed with industry insiders. In the end, the regulatory movement failed since the regulated industry invariably benefited, rather than the public. Eventual disillusionment surfaced with the entire system of government regulation—especially regarding price. It would not, however, be until the deregulation movement of the Jimmy Carter (served 1977–1981) and Ronald Reagan (served 1981–1989) years that a more competition-enhancing FCC appeared dedicated to expanding broadcasting opportunities. Meanwhile, even though by the end of the twentieth century the economy of scarcity—utilizing as it does government regulation as the instrument to restrict competition—had been discredited, various health and safety or environmental protections continue to remain in place.

Significance

The television industry inherited many of the competitive restrictions on broadcasting that had earlier been established for commercial radio. Even though the technology had largely been available, this is why television grew so slowly: it was hampered by a federal government that was slow to respond to the new demands of the media. Part of the problem was ideological. Television constituted such a potentially powerful tool that the government was fearful that broadcast rights might fall into the hands of "unsavory types." Accordingly, those applying for station licenses were thoroughly screened. The extensive background checks contributed to the seemingly endless delays in approval. Not until the early 1980s, when the deregulation movement was in full stride and when ultra-high resolution and cable channels were mushrooming, did the process of obtaining a license become easier.

Nonetheless, around 1950, licenses were difficult to obtain, and the federal government was determined to protect broadcasters from what was deemed "excessive competition" by limiting the number if television channels in any given region of the country. As a result, in many areas a small number of license holders obtained virtual monopolies and then lobbied hard to prevent rivals from entering their market. Patronage and cronyism played a major role in the granting of licenses. Elsewhere, the limited range of television broadcast signals (less than AM radio) served to isolate markets and hence enforce government-created monopolies—to the detriment of customers who were denied a wider range of programming.

Meanwhile, other federal government broadcast policies impacted viewers—often in a negative fashion. For instance, the spread of color television was delayed for almost a generation. CBS had patented a better color system that required viewers to purchase a separate color-only television set that actually produced a better picture. Instead, the FCC accepted NBC's technology that utilized existing black-and-white television sets to receive color signals. Curiously enough, by the twentieth century's end, a similar decision had been rendered regard-

An NBC television station control room in Burbank, California, 1955. Proliferation of the television medium was hampered by federal government regulation in the early 1950s. AP/WIDE WORLD PHOTOS. REPRODUCED BY PERMISSION.

ing the introduction of the next round of technology: high-definition television.

Primary Source

"Television's Big Boom: Still to Come"

SYNOPSIS: Although the technology was available by 1950, many regions of the country were slow to have access to television. The federal government strictly limited broadcast licenses and, as a result, for more than a decade a viewers in some areas could receive only one or two channels. The following April 1951 article, filled with optimism regarding the anticipated swift spread of television, underestimates the government's intention to restrict broadcast competition.

New Channels Will Open the Entire Country

Television, penned in by Government edict, now is able to reach only a part of the American people. A still smaller part of the public enjoys good reception and a choice of stations.

TV expansion, however, is about to begin in a gradual manner. The first moves now are being made to lift the federal restrictions that have held it down. Removal of those restrictions is to open television to a great, new growth that will bring all regions and hundreds of additional communities within range of TV stations.

At the moment, the number of television stations is limited to 109—107 of them operating, 2 under construction. The map on this page shows how they are concentrated in the East and North and scattered sparsely through the rest of the country. Large areas in the West and Midwest have no TV service at all.

Once the Federal Communications Commission hoists the signal, the television industry expects to start multiplying to at least 1,000 stations. In time, there may be 2,000. Existing stations will be allowed to increase their power and raise their antennas for clearer and more distant transmission.

The 12 million receiving sets now in the hands of the public probably will jump to 30 or 35 million sets in the years just ahead. Within this same period, the area served by television stations may spread to include 135 million or more inhabitants, instead of the present 90 million.

More stations and more receiving sets will call for more jobs in the fields of construction, operations, manufacturing, entertaining. A larger audience is expected to lead to larger advertising volume for an industry that quadrupled its broadcasting revenues in 1949, tripled them in 1950, but still remained in the red.

That is the bright picture that industry and Government authorities see for the future. But they also see an expansion by stages, rather than a sudden, dramatic growth.

Delays still lie ahead, in many instances. All the FCC has done so far is to produce a plan, and a prediction that it may be able to thaw by October the freeze it put on TV expansion in the autumn of 1948.

This freeze was imposed primarily because of a scramble after the war for the limited space in 12 broadcast channels reserved for TV. All these channels are in the very-high-frequency band. Now the FCC proposes to open up the ultra-high frequencies, hitherto used only for experimental TV operations.

The Government agency has figured out a formula for adding 1,805 stations—200 of them for educational purposes only—to the present 109. Some cities would get both VHF and UHF stations, some would get VHF or UHF alone.

Some of the 1,805 new stations are years away. FCC has set aside channels for towns which do not even have radio yet. And it is likely to be 18 to 24 months before many new stations get into operation. Stations for which there are only single applicants might get a quicker start, but there will have to be hearings in cases in which there is competition. Then, too, it takes 10 to 12 months to build and test a station after the FCC has approved it. Materials and man-power shortages could interfere.

In general, competition is likely to be keenest for the relatively few very-high-frequency channels still available. UHF is a new field. Old TV sets will require converters and probably additions to antennas to bring in UHF. A converter may cost $25 to $150. There is a question whether a UHF station could get enough customers in an area where VHF television is well established.

The story may be different in areas that have no TV, where UHF transmitting and receiving can start together.

Barring all-out war, the big new boom, both for UHF and VHF, appears likely to develop late in 1952 and early in 1953. That is just about the time the Government counts on plenty of materials to meet a substantial civilian demand along with military needs. And TV, ready and eager to expand, is set-

ting its sights on becoming another billion-dollar industry.

Further Resources

BOOKS

Barnouw, Erik. *Tube of Plenty: The Evolution of American Television.* New York: Oxford University Press, 1990.

Murray, Michael D., and Donald G. Godfrey, eds. *Television in America: Local Station History From Across the Nation.* Ames: Iowa State University Press, 1997.

Schilling, James Von. *The Magic Window: American Television, 1939–1953.* New York: Haworth, 2003.

"Over the Top"

Magazine article

By: *Time*

Date: December 6, 1954

Source: "Over the Top." *Time,* December 6, 1954, 102–103.

About the Publication: *Time* was founded in April 1923 by Henry R. Luce and Briton Hadden. By 1927, it was selling over 175,000 copies every week. The magazine's conservative tone originally matched that of its owner, and as a result, it was favorable toward the Republican Party. Over three thousand weekly issues later, however, it has become more liberal. Currently, it boasts a weekly circulation of 4 million in the United States and 1.4 million internationally. ■

Introduction

During the economic heyday of the 1920s, the American stock market reached its peak on September 3, 1929, when the Dow Jones Industrial Average (DJIA) closed at 381.17 points, its highest level yet. At that time, this number—an average of certain leading stocks on the New York Stock Exchange—seemed staggeringly high, corresponding with the culmination of a decade-long economic boom throughout the country. Yet the number also represented a period of exuberance among investors, who were perhaps overconfident in the stock market's strength and resilience. Fueling the stock market rise was speculation that earnings and dividends would continue to increase.

As history will tell, however, the high Dow average was quickly followed by a drastic fall in October 1929, when confidence in the stock market faltered and the Dow plunged. Known as the Wall Street Crash of 1929, the events of October resulted in a Dow diminished by nearly 50 percent. A long period of economic uncertainty and hardship ensued when the country entered the Great Depression (1930–1939). The Dow bottomed out at about 44 points in 1934—the same year that an important New Deal legislation introduced the Securities and Exchange Commission, which was designed to regulate stock market stability and prevent future crashes.

It was not until the economic stimulus of military production during World War II (1939–1945) that the country's economy regained its footing and the stock market began to rebound. In 1954—a full quarter-century after the crash of 1929—the Dow finally reached, and then surpassed, the 1929 high. When the Dow closed at 382.74 on November 23, the news made headlines across the nation. The stock market's upward climb had taken 20 years to reach this point, and had come during a newly prosperous decade in American history.

Significance

The nation's reaction to the 1954 stock market rally was a complicated one; the news was not greeted by all as a cause for celebration. When the Dow passed 1929's high of 381.17 points, the psychological impact was enormous. While some believed that the Dow rise affirmed the country's economic strength and boded well for the future, many others feared that history would repeat itself, and that another crash—and more economic chaos—were lurking right around the corner.

In actuality, the crash of October 1929 had little to do with the Depression that had lasted a full decade. But the two events, so closely related in time, had become intertwined in the American people's minds. Investors and the public saw market stability as the primary goal, and regarded wild stock market fluctuations with a deep-seated suspicion.

A return to prosperity during the wartime 1940s had done little to alleviate public fears that another Depression would strike come peacetime. Investors had restrained any excessive exuberance, keeping a close watch on market activity. Even as late as the fall of 1952, Democratic Party presidential candidate Adlai E. Stevenson had spoken approvingly of the great progress the nation had achieved toward eliminating the "boom and bust" cycle. For many, the Dow rise of 1954 indicated a return to that cycle.

These naysayers, however, were largely proven wrong. Dire predictions of a renewed Depression failed to materialize. The mid-1950s turned out to be years of unprecedented prosperity. In 1955, General Motors, the world's largest automobile maker, posted a record profit of $1 billion. Signs of an economic boom were everywhere, and a strong Dow average ultimately boosted investor and public confidence in the market and the economy. In retrospect, one might even conclude that the Dow's record-high close of November 23, 1954, finally exorcised the demons of October 1929.

Primary Source

"Over the Top" [excerpt]

SYNOPSIS: The DJIA closed at a new record high of 328.74 on November 23, 1954, eclipsing the pre-

Traders work the floor of the New York Stock Exchange in 1955. The Dow Jones Industrial Average did not reach a new high until November 1954, twenty-five years after the previous high. © JERRY COOKE/CORBIS. REPRODUCED BY PERMISSION.

vious all-time high reached on September 3, 1929, of 381.17. Although statistically somewhat misleading, the psychological impact of the plateau was enormous. Demons from the Great Depression were finally laid to rest as the country boomed ahead with Eisenhower-era prosperity that appeared to be the new norm for a nation that many felt would still one day revert to hard times.

For more than 25 years, one statistic has spelled for Wall Streeters the excitement and romance of the Roaring Twenties. The figure was 381.17, the highest closing point reached by the Dow-Jones industrial average in the 1929 bull market. In all the years since, investors hardly expected the market to reach such a peak again—until this year. Last week the big bull market of 1954, which has been surging up for five straight weeks, finally crashed through the 1929 industrial high.

As volume hit 3,000,000 shares or better every day, the floor of the N.Y. Stock Exchange swarmed with traders bidding for stock. The heavy buying shot up the motors and steels, then spread to the oils, railroads and chemicals. Standard Oil Co. (N.J.)

leaped 7 points to $^{107}\!/_{58}$; U.S. Steel 3 to $^{69}\!/_{58}$; New York Central 1½ points to 25¼; Union Carbide $^4\!/_{38}$ to 84¾. By week's end, the Dow-Jones industrial average was up nearly 10 points to 387.79, rounding off a post-election rise of 33.83 points. Since the beginning of the year, the average had risen more than 100 points, or some 35%.

Average v. Market

What did the new high in the average index mean? Said one Wall Streeter: "The Dow is back to 1929, but I don't know whether the market is." Some of the other indicators showed just what he meant. The Dow-Jones rail average, though at a high for the year (up 2.55 points last week to 132.27), was still almost 60 points below its 1929 peak; the utility average (up a fraction of a point to 60.75) was more than 80 points below its high. Among other standard Wall Street guides, there were similar discrepancies. The New York *Times* average of 50 representative stocks, at 253.55, was 50 points below the 1929 high, while the *Herald Tribune* average of 100 stocks, at 175.72 was 33.15 points below its top. On the other hand, Standard & Poor's index of 50 stocks, which had been setting new highs for three years, was 100 points above the old peak of 1929.

There was good reason why the indicators did not jibe. Each uses stocks of its own choosing, dropping them when they become inactive or cease to be representative of an industry, and substituting new ones. Of the 30 stocks that make up the Dow-Jones average today, more than one-third were not on the list in 1929. Among the newcomers are such giants as Du Pont, United Aircraft and A.T. & T. Among those dropped, for varying reasons: American Sugar Refining, Mack Truck, North American Corp. As an example of what such omissions and substitutions can mean statistically, it has been figured that if the inactive stock of International Business Machines, once on the Dow-Jones list, were still included, the industrial average would be over 400. . . .

That is why Wall Streeters turn to other gauges to determine how high the market really is. Even without allowing for the 50% depreciation of the dollar, almost all indicators show that the market is still low when compared to 1929. One such measure is the dividend yield of stocks, now at 4.85% v. 3.3% in 1929. Compared with the yield of corporate bonds, stocks are in an even stronger position. They pay one-third more than bonds now, v. only two-thirds as much at the market's peak in 1929. Furthermore,

there are still many companies whose stocks would be worth more dead than alive, *i.e.*, their liquidation value per share, based on assets, is greater than the market price. Another yardstick: stocks now sell at an average of 13 times their earnings per share *v.* 21 times in 1929.

Bulls & Bears

No one in Wall Street last week thought that the stock market had become a one-way street. But for the moment, at least, the bulls were roaring. One bullish factor, paradoxically, was supplied by the bears. It was the near record short-interest figure of 3,100,000 shares (the number of shares sold short in anticipation of a market dip). Though much of this represented investors protecting longterm gains, any decline was bound to be cushioned by the shorts buying to cover their sales. . . .

Wall Streeters could differ last week over their indices and statistics. But one thing was clear. In its spectacular rise, the stock market reflected the nationwide confidence of investors that the U.S. would continue to prosper.

Further Resources

BOOKS

Pierce, Phyllis S., ed. *The Dow Jones Averages, 1885–1995.* Chicago: Irwin, 1996.

WEBSITES

"The Dow Jones Indexes: History and Explanations." Equity Analytics, Ltd. Available online at http://www.e-analytics .com/f13.htm; website home page: http://www.e-analytics.com (accessed May 3, 2003).

"Market Crashes Through the Ages." BBC News. Available online at http://news.bbc.co.uk/1/hi/business/2131739.stm; website home page: http://news.bbc.co.uk (accessed June 16, 2003).

"What the Public Thinks About Big Business"

Magazine article

By: Gardner Cowles

Date: February 8, 1955

Source: Cowles, Gardner. "What the Public Thinks About Big Business." *Look* 19, no. 3, February 8, 1955, 19–21.

About the Author: Gardner Cowles (1903–1985) came from a prominent family of Midwestern publishers. His father, Gardner Cowles, Sr., purchased the Des Moines, Iowa, *Register* in 1903. Cowles continued the family tradition of excellence in journalism and, after working for the family newspaper, became an editor of *Look,* one of the nation's great mass-circulation monthlies. ■

Introduction

American public attitudes about big business have changed over time. During the Great Depression of the 1930s, many Americans adopted a negative attitude, only turning to a more positive view during the mobilization for World War II. In the postwar years, business leaders and large corporations were seen from a positive perspective as noted in this 1955 social science survey. With the return of prosperity and economic growth, productivity and wages climbed throughout the 1950s. Scholars and social commentators wrote about the "abundant society" made possible due to the work of big businesses. Corporate managers proclaimed the existence of "people's capitalism" with a newfound sense of social responsibility. Business mergers and acquisitions in the decade continued the long-term trend toward increased concentration of manufacturing capacity, helped along with lax enforcement of antitrust laws by the U.S. Department of Justice.

The 1920s ideal of a mass production, mass consumption economy filtering into the broader society and culture became a reality in the lives of millions of postwar Americans. As this survey conducted by the highly respected Opinion Research Corporation shows, Americans held a much more favorable attitude about big business than organized labor during the Eisenhower years. People of all income levels, men and women, Republicans and Democrats, union members and nonunion members, all gave high marks to corporations for creating jobs, lowering prices, and providing for national defense during the Cold War. The majority of Americans credited big business with creating a new middle class consumer republic. By expanding the American pie through productivity gains that created dramatic economic growth, big business earned the admiration, trust, and support of the public and regained its positive image from the 1920s. While some Americans remained concerned about federal regulation of big business, the impact of corporate competition on small businesses, and the potential for abuse of power, these fears were relatively minor during the 1950s.

Significance

Since the rise of big business in the late nineteenth century, American attitudes about the nature, role, and human impact of big business had gone through major changes. Between the 1870s and 1910, many Americans feared that big businesses would not only destroy traditional economic values of free enterprise, competition, and small business but would also undermine the political system of republican democracy. As the big business

model of large-scale corporations moved beyond the core of basic industries, more people experienced the benefits of business growth. Jobs that paid well and lasted for decades appealed to working Americans used to three or four months of unemployment every year in good times and more in bad times. Rising wages meant more Americans could purchase necessities once available only to monarchs, aristocrats, or very wealthy individuals or families. High quality products could be sold by big businesses for relatively low prices making them more widely available to ordinary people. Consumers could rely on mass produced goods to hold up over time, while service, repair, and replacement was handled efficiently and competently by large firms.

By the 1950s, the vast majority of Americans trusted big business as the most important institution in the U.S. economy—much more trusted than agriculture, organized labor, or the federal government. Although public attitudes tended to rise and fall with changes in the regular movements of the business cycle, overall Americans came to think of the postwar years as the culmination of the American system of advanced industrial manufacturing that became the envy of much of the rest of the world. Not surprisingly, a majority now perceived big business as improving the quality of life in modern America. What had begun as an economic phenomenon had grown so extensive that the broader society and culture of the postwar United States now centered on consumption of goods and services.

Primary Source

"What the Public Thinks About Big Business" [excerpt]

> **SYNOPSIS:** Cowles, an editor of *Look* magazine, reports that the American people overwhelmingly approve of the manner in which corporate America in 1955 conducts its affairs. This excerpt, containing the results of a public opinion survey of people's attitudes toward big business, serves as a ringing endorsement for the American capitalist system during the heyday of the conservative Eisenhower era.

A nationwide survey finds that the people, 10-to-1, endorse the idea of large corporations

An overwhelming majority of American adults today accept—and endorse—the viewpoint that big business is a good thing for the country. Those who approve outnumber those who disapprove by a proportion of ten to one. This approval is strengthened because the majority can, and do, cite specific reasons for their attitude.

These are major findings in a nationwide survey recently conducted for *Look* by the Opinion Research

The majority of Americans overwhelmingly approved of the manner in which corporate America, including such big business as General Motors, conducted its affairs in 1955. © LAKE COUNTY MUSEUM/CORBIS. REPRODUCED BY PERMISSION.

Corporation of Princeton, N. J. The survey reached into 83 communities in all parts of the country and sampled the opinions of all political and economic groups. Those who answered constitute a statistically accurate profile of the U.S. voting population.

For a new Congress, it may be politically significant that the survey shows general satisfaction with present laws regulating big business. The findings also establish that three times as many people worry about the power of big labor unions as worry about the power of big business.

Bigness in government itself causes concern to just as many people as does bigness in business, the survey indicates.

Despite disclosing a generally favorable attitude toward big business, and an impressively large acceptance of the idea that it is good for the country, the survey provides no sweeping mandate for big business to extend its political or economic influence. As tables and figures which follow indicate, sizable groups have criticisms of some business methods—although not of the concept of bigness in business itself.

The Opinion Research Corporation report closely follows a period in which considerable attention has been paid by the press and some agencies of government to several mergers of sizable industrial enterprises. It was likewise a period in which some elements in the Congress were announcing plans for active investigations into mergers and alleged tendencies toward monopoly. Yet, only one in a hundred of all those surveyed raised any question voluntarily about mergers, and less than a fourth expressed any fear of a tendency toward monopoly.

The ORC report, however, speaks for itself, and readers may draw their own conclusions from the factual material here presented. It has been abstracted from a series of detailed statistical tables.

This was the first question asked in the survey: "In general, do you think that big business has been a good thing, or not, for the country?" It produced these responses:

Good for the nation. 80%

Not good 8%

Both good and bad. 7%

No opinion 5%

This basic idea that big business is good, rather than bad, cuts across the boundaries of the nation's accepted political and economic groupings.

Per Cent Saying Big Business Good

Upper income	84%
Middle income	82%
Lower income	75%
Men	84%
Women	76%
Republicans	84%
Democrats	79%
Independents	79%
Union members	79%
Nonmembers	81%

Conductors of the survey went beyond this general question to find reasons for the attitudes expressed. They asked for volunteer comments on what was good or bad about big business. They then presented a series of statements on each side of the question and recorded agreement with statements. Then they asked which two or three of the comments seemed most important in each case. Here are some of those findings:

1. Big business provides many jobs—37% volunteered this as the greatest contribution of big business; 63% ranked this among the most important factors; 90% agreed when the statement was read to them. It was the most important pro-business factor in all three measurements.

2. It lowers prices through mass production—25% volunteered; 41% ranked it of highest importance; 83% agreed.

3. It promotes research—12% volunteered the observation; 40%—the third largest group—called it a most important factor; 87% agreed.

4. It is the backbone of defense production—only 3% volunteered this point about national role of big business, 27% ranked this in the most important factors; but 79%—the fourth largest group—agreed with it.

5. It helps the nation's growth and prosperity—13% volunteered; 26% ranked it in the most important list; 79% agreed with it.

6. It improves our standard of living—12% volunteered this comment; another 14% cited better wages and benefits, and 20% mentioned that it provided more and better products. Two out of three agreed that big business provided better wages and benefits, and 57% agreed on the benefits of mass production.

Against this background, the survey then sought out attitudes on the regulation of business. Two out of every three persons felt that present laws regulating business were sufficiently broad and strong, and more than half felt that these laws were being adequately enforced. Nearly two thirds thought a good job has been done in regulating big business, and three out of four thought that regulation in the present form was necessary and proper.

In this connection, the comment of a beauty-parlor operation in Missouri was one of many which seemed to sum up the attitude found in the survey: "I see no reason why they should be broken up by the Government if they are not infringing the laws. Let the Government stay out. If the business is law-abiding, why should the Government interfere?" On the question whether big business should be broken up, 84% favored keeping a close watch on them, only 10% favored breaking them up.

Against the feeling that a good job had been done in regulating big business, only 35% felt a good job had been done in keeping labor unions under control, while 56% thought that big labor unions were getting out of hand and this attitude cut across economic and political lines:

	Unions Under control	Unions Out of hand
Upper income	31%	64%
Middle income	34%	57%
Lower income	41%	48%
	Unions Under control	Unions Out of hand
Republicans	26%	68%
Democrats	43%	47%
Independents	34%	54%

Principal fears about big business are: It may harm small business or it may abuse its great economic power. Volunteered comments showed that 28% felt that the pressure on small business was the greatest problem, 24% that big business tended to become monopolistic and 15% that it represented too much power. When similar statements were read to people, a majority agreed that these are the major problems arising from big-business operations.

Further Resources

BOOKS

Beatty, Jack. *Colossus: How the Corporation Changed America.* New York: Broadway, 2001.

Diggins, John Patrick. *The Proud Decades: America in War and Peace, 1941-1960.* New York: W.W. Norton, 1988.

Potter, David. *People of Plenty: Economic Abundance and the American Character.* Chicago: University of Chicago Press, 1954.

Sobel, Robert. *The Age of Giant Corporations: A Microeconomic History of American Business, 1914–1984.* Westport, Conn.: Greenwood, 1984.

Whyte, William Hollingsworth. *The Organization Man.* New York: Simon and Schuster, 1956.

"How to Make a Billion: Fables of Texas Oil"

Magazine article

By: Harvey O'Connor

Date: February 26, 1955

Source: O'Connor, Harvey. "How to Make a Billion: Fables of Texas Oil." *The Nation,* February 26, 1955, 175–177.

About the Author: Harvey O'Connor (1897–1987), longtime business and labor journalist, brought a passion for social justice and a taste activism to his various writings. An expert on the inner-workings of the American petroleum industry, O'Connor is perhaps best known for his 1955 book *The Empire of Oil.* ∎

Introduction

The United States has produced a variety of colorful entrepreneurs over time. Few, however, have been more captivating than the legendary Texas oilmen. Americans have long been fascinated by the unique, down to earth, millionaire personality associated with Texas oilmen. Under the expensive suits, cowboy hats and boots, and plain speaking of the stereotype, however, there lie the minds of very cunning businessmen eager to protect and promote their wealth.

Contrary to common conception, the American oil industry did not originate in Texas. In fact, petroleum exploration came relatively late to the Lone Star State. The birthplace of oil exploration was Pennsylvania in 1859. Quaker State and Pennzoil are among the few remaining oil companies from the birthplace of American oil exploration. It was not until the turn of the century that oil exploration shifted to Texas and California.

From 1859 to 1945 the United States led the world in oil production and exports. After World War II (1939–45), however, the amount of petroleum deposits discovered in the Middle East and Soviet Union dwarfed the reserves in the United States. What the United States lacked in petroleum deposits, however, it made up for in technology. Despite having a smaller supply of petroleum, the United States, particularly Houston, Texas, still managed to dominate the oil exploration and refinery industry by virtue of its technology and business acumen. Texas enjoyed tremendous success in the oil industry by controlling drilling, pipeline construction, and refinery construction.

Significance

Despite the Texas oilman's reputation as a rugged individual, leaders of the oil industry relied heavily on government support for much of its success in the marketplace. Generous subsidies and tax breaks were granted to oil companies, often at the expense of other public programs. The growth of the oil exploration and refinery network in Texas also enabled powerful members of the industry to influence U.S. foreign policy, particularly U.S. policy toward the Middle East.

In 1953, for example, the United States became involved in the overthrow the existing Iranian government, which had recently nationalized the oil industry. The United States helped establish a government, headed by the Shah of Iran, who was less intent on developing Iran's oil industry than his predecessor. The United States became involved in large part to strengthen its position in the global oil market.

Oil barons also played an important role in the development of U.S. domestic policy. It is difficult for either a Democratic or Republican presidential candidate to win a majority of electoral college votes without winning the state of Texas. Out of fear of losing the support of Texas voters, both Democratic and Republican presidential candidates were reluctant to propose policies that might hinder the oil industry. Leaders of the oil industry would also throw their support behind key congressional candidates to strengthen their influence over domestic affairs. Among the policies that oil barons were able to influence was the implementation of certain tax laws that were softer on oil exploration enterprises than other businesses.

Primary Source

"How to Make a Billion: Fables of Texas Oil"
[excerpt]

> **SYNOPSIS:** Journalist Harvey O'Connor sheds light on the political machinations of America's most powerful and super rich: the Texas oilmen. In the following selection, O'Connor relates how these self-styled modern-day "cowboys" preach the philosophy of "rugged individualism" and self-reliance but, in actuality, shrewdly manipulate the government—in particular, the tax codes—to enhance their wealth.

On the theory that the more you take out of an oil well the less you have left, an ingenious tax theory has been evolved to assure the production of the biggest and most blatant crop of millionaires that the nation has seen since the "robber barons" flourished in the late nineteenth century.

The gimmick is "depletion allowance." The Treasury Department says it is the biggest of all loopholes in the tax laws, accounting for a loss of revenue of more than $500,000,000 a year on oil alone. The tall fortunes of the Texas tycoons—some estimated up to half-billion—garnered in the past twenty-five years come out of the deep holes of depletion allowance. In some cases Uncle Sam finds himself unable to pry a penny from the income of these nouveaux riches. If a well is a "dry hole," that is a deductible loss; if it produces, then 27½ per cent can be deducted on *gross* income. When the accountants get through with the books, there is often little left for the Bureau of Internal Revenue to figure on.

So it is that Hugh Roy Cullen, Haroldson Lafayette Hunt, Clint Murchison, and Sid Richardson have been able to accumulate in a brief span of years what it took John D. Rockefeller half a lifetime of patient planning to pocket. Rockefeller was obliged to organize an oil empire the hard way; if the present-day Croesuses have enough holes drilled into Mother Earth, a rigged tax structure assures them opulence. If Lady Luck smiles, they come within an ace of being able to buy up the entire United States. The country's only safety from such fate is that nothing pays off like an oil well; Eastern railroads, international airlines, Babylonian hotels—these are desired more as a pride of pomp and power than a source of income.

The "Four Hundred" of Houston, and the flanking millionaires of Dallas, Fort Worth, Tulsa, and other Southwestern towns, are personal testimonials to the efficacy of depletion allowance. But the major oil companies—Esso's Humble, Socony's Magnolia, Gulf, Texaco—and a score of minor companies specializing in exploration and drilling owe their amazing profits to tax-deductible holes in the ground, sources of wealth whether they run rich with crude oil or "dry" with salt water. The smaller companies, unencumbered by the losses sustained by the majors in marketing, reveal the true delights of tax favoritism; Argo, Honolulu, Louisiana Land and Exploration, Midwest, Pacific Western, Texas Gulf Producing, Texas Pacific Coal and Oil regularly report net income ranging from 30 to 80 per cent of gross income. Add to these the unreported incomes of a hundred family or personal corporations, such as the Cullens' Quintana and the Murchisons' Delhi, and it is easy to see why the Texas crowd of "filthy rich"—so well celebrated in Edna Ferber's "Giant"—are elbowing polished Easterners out of Wall Street.

These men operate in a jungle of "wildcats." A wildcat is a well drilled in territory where oil has not

Oilmen such as Hugh Roy Cullen benefited from loopholes in the tax codes to gain enormous wealth. © BETTMANN/CORBIS. REPRODUCED BY PERMISSION.

been discovered. On the average, says the American Petroleum Institute, eight out of nine wildcats are "dusters"—dry holes. It sounds like an unpromising way to earn money.

Here is where the tax laws come in. If the man behind the wildcat is in the bracket where 90 per cent of his income would go into the federal treasury, then wildcatting is Open Sesame! He can hardly lose so long as he keeps on drilling. The money he spends drilling eight "dusters" is deductible from his gross income. The income from his ninth well, a producer, is pretty much velvet, for all the "intangible" expenses, such as the preliminary geological work, and all the labor, equipment, and fuel costs of drilling are deductible. On top of that he can deduct 27½ per cent of his gross income on the well. . . .

"I know of no loophole in the laws so inequitable as the excessive depletion exemptions now enjoyed by oil and mining interests," said former President Truman. Senator Hubert Humphrey of Minnesota estimated that if depletion allowance had been dropped for ordinary depreciation, the entire tax increase on those earning less than $4,000 a year could have been avoided in the 1951 tax bill. In

The skyline of Houston, Texas, circa 1949. Houston dominated the oil-exploration and oil-refining industry by virtue of its technology and business acumen in the 1950s. **THE LIBRARY OF CONGRESS.**

1947 oil companies were able to deduct thirteen times more through depletion than they would have been allowed through the depreciation claimed by other industries. While most big industries are paying taxes at close to 70 per cent of their operating income, the oil industry is being tapped for about 25 per cent. The National Oil Marketers Association, feuding with the crude producers in 1953, estimated that the government could get a billion more in revenue by allowing "true" depletion instead of the flat figure of 27½ per cent.

For the oil magnates depletion allowance is the gateway to their private paradise, the touchstone of their national policy now that they have got the "tidelands." Before the portals stand guard the Texas Congressmen and their Southwestern confederates. When Robert Doughton, the conservative North Carolina Democrat, as chairman of the House Ways and Means Committee wanted to slice depletion allowance from 27½ per cent to 15 per cent, Speaker Sam Rayburn, a Texan, leaped into the breach. "The Speaker," said Doughton, "was terribly against any change in the oil-depletion-allowance provision. I know he made that plain to other members of the committee. Personally, I thought that loophole ought to be closed, that it was wrong, but the others were so much for keeping it that nothing could be done."

As a result, the stocks of companies specializing in crude-oil production are the darlings of Wall Street. Financial consultants refer to oil stocks as "tax-sheltered investments," an observation that recently led the treasurer of Humble Oil and Refining, the biggest Texas producer, to complain that the stock tipsters were doing a "disservice" to the industry. . . .

Depletion allowance is the deepest taproot of reaction in the United States. The hard-faced political primitives of Houston and Dallas, fortified by these easy millions, can guarantee that the Democratic Party, if it tries to be progressive, will be ruined. They can damn the middle-of-the-road Stevenson as a "creeping socialist" and split the solid South in two. They can do the same to Eisenhower, and are doing it, and can rejoice when the Republican Party is torn in twain. H. L. Hunt, barely noticing the expenditure, finances Facts Forum, the nation-wide radio and TV enterprise that equates moderation with communism. Roy Cullen can take a flier with the Liberty radio network, where John T. Flynn painted the United Nations as the minion of Moscow. To fantastic hundred-thousand-acre ranches hidden away in western Texas and Mexico by these beneficiaries of depletion allowances come the leaders of native facism in the United States Senate and House, for physical refreshment; in the deep pockets of these crude-oil kings can be found financial refreshment not only for election campaigns but for the bizarre crusades that bedevil American politics.

Further Resources
BOOKS

Donahue, Jack. *The Finest in the Land: The Story of the Petroleum Club of Houston.* Houston: Gulf, 1984.

Olien, Roger M., and Diana Davids Olien. *Wildcatters: Texas Independent Oilmen.* Austin: Texas Monthly Press, 1984.

Presley, James. *A Saga of Wealth: The Rise of the Texas Oilmen.* New York: Putnam, 1978.

"Consumer Credit: High But Safe"

Magazine article

By: *Newsweek*

Date: March 14, 1955

Source: "Consumer Credit: High But Safe." *Newsweek,* March 14, 1955, 75.

About the Publication: Thomas J. C. Martyn published the first issue of *Newsweek* in February 1933. In 1961, it was bought by the Washington Post Company. It's circulation is 3.1 million in the United States and over 900,000 internationally. ■

Introduction

Economists have long pondered the question of scarcity—will human beings ever have enough resources to fulfill basic needs? For most of U.S. history, scarcity economics dominated the thinking of scholars and the day-to-day lives of most Americans. In the 1920s, business leaders began talking about a "New Era" of economic activity based on mass production, mass consumption, and high wages. By the end of that decade, this hint of modern consumer culture was swept away by the Great Depression. This vision of a consumer economy and culture reemerged in the postwar years as more Americans entered the middle class due to rising productivity, growth, and income.

The great lesson of the 1920s seemed to be that employees had to have relatively high wages or salaries to engage in mass consumption. While much of the prosperity of the 1950s came from increased pay, a growing source also included the rapidly expanding consumer credit industry. In 1950, Diners' Club introduced the first credit card accounts, allowing Americans to purchase goods and services using money they would earn in the future. American Express and Sears Roebuck soon followed suit. With the expansion of consumer credit, many Americans could enjoy the material rewards of the consumer culture in their daily lives without having to worry about payment at the time of purchase.

Yet as this 1955 *Newsweek* article shows, consumer credit created complex tensions in American life. Bankers, financiers, car dealers, and appliance stores wanted to sell their products to more Americans. Buying an automobile, a TV, a refrigerator, a range, or a vacuum cleaner on the installment plan required a change in values held by Americans since the colonial period. Producers, employees, and consumers—often the same people—had to overcome historic distrust of spending, leisure, and mass consumption beyond the current paycheck. Lenders had to develop new ways of evaluating consumer risk before offering credit lines that would not strain individual or family budgets. If

they extended too much credit too soon, lenders could find customers defaulting on their debts. The problem of consumer debt emerged as a new facet of U.S. economic life.

Significance

For most of U.S. history, Americans had learned to save their money, keep their expenditures low, and internalize the values of hard work, thrift, and living within their means. Emergence of the mass production economy led to a growing reliance on huge amounts of consumer purchasing. This in turn required marketing and advertising, which had become an important part of the overall economy as early as the 1920s. Some U.S. corporations adopted credit plans such as the General Motors Acceptance Corporation, created in the 1920s. Allowing consumers to buy large ticket items such as cars and household appliances became even more significant in the postwar years. As the economy went through stages of the business cycle, lenders, consumers, manufacturers, and workers learned to adjust their production and consumption habits to fit the circumstances of the moment.

This was something new in the lives of most Americans even as late as the 1950s, as seen in the ambivalent discussion of consumer credit in this article. By that time, many American families found that the only way they could afford items once considered luxuries was to buy on credit or expand the family income with two-earner households that included husband and wife. By the end of the 1950's, Americans bought the overwhelming majority of their radios, television sets, kitchen appliances, and other consumer durables with lines of credit or the new credit cards offered by mass retailers, chain stores, and department stores. What had once been considered luxuries by earlier generations of Americans now came to be thought of as essentials. Americans outfitted their homes, cars, families, and recreational activities with all sorts of material goods that created, for the first time in U.S. history, a truly national culture defined by the acquisition of products flowing from the cornucopia of American abundance. Consumer indebtedness in the 1950s rose from $73 billion to $196 billion. Credit had become part of the American way of life.

Primary Source

"Consumer Credit: High But Safe"

> **SYNOPSIS:** The 1950s witnessed the introduction of the credit card as a preferred method of payment that soon replaced the then-existing patchwork arrangement of consumer finance options. For the American people, often weaned on advice to avoid debt, this revolution in consumer finance created some lingering anxiety. As the following excerpt

The prosperity of the 1950s was fueled in large part by huge consumer demand stimulated by easy consumer credit. © BETTMANN/CORBIS. REPRODUCED BY PERMISSION.

describes, however, American citizens showed no reluctance to continue spending.

In Washington last week, a young man with a good credit rating walked into a used-car lot and looked over a 1950 convertible. The price: $595. The down payment: Nothing. The result: A quick sale and 595 more dollars poured into the massive, moving stream of the nation's consumer credit.

Consumer credit was off on a new boom in Washington and all over the nation. As was the case with the stock market, the big question on credit was: Is it rising too fast or too high to be a healthy influence on the economy?

Government officials, who might have answered "maybe" in the case of stocks, were inclined to say "probably not" as far as credit was concerned. As one Administration economist put it: "You have to expect a bulge in consumer credit with good business."

Stimulants

There was no doubt that a credit bulge was developing, stimulated by the marked upturn in business activity and personal income. After a slow increase through most of last year, the credit level swelled almost $1 billion in December to a new all-time high of $30.1 billion. In January, strong upward pressure virtually wiped out the seasonal decline that usually comes after the flush of Christmas installment purchases.

A big reason for the increase, in addition to economic prosperity, was a buyers' (or borrowers') market at nearly every source of consumer credit. Banks, which found that the Administration's "loose money" policy gave them more funds than they could lend out, have supported the trend by easing up on their loan requirements.

With auto dealers pressing to keep sales up with booming production, "no down payment" and "three years to pay" deals have burgeoned in the auto-loan field (which accounts for about a third of all consumer credit). In a year and a half, the average auto-loan term has increased from sixteen to 22 months.

No Extremes

Nearly all businessmen agree with government observers that credit is neither too high nor rising too fast. They argue that credit, by stimulating buying, stimulates production and keeps business forging ahead. "Consumer debt can be 'too high' only to the extent that it includes debt which should never have been incurred in the first place," says Arthur Dietz, president of the C.I.T. Financial Corp.

Others, like H.H. Heimann, executive vice president of the National Association of Credit Men, agree that the picture is generally sound but warn of inherent dangers. Heimann points to the lengthening of auto-loan terms and an increase in defaults on TV and appliance purchases as signs of overextension in borrowing, although he doesn't think the trends are "too alarming." He is more concerned about "the philosophy that debt doesn't mean anything. You can only afford this philosophy when times are good." If an economic recession suddenly cut consumer income, repayment of old obligations would remove from the markets the very money needed to aid a business recovery, he says.

But A.L. Trotta, top credit man of the National Retail Dry Goods Association, believes that consumer credit has a built-in safety valve. People, he claims, "pace themselves [in their use of credit] according to what they believe the economy is going to do."

Important Difference

Bankers feel that consumer debt is still at a reasonable level in relation to disposable personal income—the figure which measures ability to pay. Right now, the average American is in hock for about 11½ per cent of his pay; the ratio has edged up from 10.3 per cent in 1950–51. The important difference, however, is in the lengthening of terms. Longer terms make more money available month to month for new spending, bolster the economy, one financier claims.

Pondering the old puzzler that plagues economists—"how high is up?," a government official puts it this way: "Credit probably won't look too heavy unless we get into another recession—but it's a situation worth watching."

Further Resources
BOOKS

Calder, Lendol Glen. *Financing the American Dream: A Cultural History of Consumer Credit.* Princeton, N.J.: Princeton University Press, 1999.

Cohen, Lizabeth. *A Consumers' Republic: The Politics of Mass Consumption in Postwar America.* New York: Alfred A. Knopf, 2003.

Horowitz, Daniel. *The Morality of Spending: Attitudes Toward the Consumer Society in America, 1870-1940.* Baltimore: Johns Hopkins University Press, 1985 and Chicago: Ivan R. Dee, 1992.

Klein, Lloyd. *It's in the Cards: Consumer Credit and the American Experience.* Westport, Conn.: Praeger, 1999.

Mandell, Lewis. *The Credit Card Industry: A History.* Boston: Twayne, 1990.

"The South Bets on Industry"
Magazine article

By: George M. MacNabb

Date: January 1957

Source: MacNabb, George M. "The South Bets on Industry." *American Mercury* 84, no. 396, January 1957, 14–19. ∎

Introduction

After the Civil War (1861–1865), when many southerners wished to return to their predominantly rural way of life, others decided to promote industrial and commercial growth such as that in the North. Accordingly, there emerged after the Civil War the so-called New South movement, which stressed economic development while retaining some older facets of traditional southern society, in particular those involving racial issues.

The South has always been potentially attractive to outside investors. The region contains abundant raw materials, comparatively low labor costs, and business-friendly state and local governments, along with an absence of troublesome labor unions. Despite these assets, however, the region remained economically underdeveloped until after World War II (1939–1945). Indeed, the situation had been so bleak that, as late as 1937, President Franklin Roosevelt (served 1933–1945) had labeled the South as the nation's "number one" economic problem.

The southern situation began to improve markedly during and after World War II. The stunning success of the Congress of Industrial Organizations' (CIO) union organizing campaign, which swept through the North from 1935 to 1940, created an even more pronounced wage differential between the two regions. While the failure by 1950 of the CIO's ambitious southern labor union recruitment strategy, Operation Dixie, served to underscore this fact, the South received economic help from the federal government. The federal government adopted a conscious strategy to flood the South with public works projects, including the construction and maintenance of military installations, which significantly boosted employment and development in the region. The South, predominantly Democratic, also benefited from the fact that the U.S. Congress at that time experienced Democratic majorities, with many southern committee chairmen in position to help out their states when need be.

Significance

By the late 1950s, the South had reached a crossroads in its economic development campaign. The signs of change were everywhere: new industry, connections to national markets, and a burgeoning basis in national retail chains. Elsewhere, the interstate highway system authorized in 1956 promised to facilitate the movement of goods and services and to break down some of the geographic isolation of the predominantly agricultural region from the rest of the nation. The advent of television also helped to challenge provincial values with a stream of images depicting a more urban, northern-based culture. All told, after eighty years, the New South finally appeared ready to materialize.

A large, unspoken issue involving southern industrialization was that of race. The South in the 1950s was very much segregated and increasingly tense. White business owners relied on cheap African American labor to handle menial tasks and offered little to no chance of advancement. In contrast, racism was less pronounced in the North, wages were higher, and African Americans could participate more actively in the region's economy. Forging stronger economic and political ties to the North would invariably place the increasingly visible southern race problem on the national agenda, as many businesses would be apt to take advantage of the cheap labor in the South, creating job loss in the North. In the end, however, the wave of technology and industrialization could not be turned back from the South.

Primary Source

"The South Bets on Industry" [excerpt]

SYNOPSIS: Nearly a century after the devastation of the Civil War and after much "booster" talk of a re-

born, industrialized New South, the region finally began to break out of its traditional agricultural mold during the 1950s. Indeed, as author George M. MacNabb notes, "The South Bets on Industry" to modernize and uplift the standard of living for its largely impoverished citizens.

John H. Jones, an industrial engineer, realized his life-long dream last spring when he left the New Jersey home he had occupied for 15 years and returned to his native South Carolina.

Jones had always wanted to live in the pleasant climate of his homeland, but had found no opportunities there and had trekked northward. Now his company had completed a branch plant in South Carolina, and he could go home as plant manager. At last he could in some measure repay his State for the education it had given him.

Jones had become a part of the "revolution" that is happening in the Southern States today—perhaps the fastest transformation of a society ever witnessed by man. . . .

With the approach of the centennial decade of the Civil War, attitudes in the South are once again Page One material for the nation and the world. The South maintains that its attitude toward segregation is not understood and that the nation's press should take more pains to explore the background and basis for its beliefs.

With all the thousands of articles and editorials that have followed the Supreme Court's integration decision, the economic side of the picture is receiving scant attention. Yet there is a very clear connection between the march of industry southward and the great question of segregation.

Many thoughtful Southerners have long held that the Negro's plight is largely an economic one. The Negro, they say, can find his true place in society only when his standards of living have been raised.

Curiously enough, the South has been under sharp attack for the very activity which may serve later to ease all the pains. Leaders of the southern states have not been standing by idly to await the coming of industry. They have been engaged for years in a vigorous campaign to go out and bring it in. In doing so, of necessity they have entered the great industrial centers where thousands depend on industry for a livelihood. There they have been greeted with an age old cry, "stop, thief!"

Union leaders and government officials have variously described these southern salesmen as burglars, pirates, ghouls, and carpetbaggers-in-reverse.

A towboat approaches a power plant on the Ohio River in West Virginia in 1959. By the late 1950s, southern states' move to industrialization began to modernize and uplift the standard of living for its largely impoverished citizens. © CHARLES E. ROTKIN/CORBIS. REPRODUCED BY PERMISSION.

On their side the southerners have paid little attention—they've been too busy building a new world.

Is it true what they say—that Dixie is plundering the northern states of industry by offering spectacular, if unfair, inducements? Is industry growing fat in the South because of sweat-shop labor, tax give-aways, and political handouts? . . .

The National Planning Association, in its 1949 study, "Why Industry Moves South," queried 88 new industries, found that, " . . . with few exceptions, company executives pointed out that they could not justify a large investment based only on such an uncertain matter as a North-South wage differential."

"Our survey," said the report, "indicates that three-fourths of the new southern plants investigated were attracted to that region . . . by the market and materials."

Concessions? Inducements? It is true that some manufacturers, in nearly every case smaller ones whose credit is strained, come South looking for bargains? . . .

Through these and other business-like methods, the South is seeking to raise itself by its own boot-straps and to become a more vital part of the nation's economy. Until the incomes of all its people are nearer the national average, it will always be a region apart.

And until the day comes when Georgia and Alabama are as well off as Kansas and Connecticut, the South must concentrate on its economic problems, in the firm belief that they are more important to all its people than the painful question of segregation.

Can the south hope for continued economic gains?

Here's what a northerner has to say of this point. Harold F. Clark, professor of education economics at Teachers College, Columbia University, has said:

> There is no reason why within a century South Carolina, Mississippi, and Arkansas should not become the three richest states in the union. They are better supplied with water than almost any other state. This could easily become a decisive advantage in the period just ahead.
>
> A dependable supply of water is going to be crucial for agriculture. Many industries are already drastically limited because of the growing shortage of water. If you couple these factors with a climate mild enough for workers to spend their leisure time outdoors almost the year around, you have the basic requirements for an extraordinary economic expansion.

Further Resources

BOOKS

Griffith, Barbara S. *The Crisis of American Labor: Operation Dixie and the Defeat of the CIO.* Philadelphia: Temple University Press, 1988.

Newman, Harvey K. *Southern Hospitality: Tourism and the Growth of Atlanta.* Tuscaloosa: University of Alabama Press, 1999.

"Convention Expels Teamsters"

Journal article

By: *American Federationist*

Date: January 1958

Source: "Convention Expels Teamsters." *American Federationist,* January 1958, 18–19. ∎

Introduction

During the industrial union organizing drives of the late 1930s, union activists had used the sit-down strike as a successful tactic. Many middle class Americans, however, saw this as willful violation of the law. During mobilization for World War II (1939–1945), quickie strikes and major coal strikes led by John L. Lewis of the United Mine Workers furthered soured public opinion on unions. After passage of the Taft-Hartley Act in 1947, labor leaders and unions had to follow increasingly complicated federal rules, including signing an anticommunist pledge, to use government agencies in labor disputes. By the middle of the 1950s, organized labor had passed its peak years to begin a long-term decline in membership as a percentage of the non-agricultural work force.

Antiunion activity by some employers, postwar prosperity, the use of collective bargaining, and a shift from blue collar physical labor to white collar and service work further eroded organized labor. By 1955, feuding unions in the competing American Federation of Labor (AFL) and the Congress of Industrial Organizations (CIO) patched up their differences to unite under the banner of a merged labor federation, the AFL-CIO. As had happened in the prosperous 1920s, organized labor went on the defensive in the abundant 1950s.

Public attention to organized labor centered on the problem of corruption in union leadership and the growing bureaucratic complexities of union organizations rather than on improving the quality of life for rank and file members. When the U.S. Senate Select Committee on Improper Activities in the Labor or Management Field under conservative Senator John L. McClellan (D-Ark.) began hearings in 1957, it focused on the corrupt practices of leaders of the International Brotherhood of Teamsters, Chauffeurs, Warehousemen, and Helpers (IBT) union, part of the AFL-CIO, commonly known as the Teamsters. Under the direction of Dave Beck and his successor, Jimmy Hoffa, the Teamsters organized over-the-road truck drivers, often using the muscle of organized crime to fight union drives in a highly competitive and corrupt sector of the economy.

This 1958 article from the AFL-CIO's official journal, *American Federationist*, describes AFL-CIO leadership action under president George Meany to expel the Teamsters from the house of labor. The McClellan Committee hearings had revealed extensive corruption in the form of bribery, kickbacks, ties with organized crime, and embezzlement of regional Teamster funds by president Dave Beck and regional conference leader Jimmy Hoffa.

Significance

During the prosperous Fifties, organized labor experienced hard times, while many workers joined the abundant society. Amidst Cold War charges of communist espionage, antiunion drives by many employers, and ongoing competition among various unions, labor union membership hit an all-time peak in the mid-1950s. Many of the affiliated unions of the newly merged AFL-CIO (1955) had allied with the Democratic Party in the 1930s.

When conservatives in Congress targeted unions for investigation under racketeering laws in the late 1950s, they fixed on one of the few Republican-allied unions, the International Brotherhood of Teamsters. Finding fault with corrupt leaders such as Dave Beck and Jimmy Hoffa came easily to McClellan Committee counsel Robert F. Kennedy. The hearings began a long-running feud between Kennedy and Hoffa, the Democratic Party and Teamsters leadership, and the Teamsters union and the AFL-CIO. After extensive hearings, Congress passed the Landrum-Griffin Act in 1959 that imposed further restrictions, more complicated rules, and more narrow labor-management relations on all unions in the name of "labor reform."

The Teamsters and organized labor as a whole came under increasing criticism by conservative politicians and the broader public partly in reaction to the huge popularity of big business during the 1950s. Ironically, Teamsters leaders Beck and Hoffa proved very popular with rank and file truck drivers who liked the higher wages, paid holidays, health insurance, and other benefits union membership brought. Just as unions followed in corporate footsteps to create large bureaucracies, rank and file workers entered a period of relative prosperity for themselves.

After the Teamsters were expelled from the AFL-CIO, organizers went after new members in now competing AFL-CIO unions to make the Teamsters the largest and most powerful labor union by the middle of the 1960s. The earlier reform idealism of industrial unionists had become the more narrowly cast bread and butter unionism of the postwar era that improved members' lives, often failed to organize unorganized workers, and further extended the growing gap between working class and middle class Americans caught up in postwar prosperity.

Primary Source

"Convention Expels Teamsters"

> **SYNOPSIS:** As discussed in the following article, the leadership of the nation's largest union federation, the AFL-CIO, led by Meany, takes a strong stand against racketeering by voting to suspend the wayward Teamsters Union, led by Hoffa. In the end, the solidarity of organized labor is shattered as the Teamsters reject cries for reform and decide to strike out on their own.

Jimmy Hoffa was leader of the Teamsters Union from 1957 to 1971. **ARCHIVE PHOTOS, INC. REPRODUCED BY PERMISSION.**

Expulsion of the International Brotherhood of Teamsters was voted by the AFL-CIO convention on the basis of findings that the union was substantially controlled or dominated by corrupt elements. Expulsion came on a roll-call vote after a three-hour debate on an Appeals Committee report sustaining the Executive Council decision that the union had failed to oust unethical and corrupt officers or investigate their conduct and had otherwise defied the ethical standards of the AFL-CIO.

Just before the roll-call, AFL-CIO President George Meany repudiated any suggestion of a "war" with the Teamsters following expulsion.

"There is no plan for a war at all," he said. "We hope it will never come."

Mr. Meany made it clear that the door was open for the union's return to the AFL-CIO as soon as it complies with the directives.

The vote in favor of expulsion was 10,458,598. Voting against the Appeals Committee recommendation were 2,266,497. Under the constitution a two-thirds majority was required for ouster.

Delegates of ninety-four international affiliates cast votes in favor of expulsion, twenty-one internationals voted against and four split their votes. Eight other internationals either did not attend the convention or failed to answer on the roll-call.

Discussion Precedes Balloting

The convention voted after Alex Rose, chairman of the Appeals Committee and president of the Hatters, and President Meany had spoken in favor of expulsion and spokesmen and supporters of the Teamsters had spoken against such action.

The Appeals Committee report was presented by Secretary John J. Murphy, general secretary of the Bricklayers. The committee held that the Teamsters had been given "adequate opportunity" to respond to charges and correct abuses and had "refused to do so." The report therefore recommended that findings of corrupt influences be confirmed and that the union be expelled from the AFL-CIO.

Vice-President Einar O. Mohn of the Teamsters made the official reply for his union, arguing that "sin is universal and ever-recurring." Speaking of Senator John L. McClellan, chairman of the Senate special committee investigating labor-management improprieties, Mohn said Senator McClellan's record and recent public statements "compel me to believe that the field he seeks to clean up will emerge torn asunder, bloody and weak—but perhaps ethical."

The Teamsters are a highly decentralized union, Mohn declared, and any conclusion that it is "substantially influenced by corrupt influences" fails to show "an understanding of our makeup."

Secretary-Treasurer John F. English of the Teamsters repeated in debate much of the defense of his union and President-elect James R. Hoffa, a principal target of corruption charges, he had made at the Teamsters' convention at Miami Beach which elected Hoffa.

Hoffa has "done more for the Teamsters than any other man, including myself," English claimed.

"The penalty urged against the union is too severe," he said, adding that the expulsion proposal "makes my blood run cold."

A large delegation of the Teamsters, including members both of the old and the recently elected executive boards, sat as guests of the convention while the debate took place and heard spokesmen of six other unions rise to speak against the expulsion recommendation.

These included President Sal B. Hoffmann, Upholsterers; President Joseph P. McCurdy, United Garment Workers; Secretary-Treasurer Edward F. Carlough, Sheet Metal Workers; President Woodruff Randolph, Typographical Union; President George Q. Lynch, Pattern Makers, and Secretary-Treasurer Patrick E. Gorman, Meat Cutters.

Chairman Rose led the debate for the Appeals Committee by saying it was "precisely because we know the great role the Teamsters can play that we want a fraternal, clean Teamsters' organization as part of the labor movement."

"We are condemning a system which does not bring forward the best and work for the benefit of that organization but to the benefit of Dave Beck and Jimmy Hoffa," he told the convention.

He didn't want to contradict Mohn about the McClellan committee. Mr. Rose said, "but I don't know whether the proceedings of the Teamsters' convention—the behavior, the arrogance, the defiance—were not even worse from the point of view of labor interests."

Defiance by the Teamsters' convention in electing Hoffa was "not an act of courage," Mr. Rose said. He added:

It was defiance as an act of vulgarity and irresponsibility.

The Executive Council found the International Brotherhood of Teamsters guilty of a rejection of the basic principle set forth in the AFL-CIO's constitution, to which the Teamsters subscribed in 1955, that the AFL-CIO must be free from any corrupt influences.

The Teamsters could have remained in affiliation with the AFL-CIO by carrying out instructions to eliminate from international union office those who constitute corrupt influences and by accepting a special committee, appointed by the Council, with "authority to direct such further actions by the Teamsters Union" as might be required to wipe out corrupt influences.

The Appeals Committee told the convention:

The Executive Council's action in suspending the Teamsters Union and its recommendation that the Teamsters Union be expelled is in no sense discriminatory and does not subject the Teamsters Union to unequal or unfair treatment. Indeed, any other action than that taken by the Council would, in the view of this committee, be unequal and unfair.

The Teamsters Union was given adequate opportunity to respond to the charges against it on their merits. It refused to do so. The Teamsters Union was given adequate opportunity to correct the abuses and to eliminate the corrupt influences found by the Executive Council. It refused to do so. Any course other than that taken by the Council and recommended by it would be grossly unfair to other unions which have attempted both to answer the charges against them and to correct the conditions found by the Council to exist.

President Meany, closing the debate, answered briefly two charges from the floor—that the procedure had been faulty and that the Executive Council had acted as a "dictatorship." He also responded to Delegate Gorman of the Meat Cutters, who had spoken of his efforts to bring Hoffa and Mr. Meany together.

"That's true," the AFL-CIO president said.

But Hoffa never showed up.

"I am for the teamster," Mr. Meany told the convention. "I am for getting the teamster away from this corrupt control. And I say to you, right here and now, I have the door open. It was open until 11 o'clock last night. It will be open after you finish voting."

Further Resources

BOOKS

Brill, Steven. *The Teamsters.* New York: Simon and Schuster, 1978.

Dubofsky, Melvyn and Warren Van Tine, eds. *Labor Leaders in America.* Urbana: University of Illinois Press, 1987.

Hutchinson, John. *The Imperfect Union: A History of Corruption in American Trade Unions.* New York: Dutton, 1970.

Moldea, Dan E. *The Hoffa Wars: Teamsters, Rebels, Politicians, and the Mob.* New York: Paddington Press distributed by Grosset & Dunlap, 1978.

Russell, Thaddeus. *Out of the Jungle: Jimmy Hoffa and the Remaking of the American Working Class.* New York: Knopf, 2001.

Sloane, Arthur A. *Hoffa.* Cambridge, MA: MIT Press, 1991.

"Why the Edsel Laid an Egg: Research vs. the Reality Principle"

Journal article

By: Samuel Ichiye Hayakawa

Date: Spring 1958

Source: Hayakawa, Samuel Ichiye. "Why the Edsel Laid an Egg: Research vs. the Reality Principle." *ETC: A Review of General Semantics,* Spring 1958, 217–221.

About the Author: Samuel Ichiye Hayakawa (1906–1992), Canadian-born, was a world-renowned author, scholar, and
expert in semantics (the study of language and meaning). After a brilliant career as a university professor and administrator, Hayakawa, a conservative Republican, was elected in a stunning upset as a U.S. senator from California in 1976. He served in Washington, D.C., from 1977 to 1983. ∎

Introduction

Despite its reputation for being the single worst automobile ever manufactured, the Edsel may not quite deserve this dubious distinction. The Ford Pinto, for example, which contained its gasoline tank in the rear causing it to explode on impact, could be considered a worse vehicle in terms of safety standards. Likewise, the Corvair Monza was known to spin out of control for no apparent reason. The Chevrolet Vega could also be in the running for worst cars ever manufactured, given the body's tendency to virtually begin corroding on the showroom floor. Still, justly or unjustly, the Edsel will likely go down in history as the ultimate example of automotive miscalculation.

The problem for the Edsel may have originated with its name. Henry Ford, the founder of Ford Motor Company, named the car after his favorite son and heir-apparent to the family business, who died prematurely in 1943. Ford's tribute to his late son turned out to be a marketing disaster due to its lack of aesthetic appeal. Comics sarcastically inquired why the care was not named "Willard" or "Norbert."

Apart from its unappealing name the Edsel's styling also contributed to is poor reception. The car was described as the "poor man's Cadillac," which placed it somewhere between a luxury sedan and an economical middle-class car. Although the engineers' goal was to appeal to both the luxury sedan and middle-class car shoppers with the body style, they managed to satisfy neither. The Edsel's front end featured an atrocious "toilet-seat" grille, which managed to repulse car shoppers from all walks of life.

Significance

The 1958 Edsel was a tremendous marketing failure. Critics of the American automobile industry, already biased against 1958 model cars, watched the Edsel's downfall with great anticipation. Ford's failure to attract buyers to later models of the Edsel (1959 and 1960) cemented the car's inglorious fate. To a certain extent the Edsel was a casualty of larger forces at work in American society. By 1958 the automobile market had been saturated with large, ornate vehicles. The size of American automobiles had reached monstrous proportions and featured space-age styling, complete with aerodynamic fins. These large, opulent body styles may have been a reflection of the United States' enthusiasm for air travel and the recently inaugurated space program. (In response to the former

They'll know you've *arrived*

when you drive up in an Edsel

Step into the 1958 Edsel and you'll soon find out where the excitement is this year.

Drivers coming toward you spot that classic vertical grille a block away. And as you pass, they glance into their rear-view mirrors for another look at this year's most exciting car.

On the open road, your Edsel is watched eagerly for the already-famous performance of its big, new V-8 Edsel Engine.

And parked in front of your home, your Edsel gets even more attention—because it always says a lot about you. It says you chose elegant styling, luxurious comfort and such exclusive features as Edsel's famous Teletouch Drive— only shift that puts the buttons where they belong, on the steering-wheel hub.

Your Edsel also means you made a wonderful buy. For of all medium-priced cars, this one really new car is actually priced the lowest.* See your Edsel Dealer this week.

Based on actual comparison of suggested retail delivered prices of the Edsel Ranger and similarly equipped cars in the medium-price field.

EDSEL DIVISION • FORD MOTOR COMPANY

Above: Edsel Citation 2-door Hardtop. Engine: the E-475, with 10.5 to one compression ratio, 345 hp, 475 ft.-lb. torque. Transmission: Automatic with Teletouch Drive. Suspension: Ball-joint with optional air suspension. Brakes: self-adjusting.

1958 EDSEL

Of all medium-priced cars, the one that's really new is the lowest-priced, too!

An advertisement for the 1958 Ford Edsel. The Edsel's marketing did little to bolster sales as Americans began developing a suspicion for flashy advertising campaigns. **THE ADVERTISING ARCHIVE LTD. REPRODUCED BY PERMISSION.**

Soviet Union's launch of *Sputnik* in 1957, the United States launched its first satellite on January 31, 1958.)

The Edsel might be seen as an extreme example of a style that was weakening in the marketplace. In addition, larger automobiles were falling out of favor with the environmentally conscious, who saw the heavy gas-guzzling machines as pollution generators. In many ways 1958 model cars signified waste, gaudiness, and a lack of civic responsibility, and the Edsel's failure may have partially been a reaction against this excess.

The Edsel's slick marketing campaign did little to bolster sales. The absence of brand-name loyalty required Ford to generate demand for the vehicle with an aggressive advertising campaign. Unfortunately for Ford, Americans were developing a suspicion for flashy advertising campaigns thanks to the 1957 publication of Vance Packard's best-selling exposé of the advertising industry and its chicanery, *The Hidden Persuaders*. The Edsel was therefore not only up against an American consumer who was tired of over-sized gaudy vehicles, but one who was suspicious of being swindled by a "hidden persuader."

In addition to these difficulties the Edsel ran up against a small but formidable competitor in the marketplace. At approximately the same time Ford Motor Company introduced the Edsel to the American pubic, the German-made Volkswagen Beetle (the "Bug") was making its debut in the United States. The contrast, in the critics' estimation, did not work to the Edsel's advantage. The sensible little Beetle—small, lightweight, fuel-efficient, and stylistically unpretentious—seemed the antithesis of the behemoth Edsel. In response to the Beetle, American manufactures began introducing smaller vehicles in 1959. In hindsight, the diminutive European import marked a turning point in the automobile market, transitioning consumers from large and gaudy to compact and economical cars.

Primary Source

"Why the Edsel Laid an Egg: Research vs. the Reality Principle" [excerpt]

SYNOPSIS: The Ford Edsel has been, and will likely continue to be, considered one of the most notable marketing failures in automotive history. However, on closer examination, the 1958 Ford Edsel may simply have been the wrong car at the wrong time. In the following excerpt, Samuel Ichiye Hayakawa seeks to explain more precisely why this supposedly innovative automobile was received so poorly by the American public, despite Detroit's best advertising and public relations efforts.

The automobile is certainly one of the most important nonlinguistic symbols in American culture.

As the advertisements keep telling us, it is one of our ways of telling others who we are, from Cadillac as a "symbol of achievement," to Ford as a symbol of "young-mindedness," to Plymouth, which says, according to a recent ad, "We're not the richest people in town, but we're the proudest. We're the kind of family that gets a big bang out of living." Even those who simply want transportation, with no fads or frills or nonsense, can buy a Jeep and "say" so. . . .

Different people have different needs, with respect both to transportation and self-expression. Hence there should be, in a rich economy like that of the United States, variety in automobiles no less than in other facets of life. Hence I believe that manufacturers should build *some* cars of very high horsepower for those who need such cars, whether for practical or psychological reasons. I do not object to *some* cars being styled to allay unconscious sexual anxieties or to provoke space-ship fantasies, if people want such cars. *Some* cars should be little and unpretentious, because there are many modest, unassuming people in the U.S., hard as this may be to believe on the basis of car ads. And since, as one obscene cigarette ad puts it, some people "like their pleasure BIG," *some* cars, whether for practical or psychological reasons, should be big. Some people love ostentation; hence it is inevitable and necessary in the free economy that manufacturers produce for their benefit *some* huge and suitably dazzling ostentation wagons.

My quarrel with the American automobile industry in 1957 was not that it produces overpriced, overpowered, oversized, and over-elaborate cars, but that it produces them almost to the exclusion of all other kinds. Except for some interesting experiments at the fringes of the market by American Motors and Studebaker, the dominating forces in the industry—General Motors, Ford, and Chrysler—are still carrying on in 1958 their assault on consumer intelligence. The "Big Three" are producing no cars that are not expensive, hideous, and (except for a few sixes) costly to operate and powered far beyond the needs of the ordinary motorist. . . .

Again we are being told that what we need is power ("Try the B-12,000 engine. It puts 12,000 pounds of thrust behind every engine stroke!"), Gull-Wing fenders, Swept-Wing styling, with Turbo-Flash performance, in Firesweep Corsair Star Chief hardtops with that Bold New Look. Again the explicit statement of the sex theme, "Hot, Handsome, a Honey to Handle."

For what? For Father to commute 17 miles to work—a distance which, with favorable traffic conditions (and they are not always favorable), he will cover at an average rate of 30 m.p.h. For Mother to drop Chrissie off at dancing school, stopping at the supermarket and the public library on the way back. For Doug, the candy salesman, to make his calls on neighborhood stores. For Florence, the social caseworker, to visit her clients. For Pete, the insurance adjuster; for Stanley, the instructor at the university extension center; for Andy, the television repair man—all of whom need their cars for their work and their occasional holiday week-ends.

It does not come altogether as a surprise, therefore, that in the spring of 1958 the volume of new automobile sales is crushingly disappointing to the trade. The Edsel has laid a colossal egg. *Time* . . . (March 31, 1958) reports that the sale of "medium-priced" cars has fallen disastrously. The manufacturers blame the recession. . . .

The trouble with car manufacturers (who, like other isolated people in underdeveloped areas, are devout believers in voodoo) is that they have been listening too long to the motivation research people. Motivation researchers are those harlot social scientists who, in impressive psychoanalytic and/or sociological jargon, tell their clients what their clients want to hear, namely, that *appeals to human irrationality are likely to be far more profitable than appeals to rationality.* This doctrine appeals to moguls and would-be moguls of all times and places, because it implies that if you hold the key to people's irrationality, you can exploit and diddle them to your heart's content and be loved for it.

The Great Gimmick of the motivation researchers, therefore, is the investigation of irrationality, of which we all have, goodness knows, an abundance. Many people (perhaps most) have sexual anxieties and fears of impotence, as the motivation researchers say. Many upward-strivers (most, I am sure) like to impress their neighbors with the display of costly status symbols. Many people (surely not most!) allay their feelings of inadequacy with space-ship fantasies. . . .

Motivation researchers seem not to know the difference between the sane and the unsane. Having learned through their "depth" techniques that we all have our irrationalities (no great discovery at this date), they fatuously conclude that we are equally governed by those irrationalities at *all* levels of consumer expenditure—although it doesn't take a social science genius to point out that the more

expensive an object is, the more its purchase compels the recognition of reality. The fact that irrationalities may drive people from Pall Mall cigarettes to Marlboro or vice versa proves little about what the average person is likely to do in selecting the most expensive object (other than a house) that he ever buys.

The trouble with selling symbolic gratification via such expensive items as the Phallic Ford, the Edsel Hermaphrodite, and the Plymouth with the Rear-End Invitation is the competition offered by much cheaper forms of symbolic gratification, such as *Playboy* (50 cents a copy), *Astounding Science Fiction* (35 cents a copy), and television (free). When, on the advice of their voodoo men, auto-makers abandon their basic social function of providing better, safer, and more efficient means of transportation in favor of entering the business of selling dreams (in which the literary and entertainment industries have far more experience and resources), they cannot but encounter competition which they are not equipped to meet.

The consumer rush to the little foreign cars does not appear to me a passing fad, although Detroit is trying to reassure itself by saying that the foreign-car trend has reached its peak. The Morris Minor, the English Fords, the Hillman, the Simca, the Volkswagen, the Volvo, the Fiat, and all the other lovely little bugs that we see today in increasing numbers are cheap to operate. As for what they "communicate," they give out simple, unassuming messages devoid of delusions of grandeur. Their popularity indicates a widespread reassertion of an orientation towards reality, which says that $1600 is less than $2800, that 30 miles per gallon is cheaper transportation than 8 to 13 miles per gallon, that a 155′ Renault is easier to park than a 214′ Dodge. The very people who are writing the ads for Plymouth, Ford, and Chevrolet are driving DKW's, MG's, and Triumphs, while their bosses, the agency heads, ride around in Jaguars and Bentleys. It will take the American auto industry five years, if not a decade or two, to regain the respect and confidence of their best friend, the American consumer.

Further Resources

BOOKS

Brooks, John. *The Fate of the Edsel and Other Business Adventures.* New York: Harper and Row, 1963.

Deutsch, Jan G., ed. *Selling the People's Cadillac: The Edsel and Corporate Responsibility.* New Haven, Conn.: Yale University Press, 1976.

Warnock, C. Gayle. *The Edsel Affair: . . . What Went Wrong? A Narrative.* Paradise Valley, Ariz.: Pro West, 1980.

"The 'Invisible' Unemployed"

Magazine article

By: Daniel Bell

Date: July 1958

Source: Bell, Daniel. "The 'Invisible' Unemployed." *Fortune,* July 1958, 105–109, 198, 202.

About the Author: Daniel Bell (1919–) was one of the twentieth century's most influential American sociologists and political observers. A Columbia University professor, Bell authored numerous books, including his two signature works, *The End of Ideology: On the Exhaustion of Political Ideas in the Fifties* (1960) and *The Cultural Contradictions of Capitalism* (1976). A one-time staunch liberal, Bell became a leader of the emerging neoconservative movement of the 1970s. ∎

Introduction

The Great Depression fundamentally altered the American public's fundamental perception of the proper role that the U.S. government should play in the economy. Consensus emerged during this era that the government should regulate and stimulate business from the sidelines, thus rejecting full-blown socialism based on government ownership. The state exerted a gentle (and, at times, not so gentle) guiding hand largely from behind the scenes. This system might be characterized as government-regulated capitalism. The overriding purpose of this arrangement was to promote stability, taming the heretofore unpredictable business cycle in order to forestall the traditional episodes of "boom and bust."

In actuality, the United States has never suffered another economic downturn as severe as that of the 1930s. Most of the economic downswings since the Great Depression have been recessions. A recession is a downturn in the business cycle that occurs when the total output of goods and services by the U.S. population declines for six months to a year. Main characteristics of a recession are a decrease in employment, income, trade, and production output. A longer lasting and more severe economic crisis is termed a depression. The worst rate during the Great Depression of the 1930s was 30 percent. Since that juncture, no unemployment rate has remotely approached this figure. The 11 percent unemployment rate of 1982 remains the high point in post–Great Depression times.

Significance

Despite the widespread perception that the presidency of Dwight Eisenhower (served 1953–1961) was a period of prosperity, it did experience the 1957–1958 recession. It was the first recession following World War II (1939–1945) to impact the so-called Rustbelt, the

Blue-collar workers were laid off in great numbers during the 1958 recession. © **CHARLES E. ROTKIN/CORBIS. REPRODUCED BY PERMISSION.**

northern and midwestern industrial states. The signs of long-term economic decline in 1957–1958 were already self-evident and provided a glimpse of the future downsizing and deindustrialization of the region that became conspicuous after 1970.

Rustbelt industry relied too heavily on outmoded plants and equipment and exhibited reluctance to invest capital in new technology. Powerful unions had saddled firms with huge fixed labor costs. The relocation of industry to the nonunion Sunbelt was more or less inevitable. Then, too, the Rustbelt economy, which was based on coal, steel, and railroads, was vulnerable to changing trends. Oil and natural gas soon became the preferred fuels for environmental reasons, lighter weight aluminum and plastics replaced steel, and the airlines and trucks (aided by the construction of the country's Interstate Highway System) took passengers and freight away from the railroads.

In retrospect, it is curious that few observers in 1957–1958 saw what was coming. In the words of social critic Daniel Bell, the American unemployed, at this juncture, tended to be regarded as "invisible." Moreover, after 1960, in addition to the Rustbelt problems listed previously, cheap foreign-made products began flooding the country. The rest of the industrialized world had been seriously damaged during World War II, thus ensuring American economic hegemony throughout the 1950s. But the foreign economic revival shifted into high gear after 1960. Sporting new factories, the latest technology, and blessed with significantly lower labor costs, foreign nations flooded the United States with cheap imported goods. This slew of inexpensive imports proved extremely popular with the American public.

Primary Source

"The 'Invisible' Unemployed" [excerpt]

> **SYNOPSIS:** The sharp, but brief economic downturn of 1957–1958 was the first recession of the post–Great Depression. This recession draws the attention of Bell, who enumerates many of the structural problems that will lead to the massive deindustrialization in many regions of the country in the coming decades.

One of the mysteries of the 1957–58 recession is that during the months unemployment was most talked about it was very difficult to see. A Congress that in February had been alarmed enough for a tax cut returned after the Easter recess considerably puzzled; despite the rising statistics of unemployment, there seemed to be little evidence of any real distress. Even in mid-May, when unemployment had leveled out at slightly less than five million, and nearly one million people had exhausted unemployment benefits, the unemployed were still hard to find.

For this has been a peculiarly stratified recession. Unlike the depression of the early Thirties, when almost every group was severely affected, this has been primarily a blue-collar slump, hitting industrial workers rather than the white-collar, professional, or managerial groups. And even among the blue-collar workers some industries and some geographical areas have been almost unscathed. The slump is concentrated principally in the metalworking industries. It is centered in the industrial complexes of the Great Lakes and Atlantic tidewater areas. And it has affected primarily the Negro, the unskilled, and the young—groups least able to express their dismay.

Nationally, the unemployed could hardly make much of an impression; they form 7½ per cent of the labor force vs. a "normal" minimum of 2 or 3 per cent unemployed. And more than 60 million Americans, after all, are still at work. Yet even where the unemployed are concentrated, they are curiously unobtrusive. In a town as hard hit as Gary, Indiana,

where one out of every five steelworkers is unemployed, few individuals loiter; some gather at the union hall, but in most instances the men are at home, usually watching TV all day. Elsewhere they are either swallowed up in the sprawling industrial countryside or as at Gary they retreat to the privacy of their homes.

It may well be that by the end of the year unemployment will have receded below the five-million high-water mark. But it is unlikely to go below four million this year even if business turns up fairly briskly in the second half because the labor force will have grown by about 900,000 during 1958. And whatever the course of business recovery, it seems clear that the recession has already administered a psychological shock. Despite the relatively small number of unemployed, the effects may be far reaching:

> The recession may be altering the newly formed middle-class buying habits of the well-paid worker, habits that had gone far to shape the new markets of the 1950's. In the mid-Fifties, the production worker, because he could earn $100 a week and buy the appurtenances of middle-class life, began to think of himself as a middle-class person. This feeling may be changing, at least among workers in hard-hit industries like steel and auto, and their psychology might spread to other industrial workers.
>
> The recession may bring about a renewed dependence and loyalty to the union among workers who had begun to be skeptical, or cynical about the union leadership.
>
> It may precipitate a Democratic sweep in November, and increase the possibility of a Democratic presidential victory in 1960.
>
> It may result in the permanent beaching of a number of the unemployed. New efficiencies, tightening of standards, increased mechanization, and discard of old plant will reduce the number of jobs in particular areas. Some of this loss will be offset by increased jobs elsewhere. Yet the process may create new "distressed areas" that will act as a drag on the economy.

Feeling the Blues

What the 1958 recession has done is to emphasize, particularly to the young, that workers do not have middle-class security. Companies severely hit rarely laid off the white-collar worker—at worst, as at Philco or Chrysler, the salaried group took 2 to 10 per cent pay cuts. But blue-collar workers were laid off in great numbers—and quickly; in steel, between 33 and 39 per cent of all production workers have been furloughed, compared with 3 to 4 per cent of the salaried group. At Chrysler's Jefferson assembly plant, by May, about 3,500 of the 10,000 production workers had been laid off, while none of the 600 white-collar employees had been laid off (about 100 either had been transferred to other Chrysler plants or had left voluntarily).

Among the blue-collar workers, the hardest hit have been the unskilled and semiskilled groups. In May, about one out of every six unskilled workers was unemployed, as against one in eight for the semiskilled, one in eleven for the skilled, one in twenty-two for sales and clerical, and only one out of sixty in the technical and professional group.

Those best protected were workers over fifty-five; about one out of seventeen of these older workers was unemployed. In most instances, union seniority rules had saved their jobs. By the same token, the first ones to go were the younger men, and the largest concentration of unemployed (apart from the new entries into the labor market) is among the men between twenty-five and thirty-five. . . .

In almost every city the heaviest burdens in the recession have fallen upon the Negro. While one out of every fifteen white workers was unemployed, one out of every seven Negroes was jobless. The Negroes out of work in April numbered about 1,024,000, or 20 per cent of the 5,200,000 unemployed. The reasons lay in the fact that the Negroes constitute the higher proportions of the unskilled, and they have the lowest seniority. . . .

The Index of Resentment

Most of the other hard-hit communities share the same mood, but nerves are becoming a little frayed. A new form of "grotesque" joke, tailored to the recession, has made its appearance and spread rapidly. For example: An unemployed father is playing baseball with his sons. One of them asks: "Daddy, are we going to have time for another game?" And the father says cheerfully: "Yes, we will. We're not having any dinner tonight." In Detroit, men of sixteen years' seniority are now running out of unemployment compensation, and day-old bread graces the table. Youngsters' allowances are eliminated. The crime rate is rising, particularly among Negroes. One shop owner in Detroit, dismayed by increasing petty thievery, had his counters caged in

with screening wire, and pushes the candy bar under the opening to the customers. . . .

The older men, many of whom until now have fared relatively well, have begun to feel qualms, not about layoffs, to which they are are better conditioned than the younger men, but about the "downgrading" of jobs as layoffs increased. For as the number of workers was cut, senior men took on menial tasks at lower pay. The downgrading seems to have affected the men more than any other blow. . . .

Even if the U.S. economy by the end of 1958 reaches the levels of production it touched in 1955–57, it seems likely that some areas will remain distressed for varying periods of time. One reason is that many firms, because of tightened standards, better planning, cost control, and mechanization, will rehire fewer workers than before, and achieve the same output with fewer hands. The net result of the recession, therefore, may be to shake out several hundred thousand jobs within manufacturing.

Further Resources

BOOKS

Galbraith, John Kenneth. *The Affluent Society.* Boston: Houghton Mifflin, 1958.

Vedder, Robert K., and Lowell Gallaway. *Out of Work: Unemployment and Government in Twentieth-century America.* New York: Holmes and Meier, 1993.

"It's a Smaller World"

Magazine article

By: *Newsweek*

Date: October 20, 1958

Source: "It's a Smaller World." *Newsweek,* October 1958, 93–94, 96.

About the Publication: Thomas J. C. Martyn published the first issue of *Newsweek* in February 1933. In 1961, it was bought by the Washington Post Company. It's circulation is 3.1 million in the United States and over 900,000 internationally. ∎

Introduction

The calendar year 1958 proved to be a most auspicious occasion for the development of the U.S. aerospace industry. In January, the United States launched into Earth-orbit its first satellite, the *Explorer I* probe. Later in the year, the advent of commercial jetliners transformed the passenger airline business. Indeed, in these two ways, the world became, in the judgment of *Newsweek,* a much "smaller" place.

Along with the DC-8, the Boeing 707, shown above, ushered in the jet age. © MUSEUM OF FLIGHT/CORBIS. REPRODUCED BY PERMISSION.

A pair of innovative American aerospace corporations engaged in a furious race to transfer jet plane technology, which had been developed originally for military aircraft, to the commercial passenger plane realm. These two companies were Boeing Aircraft of Seattle, Washington, maker of the Boeing 707, and Douglas Aircraft of southern California, maker of the DC-8. Together, these two corporations and their planes revolutionized air transportation in the United States.

American aircraft manufacturers also faced competition from Europeans bent on gaining domination of the skies through jetliner service. As far back as 1952, the de Haviland Comet I, a British aircraft, inaugurated passenger jet travel. Eventual problems of airworthiness led to the grounding of all Comets from 1954 to 1957. In the interim, the British lost their lead in the development of commercial jetliners. Meanwhile, in addition to the Boe-

ing 707 and the Douglas DC-8 as rivals, the French jetliner, the Caravelle I, debuted in 1959. Nonetheless, the United States wound up dominating the early jet age with its two entries into the jetliner sweepstakes.

In contrast with the British Comet I, which was plagued with financial and mechanical problems from the outset, the Boeing 707 and the DC-8 appeared at a most propitious moment when the technological feasibility of safe commercial jet travel meshed with practical economic considerations. Thus, the modern jet age was launched.

Significance

What were the economic implications of the jetliner revolution? First, this transformation seriously challenged passenger railway transportation, which had already been in a state of decline. In addition, the passenger liner died as a means of oceanic travel. Henceforth, cruise ships were restricted to pleasure and recreation—not to business. Meanwhile, air travel quickly came to the masses, thereby altering the travel habits of the American people.

The airlines became the glamour industry that received the red carpet treatment. Newly constructed and enlarged existing airports were lavished with subsidies and tax breaks. The term "jet set" quickly came into vogue as long-distance flights whisked Americans to European playgrounds and vice versa. Both the Atlantic and the Pacific oceans shrank to a manageable size, so that by the 1960s millions of Americans were visiting Europe and Asia.

On another front, the jet age placed a premium on airline safety, as larger planes loaded with increasing numbers of passengers made for more spectacular (and deadlier) crashes. During the old propeller-driven era, the airlines (and the federal government) had taken a rather lax approach to safety. Beginning in 1959 with the beginning of the jet age, however, the number and deadliness of accidents increased for years to come. In fact, it would not be until the 1980s that airliner crashes became something of a rarity.

Finally, the jet age fostered suburban development. Huge new airports were required to accommodate the larger jets. Requiring large tracts of land, these airports were built in the suburbs—indeed, often in the raw countryside. This was symptomatic of a greater trend where urban wealth was drained away as money and resources shifted to the suburbs from the central cities. Older, urban commercial airports declined and were often abandoned in favor of the newer airports that could more easily accomodate jet liners.

Primary Source

"It's a Smaller World" [excerpt]

> **SYNOPSIS:** The start of commercial jetliner service in the United States began in 1958. Led by the Boeing 707 and the Douglas DC-8, passengers could now travel faster and in far more comfort than ever before. The considerable economic impact of this jetliner revolution is examined in the following *Newsweek* article.

Phones jangled in airline offices this week, and questions flew at the speed of sound. "Any openings on the next jet flight to London?" "How long will it take to go from New York to Los Angeles?" "When will jets be flying to Chicago?" "Will the fares be the same?"

For the ordinary traveler, the jet age had finally arrived—and suddenly the world was 40 per cent

smaller. British Overseas Airways, which staked its claim as a jet-age pioneer with its ill-fated Comet I's six years ago, now had renewed its claim with the first transatlantic flights of its Comet IV. "First jets to Europe," cried its double-truck ads. But Pan American World Airways was not far behind. Getting ready for this week's inaugural European flight of its giant Boeing 707 (to be christened in Washington by Mamie Eisenhower), Pan Am streamed out its own publicity contrails: Where BOAC was offering weekly service, Pan Am was starting daily jet flights to Europe.

Already Pan Am could count up 3,100 winter bookings for its jet service to Rome, London, and Paris—more than three times as many passengers as had been booked at this time last year. As other airlines impatiently awaited arrival of their own jets, they did their best to rhapsodize about piston planes (the "one occasional complaint from passengers," said Alitalia of its Rome service: "They wish the trip took longer"). . . .

That Empty Feeling

But for all their enthusiasm, the jet passengers present a problem for the airlines: Will there be enough of them? With one jet—because of its size and speed—capable of carrying as many transatlantic passengers as five of the biggest piston planes, the current 15 per cent annual growth of international travel will never fill the jet seats. And the operators already have loaded themselves with huge debts to pay for the new planes.

"One does not buy a $5 million jet as if it were a new bicycle," said director general Sir William Hildred of the International Air Transport Association. Furthermore. Sir William fears, the bill for new maintenance equipment, training, fueling, and other ground chores may run as high as the cost of the jets themselves. The U.S. carriers, which alone have committed themselves to buy about $2.5 billion worth of planes, are just beginning to tot up their other bills. United, for example, has laid out $1.6 million for a jet simulator to train crews, plus another $16 million for an electronic reservation system.

To cut the debt load, operators have had to chart new financial flight plans. American Airlines, for instance, arranged to lease some of its engines from the manufacturer. The reason was plain—one jet engine costs about $100,000 (about the price of a prewar DC-3); the propellers retail at about $23,000 apiece. Some of the smaller lines in Europe are pooling resources—SAS, itself an amalgam of the three

Scandinavian national airlines, has teamed up with Swissair for its planned Caravelle, DC-8, and Convair 880 operations.

Turbine-Driven Profits

The hoped-for payoff lies in the superior performance of the turbine engine. Because it has fewer parts, theoretically it should need less maintenance—and thus less time on the ground between flights. Another factor, particularly for the bigger American planes, is their enormous seating capacity (up to 180 passenger vs. a DC-7's 99), which is supposed to reduce the seat-mile costs. Boeing has calculated that piston planes cost at least 2.5 cents a seat-mile to operate; its 707s, 1.9 to 2.1 cents.

To make these paper figures prove out, the airlines will bend every effort to keep their jets in the air. For the DC-8s it plans to put into service next October, Delta Air Lines has worked out this sample "day" . . . : Atlanta to New York, to Houston, to Chicago, to Miami, and to Atlanta—a total distance of 4,986 miles in fifteen hours, eleven of them in the air. Delta, like all its competitors, knows that keeping a 707 on the ground for just one hour will cost it roughly $135 in depreciation.

Everywhere they turn, it seems, the jet operators bump right into another problem. None of the U.S. line now getting jets, for instance, has a contract with the airline pilots' union to cover jet operations. And the union is now demanding a third pilot in every jet cockpit—plus new top salaries of $45,000 a year vs. the present $22,200. (Pan Am will start its jet service with non-union pilot-executives.) . . .

In vaulting the multifarious problems that confront them, the airlines keep coming back to the No. 1 question of them all—whether the jet travelers are there in large enough numbers. They think they are—but they may not be traveling right now.

Fewer than 1 per cent of Americans, for instance, have traveled outside the country—and fewer than 30 per cent have ever set foot in a plane. In tapping this reservoir, airline competition, already as hot as a jet blast, will go to full throttle. The battle, in fact, has already started. After BOAC's jets beat Pan Am to the transatlantic routes, both lines denied any "race"—but there was a quiver in Pan Am's stiff upper lip.

Referring to the scramble for new passengers this week, one airline executive put it this way: "We've taken them off the trains and there are only so many on the buses. To pay for these things, we're going to have to get them out of the automobiles."

Further Resources

BOOKS

Heppenheimer, T. A. *Turbulent Skies: The History of Commercial Aviation.* New York: Wiley, 1995.

Rodgers, Eugene. *Flying High: The Story of Boeing and the Rise of the Jetliner Industry.* New York: Atlantic Monthly Press, 1996.

Solberg, Carl. *Conquest of the Skies: A History of Commercial Aviation in America.* Boston: Little, Brown, 1979.

"The Challenge of Inflation"

Magazine article

By: Howard Buffett

Date: March 28, 1959

Source: Buffett, Howard. "The Challenge of Inflation." *National Review* 6, no. 22, March 28, 1959, 613, 616.

About the Author: Howard Buffett (1903–1964), a staunchly conservative Republican Party political activist, served in the U.S. House of Representatives from 1943 to 1949 and again from 1951 to 1953. He wrote and spoke frequently about fiscal matters, including the dangers of inflation. ■

Introduction

The consistent reliability of a nation's currency is a cornerstone of social, political, and economic stability. When a nation's currency is undermined by inflation it could potentially lead to the unraveling of the institutions that hold society together. Inflation refers to an increase in the cost of goods and services in a society, causing a decrease in the purchasing power of a given currency. In contemporary American society the threat of inflation generally goes unnoticed apart from recognizing that you may be paying slightly more for a pair of blue jeans now than you did a few years ago. This, however, was not always the case.

Inflation has historically been a constant threat to economic stability in developing as well as advanced capitalist countries. Entire economic systems have collapsed as a result of a government's inability to control inflation. The collapse of Germany's first experiment with democracy prior to World War II (1939–1945) (the Weimar Republic) can partially be blamed on rampant inflation. At the time, there were stories of people taking bushel baskets full of currency to the store to buy a loaf of bread.

Although the threat of inflation in the United States has been contained in recent years it is always closely monitored and taken very seriously as a measure of the economy's health. There are two general methods that

President Dwight Eisenhower meets with labor leaders at the White House in 1958. Eisenhower looked to avoid inflation which would disrupt growth in the economy. © BETTMANN/CORBIS. REPRODUCED BY PERMISSION.

the U.S. government uses to manage the economy and offset inflation: monetary policy and fiscal policy. Monetary policy refers to managing interest rates by the Federal Reserve Board. If the Federal Reserve Board believes the economy is overheating and inflation is on the rise, it will raise interest rates in an effort to decrease the flow of money in the economy. On the other hand if the Federal Reserve Board determines that the economy is too sluggish and the costs of goods and services are declining (called deflation) they will lower interest rates in an effort to increase cash flow in the economy. This has proven to be an effective measure to keep inflationary forces in check in recent years.

Fiscal policy refers to the implementation of programs by the federal government to rectify imbalances in the economy. Generally speaking, fiscal policy refers to the way the government spends tax dollars to influence the economy. Prior to WWII Democrats and Republicans debated the extent to which the federal government should become involved in economic affairs. Democrats tended to favor a more active role while Republicans generally adopted a more hands-off approach to economic affairs.

The Great Depression marked a turning point in the way the role of the federal government in economic affairs was viewed. In an effort to combat the effects of the

Great Depression, President Roosevelt enacted a series of social programs (called the "New Deal") designed to revitalize a desperate economy. New Deal initiatives such as restoring confidence in the banking industry by creating the Federal Deposit Insurance Corporation (FDIC), subsidizing the agriculture industry, establishing a minimum wage, and creating the Social Security system channeled funds into the economy. The perceived success of Roosevelt's programs led to a consensus among policy makers that the federal government had a responsibility to play a more active role in economic affairs.

Significance

There is an important difference in the way Democrats and Republicans approach fiscal policy. Democrats tend to focus on the demand side of the economy—favoring firm regulation of business practices and establishing a strong safety net for the less fortunate. Republicans place more emphasis on the supply side in their approach to fiscal policy by designing programs that favor business growth.

In contemporary American politics the debates over fiscal policy revolve around which programs should receive federal tax dollars (rather than whether the money should be spent at all). After WWII a heated debate emerged regarding how much federal tax dollars, if any, should be spent on stimulating the economy. There was a fear among some conservatives that if the federal government continued flooding the marketplace with tax dollars inflation would eventually cause the economy to collapse.

Primary Source

"The Challenge of Inflation" [excerpt]

SYNOPSIS: Former congressman Howard Buffet takes pains to remind readers that the specter of inflation, although seemingly under control under the tight-money regimen imposed by the prudent Eisenhower administration, could come roaring back at any moment.

Why are we menaced by ruinous inflation? Because, says a former member of Congress, the American people have lost control of a spendthrift government

Lenin is said to have declared that the best way to destroy the Capitalist System was to debauch the currency. By a continuing process of inflation, governments can confiscate, secretly and unobserved, an important part of the wealth of their citizens.

John Maynard Keynes

The top protagonists of Communism, Lenin and Stalin, recognized America as the key stronghold of capitalism and individual liberty. If they were alive today, how would they regard the situation in the U.S.? It requires little imagination to conclude that they would be well satisfied. For our government is herding us down the road to inflation, debauching the currency, devaluing the savings of the people, and thus undermining the economic, political and moral foundations on which the nation was built. Unpleasant as this appraisal may sound, it is buttressed by sobering evidence.

One event of 1957 illustrates the gravity of the situation. The President sent a budget to Congress calling for the expenditure of $72 billion in the fiscal year beginning July 1 of that year—a budget 80 per cent larger than that of his Democratic predecessor, President Truman, just ten years earlier.

A grass-roots protest quickly spread across America against the spending plans of the Administration, totaling $200 million dollars a day for every day of the year. Thousands of letters and telegrams poured into the offices of congressmen and senators, demanding a substantial reduction in federal spending. Veteran Capital reporters, who had seen previous economy drives blossom and fade, were amazed at the size and duration of the taxpayers'

protest of 1957. The immediate result was that leaders in both parties solemnly pledged that federal spending would be reduced.

That was the promise. What was the performance?

Instead of going down, federal spending went up! During the fiscal year ended June 20, 1958, it came to almost $72 billion—$2,463 million in excess of spending during the previous fiscal year. A $2,800 million deficit was recorded. These figures show the futility of letter-writing campaigns as a defense against inflationary spending.

Pressure Groups

What explains this failure? The simple truth seems to be that the American people have lost control over their government. Both political parties are no longer responsible to the people. Instead they are subservient to pressure groups which profit from socialist spending policies that depress the value of the dollar.

What is more important, in the process the lights of human liberty in America are going out one by one. That is the history of the inflation sequence: liberty disappears simply because the vast majority become in one way or another dependent on government favors or subsidies. That is the danger, and that is the prospect unless conservative leadership develops an effective cure for inflation and makes national acceptance of that cure the paramount goal of all its political efforts.

The words "paramount goal" mean just that. Those who defend continuing inflation plead the hostility between the United States and Russia. We are brainwashed into believing that unrestrained spending at home and overseas is the necessary answer to the Russian threat. Yet the actual truth seems to be that inflation, unless it is soon brought under control, will lead to a complete victory for Communism in America—whether from within or without is of little importance. . . .

That tragedy need not happen. It will not happen if American conservatives have the wisdom to concentrate their patriotic efforts on the decisive issue—sound money. Victory on this battlefront is the key to America's future as a free land.

Further Resources

BOOKS

Baker, Clayton. *Depression and Inflation.* New York: Vantage, 1963.

Whitney, Simon Newcomb. *Inflation Since 1945: Facts and Theories.* New York: Praeger, 1982.

"Success by Imitation"

Magazine article

By: Alan Harrington

Date: July 1959

Source: Harrington, Alan. "Success by Imitation." *The Atlantic Monthly* 201, no, 1, July 1959, 37–39.

About the Author: Alan Harrington (1919–1997), a novelist, satirist, and journalist, enjoyed exposing the pretensions of the rich and powerful. A frequent critic of the conformity present in the corporate ethos of the 1950s, Harrington often unleashed his irreverent brand of humor against social convention that he found dysfunctional. ∎

Introduction

In the years following the Great Depression (1930–1939), American businesses rebounded, and many Americans looked to these companies as a source of dependable work in the 1940s and '50s. Yet the anxiety of the Depression years—a fear of joblessness and economic chaos—had not dissipated. It was perhaps this anxiety that led the average "company man" to approach his job with a degree of timidity. By conforming to corporate rules, rather than cultivating individualism, 1950s businessmen and women seemed assured of long-term employment and security—something hard to come by just two decades earlier.

Indeed, children born in the Depression years came of working age in the 1950s, and the era's psychological effects were perhaps most pronounced in this new generation. As they entered college, Depression-born students were often reluctant to express personal opinions—a quirk that earned them the nickname of the "silent era" generation. Security and stability were chief goals for many of these young people. One story making the rounds during the decade describes the experience of corporate recruiters from one firm who visited a number of campuses in search of new employees. The students seemed inordinately interested in the firm's retirement plans—this before most of them had ever held their first real jobs!

Of course, not all subscribed to the rules of corporate conformity. Numerous books and articles published during the 1950s—including William H. Whyte's classic study *The Organization Man* (1956)—railed against this emerging trend. Sloan Wilson's best-selling 1955 novel, *The Man in the Gray Flannel Suit,* whose protagonist rejects a dehumanizing rat race and begins a voyage of self-discovery, surfaced as a scathing indictment of corporate culture.

Significance

Paradoxically, the rise of corporate conformity existed alongside the great American ideal of rugged indi-

vidualism. This ideal was ingrained in the American psyche, and was not easily vanquished. A tension between the conformity trend and the individualist ideal played itself out not just in books and articles but also in popular culture. Recording artists and comics of the era—such as Tom Lehrer, Stan Freberg, and Bob Newhart—created brilliant spoofs of the 1950s corporate ethos.

While some satirized the corporate trend, others looked to reconcile the differences between corporate life and American idealism. Even Whyte's *Organization Man* provided sage advice to would-be corporate job seekers about how to outsmart the personality tests that were administered by psychologists. These multiple-choice tests were coming into frequent use as a means of weeding out candidates who did not "fit in" or who exhibited too much independent thinking. Tests like these could make or break candidates' potential careers. Whyte advised test-takers to choose answers that emphasized the qualities of safety and subordination, rather than those that revealed a tendency toward risk-taking and independence.

Throughout the 1950s, advocates of individualism chafed against a corporate mentality that seemed at odds with the American way of life. It was at this time that a spirit of rebellion began to brew, and the seeds of the 1960s counterculture were planted. The tensions of the 1950s led to a cultural explosion in the following decade, when free-spiritedness prevailed over conformity.

Primary Source

"Success by Imitation" [excerpt]

SYNOPSIS: Many social critics deplored the stale conformity everpresent in 1950s' American corporate culture. There were others, however, who felt that there were ways to make the best of the then current business climate. In the following excerpt, Alan Harrington provides advice about how to outsmart stifling bosses and play the corporate game to win.

Corporate practices involve a fundamental inconsistency. Management wants simultaneously (a) performance from everyone and (b) protection for everyone. But the impulse to perform and the impulse to protect yourself cannot exist as equals. One must gain ascendancy over the other. To perform, move, swing, the self goes out and takes chances. The reflex of self-protection produces subservience to the group, a willingness to spread responsibility until it doesn't exist, a binding horror of chance-taking, and obeisance to the system. How can these two drives exist together in equal strength?

The corporation is, therefore, schizophrenic. At the headquarters of a company I shall call the Crystal

Many social critics deplored the stale conformity everpresent in 1950s American corporate culture. © **BETTMANN/CORBIS. REPRODUCED BY PERMISSION.**

Palace, we think we are staffed with hundreds of red-blooded free-enterprisers. But in fact, if we took samples and tapped a few kneecaps, it would be found that a large percentage of us have the circulative apparatus of bureaucrats. Instead of blood in our veins we have grapefruit juice. So far as our jobs are concerned, we would be perfectly at home in the most stifling government office in Washington. . . .

Theory: we are all in there pitching for the company, doing the best we know how. Fact: the "method" requires that we not do our best, because it would make the boss look bad. In other words, the inefficient boss's security is more important than getting the job done. Getting the job done is supposedly the law governing promotions. But the sad truth, as I have seen it work out in practice, is that in a crisis most of us are far more loyal to our pension programs than we are to doing a job in what we believe to be the best way. Sometimes for us the most rewarding decision is no decision—anything to avoid the lonely prominence of commitment.

The grand misconception here is that "organization is all." This has led to all the propaganda on the virtues of team play. Following from the team-play concept is the corporate emphasis on experience. It

will be said of some dunderhead that he has been seasoned for twenty years in his department. This is like a football coach with a rotten team last year looking forward with confidence to the fall campaign because he has "twenty lettermen returning." That impresses me not at all. Preserve us from such lettermen. If they were no good last year, particularly in the upper age brackets, they will be worse this year. No, I think any organization must make room for stars; otherwise we will have to face up to the space age with a bunch of turnips on our payroll. . . .

But the plain fact is, and the gentlemen on executive development committees must know it, that the corporation employs scores of individuals with mediocre intelligences, the motivations of squirrels, and the relating powers of amiable zombies. The Executive Development program does not visualize people as they really are. It assumes that people are natural spirits and ignores the strongest motivating force in our private civil-service state, which is self-preservation.

For this reason we model ourselves in the image of our superiors, as we follow in their footsteps, and expect subordinates to model themselves on us. This much is human nature: an executive is going to file a good report on an underling who thinks and acts more or less in the way he does. And he will tend to give a lesser rating to someone who thinks and acts differently. . . .

Once upon a time free enterprise invoked the principle of the survival of the fittest. Today we have the survival (or rather the promotion) of the most imitative. The question before the executive development committee when promotion time comes is how snugly you will fill the shoes of the man above you.

In surveying his team, almost any executive is going to appraise it so that the men below who might challenge his method of doing things will be put in their proper places. His instinct, if not his conscious aim, will be to favor those below him who appear to be smaller replicas of himself.

Can a corporation man properly appraise a subordinate more intelligent than he is? If not, what can the subordinate do, particularly in the early stages of his career, to get around inadequate appraisals which affect not only his present status but also his future? He can do nothing. He is like a man on a slow escalator with someone in front of him who will not move.

Further Resources
BOOKS

Halberstam, David. *The Fifties.* New York: Villard, 1993.

Harrington, Alan. *Life in the Crystal Palace.* New York: Knopf, 1959.

Whyte, William Hollingsworth. *The Organization Man.* New York: Simon and Schuster, 1956.

3

EDUCATION

KRISTINA PETERSON

Entries are arranged in chronological order by date of primary source. For entries with one primary source, the entry title is the same as the primary source title. Entries with more than one primary source have an overall entry title, followed by the titles of the primary sources.

Important Events in Education, 1950–1959

1950

• 29.8 million elementary and secondary students and 2.3 million college and professional-school students attend school.

• On April 16, Congress creates the National Science Foundation (NSF). The NSF promotes science education and research.

• On July 1, the New Orleans Board of Education in Louisiana grants full privileges to married teachers, including the right to promotion (not granted since the Depression).

• On October 16, the New Jersey Supreme Court upholds the practice of reading five verses of the Old Testament every day in all public schools.

1951

• On August 18, the Associated Press reports college costs up 400 percent from fifty years ago. Average tuition for one year is eighteen hundred dollars.

• On September 18, Pope Pius XII states his opposition to sex education in schools.

• On October 19, Yale University celebrates its 250th anniversary.

1952

• Baby boomers enter school in record numbers.

• Twenty percent of college and 10 percent of elementary- and secondary-school students are in desegregated classrooms.

• On March 2, the U.S. Supreme Court rules that states may bar members of the communist party from teaching;

• On April 6, the University of Florida student honor court resigns over reinstatement of two hundred students, including several football players, accused of cheating.

• On April 29, the University of Rochester in New York ends a 107-year policy of separate colleges for men and women with the opening of a coeducational College of Arts and Sciences.

• On July 2, the Stevens Institute of Technology in Hoboken, New Jersey, allows students to pay tuition in installments.

1953

• On January 14, President Harry S. Truman states that federal spending on education has doubled since 1929.

• On February 9, Williams College's Phi Delta Theta fraternity is suspended for pledging a Jewish student.

• On February 11, the National Council for Financial Aid to Education is formed to help colleges and universities recruit funds from business and industry.

• On April 3, Fisk University in Nashville, Tennessee, establishes the first Phi Beta Kappa chapter at a black college.

• On April 11, Congress creates the Department of Health, Education, and Welfare at the request of President Dwight D. Eisenhower.

• On June 11, Harvard University Law School confers its bachelor of law degree on women for the first time, eleven that year.

• On August 21, fourteen universities decline to renew contracts with the U.S. Armed Forces Institute for correspondence courses for the military to protest a federal clause permitting government "disapproval" of faculty members.

• In December, the National Education Association's membership surpasses five hundred thousand.

• On December 6, the National Educational Association (NEA) reports that American school children, particularly urban students, are less fit than Italian and Austrian children due to lack of exercise.

1954

• On January 7, President Dwight D. Eisenhower urges each state to hold a conference on education. Congress appropriates nine hundred thousand dollars for this purpose.

• On February 21, Columbia University reports that 10 percent of American public-school students suffer from emotional disturbances.

• On May 17, the U.S. Supreme Court in *Brown v. Board of Education of Topeka, Kansas* overturns the "separate but equal" doctrine of *Plessy v. Ferguson* (1896). The court declares segregated public schools unconstitutional.

• In June, the NEA National Convention endorses integration (Mississippi and South Carolina vote against the measure), stating, "All problems of integration . . . are capable of solution by citizens of intelligence, saneness and reasonableness working together. . . ."

• In September, Fort Myers Elementary School becomes the first public school in Virginia to integrate.

• On November 19, the U.S. Tax Court exempts grants by philanthropic agencies for research and study fellowships from taxes.

1955

• The National Merit Scholarship Corporation is formed.

• The College Entrance Examination Board assumes control of the Advanced Placement Program.

• On January 18, Harvard Divinity School announces the admission of women for fall 1955.

- On May 10, the New York City Board of Education reports an "end to social promotion." Schools must retain pupils who are two years or more behind in reading.

- In June, President Dwight D. Eisenhower convenes the first White House conference on education.

- On July 2, the U.S. Supreme Court orders public schools to integrate "with all deliberate speed." The vagueness of the phrase allows white segregationists to flout the order.

- On September 2, the U.S. Census Bureau reports that male college graduates can expect one hundred thousand dollars more in lifetime income than high-school graduates.

1956

- In January, President Dwight D. Eisenhower creates the President's Committee on Education Beyond the High School. The committee urges high school graduates to pursue additional education at a community college, college or university as a way of improving their career prospects.

- On February 1, Congress increases the Civilian Conservation Corps school-lunch milk fund to $60 million.

- In March, President Dwight D. Eisenhower admits his displeasure with the U.S. Supreme Court's decision to integrate public schools.

- In August, President Dwight D. Eisenhower urges states to improve the quality of schools for Native American children.

- On September 21, twelve-year-old Fred Safier of Berkeley, California, enrolls in Harvard College to study physics.

- On November 3, the U.S. Office of Education reports that 11 percent of the thirty-three hundred students surveyed are left-handed.

- On November 26, a study by the Fund for the Republic reveals that African Americans show no inherent inferiority to whites in intelligence tests.

1957

- On April 4, the National Education Association celebrates its one hundredth anniversary.

- In June, the Carnegie Foundation estimates that nonpublic school enrollment has doubled since 1944.

- In September, Arkansas Governor Orval Faubus orders the Arkansas National Guard to block the entry of black students to Like Rock's Central High School. Late in the month, Faubus withdrew the National Guard on the order of a federal judge.

- In October, President Dwight D. Eisenhower, despite personal misgivings, sends U.S. Army paratroopers to Little Rock's Central High School to protect African American children from white mobs attempting to prevent their entrance to school.

- In October, the Soviet Union launches *Sputnik* raising fears that Soviet schools are better than U.S. schools in teaching science and mathematics.

- On December 7, a study reports that American workers average 11.8 years of schooling (9 percent completed college) compared to 9.3 years (6.4 percent completed college) in 1940.

1958

- On March 10, the Vatican Sacred Congregation of Religious Studies calls for the separation of boys and girls in sports, study halls, and classrooms even in coeducational schools.

- On May 6, Public Law 926 requires public schools to establish programs for mentally retarded students.

- In September, the school board in Little Rock, Arkansas closes its public schools for the rest of the year to prevent integration. Schools in Virginia and South Carolina follow Little Rock's example.

- On September 2, Congress passes the National Defense Education Act, granting public schools money to strengthen science and mathematics education in an effort to build a critical mass of scientists, mathematicians and engineers.

- On December 1, a fire kills ninety students and three nuns at Our Lady of the Angels school in Chicago.

- On December 12, President Dwight D. Eisenhower favors the addition of a year or two of junior college (or a similar program) to high-school curricula to repair deficiencies in American education.

1959

- School enrollment totals 42.7 million elementary and secondary students and 3.4 million college and professional students.

- On October 20, schools, colleges and universities celebrate the centennial of John Dewey's birth. Dewey had distinguished himself as a philosopher and educator.

- On October 24, the Department of Health, Education, and Welfare pledges to rid the United States of "college-degree mills," which grant degrees but do not require courses.

Doremus et al. v. Board of Education of Borough of Hawthorne et al.

Court case

By: Supreme Court of New Jersey

Date: October 16, 1950

Source: *Doremus et al. v. Board of Education of Borough of Hawthorne et al.* 5 N.J. 435, 75 A 2d 880 (1950). ■

Introduction

The framers of the Constitution and the Bill of Rights sought to secure religious freedom against encroachment by the state through the First Amendment to the Constitution. The First Amendment states that "Congress shall make no law respecting an establishment of religion, or prohibiting the free exercise thereof." Put simply, this statement provides the basis for the separation of church and state.

In the early nineteenth century, those working toward a system of publicly funded and universally attended common schools had to address the issues of religious diversity and separation of church and state. For most people at the time, education meant moral and character training within the context of a particular religion. Yet, if schools were to be tax supported and attended by all, they had to be free of the influence of any religious sect. School reformer Thomas Mann maintained that schools had to teach a set of nonsectarian moral values common to all.

It was not, at the time, contemplated that schools would be free of any religious instruction, only that such instruction would be "nonsectarian," that is, shared by all Protestant Christians. As the common schools developed, Bible reading and prayer were almost universal. While Catholics and Jews protested that the Protestant Bible was a sectarian book, the practice continued in public schools well into the twentieth century.

In 1950, *Doremus v. Board of Education* came before the New Jersey Supreme Court. The appellants, Donald R. Doremus, a taxpayer, and a mother (identified only as "Klein") of a child enrolled in Hawthorne High School, objected to a New Jersey statute requiring daily readings from the Old Testament and permitting the repetition of the Lord's Prayer in public schools. Students could be excused from the reading and prayer on request. The appellants protested these practices in public schools on the grounds that they constituted sectarian instruction and were, therefore, in violation of the First Amendment.

Significance

The New Jersey Supreme Court affirmed the judgment of a lower court that the practices did not violate the establishment of religion clause of the First Amendment, arguing that the Bible and the Lord's Prayer were common to all Christian faiths and the Jewish religion and, therefore, not "sectarian." Citing numerous instances, from the references to God in the Constitution to the presence of state-supported chaplains in Congress, the court asserted that the U.S. government was founded on religious belief. The First Amendment, the court stated, was not intended to negate the existence of God.

The decision in *Doremus* represented a continuation of religious content in the public schools during the 1950s accompanied by constitutional challenges to such practices. The U.S. Supreme Court refused to consider an appeal in *Doremus* on the grounds that Doremus's and Klein's interests as taxpayers, and Klein's additional interest as the mother of a child who, by that time, had already graduated from high school, were insufficient.

Thus, the question of the constitutionality of prayer and Bible reading in public schools was delayed until 1962 when the Supreme Court ruled in *Engel v. Vitale* that "nondenominational" prayer read in public schools violated the establishment clause of the First Amendment. The 1963 Supreme Court decisions in *School District of Abington Township v. Schempp* and *Murray v. Curlett* found a state law requiring prayer and Bible reading in public schools to be unconstitutional.

A three-part "Lemon Test" was established in the 1971 Supreme Court case *Lemon v. Kurtzman* to determine whether state law violates the establishment clause. The law "must have a secular legislative purpose," "its principal or primary effect must be one that neither advances nor inhibits religion," and "the statute must not foster 'an excessive government entanglement with religion.'"

Primary Source

Doremus et al. v. Board of Education of Borough of Hawthorne et al. [excerpt]

SYNOPSIS: This excerpt from the New Jersey Supreme Court's decision in *Doremus* summarizes the facts of the case and outlines the reasoning behind the court's decision: the Bible and the Lord's Prayer are not sectarian and, therefore, their use in schools does not constitute an "establishment of religion" in violation of the First Amendment. The case was argued on September 18, 1950, and was decided on October 16, 1950.

Action under the Declaratory Judgment Act by a proceeding in lieu of prerogative writ by Donald R. Doremus and another against Board of Education of the Borough of Hawthorne and the State to test the constitutionality of statutes requiring at least five verses from Old Testament of Bible to be read in public schools each day and permitting repetition of Lord's Prayer in such schools. On cross motions for summary judgment on the pleadings. The Superior Court, Law Division, 7 N.J.Super, 442, 71 A.2d 732, granted the defendants' motion for summary judgment and denied the plaintiffs' motion and the judgment and the appeal was brought to the Supreme Court on its certification. The Supreme Court, Case, J., held that the statutes did not contravene the establishment of religion clause of First Amendment and privileges and immunities clause of Fourteenth Amendment, since such reading and repetition are not designed to inculcate any particular dogma, creed, belief, or mode of worship.

Judgment affirmed. . . .

The Old Testament of the Bible, because of its antiquity, its contents and its wide acceptance, is not a "sectarian book" within prohibition of establishment of religion clause of First Amendment, and reading thereof without comment in public schools does not constitute "sectarian instruction." U.S.C.A. Const. Amends. 1, 14. . . .

Subject to constitutional limitations, legislature has exclusive jurisdiction over matters of public policy. . . .

A statute which has been in force without any substantial challenge for many years cannot be declared unconstitutional unless its unconstitutionality is obvious. . . .

A cardinal rule in construction of constitutional and statutory enactments is that provision made by way of remedy shall be studied in light of evil against which remedy was erected. . . .

Statutes requiring at least five verses from Old Testament of Bible to be read in public schools each day and permitting repetition of Lord's Prayer in such schools do not contravene establishment of religion clause of First Amendment and privileges and im-

Third grade students at McLain Grammar School in Rockland, Maine. Some public school students began the school day with a recitation from a passage from the Bible known as the Lord's prayer. **THE LIBRARY OF CONGRESS.**

munities clause of Fourteenth Amendment, since such reading and repetition are not designed to inculcate any particular dogma, creed, belief or mode of worship. R.S. 18:14–77, 78; R.S. 18:14–77, 78, N.J.S.A.; U.S.C.A. Const. Amends. 1, 14.

Further Resources

BOOKS

Alexander, Kern, and M. David Alexander. *American Public School Law,* 5th ed. Belmont, Calif.: Wadsworth/Thomson Learning, 2001.

Gaddy, Barbara B., T. William Hall, and Robert J. Marzano. *School Wars: Resolving Our Conflicts Over Religion and Values.* San Francisco: Jossey-Bass, 1996.

Hunt, Thomas C., and James C. Carper, eds. *Religion and Schooling in Contemporary American: Confronting Our Cultural Pluralism.* New York: Garland, 1997.

Nord, Warren A. *Religion and American Education: Rethinking a National Dilemma.* Chapel Hill: University of North Carolina Press, 1995.

Spurlock, Clark. *Education and the Supreme Court.* Urbana: University of Illinois Press, 1955.

WEBSITES

"Religion and Public Schools." U.S. Department of Education. Available online at http://www.ed.gov/inits/religionandschools

/index-archive.html; website home page: http://www.ed.gov /index.jsp (accessed May 1, 2003).

"Religion in the Public Schools: A Joint Statement of Current Law." American Civil Liberties Union Online Archives. Available online at http://archive.aclu.org/issues/religion/re-lig7.html; website home page: http://archive.aclu.org/ (accessed May 1, 2003)

"Religion in the Public Schools." Anti-Defamation League. Available online at http://www.adl.org/religion_ps/default .asp; website home page: http://www.adl.org/adl.asp (accessed May 1, 2003)

"8 Teacher Ousters in Communist Case Asked by Examiner"

Newspaper article

By: Murray Illson

Date: December 13, 1950

Source: Illson, Murray. "8 Teacher Ousters in Communist Case Asked by Examiner." *The New York Times,* December 13, 1950, 1, 26.

About the Author: Murray Illson (1913–) received a bachelor's from New York University. He worked as a writer and reporter for the *New York Times* beginning in 1937, leaving to serve in World War II (1939–1945). In 1941, he resumed his position as a writer and reporter for the *Times,* where he worked until his retirement in 1978. ∎

Introduction

After World War I (1914–1918), as Americans watched the unfolding of the Russian Revolution and the subsequent spread of socialist ideas in Europe, the United States was swept by a wave of nationalism and suspicion of anything foreign or radical. The "Red Scare" was characterized by a fear that communists were infiltrating American institutions, including schools, and plotting the overthrow of the U.S. government. The perceived need to protect children from communist propaganda led to dismissals of many teachers at all levels of education for infractions such as failing to take "loyalty oaths," belonging to subversive organizations, or even being suspected of having communist ideas.

After World War II, a second Red Scare emerged in the context of concern about the rapidly developing military and technological capacity of the Soviet Union. The 1950s saw another round of teacher dismissals and renewed interest in loyalty oaths and monitoring teacher membership in "subversive organizations."

A controversial New York State law, known as the Feinberg Law, was passed in 1949 for the purpose of pre-venting individuals who advocated the illegal overthrow of the U.S. government, or belonged to organizations with this objective, from holding positions in the public schools. On the basis of this law, eight New York City public school teachers were suspended without pay in May 1950 for refusing to answer questions regarding their membership in the Communist Party. One teacher, David Friedman, was also charged with known Communist Party membership.

Trials were held, and in December 1950 the trial examiner recommended that all eight be fired. The board of education followed this recommendation and dismissed the eight teachers in February 1951. No evidence of subversive activities or ideas was found for seven of the eight teachers. Only Friedman was found to have actually been a member of the Communist Party. Suspicion of subversive activities as a result of the refusal to answer questions regarding organizational membership was the sole ground for the seven's dismissal.

Significance

The Feinberg Law and the teacher dismissals in New York City were part of a nationwide push in the 1950s to ferret out communists at all levels of education, especially higher education. Many victims of the Red Scare took legal action.

A group of teachers, led by Irving Adler, challenged the law on the grounds that it violated their rights of free speech and assembly. However, in *Adler v. Board of Education* (1952), the U.S. Supreme Court ruled the Feinberg Law to be constitutional on the grounds that individuals were free to join subversive organizations, but they had "no right to work for the State in the school system on their own terms." Schools, the Court ruled, have the right to screen their employees regarding their fitness for the job.

In 1967, however, the Supreme Court in *Keyishian v. Board of Regents* overturned the Feinberg Law. The Court ruled that a teacher may not be sanctioned for mere "knowing membership" in an organization advocating the overthrow of the government; the individual must actually intend to advance this agenda. Teachers cannot be forced to give up their constitutional rights as a condition of employment. In addition, laws of this type must be clear and unambiguous regarding the type of acts and organizations proscribed. The Court stressed the importance of academic freedom: "Scholarship cannot flourish in an atmosphere of suspicion and distrust. Teachers and students must always remain free to inquire, to study and to evaluate, to gain new maturity and understanding; otherwise our civilization will stagnate and die."

Primary Source

"8 Teacher Ousters in Communist Case Asked by Examiner"

SYNOPSIS: This *New York Times* article details the outcome of the trial of the "New York Eight" and the events leading up to the trial. The reasoning of the trial examiner and the response of the Communist Party are discussed.

8 Teacher Ousters in Communist Case Asked by Examiner

Kiendl Finds for Dismissal of Friedman and 7 Who Balked at Queries on Red Ties

Board to Pass on Verdict

No Action Is Expected Within 30 Days—Party Sees Way Opened for Witchhunt

Theodore Kiendl, trial examiner for the Board of Education, recommended yesterday the outright dismissal of eight teachers who refused to tell the Superintendent of Schools whether they were members of the Communist party.

He also held that the Corporation Counsel had proved that the Communist party stood for the violent overthrow of the Government and that David L. Friedman, one of the eight, had been a party member and thus was unfit to teach in the city's public schools.

In separate reports for each of the eight, he found all guilty of insubordination and conduct unbecoming teachers because they refused to answer or evaded questions about alleged party membership put to them by Dr. William Jansen, the superintendent. Mr. Friedman was the only one of the group to face the additional charge of party membership.

Would Continue Suspensions

The trial examiner also recommended that the teachers' suspensions from their school duties, in effect since last May 3, be continued pending final action on his reports by the Board of Education. The nine-man board, which may accept, modify or reject the trial examiner's recommendations, is not expected to act upon them before the next thirty days. This is to give the teachers time to submit additional arguments or counter-proposals.

In a supplemental report, Mr. Kiendl took note of Monday's unanimous decision of the United States Supreme Court that witnesses before a Federal grand jury could refuse to answer questions concerning alleged Communist party affiliations if they pleaded possible self-incrimination.

A 1953 editorial cartoon by John R. Fischetti criticizes physicist Albert Einstein after he wrote an open letter to a New York high school teacher. In the letter Einstein urged intellectuals to refuse to testify before the Congressional hearings conducted to seek out communists. **THE LIBRARY OF CONGRESS.**

Mr. Kiendl said that the court's decision was not applicable to Mr. Friedman's case for the following reasons:

1. The teacher was not under subpoena nor was he sworn as a witness.

2. Mr. Friedman was "a teacher in the public service being interrogated by his superior regarding his qualifications for continuance in that position."

3. "The respondent here, in refusing to answer regarding his membership and activities in the Communist party, did not do so upon the ground of self-incrimination. It may well be that his failure to assert the privilege was due to the fact that the Charter of New York expressly provides, in Section 903, that the assertion of such privilege by a city employe automatically forfeits his employment. The section has been specifically applied to an employe of the Board of Education and its constitutionality sustained."

Trials Lasted Twenty Days

Mr. Kiendl's decisions against the eight teachers came after twenty days of departmental trials that ended last Oct. 25. He was not present at the Board of Education's headquarters, 110 Livingston

Street, Brooklyn, when his recommendations were made public yesterday. Representing him was William R. Meagher, an associate in the law firm of Davis, Polk, Wardwell, Sunderland & Kiendl.

Also present were three of the suspended teachers, Abraham Lederman, who also is president of the Teachers Union, Local 555, United Public Workers; Mrs. Celia L. Zitron, the union's executive secretary, and Abraham Feingold. Accompanying them were State Senator Fred G. Moritt, Democrat of Brooklyn, who is Mr. Lederman's attorney, and Harold I. Cammer of the law firm of Witt & Cammer, which represented five of the eight teachers.

After the recommendations were made known, Mr. Lederman, speaking for the eight, all of whom are executive members of the Teachers Union, declared that the cases would be appealed to the United States Supreme Court if necessary.

He charged that the verdict gave the Superintendent of Schools "sweeping and dangerous powers and destroyed academic freedom and teacher tenure laws." He also asserted that the teaching records of the eight, "averaging over twenty years of excellent service," had been conceded by the Superintendent and the trial examiner but, as a result of the decisions, the suspended group would lose all pension rights.

Friedman Case Decisive

The cases against the eight hinged to a large extent upon Mr. Kiendl's decision in the case against Mr. Friedman, who taught English in Public School 64, Manhattan, and who was the first of the group to be tried. On several occasions in the hearings Mr. Kiendl announced that he would not sustain the charges against the teachers unless the Corporation Counsel proved that the Communist party was dedicated to the violent overthrow of the government.

In his decision on the Friedman case, which also is expected to set a precedent for similar action by the Board of Education against an undisclosed number of other city teachers, Mr. Kiendl relied heavily on the recent ruling of the United States Court of Appeals upholding the conviction of eleven Communist party officials. The party officials were charged with conspiring to teach and advocate the violent overthrow of the government.

Mr. Kiendl's decision also was founded on the testimony by former Communist party officials who appeared for the prosecution against Mr. Friedman and on the basis of sixty-five documentary exhibits placed in the record.

From the foregoing, he said, he came to the conclusion "that the Communist party was at all pertinent times dedicated to the advocacy of the violent overthrow of the Government of the United States."

Red Allegiance Condemned

Mr. Kiendl also found that the evidence showed that Mr. Friedman "as an active member of that party is conclusively presumed to have been bound to adhere to its 'party line' and to have been committed to unquestioning obedience to its leadership" as was charged by the Superintendent of Schools. The trial examiner declared that "such adherence and obedience are manifestly inconsistent with the standards of conduct the public has every right to expect and demand from its school teachers in this city."

"The 'cold war' has become a shooting war which threatens to engulf all mankind," Mr. Kiendl said. "In these critical circumstances, it would be inexcusable to place American children in daily contact with a teacher who advocates the violent overthrow of our Government."

Mr. Kiendl said he was "wholly unable to accept the proposition that even a most imposing teacher-record immunizes a teacher from what should be the obvious consequences of becoming a member of a subversive organization."

Mr. Kiendl held that the questions about Communist party membership put by Dr. Jansen to Mr. Friedman were "perfectly proper." He declared that the questions went "to the very heart" of Mr. Friedman's qualifications as a public school teacher "and his contumacious refusal to answer them constituted insubordination." The trial examiner said that it was Mr. Friedman's "clear duty to answer, just as it was the clear duty of the Superintendent of Schools to ask the very questions propounded."

With respect to the defense contention that academic freedom was being infringed by inquiries into a teacher's political affiliations and activities outside the classroom, Mr. Kiendl said:

> If and when academic freedom is relied on to permit the existence of a clear and present danger of the injection into youthful minds of any subversive doctrine, it is no longer academic freedom but unrestrained academic license parading under the name of academic freedom.

Other Decisions Similar

The decision against the seven other teachers, who were charged only with insubordination and unbecoming conduct, were similar in content. Mr. Kiendl noted that the cases "proved beyond any doubt" that the respondents repeatedly refused to answer the Superintendent's questions concerning past or present membership in the Communist party even though the Superintendent had warned that such failure to answer would be considered an act of insubordination.

In addition to Mr. Friedman, Mr. Lederman, Mrs. Zitron and Mr. Feingold, the suspended teachers are Miss Alice B. Citron, Mark Friedlander, Louis Jaffe and Isadore Rubin.

Commenting on the recommendations, Corporation Counsel John P. McGrath urged that "vigorous measures" be taken "to rid not only the school system but all government agencies of communists." The cases against the eight teachers were handled by Michael A. Castaldi, assistant corporation counsel in charge of the education division. He was assisted by Daniel T. Scannell, assistant corporation counsel.

Communists Denounce Findings

For its part, the New York State Communist party last night termed the recommendations "a brazen thought-control decision" and "a deadly blow [that] has been struck at academic freedom, teachers' tenure and the right of our children to a free, democratic education."

The party also termed Mr. Kiendl as "this corporation lawyer on loan for the specific purpose of assisting the Board of Education in its witch hunt [who] arrogated unto himself the right to pass upon the doctrine of the Communist party while denying it even the elementary right to be heard."

"We warn," the party said, "that Mr. Kiendl's decision, unless immediately fought, will open the floodgates of a vast witch hunt aimed at teachers of all political affiliations and at the whole people of free, democratic education. Either academic freedom for all, including Communists, or there will be no security for any teacher."

Further Resources

BOOKS

Alexander, Kern, and M. David Alexander. *American Public School Law*, 5th ed. Belmont, Calif.: Wadsworth/Thomson Learning, 2001.

Heale, M. J. *McCarthy's Americans: Red Scare Politics in State and Nation, 1935–1965.* Athens: University of Georgia Press, 1998.

Spurlock, Clark. *Education and the Supreme Court.* Urbana: University of Illinois Press, 1955.

Defining "Equal" in Higher Education

Sweatt v. Painter

Supreme Court decision

By: Fred M. Vinson

Date: 1950

Source: *Sweatt v. Painter.* 339 U.S. 629, 70 Sup. Ct. 848 (1950). Reproduced in Knight, Edgar W., and Clifton L. Hall. *Readings in American Educational History.* New York: Appleton-Century-Crofts, 1951, 698–700.

McLaurin v. Oklahoma State Regents

Supreme Court decision

By: Fred M. Vinson

Date: 1950

Source: *McLaurin v. Oklahoma State Regents.* 339 U.S. 637, 70 Sup. Ct. 851 (1950). Reproduced in Knight, Edgar W., and Clifton L. Hall. *Readings in American Educational History.* New York: Appleton-Century-Crofts, 1951, 698–700.

About the Author: Fred M. Vinson (1890–1953) received undergraduate and law degrees from Center College and began a law practice in Kentucky. In 1924, he was elected to the U.S. House of Representatives and served six terms. In 1945, Vinson was appointed as secretary of the treasury. In 1946, he was nominated by President Harry S. Truman (served 1945–1953) for chief justice of the U.S. Supreme Court, a position he held until his death in 1953. ∎

Introduction

The Fourteenth Amendment, ratified in 1868, guaranteed the rights of individuals, regardless of race, to "equal protection of the laws." Nonetheless, the U.S. Supreme Court permitted states to pass Jim Crow laws, thereby legalizing segregation. In 1896, legal segregation in the South was greatly strengthened by the Court's decision in *Plessy v. Ferguson* that a Louisiana law requiring segregated train cars was constitutional as long as equal accommodations were furnished.

By the 1940s, things were beginning to change. In 1945, Heman Marion Sweatt, an African American college graduate and mail carrier in Houston, applied to the University of Texas Law School, which accepted only white students. In 1946, Sweatt attempted to register and was denied admission on the basis of race. A Texas court ordered the state to provide a law school for African Americans. When the school was opened, Sweatt refused to register for that school, citing that the new school was inferior to University of Texas Law School. In 1950, the case reached the Supreme Court and, in *Sweatt v. Painter,* the Court ordered the University of Texas Law School to

Postal worker and law student Heman Sweatt's application to the all-white University of Texas Law School eventually led to the integration of that school. © BETTMANN/CORBIS. REPRODUCED BY PERMISSION.

admit African Americans because the black school was clearly not equal both in terms of measurable aspects, such as the variety of courses, and in intangibles, such as reputation and prestige.

On the same day as the Court's decision in *Sweatt,* the Court also ruled on *McLaurin v. Oklahoma State Regents* that the University of Oklahoma could not treat African American and white students differently. G. W. McLaurin, an African American student attending a doctoral program at the University of Oklahoma, was forced to sit in special areas that were reserved for "Colored people" in the library, classrooms, and the cafeteria. The Court held that without the opportunity to associate freely with his classmates, McLaurin was deprived of a substantial educational advantage afforded white students.

Significance

In both *Sweatt* and *McLaurin,* the Court further defined the term "substantially equal." Considering factors beyond the quality of buildings and the number of volumes in the library, the decisions resulted in a weakening of the "separate but equal" doctrine. Although in neither case did the Court directly consider or overturn *Plessy,* the decisions called into question the very possi-

bility that schools could be both racially separate and equal. In *Sweatt,* the Court noted that students attending the black law school would be unable to build relationships with most of the judges and lawyers with whom they would later work, and in *McLaurin,* the importance of the "exchange of views" with other students was acknowledged. Affording these types of opportunities to African American students was now a condition of providing "substantially equal" education, yet impossible to accomplish under segregation.

The rulings in these two cases had an important impact on the decision in *Brown v. Board of Education* (1954) when the Court overturned *Plessy.* The Court cited both *Sweatt* and *McLaurin* in the *Brown* ruling, noting that the decisions resting on the finding of inequality in terms of "intangible" aspects of education were directly applicable to the provision of public K–12 education. *Sweatt* and *McLaurin* were landmark cases that contributed to the eventual rejection of "separate but equal" education as a violation of the "equal protection" clause of the Fourteenth Amendment.

Primary Source

Sweatt v. Painter [excerpt]

> **SYNOPSIS:** In the following excerpt, Chief Justice Fred M. Vinson states that an African American student must be admitted to the University of Texas Law School since the black law school provided is unequal in both tangible and intangible factors.

Mr. Chief Justice Vinson delivered the opinion of the Court. . . .

In the instant case, petitioner filed an application for admission to the University of Texas Law School for the February, 1946 term. His application was rejected solely because he is a Negro. Petitioner thereupon brought this suit for mandamus against the appropriate school officials, respondents here, to compel his admission. At that time, there was no law school in Texas which admitted Negroes.

The state trial court recognized that the action of the State in denying petitioner the opportunity to gain a legal education while granting it to others deprived him of the equal protection of the laws guaranteed by the Fourteenth Amendment. The court did not grant the relief requested, however, but continued the case for six months to allow the State to supply substantially equal facilities. At the expiration of the six months, in December, 1946, the court denied the writ on the showing that the authorized university officials had adopted an order calling for the opening of a law school for Negroes the following

G. W. McLaurin, a 54-year old African American, sits outside a classroom, apart from the white students, as he attends class at the University of Oklahoma in 1948. © BETTMANN/CORBIS. REPRODUCED BY PERMISSION.

February. While petitioner's appeal was pending, such a school was made available, but petitioner refused to register therein. The Texas Court of Civil Appeals set aside the trial court's judgment and ordered the cause "remanded generally to the trial court for further proceedings without prejudice to the rights of any party to this suit." . . .

The University of Texas Law School, from which petitioner was excluded, was staffed by a faculty of sixteen full-time and three part-time professors, some of whom are nationally recognized authorities in their field. Its student body numbered 850. The library contained over 65,000 volumes. Among the other facilities available to the students were a law review, moot court facilities, scholarship funds, and Order of the Coif affiliation. The school's alumni occupy the most distinguished positions in the private practice of the law and in the public life of the State. It may properly be considered one of the nation's ranking law schools.

The law school for Negroes which was to have opened in February, 1947, would have had no independent faculty or library. The teaching was to be carried on by four members of the University of Texas Law School faculty, who were to maintain their of-

fices at the University of Texas while teaching at both institutions. Few of the 10,000 volumes ordered for the library had arrived; nor was there any full-time librarian. The school lacked accreditation.

Since the trial of this case, respondents report the opening of a law school at the Texas State University for Negroes. It is apparently on the road to full accreditation. It has a faculty of five full-time professors; a student body of 23; a library of some 16,500 volumes serviced by a full-time staff; a practice court and legal aid association; and one alumnus who has become a member of the Texas Bar.

Whether the University of Texas Law School is compared with the original or the new law school for Negroes, we cannot find substantial equality in the educational opportunities offered white and Negro law students by the State. In terms of number of the faculty, variety of courses and opportunity for specialization, size of the student body, scope of the library, availability of law review and similar activities, the University of Texas Law School is superior. What is more important, the University of Texas Law School possesses to a far greater degree those qualities which are incapable of objective measurement but which make for greatness in a law school. Such qualities, to name but a few, include reputation of the faculty, experience of the administration, position and influence of the alumni, standing in the community, traditions and prestige. It is difficult to believe that one who had a free choice between these law schools would consider the question close. . . .

In accordance with these cases, petitioner may claim his full constitutional right: legal education equivalent to that offered by the State to students of other races. Such education is not available to him in a separate law school as offered by the State. We cannot, therefore, agree with respondents that the doctrine of *Plessy v. Ferguson* . . . requires affirmance of the judgment below. Nor need we reach petitioner's contention that *Plessy v. Ferguson* should be reexamined in the light of contemporary knowledge respecting the purposes of the Fourteenth Amendment and the effects of racial segregation. . . .

We hold that the Equal Protection Clause of the Fourteenth Amendment requires that petitioner be admitted to the University of Texas Law School. The judgment is reversed and the cause is remanded for proceedings not inconsistent with this opinion.

Reversed.

Primary Source

McLaurin v. Oklahoma State Regents [excerpt]

SYNOPSIS: In this excerpt, Vinson states the Court's decision that a black student may not be segregated within the University of Oklahoma.

Mr. Chief Justice Vinson delivered the opinion of the Court.

In this case, we are faced with the question whether a state may, after admitting a student to graduate instruction in its state university, afford him different treatment from other students solely because of his race. . . .

Appellant is a Negro citizen of Oklahoma. Possessing a Master's Degree, he applied for admission to the University of Oklahoma in order to pursue studies and courses leading to a Doctorate in Education. At that time, his application was denied, solely because of his race. The school authorities were required to exclude him by the Oklahoma statutes, . . . which made it a misdemeanor to maintain or operate, teach or attend a school at which both whites and Negroes are enrolled or taught. Appellant filed a complaint requesting injunctive relief, alleging that the action of the school authorities and the statutes upon which their action was based were unconstitutional and deprived him of the equal protection of the laws. . . .

A statutory three-judge District Court held that the State had a constitutional duty to provide him with the education he sought as soon as it provided that education for applicants of any other group. It further held that to the extent the Oklahoma statutes denied him admission they were unconstitutional and void. On the assumption, however, that the State would follow the constitutional mandate, the court refused to grant the injunction, retaining jurisdiction of the cause with full power to issue any necessary and proper orders to secure McLaurin the equal protection of the laws.

Following this decision, the Oklahoma legislature amended these statutes to permit the admission of Negroes to institutions of higher learning attended by white students, in cases where such institutions offered courses not available in the Negro schools. The amendment provided, however, that in such cases the program of instruction "shall be given at such colleges or institutions of higher education upon a segregated basis." Appellant was thereupon admitted to the University of Oklahoma Graduate School. In apparent conformity with the amendment, his admission was made subject to "such rules and regulations as to segregation as the President of the University shall consider to afford to Mr. G. W. McLaurin substantially equal educational opportunities as are afforded to other persons seeking the same education in the Graduate College," a condition which does not appear to have been withdrawn. Thus he was required to sit apart at a designated desk in an anteroom adjoining the classroom; to sit at a designated desk on the mezzanine floor of the library, but not to use the desks in the regular reading room; and to sit at a designated table and to eat at a different time from the other students in the school cafeteria.

To remove these conditions, appellant filed a motion to modify the order and judgment of the District Court. That court held that such treatment did not violate the provisions of the Fourteenth Amendment and denied the motion. . . . This appeal followed.

In the interval between the decision of the court below and the hearing in this Court, the treatment afforded appellant was altered. For some time, the section of the classroom in which appellant sat was surrounded by a rail on which there was a sign stating, "Reserved For Colored," but these have been removed. He is now assigned to a seat in the class-room in a row specified for colored students; he is assigned to a table in the library on the main floor; and he is permitted to eat at the same time in the cafeteria as other students, although here again he is assigned to a special table.

It is said that the separations imposed by the State in this case are in form merely nominal. McLaurin uses the same classroom, library and cafeteria as students of other races; there is no indication that the seats to which he is assigned in these rooms have any disadvantage of location. He may wait in line in the cafeteria and there stand and talk with his fellow students, but while he eats he must remain apart.

These restrictions were obviously imposed in order to comply, as nearly as could be, with the statutory requirements of Oklahoma. But they signify that the State, in administering the facilities it affords for professional and graduate study, sets McLaurin apart from the other students. The result is that appellant is handicapped in his pursuit of effective graduate instruction. Such restrictions impair and inhibit his ability to study, to engage in discussions and exchange views with other students, and, in general, to learn his profession.

Our society grows increasingly complex, and our need for trained leaders increases correspondingly. Appellant's case represents, perhaps, the epitome of that need, for he is attempting to obtain an advanced degree in education, to become, by definition, a leader and trainer of others. Those who will come under his guidance and influence must be directly affected by the education he receives. Their own education and development will necessarily suffer to the extent that his training is unequal to that of his classmates. State-imposed restrictions which produce such inequalities cannot be sustained.

It may be argued that appellant will be in no better position when these restrictions are removed, for he may still be set apart by his fellow students. This we think irrelevant. There is a vast difference—a Constitutional difference—between restrictions imposed by the state which prohibit the intellectual commingling of students, and the refusal of individuals to commingle where the state presents no such bar. . . . The removal of the state restrictions will not necessarily abate individual and group predilections, prejudices and choices. But at the very least, the state will not be depriving appellant of the opportunity to secure acceptance by his fellow students on his own merits.

We conclude that the conditions under which this appellant is required to receive his education deprive him of his personal and present right to the equal protection of the laws. See *Sweatt v. Painter.* . . . We hold that under these circumstances the Fourteenth Amendment precludes differences in treatment by the state based upon race. Appellant, having been admitted to a state-supported graduate school, must receive the same treatment at the hands of the state as students of other races. The judgment is

Reversed.

Further Resources

BOOKS

Alexander, Kern, and M. David Alexander. *American Public School Law,* 5th ed. Belmont, Calif.: Wadsworth/Thomson Learning, 2001.

Howard, John R. *The Shifting Wind: The Supreme Court and Civil Rights from Reconstruction to "Brown."* Albany: State University of New York Press, 1999.

Spurlock, Clark. *Education and the Supreme Court.* Urbana, Ill.: University of Illinois Press, 1955.

Tushnet, Mark V. *The NAACP's Legal Strategy Against Segregated Education, 1925–1950.* Chapel Hill: University of North Carolina Press, 1987.

WEBSITES

"'Courage and the Refusal to Be Swayed': Heman Marion Sweatt's Legal Challenge that Integrated the University of Texas." TxTell UT Stories, University of Texas, Austin. Available online at http://txtell.lib.utexas.edu/stories/s0010-full.html; website home page: http://txtell.lib.utexas.edu/index.html (accessed April 30, 2003).

"*Sweatt v. Painter* Archival and Textual Sources." University of Denver College of Law. Available online at http://www.law.du.edu/russell/lh/sweatt/; website home page: http://www.law.du.edu/ (accessed April 30, 2003).

God and Man at Yale: The Superstitions of "Academic Freedom"

Memoir

By: William F. Buckley Jr.

Date: August 1951

Source: Buckley, William F., Jr. *God and Man at Yale: The Superstitions of "Academic Freedom."* Chicago: Regnery, 1986, lvii–lxiii.

About the Author: William F. Buckley Jr. (1925–), author and television personality, founded the *National Review* in 1955 and served as its editor-in-chief. A well-known conservative, he hosted the television discussion program *Firing Line* from 1966 to 1999. Buckley is the author of a series of spy novels and is a syndicated columnist. He is also the author of *Nearer My God: An Autobiography of Faith* (1997). ∎

Introduction

William F. Buckley Jr.'s undergraduate experience at Yale University in the late 1940s and early 1950s was not what he had expected. While fond of Yale for a variety of other reasons, he was disturbed by what he saw as a bias of the faculty toward atheist and socialist ideals. An advocate of Christianity and individualism, Buckley expected to find these values and beliefs reflected in the curriculum of Yale. The history of the institution provides a partial explanation for these expectations.

Yale, along with other early colleges such as Harvard University, the College of William and Mary, and Princeton University, was founded by a particular Christian sect to promote the beliefs of the denomination and to train ministers for its churches. However, over the course of the nineteenth century, the general trend for institutions of higher education in the United States was toward a more secular, scientific, and practical curriculum. By the early twentieth century, Yale, along with many other colleges originally founded by religious groups, was no longer under church control.

Although professors at these previously denominational institutions, as well as public colleges and universities, were no longer expected to teach or espouse a particular set of religious beliefs, they experienced other forms of censorship. Particularly during the time periods after World War I (1914–1918) and World War II (1939–1945), college teachers proposing radical social, political, or economic ideas risked dismissal or other disciplinary action. Calls from benefactors, trustees, alumni, politicians, or the general public to "weed out" communists or other radicals were answered by faculty with arguments in favor of academic freedom: Professors had to be allowed to pursue knowledge free of outside pressure and intimidation. The unbiased search for truth benefited the larger society, and, at the same time, unfettered classroom inquiry benefited students.

Significance

In *God and Man at Yale: The Superstitions of "Academic Freedom,"* Buckley regarded such "academic freedom" as unattainable and indefensible. Teachers are inevitably basing their ideas on certain values, beliefs, and assumptions. Indeed, the ideal of impartiality is not desirable. The faculty, Buckley asserted, is responsible to the trustees who are, in turn, responsible to those who pay the bills: parents and alumni. He stated that faculty should teach the values and beliefs of Christianity and

individualism held by the founders of the college and the majority of the trustees and alumni.

Buckley represented an important voice in the ongoing controversy over academic freedom. To whom was the American university or college responsible? What were the purposes of institutions of higher learning in American society? The American Association of University Professors argued in a 1915 report on academic freedom that universities receiving public funds, including those formerly under denominational control such as Yale, are accountable to the public for the production of knowledge that is the result of unbiased inquiry and "not echoes of the opinions of the lay public" or of the individuals who endow or manage universities. Faculty are the appointees, but not the employees, of the board of trustees. The purposes of the university are to advance knowledge, teach students, and produce experts for public service. All of these functions, the report asserted, are only possible under conditions of academic freedom.

For Buckley, university professors should be considered accountable to parents who pay their child's tuition and alumni who support the university. These groups have a right to expect that the beliefs and values they hold dear will be transmitted to students. The faculty are, from Buckley's viewpoint, employees of the trustees who are morally bound to serve the interests of alumni and parents. He stated that the university owes the public not unbiased scholarship, but the production of morally upstanding citizens with a respect for American traditions and institutions.

Primary Source

God and Man at Yale: The Superstitions of "Academic Freedom" [excerpt]

SYNOPSIS: Buckley outlines his argument that Yale, as well as other universities and colleges, has a moral responsibility to transmit to students the beliefs and values held by its founders and benefactors. The vast majority of trustees and alumni of Yale are committed to Christianity and traditional American values. That the faculty of Yale should be teaching students opposing values is, Buckley asserts, absurd and wrong.

During the years 1946 to 1950, I was an undergraduate at Yale University. I arrived in New Haven fresh from a two-year stint in the Army, and I brought with me a firm belief in Christianity and a profound respect for American institutions and traditions. I had always been taught, and experience had fortified the teachings, that an active faith in God and a rigid adherence to Christian principles are the most powerful influences toward the good life. I also believed, with only a scanty knowledge of economics, that free enterprise and limited government had served this country well and would probably continue to do so in the future.

These two attitudes were basic to my general outlook. One concerned the role of man in the universe; the other, in all its implications, the role of man in his society. I knew, of course, of the existence of many persons who had no faith in God and even less in the individual's capacity to work out his own destiny without recourse to the state. I therefore looked eagerly to Yale University for allies against secularism and collectivism.

I am one of a small group of students who fought, during undergraduate days, in the columns of the newspaper, in the Political Union, in debates and seminars, against those who seek to subvert religion and individualism. The fight we waged continues even though little headway was made. The struggle was never more bitter than when the issue concerned educational policy.

As opportunity afforded, some of us advanced the viewpoint that the faculty of Yale is morally and constitutionally responsible to the trustees of Yale, who are in turn responsible to the alumni, and thus duty bound to transmit to their students the wisdom, insight, and value judgments which in the trustees' opinion will enable the American citizen to make the optimum adjustment to the community and to the world. I contended that the trustees of Yale, along with the vast majority of the alumni, are committed to the desirability of fostering both a belief in God, and a recognition of the merits of our economic system. I therefore concluded that as our educational overseers, it was the clear responsibility of the trustees to guide the teaching at Yale toward those ends.

The reaction to this point of view has been violent. A number of persons affiliated with the University, all the way from President-emeritus Charles Seymour to a host of students, have upheld what they call "academic freedom," by which they mean the freedom of the faculty member to teach what he sees fit as he sees fit—provided, of course, he is "honest" and "professionally competent." Here the argument rested when I left Yale.

A number of persons sympathetic to this point of view have urged me to deal at greater length with the problem. I was not disposed to do this, in part because I lack the scholarly equipment to deal with it adequately, in part because I was unwilling to

Conservative activist, author, and editor William F. Buckley attended Yale University. Buckley argued that Yale and the higher education system promoted liberal policies and values. GETTY IMAGES. REPRODUCED BY PERMISSION.

spend the necessary time. I finally decided to make an attempt, largely because I fell victim to arguments I have so often utilized myself: that the so-called conservative, uncomfortably disdainful of controversy, seldom has the energy to fight his battles, while the radical, so often a member of the minority, exerts disproportionate influence because of his dedication to his cause.

I *am* dedicated to my cause. At the same time, I cannot claim to have approached this project with the diligence and patience of a professional scholar. As far as pure scholarship is concerned, it is best said of me that I have the profoundest respect for it, and no pretension to it. As witness to this, I propose, in the nontheoretical portion of this book, to confine myself to Yale. Ideally, my observations would be based on an exhaustive study of the curricula and attitudes of a number of colleges and universities. Instead, I have confined myself to the university that I know first hand.

I do this confidently, let me add, because Yale, I judge deservedly, has earned a reputation as a citadel of "triumphant conservatism," as *Time* magazine recently put it. By comparison with many others, I believe it is. This would suggest that what is amiss at Yale is more drastically amiss in other of our great institutions of learning. Yet on this point I will not insist. It is not here my concern. I propose, simply, to expose what I regard as an extraordinarily irresponsible educational attitude that, under the protective label "academic freedom," has produced one of the most extraordinary incongruities of our time: the institution that derives its moral and financial support from Christian individualists and then addresses itself to the task of persuading the sons of these supporters to be atheistic socialists.

I ought to add that what little experience I have had with the purposefulness and tenacity of the mid-twentieth-century conservative gives me few grounds for hope that this paradox will be remedied. So it is that for consolation I have turned frequently to a few sentences of Arthur Koestler:

> Art is a contemplative business. It is also a ruthless business. One should either write ruthlessly what one believes to be the truth, or shut up. Now I happen to believe that Europe is doomed. . . . This is so to speak my contemplative truth. . . . But I also happen to believe in the ethical imperative of fighting evil, even if the fight is hopeless. . . . And on this plane my contemplative truth becomes defeatist propaganda and hence an immoral influence.

I have some notion of the bitter opposition that this book will inspire. But I am through worrying about it. My concern over present-day educational practice stems from my conviction that, after each side has had its say, we are right and they are wrong; and my greatest anguish is not in contemplation of the antagonism that this essay will evoke from many quarters, but rather from the knowledge that they are winning and we are losing.

I shall insert here what may seem obvious. I consider this battle of educational theory important and worth time and thought even in the context of a world-situation that seems to render totally irrelevant any fight except the power struggle against Communism. I myself believe that the duel between Christianity and atheism is the most important in the world. I further believe that the struggle between individualism and collectivism is the same struggle reproduced on another level. I believe that if and when the menace of Communism is gone, other vital battles, at present subordinated, will emerge to the foreground. And the winner must have help from the classroom.

I should also like to state that I am not here concerned with writing an *apologia* either for Christianity or for individualism. That is to say, this essay will not attempt to prove either the divinity of Christ or to defend the advantages of conducting our lives with reference to divine sanctions. Nor shall I attempt to demonstrate the contemporary applicability of the principal theses of Adam Smith.

Rather, I will proceed on the assumption that Christianity and freedom are "good," [In point of fact, the argument I shall advance does not even require that free enterprise and Christianity be "good," but merely that the educational overseers of a private university should *consider* them to be "good."] without ever worrying that by so doing, I am being presumptuous.

The first duty, of course, is to arrive at a judgment as to whether or not there exists at Yale an atmosphere of detached impartiality with respect to the great value-alternatives of the day, that is, Christianity *versus* agnosticism and atheism, and individualism *versus* collectivism. My belief is that such impartiality does not exist. I shall document this opinion. What is more, for practical reasons I have restricted my survey to the undergraduate school, even though some of the graduate departments, the Yale Law School in particular, would provide far more flamboyant copy.

The question then arises: If there is a bias does it coincide with the bias of the educational trustees of Yale? In other words, if there is not impartiality, does the net impact of Yale education encourage those values probably held by the alumni? My opinion is that on the contrary, the emphases at Yale are directly opposed to those of her alumni.

I shall then ask if impartiality—assuming it to be possible—is desirable in classroom treatment of conflicting ideologies. I shall go on to question what so many persons consider axiomatic, namely the proposition that "all sides should be presented impartially," that the student should be encouraged to select the side that pleases him most. I hope to point out that this attitude, acknowledged in theory by the University, has never been practiced, and in fact, can never and ought never to be practiced.

In one respect, I have spared no pains. Although some of the matter that appears in this book is elusive, I have made every effort to be accurate. In fact, several friends, intimately associated with Yale over the past few years, believe I have bent over backwards almost grotesquely in my effort to avoid distortion. Be that as it may, I have worked with the clear realization that exaggeration would bring only unwarranted damage to an institution of which I am almost irrationally fond, and personal humiliation to myself.

Nor should this book be interpreted as a comprehensive indictment of Yale life. Volume after volume, each many times the bulk of this one, could justly be written commending the virtues of countless aspects of Yale's education. But it is not the diligence or patience of her scholars, or the kindness and understanding of her administrators, or the joys and sustaining pleasures of the friendships she makes possible that are the subject matter of this book. These deserve tribute, and I give mine without reservation. Notwithstanding, something greater, I think, is at stake: the net impact of Yale education. It is to this problem that I address myself.

I have made extensive use of an Appendix for documentation, for theoretical but pertinent digressions, and for references of various kinds. It is naturally the hope of every writer that the Appendix should be consulted fastidiously. Notwithstanding, many, including myself, must admit that an understanding of the thesis does not require familiarity with appendix material.

Finally, I must ask indulgence for the frequent references in the text to myself and my personal experiences at Yale. If there were a way out, I should willingly have taken it. But a great deal of the material that I have summoned, and of the insights that I have received, have been a result of personal experiences. To avoid mention of these would be not only coy, but restrictive. For these reasons I ask patience; and further, I approach my thesis with profound humility and with the desperate hope that even those who disagree emphatically will acknowledge that I could have no motive other than a devotion to Yale, a recognition of Yale's importance, and a deep concern for the future of our country.

W.F.B., Jr.
Sharon, Conn.
August, 1951

Further Resources

BOOKS

Butts, R. Freeman, and Lawrence Cremin. *A History of Education in American Culture.* New York: Henry Holt, 1953.

Lucas, Christopher J. *American Higher Education: A History.* New York: St. Martin's, 1994.

Metzger, Walter P. *Professors on Guard: The First AAUP Investigations.* New York: Arno, 1977.

PERIODICALS

Burgan, Mary. "Academic Freedom in a World of Moral Crisis." *The Chronicle of Higher Education* 49, no. 2, September 6, 2002, B20.

WEBSITES

American Association of University Professors. Available online at http://www.aaup.org/ (accessed May 1, 2003).

What Educational TV Offers You
Pamphlet

By: Jack Mabley

Date: 1954

Source: Mabley, Jack. *What Educational TV Offers You.* Public Affairs Pamphlet no. 203. New York: The Public Affairs Committee, 1954.

About the Author: Jack Mabley (1915–) earned a degree from the University of Illinois in 1938. He was a columnist, reporter, and television editor with the *Chicago Daily News* from 1938 to 1961, and then a columnist and editor for the *Chicago American* and later the *Chicago Tribune.* In 2003, Mabley was a columnist for the *Daily Herald,* in Arlington Heights, Illinois. ∎

Introduction

The 1950s saw a tremendous expansion of television viewing. While some had already become leery of the potential negative effects of television, many had high hopes for the educational possibilities of the new technology. Here was a way for everyone to be able to access the best in education and culture—the medium could be the tool that would finally bring educational equality to the masses. Everything from arts events to "how to" programs to language courses could be made available to the general population regardless of income or location. Educational uses for television developed during the 1950s included classroom instruction, education for homebound students, college courses, and general educational programming for the community.

Yet, during the 1950s commercial television already dominated the broadcasting scene, and some were voicing concerns about less-than-worthwhile programs, unwholesome content, lack of parental screening and control of children's viewing, and a negative impact on school achievement, especially in reading. Television viewing hours were quickly filling time previously devoted to reading, active play, family interaction, and homework.

In this context, Jack Mabley, in the 1954 pamphlet *What Educational TV Offers You,* advocated for the development of educational television stations in order to fulfill television's potential as "the nation's greatest teacher." Mabley stated that there is a place for educational programming: a significant segment of the population did not own a television set and, of those who did, 20 to 30 percent had the sets turned off on any given evening. This represented a large potential audience for educational programming. Mabley asserted that the promise for equal educational opportunity and the general uplift of the American society must not be wasted.

Significance

Mabley's optimism was shared by many in the 1950s. Television technology, with its ability to transmit auditory and visual information to an almost unlimited number of people, seemed to have awesome potential for education. But while educational programming has expanded tremendously in the last half century, most notably through the Public Broadcasting Service, concerns about negative effects on children's learning have intensified.

The culture of American television viewing today contrasts starkly with that of the 1950s. The proportion of Americans that are nonviewers or who do not own a television has shrunk to insignificance. Ninety-eight to 99 percent of households own a set and the television is on for an average of nearly seven hours each day. Children watch an average of fifteen hundred hours of television per year, compared to spending an average of nine hundred hours in school. Hundreds of channels offer twenty-four-hour programming. In addition, commercial television, in the form of Channel One, has entered the classroom to the dismay of many.

Television viewing has been linked in research studies to lower reading scores, shorter attention spans, and a need to be constantly entertained in the classroom. Some critics maintain that the passivity of the television viewing experience makes it inherently noneducational. "Lecture-style" education has lost popularity in favor of more interactive learning, which is difficult or impossible to accomplish via television. Others note that the medium's visual character restricts educational shows to certain types of content. Some research, however, shows positive educational effects resulting from educational programming such as *Reading Rainbow, Sesame Street,* and *Between the Lions.*

Parents and educators today have a much larger variety of quality educational programs to choose from but are far more cautious and less optimistic about the educational benefits of television than many were in the 1950s. Recent research suggesting both benefits and drawbacks of television for learning has led many to advocate a more careful and balanced approach to educational television.

Primary Source

What Educational TV Offers You [excerpt]

SYNOPSIS: Mabley discusses the need for educational television in the context of excessive commercial television viewing and the lack of worthwhile programming. The potential audience is vast, Mabley contends, as is the potential for a positive educational impact. Educational television stations will need courage and imagination to move forward and compete with commercial television.

The appeal of educational TV is as great as the imaginations of Americans. Some parents want it because of the shortcomings of commercial television. But educational television doesn't need negative appeal. Not when it's going to bring great symphony orchestras into our living rooms. Symphony orchestras and ten-year-old pianists. Courses in psychology and championship track meets. How to fight corn borers and how to enjoy ballet. Understanding Shakespeare and understanding the gasoline engine. Child psychology and leisure time after 65.

All of the extravagant adjectives which were used when commercial television was beginning to flower may be transferred to educational television.

Commercial television has become the nation's greatest salesman. Educational television will be the nation's greatest teacher.

The Need for Educational T.V.

What is the need for educational TV? Consider it only as it will be considered in most American homes—as an adjunct to commercial television.

The benefits of watching commercial television are debatable. There are wonderful and worth-while programs, but what a pitifully small percentage of parents take the trouble to supervise their children's viewing habits! A mother and father who wouldn't think of sending their youngsters to see a Saturday afternoon movie without first checking to be sure that the film was clean and suitable for children will turn the same kids loose in front of a TV set for 15, 18, or 20 hours a week, and have little or no conception of what is being soaked into the little minds.

Some optimists were surprised that families spent 20 to 22 hours a week watching their TV sets in their first year of ownership. They predicted the novelty would wear off, that families would turn back to reading and activities in the home.

It hasn't worked out that way.

We have become a nation of televiewers, of sitters.

A high school principal rehearses for the pilot of an educational television program to instruct Little Rock High School students. © BETTMANN/CORBIS. REPRODUCED BY PERMISSION.

Many children spend more time in front of TV sets than they spend in front of their school teachers. There is no evidence that their viewing is lessening. Individuals taper off some when they get in their late teens, but after marriage the TV set in the living room is as much a part of family life as kids, cars, and mortgage. . . .

A vast potential audience

In a city with 1,000,000 television sets, as many as 50 or 55 per cent of the sets may be tuned to *I Love Lucy* on a Monday night. But at this or any given hour, 20 or 30 per cent of the sets may be turned off. There is a vast potential audience even if the viewers who now watch commercial TV never tune in the educational brand.

Dr. W. R. G. Baker, vice president of General Electric, was discussing a course in elementary psychology presented by the University of Houston station. The course was on the air at 8 p.m., five nights a week. It had between eight and ten thousand viewers.

"To be frank about it," Dr. Baker said, "this is not an amazing figure when we consider that some commercial programs will draw as much as 36 per cent of the set-owning public in any one city.

"What is amazing is that this program created the largest single group of students for any class in elementary psychology ever taught, anywhere, any time."

Big adjectives are in order. This awesome accomplishment was made by the first educational TV station during its first months on the air.

Multiply this record by 100 educational stations, add experience, add a variety of programs, add a growing public awareness of what educational TV stations can offer them, and educational television becomes a very exciting national asset.

Educational television stations are not going to fit any fixed pattern, any more than all commercial stations are alike. Television stations, like newspapers, have personalities. Almost any newspaper worth the reading reflects an individual personality—sometimes that of the publisher, or the editor, or even of a group of men influential in running the paper.

TV stations, too, are being found to have personalities of their own. The dominating trait may be super-salesmanship, dullness, imagination, old time-showmanship, public spirit, or greed.

The educational stations will have personalities. The worst sin will be stodginess, reflecting unimaginative and over-conservative thinking. Some stations may start that way. They're unlikely to remain stodgy for long. It is an expensive luxury. . . .

Kinds of Programs

In the arguments before the FCC, educational institutions indicated the types of programs the public could expect on the non-commercial channels:

1. Classroom instruction for public schools.
2. Direct adult education.
3. Community programming.
4. Out-of-school programs for children.
5. General cultural and entertainment programs.

Courage Needed

Probably courage will be the most important asset. Teachers have become timid in the face of criticism, before political pressures, both on a national and local level.

Tax fighters and economic-minded groups will continue to attack educational television. A large percentage of the American public will say the programs are stuffy, that people want to be entertained, not educated.

Newspaper critics, judging by the standards of national network programs, are likely to be less kind than some were in helping to campaign for educational channels.

Commercial experts will offer easy formulas to replace those that fail to hold large audiences. Timid educators may grasp at the formulas to avoid pressures and criticism.

—and imagination

Next to courage will come imagination. It doesn't take much of that to realize that in the educational telecasters' hands has been placed the greatest instrument for the culture and improvement of the people in American history. "Equal opportunity" can have a meaning as never before. The greatest teachers in the land, the facilities of the finest universities will be accessible to areas of cultural impoverishment.

It was concisely put by a man who helped lead the fight for educational television:

Through educational television the mass medium could be used to put an end to the mass man.

Many organizations cooperating

No less than sixty-two national organizations are actively participating in the Advisory Committee of the National Citizens Committee for Educational Television in the necessary effort to make this dream a reality. These national organizations have been carefully selected to insure representation from all segments of American public opinion. They include women's organizations, business, youth, medical, religious, Negro, cultural, social service, veteran, educational, and farming interests.

Similarly representative advisory committees have been set up in Pittsburgh, Los Angeles, and other cities where educational television stations are coming into being. The KTHE advisory board in Los Angeles, for instance, has seven representatives from colleges and universities, seven from the school system, and six from community organizations. This wide representation should assure not only that our educational TV stations be democratically controlled but that they become truly reflective of the basic educational needs of the American people.

Further Resources

BOOKS

Alter, Henry C. *Of Messages and Media: Teaching and Learning by Public Television.* Brookline, Mass.: Center for the Study of Liberal Education for Adults at Boston University, 1968.

Bianculli, David. *Teleliteracy: Taking Television Seriously.* Syracuse, N.Y.: Syracuse University Press, 2000.

Channel One: Are Schools Trading Captive Student Audiences for Free Equipment? Washington, D.C.: U.S. Dept. of Education, Office of Educational Research and Improvement, Educational Resources Information Center, 1990.

Fox, Roy F. *Harvesting Minds: How TV Commercials Control Kids.* Westport, Conn.: Praeger, 2000.

Jones, Glenn R. *Cyberschools: An Education Renaissance,* 2nd ed. Englewood, Colo.: Cyber, 2000.

Mander, Jerry. *Four Arguments for the Elimination of Television.* New York: Morrow, 1978.

Postman, Neil. *Amusing Ourselves to Death: Public Discourse in the Age of Show Business.* New York: Viking, 1985.

WEBSITES

ChannelOne.com. Available online at http://www.channelone.com/ (accessed May 1, 2003).

"Channel One News: The Most Controversial Show on Television." Obligation, Inc. Available online at http://www.obligation.org/ch1.html; website home page: http://www.obligation.org/ (accessed May 1, 2003).

Public Broadcasting Service. Available online at http://www .pbs.org/ (accessed May 1, 2003).

TV-Turnoff Network. Available online at http://www.tvfa.org/ (accessed May 1, 2003).

Why Johnny Can't Read— and What You Can Do About It

Nonfiction work

By: Rudolf Flesch

Date: 1955

Source: Flesch, Rudolf. *Why Johnny Can't Read—and What You Can Do About It.* New York: Harper, 1955. Reprint, Harper and Row, 1986, 4–18.

About the Author: Rudolf Flesch (1911–1986), an Austrian-born educator, was the author of a number of books on speaking, reading, and writing including *The Art of Plain Talk* (1946), *The Art of Readable Writing* (1949), and *The Art of Clear Thinking* (1951). Flesch was best known as an advocate for the phonics method of reading instruction. ■

Introduction

When Rudolf Flesch's grandson, "Johnny," was having trouble with reading, Flesch began to work with him and found, to his surprise, that the twelve-year-old did not know the sounds associated with the letters of the alphabet and could not "sound out" words. Rather, he attempted to guess each word. Within a few months, Flesch taught him to read using a phonic approach. Starting with the sounds of the language and matching them to letters or letter combinations, he taught Johnny to decode words.

Meanwhile, Flesch began to investigate the way reading was taught in American schools. Flesch found that the method being used in most U.S. schools was the "look-say" method, also known as the "guesswork method," or, more recently, "whole language." Flesch referred to the approach as the "Chinese word-learning system" because children are told the meaning of the word and then memorize it, as if English were like the Chinese language with a different symbol for each word, rather than a phonetic language (based on an alphabet). Students were also taught to use cues, such as pictures, in order to guess the meaning of words.

Phonics was the dominant approach to reading instruction in American schools until the 1920s, yet the look-say method had origins in the early nineteenth century. Thomas Hopkins Gallaudet, the founder of the Hartford School for the Deaf, developed the look-say method as a way to teach reading to students with hearing impairments who had never heard spoken language and, therefore, could not associate sounds with letters in order to "sound out" a word. The method was eventually adopted for students without hearing impairments. Horace Mann introduced Gallaudet's method for all children in the Boston schools in the 1830s, but the unsuccessful experiment was discontinued in 1844. The first look-say textbooks were published in 1914, and the method gained popularity in the 1920s and 1930s. By the 1950s, look-say was the dominant approach to reading instruction in American schools.

Significance

The 1955 publication of *Why Johnny Can't Read—and What You Can Do About It,* a best seller, created instant public debate. Many parents had been uneasy with the new reading methods and found an advocate in Flesch. Educators and academics, on the other hand, were furious. Adding to the controversy was Flesch's suggestion that look-say was the result of an educational conspiracy. With look-say, children are unable to read real children's literature because they cannot decode unfamiliar words; instead, graded readers using controlled vocabulary must be purchased. Flesch pointed out that textbook companies, and the academics who serve as lead authors, profit enormously from the use of this method. It is this profit, Flesch believed, that prevents research showing the effectiveness of the phonic approach from impacting the way reading instruction is carried out in the schools.

Advocates of look-say, now called whole language, assert that reading is a natural learning process similar to speech development. Children will learn to read on their own if surrounded by a print-rich environment and interesting and exciting reading matter. The approach emphasizes meaning over decoding skills. Noting that skilled readers read words as units, whole language teaches beginning readers to recognize whole words rather than breaking them down into letters and their corresponding sounds.

Although the debate continues, recent research suggests that all beginning readers should receive phonics instruction within the context of exposure to the enjoyment of meaningful literature.

Primary Source

Why Johnny Can't Read—and What You Can Do About It [excerpt]

> **SYNOPSIS:** Flesch introduces his main premise: that schools no longer teach children to decode words based on the sounds of letters but, rather, teach them to memorize whole words. This system, Flesch believes, is illogical and ineffective. Children are unable

Two young students receive special lessons in speech and reading. © **BETTMANN/CORBIS. REPRODUCED BY PERMISSION.**

to read real literature, and schools must, therefore, purchase expensive graded readers with carefully controlled vocabulary. Academics and textbook publishers benefit, Flesch states, but not students.

Our system of writing—the alphabet—was invented by the Egyptians and the Phoenicians somewhere around 1500 B.C. Before the invention of the alphabet there was only picture writing—a picture of an ox meant "ox," a picture of a house meant "house," and so on. (The Chinese to this day have a system of writing with symbols that stand for whole words.) As soon as people had an alphabet, the job of reading and writing was tremendously simplified. Before that, you had to have a symbol for every word in the language—10,000, 20,000 or whatever the vocabulary range was. Now, with the alphabet, all you had to learn was the letters. Each letter stood for a certain sound, and that was that. To write a word—any word—all you had to do was break it down into its sounds and put the corresponding letters on paper.

So, ever since 1500 B.C. people all over the world—wherever an alphabetic system of writing was used—learned how to read and write by the simple

process of memorizing the sound of each letter in the alphabet. . . .

Except, as I said before, twentieth-century Americans—and other nations in so far as they have followed our example. And what do we use instead? Why, the only other possible system of course—the system that was in use before the invention of the alphabet in 1500 B.C. We have decided to forget that we write with letters and learn to read English as if it were Chinese. One word after another after another after another. If we want to read materials with a vocabulary of 10,000 words, then we have to memorize 10,000 words; if we want to go to the 20,000 word range, we have to learn, one by one, 20,000 words; and so on. We have thrown 3,500 years of civilization out the window and have gone back to the Age of Hammurabi.

You don't believe me? I assure you what I am saying is literally true. Go to your school tomorrow morning—or if Johnny has brought home one of his readers, look at it. You will immediately see that all the words in it are learned by endless repetition. Not a sign anywhere that letters correspond to sounds and that words can be worked out by pronouncing the letters. No. The child is told what each word means and then they are mechanically, brutally hammered into his brain. Like this:

> "We will look," said Susan. "Yes, yes," said all the children. "We will look and find it." So all the boys and girls looked. They looked and looked for it. But they did not find it.

Or this:

> "Quack, quack," said the duck. He wanted something. He did not want to get out. He did not want to go to the farm. He did not want to eat. He sat and sat and sat.

All the reading books used in all our schools, up through fourth and fifth and sixth grade, are collections of stuff like that. Our children learn the word *sat* by reading over and over again about a duck or a pig or a goat that sat and sat and sat. And so with every word in the language.

Every word in the language! You know what that means? It means that if you teach reading by this system, you can't use ordinary reading matter for practice. Instead, all children for three, four, five, six years have to work their way up through a battery of carefully designed readers, each one containing all the words used in the previous one plus a strictly limited number of new ones, used with the exactly "right" amount of repetition. Our children don't read Andersen's *Fairy Tales* any more or *The Arabian Nights* or Mark Twain or Louisa May Alcott or the Mary Poppins books or the Dr. Doolittle books or *anything* interesting and worth while, *because they can't.* It so happens that the writers of these classic children's books wrote without being aware of our Chinese system of teaching reading. So *Little Women* contains words like *grieving* and *serene,* and *Tom Sawyer* has *ague* and *inwardly,* and Bulfinch's *Age of Fable* has *nymph* and *deity* and *incantations.* If a child that has gone to any of our schools faces the word *nymph* for the first time, he is absolutely helpless because nobody has ever told him how to sound out *n* and *y* and *m* and *ph* and read the word off the page.

So what does he get instead? He gets those series of horrible, stupid, emasculated, pointless, tasteless little readers, the stuff and guff about Dick and Jane or Alice and Jerry visiting the farm and having birthday parties and seeing animals in the zoo and going through dozens and dozens of totally unexciting middle-class, middle-income, middle-I.Q. children's activities that offer opportunities for reading "Look, look" or "Yes, yes" or "Come, come" or "See the funny, funny animal." During the past half year

I read a good deal of this material and I don't wish that experience on anyone.

Who writes these books? Let me explain this to you in detail, because there is the nub of the whole problem.

There are one or two dozen textbook houses in America. By far the most lucrative part of their business is the publication of readers for elementary schools. There are millions of dollars of profit in these little books. Naturally, the competition is tremendous. So is the investment; so is the sales effort; so is the effort that goes into writing, editing, and illustrating these books. . . .

Naturally, the stupendous and frighteningly idiotic work of concocting this stuff can only be done by tireless teamwork of many educational drudges. But if the textbook house put only the drudges on the title page, that wouldn't look impressive enough to beat the competition. So there has to be a "senior author"—someone with a national reputation who teaches how to teach reading at one of the major universities.

And that's why each and every one of the so-called authorities in this field is tied up with a series of readers based on the Chinese word-learning method. As long as you used that method, you have to buy some $30 worth per child of Dr. So-and-so's readers; as soon as you switch to the common-sense method of teaching the sounds of the letters, you can give them a little primer and then proceed immediately to anything from the *Reader's Digest* to *Treasure Island.* . . .

Consequently it's utterly impossible to find anyone inside the official family of the educators saying anything even slightly favorable to the natural method of teaching reading. Mention the alphabetic method or phonetics or "phonics" and you immediately arouse derision, furious hostility, or icy silence.

For instance, in the May 1952 *Catholic Educator,* Monsignor Clarence E. Elwell published an article "Reading: The Alphabet and Phonics." Monsignor Elwell is Superintendent of Schools of the Diocese of Cleveland and knows what he is talking about. He says:

> In a language based on an alphabetic (that is, phonetic) method of coding the spoken word, the only sensible way to teach how to decode the written symbols is (1) by *teaching the phonetic code,* that is, the alphabet, and (2) the manner of coding—letter by letter, left to right. It is as nonsensical to use a whole word method for beginning reading as it would

be to teach the Morse code on a whole word basis. . . . A child who has been taught the code and how to use it . . . gains a confident habit in attacking words. Instead of guessing when he comes to a new word, as he did when taught by the sight word method, he now works through a word and to the surprise of the teachers usually comes up with the right answer. . . . After four years' experiment with the introduction of a strong program of phonics at the very beginning of grade one, the experimenter finds teachers convinced and children apparently happier in their success.

What do you think happened when Monsignor Elwell said publicly that our whole system of teaching reading is nonsense? Absolutely nothing. So far as I know, none of the reading "experts" has paid the slightest attention to the Cleveland experiment. . . .

And how do you convince thousands of intelligent young women that black is white and that reading has nothing to do with letters and sounds? Simple. Like this:

First, you announce loudly and with full conviction that our method of writing English is *not* based on pronunciation. Impossible, you say? Everybody knows that all alphabetic systems are phonetic? Oh no. I quote from page 297 of *Reading and the Educative Process* by Dr. Paul Witty of Northwestern University: "English is essentially an unphonetic language."

This is so ridiculous that it should be possible to just laugh about it and forget it. But the reading "experts" have created so much confusion that it's necessary to refute this nonsense. Well then: *All* alphabetic systems are phonetic; the two words mean the same thing. The only trouble is that English is a little more irregular than other languages. How much more has been established by three or four independent researchers. They all came up with the same figure. About 13 per cent of all English words are partly irregular in their spelling. The other 87 per cent follow fixed rules. Even the 13 per cent are not "unphonetic," as Dr. Witty calls it, but usually contain just one irregularly spelled vowel: *done* is pronounced "dun," *one* is pronounced "wun," *are* is pronounced "ar," and so on.

So our English system of writing is *of course* phonetic, but has a few more exceptions to the rules than other languages. . . .

What does all this add up to? It means simply and clearly that according to our accepted system of instruction, reading isn't taught at all. Books are

put in front of the children and they are told to guess at the words or wait until Teacher tells them. But they are *not* taught to read—if by reading you mean what the dictionary says it means, namely, "get the meaning of writing or printing."

Now you will say that all this applies only to first grade. Not at all. If you think that after this preparatory guessing game reading begins in earnest in second grade, or in third, or in fourth, you are mistaken. Reading *never* starts. The guessing goes on and on and on, through grade school, through high school, through college, through life. It's all they'll ever know. They'll never really learn to read.

Further Resources

BOOKS

Balmuth, Miriam. *The Roots of Phonics: A Historical Introduction.* New York: McGraw-Hill, 1982.

Berliner, David C., and Bruce J. Biddle. *The Manufactured Crisis: Myths, Fraud, and the Attack on America's Public Schools.* Reading, Mass.: Addison-Wesley, 1995.

Chall, Jeanne S. *Learning to Read: The Great Debate.* New York: McGraw-Hill, 1983.

Flesch, Rudolf. *Why Johnny Still Can't Read.* New York: Harper and Row, 1981.

McGuinness, Diane. *Why Our Children Can't Read, and What We Can Do About It: A Scientific Revolution in Reading.* New York: The Free Press, 1997.

National Academy of Education Commission on Reading. *Becoming a Nation of Readers: The Report of the Commission on Reading.* Pittsburgh, Pa.: National Academy of Education, 1985.

PERIODICALS

Sawyer, Diane J. "Whole Language in Context: Insights into the Current Great Debate." *Topics in Language Disorders* 11 no. 3, May 1991, 1–13.

Teale, William H. "Young Children and Reading: Trends Across the Twentieth Century." *Journal of Education* 177, no. 3, 1995, 95–127.

Venezky, Richard L. "A History of the American Reading Textbook." *Elementary School Journal* 87 no 3, January 1987, 247–265.

WEBSITES

"History of Reading Instruction." Educational Resources Information Center, Indiana University. Available online at http://www.indiana.edu/~eric_rec/ieo/bibs/histread.html; website home page: http://www.indiana.edu/~eric_rec/ (accessed May 1, 2003).

International Reading Association. Available online at http://www.reading.org/ (accessed May 1, 2003).

The National Right to Read Foundation. Available online at http://www.nrrf.org/ (accessed May 1, 2003).

A Report to the President: The Committee for the White House Conference on Education—Full Report.

Report

Date: April 1956
Source: *A Report to the President: The Committee for the White House Conference on Education—Full Report.* Washington, D.C., April 1956, 3342–3347. ∎

Introduction

Throughout the nineteenth century and the first half of the twentieth, strong opposition to U.S. government involvement in education was an obstacle to passing federal legislation or allocating federal funds. Some contended that such involvement was unconstitutional. For example, the Tenth Amendment reserves to the states any powers not specifically granted to the federal government—education is not mentioned in the Constitution. Others argued that federal funding meant federal control in opposition to the long-cherished tradition of local control of education in United States. Since every locality is different, it was asserted, the local authorities are in the best position to make decisions for local schools. Many feared the development of a national school system controlled by federal bureaucrats far removed from the concerns and needs of individual communities. Of particular concern to many was the possibility that federal funds would mean demands for school desegregation.

The Great Depression and World War II (1939–1945) brought a new or larger role for the federal government in many spheres of life. Americans became accustomed to this expanded role, and resistance to federal aid to schools declined somewhat. In addition, the Cold War seemed to call for new approaches.

In this context, the first White House Conference on Education, established by President Dwight Eisenhower (served 1953–1961), was held in November and December 1955. The conference task force recommended the identification and development of talent, especially in science and engineering, broad vocational education applicable to multiple trades, flexibility for students wanting to change programs, and a role for schools in character development. The committee endorsed the multiplication of educational goals as well as schools' attempts to ensure "that all needs of all children be met, one way or another." It also advocated federal aid to states and localities for general educational purposes.

Significance

Rather than breaking new ground or proposing radical changes, the White House conference report generally confirmed and bolstered important trends already in progress. For example, the "mining and refining of all human talents," especially in math and science, had been a concern since Cold War competition with the Soviet Union began shortly after World War II. The report also affirmed a long-standing trend toward a broadened curriculum addressing all needs of students, whether intellectual, social, psychological, emotional, or physical. In general, the report applauded past efforts and progress and called for more improvements along the same lines.

Itself an important step toward federal involvement in education, one purpose of the conference was to determine the appropriate role of the U.S. government in American education. The conference report recommended federal aid for schools, thus confirming a post–World War II trend toward greater federal involvement and prefiguring future participation. A greatly expanded role for the federal government in education developed between the 1950s and the 1970s. Important examples are the 1958 National Defense Education Act, the 1965 Elementary and Secondary Education Act, and the 1975 Education for all Handicapped Children's Act (later renamed the Individuals with Disabilities Act).

Primary Source

A Report to the President: The Committee for the White House Conference on Education—Full Report. [excerpt]

SYNOPSIS: In this excerpt from the White House Conference on Education's report, the committee endorses the expansion of school goals and the broadening of the curriculum to include greater attention to gifted education and a focus on serving the needs of all children. While great improvements in the education system have been made in positive directions, much more must be done to make the ideal of American education a reality.

From the work of the Committee for the White House Conference on Education, one fundamental fact emerges: schools now affect the welfare of the United States more than ever before in history, and this new importance of education has been dangerously underestimated for a long time.

Some of the reasons for the rapidly increasing importance of the schools have been often noted. Ignorance is a far greater handicap to an individual than it was generation ago, and an uneducated populace is a greater handicap to a nation. This trend is obviously going to continue and quicken.

An equally important and less frequently mentioned reason for the growing importance of education is the plain fact that the schools have become the chief instrument for keeping this Nation the fabled land of opportunity it started out to be. In other decades, the opportunities of America lay primarily in escape from the rigid class barriers of Europe, the availability of free land at the frontier, and the excitement of a violently growing nation, where farms often became villages and villages became cities within the span of one human life. When the frontier was closed, it would have been easy for opportunities to dry up in this Nation, and for rigid class barriers to develop. It has been primarily the schools which have prevented this from happening. As long as good schools are available, a man is not frozen at any level of our economy, nor is his son. Schools free men to rise to the level of their natural abilities. Hope for personal advancement and the advancement of one's children is, of course, one of the great wellsprings of human energy. The schools, more than any other agency, supply this hope in America today. By providing a channel for ambition, they have taken the place of the frontier, and in a highly technical era, have preserved the independent spirit of a pioneer nation. The schools stand as the chief expression of the American tradition of fair play for everyone, and a fresh start for each generation.

It is this fundamental conception of schools designed to give a fresh start to each generation that has broadened the ideals of education in America so much in the past 25 years. It is no longer thought proper to restrict educational programs to the skills of the mind, even though those skills remain of fundamental importance. Schools also attempt to improve children's health, to provide vocational training, and to do anything else which will help bring a child up to the starting line of adult life as even with his contemporaries as native differences in ability permit.

The most practical aspect of this new concept of education is that it calls for the most careful mining and refining of all human talents in the land—it is in itself a kind of law against waste. This new educational ideal represents the fullest flowering of the long western tradition of emphasizing the dignity of the individual. Many difficulties, of course, attend its development, but the members of this Committee believe that in essence it is noble and right, and that in the long run it will prove to be one of the great strengths of America.

It is, of course, obvious that much progress has been made toward realizing this new educational ideal in the United States during the recent past. It is the belief of this Committee, however, that improvement has been nowhere near fast enough. The onrush of science has outstripped the schools. What is even more important, ideals of human conduct have in some areas advanced as rapidly as technology. Many a school which seemed good enough a generation ago now seems a disgrace to the community where it stands.

The schools have fallen far behind both the aspirations of the American people and their capabilities. In the opinion of this Committee, there is growing resolve throughout the Nation to close the gap between educational ideals and educational realities. . . .

What Should Our Schools Accomplish?

What should our schools accomplish? No attempt has been made to answer from the point of view of ultimate philosophical objectives which could be read into the question. The Committee has deliberately limited its considerations to the responsibilities of elementary and secondary schools in the contemporary American scene. As a lay group, the Committee has felt it inappropriate to undertake a discussion of curriculum content in specific detail. It has sought instead to reaffirm those current objectives of our schools that it believes to be desirable and to suggest those new emphases which will enable our schools to adjust to the changing needs of our society.

It is relatively easy to observe what the schools *try* to accomplish. The list is startling to anyone who remembers schools a generation back, even more startling to historians who recall the original task assigned to schools: the teaching of reading and ciphering. What schools try to do varies widely. People in suburbs demand different services from those expected by residents in rural areas. In spite of this, it is not difficult to draw up a list of purposes shared by most schools, however widely the technique for fulfilling them may vary. For good or ill, most modern school systems are normally asked to provide something like the following:

1. A general education as good as or better than that offered in the past with increased emphasis on the physical and social sciences.

2. Programs designed to develop patriotism and good citizenship.

3. Programs designed to foster moral, ethical, and spiritual values.

President Dwight D. Eisenhower speaks to the graduating class of Pennsylvania State University on June 11, 1955. AP/WIDE WORLD PHOTOS. REPRODUCED BY PERMISSION.

4. Vocational education tailored to the abilities of each pupil and to the needs of community and Nation.

5. Courses designed to teach domestic skills.

6. Training in leisure-time activities such as music, dancing, avocational reading, and hobbies.

7. A variety of health services for all children, including both physical and dental inspections, and instruction aimed at bettering health knowledge and habits.

8. Special treatment for children with speech or reading difficulties and other handicaps.

9. Physical education, ranging from systematic exercises, physical therapy, and intramural sports, to interscholastic athletic completion.

10. Instruction to meet the needs of the abler students.

11. Programs designed to acquaint students with countries other than their own in an effort to help them understand the problems America faces in international relations.

12. Programs designed to foster mental health.

13. Programs designed to foster wholesome family life.

14. Organized recreational and social activities.

15. Courses designed to promote safety. These include instruction in driving automobiles, swimming, civil defense, etc.

The Growth of School Goals

During the past two generations, this list of school goals has grown with increased speed. This is a phenomenon which has excited both admiration and dismay. After several decades of experimentation, should this broadening of the goals be recognized as legitimate?

This Committee answers *Yes.* Nothing was more evident at the White House Conference on Education than the fact that these goals, representing as they do an enormously wide range of purposes, are the answer to a genuine public demand. These goals have, after all, been hammered out at countless school board meetings during the past quarter-century throughout the land. The basic responsibility of the schools is the development of the skills of the mind, but the overall mission has been enlarged. Schools are now asked to help children to acquire any skill or characteristic which a majority of the community deems worthwhile. The order given by the American people to the schools is grand in its simplicity: In addition to intellectual achievement, foster morality, happiness, and any useful ability. The talent of each child is to be sought out and developed to the fullest. Each weakness is to be studied and, so far as possible, corrected. This is truly a majestic ideal, and an astonishingly new one. Schools of that kind have never been provided for more than a small fraction of mankind.

Although it is new, this ideal of schools which do everything possible for all children is a natural development in the United States. The moving spirit of this Nation has been from the beginning a sense of fairness. Nowadays equality of opportunity for adults means little without equality of educational opportunity for children. Ignorance is a greater obstacle than ever to success of most kinds. The schools have become a major tool for creating a Nation without rigid class barriers. *It is primarily the schools which allow no man's failure to prevent the success of his son.*

In still another way, this new ideal for the schools is a natural development of this country: it recognizes the paramount importance of the individual in a free society. Our schools are asked to teach skills currently needed by the Nation, but never at the expense of the individual. This policy of encouraging each child to develop his individual talents will be of the greatest use to the Nation, for in the long run, if no talent is wasted in our land, no skill will be lacking. . . .

Recommendations

1. As the duties of the schools expand, the establishment of priorities in education should be studied by every board of education. This Committee believes that the development of the intellectual powers of young people, each to the limit of his capacity, is the first responsibility of schools. Beyond this basic task, all kinds of instruction are not equally important for all children, and their importance varies from community to community. This Committee also recognizes the need to invoke priorities in extracurricular activities. Athletics must be controlled, for instance, so that they serve young people rather than use them to enhance the competitive standing of a school or community. A primary responsibility of any local school authority is to establish priorities of significance among basic general education, specialized education of all kinds, and extracurricular activities.

In this era of international stress, the United States has unusual demands for good scientists and engineers, in addition to other specialists. There is a necessity for broad understanding of the meaning of citizenship in the United States. America must have citizens who know something of other nations and are equipped to understand their own Nation's role in international affairs. These special needs can be assigned a high priority by schools which are pursuing the broad list of objectives currently demanded by the people. In adding new, worthwhile activities to the curriculum, nothing of value has to be subtracted if a proper sense of proportion is maintained and enough resources are provided.

2. Overspecialization of vocational education should be avoided. There are almost 50,000 trades in this country, and specialized instruction for all of them cannot be provided. Broadly conceived programs of vocational education must be maintained which are not likely to be outmoded rapidly by technological change and which offer basic instruction that can be useful in many jobs.

3. Just as good schools permit flexibility in this whole Nation by allowing individuals to achieve the level of accomplishment their abilities deserve, the school system must be flexible within itself. Pupils should be able to shift from one program to another as they grow and change in interests and abilities. This Committee thinks that for every child to have, throughout his school career, the chance to change to the kind of education found best for him is more important than the time saved by choosing a few pupils early in their lives for accelerated, specialized programs, as is often done in Europe. The American people have time as well as the physical resources to allow this kind of flexibility.

4. Educational programs which fully exercise and develop the abilities of especially brilliant students must be maintained. A system which wastes the talents of those who have the most to offer has no part in the new American ideal for the schools. Social equality can be maintained by the schools without hampering the intellectual progress of the unusually able. Increased stress must be placed on meeting the challenge of those students who have the capacity for the greatest intellectual growth. Improved provision for these talented young people should be the next great advance in our public school system. This Committee believes it possible to achieve this goal and still handle the tidal wave of new students which is expected. The real and fundamental manpower scarcity at the present time is a scarcity of quality and not of numbers. Consequently, the identification and careful handling of talented youth are urgent and commanding requirements.

5. School leaders should *help* foster all desirable characteristics in children, but they should not be tempted to consider themselves the only agency in the field. The major influence upon children is their home and the whole community in which they are raised. It is right for people to expect the schools to help forward all worthy causes, but entirely wrong to abnegate responsibility in hope that the schools will take up the slack. Schools can never take the place of a warm family life, a vigorous church, and a wholesome community, although they must be strong allies. Where other good influences are lacking, schools should and do try to repair the damage, but they cannot do the job alone.

In conclusion, this Committee believes that the new goals for the schools demanded by the American people reflect a determination to leave nothing that can be done for each generation of children undone. Far from seeking the abandonment of the ideals of the past, the people have called for a quickened pursuit of those ideals. At the same time, they have decided to use the schools in a variety of new ways, sometimes as an ally of other agencies, sometimes as a replacement for other agencies which have failed. Controversy has often surrounded questions of procedure and relative importance, but the nobility of intent implicit in this new concept is beyond doubt. There is far more to be proud of in today's schools than there is to criticize. Their weaknesses usually stem from a lack of means, rather than any defect in their goal. Efforts to work out ways in which school, family, church, and many other agencies can best work together for the fullest development of every child must be a continuous process in every community. To avoid a general dilution of education, the multiplication of school duties must be accompanied by a proportionate increase of school resources. We must never lose sight of the insistent need to increase the excellence of our schools while increasing their scope; the two goals are not incompatible except under conditions of bad management or inadequate resources. The problems of the schools are great, but they never should be allowed to obscure the worthiness of their goals. In the judgment of this Committee, the people will probably continue to insist that all needs of all children be met, one way or another. The attempt to provide schools capable of playing their full part in making that ideal a reality may well prove to be one of the wisest decisions ever made by the American people.

Further Resources

BOOKS

Bendiner, Robert. *Obstacle Course on Capitol Hill.* New York: McGraw-Hill, 1964.

Berke, Joel S., and Michael W. Kirst. *Federal Aid to Education: Who Benefits? Who Governs?* Lexington, Mass.: Lexington, 1972.

Butts, R. Freeman, and Lawrence Cremin. *A History of Education in American Culture.* New York: Henry Holt, 1953.

Kaestle, Carl F. "Federal Aid to Education Since World War II: Purposes and Politics." In *The Future of the Federal Role in Elementary and Secondary Education.* Jack Jennings, ed. Washington, D.C.: Center for Education Policy, 2001.

Lee, Gordon C. *The Struggle for Federal Aid, First Phase: A History of the Attempts to Obtain Federal Aid for the Common Schools, 1870–1890.* New York: Teachers College, Columbia University, 1949.

Education of Mentally Retarded Children Act

Law

Date: September 6, 1958

Source: *Education of Mentally Retarded Children Act. U.S. Statutes at Large* 72 (1958), 1777. ■

Introduction

The development of common schools in the early nineteenth century was based on the ideal of providing publicly funded education for all children. Certain groups of children, including those with disabilities, were routinely excluded, and the ideal of "schools for all" did not become a reality until the 1970s.

In the nineteenth century and well into the twentieth century, students with disabilities had limited choices. Often denied education in the public schools, most had a choice between staying at home or institutionalization. Some students had access to boarding schools for specific disabilities, such as for the blind or deaf. These specific schools were supported by private donations or, sometimes, by state or federal funds. By 1900, a few states had public school programs serving students with certain types of disabilities. And even though compulsory education laws were in place nationwide near the end of the first decade of the twentieth century, public schools were still permitted to refuse students who were deemed "uneducable."

Little progress was made in disability education until the 1950s. A catalyst for change in the education of students with disabilities was the U.S. Supreme Court de-

A teacher supervises her class of young children with special needs in Letchworth Village, New York. © BETTMANN/CORBIS. REPRODUCED BY PERMISSION.

cision in *Brown v. Board of Education* in 1954. This ruling, although applying specifically to the rights of minority children, established equal education as a civil right for all children. In addition, the passage of the National Defense Education Act (NDEA) in 1958 paved the way for expanded federal involvement in public education. After the passage of the NDEA, the question was no longer whether the federal government would be involved, but what direction that involvement would take.

President Dwight Eisenhower (served 1953–1961) signed the Education of Mentally Retarded Children Act just days after signing the NDEA. The act, while not providing funding directly to schools for the education of students with disabilities, did assist colleges and universities in training teachers for students with mental retardation. Initially limited to mental retardation, the act was broadened in 1963 to include education for teachers specializing in other disabilities as well as for research.

Significance

The Education of Mentally Retarded Children Act marked the beginning of a greatly expanded federal role in education for students with disabilities. Advocacy groups formed by parents of children with disabilities were instrumental in the passage of laws from the late

1950s through the mid-1970s that gave children with disabilities "appropriate, equal educational opportunity." Important victories in the 1960s for the educational rights of children with disabilities include the passage in 1965 of the Elementary and Secondary Education Act, which provided federal funds for the education of students with disabilities in state-operated schools. The Handicapped Children's Early Education Assistance Act was passed in 1968 to fund educational programs for children with disabilities from birth to age six.

Two federal court decisions, *Pennsylvania Association for Retarded Children v. Commonwealth of Pennsylvania* (1971) and *Mills v. Board of Education of the District of Columbia* (1972), ruled that under the equal protection clause of the Fourteenth Amendment schools must provide equal access to education for students with disabilities. These cases set the stage for landmark federal legislation in 1975.

With the passage of the Education for All Handicapped Children's Act in 1975, students with disabilities were finally guaranteed a free appropriate education. In addition, the law established the rights of students to an education in the least restrictive environment, allowing many more students to receive special education services within the regular classroom. The act was amended a number of times, and the name was changed in 1990 to the Individuals with Disabilities Act. The Americans with Disabilities Act, passed in 1990, reinforced the rights of people with disabilities to equal opportunity and access in schools.

Primary Source

Education of Mentally Retarded Children Act

SYNOPSIS: The text of the Education of Mentally Retarded Children Act states the purpose of the act—to assist colleges and universities in training teachers of students with mental retardation—and outlines the procedures for the distribution of funds. The key terms, "nonprofit institution" and "state educational agency," are defined for the purposes of the act.

An Act

To encourage expansion of teaching in the education of mentally retarded children through grants to institutions of higher learning and to State educational agencies.

Be it enacted by the Senate and House of Representatives of the United States of America in Congress assembled, That the Commissioner of Education is authorized to make grants to public or other nonprofit institutions of higher learning to assist them in providing training of professional personnel to conduct training of teachers in fields related to education of mentally retarded children. Such grants may be used by such institutions to assist in covering the cost of courses of training or study for such personnel and for establishing and maintaining fellowships, with such stipends as may be determined by the Commissioner of Education.

Sec. 2. The Commissioner of Education is also authorized to make grants to State educational agencies to assist them in establishing and maintaining, directly or through grants to public or other nonprofit institutions of higher learning, fellowships or traineeships for training personnel engaged or preparing to engage in employment as teachers of mentally retarded children or as supervisors of such teachers.

Sec. 3. Payments of grants pursuant to this Act may be made by the Commissioner of Education from time to time, in advance or by way of reimbursement, on such conditions as the Commissioner may determine. Such payments shall not exceed $1,000,000 for any one fiscal year.

Sec. 4. Each State educational agency and each public or other nonprofit institution of higher education which receives a grant under this Act during a fiscal year shall after the end of such fiscal year sub-

mit a report to the Commissioner of Education. Such report shall contain a detailed financial statement showing the purposes for which the funds granted under this Act were expended.

Sec. 5. For purposes of this Act—

a. The term "nonprofit institution" means an institution owned and operated by one or more corporations or associations no part of the net earnings of which inures, or may lawfully inure, to the benefit of any private shareholder or individual.

b. The term "State educational agency" means the State board of education or other agency or officer primarily responsible for State supervision of public elementary and secondary schools in the State.

Sec. 6. The Commissioner of Education is authorized to delegate any of his functions under this Act, except the making of regulations, to any officer or employee of the Office of Education.

Sec. 7. This Act shall continue in effect until a date ten years after the date of the enactment of this Act.

Approved September 6, 1958.

Further Resources

BOOKS

Alexander, Kern, and M. David Alexander. *American Public School Law,* 5th ed. Belmont, Calif.: Wadsworth/Thomson Learning, 2001.

Ballard, Joseph, Bruce A. Ramirez, and Frederick J. Weintraub, eds. *Special Education in America: Its Legal and Governmental Foundations.* Reston, Va.: Council for Exceptional Children, 1982.

Longmore, Paul K., and Lauri Umansky. *The New Disability History: American Perspectives.* New York: New York University Press, 2001.

Safford, Philip L., and Elizabeth J. Safford. *A History of Childhood and Disability.* New York: Teachers College Press, 1996.

Winzer, M. A. *The History of Special Education: From Isolation to Integration.* Washington, D.C.: Gallaudet University Press, 1993.

WEBSITES

Americans with Disabilities Act Home Page, U.S. Department of Justice. Available online at http://www.usdoj.gov/crt/ada/adahom1.htm (accessed May 1, 2003).

"The Office of Special Education and Rehabilitative Services." U.S. Department of Education. Available online at http://www.ed.gov/offices/OSERS/; website home page: http://www.ed.gov/index.jsp (accessed May 1, 2003).

Pacer Center. Available online at http://www.pacer.org/ (accessed May 1, 2003).

The Cold War's Effect on U.S. Education

Summary of Major Provisions of the National Defense Education Act of 1958

Summary

By: Elliot Lee Richardson

Date: 1958

Source: *National Defense Education Act. U.S. Statutes at Large* 72 (1958), 1580–1605. Summary of the act by the Center for the Studies of Higher Education. Available online at http://ishi.lib.berkeley.edu/cshe/ndea/ndea.html; website home page: http://ishi.lib.berkeley.edu/cshe/ndea/index.html (accessed June 5, 2003).

About the Author: Elliot Lee Richardson (1920–1999) earned degrees from Harvard University and Harvard Law School. He was the lieutenant governor and attorney general of Massachusetts. Richardson held a number of high-level positions in the federal government, including secretary of health, education, and welfare; secretary of defense; U.S. attorney general; and ambassador to Great Britain. He was the author of several books.

Soviet Commitment to Education: Report of the First Official U.S. Education Mission to the U.S.S.R.

Report

By: Lawrence G. Derthick

Date: 1959

Source: U.S. Education Mission to the U.S.S.R. *Soviet Commitment to Education: Report of the First Official U.S. Education Mission to the U.S.S.R.* Office of Education Bulletin, no. 16. Washington, D.C.: U.S. Department of Health, Education, and Welfare, Office of Education, 1959, 1–4.

About the Author: Lawrence G. Derthick (1905–1992) earned a bachelor's degree from Milligan College, a master's degree from George Peabody College for Teachers, University of Tennessee, and a doctorate from Teachers College, Columbia University. He was a high school principal, superintendent of schools, and a professor of education at East Tennessee State College. Derthick served as the U.S. commissioner of education from 1956 to 1961. ■

Introduction

Events at the close of World War II (1939–1945) brought the beginning of the hostile and wary relations between the United States and the Soviet Union known as the Cold War. The presence of nuclear weapons on both sides heightened the anxiety considerably. In this uneasy context, the Soviets launched *Sputnik*, the world's first man-made satellite, in October 1957. *Sputnik*, a bushel-basket-sized object, was carried into space by an R-7 rocket. A month later, *Sputnik 2* was launched. This time, a passenger—a dog named Laika—was sent up with the satellite. These events stunned the United States. The Soviets, it seemed, had surpassed Americans in technological and, more importantly, military prowess. The Sputnik program brought home to Americans the alarming fact that the Soviets possessed rockets which could launch a nuclear weapon from the Soviet Union and strike the United States within minutes.

Critics and American popular opinion placed the blame on U.S. education. It appeared to Americans that the Soviet education system, with its hard-nosed emphasis on math and science, had allowed the Soviet Union to attain its supremacy. The dominance of the progressive education philosophy in the United States over the preceding decades had resulted in schools that promoted self-esteem, life-adjustment, social skills and "creative movement" classes at the expense of serious academic work in science, mathematics, and foreign language. Schools lacked the discipline and rigor necessary to produce the quantity and quality of skilled individuals needed for national defense. Furthermore, the nation's greatest natural resource, human talent, was being squandered: Many gifted students were not challenged to work up to their capabilities, and highly intelligent but needy students were denied access to higher education. The United States had to find and appropriately educate its "best and brightest," especially in science, math, and foreign language.

Less than a year after *Sputnik 1,* Congress passed the National Defense Education Act (NDEA), a landmark piece of legislation. The NDEA authorized federal funding for an array of educational programs designed to address the national "educational emergency." Efforts to improve education at home were accompanied by increasing American interest in Soviet education. What was the Soviet Union doing right? Could, and should, the Soviet approach be duplicated in U.S. schools? The answers to these questions would partially depend on a detailed knowledge of the Soviet educational approach. To help achieve this, an exchange agreement between the two countries was signed on January 27, 1958, authorizing "exchanges in cultural, technical, and educational fields to promote mutual understanding between the people of the United States and the Soviet Union." The first U.S. education mission to the Soviet Union took place from May to June 1958. Nine Soviet educators visited the United States from November to December 1958.

Significance

One goal of the exchange mission was to improve U.S.-Soviet relations. The second goal was "to secure first-hand information on the operation and accomplishments of Soviet schools." The mission observed and reported on the Soviet administrative system, preschool education, general education, extracurricular activities, arts education, technical training, teacher education, and higher education. The report reflected an issue important in the public debates: Was the Soviet model of authoritarian, regimented, and centrally controlled education an appropriate one to transplant in an American democracy? On the other hand, if such a system was the secret to Soviet success, could the United States afford not to? Americans faced the dilemma of wanting educational freedom and flexibility on the one hand and discipline and rigor on the other.

The members of the mission found a Soviet people dedicated to education and willing to give up much in the pursuit of self-improvement for the betterment of the state. In the foreword of the report, U.S. commissioner of education Lawrence G. Derthick posed the question: "Will we Americans work and sacrifice to extend to all our youth the best in American schools?"

The NDEA poured $887 million over four years into programs intended to develop American talent in fields relevant to national defense. The act was a major milestone in expanding the federal role in public education and opened the door to further federal involvement. For several years prior to *Sputnik 1,* Congress had debated the issue of expanding federal support for public schools. The strong American tradition of state and local control of schools proved difficult to overcome. The launch of *Sputnik 1,* however, cleared away obstacles and opposition—national security was now the number-one priority.

The NDEA was expanded in 1963 by two amendments extending the act, directing more aid to the student loan program, and allocating funds for construction of new facilities and libraries for colleges and universities.

Despite a statement under Title I that the NDEA did not allow federal government "direction, supervision, or control" of schools, the fact that the funds were subject to certain conditions did have the effect of fostering some federal influence on public schools. Individuals administrating programs were obligated to sign a loyalty oath, plans for spending the funds required federal approval, and federal regulations had to be followed. And, inevitably, the channeling of funds to certain types of programs, in preference to others, changed the face of American education.

Primary Source

Summary of Major Provisions of the National Defense Education Act of 1958

> **SYNOPSIS:** This summary of the major provisions of the NDEA lists the types of programs funded, de-

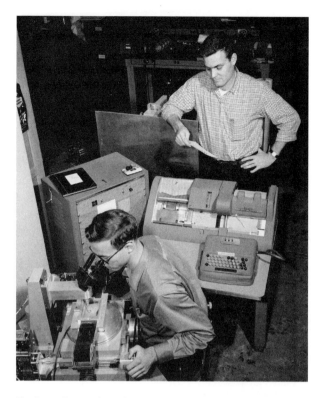

Physics graduate students observe cascade particles and anti-protons with a digitized microscope at the Berkeley Laboratory in California, 1958. Students like these received grants and loans to pursue science degrees as a result of the National Defense Education Act. ERNEST ORLANDO LAWRENCE BERKELEY NATIONAL LABORATORY. REPRODUCED BY PERMISSION.

scribes how the money will be allocated, and outlines the conditions that must be met. The programs include student loans, aid for curriculum development in defense-related subjects, fellowships, testing and guidance for bright students, language training institutes, research and development of audiovisual materials for education, vocational programs relevant to national defense, and the creation of the science information service.

Title I. General Provisions

A. Findings and Declaration of Policy

The Congress finds that an educational emergency exists and requires action by the federal government. Assistance will come from Washington to help develop as rapidly as possible those skills essential to the national defense.

B. Federal Control of Education Prohibited

Nothing in this act shall be construed to authorize any agency or employee of the United States to exercise any direction, supervision, or control over the curriculum, program of instruction, administration, or personnel of any educational institution or school system.

Title II. Loans to Students in Institutions of Higher Education

A. Appropriations Authorized

To help establish student loan funds at colleges and universities, the federal government is authorized to pay $47.5 million for fiscal 1959, $75 million for fiscal 1960, $82.5 million for fiscal 1961, and $90 million for fiscal 1962. The United States Commissioner of Education can provide whatever funds may be necessary in fiscal 1963, 1964, 1965, and 1966 to allow students in the program to complete their education.

B. Allotments to States

Each state's ratio will be based on the number of students enrolled full time in colleges and universities when compared with national figures.

C. Payment of Federal Capital Contributions

Individual institutions will file application for a portion of their state's allotment. No institution will receive more than $250,000 in a single fiscal year.

D. Conditions of Agreements

The institution must contribute 10 percent of the total loan fund. The institution must give preference to students who are superior academically and who indicate a desire to teach in elementary or secondary schools. The institution must also give preference to students with a superior capacity for or preparation in science, mathematics, engineering, or a modern foreign language.

E. Terms of Loans

No student may receive more than $1,000 per year or more than $5,000 from the loan fund. To be eligible, a student must be in need and enrolled in or accepted at the institution. Also, the institution must judge that the student is capable of maintaining a good academic standing.

The borrower begins repayment of the loan one year after he ceases full time enrollment. The 3 percent interest charge begins only after he ceases study or completes up to three years of service in the military. Repayment may take up to ten years.

F. Loans to Institutions

If an institution is unable to raise its share of the loan fund, the commissioner may loan up to $25 million to the institution. He will determine the interest rate charged and also the repayment period.

Title III. Financial Assistance for Strengthening Science, Mathematics, and Modern Foreign Language Instruction

A. Appropriations Authorized

A total of $70 million each year for fiscal 1959, 1960, 1961, and 1962 is authorized to the states as grants for purchase of equipment and as loans to private schools to purchase equipment. During the same four fiscal years, a total of $5 million each year is authorized to enable the states to expand or improve supervisory services in these subject areas.

B. Allotments to States

A formula will be devised based on the state's school-age population when compared with national figures and each state's income per school-age child. Twelve percent of the $70 million each year will be set aside for the private school loans.

C. Payments to States

After approval of each state's plan by the commissioner, he will pay one-half of the cost of the plan. The other half must come from state funds.

D. Loans to Nonprofit Private Schools

Each state will receive all amount based on its private school population when compared with national figures. The commissioner will decide the conditions of these loans, but they must be repaid within ten years.

Title IV. National Defense Fellowships

A. Number of Fellowships

There will be 1,000 fellowships in fiscal 1959 and 1,500 each year in fiscal 1960, 1961, and 1962. These fellowships cover three years of study.

B. Award of Fellowships and Approval of Institutions

Individuals may receive fellowships only after they are accepted into an approved program. To receive approval from the commissioner, a program must be new or an expansion of an existing graduate program at a university. Approved programs must aim at promoting a wide geographical distribution of graduate education in the country. They must also give preference to individuals who are interested in becoming college teachers.

C. Fellowship Stipends

Each fellow will receive $2,000 for the first academic year of study, $2,200 for the second, and $2,400 for the third. He will also receive $400 per year for each dependent. The commissioner will pay $2,500 per fellowship per year to the institutions. These stipends will continue only if the fellow enrolls full time in his studies.

Title V. Guidance, Counseling, and Testing: Identification and Encouragement of Able Students

Part I. State Programs

A. Appropriations Authorized

During fiscal 1959, 1960, 1961, and 1962, a total of $15 million a year will go to the states for secondary school programs. These programs will consist of testing to identify abilities and counseling and guidance to encourage students to develop their aptitudes and attend college.

B. Allotments to States

Each state will receive funds according to the proportion of the national school-age population it has. No state will receive less than $20,000 per year.

C. Payments to States

The commissioner will pay the full cost of the programs for fiscal 1959 and one-half of the cost for the remaining three years. If, because of its laws, any state cannot pay for testing in private schools, the commissioner will arrange and pay for these in full for fiscal 1959 and one-half in fiscal 1960, 1961, and 1962.

Part II. Counseling and Guidance Training Institutes

The commissioner will contract with universities to operate institutes for training secondary school guidance counselors. During fiscal 1959, the institutions will receive $6.25 million. For each of the following three fiscal years, they will receive $7.25 million. Public school personnel who attend these institutes will receive stipends of $75 per week of attendance and $16 per week for each dependent.

Title VI. Language Development

Part I. Centers and Research and Studies

A. Language and Area Centers

The commissioner will contract with colleges and universities for the establishment of institutes to teach modern foreign languages if such instruction is not readily available to individuals in government, business, or education. If understanding of a foreign region is necessary, these centers will also teach the history, economics, geography, and so on of the region. The commissioner will pay one-half of the cost of establishing and operating such centers. If a student at one of these institutes agrees to teach modern foreign languages in college or go into government service, the commissioner will pay stipends of unspecified amount to him and also provide allowances for dependents.

B. Appropriations Authorized

A total of $8 million a year is available for fiscal 1959, 1960, 1961, and 1962.

Part II. Language Institutes

Anyone teaching or preparing to teach any modern foreign language in any elementary or secondary school may attend institutes for training in new methods and materials. These institutes will take place at universities that. have contracts with HEW. A total of $7.26 million each year will be available to operate these institutes in fiscal 1959, 1960, 1961, and 1962. If one teaches in public schools, one may receive a stipend of $75 per week and $15 per week for each dependent during the time of attendance.

Title VII. Research and Experimentation in More Effective Utilization of Television, Radio, Motion Pictures, and Related Media for Educational Purposes

Part I. Research and Experimentation

The commissioner, assisted by the Advisory Committee oil New Educational Media in the Office of Education, will provide grants or contracts to foster new audiovisual techniques for teaching. The grants will go to nonprofit agencies and the contracts to public or private agencies or organizations.

Part II. Dissemination of Information on New Educational Media

The commissioner may authorize studies to determine the need for audiovisual media in education. He shall prepare and publish information to encourage use of such media.

Part III. General Provisions

A new Advisory Committee on New Educational Media will be established. In addition to the commissioner, it will include a representative of the National Science Foundation and twelve other members from the communications media, elementary and secondary fields, and college and university fields. The committee will review all activities of this title and will approve projects with the commissioner. A total of $3 million is authorized for this title for fiscal 1959. In each of the succeeding fiscal years, $5 million will be available.

Title VIII. Area Vocational Programs

A. Amendment to Vocational Education Act of 1946 (George-Barden Act) Known as Title III

The purpose of the amendment is to meet the needs of national defense for technicians trained in science and technology and to offer vocational education to areas not adequately served by this program The states will receive funds on the same basis of allotment as specified in other parts of the George-Barden Act.

B. Appropriations Authorized

For fiscal 1959, a total of $15 million is authorized, and the same amount for fiscal 1960, 1961, and 1962. These funds must be matched each year by an equal amount from state and local sources.

Title IX. Science Information Service

The new Science Information Service will be under the auspices of the National Science Foundation. The service will have the advice of a Science Information Council. Fifteen members will be appointed by the Director of the National Science Foundation, with several other members from other agencies of government. Such sums as may be necessary are authorized to carry out this title.

Title X. Miscellaneous Provisions

A. Loyalty Oath and Affidavit

No individual may receive funds under this act unless he first files with the commissioner an affidavit "that he does not believe in, and is not a member of and does not support any organization that believes in or teaches, the overthrow of the United States Government by force or violence or by any illegal or unconstitutional methods." Also, he must swear an oath of allegiance to the United States.

B. Administration of State Plans

No state plan will be approved to receive funds unless the commissioner decides that he will have adequate reporting by the state of administration of the plan. If the commissioner decides that a state plan has changed and no longer complies with the provisions of the act or that the state is not administering the plan successfully, he will notify the state that payments will cease until the program is satisfactory to him.

C. Judicial Review

Any state that is dissatisfied with action by the commissioner may, within sixty days of his action, file in United States district court a petition for review. The commissioner must then file his record of proceedings with the court, and the court will take whatever action it deems proper.

D. Improvement of Statistical Services of State Educational Agencies

The commissioner will make grants to the states of undetermined sums for four fiscal years: 1959, 1960, 1961, and 1962. The states will match these grants with sums of their own. No state shall receive more than $50,000 for any year. They will establish new programs or expand existing ones that will improve the reliability of educational statistics and expedite the processing and reporting of such data.

Primary Source

Soviet Commitment to Education: Report of the First Official U.S. Education Mission to the U.S.S.R. [excerpt]

> **SYNOPSIS:** The first chapter of the report of the first education mission to the Soviet Union discusses the strong impression of members of the team that the Soviet people are highly committed to education and are willing to work hard to "reach and over-reach America." General impressions of life and education in the Soviet Union are offered.

I. A Nation Committed

The one fact that most impressed us in the U.S.S.R. was the extent to which the Nation is committed to education as a means of national advancement. In the organization of a planned society in the Soviet Union, education is regarded as one of the chief resources and techniques for achieving social, economic, cultural, and scientific objectives in the national interest. Tremendous responsibilities are therefore placed on Soviet schools, and comprehensive support is provided for them by all segments and agencies of Soviet society.

One of the leading Soviet educators told us: "We believe in a planned society, you in individual initiative. Let time tell." They are convinced that time is on their side and that through education and hard work they can win their way to world acceptance of Communist ideology.

Everywhere we went in the U.S.S.R. we were struck by the zeal and enthusiasm which the people have for education. It is a kind of grand passion with them.

Wherever we turned we heard the slogan: "Reach and over-reach America." And everywhere, the people seem to respond in the conviction that education, in addition to hard work and the postponement of many creature comforts, is the best means of winning world supremacy.

Education reaches far beyond school-age children and youth and is eagerly sought by hundreds of thousands of full-time workers who are also full-time students; hundreds of thousands of others take correspondence courses. Many of these correspondence students also hope to qualify for university entrance. They do this because being well educated is the key to advancement. We are sure that the Soviet people anticipate the day when their present sacrifice for knowledge will bring them many rewards, but right now, as we see it, they regard good schools and universities as the necessities in their race for world supremacy.

And they have been building schools and universities at a rapid pace. Down on the borders of China where only a half-century ago the people were almost 100 percent illiterate, we saw thriving schools, an impressive scientific academy, and other institutions that have reduced illiteracy and advanced knowledge to an astonishing degree. From the shores of the Black Sea to remote Siberia we found the attitude summed up in the expression of a Soviet education official: "A child can be born healthy, but he can't be born educated."

We have the impression that most people in the U.S.S.R. feel that conditions are improving gradually, that they are looking ahead for 5, 10, 15, or 20 years. They appear to be completely confident about achieving a quality of life and a standard of living fully as high as ours but realize that it will take time, sacrifice, and hard work.

There is still a considerable shortage of buildings resulting in part from tremendous damage during World War II. Very likely few people in the United States are familiar with the extent of the damage to both cities and rural communities in the Soviet Union in World War II—we were shown films of whole cities

Soviet students participate in a chemistry lab in Tashkent, Uzbekistan, in the Soviet Union, 1958. During the Cold War, the United States felt it was falling dangerously behind the Soviet Union in technology due to its science and math education programs. © BETTMANN/CORBIS. REPRODUCED BY PERMISSION.

in ruins. Although whole cities have been rebuilt in less than 15 years, the normal supply of building and housing replacements, always low, has necessarily fallen behind. Housing is scarce, though relatively cheap.

People appear to be well fed and to have ample access to food stores and restaurants. Food is abundant, though not of much variety, and it is expensive. Clothing seemed to us to be very expensive and not readily available. In general, however, people seemed to be neatly, if not stylishly, dressed, by American standards.

There seems to be complete equality between men and women. The relationship between boys and girls in school appears to be characterized by dignity and mutual respect for each other. At each desk there is usually one boy and one girl. A professor at the University of Leningrad said: "With us, boys and girls, men and women, are partners. We are partners in education, partners in love, and partners in work."

A woman is expected to do any job as well as a man. Many women have entered the professions, particularly medicine. We saw women working with electrical crews, repairing telephone equipment, operating streetcars and busses, and working in factories. We noticed that many women specialized in mathematics and physics.

Education has been and is recognized as the source of past accomplishments and as the way to the future. The developments in the organization and practices of education at all levels during the past half century have been impressive both for their speed and for their extent. Wherever we went our hosts described with pride the contrasts between the present conditions and those existing before the revolution. That we returned with our faith renewed in the superiority of the American system for our society does not discount the tremendous efforts the Soviets are exerting to advance their kind of education to strengthen the Communist system. They tell many dramatic stories of the progress of their education, and all credited education with the improvement in their condition. The story summarized below, which we heard at the Ministry of Education in the Uzbek Republic, is one of the more dramatic but perhaps typical.

This is a highly developed agricultural and industrial region now, but before the revolution it was a colony of Czarist Russia and was much retarded. Agriculture was primitive, crops were small, and the country was underdeveloped. Only 2 percent of the population was literate; there were no institutions of higher education, and the 160 schools were attended by 17,300 children of privileged families. There were no engineers, doctors, or teachers with higher education.

Opportunity for education came immediately after the revolution, although schools were developed gradually. On December 2, 1920, Lenin decreed the establishment of the University of the Republics of Asia. In 1919 a decree on the elimination of illiteracy was published, and shortly afterward literate people began to teach the illiterate. Now we have an academy of science, an academy of agricultural sciences, 34 higher education establishments, 100 technicums, 50 special technical schools, 5,800 general or 10-year schools, 12 pedagogical institutes to prepare teachers, and 1,400 kindergartens. We have schools for people of each nationality in their own tongue, and we also have inservice education establishments. Altogether 1,300,000 children of all nationalities have an opportunity for education. More than 50 percent of our 80,000 teachers have higher education.

We have many establishments to develop the interests of children. We work out our own courses of study for schools. Each Republic develops curriculums for itself because of differences in language.

We have enough money to expand our education programs and buildings. Our people are rich; they like to work. All our people want peace. *We are sure we are able to meet the problems we face.*

As is indicated earlier, Uzbekistan is not an isolated example; we heard similar stories in other places—the description of similar accomplishments in the Tatar Republic, for example, was equally impressive. Such progress is dramatized for the people of the U.S.S.R. continuously by the State and the Party. In every possible way—particularly through art, music, and literature—the people are reminded of what has been done. Everywhere, in every school we visited, we saw pictures or statues of Lenin, and less frequently, Marx and Stalin, even in kindergartens. From infancy, children are taught that the highest good is to serve the State; school children through their clubs or circles, in classes, and in games are taught to identify all good things with the State; on class excursions and tours of museums, shrines, factories, they are taught the history of the revolution and to honor its heroes, underplaying the prerevolutionary achievements and emphasizing Soviet progress.

What we observed of Soviet education gave us the impression that the entire operation was being carried out on a systematically planned basis to achieve Communist objectives. To be sure, there were some excellent prerevolutionary foundations, institutions, and traditions of Russian education on which to build the Soviet structure—the academic secondary school of Imperial Russia; the Ballet School in Leningrad, over 200 years old; the great universities, especially in Leningrad and Moscow; the National Academy of Sciences; and the School for the Blind in Moscow that celebrated its 75th anniversary in 1947. These are just a few of the substantial roots from the past, and they should not be overlooked. It was always stressed, however, that education was restricted in prerevolutionary days to a very small proportion of the population of the vast area—one-sixth of the earth's surface—that today is the U.S.S.R.

Today, of course, education is planned, financed, controlled, and administered by the State. Even though education in the U.S.S.R. is controlled by the Government and is therefore standardized and regimented, there is some flexibility of operation. Furthermore decisions on policy, on textbooks, on teacher training, on curriculum, and on similar matters are not always made arbitrarily. We found fairly widespread evidence that before making decisions on education, the Government seeks opinions from specialists at all levels of education, from teachers throughout the country, and information based on research and experience. And it seems to get willing cooperation.

Few nations or people are today more passionately committed to education than the Soviet Union and the Soviet people are. The Soviets see what has already been accomplished and are confident of the future.

Further Resources

BOOKS

Avis, George, ed. *The Making of the Soviet Citizen: Character Formation and Civic Training in Soviet Education.* New York: Croom Helm, 1987.

Benton, William. *The Teachers and the Taught in the U.S.S.R.* New York: Atheneum, 1966.

Clowse, Barbara Barksdale. *Brainpower for the Cold War: The Sputnik Crisis and National Defense Education Act of 1958.* Westport, Conn.: Greenwood, 1981.

Dickson, Paul. *Sputnik: The Shock of the Century.* New York: Walker, 2001.

Douglass, John. "A Certain Future: Sputnik, American Higher Education and the Survival of a Nation." In Roger D. Launius, John M. Logsdon, and Robert W. Smith, eds, *Reconsidering Sputnik: Forty Years Since the Soviet Satellite.* London: Routledge, 2002.

Dow, Peter B. *Schoolhouse Politics: Lessons From the Sputnik Era.* Cambridge, Mass.: Harvard University Press, 1991.

Holmes, Larry E. *The Kremlin and the Schoolhouse: Reforming Education in Soviet Russia, 1917–1931.* Bloomington: Indiana University Press, 1991.

Matthews, Mervyn. *Education in the Soviet Union: Policies and Institutions Since Stalin.* Boston: Allen and Unwin, 1982.

Pearson, Landon. *Children of Glasnost: Growing up Soviet.* Seattle: University of Washington, 1990.

Zajda, Joseph I. *Education in the U.S.S.R.* New York: Pergamon, 1980.

Education and Liberty: The Role of the Schools in a Modern Democracy

Nonfiction work

By: James Bryant Conant

Date: 1958

Source: Conant, James Bryant. *Education and Liberty: The Role of the Schools in a Modern Democracy.* Cambridge: Harvard University Press, 76–87.

About the Author: James Bryant Conant (1893–1978) earned a bachelor's and doctorate in chemistry from Harvard University, where he later taught. He was president of Harvard from 1933 to 1953. Conant was the chairman of the National Defense Research Committee and served as the U.S. high commissioner to West Germany. He conducted a study of U.S. high schools for the Carnegie Corporation, and the report was published as *The American High School Today: A First Report to Interested Citizens* (1959). Conant was the author of many books. ∎

Introduction

During the first half of the nineteenth century, one of the arguments in favor of the development of tax-supported schools for all children was that such schools would unify the diverse population of the new country. Common schools could instill patriotism and loyalty to the United States and teach children to think of themselves as Americans rather than, for example, Germans, southerners, or Virginians. Common school reformers asserted that the survival of the new nation depended on promoting loyalty and unity among Americans.

Some religious groups resisted tax-supported schools, charging that the "nondenominational" curriculum was of a clearly Protestant Christian character. Some of these groups, notably Roman Catholics, developed parallel systems of private religious schools to ensure that their children were educated according to the values and beliefs of their faith.

The right of parents to choose private schools for their children was threatened by a 1922 Oregon law requiring children to attend a public school. Supporters of the law argued that attending school together would unify diverse groups and that the state must have a means of fostering loyalty among its citizens and preventing subversive groups from starting private schools. The law was challenged by two private schools, and the Supreme Court ruled in *Pierce v. Society of Sisters* (1925) that the law violated the rights of parents to choose the type of education their children will receive.

While the decision in *Pierce* ensured the continued existence of private schools, events of the 1950s again brought them under attack. An atmosphere of heightened nationalism and fear of socialism and communism resulted in a concern for patriotism and American unity. In addition, private religious schools began seeking tax support and increasing their enrollments. Public school advocates argued that society has to continue educating together the majority of children from diverse groups or risk dividing the people and thus weakening the nation. Diverse public schools, many contended, are the best place to teach loyalty and the ideals of American democracy.

Hill House at the Choate Preparatory School in Wallingford, Connecticut. Some argued that the existence of private schools, including exclusive East coast prep schools such as Choate, did not suit a true democratic society. © BETTMANN/CORBIS. REPRODUCED BY PERMISSION.

Significance

While some private school opponents called for a reevaluation of the *Pierce* decision, James Bryant Conant, in *Education and Liberty: The Role of the Schools in a Modern Democracy* (1958), did not question the rights of parents to send their children to private schools. Rather, he sought to curb the expansion of private schools by strengthening public schools, opposing the use of public funds for private schools, and urging parents and citizens to support public schools.

The comprehensive high school, for Conant, is the answer to many problems of public schooling. Comprehensive high schools can serve the children of all groups by providing a variety of programs, vocational as well as college preparatory. Gifted children, Conant asserted, must be adequately challenged in public schools or parents are justified in buying a better education elsewhere. Public schools must improve or risk the expansion of private schooling. Such an expansion, Conant argued, will result in the reinforcement of class and economic distinctions and reduce unity and understanding among the various groups of American society.

Conant's ideas had a significant impact on the development of American secondary education. However,

while the comprehensive high school did become a familiar feature of the educational landscape, many questioned the degree to which these schools actually foster unity among diverse groups in American society. Some charged that tracking impedes interaction between the college-bound and vocational students. Bias in testing and tracking procedures ensures racial segregation within schools. The belief that placing the various groups together in the same school automatically results in harmony and understanding has proved largely to be incorrect. Educators must work to reduce segregation within schools as well as to actively foster interaction and dialogue among diverse groups of students.

Primary Source

Education and Liberty: The Role of the Schools in a Modern Democracy [excerpt]

> **SYNOPSIS:** Conant argues that the United States must preserve the pattern of educating the majority of children of all classes in the public schools in order to minimize class distinctions, encourage unity, and allow movement between classes. He urges support for public schools and opposition to public funding for private schools. Public schools must be strengthened if they are to compete with private schools. Comprehensive high schools are the answer to serving the needs of all students in one school.

Unity and Diversity in Secondary Education

. . . [The] American pattern of education is quite different from that which has evolved in the other English-speaking nations. We have already noted the high percentage of the youth attending school in this country on a full-time basis; in addition, our pattern is characterized by the small numbers attending private schools. The absence of tax-supported denominational schools is in contrast with England and Scotland. Is this American pattern now so widely accepted that one need not argue for its preservation? Twenty or thirty years ago I think the answer would have been in the affirmative. But not so today. Any frank discussion of the future of education in the United States must recognize the existence of many powerful church leaders who do not accept the present pattern as a permanent feature of American life. One must likewise realize that while only some 10 per cent of the youth of the country now in school attend private schools, in some cities the figure is as high as 40 per cent. Furthermore, the percentage of students attending private schools is increasing in certain sections of the country. Therefore I believe it of importance for all citizens to consider carefully the basic issue—the continuance of the American pattern.

I shall not detain the reader by reciting the attacks on the public schools that have taken place in the last few years (1949 to 1952). The formation in many localities of citizens' groups to defend the public schools is clear evidence of the devotion to them of a vast majority of the citizens of most towns and cities. Irresponsible attacks will certainly be warded off, and though some damage will be done, one need not fear the drastic alteration of the American pattern from violent, prejudiced criticism. But I am convinced that it is wise to discuss the fundamental criticisms of the American pattern of public education and to explore the alternative patterns which some critics favor. As a matter of convenience I shall call them the Australian and English patterns. In the one, a large proportion of the youth attending school at ages 15 to 17 is enrolled in church-connected private schools financed *without* tax support; in the other, the private school—church-connected or not—may receive tax money. . . .

Public funds are used to assist private schools including denominational schools in England and Scotland. No one can object to an open advocacy of the adoption of the English pattern here in the United States. Indeed, for those who believe that education divorced from denominational control is bad education, such an advocacy would seem highly logical. It is important for every American citizen to examine this issue as unemotionally as possible and see where he or she stands. For there is more than one way of changing a social pattern; we could easily drift by slow stages into a situation where in some states the adoption of the English pattern would be inevitable. If in a number of cities and towns the public high schools no longer received popular support, their successful rivals—the private schools—would be logical recipients of tax money. By one method or another the present constitutional barriers against the use of public funds for religious schools would be swept aside.

During the past seventy-five years all but a few per cent of the children in the United States have attended public schools. More than one foreign observer has remarked that without these schools we never could have assimilated so rapidly the different cultures which came to North America in the nineteenth century. Our schools have served all creeds and all economic groups within a given geographic area. I believe it to be of the utmost importance that this pattern be continued. To this end

the comprehensive high school deserves the enthusiastic support of the American taxpayer. The greater the proportion of our youth who fail to attend our public schools and who receive their education elsewhere, the greater the threat to our democratic unity. To use taxpayers' money to assist private schools is to suggest that American society use its own hands to destroy itself. This is the answer I must give to those who would advocate the transformation of the American pattern into that of England.

What is the basic objection to the Australian or English pattern, you may ask. Or, to put it the other way around—what are the advantages of free schools for all? To ask these questions is almost to give the answers. If one accepts the ideal of a democratic, fluid society with a minimum of class distinction, the maximum of fluidity, the maximum of understanding between different vocational groups, then the ideal secondary school is a comprehensive public high school. Of this much there can be no doubt: If one wished generation after generation to perpetuate class distinction based on hereditary status in a given society, one would certainly demand a dual system of schools; this is the case in the Province of Quebec where a majority of the people wish to perpetuate two different cultural groups. A dual system serves and helps to maintain group cleavages, the absence of a dual system does the reverse. This is particularly true of the secondary schools. Indeed, I would plead with those who insist as a matter of conscience on sending their children to denominational schools that they might limit their insistence on this type of education to the elementary years.

In terms of numbers involved, the dual nature of our present pattern may seem slight—about 92 per cent of our secondary school pupils are in public schools. In terms of a stratification of society on economic and religious lines, however, the duality is marked. In socio-economic terms we are not as far from the English "Public School" system as we sometimes like to think. Chancellor McConnell of the University of Buffalo, reporting on English education, notes the predominance of "Public School" graduates over grammar school graduates in the entrants to Oxford in 1948. A half dozen of the best-known Eastern colleges in the United States would show a similar social phenomenon; they enroll something like half their students from private Protestant schools which encompass only a few per cent of an entire age group. But it is only fair to point out that these same colleges have been trying desperately hard in the last twenty-five years to attract a larger number of public high-school graduates. They aim to be national in terms of geography and representative of all income groups; that they have to some degree succeeded in moving nearer their goal is, to me, a hopeful sign.

I cannot help regretting that private schools have been established in the last twenty years in certain urban areas where a generation ago a public high school served *all* the youth of the town or city. In some of our Western cities in particular, the trend toward private education for the sons and daughters of the well-to-do has recently been pronounced, but there is no use for those of us who are committed to public high schools as schools for all to denounce or bemoan the growth of private secondary schools. The founding of a new independent school in a locality is a challenge to those connected with public education. Granted the "snob appeal" of some of these new independent schools, nevertheless I feel sure in many cases they would never have come into existence if the management of the local high school had been wiser. Education is a social process. This is a free country and people will not be pushed around by educators. What is required is for those concerned to improve the high schools; public school administrators must recognize the validity of some of the criticisms now directed against them in terms of the failure of the high school to provide adequate education for the gifted. The problem is especially acute in metropolitan areas. The success of the private school in Australian cities should be a reminder of where we may be headed.

Private schools exist and will continue to exist in the United States. Parents have the privilege of deciding whether to send their children to private or public schools. If they have doubts about the ability of secular schools to promote the growth of moral and spiritual values, then these doubts must be weighed against the advantages of a pupil's attending a free school for all denominations. Similarly, if a family questions the ability of the local high school to prepare a gifted boy or girl adequately for university work (and the question unfortunately must be raised in many communities today), the family will have to balance these misgivings against the advantage of mixing with all sorts of people while at school. It is hardly worth debating whether or not under ideal conditions in the United States all the public high schools would be so excellent that there would be no room for the private nonsectarian school. Many of those actively engaged in teaching

in private schools hope that their efforts will so challenge the public schools that fewer and fewer parents will have to decide in favor of the private school for the gifted child.

Within limits, competition between private schools and public schools can be of advantage to the latter. I have used the phrase "competition within limits" advisedly, for it is difficult to run a private school without continuously recruiting students and it is difficult to recruit students without undermining public confidence in the tax-supported schools. Since the amount of money available for public education depends largely on the enthusiasm of the taxpayer, a chain reaction inimical to public education in a community may easily be started by zealous proponents of a private school. This is obvious in regard to a denominational school. If a religious group starts a school in a community, it is difficult for the promoters to avoid showing a derogatory attitude towards the rival public school. Thus even if the members of the denomination in question have no desire to receive tax money for their own private school, their criticism of the public schools may often tend to discourage the taxpayer. The same thing may happen as a result of schools that draw sons and daughters from well-to-do homes. That the growth of private schools, quite apart from the numbers enrolled, may endanger public education in a community is a fact often overlooked by those actively concerned with private education. . . .

We Americans desire to provide through our schools unity in our national life. On the other hand, we seek the diversity that comes from freedom of action and expression for small groups of citizens. We look with disfavor on any monolithic type of educational structure; we shrink from any idea of regimentation, of uniformity as to the details of the many phases of secondary education. Unity we can achieve if our public schools remain the primary vehicle for the education of our youth, and if, as far as possible, all the youth of a community attend the same school irrespective of family fortune or cultural background. Diversity in experimentation we maintain by continued emphasis on the concept of local responsibility for our schools. Both these ideas are to a considerable degree novel in the development of civilization; a combination of them is to be found nowhere in the world outside of the United States.

By organizing our free schools on as comprehensive a basis as possible, we can continue to give our children an understanding of democracy. Religious tolerance, mutual respect between vocational groups, belief in the rights of the individual are among the virtues that the best of our high schools now foster. An understanding of the political machinery of our federal union, of the significance of the Anglo-Saxon tradition of the common law, of the distinction between decisions arrived at by "due process" and those obtained by social pressures and by duress, all this is now being achieved to some degree in the free tax-supported schools of this country.

What the great "Public Schools" of England accomplished for the future governing class of that nation in the nineteenth century the American high school is now attempting to accomplish for those who govern the United States, namely, all the people. Free schools where the future doctor, lawyer, professor, politician, banker, industrial executive, labor leader, and manual worker have studied and played together from the ages of 15 to 17 are a characteristic of large sections of the United States; they are an American invention. That such schools should be maintained and made even more democratic and comprehensive seems to me to be essential for the future of this republic.

Those who would grant all this but still question our free schools on religious grounds I would refer to a recent publication on "Moral and Spiritual Values in the Public Schools." There is set forth in strong terms the belief of many of us that in spite of their nondenominational character, our tax-supported schools have had as a great and continuing purpose the development of moral and spiritual values.

Diversity in American secondary education will be assured if we continue to insist on the doctrine of local control. We have few restrictions on the variety of approaches to secondary education presented by our thousands of local boards. Indeed, to an outsider I should think our diversity would look like educational chaos. But this is a characteristic of our flexible decentralized concept of democracy. The time may conceivably come when a state or the Federal Government may jeopardize this concept, but as far as secondary education is concerned, I do not detect any danger signals in that direction. The National Youth Administration threat, which was real in the 1930's, has almost been forgotten. In short, the answer to the question, "Can we achieve national unity through our public schools and still retain diversity?" is that we can if we so desire. My own personal answer would be that we must.

And now one final look ahead. In spite of the inadequacies of many of our high school programs and the undeveloped nature of our two-year community colleges, we have made great progress in the last twenty-five years in our attempt to provide adequate schools for *all* American youth. For the future we must endeavor to combine the British concern for training the "natural aristocracy of talents" with the American insistence on general education for *all* future citizens. If we can do that, then our industrialized society will prosper and at the same time the necessary degree of instruction will be provided for all the people so that in their hands "our liberties will remain secure."

Further Resources

BOOKS

Angus, David L., and Jeffrey E. Mirel. *The Failed Promise of the American High School, 1890–1995.* New York: Teachers College Press, 1999.

Butts, R. Freeman, and Lawrence Cremin. *A History of Education in American Culture.* New York: Henry Holt, 1953.

Conant, James Bryant. *The American High School Today: A First Report to Interested Citizens.* New York: McGraw-Hill, 1959.

————. *The Comprehensive High School: A Second Report to Interested Citizens.* New York: McGraw-Hill, 1967.

————. *My Several Lives: Memoirs of a Social Inventor.* New York: Harper and Row, 1970.

————. *The Revolutionary Transformation of the American High School.* Cambridge, Mass.: Harvard University Press, 1959.

The Long Shadow of Little Rock: A Memoir

Memoir

By: Daisy Bates

Date: 1962

Source: Bates, Daisy. *The Long Shadow of Little Rock: A Memoir.* New York: David McKay Company, Inc., 1962.

About the Author: Daisy Bates (1914–1999) was born in Huttig, Arkansas, where she attended segregated public schools. In 1952 Bates became president of the Arkansas branch of the National Association for the Advancement of Colored People (NAACP). She is most famous for serving as an advocate for the Little Rock Nine—the African American students who entered all-white Central High in 1957. She continued to play an active role in community organizations until her death. ∎

Introduction

The middle of the twentieth century was a period of sweeping changes in American history, as civil rights activists worked toward equality for African Americans.

The 1954 Supreme Court ruling, *Brown v. Board of Education,* was an important move toward equality. That ruling found school segregation (separate schools for African Americans and whites) unconstitutional, paving the way for desegregation throughout society.

Many people, especially in the southern United States, opposed the *Brown* ruling and tried to prevent desegregation from happening. The vast majority of southern congressional representatives and senators signed the "Southern Manifesto," which urged white southerners to "resist forced integration by any lawful means." Some state governments declared the *Brown* ruling invalid; imposed new, stricter segregation laws; and penalized schools that tried to desegregate. Violence against African Americans in the South rose, as did membership in the Ku Klux Klan and other violent racist organizations.

The results of all this were struggles at one southern school after another. Mobs of angry whites—often helped by the police and public officials—would try to keep African American children from attending all-white schools. The 1957 Little Rock school desegregation showdown was the nation's most closely watched.

On September 3, 1957, nine African American students (called the "Little Rock Nine") were scheduled to begin classes at all-white Central High in Little Rock, Arkansas. The night before, Arkansas's segregationist governor Orval Faubus declared on TV that it would "not be possible to restore or to maintain order . . . if forcible integration is carried out tomorrow." He claimed that "blood will run in the streets if Negro pupils should attempt to enter Central High School." Faubus ordered 250 members of the Arkansas National Guard to surround the school, supposedly to keep the peace, but really to keep the Little Rock Nine out.

With the assistance of Daisy Bates and NAACP lawyers, on September 3, the students obtained a federal court order granting them admission to the school. The next morning, they made their first attempt to enter Central High. National Guardsmen and an obscenity-screaming mob turned them away. Not until September 23, after President Eisenhower had ordered the National Guardsmen removed, were the children able to enter the school. Even then the police later removed them from the school, to protect them from an angry mob outside. Eisenhower then sent in troops from the Army to protect the African American students. This enabled them to attend school for the rest of the year but did not prevent them from being abused physically and verbally by their classmates in an attempt to drive them out.

Significance

The excerpt here illustrates the difficulty of implementing the *Brown* decision. Events in Little Rock started a chain reaction. When Daisy Bates led the Little Rock Nine through jeering crowds, and when Elizabeth Eckford faced the mob alone, television cameras and newspaper reporters captured the action for the world to see. The publicity created pressure on public officials to protect these youngsters and spurred on the long process of school integration. In fact, desegregation was a long, painful process. In 1968, only 32 percent of African American school children in the South were attending desegregated schools; by 1972 that percentage had risen to 46.

Many people were surprised to see the violence in Little Rock, which had previously seemed to have good race relations. One explanation is that protesters came from throughout the South. Eyewitnesses saw many cars with out-of-state license plates. There was definitely strong local opposition to desegregation, however. In 1958, the entire Little Rock school district was shut down to prevent it from being integrated. It was not until 1959 that Little Rock schools reopened and began accepting students of all races.

As Bates wrote in her memoir: "Events in history occur when the time has ripened for them, but they need a spark. Little Rock was the spark at that stage of the struggle of the American Negro for justice."

Primary Source

The Long Shadow of Little Rock: A Memoir
[excerpt]

SYNOPSIS: In this excerpt, Elizabeth Eckford, one of the Little Rock Nine, vividly describes her experience of walking alone into Central High on the morning of September 4, 1957. Since Eckford's home did not have a phone, she had been unaware that Daisy Bates and the NAACP lawyers had planned for all nine students to meet several blocks from the school ahead of time. The other eight students of the Little Rock Nine had arrived at the school in a group, with NAACP escorts, but Elizabeth walked in alone.

Elizabeth, whose dignity and control in the face of jeering mobsters had been filmed by television cameras and recorded in pictures flashed to newspapers over the world, had overnight become a national heroine. During the next few days' newspaper reporters besieged her home, wanting to talk to her. The first day that her parents agreed she might come out of seclusion, she came to my house where the reporters awaited her. Elizabeth was very quiet, speaking only when spoken to. I took her to my bedroom to talk before I let the reporters see her. I asked how she felt now. Suddenly all her pent-up emotion flared.

Daisy Bates (left) speaks with four high school students in her home. Little Rock, Arkansas, 1959. **AP/WIDE WORLD PHOTOS. REPRODUCED BY PERMISSION.**

"Why am I here?" she said, turning blazing eyes on me. "Why are you so interested in my welfare now? You didn't care enough to notify me of the change of plans—"

I walked over and reached out to her. Before she turned her back on me, I saw tears gathering in her eyes. My heart was breaking for this young girl who stood there trying to stifle her sobs. How could I explain that frantic early morning when at three o'clock my mind had gone on strike?

In the ensuing weeks Elizabeth took part in all the activities of the nine—press conferences, attendance at court, studying with professors at nearby Philander Smith College. She was present, that is, but never really a part of things. The hurt had been too deep.

On the two nights she stayed at my home I was awakened by the screams in her sleep, as she relived in her dreams the terrifying mob scenes at Central. The only times Elizabeth showed real excitement were when Thurgood Marshall met the children and explained the meaning of what had happened in court. As he talked, she would listen raptly, a faint smile on her face. It was obvious he was her hero.

Little by little Elizabeth came out of her shell. Up to now she had never talked about what happened to her at Central. Once when we were alone in the downstairs recreation room of my house, I asked her simply, "Elizabeth, do you think you can talk about it now?"

She remained quiet for a long time. Then she began to speak.

"You remember the day before we were to go in, we met Superintendent Blossom at the school board office. He told us what the mob might say and do but he never told us we wouldn't have any protection. He told our parents not to come because he wouldn't be able to protect the children if they did.

"That night I was so excited I couldn't sleep. The next morning I was about the first one up. While I was pressing my black and white dress—I had made it to wear on the first day of school—my little brother turned on the TV set. They started telling about a large crowd gathered at the school. The man on TV said he wondered if we were going to show up that morning. Mother called from the kitchen, where she was fixing breakfast, 'Turn that TV off!' She was so upset and worried. I wanted to comfort her, so I said, 'Mother, don't worry.'

"Dad was walking back and forth, from room to room, with a sad expression. He was chewing on his pipe and he had a cigar in his hand, but he didn't light either one. It would have been funny, only he was so nervous.

"Before I left home Mother called us into the living-room. She said we should have a word of prayer. Then I caught the bus and got off a block from the school. I saw a large crowd of people standing across the street from the soldiers guarding Central. As I walked on, the crowd suddenly got very quiet. Superintendent Blossom had told us to enter by the front door. I looked at all the people and thought, 'Maybe I will be safer if I walk down the block to the front entrance behind the guards.'

"At the corner I tried to pass through the long line of guards around the school so as to enter the grounds behind them. One of the guards pointed across the street. So I pointed in the same direction and asked whether he meant for me to cross the street and walk down. He nodded 'yes.' So, I walked across the street conscious of the crowd that stood there, but they moved away from me.

"For a moment all I could hear was the shuffling of their feet. Then someone shouted, 'Here she comes, get ready!' I moved away from the crowd on the sidewalk and into the street. If the mob came at me I could then cross back over so the guards could protect me.

"The crowd moved in closer and then began to follow me, calling me names. I still wasn't afraid. Just a little bit nervous. Then my knees started to shake all of a sudden and I wondered whether I could make it to the center entrance a block away. It was the longest block I ever walked in my whole life.

"Even so, I still wasn't too scared because all the time I kept thinking that the guards would protect me.

"When I got right in front of the school, I went up to a guard again. But this time he just looked straight ahead and didn't move to let me pass him. I didn't know what to do. Then I looked and saw that the path leading to the front entrance was a little further ahead. So I walked until I was right in front of the path to the front door.

"I stood looking at the school—it looked so big! Just then the guards let some white students go through.

"The crowd was quiet. I guess they were waiting to see what was going to happen. When I was able to steady my knees, I walked up to the guard who had let the white students in. He too didn't move. When I tried to squeeze past him, he raised his bayonet and then the other guards closed in and they raised their bayonets.

"They glared at me with a mean look and I was very frightened and didn't know what to do. I turned around and the crowd came toward me.

"They moved closer and closer. Somebody started yelling, 'Lynch her! Lynch her!'

"I tried to see a friendly face somewhere in the mob—someone who maybe would help. I looked into the face of an old woman and it seemed a kind face, but when I looked at her again, she spat on me.

"They came closer, shouting, 'No nigger bitch is going to get in our school. Get out of here!'

"I turned back to the guards but their faces told me I wouldn't get help from them. Then I looked down the block and saw a bench at the bus stop. I thought, 'If I can only get there I will be safe.' I don't know why the bench seemed a safe place to me, but I started walking toward it. I tried to close my mind to what they were shouting, and kept saying to myself, 'If I can only make it to the bench I will be safe.'

"When I finally got there, I don't think I could have gone another step. I sat down and the mob crowded up and began shouting all over again. Someone hollered, 'Drag her over to this tree! Let's take care of the nigger.' Just then a white man sat down beside me, put his arm around me and patted my shoulder. He raised my chin and said, 'Don't let them see you cry.'

"Then, a white lady—she was very nice—she came over to me on the bench. She spoke to me but I don't remember now what she said. She put me on the bus and sat next to me. She asked me my name and tried to talk to me but I don't think I answered. I can't remember much about the bus ride, but the next thing I remember I was standing in front of the School for the Blind, where Mother works.

"I thought, 'Maybe she isn't here. But she has to be here!' So I ran upstairs, and I think some teachers tried to talk to me, but I kept running until I reached Mother's classroom.

"Mother was standing at the window with her head bowed, but she must have sensed I was there because she turned around. She looked as if she had been crying, and I wanted to tell her I was all right. But I couldn't speak. She put her arms around me and I cried."

Further Resources

BOOKS

African Americans: Voices of Triumph: Perseverance. Alexandria, Va.: Time-Life Books, 1993..

Beals, Melba Pattillo. *Warriors Don't Cry: A Searing Memoir of the Battle to Integrate Little Rock's Central High.* New York: Pocket Books, 1994.

Kluger, Richard. *Simple Justice: The History of "Brown v. Board of Education" and Black America's Struggle for Equality.* New York: Vintage Books, 1975.

Levy, Peter B. *The Civil Rights Movement.* Westwood, Conn.: Greenwood Press, 1998.

Williams, Juan. *Eyes on the Prize: America's Civil Rights Years, 1954–1965.* New York: Penguin Books, 1987.

PERIODICALS

Martin, Douglas. "Daisy Bates, Civil Rights Leader, Dies at 84." *The New York Times,* November 5, 1999, B11.

Molotsky, Irvin. "U.S. Honors 9 Civil Rights Heroes, and Memory of 10th." *The New York Times,* November 10, 1999, A16.

WEBSITES

"The Little Rock Nine." *Little Rock Central High.* Available online at http://www.centralhigh57.org/The_Little_Rock _Nine.html; website home page: http://www.centralhigh57 .org (accessed June 6, 2003).

"The 1957-58 School Year." *Little Rock Central High.* Available online at http://www.centralhigh57.org/1957-58.htm; website home page: http://www.centralhigh57.org (accessed June 6, 2003).

AUDIO AND VISUAL MEDIA

Fighting Back 1957–1962." *Eyes on the Prize: America's Civil Rights Years.* Boston: Blackside, Inc., 1986.1

FASHION AND DESIGN

JESSIE BISHOP POWELL

Entries are arranged in chronological order by date of primary source. For entries with one primary source, the entry title is the same as the primary source title. Entries with more than one primary source have an overall entry title, followed by the titles of the primary sources.

Important Events in Fashion, 1950–1959

1950

- William J. Levitt expands his mass-production techniques of building identical boxlike houses in Levittown, New York, assembled by crews using precut materials, thus accelerating the rush to suburbia.

- The White House is gutted and remodeled during the first year of a three-year project. Only the outside walls remain unchanged during the rebuilding.

- New York's United Nations Secretariat building, featuring all-glass east and west facades, is completed to provide offices for the UN's thirty-four hundred employees on land overlooking the East River.

- The "Sun House" at Dover, Massachusetts, heated solely by stored-up rays of the sun and erected by the Massachusetts Institute of Technology, is occupied in comfort by a New England family throughout the winter, opening up the possibilities of solar heat for house warming.

- Miss Clairol hair coloring is introduced; it takes only half the application time needed by other hair colorings.

- Sales of at-home leisure wear grow with the increased number of television sets purchased for entertainment.

- Orlon is introduced by E.I. du Pont de Nemours, which had begun developing the wool-like fiber in 1941.

- Cotton's share of the U.S. textile market falls to 65 percent, down from 80 percent in 1940, and man-made fibers—mostly rayons and acetates—increase their share to more than 20 percent.

1951

- The first all-glass-and-steel apartment building, designed by Ludwig Mies van der Rohe, is completed on Lake Shore Drive in Chicago.

- The American Association of Textile Chemists and Colorists proclaims that a "full-fledged textile revolution"—production and demand for man-made fibers—is in progress.

- The popularity of tubular metal furniture grows.

- The Chemise Lacoste is exported to the United States for the first time by the French Izod Company. The long-tailed all-cotton "alligator" tennis shirt is soon to become a U.S. status symbol.

- Victor Gruen Associates is founded by Austrian-American architect Victor Gruen. Gruen's architecture, engineering, urban-planning firm will have a major impact on U.S. building design and city planning.

- A second Levittown is started by Levitt and Sons for seventeen thousand families in Bucks County, Pennsylvania, with schools and churches to be built on land donated by the developers. The inexpensive three- or four-bedroom houses (the price includes major appliances) encourage thousands of Americans to leave the city and move into suburban developments as scores of builders adopt the methods pioneered by Levitt.

1952

- The McDonald's Golden Arches, modeled on the flamboyant "coffee house" architecture of California, is designed.

- The inventor Buckminster Fuller displays at the Museum of Modern Art in New York his strong but lightweight geodesic dome, which eventually revolutionized construction.

- Revolutionary new materials such as melamine, a lightweight plastic, are introduced for use in furniture and dinnerware.

- Strongly modern furniture designs account for 60 percent of all new furniture patterns.

- Entirely new synthetic yarns are introduced; viscose rayon, acetate, and nylon production reach new highs.

- Femininity triumphs in women's wear as cinched waistlines, molded bodices, and yards of wide skirts worn over stiff petticoats are "in."

- Four-inch stiletto heels are introduced, much to the dismay of floor manufacturers.

- "Never wear a white shirt before sundown," says ads for Hathaway shirts. Four out of five shirts sold to men in America are white, but the ratio will fall to two out of five in the next fifteen years, and all-cotton shirts will give way to blends of cotton and synthetic fibers.

- On April 29, New York City's Lever House opens on Park Avenue. The heat-resistant glass windows in the twenty-four-story glass-walled building are sealed, and the centrally air-conditioned building uses an enormous amount of energy. It becomes an example for energy-wasting architecture.

1953

- Architects of America designs new "super" shopping centers that spread throughout suburbia.

- Plastic women's shoes become popular after Marilyn Monroe wears them in the film *How to Marry a Millionaire.*

- Bermuda shorts for men appear in offices and are even worn by some executives.

1954

- A major technological conference on plastic as a building material is held.

- Seamless nylon stockings are introduced.

- French designer Christian Dior ignites another fashion firecracker in America with his popular "H" look.

- Americans move into single-family homes—most in the suburbs—at an astounding rate; the numbers are up 33 percent over those of 1953.
- Geodesics, Inc., and Synergetics, Inc., are established to produce seven-room circular aluminum Dymaxion houses and geodesic domes designed by Buckminster Fuller.
- In March, the world's largest shopping center, with one hundred stores opens at Detroit's Northland.

1955

- No-iron Dacron is put on the market by DuPont.
- A patent for Velcro is granted to engineer George deMestral.
- Minnie and Mickey Mouse and other Disney motifs are stamped on millions of T-shirts, bags.

1956

- Elvis Presley's blue suede shoes, black leather jackets, doubled-high collars, side-burns, and long, greased hair are copied by masses of American teenage boys.
- "Does she or doesn't she?" ask advertisements for Miss Clairol hair coloring. The ads picture children with mothers to show that nice women can color their hair, too.
- Eero Saarinen's TWA Terminal at Kennedy Airport in New York opens. Saarinen also completes his seven-year project of designing the General Motors Technical Center in Michigan.
- Plastic invades the furniture industry.
- The National Automobile Show is reestablished after a lapse of sixteen years, giving U.S. car designers a showplace for new models.

1957

- Japanese architectural influence begins to be seen in America as some U.S. builders import top Japanese architects.
- Los Angeles adopts a revised building code that permits construction of high-rise buildings. The code reflects earthquake-stress engineering technology.
- Christian Dior introduces the popular chemise dress (also known as "the sack")—his concession to comfort.
- Blue jeans surge in popularity as a symbol of teen revolt in the wake of Jack Kerouac's *On The Road.*
- "Beatnik" clothing, featuring khaki pants, sweaters, sandal.
- In May, The American Institute of Architects celebrates its one hundredth birthday.

1958

- Buckminster Fuller's geodesic dome at Baton Rouge is unveiled.
- Full-skirted "rock 'n' roll" dresses layered with petticoats become fashionable for teenage girls.
- The new "trapeze" dresses designed by Frenchman Yves St. Laurent, the successor to Christian Dior, are a hit.
- The U.S. textile industry consolidates and moves south. Some 90 percent of all cotton fabrics, as well as 73 percent of man-made fabrics, are produced in the South by early 1958. Within two years, man-made fabrics increase their share of the market to 28 percent, with polyesters taking 11 percent of the market.

1959

- The first Barbie Doll is introduced.

Marlon Brando in *A Streetcar Named Desire*

Movie still

By: Warner Brothers

Date: 1951

Source: Marlon Brando in *A Streetcar Named Desire*. Movie still. 1951. The Kobal Collection/Warner Bros. Image number STR001BM. ∎

Introduction

Youth fashion in the 1950s can be described entirely with the word "commercial." Designers marketed and sold heavily to teens, who for the first time had large amounts of disposable income to spend. Moreover, teens were influenced in their clothing choices by movies, television, and rock stars. They strove to imitate their heroes and each other. In so doing, they conformed to social expectations in a way that was not entirely unlike the overall conformity of the adult world in the 1950s, though many of them claimed to be rebelling against their parents' stilted values.

Most adolescent girls chose between the poodle skirt and the greaser looks. The poodle skirt crowd wore calf-length frilly skirts with layers of crinoline underneath, bobby socks, and saddle shoes. Girls' fashions emphasized small waists, meaning their poodle skirts usually came equipped with wide belts. These girls often accessorized with cat-eye glasses. Denim was more popular with the greaser girls, who imitated the rebels they saw on TV and in the movies. They tended to wear short skirts (still scandalous by 1950s standards) and heavy makeup.

Boys, too, chose between two popular looks. They either attempted to project affluence by imitating prep school dress codes, or they wore rebellion on their sleeves, imitating Marlon Brando in *Streetcar Named Desire* and *The Wild One*. The prep school imitators sported V-necked sweaters over white button-up shirts and loose-fitting pants. They might also wear letter jackets (especially handy for lending to your girlfriend at the drive-in movies).

Marlon Brando as Stanley Kowalski

A Streetcar Named Desire was written, first as a play and then adapted for the big screen, by Thomas Lanier (Tennessee) Williams. Williams, who was born in 1911, became one of America's greatest playwrights and was extremely popular in the post-World War II era. The starring male role in *Streetcar* was the rough, working-class, highly charged Stanley Kowalski, played by Marlon Brando, who was at the time establishing himself as a youth icon. Brando was a Method actor, a proponent of the style of acting developed in the Actor's Studio, founded by Elia Kazan. The school was based on a psychological approach to acting, in which the actor strove to *become* his or her character and to feel and portray all the character's emotions. This kind of emotional display had been rare in acting prior to *Streetcar,* but Brando, directed by Kazan, held nothing back. Although Brando's character, Stanley Kowalski, was a very flawed and violent person, he was nothing like the heroes of more typical Hollywood movies. With Brando's brilliant performance, Kowalski's manner and style were magnetic. The performance had a profound effect on films to come. Soon other actors, such as James Dean and Montgomery Clift, followed in similar types of "troubled young men" roles that appealed strongly to rebellious teens of the 1950s.

Significance

The rich-kid look stayed popular with the genuinely affluent. However, the male fashion statement of the 1950s that would carry forward was the hipster greaser look. Best captured (and promoted) by Marlon Brando, a hero to rebellious youths nationwide, the look featured T-shirts and blue jeans or tight fitting sleek black pants, a leather jacket, hair slicked back into a D.A. (for "duck's ass"), and a perpetual sneer. Hipsters smoked. They drank. They rode motorcycles. And they were angry with the world. The obvious sexuality of the clothing—tight jeans for guys, heavy makeup and short skirts for girls, had the added appeal of horrifying the older generation.

Also influential to 1950s fashion were the rising "beat generation," headed by authors like Jack Kerouac and Allen Ginsberg, and by other artists and musicians from New York's Greenwich Village. This group wore tight leather Levis and Converse sneakers. Their beatnik look played heavily into hipster greaser culture, and carried its appeal to college students as well.

The American clothing culture was significantly changed by the new look of the rebel teens. T-shirts, in-

Primary Source

Marlon Brando in *A Streetcar Named Desire*

SYNOPSIS: Marlon Brando was nominated for an academy award for his performance in *A Streetcar Named Desire*. Brando's name became synonymous with rebellion in the 1950s, and his Stanley Kowalski was a brilliantly tortured soul. Angst-ridden youth may have identified with Brando, but what they loved was his *look* in his plain workman's T-shirts and blue jeans. His attire in *Streetcar* was by no means his only contribution to youth fashion. He would cement his association with the hipster look when he played Johnny in *The Wild One* in 1954. THE KOBAL COLLECTION/WARNER BROS. REPRODUCED BY PERMISSION.

vented to be worn by GIs in the South Pacific, quickly became popular as outerwear, not just for rebellious youth and blue-collar workers, but for men, women, boys, and girls from all age groups and economic backgrounds. Blue jeans also developed enormous popularity, quickly coming into fashion, especially as women escaped their skirts and looked for comfortable pants to wear. Sneak-

ers have bounded into the mainstream as well, with Nike and Adidas controlling popular teen looks every bit as much as Levi or Lee jeans.

Further Resources

BOOKS

Cawthorne, Nigel. *Key Moments in Fashion: The Evolution of Style*. London: Hamlyn, 1998.

Ettinger, Roseann. *50s Popular Fashions for Men, Women, Boys and Girls, with Price Guide.* Atglen, Pa.: Schiffer Publishing, 1995.

Fashion Advertising Collection, 1942–1982: A History in Illustration from 200 North American Newspapers. Eastchester, N.Y.: J. Alper, 1986.

Martin, Linda. *The Way We Wore: Fashion Illustrations of Children's Wear, 1870–1970.* New York: Charles Scribner's Sons, 1978.

McRobbie, Angela. *Zoot Suits and Second-hand Dresses: An Anthology of Fashion and Music.* Boston: Unwin Hyman, 1988.

Peacock, John. *The 1950s.* London: Thames and Hudson, 1997.

Skinner, Tina. *Fashionable Clothing from the Sears Catalogs: Mid-1950s.* Atglen, Pa.: Schiffer Publishing, 2002.

WEBSITES

"American Boyhood Clothes: Texas in the 1950s–60s—My Brother." Historical Boys' Clothing. Available online at http://histclo.hispeed.com/country/us/co-us-1950602bro.html; website home page: http://histclo.hispeed.com/index2.html (accessed March 26, 2003).

"History of Fashion, 1950–1960." Vintage Blues. Available online at http://www.vintageblues.com/history5.htm; website home page: http://www.vintageblues.com/vintage.htm (accessed March 26, 2003).

Maginnis, Tara. *The Costumer's Manifesto—Costumes.org* Available online at http://www.costumes.org/pages/1950inks.htm (accessed March 26, 2003).

Suburban Homes

"The Houses Women Would Like— And the Houses They Get"

Magazine article

By: *U.S. News and World Report*

Date: May 4, 1956

Source: "The Houses Women Would Like—And The Houses They Get." *U.S. News & World Report.* May 4, 1956, 54, 56.

About the Publication: In 1933, David Lawrence founded the weekly newspaper *United States News.* Six years later, he established the magazine *World Report.* He merged these two publications in 1948 to create the *U.S. News and World Report.* Beginning the in the 1980s, it started its annual rankings of U.S. colleges in universities. Besides reporting on current news events around the world, it also publishes the annuals *America's Best Colleges* and *America's Best Graduate Schools.*

"Ranch Dwellings Open in Woodmere"

Newspaper article; Floor plan

By: *The New York Times*

Date: May 25, 1952

Source: "Ranch Dwellings Open in Woodmere." *The New York Times,* May 25, 1952, R10.

"94 Homes Are Set in Jersey Colony"

Newspaper article; Floor plan

By: *The New York Times*

Date: November 29, 1959

Source: "94 Homes Are Set in Jersey Colony." *The New York Times,* November 29, 1959, R6.

About the Publication: *The New York Times,* founded in 1851 as the *Daily Times,* was originally a relatively obscure local paper. When publisher Adolph S. Ochs acquired controlling ownership of the *Times* for $75,000 in 1896, its circulation was 9,000. Ochs made dramatic changes, and the circulation soared. By the early part of the twentieth century, it had grown into a widely known, well-respected news source. Among the many new features introduced to the paper was the *Fashions of the Times* magazine, starting in 1946, which was a huge success. The *Times* banner, reading "All the News That's Fit to Print," is today recognized across the United States and indeed throughout the world. ∎

Introduction

Though living in a single family home in the suburbs is taken for granted by many Americans today, this has only been a possibility for most of the population since the 1950s. Until the end of World War II (1939–1945), a significant portion of Americans never dreamed of owning a suburban home. Prior to the war in the 1930s, most people lived in the city. Some owned or rented homes, but most lived in apartments. A high percentage of people lived in rural areas as well, often lacking modern conveniences like electricity. Throughout the early twentieth century many people had trouble saving enough money to buy a house, as banks generally required a substantial down payment. A significant number of those lucky enough to own homes in the 1920s lost them during the Depression. More would have lost their homes, but the federal government stepped in with the Home Owners Loan Corporation to carry urban mortgages. The Federal Housing Authority also originated in this era to help people with mortgages and houses.

During World War II, the largest consumer in the United States was the federal government, and wartime rationing kept most people from buying new goods. Few new homes were built, because supplies and manpower were lacking. When the war ended, the workforce, which had been largely female during the war, quickly shifted back to being mostly men. The majority of women were once more relegated to the home. Many businesses were in excellent shape, having made huge profits from their government grants. The government started buying less, leaving businesses to find new ways to maintain their profitability. They found a good market in the American public. During the war, most people had saved money, and when the war ended, they found themselves suddenly with reasonably large disposable incomes and an increasing variety of things to spend them on. In particular, people began buying houses, rushing to the suburbs in droves.

Significance

The 1950s rush to the suburbs took place for a number of reasons. Middle-class Americans fled crowded cities to get more privacy and larger houses. Cheap prefabricated homes were easily available and banks began offering loans with smaller down payments. The great exodus brought about racial disparities in many cities, since most of the people leaving the cities were white. Banks and the government frequently refused loans to African American applicants. Hence, the middle-class flight is also known as the "white flight" to the suburbs. This caused problems, since school district funding was based on property taxes, and tax funding for city schools dropped as people fled to the suburbs. The inner city schools deteriorated, and this situation still exists today as a direct result of the 1950s flight to the suburbs.

Suburban life in the 1950s began to take on a new essence. In the suburbs, people had a sense of being more secure. The new highway system that began emerging towards the middle of the decade ensured people an easy commute to work in the cars they were able to buy on easily obtained credit. Often the houses in a community looked alike, after the success of planned communities like Levittown, a suburb of New York developed to accommodate the returning GIs and their families after the war. Levittown and towns like it offered affordable small, detached, single-family houses.

The two most popular house plans that arose from the era were easily the cape cod and the ranch. Cape cods were one-and-a-half-story dwellings that had been around since the seventeenth century. They generally featured steep roofs with symmetrical dormer windows jutting out over a central front door. Ranch houses, by contrast, were asymmetrical and only one story, with a layout that usually featured an L or U shape, with an open floor plan and an attached garage. Heavily influenced by Frank Lloyd Wright and the Prairie School style of low buildings with open interiors, and horizontal lines, they generally had rambling floor plans and sliding glass doors leading out to a patio.

Primary Source

"The Houses Women Would Like—And The Houses They Get"

SYNOPSIS: This article outlines what middle class American housewives generally looked for in a new home in the 1950s. They were mostly interested in having more and larger rooms, including additional bathrooms, bedrooms, and rooms for a television and for laundry. They also wanted to have a distinctive looking home, on a curved and pleasantly shaded street. As the article points out, only some of these features were being included by builders in 1956, but it correctly predicts that many of them will become common in future years.

Latest check on what women want in a new home shows this—

They want, and usually get: 3 bedrooms, 1½ baths, more space. Most want, but do not get: a family room, a utility room.

They do not want: viewless picture windows, look-alike houses, curveless streets, extreme appearance, gadgets in lieu of space.

Gaining in popularity: masonry walls, flush doors, aluminum windows.

It is possible now to size up, in some detail, what the American housewife wants in a new home—and what she is getting.

That there are differences between what builders offer and what women demand in a home is shown by a pair of studies conducted by Government agencies.

The Housing and Home Finance Agency has been looking into the housewife's tastes in home design. The Labor Department's Bureau of Labor Statistics has made a survey of the kinds of houses being built around the country.

The studies disclose that, to some extent, the desires of the public are changing the patterns of home building.

American women are demanding more floor space, and the trend in new homes is toward more. They want three bedrooms, and most new homes are being built with three. They want at least one and a half baths, and most new homes have that many. But on many points the homes now being built still do not measure up to the demands of the American housewife.

A cross section of the housing preferences of American women is provided in views expressed by 100 housewives from all parts of the country at a conference called by Albert M. Cole, HHFA Administrator.

New Tastes

The views of these women differ on a number of things. But they are in agreement that, even in the price range of $10,000 to $15,000, a new house should contain a third bedroom, an additional half bath, and a number of other features they regard as minimal.

These housewives believe a new house should be designed so the living room will be a quiet area, a parlor—without television—for receiving guests, for reading, music, conversation. They also want a regular dining room or, at the least, a separate dining area where the entire family can sit down together at mealtime.

A nook in the kitchen for breakfast and snacks still is favored, but not as a substitute for the dining room. The housewives differ on kitchen arrangements, but believe more attention should be paid to such points as the height of the sink and working counter.

Family Room

Regarded as a "must' item by most of these housewives is a family room for television viewing, for games, for the children to romp in.

A virtually universal demand of American women—for more storage space—was echoed at the housing conference. The women want more storage space anywhere it an be located. If the plans include a garage, they want it built extra long, to provide storage in the rear.

Reflecting differences with present building practices is a demand for a separate utility-laundry room on the ground floor, adjacent to the kitchen. Most of the housewives say they don't want the washer and dryer either in the kitchen or downstairs in the basement. They would put them in this utility room, which would be a place to remove muddy shoes and wet raincoats.

Not Wanted

There are other points on which the women say that what they want often isn't what the builder thinks they want.

They don't want picture windows unless there's really a view to look at. They don't want houses that resemble the neighbors' except for minor exterior variations. They would rather have more space than gadgets that they could add later. They want the original trees on the lot saved, except for those removed to make room for the house. They want curved streets, not ones laid out in gridiron patterns. They don't like extremes in exteriors.

Some of the things being demanded most vigorously by women already are showing up in home-building trends.

Figures compiled by the FHA show that, of all homes in the country, less than half have three bedrooms. But, of the plans for new homes approved by FHA, 73.8 per cent call for three bedrooms.

A sampling by the National Association of Home Builders around the country shows that most builders are concentrating on houses with three bedrooms and with one and a half baths, or more.

Size, Price Increasing

A survey by the Labor Department's Bureau of Labor Statistics shows both floor space and prices up for new homes.

More homes are being built to sell for $12,000 to $20,000, and there is a sharp decline in houses priced at $7,000 or less. There are increases in the proportion of homes having 1,000 to 1,500 square feet of floor space, decreases in those with 800 square feet or less.

The BLS survey shows some other patterns that parallel the demands being expressed by American women. There's a strong uptrend in the use of masonry to create outside walls that require little or no painting expense, although three fourths of new homes continue to be of frame construction.

Windows with aluminum frames are being used in about a fourth of all new homes, although wooden frames still are used in windows of more than half. As for type, the double-hung window is used in more than half of new houses, but horizontal slide, awning and jalousie windows are gaining in popularity. The picture window is slipping a bit.

Flush Doors Take Over

The survey by BLS discloses that the flush door is rapidly displacing the panel door inside new homes. In new houses costing $12,000 or more, the panel door has virtually disappeared.

Fireplaces are being included in only about one third of new homes. A fireplace seems to be a matter of cost. Very few low-priced homes have fireplaces, but the percentage goes up rapidly in higher price ranges.

As reflected in the views of the housewives at the conference, a basement in a new home is more a matter of geography and cost than of taste. More than half of new houses are being built without basements. The percentage of homes with basements runs higher in cold areas, and in more-expensive homes.

One demand of the housewives—for a laundry-utility room—apparently isn't being met to any great extent. The BLS survey shows that about one third of new homes are being built with what are called utility rooms. But these rooms mostly are designed to accommodate a water heater and furnace and little else. What the women want is a utility room big enough for sewing, for doing the laundry, with space perhaps left over for a hobby bench for the man of the house.

More Changes Coming

With the market for new houses sagging and builders anxious to please the women who in most cases will have a deciding voice in purchases, more shifts in building patterns can be expected.

Primary Source

"Ranch Dwellings Open in Woodmere": Newspaper article

SYNOPSIS: The following announcement of housing development openings appeared in *The New York Times* in 1952. Note the sprawling nature of the house in these plans. The garage is set down in a corner and one hall connects the living rooms and kitchens, as well as the stairs to the attic and basement, to the three bedrooms.

Builder Plans Twenty Houses in $27,000 Price Range in Program for This Year

Two model homes have been completed and are open for inspection on Fiske Street, near Longacre Avenue, in Woodmere, L. I., where Philip Brous, builder, expects to complete a group of twenty dwellings this year. The builder, who is also an architect, designed the houses to sell in the $27,000 price range.

Mr. Brous said he mailed questionnaires to 2,500 families on Long Island's South Shore so as to be able to incorporate any ideas on exterior design and interior appointments in the plans.

In the ranch style, the houses occupy plots of 70 by 100 feet and feature center halls and vestibules. They have an L-shaped living-dining area,

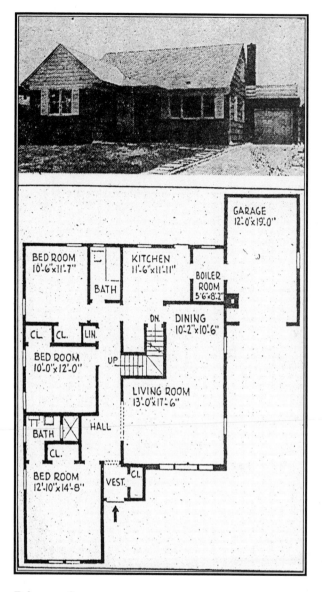

Primary Source

"Ranch Dwellings Open in Woodmere": Floor plan

This Long Island home was built to sell in the $27,000 price range. "RANCH DWELLINGS OPEN IN WOODMERE." *THE NEW YORK TIMES*, MAY 25, 1952, R10

with sleeping quarters confined to one wing of the house and consisting of three bedrooms and two bathrooms.

Kitchens are complete with electrical appliances and cabinets in solid birch with butternut finish. Bedrooms and kitchens have sliding doors and the exteriors of the houses are of stone and shingle or brick and shingle.

A laundry of the kitchen, fully insulated attic convertible to two extra bedrooms, and a third bath are

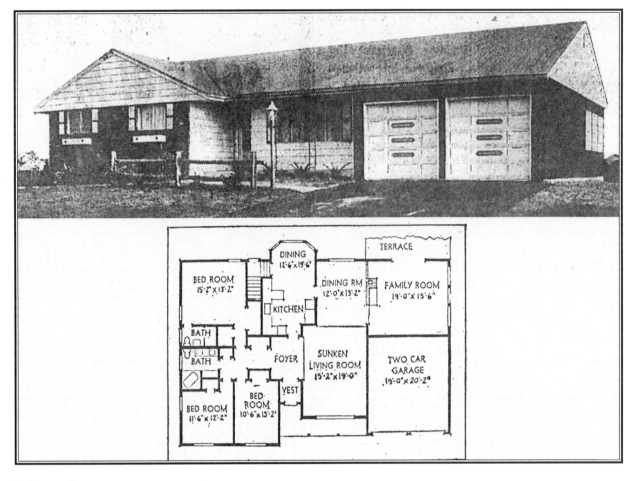

Primary Source

"94 Homes Are Set in Jersey Colony": Floor plan

SYNOPSIS: Some New York City workers settled in the developing northern New Jersey suburbs in homes such as this one in Saddle River Heights. This home was priced to sell at around $38,000. "94 HOMES ARE SET IN JERSEY COLONY." REPRINTED FROM *THE NEW YORK TIMES,* NOVEMBER 29, 1959, R6.

among other features of the houses, which are being erected on fully landscaped plots.

Primary Source

"94 Homes Are Set in Jersey Colony": Newspaper article

> **SYNOPSIS:** This article on new houses in New Jersey appeared in *The New York Times* in 1959. The house plan featured is uniformly boxy with few halls connecting rooms. Instead, the living room, dining room, family room, kitchen, and garage all open into each other, with only the bedrooms requiring any hall space at all.

Ranch Model at $24,790 Is Opened at Emerson— Other Developments

Ninety-four houses are planned at Overlook Park in the Oradell Hill section of Emerson, N. J., where

a ranch model with six rooms and two bathrooms has been opened to visitors. The houses are priced from $24,790.

The ranch model is on Munsey Road, off Soldier Hill Road, and has an exterior of cedar shakes. It contains a living room with picture window, a dining room with double window and a kitchen with wall oven and counter-top range.

The bedroom wing has a master bedroom with two closets and an adjoining bathroom with stall shower and two other bedrooms. Stairs from the living room lead down to a basement with a laundry area. The house has a two-car garage with direct entrance to the basement.

Washington Township

A ranch house with six rooms and one and one-half bathrooms is one of two models that have been introduced at Rolling Ridge on Cleveland Avenue, off Washington Avenue. It is priced at $23,990, and has an exterior of cedar shingles. A brick exterior is optional. The ranch model has a living room with picture window, a dining room and a kitchen with separate breakfast area and door leading to the yard. A split-level model with seven rooms and one and one-half bathrooms is priced at $23,490.

Norwood

A six-room ranch model has been introduced at The Glens, on Kenyon Place, off Tappan Road. It is priced at $22,990, and has a living room with a picture window, a dining room, and a kitchen with breakfast area. The kitchen has a wall oven and a counter-top range. A door from the kitchen leads to the yard.

Rivervale

A ranch house with six rooms, and a split-level containing eight rooms, have been opened at Rivervale Woods on Blue Hill Road, off River Vale Road. The rancher is priced at $22,490. It has an exterior of wood shingles and a covered entrance into a foyer with a guest closet. The split-level sells for $25,990, and has an exterior of partial brick and wood shingles. It has a covered entrance at garden level and a recreation room with a direct entrance to a two-car garage.

Linden

Twenty houses are planned in a colony called Edlyn Estates on a tract off St. George Avenue. A split-level model priced from $20,990 has a front entrance with brick planter, a ground-level foyer with guest closet, a living room with picture window, a separate dining room and a kitchen with dining area.

Ridgewood

Charles Baldanza, builder, plans ten ranch, split-level and Colonial dwellings on Bingham Road, off East Saddle River Road. The houses are priced from $32,900 and have three and four bedrooms, two and one-half bathrooms and two-car garages.

East Brunswick

A second section of sixteen homes has been started at Marc Ridge, a colony of forty-one houses in the Colonial and split-level styles on Rues Lane, off Route 18. A split-level model with eight rooms is priced at $17,990 and has an entrance foyer, large family room, kitchen with dining area and one and one-half bathrooms.

Further Resources

BOOKS

Donaldson, Scott. *The Suburban Myth.* New York: Columbia University Press, 1969.

Jackson, Kenneth T. *Crabgrass Frontier: The Suburbanization of the United States.* New York: Oxford University Press, 1985.

Kelly, Barbara M. *Expanding the American Dream: Building and Rebuilding Levittown.* Albany: State University of New York Press, 1993.

Whitford, Frank. *Bauhaus.* London: Thames and Hudson, 1984.

Wolfe, Tom. *From Bauhaus to Our House.* New York: Farrar, Straus, Giroux, 1981.

WEBSITES

Bauhaus-archiv. Museum of Design. Available online at http://www.bauhaus.de/english/ (accessed March 22, 2003).

Biography: Charles and Ray Eames. Eames Office. Available online at http://www.eamesoffice.com/resources/bio.html (accessed March 22, 2003).

"House Styles: A-frame Style." Architecture: About.com. Available online at http://architecture.about.com/library/bl-aframe.htm (accessed March 22, 2003).

"House Styles: Cape Cod Houses." Architecture: About.com. Available online at http://architecture.about.com/library/bl-capecod.htm (accessed March 22, 2003).

"House Styles: Ranch Houses." Architecture: About.com. Available online at http://architecture.about.com/library/bl-ranch.htm (accessed March 22, 2003).

"Laminate." Design Source Connection. American Society of Interior Designers. Available online at http://www.designsourceconnection.com/laminate.htm; website home page: http://www.designsourceconnection.com/index.htm (accessed March 22, 2003).

"1950 House." Shelburne Museum. Available online at http://www.shelburnemuseum.org/htm/museum/buildings_collections/buildings/1950s_house/fifties.htm; website home page: http://www.shelburnemuseum.org/index.htm (accessed March 22, 2003).

"Our Architecture Is Our Portrait"

Magazine article

By: John McAndrew

Date: January 18, 1953

Source: McAndrew, John. "Our Architecture Is Our Portrait." *The New York Times Magazine,* January 18, 1953, 12–14.

About the Author: John McAndrew (1904–1978) was born in New York and graduated from Harvard University at the age of nineteen. He became the architecture curator of New York's Museum of Modern Art in 1937 and completed his master's degree in architecture in 1940. For the majority of his career, from 1945 to 1968, he taught in Wellesly College's art department. After his retirement, when he learned that the city of Venice needed major architectural repairs to avoid sinking into the sea, he founded Save Venice, Inc. to preserve the city. ∎

Introduction

Bauhaus architecture was widely popular in both industrial and private settings across the United States in the 1950s. Its most famous architect, Mies Van Der Rohe, and his many imitators created buildings with large quantities of visible steel, rows of wide, open windows, and offices broken up by dividers rather than walls. In homes, Bauhaus was most often seen in the furniture; the kitchen chairs with exposed metal frames and practical unadorned seats were especially popular. The Bauhaus school of architecture produced works characterized by an anti-bourgeoisie attitude that led to stripped-down designs and an absence of ornamentation. Rather than contrasting one material with another, Bauhaus architects left base materials visible and arranged them into aesthetically pleasing designs.

In direct contrast to the spare, exposed nature of Bauhaus, was Frank Lloyd Wright's "organic architecture." Wright did not intend for organic architecture to mimic nature in its looks so much as in its function. He believed that architecture was like nature, an organic part of human life that should link people together within their environment and allow them to evolve. Thinking along these lines, Wright developed some of the most radical and controversial buildings of the twentieth century. With the popularity of Bauhaus and the overall tendency toward conformity in the United States in the 1950s, it might seem that radical designs like Wright's would have fallen out of fashion. However, Wright was a recognized master, and his individualistic architecture was highly respected throughout the 1950s and well beyond.

Indeed, taken together, the two forms, Bauhaus and organic architecture, were considered the essence of modern architecture by recognized 1950s experts like John McAndrew. Though Wright and Van Der Rohe got along well enough personally, they saw their designs as radically opposed to each other. The general public and even some architects of the era, on the other hand, used the two concepts side by side. A ranch home with an open floor plan a la Wright might be populated with Bauhaus furniture and might carry through with the Bauhaus ideal of minimal ornamentation. An office built in true Bauhaus steel would have rooms of Wright-esque proportions with Bauhaus dividers, rather than walls, to curtain the space.

Significance

Modern architecture appealed to businesses and individuals alike because it seemed both practical and economical. Buildings with large rooms lit by banks of windows and divided only by partitions offered significant cost savings to companies. Mass production of identical materials lowered production costs, making new homes accessible to average people, who were fleeing to the suburbs in droves. Most popular among the new home styles were ranches and cape cods, still seen today. When furnishing their new homes, many chose practical, economical, mass-produced Bauhaus-style furniture.

McAndrew is critical of mass production in his 1953 article below, considering it a detraction to the artistic value of modern architecture. But this same detail made modern architecture available to the average individual. Thus, mass production also guaranteed that the two main forms of architecture were available to the public, not just the academic and elite, memory of this country. In keeping with this, the new, planned suburban communities evolved, beginning in Long Island, New York, after World War II (1939–1945). In 1947, Levittown, New York—a community planned to provide affordable houses to returning GIs and their families—was opened to the rapidly growing house-buying public. It was comprised of houses approximately sixty feet apart, built from pre-assembled components onto concrete slabs in an assembly-line routine. Prior to the mass production of houses of the 1950s, few Americans even considered the possibility of owning a single-family home in the suburbs. Planned housing communities such as Levittown were a smashing success.

The homes and furniture built in the 1950s are still with us today, not just in memory, but in actual form, and not just as artifacts in museums, but as actual, functional pieces of our lives. Levittown itself still stands as a functioning community. Homes built in the 1950s, though many must be renovated to meet modern needs (particularly in the number of bathrooms they have) are still generally sturdy and habitable. Those metal-framed kitchen chairs remain enormously popular as furniture (though some have doubtless been turned into artworks). The modern architecture of the 1950s has had a lasting impact on American culture, and it continues to shape the designs of the new millennium.

Primary Source

"Our Architecture Is Our Portrait"

SYNOPSIS: In this article John McAndrew, a well-respected teacher and curator of architecture, first asks if modern designs will work for all types of buildings and if it will express anything unique about America. He answers "yes" to both questions, and later determines that American modern architecture is equal to the great architecture of other countries and eras.

A critic finds a valid expression of the energy and excitement of our business and technological skills in striking new buildings

Has modern architecture by now put down healthy roots and become a valid kind of American art comparable to our best paintings and sculpture? Is modern design suitable to all types of building or successful only in a special few? Does it express, as did great styles of the past, anything of ourselves and our particular world?

The exhibition of post-war American architecture, which opens Wednesday at the Museum of Modern Art, provokes such questions and suggests some answers.

The first question is easy: yes, modern architecture certainly has taken root. A big new sham-Gothic structure is a far more exotic rarity now than a big new modern one. In 1953 a good modern building can look natural almost anywhere in America; if it looks jarring that is not because it is "modern" or not "American" enough, but because it is simply not good enough. Now young architects design only in a contemporary vocabulary.

But although modern architecture has come of age, there are still many more unimaginative and sloppily designed buildings going up than admirable ones. There are not enough good architects to go around—there never have been, not even in the best days of Athens or Florence. And speculative builders cut so many corners that their styleless "ranch-house-type houses" come into the world and proliferate without benefit of any architect at all. However, one judges the quality of modern architecture by its positive accomplishments rather than by the failures of unenlightened builders.

In *quantity* there are more positive accomplishments among the many new houses than in any other kind of modern building. Since the war they have come to be accepted in nearly every community and are eagerly sought by bright young couples faced with the very problems of simplified servant-less housekeeping which modern planning has most successfully vanquished, the very kind of planning which is one of the qualities that makes a modern house a modern house. It is easier to generalize about such planning than about the whole design, but it is only by the whole design that we judge a house as architecture and not just as a "machine for living" or a "good buy."

The 25-story Lake Shore Drive Apartments in Chicago, designed by Mies van der Rohe, embrace "simplification, regularity and precision," important values in modern-era architecture. © UNDERWOOD & UNDERWOOD/CORBIS. REPRODUCED BY PERMISSION.

There is no modern "look" as standard as the regular ranch-house "look." Good modern houses are hardly ever mass-produced (which leads to entirely standardized forms) and good modern design is not a preconceived set of forms into which an architect fits the necessities of living, but rather a sort of ordering and enhancing of the needed elements to make them achieve new status as something which is handsome in its own right. The beautiful is largely made out of the necessary, and the necessary is very variable. The necessary is not a necessary evil or nuisance (as it has sometimes been in monumental styles of the past) but has become one of the sources or even integers of modern architectural design.

The variety of design in our houses makes them hard to classify. Most stand somewhere along the middle ground between two opposed points of view: the classic, intellectual or predominantly formal one (at its best in two famous glass houses, the Farnsworth House in Illinois by the leader of the trend, Mies van der Rohe, and the house that his disciple Philip Johnson has built for himself in Connecticut) and the romantic, instinctive or informal one (which finds its happiest expression in many of the houses of Frank Lloyd Wright).

Most good modern houses, for example those by architects as far apart as Breuer in Connecticut, Stubbins or Gropius' Architects' Collaborative in Massachusetts, Rudolph in Florida or Neutra in California, lie somewhere between these poles, finding their own particular equation between the simplified and not very formal way of living of most clients and some sense of order and clarity in the organization of the design. They often manage to achieve a classic simplicity of form and to imbue it with warm and even romantic feeling.

But while houses may be more interesting to more people than other kinds of architecture, it does not seem to this writer that one finds the most stimulating examples of post-war work among them. Despite the gratifying number of houses of gratifying quality, there are none to rival Mr. Wright's sixteen-year-old Fallingwater, a house as secure in its position as a masterpiece as any building of the twentieth century. It may well be that our latest masterpieces, if we have any, are not domestic, but commercial and industrial. Henry Russell Hitchcock observed a few years ago: "In America we house our machines and people when at work with a surer hand than we house them when they are at home."

For example, consider Eero Saarinen's Technical Center for General Motors. This laboratory for improving industrial products looks like a highly improved industrial product itself, improved in a way that lifts it into the realm of fine art. Its clean forms are marshaled with apparent logic into a clear and forceful statement, reinforced by strong dramatic color (rust, light blue and blue-black stand out against deep green glass and gray brick). The architect has not only displayed superlative common

sense in solving his immediate structural and functional problems (some of them of highly complex technical nature), and sure taste in the visible forms his solution takes, but he has somehow enlivened these forms with irresistible suggestions of the excitement of the mammoth machines in a power plant, of the miracles of precision techniques, of the mystery of invisible forces, and, above all, of the exhilaration of man's consummate expertness in dominating them and making them work purposefully. The neat industrial forms have been given a vivid dramatic content and one essentially suited to them. They do not represent something dramatic; they *are* dramatic in themselves.

Since the war, striking modern skyscrapers have risen in many cities. We are not now quite so sure that they are just what we want for almost any purpose in almost any place as we were in the Twenties, when they seemed the bandy and showy answer to so many boom building problems. We build fewer now, and we try not to put them up just anywhere, but only where they can be assured of a modicum of air and light around them (as Le Corbusier told us to do thirty years ago).

There has, of course, been technical progress: welding has made possible steel frames both lighter and stronger than before, and in Pittsburgh the first all-aluminum skyscraper has just been finished. Mr. Wright has built an extraordinary tower in Racine, Wis., like a great reinforced concrete tree, with a tap-root foundation, and a trunk (containing elevators, heating and plumbing) which branches out to support the floors.

Technical progress and modified building codes—glass is now allowed for the entire exterior sheath—have been accompanied by striking changes in design. The skyscrapers here illustrated all show a refining of proportions and simplification of all-over form far greater than in pre-war work; sleek surfaces are exploited and derive their rhythmical organization from the frames they envelop. Wrapped in its glossy membrane rather than encased in a heavy masonry shell, the new skyscraper seems almost weightless. We are so little concerned with the pull of gravity that no one seems worried to see the main front of the Lever Tower apparently unsupported. In fact, many think it should have been even more daring in order not to conflict with the horizontal sweep of the low wing in front.

Although we have been building them for a century, we have not developed any specialized form for the apartment house, but rather have borrowed the crate-like blocks of commerce as though we had thought it worth while to invent a kind of building for the conducting of business but not for the raising of families. For example, Mies' twin glass towers by Chicago's lake are really glorified loft buildings ("glorified" here in its real meaning). The bare essentials of construction have been single-mindedly purified into a glittering Platonic ideal diagram. Simplification, regularity and precision, all important esthetic means in modern architecture, may here seem to be dangerously close to aridity, or may seem a supremely beautiful exploitation of modern techniques, or may seem to be both at once. This is not a problem confined to this building alone, as we shall see.

All these skyscrapers have a great deal in common; they even look something alike. Not only highbrows but many middlebrows find them handsome and sense that their handsomeness is casually related to their expert construction and their general efficiency. Handsome, durable and well suited to their purposes—could anyone ask more? Surprisingly enough some can and do. Some want us to do more than flex our structural muscles and show off our technical swank. They seem to want what they often find in many of the great buildings of the past: an expression of man's ideals about himself and the world.

Is this to be found in our domestic architecture, greater in quantity and equal in quality to that of any country? To a considerable degree, yes. We are able to achieve forms which emanate ease and security, a beneficent spiritual climate in which we are glad to live and bring up our children. We can achieve a confident intimacy with nature, often by welcoming her into our rooms through wall-size windows. (In fact we sometimes even sacrifice some privacy in this way, as well as in our preference for large free-flowing spaces rather than smaller walled-in rooms.) We delight in the ease given by almost magic labor-saving machinery and easily cleaned sleek surfaces, and show our enthusiasm in trim and efficient-looking design even where there is no need for efficiency. A good house is really not only a group portrait of its inhabitants but also of their ideal of daily family life.

Is any equivalent expression to be found in our commercial and industrial architecture, in which we now lead the world? Our superb techniques, love of order and efficiency, even our liking for neat packaging can work together to produce unforgettable monuments characteristic of our time and our time only. When it was still new, Louis Sullivan said that the skyscraper should be "a proud and soaring

thing." Of course it really does not have to be: nothing in the soap or wax business demands it. But if the architect is going to make a work of art of it (and is fortunate enough to have a princely client who wants one) it *must* have some such quality.

This writer finds Lever House and Mr. Wright's Laboratory masterpieces, because they both go beyond a simple and handsome solution of their particular problems and turn their simplicity into clarity, efficiency into elegance, lightness into buoyancy, and thus somehow make a valid artistic expression out of something which is in itself not artistic at all: the know-how, energy and excitement of American business and technology.

Maybe this is a very limited expression, optimistically glorifying successful free enterprise and technical skill while ignoring the anxieties that beset the age. But it is almost impossible for architects to express feelings such as the doubt and insecurity that everyday's news makes it impossible to escape for very long. Except perhaps for some of Michelangelo's first architectural designs and some thoroughly unarchitectural Expressionist buildings of post-World War I Germany, major architecture does not seem capable of embodying such essentially personal and negative feelings.

Much new American painting seems to be disturbed by our present anxiety, but our architecture does not. Is there any valid reason why it should be? Painting can be, and now usually is, the expression of one individual's reactions, reactions of almost any kind. Architecture has to be a less individual and more social art, involved almost always with groups, groups ranging from the family or the business to assemblages for entertainment, religion or government. While individual despair does not seem to have a place in such buildings, the aspirations of the group can demand monumental expression.

Do the visible forms of its buildings express something of what the work of the United Nations means to free people? (Or do they seem merely, as the chief architect said he intended, to be a workshop?) Can a group of buildings express ethical aspirations so broad and deep? Once they could. Surely the Cathedral of Amiens is as noble and as moving as the utterances of St. Thomas Aquinas, and are not the great German baroque churches worthy companions to the lofty music Bach wrote for some of them? But now we seem to find that the offices of a soap company and the laboratories of a wax company are far more exhilarating—one can even say more poetic—than the buildings which could be meant to incarnate the conscience of the world. Granting that the last problem is as difficult as any a modern architect has had to face, is there anything in the nature of modern architecture itself which contributes to the difficulty? It is probable that there is.

Remember that the skyscraper was born of business needs for more office space for less money on less land, that the skyscraper evolved in a series of business buildings at a time which had a firm faith in technology as something which could give nearly everyone a better life if technology were given a chance. Our architecture really is a portrait of us, and it shows some clear characteristics inherited from the generation before the Depression. We have inherited the architectural vocabulary of their optimistic industrial civilization, and cannot force that vocabulary to take on quite different symbolic meanings. It is not just the United Nations buildings which seem to lack spiritual content: we do not build very many convincing churches either. We certainly cannot do everything, but we do do some things well. Architecturally this is a rewarding time to live in, perhaps more so than any time since the eighteenth century.

Further Resources

BOOKS

Blaser, Werner. *Mies Van Der Rohe*. Boston: Birkhauser, 1997.

Donaldson, Scott. *The Suburban Myth*. New York: Columbia University Press, 1969.

Drexler, Arthur. *Ludwig Mies Van Der Rohe*. New York: G. Braziller, 1960.

Jackson, Kenneth T. *Crabgrass Frontier: The Suburbanization of the United States*. New York: Oxford University Press, 1985.

Kaufmann, Edgar, Christopher Little, and Thomas A Heinz. *Fallingwater: A Frank Lloyd Wright Country House*. New York: Abbeville Press, 1986.

Kelly, Barbara M. *Expanding the American Dream: Building and Rebuilding Levittown*. Albany: State University of New York Press, 1993.

Whitford, Frank. *Bauhaus*. London: Thames and Hudson, 1984.

WEBSITES

"Bauhaus Architecture." Art and Culture Network. Available online at http://www.artandculture.com/cgi-bin/WebObjects/ACLive.woa/wa/movement?id=21; website home page: http://www.artandculture.com/about/index.html (accessed March 23, 2003).

Bauhaus-archiv. Museum of Design. Available online at http://www.bauhaus.de/english/ (accessed March 22, 2003).

Frank Lloyd Wright: Resources—Web Links. PBS. Available online at http://www.pbs.org/flw/resources/web_links.html; website home page: http://www.pbs.org (accessed March 25, 2003).

The Guggenheim Museum. Available online at http://www.guggenheim.org/ (accessed March 23, 2003).

"House Styles: Cape Cod Houses." Architecture: About.com. Available online at http://architecture.about.com/library/bl-capecod.htm (accessed March 22, 2003).

"House Styles: Ranch Houses." Architecture: About.com. Available online at http://architecture.about.com/library/bl-ranch.htm (accessed March 22, 2003).

"Frank Lloyd Wright Talks of His Art"

Magazine article

By: Frank Lloyd Wright

Date: October 4, 1953

Source: Wright, Frank Lloyd. "Frank Lloyd Wright Talks of His Art." *The New York Times Magazine*, Oct 4, 1953, 26–7, 47.

About the Author: Frank Lloyd Wright (1867–1959) was born in rural Wisconsin, but moved to Madison as a boy, where he attended high school. He spent summers on his uncle's Wisconsin farm. He left high school before graduating to work for the dean of the University of Wisconsin's engineering department. Wright took some courses in civil engineering at the university before leaving Wisconsin—at the age of twenty—to work for an architect in Chicago. He soon became a draftsman at one of the nation's leading architectural firms, which was known for its innovative skyscrapers, and rose to become its chief designer. He had gained considerable success as an architect in the early part of the twentieth century. Wright's success came at a high personal cost. By 1910, he found himself increasingly distant from his wife and eventually went off to Germany with a married woman named Mamah Cheney. Wright and Cheney then lived together at Taliesin, his famous home in Wisconsin, which he designed himself. In 1913 both Cheney and her two children were murdered by an insane cook, who then burned down most of Taliesin. Wright eventually married two more times. Along with being a prolific designer of residential, commercial, and public buildings, he was a writer and a teacher of architects, and had a profound effect on American architecture. Wright worked until he died at the age of ninety-one. Some of his greatest works, like the Guggenheim Museum, were built in the 1950s, near the end of his life. ■

Introduction

Frank Lloyd Wright was part of a group of architects known as the Prairie School, founded by his mentor, architect Louis Sullivan. This group rejected the older European models of design. Prairie School style houses, popular from the turn of the century into the 1920s, were originally designed to blend into a prairie landscape and usually featured low-pitched roofs, horizontal lines, and open interiors. Wright's designs had become popular in the 1910s and 1920s. He was gaining recognition as an architectural genius, but he was already moving on from the Prairie School group, whom he found cliquish and limiting. "Organic architecture," his own conception of combining form and function, became his guiding principal. In his designs, Wright took into consideration the site of the building as well as the times in which it was being built, creating a harmony among all the different human and natural elements.

Wright traveled to Germany in 1910 and published two books that changed the course of European architecture. In the teens, Wright began studying earthquake principles, and, having determined that a flexible structure was the only one that could survive such a disaster, in 1922 he completed the Imperial Hotel for a Japanese group. The following year, the structure survived both a fire and an earthquake. During the Great Depression, Wright wrote his autobiography. In the late 1930s, he began taking apprentices at the rebuilt Taliesin and in Taliesin West in Arizona, training a new generation of American architects. He was by then building houses in what he called the Usonian style. (The name Usonian was meant to conjure images of the United States.) In the 1940s, he began experimenting with arcs and circular buildings oriented to allow for sunlight in the design. He also developed the first of his plans for a museum to exhibit Solomon Guggenheim's collection, though wartime shortages would delay actual building until the 1950s.

Significance

Frank Lloyd Wright's organic architecture was in many ways directly opposed to the spare, exposed nature of Bauhaus architecture. Organic architecture was based on his belief that architecture was an organic part of human life and should be incorporated into society in order to link people together and allow them to evolve. His philosophy of architecture was political—he conceived it as the art of a democracy—and it was national, specifically American in style. It was also spiritual. Using his concept, he developed some of the most radical and controversial buildings of the twentieth century. With Bauhaus styles so popular and with an overwhelming trend of conformity in the United States in the 1950s, it might seem that radical designs like Wright's would have fallen out of fashion. However, Wright was a recognized master, and his architecture continued to achieve respect. Indeed, American architects were influential worldwide in the 1950s, and experts agree that Wright was the architect with the most lasting influence of the period. His use of "open" floor plans, carports, and living rooms contributed directly to house designs still in use today.

Two of Wright's most famous buildings were completed in the 1950s, when Wright was in his eighties. In

Architect Frank Lloyd Wright's designs created open living spaces, in contrast to box-shaped rooms that had prevailed until then. **GETTY IMAGES. REPRODUCED BY PERMISSION**

the early part of the decade, he began work on the Price Tower (1953–1956), a skyscraper in Bartlesville, Oklahoma. Normally more interested in works that stayed closer to the ground, like much of nature, Wright was posed with a challenge when designing a skyscraper. Thus, his natural inspiration came from the tree. He originally designed the building in 1929, as the St. Mark's tower, but it was not built until the 1950s. Wright's Solomon R. Guggenheim Museum (1956–1959) was designed with a continuing spiraling ramp wound around the inside of the building to allow the ideal setting for art viewing. The design was controversial, both because New Yorkers couldn't decide exactly what it looked like, and because its arcing shape contrasted enormously with the rest of rectangular Manhattan.

Primary Source

"Frank Lloyd Wright Talks of His Art" [excerpt]

SYNOPSIS: In this excerpt, Wright discusses his early days as an architect and describes some of his guiding principals, including organic architecture. He takes a dig at Bauhaus architecture, claiming that exposing the underlying structure of a building is "indecent exposure." He also discusses the process of designing the Imperial Hotel in the 1920s, defends the Guggenheim's revolutionary design, and affirms that architecture is art.

Around 1909, Kuno Francke, German exchange Professor of Esthetics at Harvard, heard of those Prairie Houses and he came to investigate. He saw one and got my name as the architect; he saw another and got the same name. Finally he came to the Oak Park studio and stayed three days. He felt something was being created which was being wasted on my country and he tried to persuade me to go to Germany. He told me Germany was ready for what I had. But I had no intention of going: I didn't speak German and I wasn't sure I wanted to work for the Germans. I liked my own people.

But nine months later the Wasmuth publishing house said they wanted to publish all my work if I would come to supervise it. The portfolio appeared in 1910. It changed the course of architecture in Europe. Europe was ready for it.

But the principles of construction that made the countenance of that architecture what it was, seem never to have been grasped. Louis Sullivan, "Lieber Meister," and I used to talk of it as organic, and this concept of architecture—both ridiculed and admired—was the result of these principles.

Organic architecture is distinguished from the facade-making which passes for modern architecture today, as you can see in our home, Taliesen West. Organic architecture believes in the destruction of what the so-called International Style has maintained as the box. We had a feeling that since the nature of social life was a profession of freedom, there should be a free expression in building. The box was merely an inhibition and a constraint. All architecture had been the box—a decorated box, or a box with its lid exaggerated or a box with pilasters, but always a box.

And the box did not fulfill the possibilities of steel and glass. Steel—the new material—allowed tenuity. Now you could make the building tough with tensile strength. If the idea was to do away with the box, here was the means.

There now came the cantilever. You could put the load under the center of the beam or you could reduce the span between the corners by moving the supports inward and leaving the corner open. In that single circumstance—what I suppose would be called engineering—came the opportunity to destroy the box. Now the walls could be merely screens and the corners could be knocked out. Man could look out of the corner where he had never looked before.

What could happen horizontally could also happen to the vertical corner. The essential nature of the box could be eliminated. Walls could be screens independent of each other; the open plan appeared naturally the relationship of inhabitants to the outside became more intimate; landscape and building became one, more harmonious; and instead of a separate thing set up independently of landscape and site, the building with landscape and site became inevitably one. So the life of the individual was broadened and enriched by the new concept of architecture, by light and freedom of space.

And another thought at that time was that the proper scale for a building was the human being, the human scale "Grandomania," as I called it then and still do, seemed intended to give man an inferiority complex; "monumentality" was so he could be reduced by the systems of authority.

But instead of understanding the principle involved in organic architecture, what went around the world was the corner window and the cantilever—without any sense of the release of space which had inspired them. Architects who thought they were modern concentrated on the box and the exposure of structure. Why should you always expose structure? I call it "indecent exposure."

Here, in the Larkin Building in Buffalo in 1904, was the first great assertion that the machine in the artist's hands is a great tool and will give works of art. But only if it is in the hands of the creative artist. The speech I made about the machine in 1901 at Hull House, pointing out the machine could be used for freedom and to emancipate the artist from the petty structural deceit of making things seem what they are not well. . . .

It is an interesting item that I, an architect supposed to be concerned with the esthetic sense of the building, should have invented the hung wall for the w.c. (easier to clean, under), and adopted many other innovations like the glass door, steel furniture, air conditioning and radiant or "gravity heat." Nearly every technological innovation used today was suggested in the Larkin Building in 1904.

The Unity Temple of 1906 was reinforced concrete. It was the first building to come complete as architecture from forms cast. The idea of the reality of the building as the space within had found tangible expression. I was quite pleased with myself in the Unity Temple. I thought I was prophetic and had made a statement bound to re-create the world of architecture.

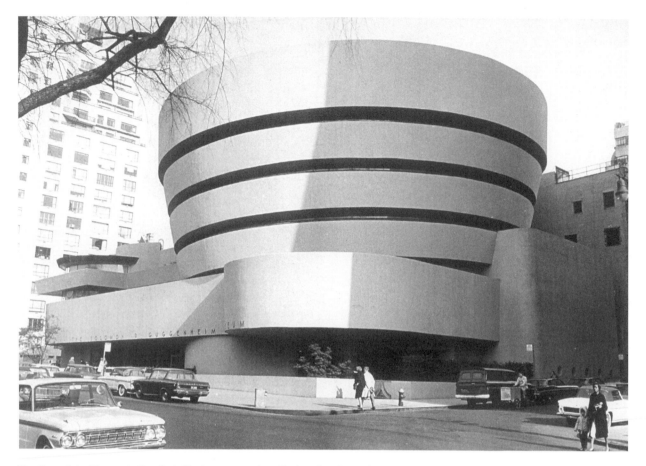

The Guggenheim Museum in New York City houses a premier collection of modern and contemporary art. Inside a spiral walking ramp surrounds open space so much of the museum can be seen from any one location. **GETTY IMAGES. REPRODUCED BY PERMISSION.**

The significance was the emphasis on what is called the third dimension. It is not thickness, but depth, a sense of space. All this added up to a new dispensation as to what might constitute the life of a building. It could parallel the life of the free individual.

What they call non-objective art—in Kandinsky and Mondrian and Leger—can be seen in patterns we designed for the Midway Gardens in 1912. Such as in this detail of a mural called "City by the Sea": But we had been making such abstract designs for fifteen years. This principle of design was natural, inevitable for us. Whether in glass or textile or whatever, it is based on the straight-line technique of the T-square and the triangle. It was inherent in the Froebel system of kindergarten training given me by my mother for I built many designs and buildings on the kitchen table out of the geometric forms of those playthings. Out of this came the straight-line patterns that are used today in textiles, linoleums and so on. But it grew out of my own limitations, by way of the T-square and the triangle and the compass.

Now in 1914 came an expedition from Japan looking for an architect to build their new Imperial Hotel. They came around the world by way of Europe and on their way to America they heard my name and knew the German publication of my work. They heard the name again and again in Europe and decided to look me up. They saw the buildings and said, "Well, not Japanese, not at all, but will look well in Japan."

Thereupon, I spent six years on studies of earthquake conditions. It never left my consciousness. And we solved the problem of the menace of the quake by concluding that rigidity couldn't be the answer, and that flexibility and resiliency must be the answer. So we built [a] building [that] could flex and return to normal. And it did withstand the great quakes.

But also for the first time in the history of Japan a foreigner had taken off his hat to her culture and tried to build with Western technology without losing what was precious and beautiful in her own culture. The Imperial Hotel had not only to withstand the

"Naughty Nautilus"

Build thee more stately mansion, O my soul,
   As the swift seasons roll!
   Leave thy low-vaulted past!
Let each new temple, nobler than the last,
  . . . Shut thee from heaven with a dome more
vast . . . .

       —*Oliver Wendell Holmes,* The Chambered Nautilus

For the better part of his 84 years, Frank Lloyd Wright, the grand, infuriating and tireless old nautilus of U.S. architecture, has built ever more amazing mansion, put ever vaster domes over such projects as a mortuary in San Francisco, a chapel for Florida Southern College, a laboratory tower for Johnson's Wax. When the Guggenheim Foundation asked him in 1945 to build an art museum for Manhattan's upper Fifth Avenue, he designed what might be taken as a monument to himself. It would be shaped, he said, "like the chambered nautilus." The picture gallery would consist of a quarter-mile ramp, slowly rising in a spiral to a height of 72 ft. where it would culminate in a huge dome.

The Guggenheim Foundation accepted his design (cost: $2,000,000), but New York City authorities prosaically declared that the museum would violate building laws: among other things, the building's 6-ft. overhang was against regulations. Last week Wright, who has described the building code as being "for fools," showed up at a hearing in Manhattan. He grandly agreed to eliminate the overhang, made plans to appeal the other objections.

Later, he explained his position: "Here is one floor for one building, going indefinitely up. There is no building just like this." It is "democratic" in design, unlike the "fascist" pattern of the usual skyscrapers, said he. "This building is neither Communist nor Socialist, but characteristic of the new aristocracy born of freedom to maintain it. The reactionary . . . will not really like it."

SOURCE: "Naughty Nautilus." *Time,* August 10, 1953, 70.

earthquake but also to be worthy to stand without annoyance and insolence in Japan.

There was the conviction that under modern conditions the telephone, the car, the airplane man must make use of the technological developments to make them a human blessing instead of a disadvantage. Even the detail shows Broadacres City project of 1932 as the expansion of humanity by way of man's own prowess. . . .

My father a preacher and a minister taught me to regard a symphony as an edifice of sound. And ever since, as I listen to Bach and Beethoven and Mozart, I have watched the builder build and learned many valuable things from music another phase of understanding nature.

And as a preparation for organic architecture a knowledge derived from nature, not only observation but constant association with the elements of nature well, these are the basis of an architectural education.

The first expression of the tree-like, mast structure was in a project for St Marks-in-the-Bouwerie in 1923. The skyscraper was indeed the product of modern technology, but it was not suitable if it increased congestion, which it inevitably would unless it could stand free in the country. There was one which was a feature of Broadacre City so these from the city wouldn't feel lost in that vision of the country, and the Johnson Tower is another such. But it was an idea that had to wait over thirty years for full realization. Here it is shown in a drawing at the bottom of the page. But it is actually being built now by H. C. Price in Bartlesville, Okla. The total weight of the building will be about 6.10 of the conventional structure of the Rockefeller Center type, due to the construction of cantilever and continuity. Now the skyscraper will come into its own on the rolling plains of Oklahoma.

The proposed new building for the Guggenheim Museum which you see in my drawing at the top of the page, is the latest sense of organic, architecture. Here we are not building a cellular composition of compartments, but one where all is one great space on a single continuous floor.

The eye encounters no abrupt change, but is gently led and treated as if at the edge of the shore watching an unbreaking wave or is that too fancy a phrase.

You ask what I would advise a young man going into architecture. Well in my new book there is a lecture I gave in Chicago in 1931 and these are the things I told him concerning ways and means.

To forget the architectures of the world except as something good in their way and in their time, not to go into architecture to get a living unless they loved it as a principle at work, to beware of architectural school except as an exponent of engineering, to go into the field to see the machines and methods at work that make modern buildings.

I said they should immediately form the habit of thinking "why" concerning effects challenge every feature, learn to distinguish the curious from the beautiful and get the habit of analysis.

I told them to "think in simples" as my old master used to say meaning to reduce the whole to its arts. And to abandon as poison the American idea of the "quick turnover," to avoid getting into practice "half-baked" and to take time to prepare even ten years.

The physician can bury his mistakes, but the architect can only advise his client to plant wines so they should go as far as possible from horse to build their first buildings. I said also to regard it just as desirable to build a chicken-house as a cathedral quality is what counts. And to stay out of architectural competitions, except as a novice and to beware of the "shopper for plans." In architecture the job should find the man. And to keep their own ideal of honesty so high that they would never quite be able to reach it.

What the American people have to learn is that architecture is the great mother art the art behind which all the others are definitely, distinctly and inevitably related. Until the time comes that when we speak of Art we immediately think of buildings, we will have no culture of our own.

Further Resources

BOOKS

Kaufmann, Edgar, Christopher Little, and Thomas A Heinz. *Fallingwater: A Frank Lloyd Wright Country House.* New York: Abbeville Press, 1986.

Larkin, David, and Bruce Brooks Pfeiffer. *Frank Lloyd Wright: The Masterworks.* New York: Rizzoli, 1993.

Levine, Neil. *The Architecture of Frank Lloyd Wright.* Princeton, N.J.: Princeton University Press, 1996.

Seacrest, Meryle. *Frank Lloyd Wright.* New York: Knopf, 1992.

Wright, Frank Lloyd. *An Autobiography.* New York: Horizon Press, 1932, 1977.

WEBSITES

Elman, Kimberly. "Frank Lloyd Wright and the Principles of Organic Architecture." PBS. Available online at http://www.pbs.org/flw/legacy/essay1.html; website home page: http://www.pbs.org (accessed March 25, 2003).

Frank Lloyd Wright: Resources—Web Links. PBS. Available online at http://www.pbs.org/flw/resources/web_links.html; website home page: http://www.pbs.org (accessed March 25, 2003).

The Guggenheim Museum, New York. Available online at http://www.guggenheim.org/new_york_index.html; website home page: http://www.guggenheim.org/ (accessed March 25, 2003).

"The Price Tower." The Great Buildings Collection. Available online at http://www.greatbuildings.com/buildings/Price _Tower.html; website home page: http://www.greatbuildings .com/gbc.html (accessed: March 25, 2003).

What Shall I Wear? The What, Where, When, and How Much of Fashion

Nonfiction work

By: Claire McCardell

Date: 1956

Source: McCardell, Claire. *What Shall I Wear? The What, Where, When, and How Much of Fashion.* New York: Simon and Schuster, 1956.

About the Author: Claire McCardell, a leading fashion designer during the 1940s and 1950s, was born in Frederick, Maryland, in 1905. She graduated from Parsons School of Design in New York in 1928 and began her career as a model and assistant designer in 1929. McCardell lived an active life style, traveling, golfing, and skiing and understood the need for a minor revolution in women's fashions. She came to be known as the pioneer of women's sportswear for forging lines of women's clothes that were comfortable and allowed for easy movement, while maintaining clean lines and a sense of fashion. She was also a pioneer in her rejection of European models of fashion, creating a uniquely American style of casual dress. Some of her most popular items were her wrap-around sashes, pedal pushers, and mix-and-match separates. McCardell died in 1958. ■

Introduction

Clothing designers in the 1950s catered largely to women, changing their styles annually to ensure that consumers would continue buying new clothes, even if the old ones were still perfectly serviceable. In the early part of the decade, fashion design was marketed with the rigid gender roles that were in place in the postwar United States. Although they had been temporarily included in the work force during World War II (1939–1945), society expected them to return home to their "appropriate places" after its conclusion. In order to maintain that "appropriate place", a women had to support several gender stereotypes, among them that of women as happy homemakers, and that of women having perfect figures. Magazines, billboards, and the television all showed women with hourglass figures, wearing perfectly tailored dresses, and cheerfully performing household tasks. Very few women maintained jobs outside of their homes, and society held them to rigid expectations as well, especially in the area of clothing, where they were expected to dress both conservatively and professionally, while still somehow maintaining variety in their wardrobes.

European designers (particularly Parisians) still heavily controlled American tastes in the beginning of the decade, as they had done since the nineteenth century. However, as the 1950s wore on, American designers with their own unique styles began to emerge. Most significant among these was Claire McCardell, who formally began her career as a designer with Townley Frocks in 1931.

Though she did train for a year in Paris, and though this influence was certainly visible in her clothing lines, McCardell's focus on the needs of American women dominated her designs. Particularly unique in McCardell's work was the way she avoided adding extra padding or understructures to emphasize the female form. Instead, she relied on the cut of the material to shape a piece of clothing to a woman's body. She believed women's clothing should be practical above all, but also feminine and comfortable. And, unlike many designers of the time, she did not consider these three goals to be mutually exclusive.

Significance

McCardell was unique among designers, American and European, in her focus on the average woman. Designing clothing based upon her own needs and instincts, and believing correctly that most women had needs similar to her own, McCardell chose not to mimic Paris fashion but to strike out into her own territory. Her clothing was reasonably priced and ready to wear. Recognizing the changes cars and airplanes had wrought on American women, she made clothing travel-wear resistant.

McCardell was in tune with the new social world that emerged after World War II, after many American women had temporarily experienced the working world for the first time. In the war years, when many servants went to work in factories, their former mistresses found themselves taking over the household labor themselves. The frock McCardell designed for them to wear over their regular clothing while working around the house evolved into her popular hostess dresses in the 1950s. Where French designers like Christian Dior displayed postwar lines that gloried in luxury and excess fabric, McCardell made her clothing practical and suitable to be worn by a woman from any class. She made denim into a dress fabric, used dirndl skirts to good advantage, and designed separates that women could mix and match to form their outfits. Where Dior's wasp-waisted look required many a girdle, McCardell's fashions imitated the look with the clever use of sashes and belts.

McCardell can be credited with creating the "American look" in women's clothing. Because she designed

for ordinary women and priced her clothing reasonably, it appealed heavily to suburban women. Her fashion line grew rapidly in popularity and influence, winning awards as early as 1943, when *Madamoiselle* awarded her its merit award. Her work inspired other American designers to resist imitating Parisian fashions and to develop their own creativity. Indeed, as the American look grew in influence, European designers began taking their cues from America, rather than the other way around.

Primary Source

What Shall I Wear? The What, Where, When, and How Much of Fashion [excerpt]

SYNOPSIS: In this excerpt from her book, McCardell discusses her concept of fashion. Where designers like Dior and Lauren focus on color and texture, McCardell's first concern is that fashion be fun. She states clearly that she wants her clothing to be enjoyed by real women who may have less than perfect figures. She says fashion is a matter of proportion, exploration, timing, influence, and choice that can be contradictory. She cautions readers to pay attention to their needs and audience, not just to what looks nice in the store.

"What Is Fashion?"

What is Fashion? What do I really know about it? And who am I to tell about it?

I who love some twenty-year-old dresses far better than the latest look. I who must nevertheless have new clothes, and want them, and look forward to everything that goes with them. The excitement of a new line . . . the feel of the right color . . . the eternal chances I know I'm going to take with material and texture and places and people—all mixed up with clothes. And the fun of it all.

Fashion should be fun and whenever I am tempted to take it too seriously, if I design something that asks for a pedestal in the Museum of Modern Art, I am tumbled down to earth by the blunt voice of a buyer: "Where would you wear it?" And mentally I applaud because I believe that clothes are for real live women, not for pedestals. They are made to be worn, to be lived in. Not to walk around on models blessed with perfect figures.

But to go on trying to find what Fashion is:

Fashion Is Elusive

Some people have it without knowing it—some people know it without having it. Consider the peasant girl who knows how to tie her kerchief. Consider the art student who doesn't—even though she's majoring in Fashion Design.

What you do with Fashion makes it Fashion. The right proportion, this much red, this much white, Fashion wouldn't want it that way—and the truly fashionable woman couldn't be that way. Everything in Fashion is *how much, how little,* not *too much, too little*–whether color or jewelry or fur or crinolines or the brim of your hat.

Everything in Fashion is also *when and where,* which will bear repeating in every chapter in this book. "I hate crinolines," I said passionately one day. Then I stopped to think. "I don't really hate crinolines. I just hate them in a crowded elevator in the middle of a busy day. And I hate them when they look uneven and sloppy—holding out a horrible fabric never meant to go over so much stiffness." If you try to make the current fashion work everywhere, it will defeat you. And instead of fun, it will be a worry and an embarrassment.

Do you fall in love with a dress just because it is shown in a glossy fashion magazine? Don't forget that a fashion magazine is more or less a dream book. Take a good look at the model who is wearing the dress. Can your figure compete with hers? Are you as impeccably groomed? Will your husband worry about the neckline? Where is *she* wearing it? In a fashion magazine! Where would you wear it?

Fashion Should Be Explored

And now having warned you to be cautious, I shall urge you to be brave. Look at new fashions and see if they can be yours. Test the way they fit, feel, look—how they are supposed to be worn—how you will wear them. You'll find you have enormous choice. Gingham and calico vs. satin and mink. Usually not to be mated otherwise—although jersey and flannel have been known to invite a satin touch, and silk often asks for a wool jersey sash. Temperament plays a part here. I happen to like black jersey and caviar. You may like black satin and caviar. Wear the fabric you feel best in. That's a number-one rule. (A small word of caution though. While caviar is both a lunchtime and cocktail hour delicacy, black satin is too dressed up for lunch.)

Explore Fashion and say No if you are temperamentally incapable of starting a trend. Wait for the first wave of big hats if you are afraid you might duck. But if you do decide to dare the "wild hat"— remember to hold your head high in spite of the whistles and giggles that may greet it. Later your friends will probably say, "You know, you were the first to wear it, and now everybody's got one."

Hats were a popular accessory for women in the 1950s. **HULTON ARCHIVE/GETTY IMAGES. REPRODUCED BY PERMISSION.**

You can also wait too long to buy a new idea— it may be "old hat" by the time you discover it, which can result in a very bad investment. Part of the fun of Fashion is the excitement of change. And Fashion isn't meant to be taken too seriously. Sometimes it is a whim, frivolous and silly on purpose. But if you are afraid of looking silly or *feeling* silly in the hat with the butterflies perched on the crown, the hat is not for you. Not even if it wears the label of a famous designer and costs enough to prove that Fashion is big business.

Even the Fashion magazines (whose whole reason for being depends on Fashion) are willing to wink at it. How often they show you its gay side, write about it with humor, pose it amusingly. A model vamps you with a fantastic umbrella or a provocatively placed mole. She is quite openly kidding Fashion. And Fashion can take it—even thrives on it. . . .

Fashion Is an Influence

You may set a trend, you may be a mouse, you may invest in smart clothes because of your job, or

"Tailored Classic" —Combed woven cotton by Burlington's-Mooresville. Sizes 12-20; 14½-24½. Blue, Pink, Lilac, or Green Plaids.

Accepted By **Fashion Wise Women** *Everywhere*

Bea Young

"Casual Charmer" Smart shirtwaist in all-combed lustrous finish chambray. Sizes 10-20; 14½-22½. Rose, Blue, Grey, and Brown.

$5.98*

"Trim CoatDress" —Lace trimmed biased bands in baby checked combed woven cotton. Sizes 12-20; 14½-24½. Pink, Blue, Red, and Yellow.

"Cardigan CoatDress" —Peg pocket sheath with silk hanky. In combed tone on tone woven cotton. Sizes 12-20; 14½-24½. Blue, Pink, Cognac, and Lilac.

* Prices slightly higher on West Coast

Photos by Leigh Charell

America's greatest dress values . . . styled in famous American fabrics!

See Bea Youngs on display at better stores everywhere. For the name of the store nearest you, call **Western Union Operator 25.**

Glamour gift . . . for giving or getting. Smartly styled with quality details and tailoring— cut for perfect fit—designed for every style and age. Every Bea Young is machine washable with less than 2% residual shrinkage. Generous hems for easy adjustability. For smart living from now through spring—make friends with Bea Young soon!

NECESSITY OF LIFE FASHIONS • product of SMOLER BROS., Inc. • CHICAGO, NEW YORK, LOS ANGELES, DALLAS

These Bea Young dresses were marketed towards women on a budget who favored the lady-like fashions that were chic in the 1950s. **THE ADVERTISING ARCHIVE, LTD. REPRODUCED BY PERMISSION.**

give up smart clothes because of your husband. But one thing you can be sure of: what you wear is going to influence your life and what others think about you.

Some people have the touch—they can absorb new ideas and make them their own. Others are lost and afraid. They don't even realize a change until it is two years old. Sometimes it is better to be a mouse, to fade into your own background. And you won't really envy the woman who dresses for instant recognition value because you like your own background best. There is a great deal to be said for the woman who *knows* what she should wear. Some jobs, some temperaments, some husbands, like the latest thing in Fashion. I think of myself as a continuous experiment, a testing ground for ideas. That's why you'll find a black peasant-cape in my wardrobe, picked up in the store in Paris where the peasants go to buy their capes. Naturally I don't wear it in the fields. I wear it over my ski clothes, to football games—and sometimes on a rainy night to the theater.

And now, perhaps, we come to the question of who am I to write about Fashion? First of all, I am a woman. Quite secondarily, I am a designer. Sometimes I am a hostess. Sometimes I am a guest. I have a job to go to. I have a market list to plan. I *love* clothes. I have loved them since the days when I cut paper dolls from the Fashion magazines, and I think the way the scissors followed the lines of Fashion had a great deal to do with my Fashion education.

I have seen Fashion as business.

Sizes—colors—buyers—models—salesmen—saleswomen—swatches—piece goods—stores—fashion magazines. I have also seen Fashion in action—how it looks when you move—walking, traveling, flying, hitting a golf ball, skiing and sailing. I have seen Fashion in tune with background—place, climate, occasion. And I have asked myself the thousands of questions that anything to do with Fashion will always pose.

What shall I wear? Where would I wear *that*? What is my size—and does it fit? Where is my waistline today? How short is too short? How long is a train? What color with what? Am I the type? Is anyone?

Fashion Lets You Choose

Don't try to live up to Fashion. First of all, stay firmly *you*. And if Fashion seems to be saying something that isn't right for you, ignore it. Make your own mixtures—in jewelry as in jackets. Don't try to be a type. Too often you have heard the word *type* and have tried to wriggle yourself into the definition. Pretty type. Smart type. Casual type. Arty type. Each implies overemphasis. And if you academically try to choose which is you, you are going to find yourself in trouble.

When pretty is too pretty, your audience is going to be conscious of flutter and lace and every-

thing trailing, including probably your overcurled hair. Too smart may be as coldly impersonal as a decorator's showroom where even the matchbox must stay in place. Overemphasis can be disastrous and true this much blue; it makes flags and it makes well-dressed women. The right combination counts. And you can't look it up in the dictionary. The right shoes, the right hat, the right bag, the extra color, the necklace or scarf—or the thing that made you think of it all. There are no permanent rules. A fashion that is here today may be gone tomorrow—and back the next day. But I can promise you that if you use your eyes, *train* your eyes, you will soon learn to recognize the woman with a sense of Fashion.

Fashion Is Contradictory

I hate anything that looks too new in a brassy sense—but I can't imagine not trying new color combinations, new ways to tie a sash, new hats, new angles . . . even new postures. Moving my waistline around—up, down—or deciding to have none at all.

Fashion Makes Rules.

Hems—by day, by night, when short, when long, in what year? And does eight inches or twelve from the floor look the same on all women no matter what shape they are, what heel-height they're wearing? Of course not. So . . .

Fashion Breaks Rules

Be flexible, it warns you. Keep a stern eye on yourself. Where do jackets end in the Fashion magazines? Where *should* they end on *you*? Waist-length, hip-length, finger-tip, tunic? Obviously something besides Fashion reportage enters into your choice of clothes. The Fashion magazines might not have mentioned the bolero—but this short little miracle that avoids the waistline is a wonderful way to disguise the less-than-perfect dimension.

Fashion Is a Calendar, a Clock, a Date-book, a Quiz Program.

Short gloves, eight-button, twelve-button—and don't forget the really long white ones for a ball. Fashion tells you which to buy for when, for where. What goes with what. But *why*? And who says so? The last question is important. People without a sense of fun, of dash, of whim, may misunderstand Fashion. If your maiden aunt finds a ladybug on the lapel of your suit unamusing, don't blame the maiden aunt. Blame yourself. You have worn the ladybug for the wrong audience. And how stern is your eye on yourself? Are you tea-dancing in the supermarket? Are you a secretary dressing like a siren? Is your mink a rat? Is your Hunting Pink really Shocking? Is your age *really* a secret? And are you by any chance trying to dress for a fashion-magazine audience instead of your husband? Beware if he says: "Well, who are you trying to impress tonight?" Stunning is all right—but who wants to be stunning if it's going to stun—not only your husband but everyone who knows you?

Further Resources

BOOKS

Buckley, Cheryl, and Hilary Fawcett. *Fashioning the Feminine: Representation and Women's Fashion from the Fin de Siecle to the Present.* London: I.B. Tauris, 2002.

Byrde, Penelope. *The Twentieth Century.* London: Batsford, 1986.

Dorner, Jane. *Fashion in the Forties and Fifties.* New Rochelle, N.Y.: Arlington House Publishers, 1975.

Ettinger, Roseann. *50s Popular Fashions for Men, Women, Boys and Girls: with Price Guide.* Atglen, Pa.: Schiffer, 1995.

Fifties' Fit & Flair: Dress to Sew with Three Neckline Options & Stole to Knit. San Rafael, Calif.: Folkwear, 1986.

Impey, Janet. *Style Made Simple: Fashion and Beauty Know-how.* London: Century, 1988.

Sichel, Marion. *History of Women's Costume.* New York: Chelsea House, 1984.

Yohannan, Kohle. *Claire McCardell: Redefining Modernism.* New York: Harry N. Abrams, 1998.

WEBSITES

"History of Fashion, 1950–1960." Vintage Blues. Available online at http://www.vintageblues.com/history5.htm; website home page: http://www.vintageblues.com/vintage.htm (accessed March 25, 2003).

Maginnis, Tara. *The Costumer's Manifesto—Costumes.org* [Online] http://www.costumes.org/pages/1950inks.htm (accessed March 25, 2003).

"What's Ahead in New Appliances"

Interview

By: C.K. Rieger

Date: February 15, 1957

Source: Rieger, C.K. "What's Ahead in New Appliances." *U.S. News and World Report,* February 15, 1957, 56–69.

About the Author: Charles Kreuger Rieger (1916–) was born in Kansas City, Missouri, and received an engineering degree from the University of Missouri. He was vice president of the General Electric Company (GE) in 1957, where he worked for thirty-one years. He was one of six directors of GE before leaving the company. He became the chief executive officer of a company called Ebasco in 1968. The company was voted out of existence the following year as part of a merger. ■

Introduction

One of the most dramatic and lasting interior design changes wrought by the culture of the 1950s occurred in the kitchen. Once simply a room for meal preparation, the kitchen became a center for new gadgets and appliances that changed its look dramatically. Time-saving technology was very popular; one of the key themes of the 1950s was "convenience." Having scrimped to save their money during the war, consumers of the 1950s were ready to spend a little more if it meant saving time. For a large number of people, the standard of living was increasing in the 1950s. Indeed, consumerism in this era skyrocketed, with the kitchen being one of the most popular areas for housewives to spend their money.

As many American women went from a working to a domestic role due to the return of the "boys from the front" at the end of World War II (1939–1945), stores and marketers recognized the heavy influence of women in household spending. Thus, many stores targeted what they perceived as women's desires, inviting them, basically, to buy free time by purchasing prepackaged convenience. From store-bought clothes, with trends the fashion industry changed annually to ensure that women would have to keep buying to remain in style, to household appliances, women were many manufacturers' primary targets.

In the advertising world, women were constantly pictured as nurturing homemakers who spent most of their time in the kitchen. Manufacturers found they could make a mint selling items to make Mom's life a little more simple and allow her to spend more time with her family. Some of the small appliances so popular in the 1950s grew out of wartime army efficiency. During the war, government contracts supported numerous small manufacturers, who then had to focus on public sales to maintain their success in the postwar period. Kitchens, in turn, changed in appearance as homemakers struggled to find a new place for all of their new gadgets.

Significance

Though household gadgets existed before the 1950s, they proliferated wildly in the new era of consumer culture, and manufacturers went to extremes to invent new things women would use. The dishwasher was among the newly popular appliances that drastically changed the kitchen. Dishwashers, though they existed before the 1950s, did not become fully automatic until

1940, and they weren't particularly efficient or available to the average consumer until the postwar boom in the 1950s. However, dishwashers generally had to be moved and hooked up to the sink to be operated, and they took up an awkward amount of floor space. Eventually, the search for efficiency led to dishwashers that could be hooked directly into the household water and sewer and located under the countertop. And electronic ovens, now called microwaves and found in most households, also had their beginnings in the 1950s.

When kitchen appliances could not be stored out of sight, manufacturers and homemakers tried to make them look more attractive. Companies like KitchenAid and Toastmaster developed color-coordinated toasters and electric mixers that, though they could not be hidden from guests, could certainly be made to fit in with the kitchen's color scheme. With the 1950s plastic boom came an increase in plastic kitchen storage. No longer was it necessary to store foods in glass casserole dishes. Now, you could store them in convenient plastic containers, particularly Tupperware. Indeed, the Tupperware company, founded in 1942, took off in the 1950s when housewife Brownie Wise combined the product with a door to door sales campaign. Her approach included the ubiquitous Tupperware party in which a woman would invite her friends to her home to examine and buy Tupperware items, for which she received free products. Then, she would have to attend her friends' parties and keep buying the product.

A woman shows that you can cook a 10-pound turkey in 25 minutes by using a General Electric microwave. © **BETTMANN/CORBIS. REPRODUCED BY PERMISSION.**

Primary Source

"What's Ahead in New Appliances" [excerpt]

SYNOPSIS: In this 1957 interview in *U.S. News and World Report,* GE vice president C.K. Rieger discusses the change in the use of the kitchen, with families returning to it as a gathering place. He comments on the potential for several new kitchen appliances, like the electronic (microwave) oven. He also considers the importance of electricity to the modern kitchen and the increased standard of living in the United States.

Generally speaking, Mr. Rieger, has there been a marked change in the kitchen setup in this country in the last few years?

Well, we think there is quite an evolution, which, oddly enough, is taking us back to an earlier day. You will remember that the kitchen used to be where everybody lived—that's before you had plumbing and central heating and all that. Everybody gathered around the stove in the kitchen. You even took your bath there.

And then as central heating itself changed the living habits—and better plumbing—everybody moved out of the kitchen. Many families today are at this point where you've got people living all over the house, and they have sort of left Mom out in the kitchen by herself. I think she has more or less resented it.

Then, I think, truthfully we manufacturers were a little shortsighted. We decided to make the kitchen a nice, clinical, sterile, white thing that was a little deadly, if you know what I mean.

In these last three or four years we have been questioning the housewife herself, rather than trying to make the decisions for her. And we found to our amazement that that's the last thing she wants. I think, as a result of that plus a couple of other things, there has been a terrific change in the kitchen, and the family is going back there.

Isn't that due largely to the fact that you have increased the number of appliances?

Yes, I think we have put in a lot of laborsaving devices, but primarily you have to give credit where credit is due, rather than to ourselves. I think a lot

A woman uses a mixer while creating a dessert. Mixers were one of a number kitchen appliances that became easily available to the American housewife in the 1950s. © BETTMANN/CORBIS. REPRODUCED BY PERMISSION.

of this change has been due to the fact that, with this modern type of living, the architects have begun to leave interior walls out of houses. They are beginning to let you see into the kitchen, you might say, rather than have it a room closed off.

I think another thing, probably, is the fact that servants are so hard to get. As a result, the housewife has to do a lot of this work herself, and has commanded a lot of this automation in the kitchen. This has hurried us along with such things as dishwashers and disposers and many of the newer appliances.

What have been the principal appliances that have really changed life in the kitchen?

You can't lay your finger on any one. I think possibly there are two or three that seem to be changing it. One is the garbage disposer, which keeps garbage from accumulating. You just grind up food waste as you go along and flush it down the drain. And there's no question about the dishwasher also having changed things, in this day of bigger families and more entertaining. It frees mother to be with her family and her guests more.

I think this electronic oven might well in the future make a bigger change than anything else.

What do you mean by an electronic oven?

It is simply an oven which cooks with microwaves and very rapidly. As an example, take a medium-sized four-pound roast. You could cook it in less than 30 minutes if you used an electronic oven, whereas it would take almost two and a half hours otherwise.

Hasn't the main value of the kitchen for many years been in the refrigerator?

That's right.

You know, we went out and asked a lot of women, "How would you like to hang your refrigerator on the wall?" and they thought we were crazy.

To be frank with you, when we actually showed it to women, they jumped at it. They said, "This is what we want." But we couldn't describe it to them in advance.

What do you mean by a wall refrigerator?

Well, instead of letting it sit on the floor and running up and down, it hangs on the wall just like a cabinet. As a matter of fact, if you would visualize three or four kitchen cabinets put together, you'd have a wall refrigerator.

We made a rather interesting survey and found out that what a woman really wants is to stoop down about 15 inches and never to reach higher than about 65 inches. And if you could put everything in that narrow band it would be ideal. But we didn't know quite how to do it until we started on some of this—just changing everything.

What about the freezing capacity of the refrigerator! Hasn't that been rather revolutionary?

Yes, it has increased tremendously and is greatly simplified. All of us manufacturers now put much larger content into the freezing compartment. For example, we have now a refrigerator that will hold 10 cubic feet of fresh food—that is just the regular part of the refrigerator. Then, where we used to have maybe 1 cubic foot of capacity in the freezer section now we have up to 5 cubic feet. It looks to us as if the trend toward more freezer capacity is going on up, too. You know we already have freezers with as much as 18 cubic feet capacity. There's no question but that this is growing rapidly.

Do you think this means the so-called freezer by itself will get less and less popular and the combination will be more popular?

No, I don't think so. Just the opposite, in fact. The combination has gotten about as big as you would want it and has about reached the peak of its popularity. We think that the upright freezer, which is designed to match the refrigerator in looks and make an attractive pair, will have a lot of consumer acceptance.

Well, has the effect of all this been to preserve foods for a greater length of time?

Yes, that's right.

Has it had anything to do with the preservation of the quality of the food?

Well, when you get down to zero or below, the quality is preserved much better than it is in the so-called old type of refrigeration, where the freezer section was just for freezing ice cubes and was certainly not for preserving foods for any length of time.

Actually, the main thing about freezing is the help it gives the housewife. She can shop once a week and freeze some of her purchases. She's encouraged to plan more diverse menus. She can make special dishes in advance of a party, freeze them, and then heat them whenever she wants. And frozen foods are a great convenience. You know their sales have tripled in the last 10 years.

"Creative" Cooking

What is coming in the future? What do you see ahead in the next few years? Women keep asking, "Is there something where you can push a button and leave a few instructions and then forget it?"

Well, first let's tell you what's not coming, and then I'll tell you—I'll make a guess on what's coming.

We have made some mistakes in the past as an industry. I think probably one of the worst ones we made was trying to visualize a so-called fully automatic kitchen. And we have been building along that line, but we have come to realize that the worst thing we could ever do was to use some device which by the push of a button would put out a meal. For, if you ever get that, all the meals in Mrs. Smith's house and in Mrs. Jones's house and all the others would taste the same, and I don't think people want that. Also, cooking ought to be a creative thing, and you don't want to take that away from women.

What we are trying to do is to eliminate the drudgery and yet not eliminate the individual from the kitchen. At least we think that's the way people will want it for quite a few years.

What do you see coming in the way of improved gadgets?

Well, let's look at it, product by product. As I have explained, I think electronic cooking will become important within the next few years. And I think

from there would come logical progress in combining certain conveyers, etc., maybe on a time cycle, so as to move pre-prepared dishes from the freezer into the oven for quick cooking. You might say it is an automatic meal, but always, we believe, one that has been individually prepared and put in the freezer to be kept for as long as you want.

Now, to match this I believe it is quite necessary to redevelop surface units which will go along with the oven, because it is not good enough just to have high-speed ovens—you have to have high-speed surface units with it. By that I mean the thing on which, for example, you would fry bacon or boil your vegetables, and so on. So there are a lot of advances coming in that.

Also, the important thing is to make them completely automatic so that you don't have to watch to see if something is burning. That the complete automatic surface unit is well on its way there is no question, and there are even a few on the market now, limited in their possibilities but still there.

New Place for Ice Cubes

Let's take refrigeration next—

We think that, in addition to the "square look" refrigerator as you and I know it today, there are possibly two things going to happen. One: We seriously question that a refrigerator is the proper place to make ice cubes, because you never use ice cubes in a refrigerator, actually. We think that someday the ice-cube machine, if you want to call it that, will come into its own and will probably use part of the sink combination, where it is used, when finally it gets away from the refrigerator. We think it should be made where it's used and stored where it's used.

I expect, also, there probably will be a third zone of refrigeration in addition to the freezing and the so-called fresh food, and that is a zone that will be—oh, maybe 32.5 degrees or 33.5 degrees, slightly above freezing, very slightly, and very humid, so that you can keep fresh fruit and vegetables for a long time. We are becoming more and more convinced that this is a complete new thing that should be coming along.

Now at present we are proud of the fact that you can put the dirty dishes under the counter and they will come out shining and clean, and so forth, but, very frankly, the dishwashers of today require some work. So I think the logical thing is to combine the garbage disposer with the dishwasher—put the two together and then you won't have to scrape your dishes ahead of time.

Has this been perfected yet?

Yes, it has. As a matter of fact, we started on it this year. This year's model has it, but I think it is only the beginning. The thing we are working on rapidly will not only do all of the hard work of scraping and cleaning and washing, which you can pretty well do now, but also automatically store them. Having cleaned the dishes, some of the housewives are now complaining that they have to unload the dishwashers. Well, we started to think about it, and we decided how silly it was, because this was a natural storage place anyway, so we are working on automatic storage.

Further Resources

BOOKS

Avery, Arthur C. *A Modern Guide to Foodservice Equipment*, rev. ed. New York: CBI Book, 1985.

Brooke, Sheena. *Hearth and Home: A Short History of Domestic Equipment*. London: Mills and Boon, 1973.

Frost & Sullivan. *Convenience Foods and Associated Microwave Ovens and Packaging Markets*. New York: Frost & Sullivan, 1978.

Leach, Margaret. *Freezer Facts*. London: Forbes Publications, 1975.

Lifshey, Earl. *The Housewares Story: A History of the American Housewares Industry*. Chicago: National Housewares Manufacturers Association, 1973.

Stout, Gerald John. *Home Freezers*. New York: Van Nostrand, 1954.

WEBSITES

"The History of the Refrigerator and Freezer." About.com. Available online at http://inventors.about.com/library/inventors/blrefrigerator.htm (accessed March 26, 2003).

"Who Invented Microwaves?" Available online at http://www.gallawa.com/microtech/history.html (accessed March 26, 2003).

AUDIO AND VISUAL MEDIA

Freezer Living—Freezing Techniques for Modern Living and Entertaining. Animatic Productions. Videocassette, 1964.

David Halberstam's the Fifties. History Channel: A & E Entertainment. Videocassette, 1997.

Christian Dior and I

Autobiography

By: Christian Dior

Date: 1957

Source: Dior, Christian. *Christian Dior and I*. Trans. by Antonia Fraser. New York: E.P. Dutton, 1957.

About the Author: Christian Dior (1905–1957) was born in Normandy, France. He began developing his fashion lines in Paris in the mid 1930s. During the early part of World War II he served in the French army and then worked for two different design houses during the German occupation of Paris. Dior began his own clothing line in 1946, backed by textile manufacturer Marcel Boussac. In 1947, he launched the "new look" of feminine luxury, and in the 1950s, he created the Y, H, and A lines. He died of a sudden heart attack in 1957. ∎

Introduction

In the early 1950s, many American women took their fashion cues from Europeans, particularly from the French. And no French designer ranked higher than Christian Dior. Dior began establishing himself in French design in the mid 1930s in Paris. His work was temporarily interrupted by World War II (1939–1945), but he was able to work productively in Paris during the German Occupation. (While many French cities were destroyed by the Germans, Paris was able to maintain a fairly normal business life.) Thus, he was prepared, at the end of the war, to launch his own clothing house.

His base of operations, 30 Avenue Montaigne, near the Champs-Elysées, quickly became known simply as "House Dior" as his styles achieved enormous popularity. Because cloth was rationed throughout France during the war, Dior's Corolle line wasn't launched until 1947, when restrictions were lifted. The line contrasted sharply with the difficult living conditions in France, focusing attention on luxurious femininity and featuring narrow, rounded shoulders, cinched "wasp" waists, and full calf-length skirts. *Life* magazine dubbed the Corolle line the "new look," and the moniker stuck.

In the United States, most women left their factory jobs and returned to lives of domesticity at the end of the war. Social mores of the era encouraged them to be homemakers and to maintain attractive figures. Advertisements featured women adorned in thin-waisted "house" dresses—sometimes even wearing the stereotypical strings of pearls—performing housework as if their lives were fulfilled by clean dishes and vacuumed floors. Few women maintained careers, and those who did so also adhered to strict fashion rules. The "ideal" woman of the time was possessed of an hourglass figure resplendent with curves at the bosom and hip. Thus, Dior's luxurious feminine designs, with their emphasis on the hourglass figure, appealed heavily to American women in the first three years of the 1950s.

Significance

Though the day was quickly approaching when American women would begin looking to American designers for their style, Dior was firmly entrenched as a respected fashion leader in the early years of the decade.

That his cinched waistlines required many women to wear a girdle was accepted as a fashion necessity rather than being considered unnatural cruelty.

In the 1950s, all of Dior's collections had a theme, the two most famous of which were the H and Y lines. The H line featured flat chested dresses with lowered breast lines designed to look pretty on small chested women. American women were not universally impressed. Not a few Hollywood stars were critical of the line, which contributed to some of the dramatic changes in Dior's 1955 Y line. Shaped like an upside down Coke bottle, Y-line dresses flattered the bosom and appealed to the same consumers who had been so taken, in the early 1950s, with his Oblique dresses and their asymetrical lines.

In 1956, Dior introduced the A line, also known as the sack dress, which was shaped something like the letter A, with the two sides angling out from the bust line. The A's were as unpopular as the H's had been, and did not gain popularity until the 1960s when, with slight modifications, Jacqueline Kennedy brought new life and popularity to the line.

Dior's significance lay not only in his specific designs, but also in some of his contributions to the field of fashion. Product licensing was unheard of in the late 1940s. Together with his partner Jacques Rouen, Dior pioneered this field to maintain control over his own line by only allowing it to be sold in places of his choosing. Today, product licensing is the sustaining practice of many design houses. Dior also hired a twenty-one-year-old designer named Yves Saint Laurent in 1921, who would go on to develop his own internationally acclaimed fashion line. Indeed Saint Laurent would briefly take the designing reigns in hand at "House Dior" following Dior's unexpected death by heart attack while in Italy in 1957.

Primary Source

Christian Dior and I [excerpt]

SYNOPSIS: In this section of his autobiography, Dior discusses the process of finalizing his lines. He first introduces the importance of which "mannequin" (model) is to wear which dress, and then goes on to discuss the importance of the material the dress will be made of. He explains how he chooses a particular fabric and suits it to a particular model.

Too often people believe that a collection develops in bursts of enthusiasm and caprice, without any co-ordinated plan. In point of fact, it is always built up along lines that have been established well in advance. Mme Raymonde draws up a complete chart of the collection on several large sheets of paper; she maps out space for a certain number of

Christian Dior does a take on the "little girl" dress. Puffed sleeves, a bow, and a thin, flat-chested torso give way to a bouffant skirt starting low at the hips. © BETTMANN/CORBIS. REPRODUCED BY PERMISSION.

daytime dresses, suits, coats and evening dresses. I force myself to reduce this skeleton plan to the minimum, knowing perfectly well that sooner or later we will break out of it. I try to be wary of the seductive pleasures of invention, luring me on toward fresh creations, for I know that certain materials and embroideries, which I have had set aside for me, will need new designs. I also know that there will always be some last-minute dresses. They are born of various impulses; in some cases I want to appeal to a type of woman or occasion I have involuntarily neglected;

A Dior dress with a plunging neckline emphasizes the upper body. Dior had stated that his collection of dresses catered to women of all shapes. © BETTMANN/CORBIS. REPRODUCED BY PERMISSION.

every country there are women thin and fat, dark and fair, subdued and flamboyant. There are some women with a beautiful *decollétage,* and others whose aim is to disguise their hips. Some are too tall, others too short. The world is wonderfully full of beautiful women whose shapes and tastes offer an inexhaustible diversity. My collection must cater to each one of them, and if I really wanted to satisfy them completely, I should have to design not 170 models but at least twice as many. Fortunately, the chart of my collection is there to keep me in check, even though it seems to be acting like a strait jacket on my imagination.

At last the moment has come actually to decide. The *toiles* which have been judged worthy of transformation into actual models have been classified, described, numbered and roughly sketched by Mme Raymonde. Now I have them paraded singly in front of me for one last time. The next step is to indicate which mannequin will wear which model, and the material in which it is to be made.

The dress and the mannequin are often as inseparable as the dress and the material. Of the dozen girls who present my collection, three or four can show anything to advantage. But for the others who have a more individual type of beauty, I have to be careful to choose models which will harmonize with their figures and styles. Yet I must reconcile this choice with the problem of simple arithmetic. For unless there are to be empty spaces in the final parade, each mannequin has to show approximately the same number of dresses.

Then, too, each girl must be given a balanced number of daytime dresses, cocktail dresses and evening gowns. It is obviously impossible to work this out exactly, and I am frequently made miserable during a show when I see a woolen suit parade in the midst of a series of more formal dresses, or a short evening dress in the midst of full-length gowns. The most successful model cannot stand up to such unfair competition.

And if the choice of mannequin is important, that of the material is even more so because, once chosen, it is very hard to remedy a mistake. This very important operation of choosing the material has several stages. Every couturier has his own work method; a few are inspired by the material to create their dresses but the majority proceed from a *toile* which has been cut from a sketch or from the designer's instructions. Personally, whatever the variety, beauty or novelty of the materials displayed to me, they are always a secondary consideration.

in others I want to underline some detail of the cut or design that I find insufficiently illustrated in the other dresses in the collection.

Even my most fanatical clients agree that there are always too many models in any one collection. They are absolutely right. A two-hour show without an intermission *is* far too long. Besides, it is always too hot in the salons. But though it is true that there are far too many dresses for each individual woman, you must remember that I serve professional buyers and private customers of vastly different needs. In

When work on the new collection is nearing completion, and the new line is definitely formulated, I do allow myself occasionally to be tempted by the texture, color or pattern of a particular material. I drape it in folds there and then, as long as I am convinced that there already exists a satisfactory basic design on which the dress can be founded.

My prime inspiration is the form of the female body. Since the female form is the point of departure, the art of the couturier consists of using the materials at his disposal so as to enhance its natural beauty. I have no wish to deprive fashion (and the ladies) of the added allure and charm of color, but I could perfectly well design a whole collection in black or white and express all my ideas to my complete satisfaction. Color cannot transform a failure into a success; it merely plays a supporting role in a cast where the cut is the star performer.

In order to relate materials to the general background of *haute couture,* I must digress a little. Two months before I even rough out my first sketch I have to make a preliminary selection. For that is when the dealers in silk and wool, the lacemakers, men who in the time of the French kings had the same privileges as nobles, call upon me. They come from all over the world, from Paris, London, Roubaix, Lyons, Milan and Zurich, and they bring with them the wealth of the low Countries and the richness of the Orient.

I await them with my two assistant designers, Mme Raymonde and my piece-goods staff at my side. It is like receiving an embassy. Rising to our feet to greet the ambassadors, we solemnly shake hands, and in order not to get to the subject of the materials piled up in the corridor too quickly, we chat politely about the preceding season. We recall the materials which have "gone well," and we tell of the sales of the models which were made from them, exactly as if we were friends imparting news of mutual acquaintances whom they have not seen for some time. Then the show starts, and each manufacturer has his characteristic method of display. Some, respectful of the great traditions of the past, are accompanied by a procession of seven or eight trunks which are carried in by bearers, like gifts brought from far-off countries by Oriental potentates. They are set down and opened; then with the deftness of a magician, the bearer spills out the multicolored pieces. I have before me a rainbow of colors, all equally tempting.

Others arrive with small dispatch cases, like peddlers selling their wares on the street. Out of them they prodcue tiny samples, often only the size of postage stamps, and one has to rummage to find treasure. In the spring, when the prints run riot amid the plain materials which are the basis of the collection, all this leads to a delicious confusion.

As in the world of dressmaking, it is the big firms that supply the best quality, color and design. The fabrics they put forward naturally influence the collection which is to come, but these fabrics have themselves been suggested by the past collection, so they insure the continuity of fashion from one season to the next.

At this moment I have no idea what materials I shall be wanting in two months' time. Paradoxically enough, this makes it quite easy for me to choose. Instead of hesitating between what I think will be useful and what I think I want, I am able to decide between what pleases me and what doesn't. I give way to my instinctive reactions.

Contrary to popular belief, a designer very rarely commissions a material from the manufacturer. Of course materials can be inspired by stray conversation between the two men, and by desires vaguely expressed several months before. For that very reason I am always very careful to avoid proposing precise themes, material or shades of color in our casual chats. For one thing, I am well aware of the impermanence of my own whims; for another, in such an essentially collective business as fashion design, I do not want to lose the benefit of the interaction of many different ideas and views.

It is from this profusion of materials which I have selected two months before that I have to make my first choice, in the interval between the display of the sketches and the emergence of the *toiles;* I go back a second time for the printed fabrics. First of all I eliminate everything which definitely does not please me and which is therefore incumbering the studio to no purpose. (The rest of the materials continue to submerge it with their mounting waves.) I then mark my favorites with a cross and have them put in special cases. Of course I know perfectly well that I shall find new favorites every day. Nevertheless, the foundations of my selection have been laid, and all these glistening, alluring rolls, dangerous by their very beauty, are now listed and catalogued by color and type and also, if possible, by manufacturer. They inundate my studio. They also illuminate it.

Surrounded by my staff, I now concentrate entirely on the problem of the mannequin still in her *toile.* Among all these engulfing materials, there must be one which suits both the dress and the girl. I have to resist many insidious temptations; sometimes it is the color which attracts me, sometimes the texture of the material. Of the two, the latter is the more likely to captivate me because I never choose a material solely because of its exquisite shade; it must have a texture that seems exactly right for the effect I want to achieve. Many factors have to be taken into consideration: the suppleness or the "body" of the cloth, the weight or the thickness. The material is stretched out straight and on the bias. It is weighed; stroked—for it must not scratch the skin; rubbed—for the dye must not come off; and examined in the light—for the color must suit the complexion of the mannequin who is going to wear it. How many examinations, such tests it must pass! But none is useless, because in the long run the form of a model will depend almost as much on the way the fabric behaves as on the cut itself.

There are probably eight or nine of us together in the studio. Facing me is a lone mannequin in white muslin standing in front of a large mirror; behind me are two designers. Mme Raymonde with the help of Claude, her assistant, is busy hunting for the material most nearly corresponding to my scarcely formulated desire. Mme Marguerite is supposed to remain at my side, but cannot sit still on her chair. Unable to mask her impatience, she runs up and down between the model and the seat to which I keep recalling her. Next to the mannequin stands the *première* or the tailor who is responsible for making the *toile*. In a corner stands Jeanine, nicknamed "Boutonnette," who is in charge of accessories (her hour has not yet come), and Frontine, pencil in air, ready to make out cutting tickets for the piece-goods department. From time to time Mme Bricard emerges from her hatboxes, sails in magnificently, gives one definitely adverse comment, condemns an unfortunate fabric with a look, or suddenly plumps for a daring color.

But most of the time this ritual, which would baffle an outsider, consists of choosing from among thirty black woolen materials, of excellent quality, the only one that is really right. As I hesitate between the rival claims of the various wools submitted to me, and try to get an idea, the pieces of material are draped over the shoulder of the mannequin, so that I can judge the softness and fall, in relation to the *toile* which is still visible on the other shoulder.

Certain combinations are obviously unsuitable.

"Oh, no—take that away at once."

And I point to another piece. This one, instead of immediately sliding off the mannequin's bust, stays there. We all look at it. Does it really suit her? It certainly seems to. . . . But after all, perhaps not. So I ask anyone at random "What do *you* think of it?"

They all know perfectly well that I don't really want to hear their opinion, and so they hardly bother to give me a serious reply. All the same, their mere presence is of assistance to me. A reply, whatever it is, crystallizes my doubts. I press them further: "And you, Boutonnette, what do *you* think of it?"

Boutonnette nods her head without committing herself; then it is Claude's turn, and in this way the whole room joins in, from Mme Marguerite down to the mannequin, who, as the debate continues, begins to feel the first prickings of fatigue. The choice is made at the price of universal tension. It needs only the indifference of one person to destroy the whole climate of passionate collective concentration. Sometimes the decision is made almost at once; sometimes there are dozens of false tries. In the end, we may revert to something we had previously dismissed as hopeless, after rummaging among the discarded pieces of material. Wretched fabric! Once again it is draped, redraped, examined and reexamined. It is never manipulated by the same hand twice; a dozen hands are there to wreak their will upon it.

Further Resources

BOOKS

Dior, Christian. *Talking About Fashion.* New York: Putnam, 1954.

Giroud, Françoise, and Sacha Van Dorssen. *Dior: Christian Dior, 1905–1957.* New York: Rizzoli, 1987.

Keenan, Brigid. *Dior in Vogue.* New York: Harmony Books, 1981.

Martin, Richard, and Harold Koda. *Christian Dior.* New York: Metropolitan Museum of Art, 1996.

Pochna, Marie France. *Christian Dior: The Man Who Made the World Look New.* New York: Arcade Publishing, 1996.

WEBSITES

"A-line dress." Yesterdayland. Available online at http://www.yesterdayland.com/popopedia/shows/fashion/fa1013.php; website home page: http://www.yesterdayland.com/ (accessed March 20, 2003).

Benaïm, Laurence. "The Great Names of Haute Couture: Christian Dior." Label France N°23. Available online at http://www.france.diplomatie.fr/label_france/ENGLISH/DOSSIER/MODE/dio.html; website home page: http://www.france.diplomatie.fr/label_france/ENGLISH/INDEX/i23.html (accessed March 20, 2003).

Krebs, Jost. "Christian Dior: The Most Recognized Name in Fashion." Available online at http://www.unibw-muenchen

.de/campus/WOW/v1041/hyper/dior.html (accessed March 20, 2003).

"1950s Glamour: Dior's New Look of 1947." Fashion-era.com. Available online at http://www.fashion-era.com/1950s _glamour.htm#Dior's%20New%20Look%201947; website home page: http://www.fashion-era.com (accessed March 20, 2003).

"Pretty Way To Go"
Magazine advertisement

By: Revlon

Date: April 1958

Source: Revlon. "Pretty Way to Go." Printed in *Mademoiselle*, April 1958, 156.

About the Organization: Founded in 1932, the Revlon Company achieved rapid success despite the poor economy nationwide. The company, named by combining the last name of founders Charles and Joseph Revson with the "L" from founder Joseph Lachman's name, began with only one product: a nail enamel. The company quickly expanded into cosmetics, skin care, fragrance, and personal care. By the 1950s Revlon had added television advertising to its corporate agenda. In the 1960s, the company began international marketing. After a change in ownership in the 1980s, it still holds formidable influence in the fashion world in the early 2000s. ■

Introduction

A discussion of fashion in 1950s America would be incomplete unless it included the ultimate fashion accessory—makeup. Hardly new to the era, women's cosmetics nonetheless took on a new life in the consumer market that followed the end of World War II (1939–1945). As clothing, appliance, and even home designers heavily targeted female consumers—especially housewives—the path was already paved for the cosmetics industry to attract women to its counters.

Even before the 1950s brought consumerism to American culture in full force, most women owned some sort of cosmetics. Even poor working girls could afford a little bit of perfume before the Great Depression. In the 1950s, cosmetic surgery was still rarely performed, even on the rich and famous, and there was every danger of its leaving obvious scars. This meant women of the era had to hide their imperfections. Makeup was the ultimate concealer, the best way for a woman to hide skin flaws and blemishes.

Like most things in the 1950s in America, conformity to the standard was at the core of the pervasive concept of beauty. Women were expected to have hourglass figures and movie star faces. As sitcom moms Donna

Reed and June Cleaver trotted around their homes in high heels, many American women tried to imitate the look, from dress to hairstyle. Cosmetic companies thrived (and still thrive) on women's desires to look like the stars, and most companies carried ads implying that their product could transform any girl into a starlet.

Significance

Seeing beautiful stars on television wasn't the only thing that motivated women to purchase cosmetics. With the advent of television, cosmetic companies had a highly effective medium to advertise their products, which they invariably did by using beautiful models. If 1950s makeup ads weren't all selling sex, as most do today, they *were* selling the idea that beauty can be purchased. (In fact, in the following advertisement, Revlon says beauty can bought in a bag and that Revlon, specifically, makes that bag.) Many print ads in the 1950s were created to look like magazine articles. Where such ad/articles today are required to carry fairly prominent disclaimers, there were no such expectations in the 1950s, and the unwary consumer might well have mistaken the Revlon ad below for just another of *Mademoiselle's* fashion articles.

Cosmetics manufacturers also developed a new tactic in the 1950s, with many of them releasing their new colors to coincide with (not to mention harmonize with) seasonal clothing fashions. As the clothing fashion industry boomed in the 1950s, this practice helped makeup companies thrive as well.

Where cosmetics today often come in sleek cases with appealing shapes, cosmetic bottles of the 1950s were oddly ungainly. Though some products came in shapes implying, for example, a woman with an hourglass figure, most containers were merely practical, designed only to hold and dispense the product.

The attitudes about women's beauty fostered by fashion attitudes of the 1950s are still with us today. Makeup companies, clothing designers, and the entertainment industry still promote the ideal of a skinny, blemish-free woman-child. If anything, even as women have increasingly joined the work force and worked for equal rights, the standard images of beauty in cosmetics marketing—with anorexic models and the selling of sex—have become even more extreme.

Primary Source

"Pretty Way to Go"

SYNOPSIS: This Revlon advertisement appeared in *Mademoiselle* magazine in 1958, thinly veiled as an informative article. The text carries two implied messages. First, the ad implies that by buying Revlon's line of cosmetics, the average woman can be as

MARILYN MONROE
In 20th Century Fox Production
"RIVER OF NO RETURN"
CinemaScope. Color by Technicolor.

WESTMORE brings you...

"CLOSE-UP PERFECT" complexion beauty

Proved in giant-screen close-ups by movie stars...

WESTMORE
Tru-Glo
liquid make-up
'59¢*

Wonderful Tru-Glo all-day make-up shows how smoothly alluring your complexion can be! PROVED by movie stars in giant-screen close-ups where make-up must be perfect to keep skin looking perfectly smooth, lines and imperfections invisible.

Because others see you in close-up always, you need Tru-Glo to look your loveliest. Made for you and movie stars

by the Westmore brothers, world's most famous make-up artists, originators of liquid make-up.

SEE the thrilling difference on your skin: Simply dot on creamy Tru-Glo, blend in evenly, pat off with tissue. Now you have "close-up perfect" complexion beauty, possible only with Tru-Glo! For all types of skin—in a perfect-for-YOU shade. Get Westmore Tru-Glo now!

WESTMORE
Party Puff
creamy powder make-up

FOR INSTANT BEAUTY, carry Party Puff as movie stars do on the set, at play and evenings. Powder and base all-in-one, in gorgeous mirror compact with puff. Choose the perfect-for-YOU shade.

$1*

WESTMORE
Kiss-Tested lipstick

PROVED BEST in movie close-ups where lipstick MUST NOT SMEAR, even after kissing, eating, working under hot lights. Non-drying! Perfect-for-YOU shades.

59¢* and 29¢*

At all variety and drug stores.
Prices plus tax. Slightly higher in Canada
House of Westmore, Inc., New York 11 • Hollywood

Tru Glo makeup markets its foundation and lipsticks to those who may have admired Marilyn Monroe's clear complexion while at the movies. THE ADVERTISING ARCHIVE, LTD. REPRODUCED BY PERMISSION.

"cute tomata"!
by CUTEX

NEW...the FRESHEST, RIPEST RED ever Cultivated...
Prettiest Pick for Lips and Fingertips!

Warning to bachelors! Here comes the gayest, brightest, cutest breath of spring that ever breezed into town! It's *YOU* ... flaunting this season's fresh and flirty new red ..."CUTE TOMATA" by Cutex ...

a stop, look and whistle red ...
that's just your dish for spring!

Separates by
Cole of California;
Fabric by A.B.C.;
Look for "Cute Tomata"
fashions when you shop!

Help Yourself to "Cute Tomata"... in
Chip-Pruf Cutex, America's best-wearing nail polish, 25¢
Pearl Cutex, new iridescent polish—the last word in luxury, 39¢
Cutex Stay Fast, creamiest, longest-lasting lipstick ever created, 59¢
Cutex Duo Vanity Stand with Pearl Cutex and Stay Fast Lipstick, 98¢.

Prices plus tax

Cutex advertises their new tomato red nail polish. THE ADVERTISING ARCHIVE, LTD. REPRODUCED BY PERMISSION.

beautiful and look as young as a nineteen-year-old-ballerina. A second implication is that beauty comes in a bag (the "Celebrity bag"), and that only Revlon sells that bag.

A Word About Beauty

Looks like a heap to carry, does it not? That line-up below of the beauty-makers prescribed by Revlon for Susan Borree's five-month European tour with the American Ballet Theatre.

But everything's *needed*. What's more, everything will fit—with space to spare—into the snappy Celebrity Air Flite bag

Some of the preparations have been transferred to the bubble-weight containers that are such an intelligent part of this cosmetic case. Others travel as is, being either already in lightweight plastic containers or—like the aerosols of hair spray and cologne—nontransferable. Extra bottles, jars and even spray-topped containers of polyethylene are available separately if Susan should want or need more.

All twelve of the American Ballet Theatre troupe of young dancers were, like Susan, skin-analyzed and "color-cast" by the Revlon expert. All have similar bags to carry their beauty loot.

Prescribed for Susan's nineteen-year-old skin, part-dry, part-oily: White Sable cleanser; Liquid Asset (an aci-alkaline "balancer"); Moondrops Moisture Balm; Aquamarine Lotion for hands and all over.

For freshness, skin-and-hair division: Aquamarine soap, lotion deodorant, talc, shampoo and Spray Mist Eau de Cologne Forte.

For warming her fair, slightly pale complexion, the shade Creamy Peach. This in Touch and Glow foundation, loose and pressed powder.

For lips, three color families to alternate as tenants of a silvery Futurama case: Pink Vanilla, Orange Flip, Say It with Rubies. And to glow the cheeks, a tint-hint of Coral Orange liquid rouge. On hand, one shade only—it agrees with simply everything, that delicacy of color, Pink Platinum Nail Enamel.

For Susan's eyes (blue), dark brown eyebrow pencil and—to deepen as well as darken—dark brown eye-liner. Two shades of Frosted eye shadow, blue and green. Mascara, black. And for her more glittery evenings, Revlon gave Susan mascara and eye-liner in blue and green.

The line-up below shows almost all of her Revlon goodies. (A few were added after these had had their picture taken—lip brush, orange sticks, nail-enamel remover, extra eye make-up.) That all, and very much

more, will fit more easily into her Celebrity bag than they do on our page. And since the case travels over her arm, she can keep suitcase space and weight down (her luggage weighed in several pounds *below* the maximum of 44). Light-footed traveling, this is, and a pretty way to get off the ground.

Further Resources

BOOKS
Brownmiller, Susan. *Femininity.* New York: Simon and Schuster, 1984.

De Castelbajac, Kate, Nan Richardson, and Catherine Chermayeff. *The Face of the Century: 100 Years of Makeup and Style.* New York: Rizzoli, 1995.

Eaton, Ann, M.C. Dip, and F. Openshaw. *Cosmetic Makeup and Manicure: The Art and the Science.* Harlow, Essex, England, 1988.

Friday, Nancy. *The Power of Beauty.* New York: HarperCollins Publishers, 1996.

Hansen, Joseph, and Evelyn Reed. *Cosmetics, Fashions, and the Exploitation of Women.* New York: Pathfinder Press, 1986.

Peiss, Kathy Lee. *Hope in a Jar: The Making of America's Beauty Culture.* New York: Metropolitan Books, 1998.

WEBSITES
Madrano, Autumn. "A Colorful History." Available online at http://influx.uoregon.edu/1999/makeup/history.html (accessed March 27, 2003).

Interior Design

Room Setting for a Child's Room; Room Setting at the Design Center for Interiors

Photographs

By: AP/Wide World

Date: May 28, 1959; June 25, 1959

Source: Room Setting for a Child's Room. May 28, 1959; Room Setting at the Design Center for Interiors, New York. June 25, 1959. AP/Wide World Photos. Available online at http://www.apwideworld.com (accessed March 27, 2003). ■

Introduction

Interior design was, in the 1950s, a new concern for the average individual. Prior to the decade, a lack of money and supplies had limited the way most people organized their houses. During the Great Depression in the 1930s, few had the funds to worry about the organization of furniture or the coloration of rooms and during

Primary Source

Room Setting for a Child's Room

SYNOPSIS: These images exhibit both the strong Bauhaus leaning of furniture in the 1950s and the era's focus on practical items. This room setting for a child's room from the 1950s exhibits the popular Bauhaus style of the decade, and its emphasis on practical items. The room is designed for attractiveness and ease of care—all of the furniture is washable, the round table and floor being spill-proof. The table and floor are covered with wedges of multi-colored vinyl. The sliding doors of the hanging cabinet are cane on one side, yellow on the other. AP/WIDE WORLD PHOTOS. REPRODUCED BY PERMISSION.

Primary Source

Room Setting at the Design Center for Interiors

SYNOPSIS: A Bauhaus style room setting at the Design Center for Interiors in New York. Black table and three cane back chairs in an ebony finish; white leather chair and sofa, white tables, and rug. The painting on the rug on the wall is a stylized crown motif in gold, white and grey. Room setting by Everett Brown, who designed the rug for Edward Fields. AP/WIDE WORLD PHOTOS. REPRODUCED BY PERMISSION.

"How to Give Tiny Rooms Extra Inches"

How to make a single small room function well twenty-four hours a day is a problem that faces many New Yorkers. That this can be achieved—and attractively—is demonstrated by a series of furnished one-room apartments just completed at 415 East Sixty-fourth Street.

The apartments are in a fifty-year-old building originally designed as a low-cost private housing project. The project received commendation when it was built because an unexpectedly large number of tiny rooms were crammed into a small area. But because today's preference is for fewer rooms and larger ones, the inside of the building has been "gutted" and most non-structural partitions removed.

The design and furnishings of the apartments in this renovated building provide a series of lessons that homemakers faced with limited space may adapt to their own use. Emily Malino executed both the interior design and decoration.

Elimination of doors wherever possible is one way to add usable space. Closets, for example, have sliding panels because ordinary doors often interfere with a chest placed directly next to a closet. Kitchens are hidden from sight by devices other than doors: Venetian blinds in some cases, in others a new metal folding door that works like an accordion.

All the furniture is modern. Much of it is Scandinavian in design, not a surprising fact when one remembers the small living-bedrooms typical of Denmark and Sweden. There is a judicious use of metal-based pieces, both black and white, a type of furniture that looks lighter than wood because it has less bulk.

The sofa beds are foam-rubber slabs placed on wood bases that are raised off the floor several inches, a device that makes a room look larger because the entire floor area is exposed to the eye.

Coffee tables in front of the sofa beds have been avoided. Instead, there are extremely commodious end tables, many of them with glass tops and cane shelves, two materials with a clean, airy look. Lighting fixtures attached to the ceiling over tables, or affixed to the wall over sofas, eliminate the need for extra lamps, which would clutter up the room.

Shelves and storage units hung on the walls save floor space. Plain wall-to-wall carpeting, and simple ceiling-to-floor draperies at the windows, enhance the illusion of serenity and size.

Color adds interest to the simple décor. Miss Malino has used three color schemes: one based on orange, another on yellow, a third on an intense clear blue. In each case the bright color is used for one or two walls, for plastic surfaces in the kitchen, for pillows, for one chair seat, possibly for a single modern lacquered chest. The draperies repeat the brilliant color, usually in a widely spaced print on sheer white.

SOURCE: Pepis, Betty. "How to Give Tiny Rooms Extra Inches." *The New York Times*, July 6, 1955, 22.

World War II (1939–1945) supply rationing restricted attempts to update homes. After the war, however, people began to spend their wartime savings on their own homes.

Several changes at the end of World War II fostered an intense interest in home furnishings and interior design among middle-class Americans. First and foremost was the relative prosperity enjoyed nationwide. Second, many companies that had been fully occupied fulfilling their government contracts during the war were compelled to shift their interests back to the private sector. These companies needed to market heavily to the public in order to continue the level of success they had achieved during the war. Third, white middle-class people were moving to the suburbs in droves, where they had new homes to decorate and arrange. Women, many having returned to roles as homemakers after holding jobs and working in factories during the war, were largely responsible for organizing and arranging their new dwellings.

Television's influence played an enormous role in how homes looked, with sitcom moms June Cleaver (*Leave It to Beaver*) and Donna Reed dominating the airwaves and exhibiting their own perfect homes (while they vacuumed in strings of pearls). Stores extended credit lines and allowed people to pay in installments, further extending families' ability to furnish their homes.

Significance

And what did they choose? By and large, houses were furnished along Bauhaus lines. American homes constructed in the 1950s had lot of open space. In the name of open space, and heavily influenced by Frank Lloyd Wright's Prairie School architecture, walls separating rooms were scarce. Dining rooms flowed into living rooms into family rooms, so that large portions of a home might be partitioned only by arches and the suggestions of doorways. Furniture became a key element to identifying one room from the other. Bedrooms and bathrooms retained their walls, largely because architects admitted the need for privacy in them, but the rest of the house was opened out. Taking the concept of open space to its extreme, architect Philip Johnson even designed an entire glass house, with only a bricked in bathroom and fireplace.

Walls and furniture were generally bright in color, and space was sometimes partitioned with screens, accordion-style doors, and curtains. Popular designer furniture pieces included the Van Der Rohe leather on chrome variety, and ornamentation, which took up space, was minimal. Charles Eames' famous Eames chair exhibited the simplicity associated with furniture of the era. What little ornamentation people did use included lamps and clocks. People were particularly fond of bubble-shaped items, from George Nelson's marshmallow sofa to bubble lamps and ball clocks.

Further Resources

BOOKS

Fehrman, Cherie, and Kenneth Fehrman. *Postwar Interior Design, 1945–1960*. New York: Van Nostrand Reinhold, 1987.

Massey, Anne. *Interior Design of the 20th Century*. New York: Thames and Hudson, 1990.

Parish, Mrs. Henry II, Albert Hadley, and Christopher Petkanas. *Parish-Hadley: Sixty Years of American Design*. Boston: Little, Brown, 1995.

WEBSITES

Architecture and Interior Design for 20th Century America, 1935–1955. American Memory digital primary source collection, Library of Congress. Available online at http://memory.loc.gov/ammem/gschtml/gotthome.html; website home page: http://memory.loc.gov/ammem/ammemhome.html (ac-cessed March 27, 2003).

Interior Design. Available online at http://www.interior design.net/index.asp?layout=id_front_page&webzine=id &publication=id; website home page: http://www.interior design.net/ (accessed March 27, 2003).

"Kitsch and Retro." Kitsch Shop. Available online at http://www.kitsch.co.uk/ (accessed March 27, 2003).

"Laminate." Available online at http://www.designsourcecon nection.com/laminate.htm (accessed March 27, 2003).

AUDIO AND VISUAL MEDIA

The Power of Color. Learning Zone Express. Videocassette, 2000.

Environmental Interiors Ancient Through Contemporary. J/B Associates. Videocassette, 1983.

"Patterns Spark Fall Rainwear"

Magazine article

By: William J. Ullmann

Date: August 21, 1959

Source: Ullmann, William J. "Patterns Spark Fall Rainwear." *Men's Wear*, August 21, 1959, 43–45. ■

Introduction

Men's fashion in the 1950s was, not surprisingly, business oriented and extremely conformist. Men's and women's roles were rigidly defined in the 1950s. Marriage was expected of all (single people were as worrisome as communists, almost); women were expected to become mothers and homemakers; men were expected to be wage earners and family providers. The fashion industry catered largely to the homemakers and not the wage earners. It would be a decade or two before men's fashion developed any sort of flair.

Specifically, businessmen wore conservative suits with cuffed, rarely pleated, pants and narrow jackets. The jackets usually had two to four buttons on their small lapels. Ties were narrow and conservative and were matched to the suit, and shirts were generally white or pale blue. (Pale pink, though it appeared on the casual scene, was considered entirely too effeminate in the corporate world.) With their short buzz haircuts, men in their hats and overcoats closely resembled the stereotypical image of J. Edgar Hoover's FBI "Untouchables." Indeed, the hats were generally fedoras or others of the narrow-brimmed, pinched-crown variety. Blue-collar workers were in a somewhat better position. Though still generally expected to wear a uniform, their attire usually matched their job's needs, generally allowing for more comfort.

Perhaps because they were so constrained in their work wardrobe, men in the 1950s sometimes chose quite vivid casual wear. The decade began the reign of Bermuda shorts, Hawaiian shirts (complete with wooden buttons), and outrageously decorative sports jackets. Men might also choose to wear a cabana set—a loose long shirt that hung around the thighs with matching shorts that came down to the middle of the thigh. Some men also wore string ties and T-shirts, though these were generally more popular among teenage boys. Even with these options, though, the conservative image projected by the famous sitcom father, Ward Cleaver (from *Leave It to Beaver*), who apparently wore his suit at home most days, also prevailed.

Significance

Menswear in the 1950s was one of the most visible images of the larger pattern of conformity associated with the era. Though boys and blue-collar workers were slowly breaking out of the mold—wearing T-shirts as something more than undershirts and heading out to sock hops and barbecues in their blue jeans—suburban white-collar workers were usually far more restricted in their choice of outfit.

In 1956 writer Sloan Wilson wrote his novel, *The Man in the Gray Flannel Suit*, which criticizes 1950s corporate greed. The novel's man in a three-piece gray flannel suit has carried forward as the image of the stereotypical businessman. Corporate culture called upon its employees to project confidence, honesty (even if the company's dealings were far less than honest), company image, and, most of all, Americanism. Apparently the overall view was that only one image could project that American business ideal, and so white-collar employees strove to emulate their managers as closely as possible, particularly in dress.

Indeed, a certain amount of the attitude fostered towards men's fashion in the 1950s carries into the present day. Most men update their wardrobes far more frequently than they would have done fifty years ago, and men's suits have developed extraordinary degrees of subtlety. However, even today men's wardrobe concerns are far fewer than those of their female counterparts.

Primary Source

"Patterns Spark Fall Rainwear"

SYNOPSIS: In the following article, Ullmann describes men's rainwear in terms of bold patterns and subtle colors, but he is really describing coats which, with the exception of their color, were easily interchangeable. Drip-dry and knee length, men's rainwear was as conformist as the suits. After all, it had to be worn into the office. The hats were all brimmed, though some had a jaunty lilt in them with half the brim pointing up and the other half pointing down.

Several important developments have manifested themselves in the rainwear that will be sold for fall 1959. Dark iridescents have become anathema to the makers of quality garments. There is a definite leveling off in the demand for "over-designed" models, and—most important—bold patterns in subtle colors show signs of becoming a very active market factor. With dark iridescents retailing at $14.95 and less, better makers have shifted fabric emphasis to the lighter shades. Soft greens are getting a lot of attention in many lines. Black is another color that has picked-up strength after the initial showings. However, these are flat blacks, not iridescents. Medium tones are moving well, too, but it is pointed out that these must have some "life" to them.

While the array of styles and models is as large as ever, the demand for "gimmicked-up" styles has fallen off to a considerable extent. Lengths ranging from 43-inches to 41-inches have met with ready acceptance and the Continental tag is applied to almost everything, other than the classic balmacaan models.

Conservative trench coats were favored by men in the 1950s. HULTON ARCHIVE/GETTY IMAGES. REPRODUCED BY PERMISSION.

Split-raglans are still the top numbers in some lines while other makers observe that set-in sleeves in some cases and full raglans in others are now best.

Double-breasted raincoats (other than trench coats) in the shorter lengths are moving well. Made both plain and belted (most belts are detachable), the double-breasteds show up in many models—some resembling the Short Warm-type overcoats, others keyed to the Continental concepts. Fur collars, pile collars and trims, as well as a tremendous variety of liners, are getting good response from retailers.

Patterned raincoats stressing large glen plaids, tatersall checks, houndstooth checks and miniature pin-checks have suddenly come to life. For the most part, colorings in this group are muted greens, grays and browns. They look new and manufacturers who have them say that patterns may be the "hottest" item for fall.

Further Resources

BOOKS

Ettinger, Roseann *50s Popular Fashions for Men, Women, Boys and Girls, with Price Guide.* Atglen, Pa.: Schiffer Publishing, 1995.

Hochswender, Woody, and Kim Johnson Gross. *Men in Style: The Golden Age of Fashion from Esquire.* New York: Rizzoli, 1993.

Reilly, Maureen E. Lynn *Swing Style: Fashions of the 1930s–1950s.* Atglen, Pa.: Schiffer Publishing, 2000.

Salamone, Frank. *A Popular Culture in the Fifties.* Lanham, Md.: University Press of America, 2001.

Steele, Valerie. *Fifty Years of Fashion: New Look to Now.* New Haven, Conn.: Yale University Press, 1997.

Warren, Geoffrey. *Fashions and Accessories, 1840 through 1980.* Atglen, Pa.: Schiffer Publishing, 1997.

WEBSITES

"History of Fashion, 1950–1960." Vintage Blues. Available online at http://www.vintageblues.com/history5.htm; website home page: http://www.vintageblues.com/vintage.htm (accessed March 26, 2003).

"The History of Menswear: 1800–Present Day." The Costume Gallery. Available online at http://www.costumegallery.com/men.htm; website home page: http://www.costumegallery.com (accessed March 27, 2003).

Maginnis, Tara. *The Costumer's Manifesto—Costumes.org* Available online at http://www.costumes.org/pages/1950inks.htm (accessed March 26, 2003).

American Automobiles

"What Does the Lark Have That the Others Do Not?"

Newspaper advertisement

By: Studebaker

Date: November 3, 1959

Source: "What Does the Lark Have That the Others Do Not?" *Cincinnati Enquirer.* Nov. 3, 1959, 3-C.

About the Organization: Studebaker, founded in 1852, was the only wagon manufacturer to successfully make the transition into the automobile industry at the turn of the twentieth century. The H & C Studebaker blacksmith shop opened in 1858 in South Bend, Indiana. It became the largest wagon manufacturer in the world. The company introduced an electric car in 1902 and a gasoline-powered car two years later, although it continued to manufacture wagons until the 1920s. After struggling to survive during the Depression, Studebaker rose to fame when modern industrial design pioneer Raymond Loewy began designing its cars in 1938. As an independent automaker, however, Studebaker faced a constant struggle to compete, and the company folded in 1966.

"Announcing the New Low Prices for All 1960 Mercury Country Cruisers"

Newspaper advertisement

By: Lincoln-Mercury Division of the Ford Motor Company

Date: November 3, 1959

Source: "Announcing the New Low Prices for All 1960 Mercury Country Cruisers." *Cincinnati Enquirer.* Nov. 3, 1959, 3-D

About the Organization: The Lincoln-Mercury division of the Ford Motor Company has undergone several incarnations over the course of its life. Lincoln Motor Company was created by Henry Leland to build aircraft for the U.S. military during World War I. The company later switched to producing high-quality, high-end automobiles. Ford bought the company in the 1920s and created a line of luxury cars under the Lincoln name. Because there was a considerable difference between Ford's economy cars and its Lincolns, in the 1930s, Ford created the Mercury line of mid-priced cars, associated with the Lincoln division. Throughout the 1940s and 1950s, Ford tried several identity changes, including a complete separation of the Lincoln and Mercury divisions in 1955. At one time, the two names were also briefly paired with the disastrously unsuccessful Ford Edsel. ∎

Introduction

In the early 1950s, people began to slowly shed the thrifty habits they had acquired during World War II (1939–1945). Many were quite willing to spend significant amounts of money, especially when their purchases could save them time. The mass-produced automobiles coming out of Detroit proved to be the ultimate time-savers, allowing people to commute to city jobs from suburban homes. Increasingly affordable and sold on credit, they came to be perceived not as a luxury but a necessity.

Manufacturers adorned even the most basic auto models with huge fins and outrageous amounts of chrome, transforming nearly every car into a luxury model. Automakers in the 1950s were far more concerned with marketing their products than with consumer safety. Even though studies as early as 1954 showed that seat belts reduced deaths from automobile accidents, carmakers only offered these items as expensive optional items. They were far more concerned with flashy ornamentation that often reduced the safety of their cars. Low-riding cars' gas tanks were dangerously exposed in collisions, and useless gadgets in the cab could be deadly to passengers in a crash. Tires remained unchanged even as car bodies grew, creating less safe vehicles.

If the American love of the car was not already complete in 1956, the government's National Defense Highway Act in that year ensured the automobile's future success. At that time mass transit—such as trains—was still preferred for most long-distance travel. Though America already had large spans of roadways, many cities were not connected by consistently reliable roads. That began to change when federal dollars were allotted to connect the country from north to south and east to west. Ostensibly enacted as a national safety measure, these national highways guaranteed motorists easy cross-country travel in their individual cars.

Significance

The car industry was dominated by the triumvirate of Ford, General Motors (GM), and Chrysler, allowing little room for competition from independent carmakers. One successful independent, for at least the early part of the decade, was Studebaker. Begun as a wagonmaking business in 1852, Studebaker celebrated its centennial in 1952 as a successful automobile manufacturer. The best remembered Studebakers of the 1950s were the bullet nosed models, which had an extra point sticking out between the headlights, bearing the Studebaker logo.

The decade was dominated by big gas-guzzling cars with few safety features. As city streets and highways began to get crowded, analysts increasingly argued that a reduction in car size would result in less crowding. As an added incentive for Detroit to make smaller cars, another independent manufacturer, German automaker Volkswagen (VW; literally, the people's car) was making great strides with their tiny Beetles. Minuscule by comparison to the American carmakers' monsters, VW Beetles could park in smaller spaces and zip through heavy traffic, leaving owners of larger cars gazing longingly after.

Of course, with the engine in back, and therefore closer to the passengers, the Beetle was eventually determined to have as many safety hazards as its larger counterparts, but its popularity made a huge impact on American carmakers. By the end of the 1950s, they were slowly starting to decrease the size of their vehicles. In at least one instance, that of the quick-to-flip Corvair, they did so with a continued lack of concern for safety. The trend to reduce car size allowed Studebaker one last competitive car—its Lark. These "smaller" cars were not anywhere near as small as Beetles. Detroit was distinctly conservative in its move to the small car market, and it was the 1980s before an American car maker would make a truly competitive small car.

Primary Source

"What Does the Lark Have That the Others Do Not?"

SYNOPSIS: This advertisement for the 1960 Studebaker Lark emphasizes the car's versatility, including its many options. The ad praises the Lark as having all of the advantages of "new dimension cars," meaning relatively small cars, while also taking pains to indicate how spacious and powerful a vehicle it still is.

It Has Six Body Styles

New convertible, new 4-door and 2-door station wagon, hardtop, 4-door and 2-door sedan! Selection of seven sophisticated colors. Interiors handsomely appointed in distinctive pleated vinyl or cloth upholstery. Nobody else has them. Why settle for less?

It Has a Powerful, Thrifty V-8 or Super Economical "6"

The Lark V-8 topped all other eights in last year's Mobilgas Economy Run. It's one of the fastest accelerating cars in the U.S.A. and is still more economical than some "sixes." Have your cake and eat it, too. The V-8 Lark (costs just a litle more than the "6") offers all the advantages of new dimension cars plus potent performance matched to economy. The "six" offers spirited performance with, of course, greater fuel economy. Why be limited? Choose with The Lark! *(Important! The Lark couples safety with power . . . V-8, brakes are biggest in field.)*

It Has a Choice of Three Terrific Transmissions

Automatic, three-speed stick shift, three-speed stick with overdrive. Lark automatic transmission has a full range of speeds including Park, Neutral, Drive, Low, Reverse. Low and Reverse are purposely placed together for rocking the car out of snow, ice or mud. Lark three-speed synchromesh is smooth, decisive, sure and, with overdrive, the engine loafs at cruising speed and cuts your gas bills even more. Which one suits you best? The Lark offers this choice—plus a selection of 7 axle ratios—the *others* do not!

It Has Many Unusual Features

For example, reclining seats that make into beds, front seat headrests, hillholder, Twin Traction (for driving through snow, sand, ice or mud), air conditioning, 4-barrel carburetor and dual exhausts . . . many, many more. None of the *others* have this wide variety of optional features from which to choose.

It Has Proven Performance Without Recourse to Experimental Runs

130,000 Lark owners have driven a total of over 750 million miles under every conceivable road and weather condition. Result is: no "bugs" to iron out, no "hidden" mechanical faults . . . no problems for new owners. Dealers and service men everywhere know The Lark. Studebaker-Packard corporate records clearly show that Lark service and maintenance costs are one third of the automobile industry average. How can you go wrong on that?

Primary Source

"Announcing the New Low Prices for All 1960 Mercury Country Cruisers"

SYNOPSIS: This advertisement for the 1960 Mercury Country Cruiser emphasizes the car's large dimensions and its "low price." Mercury was well known for making "mid-price" cars, so the ad encourages readers to think that buying the Mercury Country Cruiser for only a little more than a "low-price" brand is a good bargain.

Now only $50 more than wagons with "low-price" names

Besides New Low Prices, Look at Mercury's Extra Values

Handsome Hardtop Styling

There's no hemmed-in feeling, no need to play peekaboo with pillars. Notice how one side pillar takes the place of the usual three.

Unique Road-Tuned Ride

This great advance in riding comfort takes the bounce out of bumps—makes the Country Cruiser ride like a limousine.

Retractable Rear Window

It takes the place of the old-fashioned liftgate. There's nothing to bump your head on when loading. And it's better looking, permits easier ventilation.

Most Usable Cargo Space

Biggest in any wagon—over 101 cubic feet behind the front seat.

Front-Facing, Self-Storing 3rd Seat

Optional for all models. There's no need for passengers to sit backwards.

■ ■ ■

You might expect to pay a lot more for a wagon that offers so much more. While other station wagon prices are going up, Mercury announces new low prices for the Country Cruisers. The Commuter, for example, is priced $88 lower than last year. It now costs only $1.60 more a month than station wagons with "low-price" names. Why not see for yourself at our showroom.

Every Model Now at New Low Prices . . . Don't Buy Any Car Until You've Driven the Road-tuned 1960 Mercury

Further Resources

BOOKS

Finch, Christopher. *Highways to Heaven: The Auto Biography of America.* New York: American Heritage, 1977.

Flink, James J. *The Automobile Age.* Cambridge, Mass.: MIT Press, 1988.

Miller, Douglas T., and Marion Nowack. *The Fifties: The Way We Really Were.* New York: Doubleday, 1977.

Rae, John Bell. *The American Automobile: A Brief History.* Chicago: University of Chicago Press, 1965.

Yasutoshi, Ikuta. *Cruise-o-matic.* San Francisco: Chronicle Books, 1988.

PERIODICALS

Thompson, Neal. "Passengers on the 100-Year Ride." *Bergen Record,* June 11, 1996.

WEBSITES

Liegl, Paula. "The 1950s: Industry Retools in the Postwar Period." Available online at http://www.achrnews.com (accessed March 22, 2003).

Ritzinger, André. Studebaker Lark 1960. Ritzsite. Available online at http://www.ritzsite.demon.nl/Lark/Lark.htm; website home page: http://www.ritzsite.net/index.htm#Add_Lark (accessed March 23, 2003).

Vargas, Gabriel. "50s Cars Changed American Lifestye." Borderlands: An El Paso Community College Local History Project. Available online at http://www.epcc.edu/ftp/Homes/monicaw/borderlands/13_50s_cars.htm (accessed March 23, 2003.)

What We Wore
Interviews

By: Ellen Melinkoff

Date: 1984

Source: Melinkoff, Ellen. *What We Wore.* New York: William Morrow, 1984.

About the Author: Ellen Melinkoff (1944–) was born in the state of New York, but she has since moved to Los Angeles, California. She received her B.A. in history from University of California at Los Angeles and is a full-time freelance writer. Her books include *The Working Parents' Handbook, The Flavor of L.A.: A Guide to Ethnic Restaurants and Markets,* and *What We Wore.* ■

Introduction

Before the end of World War II (1939–1945), adolescents had little personal disposable income. The words "teen age" to refer to this age group appeared in the early 1920s, but it was the late 1930s or early 1940s before the term shifted to the current word "teenager." Due to financial and social constrictions, teens had little choice in the matter of their own clothing in the early twentieth century. Girls, in particular, were restricted to a dress code enforced by their mothers.

Moreover, "store-bought" clothes in the early part of the twentieth century were a luxury few families could really afford. It was far more likely that parents would buy new fabric to make clothes than to buy the clothes ready made or from a tailor. In the 1920s, young women in their twenties began to push the boundaries of fashion, dressing as flappers. But this trend did not filter down to adolescents whose clothing choices were still safely controlled by their parents.

However, after World War II came to a close, television and print ads began marketing heavily to youth. Where their parents had grown up in the thrifty years of the Depression, these youngsters grew up in the heady days of postwar consumerism. Moreover, even as they unknowingly clung to their parents' patterns of conformity, many teens wanted to rebel. Listening to rock and roll music that horrified their elders, 1950s teens wanted to be seen as different from their parents. Fashion manufacturers recognized the potential of this new market and set to work.

Significance

While many young girls in the 1950s dressed like Dale Evans, a feminine cowgirl if ever there was such, their adolescent sisters wore calf-length frilly skirts and bobby socks, and listened to rock and roll music. Girls' fashions in the 1940s translated into fashions for the 1950s as well. Where wartime nylon rationing had resulted in adult women painting their legs to look as though they had on stockings, younger American girls adopted the British habit of wearing white ankle-length socks (called "bobby socks" after the British police) with their saddle shoes. The saddle shoes, first developed in 1906 by the Spalding Sport Company, had reinforced insteps ("saddles") that helped ease running. Originally a college trend, the shoes quickly spread to adolescents. Since saddle shoes became associated with rock and roll and rebellion, parents originally considered the footwear quite controversial.

Despite the new look, though, teenage girls were for the most part imitating their parents in their own way. Bobby socks and saddle shoes represented a conformity of their own, worn by the teenage masses. Hand in hand with their bobby socks and saddle shoes, teenaged girls also wore poodle skirts. And where else did you display your bobby socks and poodle skirt but at a sock hop! Generally held in gymnasiums, sock hops were so called because the dancers had to remove their saddle shoes to protect the gym floor. Generally made from stiff wool felts, poodle skirts sported an appliqué poodle on the front and layers of crinoline underneath. The crinolines and petticoats, a real symbol of the removal of postwar fabric rationing, lifted poodle skirts out to show the appliqué to its best advantage. Girls' fashions imitated women's fashions, in that they emphasized a small waist, and poodle skirts usually came equipped with wide belts for this

A model wears a full skirt with a beaded umbrella that doubles as a pocket. The poodle skirt made appliqued skirts very popular in America in the 1950s. © UNDERWOOD & UNDERWOOD/CORBIS. REPRODUCED BY PERMISSION.

reason. Girls might also accessorize with cat-eye glasses, which have faded in and out of popularity since that time.

Primary Source

What We Wore [excerpt]

SYNOPSIS: In this series of quotations compiled in Ellen Melinkoff's book, women reminisce about being teens in the 1950s. They talk about the importance of wearing full skirts to fit in with peers. Particularly, they focus on the layers of petticoats and crinolines important to keeping the skirts standing out. They also remember being concerned with their small waists and suffering the itchiness of all those layers for the sake of looking good.

We moved to California when I was in the sixth grade (1956). My family had a lot of kids and we couldn't always afford the latest fashions. My older cousin made a hoop for me out of wire coat hangers twisted together. Unfortunately, I wasn't up on all the techniques of wearing a hoop and my first experience with it was in crowded quarters, negotiating the aisle of the school bus, at which time the ends of two hangers disconnected and my hoop went totally awry. After suffering intense humiliation, I tried it one more time. Going between the desks in the classroom, I suffered the same consequences. I went to the girls' rest room at recess and took the damn thing off and threw it away. So much for high fashion!

Michele Burgess

In junior high, 1955–1956, multiple petticoats were in full swing, so to speak. I remember trying to convince my mother that three or four of these were barely a decent minimum. It was critical that the skirt stand out like a longer version of the ballerina's tutu. As I recall, there were two kinds of petticoats: the net one which scratched your legs and the cotton lace, all seven or eight yards of which had to be ironed.

One day I lost my bottom petticoat. Of course, it was one that was really ratty and probably, knowing me at the time, not real clean. It had a button at the waist which apparently came off. As I began walking out of class, there was this ratty petticoat draped about my feet. I was paralyzed with embarrassment, and around me boys were snickering. The homeroom teacher was male, of course. The boy walking behind me—who undoubtedly had sisters—calmly bent down, untangled my legs from the petticoat, handed it to me, and walked out. I spent the next two periods or so in the girls' room—dying.

Gloria Casvin

In the fifth grade, 1957, full skirts hit. The fuller, the better. So we wore not one, not two, but three or more petticoats, starched stiff. When that wasn't enough, we learned to wear a hoopskirt. I say learned because it took practice to learn to seat yourself without the hoop flying up in front of you. I remember my mother suggesting that I *could* wear just one petticoat. Couldn't I see how much more graceful it looked, wearing just one? Of course not. What was the point of wearing just one? The fuller, the better. The beginning, for me, of extreme styles, of sacrificing comfort for design. For the next ten years, I would eagerly follow almost every new fad, no matter how strange.

Lyn Messner

The bottommost layer was stiff net and resulted in symptoms akin to poison ivy as we scratched our way through the day.

Linda Dahl

"Stand-out" petticoats are what I called them. Those horribly stiff, scratchy net things my mother thought were so necessary but were the epitome of

discomfort. I had to wear them to church under my Sunday dresses. Before I would sit down in the pew, I would reach behind me and under the petticoats, lift them up almost to the height of my head, and sit down—bare legs against cold pew. I'm sure it looked pretty odd, but there was no way I was going to sit on three or more layers of scratchy netting for an hour.

Pamela J. Baergen

I ironed some of my petticoats with wax paper to stiffen them, and starched everything that could be starched. The feel of those crinolines was simply heavenly. I think in West Virginia we all felt just like Scarlett O'Hara, and I particularly liked having my small waist emphasized as I was getting fairly plump in the hips at that point.

Sara B. Chase

I would wear two or three slips at a time. When I washed them I would dip them in a starch solution and then set them out to dry. Then I would iron them with spray starch so that they would be even fuller.

Eileen Fond

My favorite crinoline was one made of two layers of pink net that could be pulled apart for volume so it didn't need starching so often.

M. Miller

. . .

In junior high, 1959 or so, I remember wearing two or three crinolines at a time and being so hot and itchy from all the net. Then styles went to the other extreme of being very tight, straight skirts with kick pleats. Even girls weighing under one hundred pounds, as I did, had to wear girdles as part of the fashion.

Linda Finch

My first day of high school in 1962, I wore so many crinolines, my skirt stood straight out. I remember counting them in the girls' bathroom with my friends to see who had the most. My hair was a big bouffant. Oh, it was horrible! I thought I looked so great. At the time, I *knew* everyone looked at me because I looked so good. Now, I wonder. . . .

Sherry Alberoni

The hoop slip was never fun. It was breezy and one had to be very careful when taking a seated position so that the skirt did not pop up in one's face.

Carolyn Zucker

Brand-new or freshly starched tulle petticoats snagged nylon stockings at knee level like mad, rendering nylons unwearable. That made nylons an even more precious commodity because your mother wouldn't buy you replacement ones.

Nancy Kinney

Crinolines itched and those hoopskirts made sitting a problem until you got the hang of lifting the rear up before you sat down.

Sandy Whitehurst

When I was ten, I had a mambo skirt. It was lavender felt, a full circle, with footprint directions for the mambo across the front. Lavender was considered a daring color then.

Ellen Ekman

From my earliest recollections of pink dresses and patent leather shoes, clothes were important to me. My early years were at the end of an era when clothes symbolized steps in growing up—boys wearing their first long pants and girls wearing girdles (or should I say foundation garments) and nylon stockings. Though we weren't exactly poor, day-to-day life was not very glamorous or necessarily luxurious, and growing up represented attaining status (children in those days were seen and not heard). It was nebulously implied that growing up also included the longed-for luxuries of life. We could hardly wait!

Clothes also represented status to us that the modes of dress drastically separated the educated and the noneducated, the "blue collar" worker and the "white collar" worker success story, and we wanted desperately to be identified with the next higher standard of living. So we "wouldn't be caught dead" without the right shoes or matching bags, or wearing white after Labor Day, or without hats and gloves.

Nancie L. Porter

In elementary school I always wore dresses. Dresses were for school. It never occurred to me or anyone else to have the girls wear pants, despite skinned knees and later being inhibited on the playground because of wearing a skirt. It wouldn't be until after I graduated from high school in 1965 that girls would begin to wear pants to school.

Lyn Messner

. . .

Nineteen fifty was the year I turned twelve, and at that point (seventh grade, big junior high), clothes became very important to me and my memory of them is clear. We wore white dickey collars or small silk scarves tied in a square Girl Scout knot. I felt snappiest in a navy wool skirt (very

straight), burgundy sweater set, white dickey with a tiny cutwork motif, and boxy, navy-and-white small-check jacket.

Sara B. Chase

In junior high, one of my favorite outfits was a full-skirted, scoopnecked black jumper and a white, round-collared, puffy-sleeved blouse which I accessorized with white knee socks and black flats. I thought it was "dreamy." One morning when I was dressed in my dynamite outfit, waiting for the school bus, somebody called me "Alice." I replied that my name wasn't Alice. The boy replied, "Well, you look like Alice in Wonderland." It was the last time I ever wore *that* outfit. I was furious that some dumb boy had ruined it for me. What did he know? Nothing about "Fashion" (as I saw it) and too much about Lewis Carroll.

Ellen Ekman

In the sixth grade, I *finally* convinced my mother to let me have a plaid skirt and sweater. Red, green, and navy plaid and a red pullover sweater. Up till then it had been dresses, and I felt so babyish. But skirts and sweaters were definitely big girl and, after all, I *was* in the graduating class. We had a lot of boy-girl parties, but it's funny that what I wore doesn't stand out in my mind at all. It's more that skirt and sweater that I wore to school. I guess I remember it because *I*, not my mother, chose it.

Susan Stern

What I chiefly remember about my clothes in the fifties is how formal they seemed. I have a picture of me in 1957, taken on my way to some get-together of senior high girls. If you can believe it, I wore white gloves and a string of pearls. Today such an event among my daughter's friends would produce an entire roomful of blue jeans.

Caroline Latham

While I was a product of the times and the rules were clearly defined and it never entered our heads to question them, or not to go along with them, I think clothes have always meant more to me than to my contemporaries. I could never stand being submerged in a group. Back then, I used clothes as a way of standing out, or at-specification. The gaggiest thing a girl could possibly wear with her formal was lace or net mitts, those fingerless above-the-elbow gloves.

Nancy Kinney

To the senior prom, 1956 in Massapequa, we wore strapless tops, big long skirts of tulle. Mine was white with four or five tiers of tulle ruffles over crinolines and a hoop. I found out somehow that another girl had bought the same dress. Disaster! But Mother and a neighbor changed it at the last minute with a pink sash.

Peggy Byrnes

At our high school prom, the nuns had a rule against girls wearing spaghetti-strap dresses. The straps had to be at least one inch wide. (Strapless, never!) My friend Celeste and I had the same dress. It came with spaghetti straps and I had special straps made to regulation. Celeste, who later became a nun, didn't and she got away with it.

Rose Mary Kimble

The *pièce de résistance* of those high school years was a luscious evening gown I wore to my senior prom and later to a few dances in college. It was very sophisticated for me in those days—black cotton lace over white taffeta, spaghetti straps and all. Nobody else had a black-and-white dress for the prom; everyone had those stickysweet, ice cream pastels, and I really like being different than the rest of the pack. I still have this dress. Maybe I'll wear it again someday.

Annette Swanberg

One could own formal after formal in high school—but to own a BLACK COCKTAIL DRESS was really the last word. Mine was a sheath with an interesting draped neckline, sleeveless, in some wonderful, drapy, crepy fabric. Not low, but off the shoulder somehow. The world was mine when I wore it.

Nancy Kinney

Further Resources

BOOKS

Bolino, Monika. *Fashion.* San Diego, Calif.: Greenhaven, 2002.

Cunningham, Patricia, and Susan V. Lab. *Dress and Popular Culture.* Bowling Green, Ohio: Bowling Green University Popular Press, 1991.

Boone, Pat. *'Twixt Twelve and Twenty.* Englewood Cliffs, N.J.: Prentice-Hall, 1958.

Miller, Douglas T., and Marion Nowak. *The Fifties: The Way We Really Were.* Doubleday: 1977.

Steele, Valerie. *New Look to Now.* New Haven: Yale University Press, 1997.

WEBSITES

Dilly, Neysa, Annette Romero, and Ruth Beltran. "Teenage Fashion of the Nifty Fifties." Borderlands: An El Paso Community College Local History Project. Available online at http://www.epcc.edu/ftp/Homes/monicaw/borderlands/12_teenage_fashions.htm; website home page: http://www.epcc.edu/ftp/Homes/monicaw/borderlands/border_index.htm (accessed March 26, 2003).

"Fashion from the 50s." Yesterdayland. Available online at http://www.yesterdayland.com/popopedia/shows/decades/fashion_1950s.php; website home page: http://www.yesterdayland.com/ (accessed March 26, 2003).

"Fifties Skirts: Fashions of the Fifties." Fifties Website. Available online at http://www.fiftiesweb.com/fashion/fashion-ws.htm; website home page: http://www.fiftiesweb.com/fifties.htm (accessed March 26, 2003).

Passalaqua, Carolyn. *Boomer's Fifties Teen Idol Magazine: A Look Back at Fifties Teen Magazines.* Available online at http://home.att.net/~boomers.fifties.teenmag/ (accessed March 26, 2003).

Rich, Candace. "At the Hop." Fifties Website. Available online at http://www.fiftiesweb.com/atthehop.htm website home page: http://www.fiftiesweb.com/fifties.htm (accessed March 26, 2003).

"Sock Hop." The Iceburg.com. Available online at http://www.theiceberg.com/radio/sock_hop/ (accessed March 26, 2003).

5

GOVERNMENT AND POLITICS

DAN PROSTERMAN

Entries are arranged in chronological order by date of primary source. For entries with one primary source, the entry title is the same as the primary source title. Entries with more than one primary source have an overall entry title, followed by the titles of the primary sources.

Important Events in Government and Politics, 1950–1959

1950

- J. Edgar Hoover, Director of the FBI, publicly opposes the creation of a national police agency to control domestic communists.

- On January 25, Alger Hiss, the State Department official under investigation for his communist ties, receives a five-year prison sentence for perjury.

- On February 9, at Wheeling, West Virginia, the politically obscure senator Joseph McCarthy (R-Wis.) charges that there are "a lot" of communists working and making policy in the United States State Department.

- On March 8, Senator McCarthy lists fifty-seven communists he claims are employed in the State Department.

- On March 28, President Harry S. Truman launches an investigation into officials cited by Senator McCarthy as communists.

- On June 6, Senator McCarthy claims that at least three top officials in the State Department are communists.

- On June 15, David Greenglass confesses to providing the Soviet Union with information on the U.S. atomic bomb program.

- On July 5, for the first time since World War II, American troops go into battle in an effort to stop communist North Korea from overwhelming South Korea.

- On July 17, Julius Rosenberg, a former Army Signal Corps engineer, is arrested by the FBI on the charge of atomic espionage for the Soviet Union.

- On August 11, Ethel Greenglass Rosenberg, the wife of Julius and sister of David Greenglass, is arrested by the FBI for allegedly conspiring to give atomic secrets to the Soviet Union.

- On October 18, David Greenglass pleads guilty to passing atomic secrets to the Soviet Union while working at the Los Alamos, New Mexico, atom bomb installation.

- On November 1, Puerto Rican nationalists Griselio Torresola and Oscar Collanzo attempt to assassinate President Truman in Washington, D.C. The president is unharmed, but Torresola is killed and Collanzo wounded.

1951

- On February 26, the Twenty-second Amendment to the United States Constitution, barring a president from serving

more than two terms in office, goes into effect after Nevada becomes the thirty-sixth state to ratify it.

- On March 7, General Douglas MacArthur warns President Truman that a stalemate will develop in Korea unless United Nations troops are permitted to move against China.

- On April 5, Julius and Ethel Rosenberg receive death sentences for transmitting U.S. atomic bomb information to the Soviet Union.

- On April 5, General MacArthur advocates using Chiang Kai-shek's Nationalist Chinese (based in Taiwan) to open a front against the mainland Red Chinese in the Korean War.

- On April 11, President Truman dismisses General MacArthur from command of UN, Allied, and U.S. forces in the Far East.

1951

- On April 19, General MacArthur defends his position to widen the Korean War in a speech before a joint session of Congress. In the speech, he states that the Joint Chiefs of Staff share his views toward defeating the communist menace in the Far East.

- On April 20, President Truman attends opening day of the Washington Senators baseball season. When he throws out the first ball, McArthur supporters in the crowd boo him.

- On August 6, Senator William Benton (D-Conn.) sponsors a resolution calling for an investigation of Senator McCarthy to decide whether he should be expelled from Congress.

- On August 9, Senator McCarthy, speaking before the Senate, names twenty-six members of the State Department who he suspects of disloyalty.

- On September 20, former First Lady Eleanor Roosevelt denounces McCarthy as "the greatest menace to freedom because he smears people without the slightest regard for the facts."

- On September 28, Senator Benton calls upon his senatorial peers to expel or censure Senator McCarthy, accusing the senator from Wisconsin of being "an amoral man who uses the lie as an instrument of policy" and follows a "pattern of distortion and deceit."

- On October 22, Senator Robert Taft (R-Ohio), who is considering running for president in 1952, commends Senator McCarthy for calling attention to widespread infiltration of communists in government.

1952

- On March 26, Senator McCarthy sues Senator Benton for $2 million for libel and slander in Benton's attempt to remove McCarthy from the Senate.

- On March 29, President Truman announces at a Jefferson-Jackson Day dinner that he will not be a candidate for re-election.

- On April 11, Elia Kazan, the famous Hollywood director, tells the House Un-American Activities Committee that he was a communist along with others from The Group Theater of New York.

- On May 30, the United States Socialist Party meeting in Cleveland nominates Darlington Hoopes for president and Samuel Friedman for vice president.

- From June to July 7, General Dwight D. Eisenhower builds support for his presidential nomination for the Republican Party in the 1952 election, winning the nomination on July 7. Richard Nixon is nominated as the vice presidential candidate.

- From July 21 to July 24, the Democratic National Convention nominates Illinois governor Adlai E. Stevenson for president. Senator John Sparkman of Alabama is nominated for vice president

- On September 23, vice president candidate Nixon, responding to media reports that he had pocketed a political expense fund, makes a powerful televised appeal to the public in which he states, "I'm not a quitter," and in which he observes that the only gift his family received from his life in politics was a cocker spaniel named Checkers.

- On October 24, Republican presidential nominee Eisenhower promises to go to Korea to seek "an early and honorable end" to the war.

- On November 4, Eisenhower wins election by a popular vote of 32.9 million to 26.5 million and carries thirty-nine states to Stevenson's nine.

1953

- On January 2, the United States Senate ends its eighteen month investigation of Senator McCarthy's fitness to remain in elective office. In a four-hundred-page report, the Senate concludes that McCarthy deliberately tried to circumvent the investigation.

- On March 15, Senate Majority Leader Robert A. Taft states that the entire staff of the Voice of America radio-broadcasting station should be fired for being communist sympathizers.

- On June 19, the convicted Soviet spies Julius and Ethel Rosenberg are executed after President Eisenhower rejects their pleas for clemency.

- On July 27, after three years and thirty-two days of war, an armistice is finalized in Korea, leaving the country divided along the 38th parallel. The United States guarantees economic aid and military security to South Korea.

1954

- On February 18, Senator McCarthy assails Brigadier General Ralph W. Zwicker, a decorated war hero of the D-Day landing in Normandy, for harboring communists in the army.

- On February 20, Army Secretary Robert T. Stevens orders Brigadier General Zwicker not to answer McCarthy's summonses to appear before his investigating committee.

- On March 1, Puerto Rican nationalists shoot five members of Congress in the House of Representatives.

- On April 12, the Atomic Energy Commission charges atomic scientist J. Robert Oppenheimer with being a security risk for his associations with communists.

- On May 17, the United States Supreme Court, in *Brown v. Board of Education,* rules segregation is illegal in public schools.

- On May 28, President Eisenhower signs legislation inserting the words "under God" into the pledge of allegiance to the flat.

- On June 17, the United States Senate ends its eight-week probe into the dispute between Senator McCarthy and the United States Army.

- On August 24, President Eisenhower signs into law the Communist Control Act.

- On September 27, the United States Senate Select Committee recommends the censure of Senator McCarthy for contempt of the Senate Privileges and Elections Subcommittee for verbally abusing Brigadier General Zwicker.

- On November 27, Alger Hiss is released from prison after serving forty-four months of his five year sentence.

- On December 2, the United States Senate, on a vote of 67-22 does not censure, but rather condemns, Senator McCarthy.

1955

- The eighty-fourth Congress has a record eighteen women (sixteen in the House, one in the Senate, and one nonvoting delegate from Hawaii).

- On June 17, fifty-three cities participate in Operation Alert, a three-day mock H-bomb drill. The alert ends with a broadcast by President Eisenhower from his secret underground bunker near Washington, D.C.

- On July 11, President Eisenhower signs legislation requiring the words "In God We Trust" on all American currency.

- On September 24, President Eisenhower suffers a heart attack while vacationing in Colorado. He is released from a Denver army hospital on November 11.

- On December 5, a boycott of the Montgomery, Alabama, city bus lines begins after Rosa Parks, an African American woman, is fined for refusing to give up her seat to a white passenger.

1956

- On February 4, a House banking subcommittee charges that the slum clearance and urban redevelopment programs are bogged down by the Eisenhower administration's bungling, roadblocks, and strangling red tape.

- On February 25, Senator Harry F. Byrd (D-Va.) calls on southern states to organize "massive resistance" to the United States Supreme Court's school desegregation decision.

- On June 10, the United States Socialist Party National Convention meeting in Chicago nominates Darlington Hoopes for president and Samuel Friedman for vice president.

- On June 26, President Eisenhower signs the $33.5 billion federal highway act, which creates the federal interstate highway system. This act initiates the largest public works project in history.

- On July 22, the United States detonates its tenth nuclear explosion of its current test series in the Pacific.

- On August 16, the Democratic National Convention nominates Adlai Stevenson and Estes Kefauver for president and vice president, respectively, in the fall elections.

• On August 22, the Republican National Convention in San Francisco renominates Dwight Eisenhower and Richard Nixon for president and vice president, respectively, in the fall elections.

• On October 11, Stevenson's proposal to end hydrogen bomb testing becomes the defining campaign issue.

• On November 6, President Eisenhower and Vice President Nixon are reelected in a landslide victory over Stevenson and Kefauver (457 electoral votes to 74; 33.2 million popular votes to 24.1 million).

1957

• On January 3, the Eighty-fifth Congress convenes with the Democrats controlling both houses of Congress (233–200 in House; 49–46 in the Senate).

• On May 2, Senator Joseph McCarthy dies at the age of forty-eight from the effects of chronic alcoholism.

• On August 29, Senator Strom Thurmond (D-S.C.) filibusters a civil rights bill on the Senate floor for a record 24 hours, 18 minutes. Nevertheless, the bill is passed and sent to President Eisenhower for signing.

• On September 24, President Eisenhower orders United States Army paratroopers to prevent interference with racial integration at Central High School in Little Rock, Arkansas.

• On November 5, Secretary of State John Foster Dulles admits that the Soviets have outdistanced the United States in certain aspects of missile development; the *New York Herald Tribune* reports that the U.S. government has asked U.S. companies for plans for rockets capable of reaching the moon.

1958

• On April 30, the U.S. Senate votes for aid in the form of guaranteed loans to the nation's financially pressed railroads.

• On May 8, President Eisenhower orders federalized Arkansas National Guardsmen removed from Central High School in Little Rock, Arkansas.

• On August 26, the residents of Alaska approve statehood.

1959

• On February 5, President Eisenhower asks Congress to enact a seven-point civil rights program.

• On March 12, Congress passes legislation making Hawaii the fiftieth state.

• On June 16, the Federal Communications Commission upholds the "equal time" rule for political candidates.

• On October 11, Governor Ernest Hollings of South Carolina, a staunch states rights supporter and segregationist, announces that he will quit the Democratic Party if the party chooses an "unacceptable" presidential candidate in 1960.

• On November 16, the Justice Department initiates a law suit in U.S. District Court to end "white primaries" in Tennessee, where African Americans had been prohibited from voting.

• On December 29, President Eisenhower says that the United States is no longer bound by the unilateral nuclear test suspension and is "free to resume . . . testing."

Speech at Wheeling, West Virginia

Speech

By: Joseph McCarthy

Date: February 9, 1950

Source: McCarthy, Joseph. "Speech at Wheeling, West Virginia." February 9, 1950. Reprinted in *Congressional Record of the Senate*, February 20, 1950. Available online at http://azimuth.harcourtcollege.com/history/ayers/chapter27/27.4.mccarthy.html; website home page: http://www.azimuth.harcourtcollege.com (accessed June 18, 2003).

About the Author: Joseph McCarthy (1908–1957), born in Appleton, Wisconsin, earned his law degree from Marquette University. When World War II (1939–1945) erupted, he served as an intelligence officer. He returned from the war to successfully run for the U.S. Senate. McCarthy became one of the most notorious senators in U.S. history as his pursuit of American communists led to his eventual downfall. ∎

Introduction

Following the end of World War II, the United States entered into a struggle for global supremacy with its former ally, the Soviet Union. Between the war's end in 1945 and 1950, this Cold War escalated to such an extent that it influenced all sectors of American policy making. By the beginning of 1950, according to growing numbers of anticommunists in government and the mass media, the communist specter had encircled the globe and threatened to destroy American gains abroad and its security at home. The Soviet Union's successful test of its first atomic bomb in August 1949 and the victory of the Chinese Communist Party in October 1949 only heightened domestic fears that the United States faced a threat more powerful than the Axis of World War II.

Less than two weeks before Senator Joseph McCarthy's address in West Virginia, one of the most famous anticommunist trials ended with former State Department official Alger Hiss receiving a five-year prison sentence for lying about his previous association with communists. In this context, domestic persecution of suspected communists increased dramatically. Both Democrats and Republicans recognized that the number-one political issue of the day concerned communism, and members of both parties strove to outdo the other in anti-communist word and deed.

Significance

McCarthy's speech at the Women's Republican Club in Wheeling, West Virginia, catapulted the junior senator's career. Elected to the U.S. Senate in 1946, he enjoyed little respect from his colleagues, and he struggled to possess any legislative influence. This speech, however, resurrected his political career and put him on the path to being one of the most controversial government officials in U.S. history. The speech gained national attention not for his general denunciation of communism, but for his specific declaration that communists had infiltrated the State Department and threatened to aid the Soviet Union's supposed plans for global conquest.

Much as he would do in the coming years, McCarthy eagerly named specific individuals he believed to be aiding the enemy. He focused in particular on Secretary of State Dean Acheson. These charges proved characteristic of his tactic to attack his political enemies relentlessly in the name of national security and patriotism. According to McCarthy and other red-baiters, anyone who challenged such assaults in effect gave comfort to the enemy as well. Thus, by their very nature, these charges became self-justifying and quite difficult to counter lest one risked being charged as a communist sympathizer. Buttressed by the growing popularity he received in the months after the Wheeling address, McCarthy won reelection in a landslide in 1952. He soon dramatically increased his powers in the Senate, leading to his notorious investigations of supposed communist infiltration in the federal government in 1953–1954.

Primary Source

"Speech at Wheeling, West Virginia" [excerpt]

SYNOPSIS: McCarthy entered the Wheeling speech into the *Congressional Record of the Senate* on February 20, 1950. Interestingly, he revised the address to read that 57, rather than 205, Communist Party loyalists worked in the State Department. This change proved typical of most of the senator's assertions. He never actually possessed such a list and freely manipulated the figures from speech to speech. Nevertheless, McCarthy's supposed list pushed him to the forefront of the anticommunist movement.

Ladies and gentlemen,

Tonight as we celebrate the one hundred and forty-first birthday of one of the greatest men in American history, I would like to be able to talk about what a glorious day today is in the history of the world. As we celebrate the birth of this man who with his whole heart and soul hated war, I would like to be able to speak of peace in our time, of war being outlawed, and of world-wide disarmament. These would be truly appropriate things to be able to mention as we celebrate the birthday of Abraham Lincoln. . . .

Five years after a world war has been won, men's hearts should anticipate a long peace, and men's minds should be free from the heavy weight that comes with war. But this is not such a period—for this is not a period of peace. This is a time of the "cold war." This is a time when all the world is split into two vast, increasingly hostile armed camps—a time of great armaments race. . . .

Six years ago, at the time of the first conference to map out the peace—Dumbarton Oaks—there was within the Soviet orbit 180,000,000 people. Lined up on the antitotalitarian side there were in the world at that time roughly 1,625,000,000 people. Today, only 6 years later, there are 800,000,000 people under the absolute domination of Soviet Russia— an increase of over 400 percent. On our side, the figure has shrunk to around 500,000,000. In other words, in less than 6 years the odds have changed from 9 to 1 in our favor to 8 to 5 against us. This indicates the swiftness of the tempo of Communist victories and American defeats in the cold war. As one of our outstanding historical figures once said, "When a great democracy is destroyed, it will not be because of enemies from without, but rather because of enemies from within."

The truth of this statement is becoming terrifyingly clear as we see this country each day losing on every front.

At war's end we were physically the strongest nation on earth and, at least potentially, the most powerful intellectually and morally. Ours could have been the honor of being a beacon on the desert of destruction, a shining living proof that civilization was not yet ready to destroy itself. Unfortunately, we have failed miserably and tragically to arise to the opportunity.

The reason why we find ourselves in a position of impotency is not because our only powerful potential enemy has sent men to invade our shores, but rather because of the traitorous actions of those who have been treated so well by this Nation. It has not been the less fortunate or members of minority groups who have been selling this Nation out, but rather those who have had all the benefits that the wealthiest nation on earth has had to offer—the

Senator Joseph McCarthy (left) during a 1951 HUAC hearing. © **BETTMANN/CORBIS. REPRODUCED BY PERMISSION.**

finest homes, the finest college education, and the finest jobs in Government we can give.

This is glaringly true in the State Department. There the bright young men who are born with silver spoons in their mouths are the ones who have been the worst. . . .

Now I know it is very easy for anyone to condemn a particular bureau or department in general terms. Therefore, I would like to cite one rather unusual case—the case of a man who has done much to shape our foreign policy.

When Chiang Kai-shek was fighting our war, the State Department had in China a young man named John S. Service. His task, obviously, was not to work for the communization of China. Strangely, however, he sent official reports back to the State Department urging that we torpedo our ally Chiang Kai-shek and stating, in effect, that communism was the best hope of China.

Later, this man—John Service—was picked up by the Federal Bureau of Investigation for turning over to the Communists secret State Department information. Strangely, however, he was never prosecuted. However, Joseph Grew, the Under Secretary

A Declaration of Conscience

[In June 1950, Republican senator Margaret Chase Smith responded to the red-baiting rampant in the Cold War political discourse with a "Declaration of Conscience." Signed by six other moderate Republican senators, this declaration repudiated McCarthy's tactics while also attacking the administration of Harry Truman (served 1945–1953) and other Democrats for offering ineffective leadership against the Soviet Union. The following excerpt charges that both sides aide the enemy, and, in effect, replicates the strategy it seeks to rebuke.]

It is with these thoughts that I have drafted what I call a Declaration of Conscience. I am gratified that the Senator from New Hampshire [Mr. Tobey], the Senator from Vermont [Mr. Aiken], the Senator from Oregon [Mr. Morse], the Senator from New York [Mr. Ives], the Senator from Minnesota [Mr. Thye], and the Senator from New Jersey [Mr. Hendrickson] have concurred in that declaration and have authorized me to announce their concurrence.

The declaration reads as follows:

Speech of Senator Margaret Chase Smith, 1950 [excerpt]

Statement of Seven Republican Senators

1. We are Republicans. But we are Americans first. It is as Americans that we express our concern with the growing confusion that threatens the security and stability of our country. Democrats and Republicans alike have contributed to that confusion.

2. The Democratic administration has initially created the confusion by its lack of effective leadership, by its contradictory grave warnings and optimistic assurances, by its complacency to the threat of communism here at home, by its oversensitiveness to rightful criticism, by its petty bitterness against its critics.

3. Certain elements of the Republican Party have materially added to this confusion in the hopes of riding the Republican Party to victory through the selfish political exploitation of fear, bigotry, ignorance and intolerance. There are enough mistakes of the Democrats for the Republicans to criticize constructively without resorting to political smears.

4. To this extent, Democrats and Republicans alike have unwittingly, but undeniably, played directly into the Communist design of "confuse, divide and conquer."

5. It is high time that we stopped thinking politically as Republicans and Democrats about elections and started thinking patriotically as Americans about national security based in individual freedom. It is high time that we all stopped being tools and victims of totalitarian techniques—techniques that, if continued here unchecked, will surely end what we have come to cherish as the American way of life.

Margaret Chase Smith, Maine.
Charles W. Tobey, New Hampshire.
George D. Aiken, Vermont.
Wayne L. Morse, Oregon.
Irving M. Ives, New York.
Edward J. Thye, Minnesota.
Robert C. Hendrickson, New Jersey.

SOURCE: Smith, Margaret Chase. "Speech of Senator Margaret Chase Smith, 1950." *Congressional Record of the Senate,* 81st Cong., 2nd sess., June 1, 1950. Available online at http://azimuth.harcourtcollege.com/history/ayers/chapter27/27.4.mcsmith.html; website home page: http://azimuth.harcourtcollege.com (accessed June 18, 2003).

---

of State, who insisted on his prosecution, was forced to resign. Two days after Grew's successor, Dean Acheson, took over as Under Secretary of State, this man—John Service—who had been picked up by the FBI and who had previously urged that communism was the best hope of China, was not only reinstated in the State Department but promoted. And finally, under Acheson, placed in charge of all placements and promotions.

Today, ladies and gentlemen, this man Service is on his way to represent the State Department and Acheson in Calcutta—by far and away the most important listening post in the Far East. . . .

Then there was a Mrs. Mary Jane Kenny, from the Board of Economic Warfare in the State Department, who was named in an FBI report and in a House committee report as a courier for the Communist Party while working for the Government. And where do you think Mrs. Kenny is—she is now an editor in the United Nations Document Bureau. . . .

This, ladies and gentlemen, gives you somewhat of a picture of the type of individuals who have been helping to shape our foreign policy. In my opinion the State Department, which is one of the most important government departments, is thoroughly infested with Communists.

I have in my hand 57 cases of individuals who would appear to be either card carrying members or certainly loyal to the Communist Party, but who nevertheless are still helping to shape our foreign policy. . . .

This brings us down to the case of one Alger Hiss who is more important not as an individual any more, but rather because he is so representative of a group in the State Department. . . .

If time permitted, it might be well to go into detail about the fact that Hiss was Roosevelt's chief advisor at Yalta when Roosevelt was admittedly in ill health and tired physically and mentally. . . .

According to the then Secretary of State Stettinius, here are some of the things that Hiss helped to decide at Yalta. (1) The establishment of a European High Commission; (2) the treatment of Germany—this you will recall was the conference at which it was decided that we would occupy Berlin with Russia occupying an area completely circling the city, which, as you know, resulted in the Berlin airlift which cost 31 American lives; (3) the Polish question; . . . (6) Iran; (7) China—here's where we gave away Manchuria; (8) Turkish Straits question; (9) international trusteeships; (10) Korea. . . .

As you hear this story of high treason, I know that you are saying to yourself, "Well, why doesn't the Congress do something about it?" Actually, ladies and gentlemen, one of the important reasons for the graft, the corruption, the dishonesty, the disloyalty, the treason in high Government positions—one of the most important reasons why this continues is a lack of moral uprising on the part of the 140,000,000 American people. In the light of history, however, this is not hard to explain.

It is the result of an emotional hang-over and a temporary moral lapse which follows every war. It is the apathy of evil which people who have been subjected to the tremendous evils of war feel. As the people of the world see mass murder, the destruction of defenseless and innocent people, and all of the crime and lack of morals which go with war, they become numb and apathetic. It has always been thus after war.

However, the morals of our people have not been destroyed. They still exist. This cloak of numbness and apathy has only needed a spark to rekindle them. Happily, this spark has finally been supplied.

As you know, very recently the Secretary of State proclaimed his loyalty to a man [Hiss] guilty of what has always been considered as the most abominable of all crime—of being a traitor to the people who gave him a position of great trust. The Secretary of State in attempting to justify his continued devotion to the man who sold out the Christian world to the atheistic world, referred to Christ's Sermon on the Mount as a justification and reason therefor, and the reaction of the American people to this would have made the heart of Abraham Lincoln happy.

This cartoon shows a dismayed Secretary of State, John Foster Dulles, after finding Senator McCarthy in his desk drawer. The U.S. State Department was a frequent target of McCarthy's hunt for communists and communist sympathizers in the U.S. government. **THE LIBRARY OF CONGRESS.**

When this pompous diplomat in striped pants, with a phony British accent, proclaimed to the American people that Christ on the Mount endorsed communism, high treason, and betrayal of a sacred trust, the blasphemy was so great that it awakened the dormant indignation of the American people.

He has lighted the spark which is resulting in a moral uprising and will end only when the whole sorry mess of twisted, warped thinkers are swept from the national scene so that we may have a new birth of national honesty and decency in Government.

Further Resources

BOOKS

Fried, Richard M. *The Russians Are Coming! The Russians Are Coming!* New York: Oxford University Press, 1998.

Oshinsky, David M. *A Conspiracy So Immense: The World of Joe McCarthy.* New York: The Free Press, 1983.

Powers, Richard Gid. *Not Without Honor: The History of American Anticommunism.* New Haven, Conn.: Yale University Press, 1995.

Reeves, Thomas C. *The Life and Times of Joe McCarthy.* Lanham, Wisc.: Madison, 1997.

Schrecker, Ellen. *Many Are the Crimes: McCarthyism in America.* Princeton, N.J.: Princeton University Press, 1998.

WEBSITES

Oshinsky, David M. "McCarthy, Joseph." *American National Biography Online.* Available online at http://www.anb .org/articles/07/07-00188.html; website home page: http:// www.anb.org/ (accessed June 18, 2003) *This website is a subscription-based service that is available for free through most libraries.*

Presidential Reactions to Joseph McCarthy

Reaction of President Harry Truman to Loyalty Investigation, News Conference at Key West

News conference

By: Harry Truman

Date: March 30, 1950

Source: Truman, Harry. Reaction of President Harry Truman to Loyalty Investigation, News Conference at Key West. March 30, 1950. In Schlesinger, Arthur M., Jr., and Rodger Burns, eds. *Congress Investigates: A Documentation of History, 1792–1974.* New York: Chelsea House, 1975, 80–83. Available online at http://trumanlibrary.org/publicpapers/ (accessed August 6, 2003).

About the Author: Harry Truman (1884–1972) was elected to the U.S. Senate in 1934 and then served as President Franklin Roosevelt's (served 1933–1945) vice president in 1945. Following Roosevelt's death on April 12, 1945, Truman was sworn in as the thirty-third U.S. president. After World War II (1939–1945), he directed the United States to become the world's dominant power in the postwar era, which led to the Cold War struggle between the United States and the Soviet Union.

Letter to Harry Bullis

Letter

By: Dwight Eisenhower

Date: May 18, 1953

Source: Eisenhower, Dwight. Letter to Harry Bullis. May 18, 1953. Available online at http://www.eisenhower.utexas .edu/dl/McCarthy/Mccarthydocuments.html; website home page: http://www.eisenhower.utexas.edu (accessed June 18, 2003).

About the Author: Dwight Eisenhower (1890–1969) graduated from West Point in 1915. By 1940, he rose to the rank of lieutenant colonel. With the eruption of World War II (1939–1945), he swiftly advanced to four-star general in 1943. That same year, Eisenhower received the assignment to lead one of the largest military campaigns in world history: the D day invasion of June 6, 1944. After the war, he went

into politics and served as the thirty-fourth U.S. president from 1953 to 1961. ■

Introduction

In the early months of his presidency, Harry Truman oversaw a series of momentous events: the German surrender on May 7, 1945, the successful Trinity atomic bomb test in July, the Potsdam Conference with Britain and the Soviet Union in July and August, the atomic bombings of Hiroshima and Nagasaki in August 6 and 9, followed by the end of World War II with the Japanese surrender on August 15. Furthermore, Truman called for significant monetary investments in Europe and East Asia to thwart what he perceived as a growing communist threat to U.S. global hegemony.

Despite growing worries about his Cold War policies abroad and an economic recession at home, Truman surprised many by winning a second term in 1948. The president, who raised the stakes of the United States' competition with the so-called Red menace, soon became the victim of the sort of vehement anticommunism he had initiated. During his second term, he suffered a series of stinging defeats abroad that decimated his approval ratings: the Soviet Union successfully tested its first atomic bomb in August 1949, communists gained control of China in October 1949, and communist North Korea invaded South Korea in June 1950.

On the home front, the economy worsened, and Truman faced mounting criticism that his administration harbored communist spies and sympathizers. Senator Joseph McCarthy issued the most stinging assaults, especially his speech before the Women's Republican Club in Wheeling, West Virginia, in February 1950, in which he criticized the Truman administration for inadequate investigations into supposed communists within its ranks. McCarthy sparked a wave of anticommunist railings against the Truman administration from Republicans and Democrats alike. The red-baiting, almost entirely based on supposition and outright deceit, enabled conservatives in both parties to block Truman's relatively liberal Fair Deal legislative agenda, including proposals concerning civil rights and national health care insurance.

Significance

In his March 30, 1950, press conference, Truman countered McCarthy directly by attempting to out red-bait the nation's leading anticommunist. Truman, who ushered in the Cold War with virulent anticommunist domestic and foreign policies in the late 1940s, now struggled to protect his stature from an upstart senator who gained increasing national attention for levying a relentless barrage of anticommunist attacks on his political enemies.

Squarely framing McCarthy's charges as political in nature, Truman concluded that Republican obstruction of his policies was "just as bad as trying to cut the Army in time of war" or "shoot[ing] our soldiers in the back in a hot war." This rhetoric certainly fought fire with fire, but it also further heightened domestic Cold War tensions and, implicitly, justified red-baiting as an acceptable political tactic.

Butressed by his high-profile battles with the Truman administration, McCarthy's influence grew in the coming years. By 1953, following his reelection, McCarthy had begun a series of nationally publicized investigations into communist infiltration in the federal government. The senator's attacks did not diminish, even with the installation of Dwight Eisenhower (served 1953–1961), a Republican war hero, as president.

Eisenhower rose to the White House in 1952 on a wave of public discontent with the Truman administration. Faced with McCarthy's continuing criticism of the federal government, many called on Eisenhower to publicly rebuke the senator and put the full weight of the presidency behind a defense of the victims of red-baiting.

As conveyed in his letter May 18, 1953, to his friend Harry Bullis, Eisenhower believed that it would demean his high office to engage in a public argument with McCarthy. At the same time, Eisenhower acknowledged that he believed in many of the core justifications for the investigations in the first place. Like Truman, Eisenhower depicted McCarthy as someone desperate for attention and overreliant on anticommunism as a means of selfishly advancing his career.

President Harry Truman speaks to the press from the White House.
© BETTMANN/CORBIS. REPRODUCED BY PERMISSION.

Primary Source

Reaction of President Harry Truman to Loyalty Investigation, News Conference at Key West

SYNOPSIS: Two days after his Wheeling address, McCarthy wrote Truman urging him to begin an immediate investigation into communist subversion in the State Department. He warned Truman that "[f]ailure on your part will label the Democratic Party of being the bedfellow of international communism." Truman decided to reply publicly to the senator's charges in a press conference at his vacation home, the "Little White House," in Key West, Florida. After having a picnic with reporters on a sunny afternoon, Truman bluntly chastised McCarthy and his Republican allies.

Mr. President, do you think Senator McCarthy is getting anywhere in his attempt to win the case against the State Department?
What's that?

Do you think that Senator McCarthy can show any disloyalty exists in the State Department?

I think the greatest asset that the Kremlin has is Senator McCarthy.

Would you care to elaborate on that?
I don't think it needs any elaboration—I don't think it needs any elaboration.

Brother, will that hit page one tomorrow!

If you think we are going to bust down the fence on what you have got later, that's a pretty good starter. (Laughter)

Mr. President, could we quote that one phrase, "I think the greatest asset the Kremlin has is Senator McCarthy"?

Now let me give you a little preliminary, and then I will tell you what I think you ought to do. Let me tell you what the situation is.

We started out in 1945, when I became President, and the two wars were still going on, and the Russians were our allies, just the same as the British and the French and Brazil and the South American countries. And we won the war together.

We organized the United Nations in April 1945, and one of the first questions that was asked me, after I was sworn in at 7:00 o'clock on the 12th of April, was whether or not the San Francisco conference on the United Nations should go ahead. And I said it certainly will. It went ahead and we finally succeeded in getting a charter and getting it agreed to by I think 51 nations, if I remember correctly.

Then our objective was to—as quickly as possible—get peace in the world. We made certain agreements with the Russians and the British and the French and the Chinese. We kept those agreements to the letter. They have nearly all been—those agreements where the Russians were involved—been broken by the Russians. And it became perfectly evident that they had no intention of carrying out the fundamental principles of the United Nations Charter and the agreements which had been made at Teheran, Yalta, and Potsdam. And it became evident that there was an endeavor on the part of the Kremlin to control the world.

A procedure was instituted which came to be known as the cold war. The airlift to Berlin was only one phase of it. People became alarmed here in the United States then, that there might be people whose sympathies were with the Communist ideal of government—which is not communism under any circumstances, it is totalitarianism of the worst brand. There isn't any difference between the totalitarian Russian Government and the Hitler government and the Franco government in Spain. They are all alike. They are police state governments.

In 1947 I instituted a loyalty program for Government employees, and that loyalty procedure program was set up in such a way that the rights of individuals were respected.

In a survey of the 2,200,000 employees at that time, I think there were some 205—something like that—who left the service. I don't know—a great many of them left of their own accord.

How many, Mr. President?

Somewhere in the neighborhood of 205. Does anybody remember those figures exactly? It's a very small figure.

Very small.

An infinitesimal part of 1 percent. We will get the figures for you.

And then, for political background, the Republicans have been trying vainly to find an issue on which to make a bid for the control of the Congress for next year. They tried "statism." They tried "welfare state." They tried "socialism." And there are a certain number of members of the Republican Party who are trying to dig up that old malodorous dead horse called "isolationism." And in order to do that, they

are perfectly willing to sabotage the bipartisan foreign policy of the United States. And this fiasco which has been going on in the Senate is the very best asset that the Kremlin could have in the operation of the cold war. And that is what I mean when I say that McCarthy's antics are the best asset that the Kremlin can have.

Now, if anybody really felt that there were disloyal people in the employ of the Government, the proper and the honorable way to handle the situation would be to come to the President of the United States and say, "This man is a disloyal person. He is in such and such a department." We will investigate him immediately, and if he were a disloyal person he would be immediately fired.

That is not what they want. They are trying to create an issue, and it is going to be just as big a fiasco as the campaign in New York and other places on these other false and fatuous issues.

With a little bit of intelligence they could find an issue at home without a bit of trouble!

What would it be, Mr. President?

Anything in the domestic line. I will meet them on any subject they want, but to try to sabotage the foreign policy of the United States, in the face of the situation with which we are faced, is just as bad as trying to cut the Army in time of war.

On that question we were just kidding.

And that gave me a chance to give you an answer. To try to sabotage the foreign policy of the United States is just as bad in this cold war as it would be to shoot our soldiers in the back in a hot war.

I am fed up with what is going on, and I am giving you the facts as I see them.

Mr. President, do you consider the Republican Party as a party?

The policy of the Republican Party has endorsed the antics of Mr. McCarthy.

That affects the bipartisan—

That's what it is for—that's what it is for. They are anxious for the return of isolationism.

Do you think that this has torpedoed, then, the bipartisan—

It is an endeavor to torpedo the bipartisan foreign policy. They are not going to succeed, because the levelheaded Republicans do not believe that at all, as note Mr. Stimson, Senator Vandenberg, Senator Saltonstall, and a dozen others I could name, who know exactly what is going on and are trying their best to cooperate. And I am going to try to help them prevent it going under.

Well, Mr. President, to carry that out to its logical conclusion, when Dean Acheson will go down in history as one of the great Secretaries of State, nothing that the Democratic Party can do except simply to sit on the sidelines and say, "Well?"

Well, it's too bad. It's a dangerous situation, and it has got to be stopped. And every citizen in the United States is going to find out just exactly what the facts are when I get through with this thing.

You will stand up on one side, and they will stand up on the other?

There's only one side that the people will stay on, and that is the side that will lead to peace. That is all we are after. This is just another fiasco to find an issue. This is not it.

Mr. President, would you like to name any others besides Senator McCarthy who have participated in this attempt to sabotage our foreign policy?

Senator Wherry.

Yes, sir?

Senator Bridges.

Yes, sir?

That's about as far as I care to go.

Okay, sir.

Now, what I forgot to say was would you like to say anything about Mr. Acheson and Mr. Lattimore, and—what's his name—the Ambassador at Large?

Jessup. I think I made myself perfectly clear that I think Dean Acheson will go down in history as one of the great Secretaries of State. You know very well that Mr. Jessup is as able and distinguished a citizen as this country has ever produced. Lattimore is a member of the faculty of Johns Hopkins University and is a very well informed person on foreign affairs.

You don't believe he is a spy?

Why of course not. It's silly on the face of it.

Mr. President, don't you think the American people recognize this for what it is?

There is no doubt about it. I am just emphatically bringing it to their attention.

For direct quotes, could we have that, "I think the greatest asset—

I would rather you would say that the greatest asset the Kremlin has is the present approach of those in the Senate who are trying to sabotage the bipartisan foreign policy.

Could we have that read back to us?

Sure. Jack?

Mr. Romagna: I'm all balled up.

Take your time—take your time.

The greatest asset that the Kremlin has is the partisan attempt in the Senate to sabotage the bipartisan foreign policy of the United States.

This may seem redundant, but this is just for the record. The partisan effort, of course, is the effort by the Republicans in the Senate—

Well now, I didn't say that, "partisan effort." Leave it at that. Draw your own conclusions.

Primary Source
Letter to Harry Bullis

SYNOPSIS: In the following letter, Eisenhower presents his reasons to Bullis for refusing to confront McCarthy, but he notes that he might change his mind on the issue. In the fall of 1953, McCarthy began hearings on supposed communist infiltration in the U.S. Army that would do just that. The charges enraged the former general to such an extent that he openly encouraged a congressional investigation into McCarthy's investigations. The Army-McCarthy hearings of 1954 destroyed the senator's public stature and resulted in his censure by the Senate.

May 18, 1953

Dear Harry:

I emphatically agree with most of what you have to say in your letter of May ninth. I shall certainly take seriously your observation about the Judd case.

With respect to McCarthy, I continue to believe that the President of the United States cannot afford to name names in opposing procedures, practices and methods in our government. This applies with special force when the individual concerned enjoys the immunity of a United States Senator. This particular individual wants, above all else, publicity. Nothing would probably please him more than to get the publicity that would be generated by public repudiation by the President.

I do not mean that there is no possibility that I shall ever change my mind on this point. I merely mean that as of this moment, I consider that the wisest course of action is to continue to pursue a steady, positive policy in foreign relations, in legal procedures in cleaning out the insecure and the disloyal, and in all other areas where McCarthy seems to take such a specific and personal interest. My friends on the Hill tell me that of course, among other things, he wants to increase his appeal as an after-dinner speaker and so raise the fees that he charges.

It is a sorry mess; at times one feels almost like hanging his head in shame when he reads some of the unreasoned, vicious outbursts of demagoguery that appear in our public prints. But whether a Presidential "crack down" would better, or would actually worsen, the situation, is a moot question.

With all the best,
As ever,
[Dwight D. Eisenhower]
Mr. Harry Bullis,
General Mills Incorporated,
400 Second Avenue South,
Minneapolis 1, Minnesota.

Further Resources

BOOKS

Ambrose, Stephen E. *Eisenhower: The President.* New York: Simon and Schuster, 1984.

Griffin, Robert, and Athan Theoharis. *The Specter: Original Essays on the Cold War and the Origins of McCarthyism.* New York: New Viewpoints, 1974.

Hogan, Michael J. *A Cross of Iron: Harry S. Truman and the Origins of the National Security State, 1945–1954.* Cambridge: Cambridge University Press, 1999.

Reeves, Thomas C. *The Life and Times of Joe McCarthy.* Lanham, Wisc.: Madison, 1997.

WEBSITES

"McCarthyism or 'The Red Scare.'" Dwight D. Eisenhower Library. Available online at http://www.eisenhower.utexas.edu /dl/McCarthy/Mccarthydocuments.html; website home page: http://www.eisenhower.utexas.edu/ (accessed June 18, 2003).

NSC-68: United States Objectives and Programs for National Security

Policy

By: Paul H. Nitze

Date: April 14, 1950

Source: Nitze, Paul H. *NSC-68: United States Objectives and Programs for National Security.* April 14, 1950. Available online at http://www.fas.org/irp/offdocs/nsc-hst/nsc-68 .htm; website home page: http://www.fas.org (accessed June 18, 2003).

About the Author: Paul H. Nitze (1907–) authored one of the most influential policies of the Cold War: National Security Council Document 68 (NSC 68). Graduating from Harvard University in 1927, Nitze worked in a number of federal government positions during and after World War II (1939–1945). Since the end of the Cold War, Nitze has strengthened his views toward nonproliferation and now concludes that nuclear weapons are no longer necessary in world affairs. ■

Introduction

The end of World War II brought only a temporary sense of safety for the American public. With the atomic bombings of Hiroshima and Nagasaki in August 1945, the United States ended the war and began a new conflict with the Soviet Union. The Cold War emerged from the devastation of World War II as the wartime allies competed to fill the void left by Germany in Europe and Japan in East Asia. Over the next five years, policy makers, the press, and many common citizens declared that a new menace threatened global security even more than the rise of fascism in the 1930s. The battle between communism and capitalism would impact every corner of the globe for much of the next half century.

Communism, supposedly directed by the Soviet Union, challenged U.S. hegemony in Europe and Asia. President Harry Truman (served 1945–1953) directed policies that provided enormous amounts of economic aid, and a significant U.S. military presence, to nations still reeling from the devastation wrought during the previous decade. The Truman doctrine (1947) distilled these new policies into a single ideology under which the United States must intervene in other countries to prevent the establishment of communist regimes. If the United States did not act immediately and strongly, the communist menace would soon spread from nation to nation, eventually isolating and likely invading the United States in a final push for Soviet world domination. The specific guidelines concerning why, when, and how the United States should develop its military force for possible engagement with the Soviet Union waited to be determined. Also in 1947, Truman expanded the federal government's anticommunist infrastructure with the National Security Act. This policy created the Central Intelligence Agency, the Department of Defense, and the National Security Council. As their names reflected, these agencies' primary purpose concerned protecting the United States against the communist threat.

Significance

Written in 1950, NSC 68 presented the Truman administration with a comprehensive strategy for confronting the Soviet Union and winning the Cold War. The document begins with a detailed analysis of the origins of the Cold War and presents a clear, forceful rationalization of global anticommunist action. NSC 68 portrays the United States as a protector of the free world, while the Soviet Union, bent on total domination, was the opposite. Lest anyone conclude that the Soviet Union did not in fact represent the most significant threat to the United States in its history, the NSC 68 emphasizes that "the cold war is in fact a real war in which the survival of the free world is at stake."

Following this conclusion, NSC 68 urges a massive increase in U.S. military spending and economic aid to nations menaced by communism. Contrary to the isolationist policies of the 1930s, which many had concluded led to the rise of Germany and Japan, the United States must intervene throughout the world with displays of strength, unity, and dedication to protect its own national security. Yet, NSC 68 does not call for direct, armed assaults on the Soviet Union. The communist nation already possessed sufficient weaponry to defend itself and subject the United States to heavy losses. Rather, this policy paper calls for the containment and isolation of global communism.

Despite the immediate action urged by NSC 68, many believed that the American public would not support billions of dollars to be spent in a war in which the United States had not been directly attacked. As Senator Arthur Vandenburg emphasized, the Truman administration would need to "scare the hell out of the American people" to get them to support massive military and foreign policy expenditures in the midst of a domestic economic recession. Just such an event occurred on June 25, 1950, when communist North Korean forces invaded South Korea, beginning the Korean War (1950–1953). Thereafter, many skeptics of NSC 68 reversed their opinion in the context of a communist takeover of South Korea and supported U.S. involvement in the war.

Primary Source

NSC-68: United States Objectives and Programs for National Security [excerpt]

SYNOPSIS: NSC 68 may be viewed as a document with specific foreign and domestic goals, as the Truman administration attempted to strengthen itself on the domestic front as it attempted to do the same internationally. The Korean War would soon call for many of the following recommendations, cementing NSC 68's stature as one of the most significant policy statements of the Cold War.

"Conclusions and Recommendations"

Conclusions

The foregoing analysis indicates that the probable fission bomb capability and possible thermonuclear bomb capability of the Soviet Union have greatly intensified the Soviet threat to the security of the United States. This threat is of the same character as that described in NSC 20/4 (approved by the President on November 24, 1948) but is more immediate than had previously been estimated. In particular, the United States now faces the contingency that within the next four or five years the Soviet Union will possess the military capability of delivering a surprise atomic attack of such weight that the United States must have substantially increased general air, ground, and sea strength,

Paul Nitze served as the U.S. Department of State's Chief Policy Planner in the early 1950s. AP/WIDE WORLD PHOTOS. REPRODUCED BY PERMISSION.

atomic capabilities, and air and civilian defenses to deter war and to provide reasonable assurance, in the event of war, that it could survive the initial blow and go on to the eventual attainment of its objectives. In return, this contingency requires the intensification of our efforts in the fields of intelligence and research and development.

Allowing for the immediacy of the danger, the following statement of Soviet threats, contained in NSC 20/4, remains valid:

14. The gravest threat to the security of the United States within the foreseeable future stems from the hostile designs and formidable power of the USSR, and from the nature of the Soviet system.

15. The political, economic, and psychological warfare which the USSR is now waging has dangerous potentialities for weakening the relative world position of the United States and disrupting its traditional institutions by means short of war, unless sufficient resistance is encountered in the policies of this and other non-communist countries.

16. The risk of war with the USSR is sufficient to warrant, in common prudence, timely and adequate preparation by the United States.

    a. Even though present estimates indicate that the Soviet leaders probably do not intend deliberate armed action involving the United States at this time, the possibility of such deliberate resort to war cannot be ruled out.

    b. Now and for the foreseeable future there is a continuing danger that war will arise either through Soviet miscalculation of the determination of the United States to use all the means at its command to safeguard its security, through Soviet misinterpretation of our intentions, or through U.S. miscalculation of Soviet reactions to measures which we might take.

17. Soviet domination of the potential power of Eurasia, whether achieved by armed aggression or by political and subversive means, would be strategically and politically unacceptable to the United States.

18. The capability of the United States either in peace or in the event of war to cope with threats to its security or to gain its objectives would be severely weakened by internal development, important among which are:

    a. Serious espionage, subversion and sabotage, particularly by concerted and well-directed communist activity.

    b. Prolonged or exaggerated economic instability.

    c. Internal political and social disunity.

    d. Inadequate or excessive armament or foreign aid expenditures.

    e. An excessive or wasteful usage of our resources in time of peace.

    f. Lessening of U.S. prestige and influence through vacillation of appeasement or lack of skill and imagination in the conduct of its foreign policy or by shirking world responsibilities.

    g. Development of a false sense of security through a deceptive change in Soviet tactics.

Although such developments as those indicated in paragraph 18 above would severely weaken the capability of the United States and its allies to cope with the Soviet threat to their security, considerable progress has been made since 1948 in laying the foundation upon which adequate strength can now be rapidly built.

The analysis also confirms that our objectives with respect to the Soviet Union, in time of peace as well as in time of war, as stated in NSC 20/4 (para. 19), are still valid, as are the aims and measures stated therein (paras. 20 and 21). Our current security programs and strategic plans are based upon these objectives, aims, and measures:

19.

    a. To reduce the power and influence of the USSR to limits which no longer constitute a threat to the peace, national independence, and stability of the world family of nations.

    b. To bring about a basic change in the conduct of international relations by the government in power in Russia, to conform with the purposes and principles set forth in the UN Charter.

        In pursuing these objectives, due care must be taken to avoid permanently impairing our economy and the fundamental values and institutions inherent in our way of life.

20. We should endeavor to achieve our general objectives by methods short of war through the pursuit of the following aims:

    a. To encourage and promote the gradual retraction of undue Russian power and influence from the present perimeter areas around traditional Russian boundaries and the emergence of the satellite countries as entities independent of the USSR.

    b. To encourage the development among the Russian peoples of attitudes which may help to modify current Soviet behavior and permit a revival of the national life of groups evidencing the ability and determination to achieve and maintain national independence.

    c. To eradicate the myth by which people remote from Soviet military influence are held in a position of subservience to Moscow and to cause the world at large to see and understand the true nature of the USSR and the Soviet-directed world communist party, and to adopt a logical and realistic attitude toward them.

    d. To create situations which will compel the Soviet Government to recognize the practical undesirability of acting on the basis of its present concepts and the necessity of behaving in accordance with precepts of international conduct, as set forth in the purposes and principles of the UN Charter.

21. Attainment of these aims requires that the United States:

a. Develop a level of military readiness which can be maintained as long as necessary as a deterrent to Soviet aggression, as indispensable support to our political attitude toward the USSR, as a source of encouragement to nations resisting Soviet political aggression, and as an adequate basis for immediate military commitments and for rapid mobilization should war prove unavoidable.

b. Assure the internal security of the United States against dangers of sabotage, subversion, and espionage.

c. Maximize our economic potential, including the strengthening of our peacetime economy and the establishment of essential reserves readily available in the event of war.

d. Strengthen the orientation toward the United States of the non-Soviet nations; and help such of those nations as are able and willing to make an important contribution to U.S. security, to increase their economic and political stability and their military capability.

e. Place the maximum strain on the Soviet structure of power and particularly on the relationships between Moscow and the satellite countries.

f. Keep the U.S. public fully informed and cognizant of the threats to our national security so that it will be prepared to support the measures which we must accordingly adopt.

In the light of present and prospective Soviet atomic capabilities, the action which can be taken under present programs and plans, however, becomes dangerously inadequate, in both timing and scope, to accomplish the rapid progress toward the attainment of the United States political, economic, and military objectives which is now imperative.

A continuation of present trends would result in a serious decline in the strength of the free world relative to the Soviet Union and its satellites. This unfavorable trend arises from the inadequacy of current programs and plans rather than from any error in our objectives and aims. These trends lead in the direction of isolation, not by deliberate decision but by lack of the necessary basis for a vigorous initiative in the conflict with the Soviet Union.

Our position as the center of power in the free world places a heavy responsibility upon the United States for leadership. We must organize and enlist the energies and resources of the free world in a positive program for peace which will frustrate the Kremlin design for world domination by creating a situation in the free world to which the Kremlin will be compelled to adjust. Without such a cooperative effort, led by the United States, we will have to make gradual withdrawals under pressure until we discover one day that we have sacrificed positions of vital interest.

It is imperative that this trend be reversed by a much more rapid and concerted build-up of the actual strength of both the United States and the other nations of the free world. The analysis shows that this will be costly and will involve significant domestic, financial, and economic adjustments.

The execution of such a build-up, however, requires that the United States have an affirmative program beyond the solely defensive one of countering the threat posed by the Soviet Union. This program must light the path to peace and order among nations in a system based on freedom and justice, as contemplated in the Charter of the United Nations. Further, it must envisage the political and economic measures with which and the military shield behind which the free world can work to frustrate the Kremlin design by the strategy of the cold war; for every consideration of devotion to our fundamental values and to our national security demands that we achieve our objectives by the strategy of the cold war, building up our military strength in order that it may not have to be used. The only sure victory lies in the frustration of the Kremlin design by the steady development of the moral and material strength of the free world and its projection into the Soviet world in such a way as to bring about an internal change in the Soviet system. Such a positive program—harmonious with our fundamental national purpose and our objectives— is necessary if we are to regain and retain the initiative and to win and hold the necessary popular support and cooperation in the United States and the rest of the free world.

This program should include a plan for negotiation with the Soviet Union, developed and agreed with our allies and which is consonant with our objectives. The United States and its allies, particularly the United Kingdom and France, should always be ready to negotiate with the Soviet Union on terms consistent with our objectives. The present world situation, however, is one which militates against successful negotiations with the Kremlin—for the terms of agreements on important pending issues would reflect present realities and would therefore be unacceptable, if not disastrous, to the United States and the rest of the free world. After a decision and a start on building up the strength of the free world has been made, it might then be desirable for the United States to take an initiative in seeking negotiations in the hope that it might facilitate the process of accommodation by the Kremlin to the new situation. Failing that, the unwillingness of the Kremlin to accept equitable terms or its bad faith in observing them would assist in consolidating popular opinion in the free world in support of the measures necessary to sustain the build-up.

In summary, we must, by means of a rapid and sustained build-up of the political, economic, and military strength of the free world, and by means of an affirmative program intended to wrest the initiative from the Soviet Union, confront it with convincing evidence of the determination and ability of the free world to frustrate the Kremlin design of a world dominated by its will. Such evidence is the only means short of war which eventually may force the Kremlin to abandon its present course of action and to negotiate acceptable agreements on issues of major importance.

The whole success of the proposed program hangs ultimately on recognition by this Government, the American people, and all free peoples, that the cold war is in fact a real war in which the survival of the free world is at stake. Essential prerequisites to success are consultations with Congressional leaders designed to make the program the object of nonpartisan legislative support, and a presentation to the public of a full explanation of the facts and implications of the present international situation. The prosecution of the program will require of us all the ingenuity, sacrifice, and unity demanded by the vital importance of the issue and the tenacity to persevere until our national objectives have been attained.

Recommendations

That the President:

a. Approve the foregoing Conclusions.

b. Direct the National Security Council, under the continuing direction of the President, and

with the participation of other Departments and Agencies as appropriate, to coordinate and insure the implementation of the Conclusions herein on an urgent and continuing basis for as long as necessary to achieve our objectives. For this purpose, representatives of the member Departments and Agencies, the Joint Chiefs of Staff or their deputies, and other Departments and Agencies as required should be constituted as a revised and strengthened staff organization under the National Security Council to develop coordinated programs for consideration by the National Security Council.

Further Resources

BOOKS

Hogan, Michael J. *A Cross of Iron: Harry S. Truman and the Origins of the National Security State, 1945-1954.* Cambridge: Cambridge University Press, 1999.

Kennan, George F. *American Diplomacy, 1900–1950.* Chicago: University of Chicago Press, 1951.

May, Ernest R., ed. *American Cold War Strategy: Interpreting NSC 68.* Boston: Bedford/St. Martin's, 1993.

Talbott, Strobe. *The Master at the Game: Paul Nitze and the Nuclear Peace.* New York: Knopf, 1988.

WEBSITES

"Nitze, Paul Henry." *The Columbia Encyclopedia,* 6th ed. Available online at http://www.bartleby.com/65/ni/Nitze-Pa.html; website home page: http://www.bartleby.com (accessed June 18, 2003).

"NSC 68: United States Objectives and Programs for National Security." National Security Council, Intelligence Resource Program, Federation of American States. Available online at http://www.fas.org/irp/offdocs/nsc-hst/nsc-68.htm; website home page: http://www.fas.org/irp/ (accessed June 18, 2003).

"Paul Nitze." Paul H. Nitze School of Advanced International Studies, Johns Hopkins University. Available online at http://www.sais-jhu.edu/faculty_bios/faculty_bio1.php?ID=46; website home page: http://www.sais-jhu.edu/ (accessed June 18, 2003).

AUDIO AND VISUAL MEDIA

The Cold War. Original release, 1998. CNN/Turner Home Video, 2002, VHS.

The Korean War

Telegram from the State Department to President Truman

Telegram

By: U.S. State Department

Date: June 24, 1950

Source: Telegram from the State Department to President Truman. June 24, 1950. Available online at http://www .trumanlibrary.org/whistlestop/study_collections/korea/large /week1/kw_1_1.jpg; website home page: http://www.truman library.org (accessed June 18, 2003).

About the Author: The U.S. State Department is the United States' leading foreign affairs agency. Led by the Secretary of State, who serves as the president's primary foreign affairs advisor, the department presents U.S. policies and aims to the rest of the world. The State Department maintains embassies and consulates in most nations to support U.S. travellers abroad and to promote U.S. interests and cultural exchanges with foreign countries to foster better relations.

Telegram to President Truman

Telegram

By: John Foster Dulles and John Allison

Date: June 25, 1950

Source: Dulles, John Foster, and John Allison. Telegram to President Truman. June 25, 1950. Available online at http:// www.trumanlibrary.org/whistlestop/study_collections/korea /large/week1/elsy_3_1.jpg; website home page: http://www .trumanlibrary.org (accessed June 18, 2003).

About the Author: John Foster Dulles (1888–1959) served in the Army during World War I before being appointed to the U.S. Senate to complete the term of ailing Senator Robert F. Wagner. After World War II, Dulles was tasked by President Harry Truman (served 1945–1953) to serve as a special representative to negotiate a peace treaty with Japan. He was appointed Secretary of State under the Dwight Eisenhower (served 1953–1961) administration and resigned in 1959 due to poor health. Shortly before his death later that year, he was awarded the Medal of Freedom.

John Allison (1905–1978) had a career in the foreign service. Throughout the 1950s he held posts as the U.S. ambassador to Japan, Indonesia, and Czechoslovakia.

"President Truman's Conversation with George M. Elsey"

Diary

By: George M. Elsey

Date: June 26, 1950

Source: Elsey, George M. "President Truman's Conversation with George M. Elsey." June 26, 1950. Available online at

http://www.trumanlibrary.org/whistlestop/study_collections /korea/large/week1/elsy_7_1.jpg; website home page: http:// www.trumanlibrary.org (accessed June 18, 2003).

About the Author: George M. Elsey (1918–?) served in the U.S. Naval Reserves before joining the White House staff in the mid-1940s. From 1949 to 1951 he served as Administrative Assistant to the President during the Harry Truman administration. Later in his career, Elsey led the American Red Cross.

Address to the American People on the Situation in Korea

Speech

By: Harry S. Truman

Date: July 19, 1950

Source: Truman, Harry S. Address to the American People on the Situation in Korea. July 19, 1950. Available online at http://www.presidency.ucsb.edu (accessed June 18, 2003).

About the Author: Harry Truman (1884–1972) was elected to the U.S. Senate in 1934 and then served as President Franklin Roosevelt's (served 1933–1945) vice president in 1945. Following Roosevelt's death on April 12, 1945, Truman was sworn in as the thirty-third U.S. president. After World War II (1939–1945), he directed the United States to become the world's dominant power in the postwar era, which led to the Cold War struggle between the United States and the Soviet Union. ∎

Introduction

In the closing days of World War II, the Soviet Union and United States rushed to control territory formerly occupied by Germany in Europe and Japan in East Asia. Japan, which had controlled the Korean Peninsula since its annexation in 1910, began to remove its forces to devote more of its resources to defending the main islands of Japan from U.S. assaults. Following the official surrender of Japan to the United States on August 15, 1945, the United States and the Soviet Union agreed to partition the newly independent Korea at the thirty-eighth parallel. The Soviet Union would aid Koreans in the removal of Japanese forces remaining in the northern half of the peninsula, while U.S. troops would do the same in the southern half.

Korean leaders soon emerged on both sides of the parallel, with the Soviet Union and the United States aiding the formation of national governments in the North and South, respectively. The official separation of Korea came in 1948, when the North installed a communist national structure and proclaimed itself the People's Democratic Republic of Korea, while citizens in the South developed a noncommunist government. In the months leading up to June 1950, tension increased on both sides of the demarcation as officials in the North and South,

American soldiers attend to a tank climbing out of a hole during the Korean War. **NATIONAL ARCHIVES AND RECORDS ADMINISTRATION.**

echoed by their counterparts in the Soviet Union and the United States, proclaimed their right to control the entire peninsula. On June 25, 1950, the North initiated a full-scale invasion of South Korea.

Significance

Late in evening of June 24, 1950, the State Department forwarded to President Truman an emergency message it had received from officers in Seoul, the capital of South Korea. The telegram described an "all out offense against" the Republic of Korea by communist forces from the North. On June 25, John Foster Dulles and John Allison provided analysis on the Korean conflict. The authors emphasized that the United States must be prepared to intervene if South Korean forces proved unable to defeat the Northern invasion force and that the refusal to do so would lead to world war. According to recollections by George M. Elsey, President Truman had reached the same conclusion by the next day. In terms that foreshadowed the domino theory, Truman argued that communists in other sections of the world, especially the Middle East, would soon attack if the United States did not counter the North Korean aggression. Thus, within a few hours of the attack, influential policy makers in the Truman administration and Truman himself had con-

cluded that the United States must immediately aid South Korea with military force.

The perspectives offered in these secret communications helped construct the president's public justification for U.S. involvement in the Korean War, given on July 19. In that address, Truman emphasized that the security of the United States and the world rested on whether the United States would enter the conflict. In the remainder of the speech, Truman described the necessity of instituting many of the policies initially supported by the National Security Council Document 68 in April 1950. The president called for massive increases in military spending, foreign aid, and domestic economic production to strengthen the United States and the global anticommunist cause. In many respects, Truman's characterization of the Korean conflict shaped the language later presidents used to persuade Americans to support intervention in Vietnam.

Primary Source

Telegram from the State Department to President Truman

SYNOPSIS: In the following document, the State Department reports to President Truman about the North Korean advance on South Korea. Even though this information is not completely digested, it appears that the invasion is well organized and can be considered to be an "all out offensive" against South Korea.

From: The State Department, Washington D.C.
The Secretary of State requested the following message be transmitted to the President:
To the President

From Seoul
To Secretary of State

No nine two five cma June two five cma one zero able mike

Nlact

Sent department nine two five cma repeated information cincfe.

According Korean army reports which partly confirmed by Kmag field adciqzr reports cma North Korean forces invaded rok territory at several points this morning. Action was initiated about four able mike Ongjin blasted by North Korean artillery fire. About six able mike North Korean infantry commenced crossing parallel in Ongjin area cma Kaesong area cma Chunchon area and amphibious landing was reportedly made south of Kangnung on East Coast. Kaesong was reportedly made captured at nine able mike with some one zero North Korean tanks participating in operation. North Korean forces cma spearheaded by tanks, reportedly closing in on Chunchon. Details of fighting in Kangnung area unclear, although it seems North Korean forces have cut highway. Am conferring with Kmag advisors and Korean officials this morning re situation. It would appear from nature of attack and manner in which it was launched it constitutes all out offensive against rok.

Primary Source

Telegram to President Truman [excerpt]

> **SYNOPSIS:** In this document, John Dulles and John Allison suggest that if in the event South Korea cannot defend itself and repulse the North Korean forces, the United States should be prepared to enter the conflict. They suggest that if the United States fails to act, it is possible that "a disastrous chain of events" may lead to another "world war."

Tokyo, June 25, 1950
[Received June 25, 1950, 10:35 a.m.]

It is possible that the South Koreans may themselves contain and repulse the attack and, if so, this is the best way. If, however, it appears that they cannot do so, then we believe that United States force should be used. . . . To sit by while Korea is overrun by unprovoked armed attack would start a disastrous chain of events leading most probably to world war. We suggest that the Security Council might call for action on behalf of the organization under Article 106 by the five powers or such of them as are willing to respond.

Primary Source

"President Truman's Conversation with George M. Elsey"

> **SYNOPSIS:** In the following document, Elsey describes the conversation he had with President Truman about the unfolding events in Korea. Though the president was concerned about South Korea, Elsey states that Truman was more worried about where the communists would attack next: the Middle East.

June 26, 1950—Monday

Subject: President Truman's conversations with George M. Elsey.

Immediately after the first statement was finished and while Charlie Ross was taking it off for mimeographing, I stayed behind to chat with the President about the significance of Korea. I expressed my very grave concern about Formosa. I said it seemed to me this was the perfect course for the Chinese communists to take.

The President walked over to the globe standing in front of the fireplace and said he was more worried about other parts of the world. He said he had ordered MacArthur to give ammunition to the Koreans, that the Air Force and the Navy were to protect the evacuation of Americans. That much was easy and clear. But what he was worried about, the President said, was the Middle East. He put his finger on Iran and said: "Here is where they will start trouble if we aren't careful."

"Korea," he said, "is the Greece of the Far East. If we are tough enough now, if we stand up to them like we did in Greece three years ago, they won't take any next steps. But if we just stand by, they'll move into Iran and they'll take over the whole Middle East. There's no telling what they'll do, if we don't put up a fight now."

The President appeared sincerely determined to go very much further than the initial orders that he had approved for General MacArthur the evening before.

Primary Source

Address to the American People on the Situation in Korea [excerpt]

SYNOPSIS: In the following excerpt, Truman provides his justifications for intervention and further emphasizes the need for national unity during this crisis. Before an armistice ended hostilities on July 27, 1953, more than thirty thousand U.S. soldiers, two million Koreans, and three hundred thousand Chinese would be killed in the conflict. The division between North and South Korea remained at the thirty-eighth parallel—the same as before the war.

My fellow citizens:

At noon today I sent a message to the Congress about the situation in Korea. I want to talk to you tonight about that situation, and about what it means to the security of the United States and to our hopes for peace in the world.

Korea is a small country, thousands of miles away, but what is happening there is important to every American.

On Sunday, June 25th, Communist forces attacked the Republic of Korea.

This attack has made it clear, beyond all doubt, that the international Communist movement is willing to use armed invasion to conquer independent nations. An act of aggression such as this creates a very real danger to the security of all free nations. The attack upon Korea was an outright breach of the peace and a violation of the Charter of the United Nations. By their actions in Korea, Communist leaders have demonstrated their contempt for the basic moral principles on which the United Nations is founded. This is a direct challenge to the efforts of the free nations to build the kind of world in which men can live in freedom and peace.

This challenge has been presented squarely. We must meet it squarely.

It is important for all of us to understand the essential facts as to how the situation in Korea came about.

Before and during World War II, Korea was subject to Japanese rule. When the fighting stopped, it was agreed that troops of the Soviet Union would accept the surrender of the Japanese soldiers in the northern part of Korea, and that American forces would accept the surrender of the Japanese in the southern part. For this purpose, the 38th parallel was used as the dividing line.

Later, the United Nations sought to establish Korea as a free and independent nation. A commission was sent out to supervise a free election in the whole of Korea. However, this election was held only in the southern part of the country, because the Soviet Union refused to permit an election for this purpose to be held in the northern part. Indeed, the Soviet authorities even refused to permit the United Nations Commission to visit northern Korea.

Nevertheless, the United Nations decided to go ahead where it could. In August 1948 the Republic of Korea was established as a free and independent nation in that part of Korea south of the 38th parallel.

In December 1948, the Soviet Union stated that it had withdrawn its troops from northern Korea and that a local government had been established there. However, the Communist authorities never have permitted the United Nations observers to visit northern Korea to see what was going on behind that part of the Iron Curtain.

It was from that area, where the Communist authorities have been unwilling to let the outside world see what was going on, that the attack was launched against the Republic of Korea on June 25th. That attack came without provocation and without warning. It was an act of raw aggression, without a shadow of justification.

I repeat that it was an act of raw aggression. It had no justification whatever.

The Communist invasion was launched in great force, with planes, tanks, and artillery. The size of the attack, and the speed with which it was followed up, make it perfectly plain that it had been plotted long in advance.

As soon as word of the attack was received, Secretary of State Acheson called me at Independence, Mo., and informed me that, with my approval, he would ask for an immediate meeting of the United Nations Security Council. The Security Council met just 24 hours after the Communist invasion began.

One of the main reasons the Security Council was set up was to act in such cases as this—to stop outbreaks of aggression in a hurry before they develop into general conflicts. In this case the Council passed a resolution which called for the invaders of Korea to stop fighting, and to withdraw. The Council called on all members of the United Nations to help carry out this resolution. The Communist invaders ignored the action of the Security Council and kept fight on with their attack.

The Security Council then met again. It recommended that members of the United Nations help the Republic of Korea repel the attack and help restore peace and security in that area.

Fifty-two of the 59 countries which are members of the United Nations have given their support to the action taken by the Security Council to restore peace in Korea.

These actions by the United Nations and its members are of great importance. The free nations have now made it clear that lawless aggression will be met with force. The free nations have learned the fateful lesson of the 1930's. That lesson is that aggression must be met firmly. Appeasement leads only to further aggression and ultimately to war.

The principal effort to help the Koreans preserve their independence, and to help the United Nations restore peace, has been made by the United States. We have sent land, sea, and air forces to assist in these operations. We have done this because we know that what is at stake here is nothing less than our own national security and the peace of the world.

So far, two other nations—Australia and Great Britain—have sent planes to Korea; and six other nations—Australia, Canada, France, Great Britain, the Netherlands, and New Zealand—have made naval forces available.

Under the flag of the United Nations a unified command has been established for all forces of the members of the United Nations fighting in Korea. Gen. Douglas MacArthur is the commander of this combined force.

The prompt action of the United Nations to put down lawless aggression, and the prompt response to this action by free peoples all over the world, will stand as a landmark in mankind's long search for a rule of law among nations. . . .

For our part, we shall continue to support the United Nations action to restore peace in the world. . . .

Furthermore, the fact that Communist forces have invaded Korea is a warning that there may be similar acts of aggression in other parts of the world. The free nations must be on their guard, more than ever before, against this kind of sneak attack.

It is obvious that we must increase our military strength and preparedness immediately. There are three things we need to do.

First, we need to send more men, equipment, and supplies to General MacArthur.

Second, in view of the world situation, we need to build up our own Army, Navy, and Air Force over and above what is needed in Korea.

Third, we need to speed up our work with other countries in strengthening our common defenses.

To help meet these needs, I have already authorized increases in the size of our Armed Forces. These increases will come in part from volunteers, in part from Selective Service, and in part from the National Guard and the Reserves.

I have also ordered that military supplies and equipment be obtained at a faster rate.

The necessary increases in the size of our Armed Forces, and the additional equipment they must have, will cost about $10 billion, and I am asking the Congress to appropriate the amount required.

These funds will be used to train men and equip them with tanks, planes, guns, and ships, in order to build the strength we need to help assure peace in the world.

When we have worked out with other free countries an increased program for our common defense, I shall recommend to the Congress that additional funds be provided for this purpose. This is of great importance. The free nations face a worldwide threat. It must be met with a worldwide defense. The United States and other free nations can multiply their strength by joining with one another in a common effort to provide this defense. This is our best hope for peace.

The things we need to do to build up our military defense will require considerable adjustment in our domestic economy. We have a tremendously rich and productive economy, and it is expanding every year. . . .

We have the resources to meet our needs. Far more important, the American people are unified in their belief in democratic freedom. We are united in detesting Communist slavery.

We know that the cost of freedom is high. But we are determined to preserve our freedom—no matter what the cost.

I know that our people are willing to do their part to support our soldiers and sailors and airmen who are fighting in Korea. I know that our fighting men can count on each and every one of you.

Our country stands before the world as an example of how free men, under God, can build a community of neighbors, working together for the good of all.

That is the goal we seek not only for ourselves, but for all people. We believe that freedom and peace are essential if men are to live as our Creator intended us to live. It is this faith that has guided us in the past, and it is this faith that will fortify us in the stern days ahead.

Further Resources

BOOKS

Cumings, Bruce. *The Origins of the Korean War.* Vol. 2, *The Roaring of the Cataract, 1947–1950.* Princeton, N.J.: Princeton University Press, 1990.

Hamby, Alonzo L. *Man of the People: A Life of Harry S. Truman.* New York: Oxford University Press, 1995.

Hogan, Michael J. *A Cross of Iron: Harry S. Truman and the Origins of the National Security State, 1945–1954.* Cambridge: Cambridge University Press, 1999.

McCulloch, David. *Truman.* New York: Simon and Schuster, 1992.

WEBSITES

"Cold War." Special Reports, CNN. Available online at http://www.cnn.com/SPECIALS/cold.war/; website home page: http://www.cnn.com/SPECIALS/ (accessed June 18, 2003).

"June 24–July 1, 1950—Outbreak of the Korean War: Week of Decision." Project WhistleStop, Truman Presidential Museum and Library. Available online at http://www.trumanlibrary.org /whistlestop/study_collections/korea/large/koreav1.htm; website home page: http://www.trumanlibrary.org/whistlestop/ (accessed June 18, 2003).

AUDIO AND VISUAL MEDIA

The Cold War. Original release, 1998. CNN/Turner Home Video, 2002, VHS.

Statement Upon Sentencing the Rosenbergs

Statement

By: Irving Kaufman

Date: April 5, 1951

Source: Kaufman, Irving. Statement Upon Sentencing the Rosenbergs. April 5, 1951. Available online at http://www .law.umkc.edu/faculty/projects/ftrials/rosenb/ROS_SENT.HTM; website home page: http://www.law.umkc.edu (accessed June 18, 2003).

About the Author: Irving Kaufman's (1910–1992) judicial career spanned five decades. By the age of twenty, he graduated from Fordham College and Fordham Law School. In 1947, Kaufman had attained a position as a U.S. District Court judge in New York City. In 1951, he presided over his most important and controversial case: *United States v. Julius Rosenberg, Ethel Rosenberg, and Morton Sobell.* In 1961, Kaufman received an appointment to the Second Circuit Court of Appeals, where he served until his retirement in 1987. ■

Introduction

In addition to dominating U.S. foreign policy following World War II (1939–1945), the Cold War emphasized the need for vigilant anticommunist activity on the home front. Anticommunists agreed that any Soviet sympathizer must be publicly exposed and punished. Through government hearings and policies designed to reveal the supposed communist menace in the United States, public officials at all levels of government contributed to a growing Red Scare that ultimately destroyed the lives of hundreds of accused "Reds." To dissent against these tribunals often brought the charge of being a communist. In this repressive atmosphere, Julius and Ethel Rosenberg were accused of stealing secret engineering information and passing it to the Soviet Union to enable the Soviets to manufacture an atomic bomb.

Julius and Ethel, who were participants in various left-wing groups during the 1930s, met in 1936 and married three years later. Julius worked in the U.S. Army Signal Corps until being expelled in February 1945 on charges that he was a communist. Ethel's brother, David Greenglass, who worked on the atomic bomb development project in Los Alamos, New Mexico, was interrogated by federal investigators. Shortly thereafter, the investigators developed a conspiracy in which Julius had passed bomb schematics from Greenglass to a Soviet agent in 1944 and 1945.

On July 15, 1950, less than one month after the beginning of the Korean War (1950–1953), Julius was arrested for conspiring with an enemy during wartime. Likely in an attempt to force a confession from Julius, Ethel was arrested on August 11. Within the past year, the Soviet Union had detonated its first atomic weapon and Alger Hiss was convicted of perjury concerning his ties to communists during his work at the U.S. State Department. These high-profile events, along with the media's thirst for anticommunist headlines, did not bode well for the Rosenbergs.

Significance

The Rosenbergs' trial began on March 6, 1951, to great publicity. Federal prosecutors, including future McCarthy assistant Roy Cohn, focused on the testimony of Greenglass to convince the jury of the defendants' guilt. The Rosenbergs argued their innocence but received little help from their attorney, who provided little examination of possible flaws in the government's case.

One month after the trial's opening, the jury returned a guilty verdict. Judge Irving Kaufman sentenced the pair to death. Kaufman's sentencing statement offers a revealing glimpse into the domestic impact of the Cold War and the extent to which anticommunism influenced the U.S. legal system in the 1950s. He viewed his actions as part of a larger struggle against a Soviet menace, a threat he found no qualms with voicing openly and passionately in court.

Global opposition to the decision, including even some limited protests in the United States, heightened in the months leading up to the execution. Some argued that the Rosenbergs had been tried unfairly, but the bulk of opposition arose over the death sentence imposed for the crime committed. After several appeals failed, Supreme Court justice William Douglas issued a temporary stay of execution on June 17, 1953, one day before the execution date. On June 19, the full Court ended the stay, with three justices dissenting. Nevertheless, later that day, Julius and Ethel were executed via the electric chair at Sing-Sing Prison in New York.

Similar to the ongoing debate concerning the execution of Nicola Sacco and Bartolomeo Vanzetti in 1927, historians continue to argue the case of Julius and Ethel Rosenberg. The tenuous consensus, if there is one, finds that Julius likely participated in espionage for the Soviet Union, though the full extent of his actions remains the subject of considerable controversy. But, the certainty of Ethel's guilt, who prosecutors argued aided her husband in fairly vague ways, has diminished considerably.

Primary Source

Statement Upon Sentencing the Rosenbergs
[excerpt]

> **SYNOPSIS:** On April 5, 1951, Judge Kaufman sentenced the Rosenbergs to death by electrocution for conspiring to pass secret information concerning the atomic bomb to the Soviet Union. As the following document demonstrates, Kaufman explicitly characterizes this death sentence as a measure to defend national security. He concludes by responding directly to arguments that the Rosenbergs should not be executed because of the impact on their two children. He tosses aside this plea and proclaims that the pair's allegiance to communism surpasses their devotion to their family.

Citizens of this country who betray their fellow-countrymen can be under none of the delusions about the benignity of Soviet power that they might have been prior to World War II. The nature of Russian terrorism is now self-evident. Idealism as a rationale dissolves. . . .

I consider your crime worse than murder. Plain deliberate contemplated murder is dwarfed in magnitude by comparison with the crime you have committed. In committing the act of murder, the criminal kills only his victim. The immediate family is brought to grief and when justice is meted out the chapter is closed. But in your case, I believe your conduct

Judge Irving Kaufman at his desk prior to sentencing Julius and Ethel Rosenberg, March 29, 1951. © **BETTMANN/CORBIS. REPRODUCED BY PERMISSION.**

in putting into the hands of the Russians the A-bomb years before our best scientists predicted Russia would perfect the bomb has already caused, in my opinion, the Communist aggression in Korea, with the resultant casualties exceeding 50,000 and who knows but that millions more of innocent people may pay the price of your treason. Indeed, by your betrayal you undoubtedly have altered the course of history to the disadvantage of our country.

No one can say that we do not live in a constant state of tension. We have evidence of your treachery all around us every day—for the civilian defense activities throughout the nation are aimed at preparing us for an atom bomb attack. Nor can it be said in mitigation of the offense that the power which set the conspiracy in motion and profited from it was not openly hostile to the United States at the time of the conspiracy. If this was your excuse the error of your ways in setting yourselves above our properly constituted authorities and the decision of those authorities not to share the information with Russia must now be obvious. . . .

In the light of this, I can only conclude that the defendants entered into this most serious conspiracy

Demonstrators, bound for Washington, D.C. with signs pleading for clemency for Ethel and Julius Rosenberg, fill Penn Station in New York City, 1953.
© BETTMANN/CORBIS. REPRODUCED BY PERMISSION.

against their country with full realization of its implications. . . .

The statute of which the defendants at the bar stand convicted is clear. I have previously stated my view that the verdict of guilty was amply justified by the evidence. In the light of the circumstances, I feel that I must pass such sentence upon the principals in this diabolical conspiracy to destroy a God-fearing nation, which will demonstrate with finality that this nation's security must remain inviolate; that traffic in military secrets, whether promoted by slavish devotion to a foreign ideology or by a desire for monetary gains must cease.

The evidence indicated quite clearly that Julius Rosenberg was the prime mover in this conspiracy. However, let no mistake be made about the role which his wife, Ethel Rosenberg, played in this conspiracy. Instead of deterring him from pursuing his

ignoble cause, she encouraged and assisted the cause. She was a mature woman—almost three years older than her husband and almost seven years older than her younger brother. She was a full-fledged partner in this crime.

Indeed the defendants Julius and Ethel Rosenberg placed their devotion to their cause above their own personal safety and were conscious that they were sacrificing their own children, should their misdeeds be detected—all of which did not deter them from pursuing their course. Love for their cause dominated their lives—it was even greater than their love for their children.

Further Resources

BOOKS

Fried, Richard M. *The Russians Are Coming! The Russians Are Coming!* New York: Oxford University Press, 1998.

Oshinsky, David M. *A Conspiracy So Immense: The World of Joe McCarthy.* New York: The Free Press, 1983.

Schrecker, Ellen. *Many Are the Crimes: McCarthyism in America.* Princeton, N.J.: Princeton University Press, 1998.

WEBSITES

Markowitz, Norman. "Rosenberg, Ethel, and Julius Rosenberg." American National Biography Online. Available online at http://www.anb.org/articles/07/07–00256.html; website home page: http://www.anb.org/ (accessed June 18, 2003) *This website is a subscription-based service that is available for free through most libraries.*

"'Old Soldiers Never Die' Address to Congress"

Speech

By: Douglas MacArthur

Date: April 19, 1951

Source: MacArthur, Douglas. "'Old Soldiers Never Die' Address to Congress." April 19, 1951. Available online at http://www.pbs.org/wgbh/amex/macarthur/filmmore/reference/primary/macspeech05.html; website home page: http://www.pbs.org (accessed June 18, 2003).

About the Author: Douglas MacArthur (1880–1964) graduated from West Point in 1903. He distinguished himself throughout his military career, including during World War I (1914–1918), as a commandant of West Point from 1919–1922, Chief of Staff of the U.S. Army commander of the Philippine military (the Phillipines were a U.S. posession at that time), and Supreme Commander of Allied Powers occupying Japan. MacArthur had obtained the rank of five-star general several years before he led the United Nations (UN) forces and repelled the North Korean invaders. Following a series of overt challenges to President Harry Truman (served 1945–1953), Truman fired him for insubordination in 1951. ∎

Introduction

Douglas MacArthur's discontent with the Truman administration's policy toward Korea began long before the Korean War's outbreak in 1950. Despite the growing strength of the Communist Party in China and the formation of the Communist People's Democratic Republic of Korea (North Korea) in 1948, MacArthur opposed significant U.S. investment in the strengthening of non-communist South Korea. This changed dramatically with the victory of the communists in the Chinese revolution of 1949. Anticommunists in the United States and MacArthur in Japan argued that Truman had "lost China" to communism.

North Korea invaded South Korea on June 25, 1950, and rapidly pushed the South Korean army and the small number of U.S. troops with them back. President Tru-

man, with the backing of the United Nations, quickly decided to commit the United States to a major effort to defend South Korea. As troop build-up began, and General MacArthur was placed in command of all UN forces in Korea. Badly outnumbered initially, MacArthur managed to hang on in South Korea long enough to orchestrate a brilliant landing behind North Korean lines at Inchon in September 1950. Cut-off from supply and fighting on two fronts, the North Korean troops were soon either defeated or forced out of the South. MacArthur's forces regained control of the thirty-eighth parallel, the demarcation boundary between North and South Korea. Pleased with this success, the Truman administration altered its strategy to support a further advancement aimed at destroying the North Korean government. However, it ordered MacArthur to keep American troops away from the border with China and placed other restrictions on his actions that it hoped would keep the communist Chinese from intervening to help North Korea. The Chinese had warned that the idea of U.S. troops near their borders was unacceptable to them.

Truman and his advisers feared the possibility of a Chinese intervention not only because it would jeopradize victory in Korea, but because it carried with it the threat of a much larger and prolonged war, even a new world war. This was something they were not prepared to risk simply in order to end communist control of North Korea. Their essential goal remained the defense of South Korea. MacArthur disagreed, seeing no reason why the United States, with its enormous military might, need fear another world war. If anything, he welcomed it as an opportunity to roll back communism, or even defeat it once and for all. He argued for bolder action but was rebuffed by Truman.

Still disinclined to follow Truman's policies, MacArthur did little to restrain his troops in their attack into North Korea. American forces were approaching the Yalu River, which divided North Korea and China, by late November, 1950. In fact, U.S. aircraft were flying over the border, and even made some attacks on the Chinese side. On November 26, Chinese forces counterattacked in great force. The U.S forces were forced to retreat all the way back into South Korean territory.

Now that China was in the war, MacArthur argued that the United States should use every means at its disposal to defeat it outright. This included the bombing of Chinese industry and cities and the use of nuclear weapons. Truman and his advisers remained adamantly opposed to such moves, as they wished to keep the war limited to Korea. MacArthur would not accept this and began to publicly criticize Truman and his policies. He also began to act increasingly independently, threatening to bomb China if it would not negotiate directly with him.

General Douglas MacArthur delivers his farewell address to Congress after being removed from command. President Truman, backed by his joint chiefs of staff, and the secretaries of state and defense, intended to replace MacArthur with someone who would be more in accord with the presidential adminstration. © BETTMANN/CORBIS. REPRODUCED BY PERMISSION.

In an April 5, 1951, letter to Representative Joseph Martin, which Martin read to Congress, MacArthur blamed Truman for the deaths of U.S. soldiers and for losing the war effort. By this point Truman had had enough. On April 11, he fired MacArthur for insubordination. On April 16, MacArthur left Japan, met at the airport by a throng of supporters. Following his return to the United States, congressional leaders provided him with an opportunity to rebuke Truman and explain his actions to the nation.

Significance

Not surprisingly, MacArthur characertized his actions in the most glowing terms. His mission was to repel communist invaders in an effort to ensure the survival of the free world—rhetoric not too different from Truman when the president justified the United States' initial involvement in the war. Just as policy makers in the Truman and Dwight Eisenhower (served 1953–1961) adminstrations had consistently argued, MacArthur viewed China's intervention as unjustified aggression against the United States. He ignored the fact that he had ordered attacks on Chinese forces north of the Yalu River as a first

step in the ultimate overthrow of the Chinese Communist Party, not simply as a means to "neutralize sanctuary protection given the enemy north of the Yalu." In declaring that "in war there can be no substitute for victory," MacArthur confronted implicitly Truman's refusal to authorize the use of nuclear bombs in North Korea and China. At the height of anticommunist fervor in the United States, many agreed with MacArthur's desire to use the United States' nuclear power to annihilate the opposition.

MacArthur concluded the address with a song reference that made the speech famous, further heightening his stature in public memory. Presenting himself as an almost spiritual figure, he acknowledged that now was his time to "just fade away." Far from fading away, he soon became swept up in the public euphoria that followed his speech. He considered a run for the Republican presidential nomination in 1952 but quickly became overshadowed by Eisenhower, an even more popular hero of World War II (1939–1945). Eisenhower rode popular discontent with Truman all the way to the White House and served two terms as president.

The Korean War dragged on into 1953, with neither side able to make much headway against the other. The armistice that ended the fighting restored the old border along the 38th parallel. A congressional investigation into Truman's firing of MacArthur vindicated the president's action. The inquiry showed that MacArthur had in fact violated the president's orders. Furthermore, popular and influential military men and World War II heros, such as Omar Bradley and George Marshall, spoke out in favor of Truman's policy of limiting the war to Korea.

Primary Source

"Old Soldiers Never Die' Address to Congress" [excerpt]

SYNOPSIS: In the following excerpt, MacArthur addresses a joint session of Congress and a nationwide television audience, who do not know what to expect from the bombastic, egotistical, yet widely revered military leader. Many will view the address as marking the final return home for a defiant World War II hero who served his country for nearly fifty years. The thirty-seven-minute speech enraptures the congressional members in attendance, who stand and cheer wildly after MacArthur's self-glorifying climax.

Mr. President, Mr. Speaker and Distinguished Members of the Congress:

I stand on this rostrum with a sense of deep humility and pride—humility in the weight of those great architects of our history who have stood here before me, pride in the reflection that this home of legislative debate represent human liberty in the purest form yet devised.

Here are centered the hopes and aspirations and faith of the entire human race.

I do not stand here as advocate for any partisan cause, for the issues are fundamental and reach quite beyond the realm of partisan considerations. They must be resolved on the highest plane of national interest if our course is to prove sound and our future protected.

I trust, therefore, that you will do me the justice of receiving that which I have to say as solely expressing the considered viewpoint of a fellow American.

I address you with neither rancor nor bitterness in the fading twilight of life, with but one purpose in mind: to serve my country.

The issues are global, and so interlocked that to consider the problems of one sector oblivious to those of another is to court disaster for the whole. While Asia is commonly referred to as the Gateway to Europe, it is no less true that Europe is the Gateway to Asia, and the broad influence of the one cannot fail to have its impact upon the other. There are those who claim our strength is inadequate to protect on both fronts, that we cannot divide our effort. I can think of no greater expression of defeatism.

If a potential enemy can divide his strength on two fronts, it is for us to counter his effort. The Communist threat is a global one.

Its successful advance in one sector threatens the destruction of every other sector. You can not appease or otherwise surrender to communism in Asia without simultaneously undermining our efforts to halt its advance in Europe. . . .

While I was not consulted prior to the President's decision to intervene in support of the Republic of Korea, that decision from a military standpoint, proved a sound one. As I said, it proved to be a sound one, as we hurled back the invader and decimated his forces. Our victory was complete, and our objectives within reach, when Red China intervened with numerically superior ground forces.

This created a new war and an entirely new situation, a situation not contemplated when our forces were committed against the North Korean invaders; a situation which called for new decisions in the diplomatic sphere to permit the realistic adjustment of military strategy. Such decisions have not been forthcoming.

While no man in his right mind would advocate sending our ground forces into continental China, and such was never given a thought, the new situation did urgently demand a drastic revision of strategic planning if our political aim was to defeat this new enemy as we had defeated the old one.

Apart from the military need, as I saw it, to neutralize sanctuary protection given the enemy north of the Yalu, I felt that military necessity in the conduct of the war made necessary the intesification of our economic blockade against China, the imposition of a naval blockade against the China coast, removal of restrictions on air reconnaissance of China's coastal area and of Manchuria, removal of restrictions on the forces of the Republic of China on Formosa, with logistical support to contribution to their effective operations against the Chinese mainland.

For entertaining these views, all professionally designed to support our forces in Korea and to bring hostilities to an end with the least possible delay and at a savings of countless American and Allied lives, I have been severely criticized in lay circles, principally abroad, despite my understanding that from a military standpoint the above views have been fully shared in the past by practically every military leader concerned with the Korean campaign, including our own Joint Chiefs of Staff.

I called for reinforcements, but was informed that reinforcements were not available. I made clear that if not permitted to destroy the enemy built-up bases north of the Yalu, if not permitted to utilize the friendly Chinese Force of some 600,000 men on Formosa, if not permitted to blockade the China coast to prevent the Chinese Reds from getting succor from without, and if there was to be no hope of major reinforcements, the position of the command from the military standpoint forbade victory.

We could hold in Korea by constant maneuver and in an approximate area where our supply line advantages were in balance with the supply line disadvantages of the enemy, but we could hope at best for only an indecisive campaign with its terrible and constant attrition upon our forces if the enemy utilized its full military potential.

I have constantly called for the new political decisions essential to a solution.

Efforts have been made to distort my position. It has been said in effect that I was a warmonger. Nothing could be further from the truth. I know war as few other men now living know it, and nothing to me—and nothing to me is more revolting. I have long advocated its complete abolition, as its very destructiveness on both friend and foe has rendered it useless as a means of settling international disputes.

Indeed, the Second Day of September, 1945, just following the surrender of the Japanese nation on the Battleship Missouri, I formally cautioned as follows:

> Men since the beginning of time have sought peace. Various methods through the ages have been attempted to devise an international process to prevent or settle disputes between nations. From the very start workable methods were found in so far as individual citizens were concerned, but the mechanics of an instrumentality of larger international scope have never been successful. Military alliances, balances of power, Leagues of Nations, all in turn failed, leaving the only path to be 'by way of the crucible of war. The utter destructiveness of war now blocks out this alternative. We have had our last chance. If we will not devise some greater and more equitable system, Armageddon will be at our door. The problem basically is theological and involves a spiritual recrudescence and improvement of human character that will synchronize with our almost matchless advances in science, art, literature and all the material and cultural developments of the past 2000 years. It must be of the spirit if we are to save the flesh.

But once war is forced upon us, there is no other alternative than to apply every available means to bring it to a swift end. War's very object is victory, not prolonged indecision.

In war there can be no substitute for victory.

There are some who for varying reasons would appease Red China. They are blind to history's clear lesson, for history teaches with unmistakable emphasis that appeasement but begets new and bloodier wars. It points to no single instance where this end has justified that means, where appeasement has led to more than a sham peace. Like blackmail, it lays the basis for new and successively greater demands until, as in blackmail, violence becomes the only other alternative. Why, my soldiers asked me, surrender military advantages to an enemy in the field? I could not answer.

Some may say to avoid spread of the conflict into an all-out war with China, others, to avoid Soviet intervention. Neither explanation seems valid, for China is already engaging with the maximum power it can commit, and the Soviet Union will not necessarily mesh its actions with our moves. Like a

cobra, any new enemy will more likely strike whenever it feels that the relativity of military and other potentialities is in its favor on a world-wide basis.

The tragedy of Korea is further heightened by the fact that its military action was confined to its territorial limits. It condemns that nation, which it is our purpose to save, to suffer the devastating impact of full naval and air bombardment while the enemy's sanctuaries are fully protected from such attack and devastation.

Of the nations of the world, Korea alone, up to now, is the sole one which has risked its all against communism. The magnificence of the courage and fortitude of the Korean people defies description. They have chosen to risk death rather than slavery. Their last words to me were: "Don't scuttle the Pacific."

I have just left your fighting sons in Korea. They have done their best there, and I can report to you without reservation that they are splendid in every way.

It was my constant effort to preserve them and end this savage conflict honorably and with the least loss of time and a minimum sacrifice of life. Its growing bloodshed has caused me the deepest anguish and anxiety. Those gallant men will remain often in my thoughts and in my prayers always.

I am closing my 52 years of military service. When I joined the Army, even before the turn of the century, it was the fullfillment of all of my boyish hopes and dreams. The world has turned over many times since I took the oath at West Point, and the hopes and dreams have all since vanished, but I still remember the refrain of one of the most popular barracks ballads of that day which proclaimed most proudly that old soldiers never die; they just fade away. And like the old soldier of that ballad, I now close my military career and just fade away, an old soldier who tried to do his duty as God gave him the light to see that duty.

Good Bye.

Further Resources

BOOKS

Cumings, Bruce. *The Origins of the Korean War.* Vol. 2, *The Roaring of the Cataract, 1947–1950.* Princeton, N.J.: Princeton University Press, 1990.

Dower, John W. *Embracing Defeat: Japan in the Wake of World War II.* New York: Norton, 1999.

Gaddis, John Lewis. *We Now Know: Rethinking Cold War History.* New York: Oxford University Press, 1997.

Hogan, Michael J. *A Cross of Iron: Harry S. Truman and the Origins of the National Security State, 1945–1954.* Cambridge: Cambridge University Press, 1999.

WEBSITES

Schaller, Michael. "MacArthur, Douglas." *American National Biography Online.* Available online at http://www.anb .org/articles/07/07–00178.html; website home page: http:// www.anb.org/ (accessed June 18, 2003) *This website is a subscription-based service that is available for free through most libraries.*

A U.S. Army soldier offers to push a Japanese youth on a swing on a playground in Sendai, Japan, in 1951. The Mutual Security Agreement between Japan and the U.S. provided rationale for U.S. military occupation of Japanese land. **AP/WIDE WORLD PHOTOS. REPRODUCED BY PERMISSION.**

Agreements Between the United States and Japan

"Security Treaty Between the United States and Japan, September 8, 1951"

Treaty

Date: September 8, 1951

Source: "Security Treaty Between the United States and Japan, September 8, 1951." Available online at http://www .yale.edu/lawweb/avalon/diplomacy/japan/japan001.htm; website home page: http://www.yale.edu (accessed June 18, 2003).

"U.S. and Japan Mutual Defense Assistance Agreement"

Treaty

Date: March 8, 1954

Source: "U.S. and Japan Mutual Defense Assistance Agreement." March 8, 1954. Available online at http://www.learner .org/channel/workshops/primarysources/coldwar/docs/usjapan .html; website home page: http://www.learner.org (accessed June 18, 2003). ∎

Introduction

In the closing days of World War II, the Soviet Union and the United States both sought control of territory formerly controlled by the Axis powers. In Europe, the United States strove to stabilize West Germany. On a larger scale, the Truman doctrine and the Marshall Plan emphasized that the United States would spend billions of dollars in order to strengthen its alliances with European nations and counter the Soviet Union's movements into Eastern Europe.

In Asia, a similar situation unfolded. After signing the surrender agreement, the United States began an occupation of Japan that lasted until 1952. During this span, U.S. officials, under the direction of General Douglas MacArthur, directed the complete reconstruction of Japanese society. In the first two years of the occupation, often described as the program's progressive period, MacArthur encouraged several liberal social, economic, and political reforms.

From a military viewpoint, however, the United States did not allow Japan to construct and maintain armed forces for the purpose of an offensive conflict. Ironically, the United States soon called for Japan to remilitarize, requesting a standing army following the onset of the Korean War (1950–1953). U.S. officials ended the period of liberal reforms and strove to make Japan a "bulwark against communism" in East Asia. To achieve this objective, many of Japan's wartime leaders were reappointed to positions of power in order to more rapidly reconstruct the nation's industrial capacity.

The reappointment of Japan's wartime leaders reveals the massive impact of the Cold War and anticommunism, where the leaders of Japan and the Japanese people themselves could be portrayed as the perfect allies in the war against communism. This was a dramatic shift from the racist propaganda that flooded the United States just five years before.

Significance

The culmination of this shift in attitude from the racist propaganda of World War II to the new objectives of the Cold War may be seen in the Security Treaty of

1951 and the Mutual Defense Assistance Agreement of 1954. These documents outlined the postwar alliance between the United States and Japan that would continue throughout the second half of the twentieth century. The Treaty of Peace, signed the same day as the Security Treaty on September 8, 1951, called for the end of U.S. occupation. Yet, as emphasized by the Security Treaty, the two nations would continue to possess a strong bond. In fact, this pact called for the continued presence of U.S. military personnel in Japan as a defense measure against possible attack. The agreement also encouraged the development of a Japanese self-defense force that would eventually enable the removal of U.S. military forces from Japan.

In the context of heightened nuclear tensions between the superpowers, the involvement of Japan in the United States' Cold War policies sparked massive protests against the military alliance. The Mutual Defense Assistance Agreement, signed on March 8, 1954, reflected Japan's desire for increased autonomy following the end of the Korean War. The pact expanded on the central economic and security elements addressed in the earlier Security Treaty and further emphasized the need for both nations to support each other not only with the promise of military protection, but also with aid in economic development. While the United States devoted billions of dollars to an arms race with the Soviet Union, protection under the U.S. defense umbrella and production orders to support U.S. personnel stationed in the region brought real economic benefits for Japan. Japan's economic policies could focus on development of consumer goods, rather than weaponry, thus enabling the nation to develop one of the world's largest economies by the end of the 1960s.

Primary Source

"Security Treaty Between the United States and Japan, September 8, 1951"

SYNOPSIS: The following document marks the beginning of a formal international alliance between the United States and Japan. In this treaty, the United States agrees to maintain a standing military force within the region to help provide security and defense from an outside aggressor. Furthermore, Japan agrees to build its own military, which will eventually take over the responsibility of national defense.

Japan has this day signed a Treaty of Peace with the Allied Powers. On the coming into force of that Treaty, Japan will not have the effective means to exercise its inherent right of self-defense because it has been disarmed.

There is danger to Japan in this situation because irresponsible militarism has not yet been driven from the world. Therefore Japan desires a Security Treaty with the United States of America to come into force simultaneously with the Treaty of Peace between the United States of America and Japan.

The Treaty of Peace recognizes that Japan as a sovereign nation has the right to enter into collective security arrangements, and further, the Charter of the United Nations recognizes that all nations possess an inherent right of individual and collective self-defense.

In exercise of these rights, Japan desires, as a provisional arrangement for its defense, that the United States of America should maintain armed forces of its own in and about Japan so as to deter armed attack upon Japan.

The United States of America, in the interest of peace and security, is presently willing to maintain certain of its armed forces in and about Japan, in the expectation, however, that Japan will itself increasingly assume responsibility for its own defense against direct and indirect aggression, always avoiding any armament which could be an offensive threat or serve other than to promote peace and security in accordance with the purposes and principles of the United Nations Charter. Accordingly, the two countries have agreed as follows:

Article I

Japan grants, and the United States of America accepts, the right, upon the coming into force of the Treaty of Peace and of this Treaty, to dispose United States land, air and sea forces in and about Japan. Such forces may be utilized to contribute to the maintenance of international peace and security in the Far East and to the security of Japan against armed attack from without, including assistance given at the express request of the Japanese Government to put down largescale internal riots and disturbances in Japan, caused through instigation or intervention by an outside power or powers.

Article II

During the exercise of the right referred to in Article I, Japan will not grant, without the prior consent of the United States of America, any bases or any rights, powers or authority whatsoever, in or relating to bases or the right of garrison or of maneuver, or transit of ground, air or naval forces to any third power.

Article III

The conditions which shall govern the disposition of armed forces of the United States of America in and about Japan shall be determined by administrative agreements between the two Governments.

Article IV

This Treaty shall expire whenever in the opinion of the Governments of the United States of America and Japan there shall have come into force such United Nations arrangements or such alternative individual or collective security dispositions as will satisfactorily provide for the maintenance by the United Nations or otherwise of international peace and security in the Japan Area.

Article V

This Treaty shall be ratified by the United States of America and Japan and will come into force when instruments of ratification thereof have been exchanged by them at Washington.

IN WITNESS WHEREOF the undersigned Plenipotentiaries have signed this Treaty.

DONE in duplicate at the city of San Francisco, in the English and Japanese languages, this eighth day of September, 1951.

Primary Source

"U.S. and Japan Mutual Defense Assistance Agreement"

SYNOPSIS: U.S. and Japanese officials have renewed this mutual security agreement every decade since the end of the U.S. occupation. These renewals often create waves of protests from Japanese discontent with their implicit role in U.S. foreign policy. Marking the agreement's renewal in 1997, the joint authors once again proclaimed the necessity of a security alliance between the United States and Japan, "Although the Cold War has ended, the potential for instability in this region has greater importance for the security of Japan."

The Government of the United States of America and the Government of Japan,

Desiring to foster international peace and security, within the framework of the Charter of the United Nations, through voluntary arrangements which will further the ability of nations dedicated to the purposes and principles of the Charter to develop effective measures for individual and collective self-defense in support of those purposes and principles;

Reaffirming their belief as stated in the Treaty of Peace with Japan signed at the city of San Francisco on September 8, 1951 that Japan as a sovereign nation possesses the inherent right of individual or collective self-defense referred to in Article 51 of the Charter of the United Nations;

Recalling the preamble of the Security Treaty between the United States of America and Japan, signed at the city of San Francisco on September 8, 1951, to the effect that the United States of America, in the interest of peace and security, would maintain certain of its armed forces in and about Japan as a provisional arrangement in the expectation that Japan will itself increasingly assume responsibility for its own defense against direct and indirect aggression, always avoiding armament which could be an offensive threat or serve other than to promote peace and security in accordance with the purposes and principles or the Charter of the United Nations;

Recognizing that, in the planning of a defense assistance program for Japan, economic stability will be an essential element for consideration in the development of its defense capacities, and that Japan can contribute only to the extent permitted by its general economic condition and capacities;

Taking into consideration the support that the Government of the United States of America has brought to these principles by enacting the Mutual Defense Assistance Act of 1949, as amended, and the Mutual Security Act of 1951, as amended, which provide for the furnishing of defense assistance by the United States of America in furtherance of the objectives referred to above; and

Desiring to set forth the conditions which will govern the furnishing of such assistance;

Have agreed as follows:

Article I

1. Each Government, consistently with the principle that economic stability is essential to international peace and security, will make available to the other and to such other governments as the two Governments signatory to the present Agreement may in each case agree upon, such equipment, materials, services, or other assistance as the Government furnishing such assistance may authorize, in accordance with such detailed arrangements as may be made between them. The furnishing and use or any such assistance as may be authorized by either Government shall be consistent with the Charter of the United Nations. Such assistance as may be made

available by the Government of the United States of America pursuant to the present Agreement will be furnished under those provisions, and subject to all of those terms, conditions and termination provisions of the Mutual Defense Assistance Act of 1949, the Mutual Security Act of 1951, acts amendatory and supplementary thereto, and appropriation acts thereunder which may affect the furnishing of such assistance.

2. Each Government will make effective use of assistance received pursuant to the present Agreement for the purposes of promoting peace and security in a manner that is satisfactory to both Governments, and neither Government, without the prior consent of the other, will devote such assistance to any other purpose.

3. Each Government will offer for return to the other, in accordance with terms, conditions and procedures mutually agreed upon, equipment or materials furnished under the present Agreement, except equipment and materials furnished on terms requiring reimbursement, and no longer required for the Purposes for which it was originally made available.

4. In the interest of common security, each Government undertakes not to transfer to any person not an officer or agent of such Government, or to any other government, title to or possession of any equipment, materials, or services received pursuant to the present Agreement, without the prior consent of the Government which furnished such assistance.

Article II

In conformity with the principle of mutual aid, the Government of Japan agrees to facilitate the production and transfer to the Government of the United States of America for such period of time, in such quantities and upon such terms and conditions as may be agreed upon of raw and semiprocessed materials required by the United States of America as a result of deficiencies or potential deficiencies in its own resources, and which may be available in Japan. Arrangements for such transfers shall give due regard to requirements for domestic use and commercial export as determined by the Government of Japan.

Article III

1. Each Government will take such security measures as may be agreed upon between the two Governments in order to prevent the disclosure or compromise of classified articles, services or information furnished by the other Government pursuant to the present Agreement.

2. Each Government will take appropriate measures consistent with security to keep the public informed of operations under the present Agreement.

Article IV

The two Governments will, upon the request of either or them, make appropriate arrangements providing for the methods and terms of the exchange of industrial property rights and technical information for defense which will expedite such exchange and at the same time protect private interests and maintain security safeguards.

Article V

The two Governments will consult for the purpose of establishing procedures whereby the Government of Japan will so deposit, segregate, or assure title to all funds allocated to or derived from any programs of assistance undertaken by the Government of the United States of America so that such funds shall not be subject to garnishment, attachment, seizure or other legal process by any person, firm, agency, corporation, organization or government, when the Government of Japan is advised by the Government of the United States of America that any such legal process would interfere with the attainment of the objectives of the program of assistance.

Article VI

1. The Government of Japan will grant

a. Exemption from duties and internal taxation upon importation or exportation to materials, supplies or equipment imported into or exported from its territory under the present Agreement or any similar agreement between the Government of the United States of America and the Government of any other country receiving assistance, except as otherwise agreed to; and

b. Exemption from and refund of Japanese taxes, as enumerated in the attached Annex E, so far as they may affect expenditures of or financed by the Government of the United States of America effected in Japan for procurement of materials, supplies, equipment and services under the present Agreement or any similar agreement between the Government of the United States of America and the Government of any other country receiving assistance.

2. Exemption from duties and exemption from and refund of Japanese taxes as enumerated in the

attached Annex E will apply, in addition, to any other expenditures of or financed by the Government of the United States of America for materials, supplies, equipment and services for mutual defense, including expenditures made in conformity with the Security Treaty between the United States of America and Japan or any foreign aid program of the Government of the United States of America under the Mutual Security Act of 1951, as amended, or any acts supplementary, amendatory or successory thereto.

Article VII

1. The Government of Japan agrees to receive personnel of the Government of the United States of America who will discharge in the territory of Japan the responsibilities of the latter Government regarding equipment, materials, and services furnished under the present Agreement, and who will be accorded facilities to observe the progress of the assistance furnished by the Government of the United States of America under the present Agreement. Such personnel who are nationals of the United States of America, including personnel temporarily assigned, will, in their relationships with the Government of Japan, operate as part of the Embassy of the United States of America under the direction and control of the Chief of the Diplomatic Mission, and will have the same privileges and immunities as are accorded to other personnel with corresponding rank in the Embassy of the United States of America.

2. The Government of Japan will make available, from time to time, to the Government of the United States of America funds in yen for the administrative and related expenses of the latter Government in connection with carrying out the present Agreement.

Article VIII

The Government of Japan, reaffirming its determination to join in promoting international understanding and good will, and maintaining world peace, to take such action as may be mutually agreed upon to eliminate causes of international tension, and to fulfill the military obligations which the Government of Japan has assumed under the Security Treaty between the United States of America and Japan, will make, consistent with the political and economic stability of Japan, the full contribution permitted by its manpower, resources, facilities and general economic condition to the development and maintenance of its own defensive strength and the defensive strength of the free world, take all reasonable measures which may be needed to develop its defense capacities, and take appropriate steps to ensure the effective utilization of any assistance provided by the Government of the United States of America.

Article IX

1. Nothing contained in the present Agreement shall be construed to alter or otherwise modify the Security Treaty between the United States of America and Japan or any arrangements concluded thereunder.

2. The present Agreement will be implemented by each Government in accordance with the constitutional provisions of the respective countries.

Article X

1. The two Governments will, upon the request of either of them, consult regarding any matter relating to the application of the present Agreement or to operations or arrangements carried out pursuant to the present Agreement.

2. The terms of the present Agreement may be reviewed at the request of either of the two Governments or amended by agreement between them at any time.

Article XI

1. The present Agreement shall come into force on the date of receipt by the Government of the United States of America of a written notice from the Government of Japan of ratification of the Agreement by Japan.

2. The present Agreement will thereafter continue in force until one year after the date of receipt by either Government of a written notice of the intention of the other to terminate it, provided that the provisions of Article I, paragraphs 2, 3 and 4, and arrangements entered into under Article III, paragraph 1 and Article IV shall remain in force unless otherwise agreed by the two Governments.

3. The Annexes to the present Agreement shall form an integral part thereof.

4. The present Agreement shall be registered with the Secretariat of the United Nations.

IN WITNESS WHEREOF the representatives of the two Governments, duly authorized for the purpose, have signed the present Agreement.

DONE in duplicate, in the English and Japanese languages, both equally authentic, at Tokyo, this eighth day of March, one thousand nine hundred fifty-four.

For the United States of America:
John M. Allison

For Japan:
Katsuo Okazaki

Further Resources

BOOKS

Bix, Herbert P. *Hirohito and the Making of Modern Japan.* New York: HarperCollins, 2000.

Dower, John W. *Embracing Defeat: Japan in the Wake of World War II.* New York: Norton, 1999.

"The Checkers Speech"

Speech

By: Richard Nixon

Date: September 23, 1952

Source: Nixon, Richard. "Richard Nixon Defending His Record, Promises To Drive 'The Crooks and the Communists' Out of Washington, Los Angeles, CA, September 23, 1952." Available online at http://www.pbs.org/greatspeeches /timeline/r_nixon_s.html; website home page: http://www .pbs.org (accessed June 18, 2003).

About the Author: Richard Nixon (1911–1994) graduated from Duke Law School in 1934. After serving in the navy during World War II (1939–1945), he pursued a career in politics. Serving as a U.S. representative and then a U.S. senator, he eventually became the vice president under President Dwight Eisenhower (served 1953–1961). He then was elected president in 1968. Nixon will probably be best remembered for the Watergate scandal, which led him to resign from office in 1974. ∎

Introduction

By the time Richard Nixon accepted the Republican nomination for vice president in 1952, he had already established a reputation for merciless campaigning that enthralled supporters and enraged opponents. In 1946, he defeated five-term incumbent Democrat Jerry Voorhis for a seat in the U.S. House of Representatives, primarily on the basis of a series of charges that Voorhis was a spoiled communist sympathizer. Red-baiting brought Nixon continued success as he led the House of Un-American Activities Committee campaign against Alger Hiss, a U.S. State Department official. Nixon gained national recognition for his battle against Hiss, who was charged and convicted of being a Soviet informant in 1948.

The Hiss investigations catapulted Nixon's bid for the U.S. Senate in 1950. During his second term in Con-

gress, the Nixon campaign smeared his liberal opponent, Representative Helen Gahagan Douglas, as "the pink lady" and easily won the contest. When the Republican National Committee searched for an aggressive vice presidential candidate to join the more moderate, reserved General Dwight Eisenhower on the presidential ticket, it settled on Senator Nixon for the position.

In the months leading up to election day, Nixon found himself embroiled in a controversy that nearly cost him the nomination. Charges emerged that he had created an $18,000 campaign slush fund to enrich himself with campaign donations. Faced with mounting support to remove him from the ticket, Nixon attempted to use media interest to his advantage and turn the tables on the opposition. On September 23, 1952, just six weeks before the election, Nixon appeared on national television to refute the charges and, more importantly, campaign for his political future.

Significance

Nixon's shrewd address marked the birth of political campaigning in the era of live television broadcasting. Rarely if ever before had a vice presidential candidate addressed a nationwide audience via television. Under the bright studio lights, he delivered an impassioned speech that saved his political career.

Concerning the charges about a campaign slush fund, he seemed to admit guilt by speaking of himself in the third and first person in the same sentence, before reversing himself. In detailing his family finances, flattering his wife, or describing his respect for Eisenhower, Nixon attempted to accomplish more than proving he had not pocketed campaign contributions. He presented himself as an honest politician, loyal patriot and husband, and champion of the common American. At the same time, he redirected the spotlight away from his own possible misdeeds and levied a series of countercharges on the Truman administration and the Democratic candidates.

He closed the speech by deriding his enemies as "crooks and Communists" and called on viewers to decide his fate. This clever maneuver turned to his advantage, when the Republican National Committee soon received hundreds of thousands of messages in Nixon's favor. He remained on the ticket, which won in November, and he served two terms as Eisenhower's vice president.

While Eisenhower continued to stay above the political fray, the aggressive Nixon thrust himself into several high-profile political fights against Democrats at home and Cold War enemies abroad. In 1958, Nixon traded barbs with Soviet premier Nikita Khrushchev during an impromptu Kitchen debate. Two years later, the vice pres-

Vice presidential nominee Richard Nixon delivers his "Checkers" speech, in which he explains his controversial $18,000 expense fund. **AP/WIDE WORLD PHOTOS. REPRODUCED BY PERMISSION.**

ident found himself outmatched by a candidate even more skillful at media manipulation. With the help of the country's first televised presidential debate, Senator John F. Kennedy defeated Nixon in the 1960 presidential contest.

Primary Source

"The Checkers Speech" [excerpt]

> **SYNOPSIS:** Throughout most of his speech, Nixon focuses directly on the camera, looking down a few times to read economic and legal reports and correspondence. He raises his hands to his face in ex-

asperation at times, but for the most part projects a sense of composure and confidence. During the closing segment concerning his future on the Republican ticket, he outstretches his hands as he pleads with the American public. Just as he seems to be concluding his speech, the broadcast feed stops as he runs over his allotted time.

My Fellow Americans,

I come before you tonight as a candidate for the Vice-Presidency and as a man whose honesty and integrity has been questioned.

Now, the usual political thing to do when charges are made against you is to either ignore them or to deny them without giving details. I believe we have had enough of that in the United States, particularly with the present Administration in Washington, D.C.

To me, the office of the Vice Presidency of the United States is a great office, and I feel that the people have got to have confidence in the integrity of the men who run for that office and who might attain them

I have a theory, too, that the best and only answer to a smear or an honest misunderstanding of the facts is to tell the truth. And that is why I am here tonight. I want to tell you my side of the case.

I am sure that you have read the charges, and you have heard it, that I, Senator Nixon, took $18,000 from a group of my supporters.

Now, was that wrong? And let me say that it was wrong. I am saying it, incidentally, that it was wrong, just not illegal, because it isn't a question of whether it was legal or illegal, that isn't enough. The question is, was it morally wrong. I say that it was morally wrong—if any of that $18,000 went to Senator Nixon, for my personal use. I say that it was morally wrong if it was secretly given and secretly handled.

And I say that it was morally wrong if any of the contributors got special favors for the contributions that they made.

And to answer those questions, let me say this: Not a cent of the $18,000 or any other money of that type ever went to me for my personal use. Every penny of it was used to pay for political expenses that I did not think should be charged to the taxpayers of the United States. . . .

The taxpayers should not be required to finance items which are not official business but which are primarily political business. . . .

I felt that the best way to handle these necessary political expenses of getting my message to the American people and the speeches I made—the speeches I had printed for the most part concerned this one message of exposing this Administration, the Communism in it, the corruption in it—the only way I could do that was to accept the aid which people in my home state of California, who contributed to my campaign and who continued to make these contributions after I was elected, were glad to make. And let me say that I am proud of the fact that not one of them has ever asked me for a special favor. I am proud of the fact that not one of them has ever

asked me to vote on a bill other than my own conscience would dictate. And I am proud of the fact that the taxpayers, by subterfuge or otherwise, have never paid one dime for expenses which I thought were political and should not be charged top the taxpayers. . . .

But then I realized that there are still some who may say, and rightly so—and let me say that I recognize that some will continue to smear regardless of what the truth may be—but that there has been, understandably, some honest misunderstanding on this matter, and there are some that will say, "well, maybe you were able, Senator, to fake the thing. How can we believe what you say—after all, is there a possibility that maybe you got some sums in cash? Is there a possibility that you might have feathered your own nest?" And so now, what I am going to do—and incidentally this is unprecedented in the history of American politics—I am going at this time to give to this television and radio audience a complete financial history, everything I have earned, everything I have spent and everything I own, and I want you to know the facts.

I will have to start early: I was born in 1913. Our family was one of modest circumstances, and most of my early life was spent in a store out in East Whittier. It was a grocery store, one of those family enterprises.

The only reason we were able to make it go was because my mother and dad had five boys, and we all worked in the store. I worked my way through college, and, to a great extent, through law school. And then, in 1940, probably the best thing that ever happened to me happened: I married Pat, who is sitting over here. We had a rather difficult time after we were married, like so many of the young couples who might be listening to us. I practiced law. She continued to teach school.

Then, in 1942, I went into the service. Let me say that my service record was not a particularly unusual one. I went to the South Pacific. I guess I'm entitled to a couple of battle stars. I got a couple of letters of commendation. But I was just there when the bombs were falling. And then I returned. I returned to the United States, and in 1946, I ran for Congress. When we came out of the war—Pat and I—Pat, [who] during the war had worked as a stenographer, and in a bank, and as an economist for a Government agency—and when we came out, the total of our savings, from both my law practice, her teaching and all the time I was in the war, the total for that entire period was just less than $10,000—every cent of that, incidentally, was in Government bonds—well, that's where we start, when I go into politics.

Now, whatever I earned since I went into politics—well, here it is. I jotted it down. Let me read the notes. First of all, I have had my salary as a Congressman and as a Senator. . . .

I owe $3,500 to my parents, and the interest on that loan, which I pay regularly, because it is a part of the savings they made through the years they were working so hard—I pay regularly 4 percent interest. And then I have a $500 loan, which I have on my life insurance.

Well, that's about it. That's what we have. And that's what we owe. It isn't very much. But Pat and I have the satisfaction that every dime that we have got is honestly ours.

I should say this, that Pat doesn't have a mink coat. But she does have a respectable Republican cloth coat, and I always tell her she would look good in anything.

One other thing I should probably tell you, because if I don't, they will probably be saying this about me, too. We did get something, a gift, after the election. A man down in Texas heard Pat on the radio mention that our two youngsters would like to have a dog, and, believe it or not, the day we left before this campaign trip we got a message from Union Station in Baltimore, saying they had a package for us. We went down to get it. You know what it was?

It was a little cocker spaniel dog, in a crate that he had sent all the way from Texas, black and white, spotted, and our little girl Tricia, the six year old, named it "Checkers."

And you know, the kids, like all kids, loved the dog, and I just want to say this, right now, that regardless of what they say about it, we are going to keep it!

It isn't easy to come before a nation-wide audience and bare your life, as I have done. But I want to say some things before I conclude, that I think most of you will agree on.

Mr. Mitchell, the Chairman of the Democratic National Committee, made this statement, that if a man couldn't afford to be in the United States Senate, he shouldn't run for Senate. And I just want to make my position clear.

I don't agree with Mr. Mitchell when he says that only a rich man should serve his Government in the United States Senate or Congress. I don't believe that represents the thinking of the Democratic Party,

and I know it doesn't represent the thinking of the Republican Party. . . .

And now I'm going to suggest some courses of conduct. First of all, you have read in the papers about other funds, now, Mr. Stevenson apparently had a couple. One of them in which a group of business people paid and helped to supplement the salaries of state employees. Here is where the money went directly into their pockets, and I think that what Mr. Stevenson should do should be to come before the American people, as I have, give the names of the people that contributed to that fund, give the names of the people who put this money into their pockets, at the same time that they were receiving money from their state government and see what favors, if any, they gave out for that. . . .

Now let me say this: I know this is not the last of the smears. In spite of my explanation tonight, other smears will be made. Others have been made in the past. And the purpose of the smears, I know, is this, to silence me, to make me let up. Well, they just don't know who they are dealing with. I'm going to tell you this: I remember in the dark days of the Hiss trial some of the same columnists, some of the same radio commentators who are attacking me now and misrepresenting my position, were violently opposing me at the time I was after Alger Hiss. But I continued to fight because I knew I was right, and I can say to this great television and radio audience, that I have no apologies to the American people for my part in putting Alger Hiss where he is today. And as far as this is concerned, I intend to continue to fight.

Why do I feel so deeply? Why do I feel that in spite of the smears, the misunderstanding, the necessity for a man to come up here and bare his soul? And I want to tell you why.

Because, you see, I love my country. And I think my country is in danger. And I think the only man that can save America at this time is the man that's running for President, on my ticket, Dwight Eisenhower.

You say, why do I think it is in danger? And I say look at the record. Seven years of the Truman-Acheson Administration, and what's happened? Six hundred million people lost to Communists.

And a war in Korea in which we have lost 117,000 American casualties, and I say that those in the State Department that made the mistakes which caused that war and which resulted in those losses should be kicked out of the State Department just as fast as we can get them out of there. . . .

Let me say this, finally. This evening I want to read to you just briefly excerpts from a letter that I received, a letter which after all this is over, no one can take away from us. It reads as follows:

Dear Senator Nixon,

Since I am only 19 years of age, I can't vote in this presidential election, but believe me, if I could, you and General Eisenhower would certainly get my vote. My husband is in the Fleet Marines in Korea. He is in the front lines. And we have a two month old son he has never seen. And I feel confident that with great Americans like you and General Eisenhower in the White House, lonely Americans like myself will be united with their loved ones now in Korea. I only pray to God that you won't be too late. Enclosed is a small check to help you with your campaign. Living on $85 a month it is all I can do.

Folks, it is a check for $10, and it is one that I shall never cash. And let me just say this: We hear a lot about prosperity these days, but I say, why can't we have prosperity built on peace, rather than prosperity built on war? Why can't we have prosperity and an honest Government in Washington, D.C. at the same time?

Believe me, we can. And Eisenhower is the man that can lead the crusade to bring us that kind of prosperity.

And now, finally, I know that you wonder whether or not I am going to stay on the Republican ticket or resign. Let me say this: I don't believe that I ought to quit, because I am not a quitter. And, incidentally, Pat is not a quitter. After all, her name is Patricia Ryan and she was born on St. Patrick's Day, and you know the Irish never quit.

But the decision, my friends, is not mine. I would do nothing that would harm the possibilities of Dwight Eisenhower to become President of the United States. And for that reason, I am submitting to the Republican National Committee tonight through this television broadcast the decision which it is theirs to make. Let them decide whether my position on the ticket will help or hurt. And I am going to ask you to help them decide. Wire and write the Republican National Committee whether you think I should stay on or whether I should get off. And whatever their decision, I will abide by it.

But let me just say this last word. (Nixon rises from chair and points to the camera.) Regardless of what happens, I am going to continue this fight.

I am going to campaign up and down America until we drive the crooks and the Communists and those that defend them out of Washington, and remember folks, Eisenhower is a great man. Folks, he is a great man, and a vote for Eisenhower is a vote for what is good for America. . . . [Nixon is cut off by the broadcasting station as he runs beyond his time allowance.]

Further Resources

BOOKS

Ambrose, Stephen E. *Nixon: The Education of a Politician, 1913–1962.* New York: Simon and Schuster, 1987.

Jameson, Kathleen Hall. *Packaging the Presidency: A History and Criticism of Presidential Campaign Advertising,* 3rd ed. New York: Oxford University Press, 1996.

WEBSITES

Oliver, Myrna. "'Ted' Rodgers, 82; Set up Nixon's 'Checkers' Speech." *Los Angeles Times,* March 27, 2003, C15. Available online at http://www.latimes.com/news/printedition /national/20030327/20030327C15.pdf; website home page: http://www.latimes.com/ (accessed June 18, 2003).

"Richard Nixon: Sounds and Pictures." EarthStation1.com. Available online at http://www.earthstation1.com/Nixon.html; website home page: http://www.earthstation1.com (accessed June 18, 2003).

Television Campaign Commercials

"Television Commercials from 1952 Presidential Campaign"

Television advertisements

By: Dwight Eisenhower and Adlai Stevenson

Date: 1952

Source: Eisenhower, Dwight, and Adlai Stevenson. "Television Commercials from the 1952 Presidential Campaign." American Museum of the Moving Image: The Living Room Candidate: A History of Presidential Campaign Commercials, 1952–2000. Available online at http://www.ammi.org/livingroomcandidate/ (accessed June 18, 2003).

"Television Commercials from 1956 Presidential Campaign"

Television advertisements

By: Dwight Eisenhower and Adlai Stevenson

Date: 1956

Source: Eisenhower, Dwight, and Adlai Stevenson. "Television Commercials from the 1956 Presidential Campaign." American

Museum of the Moving Image: The Living Room Candidate: A History of Presidential Campaign Commercials, 1952–2000. Available online at http://www.ammi.org/livingroomcandidate/ (accessed June 18, 2003).

About the Authors: Dwight Eisenhower (1890–1969) graduated from West Point in 1915. By 1940, he rose to the rank of lieutenant colonel. With the eruption of World War II (1939–1945), he swiftly advanced to four-star general in 1943. That same year, he received the assignment to lead one of the largest military campaigns in world history: the D day invasion of June 6, 1944. After the war, he went into politics and served as the thirty-fourth U.S. president from 1953 to 1961.

Adlai Stevenson (1900–1965) served in the Franklin D. Roosevelt (served 1933–1945) and the Harry Truman (served 1945–1953) administrations. In 1948, he won the Illinois governorship. He unsuccessfully ran for the U.S. presidency in both the 1952 and 1956 elections, but succeeded in being appointed as ambassador to the United Nations during the John F. Kennedy (served 1961–1963) administration. ■

Introduction

After deciding to forego a campaign with or against his former commander-in-chief in the 1948 presidential race, General Dwight Eisenhower opted to wait until 1952 to launch his bid for the White House, when the Korean War (1950–1953) and a lackluster economy resulted in Truman and his Democratic Party losing support among the public. In former general Dwight Eisenhower's elevation to Republican candidate in the 1952 presidential race, the Democrats faced stiff competition. Despite his lack of political experience and relatively unimaginative campaign speeches, Eisenhower's candidacy appeared invincible from the start. The man who led the campaign against Nazi Germany struck many as the perfect choice to defend the United States against communism and the Soviet Union. Eisenhower campaigned on his war record and many voters seemed to believe him when he declared that he would end the Korean War and communist infiltration in government if elected president.

As domestic and foreign Cold War crises enveloped the Truman administration in the early 1950s, the Democratic Party searched for a presidential candidate who could somehow overcome Truman's unpopularity and Eisenhower's status as an unassailable war hero. The Democrats did not locate such a candidate, but they did find Illinois governor Adlai Stevenson. Given little chance for victory, Stevenson enraged many liberal supporters when he selected Alabama senator John Sparkman, a staunch segregationist, as his running mate. The tactic to encourage conservative southerners to support a Democratic ticket seemingly opposed to civil rights legislation struck many as political opportunism of the worst kind. Nevertheless, Stevenson impressed crowds with his refreshing brand of wit and wisdom. In November 1952, Stevenson became the first Democrat since Al Smith in 1928 to lose a presidential election. Four years later, a

Poster endorsing democratic candidate Adlai Stevenson for the 1952 presidential election. Stevenson's intellectualism is thought to have alienated voters. © DAVID J. & JANICE L. FRENT/CORBIS. REPRODUCED BY PERMISSION.

more energetic and liberal Stevenson lost once again to Eisenhower by an even larger margin.

Significance

In addition to Republican vice presidential nominee Richard Nixon's famous Checkers speech, the 1952 campaign's most important contribution to the political process came with the development of television campaign advertising. The television ads that were created by both major political parties during that campaign, as well as the 1956 campaign, may seem dull and perhaps unconvincing, but, in many respects, these spots contain many of the basic traits of more recent political attack ads.

The 1952 Democratic commercials reminded voters of the Great Depression experienced the last time a Republican controlled the White House. The Republicans, however, offered far more biting ads. In several "Eisenhower Answers America" ads, Eisenhower responded to the questions of common Americans with consistent attacks on the Truman administration and the national peril faced during the Cold War. The ads also underscored Eisenhower's military career to emphasize how a change in leadership would turn the world's current struggles toward America's favor.

The 1956 spots expanded on many of the previous ads' core elements. Rather than simply interviewing people in a television studio about their perspectives on the election, the Republicans, such as in "Woman Voters," tried to present real people with real opinions. This format added a sense of sincerity and persuasiveness to the ad's basic message to reelect President Eisenhower. Taken as a whole, these early television ads laid the groundwork for many of the common styles of political advertising that continue to be used in the twenty-first century.

Primary Source

"Television Commercials From 1952 Presidential Campaign"

> **SYNOPSIS:** The following 1952 television commercials address a number of issues that both the Democrats and Republicans deemed to be important, while attacking the opposing candidate with what was considered then to be strong criticism. Finally, they highlight a practice that has diminished over the years: the candidate campaign song. With "Ike for President," "Let's Not Forget . . . The Farmer!" and "I Love the Gov," both sides fashioned campaign arguments into catchy tunes that could be played in television and radio broadcasts.

"I Love the Gov," 1952 Commercial for Adlai Stevenson, Democrat

I'd rather have a man with a hole in his shoe than a
  hole in everything he says,
I'd rather have a man who knows what to do when
  he gets to be the Pres.
I love the Gov, the Governor of Illinois,
He is the Gov that brings the dove of peace and joy.
When Illinois the GOP double-crossed, he was the
  one who told all the crooks, get lost.
Adlai, love you madly,
And what you did for your great state, you're gonna
  do for the rest of the forty-eight.
Didn't know much about him before he came,
But now my heart's a ballot that bears his name.
'Cause I listened to what he had to say, I know that
  on election day, we're gonna choose the Gov we
  love,
He is the Gov nobody can shove.
We'll make the Gov the President of the U, the me
  and the you SA.

"Let's Not Forget the Farmer," 1952 Commercial for Adlai Stevenson, Democrat

Old MacDonald had a farm, back in '31.
Conditions filled him with alarm, back in '31.
Not a chick-chick here or a moo-cow there,
Just broken down farmland everywhere.
And farmer Mac doesn't want to go back
To the days when there wasn't a moo or quack,
To the days of 1931,
When they didn't have bread, when the day was
  done.

Farmer Mac knows what to do,
Election day of '52,
Gonna go out with everyone in the U.S.A.
To vote for Adlai Stevenson,
To keep his farm this way.
With a vote-vote here and vote-vote there
And a vote for Stevenson everywhere,
For if it's good for Mac you see,
Then it's good for you and it's good for me.
All America loves that farm, vote Stevenson today.

"Eisenhower Answers America," 1952 Commercial for Dwight Eisenhower, Republican

Announcer: Eisenhower answers America.

Couple, woman speaking: General, both parties talk about bringing down food prices. How do we know which party to believe?

Eisenhower: Well, instead of asking what party will bring prices down, why not ask, "What party put prices up?" Then, vote for a change.

Announcer: Eisenhower answers America.

Woman 2: The Democrats have made mistakes, but aren't their intentions good?

Announcer: Well, if a driver of your school bus runs into a truck, hits a lamppost, drives into a ditch, you don't say, "His intentions are good." You get a new bus driver.

Announcer: Eisenhower answers America.

African American Man: Food prices, clothing prices, income taxes, won't they ever go down?

Eisenhower: Not with an eighty-five billion dollar budget eating away on your grocery bill, your clothing, your food, your income. (*Smirking*) Yet the Democrats say, "You never had it so good."

"Eisenhower for President," 1952 Commercial for Dwight Eisenhower, Republican

Ike for President.
Ike for President.
Ike for President.

You like Ike, I like Ike, everybody likes Ike, for
  president.
Hang up the banners, beat the drums,
We'll take Ike to Washington.

We don't want John, or Adlai (*sounding like "D"*) or
  Harry.
Let's do that big job right.
Let's get in step with the guy that's hep,
Get in step with Ike, for president.

You like Ike, I like Ike, everybody likes Ike, for
  president.
Hang up the banners, beat the drums,
We'll take Ike to Washington.

We've got to get where we are going,
Travel day and night.
There's Adlai goin' the other way,
We'll all go with Ike, for president.

You like Ike, I like Ike, everybody likes Ike, for
  president.
Hang up the banners, beat the drums,
We'll take Ike to Washington.
We'll take Ike to Washington.

Announcer (*with "Ike for president" being chanted
  in the background*): Now is the time for all good
  Americans to come to the aid of their country.

Primary Source

"Television Commercials From 1956 Presidential
Campaign"

> **SYNOPSIS:** The Republican commercial "Woman
> Voters" presents footage of people who seemingly
> stop for a moment to comment for a reporter be-
> fore continuing on their daily routines. This format
> strengthens the ad's basic message to reelect
> President Eisenhower. Following a tactic that re-
> mains popular with campaign ad makers, "How's
> That Again, General?" contrasts Eisenhower's re-
> marks given in his 1952 ads with the Democrats'
> perspective on how the president has been proven
> wrong since his election.

"How's That Again, General?" 1956 Commercial for Adlai Stevenson, Democrat

Announcer: How's that again, General? In the
  1952 campaign, the General complained
  about the cost of living. He promised his television audience,

Eisenhower, speaking on camera in a 1952 commercial: The people can afford less butter,
  less fruit, less bread, less milk. Yes, it's time
  for a change.

Announcer: How's that again, General?

Eisenhower: Yes, its time for a change.

Estes Kefauver on camera: This is Estes Kefauver. The General's promise to bring down
  prices was another broken promise. Since the
  Republicans took office, the cost of living has
  reached its highest point in history. Today,
  the consumer can buy less food, less housing, less clothing, less medical care than he
  could in 1952 for the same money. The General promised a change for the better, and we
  got short-changed for the worst. Think it
  through.

Announcer: Vote for Stevenson and Kefauver. Vote
  Democratic.

An automobile bumper sign features Eisenhower's famous campaign
slogan. © CORBIS. REPRODUCED BY PERMISSION.

"Women Voters," 1956 Commercial for Dwight Eisenhower, Republican

Announcer: This year there are fifty-four million
  women eligible to vote. Two and a half million
  more women than men: enough to decide the
  whole election.

And as November 6 draws near, you women
  are doing a lot of thinking about a lot of important things.

For instance, you're thinking about the cost of
  living. You want to see living expenses stay at
  a reasonable level. You want your family budget to be protected against inflation.

You're thinking about your family. You want to
  be as sure as you can that you will all go on
  living together in our present happiness and
  prosperity, in an America at peace.

You're thinking about your children's future.
  You want them to grow up under the best possible conditions, in terms of schools, health,
  and general welfare.

And, because they believe he represents their
  best hope of achieving these things, the

women of America are making their choice for president Dwight D. Eisenhower.

But, suppose we ask some of them what they think about the coming election.

Woman 1: My main reason for voting for Eisenhower is because I believe in his sincerity. I don't feel that he is furthering his own interests, but he is furthering the interests of the country and the people.

Woman 2: I feel he's a very big man, which is needed for that position. And also because he has not been and is not what I consider a politician.

Woman 3: I'm interested in Ike and this (*gesturing to her son*) is my one big reason why I'm interested in Ike.

Woman 4: As a woman and future homemaker and mother in America, the type of man that I want to be president is the man that I and my family and my children and those around me can look up to and respect. I think that President Eisenhower is that sort of man.

Woman 5: Inflation. We're not going to have that in the next four years if we vote right, with Ike.

Woman 6: I'm voting for Ike because I feel that he is a God-fearing man, and I think that's essential in any leader, and especially the leader of our country. . . .

Announcer: So much of our future rests with the women of our country. They're the homemakers. The whole family unit revolves around them. Everything that affects the family welfare affects them first. And everything in the family's life benefits from their influence.

They do the family buying. They see that everybody in the family circle is well clothed and well fed.

But beyond this they are the custodian of its values and aspirations for the future. In their hands lies the training of our young people, to whom they pass on the rich heritage of our nation, its love of peace and justice, and its passion for freedom.

The women of this nation swept Dwight D. Eisenhower into office four years ago. They will probably decide the election this time. And they like Ike.

And here's somebody else they like too. Ike's beloved Mamie, whose smile and modesty, and easy natural charm make her the ideal

first lady. Let's keep our first lady in the White House for four more years. November 6 vote for Dwight D. Eisenhower.

Second Announcer: The national citizens for Eisenhower-Nixon have presented this message to all thinking voters, regardless of party affiliation.

Further Resources

BOOKS

Ambrose, Stephen E. *Eisenhower: The President.* New York: Simon and Schuster, 1984.

Jameson, Kathleen Hall. *Packaging the Presidency: A History and Criticism of Presidential Campaign Advertising,* 3rd ed. New York: Oxford University Press, 1996.

Martin, John Bartlow. *Adlai Stevenson and the World: The Life of Adlai E. Stevenson.* Garden City, N.Y.: Doubleday, 1977.

WEBSITES

"1952." The 30 Second Candidate, Public Broadcasting Service. Available online at http://www.pbs.org/30secondcandidate /timeline/years/1952.html; website home page: http://www .pbs.org/30secondcandidate/ (accessed June 18, 2003).

American Museum of the Moving Image: The Living Room Candidate: A History of Presidential Campaign Commercials, 1952–2000. Available online at http://www.ammi.org /livingroomcandidate/ (accessed June 18, 2003).

AUDIO AND VISUAL MEDIA

Adlai Stevenson: The Man from Libertyville. Films for the Humanities and Sciences, 1990, VHS.

"The Row of Dominoes"
Speech

By: Dwight Eisenhower

Date: April 7, 1954

Source: Eisenhower, Dwight. "The Row of Dominoes." April 7, 1954. Available online at http://www.uiowa.edu/%7Ec030162 /Common/Handouts/POTUS/IKE.html; website home page: http://www.uiowa.edu (accessed June 18, 2003).

About the Author: Dwight Eisenhower (1890–1969) graduated from West Point in 1915. By 1940, he rose to the rank of lieutenant colonel. With the eruption of World War II (1939–1945), he swiftly advanced to four-star general in 1943. That same year, Eisenhower received the assignment to lead one of the largest military campaigns in world history: the D day invasion of June 6, 1944. After the war, he went into politics and served as the thirty-fourth U.S. president from 1953 to 1961. ■

Introduction

Although Dwight Eisenhower seems to have been the first president to compare the spread of communism

President Dwight D. Eisenhower speaks at a press conference about communist aggression in Southeast Asia, 1954. © **BETTMANN/CORBIS. REPRODUCED BY PERMISSION.**

to a row of dominoes falling, he certainly did not originate the theory's core assumptions. Following the Allied victory in World War II, the United States and Soviet Union moved quickly to consolidate and strengthen their spheres of influence throughout the world. The economic, military, political, and cultural competition that developed became known as the Cold War. During this period, many U.S. officials believed that the Soviet Union threatened to surround and ultimately invade if the United States did not counter the spread of communism in all corners of the globe.

In 1947, President Harry Truman (served 1945–1953) issued his doctrine calling for $400 million in aid to block the spread of communism in Greece and Turkey. If Greece and/or Turkey fell to communism, Truman argued, their neighbors in Europe and the Middle East would soon fall as well. The suppositions behind this policy soon led the United States into joining in the Korean War (1950–1953). Truman depicted the North Korean invasion of the South as part of the global struggle against communism, buttressed by the communist revolution in China the preceding year. If the communist North succeeded, according to Truman, communists would invade Japan, then Southeast Asia, then perhaps Australia, until they reached across the Pacific to the United States itself.

Significance

In a press conference on April 7, 1954, President Eisenhower emphasized the necessity of dealing with a new communist threat in Southeast Asia. Just as his predecessor had called for U.S. intervention to stop communists from taking over Korea, Eisenhower conveyed the horrible consequences he saw occurring if the communists succeeded in controlling Indochina, a former French colony that comprised Laos, Cambodia, and Vietnam. Since the end of World War II, French forces had competed with Vietnamese nationalists for control over the nation. In March 1954, one month before this discussion, Vietnamese troops began the final encirclement of French soldiers at Dien Bien Phu. France, which had received economic aid from the United States to continue its occupation in Vietnam since 1950, called for U.S. military support. Although Eisenhower refused, his comments at this press conference revealed that he would act to prevent communist rule of Vietnam.

In order to convey the gravity of the crisis, Eisenhower offered the "falling domino principle." This theory unified all of the reasons given for opposition to the Soviet Union into a single justification for U.S. involvement in the Cold War: communism unchecked anywhere in the world threatened the United States. At the same time, the depiction of these events as akin to dominoes falling obscured and overruled alternate interpretations of specific crises. Thus, the Vietnamese could not want independence or freedom if, as the theory concluded, they were being controlled by the Soviet Union.

Following the French surrender in May 1954, the Eisenhower administration helped structure and control a new noncommunist regime in the southern half of Vietnam. Eisenhower refused to send official military soldiers to Vietnam, but he greatly escalated U.S. economic and military aid to the South. American investment in South Vietnam eventually included full-fledged military support and the deaths of over fifty thousand American soldiers before the last of the troops left in 1975.

Primary Source

"The Row of Dominoes" [excerpt]

SYNOPSIS: In the following excerpt, President Eisenhower faces an array of questions concerning domestic and foreign developments in the Cold War. The first few questions deal with the nuclear arms race, specifically concerning the production of the hydrogen bomb and whether the Soviet Union, which detonated its first atomic bomb in 1950, would soon threaten the United States by building a bigger hydrogen bomb. Toward the end of the conference, reporters inquire whether the United States will "go it alone" in Vietnam and if the United Nations should be involved.

Robert Richards, Copley Press: Mr. President, would you mind commenting on the strategic importance of Indochina for the free world? I think there has been, across the country, some lack of understanding on just what it means to us.

The President: You have, of course, both the specific and the general, when you talk about such things. First of all, you have the specific value of a locality in its production of materials that the world needs.

Then you have the possibility that many human beings pass under a dictatorship that is inimical to the free world.

Finally, you have broader considerations that might follow what you would call the "falling domino" principle. You have a row of dominoes set up, you knock over the first one, and what will happen to the last one is the certainty that it will go over very quickly. So you could have a beginning of a disintegration that would have the most profound influences.

Now, with respect to the first one, two of the items from this particular area, that the world uses, are tin and tungsten. They are very important. There are others, of course, the rubber plantations, and so on.

Then, with respect to more people passing under this domination, Asia, after all, has already lost some 450 million of its peoples to the Communist dictatorship, and we simply can't afford greater losses.

But when we come to the possible sequence of events, the loss of Indochina, of Burma, of Thailand, of the Peninsula, and Indonesia falling, now you begin to talk about areas that no only multiply the disadvantages that you would suffer through the loss of materials, sources of materials, but now you are talking about millions and millions of people.

Finally, the geographical position achieved thereby does many things. It turns the so-called island defensive chain of Japan, Formosa, of the Philippines and to the southward; it moves in to threaten Australia and New Zealand.

It takes away, in its economic aspects, that region that Japan must have as a trading area, or Japan, in turn, will have only one place in the world to go—that is, toward the Communist areas—in order to live.

So, the possible consequences of the loss are just incalculable to the free world.

Further Resources

BOOKS

Ambrose, Stephen E. *Eisenhower: The President.* New York: Simon and Schuster, 1984.

Gettleman, Marvin E., ed. *Vietnam and America: A Documented History,* 2nd ed. New York: Grove, 1995.

Leffler, Melvyn P. *The Specter of Communism: The United States and the Origins of the Cold War, 1917–1953.* New York: Hill and Wang, 1994.

Young, Marilyn B. *The Vietnam Wars, 1945–1990.* New York: HarperCollins, 1991.

WEBSITES

"Domino Theory Principle, Dwight D. Eisenhower." Public Papers of the Presidents Dwight D. Eisenhower, Michigan State University. Available online at http://coursesa.matrix .msu.edu/~hst306/documents/domino.html; website home page: http://www.msu.edu/home/ (accessed June 18, 2003).

AUDIO AND VISUAL MEDIA

Vietnam: A Television History. American Experience, Public Broadcasting Service, 1983, VHS.

Letter to Ngo Dinh Diem

Letter

By: Dwight Eisenhower

Date: October 23, 1954

Source: Eisenhower, Dwight. Letter to Ngo Din Diem. October 23, 1954. Available online at http://www.fordham.edu /cgi-bin/getdoc.cgi?94827,12175; website home page: http:// www.fordham.edu (accessed June 18, 2003).

About the Author: Dwight Eisenhower (1890–1969) graduated from West Point in 1915. By 1940, he rose to the rank of lieutenant colonel. With the eruption of World War II (1939–1945), he swiftly advanced to four-star general in 1943. That same year, he received the assignment to lead one of the largest military campaigns in world history: the D day invasion of June 6, 1944. After the war, he went into politics and served as the thirty-fourth U.S. president from 1953 to 1961. ■

Introduction

On August 15, 1945, the same day that Japan surrendered to the United States, ending World War II, Vietnamese nationalist Ho Chi Minh issued a "Declaration of Vietnamese Independence." Ho approached the United States for assistance in ousting French imperialists. President Harry Truman (served 1945–1953) ignored Ho's request and instead supported the reinstallation of French colonial rulers following the removal of Japanese forces in Indochina. This decision began U.S. involvement in the conflict that came be known as the Vietnam War (1964–1975).

Between 1945 and 1954, the French battled to regain control over their former colony. A February 1950 National Security Council report emphasized that preventing the further spread of communism was crucial to U.S. security and that Indochina was "a key area of Southeast Asia" that was "under immediate threat."

During this period, presidents Harry Truman and Dwight Eisenhower (served 1953–1961) began to assume greater economic responsibility for France's fight, providing about $2.5 billion to help France defeat Ho's communist forces, which were based primarily in the northern half of Vietnam. The same Cold War mentality that led to U.S. intervention in the Korean War (1950–1953) led to U.S. involvement in Vietnam. Just as Truman and Eisenhower viewed the communist takeover of Korea as a threat to U.S. national security, they concluded that the same possibility existed if communists gained control of Vietnam.

By 1953, the United States paid roughly 80 percent of the French war effort. The United States had also begun to strengthen its ties with the French-installed Vietnamese leadership in the South, which had been created to compete against Ho's government in the North. When French forces were finally defeated in 1954, Eisenhower offered the "falling domino principle" to justify the necessity of further American intervention. This theory held that if one nation fell to communism, then its neighbors would automatically do likewise, eventually leading to a direct assault on the United States. The president's adherence to this ideology would lead to his refusal to support the Geneva Accords in 1954, which provided for a peaceful settlement to the Vietnam War.

Significance

The Final Declaration of the Geneva Conference presented an agreement reached by the diplomats representing France and North Vietnam, whose forces had defeated the French. The accords called for a temporary partition of Vietnam along the seventeenth parallel. In two years, elections would be held to unify the entire country under a single national government. Although representatives of other nations, including the United States and South Vietnam, attended the conference, they did not sign the final accords.

President Eisenhower's letter to Ngo Dinh Diem, whom the United States had recently installed as president of South Vietnam, revealed that he strongly opposed the terms of the Geneva agreement. Moreover, Eisenhower revealed that the United States supported the formation of a permanent state in the southern half of Vietnam. Arguing that the communists had infiltrated Vietnam and attempted to subvert the democratic process there, Eisenhower declared that the United States would not support elections involving the northern half of Vietnam. American intelligence had concluded by 1956 that Ho would receive well over a majority of the vote in the national election required by the Geneva Accords. Although the president concluded his letter with an admonition to "any who might wish to impose a foreign ideology on your free people," many historians would later conclude that the United States and the Eisenhower administration had attempted to do just that with their support of Diem's puppet regime.

Primary Source

Letter to Ngo Dinh Diem

> **SYNOPSIS:** This letter provides crucial insight into the origins of U.S. participation in the Vietnam War. Years before the first U.S. military personnel arrived in Vietnam at the end of the Eisenhower administration, U.S. officials had begun significant investments in the prevention of a communist-governed Vietnam. President Eisenhower's decision to take over France's role in supporting a noncommunist regime in the South greatly increased U.S. involvement in the conflict.

U.S. President Dwight Eisenhower shakes hands with South Vietnam President Ngo Dinh Diem, May 8, 1957. **AP/WIDE WORLD PHOTOS. REPRODUCED BY PERMISSION.**

Dear Mr. President:

I have been following with great interest the course of developments in Viet-Nam, particularly since the conclusion of the conference at Geneva. The implications of the agreement concerning Viet-Nam have caused grave concern regarding the future of a country temporarily divided by an artificial military grouping, weakened by a long and exhausting war and faced with enemies without and by their subversive collaborators within.

Your recent requests for aid to assist in the formidable project of the movement of several hundred thousand loyal Vietnamese citizens away from areas which are passing under a *de facto* rule and political ideology which they abhor, are being fulfilled. I am glad that the United States is able to assist in this humanitarian effort.

We have been exploring ways and means to permit our aid to Viet-Nam to be more effective and to make a greater contribution to the welfare and stability of the Government of Viet-Nam. I am, accordingly, instructing the American Ambassador to Viet-Nam to examine with you in your capacity as Chief of Government, bow an intelligent program of

France Makes Peace in Indochina

The following document marks the end of French military influence in Indochina. Although this declaration was hoped to have led to lasting peace, in reality, it only provided a respite when the United States decided to become more involved by sending thousands of troops to the region a decade later.

"The Final Declaration of the Geneva Conference: On Restoring Peace in Indochina, July 21, 1954" [excerpt]

1. The Conference takes note of the agreements ending hostilities in Cambodia, Laos, and Viet-Nam and organizing international control and the supervision of the execution of the provisions of these agreements.

2. The Conference expresses satisfaction at the ending of hostilities in Cambodia, Laos, and Viet-Nam. The Conference expresses its conviction that the execution of the provisions set out in the present declaration and in the agreements on the cessation of hostilities will permit Cambodia, Laos, and Viet-Nam henceforth to play their part, in full independence and sovereignty, in the peaceful community of nations. . . .

4. The Conference takes note of the clauses in the agreement on the cessation of hostilities in Viet-Nam prohibiting the introduction into Viet Nam of foreign troops and military personnel as well as of all kinds of arms and munitions. . . .

5. The Conference takes note of the clauses in the agreement on the cessation of hostilities in Viet-Nam to the effect that no military base at the disposition of a foreign state may be established in the regrouping zones of the two parties, the latter having the obligation to see that the zones allotted to them shall not constitute part of any military alliance and shall not be utilized for the resumption of hostilities or in the service of an aggressive policy. . . .

7. The Conference declares that, so far as Viet-Nam is concerned, the settlement of political problems, effected on the basis of respect for the principles of independence, unity, and territorial integrity, shall permit the Vietnamese people to enjoy the fundamental freedoms, guaranteed by democratic institutions established as a result of free general elections . . . .

11. The Conference takes note of the declaration of the French Government to the effect that for the settlement of all the problems connected with the reestablishment and consolidation of peace in Cambodia, Laos, and Viet-Nam, the French Government will proceed from the principle of respect for the independence and sovereignty, unity, and territorial integrity of Cambodia, Laos, and Viet-Nam.

12. In their relations with Cambodia, Laos, and Viet-Nam, each member of the Geneva Conference undertakes to respect the sovereignty, the independence, the unity, and the territorial integrity of the above-mentioned states, and to refrain from any interference in their internal affairs. . . .

SOURCE: "The Final Declaration of the Geneva Conference: On Restoring Peace in Indochina." July 21, 1954. Available online at http://www .fordham.edu/halsall/mod/1954-geneva-indochina.html; website home page: http://www.fordham.edu (accessed June 18, 2003).

American aid given directly to your Government can serve to assist Viet-Nam in its present hour of trial, provided that your Government is prepared to give assurances as to the standards of performance it would be able to maintain in the event such aid were supplied.

The purpose of this offer is to assist the Government of Viet-Nam in developing and maintaining a strong, viable state, capable of resisting attempted subversion or aggression through military means. The Government of the United States expects that this aid will be met by performance on the part of the Government of Viet-Nam in undertaking needed reforms. It hopes that such aid, combined with your own continuing efforts, will contribute effectively toward an independent Viet-Nam endowed with a strong government. Such a government would, I hope, be so responsive to the nationalist aspirations of its people, so enlightened in purpose and effective in performance, that it will be respected both at home and abroad and discourage any who might wish to impose a foreign ideology on your free people.

Sincerely,
Dwight D. Eisenhower

Further Resources

BOOKS

Ambrose, Stephen E. *Eisenhower: The President.* New York: Simon and Schuster, 1984.

Gettleman, Marvin E., ed. *Vietnam and America: A Documented History,* 2nd ed. New York: Grove, 1995.

Greene, Graham. *The Quiet American: Text and Criticism.* John Clark Pratt, ed. New York: Penguin, 1995.

Leffler, Melvyn P. *The Specter of Communism: The United States and the Origins of the Cold War, 1917–1953.* New York: Hill and Wang, 1994.

Young, Marilyn B. *The Vietnam Wars, 1945–1990.* New York: HarperCollins, 1991.

AUDIO AND VISUAL MEDIA

Vietnam: A Television History. American Experience, Public Broadcasting Service, 1983, VHS.

Speech by Dwight Eisenhower to the U.S. Congress, February 22, 1955

Speech

By: Dwight Eisenhower

Date: February 22, 1955

Source: Eisenhower, Dwight. Speech to the U.S. Congress. February 22, 1955. Available online at http://www.eisenhower.utexas.edu/dl/InterstateHighways/InterstateHighwaysdocuments.html; website home page: http://www.eisenhower.utexas.edu (accessed June 18, 2003).

About the Author: Dwight Eisenhower (1890–1969) graduated from West Point in 1915. By 1940, he rose to the rank of lieutenant colonel. With the eruption of World War II (1939–1945), he swiftly advanced to four-star general in 1943. That same year, he received the assignment to lead one of the largest military campaigns in world history: the D day invasion of June 6, 1944. After the war, he went into politics and served as the thirty-fourth U.S. president from 1953 to 1961. ∎

Introduction

Before the presidency of Dwight Eisenhower, the U.S. interstate highway system developed on a piecemeal basis. In 1938, President Franklin Roosevelt (served 1933–1945) signed the Federal Aid Highway Act, which proposed a nationwide network of roads akin to the eventual interstate highway system. This measure, though, did not allocate any federal funds for the project.

The 1944 Federal Aid Highway Act called for the building of the first specific stretches of this network, which would feature dedicated traffic lanes in each direction, standard widths and safety specifications, and stop light–free driving. Although the federal government again offered no monetary support, construction eventually began in 1947, but the project suffered from little federal aid and uneven state support. Yet, another Federal Aid Highway Act, passed in 1952, marked the first time the federal government actually dedicated funds for interstate roads with an authorization of $25 million. By the time of Eisenhower's inaugural address in 1953, only six thousand miles had been completed, for a total cost of over $950 million. The entrance of a moderate Republican president, who desired to reform government and roll back the New Deal domestic programs of his predecessors, did not bode well for the overbudgeted, underconstructed interstate system.

During his long military career, however, Eisenhower realized the enormous benefit to the country that could be achieved with a uniform, national network of roads. Shortly after World War I (1914–1918), in 1919, the young colonel participated in the U.S. Army's transcontinental motor convoy from Washington, D.C., to San Francisco. The cross-country journey took nearly two months, and the crews experienced myriad problems due to inadequate, and sometimes nonexistent, roads and bridges. As a general during World War II, Eisenhower admired the speed and precision with which drivers could traverse Germany using its *autobahn* highways, which had been constructed during the 1930s.

Significance

As president, Eisenhower urged a massive expansion of the nation's highways. This process began with the Federal Aid Highway Act of 1954, which provided $175 million in federal funds for the system. Eisenhower realized that this amount would not come close to covering the necessary construction costs. On February 22, 1955, he addressed Congress and the nation concerning the need to vastly improve the interstate system. From his opening sentence, he emphasized how the creation of an interstate highway system would strengthen the entire country. The United States' "unity as a nation," he argued, depended on free-flowing transportation and communication.

In addition to the economic benefits to be gained through smoother interstate travel, Eisenhower asserted that the nation needed a cohesive highway system to survive in the event of nuclear war. The freeways, in effect, could serve as escape routes in the event of atomic attacks on the nation's major cities. Thus, the ongoing struggle with the Soviet Union permeated the speech and shaped many of his primary rationales for this project. Ultimately labeled the "National System of Interstate and Defense Highways," Eisenhower's highway policy underlined the Cold War's far-reaching impact on American society during the 1950s.

Although Eisenhower initially called for the network's completion by 1964, interstate roads would continue to be built into the twenty-first century. The bulk of the system, however, was completed by 1990, when President George H.W. Bush renamed the system the "Dwight D. Eisenhower System of Interstate and Defense Highways." Eisenhower's highway policy developed into the nation's single largest project and, according to certain officials, the biggest public works endeavor in world history—ironic for a president not known for domestic policy. Early in the twenty-first century, the network contained more than forty-six thousand miles of roads and sustains one-fifth of the nation's daily traffic. By restructuring how Americans live, work, and spend their vacations, the interstate system has fundamentally altered life in the United States.

Primary Source

Speech by Dwight Eisenhower to the U.S. Congress, February 22, 1955 [excerpt]

SYNOPSIS: In the following speech, Eisenhower justifies an enormous public works program in the name of national defense and economic security at the height of the Cold War. He transmits to Congress General Lucius D. Clay's report concerning the need for an advanced interstate highway system, which calls for the federal government to contribute $27 billion to the project. Though Congress defeated the plan in 1955, Eisenhower signed a modified Federal Aid Highway Act in 1956. In effect, this policy created the modern interstate network.

To the Congress of the United States:

Our unity as a nation is sustained by free communication of thought and by easy transportation of people and goods. The ceaseless flow of information throughout the Republic is matched by individual and commercial movement over a vast system of inter-connected highways criss-crossing the Country and joining at our national borders with friendly neighbors to the north and south.

Together, the uniting forces of our communication and transportation systems are dynamic elements in the very name we bear—United States. Without them, we would be a mere alliance of many separate parts.

The Nation's highway system is a gigantic enterprise, one of our largest items of capital investment. Generations have gone into its building. Three million, three hundred and sixty-six thousand miles of road, travelled by 58 million motor vehicles, comprise it. The replacement cost of its drainage and bridge and tunnel works is incalculable. One in every seven Americans gains his livelihood and supports his family out of it. But, in large part, the network is inadequate for the nation's growing needs.

In recognition of this, the Governors in July of last year at my request began a study of both the problem and methods by which the Federal Government might assist the States in its solution. I appointed in September the President's Advisory Committee on a National Highway Program, headed by Lucius D. Clay, to work with the Governors and to propose a plan of action for submission to the Congress. At the same time, a committee representing departments and agencies of the national Government was organized to conduct studies coordinated with the other two groups.

All three were confronted with inescapable evidence that action, comprehensive and quick and

The Federal Aid Highway Act signed by Dwight Eisenhower set construction of modern interstate highways in motion. Eisenhower was convinced for the need of interstate highways after seeing the German Autobahn during World War II. THE LIBRARY OF CONGRESS.

forward-looking, is needed.

First: Each year, more than 36 thousand people are killed and more than a million injured on the highways. To the home where the tragic aftermath of an accident on an unsafe road is a gap in the family circle, the monetary worth of preventing that death cannot be reckoned. But reliable estimates place the measurable economic cost of the highway accident toll to the Nation at more than $4.3 billion a year.

Second: The physical condition of the present road net increases the cost of vehicle operation, according to many estimates, by as much as one cent per mile of vehicle travel. At the present rate of travel, this totals more than $5 billion a year. The cost is not borne by the individual vehicle operator alone. It pyramids into higher expense of doing the nation's business. Increased highway transportation costs, passed on through each step in the distribution of goods, are paid ultimately by the individual consumer.

Third: In case of an atomic attack on our key cities, the road net must permit quick evacuation of

Highway 40, under construction in Vallejo, California, in 1958. The enactment of the Federal-Aid Highway Act of 1956 led to funding of the interstate system. **AP/WIDE WORLD PHOTOS. REPRODUCED BY PERMISSION.**

target areas, mobilization of defense forces and maintenance of every essential economic function. But the present system in critical areas would be the breeder of a deadly congestion within hours of an attack.

Fourth: Our Gross National Product, about $357 billion in 1954, is estimated to reach over $500 billion in 1965 when our population will exceed 180 million and, according to other estimates, will travel in 81 million vehicles 814 billion vehicle miles that year. Unless the present rate of highway improvement and development is increased, existing traffic jams only faintly foreshadow those of ten years hence.

To correct these deficiencies is an obligation of Government at every level. The highway system is a public enterprise. As the owner and operator, the various levels of Government have a responsibility for management that promotes the economy of the nation and properly serves the individual user. In the case of the Federal Government, moreover, expenditures on a highway program are a return to the highway user of the taxes which he pays in connection with his use of the highways.

Congress has recognized the national interest in the principal roads by authorizing two Federal-aid systems, selected cooperatively by the States, local units and the Bureau of Public Roads.

The Federal-aid primary system as of July 1, 1954, consisted of 234,407 miles, connecting all the principal cities, county seats, ports, manufacturing areas and other traffic generating centers.

In 1944 the Congress approved the Federal-aid secondary system, which on July 1, 1954, totalled 482,972 miles, referred to as farm-to-market roads—important feeders linking farms, factories, distribution outlets and smaller communities with the primary system.

Because some sections of the primary system, from the viewpoint of national interest are more important than others, the Congress in 1944 authorized the selection of a special network, not to exceed 40,000 miles in length, which would connect by routes, as direct as practicable, the principal metropolitan areas, cities and industrial centers, serve the national defense, and connect with routes of continental importance in the Dominion of Canada and the Republic of Mexico.

This National System of Interstate Highways, although it embraces only 1.2 percent of total road mileage, joins 42 State capital cities and 90 percent of all cities over 50,000 population. It carries more than a seventh of all traffic, a fifth of the rural traffic, serves 65 percent of the urban and 45 percent of the rural population. Approximately 37,600 miles have been designated to date. This system and its mileage are presently included within the Federal-aid primary system.

In addition to these systems, the Federal Government has the principal, and in many cases the sole, responsibility for roads that cross or provide access to Federally owned land—more than one-fifth the nation's area.

Of all these, the Interstate System must be given top priority in construction planning. But at the current rate of development, the Interstate network would not reach even a reasonable level of extent and efficiency in half a century. State highway departments cannot effectively meet the need. Adequate right-of-way to assure control of access; grade separation structures; relocation and realignment of present highways; all these, done on the necessary scale within an integrated system, exceed their collective capacity.

If we have a congested and unsafe and inadequate system, how then can we improve it so that ten years from now it will be fitted to the nation's requirements?

A realistic answer must be based on a study of all phases of highway financing, including a study of the costs of completing the several systems of highways, made by the Bureau of Public Roads in cooperation with the State highway departments and local units of government. This study, made at the direction of the 83rd Congress in the 1954 Federal-aid Highway Act, is the most comprehensive of its kind ever undertaken.

Its estimates of need show that a 10-year construction program to modernize all our roads and streets will require expenditure of $101 billion by all levels of Government. . . .

In its report, the Advisory Committee recommends:

1. That the Federal Government assume principal responsibility for the cost of a modern Interstate Network to be completed by 1964 to include the most essential urban arterial connections; at an annual average cost of $2.5 billion for the ten year period.

2. That Federal contributions to primary and secondary road systems, now at the rate authorized by the 1954 Act of approximately $525 million annually, be continued.

3. That Federal funds for that portion of the Federal-aid systems in urban areas not on the Interstate System, now approximately $75 million annually, be continued.

4. That Federal funds for Forest Highways be continued at the present $22.5 million per year rate. . . .

The extension of necessary highways in the Territories and highway maintenance and improvement in National Parks, on Indian lands and on other public lands of the United States will continue to be treated in the budget for these particular subjects.

A sound Federal highway program, I believe, can and should stand on its own feet, with highway users providing the total dollars necessary for improvement and new construction. Financing of interstate and Federal-aid systems should be based on the planned use of increasing revenues from present gas and diesel oil taxes, augmented in limited instances with tolls.

I am inclined to the view that it is sounder to finance this program by special bond issues, to be paid off by the above-mentioned revenues which will be collected during the useful life of the roads and pledged to this purpose, rather than by an increase in general revenue obligations.

At this time, I am forwarding for use by the Congress in its deliberations the Report to the President made by the President's Advisory Committee on a National Highway Program. This study of the entire highway traffic problems and presentation of a detailed solution for its remedy is an analytical review of the major elements in a most complex situation. In addition, the Congress will have available the study made by the Bureau of Public Roads at the direction of the 83rd Congress.

These two documents together constitute a most exhaustive examination of the National highway system, its problems and their remedies. Inescapably, the vastness of the highway enterprise fosters varieties of proposals which must be resolved into a national highway pattern. The two reports, however, should generate recognition of the urgency that presses upon us; approval of a general program that will give us a modern safe highway system; realization of the rewards for prompt and comprehensive action. They provide a solid foundation for a sound program.

Dwight D. Eisenhower
The White House,
February 22, 1955.

Further Resources

BOOKS

Jackson, Kenneth T. *Crabgrass Frontier: The Suburbanization of the United States.* New York: Oxford University Press, 1985.

Lewis, Tom. *Divided Highways: The Interstate Highway System and the Transformation of American Life.* New York: Viking, 1997.

WEBSITES

"Interstate Highway System." Dwight D. Eisenhower Library. Available online at http://www.eisenhower.utexas.edu/dl /InterstateHighways/InterstateHighwaysdocuments.html; website home page: http://www.eisenhower.utexas.edu (accessed June 18, 2003).

Weingroff, Richard F. "Federal-Aid Highway Act of 1956: Creating the Interstate System." Turner-Fairbank Highway Research Center. Available online at http://www.tfhrc.gov /pubrds/summer96/p96su10.htm; website home page: www .tfhrc.gov (accessed June 18, 2003).

AUDIO AND VISUAL MEDIA

Divided Highways: The Interstates and the Transformation of American Life. By Tom Lewis and Lawrence Hott. Films for the Humanities and Sciences, 1997, VHS.

African American and Women Voters in the 1950s

"The Negro Voter: Can He Elect a President?"

Magazine article

By: Theodore White

Date: August 17, 1956

Source: White, Theodore H. "The Negro Voter: Can He Elect a President?" *Collier's,* August 17, 1956. Available online at http://historymatters.gmu.edu/d/6331/ (accessed June 18, 2003).

About the Author: Theodore H. White (1915–1986) started his career in journalism by writing for *Time* magazine. By the mid-1950s, he focused on political coverage for *Collier's.* After covering the 1956 presidential campaign, he eventually wrote *The Making of the President, 1960* (1961). In 1962, the study received the Pulitzer Prize. He wrote subsequent editions of *The Making of the President* series, covering the 1964, 1968, and 1972 campaigns.

"Where Men Go Wrong About Women Voters"

Magazine article

By: Walter Davenport

Date: September 14, 1956

Source: Davenport, Walter. "Where Men Go Wrong About Women Voters." *Collier's,* September 14, 1956. Available online at http://historymatters.gmu.edu/d/6563/ (accessed June 18, 2003).

About the Author: Walter Davenport (1889–1971) was the first editor of *Liberty.* Later in his life, he worked for *Collier's.* ∎

Introduction

Voting practices and voter demographics changed subtlely but substantially in the 1950s. When Dwight Eisenhower (served 1953–1961) won the 1952 presidential election, increasing numbers of women and African Americans went to the polls during the decade. The Cold War dominated foreign and domestic policy, and both groups perceived important changes underway that would influence their lives in the near future.

Furthermore, the economic boom of the mid-1950s increased the standard of living and the incomes of millions of American voters. The jobs created during this period enabled even greater numbers of African Americans to move north, continuing the Great Migration of African Americans from the South that began in the 1910s. While most women continued to work as homemakers during the 1950s, they also advanced their political participation to unprecedented levels. In order to gauge the impact these populations would have on the 1956 presidential election, *Collier's* sent Walter Davenport and Theodore White to the Midwest to investigate this question, as well as to examine why black and female voters might support one candidate over another.

Significance

While a far smaller population than the total number of women, most African Americans settled in urban centers throughout the North following their migration from the South. In "The Negro Voter: Can He Elect a President?" White examined the changes wrought by this mass movement on the American political landscape. Many of the primarily Democratic respondents expressed a growing dissatisfaction with the Democratic Party's reliance on southern segregationist support. These tensions within the party exploded in the political and social upheavals of the 1960s, when millions of white southerners began to leave the Democratic Party in response to its support of the civil rights movement. By focusing his research in Chicago, White also conveyed the growing power African Americans held in northern metropolitan areas. His closing predication that whichever party supported civil rights would receive the overwhelming support of African Americans came four years too soon. In the election of 1956, the majority of African American voters supported President Eisenhower, despite his lack of support for the *Brown v. Board of Education* decision, which outlawed segregation in public schools.

An African American man registers to vote in Montgomery, Alabama, in 1958. AP/WIDE WORLD PHOTOS. REPRODUCED BY PERMISSION.

In "Where Men Go Wrong About Women Voters," Davenport mistakenly proposed that "voting females" were a "new political phenomenon." Still, his focus correctly reflected the growing participation of women in elections. Davenport argued that women cared first and foremost about their families and thus supported candidates whose policies would best protect the welfare of women's husbands and children. Yet, in various interviews excerpted throughout the report, Davenport portrayed typical female voters as perceptive, unfazed by political showmanship, and eager to throw ineffective and corrupt politicians out of office. Although women's rights did not top the Democratic or Republican agendas in 1956, the precursor to the mass movement of the 1960s and 1970s may have been foreshadowed in the reformist arguments and latent discontent expressed by many of the subjects for this article.

Primary Source

"The Negro Voter: Can He Elect a President?" [excerpt]

> **SYNOPSIS:** The following article provides modern readers with an intriguing insight into how African American voters conceived of presidential politics during the 1950s, as well as how journalists perceived this group in the process.

Negroes now hold the political balance of power in America's five biggest cities. These cities in turn dominate states that cast 156 electoral votes, three fifths the number needed to elect a President. The drama of this month' s national conventions will revolve in large part around the efforts of both major parties to convince American Negroes that politically they do not stand trapped, as one of their leaders has said, "between the known Devil and the suspected Witch." Whichever party succeeds best may well swing the crucial Negro vote—and the 1956 election—next November. . . .

Chicago, evening on the South Side, in the black belt, and the 2d Ward Republicans are meeting in the made-over store that holds their clubroom. Outside, through the open door on 35th Street, the sound of loiterers, chatterers, high-pitched laughter. Inside, 50 or so people on the shabby folding chairs, watching television, waiting.

The meeting opens with a hymn ("Pass Me Not, O Gentle Saviour"), and the Reverend King S. Rains rises to talk. He's just been down to Memphis on a "mother-trip," the way he has gone to see his mother down South every year for 30 years.

"Been to a meeting down there of ministers," proclaims the Reverend Rains; "heard more talk about voting in two hours than I've heard in Chicago in two years. Down there, they're pledging themselves to get 70,000 more votes than ever before and they said to me, 'What you doing in Chicago?' I said we're raising money to send to the bus strike in Alabama. You know what they said to me? They said to me, 'You Northern Negroes don't know what you're doing. You're like a man running to put out a fire with a bucket of water in one hand, bucket of gasoline in the other. That's what you're doing, raising money for the strikers in Alabama with one hand, voting Democratic with the other.'"

Long pause.

"And they're right," says the Reverend, his voice rising and breaking. "What are we doing up here? These knock-kneed ministers, eating chicken, getting fat, telling people to vote Democrat—and people listen to them! They know they're lying when they tell the people to vote Democrat." (Audience groans, murmurs, "That's right.") "Do you know we've got the balance of power in our votes? What are we going to do with it? The president of the NAACP, he told you the other day, he said we're between the Devil and the Witch. He couldn't come right out and say it because of his job. But I tell you what he meant—he meant you've got to vote Republican. I say so."

The meeting goes on and I wander out. It is a long way from Chicago to the deep South—Eastland and Talmadge, Emmett Till and Autherine Lucy, bus boycotts in Montgomery and Tallahassee, all far away. But the winds blow hot off the embers of hate and carry strong to the North. How strong, one asks? Are they strong enough for the 2d Ward Republicans to stir a revolt of Negroes against Democrats in Chicago because Democrats in the South savage their kinfolk? . . .

Few of the Democratic delegates who assemble in Chicago this month will have the time to wander the pavings of 35th Street less than a mile away from the stockyards convention hall. But their actions and decisions will be magnetized, nonetheless, by such rumblings as stir the 2d Ward. For these are questions that reach far beyond Chicago's 2d Ward, or the parishes and hill counties of the South. The relations of white man and black man in our country have become in this year, 1956, for the first time since the Civil War, one of the central imponderables in the great struggle for our Presidency.

In the past 10 years, all American politics have buckled under one of the great movements of history—the mass migration of millions of American Negroes from the lands of humiliation in the South to the democracy of the big cities of the North. Here, bewildering and perplexing the crowded cities, they have found finally the power to alter the shape of American life.

The new political power of the Northern Negro rests upon two things: his irresistible growth in numbers, and a fresh, superbly gifted leadership. . . .

Potential power as great as this is too stupendous a fact to be concealed—least of all from those who shape and lead it

And what has happened is that American Negro leaders have become aware of their strength; and they are determined to use it this year.

Any white American in whose mind the image of Negro leadership is still yesterday's fuzzy picture of Booker T. Washington is today completely out of touch with reality. A whole constellation of action groups has matured among Negroes of the North in the past 10 years of progress; they operate on every front of what Negro leaders like to call "the power structure of America." The NAACP is the senior, legal arm, prying open opportunity after opportunity through the courts; the Urban League fights on the industrial front, wrenching open closed jobs in field after field; the Negro church has come alive, vibrant, passionate, inflaming politics with religion; prosperity has brought the Negro community businessmen of wealth and prominence; the labor unions have trained and educated men of depth and drive; a Negro press of constant and effective indignation amplifies and magnifies them all among their own people.

At the summit of these groups stand leaders too brilliant and diverse to be capped by any single figure: Thurgood Marshall of the NAACP, victor of the historic Supreme Court decision on school integration, tall, sardonic, gay, almost mischievous; Roy Wilkins, executive secretary of NAACP, polished phrase maker, eloquent, calculating; Alex Fuller, the solid, burly, easygoing vice-president of the Wayne County CIO; bitter brooding, delicately handsome Edwin Berry of the Chicago Urban League; the grave, solemn, grizzled veteran Julius Thomas of the National Urban League; Congressman the Reverend Adam Clayton Powell, Jr., flamboyant, graceful; or City Councilor the Reverend Marshall Shepard of Philadelphia, dedicated, robust, untiring; and others, too many to note. . . .

These men know their strength and they recognize their moment. For, in the past two years, there has been a flare-up of Negro emotions in America unprecedented since the days of Reconstruction. This flare-up dates precisely from the Supreme Court's decision to desegregate the public schools of America; which, in turn, provoked the last-ditch reaction of the white South—the murders in Mississippi, the white Citizens' Councils—which, finally, has shaken Negroes North and South to the resistance and reaction that now daily make headlines all across the country.

In Chicago, a Negro social worker organizes a handful of Negro housewives in a voter-registration campaign. Her pamphlets say: "Don't Get Mad—Get Smart, Register!"; and in two years her volunteer committee has jabbed Negro registration in the South Side up from 200,000 to 275,000. In Detroit, a Negro doctor decides to invite a few friends for dinner to raise money for the Montgomery strike; the dinner grows in a few weeks to a community affair and $32,000 is raised in an evening. Says Senator Jim Watson, New York's only Negro state senator, "Why, I'll be walking down Amsterdam Avenue and a stranger will grab my arm and say, 'What'cha gonna do about that Miss Lucy girl, man?'" Pastor Martin Luther King, hero of the Montgomery bus strike, comes to speak in Brooklyn and thousands crowd the church to overflow the sidewalks outside. The temper shakes family loyalties.

In Detroit, the aged and ailing father of Congressman Charles Diggs, Jr., tells me, "We've got to get rid of Eastland and I don't care how—even if it costs my son his seat."

The temper goes deep. Traditional political loyalties teeter-totter in slums, at bars, in poolrooms, on street corners. In one day's doorbell ringing on the South Side, I interviewed 21 people (too fragmentary a cut from which to draw final political conclusions, but one learns that the Negroes are disturbed). Five weren't going to vote or wouldn't say ("Neither party is worth a damn," said one auto worker on the street corner), nine thought they'd stay Democratic, seven thought the Republicans would do more for civil rights ("I read everything I can get my hands on," said one. "I'm a Democrat, but I'll go for Ike nationally. We got to do something about this Eastland; and that Talmadge, he's worse."). . . .

Basically, for the Negro, what is at issue in this campaign is not principle, but timing—which party's candidate will go faster, which will move sooner. Nor are the Negroes themselves insistent on explosive immediacy. "We walk a tightrope," said Roy Wilkins. "We want to move, but there must be no explosion, no bloodshed. If there's bloodshed, our people down South get hurt worst of all. There mustn't be bloodshed. If there's bloodshed, it's disaster, for it wipes out all the middle ground of white good will down South, the very people we need as friends if we're to succeed."

It would be missing part of the enormous drama of American life if the Negro surge of 1956 were seen only in terms of one campaign. To see its historic meaning one must draw back and see the Negro migrant to the Northern city against the political development of all the migrant groups who have gone before. For the Northern cities of America, with all their squalor and violence, have been radiant centers of freedom and democracy for all the world. Each immigrant group that has found dignity and freedom there has been educated to use its power to give the same values to its folk at home. Thus did the Germans of the 1848 migration work for the freedom of Germany; so did the Irish of Boston, New York and Chicago help to create a free Ireland; so did the Jews of the East Coast help to create a free Israel; indeed, in Pittsburgh in 1917 the Czechs of Pennsylvania actually outlined the structure of the first free Czechoslovakia. Each group has used its vote and power to sway American support for American ideals everywhere in the world. And now the

Northern Negro is using his vote and power to do in America what other minority groups have done for their brethren overseas.

Primary Source

"Where Men Go Wrong About Women Voters" [excerpt]

SYNOPSIS: This article emphasizes the likely possibility of massive shifts in voting patterns in the coming years. In every presidential election since 1956, women have disproportionately supported Democratic candidates primarily because of this party's support for liberal social policies favored by women.

A cross section of that new political phenomenon—voting females—is quizzed by a *Collier's* editor. He got told, and now tells you, why the ladies are voting much more and much differently than expected. . . .

We were going to Indianapolis, Indiana, to ask women why they vote as they do, why they are voting in ever-increasing numbers, why they are overtaking and even passing men in their interest and activity in politics. Thus, the bare bones of our mission. Before we finished the job or, perhaps more accurately, got as far as anyone was likely to get, we saw a great light.

Up to a certain but never fixed point, the woman voter is a lady. Pushed beyond that by the candidate's stale burblings on time-tattered issues and/or by his blind and unimaginative adherence to a creaking political machine, she is more than likely to become a Nemesis—particularly his—and ballot him back to whatever he was doing before he decided to become a public payrollee.

"It is not hard to explain in a sort of vague way," said our survivor of the political wars. "Every so often," he explained, reaching into his capacious bag of memories, "women get causy. You can gentle them around for just so long. The old sweet-nothings stuff, if you get what I mean. And then someone will come along with a ringing call to arms, a cause. And suddenly," he concluded with a sigh, "they'll throw party affiliations and party leaders—bosses, some call them—out the window. Believe me, sir, a woman with a cause can be a fearsome thing." (Later, when we got out in the field, we indeed found women less tolerant, to put it gently, of party hacks and political clichés than their shoulder-shrugging husbands.) . . .

In a job like this you knock on any door. That's how we met Mrs. Vivian Wells, an industrial worker's

wife and, incidentally, a persistent demander for Plain Answers to Simple Questions, an unorganized but rapidly growing movement among women voters.

In her precinct, Mrs. Wells said, "Women voters outnumbered the men two to one at the latest elections." Why? Hard to say exactly. But the men are inclined to shrug things off, don't see what can be done about a lot of things that need to be done. But women are all house cleaners at heart. Sort of look upon brooms, mops, dusters and disinfectants as weapons peculiar to their sex. "Understand?" We nodded.

Well, in the latest local elections the women had a slogan: Scratch the Hacks. Here was that Cause we'd heard about in Washington. And the women need nothing more. Scratch the Hacks.

The slaughter of the hacks—the interminables who grew potbellied, waffle-tailed and bag-eyed in public office—can be compared to one of those cellar-to-attic house cleanings, the kind that jars and confuses the easygoing male.

Women, Mrs. Wells went on, are born ticket splitters. They may be registered Republicans or registered Democrats but let them get together to talk things over, and they'll emerge from the kitchen on Election Day and leap party fences. Scratching hacks? Mister, it's a pleasure. . . .

A Mrs. Annie Furrmann had something to say about the feminine fondness for ticket splitting. She said she doesn't know "one solitary woman who votes a straight ticket unless she has a political job." It is—well, sort of woman's nature. Let's say (she said) she's got two children, a boy and a girl. Let's say one of them gets out of line—disobeys, or something. That one gets a clout or is fined a week's allowance, or something. Anyway, a stern warning. Punished. Well, that's the way she feels about politicians and parties. Clout the bad ones regardless of sex or party or personal pre-disposition. She asked us whether her theory sounded screwy. We hedged; said only another woman could answer that. She flapped her hand at us.

In Indianapolis and on Marion County's farms we talked to scores of women. Without exception, all derided the predictions so frequently made in 1920, when the Nineteenth Amendment to the Constitution became effective, that government would become cleaner and more efficient as the woman vote increased. Also, that the quality of male candidates would consequently improve. Nonsense, they said. Rot. Bunk. Short snorts like that. The woman voter, they said, is still a human being, with all the ability of the male to vote for the wrong candidate and be bamboozled by well-constructed but false propaganda. But, they added, it is extremely dangerous to tell a woman the same lie twice.

Only two women foresaw the day when a woman would become a Presidential candidate. Neither said that she'd necessarily vote for her. Both denied with some heat that this latter is due to the familiar male theory that jealousy deprives many female candidates of the votes of her sisters. Rather, they agreed, a woman lacks the administrative qualities of a man.

But, said Mrs. Lydia Wellcome, a woman as President might be "influenced in big things by what men regard as little things—the kids, for example, or primary schools or TV shows."

You may accept it as a fact that, in a manner of speaking, women carry the simple problems of their individual homes with them as they enter the polling booths. Men, to the contrary, vote with their business affairs uppermost in mind. This is as true as it is trite. . . .

Mrs. Margaret Jones, a housewife, was certain the days are vanishing when husband and wife voted "hand in hand." In that fading past the precinct worker took it for granted that the men in the family guided or even dictated the votes of their women. Suddenly, it seemed, women's political discussion groups sprang into being—"like overnight." Come to think of it, these groups multiplied fast "during the second World War and Korea while the men were overseas fighting." Or maybe it began before that—in the early thirties, when the government began doing things to alleviate the family privations of the Great Depression. Women, Mrs. Jones said, were thinking in terms of food and shelter, and women were thankful for the aid Mr. Roosevelt brought to their doors. Anyway, the more women talked among themselves, the more convinced they became that they needed no mere male to lead them to the polls. . . .

Thus far we had turned up very little to substantiate what professional male politicians had said when we told them what we were planning to write about. Sure, here and there a woman would give us to suspect that her "emotions" dictated her vote. But our own experience in digging into American voting habits told us that emotion-voting is not exclusively a feminine quality. Very far from it.

If there is any reason to believe that the farm woman's voting motivations are different from the city woman's, we didn't find it. Each apparently votes

in the interests of family security as she sees it; although today, as ever, the farmer's wife is more concerned with teetering farm produce prices than her city sister is with, say, stocks and bonds or even union wage scales.

Nor did we find anything to back up the oft-repeated male contention that the woman voter is highly susceptible to the matinee-idol type of candidate. "That sort of male thinking," one woman said, "is more directly than indirectly the reason we are voting in greater numbers. It's old, old stuff. Antique-shop junk. It's evidence that the male politician has not changed his frayed brand of thinking. And because he hasn't, because his campaign methods and phrases are just about the same as his grandfather's, the demand calls for something new. And I believe we women are supplying that."

. . . "Listen," said Mrs. Boland, "write this down. Us women can understand what's going on in our precincts. Even in the city. Like graft, overcrowded schools, holes in the streets, curfews for the kids, and stuff like that. But when we listen to those people in Washington about what's going on outside the country and why we ought to agree that what they're doing about it is okay—well, it doesn't make sense. Straight talk in simple language. That's what we want."

In the eye of the Indiana political whirlpool, the Claypool Hotel, we had a leave-taking chat with a State senator—male. "So all you had to do," said he, "was find out why women vote like they do."

"What do you mean 'all we had to do'?" we demanded.

"I could have told you without all the fuss," he replied. "It's because they're women."

Further Resources

BOOKS

White, Theodore H. *The Making of the President, 1960.* New York: Atheneum, 1961.

———. *The Transformation of American Politics: The Making of the President, 1956–1980.* New York: Harper and Row, 1982.

WEBSITES

Sogge, Paul. "White, Theodore H." American National Biography Online. Available online at http://www.anb.org/articles/16/16–02823.html; website home page: http://www.anb.org/ (accessed June 18, 2003). *This website is a subscription-based service that is available for free through most libraries.*

The Little Rock Crisis

Address to the American People on the Situation in Little Rock

Speech

By: Dwight Eisenhower

Date: September 24, 1957

Source: Eisenhower, Dwight. Address to the American People on the Situation in Little Rock. September 24, 1957. Available online at http://eisenhower.archives.gov/dl/Little Rock/littlerockdocuments.html; website home page: http://eisenhower.archives.gov (accessed June 18, 2003).

About the Author: Dwight Eisenhower (1890–1969) graduated from West Point in 1915. By 1940, he rose to the rank of lieutenant colonel. With the eruption of World War II (1939–1945), he swiftly advanced to four-star general in 1943. That same year, he received the assignment to lead one of the largest military campaigns in world history: the D day invasion of June 6, 1944. After the war, he went into politics and served as the thirty-fourth U.S. president from 1953 to 1961.

Telegram to President Dwight Eisenhower

Telegram

By: Richard B. Russell

Date: September 27, 1957

Source: Russell, Richard B. Telegram to President Dwight Eisenhower. September 27, 1957. Available online at http://eisenhower.archives.gov/dl/LittleRock/littlerockdocuments.html; website home page: http://eisenhower.archives.gov (accessed June 18, 2003).

About the Author: Richard B. Russell (1897–1971) began his political career in the Georgia House of Representatives before being elected governor. He went on to serve multiple terms in the U.S. Senate, becoming a powerful figure in Washington politics. Russell was considered as a presidential candidate in the 1952 election, but Democratic Party officials determined that his unwavering support for segregation would alienate many voters in the North. Adlai Stevenson was placed on the ticket instead. Russell remained in the Senate and continued to support segregation, participating in the effort to block President Lyndon Johnson's (served 1963–1969) civil rights legislation in the 1960s.

Letter to Richard B. Russell

Letter

By: Dwight Eisenhower

Date: September 27, 1957

Source: Eisenhower, Dwight. Letter to Richard B. Russell. September 27, 1957. Available online at http://eisenhower.archives.gov/dl/LittleRock/littlerockdocuments.html; website

home page: http://eisenhower.archives.gov (accessed June 18, 2003). ■

Introduction

In the fall of his first year in office, President Dwight Eisenhower appointed California governor Earl Warren, a Republican, to be chief justice of the Supreme Court following the death of Chief Justice Fred Vinson. Eisenhower never suspected that Warren, a seemingly loyal Republican who campaigned for Eisenhower in 1952, would later direct the Court through its most liberal period in U.S. history. Soon after receiving an on-the-job confirmation by the Senate in 1954, Warren offered his most famous decision: *Brown v. Board of Education of Topeka* (1954). This landmark ruling held that "separate but equal has no place" in public education. Thus, the Supreme Court, under Warren's direction, unanimously decided that segregation in public shools was "inherently" unconstitutional. The decision buttressed the burgeoning civil rights movement and ushered in a period of dramatic clashes over whether Americans, President Eisenhower in particular, would endorse or oppose racial equality in the United States.

Segregationists responded to the court's ruling by increasing the number of segregated schools. Faced with growing opposition and outright refusals to abide by *Brown,* the Supreme Court took the unusual step of issuing *Brown v. Board of Education of Topeka II* (1955), which asserted that the Court's orders must be carried out "with all deliberate speed." Early in 1956, ninety-six members of Congress—seventy-seven House members and nineteen senators representing eleven states—responded to the Court's demand with the Southern Manifesto. These segregationist legislators declared the *Brown* decision unconstitutional and implicitly encouraged their constituents to block integration. With two branches of government seemingly pitted against one another, Americans looked to President Eisenhower to decide the fate of segregation. Eisenhower, who privately supported segregation, struggled to avoid any direct action concerning civil rights. When Arkansas governor Orval Faubus ordered the state's National Guard to block nine African American children from attending Central High School in 1957, the president finally entered the fray.

Significance

On September 24, 1957, Eisenhower issued Executive Order 10730, which federalized the Arkansas National Guard, and ordered it to permit the students' entrance into Central High. He also dispatched the 101st Airborne Division to protect the "Little Rock Nine." That evening, Eisenhower justified his decision in a nationally televised statement. He argued that his actions were necessary to maintain constitutional order, but he refused to support integration and did not mention the term anywhere in his address. Throughout the address, he justified his decision to use military force to integrate Central High School as a matter of law, order, and national security.

To bolster his argument, Eisenhower reminded his audience of the global context in which these events took place. Governor Faubus and other "extremists," according to Eisenhower, threatened national security by providing aid to the Soviet Union's propaganda campaign against the United States. In line with his other domestic policy statements, he called for national unity to defeat a common enemy. This rhetoric served to quell dissent during the Cold War at the same time that it allowed Eisenhower a justification for his order that did not explicitly endorse civil rights.

Nonetheless, segregationists raged against the president's decision to intervene in the Little Rock crisis. Georgia senator Richard B. Russell, the chairman of the Senate Armed Services Committee, telegrammed the White House to show his displeasure with Eisenhower's decision. Furthermore, he believed the federal actions were putting state and individual liberties at stake.

Eisenhower's September 27 response to Russell's diatribe offered the same rationale as given in his earlier speech. But he went further by explaining that his actions were required by the office of the presidency.

Governor Faubus shut down Little Rock's high schools the following year, and segregationist sentiment actually increased over the next few years. Eisenhower backed the Civil Rights Acts of 1957, but this toothless act did not provide sufficient federal enforcement provisions to make any real headway in the areas of African American voting or civil rights.

Primary Source

Address to the American People on the Situation in Little Rock

SYNOPSIS: Eisenhower skillfully utilized the new medium of television to his advantage as the television industry boomed during the 1950s. He offered the first televised presidential press conference and often addressed the nation in live broadcasts. And so, as the nation learns of his decision to order the Arkansas National Guard to protect the nine students integrating a public school in Little Rock, Eisenhower gives this address to explain his decision and to persuade the public to support him and his controversial tactic.

My Fellow Citizens:

For a few minutes I want to speak to you about the serious situation that has arisen in Little Rock.

For this talk I have come to the President's office in the White House. I could have spoken from Rhode Island, but I felt that, in speaking from the house of Lincoln, of Jackson and of Wilson, my words would more clearly convey both the sadness I feel in the action I was compelled today to take and the firmness with which I intend to pursue this course until the orders of the Federal Court at Little Rock can be executed without unlawful interference.

In that city, under the leadership of demagogic extremists, disorderly mobs have deliberately prevented the carrying out of proper orders from a Federal Court. Local authorities have not eliminated that violent opposition and, under the law, I yesterday issued a Proclamation calling upon the mob to disperse.

This morning the mob again gathered in front of the Central High School of Little Rock, obviously for the purpose of again preventing the carrying out of the Court's order relating to the admission of Negro children to the school.

Whenever normal agencies prove inadequate to the task and it becomes necessary for the Executive Branch of the Federal Government to use its powers and authority to uphold Federal Courts, the President's responsibility is inescapable.

In accordance with that responsibility, I have today issued an Executive Order directing the use of troops under Federal authority to aid in the execution of Federal law at Little Rock, Arkansas. This became necessary when my Proclamation of yesterday was not observed, and the obstruction of justice still continues.

It is important that the reasons for my action be understood by all citizens.

As you know, the Supreme Court of the United States has decided that separate public educational facilities for the races are inherently unequal and therefore compulsory school segregation laws are unconstitutional.

Our personal opinions about the decision have no bearing on the matter of enforcement; the responsibility and authority of the Supreme Court to interpret the Constitution are clear. Local Federal Courts were instructed by the Supreme Court to issue such orders and decrees as might be necessary to achieve admission to public schools without regard to race—and with all deliberate speed. . . .

It was my hope that this localized situation would be brought under control by city and State authorities. If the use of local police powers had been sufficient, our traditional method of leaving the problem

White students look on as African American students are escorted into Little Rock's Central High School by federal troops. © BETTMANN/CORBIS. REPRODUCED BY PERMISSION.

in those hands would have been pursued. But when large gatherings of obstructionists made it impossible for the decrees of the Court to be carried out, both the law and the national interest demanded that the President take action. . . .

The very basis of our individual rights and freedoms is the certainty that the President and the Executive Branch of Government will support and insure the carrying out of the decisions of the Federal Courts, even, when necessary with all the means at the President's command.

Unless the President did so, anarchy would result.

There would be no security for any except that which each one of us could provide for himself.

The interest of the nation in the proper fulfillment of the law's requirements cannot yield to opposition and demonstrations by some few persons.

Mob rule cannot be allowed to override the decisions of the courts. . . .

The proper use of the powers of the Executive Branch to enforce the orders of a Federal Court is limited to extraordinary and compelling circumstances. Manifestly, such an extreme situation has been created in Little Rock. This challenge must be

met with such measures as will preserve to the people as a whole their lawfully protected rights in a climate permitting their free and fair exercise.

The overwhelming majority of our people in every section of the country are united in their respect for observance of the law—even in those cases where they may disagree with that law. . . .

In the South, as elsewhere, citizens are keenly aware of the tremendous disservice that has been done to the people of Arkansas in the eyes of the nation, and that has been done to the nation in the eyes of the world.

At a time when we face a grave situation abroad because of the hatred that Communism bears toward a system of government based on human rights, it would be difficult to exaggerate the harm that is being done to the prestige and influence, and indeed to the safety, of our nation and the world.

Our enemies are gloating over this incident and using it everywhere to misrepresent our nation. We are portrayed as a violator of those standards of conduct which the peoples of the world united to proclaim in the Charter of the United Nations. There they affirmed "faith in fundamental human rights and in the dignity of the human person" and did so "without distinction as to race, sex, language or religion."

And so, with confidence, I call upon citizens of the State of Arkansas to assist in bringing to an immediate end all interference with the law and its processes. If resistance to the Federal Court orders ceases at once, the further presence of Federal troops will be unnecessary and the City of Little Rock will return to its normal habits of peace and order and a blot upon the fair name and high honor of our nation in the world will be removed.

Thus will be restored the image of America and of all its parts as one nation, indivisible, with liberty and justice for all.

Primary Source

Telegram to President Dwight Eisenhower

SYNOPSIS: In this telegram to Eisenhower, Russell compares the National Guard's actions to the terrorism employed in Nazi Germany. For Russell and other so-called state's rights activists, federal actions to promote integration unconstitutionally infringe on the liberties of individuals and the states—virtually the same argument used to condone segregation and slavery in previous decades.

The President
The White House

As a citizen, as a Senator of the United States, and as Chairman of the Senate Committee on Armed Services, I must vigorously protest the highhanded and illegal methods being employed by the Armed Forces of the United States under your command who are carrying out your orders to mix the races in the public schools of Little Rock, Arkansas. If reports of reputable press associations and news writers are to be believed, these soldiers are disregarding and overriding the elementary rights of American citizens by applying tactics which must have been copied from the manual issued the officers of Hitler's Storm Troopers. The overpowering military might you have assembled there makes such actions as these newspaper accounts describe completely inexcusable unless the purpose be to intimidate and overawe all the people of the country who are opposed to mixing the races by force.

These dispatches agree that an unarmed citizen had his head cracked by a rifle butt while standing peacefully on private property more than one block removed from the school after he had told your troopers that he was there with the consent of the owner of the property.

Another account relates that three or more citizens were pushed down a street, with bayonets at their throats, while a bellicose sergeant shouted again and again quote keep the bayonets at their throats unquote.

An Associated Press dispatch from Little Rock dated today states that eight persons arrested by your troopers at Central High School yesterday had been held in jail incommunicado overnight without any charges having been filed against them and had been denied the right to call a lawyer. The dispatch further states that efforts to find out what would be done with the eight people were fruitless, and both the FBI and the United States Marshal disclaimed any knowledge of the case.

The present Supreme Court has in a number of cases freed confessed Negro rapists and murderers because they were not arraigned within the period of time that these eight people have been imprisoned and denied the right of counsel by military might.

Under the decision of Ex-parte Milligan, military courts have no jurisdiction where civil courts are available. I would not challenge any contention that the present Supreme Court would reverse this decision in any case involving school integration, but they have not yet done so, and under existing law these eight men, whatever may have been their crime, have been clearly denied their constitutional rights.

I do not have first hand information of the feeling of the majority of the people in Little Rock. The attendance in this school would indicate that a majority of the people do not have very strong feelings against integrating the school but if a minority of one who has confessed the crime of rape and murder is entitled to early arraignment and counsel, the eight dissenters at Little Rock should not be denied their rights merely because the President of the United States saw fit to place the school under military control.

The laws of this country give ample authority to United States Marshals to deputize a posse of sufficient strength to maintain order and carry out any decision of the courts. It has never contemplated that such a great aggregation of military might would be diverted for this purpose.

However, since you have seen fit to order the troopers into action, they should observe the elementary rights of American citizens who are violating no federal law, especially in the absence of a declaration of martial law.

There are millions of patriotic people in this country who will strongly resent the strong armed totalitarian police-state methods being employed at Little Rock. The fact that these tactics are unnecessary makes it even more tragic.

There are a number of other aspects of this case as reported in the press which do not reflect credit upon those in command of this army of troopers. Unless corrected this will bring the armed services into disrepute. I earnestly insist that orders be issued prohibiting these acts of violence which are wholly unnecessary, especially in view of the facts that the Negro children have a large armed personal escort to and from the school; that armed troopers patrol the corridors and classrooms; and that a cordon of armed troopers surrounds the school.

The United States government is undoubtedly liable in pecuniary damages for any attacks upon unoffending citizens. We have surrendered an American soldier accused of an attack of violence against a Japanese National to the Japanese courts for trial. We cannot do less than investigate these attacks and properly punish all of those who may have been guilty of unnecessary violence against inoffensive and peaceable American citizens.

Richard B. Russell

Primary Source

Letter to Richard B. Russell

SYNOPSIS: In this letter, Eisenhower remains "saddened" by recent events. He explains why he is required, by his office, to react to the Arkansas governor's misuse of police powers. In his private correspondence, he characterized his actions as being obligations rather than decisions that the duties of the presidency "required" him to carry out. Eisenhower again attempted to draw a fine line between appearing as an integrationist or a segregationist, in the process frustrating leaders of and against the civil rights movement.

Newport, Rhode Island, September 27, 1957

The Honorable Richard B. Russell
United States Senate
Washington, D.C.

Few times in my life have I felt as saddened as when the obligations of my office required me to order the use of force within a state to carry out the decisions of a Federal Court. My conviction is that had the police powers of the State of Arkansas been utilized not to frustrate the orders of the Court but to support them, the ensuing violence and open disrespect for the law and the Federal Judiciary would never have occurred. The Arkansas National Guard could have handled the situation with ease had it been instructed to do so. As a matter of fact, had the integration of Central High School been permitted to take place without the intervention of the National Guard, there is little doubt that the process would have gone along quite as smoothly and quietly as it has in other Arkansas communities. When a State, by seeking to frustrate the orders of a Federal Court, encourages mobs of extremists to flout the orders of a Federal Court, and when a State refuses to utilize its police powers to protect against mobs persons who are peaceably exercising their right under the Constitution as defined in such Court orders, the oath of office of the President requires that he take action to give that protection. Failure to act in such a case would be tantamount to acquiescence in anarchy and the dissolution of the union.

I must say that I completely fail to comprehend your comparison of our troops to Hitler's storm troopers. In one case military power was used to further the ambitions and purposes of a ruthless dictator; in the other to preserve the institutions of free government.

You allege certain wrong-doings on the part of individual soldiers at Little Rock. The Secretary of the Army will assemble the facts and report them directly to you.

With warm regard,
Dwight D. Eisenhower

Further Resources

BOOKS

Ambrose, Stephen E. *Eisenhower: The President.* New York: Simon and Schuster, 1984.

Burk, Robert F. *The Eisenhower Administration and Black Civil Rights.* Knoxville: University of Tennessee Press, 1984.

Dudziak, Mary L. *Cold War Civil Rights: Race and the Image of American Democracy.* Princeton, N.J.: Princeton University Press, 2000.

Kluger, Richard. *Simple Justice: The History of "Brown v. Board of Education" and Black America's Struggle for Equality.* New York: Knopf, 1976.

WEBSITES

"Little Rock School Integration Crisis." Dwight D. Eisenhower Library. Available online at http://eisenhower.archives.gov /dl/LittleRock/littlerockdocuments.html; website home page: http://eisenhower.archives.gov (accessed June 18, 2003).

Creation of NASA

U.S. Objectives in Space Exploration and Science

Report

By: S. Everett Gleason

Date: March 7, 1958

Source: Gleason, S. Everett. Discussion, 357th Meeting of the National Security Council Concerning "U.S. Objectives in Space Exploration and Science." March 6, 1958. Available online at http://www.eisenhower.utexas.edu/dl/Sputnik /Sputnikdocuments.html; website home page: http://www .eisenhower.utexas.edu (accessed June 18, 2003).

About the Author: S. Everett Gleason served as deputy executive secretary of the National Security Council. Together with William L. Langer, Gleason wrote the book *The Challenge of Isolation: The World Crisis of 1937–1940 and American Foreign Policy* (New York: Harper Brothers, 1952).

National Aeronautics and Space Act of 1958

Law

By: U.S. Congress

Date: July 29, 1958

Source: *National Aeronautics and Space Act of 1958.* Available online at http://www.hq.nasa.gov/office/pao/History /spaceact.html; website home page: http://www.hq.nasa.gov. (accessed June 18, 2003). ∎

Introduction

The Cold War conflict between the United States and the Soviet Union impacted both nations militarily, culturally, economically, and, with the space race especially, scientifically. From the launch of *Sputnik* in 1957 until the successful Moon landing of *Apollo 11* in 1969, the superpowers competed with one another for the supremacy of space.

With the threat of global nuclear warfare heightening yearly during the 1950s, the launch of *Sputnik* in October 1957 created hysteria for many Americans. Although the tiny craft orbited Earth for only two months, it made clear the Soviet Union's power in space. To many, the launch of *Sputnik* meant that the Soviet Union could just as easily send a barrage of atomic weapons toward the United States. In this context, the Eisenhower administration immediately sought to counter the Soviet Union and strengthen American resolve.

In a nationwide address on October 9, 1957, Eisenhower congratulated the Soviet Union for its success and comforted the American public by emphasizing that the United States' commitment to space exploration

continued to develop with Project Vanguard. While he attempted to allay the fears of the American public, secret intelligence reports discussed in the days after the launching acknowledged that the Soviets were planning to launch either a satellite or an intercontinental ballistic missile.

Like many common Americans, government officials worried that the rocket thrust and precision necessary to launch *Sputnik* posed the very real problem of defense against a Soviet missile attack. These worries increased the following month when the Soviets launched another successful satellite, *Sputnik II,* which carried a dog, Laika, into orbit. While *Sputnik* weighed less than two hundred pounds, the hefty sequel weighed more than one thousand pounds. American scientists raced to counter these high-profile Soviet triumphs, and the United States sent its first orbiter into space in January 1958.

Significance

In a National Security Council (NSC) meeting in March 1958, presidential science advisor James R. Killian outlined the central motives behind American space exploration, which were a combination of "human curiosity," "military considerations," and "scientific observation and experiment."

The National Aeronautics and Space Act of 1958 reflected the duties set forth in the NSC March 1958 meeting, while emphasizing the civilian organization of the new space agency. Seeking to distinguish NASA from the Soviet space program, which operated under direct military oversight, the act presented again and again NASA's objectives as "peaceful." Although the minutes of the earlier NSC meeting stressed the military objectives girding space research, the act underlined NASA's status as a civilian-controlled agency, with specific guidelines for interaction between it and the armed services.

NASA started operations on October 1, 1958, and its fortunes grew as the space race escalated in the coming years. Eisenhower's successor, John F. Kennedy (served 1961–1963), called for massive increases in expenditures for space exploration. The Soviet Union achieved another milestone when Yuri Gagarin successfully orbited Earth in April 1961. U.S. astronaut Alan B. Shepard reached space in May 1961, three weeks after Gagarin, but did not complete an orbit. John Glenn became the first American to orbit the planet in space flight in February 1962. The *Apollo 11* mission to the Moon marked NASA's pinnacle achievement in July 1969. Despite a series of interplanetary research missions and numerous scientific innovations since the Moon landing, NASA's stature has diminished, in part, due to a détente with the Soviet Union and the ultimate end of the Cold War. Throughout its history, NASA has maintained a tenuous existence, which

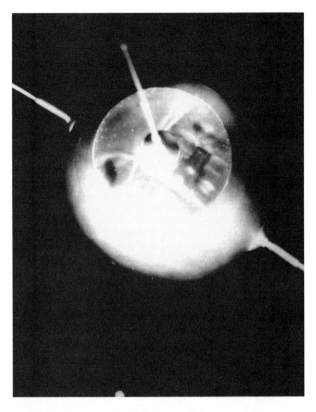

Model of the Soviet satellite, Sputnik 1, on display at an exhibition in Prague, Czechoslovakia, three days after the launch of the original. **AP/WIDE WORLD PHOTOS. REPRODUCED BY PERMISSION.**

many attribute to its complex assortment of objectives framed by the Cold War. This conflict provided many of the core objectives behind the agency, and once the Cold War ended, so, too, did a great deal of support for space exploration.

Primary Source

U.S. Objectives in Space Exploration and Science

> **SYNOPSIS:** On February 4, 1958, President Eisenhower requested that Killian research the best means of developing a national space program. Two days later, the U.S. Senate established a Special Committee on Space and Astronautics to form a permanent space agency. The 357th Meeting of the National Security Council occurred one month later, providing Killian the opportunity to present his analysis of American space objectives that would ultimately set many of the guidelines for the creation of a government agency devoted to space technology and exploration.

General Cutler introduced Dr. Killian, who stated initially that the reports to be given by himself, Dr. Purcell and Dr. York were in the nature of informal reports and would not contain specific recommendations. Next, Dr. Killian undertook to explain the main motives behind the development of space technology and space exploration. There he listed as, first, natural human curiosity about the nature of the universe; secondly, military considerations; third, U.S. prestige vis-a-vis the Soviet Union and other countries; and fourth, scientific observation and experiment. Space travel, thought Dr. Killian, may or may not have material and practical values, but the space programs that would be discussed at this time must, all of them, be based on the above-mentioned four motivating factors.

Dr. Killian then indicated that various programs of differing size, shape and cost would be presented to the Council in order to provide the basis for a subsequent choice of a U.S. national outer space program. Dr. Killian, in this context, pointed out the need for a balanced outer space program—one which would take into due account the other great national security programs, inasmuch as any affective outer space program was bound to prove very costly.

Thereafter Dr. Killian called on Dr. Purcell, who discussed with the Council his views on space science and the objectives of space science. At the end of his discussion, these objectives were summarized on a chart which was divided into three time-periods: Early (first years), Later (two to five years), and Still Later (five to fifteen years). Dr. Purcell concluded his remarks with comments on the military application of space exploration. He listed on a chart (1) communications; (2) reconnaissance (optical, radio, infrared); (3) early warning; (4) meteorological.

At the conclusion of Dr. Purcell's remarks, the President inquired whether Dr. Purcell thought it would be a good idea if there could be more public education with respect to the matters in his report. The general view seemed to be in the affirmative.

The President then inquired of Dr. Purcell whether the distant planets of which he had spoken rotated on their own axis as did our earth. Dr. Purcell replied that most of them did, but that there were some we could hardly see and could not determine whether they rotated or not.

Dr. Killian next introduced Dr. York, who, he indicated, would discuss various illustrative space science programs designed to achieve the objectives of space science which had just been outlined by Dr. Purcell.

Dr. York spoke first, using a chart, of the vehicles which would be used in the exploration of outer space. The first usable vehicles would be the

IRBMs—Jupiter and THOR—with added stages. Such vehicles would be available late in 1958 or early in 1959. They would eventually be able to carry a payload (instrumentation, etc.) weighting 500 pounds.

Later on in the process, Dr. York indicated that ICBM vehicles would become available for space exploration. Either TITAN or ATLAS could be used, perhaps in 1961, with a third stage added to them. The pay-load carried by these vehicles would be much larger than that which the IRBMs would carry. The pay-load for an earth satellite could be as large as 6500 pounds if fluorine were used for fueling, or 3800 pounds if the ICBM were fueled with liquid oxygen (lox). For a moon-hit or a Mars-hit, a pay-load of 2150 pounds with fluorine and 1000 pounds with lox could be carried.

Dr. York cautioned that even an ICBM vehicle was not sufficiently powerful to get a man to the moon. To do this we would have to construct a very large new rocket with a weight of 1.5 million pounds gross. He estimated the cost of developing such a new rocket as lying somewhere between $500 million and $1 billion.

After describing the various sample or illustrative space science and exploration programs, Dr. York turned to the subject of the approximate costs of such programs. The cost of any effective space exploration program would begin at $275 million a year, and would be likely to reach a cost of $650 million a year by 1965. Such figures, moreover, said Dr. York, were minimal.

Dr. York pointed out that a probing of the planet Mars, which might be achieved by the United States in 1962, would probably be the first achievement we could count on doing before the Russians, because they were so far ahead of us in big boosters.

The final section of Dr. York's report dealt with the possible effects to be achieved by exploiting very large megaton bombs at various heights above the earth's atmosphere. If sufficiently powerful, such explorations, he believed, could inhibit all space travel, including intercontinental ballistic missiles.

In bringing the report to a close, Dr. Killian, followed by Secretary Charles, stressed the security aspects of the information which had been provided for the Council, most particularly with respect to the final portion of Dr. York's presentation. Dr. Killian also indicated that time would not permit him to go on with a discussion of the organizational aspects of a U.S. program for space science and exploration. This subject would be discussed by Dr. Killian at a subsequent Council meeting.

The National Security Council:

a. Noted and discussed a report by the Special Assistant to the President for Science and Technology, assisted by Drs. Edward Purcell and Herbert York of the President's Science Advisory Committee, prepared pursuant to NSC Action No. 1859-b, on U.S. objectives in space exploration and science, and examples of possible programs designed to achieve these objectives.

b. Noted that the Special Assistant to the President for Science and Technology would make a subsequent report to the Council on the organizational aspects involved in pursuing U.S. objectives in space exploration and science.

Note: The action in b above, as approved by the President, subsequently transmitted to the Special Assistant to the President for Science and Technology.

Primary Source

National Aeronautics and Space Act of 1958 [excerpt]

SYNOPSIS: On April 2, 1958, Eisenhower addressed Congress to urge passage of the National Aeronautics and Space Act—a measure he signed on July 29. The sections of the act included here discuss the establishment of NASA, specifically its purposes and responsibilities concerning both scientific research and military preparedness. Less than one year after *Sputnik,* NASA began work in October 1958.

An Act to provide for research into problems of flight within and outside the earth's atmosphere, and for other purposes.

Be it enacted by the Senate and House of Representatives of the United States of America in Congress assembled,

Title I—Short Title, Declaration of Policy, and Definitions

Short Title

Sec. 101. This act may be cited as the "National Aeronautics and Space Act of 1958."

Declaration of Policy and Purpose

Sec. 102. (a) The Congress hereby declares that it is the policy of the United States that activities in space should be devoted to peaceful purposes for the benefit of all mankind.

(b) The Congress declares that the general welfare and security of the United States require that adequate provision be made for aeronautical and space activities. The Congress further declares that such activities shall be the responsibility of, and shall be directed by, a civilian agency exercising control over aeronautical and space activities sponsored by the United States, except that activities peculiar to or primarily associated with the development of weapons systems, military operations, or the defense of the United States (including the research and development necessary to make effective provision for the defense of the United States) shall be the responsibility of, and shall be directed by, the Department of Defense; and that determination as to which such agency has responsibility for and direction of any such activity shall be made by the President in conformity with section 201 (e).

(c) The aeronautical and space activities of the United States shall be conducted so as to contribute materially to one or more of the following objectives:

(1) The expansion of human knowledge of phenomena in the atmosphere and space;

(2) The improvement of the usefulness, performance, speed, safety, and efficiency of aeronautical and space vehicles;

(3) The development and operation of vehicles capable of carrying instruments, equipment, supplies and living organisms through space;

(4) The establishment of long-range studies of the potential benefits to be gained from, the opportunities for, and the problems involved in the utilization of aeronautical and space activities for peaceful and scientific purposes.

(5) The preservation of the role of the United States as a leader in aeronautical and space science and technology and in the application thereof to the conduct of peaceful activities within and outside the atmosphere.

(6) The making available to agencies directly concerned with national defenses of discoveries that have military value or significance, and the furnishing by such agencies, to the civilian agency established to direct and control nonmilitary aeronautical and space activities, of information as to discoveries which have value or significance to that agency;

(7) Cooperation by the United States with other nations and groups of nations in work done pursuant to this Act and in the peaceful application of the results, thereof; and

(8) The most effective utilization of the scientific and engineering resources of the United States, with close cooperation among all interested agencies of the United States in order to avoid unnecessary duplication of effort, facilities, and equipment. . . .

Title II—Coordination of Aeronautical and Space Activities

National Aeronautics and Space Council

Sec. 201. (a) There is hereby established the National Aeronautics and Space Council (hereinafter called the "Council") which shall be composed of—

(1) the President (who shall preside over meetings of the Council);

(2) the Secretary of State;

(3) the Secretary of Defense

(4) the Administrator of the National Aeronautics and Space Administration;

(5) the Chairman of the Atomic Energy Commission;

(6) not more than one additional member appointed by the President from the departments and agencies of the Federal Government; and

(7) not more than three other members appointed by the President, solely on the basis of established records of distinguished achievement from among individuals in private life who are eminent in science, engineering, technology, education, administration, or public affairs. . . .

National Aeronautics and Space Administration

Sec. 202. (a) There is hereby established the National Aeronautics and Space Administration (hereinafter called the "Administration"). The Administration shall be headed by an Administrator, who shall be appointed from civilian life by the President by and with the advice and consent of the Senate, and shall receive compensation at the rate of $22,500 per annum. Under the supervision and direction of the President, the Administrator shall be responsible for the exercise of all powers and the discharge of all duties of the Administration, and shall have authority and control over all personnel and activities, thereof. . . .

Functions of the Administration

Sec. 203. (a) The Administration, in order to carry out the purpose of this Act, shall—

(1) plan, direct, and conduct aeronautical and space activities;

(2) arrange for participation by the scientific community in planning scientific measurements and observations to be made through use of aeronautical and space vehicles, and conduct or arrange for the conduct of such measurements and observations; and

(3) provide for the widest practicable and appropriate dissemination of information concerning its activities and the results thereof. . . .

Civilian-Military Liaison Committee

Sec. 204 (a) There shall be a Civilian-Military Liaison Committee consisting of—

(1) a Chairman, who shall be the head thereof and who shall be appointed by the President, shall serve at the pleasure of the President, and shall receive compensation (in the manner provided in subsection (d)) at the rate of $20,000 per annum;

(2) one or more representatives from the Department of Defense, and one or more representatives from each of the Departments of the Army, Navy, and Air Force, to be assigned by the Secretary of Defense to serve on the Committee without additional compensation; and

(3) representatives from the Administration, to be assigned by the Administrator to serve on the Committee without additional compensation, equal in number to the number of representatives assigned to serve on the Committee under paragraph (2).

(b) The Administration and the Department of Defense, through the Liaison Committee, shall advise and consult with each other on all matters within their respective jurisdictions relating to aeronautical and space activities and shall keep each other fully and currently informed with respect to such activities.

(c) If the Secretary of Defense concludes that any request, action, proposed action, or failure to act on the part of the Administrator is adverse to the responsibilities of the Department of Defense, or the Administrator concludes that any request, action, or proposed action, or failure to act on the part of the Department of Defense is adverse to the responsibilities of the Administration, and the Administrator and the Secretary of Defense are unable to reach an agreement with respect thereto, either the Administrator or the Secretary of Defense may refer the matter to the President for his decision (which shall be final) as provided in section 201 (e). . . .

International Cooperation

Sec. 205. The Administration, under the foreign policy guidance of the President, may engage in a program of international cooperation in work done pursuant to the Act, and in the peaceful application of the results thereof, pursuant to agreements made by the President with the advice and consent of the Senate.

Further Resources

BOOKS

Divine, Robert A. *The Sputnik Challenge.* New York: Oxford University Press, 1993.

Killian, James R., Jr. *Sputnik, Scientists, and Eisenhower: A Memoir of the First Special Assistant to the President for Science and Technology.* Cambridge: MIT Press, 1977.

McDougall, Walter A. *The Heavens and the Earth: A Political History of the Space Age.* New York: Basic, 1985.

WEBSITES

Gorn, Michael H. "Hugh L. Dryden's Career in Aviation and Space." Dryden Flight Research Center, National Aeronautics and Space Administration. Available online at http://www.dfrc.nasa.gov/History/Publications/PDF/Dryden.pdf; website home page: http://www.dfrc.nasa.gov/ (accessed June 18, 2003).

"James Killian." History Office, National Aeronautics and Space Administration. Available online at http://www.hq.nasa.gov/office/pao/History/sputnik/killian.html; website home page: http://www.hq.nasa.gov/office/pao/History/ (accessed June 18, 2003).

"Sputnik and the Space Race." Dwight D. Eisenhower Library. Available online at http://www.eisenhower.utexas.edu/dl/Sputnik/Sputnikdocuments.html; website home page: http://www.eisenhower.utexas.edu (accessed June 18, 2003).

"The Kitchen Debate"
Debate

By: Richard Nixon and Nikita Khrushchev
Date: July 25, 1959
Source: Nixon, Richard, and Nikita Khrushchev. "The Kitchen Debate." July 25, 1959. Available online at http://teachingamericanhistory.org/library/index.asp?document=176; website home page: http://teachingamericanhistory.org (accessed June 18, 2003).

About the Authors: Richard Nixon (1911–1994) graduated from Duke Law School in 1934. After serving in the navy during World War II (1939–1945), he pursued a career in politics. Serving as a U.S. representative and then a U.S. senator, he eventually became the vice president for President Dwight Eisenhower (served 1953–1961). Defeated for the presidency in 1960, he ran again in 1968 and won. He is best remembered for the Watergate scandal, which led to him resigning from office in 1974.

Nikita Khrushchev (1894–1971) started out as a worker in heavy industry. He eventually rose through the ranks of the Communist Party to lead the Soviet Union in the 1950s and early 1960s. Proclaimed as *Time* magazine's "Man of the Year" in 1957, he attained the premiership in March 1958, at the height of the space race with the United States. In 1964, conservatives in the Party removed him from office, frustrated by his desire for domestic reform and his perceived weakness towards the United States. ■

Introduction

Just as American politicians faced the difficult task of appearing forceful to constituents and political opponents at home during the Cold War, Nikita Khrushchev straddled a tenuous line between warm and cold relations with the United States. With this in mind, he permitted, in the summer of 1959, the establishment of a U.S. Trade and Cultural Fair that was designed to depict life in the United States to the people of Moscow. While touring the American National Exhibition, which featured a presentation of an American kitchen, Khrushchev met U.S. vice president Richard Nixon. The ensuing, unscripted exchange became a stunning, and often hilarious, battle of wills between two representatives of the most powerful nations on Earth.

With television and tape recorders rolling, Khrushchev and Nixon entered the kitchen exhibit and stood next to a washer-dryer. The off-the-cuff debate saw each leader present his view of capitalism, communism, and the societies these ideologies had spawned in the United States and the Soviet Union. Khrushchev and Nixon sparred for several minutes, as each offered startlingly blunt assessments of the other. Both leaders refused to concede any point, and both could agree only that the other should change.

Significance

"The Kitchen Debate," as it became known, proved a fitting end to the 1950s. The decade had seen the emergence of the Cold War as the dominant force in international and domestic affairs in both the Soviet Union and the United States. In the United States, politicians such as Nixon manipulated anticommunist hysteria to advance their political careers. In Europe, East Asia, and elsewhere, the United States attempted to strengthen its allies to fend off the perceived Soviet menace. And finally, all of the decade's investigations, treaties, and arguments culminated in this debate between representatives of the two superpowers. Far from providing future generations with an intellectual discussion of the Cold War, Nixon and Khrushchev bickered with one another like opponents in a high school debate.

Nixon, though, received enormous popular approval for what the press described as his taking Khrushchev to task on the merits of capitalism over communism. The

man who made a name for himself with guile and prosecutorial zeal once again rode a public confrontation to national attention. Nixon's anticommunism, however, was soon out-matched by the rhetorical flights of John F. Kennedy (served 1961–1963).

Kennedy's anticommunism followed a fine line between comforting the public and preparing it for continued struggle in the Cold War. The best example of this was in his 1961 inaugural address, where he pledged on the one hand to "never fear to negotiate" and on the other to "pay any price, bear any burden, meet any hardship, support any friend, oppose any foe, in order to assure the survival and the success of liberty." The Cuban missile crisis of 1962 tested the resolve of both Kennedy and Khrushchev as the superpowers approached the brink of nuclear war, only to stand down at the last possible moment.

Primary Source

"The Kitchen Debate"

SYNOPSIS: When Nixon and Khrushchev encountered one another while touring the American National Exhibition on July 25, 1959, none of the Russian or American observers expected what happened next. The two refused to back down from the other's challenges, with the resulting debate providing another clear example of the continuing polarization between the superpowers. Yet, by agreeing to disagree at the meeting's conclusion, the pair's closing foreshadowed, in a certain respect, the détente policies later encouraged by President Nixon in the 1970s.

(*Both men enter kitchen in the American exhibit.*)

Nixon: I want to show you this kitchen. It is like those of our houses in California. (Nixon *points to dishwasher.*)

Khrushchev: We have such things.

Nixon: This is our newest model. This is the kind which is built in thousands of units for direct installations in the houses. In America, we like to make life easier for women. . . .

Khrushchev: Your capitalistic attitude toward women does not occur under Communism.

Nixon: I think that this attitude towards women is universal. What we want to do, is make life more easy for our housewives. . . .

Nixon: This house can be bought for $14,000, and most American [veterans from World War II] can buy a home in the bracket of $10,000 to $15,000. Let me give you an example that you can appreciate. Our steel workers, as you

Soviet premier Nikita Khrushchev (center) and U.S. vice president Richard Nixon during their famous "Kitchen Debate" at the American National Exhibition in Moscow. AP/WIDE WORLD PHOTOS. REPRODUCED BY PERMISSION.

know, are now on strike. But any steel worker could buy this house. They earn $3 an hour. This house costs about $100 a month to buy on a contract running 25 to 30 years.

Khrushchev: We have steel workers and peasants who can afford to spend $14,000 for a house. Your American houses are built to last only 20 years so builders could sell new houses at the end. We build firmly. We build for our children and grandchildren.

Nixon: American houses last for more than 20 years, but, even so, after 20 years, many Americans want a new house or a new kitchen. Their kitchen is obsolete by that time. . . . The American system is designed to take advantage of new inventions and new techniques.

Khrushchev: This theory does not hold water. Some things never get out of date—houses, for instance, and furniture, furnishings—perhaps—but not houses.

I have read much about America and American houses, and I do not think that this exhibit and what you say is strictly accurate.

Nixon: Well, um. . . .

Khrushchev: I hope I have not insulted you.

Nixon: I have been insulted by experts. Everything we say [on the other hand] is in good humor. Always speak frankly.

Khrushchev: The Americans have created their own image of the Soviet man. But he is not as you think. You think the Russian people will be dumbfounded to see these things, but the fact is that newly built Russian houses have all this equipment right now.

Nixon: Yes, but. . . .

Khrushchev: In Russia, all you have to do to get a house is to be born in the Soviet Union. You are entitled to housing. . . . In America, if you don't have a dollar you have a right to choose between sleeping in a house or on the pavement. Yet you say we are the slave to Communism.

Nixon: I appreciate that you are very articulate and energetic. . . .

Khrushchev: Energetic is not the same thing as wise.

Nixon: If you were in the Senate, we would call you a filibusterer! You—(Khrushchev *interrupts*)—do all the talking and don't let anyone else talk.

This exhibit was not designed to astound but to interest.

Diversity, the right to choose, the fact that we have 1,000 builders building 1,000 different houses is the most important thing. We don't have one decision made at the top by one government official. This is the difference.

Khrushchev: On politics, we will never agree with you. For instance, Mikoyan likes very peppery soup. I do not. But this does not mean that we do not get along.

Nixon: You can learn from us, and we can learn from you. There must be a free exchange. Let the people choose the kind of house, the kind of soup, the kind of ideas that they want.

(*Translation lost as both men enter the television recording studio.*)

Khrushchev: (*in jest*) You look very angry, as if you want to fight me. Are you still angry?

Nixon: (*in jest*) That's right!

Khrushchev: . . . And Nixon was once a lawyer? Now he's nervous.

Nixon: Oh yes, (Nixon *chuckling*) he still is [a lawyer].

Other Russian speaker: Tell us, please, what are your general impressions of the exhibit?

Khrushchev: It's clear to me that the construction workers didn't manage to finish their work and the exhibit still is not put in order. . . . This is what America is capable of, and how long has she existed? 300 years? 150 years of independence and this is her level.

We haven't quite reached 42 years, and in another 7 years, we'll be at the level of America, and after that we'll go farther. As we pass you by, we'll wave "hi" to you, and then if you want, we'll stop and say, "please come along behind us."

. . . If you want to live under capitalism, go ahead, that's your question, an internal matter, it doesn't concern us. We can feel sorry for you, but really, you wouldn't understand. We've already seen how you understand things.

Other U.S speaker: Mr. Vice President, from what you have seen of our exhibition, how do you think it's going to impress the people of the Soviet Union?

Nixon: It's a very effective exhibit, and it's one that will cause a great deal of interest. I might say that this morning I, very early in the morning, went down to visit a market, where the farmers from various outskirts of the city bring in their items to sell.

I can only say that there was a great deal of interest among these people, who were workers and farmers, etc. . . . I would imagine that the exhibition from that standpoint would, therefore, be a considerable success.

As far as Mr Khrushchev's comments just now, they are in the tradition we learned to expect from him of speaking extemporaneously and frankly whenever he has an opportunity.

I can only say that if this competition which you have described so effectively, in which you plan to outstrip us, particularly in the production of consumer goods. . . . If this competition is to do the best for both of our peoples and for people everywhere, there must be a free exchange of ideas.

There are some instances where you may be ahead of us—for example in the development of the thrust of your rockets for the investigation of outer space. There may be some instances, for example, color television, where we're ahead of you. But in order for both of us benefit. . . .

Khrushchev: (*interrupting*) No, in rockets we've passed you by, and in the technology. . . .

Nixon: (*continuing to talk*) You see, you never concede anything.

Khrushchev: We always knew that Americans were smart people. Stupid people could not have risen to the economic level that they've reached. But as you know, "we don't beat flies with our nostrils!" In 42 years we've made progress.

Nixon: You must not be afraid of ideas.

Khrushchev: We're saying it is you who must not be afraid of ideas. We're not afraid of anything. . . .

Nixon: Well, then, let's have more exchange of them. We all agree on that, right?

Khrushchev: Good. (Khrushchev *turns to translator and asks*): Now, what did I agree on?

Nixon: (*interrupts*) Now, let's go look at our pictures.

Khrushchev: Yes, I agree. But first I want to clarify what I'm agreeing on. Don't I have that right? I know that I'm dealing with a very good lawyer. Therefore, I want to be unwavering in my miner's girth, so our miners will say, "He's ours and he doesn't give in!"

Nixon: No question about that.

Khrushchev: You're a lawyer of Capitalism, I'm a lawyer for Communism. Let's kiss.

Nixon: All that I can say, from the way you talk and the way you dominate the conversation, you would have made a good lawyer yourself.

What I mean is this: Here you can see the type of tape which will transmit this very conversation immediately, and this indicates the possibilities of increasing communication. And this increase in communication, will teach us some things, and you some things, too. Because, after all, you don't know everything.

Khrushchev: If I don't know everything, then you know absolutely nothing about Communism, except for fear!

But now the dispute will be on an unequal basis. The apparatus is yours, and you speak English, while I speak Russian. Your words are taped and will be shown and heard. What I say to you about science won't be translated, and so your people won't hear it. These aren't equal conditions.

Nixon: There isn't a day that goes by in the United States when we can't read everything that you say in the Soviet Union. . . . And, I can assure you, never make a statement here that you don't think we read in the United States.

Khrushchev: If that's the way it is, I'm holding you to it. Give me your word. . . . I want you, the Vice President, to give me your word that my speech will also be taped in English. Will it be?

Nixon: Certainly it will be. And by the same token, everything that I say will be recorded and translated and will be carried all over the Soviet Union. That's a fair bargain.

(*Both men shake hands and walk off stage, still talking.*)

Further Resources

BOOKS
Ambrose, Stephen E. *Nixon: The Education of a Politician, 1913–1962.* New York: Simon and Schuster, 1987.

WEBSITES
Hoff, Joan. "Nixon, Richard Milhous." American National Biography Online. Available online at http://www.anb.org/articles /07/07–00684.html; website home page: http://www.anb .org/ (accessed June 18, 2003) *This website is a subscription-based service that is available for free through most libraries.*

6

LAW AND JUSTICE

SCOTT A. MERRIMAN

Entries are arranged in chronological order by date of primary source. For entries with one primary source, the entry title is the same as the primary source title. Entries with more than one primary source have an overall entry title, followed by the titles of the primary sources.

Important Events in Law and Justice, 1950–1959

1950

- The Federal Bureau of Investigation releases its first Ten Most Wanted list.

- On January 21, Alger Hiss, a former State Department official, is found guilty of perjury by a federal jury in New York.

- On February 20, the Supreme Court upholds the legality of warrantless searches of a lawfully arrested person and the immediate premises where the arrest occurred.

- On April 10, the Supreme Court upholds the convictions of Hollywood screenwriters John Howard Lawson and Dalton Trumbo for contempt of Congress.

- On April 24, the Supreme Court reverses a criminal conviction based on an indictment by a grand jury that excluded African Americans.

- On May 8, the Supreme Court upholds provisions of the Taft-Hartley Labor Act which deny unions access to the National Labor Relations Board if their officers refuse to swear they are not affiliated with the Communist party.

- On June 5, the Supreme Court unanimously holds in *Sweatt v. Painter* that a state may not bar an African American male admission to its law school despite a "black" law school being available.

- On November, two Puerto Rican nationals try to assassinate President Truman. One of the pair is killed in the attempt.

1951

- On January 4, the Supreme Court upholds convictions under the Smith Act of Communist party leaders. The Smith Act made it unlawful to knowingly conspire to teach and advocate the overthrow or destruction of the U.S. government. The Supreme Court ruled in *Dennis v. United States* that the Smith Act did not violate the First Amendment.

- On January 15, the Supreme Court finds a New York City ordinance barring worship services on public streets without a permit unconstitutional.

- On March 8, Martha Beck and Raymond Fernandez, the Lonely Hearts Killers, are executed for three murders; they likely committed seventeen more.

- On March 29, Julius and Ethel Rosenberg are convicted of violating the Espionage Act of 1917 by passing atomic secrets to the Soviet Union. On April 5, they receive death sentences.

- On June 4, the Supreme Court finds that restraints on speeches advocating the forceful overthrow of the government do not abridge First Amendment rights. The court also upholds a law requiring public employees to take a loyalty oath.

1952

- The police force of Milwaukee, Wisconsin, becomes the first to recruit and train officers using the cadet system.

- On January 2, the Supreme Court rules in *Rochin v. California* that police officers' use of a stomach pump on an unconsenting suspect to extract evidence of drugs violates Fourth Amendment protection against unreasonable search and seizure.

- On April 28, the Supreme Court holds in *Zorach v. Clauson* that "released time" programs allowing students to be dismissed from classroom activities to participate in religious instruction elsewhere did not violate the Establishment Clause of the First Amendment.

- On May 26, the Supreme Court overturns a lower court's ban of the film *The Miracle,* thus establishing that movies are a constitutionally protected form of expression.

- On June 2, the Supreme Court rules in *Youngstown Sheet and Tub Co. v. Sawyer* that President Truman did not have the constitutional authority to authorize the secretary of commerce to seize and operate the nation's steel mills during the Korean War.

- On November 12, an all-white jury in North Carolina convicts an African American man of assault for leering at a white woman 75 feet away.

1953

- On May 4, the Supreme Court finds that Texas's Jaybird party primary excluded African Americans, violating the Fifteenth Amendment's guarantee of voting rights to all citizens regardless of race.

- On June 19, Julius and Ethel Rosenberg are executed after the Supreme Court lifts a stay of execution.

- On August 25, the American Bar Association adopts a resolution to oust Communists from the legal profession.

- On September 8, Chief Justice of the United States Fred Vinson dies of a heart attack.

- On September 30, Earl Warren is appointed chief justice of the U.S. He takes office on October 5.

1954

- On March 1, five Puerto Rican nationalists open fire in the gallery of the House of Representatives; five congressmen are wounded.

- On May 3, the Supreme Court rules that the systematic exclusion of Mexican Americans from jury duty in Texas violates the Fourteenth Amendment.

- On May 17, in *Brown v. Board of Education,* the Supreme Court unanimously rules that separate public schools for white and black students violate the equal protection clause of the Fourteenth Amendment, expressly overruling the "separate but equal" doctrine as applied to public schools.

• On August 24, President Eisenhower signs the Communist Control Act, effectively outlawing the Communist party.

• On October 9, Robert H. Jackson, associate justice of the Supreme Court, dies.

1955

• On March 28, John Marshall Harlan is sworn in as an associate justice to the Supreme Court.

• On May 17, former associate justice of the Supreme Court Owen J. Roberts dies. Roberts served on the court from 1930 to 1945.

• On May 31, in a subsequent ruling on *Brown v. Board of Education,* the Supreme Court relegates school desegregation to local school districts and the courts which originally heard the segregation cases, stipulating that local school officials must proceed toward desegregation "with all deliberate speed."

• On June 3, convicted murderer Barbara Graham is executed. In 1958 her story is made into the movie *I Want to Live!* starring Susan Hayward.

• On June 23, the U.S. Court of Appeals upholds the natural right of all citizens to travel abroad, ruling that the State Department could not refuse a citizen a passport without due process.

• On August 28, Emmett Till, an African American teenager, is abducted from his uncle's home in Mississippi by two whites. Till allegedly whistled at a white woman. He is found murdered three days later.

• On September 23, in Mississippi, Roy Bryant and J.W. Milam are acquitted by an all-male, all-white jury of murdering Emmett Till. The two later confess to the murder.

• On November 1, John Gilbert Graham, in an attempt to collect on his mother's life-insurance policy, places a bomb in the airplane she is boarding; the resulting explosion kills her and forty-three others.

• On November 7, the Supreme Court rules that a civilian cannot be tried by court martial for crimes he committed while in the service.

• On December 1, African American Rosa Parks refuses to give up her seat to a white man on a bus in Montgomery, Alabama, resulting in her arrest and a year-long boycott of the buses.

1956

• On January 12, the FBI announces that it has arrested six men in the Brinks robbery.

• On April 5, New York labor columnist Victor Riesel is blinded when acid is thrown in his face by thugs allegedly acting at the behest of Teamsters Union vice president Jimmy Hoffa.

• On April 26, the Supreme Court rules that a defendant should not be denied the right to a transcript of his trial because he could not afford to pay for it.

• On June 11, the Supreme Court rules that only federal employees in sensitive jobs could be dismissed as security risks.

• On September 7, Supreme Court Justice Sherman Minton announces his retirement due to poor health. He retires on October 15. On September 29, President Eisenhower names William J. Brennan, Jr., as Minton's replacement on the Supreme Court.

• On November 15, Brennan is sworn in as an associate justice of the Supreme Court.

• On November 13, the Supreme Court rules that an Alabama law and a Montgomery, Alabama ordinance requiring racial segregation on interstate buses are unconstitutional.

1957

• On January 22, police in Waterbury, Connecticut arrest George Metesky, the "Mad Bomber" who had left more than thirty bombs around New York City over sixteen years.

• On February 25, Associate Justice Stanley Reed retires.

• On March 2, Judge Charles E. Whittaker of Missouri is nominated to the Supreme Court by President Eisenhower to replace Justice Reed. He is sworn in on March 25.

• On June 17, the Supreme Court holds that prosecutions of persons under the Smith Act for advocating the violent overthrow of the government must be based on more than accusations. This reverses the convictions of five persons and orders new trials for nine others.

• On June 24, the Supreme Court finds that obscene material is not protected by the First Amendment guarantees of freedom of speech and the press.

• On September 4, Arkansas Governor Orval Faubus summons the National Guard to prevent nine African American students from entering a Little Rock high school.

• In November, mass murderer Ed Gein, whose exploits inspire the movies *Psycho* and *The Texas Chainsaw Massacre,* is arrested in Plainfield, Wisconsin.

1958

• In March, Nathan Leopold is paroled thirty-four years after the murder of Bobby Franks.

• On March 31, in *Trop v. Dulles,* the Supreme Court rules that the Eighth Amendment forbids depriving a native-born American of his citizenship for deserting the armed forces.

• On April 4, Cheryl Crane, the 14-year-old daughter of actress Lana Turner, stabs Turner's husband, gangster Johnny Stompanato, after she overhears Stompanato threaten her mother. The killing is ruled a justifiable homicide.

• On June 16, the Supreme Court rules in *Kent v. Dulles* that American citizens have a liberty interest in the right to travel, and that a citizen cannot be denied a passport based on suspicion of his or her communist ties.

• On June 30, the Supreme Court rules that a state order requiring the NAACP to produce its membership lists is a violation of free speech and assembly rights.

• On August 25, Chief Justice Warren calls a special session of the Supreme Court to rule on the integration of Central High School in Little Rock, Arkansas.

- On September 4, the Department of Justice invokes the powers of the 1957 Civil Rights Act for the first time to stop alleged violations of African American voting rights in Terrell County, Georgia.
- On September 12, in *Cooper v. Aaron,* the Supreme Court denounces Arkansas officials for delaying desegregation mandates.
- On September 29, Governor James Folsom of Alabama commutes to life imprisonment the death sentence of an African American man convicted of robbing a woman of less than two dollars.
- On October 7, President Eisenhower appoints Potter Stewart to replace retiring Supreme Court Justice Harold Burton, who retires on October 13.

1959

- The Supreme Court rules that state and federal governments can each prosecute a criminal for the same crime.

- On January 2, the Teamsters Union announces it is abandoning plans to organize the New York City police force.
- On June 25, nineteen-year-old Charles Starkweather is electrocuted for the eleven murders he and Caril Ann Fugate committed during a week-long murder spree.
- On July 20, Federal judge Frederick van Pelt Bryan overrules the postmaster general's ban on D.H. Lawrence's *Lady Chatterley's Lover.*
- On September 18, Teamsters Union president Jimmy Hoffa is ordered by the Department of Labor to remove all union officials with criminal records.
- On November 8, undercover detectives disguised as beatniks arrest more than one hundred people in narcotics raids in New York City.

Henderson v. U.S.

Supreme Court decision

By: Harold Burton

Date: June 5, 1950

Source: Burton, Harold. *Henderson v. United States,* 339 U.S. 816. Available online at http://caselaw.lp.findlaw.com /scripts/getcase.pl?court=US&vol=339&invol=816; website home page: http://www.findlaw.com (accessed March 3, 2003).

About the Author: Harold Burton (1888–1964), a native of Boston, received his law degree from Harvard. He later moved to Ohio and became mayor of Cleveland. He served as senator from Ohio from 1941 to 1945. Even though he was a Republican, he was appointed to the Supreme Court by President Harry S. Truman (a Democrat). He retired in 1958 for health reasons. ■

Introduction

When slavery was abolished by the Thirteenth Amendment, racial discrimination did not end with it. After the Civil War (1861–1865) and the ensuing Reconstruction Era (when the defeated Southern states reorganized without slavery but with a federal mandate for equal rights for all citizens), Southern whites regained power and imposed a system of segregation throughout the South with Jim Crow laws. Schools, courtrooms, theaters, and railroads were all segregated. The U.S. Supreme Court put its stamp of approval upon this practice in 1896 in *Plessy v. Ferguson,* which allowed separate facilities as long as they were equal. The equality requirement, however, was not regularly met.

In most railroad cars in the early part of the twentieth century, there were no dining facilities for African Americans. In the 1930s and 1940s, public pressure forced the railroads to provide some dining facilities, and the carriers set up one or two curtained-off tables for African Americans—the only place they were allowed to eat, regardless of how many needed to be served. Very often "white" tables sat empty while African Americans went hungry, as their dining tables were occupied throughout the dinner hours. On May 17, 1942, Elmer Henderson, an African American first-class passenger on the Southern Railroad, was denied dining car service be-

cause white passengers were using the tables set aside for serving African American passengers. There was a seat available at those tables, but Henderson was offered dinner at his Pullman seat and declined service in the dining car. Henderson hired an attorney and challenged the Interstate Commerce Commission for its approval of railroad segregation policies. The case was taken to the Supreme Court and was notable because the solicitor general of the United States took the unique step of appearing before the Supreme Court to argue against "separate but equal" segregation policies.

Significance

At stake in the *Henderson* case was not only the violation of the Interstate Commerce Act, which prohibits undue racial discrimination on railroads, but also the Supreme Court's ruling in *Plessy v. Ferguson,* which held that "separate but equal" segregation policies were constitutional. The Supreme Court in *Henderson* ruled in favor of African American railroad passengers, holding that the seating practice in dining cars violated the *Interstate Commerce Act.* The Court did not rule in this case on the constitutionality issue. This followed a decision four years earlier in which a Virginia law requiring segregation on interstate bus routes was held to be unconstitutional. In *Mitchell v. U.S.* (1941) the Court ruled that the ICC was in violation of the act when a Pullman seat was denied to a first-class African American passenger, although seats were available, because the seats reserved for African American passengers were occupied. The Interstate Commerce Commission followed up these court rulings by ordering, in 1955, the desegregation of interstate buses and trains and bus and train facilities. These orders, though, were not always enforced, and President Dwight D. Eisenhower's administration (served 1953–1961) did not give a high priority to the promotion of civil rights.

In the early 1960s, sit-ins and freedom rides drew attention to the continuing segregation in the South, and President John F. Kennedy (served 1961–1963) sent federal marshals to escort the freedom riders. Kennedy proposed civil rights legislation, which, after his assassination, became the *Civil Rights Act of 1964.* Massive civil rights protests, led by Martin Luther King Jr. and others, kept attention on the issue as well. The 1964 act mandated desegregation in all public accommodations and went a long way toward desegregating the South.

Primary Source

Henderson v. U.S. [excerpt]

SYNOPSIS: Justice Harold Burton surveys the Southern Railway Company's practices in segregating its dining cars. He holds that the Supreme Court does have jurisdiction over this matter. It is unconstitutional to deny Henderson a seat in the dining car because he is an African American.

Mr. Justice Burton delivered the opinion of the Court.

The question here is whether the rules and practices of the Southern Railway Company, which divide each dining car so as to allot ten tables exclusively to white passengers and one table exclusively to Negro passengers, and which call for a curtain or partition between that table and the others, violate 3 (1) of the Interstate Commerce Act. That section makes it unlawful for a railroad in interstate commerce "to subject any particular person . . . to any undue or unreasonable prejudice or disadvantage in any respect whatsoever . . ." We hold that those rules and practices do violate the Act.

This issue grows out of an incident which occurred May 17, 1942. On that date the appellant, Elmer W. Henderson, a Negro passenger, was traveling on a first class ticket on the Southern Railway from Washington, DC, to Atlanta, Georgia, en route to Birmingham, Alabama, in the course of his duties as an employee of the United States. The train left Washington at 2 p.m. At about 5:30 p.m., while the train was in Virginia, the first call to dinner was announced and he went promptly to the dining car. In accordance with the practice then in effect, the two end tables nearest the kitchen were conditionally reserved for Negroes. At each meal those tables were to be reserved initially for Negroes and, when occupied by Negroes, curtains were to be drawn between them and the rest of the car. If the other tables were occupied before any Negro passengers presented themselves at the diner then those two tables also were to be available for white passengers, and Negroes were not to be seated at them while in use by white passengers. When the appellant reached the diner, the end tables in question were partly occupied by white passengers but at least one seat at them was unoccupied. The dining-car steward declined to seat the appellant in the dining car but offered to serve him, without additional charge, at his Pullman seat. The appellant declined that offer and the steward agreed to send him word when space was available. No word was sent and the appellant was not served, although he twice returned to the diner before it was detached at 9 p.m.

In October, 1942, the appellant filed a complaint with the Interstate Commerce Commission alleging especially that the foregoing conduct violated 3 (1)

Supreme Court Justice Harold Burton. © BETTMANN/CORBIS. REPRODUCED BY PERMISSION.

of the Interstate Commerce Act. Division 2 of the Commission found that he had been subjected to undue and unreasonable prejudice and disadvantage, but that the occurrence was a casual incident brought about by the bad judgment of an employee. The Commission declined to enter an order as to future practices. . . . A three-judge United States District Court for the District of Maryland, however, held that the railroad's general practice, as evidenced by its instructions of August 6, 1942, was in violation of 3 (1). Accordingly, on February 18, 1946, it remanded the case for further proceedings. . . . Effective March 1, 1946, the company announced its modified rules which are now in effect. They provide for the reservation of ten tables, of four seats each, exclusively and unconditionally for white passengers and one table, of four seats, exclusively and unconditionally for Negro passengers. Between this table and the others a curtain is drawn during each meal.

On remand, the full Commission, with two members dissenting and one not participating, found that the modified rules do not violate the Interstate Commerce Act and that no order for the future was necessary. . . . The appellant promptly instituted the present proceeding before the District Court, constituted of the same three members as before, seeking to have the Commission's order set aside and a cease and desist order issued. . . . With one member dissenting, the court sustained the modified rules on the ground that the accommodations are adequate to serve the average number of Negro passengers and are "proportionately fair." . . . The case is here on direct appeal. . . . In this Court, the United States filed a brief and argued orally in support of the appellant.

It is clear that appellant has standing to bring these proceedings. He is an aggrieved party, free to travel again on the Southern Railway. Having been subjected to practices of the railroad which the Commission and the court below found to violate the Interstate Commerce Act, he may challenge the railroad's current regulations on the ground that they permit the recurrence of comparable violations. . . .

The material language in 3 (1) of the Interstate Commerce Act has been in that statute since its adoption in 1887. . . . From the beginning, the Interstate Commerce Commission has recognized the application of that language to discriminations between white and Negro passengers. . . . That section recently was so applied in *Mitchell v. United States,* supra.

The decision of this case is largely controlled by that in the *Mitchell* case. There a Negro passenger holding a first-class ticket was denied a Pullman seat, although such a seat was unoccupied and would have been available to him if he had been white. The railroad rules had allotted a limited amount of Pullman space, consisting of compartments and drawing rooms, to Negro passengers and, because that space was occupied, the complainant was excluded from the Pullman car and required to ride in a second-class coach. This Court held that the passenger thereby had been subjected to an unreasonable disadvantage in violation of 3 (1).

The similarity between that case and this is inescapable. The appellant here was denied a seat in the dining car although at least one seat was vacant and would have been available to him, under the existing rules, if he had been white. The issue before us, as in the *Mitchell* case, is whether the railroad's current rules and practices cause passengers to be subjected to undue or unreasonable prejudice or disadvantage in violation of 3 (1). We find that they do.

The right to be free from unreasonable discriminations belongs, under 3 (1), to each particular person. Where a dining car is available to passengers holding tickets entitling them to use it, each such passenger is equally entitled to its facilities in accordance with reasonable regulations. The denial of dining service to any such passenger by the rules before us subjects him to a prohibited disadvantage. Under the rules, only four Negro passengers may be served at one time and then only at the table reserved for Negroes. Other Negroes who present themselves are compelled to await a vacancy at that table, although there may be many vacancies elsewhere in the diner. The railroad thus refuses to extend to those passengers the use of its existing and unoccupied facilities. The rules impose a like deprivation upon white passengers whenever more than 40 of them seek to be served at the same time and the table reserved for Negroes is vacant.

We need not multiply instances in which these rules sanction unreasonable discriminations. The curtains, partitions and signs emphasize the artificiality of a difference in treatment which serves only to call attention to a racial classification of passengers holding identical tickets and using the same public dining facility. . . . They violate 3 (1).

Our attention has been directed to nothing which removes these racial allocations from the statutory condemnation of "undue or unreasonable prejudice or disadvantage. . . ." It is argued that the limited demand for dining-car facilities by Negro passengers justifies the regulations. But it is no answer to the particular passenger who is denied service at an unoccupied place in a dining car that, on the average, persons like him are served. As was pointed out in *Mitchell v. United States,* . . . "the comparative volume of traffic cannot justify the denial of a fundamental right of equality of treatment, a right specifically safeguarded by the provisions of the Interstate Commerce Act." . . .

That the regulations may impose on white passengers, in proportion to their numbers, disadvantages similar to those imposed on Negro passengers is not an answer to the requirements of 3 (1). Discriminations that operate to the disadvantage of two groups are not the less to be condemned because their impact is broader than if only one were affected. . . .

Since 3 (1) of the Interstate Commerce Act invalidates the rules and practices before us, we do not reach the constitutional or other issues suggested.

The judgment of the District Court is reversed and the cause is remanded to that court with directions to set aside the order of the Interstate

Commerce Commission which dismissed the original complaint and to remand the case to that Commission for further proceedings in conformity with this opinion.

It is so ordered.

Mr. Justice Douglas concurs in the result.

Mr. Justice Clark took no part in the consideration or decision of this case.

Further Resources

BOOKS

Berry, Mary Frances. *Stability, Security, and Continuity: Mr. Justice Burton and Decision-making in the Supreme Court, 1945–1958.* Westport, Conn.: Greenwood Press, 1978.

Urofsky, Melvin I. *Division and Discord: The Supreme Court Under Stone and Vinson, 1941–1953.* Columbia: University of South Carolina Press, 1997.

PERIODICALS

Atkinson, David N. "American Constitutionalism Under Stress: Mr. Justice Burton's Response to National Security Issues." *Houston Law Review* 9, no.1, September 1971, 271–288.

Forrester, Ray. "Mr. Justice Burton and the Supreme Court." *Tulane Law Review* 20, no.1, October 1945, 1–21.

Levy, Claudia. "Elmer Henderson Dies: Integrated Rail Cars." *Washington Post,* July 18, 2001, B-7.

Stout, David. "Elmer Henderson Dies: Father of Major Case." *New York Times,* July 18, 2001.

WEBSITES

"Arguments Before the Court." Reprinted from *The United States Law Week* 18, no. 39, April 11, 1950, 3277. Available online at http://www.law.du.edu/russell/lh/sweatt/uslw/uslw41150.html; website home page: http://www.law.du.edu (accessed March 4, 2004).

"Racial Justice." American Civil Liberties Union of Florida. Available online at http://www.aclufl.org/body_11.html; website home page: http://www.aclufl.org (accessed March 4, 2003).

Sweatt v. Painter

Supreme Court decision

By: Fred M. Vinson

Date: June 6, 1950

Source: Vinson, Fred M. *Sweatt v. Painter.* 339 U.S. 629 (1950). Available online at http://caselaw.lp.findlaw.com/scripts/getcase.pl?court=US&vol=339&invol=629; website home page: http://www.findlaw.com (accessed March 5, 2003).

About the Author: Fred M. Vinson (1890–1953) was an eight-term congressman, serving on numerous congressional committees, including the Ways and Means Committee. He also served on the U.S. Court of Appeals for the District of Columbia and headed the Office of War Mobilization. He was chief justice of the Supreme Court from 1946 until his death. ■

Introduction

Even though slavery was outlawed after the Civil War (1861–1865) by the Thirteenth Amendment, many vestiges of slavery, including racial discrimination, lingered long after the war. During the Reconstruction era, Southern states were reorganized under the Fourteenth Amendment, which prohibited states from denying any person equal protection under its laws. But as Southern white leaders took back political domination, they imposed a system of racial segregation known as Jim Crow. Under Jim Crow, everything in the South was segregated, from drinking fountains to bathrooms to theaters. In 1896, the Supreme Court upheld this practice in *Plessy v. Ferguson,* reinforcing the Jim Crow concept of "separate but equal" by ruling that separate facilities for African Americans and whites were legal as long as they were equal. Of course, these separate facilities were not equal, particularly in the realm of higher education. Most African Americans did not have a chance to get into college—assuming they could even afford it—because of all-white admissions policies. If they wanted to go to a graduate school in the South, there were just a few open to them, including Howard University in Washington, D.C., and Meharry Medical College in Nashville, Tennessee. In addition, the colleges open to African Americans were generally very small. For instance, the only state-supported college for African Americans in Kentucky had 138 students in 1930. The University of Kentucky, by contrast, had 3,245.

The National Association for the Advancement of Colored People (NAACP) began to sponsor lawsuits to open up higher education to African Americans. Its first victory came in 1938, in *Missouri ex. rel. Gaines v. Canada,* in which Missouri's practice of sending its qualified African American students to law schools in neighboring states was brought before the Supreme Court. The Court ordered the state to provide a law school for African American students in Missouri instead of offering to pay their tuition to go out of state. Later, Texas, in response to the *Gaines* case, began looking into setting up a law school for African Americans.

In 1946, Heman Marion Sweatt, an African American postal worker from Houston, was denied admission to the University of Texas School of Law because of the school's policy barring African American students from enrollment. At the time, there was no other law school in Texas he could attend. Sweatt sued the state of Texas in an attempt to force the university to accept him. In February 1947, the School of Law of the Texas State University for Negroes was established. Sweatt was offered enrollment in the new school but did not register. While

NAACP leaders Roy Wilkins (left), Robert L. Carter (right), and plaintiff Heman Sweatt (center) give a press conference at NAACP headquarters in New York City, 1950. **THE LIBRARY OF CONGRESS.**

law schools for African Americans presented an opportunity, he believed it clearly was not an *equal* opportunity. Texas courts disagreed, ruling that the new law school would provide Sweatt with an education equivalent to that offered by the University of Texas Law School. In 1950, an NAACP team of attorneys led by Thurgood Marshall brought Sweatt's case before the Supreme Court.

Significance

In *Sweatt v. Painter,* the Supreme Court reversed the Texas courts' findings. The Court held that the University of Texas Law School was much better than the new state law school for African Americans. The University of Texas had an unquestionably bigger and more well-rounded faculty, a much larger library, better buildings and resources, and more prestige. While it did not rule segregation unconstitutional, the Supreme Court clearly did *question* its constitutionality, and it imposed a tough

standard for determining what constituted separate and truly equal systems.

The *Sweatt* case was used as precedent four years later, in 1954, when the Supreme Court declared educational segregation unconstitutional in the landmark ruling *Brown v. Board of Education.* The *Brown* decision provoked a firestorm of criticism from Southern legislators. Most Southern Congressmen signed the Southern Manifesto, which declared *Brown* unconstitutional and vowed "massive resistance." Even after *Brown,* many parts of the South took a long time to become integrated. It wasn't until 1967, for example, that an African American played collegiate football in the Southeastern Conference. Southern resistance to *Brown* reached a historic turning point in 1957, when Governor Orval Faubus of Arkansas refused to allow nine African American students to attend Little Rock High School. When the courts ordered Faubus to step aside, a mob blocked the students' entry. It was not until President Dwight D. Eisenhower (served 1953–1961) reluctantly dispatched federal troops that the students were able to enter.

Real gains for African American students came in the 1960s. The 1964 *Civil Rights Act* gave the federal government more power to force integration. The new educational programs of the Great Society—the plan of President Lyndon B. Johnson (served 1963–1969) for an American society based on economic and racial equality—had large amounts of money attached that was to be withheld from schools that discriminated against minority students. Both of these factors accelerated the rate of desegregation in the United States. Although racial conflicts still remained in the early twenty-first century, it is in large part because of the rulings in *Sweatt*—and, later, *Brown*—that graduate education was much more representative of the nation in the early twenty-first century than it was in Heman Sweatt's time.

Primary Source

Sweatt v. Painter [excerpt]

SYNOPSIS: In stating the opinion of the Supreme Court, Chief Justice Fred Vinson first notes that the case will be decided on a narrow basis of the particulars of the case rather than by considering the constitutional issue. Vinson then notes the differences between the University of Texas Law School and the proposed law school for African Americans. He states that the two schools are not in any way equal and, even with effort, cannot be made equal in terms of intangibles such as reputation, experience, and community standing.

Mr. Chief Justice Vinson delivered the opinion of the Court.

This case and *McLaurin v. Oklahoma State Regents* . . . present different aspects of this general question: To what extent does the Equal Protection Clause of the Fourteenth Amendment limit the power of a state to distinguish between students of different races in professional and graduate education in a state university? Broader issues have been urged for our consideration, but we adhere to the principle of deciding constitutional questions only in the context of the particular case before the Court. We have frequently reiterated that this Court will decide constitutional questions only when necessary to the disposition of the case at hand, and that such decisions will be drawn as narrowly as possible. *Rescue Army v. Municipal Court,* . . . and cases cited therein. Because of this traditional reluctance to extend constitutional interpretations to situations or facts which are not before the Court, much of the excellent research and detailed argu-

ment presented in these cases is unnecessary to their disposition.

In the instant case, petitioner filed an application for admission to the University of Texas Law School for the February, 1946 term. His application was rejected solely because he is a Negro. Petitioner thereupon brought this suit for mandamus against the appropriate school officials, respondents here, to compel his admission. At that time, there was no law school in Texas which admitted Negroes.

The state trial court recognized that the action of the State in denying petitioner the opportunity to gain a legal education while granting it to others deprived him of the equal protection of the laws guaranteed by the Fourteenth Amendment. The court did not grant the relief requested, however, but continued the case for six months to allow the State to supply substantially equal facilities. At the expiration of the six months, in December, 1946, the court denied the writ on the showing that the authorized university officials had adopted an order calling for the opening of a law school for Negroes the following February. While petitioner's appeal was pending, such a school was made available, but petitioner refused to register therein. The Texas Court of Civil Appeals set aside the trial court's judgment and ordered the cause "remanded generally to the trial court for further proceedings without prejudice to the rights of any party to this suit."

On remand, a hearing was held on the issue of the equality of the educational facilities at the newly established school as compared with the University of Texas Law School. Finding that the new school offered petitioner "privileges, advantages, and opportunities for the study of law substantially equivalent to those offered by the State to white students at the University of Texas," the trial court denied mandamus. The Court of Civil Appeals affirmed. . . .

The University of Texas Law School, from which petitioner was excluded, was staffed by a faculty of sixteen full-time and three part-time professors, some of whom are nationally recognized authorities in their field. Its student body numbered 850. The library contained over 65,000 volumes. Among the other facilities available to the students were a law review, moot court facilities, scholarship funds, and Order of the Coif affiliation. The school's alumni occupy the most distinguished positions in the private practice of the law and in the public life of the State. It may properly be considered one of the nation's ranking law schools.

The law school for Negroes which was to have opened in February, 1947, would have had no independent faculty or library. The teaching was to be carried on by four members of the University of Texas Law School faculty, who were to maintain their offices at the University of Texas while teaching at both institutions. Few of the 10,000 volumes ordered for the library had arrived; nor was there any full-time librarian. The school lacked accreditation.

Since the trial of this case, respondents report the opening of a law school at the Texas State University for Negroes. It is apparently on the road to full accreditation. It has a faculty of five full-time professors; a student body of 23; a library of some 16,500 volumes serviced by a full-time staff; a practice court and legal aid association; and one alumnus who has become a member of the Texas Bar.

Whether the University of Texas Law School is compared with the original or the new law school for Negroes, we cannot find substantial equality in the educational opportunities offered white and Negro law students by the State. In terms of number of the faculty, variety of courses and opportunity for specialization, size of the student body, scope of the library, availability of law review and similar activities, the University of Texas Law School is superior. What is more important, the University of Texas Law School possesses to a far greater degree those qualities which are incapable of objective measurement but which make for greatness in a law school. Such qualities, to name but a few, include reputation of the faculty, experience of the administration, position and influence of the alumni, standing in the community, traditions and prestige. It is difficult to believe that one who had a free choice between these law schools would consider the question close.

Moreover, although the law is a highly learned profession, we are well aware that it is an intensely practical one. The law school, the proving ground for legal learning and practice, cannot be effective in isolation from the individuals and institutions with which the law interacts. Few students and no one who has practiced law would choose to study in an academic vacuum, removed from the interplay of ideas and the exchange of views with which the law is concerned. The law school to which Texas is willing to admit petitioner excludes from its student body members of the racial groups which number 85% of the population of the State and include most of the lawyers, witnesses, jurors, judges and other officials with whom petitioner will inevitably be dealing when he becomes a member of the Texas Bar. With such a substantial and significant segment of society excluded, we cannot conclude that the education offered petitioner is substantially equal to that which he would receive if admitted to the University of Texas Law School.

It may be argued that excluding petitioner from that school is no different from excluding white students from the new law school. This contention overlooks realities. It is unlikely that a member of a group so decisively in the majority, attending a school with rich traditions and prestige which only a history of consistently maintained excellence could command, would claim that the opportunities afforded him for legal education were unequal to those held open to petitioner. That such a claim, if made, would be dishonored by the State, is no answer. "Equal protection of the laws is not achieved through indiscriminate imposition of inequalities." *Shelley v. Kraemer*. . . .

It is fundamental that these cases concern rights which are personal and present. This Court has stated unanimously that "The State must provide [legal education] for [petitioner] in conformity with the equal protection clause of the Fourteenth Amendment and provide it as soon as it does for applicants of any other group." *Sipuel v. Board of Regents*. . . . That case "did not present the issue whether a state might not satisfy the equal protection clause of the Fourteenth Amendment by establishing a separate law school for Negroes." *Fisher v. Hurst*. . . . In *Missouri ex rel. Gaines v. Canada*, . . . the Court, speaking through Chief Justice Hughes, declared that "petitioner's right was a personal one. It was as an individual that he was entitled to the equal protection of the laws, and the State was bound to furnish him within its borders facilities for legal education substantially equal to those which the State there afforded for persons of the white race, whether or not other negroes sought the same opportunity." These are the only cases in this Court which present the issue of the constitutional validity of race distinctions in state-supported graduate and professional education.

In accordance with these cases, petitioner may claim his full constitutional right: legal education equivalent to that offered by the State to students of other races. Such education is not available to him in a separate law school as offered by the State. We cannot, therefore, agree with respondents that the doctrine of *Plessy v. Ferguson* . . . requires affirmance of the judgment below. Nor need we reach petitioner's contention that *Plessy v. Ferguson* should be reexamined in the light of contemporary knowledge respecting the purposes of the Fourteenth Amendment and the effects of racial segregation. . . .

We hold that the Equal Protection Clause of the Fourteenth Amendment requires that petitioner be admitted to the University of Texas Law School. The judgment is reversed and the cause is remanded for proceedings not inconsistent with this opinion.

Reversed.

Further Resources

BOOKS

Franklin, John Hope, and August Meier, eds. *Black Leaders of the Twentieth Century.* Urbana, Ill.: University of Illinois Press, 1982.

Palmer, Jan. *The Vinson Court Era: The Supreme Court's Conference Votes—Data and Analysis.* New York: AMS, 1990.

St. Clair, James E., and Linda C. Gugin. *Chief Justice Fred M. Vinson of Kentucky: A Political Biography.* Lexington, Ky.: University Press of Kentucky, 2002.

University of Texas, Sweatt vs. Painter: Correspondence, 1945–50. Frederick, Md.: University Publications of America, 1986.

Urofsky, Melvin I. *Division and Discord: The Supreme Court Under Stone and Vinson, 1941–1953.* Columbia, S.C.: University of South Carolina Press, 1997.

PERIODICALS

Entin, Jonathan L. "*Sweatt v. Painter,* the End of Segregation, and the Transformation of Education Law." *The Review of Litigation* 5, no.1, 1980, 3–71.

WEBSITES

"*Sweatt v. Painter:* Archival and Textual Sources." University of Denver Law School. Available online at http://www.law.du.edu/russell/lh/sweatt; website home page: http://www.law.du.edu (accessed March 5, 2003).

Dennis v. U.S.

Supreme Court decision

By: Fred M. Vinson, Hugo L. Black

Date: June 4, 1951

Source: Vinson, Fred M. and Hugo L. Black *Dennis v. United States,* 341 U.S. 494 (1951). Available online at http://caselaw.lp.findlaw.com/cgi-bin/getcase.pl?navby =case&court=us&vol=341&invol=494; website home page: http://www.findlaw.com (accessed February 21, 2003).

About the Authors: Fred M. Vinson (1890–1953) worked his way through law school and was an eight-term congressman, serving on numerous congressional committees, including the Ways and Means Committee. He also served on the U.S. Court of Appeals for the District of Columbia and headed the Office of War Mobilization. He was chief justice of the Supreme Court from 1946 until his death.

Hugo L. Black (1886–1971) was appointed to the Supreme Court in 1937, after serving two terms as a U.S. senator from Alabama. He was nominated to the Court by President

Franklin D. Roosevelt (served 1933–1945). Black served on the Supreme Court for thirty-four years, retiring one week before his death. His tenure was generally distinguished by his support of civil rights. ∎

Introduction

The United States has long been concerned with radical organizations seeking to undermine or overthrow the government. In the years before World War I (1914–1918), much effort went into ridding the country of anarchists and others who were perceived as a threat to the government. During World War I, many of those arrested under a number of wartime laws were radicals. After the success of the 1917 Russian Revolution, anticommunist sentiment grew in the United States, and efforts were made—some partially successful—to deport large numbers of radicals. The post-World War I "Red Scare" revolved around many Americans' fear that the country was being overrun by communists. In the 1920s, immigration restrictions were passed to keep communists and other radicals out of the country.

Communist hysteria abated somewhat during the 1930s, as the United States coped with the Great Depression. During World War II (1939–1945), with the United States allied with Communist Russia, the level of anticommunist rhetoric in Washington was necessarily toned down. But the fear hadn't gone away. In 1940, the government passed the *Smith Act,* making it a crime to teach or advocate the forcible overthrow of the government. But questions remained as to what types of speech could be criminalized. The Supreme Court maintained its World War I standard, requiring a "clear and present danger" before any speech could be banned. But as the 1940s progressed, the lower courts expanded their views on what presented a "danger" to the country, encompassing an increasing number of different types of speech. With the rise of the Cold War, communism became publicly feared again, and in 1948 eleven (some sources say twelve) U.S. Communist Party leaders were arrested under the *Smith Act.* Eugene Dennis, the general secretary of the U.S. Communist Party, was among the leaders arrested. They were convicted in 1949. *Dennis v. U.S.* was one of only a few cases that made it on appeal to the Supreme Court in 1951.

Significance

In *Dennis v. U.S.,* the important question before the court was whether the *Smith Act* violated the First Amendment and other provisions of the Bill of Rights. In dispute was whether the act could ban speech that merely suggested a need to get rid of the government or if, under the First Amendment, speech could only be banned when it advocated an act that would cause the overthrow of the government. If speech could be banned for suggesting an idea, then, in effect, all Communist Party leaders were criminals under the *Smith Act.*

The majority opinion of the Supreme Court upheld the *Smith Act,* determining that language could be criminalized if, in the minds of the government and the jury, it constituted a "clear and present danger." The two dissenters, Justices Hugo Black and William Orville Douglas, pointed out that there had been no known attempt to overthrow the government, nor had there been any planning for such an attempt. What had been uncovered, though, was the use of speech advocating the overthrow of the government. Black and Douglas maintained that a conviction based on speech alone was a limitation of the First Amendment. Their opinion was not shared by the rest of the Court—or by most of the country, for that matter. At the time, the United States was in the middle of its second Red Scare, as Joseph McCarthy, U.S. senator from Wisconsin, whipped the nation into a frenzy with charges that he knew of communists in the government. McCarthy's claims were wholly unsubstantiated, but amid the communist hysteria and fears of being labeled communists themselves, very few people dared dispute his assertions.

In 1957, as the McCarthy era came to an end, the Supreme Court ruled on the *Yates v. U.S.* case, holding that if someone advocates an idea, even the idea that the U.S. government needs to be overthrown, that alone is not illegal. It is only when it becomes advocacy of a specific illegal act, such as taking over a federal building, that such speech becomes illegal. The *Yates* ruling overturned the convictions of several lower-level communist officials. Significantly, prosecutions under the *Smith Act* almost ceased after the decision. Free speech was further expanded in 1969, when the Supreme Court held that only advocacy aimed at "inciting or producing imminent lawless action" that was likely to succeed could be banned. This was the widest definition of political free speech to date and, for the most part, the one still used in the early twenty-first century.

Primary Source

Dennis v. U.S. [excerpt]

SYNOPSIS: In this excerpt, Chief Justice Fred Vinson argues that the purpose of the *Smith Act* is to protect the government against revolution and that it is aimed "at advocacy, not discussion." Vinson admits that speech is involved but holds that speech, though protected by the First Amendment, may be restricted when it presents "a clear and present danger." Justice Hugo Black dissents, arguing that those convicted were not indicted for advocating the government's overthrow, and that the right to free speech must prevail in this case.

Mr. Chief Justice Vinson announced the judgment of the Court and an opinion in which Mr. Justice Reed, Mr. Justice Burton, and Mr. Justice Minton join. . . .

The obvious purpose of the statute is to protect existing Government, not from change by peaceable, lawful and constitutional means, but from change by violence, revolution and terrorism. That it is within the power of the Congress to protect the Government of the United States from armed rebellion is a proposition which requires little discussion. Whatever theoretical merit there may be to the argument that there is a "right" to rebellion against dictatorial governments is without force where the existing structure of the government provides for peaceful and orderly change. We reject any principle of governmental helplessness in the face of preparation for revolution, which principle, carried to its logical conclusion, must lead to anarchy. No one could conceive that it is not within the power of Congress to prohibit acts intended to overthrow the Government by force and violence. The question with which we are concerned here is not whether Congress has such power, but whether the means which it has employed conflict with the First and Fifth Amendments to the Constitution. . . .

The very language of the *Smith Act* negates the interpretation which petitioners would have us impose on that Act. It is directed at advocacy, not discussion. . . . Congress did not intend to eradicate the free discussion of political theories, to destroy the traditional rights of Americans to discuss and evaluate ideas without fear of governmental sanction. Rather Congress was concerned with the very kind of activity in which the evidence showed these petitioners engaged.

But although the statute is not directed at the hypothetical cases which petitioners have conjured, its application in this case has resulted in convictions for the teaching and advocacy of the overthrow of the Government by force and violence, which, even though coupled with the intent to accomplish that overthrow, contains an element of speech. For this reason, we must pay special heed to the demands of the First Amendment marking out the boundaries of speech.

We pointed out in *Douds* . . . that the basis of the First Amendment is the hypothesis that speech can rebut speech, propaganda will answer propaganda, free debate of ideas will result in the wisest governmental policies. It is for this reason that this Court has recognized the inherent value of free

Eugene Dennis (third from left) and other top officials of the American Communist Party leave a New York City federal court after posting $5000 bail each, following their arrest under the *Smith Act,* July 21, 1948. © BETTMANN/CORBIS. REPRODUCED BY PERMISSION.

discourse. An analysis of the leading cases in this Court which have involved direct limitations on speech, however, will demonstrate that both the majority of the Court and the dissenters in particular cases have recognized that this is not an unlimited, unqualified right, but that the societal value of speech must, on occasion, be subordinated to other values and considerations.

No important case involving free speech was decided by this Court prior to *Schenck v. United States.* . . . Writing for a unanimous Court, Justice Holmes stated that the "question in every case is whether the words used are used in such circumstances and are of such a nature as to create a clear and present danger that they will bring about the substantive evils that Congress has a right to prevent." . . . The fact is inescapable, too, that the phrase bore no connotation that the danger was to be any threat to the safety of the Republic. The charge was causing and attempting to cause insubordination in the military forces and obstruct recruiting. The objectionable document denounced conscription and its most inciting sentence was, "You must do your share to maintain, support and uphold the rights of the people of this country." . . . Fifteen thousand copies were

printed and some circulated. This insubstantial gesture toward insubordination in 1917 during war was held to be a clear and present danger of bringing about the evil of military insubordination. . . .

And in *American Communications Assn. v. Douds,* . . . we suggested that the Holmes-Brandeis philosophy insisted that where . . . there was a direct restriction upon speech, a "clear and present danger" that the substantive evil would be caused was necessary before the statute in question could be constitutionally applied. And we stated, "[The First] Amendment requires that one be permitted to believe what he will. It requires that one be permitted to advocate what he will unless there is a clear and present danger that a substantial public evil will result therefrom." . . . But we further suggested that neither Justice Holmes nor Justice Brandeis ever envisioned that a shorthand phrase should be crystallized into a rigid rule to be applied inflexibly without regard to the circumstances of each case. Speech is not an absolute, above and beyond control by the legislature when its judgment, subject to review here, is that certain kinds of speech are so undesirable as to warrant criminal sanction. Nothing is more certain in modern society than the principle that there are no absolutes, that a name, a phrase, a standard has meaning only when associated with the considerations which gave birth to the nomenclature. . . . To those who would paralyze our Government in the face of impending threat by encasing it in a semantic strait-jacket we must reply that all concepts are relative.

In this case we are squarely presented with the application of the "clear and present danger" test, and must decide what that phrase imports. We first note that many of the cases in which this Court has reversed convictions by use of this or similar tests have been based on the fact that the interest which the State was attempting to protect was itself too insubstantial to warrant restriction of speech. . . . Overthrow of the Government by force and violence is certainly a substantial enough interest for the Government to limit speech. Indeed, this is the ultimate value of any society, for if a society cannot protect its very structure from armed internal attack, it must follow that no subordinate value can be protected. If, then, this interest may be protected, the literal problem which is presented is what has been meant by the use of the phrase "clear and present danger" of the utterances bringing about the evil within the power of Congress to punish.

Obviously, the words cannot mean that before the Government may act, it must wait until the putsch is about to be executed, the plans have been laid and the signal is awaited. If Government is aware that a group aiming at its overthrow is attempting to indoctrinate its members and to commit them to a course whereby they will strike when the leaders feel the circumstances permit, action by the Government is required. The argument that there is no need for Government to concern itself, for Government is strong, it possesses ample powers to put down a rebellion, it may defeat the revolution with ease needs no answer. For that is not the question. Certainly an attempt to overthrow the Government by force, even though doomed from the outset because of inadequate numbers of power of the revolutionists, is a sufficient evil for Congress to prevent. The damage which such attempts create both physically and politically to a nation makes it impossible to measure the validity in terms of the probability of success, or the immediacy of a successful attempt. . . . We must therefore reject the contention that success or probability of success is the criterion.

The situation with which Justices Holmes and Brandeis were concerned in *Gitlow* was a comparatively isolated event, bearing little relation in their minds to any substantial threat to the safety of the community. . . . They were not confronted with any situation comparable to the instant one—the development of an apparatus designed and dedicated to the overthrow of the Government, in the context of world crisis after crisis.

Chief Judge Learned Hand, writing for the majority below, interpreted the phrase as follows: "In each case [courts] must ask whether the gravity of the 'evil,' discounted by its improbability, justifies such invasion of free speech as is necessary to avoid the danger." . . . We adopt this statement of the rule. As articulated by Chief Judge Hand, it is as succinct and inclusive as any other we might devise at this time. It takes into consideration those factors which we deem relevant, and relates their significances. More we cannot expect from words.

. . . If the ingredients of the reaction are present, we cannot bind the Government to wait until the catalyst is added. . . .

. . . The judgments of conviction are

Affirmed. . . .

Mr. Justice Black, dissenting. . . .

At the outset I want to emphasize what the crime involved in this case is, and what it is not. These petitioners were not charged with an attempt to overthrow the Government. They were not charged with overt acts of any kind designed to overthrow the Government. They were not even charged with saying anything or writing anything designed to overthrow the Government. The charge was that they agreed to assemble and to talk and publish certain ideas at a later date: The indictment is that they conspired to organize the Communist Party and to use speech or newspapers and other publications in the future to teach and advocate the forcible overthrow of the Government. No matter how it is worded, this is a virulent form of prior censorship of speech and press, which I believe the First Amendment forbids. I would hold 3 of the *Smith Act,* authorizing this prior restraint unconstitutional on its face and as applied.

But let us assume, contrary to all constitutional ideas of fair criminal procedure, that petitioners although not indicted for the crime of actual advocacy, may be punished for it. Even on this radical assumption, the other opinions in this case show that the only way to affirm these convictions is to repudiate directly or indirectly the established "clear and present danger" rule. This the Court does in a way which greatly restricts the protections afforded by the First Amendment. The opinions for affirmance indicate that the chief reason for jettisoning the rule is the expressed fear that advocacy of Communist doctrine endangers the safety of the Republic. Undoubtedly, a governmental policy of unfettered communication of ideas does entail dangers. To the Founders of this Nation, however, the benefits derived from free expression were worth the risk. They embodied this philosophy in the First Amendment's command that "Congress shall make no law . . . abridging the freedom of speech, or of the press. . . ." I have always believed that the First Amendment is the keystone of our Government, that the freedoms it guarantees provide the best insurance against destruction of all freedom. At least as to speech in the realm of public matters, I believe that the "clear and present danger" test does not "mark the furthermost constitutional boundaries of protected expression" but does "no more than recognize a minimum compulsion of the Bill of Rights. . . ."

Public opinion being what it now is, few will protest the conviction of these Communist petitioners. There is hope, however, that in calmer times, when present pressures, passions and fears subside, this or some later Court will restore the First Amendment liberties to the high preferred place where they belong in a free society.

Further Resources

BOOKS

Boxly, George T. *The Twelve: A Lawyer Looks at the Case.* New York: New Century, 1949.

Dennis, Eugene. *Letters From Prison.* New York: International, 1956.

Palmer, Jan. *The Vinson Court Era: The Supreme Court's Conference Votes—Data and Analysis.* New York: AMS, 1990.

St. Clair, James E., and Linda C. Gugin. *Chief Justice Fred M. Vinson of Kentucky: A Political Biography.* Lexington, Ky.: University Press of Kentucky, 2002.

Urofsky, Melvin I. *Division and Discord: The Supreme Court Under Stone and Vinson, 1941–1953.* Columbia, S.C.: University of South Carolina Press, 1997.

Adler v. Board of Education

Supreme Court decision

By: Sherman Minton, Hugo L. Black, William O. Douglas

Date: March 3, 1952

Source: Minton, Sherman, Hugo L. Black, and William O. Douglas. *Adler v. Board of Education.* 342 U.S. 485 (1952). Available online at http://laws.lp.findlaw.com/getcase/US/342 /485.html; website home page: http://www.findlaw.com (accessed June 13, 2003).

About the Authors: Sherman Minton (1890–1965) served in the U.S. Senate and the U.S. Court of Appeals prior to being appointed to the Supreme Court by President Harry S. Truman (served 1945–1953), a good friend, in 1949. A New Deal liberal, he surprised many when he began ruling against civil liberties and adopting some of the repressive opinions of the Cold War era. He served until 1956.

Hugo L. Black (1886–1971) served two terms as a U.S. senator from Alabama and was known as a New Deal liberal. His 1937 appointment to the Supreme Court roused controversy when his past membership in the Ku Klux Klan became public, although he had long ago left the group. His term was generally distinguished by his support of civil rights.

William O. Douglas (1898–1980) chaired the Securities and Exchange Commission in 1939, when he became, at forty, one of the youngest men ever appointed to the Supreme Court. He served over thirty-six years, the longest of any justice, retiring in 1975. Many thought Douglas would be pro-business, but he devoted himself to the defense of the Bill of Rights and freedom of speech. ■

Introduction

Freedom of speech as protected under the First Amendment has at times not extended to teachers in public institutions. During World War I (1914–1918) many schoolteachers and college professors were dismissed from their jobs for voicing opposition to the war. College professors, as a response to these firings, developed the idea of tenure, which meant that after receiving tenure approval from an advisory committee, a professor could only be fired for gross misconduct. But the issue of firing a teacher for expressing certain political opinions returned with a vengeance at the start of the Cold War after World War II (1939–1945). States and the federal government began investigations to find educators with previous ties to the Communist Party. These people were often fired. Tenure proved little protection to college professors, as the administration often ignored its existence, and no one wanted to stand up for ex- or current communists. In order to keep their jobs, many teachers were required to take an oath, swearing they were not members of the Communist Party.

In 1949, New York enacted the Feinberg law, which authorized the public school authorities to fire employees who were found to advocate the overthrow of the government by unlawful means or were unable satisfactorily to explain membership in certain subversive organizations. A group of concerned taxpayers and teachers represented by Irving Adler challenged the law. New York courts upheld the Feinberg law, and the case went to the Supreme Court.

Significance

In *Adler v. Board of Education* the Court took a very narrow view of the issue. Part of this was undoubtedly due to the fact that the Cold War was in full swing in the early 1950s. At this time of the Red Scare, politicians saw communists under every bed in Washington. The majority opinion of the Court was that communists and communism were a threat and that while one had a right to be a communist, one did not have a right to be a schoolteacher. Thus, the requirement that one not be a communist to be a schoolteacher did not violate anyone's rights. The dissenters held that schoolteachers had the same rights as anyone else, and so the requirement that they not be communists was unconstitutional.

The view of the majority in *Adler*—that institutions can discharge people for being communists or members of other "dangerous" organizations—held sway throughout most of the 1950s. Professors were discharged from colleges, and their dismissals were generally upheld. The court did require adequate procedural safeguards for these firings and overturned some that did not have these safeguards. In the 1960s, however, teachers developed increased union protection and the Court turned more liberal. As the Red Scare passed, many state programs, including loyalty oaths (where one had to swear loyalty to the country and against the Communist Party) and the requirement that one not be a communist, were struck down. Generally these holdings have prevailed since that time.

Primary Source

Adler v. Board of Education [excerpt]

SYNOPSIS: Justice Sherman Minton summarizes the purpose of the Feinberg law, which is to keep people who have advocated the overthrow of the government from passing propaganda amongst students. Justice Hugo L. Black dissents, arguing that once the government starts deciding what teachers can think and say, the free exchange of ideas will cease. Justice William O. Douglas dissents as well, upholding teachers' freedom of thought and association.

Mr. Justice Minton delivered the opinion of the Court. . . .

. . . It is the purpose of the Feinberg Law to provide for the disqualification and removal of superintendents of schools, teachers, and employees in the public schools in any city or school district of the State who advocate the overthrow of the Government by unlawful means or who are members of organizations which have a like purpose. . . .

It is first argued that the Feinberg Law and the rules promulgated thereunder constitute an abridgment of the freedom of speech and assembly of persons employed or seeking employment in the public schools of the State of New York.

It is clear that such persons have the right under our law to assemble, speak, think and believe as they will. . . . It is equally clear that they have no right to work for the State in the school system on their own terms. . . . They may work for the school system upon the reasonable terms laid down by the proper authorities of New York. If they do not choose to work on such terms, they are at liberty to retain their beliefs and associations and go elsewhere. Has the State thus deprived them of any right to free speech or assembly? We think not. Such persons are or may be denied, under the statutes in question, the privilege of working for the school system of the State of New York because, first, of their advocacy of the overthrow of the government by force or violence, or, secondly, by unexplained membership in an organization found by the school authorities, after notice and hearing, to teach and advocate the overthrow of the government by force or violence, and known by such persons to have such purpose.

The constitutionality of the first proposition is not questioned here. . . .

As to the second, it is rather subtly suggested that we should not follow our recent decision in *Garner v. Los Angeles Board.* We there said:

We think that a municipal employer is not disabled because it is an agency of the State from inquiring of its employees as to matters that may prove relevant to their fitness and suitability for the public service. Past conduct may well relate to present fitness; past loyalty may have a reasonable relationship . . . to present and future trust. Both are commonly inquired into in determining fitness for both high and low positions in private industry and are not less relevant in public employment.

We adhere to that case. A teacher works in a sensitive area in a schoolroom. There he shapes the attitude of young minds towards the society in which they live. In this, the state has a vital concern. It must preserve the integrity of the schools. That the school authorities have the right and the duty to screen the officials, teachers, and employees as to their fitness to maintain the integrity of the schools as a part of ordered society, cannot be doubted. One's associates, past and present, as well as one's conduct, may properly be considered in determining fitness and loyalty. From time immemorial, one's reputation has been determined in part by the company he keeps. In the employment of officials and teachers of the school system, the state may very properly inquire into the company they keep, and we know of no rule, constitutional or otherwise, that prevents the state, when determining

Justice Sherman Minton delivered the opinion of the court for *Adler v. Board of Education*. **AP/WIDE WORLD PHOTOS. REPRODUCED BY PERMISSION.**

the fitness and loyalty of such persons, from considering the organizations and persons with whom they associate.

If, under the procedure set up in the New York law, a person is found to be unfit and is disqualified from employment in the public school system because of membership in a listed organization, he is not thereby denied the right of free speech and assembly. His freedom of choice between membership in the organization and employment in the school system might be limited, but not his freedom of speech or assembly, except in the remote sense that limitation is inherent in every choice. Certainly such limitation is not one the state may not make in the exercise of its police power to protect the schools from pollution and thereby to defend its own existence. . . .

Membership in a listed organization found to be within the statute and known by the member to be within the statute is a legislative finding that the member by his membership supports the thing the organization stands for, namely, the overthrow of government by unlawful means. We cannot say that such a finding is contrary to fact or that "generality

of experience" points to a different conclusion. Disqualification follows therefore as a reasonable presumption from such membership and support. Nor is there here a problem of procedural due process. The presumption is not conclusive but arises only in a hearing where the person against whom it may arise has full opportunity to rebut it. . . .

Where, as here, the relation between the fact found and the presumption is clear and direct and is not conclusive, the requirements of due process are satisfied. . . .

We find no constitutional infirmity in 12-a of the Civil Service Law of New York or in the Feinberg Law which implemented it, and the judgment is

Affirmed. . . .

Mr. Justice Black, dissenting.

While I fully agree with the dissent of Mr. Justice Douglas, the importance of this holding prompts me to add these thoughts.

This is another of those rapidly multiplying legislative enactments which make it dangerous—this time for school teachers—to think or say anything except what a transient majority happen to approve at the moment. Basically these laws rest on the belief that government should supervise and limit the flow of ideas into the minds of men. The tendency of such governmental policy is to mould people into a common intellectual pattern. Quite a different governmental policy rests on the belief that government should leave the mind and spirit of man absolutely free. Such a governmental policy encourages varied intellectual outlooks in the belief that the best views will prevail. This policy of freedom is in my judgment embodied in the First Amendment and made applicable to the states by the Fourteenth. Because of this policy public officials cannot be constitutionally vested with powers to select the ideas people can think about, censor the public views they can express, or choose the persons or groups people can associate with. Public officials with such powers are not public servants; they are public masters.

I dissent from the Court's judgment sustaining this law which effectively penalizes school teachers for their thoughts and their associates. . . .

Mr. Justice Douglas, with whom Mr. Justice Black concurs, dissenting.

I have not been able to accept the recent doctrine that a citizen who enters the public service can be forced to sacrifice his civil rights. I cannot for example find in our constitutional scheme the power of a state to place its employees in the category of second-class citizens by denying them freedom of thought and expression. The Constitution guarantees freedom of thought and expression to everyone in our society. All are entitled to it; and none needs it more than the teacher.

The public school is in most respects the cradle of our democracy. The increasing role of the public school is seized upon by proponents of the type of legislation represented by New York's Feinberg law as proof of the importance and need for keeping the school free of "subversive influences." But that is to misconceive the effect of this type of legislation. Indeed the impact of this kind of censorship on the public school system illustrates the high purpose of the First Amendment in freeing speech and thought from censorship.

The present law proceeds on a principle repugnant to our society—guilt by association. A teacher is disqualified because of her membership in an organization found to be "subversive." The finding as to the "subversive" character of the organization is made in a proceeding to which the teacher is not a party and in which it is not clear that she may even be heard. To be sure, she may have a hearing when charges of disloyalty are leveled against her. But in that hearing the finding as to the "subversive" character of the organization apparently may not be reopened in order to allow her to show the truth of the matter. The irrebuttable charge that the organization is "subversive" therefore hangs as an ominous cloud over her own hearing. The mere fact of membership in the organization raises a prima facie case of her own guilt. She may, it is said, show her innocence. But innocence in this case turns on knowledge; and when the witch hunt is on, one who must rely on ignorance leans on a feeble reed.

The very threat of such a procedure is certain to raise havoc with academic freedom. Youthful indiscretions, mistaken causes, misguided enthusiasms—all long forgotten—become the ghosts of a harrowing present. Any organization committed to a liberal cause, any group organized to revolt against an hysterical trend, any committee launched to sponsor an unpopular program becomes suspect. These are the organizations into which Communists often infiltrate. Their presence infects the whole, even though the project was not conceived in sin. A teacher caught in that mesh is almost certain to stand condemned. Fearing condemnation, she will tend to shrink from any association that stirs controversy. In that manner freedom of expression will be stifled.

But that is only part of it. Once a teacher's connection with a listed organization is shown, her views become subject to scrutiny to determine whether her membership in the organization is innocent or, if she was formerly a member, whether she has bona fide abandoned her membership.

The law inevitably turns the school system into a spying project. Regular loyalty reports on the teachers must be made out. The principals become detectives; the students, the parents, the community become informers. Ears are cocked for tell-tale signs of disloyalty. The prejudices of the community come into play in searching out the disloyal. This is not the usual type of supervision which checks a teacher's competency; it is a system which searches for hidden meanings in a teacher's utterances. . . .

What happens under this law is typical of what happens in a police state. Teachers are under constant surveillance; their pasts are combed for signs of disloyalty; their utterances are watched for clues to dangerous thoughts. A pall is cast over the classrooms. There can be no real academic freedom in that environment. Where suspicion fills the air and holds scholars in line for fear of their jobs, there can be no exercise of the free intellect. Supineness and dogmatism take the place of inquiry. A "party line"—as dangerous as the "party line" of the Communists—lays hold. It is the "party line" of the orthodox view, of the conventional thought, of the accepted approach. A problem can no longer be pursued with impunity to its edges. Fear stalks the classroom. The teacher is no longer a stimulant to adventurous thinking; she becomes instead a pipe line for safe and sound information. A deadening dogma takes the place of free inquiry. Instruction tends to become sterile; pursuit of knowledge is discouraged; discussion often leaves off where it should begin.

This, I think, is what happens when a censor looks over a teacher's shoulder. This system of spying and surveillance with its accompanying reports and trials cannot go hand in hand with academic freedom. It produces standardized thought, not the pursuit of truth. Yet it was the pursuit of truth which the First Amendment was designed to protect. A system which directly or inevitably has that effect is alien to our system and should be struck down. Its survival is a real threat to our way of life. We need be bold and adventuresome in our thinking to survive. A school system producing students trained as robots threatens to rob a generation of the versatility that has been perhaps our greatest distinction. The Framers knew the danger of dogmatism; they also knew the strength that comes when the mind is free, when ideas may be pursued wherever they lead. We forget these teachings of the First Amendment when we sustain this law.

Of course the school systems of the country need not become cells for Communist activities; and the classrooms need not become forums for propagandizing the Marxist creed. But the guilt of the teacher should turn on overt acts. So long as she is a law-abiding citizen, so long as her performance within the public school system meets professional standards, her private life, her political philosophy, her social creed should not be the cause of reprisals against her.

Further Resources

BOOKS

American Municipal Association. *Loyalty Oaths For Municipal Employees: Report of an Inquiry to State Leagues and Associations of Municipalities.* Chicago [no publisher], 1954.

Bryson, Joseph E. *Legality of Loyalty Oath and Non-Oath Requirements for Public School Teachers.* Boone, N.C. [no publisher], 1963.

Ellis, Charley. *If We Remain Silent. . . .* Los Angeles: United Defense Committee Against "Loyalty" Checks, 1950.

Gugin, Linda C., and James E. St. Clair. *Sherman Minton: New Deal Senator, Cold War Justice.* Indianapolis: Indiana Historical Society, 1997.

Hyman, Harold Melvin. *To Try Men's Souls: Loyalty Tests in American History.* Berkeley, Calif.: University of California Press, 1960.

Radcliff, William Franklin. *Sherman Minton: Indiana's Supreme Court Justice.* Indianapolis, Ind.: Guild Press of Indiana, 1996.

PERIODICALS

Atkinson, David N. "Justice Sherman Minton and the Protection of Minority Rights." *Washington and Lee Law Review* 34, no.1, Winter 1977, 97–117.

Beauharnais v. Illinois

Supreme Court decision

By: Felix Frankfurter, Hugo L. Black, William O. Douglas

Date: April 28, 1952

Source: Frankfurter, Felix, Hugo L. Black, and William O. Douglas. *Beauharnais v. Illinois.* 343 U.S. 250 (1952). Available online at http://caselaw.lp.findlaw.com/scripts/getcase.pl?navby=case&court=us&vol=343&invol=250; website home page: http://www.findlaw.com (accessed February 28, 2003).

About the Authors: Felix Frankfurter (1882–1965) was a Harvard Law professor and advisor to President Franklin D.

Roosevelt (served 1933–1945). A longtime friend of justices Louis D. Brandeis and Oliver Wendell Holmes, he served on the Supreme Court 1939–1962 and was known for his vigorous defense of civil rights and his scholarly writings.

Hugo L. Black (1886–1971) served two terms as a U.S. senator from Alabama and was known as a New Deal liberal. His 1937 appointment to the Supreme Court roused controversy when his past membership in the Ku Klux Klan became public, although he had long ago left the group. His term was generally distinguished by his support of civil rights.

William O. Douglas (1898–1980) chaired the Securities and Exchange Commission in 1939, when he became, at forty, one of the youngest men ever appointed to the Supreme Court. He served over thirty-six years, the longest of any justice, retiring in 1975. Many thought Douglas would be pro-business, but he devoted himself to the defense of the Bill of Rights and freedom of speech. ■

Introduction

Freedom of expression, in speech and press, has a long history as one of America's most valued—and protected—rights. The First Amendment was added to the Constitution with the Bill of Rights in 1791, stating "Congress shall make no law respecting an establishment of religion, or prohibiting the free exercise thereof; or abridging the freedom of speech, or of the press; or the right of the people peaceably to assemble, and to petition the government for a redress of grievances."

Freedom of the press in the United States, like freedom of speech, has never been absolute. Nearly all states at the time of the Constitution excluded libel, or the defamation of an individual, from First Amendment protection. Over the years other exceptions to the protection of speech and press from First Amendment rights have arisen. Most of the early examples were obscenity cases. Later, freedom of the press was infringed during World War I (1914–1918) when the Supreme Court allowed the censorship of certain newspapers and periodicals as a part of the war effort. In 1925, the Supreme Court upheld the conviction of Benjamin Gitlow for his role in publishing a document called "The Left-Wing Manifesto," ruling that it presented a "clear and present danger" to the government. *Gitlow* was notable as the first time that the Supreme Court had held that First Amendment protection of speech and press applied against state laws as well as federal, since the Fourteenth Amendment stipulates that no state can make any law that limits the rights assured to individual citizens by the federal government. In 1942, in *Chaplinsky v. New Hampshire*, the Supreme Court held that "fighting words" were not protected under the First Amendment, stating that words that inflict injury or incite an immediate breach of the peace are not protected.

Hate speech or press has traditionally been protected under the First Amendment, but this has generated considerable debate. Could hate speech—which is similar to libel but directed at a group—be excluded from protection under the First Amendment in the way that libel against an individual is excluded? Speech advocating issues such as segregation of the races, though, falls into the category of political discussion. Protecting the right to freely discuss ideas is vital under the Bill of Rights. This debate arose in 1950, at a time of great racial tension in Illinois. Joseph Beauharnais, the president of a white supremacy group, distributed a leaflet calling for white people to unite in an all-out effort to stop African Americans from residing and intermingling with whites. Beauharnais was arrested under an Illinois criminal libel law which prohibited any published material that "portrays depravity, criminality, unchastity, or lack of virtue of a class of citizens, of any race, creed, color, or religion which said publication or exhibition exposes the citizens of any race, color, creed, or religion to contempt, derision, or obloquy or which is productive of breach of the peace or riots." When the Illinois courts upheld Beauharnais's conviction, the case went to the Supreme Court to determine whether the Fourteenth Amendment restricted the power of Illinois to prohibit speech or press that promoted friction among racial groups.

Significance

The Supreme Court narrowly upheld the Illinois criminal libel law in *Beauharnais v. Illinois.* Frankfurter argued that since an individual can be prohibited from using fighting words against an individual, he or she can also be prohibited from using them against a group. His decision used a sort of "balancing" test, balancing the rights of the individual against the rights of the state to keep peace. The dissent, however, argued that the First Amendment either allowed no infringements, or should only be abridged when no other way could be found to achieve the government's vital interest. Although *Beauharnais* has never been overturned, the decision was heavily criticized, particularly because Frankfurter's argument was so heavily based on the historical circumstances of racial conflict in Chicago at the time of the case. Later cases did not follow its lead.

Since *Beauharnais,* protection of hate speech under the First Amendment has been upheld in several cases. In *Collin v. Smith* (1978), for example, the U.S. Court of Appeals affirmed that the village of Skokie could not deny a group of Nazis the right to march through the town or prohibit the dissemination of materials that would promote hatred toward persons on the basis of their heritage. In the 1992 case *R.A.V. v. City of St. Paul,* which involved the burning of a cross in an African American family's yard, the Supreme Court struck down a city ordinance that outlawed symbolic speech, specifically including cross burning and swastikas.

Fears about limiting freedom of expression were somewhat assuaged in the 1964 case of *The New York Times v. Sullivan. The New York Times* had been sued for an advertisement that it ran containing some false statements about police treatment of civil rights protesters in Alabama. L.B. Sullivan, a county commissioner, had taken the *Times* to court and won a $5 million settlement. The Supreme Court overturned the verdict, holding that Sullivan must prove that the statement had been published by the *Times* "with knowledge that it was false or with reckless disregard of whether it was false or not." Thus, libel was "not categorically excluded from constitutional protection." This ensures individuals and publications the right to freely criticize public figures, in speech or in publication, as long as what they express about these figures is not knowingly false. This rule has generally been sustained by courts.

Primary Source

Beauharnais v. Illinois [excerpt]

SYNOPSIS: In his majority opinion, Justice Felix Frankfurter states that Illinois can punish speech that creates racial hatred. Justice Hugo L. Black dissents, holding that the court's decision allowing the abridgment of freedom of speech threatens all freedoms. Justice William O. Douglas dissents as well, arguing that the founding fathers wanted the United States to have free speech.

Mr. Justice Frankfurter delivered the opinion of the Court. . . .

The precise question before us, then, is whether the protection of "liberty" in the Due Process Clause of the Fourteenth Amendment prevents a State from punishing such libels . . . directed at designated collectivities and flagrantly disseminated. . . . We cannot say, however, that the question is concluded by history and practice. But if an utterance directed at an individual may be the object of criminal sanctions, we cannot deny to a State power to punish the same utterance directed at a defined group, unless we can say that this is a willful and purposeless restriction unrelated to the peace and well-being of the State.

. . . we would deny experience to say that the Illinois legislature was without reason in seeking ways to curb false or malicious defamation of racial and religious groups, made in public places and by means calculated to have a powerful emotional impact on those to whom it was presented. . . .

We are warned that the choice open to the Illinois legislature here may be abused, that the law may be discriminatorily enforced; prohibiting libel of a creed or of a racial group, we are told, is but a step from prohibiting libel of a political party. Every power may be abused, but the possibility of abuse is a poor reason for denying Illinois the power to adopt measures against criminal libels sanctioned by centuries of Anglo-American law. "While this Court sits" it retains and exercises authority to nullify action which encroaches on freedom of utterance under the guise of punishing libel. Of course discussion cannot be denied and the right, as well as the duty, of criticism must not be stifled. . . .

We find no warrant in the Constitution for denying to Illinois the power to pass the law here under attack. But it bears repeating—although it should not—that our finding that the law is not constitutionally objectionable carries no implication of approval of the wisdom of the legislation or of its efficacy. These questions may raise doubts in our minds as well as in others. It is not for us, however, to make the legislative judgment. We are not at liberty to erect those doubts into fundamental law.

Affirmed. . . .

Mr. Justice Black, with whom Mr. Justice Douglas concurs, dissenting. . . .

That Beauharnais and his group were making a genuine effort to petition their elected representatives is not disputed. . . . Without distortion, this First Amendment could not possibly be read so as to hold that Congress has power to punish Beauharnais and others for petitioning Congress as they have here sought to petition the Chicago authorities. . . . And we have held in a number of prior cases that the Fourteenth Amendment makes the specific prohibitions of the First Amendment equally applicable to the states.

In view of these prior holdings, how does the Court justify its holding today that states can punish people for exercising the vital freedoms intended to be safeguarded from suppression by the First Amendment? The prior holdings are not referred to; the Court simply acts on the bland assumption that the First Amendment is wholly irrelevant. It is not even accorded the respect of a passing mention. This follows logically, I suppose, from recent constitutional doctrine which appears to measure state laws solely by this Court's notions of civilized "canons of decency," reasonableness, etc. . . . Under this "reasonableness" test, state laws abridging First Amendment freedoms are sustained if found to have a "rational basis." . . .

It is now a certainty that the new "due process" coverall offers far less protection to liberty than would adherence to our former cases compelling states to abide by the unequivocal First Amendment command that its defined freedoms shall not be abridged.

The Court's holding here and the constitutional doctrine behind it leave the rights of assembly, petition, speech and press almost completely at the mercy of state legislative, executive, and judicial agencies. . . . My own belief is that no legislature is charged with the duty or vested with the power to decide what public issues Americans can discuss. In a free country that is the individual's choice, not the state's. State experimentation in curbing freedom of expression is startling and frightening doctrine in a country dedicated to self-government by its people. I reject the holding that either state or nation can punish people for having their say in matters of public concern. . . .

This statute imposes state censorship over the theater, moving pictures, radio, television, leaflets, magazines, books and newspapers. No doubt the statute is broad enough to make criminal the "publication, sale, presentation or exhibition" of many of the world's great classics, both secular and religious.

The Court condones this expansive state censorship by painstakingly analogizing it to the law of criminal libel. . . .

Prior efforts to expand the scope of criminal libel beyond its traditional boundaries have not usually met with widespread popular acclaim. . . .

Unless I misread history the majority is giving libel a more expansive scope and more respectable status than it was ever accorded even in the Star Chamber. . . .

This Act sets up a system of state censorship which is at war with the kind of free government envisioned by those who forced adoption of our Bill of Rights. The motives behind the state law may have been to do good. But the same can be said about most laws making opinions punishable as crimes. History indicates that urges to do good have led to the burning of books and even to the burning of "witches."

No rationalization on a purely legal level can conceal the fact that state laws like this one present a constant overhanging threat to freedom of speech, press and religion. Today Beauharnais is punished for publicly expressing strong views in favor of segregation. Ironically enough, Beauharnais, convicted of crime in Chicago, would probably be given a hero's reception in many other localities, if not in some parts of Chicago itself. Moreover, the same kind of state law that makes Beauharnais a criminal for advocating segregation in Illinois can be utilized to send people to jail in other states for advocating equality and nonsegregation. What Beauharnais said in his leaflet is mild compared with usual arguments on both sides of racial controversies.

We are told that freedom of petition and discussion are in no danger "while this Court sits." This case raises considerable doubt. Since those who peacefully petition for changes in the law are not to be protected "while this Court sits," who is? I do not agree that the Constitution leaves freedom of petition, assembly, speech, press or worship at the mercy of a case-by-case, day-by-day majority of this Court. I had supposed that our people could rely for their freedom on the Constitution's commands, rather than on the grace of this Court on an individual case basis. To say that a legislative body can, with this Court's approval, make it a crime to petition for and publicly discuss proposed legislation seems as farfetched to me as it would be to say that a valid law could be enacted to punish a candidate for President for telling the people his views. I think the First Amendment, with the Fourteenth, "absolutely" forbids such laws without any "ifs" or "buts" or "whereases." Whatever the danger, if any, in such public discussions, it is a danger the Founders deemed outweighed by the danger incident to the stifling of thought and speech. The Court does not act on this view of the Founders. It calculates what it deems to be the danger of public discussion, holds the scales are tipped on the side of state suppression, and upholds state censorship. This method of decision offers little protection to First Amendment liberties "while this Court sits."

If there be minority groups who hail this holding as their victory, they might consider the possible relevancy of this ancient remark:

Another such victory and I am undone.

■ ■ ■

Mr. Justice Douglas, dissenting.

Hitler and his Nazis showed how evil a conspiracy could be which was aimed at destroying a race by exposing it to contempt, derision, and obloquy. I would be willing to concede that such conduct directed at a race or group in this country could be made an indictable offense. For such a project would be more than the exercise of free speech. Like picketing, it would be free speech plus.

Supreme Court Justice Felix Frankfurter. COLLECTION OF THE SUPREME COURT OF THE UNITED STATES.

I would also be willing to concede that even without the element of conspiracy there might be times and occasions when the legislative or executive branch might call a halt to inflammatory talk, such as the shouting of "fire" in a school or a theatre.

My view is that if in any case other public interests are to override the plain command of the First Amendment, the peril of speech must be clear and present, leaving no room for argument, raising no doubts as to the necessity of curbing speech in order to prevent disaster.

The First Amendment is couched in absolute terms—freedom of speech shall not be abridged. Speech has therefore a preferred position as contrasted to some other civil rights. For example, privacy, equally sacred to some, is protected by the Fourth Amendment only against unreasonable searches and seizures. There is room for regulation of the ways and means of invading privacy. No such leeway is granted the invasion of the right of free speech guaranteed by the First Amendment. . . .

In matters relating to business, finance, industrial and labor conditions, health and the public welfare, great leeway is now granted the legislature, for there is no guarantee in the Constitution that the status quo will be preserved against regulation by government. Freedom of speech, however, rests on a different constitutional basis. The First Amendment says that freedom of speech, freedom of press, and the free exercise of religion shall not be abridged. That is a negation of power on the part of each and every department of government. Free speech, free press, free exercise of religion are placed separate and apart; they are above and beyond the police power; they are not subject to regulation in the manner of factories, slums, apartment houses, production of oil, and the like.

The Court in this and in other cases places speech under an expanding legislative control. . . . The Framers of the Constitution knew human nature as well as we do. They too had lived in dangerous days; they too knew the suffocating influence of orthodoxy and standardized thought. They weighed the compulsions for restrained speech and thought against the abuses of liberty. They chose liberty. That should be our choice today no matter how distasteful to us the pamphlet of Beauharnais may be. It is true that this is only one decision which may later be distinguished or confined to narrow limits. But it represents a philosophy at war with the First Amendment—a constitutional interpretation which puts free speech under the legislative thumb. It reflects an influence moving ever deeper into our society. It is notice to the legislatures that they have the power to control unpopular blocs. It is a warning to every minority that when the Constitution guarantees free speech it does not mean what it says.

Further Resources

BOOKS

Bollinger, Lee C., and Geoffrey R. Stone. *Eternally Vigilant: Free Speech in the Modern Era.* Chicago: University of Chicago Press, 2002.

Heumann, Milton, Thomas W. Church, and David P. Redlawsk. *Hate Speech on Campus: Cases, Case Studies, and Commentary.* Boston: Northeastern University Press, 1997.

Hockett, Jeffrey D. *New Deal Justice: The Constitutional Jurisprudence of Hugo L. Black, Felix Frankfurter, and Robert H. Jackson.* Lanham, Md.: Rowman & Littlefield, 1996.

Simon, James F. *The Antagonists: Hugo Black, Felix Frankfurter, and Civil Liberties in Modern America.* New York: Simon and Schuster, 1989.

Urofsky, Melvin I. *Felix Frankfurter: Judicial Restraint and Individual Liberties.* Boston: Twayne, 1991.

Walker, Samuel. *Hate Speech: The History of an American Controversy.* Lincoln, Nebr.: University of Nebraska Press, 1994.

PERIODICALS

Neely, Alfred S. "Mr. Justice Frankfurter's Iconography of Judging." *Kentucky Law Journal* 83, no. 2, 1993–1994, 535–573.

WEBSITES

"Hate Speech." American Library Association. Available online at http://www.ala.org/alaorg/oif/hatespeech.html; website home page: http://www.ala.org/ (accessed February 28, 2003).

Zorach v. Clauson

Supreme Court decision

By: William O. Douglas, Hugo L. Black, and Robert H. Jackson

Date: April 28, 1952

Source: Douglas, William O., Hugo L. Black, and Robert H. Jackson. *Zorach v. Clauson.* 343 U.S. 306. Available online at http://caselaw.lp.findlaw.com/scripts/getcase.pl?navby =search&court=US&case=/us/343/306.html; website home page: http://www.findlaw.com (accessed February 28, 2003).

About the Authors: William O. Douglas (1898–1980) chaired the Securities and Exchange Commission in 1939, when he became, at forty, one of the youngest men ever appointed to the Supreme Court. He served over thirty-six years, the longest of any justice, retiring in 1975. Many thought Douglas would be pro-business, but he devoted himself to the defense of the Bill of Rights and freedom of speech.

Hugo L. Black (1886–1971) served two terms as a U.S. senator from Alabama and was known as a New Deal liberal. His 1937 appointment to the Supreme Court roused controversy when his past membership in the Ku Klux Klan became public, although he had long ago left the group. His term was generally distinguished by his support of civil rights.

Robert H. Jackson (1892–1954) was U.S. attorney general when President Franklin Roosevelt (served 1933–1945) appointed him to the Supreme Court in 1941. He took a leave from the Court in 1945 to serve as U.S. chief counsel at the Nuremberg war crimes trial. He was known for his strong defense of religious freedom and civil rights. ∎

Introduction

The First Amendment to the Constitution reads, in part, "Congress shall make no law respecting an establishment of religion, or prohibiting the free exercise thereof." Thus, under the First Amendment the government is prohibited from establishing an official religion or favoring one religion over another. The government is also prohibited from interfering with an individual's practice of religion. The relationship between state and local governments and religious organizations, however, has often come into question. Since 1925 it has been held that the First Amendment protects individuals' religious freedom from state legislation as well as federal, but the degree of separation between state and church is often tested, and such cases have continually been brought before the Supreme Court.

Efforts to intensify or to create a state's support of religion grew after World War II (1939–1945), as widespread nuclear-age fears stimulated a resurgence in church attendance. Blocs of parents advocated varying levels of state support for religious instruction for their school-aged children. One way states provided such support was by reimbursing parents who transported their children to parochial (church-affiliated) schools, since the states were already transporting other public and private school pupils. This program was ruled constitutional in 1947 by the Supreme Court in *Everson v. Board of Education of Ewing Township.* A program in an Illinois school system that allowed religious education in the school buildings during school hours, however, was deemed to be too much establishment of religion by a state in *McCollum v. Board of Education* (1948).

Since the Supreme Court in *McCollum* had prohibited religious teachers from teaching in public schools during school hours, New York City decided to try a "released time program," in which children were allowed to leave school to attend religious classes away from school property (generally at parochial schools). When the program was challenged, the New York courts upheld it. In 1952 this issue was appealed to the U.S. Supreme Court in *Zorach v. Clauson.*

Significance

The Supreme Court upheld the released time program, commenting that it was different than the program allowing education in the schools, as the religious education was off school grounds and no state funds were involved. The decision was decided with a majority of six upholding and three dissenting. Justice William O. Douglas expressed the majority opinion that it was not the intent of the First Amendment to create an environment hostile to religion, and as the U.S. population is, on the whole, a religious one, efforts should be made to encourage and cooperate with religious institutions. Justice Robert H. Jackson's dissent argued that the school program promoted religion.

After the *Zorach* case, the next major controversy over freedom of religion and the separation of church and state—one that is still raging today—was over prayer and Bible reading in public schools. In the 1962 case of *Engel v. Vitale,* the Court struck down the New York practice of requiring students to begin the school day with a nondenominational prayer. The Court held that this promoted religion in general, and since part of the freedom of religion was the freedom not to have a religion, the New York practice of daily prayer in public schools vi-

A young boy holds a rosary while attending services led by Father Peyton of the Congregation of the Holy Cross, 1952. © HULTON-DEUTSCH COLLECTION/CORBIS. REPRODUCED BY PERMISSION.

olated the First Amendment right. The next year, the Court struck down a Pennsylvania law that required a daily Bible reading.

Since these decisions, many constitutional amendments have been proposed to either require or allow prayer and Bible readings in schools, but none have passed Congress. State support for religion returned to the Court in *Board of Education v. Allen* in 1968, when the Court upheld a New York program lending free textbooks to students in private (including parochial) and public schools. This was held to not be an "excessive entanglement of church and state." In 1971, the Supreme Court ruled in *Lemon v. Kurtzman* on the practice of using of state money to assist private schools by supplementing the salaries of teachers and buying textbooks and other school supplies for parochial schools. The Court established the test that still exists today for the most part— governments were allowed to act on religious issues, if the program's purpose was a secular one, if there was not an "excessive entanglement of church and state," and if the main effect did not help or hurt religion. Since that time, the court has issued varying rulings on things such as school prayer and tax credits for education that helped private schools, but the *Lemon* test, for the most part, still remains the rule.

Primary Source

Zorach v. Clauson [excerpt]

SYNOPSIS: Justice William O. Douglas summarizes the New York City public school program being challenged. With no state funding or coercion of students, he finds no constitutional bars against the program. Justice Hugo L. Black dissents, holding that the separation of church and state must be completely neutral. Justice Robert H. Jackson, also dissenting, expresses concerns that in this program the state takes upon itself the role of determining appropriate religious authorities for the program.

Mr. Justice Douglas delivered the opinion of the Court.

New York City has a program which permits its public schools to release students during the school day so that they may leave the school buildings and school grounds and go to religious centers for religious instruction or devotional exercises. A student is released on written request of his parents. Those not released stay in the classrooms. The churches make weekly reports to the schools, sending a list of children who have been released from public school but who have not reported for religious instruction.

This "released time" program involves neither religious instruction in public school classrooms nor the expenditure of public funds. All costs, including the application blanks, are paid by the religious organizations. The case is therefore unlike *McCollum v. Board of Education* . . . which involved a "released time" program from Illinois. In that case the classrooms were turned over to religious instructors. We accordingly held that the program violated the First Amendment which (by reason of the Fourteenth Amendment) prohibits the states from establishing religion or prohibiting its free exercise.

Appellants, who are taxpayers and residents of New York City and whose children attend its public schools, challenge the present law. . . . Their argument, stated elaborately in various ways, reduces itself to this: the weight and influence of the school is put behind a program for religious instruction; public school teachers police it, keeping tab on students who are released; the classroom activities come to a halt while the students who are released for religious instruction are on leave; the school is a crutch on which the churches are leaning for support in their religious training; without the cooperation of the schools this "released time" program . . . would be futile and ineffective. The New York Court of Appeals sustained the law against this claim of unconstitutionality. . . . The case is here on appeal. . . .

Those matters [on the merits of this type of "released time" program] are of no concern here, since our problem reduces itself to whether New York by this system has either prohibited the "free exercise" of religion or has made a law "respecting an establishment of religion" within the meaning of the First Amendment.

It takes obtuse reasoning to inject any issue of the "free exercise" of religion into the present case. No one is forced to go to the religious classroom and no religious exercise or instruction is brought to the classrooms of the public schools. A student need not take religious instruction. He is left to his own desires as to the manner or time of his religious devotions, if any.

There is a suggestion that the system involves the use of coercion to get public school students into religious classrooms. There is no evidence in the record before us that supports that conclusion. The present record indeed tells us that the school authorities are neutral in this regard and do no more than release students whose parents so request. If in fact coercion were used, if it were established that any one or more teachers were using their office to persuade or force students to take the religious instruction, a wholly different case would be presented. . . .

We would have to press the concept of separation of Church and State to . . . extremes to condemn the present law on constitutional grounds. The nullification of this law would have wide and profound effects. A Catholic student applies to his teacher for permission to leave the school during hours on a Holy Day of Obligation to attend a mass. A Jewish student asks his teacher for permission to be excused for Yom Kippur. A Protestant wants the afternoon off for a family baptismal ceremony. In each case the teacher requires parental consent in writing. In each case the teacher, in order to make sure the student is not a truant, goes further and requires a report from the priest, the rabbi, or the minister. The teacher in other words cooperates in a religious program to the extent of making it possible for her students to participate in it. Whether she does it occasionally for a few students, regularly for one, or pursuant to a systematized program designed to further the religious needs of all the students does not alter the character of the act.

We are a religious people whose institutions presuppose a Supreme Being. We guarantee the freedom to worship as one chooses. We make room for as wide a variety of beliefs and creeds as the spiritual needs of man deem necessary. We sponsor an attitude on the part of government that shows no partiality to any one group and that lets each flourish according to the zeal of its adherents and the appeal of its dogma. When the state encourages religious instruction or cooperates with religious authorities by adjusting the schedule of public events to sectarian needs, it follows the best of our traditions. For it then respects the religious nature of our people and accommodates the public service to their spiritual needs. To hold that it may not would be to find in the Constitution a requirement that the government show a callous indifference to religious groups. That would be preferring those who believe in no religion over those who do believe. Government may not finance religious groups nor undertake religious instruction nor blend secular and sectarian education nor use secular institutions to force one or some religion on any person. But we find no constitutional requirement which makes it necessary for government to be hostile to religion and to throw its weight against efforts to widen the effective scope of religious influence. The government must be neutral when it comes to competition between sects. It may not thrust any sect on any person. It may not make a religious observance compulsory. It may not coerce anyone to attend church, to observe a religious holiday, or to take religious instruction. But it can close its doors or suspend its operations as to those who want to repair to their religious sanctuary for worship or instruction. No more than that is undertaken here.

This program may be unwise and improvident from an educational or a community viewpoint. . . . Our individual preferences, however, are not the constitutional standard. The constitutional standard is the separation of Church and State. The problem, like many problems in constitutional law, is one of degree. . . .

In the McCollum case the classrooms were used for religious instruction and the force of the public school was used to promote that instruction. Here, as we have said, the public schools do no more than accommodate their schedules to a program of outside religious instruction. We follow the McCollum case. But we cannot expand it to cover the present released time program unless separation of Church and State means that public institutions can make no adjustments of their schedules to accommodate the religious needs of the people. We cannot read into the Bill of Rights such a philosophy of hostility to religion.

Affirmed. . . .

Mr. Justice Black, dissenting. . . .

The Court's validation of the New York system rests in part on its statement that Americans are "a religious people whose institutions presuppose a Supreme Being." This was at least as true when the First Amendment was adopted; and it was just as true when eight Justices of this Court invalidated the released time system in McCollum on the premise that a state can no more "aid all religions" than it can aid one. It was precisely because Eighteenth Century Americans were a religious people divided into many fighting sects that we were given the constitutional mandate to keep Church and State completely separate. Colonial history had already shown that, here as elsewhere zealous sectarians entrusted with governmental power to further their causes would sometimes torture, maim and kill those they branded "heretics," "atheists" or "agnostics." The First Amendment was therefore to insure that no one powerful sect or combination of sects could use political or governmental power to punish dissenters whom they could not convert to their faith. Now as then, it is only by wholly isolating the state from the religious sphere and compelling it to be completely neutral, that the freedom of each and every denomination and of all nonbelievers can be maintained. It is this neutrality the Court abandons today when it treats New York's coercive system as a program which merely "encourages religious instruction or cooperates with religious authorities." The abandonment is all the more dangerous to liberty because of the Court's legal exaltation of the orthodox and its derogation of unbelievers.

Under our system of religious freedom, people have gone to their religious sanctuaries not because they feared the law but because they loved their God. The choice of all has been as free as the choice of those who answered the call to worship moved only by the music of the old Sunday morning church bells. The spiritual mind of man has thus been free to believe, disbelieve, or doubt, without repression, great or small, by the heavy hand of government. Statutes authorizing such repression have been stricken. Before today, our judicial opinions have refrained from drawing invidious distinctions between those who believe in no religion and those who do believe. The First Amendment has lost much if the religious follower and the atheist are no longer to be judicially regarded as entitled to equal justice under law.

State help to religion injects political and party prejudices into a holy field. It too often substitutes force for prayer, hate for love, and persecution for persuasion. Government should not be allowed, under cover of the soft euphemism of "co-operation," to steal into the sacred area of religious choice. . . .

Mr. Justice Jackson, dissenting. . . .

The day that this country ceases to be free for irreligion it will cease to be free for religion—except for the sect that can win political power. The same epithetical jurisprudence used by the Court today to beat down those who oppose pressuring children into some religion can devise as good epithets tomorrow against those who object to pressuring them into a favored religion. And, after all, if we concede to the State power and wisdom to single out "duly constituted religious" bodies as exclusive alternatives for compulsory secular instruction, it would be logical to also uphold the power and wisdom to choose the true faith among those "duly constituted." We start down a rough road when we begin to mix compulsory public education with compulsory godliness.

A number of Justices just short of a majority of the majority that promulgates today's passionate dialectics joined in answering them in *Illinois ex rel. McCollum v. Board of Education*. . . . The distinction attempted between that case and this is trivial, almost to the point of cynicism, magnifying its nonessential details and disparaging compulsion which was the underlying reason for invalidity. A reading of the Court's opinion in that case along with its opinion in this case will show such difference of overtones and undertones as to make clear that the *McCollum* case has passed like a storm in a teacup. The wall which the Court was professing to erect between Church and State has become even more warped and twisted than I expected. Today's judgment will be more interesting to students of psychology and of the judicial processes than to students of constitutional law.

Further Resources

BOOKS

Ball, Howard, and Phillip J. Cooper. *Of Power and Right: Hugo Black, William O. Douglas, and America's Constitutional Revolution.* New York: Oxford University Press, 1992.

Douglas, William O. *The Court Years, 1939–1975: The Autobiography of William O. Douglas.* New York: Random House, 1980.

Murphy, Bruce Allen. *Wild Bill: The Legend and Life of William O. Douglas.* New York: Random House, 2002.

Urofsky, Melvin I. *The Warren Court: Justices, Rulings, and Legacy.* Santa Barbara, Calif.: ABC-CLIO, 2001.

Wasby, Stephen L. *"He Shall Not Pass This Way Again": The Legacy of Justice William O. Douglas.* Pittsburgh, Pa.: University of Pittsburgh Press for the William O. Douglas Institute, 1990.

PERIODICALS

Louisell, David W. "The Man and the Mountain: Douglas on Religious Freedom." *Yale Law Journal* 73, no. 6, May 1964, 975–998.

WEBSITES

"Zorach v. Clauson." The Religious Freedom Page. Available online at http://religiousfreedom.lib.virginia.edu/court/zora _v_clau.html; website home page: http://religiousfreedom .lib.virginia.edu/home.html (accessed March 3, 2003).

Ethel and Julius Rosenberg

The Final Letter From the Rosenbergs to Their Children
Letter

By: Ethel and Julius Rosenberg

Date: June 19, 1953

Source: Rosenberg, Ethel, and Julius Rosenberg. The Final Letter From the Rosenbergs to Their Children. Reprinted from *We Are Your Sons.* Meeropol, Michael, and Robert Meeropol, eds. Boston: Houghton, Mifflin, 1975. Available online at http://www.law.umkc.edu/faculty/projects/ftrials /rosenb/ROS_LTR.HTM; website home page: http://www .law.umkc.edu (accessed February 26, 2003).

About the Authors: Julius Rosenberg (1918–1953) was involved in a variety of political activities, including the Young Communist League. He worked for a time in the 1940s as a civilian employee of the U.S. Army Signal Corps, but in 1945 the Corps fired him for his past membership in the American Communist Party. In July 1950, Rosenberg was arrested and accused of committing espionage for the Soviet Union. He was executed in 1953.

Ethel Rosenberg (1915–1953) was very active in trade union politics, joining the Young Communist League and later the American Communist Party. After marrying Julius Rosenberg, she stayed home with their two young sons. She was arrested for espionage one month after her husband's arrest and executed in 1953.

"Ethel Rosenberg's Brother Admits Lying Under Oath"
Newspaper article

By: Associated Press

Date: December 5, 2001

Source: "Ethel Rosenberg's Brother Admits Lying Under Oath." *Beloit Daily News,* December 5, 2001. Available online at http://www.beloitdailynews.com/1201/rose5.htm; web-

Ethel and Julius Rosenberg during the espionage trial held in New York City, March 1951. AP/WIDE WORLD PHOTOS. REPRODUCED BY PERMISSION.

site home page: http://www.beloitdailynews.com (accessed February 26, 2003). ■

Introduction

In 1945, after the United States had dropped the world's first two atomic bombs on Japan in order to end World War II (1939–1945) in the Pacific, most scientists and public policy makers thought it would be many years before the Soviet Union would have the scientific knowledge to build an atomic weapon. However, in 1949, only four years later, the Soviets surprised the world when they tested their own atomic bomb. How the Soviets had so quickly achieved the knowledge with which to create the atomic bomb became a pressing issue.

Part of the answer came from Great Britain. In February 1950 the British arrested a German-born physicist, Klaus Fuchs, as a Soviet spy. During the war years, Fuchs had been one of the scientists working in Los Alamos, New Mexico, on the Manhattan Project, the U.S. effort to develop an atomic bomb. The arrest of Fuchs on charges of passing information to the Soviets soon led the FBI to other conspirators. Among those arrested was David Greenglass, an American machinist who had worked on the Manhattan Project while in the army. Greenglass named his sister and brother-in-law, Ethel and Julius Rosenberg, as co-conspirators.

Greenglass claimed that during his days at Los Alamos, Julius Rosenberg had urged him to deliver notes and sketches of a high-explosive lens mold that was being developed there. Either Julius or another conspirator, Harry Gold, would pick up Greenglass's notes to be passed on to a Soviet agent. Julius Rosenberg was arrested and charged with espionage in July 1950. Although there was little evidence against Ethel, she was arrested in August. Greenglass and his wife said that she had been in the room when the others were speaking about espionage and that she had typed up some of her brother's notes that were to be passed to the Soviets. The FBI hoped that by making a capital case against Ethel they could force Julius to confess his own involvement. Julius Rosenberg never admitted to any criminal act, and the case against Ethel moved forward.

Significance

The Rosenberg trial took place during particularly turbulent times. The couple was arrested just one year after the Soviets tested their atomic bomb. During the year preceding their arrest, Alger Hiss, an adviser to the president, had been found guilty of spying for the Soviet Union. Wisconsin senator Joseph McCarthy had started a national crusade against communists in his February 9, 1950, speech proclaiming that he had names (never disclosed) of 205 members of the Communist Party who were currently serving in the U.S. State Department.

The Rosenberg trial is generally remembered for its extremely harsh sentence. Though current evidence indicates that Julius was in fact guilty of the crimes he was accused of committing, he was the only person to receive the death penalty for committing such crimes. Debate remains as to whether Ethel was actually guilty of knowing about the espionage and typing her brother's notes, as charged. The death sentence for such a crime is unprecedented in any case, and the circumstances that led to her execution were quite underhanded. The government made its case against her in an attempt to get Julius to name names. Her brother, whose testimony formed the whole case against her, admitted in 2001 to having lied about her involvement to save his wife from time in jail. The methods of the government, the rush to judgment, and the execution of an innocent person in the Rosenberg trial are sobering testaments to the way emotionalism can cloud justice in situations involving national security.

Primary Source

The Final Letter From the Rosenbergs to Their Children

SYNOPSIS: Convicted and sentenced, the Rosenbergs appealed without success. Massive demonstrations changed nothing. In June 1953, the Rosenbergs' attorney, Emanuel Bloch ("Manny" in the postscripts) brought their two sons—aged ten and six—to the prison to say goodbye. Supreme Court Justice William O. Douglas then granted a stay, but it was defeated by a special session of the Court on June 19, 1953, the scheduled day of execution. This letter was written that day. The Rosenbergs were put to death only hours later.

Dearest Sweethearts, my most precious children,

Only this morning it looked like we might be together again after all. Now that this cannot be, I want so much for you to know all that I have come to know. Unfortunately, I may write only a few simple words; the rest your own lives must teach you, even as mine taught me.

At first, of course, you will grieve bitterly for us, but you will not grieve alone. That is our consolation and it must eventually be yours.

Eventually, too you must come to believe that life is worth the living. Be comforted that even now, with the end of ours slowly approaching, that we know this with a conviction that defeats the executioner!

Your lives must teach you, too, that good cannot flourish in the midst of evil; that freedom and all the things that go to make up a truly satisfying and worthwhile life, must sometime be purchased very dearly. Be comforted then that we were serene and understood with the deepest kind of understanding, that civilization had not as yet progressed to the point where life did not have to be lost for the sake of life; and that we were comforted in the sure knowledge that others would carry on after us.

We wish we might have had the tremendous joy and gratification of living our lives out with you. Your Daddy who is with me in the last momentous hours, sends his heart and all the love that is in it for his dearest boys. Always remember that we were innocent and could not wrong our conscience.

We press you close and kiss you with all our strength.

Lovingly,
Daddy and Mommy
Julie [and] Ethel

P.S. to Manny: The Ten Commandments religious medal and chain and my wedding ring—I wish you to present to our children as a token of our undying love.

David Greenglass, brother-in-law of Julius Rosenberg, is escorted into a New York City court by a U.S. marshall. July 31, 1951. **AP/WIDE WORLD PHOTOS. REPRODUCED BY PERMISSION**

P.S.—to Manny

Please be certain to give my best wishes to _____. Tell him I love and honor him with all my heart—Tell him I want him to know that I feel he shares my triumph—For I have no fear and no regrets—Only that the release from the trap was not completely effectuated and the qualities I possessed could not expand to their fullest capacities—I want him to have the pleasure of knowing how much he meant to me, how much he did to help me grow up—All our love to all our dear ones.

Love you so much—
Ethel

Primary Source

"Ethel Rosenberg's Brother Admits Lying Under Oath"

SYNOPSIS: For his part in the espionage conspiracy, David Greenglass served ten years in prison and then resumed life with his wife under an assumed name. Never an appealing character in the case, he testified against wife, sister, and brother-in-law to save himself, even lying without remorse about his sister's part in the plot. In an interview with *60 Minutes II* Greenglass recalled the Rosenbergs' highly charged trial, in which assistant prosecutor Roy Cohn—later a top McCarthy aid—urged him to lie.

New York (AP)—Nearly 50 years after convicted Soviet spy Ethel Rosenberg was executed, her brother has admitted that he lied under oath to save himself and says he is unconcerned that his perjury may have sent his sister and her husband to the electric chair.

"As a spy who turned his family in . . . I don't care," David Greenglass says in a television interview to be broadcast Wednesday. "I sleep very well."

The admission may shed new light on the Rosenberg case, one of the most infamous events of the Cold War. Julius and Ethel Rosenberg were executed in Sing Sing prison in June 1953, two years after a sensational trial on charges of conspiring to steal U.S. atomic secrets for the Soviet Union.

They were the only people ever executed in the United States for Cold War espionage, and their conviction helped give fuel to Sen. Joseph McCarthy's communist-hunting crusade.

Greenglass, now 79, makes the disclosure of false testimony in "The Brother," a new book by veteran New York Times editor Sam Roberts, and in a taped interview to be broadcast Wednesday on the CBS program "60 Minutes II."

Greenglass, Ethel's younger brother, admits in the book that he, too, was a spy who gave the Soviets information about atomic research and a detonator invented by another scientist.

When the Rosenbergs came to trial, Greenglass was also under indictment and worried that he and his wife, Ruth, would be convicted. He says Roy Cohn, an assistant prosecutor and later aide to McCarthy, encouraged him to lie.

In court, Greenglass delivered what would be the most incriminating testimony against Ethel Rosenberg—that she transcribed his spy notes destined for Moscow on a portable Remington typewriter. His wife corroborated his testimony.

But now, Greenglass tells author Roberts that he based his account entirely on his wife's recollection, not on his own. In the TV interview, he says, "I don't know who typed it, frankly, and to this day I can't remember that the typing took place. I had no memory of that at all—none whatsoever."

Roberts writes in his book, "Handwritten or typed, the notes contained little or nothing that was new. But from the prosecution's perspective, the Remington was as good as a smoking gun in Ethel Rosenberg's hands."

In the TV interview, Greenglass is asked why the Rosenbergs went to their deaths rather than admit espionage.

"One word—stupidity," Greenglass replies. Asked whether that makes Ethel responsible for her own death, he says, "Yeah."

Greenglass admits he is sometimes haunted by the Rosenberg case, but adds, "My wife says, 'Look, we're still alive.'"

Should he ever encounter the pair's two sons, Greenglass says, he would tell them he was "sorry that your parents are dead," but would not apologize for his part in their execution.

"I had no idea they would give them the death sentence," he tells "60 Minutes II."

In the book, subtitled "The Untold Story of Atomic Spy David Greenglass and How He Sent His Sister Ethel Rosenberg to the Electric Chair," Greenglass admits to further perjury in court and before a congressional committee—all aimed at gaining leniency for himself and keeping his wife out of prison.

Sentenced to 15 years, Greenglass was released in 1960. He lives in the New York area under an assumed name.

The Rosenberg case became a political cause celebre with anti-Semitic overtones. While some historians say evidence against Ethel Rosenberg was weak compared with that against her husband, the pair's refusal to admit spying for Moscow added to public fears of a nuclear showdown with the Soviets.

"This was a time when people were terrified," Roberts said in an interview with The Associated Press. "There was no way the Russians could have obtained the atomic bomb without stealing it from us."

Roberts said the late William Rogers, a deputy U.S. attorney general in 1951 and later President Nixon's secretary of state, told him the government had expected Ethel Rosenberg to save herself by providing incriminating evidence against Julius.

But in the end, "she called our bluff," Rogers said.

Some tidbits of Cold War espionage lore related by Roberts are almost comic. According to Roberts, Greenglass admitted sleeping through the first A-bomb test, using atomic implosion technology to make artificial diamonds, and being picked up while hitchhiking by Lt. Gen. Leslie Groves, head of the top-secret Manhattan Project that developed the atomic bomb.

Further Resources

BOOKS

Burnett, Betty. *The Trial of Julius and Ethel Rosenberg: A Primary Source Account.* New York: Rosen Publishing Group, 2003.

Carmichael, Virginia. *Framing History: The Rosenberg Story and the Cold War.* Minneapolis: University of Minnesota Press, 1993.

Radosh, Ronald, and Joyce Milton. *The Rosenberg File.* 2nd ed. New Haven, Conn.: Yale University Press, 1997.

Roberts, Sam. *The Brother: The Untold Story of Atomic Spy David Greenglass and How He Sent His Sister, Ethel Rosenberg, to the Electric Chair.* New York: Random House, 2001.

Rosenberg, Julius, Ethel Rosenberg, and Michael Meeropol. *The Rosenberg Letters: A Complete Edition of the Prison Correspondence of Julius and Ethel Rosenberg.* New York: Garland, 1994.

WEBSITES

Linder, Douglas, ed. "Famous American Trials: The Rosenbergs." University of Missouri–Kansas City Law School, 2002. Available online at http://www.law.umkc.edu/faculty /projects/ftrials/rosenb/ROS_LTR.HTM; website home page: http://www.law.umkc.edu (accessed February 26, 2003).

Perlin Papers On-line. Columbia University Law School Available online at http://www.columbia.edu/acis/cria/rosenberg /index.html; website home page: http://www.columbia.edu (accessed March 6, 2003).

Irvine v. California

Supreme Court decision

By: Robert H. Jackson, Thomas C. Clark, Hugo L. Black, William O. Douglas

Date: February 8, 1954

Source: Jackson, Robert H., Thomas C. Clark, Hugo L. Black, and William O. Douglas. *Irvine v. California.* 347 U.S. 128 (1954). Available online at http://caselaw.lp.findlaw.com /cgi-bin/getcase.pl?navby=case&court=us&vol=347&invol=128; website home page: http://www.findlaw.com/ (accessed March 4, 2003).

About the Authors: Robert H. Jackson (1892–1954) was the U.S. attorney general when President Franklin D. Roosevelt (served 1933–1945) appointed him to the Supreme Court in 1941. He took a leave from the Court in 1945 to serve as U.S. chief counsel at the Nuremberg war crimes trial. He was known for his strong defense of religious freedom and civil rights.

Thomas C. Clark (1899–1977) was U.S. attorney general under President Harry S. Truman (served 1945–1953). He served on the Supreme Court from 1949 to 1967. Although

Clark was noted for some conservative Cold War–era views, he supported certain civil liberties vigorously.

Hugo L. Black (1886–1971) served two terms as a U.S. senator from Alabama and was known as a New Deal liberal. Roosevelt appointed him to the Supreme Court in 1937. His term was generally distinguished by his support of civil rights. He died one week after retiring from the Court.

William O. Douglas (1898–1980) was the chairman of the Securities and Exchange Commission in 1939, when Roosevelt appointed him to the Supreme Court. At forty, he was one of the youngest men ever to be appointed. He served the longest of any justice, with over thirty-six years on the bench, and was highly regarded for his strong support of civil rights. ∎

Introduction

Unreasonable searches and seizures by policing agencies have taken place in the Americas since colonial times. Under the British crown, authorities searching out smuggled goods in the colonies were given documents called "writs of assistance," which gave them a general right to search wherever they wished and to seize whatever they found. The colonists themselves later used writs of assistance to collect taxes and recover slaves. Due to a growing sense of outrage against this practice, the Fourth Amendment was included in the Bill of Rights. The amendment reads, in part, that "the right of the people to be secure . . . against unreasonable searches and seizures, shall not be violated, and no Warrants shall issue, but upon probable cause . . . and particularly describing the place to be searched, and the persons or things to be seized." The Fourth Amendment, though, prescribes no penalty for violation, and throughout the nineteenth century courts generally allowed the use of evidence seized illegally in obtaining convictions. Victims could use the civil courts to sue the person who had violated their Fourth Amendment rights, but this was little comfort when they had to do it from jail.

In 1886, the Supreme Court overturned a conviction and excluded from a trial papers that had been seized without a warrant. It took twenty-eight more years for the Supreme Court in *Weeks v. U.S.* (1914) to create what is called the "exclusionary rule"—proclaiming that evidence seized without a warrant cannot be used in trial in a federal court. The exclusionary rule, though, was unclear as to whether it was integral to the Fourth Amendment or not. The Supreme Court was also divided as to whether the exclusionary rule applied against the states. In 1949, the Supreme Court held that the right to privacy and to not be searched without a warrant was integral to the Fourth Amendment, but the Court did not apply this rule against the states. The same question, of whether the states were required to follow the Fourth Amendment, came up again in 1954 in *Irvine v. California.*

Significance

In *Irvine,* a taping device was installed and used, without a warrant, to gather evidence against Irvine, a suspected horse race bookmaker. Once the evidence was thus gathered, it was used in court to obtain a conviction. The petitioner, Irvine, argued that the use of this evidence violated his Fourth Amendment rights, but a majority of the court ruled that, even though his rights had been violated, the evidence could be used against him. The Court held that even though the invasion of Irvine's rights was shocking, it did not follow that he, as a guilty party, should not be convicted. The exclusionary rule that the federal courts had adopted to enforce Fourth Amendment rights was not being applied to the states. The dissent in *Irvine* argued that the Fourth Amendment should be applied against the states and the exclusionary rule was the only way to enforce it. The dissenters' views did not gain a majority until 1961 in *Mapp v. Ohio,* in which a search without a warrant was conducted in the home of a bombing suspect. The search produced allegedly obscene materials that were then used to bring about an obscenity conviction. The court overturned this conviction, holding that the exclusionary rule applied to states.

Courts have generally followed *Mapp* since, but narrowed it. The Supreme Court ruled that the exclusionary rule only applied to cases brought after *Mapp.* The Court also ruled that illegally seized evidence can be used if it can be proven that the evidence would have been found in time by other police methods. They also ruled that the Fourth Amendment only applies to the person whose privacy has been violated, not to anyone else, and that the exclusionary rule only applies at trial, and not to any preliminary hearings or grand jury proceedings. Later cases have also "weighed" the rights of the accused versus the rights of society in many criminal justice areas. The exclusionary rule generally applies, even though it has been limited.

Primary Source

Irvine v. California [excerpt]

SYNOPSIS: In recounting his opinion in *Irvine,* Justice Robert H. Jackson documents the officers' misconduct in the case. He holds that even though the conduct is shocking, it does not require overturning Irvine's conviction. He raises the issue that it has only been in relatively recent times, since 1949, that the Court has applied the basic search-and-seizure prohibition to the states, and that the states have not yet had time to respond. He upholds the opinion that the states should have the discretion to decide in such cases. Justice Tom C. Clark concurs with Jackson. Justice Hugo L. Black, dissenting, argues that there should be a reversal, as the evidence was extorted from Irvine by the federal government in violation of Fifth Amendment protection

from being forced to incriminate oneself. Douglas dissents as well, stating that this conviction would seem more likely in a police state than in America.

Mr. Justice Jackson announced the judgment of the Court and an opinion in which The Chief Justice, Mr. Justice Reed and Mr. Justice Minton join. . . .

But the questions raised by the officers' conduct while investigating this case are serious. The police strongly suspected petitioner of illegal bookmaking but were without proof of it. On December 1, 1951, while Irvine and his wife were absent from their home, an officer arranged to have a locksmith go there and make a door key. Two days later, again in the absence of occupants, officers and a technician made entry into the home by the use of this key and installed a concealed microphone in the hall. A hole was bored in the roof of the house and wires were strung to transmit to a neighboring garage whatever sounds the microphone might pick up. Officers were posted in the garage to listen. On December 8, police again made surreptitious entry and moved the microphone, this time hiding it in the bedroom. Twenty days later, they again entered and placed the microphone in a closet, where the device remained until its purpose of enabling the officers to overhear incriminating statements was accomplished. . . .

Each of these repeated entries of petitioner's home without a search warrant or other process was a trespass, and probably a burglary, for which any unofficial person should be, and probably would be, severely punished. Science has perfected amplifying and recording devices to become frightening instruments of surveillance and invasion of privacy, whether by the policeman, the blackmailer, or the busybody. That officers of the law would break and enter a home, secrete such a device, even in a bedroom, and listen to the conversation of the occupants for over a month would be almost incredible if it were not admitted. Few police measures have come to our attention that more flagrantly, deliberately, and persistently violated the fundamental principle declared by the Fourth Amendment. . . . The decision in *Wolf v. Colorado,* for the first time established that "[t]he security of one's privacy against arbitrary intrusion by the police" is embodied in the concept of due process found in the Fourteenth Amendment. . . .

It is suggested, however, that although we affirmed the conviction in *Wolf,* we should reverse here because this invasion of privacy is more shocking, more offensive, than the one involved there.

Demonstration of an eavesdropping device like the one used by those involved in *Irvine v. California*. The Supreme Court ruled later, in 1967, that law enforcement may not use wiretaps without court authorization. © BETTMANN/CORBIS. REPRODUCED BY PERMISSION.

The opinions in *Wolf* were written entirely in the abstract and did not disclose the details of the constitutional violation. Actually, the search was offensive to the law in the same respect, if not the same degree, as here. . . .

We are urged to make inroads upon *Wolf* by holding that it applies only to searches and seizures which produce on our minds a mild shock, while if the shock is more serious, the states must exclude the evidence or we will reverse the conviction. We think that the *Wolf* decision should not be overruled, for the reasons so persuasively stated therein. We think, too, that a distinction of the kind urged would leave the rule so indefinite that no state court could know what it should rule in order to keep its processes on solid constitutional ground.

Even as to the substantive rule governing federal searches in violation of the Fourth Amendment, both the Court and individual Justices have wavered considerably. . . . Never until June of 1949 did this Court hold the basic search-and-seizure prohibition in any way applicable to the states under the Fourteenth Amendment. At that time, as we pointed out,

thirty-one states were not following the federal rule excluding illegally obtained evidence, while sixteen were in agreement with it. Now that the *Wolf* doctrine is known to them, state courts may wish further to reconsider their evidentiary rules. But to upset state convictions even before the states have had adequate opportunity to adopt or reject the rule would be an unwarranted use of federal power. The chief burden of administering criminal justice rests upon state courts. To impose upon them the hazard of federal reversal for noncompliance with standards as to which this Court and its members have been so inconstant and inconsistent would not be justified. . . .

It must be remembered that petitioner is not invoking the Constitution to prevent or punish a violation of his federal right recognized in *Wolf* or to recover reparations for the violation. He is invoking it only to set aside his own conviction of crime. That the rule of exclusion and reversal results in the escape of guilty persons is more capable of demonstration than that it deters invasions of right by the police. The case is made, so far as the police are concerned, when they announce that they have arrested their man. Rejection of the evidence does nothing to punish the wrong-doing official, while it may, and likely will, release the wrong-doing defendant. It deprives society of its remedy against one lawbreaker because he has been pursued by another. It protects one against whom incriminating evidence is discovered, but does nothing to protect innocent persons who are the victims of illegal but fruitless searches. The disciplinary or educational effect of the court's releasing the defendant for police misbehavior is so indirect as to be no more than a mild deterrent at best. Some discretion is still left to the states in criminal cases, for which they are largely responsible, and we think it is for them to determine which rule best serves them.

But admission of the evidence does not exonerate the officers and their aides if they have violated defendant's constitutional rights. It was pointed out in *Wolf v. Colorado,* supra, that other remedies are available for official lawlessness, although too often those remedies are of no practical avail. The difficulty with them is in part due to the failure of interested parties to inform of the offense. No matter what an illegal raid turns up, police are unlikely to inform on themselves or each other. If it turns up nothing incriminating, the innocent victim usually does not care to take steps which will air the fact that he has been under suspicion. And the prospect that the guilty may capitalize on the official wrongdoing in his defense, or to obtain reversal from a higher court, removes any motive he might have to inform. . . .

Judgment affirmed. . . .

Mr. Justice Clark, concurring.

Had I been here in 1949 when *Wolf* was decided, I would have applied the doctrine of *Weeks v. United States,* . . . (1914) to the states. But the Court refused to do so then, and it still refuses today. Thus *Wolf* remains the law and, as such, is entitled to the respect of this Court's membership. . . .

In light of the "incredible" activity of the police here, it is with great reluctance that I follow *Wolf.* Perhaps strict adherence to the tenor of that decision may produce needed converts for its extinction. Thus I merely concur in the judgment of affirmance.

Mr. Justice Black, with whom Mr. Justice Douglas concurs, dissenting.

I would reverse this conviction because the petitioner Irvine was found guilty of a crime and sentenced to prison on evidence extorted from him by the Federal Government in violation of the Fifth Amendment. . . .

I think the Fifth Amendment of itself forbids all federal agents, legislative, executive and judicial, to force a person to confess a crime; forbids the use of such a federally coerced confession in any court, state or federal; and forbids all federal courts to use a confession which a person has been compelled to make against his will. . . .

The Fifth Amendment not only forbids agents of the Federal Government to compel a person to be a witness against himself; it forbids federal courts to convict persons on their own forced testimony, whatever "sovereign"—federal or state—may have compelled it. Otherwise, the constitutional mandate against self-incrimination is an illusory safeguard that collapses whenever a confession is extorted by anyone other than the Federal Government.

So far as this case is concerned it is enough for me that Irvine was convicted in a state court on a confession coerced by the Federal Government. I believe this frustrates a basic purpose of the Fifth Amendment—to free Americans from fear that federal power could be used to compel them to confess conduct or beliefs in order to take away their life, liberty or property. For this reason I would reverse Irvine's conviction. . . .

Mr. Justice Douglas, dissenting.

The search and seizure conducted in this case smack of the police state, not the free America the Bill of Rights envisaged. . . .

The evidence so obtained was used by California to send the suspect, petitioner here, to prison.

What transpired here was as revolting as the abuses arising out of the writs of assistance against which James Otis complained. . . .

In those days courts put their sanction behind the unlawful invasion of privacy by issuing the general warrant that permitted unlimited searches. There is no essential difference between that and the action we take today. Today we throw the weight of the Government on the side of the lawless search by affirming a conviction based on evidence obtained by it. Today we compound the grievance against which Otis complained. Not only is privacy invaded. The lawless invasion is officially approved as the means of sending a man to prison.

I protest against this use of unconstitutional evidence. It is no answer that the man is doubtless guilty. The Bill of Rights was designed to protect every accused against practices of the police which history showed were oppressive of liberty. The guarantee against unreasonable searches and seizures contained in the Fourth Amendment was one of those safeguards. In 1914 a unanimous Court decided that officers who obtained evidence in violation of that guarantee could not use it in prosecutions in the federal courts. *Weeks v. United States.* . . . Lawless action of the federal police, it said, "should find no sanction in the judgments of the courts. . . ." . . .

The departure from that principle which the Court made in 1949 in *Wolf v. Colorado* . . . is part of the deterioration which civil liberties have suffered in recent years. In that case the Court held that evidence obtained in violation of the Fourth Amendment, though inadmissible in federal prosecutions, could be used in prosecutions in the state courts. . . .

Exclusion of evidence is indeed the only effective sanction. If the evidence can be used, no matter how lawless the search, the protection of the Fourth Amendment, to use the words of the Court in the Weeks case, "might as well be stricken from the Constitution." . . .

If unreasonable searches and seizures that violate the privacy which the Fourth Amendment protects are to be outlawed, this is the time and the occasion to do it. If police officers know that evidence obtained by their unlawful acts cannot be used in the courts, they will clean their own houses and put an end to this kind of action. But as long as courts will receive the evidence, the police will act lawlessly and the rights of the individual will suffer. We should throw our weight on the side of the citizen and against the lawless police. We should be alert to see that no unconstitutional evidence is used to convict any person in America.

Further Resources

BOOKS

Hockett, Jeffrey D. *New Deal Justice: The Constitutional Jurisprudence of Hugo L. Black, Felix Frankfurter, and Robert H. Jackson.* Lanham, Md.: Rowman & Littlefield Publishers, 1996.

Sullivan, John J. *A Guide to the Laws of Search and Seizure for New York State Law Enforcement Officers,* rev. ed. Flushing, N.Y.: Looseleaf Law Publications, 1996.

Wilson, Bradford P. *Enforcing the Fourth Amendment: A Jurisprudential History.* New York: Garland, 1986.

PERIODICALS

Seamon, Richard H. "*Kyllo v. United States* and the Partial Ascendance of Justice Scalia's Fourth Amendment." *Washington University Law Quarterly* 79, no. 4, 2001, 1013–1033.

Taylor, Telford. "The Nuremberg Trials." *Columbia Law Review* 55, no. 4, April 1955, 488–525.

WEBSITES

"U.S. Constitution: Fourth Amendment. Enforcing the Fourth Amendment: The Exclusionary Rule." Findlaw. Available online at http://supreme.lp.findlaw.com/constitution/amendment04/06.html; website home page: http://www.findlaw.com/ (accessed March 4, 2003).

Brown v. Board of Education

Supreme Court decision

By: Earl Warren

Date: May 17, 1954

Source: Warren, Earl. *Brown v. Board of Education.* 347 U.S. 483 (1954) Available online at http://caselaw.lp.findlaw.com/scripts/getcase.pl?navby=case&court=us&vol=347&page=483; website home page: http://www.findlaw.com (accessed March 4, 2003).

About the Author: Earl Warren (1891–1974) received his bachelor's degree from the University of California in 1912 and his law degree there two years later. After three years in private practice, he joined the army in 1917, then began a career in government as deputy city attorney for Oakland. From 1945 to 1953, he was governor of California. He became chief justice of the U.S. Supreme Court in 1953, a position he held until 1969. The Warren Court is synonymous with expansion of civil rights and civil liberties. ∎

Introduction

Slavery legally ended in the United States with the Thirteenth Amendment in 1865, but racial discrimination did not end with slavery. During the Reconstruction Era (1865–1877), the North took steps to help the former slaves and to rebuild the South. The Fourteenth Amendment, guaranteeing due process and equal protection to all citizens, and the Fifteenth Amendment, providing that the right to vote would not be denied on the basis of the color of one's skin, were passed during that era. But the North soon tired of Reconstruction, and white domination quickly returned to Southern institutions. Jim Crow laws, beginning in the 1880s, segregated all aspects of Southern life—theaters, railroad cars, schools, even public restrooms. The Supreme Court gave its stamp of approval to Jim Crow in *Plessy v. Ferguson* (1896), which held that separate facilities for African Americans and whites were constitutional as long as the facilities were equal. With whites holding political power in the South, the system never even approximated equality. Schools for African Americans were particularly bad. Most states did not have colleges for African Americans, and they provided few high schools.

The National Association for the Advancement of Colored People (NAACP) challenged segregation throughout the South, especially targeting education. Their first victory in education came in 1938 in *Missouri ex rel. Gaines v. Canada,* when the Supreme Court ruled against the state of Missouri's practice of providing scholarships for its eligible African American students to go to law school in other states rather than providing opportunities for African Americans to go to law school in Missouri. The Court held that law schools for African Americans could be separate, but they had to exist. Most states responded to this by providing token law schools for African Americans in their states. In *Sweatt v. Painter* (1950) the Court held that if separate schools existed, they had to be equal in every way, including the intangibles.

Linda Brown was an African American elementary school student living in Topeka, Kansas, in the early 1950s. Since she had a long way to travel to get to the all-African American elementary school in her district, she applied to the Board of Education of Topeka to gain admission to an all-white school closer to home. She was denied admission. Kansas state law at the time allowed school districts to maintain separate facilities for African American and white students, and Topeka had elected to do so at the elementary level. Linda Brown's parents took the Board of Education to court with NAACP attorney Thurgood Marshall handling the case. The federal court found that Linda Brown's rights had not been violated, referring to the *Plessy* doctrine of "separate but equal." The case then went to the Supreme Court, which combined *Brown* with cases from several other states that raised the same issue: that segregated schools were never equal and constituted a violation of equal protection under the laws provided in the Fourteenth Amendment.

Significance

The Supreme Court took an historic step in 1954, declaring that "separate educational facilities are inherently unequal." Segregation in education under any circumstance was deemed unconstitutional. The Court caused an uproar with this ruling. The nationwide reaction to the Court's finding was extremely powerful, whether favorable or not. The Chicago *Defender* of May 18, 1954, proclaimed: "Neither the atom bomb nor the hydrogen bomb will ever be as meaningful to our democracy as the unanimous decision of the Supreme Court of the United States that racial segregation violates the spirit and letter of our Constitution." Many in the South, which had the largest share of the nation's public schools that were segregated by legal mandate, reacted to the decision in horror and anger. On the same day, the Chicago press and many others throughout the nation lauded the *Brown* decision. The Jackson, Mississippi, *Daily News* grimly predicted: "Human blood may stain Southern soil in many places because of this decision but the dark red stains of that blood will be on the marble steps of the United States Supreme Court building." A congressional delegation of mostly Southern congressmen jointly announced the signing of the Southern Manifesto, which called for "massive resistance" against the *Brown* decision.

In 1955, the Supreme Court issued another *Brown* decision concerning the schedule and means of racially integrating the nation's schools. Compliance with the Court's ruling was very slow. In 1957, nine African American students were blocked from entering Little Rock High School until President Dwight D. Eisenhower (served 1953–1961) very reluctantly ordered the Arkansas National Guard to escort the students into the school. Ten years after *Brown,* less than 2 percent of Southern African American students attended integrated schools. The South was not the only reluctant participant in the move to desegregate. As late as 1974, a federal court ruled that the Boston School Committee had deliberately maintained racial segregation in the city's public schools and ordered the city to initiate busing programs to bring children to schools outside their own neighborhoods. Civil rights bills passed during President Lyndon B. Johnson's administration (1963–1969) provided much-needed force behind integrating the nation's schools, but racial segregation remains a reality in many parts of the nation today.

Primary Source

Brown v. Board of Education [excerpt]

SYNOPSIS: Chief Justice Earl Warren describes the Court's efforts to study the history and facts of seg-

regation in education and the Fourteenth Amendment. The Court had been ruling for several decades without directly considering the constitutionality of segregated education as a whole. With several such cases before the Court, it takes this challenge, ruling directly that segregated schools are "inherently unequal" and overruling the concept of separation laid out in *Plessy* as it applies to education.

Mr. Chief Justice Warren delivered the opinion of the Court.

These cases come to us from the States of Kansas, South Carolina, Virginia, and Delaware. They are premised on different facts and different local conditions, but a common legal question justifies their consideration together in this consolidated opinion.

In each of the cases, minors of the Negro race, through their legal representatives, seek the aid of the courts in obtaining admission to the public schools of their community on a nonsegregated basis. In each instance, they had been denied admission to schools attended by white children under laws requiring or permitting segregation according to race. This segregation was alleged to deprive the plaintiffs of the equal protection of the laws under the Fourteenth Amendment. In each of the cases other than the Delaware case, a three-judge federal district court denied relief to the plaintiffs on the so-called "separate but equal" doctrine announced by this Court in *Plessy v. Ferguson.* . . .

The plaintiffs contend that segregated public schools are not "equal" and cannot be made "equal," and that hence they are deprived of the equal protection of the laws. Because of the obvious importance of the question presented, the Court took jurisdiction. Argument was heard in the 1952 Term, and reargument was heard this Term on certain questions propounded by the Court.

Reargument was largely devoted to the circumstances surrounding the adoption of the Fourteenth Amendment in 1868. It covered exhaustively consideration of the Amendment in Congress, ratification by the states, then existing practices in racial segregation, and the views of proponents and opponents of the Amendment. This discussion and our own investigation convince us that, although these sources cast some light, it is not enough to resolve the problem with which we are faced. At best, they are inconclusive. The most avid proponents of the post-War Amendments undoubtedly intended them to remove all legal distinctions among "all persons born or naturalized in the United States." Their opponents,

George Hayes (left), standing with Thurgood Marshall (center), and James M. Nabrit (right) after the *Brown v. Board of Education* Supreme Court decision. AP/WIDE WORLD PHOTOS. REPRODUCED BY PERMISSION

just as certainly, were antagonistic to both the letter and the spirit of the Amendments and wished them to have the most limited effect. What others in Congress and the state legislatures had in mind cannot be determined with any degree of certainty.

An additional reason for the inconclusive nature of the Amendment's history, with respect to segregated schools, is the status of public education at that time. In the South, the movement toward free common schools, supported by general taxation, had not yet taken hold. Education of white children was largely in the hands of private groups. Education of Negroes was almost nonexistent, and practically all of the race were illiterate. In fact, any education of Negroes was forbidden by law in some states. Today, in contrast, many Negroes have achieved outstanding success in the arts and sciences as well as in the business and professional world. It is true that public school education at the time of the Amendment had advanced further in the North, but the effect of the Amendment on Northern States was generally ignored in the congressional debates. Even in the North, the conditions of public education did not approximate those existing today. The curriculum

was usually rudimentary; ungraded schools were common in rural areas; the school term was but three months a year in many states; and compulsory school attendance was virtually unknown. As a consequence, it is not surprising that there should be so little in the history of the Fourteenth Amendment relating to its intended effect on public education.

In the first cases in this Court construing the Fourteenth Amendment, decided shortly after its adoption, the Court interpreted it as proscribing all state-imposed discriminations against the Negro race. The doctrine of "separate but equal" did not make its appearance in this Court until 1896 in the case of *Plessy v. Ferguson,* supra, involving not education but transportation. American courts have since labored with the doctrine for over half a century. In this Court, there have been six cases involving the "separate but equal" doctrine in the field of public education. In *Cumming v. County Board of Education* . . . and *Gong Lum v. Rice* . . . the validity of the doctrine itself was not challenged. In more recent cases, all on the graduate school level, inequality was found in that specific benefits enjoyed by white students were denied to Negro students of the same educational qualifications. *Missouri ex rel. Gaines v. Canada* . . . ; *Sipuel v. Oklahoma* . . . ; *Sweatt v. Painter* . . . ; *McLaurin v. Oklahoma State Regents.* . . . In none of these cases was it necessary to re-examine the doctrine to grant relief to the Negro plaintiff. And in *Sweatt v. Painter,* supra, the Court expressly reserved decision on the question whether *Plessy v. Ferguson* should be held inapplicable to public education.

In the instant cases, that question is directly presented. Here, unlike *Sweatt v. Painter,* there are findings below that the Negro and white schools involved have been equalized, or are being equalized, with respect to buildings, curricula, qualifications and salaries of teachers, and other "tangible" factors. [In the Kansas case, the court below found substantial equality as to all such factors. In the South Carolina case, the court below found that the defendants were proceeding "promptly and in good faith to comply with the court's decree." In the Virginia case, the court below noted that the equalization program was already "afoot and progressing"; since then, we have been advised, in the Virginia Attorney General's brief on reargument, that the program has now been completed. In the Delaware case, the court below similarly noted that the state's equalization program was well under way.] Our decision, therefore, cannot turn on merely a comparison of these tangible factors in the Negro and white schools involved in each of the cases. We must look instead to the effect of segregation itself on public education.

In approaching this problem, we cannot turn the clock back to 1868 when the Amendment was adopted, or even to 1896 when *Plessy v. Ferguson* was written. We must consider public education in the light of its full development and its present place in American life throughout the Nation. Only in this way can it be determined if segregation in public schools deprives these plaintiffs of the equal protection of the laws.

Today, education is perhaps the most important function of state and local governments. Compulsory school attendance laws and the great expenditures for education both demonstrate our recognition of the importance of education to our democratic society. It is required in the performance of our most basic public responsibilities, even service in the armed forces. It is the very foundation of good citizenship. Today it is a principal instrument in awakening the child to cultural values, in preparing him for later professional training, and in helping him to adjust normally to his environment. In these days, it is doubtful that any child may reasonably be expected to succeed in life if he is denied the opportunity of an education. Such an opportunity, where the state has undertaken to provide it, is a right which must be made available to all on equal terms.

We come then to the question presented: Does segregation of children in public schools solely on the basis of race, even though the physical facilities and other "tangible" factors may be equal, deprive the children of the minority group of equal educational opportunities? We believe that it does.

In *Sweatt v. Painter,* supra, in finding that a segregated law school for Negroes could not provide them equal educational opportunities, this Court relied in large part on "those qualities which are incapable of objective measurement but which make for greatness in a law school." In *McLaurin v. Oklahoma State Regents,* supra, the Court, in requiring that a Negro admitted to a white graduate school be treated like all other students, again resorted to intangible considerations: " . . . his ability to study, to engage in discussions and exchange views with other students, and, in general, to learn his profession." Such considerations apply with added force to children in grade and high schools. To separate them from others of similar age and qualifications solely because of their race generates a feeling of inferiority as to their status in the community that may affect their hearts and minds in a way unlikely ever to be undone. The effect of this separation on their educational opportunities was well stated by a finding in the Kansas case by a court which nevertheless felt compelled to rule against the Negro plaintiffs:

> Segregation of white and colored children in public schools has a detrimental effect upon the colored children. The impact is greater when it has the sanction of the law; for the policy of separating the races is usually interpreted as denoting the inferiority of the negro group. A sense of inferiority affects the motivation of a child to learn. Segregation with the sanction of law, therefore, has a tendency to [retard] the educational and mental development of negro children and to deprive them of some of the benefits they would receive in a racial[ly] integrated school system.

[A similar finding was made in the Delaware case: "I conclude from the testimony that in our Delaware society, State-imposed segregation in education itself results in the Negro children, as a class, receiving educational opportunities which are substantially inferior to those available to white children otherwise similarly situated."]

Whatever may have been the extent of psychological knowledge at the time of *Plessy v. Ferguson,* this finding is amply supported by modern authority. Any language in *Plessy v. Ferguson* contrary to this finding is rejected.

We conclude that in the field of public education the doctrine of "separate but equal" has no place. Separate educational facilities are inherently unequal. Therefore, we hold that the plaintiffs and others similarly situated for whom the actions have been brought are, by reason of the segregation complained of, deprived of the equal protection of the laws guaranteed by the Fourteenth Amendment. This disposition makes unnecessary any discussion whether such segregation also violates the Due Process Clause of the Fourteenth Amendment.

Because these are class actions, because of the wide applicability of this decision, and because of the great variety of local conditions, the formulation of decrees in these cases presents problems of considerable complexity. On reargument, the consideration of appropriate relief was necessarily subordinated to the primary question—the constitutionality of segregation in public education. We have now announced that such segregation is a denial of the equal protection of the laws. In order that we may have the full assistance of the parties in formulating decrees, the cases will be restored to the docket, and the parties are requested to present further argument on Questions 4 and 5 previously propounded by the Court for the reargument this Term. The Attorney General of the United States is again invited to participate. The Attorneys General of the states requiring or permitting segregation in public education will also be permitted to appear as amici curiae upon request to do so by September 15, 1954, and submission of briefs by October 1, 1954.

It is so ordered.

Further Resources

BOOKS

Balkin, J.M., and Bruce A. Ackerman. *What "Brown v. Board of Education" Should Have Said: The Nation's Top Legal Experts Rewrite America's Landmark Civil Rights Decision.* New York: New York University Press, 2001.

Cray, Ed. *Chief Justice: A Biography of Earl Warren.* New York: Simon & Schuster, 1997.

Horwitz, Morton J. *The Warren Court and the Pursuit of Justice: A Critical Issue.* New York: Hill and Wang, 1998.

Kluger, Richard. *Simple Justice: The History of "Brown v. Board of Education" and Black America's Struggle for Equality.* New York: Knopf, 1976.

Patterson, James T. *"Brown v. Board of Education": A Civil Rights Milestone and Its Troubled Legacy.* Oxford: Oxford University Press, 2001.

Wilson, Paul E. *A Time to Lose: Representing Kansas in "Brown v. Board of Education."* Lawrence: University Press of Kansas, 1995.

WEBSITES

"Brown v. Board of Education: Immediate Reaction to Decision." Landmark Cases, Supreme Court. Available online at http://www.landmarkcases.org/brown/reaction.html; website home page: http://www.landmarkcases.org/index.html (accessed March 4, 2003).

"Brown v. Board of Education National Historic Site." National Park Service. Available online at http://www.nps.gov/brvb/ (accessed March 5, 2003).

"The Army-McCarthy Hearings"

Transcript

By: Joseph R. McCarthy, Joseph N. Welch

Date: 1954

Source: "The Army-McCarthy Hearings." 1954. Available online at http://historymatters.gmu.edu/d/6444/; website home page: http://historymatters.gmu.edu/ (accessed June 25, 2003).

About the Authors: Joseph R. McCarthy (1908–1957) was a little-known senator from Wisconsin in 1950, when he won

instant notoriety alleging a large network of communists within the U.S. government. Starting in 1953 he used his political position to go after a wide array of alleged communists. Facing growing opposition until the Army-McCarthy hearings, he finally lost credibility and was censured by Congress. He died a few years later of complications from alcoholism.

Joseph N. Welch (1890–1960) was a successful trial lawyer at Hale & Dorr, a large Boston law firm. In April 1954 he was appointed to his most famous case, serving as special counsel to the Department of the Army in the congressional inquiry with Senator Joseph R. McCarthy. During the televised hearings, Welch became a familiar face to the American public. He went on to appear in television programs and movies, notably as a judge in the 1959 courtroom drama *Anatomy of a Murder.* ■

Introduction

By the end of World War II (1939–1945), the Soviet Union had achieved extensive power in eastern Europe, causing great concern among the Western nations. Distrust grew to extreme proportions, triggering the Cold War, which was accompanied by a renewed and heightened anticommunist fervor in the United States. While the tension among nations was very real, there were those who manipulated American fears for political and even personal purposes. The best known of these was Joseph McCarthy, a senator from Wisconsin. McCarthy was relatively unknown until February 1950, when, in a speech, he claimed that he had in his hand a list of 205 communists who worked in the State Department. No list was ever produced, but he gained a lot of attention. For four years, McCarthy made outrageous charges and prompted numerous unnecessary investigations, always accompanied with maximum publicity and minimum evidence. His attacks were popular amid Cold War fears, though, and Republicans, with a hot campaign issue, won overwhelmingly in the 1952 elections. In 1953 McCarthy got himself appointed chairman of the Senate Committee on Government Operations and its investigative arm, the Permanent Subcommittee on Investigations. His chief counsel on the committee was Roy Cohn, who had become known for his zealous work in the prosecution of Julius and Ethel Rosenberg.

In 1954, McCarthy decided to take on the U.S. Army. When one of McCarthy's consultants, G. David Schine, was drafted, McCarthy let the army know he wanted Schine to get a special assignment. The army's refusal angered McCarthy, apparently to the point of his accusing the army of harboring communists. Several highly charged conflicts took place between McCarthy and army officials. Finally, an investigation into the charges and counter-charges was arranged. The hearings were televised live.

Significance

The two-month Army-McCarthy hearings destroyed Joseph McCarthy precisely because they were televised.

Senator Joseph McCarthy (left) confers with his chief counsel, Roy Cohn, at a Senate subcommittee hearing on the Army-McCarthy charges, April 1954. AP/WIDE WORLD PHOTOS. REPRODUCED BY PERMISSION

Twenty million television viewers watched throughout April and May 1954 as McCarthy's bad temper and irrational behavior flared. His bullying tactics and even apparent drunkenness were duly noted. Then on June 9 McCarthy confronted army counsel Joseph Welch with the fact that an attorney in his law firm, Fred Fisher, had once been a member of the National Lawyer's Guild, a group with Communist Party associations. Welch had excluded Fisher from the trial because he had known that McCarthy would use the information on his past to manipulate the trial. In his famous outburst—"Have you left no sense of decency?"—Welch brought home to the American audience the devious methods used by the senator.

McCarthy was cleared of the army's charges, but by the end of the year, the Senate voted to "condemn" him for contempt of a Senate elections subcommittee that had investigated his conduct and financial affairs in 1952 and for his abusive and insulting behavior toward several Senators. The McCarthy era was over.

Primary Source

"The Army-McCarthy Hearings" [excerpt]

SYNOPSIS: During the Army-McCarthy hearings, McCarthy's dramatic tactics fail him. When McCarthy accuses Joseph N. Welch, the army's highly respected counsel, of having an attorney on his staff who was once a member of the Lawyers Guild, a "communist front," Welch puts into perspective for the viewing audience what kind of upstanding people are being hurt by McCarthy's charges and how severe the repercussions of the McCarthy "witch-hunts" really are.

Secretary [of the Army] Stevens: Gentlemen of the committee, I am here today at the request of this committee. You have my assurance of the fullest cooperation.

In order that we may all be quite clear as to just why this hearing has come about, it is necessary for me to refer at the outset to Pvt. G. David Schine, a former consultant of this committee. David Schine was eligible for the draft. Efforts were made by the chairman of this committee, Senator Joseph R. McCarthy, and the subcommittee's chief counsel, Mr. Roy M. Cohn, to secure a commission for him. Mr. Schine was not qualified, and he was not commissioned. Selective service then drafted him. Subsequent efforts were made to seek preferential treatment for him after he was inducted.

Before getting into the Schine story I want to make two general comments.

First, it is my responsibility to speak for the Army. The Army is about a million and a half men and women, in posts across this country and around the world, on active duty and in the National Guard and Organized Reserves, plus hundreds of thousands of loyal and faithful civil servants.

Senator McCarthy: Mr. Chairman, a point of order.

Senator Mundt: Senator McCarthy has a point of order.

Senator McCarthy: Mr. Stevens is not speaking for the Army. He is speaking for Mr. Stevens, for Mr. Adams, and Mr. Hensel. The committee did not make the Army a party to this controversy, and I think it is highly improper to try to make the Army a party. Mr. Stevens can only speak for himself. . . .

All we were investigating has been some Communists in the Army, a very small percentage, I would say much less than 1 percent. And when the Secretary says that, in effect "I am speaking for the Army," he is putting the 99.9 percent of good, honorable, loyal men in the Army into the position of trying to oppose the exposure of Communists in the Army.

I think it should be made clear at the outset, so we need not waste time on it, hour after hour, that Mr. Stevens is speaking for Mr. Stevens and those who are speaking through him; when Mr. Adams speaks, he is speaking for Mr. Adams and those who are speaking through him, and likewise Mr. Hensel.

I may say I resent very, very much this attempt to connect the great American Army with this attempt to sabotage the efforts of this committee's investigation into communism. . . .

Mr. Welch: Mr. Cohn, what is the exact number of Communists or subversives that are loose today in these defense plants?

Mr. Cohn: The exact number that is loose, sir?

Mr. Welch: Yes, sir.

Mr. Cohn: I don't know.

Mr. Welch: Roughly how many?

Mr. Cohn: I can only tell you, sir, what we know about it.

Mr. Welch: That is 130, is that right?

Mr. Cohn: Yes, sir. . . .

Mr. Welch: Will you not, before the sun goes down, give those names to the FBI and at least have those men put under surveillance. . . .

Senator McCarthy: Mr. Chairman, let's not be ridiculous. Mr. Welch knows, as I have told him a dozen times, that the FBI has all of this information. The defense plants have the information. The only thing we can do is to try and publicly expose these individuals and hope that they will be gotten rid of. And you know that, Mr. Welch.

Mr. Welch: I do not know that. . . .

Cannot the FBI put these 130 men under surveillance before sundown tomorrow? . . .

Mr. Welch: Mr. Cohn, tell me once more: Every time you learn of a Communist or a spy anywhere, is it your policy to get them out as fast as possible? . . .

Mr. Welch: May I add my small voice, sir, and say whenever you know about a subversive or a Communist spy, please hurry. Will you remember those words? . . .

Senator McCarthy: . . . In view of Mr. Welch's request that the information be given once we know of anyone who might be performing any work for the Communist Party, I think we should tell him that he has in his law firm a young man named Fisher whom he recommended, incidentally, to do work on this committee, who has been for a number of years a member of an organization which was named, oh, years and years ago, as the legal bulwark of the Communist Party, an organization which always swings to the defense of anyone who dares to expose Communists. I certainly assume that Mr. Welch did not know of this young man at the time he recommended him as the assistant counsel for this committee, but he has such terror and such a great desire to know where anyone is located who may be serving the Communist cause, Mr. Welch, that I thought we should just call to your attention the fact that your Mr. Fisher, who is still in your law firm today, whom you asked to have down here looking over the secret and classified material, is a member of an organization, not named by me but named by various committees, named by the Attorney General, as I recall, and I think I quote this verbatim, as "the legal bulwark of the Communist Party." He belonged to that for a sizable number of years, according to his own admission, and he belonged to it long after it had been exposed as the legal arm of the Communist Party.

Knowing that, Mr. Welch, I just felt that I had a duty to respond to your urgent request that before sundown, when we know of anyone serving the Communist cause, we let the agency know. We are now letting you know that your man did belong to this organization for, either 3 or 4 years, belonged to it long after he was out of law school.

I don't think you can find anyplace, anywhere, an organization which has done more to defend Communists—I am again quoting the report—to defend Communists, to defend espionage agents, and to aid the Communist cause, than the man whom you originally wanted down here at your right hand instead of Mr. St. Clair.

I have hesitated bringing that up, but I have been rather bored with your phony requests to Mr. Cohn here that he personally get every Communist out of government before sundown. Therefore, we will give you information about the young man in your own organization.

I am not asking you at this time to explain why you tried to foist him on this committee. Whether you knew he was a member of that Communist organization or not, I don't know. I assume you did not, Mr. Welch, because I get the impression that, while you are quite an actor, you play for a laugh, I don't think you have any conception of the danger of the Communist Party. I don't think you yourself would ever knowingly aid the Communist cause. I think you are unknowingly aiding it when you try to burlesque this hearing in which we are attempting to bring out the facts, however. . . .

Mr. Welch: Mr. Chairman, under these circumstances I must have something approaching a personal privilege. . . .

Mr. Welch: Senator McCarthy, I think until this moment—

Senator McCarthy: Jim, will you get the news story to the effect that this man belonged to this Communist-front organization? Will you get the citations showing that this was the legal arm of the Communist Party, and the length of time that he belonged, and the fact that he was recommended by Mr. Welch? I think that should be in the record.

Mr. Welch: You won't need anything in the record when I have finished telling you this.

Until this moment, Senator, I think I never really gauged your cruelty or your recklessness. Fred Fisher is a young man who went to the Harvard Law School and came into my firm and is starting what looks to be a brilliant career with us.

When I decided to work for this committee I asked Jim St. Clair, who sits on my right, to be my first assistant. I said to Jim, "Pick somebody in the firm who works under you that you would like." He chose Fred Fisher and they came down on an afternoon plane. That night, when he had taken a little stab at trying to see what the case was about, Fred Fisher and Jim St. Clair and I went to dinner together. I then said to these two young men, "Boys, I don't know anything about you except I have always liked you, but if there is anything funny in the life of either one of you that would hurt anybody in this case you speak up quick."

Fred Fisher said, "Mr. Welch, when I was in law school and for a period of months after, I belonged to the Lawyers Guild," as you have suggested, Senator. He went on to say, "I am secretary of the Young Republicans League in Newton with the son of Massachusetts' Governor, and I have the respect and admiration of the 25 lawyers or so in Hale & Dorr."

I said, "Fred, I just don't think I am going to ask you to work on the case. If I do, one of these days that will come out and go over national television and it will just hurt like the dickens."

So, Senator, I asked him to go back to Boston.

Little did I dream you could be so reckless and cruel as to do an injury to that lad. It is true he is still with Hale & Dorr. It is true that he will continue to be with Hale & Dorr. It is, I regret to say, equally true that I fear he shall always bear a scar needlessly inflicted by you. If it were in my power to forgive you for your reckless cruelty, I will do so. I like to think I am a gentleman, but your forgiveness will have to come from someone other than me. . . .

Senator McCarthy: May I say that Mr. Welch talks about this being cruel and reckless. He was just baiting; he has been baiting Mr. Cohn here for hours, requesting that Mr. Cohn, before sundown, get out of any department of Government anyone who is serving the Communist cause.

I just give this man's record, and I want to say, Mr. Welch, that it has been labeled long before he became a member, as early as 1944—

Mr. Welch: Senator, may we not drop this? We know he belonged to the Lawyers Guild, and Mr. Cohn nods his head at me. I did you, I think, no personal injury, Mr. Cohn.

Mr. Cohn: No, sir.

Mr. Welch: I meant to do you no personal injury, and if I did, beg your pardon.

Let us not assassinate this lad further, Senator. You have done enough. Have you no sense of decency sir, at long last? Have you left no sense of decency?

Senator McCarthy: I know this hurts you, Mr. Welch. But I may say, Mr. Chairman, on a point of personal privilege, and I would like to finish it.—

Mr. Welch: Senator, I think it hurts you, too, sir.

Senator McCarthy: I would like to finish this.

Mr. Welch has been filibustering this hearing, he has been talking day after day about how he wants to get anyone tainted with communism out before sundown. I know Mr. Cohn would rather not have me go into this. I intend to, however, Mr. Welch talks about any sense of decency. If I say anything which is not the truth, then I would like to know about it.

The foremost legal bulwark of the Communist Party, its front organizations, and controlled unions, and which, since its inception, has never failed to rally to the legal defense of the Communist Party, and individual members thereof, including known espionage agents.

Now, that is not the language of Senator McCarthy. That is the language of the Un-American Activities Committee. And I can go on with many more citations. It seems that Mr. Welch is pained so deeply he thinks it is improper for me to give the record, the Communist front record, of the man whom he wanted to foist upon this committee. But it doesn't pain him at all—there is no pain in his chest about the unfounded charges against Mr. Frank Carr; there is no pain there about the attempt to destroy the reputation and take the jobs away

from the young men who were working in my committee.

And, Mr. Welch, if I have said anything here which is untrue, then tell me. I have heard you and every one else talk so much about laying the truth upon the table that when I hear—and it is completely phony, Mr. Welch, I have listened to you for a long time—when you say "Now, before sundown, you must get these people out of Government," I want to have it very clear, very clear that you were not so serious about that when you tried to recommend this man for this committee. . . .

Senator McCarthy: Let me ask Mr. Welch. You brought him down, did you not, to act as your assistant?

Mr. Welch: Mr. McCarthy, I will not discuss this with you further. You have sat within 6 feet of me, and could have asked me about Fred Fisher. You have brought it out. If there is a God in heaven, it will do neither you nor your cause any good. I will not discuss it further. . . .

Mr. Jenkins: Senator McCarthy, how do you regard the communistic threat to our Government as compared with other threats with which it is confronted?

Senator McCarthy: Mr. Jenkins, the thing that I think we must remember is that this is a war which a brutalitarian force has won to a greater extent than any brutalitarian force has won a war in the history of the world before.

Further Resources

BOOKS

Fried, Albert. *McCarthyism: The Great American Red Scare: A Documentary History.* New York: Oxford University Press, 1996.

Garber, Marjorie B., and Rebecca L. Walkowitz, eds. *Secret Agents: The Rosenberg Case, McCarthyism, and Fifties America.* New York: Routledge, 1995.

Heale, M.J. *McCarthy's Americans: Red Scare Politics in State and Nation, 1935–1965.* Athens, Ga.: University of Georgia Press, 1998.

Herman, Arthur. *Joseph McCarthy: Reexamining the Life and Legacy of America's Most Hated Senator.* New York: Free Press, 2000.

Reeves, Thomas C. *The Life and Times of Joe McCarthy: A Biography.* Lanham, Md.: Madison Books, 1997.

Rosteck, Thomas. *"See It Now" Confronts McCarthyism: Television Documentary and the Politics of Representation.* Tuscaloosa, Ala.: University of Alabama Press, 1994.

Schrecker, Ellen. *Many Are the Crimes: McCarthyism in America.* Boston: Little, Brown, 1998.

"Southern Manifesto"

Statement

By: Strom Thurmond, representing nineteen senators and seventy-seven members of the House of Representatives

Date: March 12, 1956

Source: Thurmond, Strom. "Southern Manifesto." Congressional Record, 84th Congress, Second Session. Vol. 102, part 4, March 12, 1956. Washington, D.C.: Governmental Printing Office, 1956, 4459–4460. Available online at http://www.toptags.com/aama/voices/speeches/sthmani.htm; website home page: http://www.toptags.com/aama/index.htm (accessed March 3, 2003).

About the Author: James Strom Thurmond (1902–2003) was a teacher and school superintendent in South Carolina before obtaining his law degree. He served South Carolina as a state senator before being elected governor in 1946. He ran for president as the Southern Democrat "Dixiecrat" candidate in 1948. In 1954 he won a write-in campaign to win election to the U.S Senate. In 1957, he spoke against the civil rights bill for twenty-four hours and eighteen minutes, setting a record for the longest filibuster in Senate history. He was also the longest-serving senator, retiring in 2002 at the age of 100. ∎

Introduction

When the federal courts ruled against racial segregation in *Brown v. Board of Education* in 1954, Southern leaders, wanting to nullify the ruling, raised the issue of states' rights. The rights and power of state governments over the federal government has long been disputed. Under the Articles of Confederation, which served as the constitution for Americans from 1781 until 1788, the states had more power than the federal government. Under the Constitution, the federal government clearly reigns supreme.

There have been several points in U.S. history when opposition to the supremacy of the federal government and a call for states' rights has been taken up by one political group or another. In 1798, the United States passed the *Alien and Sedition Act,* a group of repressive laws aimed largely at recent immigrants. In protest, various politicians promoted the Virginia and Kentucky Resolutions written by Thomas Jefferson and James Madison, which argued that states had the right to "nullify" unconstitutional federal laws. Later, in 1828, South Carolina returned to the idea of nullification to oppose what it called the "Tariff of Abominations," a tariff thought to favor Northern industry. Between 1850 and 1856, Northern states argued for nullification as a way to eliminate the hated Fugitive Slave Law, which made Northerners responsible for the return of escaped slaves to the South. Not surprisingly, Southern states were very much against nullification at that time.

The idea of nullification, or states having the power to overrule acts of Congress and the federal government, has come to be called "states' rights." Even though Southern states were against the most common use of states' rights in the 1850s, much mythology grew up in the decades after the Civil War (1861–1865) to the effect that the South fought the Civil War on behalf of states' rights.

The South had imposed a system of segregation on nearly all areas of life after the end of the Civil War and Reconstruction. The Supreme Court had approved this system in *Plessy v. Ferguson* (1896), holding that separate systems were allowable, as long as they were equal. The "separate but equal" system continued until *Brown v. Board of Education* (1954), in which the Supreme Court held that segregation in education was illegal. The South was outraged, believing that Southern leaders had the right to control their own educational systems, and many Southern politicians brought up "states' rights" as a defense. As an encapsulation of their ideas and protest, nearly all Southern congressmen jointly offered the Southern Manifesto, pledging "massive resistance" to integration in the South. In 1956, nineteen Southern senators and eighty-two members of the House of Representatives issued and signed the Southern Manifesto. Senator Strom Thurmond of South Carolina, who had run for president on a states' rights ticket in 1948, was largely credited with the creation and writing of the document. On March 12, 1956, Georgia Senator Walter F. George read it to Congress.

Significance

After the reading of the Southern Manifesto, the South adopted a variety of plans in order to implement their idea of "massive resistance" to the federally mandated racial integration of public schools. Seven states adopted, on a state level, resolutions declaring *Brown* unconstitutional. School boards adopted a variety of laws to thwart *Brown,* including laws allowing the redrawing of district lines to keep districts all white, laws allowing parents to send their children to private schools that were all white, "freedom of choice" plans allowing students to pick their schools, which were inevitably all white, and even closing some schools to prevent integration.

The most well-known clash over integration was in Little Rock, Arkansas, where Governor Orval Faubus used the Arkansas National Guard to block black students from entering a public school. When a court order removed the guard, a mob then prevented the students from entering. President Dwight D. Eisenhower (served 1953–1961) reluctantly sent in troops to force the desegregation. When the power of the Court's ruling over states was challenged in 1958, the Supreme Court ruled in *Cooper v. Aaron* that the states were in fact bound to uphold the Court's decisions in regard to *Brown. Cooper* was signed by all the justices (a quite unusual accord), resoundingly upholding the *Brown* decision. Desegregation proceeded slowly, though. In fact, by 1964 less than

2 percent of African American students in the former confederate states attended integrated schools.

The impact of the manifesto continued to be felt at the beginning of the twenty-first century. At the one-hundredth birthday party for James Strom Thurmond in December 2002, Senator Trent Lott made comments appearing to support Thurmond's 1950s position on segregation. Amid public uproar, Lott announced his resignation as Senate majority leader. This incident seems to indicate a large measure of public abhorrence for segregation, yet also the continued survival of racist attitudes. While legal segregation has been eliminated, factors such as residential segregation, school funding practices, and tracking perpetuate racial imbalances and inequities in schools into the fwenty-first century.

Primary Source

"Southern Manifesto"

> **SYNOPSIS:** The Southern Manifesto is a direct challenge to the Supreme Court, stating that the Court went too far in *Brown* and arguing that since all school systems existing at the time of the Fourteenth Amendment were segregated, that amendment allows segregated schools. The Manifesto claims to stand for reserved powers of the states and protection against the overzealous execution of federal judicial powers. It closes by asking the states to resist the application of *Brown* in any legal manner possible.

The Decision of the Supreme Court in the School Cases—Declaration of Constitutional Principles

Mr. President, the increasing gravity of the situation following the decision of the Supreme Court in the so-called segregation cases, and the peculiar stress in sections of the country where this decision has created many difficulties, unknown and unappreciated, perhaps, by many people residing in other parts of the country, have led some Senators and some Members of the House of Representatives to prepare a statement of the position which they have felt and now feel to be imperative.

I now wish to present to the Senate a statement on behalf of 19 Senators, representing 11 States, and 77 House Members, representing a considerable number of States likewise. . . .

Declaration of Constitutional Principles

The unwarranted decision of the Supreme Court in the public school cases is now bearing the fruit always produced when men substitute naked power for established law. The Founding Fathers gave us a Constitution of checks and balances because they realized the inescapable lesson of history that no man or group of men can be safely entrusted with unlimited power. They framed this Constitution with its provisions for change by amendment in order to secure the fundamentals of government against the dangers of temporary popular passion or the personal predilections of public officeholders.

We regard the decisions of the Supreme Court in the school cases as a clear abuse of judicial power. It climaxes a trend in the Federal Judiciary undertaking to legislate, in derogation of the authority of Congress, and to encroach upon the reserved rights of the States and the people.

The original Constitution does not mention education. Neither does the 14th Amendment nor any other amendment. The debates preceding the submission of the 14th Amendment clearly show that there was no intent that it should affect the system of education maintained by the States.

The very Congress which proposed the amendment subsequently provided for segregated schools in the District of Columbia.

When the amendment was adopted in 1868, there were 37 States of the Union. Every one of the 26 States that had any substantial racial differences among its people, either approved the operation of segregated schools already in existence or subsequently established such schools by action of the same law-making body which considered the 14th Amendment.

As admitted by the Supreme Court in the public school case (*Brown v. Board of Education*), the doctrine of separate but equal schools "apparently originated in *Roberts v. City of Boston* (1849), upholding school segregation against attack as being violative of a State constitutional guarantee of equality." This constitutional doctrine began in the North, not in the South, and it was followed not only in Massachusetts, but in Connecticut, New York, Illinois, Indiana, Michigan, Minnesota, New Jersey, Ohio, Pennsylvania and other northern states until they, exercising their rights as states through the constitutional processes of local self-government, changed their school systems.

In the case of *Plessy v. Ferguson* in 1896 the Supreme Court expressly declared that under the 14th Amendment no person was denied any of his rights if the States provided separate but equal facilities. This decision has been followed in many other cases. It is notable that the Supreme Court, speaking through Chief Justice Taft, a former President of the United States, unanimously declared in 1927 in *Lum v. Rice* that the "separate but equal" principle is "within the discretion of the State in regulating its public schools and does not conflict with the 14th Amendment."

This interpretation, restated time and again, became a part of the life of the people of many of the States and confirmed their habits, traditions, and way of life. It is founded on elemental humanity and commonsense, for parents should not be deprived by Government of the right to direct the lives and education of their own children.

Though there has been no constitutional amendment or act of Congress changing this established legal principle almost a century old, the Supreme Court of the United States, with no legal basis for such action, undertook to exercise their naked judicial power and substituted their personal political and social ideas for the established law of the land.

This unwarranted exercise of power by the Court, contrary to the Constitution, is creating chaos and confusion in the States principally affected. It is destroying the amicable relations between the white and Negro races that have been created through 90 years of patient effort by the good people of both races. It has planted hatred and suspicion where there has been heretofore friendship and understanding.

Without regard to the consent of the governed, outside mediators are threatening immediate and revolutionary changes in our public schools systems. If done, this is certain to destroy the system of public education in some of the States.

With the gravest concern for the explosive and dangerous condition created by this decision and inflamed by outside meddlers:

We reaffirm our reliance on the Constitution as the fundamental law of the land.

We decry the Supreme Court's encroachment on the rights reserved to the States and to the people, contrary to established law, and to the Constitution.

We commend the motives of those States which have declared the intention to resist forced integration by any lawful means.

We appeal to the States and people who are not directly affected by these decisions to consider the constitutional principles involved against the time when they too, on issues vital to them may be the victims of judicial encroachment.

Even though we constitute a minority in the present Congress, we have full faith that a majority of

Senator Walter F. George delivered the Southern Manifesto to Congress on March 12, 1956. **AP/WIDE WORLD PHOTOS. REPRODUCED BY PERMISSION.**

the American people believe in the dual system of government which has enabled us to achieve our greatness and will in time demand that the reserved rights of the States and of the people be made secure against judicial usurpation.

We pledge ourselves to use all lawful means to bring about a reversal of this decision which is contrary to the Constitution and to prevent the use of force in its implementation.

In this trying period, as we all seek to right this wrong, we appeal to our people not to be provoked by the agitators and troublemakers invading our States and to scrupulously refrain from disorder and lawless acts.

Signed by:

Members of the United States Senate

Walter F. George, Richard B. Russell, John Stennis, Sam J. Elvin, Jr., Strom Thurmond, Harry F. Byrd,

A. Willis Robertson, John L. McClellan, Allen J. Ellender, Russell B. Long, Lister Hill, James O. Eastland, W. Kerr Scott, John Sparkman, Olin D. Johnston, Price Daniel, J.W. Fulbright, George A. Smathers, Spessard L. Holland.

Members of the United States House of Representatives

Alabama: Frank W. Boykin, George M. Grant, George W. Andrews, Kenneth A. Roberts, Albert Rains, Armistead I. Selden, Jr., Carl Elliott, Robert E. Jones, George Huddleston, Jr.

Arkansas: E.C. Gathings, Wilbur D. Mills, James W. Trimble, Oren Harris, Brooks Hays, W.F. Norrell.

Florida: Charles E. Bennett, Robert L.F. Sikes, A.S. Herlong, Jr., Paul G. Rogers, James A. Haley, D.R. Matthews.

Georgia: Prince H. Preston, John L. Pilcher, E.L. Forrester, John James Flynt, Jr., James C. Davis, Carl Vinson, Henderson Lanham, Iris F. Blitch, Phil M. Landrum, Paul Brown.

Louisiana: F. Edward Hebert, Hale Boggs, Edwin E. Willis, Overton Brooks, Otto E. Passman, James H. Morrison, T. Ashton Thompson, George S. Long.

Mississippi: Thomas G. Abernathy, Jamie L. Whitten, Frank E. Smith, John Bell Williams, Arthur Winstead, William M. Colmer.

North Carolina: Herbert C. Bonner, L.H. Fountain, Graham A. Barden, Carl T. Durham, F. Ertel Carlyle, Hugh Q. Alexander, Woodrow W. Jones, George A. Shuford.

South Carolina: L. Mendel Rivers, John J. Riley, W.J. Bryan Dorn, Robert T. Ashmore, James P. Richards, John L. McMillan.

Tennessee: James B. Frazier, Jr., Tom Murray, Jere Cooper, Clifford Davis.

Texas: Wright Patman, John Dowdy, Walter Rogers, O.C. Fisher, Martin Dies.

Virginia: Edward J. Robeson, Jr., Porter Hardy, Jr., J. Vaughan Gary, Watkins M. Abbitt, William M. Tuck, Richard H. Poff, Burr P. Harrison, Howard W. Smith, W. Pat Jennings, Joel T. Broyhill.

Further Resources

BOOKS

Bartley, Numan V. *The Rise of Massive Resistance: Race and Politics in the South During the 1950's.* Baton Rouge, La.: Louisiana State University Press, 1969.

Lassiter, Matthew D., and Andrew B Lewis, eds. *The Moderates' Dilemma: Massive Resistance to School Desegregation in Virginia.* Charlottesville, Va.: University Press of Virginia, 1998.

Leidholdt, Alexander. *Standing Before the Shouting Mob: Lenoir Chambers and Virginia's Massive Resistance to Public-School Integration.* Tuscaloosa, Ala.: University of Alabama Press, 1997.

Modlin, Carolyn Carter. "The Desegregation of Southampton County, Virginia Schools, 1954–1970." Dissertation, Virginia Tech, 1998. Available online at http://scholar.lib.vt .edu/theses/available/etd-121098-154942 (accessed March 3, 2003).

Patterson, James T. *"Brown v. Board of Education": A Civil Rights Milestone and Its Troubled Legacy.* Oxford: Oxford University Press, 2001.

Wilson, Paul E. *"Brown v. Board of Education of Topeka: A Personal Perspective."* In *Kansas Revisited.* 2nd ed. Lawrence, Kans.: Division of Continuing Education, University of Kansas, 1998, 347–359.

Yates v. U.S.

Supreme Court decision

By: John Marshall Harlan

Date: June 17, 1957

Source: Harlan, John Marshall. *Yates v. United States,* 354 U.S. 298 (1957). Available online at http://caselaw.lp .findlaw.com/scripts/getcase.pl?court=US&vol=403 &invol=15; website home page: http://www.findlaw.com (accessed March 5, 2003).

About the Author: John Marshall Harlan (1899–1971) was grandson and namesake of another Supreme Court justice, who served from 1877 to 1911. Harlan attended Princeton University as a Rhodes scholar and earned a law degree at New York University. In 1955 he was appointed to the Supreme Court by President Dwight D. Eisenhower (served 1953–1961). Harlan believed that federal courts should not interfere unnecessarily in state and local matters, but in several important cases he upheld the majority's defense of civil rights. ■

Introduction

The First Amendment, which established freedom of speech, only specifically limited the federal government's powers to control speech and was not always perceived to control the states. Through much of early U.S. history, the federal government left most free speech issues to local governments, which enacted various laws to control what was said and written. These laws generally did not become constitutional issues. In the early twentieth century, though, there was increasing concern about threats from outside America. As these concerns grew, so did laws aiming to control speech. For instance, during World War I (1914–1918), the U.S. government itself passed several laws prohibiting people from interfering with the war effort. The only real victory for free speech was in 1925 when the Supreme Court held that the First Amendment applied to the states due to the Fourteenth Amendment, which says: "No State shall make or enforce any law which shall abridge the privileges or immunities of citizens of the United States; nor shall any State deprive any person of life, liberty, or property, without due process of law; nor deny to any person within its jurisdiction the equal protection of the laws."

In 1940, the U.S. government passed the *Smith Act,* which made it illegal to advocate or organize the violent overthrow of the government. This law was used in the late 1940s against a number of communist leaders—not for doing anything to overthrow the government, but for advocating communist doctrine. These efforts were upheld in 1951 in the case *Dennis v. U.S.,* which held that merely advocating that the government should be overthrown was enough to merit conviction. *Dennis* came to the Supreme Court at a time when the people of the United States were quite worried about the communist threat from the Soviet Union.

Six years later, when the threat had abated somewhat, the *Smith Act* once again came before the Supreme Court. In 1951, Oleta Yates and 13 other members of the U.S. Communist Party in California were convicted of violating the *Smith Act* by teaching the necessity of the forcible overthrow of the government. Yates claimed that she and her cohorts in the Communist Party were engaged in *passive* actions, while a violation of the *Smith Act* involves *active* attempts to overthrow the government. The Supreme Court agreed.

Significance

The Supreme Court in *Yates* held that mere advocacy of an idea was not illegal, but that one had to advocate a specific illegal act. Communist leaders could no longer be prosecuted for simply being communists and expressing the idea that the U.S. government should be overthrown, but had to advocate specific illegal action to overthrow the government. This reduced prosecution under the *Smith Act* to almost nothing. In the six years between *Dennis* and *Yates,* more than 100 communists were convicted; after *Yates,* there were few convictions. The Supreme Court also held that the U.S. government generally could not make communist party members register with the government. These decisions greatly increased Americans' freedom of speech and freedom of association. They also eased the way for civil rights groups, as registration was no longer required and it was more difficult to prosecute those who advocated "unwelcome" ideas, which, for much of the white South, included civil rights.

The Supreme Court continued to expand the ideas of free speech and free expression. In *Brandenburg v. Ohio* (1969), the Court ruled that only speech aimed at producing or inciting "imminent lawless action" or likely to produce or incite such action could be prosecuted under

the *Smith Act.* This greatly expanded upon *Dennis* and *Yates* and similar cases where the Court had held that a "clear and present danger" had to be present to permit the suppression of speech. The *Brandenburg* standard has continued to be upheld. The Supreme Court has steadfastly overturned laws banning flag burning and certain laws banning the burning of crosses. Focusing on the expression of one point of view, these laws violated the First Amendment's provision for freedom of speech for all viewpoints.

Primary Source

Yates v. U.S. [excerpt]

> **SYNOPSIS:** Justice John M. Harlan holds that advocacy of the type banned by the *Smith Act* does not mean mere discussion of illegal action, but means advocacy of a specific illegal act. Thus, the defendants in *Yates,* convicted under the former definition of advocacy, must have their convictions overturned. He reaffirms *Dennis,* holding that an individual must advocate the overthrow of government by forcible action to be convicted.

Mr. Justice Harlan delivered the opinion of the Court. . . .

In the view we take of this case, it is necessary for us to consider only the following of petitioners' contentions: (1) that the term "organize" as used in the Smith Act was erroneously construed by the two lower courts; (2) that the trial court's instructions to the jury erroneously excluded from the case the issue of "incitement to action"; (3) that the evidence was so insufficient as to require this Court to direct the acquittal of these petitioners; and (4) [that one of the defendant's convictions was precluded by a prior Court decision]. . . . For reasons given hereafter, we conclude that these convictions must be reversed and the case remanded to the District Court with instructions to enter judgments of acquittal as to certain of the petitioners, and to grant a new trial as to the rest.

I. The Term "Organize"

. . . Petitioners claim that "organize" means to "establish," "found," or "bring into existence," and that in this sense the Communist Party was organized by 1945 at the latest. On this basis petitioners contend that this part of the indictment, returned in 1951, was barred by the three-year statute of limitations. The Government, on the other hand, says that "organize" connotes a continuing process which goes on throughout the life of an organization, and that, in the words of the trial court's instructions to the jury, the term includes such things as "the recruiting of new members and the forming of new units, and the regrouping or expansion of existing clubs, classes and other units of any society, party, group or other organization." The two courts below accepted the Government's position. We think, however, that petitioners' position must prevail. . . .

We conclude, therefore, that since the Communist Party came into being in 1945, and the indictment was not returned until 1951, the three-year statute of limitations had run on the "organizing" charge, and required the withdrawal of that part of the indictment from the jury's consideration. . . .

II. Instructions to the Jury

Petitioners contend that the instructions to the jury were fatally defective in that the trial court refused to charge that, in order to convict, the jury must find that the advocacy which the defendants conspired to promote was of a kind calculated to "incite" persons to action for the forcible overthrow of the Government. . . .

We are thus faced with the question whether the *Smith Act* prohibits advocacy and teaching of forcible overthrow as an abstract principle, divorced from any effort to instigate action to that end, so long as such advocacy or teaching is engaged in with evil intent. We hold that it does not.

The distinction between advocacy of abstract doctrine and advocacy directed at promoting unlawful action is one that has been consistently recognized in the opinions of this Court. . . .

We need not, however, decide the issue before us in terms of constitutional compulsion, for our first duty is to construe this statute. In doing so we should not assume that Congress chose to disregard a constitutional danger zone so clearly marked, or that it used the words "advocate" and "teach" in their ordinary dictionary meanings when they had already been construed as terms of art carrying a special and limited connotation. . . . The legislative history of the *Smith Act* and related bills shows beyond all question that Congress was aware of the distinction between the advocacy or teaching of abstract doctrine and the advocacy or teaching of action, and that it did not intend to disregard it. The statute was aimed at the advocacy and teaching of concrete action for the forcible overthrow of the Government, and not of principles divorced from action.

The Government's reliance on this Court's decision in *Dennis* is misplaced. . . .

In failing to distinguish between advocacy of forcible overthrow as an abstract doctrine and advocacy of action to that end, the District Court appears to have been led astray by the holding in *Dennis* that advocacy of violent action to be taken at some future time was enough. It seems to have considered that, since "inciting" speech is usually thought of as something calculated to induce immediate action, and since *Dennis* held advocacy of action for future overthrow sufficient, this meant that advocacy, irrespective of its tendency to generate action, is punishable, provided only that it is uttered with a specific intent to accomplish overthrow. In other words, the District Court apparently thought that *Dennis* obliterated the traditional dividing line between advocacy of abstract doctrine and advocacy of action.

This misconceives the situation confronting the Court in *Dennis* and what was held there. Although the jury's verdict, interpreted in light of the trial court's instructions, did not justify the conclusion that the defendants' advocacy was directed at, or created any danger of, immediate overthrow, it did establish that the advocacy was aimed at building up a seditious group and maintaining it in readiness for action at a propitious time. In such circumstances, said Chief Justice Vinson, the Government need not hold its hand "until the putsch is about to be executed, the plans have been laid and the signal is awaited. If Government is aware that a group aiming at its overthrow is attempting to indoctrinate its members and to commit them to a course whereby they will strike when the leaders feel the circumstances permit, action by the Government is required." . . . The essence of the *Dennis* holding was that indoctrination of a group in preparation for future violent action, as well as exhortation to immediate action, by advocacy found to be directed to "action for the accomplishment" of forcible overthrow, to violence as "a rule—or principle of action," and employing "language of incitement," . . . is not constitutionally protected when the group is of sufficient size and cohesiveness, is sufficiently oriented towards action, and other circumstances are such as reasonably to justify apprehension that action will occur. This is quite a different thing from the view of the District Court here that mere doctrinal justification of forcible overthrow, if engaged in with the intent to accomplish overthrow, is punishable per se under the *Smith Act*. That sort of advocacy, even though uttered with the hope that it may ultimately lead to violent revolution, is too remote from concrete action to be regarded as the kind of indoctrination preparatory to action which was condemned in *Dennis*. As one of the concurring opinions in *Dennis* put it: "Throughout our decisions there has recurred a distinction between the statement of an idea which may prompt its hearers to take unlawful action, and advocacy that such action be taken." . . . There is nothing in *Dennis* which makes that historic distinction obsolete. . . .

In light of the foregoing we are unable to regard the District Court's charge upon this aspect of the case as adequate. The jury was never told that the *Smith Act* does not denounce advocacy in the sense of preaching abstractly the forcible overthrow of the Government. We think that the trial court's statement that the proscribed advocacy must include the "urging," "necessity," and "duty" of forcible overthrow, and not merely its "desirability" and "propriety," may not be regarded as a sufficient substitute for charging that the *Smith Act* reaches only advocacy of action for the overthrow of government by force and violence. The essential distinction is that those to whom the advocacy is addressed must be urged to do something, now or in the future, rather than merely to believe in something. At best the expressions used by the trial court were equivocal, since in the absence of any instructions differentiating advocacy of abstract doctrine from advocacy of action, they were as consistent with the former as they were with the latter. Nor do we regard their ambiguity as lessened by what the trial court had to say as to the right of the defendants to announce their beliefs as to the inevitability of violent revolution, or to advocate other unpopular opinions. Especially when it is unmistakable that the court did not consider the urging of action for forcible overthrow as being a necessary element of the proscribed advocacy, but rather considered the crucial question to be whether the advocacy was uttered with a specific intent to accomplish such overthrow, we would not be warranted in assuming that the jury drew from these instructions more than the court itself intended them to convey. . . .

We recognize that distinctions between advocacy or teaching of abstract doctrines, with evil intent, and that which is directed to stirring people to action, are often subtle and difficult to grasp, for in a broad sense, as Mr. Justice Holmes said in his dissenting opinion in *Gitlow:* "Every idea is an incitement." But the very subtlety of these distinctions required the most clear and explicit instructions with reference to them, for they concerned an issue which went to the very heart of the charges against these petitioners. The need for precise and understandable instructions on this issue is further emphasized by the equivocal character of the evidence in this record, with which we deal in Part III of this opinion. Instances of speech

Oleta Yates speaks to dock workers in San Francisco.
© BETTMANN/CORBIS. REPRODUCED BY PERMISSION.

that could be considered to amount to "advocacy of action" are so few and far between as to be almost completely overshadowed by the hundreds of instances in the record in which overthrow, if mentioned at all, occurs in the course of doctrinal disputation so remote from action as to be almost wholly lacking in probative value. Vague references to "revolutionary" or "militant" action of an unspecified character, which are found in the evidence, might in addition be given too great weight by the jury in the absence of more precise instructions. Particularly in light of this record, we must regard the trial court's charge in this respect as furnishing wholly inadequate guidance to the jury on this central point in the case. We cannot allow a conviction to stand on such "an equivocal direction to the jury on a basic issue." . . .

The judgment of the Court of Appeals is reversed, and the case remanded to the District Court for further proceedings consistent with this opinion.

It is so ordered.

Further Resources
BOOKS
In Memoriam, Honorable John Marshall Harlan: Proceedings of the Bar and Officers of the Supreme Court of the United

States. Washington, D.C.: United States Supreme Court, 1972.

Powe, L.A. Scot. *The Warren Court and American Politics.* Cambridge, Mass.: Belknap Press of Harvard University Press, 2000.

Schwartz, Bernard. *The Warren Court: A Retrospective.* New York: Oxford University Press, 1996.

Yarbrough, Tinsley E. *John Marshall Harlan: Great Dissenter of the Warren Court.* New York: Oxford University Press, 1992.

PERIODICALS

Farber, Daniel A., and John E. Nowak. "Justice Harlan and the First Amendment." *Constitutional Commentary* 2, no. 2, Summer 1985, 425–462.

Lewin, Nathan. "Justice Harlan: 'The Full Measure of the Man.'" *American Bar Association Journal* 58, no. 6, June 1972, 579–583.

Lumbard, J. Edward. "John Harlan: In Public Service, 1925–1971." *Harvard Law Review* 85, no. 2, December 1971, 372–376.

WEBSITES

Civil Liberties Docket, Vol. 3, No. 1. October 1957. Meiklejohn Civil Liberties Institute Archives. Available online at http://sunsite.berkeley.edu/meiklejohn/meik-3_1/meik-3_1-2 .html; website home page: http://bancroft.berkeley.edu /collections/meiklejohn/project.html (accessed March 5, 2003).

Watkins v. U.S.

Supreme Court decision

By: Earl Warren

Date: June 17, 1957

Source: Warren, Earl. *Watkins v. United States,* 354 U.S. 178 (1957). Available online at http://caselaw.lp.findlaw.com /scripts/getcase.pl?court=US&vol=354&invol=178; website home page: http://www.findlaw.com (accessed March 5, 2003).

About the Author: Earl Warren (1891–1974) received his bachelor's degree from the University of California in 1912 and his law degree there two years later. After three years in private practice, he joined the army in 1917, then began a career in government as deputy city attorney for Oakland. From 1945 to 1953, he was governor of California. He became chief justice of the U.S. Supreme Court in 1953, a position he held until 1969. The Warren Court is synonymous with expansion of civil rights and civil liberties. ∎

Introduction

After World War II (1939–1945), the United States found itself facing a new enemy: the Soviet Union. Although the Soviets were an ally during the war, the nation had negotiated so much power afterwards that many Westerners feared it would attempt to conquer the world. The Cold War began when the alliance with the Soviets turned into a bitter rivalry. When the Soviet Union unexpectedly exploded its own atomic bomb in 1949, the United States feared a nuclear attack. Convinced there were Soviet spies all over the United States, the U.S. government assigned many different agencies to ferret out the communists within. Congress expanded its House Un-American Activities Committee (HUAC), giving that congressional agency broad powers to investigate anyone it believed to have ties to communism. HUAC was relentless in its pursuits and notably attacked Hollywood, forcing hundreds out of the business with its blacklist and sending others to jail.

HUAC's investigative process was often considered abusive and unfair. It did not matter whether a suspect being questioned by HUAC had been a member of an organization with slight communist connections twenty years ago or was a current member. Suspects were asked: "Are you now, or have you ever been, a member of the Communist Party?" If the accused answered yes, he or she was asked to "name names" of associates who had been involved with them. The options were grim. If suspects lied, they could be indicted for perjury; if they refused to name names, they could be indicted for contempt; if they informed on friends and associates, they knew they were ruining more lives—and during this era, many careers and lives were destroyed in this manner.

As public protest against HUAC and its methods mounted, the issue of HUAC's authority appeared several times before the Supreme Court, which initially upheld the power of the committee. One of the later cases challenging HUAC's authority was *Watkins v. U.S.* John T. Watkins had been called to testify before HUAC. He had freely answered the committee's questions about his own activities, but he refused to name names and invoked the First Amendment, claiming that his freedom of expression was being infringed and that there was no basis for the committee to ask the questions. He was convicted of a misdemeanor, contempt of court, for his refusal to answer.

Significance

This Supreme Court decision, upholding the right of witnesses in certain circumstances to refuse to answer questions posed by HUAC, was one of the first decisions to place significant limitation on that committee. Chief Justice Earl Warren stated that the Court deemed the resolution creating HUAC to be too vague and so violated the due process clause of the Fifth Amendment. Most importantly, the Court ruled that, in order to demand an answer during a committee inquiry, the questioner on the committee had to demonstrate the need for the question to be asked and the question asked had to relate to a specific constitutionally granted function of Congress. These were revolutionary controls upon congressional committees.

After *Watkins,* the Supreme Court upheld several contempt citations from HUAC and similar committees. In some of those cases, the Court argued that the end of preserving the country justified any means. But as the anticommunist hysteria of the Cold War eased over the years, the Court greatly limited the intrusive methods that had been used by HUAC and other congressional investigative committees.

Primary Source

Watkins v. U.S. [excerpt]

SYNOPSIS: Chief Justice Earl Warren argues that Congress has broad powers to investigate, that people should generally cooperate, and that the courts must balance Congress's right to investigate versus individual rights. Warren next examines HUAC's charter, holding that Congress did not give it a clear mission and that this overbroad mission too easily leads to individual rights being trampled, especially since people do not know what is being investigated. Thus, the questions were not permissible and the contempt charges voided.

Mr. Chief Justice Warren delivered the opinion of the Court. . . .

We start with several basic premises on which there is general agreement. The power of the Congress to conduct investigations is inherent in the legislative process. That power is broad. . . . But, broad as is this power of inquiry, it is not unlimited. . . .

It is unquestionably the duty of all citizens to cooperate with the Congress in its efforts to obtain the facts needed for intelligent legislative action. It is their unremitting obligation to respond to subpoenas, to respect the dignity of the Congress and its committees and to testify . . . fully with respect to matters within the province of proper investigation. This, of course, assumes that the constitutional rights of witnesses will be respected by the Congress as they are in a court of justice. The Bill of Rights is applicable to investigations as to all forms of governmental action. Witnesses cannot be compelled to give evidence against themselves. They cannot be subjected to unreasonable search and seizure. Nor can the First Amendment freedoms of speech, press, religion, or political belief and association be abridged. . . .

A far more difficult task evolved from the claim by witnesses that the committees' interrogations were infringements upon the freedoms of the First Amendment. Clearly, an investigation is subject to the command that the Congress shall make no law abridging freedom of speech or press or assembly. While it is true that there is no statute to be reviewed, and that an investigation is not a law, nevertheless an investigation is part of lawmaking. It is justified solely as an adjunct to the legislative process. The First Amendment may be invoked against infringement of the protected freedoms by law or by lawmaking.

Abuses of the investigative process may imperceptibly lead to abridgment of protected freedoms. The mere summoning of a witness and compelling him to testify, against his will, about his beliefs, expressions or associations is a measure of governmental interference. And when those forced revelations concern matters that are unorthodox, unpopular, or even hateful to the general public, the reaction in the life of the witness may be disastrous. This effect is even more harsh when it is past beliefs, expressions or associations that are disclosed and judged by current standards rather than those contemporary with the matters exposed. Nor does the witness alone suffer the consequences. Those who are identified by witnesses and thereby placed in the same glare of publicity are equally subject to public stigma, scorn and obloquy. Beyond that, there is the more subtle and immeasurable effect upon those who tend to adhere to the most orthodox and uncontroversial views and associations in order to avoid a similar fate at some future time. That this impact is partly the result of non-governmental activity by private persons cannot relieve the investigators of their responsibility for initiating the reaction. . . .

Accommodation of the congressional need for particular information with the individual and personal interest in privacy is an arduous and delicate task for any court. We do not underestimate the difficulties that would attend such an undertaking. It is manifest that despite the adverse effects which follow upon compelled disclosure of private matters, not all such inquiries are barred. . . . The critical element is the existence of, and the weight to be ascribed to, the interest of the Congress in demanding disclosures from an unwilling witness. We cannot simply assume, however, that every congressional investigation is justified by a public need that overbalances any private rights affected. To do so would be to abdicate the responsibility placed by the Constitution upon the judiciary to insure that the Congress does not unjustifiably encroach upon an individual's right to privacy nor abridge his liberty of speech, press, religion or assembly. . . .

Members of the Hollywood industry who were suspected of communist activities were probed by the House Un-American Activities Committee.
© BETTMANN/CORBIS. REPRODUCED BY PERMISSION.

An essential premise in this situation is that the House or Senate shall have instructed the committee members on what they are to do with the power delegated to them. . . . The more vague the committee's charter is, the greater becomes the possibility that the committee's specific actions are not in conformity with the will of the parent House of Congress.

The authorizing resolution of the Un-American Activities Committee was adopted in 1938 when a select committee, under the chairmanship of Representative Dies, was created. Several years later, the Committee was made a standing organ of the House with the same mandate. It defines the Committee's authority as follows:

> The Committee on Un-American Activities, as a whole or by subcommittee, is authorized to make from time to time investigations of (1) the extent, character, and objects of un-American propaganda activities in the United States, (2) the diffusion within the United States of subversive and un-American propaganda that is instigated from foreign countries or of a domestic origin and attacks the principle of the form of government as guaranteed by our Constitution, and (3) all other questions in re-

lation thereto that would aid Congress in any necessary remedial legislation.

It would be difficult to imagine a less explicit authorizing resolution. Who can define the meaning of "un-American"? What is that single, solitary "principle of the form of government as guaranteed by our Constitution"? There is no need to dwell upon the language, however. At one time, perhaps, the resolution might have been read narrowly to confine the Committee to the subject of propaganda. The events that have transpired in the fifteen years before the interrogation of petitioner make such a construction impossible at this date. . . .

Combining the language of the resolution with the construction it has been given, it is evident that the preliminary control of the Committee exercised by the House of Representatives is slight or nonexistent. No one could reasonably deduce from the charter the kind of investigation that the Committee was directed to make. As a result, we are asked to engage in a process of retroactive rationalization. Looking backward from the events that transpired, we are asked to uphold the Committee's actions unless it appears that they were clearly not authorized by the charter. As a corollary to this inverse approach, the Government urges that we must view the matter hospitably to the power of the Congress—that if there is any legislative purpose which might have been furthered by the kind of disclosure sought, the witness must be punished for withholding it. No doubt every reasonable indulgence of legality must be accorded to the actions of a coordinate branch of our Government. But such deference cannot yield to an unnecessary and unreasonable dissipation of precious constitutional freedoms.

The Government contends that the public interest at the core of the investigations of the Un-American Activities Committee is the need by the Congress to be informed of efforts to overthrow the Government by force and violence so that adequate legislative safeguards can be erected. From this core, however, the Committee can radiate outward infinitely to any topic thought to be related in some way to armed insurrection. The outer reaches of this domain are known only by the content of "un-American activities." . . .

The consequences that flow from this situation are manifold. . . . The Committee is allowed, in essence, to define its own authority, to choose the direction and focus of its activities. In deciding what to do with the power that has been conferred upon them, members of the Committee may act pursuant to motives that seem to them to be the highest. Their decisions, nevertheless, can lead to ruthless exposure of private lives in order to gather data that is neither desired by the Congress nor useful to it. Yet it is impossible in this circumstance, with constitutional freedoms in jeopardy, to declare that the Committee has ranged beyond the area committed to it by its parent assembly because the boundaries are so nebulous.

More important and more fundamental than that, however, it insulates the House that has authorized the investigation from the witnesses who are subjected to the sanctions of compulsory process. There is a wide gulf between the responsibility for the use of investigative power and the actual exercise of that power. This is an especially vital consideration in assuring respect for constitutional liberties. Protected freedoms should not be placed in danger in the absence of a clear determination by the House or the Senate that a particular inquiry is justified by a specific legislative need.

It is, of course, not the function of this Court to prescribe rigid rules for the Congress to follow in drafting resolutions establishing investigating committees. . . . An excessively broad charter, like that of the House Un-American Activities Committee, places the courts in an untenable position if they are to strike a balance between the public need for a particular interrogation and the right of citizens to carry on their affairs free from unnecessary governmental interference. It is impossible in such a situation to ascertain whether any legislative purpose justifies the disclosures sought and, if so, the importance of that information to the Congress in furtherance of its legislative function. The reason no court can make this critical judgment is that the House of Representatives itself has never made it. Only the legislative assembly initiating an investigation can assay the relative necessity of specific disclosures. . . .

In fulfillment of their obligation under this statute, the courts must accord to the defendants every right which is guaranteed to defendants in all other criminal cases. Among these is the right to have available, through a sufficiently precise statute, information revealing the standard of criminality before the commission of the alleged offense. . . . this raises a special problem in that the statute defines the crime as refusal to answer "any question pertinent to the question under inquiry." Part of the standard of criminality, therefore, is the pertinency of the questions propounded to the witness.

The problem attains proportion when viewed from the standpoint of the witness who appears before a congressional committee. He must decide at the time the questions are propounded whether or not to answer. . . . An erroneous determination on his part, even if made in the utmost good faith, does not exculpate him if the court should later rule that the questions were pertinent to the question under inquiry.

It is obvious that a person compelled to make this choice is entitled to have knowledge of the subject to which the interrogation is deemed pertinent. That knowledge must be available with the same degree of explicitness and clarity that the Due Process Clause requires in the expression of any element of a criminal offense. The "vice of vagueness" must be avoided here as in all other crimes. There are several sources that can outline the "question under inquiry" in such a way that the rules against vagueness are satisfied. The authorizing resolution, the remarks of the chairman or members of the committee, or even the nature of the proceedings themselves, might sometimes make the topic clear. This case demonstrates, however, that these sources often leave the matter in grave doubt. . . .

. . . Fundamental fairness demands that no witness be compelled to make such a determination with so little guidance. Unless the subject matter has been made to appear with undisputable clarity, it is the duty of the investigative body, upon objection of the witness on grounds of pertinency, to state for the record the subject under inquiry at that time and the manner in which the propounded questions are pertinent thereto. To be meaningful, the explanation must describe what the topic under inquiry is and the connective reasoning whereby the precise questions asked relate to it. . . .

We are mindful of the complexities of modern government and the ample scope that must be left to the Congress as the sole constitutional depository of legislative power. . . . A measure of added care on the part of the House and the Senate in authorizing the use of compulsory process and by their committees in exercising that power would suffice. That is a small price to pay if it serves to uphold the principles of limited, constitutional government without constricting the power of the Congress to inform itself.

The judgment of the Court of Appeals is reversed, and the case is remanded to the District Court with instructions to dismiss the indictment.

It is so ordered.

Further Resources

BOOKS

Cray, Ed. *Chief Justice: A Biography of Earl Warren.* New York: Simon and Schuster, 1997.

Horwitz, Morton J. *The Warren Court and the Pursuit of Justice: A Critical Issue.* New York: Hill and Wang, 1998.

Powe, L.A. Scot. *The Warren Court and American Politics.* Cambridge, Mass.: Belknap Press of Harvard University Press, 2000.

Schwartz, Bernard. *The Warren Court: A Retrospective.* New York: Oxford University Press, 1996.

Urofsky, Melvin I. *The Warren Court: Justices, Rulings, and Legacy.* Santa Barbara, Calif.: ABC-CLIO, 2001.

Warren, Earl. *The Memoirs of Earl Warren.* Garden City, N.Y.: Doubleday, 1977.

WEBSITES

Gallagher, Susan E. "The History of Privacy in the United States." The Privacy Archive. Available online at http://faculty.uml.edu/sgallagher/ThePrivacyArchive.htm (accessed March 5, 2003).

Roth v. U.S.

Supreme Court decision

By: William J. Brennan Jr., William O. Douglas

Date: June 24, 1957

Source: Brennan, Jr., William J. and William O. Douglas. *Roth v. United States* 354 U.S. 476 (1957). Available online at http://caselaw.lp.findlaw.com/scripts/getcase.pl?court=US&vol=354&invol=476; website home page: http://www.findlaw.com (accessed March 5, 2003).

About the Authors: William J. Brennan Jr. (1906–1997) graduated from Harvard Law School and practiced labor law before service in World War II (1939–1945), where he became a colonel. He was appointed to New Jersey's highest court in 1952 and to the Supreme Court in 1957. Brennan was a strong defender of civil rights, equal representation, prisoners' rights, and free speech and was an opponent of the death penalty. William O. Douglas (1898–1980) chaired the Securities and Exchange Commission in 1939, when he became, at forty, one of the youngest men ever appointed to the Supreme Court. He served over thirty-six years, the longest of any justice, retiring in 1975. Many thought Douglas would be pro-business, but he devoted himself to the defense of the Bill of Rights and freedom of speech. ∎

Introduction

In the early history of the United States, legislation against and control of obscene materials was always undertaken at the local and state level. The federal government first became involved in policing obscenity with the 1873 *Comstock Act,* which prohibited "obscene" materials from being transmitted via interstate mail. The *Comstock Act* was enforced against the distributors of birth control information, as well as a number of different books and magazines. In 1925, the Supreme Court stated, in passing, that the First Amendment freedoms of speech and press applied against the states because of the Fourteenth Amendment, which states: "No State shall make or enforce any law which shall abridge the privileges or immunities of citizens of the United States; nor shall any State deprive any person of life, liberty, or property, without due process of law; nor deny to any person within its jurisdiction the equal protection of the laws." The question then became whether or not obscenity was protected by the First Amendment. In 1942, in *Chaplinsky v. New Hampshire,* the court held that obscenity was not protected under the First Amendment. The important remaining question was: what is obscenity?

Samuel Roth was convicted in 1956 of mailing obscene circulars and an obscene book in violation of a federal obscenity statute. He appealed to the Supreme Court, claiming that the federal statute under which he had been convicted, which was based on the original *Comstock Act,* was unconstitutional. The two central issues before the Court in this case were (1) whether obscenity was protected by the First Amendment; and, (2) what constituted obscenity.

Significance

Roth v. U.S. represented the first time the Supreme Court had the opportunity to define obscenity. The Court defined it as material lacking "redeeming social importance," which, when considered as a whole, using "contemporary social standards," appeals to a "prurient interest." (Prurient is probably best defined as appealing to deviant sexual interest). This definition was used by the Court until 1962, when the Court under Chief Justice Earl Warren struck down a conviction for obscenity, adding the requirement that obscene materials had to be typified by "patent offensiveness and indecency." Two years later the Court commented that obscene materials had to be "'utterly' without social importance." The Supreme Court under Chief Justice Earl Warren reversed several other convictions for obscenity as well. The difficulty of determining obscenity was noted by Justice Byron White, who said that he could not define obscenity, but "I know it when I see it." That obviously does not create an easy definition.

The Court under Chief Justice Warren Burger, which followed the Warren Court, in *Miller v. California* (1973) upheld a conviction for obscenity and issued a new, looser standard for obscenity. Obscene materials had to, under local community standards, invite a "prurient interest," not have "serious artistic, political or scientific value," and depict sexual items in a "patently offensive way." Courts since have generally upheld the *Miller* standard but have not universally upheld the convictions. A twenty-first century complication with the issue of obscenity and pornography is the Internet, where what may be obscene in the recipient's community may not be obscene in the sender's community. This makes the idea of judging obscenity by "local community standards" highly problematic. The Supreme Court struck down, in *Reno v. ACLU* (1997), an attempt to regulate the Internet, holding that the Communications Decency Act was overly broad, overly vague, and did not meet the *Miller* standards for obscenity.

Primary Source

Roth v. U.S. [excerpt]

SYNOPSIS: Justice William J. Brennan Jr. first examines obscenity, ruling that it is not protected by the First Amendment. The majority opinion of the Court upholds Roth's conviction, saying that the proper standards were used in determining what constituted obscenity. Justice William O. Douglas dissents, joined by Justice Hugo L. Black, stating that the obscenity test is too broad and that the conviction violates Roth's right to freedom of speech and press.

Mr. Justice Brennan delivered the opinion of the Court. . . .

The dispositive question is whether obscenity is utterance within the area of protected speech and press. Although this is the first time the question has been squarely presented to this Court, either under the First Amendment or under the Fourteenth Amendment, expressions found in numerous opinions indicate that this Court has always assumed that obscenity is not protected by the freedoms of speech and press. . . .

The protection given speech and press was fashioned to assure unfettered interchange of ideas for the bringing about of political and social changes desired by the people. . . .

All ideas having even the slightest redeeming social importance—unorthodox ideas, controversial ideas, even ideas hateful to the prevailing climate of opinion—have the full protection of the guaranties, unless excludable because they encroach upon the limited area of more important interests. But implicit in the history of the First Amendment is the rejection of obscenity as utterly without redeeming social importance. . . .

We hold that obscenity is not within the area of constitutionally protected speech or press. . . .

Some American courts adopted this standard but later decisions have rejected it and substituted this test: whether to the average person, applying contemporary community standards, the dominant theme of the material taken as a whole appeals to prurient interest. The *Hicklin* test, judging obscenity by the effect of isolated passages upon the most susceptible persons, might well encompass material legitimately treating with sex, and so it must be rejected as unconstitutionally restrictive of the freedoms of speech and press. On the other hand, the substituted standard provides safeguards adequate to withstand the charge of constitutional infirmity.

Both trial courts below sufficiently followed the proper standard. Both courts used the proper definition of obscenity. . . .

The judgments are

Affirmed. . . .

Mr. Justice Douglas, with whom Mr. Justice Black concurs, dissenting.

When we sustain these convictions, we make the legality of a publication turn on the purity of thought which a book or tract instills in the mind of the reader. I do not think we can approve that standard and be

J. Lee Rankin was the Solicitor General who represented the U.S. in *Roth v. U.S.* AP/WIDE WORLD PHOTOS. REPRODUCED BY PERMISSION

faithful to the command of the First Amendment, which by its terms is a restraint on Congress and which by the Fourteenth is a restraint on the States. . . .

The tests by which these convictions were obtained require only the arousing of sexual thoughts. Yet the arousing of sexual thoughts and desires happens every day in normal life in dozens of ways. Nearly 30 years ago a questionnaire sent to college and normal school women graduates asked what things were most stimulating sexually. Of 409 replies, 9 said "music"; 18 said "pictures"; 29 said "dancing"; 40 said "drama"; 95 said "books"; and 218 said "man." . . .

The test of obscenity the Court endorses today gives the censor free range over a vast domain. To allow the State to step in and punish mere speech or publication that the judge or the jury thinks has an undesirable impact on thoughts but that is not shown to be a part of unlawful action is drastically to curtail the First Amendment. As recently stated by two of our outstanding authorities on obscenity, "The danger of influencing a change in the current moral standards of the community, or of shocking or offending readers, or of stimulating sex thoughts

or desires apart from objective conduct, can never justify the losses to society that result from interference with literary freedom." . . .

If we were certain that impurity of sexual thoughts impelled to action, we would be on less dangerous ground in punishing the distributors of this sex literature. But it is by no means clear that obscene literature, as so defined, is a significant factor in influencing substantial deviations from the community standards. . . .

The absence of dependable information on the effect of obscene literature on human conduct should make us wary. It should put us on the side of protecting society's interest in literature, except and unless it can be said that the particular publication has an impact on action that the government can control. . . .

I assume there is nothing in the Constitution which forbids Congress from using its power over the mails to proscribe conduct on the grounds of good morals. No one would suggest that the First Amendment permits nudity in public places, adultery, and other phases of sexual misconduct. . . .

Thus, if the First Amendment guarantee of freedom of speech and press is to mean anything in this field, it must allow protests even against the moral code that the standard of the day sets for the community. In other words, literature should not be suppressed merely because it offends the moral code of the censor. . . .

I reject too the implication that problems of freedom of speech and of the press are to be resolved by weighing against the values of free expression, the judgment of the Court that a particular form of that expression has "no redeeming social importance." The First Amendment, its prohibition in terms absolute, was designed to preclude courts as well as legislatures from weighing the values of speech against silence. The First Amendment puts free speech in the preferred position. . . .

I would give the broad sweep of the First Amendment full support. I have the same confidence in the ability of our people to reject noxious literature as I have in their capacity to sort out the true from the false in theology, economics, politics, or any other field.

Further Resources

BOOKS

Eisler, Kim Isaac. *A Justice for All: William J. Brennan, Jr., and the Decisions That Transformed America*. New York: Simon and Schuster, 1993.

Goldman, Roger L., and David Gallen. *Justice William J. Brennan, Jr.: Freedom First.* New York: Carroll & Graf Publishers, 1994.

Harrison, Maureen, and Steve Gilbert, eds. *Obscenity and Pornography Decisions of the United States Supreme Court.* Carlsbad, Calif.: Excellent Books, 2000.

Heins, Marjorie. *Not in Front of the Children: "Indecency," Censorship and the Innocence of Youth.* New York: Hill and Wang, 2001.

Hopkins, W. Wat. *Mr. Justice Brennan and Freedom of Expression.* New York: Praeger, 1991.

Mackey, Thomas C. *Pornography on Trial: A Handbook with Cases, Laws, and Documents.* Santa Barbara, Calif.: ABC-CLIO, 2002.

Zelezny, John D. *Communications Law: Liberties, Restraints, and the Modern Media.* Belmont, Calif.: Wadsworth/Thomson Learning, 2001, 3rd edition.

WEBSITES

Roth v. United States Certiorari to the United States Court of Appeals for the Second Circuit. Available at http://www.fordhamprep.org/socstud/Cases/roth.htm (accessed March 6, 2003).

Cooper v. Aaron

Supreme Court decision

By: U.S. Supreme Court

Date: September 15, 1958

Source: U.S. Supreme Court. *Cooper v. Aaron.* 358 U.S. 1 (1958). Available online at http://caselaw.lp.findlaw.com/cgi-bin/getcase.pl?court=us&vol=358&invol=1; website home page: http://www.findlaw.com (accessed March 11, 2003).

About the Organization: The Supreme Court under Chief Justice Earl Warren (1891–1974) made some of the most revolutionary decisions of the Court's history, particularly in the areas of civil rights and the Court's powers over federal and state authorities. Presiding over some of the strongest personalities ever to sit on the bench, Warren, within a year of becoming Chief Justice, led the way to such groundbreaking decisions as *Brown v. Board of Education.* ∎

Introduction

By the 1950s, segregation in the Southern schools was drawing fire from a number of areas. The National Association for the Advancement of Colored People (NAACP) won some legal victories against discrimination and school segregation, initially at the graduate school level, in the first years of the decade. The organization won its biggest victory on the educational front in 1954, with the case *Brown v. Board of Education,* in which the Supreme Court held that "separate educational facilities are inherently unequal" and thus unconstitutional. In 1955, in a second *Brown* decision, the Court is-

sued a plan to implement the desegregation of public schools with "all deliberate speed." Southern legislators pledged "massive resistance" to the enforcement of desegregation, and most Southern congressmen joined in signing a Southern Manifesto that called *Brown* an unconstitutional decision. They claimed that the Court had overstepped its powers in making the decision and that it did not have the right to enforce its decisions within the states. In fact, at that time the Supreme Court had no real enforcement agency. Since President Dwight D. Eisenhower (served 1953–1961) did not wish to interfere with federal enforcement, the progress in integrating American schools was slow.

A showdown between the forces of the Court and the state authorities occurred in 1957, when Governor Orval Faubus of Arkansas, backed by the Arkansas National Guard, refused to allow nine African American students to enter Little Rock Central High School. When the courts ordered Faubus to step aside, a mob blocked the students' entry. Only after Eisenhower reluctantly dispatched federal troops were the students able to enter the school building. Federalized National Guardsmen remained on site to protect the children and ensure their passage. The Little Rock school board then sought an injunction in federal court to delay any further desegregation, saying that the public had become so inflamed by the situation, it had become impossible to carry on with basic schooling at Central High. They asked to remove the eight remaining African American students from the high school and place them in a segregated school. When the District Court granted the postponement of the desegregation program, a group of African Americans appealed, and the Court of Appeals reversed the District Court. The Supreme Court then met in a special session to confirm the appellate decision, resulting in the case *Cooper v. Aaron.* The decision responded to the schools board's request for a stay of the desegregation program, but also to the actions of the state of Arkansas, which had claimed it was not bound by the *Brown* decision, since it had not been party to it. The state had also argued that its governor had the same power to interpret the Constitution as did the Supreme Court, thereby challenging the power of the Court.

Significance

The Court ordered Little Rock High School to desegregate immediately. This decision was signed by all of the justices, in order to emphasize their resolve on the issue. The opinion basically restates the decision made in *Brown* and affirms that the opinions of the Court are to be followed. The justices announced with this decision that it was the Supreme Court's duty and function to be the nation's interpreter of the Constitution. After *Cooper,* the legality of segregation was no longer in question. The

Arkansas governor Orval Faubus holds a photo of federal troops with drawn bayonets hustling students from Central High School. Faubus accused the government of unwarranted use of force to integrate the school in Little Rock. © BETTMANN/CORBIS. REPRODUCED BY PERMISSION.

Court continued to order desegregation to be implemented in case after case that appeared before it. Although the process was very slow at first, the *Civil Rights Act of 1964* gave the federal government much more power to force integration and compliance with the Supreme Court's rulings.

The Warren Court broke new ground by affirming its own powers under the Constitution. Since there were many who were not pleased with the Court's decisions, the Court was—and still is—criticized for exerting too much power over the other branches of government. But many praised the Warren Court for its adherence to the principles of equality and for its efforts to ensure the constitutional rights of every American, even when that meant intervening in unconstitutional state policies.

Primary Source

Cooper v. Aaron [excerpt]

SYNOPSIS: The Court, in reviewing the series of events leading to *Cooper,* shows that certain officials of the state of Arkansas were to blame for the disruption of education in Central High. The Court holds that the civil rights of African Ameri-

cans are not to be denied because the governor and legislature of Arkansas have resisted rulings they are sworn to uphold and affirms the legal principles behind *Brown*—and behind the Supreme Court's powers.

Opinion of the Court by The Chief Justice, Mr. Justice Black, Mr. Justice Frankfurter, Mr. Justice Douglas, Mr. Justice Burton, Mr. Justice Clark, Mr. Justice Harlan, Mr. Justice Brennan, and Mr. Justice Whittaker.

As this case reaches us it raises questions of the highest importance to the maintenance of our federal system of government. It necessarily involves a claim by the Governor and Legislature of a State that there is no duty on state officials to obey federal court orders resting on this Court's considered interpretation of the United States Constitution. Specifically it involves actions by the Governor and Legislature of Arkansas upon the premise that they are not bound by our holding in *Brown v. Board of Education.* . . . That holding was that the Fourteenth Amendment forbids States to use their governmental powers to bar children on racial grounds from attending schools where there is state participation through any arrangement, management, funds or property. We are urged to uphold a suspension of the Little Rock School Board's plan to do away with segregated public schools in Little Rock until state laws and efforts to upset and nullify our holding in *Brown v. Board of Education* have been further challenged and tested in the courts. We reject these contentions. . . .

The following are the facts and circumstances so far as necessary to show how the legal questions are presented. . . .

Nine Negro children were scheduled for admission in September 1957 to Central High School, which has more than two thousand students. Various administrative measures, designed to assure the smooth transition of this first stage of desegregation, were undertaken.

On September 2, 1957, the day before these Negro students were to enter Central High, the school authorities were met with drastic opposing action on the part of the Governor of Arkansas who dispatched units of the Arkansas National Guard to the Central High School grounds and placed the school "off limits" to colored students. As found by the District Court in subsequent proceedings, the Governor's action had not been requested by the school authorities, and was entirely unheralded. . . .

On the morning of . . . September 4, 1957, the Negro children attempted to enter the high school but, as the District Court later found, units of the Arkansas National Guard "acting pursuant to the Governor's order, stood shoulder to shoulder at the school grounds and thereby forcibly prevented the 9 Negro students . . . from entering," as they continued to do every school day during the following three weeks. . . .

That same day, September 4, 1957, the United States Attorney for the Eastern District of Arkansas was requested by the District Court to begin an immediate investigation in order to fix responsibility for the interference with the orderly implementation of the District Court's direction to carry out the desegregation program. Three days later, September 7, the District Court denied a petition of the School Board and the Superintendent of Schools for an order temporarily suspending continuance of the program.

Upon completion of the United States Attorney's investigation, he and the Attorney General of the United States, at the District Court's request, entered the proceedings and filed a petition on behalf of the United States, as amicus curiae, to enjoin the Governor of Arkansas and officers of the Arkansas National Guard from further attempts to prevent obedience to the court's order. After hearings on the petition, the District Court found that the School Board's plan had been obstructed by the Governor through the use of National Guard troops, and granted a preliminary injunction on September 20, 1957, enjoining the Governor and the officers of the Guard from preventing the attendance of Negro children at Central High School, and from otherwise obstructing or interfering with the orders of the court in connection with the plan. . . . The National Guard was then withdrawn from the school.

The next school day was Monday, September 23, 1957. The Negro children entered the high school that morning under the protection of the Little Rock Police Department and members of the Arkansas State Police. But the officers caused the children to be removed from the school during the morning because they had difficulty controlling a large and demonstrating crowd which had gathered at the high school. . . . On September 25, however, the President of the United States dispatched federal troops to Central High School and admission of the Negro students to the school was thereby effected. Regular army troops continued at the high school until November 27, 1957. They were then replaced by federalized National Guardsmen who re-

mained throughout the balance of the school year. Eight of the Negro students remained in attendance at the school throughout the school year.

We come now to the aspect of the proceedings presently before us. On February 20, 1958, the School Board and the Superintendent of Schools filed a petition in the District Court seeking a postponement of their program for desegregation. Their position in essence was that because of extreme public hostility, which they stated had been engendered largely by the official attitudes and actions of the Governor and the Legislature, the maintenance of a sound educational program at Central High School, with the Negro students in attendance, would be impossible. The Board therefore proposed that the Negro students already admitted to the school be withdrawn and sent to segregated schools, and that all further steps to carry out the Board's desegregation program be postponed for a period later suggested by the Board to be two and one-half years.

After a hearing the District Court granted the relief requested by the Board. Among other things the court found that the past year at Central High School had been attended by conditions of "chaos, bedlam and turmoil." . . .

The District Court's judgment was dated June 20, 1958. The Negro respondents appealed to the Court of Appeals for the Eighth Circuit and also sought there a stay of the District Court's judgment. . . . The Court of Appeals did not act on the petition for a stay, but, on August 18, 1958, after convening in special session on August 4 and hearing the appeal, reversed the District Court, 257 F.2d 33. On August 21, 1958, the Court of Appeals stayed its mandate to permit the School Board to petition this Court for certiorari. . . . Recognizing the vital importance of a decision of the issues in time to permit arrangements to be made for the 1958–1959 school year . . . we convened in Special Term on August 28, 1958, and heard oral argument on the respondents' motions, and also argument of the Solicitor General who, by invitation, appeared for the United States as amicus curiae, and asserted that the Court of Appeals' judgment was clearly correct on the merits, and urged that we vacate its stay forthwith. . . . On September 12, 1958, as already mentioned, we unanimously affirmed the judgment of the Court of Appeals. . . .

In affirming the judgment of the Court of Appeals which reversed the District Court we have accepted without reservation the position of the School Board,

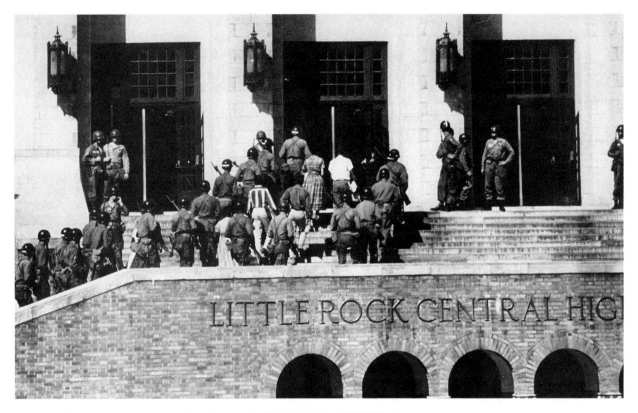

A long line of armed federal troops surround students entering Little Rock's Central High School. © **BETTMANN/CORBIS. REPRODUCED BY PERMISSION.**

the Superintendent of Schools, and their counsel that they displayed entire good faith in the conduct of these proceedings and in dealing with the unfortunate and distressing sequence of events which has been outlined. We likewise have accepted the findings of the District Court as to the conditions at Central High School during the 1957–1958 school year, and also the findings that the educational progress of all the students, white and colored, of that school has suffered and will continue to suffer if the conditions which prevailed last year are permitted to continue.

The significance of these findings, however, is to be considered in light of the fact, indisputably revealed by the record before us, that the conditions they depict are directly traceable to the actions of legislators and executive officials of the State of Arkansas, taken in their official capacities, which reflect their own determination to resist this Court's decision in the *Brown* case and which have brought about violent resistance to that decision in Arkansas. In its petition for certiorari filed in this Court, the School Board itself describes the situation in this language: "The legislative, executive, and judicial departments of the state government op-

posed the desegregation of Little Rock schools by enacting laws, calling out troops, making statements villifying federal law and federal courts, and failing to utilize state law enforcement agencies and judicial processes to maintain public peace."

One may well sympathize with the position of the Board in the face of the frustrating conditions which have confronted it, but, regardless of the Board's good faith, the actions of the other state agencies responsible for those conditions compel us to reject the Board's legal position. . . .

The constitutional rights of respondents are not to be sacrificed or yielded to the violence and disorder which have followed upon the actions of the Governor and Legislature. . . . Thus law and order are not here to be preserved by depriving the Negro children of their constitutional rights. The record before us clearly establishes that the growth of the Board's difficulties to a magnitude beyond its unaided power to control is the product of state action. Those difficulties, as counsel for the Board forthrightly conceded on the oral argument in this Court, can also be brought under control by state action.

The controlling legal principles are plain. The command of the Fourteenth Amendment is that no

"State" shall deny to any person within its jurisdiction the equal protection of the laws. . . . Thus the prohibitions of the Fourteenth Amendment extend to all action of the State denying equal protection of the laws; whatever the agency of the State taking the action. . . . In short, the constitutional rights of children not to be discriminated against in school admission on grounds of race or color declared by this Court in the *Brown* case can neither be nullified openly and directly by state legislators or state executive or judicial officers, nor nullified indirectly by them through evasive schemes for segregation whether attempted "ingeniously or ingenuously." . . .

What has been said, in the light of the facts developed, is enough to dispose of the case. However, we should answer the premise of the actions of the Governor and Legislature that they are not bound by our holding in the *Brown* case. It is necessary only to recall some basic constitutional propositions which are settled doctrine.

Article VI of the Constitution makes the Constitution the "supreme Law of the Land." In 1803, Chief Justice Marshall, speaking for a unanimous Court, referring to the Constitution as "the fundamental and paramount law of the nation," declared in the notable case of *Marbury v. Madison,* 1 Cranch 137, 177, that "It is emphatically the province and duty of the judicial department to say what the law is." This decision declared the basic principle that the federal judiciary is supreme in the exposition of the law of the Constitution, and that principle has ever since been respected by this Court and the Country as a permanent and indispensable feature of our constitutional system. It follows that the interpretation of the Fourteenth Amendment enunciated by this Court in the *Brown* case is the supreme law of the land, and Art. VI of the Constitution makes it of binding effect on the States "any Thing in the Constitution or Laws of any State to the Contrary notwith-standing." Every state legislator and executive and judicial officer is solemnly committed by oath taken pursuant to Art. VI, cl. 3, "to support this Constitution." Chief Justice Taney, speaking for a unanimous Court in 1859, said that this requirement reflected the framers' "anxiety to preserve it [the Constitution] in full force, in all its powers, and to guard against resistance to or evasion of its authority, on the part of a State." . . .

No state legislator or executive or judicial officer can war against the Constitution without violating his undertaking to support it. . . .

It is, of course, quite true that the responsibility for public education is primarily the concern of the States, but it is equally true that such responsibilities, like all other state activity, must be exercised consistently with federal constitutional requirements as they apply to state action. The Constitution created a government dedicated to equal justice under law. The Fourteenth Amendment embodied and emphasized that ideal. State support of segregated schools through any arrangement, management, funds, or property cannot be squared with the Amendment's command that no State shall deny to any person within its jurisdiction the equal protection of the laws. The right of a student not to be segregated on racial grounds in schools so maintained is indeed so fundamental and pervasive that it is embraced in the concept of due process of law. . . . The basic decision in *Brown* was unanimously reached by this Court only after the case had been briefed and twice argued and the issues had been given the most serious consideration. Since the first *Brown* opinion three new Justices have come to the Court. They are at one with the Justices still on the Court who participated in that basic decision as to its correctness, and that decision is now unanimously reaffirmed. The principles announced in that decision and the obedience of the States to them, according to the command of the Constitution, are indispensable for the protection of the freedoms guaranteed by our fundamental charter for all of us. Our constitutional ideal of equal justice under law is thus made a living truth.

Further Resources
BOOKS
Beals, Melba. *Warriors Don't Cry: A Searing Memoir of the Battle to Integrate Little Rock's Central High.* New York: Pocket Books, 1994.

Counts, I. Wilmer. *A Life Is More Than a Moment: The Desegregation of Little Rock's Central High.* (With essays by Will D. Campbell, Ernest Dumas, Robert S. McCord.) Bloomington: Indiana University Press, 1999.

Cray, Ed. *Chief Justice: A Biography of Earl Warren.* New York: Simon and Schuster, 1997.

Powe, L.A. Scot. *The Warren Court and American Politics.* Cambridge, Mass.: Belknap Press of Harvard University Press, 2000.

Roy, Beth. *Bitters in the Honey: Tales of Hope and Disappointment Across Divides of Race and Time.* Fayetteville: University of Arkansas Press, 1999.

Schwartz, Bernard. *The Warren Court: A Retrospective.* New York: Oxford University Press, 1996.

Urofsky, Melvin I. *The Warren Court: Justices, Rulings, and Legacy.* Santa Barbara, Calif.: ABC-CLIO, 2001.

WEBSITES
Little Rock Central High School 40th Anniversary. Available online at http://www.centralhigh57.org/ (accessed March 12, 2003).

7

LIFESTYLES AND SOCIAL TRENDS

SCOTT A. MERRIMAN

Entries are arranged in chronological order by date of primary source. For entries with one primary source, the entry title is the same as the primary source title. Entries with more than one primary source have an overall entry title, followed by the titles of the primary sources.

Important Events in Lifestyles and Social Trends, 1950–1959

1950

- Levittown, near Hicksville, Long Island, adds a new suburban home every fifteen minutes. The community's rules require homeowners to cut their lawns at least once a week and assign a specific day for doing the laundry.

- The average price nationally for a single-family home is $10,050. A two-bedroom, two-bath brick home in Bayside Hills, New York, can be had for $12,900.

- About 3.8 million households—9 percent of the nation's homes—have televisions. American children average twenty-seven hours a week watching TV, according to a national survey—only forty-five minutes less than they spend in school. Daniel Marsh, president of Boston University, warns, "We are destined to have a nation of morons."

- The Henry J, a domestically produced compact car, is introduced by the automaker Henry J. Kaiser.

- *Prevention* magazine, which champions folk remedies over established medical practices, debuts, helping to launch a folk-remedies craze.

- *Look Younger, Live Longer* by Gayelord Hauser is published; the book becomes a best-seller and boosts demand for "wonder foods" such as yogurt and blackstrap molasses.

- *Betty Crocker's Picture Cookbook,* based on General Mills's fictitious spokes-woman, is published.

- On January 24, a federal minimum wage of 75 cents an hour goes into effect.

- On February 9, Wisconsin senator Joseph McCarthy, in a speech to the Republican Women's Club of Wheeling, West Virginia, claims that 205 State Department employees are known members of the Communist Party. The charge creates a furor and feeds the nation's anti-Communist hysteria. A resulting four-year effort to uncover "subversives" in government and society unjustly stains the reputations and careers of countless Americans. These "witch hunts" and the smear tactics they employ become forever known as *McCarthyism.*

- In February, Frank MacNamara, head of a small finance company, launches the Diners Club card, which allows cardholders to charge meals at participating restaurants. The inspiration for his venture comes after he leaves his wallet at home and cannot pay the bill when entertaining guests at a restaurant. The first card is cardboard and lists twenty-eight participating establishments on the back.

- On July 7, the government reinstates the military draft to increase the size of the nation's armed forces.

- On July 17, a survey by the University of Michigan library shows that almost half of the U.S. population does not read books. However, illiteracy is at an all-time low of 3.2 percent.

- On September 22, UN diplomat Ralph Bunche becomes the first African American awarded the Nobel Peace Prize.

1951

- A Denver grocery store chain revives the use of trading stamps by offering S&H stamps to store customers.

- A cemetery in Sioux City, Iowa refuses to accept John Rice, a Native American soldier killed in the Korean War. President Truman sends an Air Force plane to bring the remains to Washington for burial in Arlington National Cemetery.

- Gerber Products Company starts using the flavor additive MSG (monosodium glutamate) to make its baby foods taste better to mothers. Other innovations this year include power steering in automobiles (Chrysler), remote-control garage door openers, and college courses offered on television (Marquette University).

- On February 12, the U.S. Office of Naval Research reports that purported flying saucers can almost always be attributed to high-altitude weather balloons used for cosmic ray research.

- In March, Americans are mesmerized by televised Senate hearings investigating organized crime in America. Some 2.5 million sets are tuned in as famous reputed gangsters are called to testify. By October, the hearings' TV audience reaches 30 million, equaling the ratings of the World Series that month. A Chicago department store offers a 10 percent discount when the hearings are on TV, trying to attract customers.

- On June 14, the Remington Rand Company unveils a powerful electronic digital computer in Philadelphia. Called UNIVAC (for Universal Automatic Computer), it is the first such device on the market. The first customer for the new machine will be the U.S. Census Bureau.

- On July 1, the largest unsegregated audience in Atlanta since Reconstruction meets at the convention of the National Association for the Advancement of Colored People.

- On July 12, a riot erupts when an African American family attempts to move into the Chicago suburb of Cicero. The National Guard is called out to restore order.

- On October 10, the first transcontinental telephone call completed by dialing the number instead of going through a phone company operator is made from Englewood, New Jersey.

1952

- More than fifty-two million automobiles ride American highways, up from twenty-five million in 1945.

- *Amy Vanderbilt's Complete Book of Etiquette* is published.

- The first Holiday Inn motel opens in Memphis, Tennessee.

- A contraceptive pill for women is developed by G.D. Searle laboratories in Chicago.

- On July 16, President Truman signs the Korean War GI Bill of Rights. This law provides Korean War veterans the same college education benefits, low-cost home and business loans, and other financial aid that helped millions of other veterans after World War II.

- On November 26, *Bwana Devil,* the first full-length 3-D movie requiring the use of polarized eye-glasses, premieres.

- On December 30, the Tuskegee Institute reports that 1952 was the first in seventy-one years in which no lynchings were reported.

1953

- Alfred Kinsey's *Sexual Behavior in the Human Female* is published.

- In Hollywood, the Screen Actors Guild adopts a by-law banning Communists from membership in the organization.

- In Indiana, a state education official criticizes teaching the story of Robin Hood as subversive because the hero robs the rich and gives to the poor.

- Chevrolet introduces the two-seat Corvette sports car.

- The Kellogg Company introduces Sugar Smacks breakfast cereal, which is 56 percent sugar. Sara Lee Kitchens begins to mass-market frozen cakes and pies successfully.

- Cigarette makers respond to reports of a link between smoking and cancer by introducing "safer" filter-tipped cigarettes.

- On April 14, the air force publication *Air Training* reports that one thousand flying saucer sightings were reported to the government's Air Intelligence Center during 1952.

- In May, brothers Richard and Mac McDonald reject their architect's ideas for the hamburger shops they plan to open in Phoenix and instead decide on two "golden arches" made of sheet metal to give them the "look" they are seeking.

- On October 26, the Songwriter's Protective Association reports that coin-operated jukeboxes gross nearly $1 billion annually in the United States.

1954

- C.A. Swanson and Sons introduces frozen TV dinners.

- The cha cha, based on the Cuban Chanzon, becomes a popular dance in U.S. dance halls.

- A survey reveals that 78 percent of Americans believe it is important to report relatives or friends they suspect of being Communists to the FBI.

- According to a Gallup Poll, a family of four can live on sixty dollars a week.

- From April through June, as many as 20 million Americans watch some 187 hours of televised Senate hearings investigating Senator McCarthy's charge the U.S. Army has been infiltrated by Communists.

- On May 17, the U.S. Supreme Court strikes down the long-standing practice of racial segregation in public schools. In the case of *Brown v. the Board of Education,* the justices rule that separate facilities for African American and white students do not provide an equal education for each group. The Court later orders an end to the practice, which has prevailed in the nation's schools for more than a century.

- On June 14, President Eisenhower signs legislation inserting the phrase "under God" in the Pledge of Allegiance.

- On October 27, twenty-six American publishers announce the formation of the Comics Code, regulating the contents of comic books.

- On December 2, Senator McCarthy's troubled hunt for Communists in America comes to an end when, by a vote of 67-22, his fellow senators condemn his actions and sleazy tactics of rumor, innuendo, and guilt by association. After fours years of trying, McCarthy has never convincingly unmasked one Communist, although many people's lives and careers have been ruined by his efforts.

- On December 15, the U.S. observes the first Safe Driving Day, sponsored by the Presidential Traffic Safety Commission.

1955

- Ford introduces the two-seat Thunderbird sports car. Among the year's other new products are Colonel Sanders' Kentucky Fried Chicken, "no-smear" lipstick, and roll-on deodorant.

- The Coca-Cola Company officially uses the name Coke for the first time.

- The popularity of "Davy Crockett" inspires Americans to buy $100 million in merchandise related to the show.

- On February 19, the Senate committee investigating juvenile delinquency denounces comic books as offering "short courses in crime."

- In May, Bill Haley's *Rock Around the Clock* hits number one on the record charts. Haley is not sure what to call his blend of rhythm and blues and country swing. But others are using the term *rock and roll* to describe it. Haley's song did not do well until it was included in the film *Blackboard Jungle.* The merger of rock and roll with the theme of juvenile delinquency have attracted huge numbers of teens to the movie. This has caused critics to label Haley's music— as well as that of other rock and rollers like Chuck Berry, Bo Diddley, and Little Richard—as dirty and as bad for kids as dope.

- On July 18, WED Enterprises, owned by Walt Disney, opens Disneyland in Anaheim, California, and introduces "The Mickey Mouse Club" on afternoon television.

- On August 12, the federal minimum wage increases from seventy-five cents to one dollar per hour.

1956

- Some seven thousand drive-in movies are operating around the country, more than triple the number in 1950. Some supply in-car heaters to attract moviegoers year round. Movie theaters complain that the drive-ins are stealing their business. But the high ticket prices in regular theaters—$2 in New York and $1.50 in Los Angeles—are more likely to blame.

- Elvis Presley, a former $35-a-week truck driver from Memphis, Tennessee, bursts onto the national music scene with three huge hits—*Heartbreak Hotel, Don't Be Cruel,* and *Blue Suede Shoes.* Critics call him "untalented and vulgar," but teenage fans buy seven million copies of his record this year.

• About six million cars are produced this year in the United States, the third-best year ever. Of them, 11 percent are station wagons.

• For the first time, airplanes carry as many passengers during the year as railroads do.

• After Proctor & Gamble finds that women change 25 billion baby diapers a year, it introduces Pampers, the first disposable diaper.

• On February 6, Autherine Lucy, the first African American student at the University of Alabama, is suspended after three days of violent protests rock the campus. On March 1 she is expelled.

• On May 2, the General Conference of the Methodist Church abolishes racial segregation in Methodist churches.

• On June 29, the Federal Aid Highway Act is passed by Congress, authorizing $33.5 billion to build 42,500 miles of high-speed, limited-access interstate highways.

• On November 11, the U.S. Census Bureau reports that women outnumber men in the United States by 1.381 million.

1957

• Wham-O Manufacturing introduces the Frisbee and the hula hoop.

• The German automaker Volkswagen sells two hundred thousand Beetles in the United States.

• In January, "American Bandstand," hosted by Philadelphia disc jockey Dick Clark, debuts on the ABC network.

• On January 2, the Immigration and Naturalization Service announces that 350,000 immigrants, the most since quotas were established in 1924, entered the country in 1956.

• In September, violence erupts in Little Rock, Arkansas, as authorities try to integrate the city's all-white Central High School. The governor posts National Guard outside the school to block the attempt. President Eisenhower responds by sending U.S. Army troops to the city to enforce the integration order.

1958

• Pizza Hut, eventually the largest chain of pizzerias in the United States, opens its first restaurant in Kansas City, Missouri.

• The average cost of college tuition is thirteen hundred dollars per year, more than double what it was in 1940.

• On January 18, New York City police break up a white-supremacist youth gang, with members ranging from sixteen to twenty-one years of age.

• From February 25 to March 5, wood alcohol poisoning kills twenty-seven people in New York City who drank a homemade liquor called King Kong.

• On March 19, Kentucky governor Albert B. Chandler signs into law a bill abolishing daylight savings time in the state and making it a crime to display publicly the incorrect time.

• On March 24, Elvis Presley is inducted into the U.S. Army.

1959

• The Ford Falcon, the first attempt on the part of the Big Three automakers to compete in the compact-car market, is introduced.

• Supermarkets comprise 11 percent of U.S. grocery stores but are responsible for 69 percent of the country's food sales.

• On April 3, University of Florida president S. Wayne Reitz reveals that fourteen employees were dismissed for homosexual activities.

• On May 5, Judge Jennie Loitman Barron of the Massachusetts Superior Court was named Mother of the Year by the American Mothers Committee.

• On May 19, the U.S. Public Roads Bureau reports that there are a record 68,299,408 registered vehicles on the road, approximately 1 for every 2.5 Americans.

• On July 21, D.H. Lawrence's torrid novel *Lady Chatterley's Lover* is banned from U.S. mails as obscene—some thirty one years after it was published.

• On September 7, a study reports that 64 percent of Americans belong to an organized church.

Communist Paranoia

"Declaration of Conscience"

Speech

By: Margaret Chase Smith

Date: June 1, 1950

Source: U.S. Senate. Senator Margaret Chase Smith of Maine Speaking on the Senate Floor for the "Declaration of Conscience." 82d Cong., 1st sess. *Congressional Record* June 1, 1950, 7894–7895. Reprinted in Woy, Jean L. *United States History as Seen by Contemporaries,* 10th ed. Vol. 2, *Volume II: Since 1865.* The American Spirit. Boston: Houghton, 2002, 443–444.

About the Author: Margaret Chase Smith (1897–1995) was one of the leading woman politicians in twentieth-century America. Highly independent, she served thirty-two years in the U.S. Congress as a Republican, becoming the first woman to be elected to both the House and Senate. She entered politics in 1940 to fill the seat of her Congressman husband, Clyde Smith, after his death. She won election in 1948 to the Senate, despite the refusal of the Republicans to endorse her, solely because she was a woman.

Letters to the Harvard *Crimson*

Letters

By: K.W.L and M.F.G; J.C. Peter Richardson

Date: November 1954

Source: K.W.L. and M.F.G.; J.C. Peter Richardson. Letter to the editors of the *Crimson,* November 1954. In *Harvard Crimson* November 24, 1954 and November 30, 1954. Reprinted in Woy, Jean L. *United States History as Seen by Contemporaries,* 10th ed. Vol. 2, *Volume II: Since 1865.* The American Spirit. Boston: Houghton, 2002, 445. ■

Introduction

Americans have long been scared of "radical" ideas. Anarchists were among the first to be excluded from America, and many feared radicals during World War I (1914–1918). Fear increased substantially after communists successfully assumed power in the Russian Revolution of 1917. This apprehension led to the passage of the 1924 National Origins Act, which limited immigra-

tion, especially from Eastern Europe. For a time the trepidation decreased as the Great Depression's economic concerns slowed immigration. Despite having been allies, disagreements over interpretations of the peace treaties ending World War II (1939–1945) sparked the Cold War, pitting the Soviet Union and its communist allies against the United States and its non-communist allies. Many politicians gained great fame, and frightened many, by identifying communists and their sympathizers in the United States—especially government officials allegedly "soft" on communism.

America's fears increased in 1949 when the Soviet Union developed its own atomic bomb. This event coincided closely with the communist revolution in China, led by Mao Tse-tung in 1949, and the start of the Korean War in 1950. Even President Truman fanned the hysteria by instituting a mandatory loyalty program for federal workers.

The most well-known "red hunter" was Joseph McCarthy, Republican senator from Wisconsin. Senator McCarthy accused many of being Communists, often with little proof. He was protected by governmental immunity while in the U.S. Senate, and many people feared his power and so did not protest against his and similar smears. Many people's lives, however, were ruined by the charges hurled by McCarthy and others. McCarthy effectively ended his own career by attacking the army, claiming that they were hiding communists. These charges resulted in the Army-McCarthy hearings, where McCarthy's charges were shown to be baseless. McCarthy was eventually censured—ending his reign, but the fear of communism began before McCarthy and continued long after. The national witch-hunt was not limited to McCarthy's committee, or even Congress. Hollywood blacklisted anyone who was thought to be a communist, even investigating Lucille Ball. College campuses banned professors with past communist affiliations. At the height of McCarthyism, few were willing to challenge the hysteria, as Margaret Chase Smith did. The more common reaction was to allow fear to silence any criticism, characterized by the letter dated November 24, 1954 from two Harvard students.

Significance

Margaret Chase Smith was one of the few to oppose McCarthy publicly without suffering any harm during that era. McCarthy, angered by her opposition, attempted to defeat her bid for reelection to the Senate in 1954. However, McCarthy was unsuccessful, one of his few defeats during that period. Unlike Smith, the public's thoughts on communism were reflected well in this anonymous comment: "I don't know what communism is, but there had better not be any of it in Washington."

The label "Communist" was not used just to tar politicians, those who were or had been communists or associated with radicals. The label also has been used to discredit leaders in the Civil Rights movement and the anti-war movement in the 1960s. Despite the collapse of the Soviet Union and the small number of Americans who advocate communism, the label remains an epithet to be employed against political enemies.

In the 1960s, both the courts and the public broadened their conceptions of free speech. The Supreme Court began to enlarge the First Amendment to protect unpopular ideas and to prevent the police from arresting those who pronounced those ideas. The student counterculture of the 1960s also promoted free speech as well (although sometimes not wanting to grant that freedom to their opponents). Since the 1960s, free speech has not always increased. But, on the whole, people have come to believe in free speech more and enjoy more free speech than they did in the 1950s.

Primary Source

"Declaration of Conscience" [excerpt]

SYNOPSIS: Senator Margaret Chase Smith argues that many people are being damaged by innuendo, possible only because of the constitutional grant of immunity to members of Congress. She asserts that basic freedoms, including the "right to hold unpopular ideas," are being compromised by the unseemly behavior by the Senate.

A Senator Speaks Up

I think that it is high time for the United States Senate and its Members to do some real soul searching, and to weigh our consciences as to the manner in which we are performing our duty to the people of America, and the manner in which we are using or abusing our individual powers and privileges.

I think it is high time that we remembered that we have sworn to uphold and defend the Constitution. I think it is high time that we remembered that the Constitution, as amended, speaks not only of the freedom of speech but also of trial by jury instead of trial by accusation.

Whether it be a criminal prosecution in court or a character prosecution in the Senate, there is little practical distinction when the life of a person has been ruined.

Those of us who shout the loudest about Americanism in making character assassinations are all too frequently those who, by our own words and acts, ignore some of the basic principles of Americanism—

The right to criticize.

The right to hold unpopular beliefs.

The right to protest.

The right of independent thought.

The exercise of these rights should not cost one single American citizen his reputation or his right to a livelihood, nor should he be in danger of losing his reputation or livelihood merely because he happens to know someone who holds unpopular beliefs. Who of us does not? Otherwise none of us could call our souls our own. Otherwise thought control would have set in.

The American people are sick and tired of being afraid to speak their minds lest they be politically smeared as Communists or Fascists by their opponents. Freedom of speech is not what it used to be in America. It has been so abused by some that it is not exercised by others.

The American people are sick and tired of seeing innocent people smeared and guilty people whitewashed. But there have been enough proved cases, such as the *Amerasia* case [*Amerasia* was a communist-tainted magazine that acquired confidential government documents. Judith Coplon, a Justice Department employee, and Harry Gold, a Philadelphia biochemist, were both convicted in 1950 of spying for the Soviet Union.], the Hiss case, the Coplon case, the Gold case, to cause nationwide distrust and strong suspicion that there may be something to the unproved, sensational accusations. . . .

Today our country is being psychologically divided by the confusion and the suspicions that are bred in the United States Senate to spread like cancerous tentacles of "know nothing, suspect everything" attitudes. . . .

As a United States Senator, I am not proud of the way in which the Senate has been made a publicity platform for irresponsible sensationalism. I am not proud of the reckless abandon in which unproved charges have been hurled from this [Republican] side of the aisle. I am not proud of the obviously staged, undignified countercharges which have been attempted in retaliation from the other [Democratic] side of the aisle.

I do not like the way the Senate has been made a rendezvous for vilification, for selfish political gain at the sacrifice of individual reputations and national unity. I am not proud of the way we smear outsiders from the floor of the Senate and hide behind the cloak of congressional immunity, and still place ourselves beyond criticism on the floor of the Senate.

As an American, I am shocked at the way Republicans and Democrats alike are playing directly into the Communist design of "confuse, divide, and conquer." As an American, I do not want a Democratic administration whitewash or cover-up any more than I want a Republican smear or witch hunt.

As an American, I condemn a Republican Fascist just as much as I condemn a Democratic Communist. I condemn a Democratic Fascist just as much as I condemn a Republican Communist. They are equally dangerous to you and me and to our country. As an American, I want to see our Nation recapture the strength and unity it once had when we fought the enemy instead of ourselves.

Primary Source

Letters to the Harvard *Crimson*

SYNOPSIS: Two Harvard students write that they would not sign a petition calling for the Senate to censure McCarthy because of fear that their signatures could be used eventually to attack them, if a cosigner of the petition happened to be a communist. This letter and the response by a fellow student reflect the hysteria of fear in America during that era.

To the Editors of the *Crimson:*

This afternoon my roommate and I were asked to sign a petition advocating the censure of Senator Joseph R. McCarthy. We both refused. And yet, we both hope that the censure motion is adopted.

Discussing our actions, we came to the conclusion that we did not sign because we were afraid that sometime in the future McCarthy will point to us as having signed the petition, and, as he had done to others, question our loyalty.

We are afraid that of the thousands of petition signers, one will be proved a Communist, and as a result, McCarthy, or someone like him, will say, because we were both co-signers and classmates of the Communist, that we, too, are Reds.

The fact that two college students and others like us will not sign a petition for fear of reprisal indicates only too clearly that our democracy is in danger. It is clear that McCarthy is suppressing free speech and free actions by thrusting fear into the hearts of innocent citizens.

Senator Margaret Chase Smith openly criticized Senator McCarthy.
© BETTMANN/CORBIS. REPRODUCED BY PERMISSION.

Let us hope that the Senators of the United States are not victims of the same fear that has infected us.

K. W. L. '58
M. F. G. '58

To the Editors of the *Crimson:*

The letter sent to you by two Harvard students and published yesterday can safely be said to represent the viewpoint of about one half of those who did not sign the anti-McCarthy petition.

The position taken by the authors is common and understandable, but it is by no means justifiable. In a free society, when opinions become unpopular and dangerous, it is most important that they be expressed. To yield to the climate of fear, to become a scared liberal, is to strengthen the very forces which one opposes. Courage must complement conviction, for otherwise each man will become a rubber-stamp, content to spend the rest of his life echoing popular beliefs, never daring to dissent, never having enough courage to say what he thinks, and never living as an individual, but only as part of the crowd.

Yes, our democracy is in danger, but as long as men are not afraid to express their view in spite of the consequences, it shall flourish. Only when fear is allowed to limit dissension does democracy falter.

The blame for America's present intellectual intolerance rests as heavily on those who have bowed to it as it does on those who encourage it.

Sincerely,
J. C. Peter Richardson '56

Further Resources

BOOKS

Garber, Marjorie B., and Rebecca L Walkowitz. *Secret Agents: the Rosenberg Case, McCarthyism, and Fifties America.* New York: Routledge, 1995.

Heale, M.J. *McCarthy's Americans: Red Scare Politics in State and Nation, 1935-1965.* Athens: University of Georgia Press, 1998.

Herman, Arthur. *Joseph McCarthy: Reexamining the Life and Legacy of America's Most Hated Senator.* New York: Free Press, 2000.

Navasky, Victor S. *Naming Names.* New York: Viking Press, 1980.

Schrecker, Ellen. *No Ivory Tower: McCarthyism and the Universities.* New York: Oxford University Press, 1986.

Sherman, Janann. *No Place For a Woman: A Life of Senator Margaret Chase Smith.* New Brunswick: Rutgers University Press, 2000.

Smith, Margaret Chase. *Declaration of Conscience.* New York: Doubleday, 1972.

Vallin, Marlene Boyd. *Margaret Chase Smith: Model Public Servant.* Westport, Conn.: Greenwood Press, 1998.

WEBSITES

Margaret Chase Smith Center for Public Policy. Available online at http://www.umaine.edu/mcsc; website home page: http://www.umaine.edu (accessed March 15, 2003).

Margaret Chase Smith Biography. Available online at http://www.umaine.edu/mcsc/AboutUs/Bio.htm; website home page: http://www.umaine.edu (accessed March 15, 2003).

Chesterfield Cigarettes Advertisements

Advertisements

By: Chesterfield Cigarettes

Date: 1950–1960

Source: Chesterfield cigarette advertisements 1950–1960. Reproduced from The Advertising Archive, Ltd.

About the Organization: Liggett and Myers introduced Chesterfield cigarettes, a mix of Turkish and Virginia tobacco, in 1912. One of Chesterfield's early slogans was

"They do satisfy." Chesterfields sponsored entertainment shows, including Dragnet and the Bing Crosby Show. Lucille Ball was a poster girl for Chesterfield Cigarettes, as were Jane Wyman and Donna Reed. Liggett Group sold the Chesterfield trademark in 1999 to Phillip Morris USA, who still manufactures Chesterfields. ■

Introduction

Native Americans grew tobacco long before European explorations. Tobacco was the crop that sustained Virginia's economy, and it was very popular in Europe. The tobacco market, though, proved unstable, and it was largely replaced by cotton and wheat in the early 1800s. Tobacco processing grew in the American South, particularly that of cigarettes, in the late nineteenth century. Cigarettes became a mass consumption item in the 1920s, as more people could afford them. During the 1910s and 1920s, print ads were used to sell cigarettes. During World War I (1914–1918), ads ran suggesting that war heroes would trade all of their souvenirs for one cigarette of a certain brand. Funds also were established to help buy soldiers packs of cigarettes.

After World War I, besides newspaper ads, cigarettes also got a boost from the movies. While most movies did not promote a certain brand of cigarettes, movie (and later television) stars were seen smoking, making smoking appear glamorous. Leading Hollywood stars smoked onscreen, including Humphrey Bogart in the 1940s and James Dean in the 1950s. Cigarettes were included in the army's K-rations during World War II (1939–1945). By the 1950s, however, advertisers had a number of other concerns. Since the 1920s, there were health concerns linked to smoking, and companies needed to address those concerns. Companies also wanted to be able to promote cigarettes as a good gift.

Significance

Chesterfield promoted their cigarette as safe—and this was before cigarettes had filters. Chesterfield noted that a study by a "responsible consulting organization," concluded that "nose, throat and accessory organs not adversely affected by smoking Chesterfields." Whether the medical specialists believed these findings is unknown. (Based on current medical research, either the study sample was not representative or the findings were biased.) By the 1950s, the clear medical evidence, published in major medical journals, demonstrated the negative health consequences of smoking. It was not just Chesterfield though, as other cigarette manufacturers promoted themselves as companies with "not a cough in a carload" of their smokers. These claims came back to haunt companies, as they formed the basis of later legal claims.

These ads also promoted smoking as a way of life. After all, if movie star Ronald Reagan smokes Chester-

I'M SENDING CHESTERFIELDS to all my friends. That's the merriest Christmas any smoker can have— Chesterfield mildness plus no unpleasant after-taste

Ronald Reagan

see RONALD REAGAN starring in "HONG KONG" a Pine-Thomas Paramount Production Color by Technicolor

CHESTERFIELD *"Buy the beautiful Christmas-card" carton*

Primary Source

Chesterfield Cigarettes Advertisements (1 of 2)

SYNOPSIS: A Chesterfields cigarette ad shows actor (later President) Ronald Reagan sending cartons of Chesterfields to his friends for Christmas. Another ad falsely states "nose, throat and accessory organs not adversely affected by smoking Chesterfields." It discusses a study by a "responsible consulting organization" that reached this conclusion. Two boxes of Chesterfields (regular and king size) are featured in the ad. Cigarette smoking is known to cause cancer of the mouth and throat and the link between lung cancer and smoking had been discovered in 1950. THE ADVERTISING ARCHIVE, LTD. REPRODUCED BY PERMISSION.

NOSE, THROAT,
and Accessory Organs not Adversely Affected by Smoking Chesterfields

FIRST SUCH REPORT EVER PUBLISHED ABOUT ANY CIGARETTE

A responsible consulting organization has reported the results of a continuing study by a competent medical specialist and his staff on the effects of smoking Chesterfield cigarettes.

A group of people from various walks of life was organized to smoke only Chesterfields. For six months this group of men and women smoked their normal amount of Chesterfields – 10 to 40 a day. 45% of the group have smoked Chesterfields continually from one to thirty years for an average of 10 years each.

At the beginning and at the end of the six-months period each smoker was given a thorough examination, including X-ray pictures, by the medical specialist and his assistants. The examination covered the sinuses as well as the nose, ears and throat.

The medical specialist, after a thorough examination of every member of the group, stated: "It is my opinion that the ears, nose, throat and accessory organs of all participating subjects examined by me were not adversely affected in the six-months period by smoking the cigarettes provided."

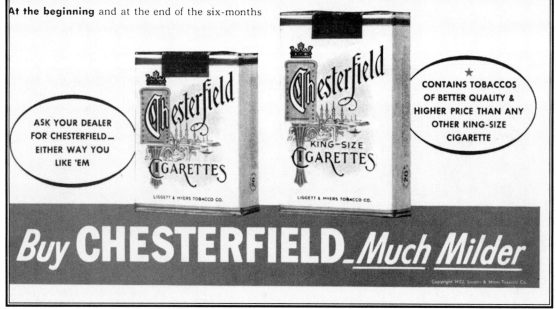

ASK YOUR DEALER FOR CHESTERFIELD — EITHER WAY YOU LIKE 'EM

CONTAINS TOBACCOS OF BETTER QUALITY & HIGHER PRICE THAN ANY OTHER KING-SIZE CIGARETTE

Buy CHESTERFIELD _Much Milder_

Primary Source

Chesterfield Cigarettes Advertisements (2 OF 2)

Chesterfield brand cigarettes—at one time the best selling cigarette brand in America—claimed that those who used their product were not adversely affected. THE ADVERTISING ARCHIVE, LTD. REPRODUCED BY PERMISSION.

fields and gives them away to his friends, should not the average person as well? Smoking also was aided by workplace policies that offered smoke breaks. Some workplaces only gave these breaks to those who smoked, encouraging the habit.

The surgeon general's report linking smoking and cancer caused smoking to come under attack in the 1960s. During the 1970s, warnings of smoking's ill effects were placed upon cigarette packages, and advertising was restricted. States also began to ban smoking in certain public places. Smokers viewed these efforts as intruding on their personal autonomy. However, recent research on the harmful effects of second-hand smoke challenges that position. People also have been forced to change their lifestyle as most private businesses, including many restaurants, prohibit smoking.

Further Resources

BOOKS

Kessler, David A. *A Question of Intent: A Great American Battle with a Deadly Industry.* New York: Public Affairs, 2001.

Schaler, Jeffery A., and Magda E. Schaler. *Smoking: Who Has the Right?* Amherst, N.Y.: Prometheus Books, 1998.

Should Tobacco Advertising Be Restricted? San Diego, Calif.: Greenhaven Press, 1998.

U.S. Senate. *Tobacco: Hearing before the Committee on Commerce, Science, and Transportation, March 3, 1998* 105th Cong., 2nd sess.

Viscusi, W. Kip. *Smoke-Filled Rooms: A Postmortem on the Tobacco Deal.* Chicago: University of Chicago Press, 2002.

WEBSITES

Center for Disease Control-Tobacco Information and Prevention Source. Available online at http://www.cdc.gov/tobacco /advcoadv.htm; website home page: http://cdc.gov (accessed March 17, 2003).

AUDIO AND VISUAL MEDIA

Jhally, Sut, Jean Kilbourne, and Richard W. Pollay. *Pack of Lies: The Advertising of Tobacco.* Northampton, Mass.: Foundation for Media Education, 1992.

"The Two-Income Family"

Magazine article

By: *Harper's Magazine*

Date: December 1951

Source: "The Two-Income Family" *Harper's Magazine,* December, 1951. Reprinted in Kennedy, David M., ed. *The American Spirit.* Vol. 2, 10th ed., Boston: Houghton Mifflin Co., 2002, 399–400.

About the Publication: *Harper's* debuted in 1850, quickly becoming a mass-market magazine featuring American

artists and the news of the period. *Harper's* has published works by significant political figures in their youth, including Winston Churchill. In the 1970s, *Harper's* was one of the first magazines to cover the My Lai massacre. *Harper's* publishing interests are now HarperCollins, and *Harper's* is now published by the Harper's Magazine Foundation, which was formed with assets from a grant from the MacArthur Foundation. ■

Introduction

Women and men have not been treated equally in the American workplace, even though historically both women and men have worked. In the early agricultural households, women worked in the house, while the men worked on the farm. With the early industries, women and men both worked out of the home. Women were not treated equally, though, as women generally were not allowed the right to vote. In the nineteenth century, middle and upper class women (without being asked) were (theoretically) put upon a pedestal and elevated into the "cult of domesticity"—assigned a special role to run the home, protect it, and elevate the morals of the home. With the rise of the middle and upper classes, women were not allowed to work in industry, and women were kept out of the professions.

Societal barriers for women began to be lowered in the early twentieth century. The Nineteenth Amendment (1920) provided that the right to vote would not be denied on the basis of sex. Women also served in the armed forces and worked in factories during World War I (1914–1919) and World War II (1939–1945). Particularly after World War II, women often did not want to return to the home or move from the factory to a lower paying job. Women, though, did not have a choice, as they were usually summarily fired and replaced by men. In the prevailing culture of the 1950s, women were supposed to gladly return to the home and allow men to work. Besides those not wanting to be homemakers, there were also those who needed to work for economic reasons.

Significance

Many Americans regard the 1950s as a time when most women stayed home, and men were the sole breadwinners. As this excerpt indicates, the decision for women to work was very often economically based. Women were working to purchase extra items for the children or a larger house. Women were also working to help provide financial security that the experience of the Great Depression caused them to doubt. The 1950s were the decade when consumerism established its hold on America—which it has never lost since. That consumerism was financed, in part, by women working.

A working mother waves goodbye to her family as she leaves to go to her job outside of the home, 1953. © BETTMANN/CORBIS. REPRODUCED BY PERMISSION.

These women, though, were not trying to change the world, and not all women worked. Further, there were only limited employment opportunities open to women. The few female law school graduates were shunted into second-class jobs. Sandra Day O'Connor, graduating near the top of her class at Stanford, could not find a job at any law firm. Women were kept out of other professions as well, and they were told to be happy being housewives. It took until the 1960s for women, at least publicly and frequently, to be crusaders for change. Despite outside employment, women were still left with most of the child-care, cleaning and cooking responsibilities. In the 1990s and 2000s, there has been a resurgence of stay-at-home moms, and even the emergence of stay-at-home dads. People began to consider whether a one-income (or a one-and-a-half-income) family was best for all concerned. A perfect solution for all still has yet to be found, as America still struggles with the "two-income" family issue.

Primary Source

"The Two-Income Family" [excerpt]

SYNOPSIS: The author opens with the observation that working is no longer a political statement, but an economic one. She then notes that men have accepted the necessity of women working in order to break even, and that men and women know that families can no longer be raised on a single income. The article closes commenting that the Great Depression and the war have convinced families that they cannot go back to having only one income.

I am a wife, a mother, and a grandmother, and I have been a continuous jobholder since I graduated from college. Besides all that, I am a dodo.

I never used to think of myself as a dodo, but it has been brought home to me by my married daughter and her contemporaries that I most certainly am. These young people have perpetrated a revolution right under the noses of my generation. There have been no parades, no crusading arguments or lectures or legislative lobbying. They did not fight for a revolution—they simply are one.

The whole argument of marriage versus a career which burned like a roaring fire when I was my daughter's age is now as dead as wet ashes. The revolution that we were so vociferous about as a matter of principle has taken place unobtrusively as a matter of hard necessity.

My daughter and her friends and the young married women who work in my office do not call themselves career women. They do not harangue about the right to develop their individual capacities. They do not discuss the primary function of woman as a homemaker. They do not argue the propriety of muscling in on the labor market. They just plain work. . . .

Under present circumstances, a single pay envelope will not meet the needs of a white-collar-class family. It is as simple as that. . . .

Through a good many years of my life I heard men say, "I'd be ashamed to let my wife work." The standard of a man's success in America was—and to some extent still is—his earning capacity. It was a symbol of his masculine prowess and an extension of his virility. To maintain his social, his economic, and his psychological position as titular head of the family by virtue of being its source of supply he often had to relinquish long-term goals for temporary advantages and to sacrifice his natural aptitudes to the demands of an immediate and steady job. No wonder Thoreau said that "most men lead lives of quiet desperation."

No wonder, then, that men jealously guarded their prerogatives. To be a "good provider" was one of the chief criteria—and in the eyes of many was *the* criterion—of man's achievement. Every woman of my generation who worked in what was called a "man's job" knew what it was to walk on eggs. With a diplomacy that would make Machiavelli look like a coal-heaver in a conference of foreign ministers the masculine ego had to be protected from the slightest scratch in both marital and occupational relations.

This often made the women of my generation hopping mad. What we did not realize was that the restrictions foisted on us by the masculine ego were not prompted by innate sex cussedness. They were imposed by a cultural code which men dared not

flout under penalty of losing face, and which they would keep women from flouting, if they could, for the same reason. But something has happened to alter this code, something that has convinced men as well as women that the rigid demarcation of their spheres of action made them both the losers. . . .

These young people were children during the great depression of the thirties. They learned the facts of economic life by experiencing or observing the collapse of financial security. They were married either just before or during or after the late war, and when their husbands were called into the armed forces the young wives had to learn to stand alone in a practical as well as an emotional sense.

Once the war was over and husbands returned, few of them had had a chance to accumulate any savings. The allotments they received from the government were insufficient to support their families in accordance with middle-class standards of living. Wives with or without children either had to produce income or throw themselves on the mercy of relatives who had problems of their own. . . .

How does a two-income family cope with the problem of bringing up young children? Not so long ago a woman of proved vocational ability was adjured to divide her life into two—or, more rarely, three—periods. She might work until she produced a baby, but then she must either bury her vocation altogether, exchanging it for that of housewife-and-mother, or else lay it away for long years with the rather feeble hope of resuscitating it after the children were grown. That picture has now changed out of all recognition. Indeed, one hears wives arguing that children, instead of constituting the unanswerable argument against the two-income family, are strong arguments in its favor.

"If it weren't for the children," said one wife to me, "I'd be tempted to try to get along on one salary, even if it meant skimping. But we need two incomes to enable us to have a house with a yard that the children can play in; to live in a neighborhood where I don't have to worry about their playmates; to provide a guitar for the musical one and dancing lessons for the one who needs to improve her muscular coordination—not to mention teeth-straightening and medical insurance and the bonds we are stowing away for their education. . . ."

The depression years, the war years, and the postwar years have cracked the old economic-social family mold. These were forces outside the control of individual women, but they have learned a lesson from circumstances. The working wives of 1951 have learned to recognize the mistakes of my generation, and are determined not to repeat them. . . .

Further Resources

BOOKS

Barnett, Rosalind C., and Caryl Rivers. *She Works/He Works: How Two-Income Families are Happier, Healthier, and Better-off.* San Francisco: HarperSanFrancisco, 1996.

Ellen Galinsky. *Ask the Children: What America's Children Really Think about Working Parents.* New York: William Morrow, 1999.

Hochschild, Arlie Russell. *The Time Bind: When Work Becomes Home and Home Becomes Work.* New York: Metropolitan Books, 1997.

Hochschild, Arlie Russell, and Anne Machung. *The Second Shift: Working Parents and the Revolution at Home.* New York: Viking, 1989.

Kimball, Gayle. *50-50 Parenting: Sharing Family Rewards and Responsibilities.* Lexington, Mass.: Lexington Books, 1988.

Meyerowitz, Joanne J. *Not June Cleaver: Women and Gender in Postwar America, 1945-1960.* Philadelphia: Temple University Press, 1994.

PERIODICALS

Townsend, Bickley, and Martha Farnsworth Riche. "Two Paychecks and Seven Lifestyles." *American Demographics,* Vol. 9, No. 8, August 1987, 24–29.

WEBSITES

Family Diversity. Available online at http://www.parenting information.org/familydiversity.htm; website home page: www.parentinginformation.org (accessed March 18, 2003).

"Homogenized Children of New Suburbia"

Magazine article

By: Sidonie Gruenberg

Date: September 19, 1954

Source: Gruenberg, Sidonie. "Homogenized Children of New Suburbia." *New York Times Magazine,* September 19, 1954. Reprinted in Kennedy, David M., ed. *The American Spirit.* Vol. 2, 10th ed., Boston: Houghton Mifflin Co., 2002, 401–402.

About the Author: Sidonie Gruenberg (1881–1974) was a graduate of Columbia University, and lectured at Columbia and New York University. He wrote over 18 works including *Sons and Daughters* and *Parents, Children and Money.* He served on a number of boards, including the National Council on Family Relations, and he was a member of the editorial board of the Junior Literary Guild. He contributed articles to several periodicals, including *Childcraft, Family Circle, Redbook,* and the *New York Times Magazine.* ■

Introduction

In America's early years, the vast majority of Americans lived in small towns or rural areas, and most Americans were connected to the farm economy. At the time of the nation's first census in 1790, nearly ninety-five percent of American citizens lived in rural areas. In the cities, only the wealthy could afford to purchase their own homes. People generally were limited to the "walking city," and this limited the geographical size of cities—in turn driving up the cost of land. Even with a horse, the commuting range was limited.

This all changed with the invention of the electric streetcar in the 1870s. Streetcars pulled by horses existed, but they were not fast enough. Electric streetcars, elevated railway, cable cars, and trolleys all developed in this period to speed transportation, and they allowed employees to move further from work. Many in the middle class, unable to afford houses in the central city, moved out to what were called "streetcar suburbs." These were America's first suburbs. With the automobile, suburbs moved even further from the cities. Access routes limited commuters, as most streets leading to the inner city had a stoplight on every block. Mortgages typically required purchasers to make a down payment of eighty percent of the homes' value, with the balance to be paid off in five years. World War II (1939–1945) drastically changed the mortgage system, as the federal government began to offer Veterans Administration mortgages with a one dollar down payment and a thirty–year payment plan.

Significance

Gruenberg points out several difficulties with suburbia, many of which still exist today. He first points out that many of the suburbs were homogenized, lacking minority populations. While more minorities have moved to the suburbs in the last half-century, there still are many suburbs, if not the majority, that still exist as largely monocultural enclaves. The suburbs, especially today with planned developments, clearly present a homogenized economic community—as houses within any development are in a certain price range, presupposing a similar economic status.

Gruenberg also pointed out the lack of culture and lack of community often found in the suburbs. These issues also continue in the present. Houses are located in one area, businesses in another, and government buildings and shopping centers in still others. Many citizens of many communities hardly ever interact with one another. In many suburbs, rather than being a community where people generally interact from front porches or backyards, they are living room communities—where people remain in their living room, watch television (or play on the Internet) and are too busy to interact with anyone.

Rows of tract housing make up Cottage Grove Township, a suburb of St. Paul, Minnesota. © MINNESOTA HISTORICAL SOCIETY/CORBIS. REPRODUCED BY PERMISSION.

Gruenberg also pointed out the lack of opportunities for women and the pressure to conform. The first has been somewhat alleviated, as most families are multi-car families and women commute into work, just like men do. Commuting times of over two hours per day are not unheard of in many areas. Mass transit systems also do not exist for most of these new suburbs, creating additional congestion and pollution issues. Thus, even though suburbs are beneficial to many, they still have many problems.

Primary Source

"Homogenized Children of New Suburbia" [excerpt]

SYNOPSIS: Gruenberg first notes that suburbs tend to be very racially and culturally homogenized. The article comments that the newer suburbs, especially developed in the 1950s, are without history or culture. Gruenberg remarks on how few older people or minorities live in the suburbs. Therefore, the sub-urbs are "homogenized" and its residents are pressured to conform. The article closes by noting how women have few opportunities in the new suburbs.

A young man who had attended an exclusive preparatory school and an Ivy League college felt that his horizon had been restricted because, during the years of his education he had met only the sons of bankers, brokers, executives, lawyers and doctors. He determined that, when the time came, *his* children would go to public school.

The time came. The young man and his wife moved out to the suburbs where their children could get fresh air and play space, go to public school and grow up with children of all kinds. "And whom do my children meet?" he asks. "The children of bankers, brokers, executives, lawyers and doctors!"

Despite the drawback that depressed this particular parent, the suburb into which he moved had certain things in its favor, besides the obvious attraction of lebensraum [A German word meaning space required for life, growth, or activity]. It was a town, one of the older suburbs. It had grown up gradually over the years with its own schools, churches and deepening civic consciousness until it had developed into a real *community* with traditions of its own.

New Suburbia is something else again. Around every major city from the Atlantic to the Pacific the new suburbs have been springing up like mushrooms in a damp season. They are sometimes created by dividing large estates—as on Long Island, in Westchester County and in areas around Chicago, Detroit and Los Angeles. More often the new suburbs are built on what had been until recently empty acreage. Whether in California or New Jersey they are typically "prefabricated" in all their details and the parts are suddenly assembled on the spot. Unlike towns and cities and the suburbs of the past, they do not evolve gradually but emerge full-blown. They are designed and constructed by corporations or real estate operators who work on mass-production principles. A hundred or a thousand houses open their doors almost simultaneously, ready for occupancy. . . .

. . . The new suburbanites take what they can afford and can get. And they pay a subtle psychological price. For one thing, the new suburb is a community only in the sense that it is an aggregate of dwellings—often identical houses. It may in time become a community, but not yet. No one has grown up in it; it has no traditions. We really don't know what effect it will ultimately have on children; we can only conjecture.

The families of New Suburbia consist typically of a young couple with one or two children, or perhaps one child and another on the way. The child living here sees no elderly people, no teenagers. Except on weekends and holidays he sees only mothers and other children of his own age. This dearth of weekday variety was remarked on by a woman who had moved to a new suburb and returned after some months to visit friends in her former city neighborhood. "Though I have lived in the city most of my life," she said, "I was actually startled to see such a variety of people, of every type and age. It seemed so long since I had seen old people and school kids, since I had seen men around in the daytime!"

If Old Suburbia is lacking in a variety of work going on that boys and girls can watch or actively share in, it at least has a garage, a movie theatre, a shoe repair shop. In New Suburbia there is often nothing but a supermarket and a gasoline station. In Old Suburbia children grow up seeing people of all ages and playing with children older than themselves—from whom each child normally learns the ways and customs appropriate to the age into which he matures day by day. In New Suburbia the children are likely to be nearly of the same age. In Old Suburbia the fathers take the train to the city each day, leaving the car with the mothers. In New Suburbia there is often no railroad station, so the fathers drive to work in their own cars or by "car pool." The mothers remain—with the house and yard and children.

The children growing up in New Suburbia run the danger of becoming "homogenized." In many of the new suburbs the white child never sees a Negro. In others the Jewish child never plays with any but Jewish children. Some of these suburbs are virtually all Catholic. In others there are no Catholics. Even without racial and religious segregation—and in these new developments groups tend to segregate themselves to an alarming degree—the pressure to conform is intense, and stultifying. . . .

Moreover, in this atmosphere children are likely to picture the good life in terms of uniform, standardized patterns; and that tends to block invention and experiment. Because nothing out of the way ever happens in these quiet, sanitary and standardized surroundings, one wonders what will arouse the imagination of these children. What spiritual equivalent will they find for the challenge and inspiration that an older generation found during childhood in city streets, on farms, in market towns? . . .

Many of the mothers in these new suburbs have had considerable training in offices or shops and some have a degree of executive ability. In New Suburbia they find no outlets for their talents and energies and they tend to focus all their efforts upon their children. Everything that the mothers do, all the little chores, tend to take on disproportionate significance, so that the children feel the pressures while the mothers cannot help feeling frustrated and discontented. This does not mean that they are unhappy with their homes and their children, for they have, essentially, what every woman wants; but they are confused and often feel that there is something lacking in the lives they lead. At the same time, their children cannot help but get a picture of adults as being constantly concerned with trivialities.

Some of the other obvious shortcomings of the new suburbs are incidental to their very newness. In time, a church will be built, perhaps several. A meeting place or assembly hall will rise. In some new suburbs the school from the very first offers a meeting place for parents. But the important question, it seems to me, is how the parents can keep the benefits of New Suburbia without paying too heavy a price. . . .

Further Resources

BOOKS

Halberstam, David. *The Fifties.* New York: Villard Books, 1993.

Hughes, Robert. *Culture of Complaint: The Fraying of America.* New York: Oxford University Press, 1993.

Jackson, Kenneth T. *Crabgrass Frontier: The Suburbanization of the United States.* New York: Oxford University Press, 1985.

Kammen, Michael G. *American Culture, American Tastes: Social Change and the 20th Century.* New York: Knopf, 1999.

Rollin, Lucy. *Twentieth-Century Teen Culture by the Decades: A Reference Guide.* Westport, Conn.: Greenwood Press, 1999.

Silverstone, Roger. *Visions of Suburbia.* London: Routledge, 1997.

Stach, Patricia Burgess. *Building the Suburbs: The Social Structure of the Residential Neighborhoods in Post-War America.* Arlington: Institute of Urban Studies, University of Texas at Arlington, 1991.

WEBSITES

Suburban Sprawl from the Sierra Club. Available online at http://www.sierraclub.org/sprawl/; website home page: http://www.sierraclub.org (accessed March 17, 2003.)

AUDIO AND VISUAL MEDIA

Jennings, Peter, et al. *The Century: America's Time. 9, Happy Days.* Princeton, N.J.: Films for the Humanities & Sciences, 1999.

Seduction of the Innocent

Nonfiction work

By: Frederic Wertham

Date: 1954

Source: Wertham, Fredric, M.D. *Seduction of the Innocent.* New York: Rinehart & Company, 1954, 4–5, 8–9, 19, 22–23, 33, 395.

About the Author: Frederic Wertham M.D. (1895–1981) graduated medical school at the University of Wurzburg. He served in a variety of posts, including the Director of the Mental Hygiene Clinic at Bellevue Hospital for ten years. He also served as the Psychiatric Consultant to U.S. Senate Ke-

fauver Subcommittee to Study Organized Crime. The author of at least a dozen books, Wertham focused on how people are "acculturated" to violence, and on the influence of television and print on violence. ∎

Introduction

Mass production of newspapers developed during the late nineteenth century. Between 1870 and 1910, newspaper circulation exploded—from just over two million to nearly twenty-five million. Mass produced novels circulated as well. These "dime" novels were produced on cheap paper and told wild tales of the old west, romantic tales, and detective stories. Many newspapers of the period included comic strips in their pages.

These newspapers and the larger cultural attractions were not without their detractors though. Many progressives believed that the way to bring about progress in society was to control what people watched in the theaters or read. One progressive argued that a play "Raffles the Amateur Cracksman" caused at least thirteen boys to become burglars. To stop these and similar youths, progressives argued that the offending plays, movies, and books should be banned. "Safe" activities like baseball and group sports should be substituted.

Comic books began to be sold in large quantities during and after World War II (1939–1945). Dr. Wertham estimated that sixty million comic books were sold every month. This high readership was the result of the era's children having more "pocket money." Dr. Wertham launched an all-out attack on comic books, blaming them for many of society's ills.

Significance

Wertham failed in his attempt to have comic books removed from society. Although he caused a great many people to become alarmed over the issue, no comic book rating system was ever developed. Comic books were not removed from many stores, at least not for extended periods of time. The whole concern over comic books causing delinquency shifted in the late 1950s, as many now attributed delinquency to a new cause, "rock and roll" music. These same concerns, ironically, were raised a decade earlier by people wishing to remove Frank Sinatra, jazz, and swing from stores, believing that those genres of music were causing the decline of the youth of that generation.

With the counterculture movement of the 1960s, many new forms of music and writings flooded America. Some argued for censoring music, art and literature in order to protect the minds of young Americans. Others argued that the music and other cultural expressions were a result of the counterculture, and not the cause of it. Censoring regulations were challenged on many campuses, with, perhaps, the most well known occurring on

Boys read 3D comic books together in 1953. © BETTMANN/CORBIS. REPRODUCED BY PERMISSION.

the University of California at Berkeley's campus with the Free Speech movement. Many of these battles over censorship intertwined with other issues, as "vulgar" messages that the government wanted to repress expressed fierce opposition to the Vietnam War (1964–1975). Rating systems were instituted for movies in 1968.

With the end of the Vietnam War and the maturing of the baby boom generation, protests lessened. But there still were many who wanted to control what the youth of America heard or read. Ratings were developed for music, and "explicit lyrics" labels were added. Tipper Gore, wife of former vice-president Al Gore, was one of the people spearheading this effort. Efforts were and continue to be made to control the Internet as well, beginning in the mid-1990s. Although the controversy has died down somewhat over comic books and the counterculture, the issue of censorship still remains.

Primary Source

Seduction of the Innocent [excerpt]

SYNOPSIS: Wertham notes that today's children have never been protected against corrupting influences. He describes the violence in many comic books, and argues that even the messages claiming, "crime does not pay," convey just the opposite message. Wertham closes by relating the story of a youth named Willie who had committed crimes because he had read too many comic books. Wertham reassured the youth's mother that it was not her fault, but the comic books' fault.

Some time ago a judge found himself confronted with twelve youths, the catch of some hundred and fifty policemen assigned to prevent a street battle of juvenile gangs. This outbreak was a sequel to the killing of a fifteen-year-old boy who had been stabbed to death as he sat with his girl in a parked car. The twelve boys were charged with being involved in the shooting of three boys with a .22-caliber zip gun and a .32 revolver. The indignant judge addressed them angrily, "We're not treating you like kids any longer. . . . If you act like hoodlums you'll be treated like hoodlums." But *were* these youths treated like "kids" in the first place? Were they protected against the corrupting influence of comic books which glamorize and advertise dangerous knives and the guns that can be converted into deadly weapons? . . .

The Lafargue Clinic has some of his [Willie's] comic books. They are before me as I am writing this, smudgily printed and well thumbed, just as he used to pore over them with his weak eyes. Here is the lecherous-looking bandit overpowering the attractive girl who is dressed (if that is the word) for very hot weather ("She could come in handy, then! Pretty little spitfire, eh!") in the typical pre-rape position. Later he threatens to kill her:

> Yeah, it's us, you monkeys, and we got an old friend of yours here. . . . Now unless you want to see somp'n FATAL happen to her, u're gonna kiss that gold goodbye and lam out of here!

Here is violence galore, violence in the beginning, in the middle, at the end:

ZIP! CRASH! SOCK! SPLAT! BAM! SMASH!

(This is an actual sequence of six pictures illustrating brutal fighting, until in the seventh picture: "He's out cold!")

Here, too, is the customary close-up of the surprised and frightened-looking policeman with his hands half-raised saying:

NO—NO! DON'T SHOOT!

as he is threatened by a huge fist holding a gun to his face. This is followed by mild disapproval ("You've gone too far! This is murder!") as the uniformed man lies dead on the ground. This comic book is endorsed by child specialists who are connected with important institutions. No wonder Willie's aunt did not trust her own judgment sufficiently.

The stories have a lot of crime and gunplay and, in addition, alluring advertisements of guns, some of them full-page and in bright colors, with four guns of various sizes and descriptions on a page:

> Get a sweet-shootin'———[gun] and get in on the fun!

Here is the repetition of violence and sexiness which no Freud, Krafft-Ebing or Havelock Ellis ever dreamed would be offered to children, and in such profusion. Here is one man mugging another, and graphic pictures of the white man shooting colored natives as though they were animals: "You sure must have treated these beggars rough in that last trip through here!" And so on. This is the sort of thing that Willie's aunt wanted to keep him from reading. . . .

Of course there are people who still fall for the contention of the comic-book industry that their products deal not with crime, but with the punishment of crime. Is not the very title of some of these books, *Crime Does Not Pay?* Here, too, adults are more readily deceived than children. Children know that in quite a number of crime comic books there is in the title some reference to punishment. But they also know that just as that very reference is in small letters and inconspicuous color, the parts of the title that really count are in huge, eye-catching type and clear sharp colors: CRIME; CRIMINALS; MURDER; LAW BREAKERS; GUNS; etc. The result of this is, of course, that when comic books are on display only the *crime* and not the punishment is visible. Often the type of the second part of the title is so arranged that in the display case it does not show at all, concealed as it is behind the tops of other comic books. These are a few examples:

LAWBREAKERS Always Lose

There Is No Escape For PUBLIC ENEMIES

The West Thunders with the Roar of GUNS

CRIME Can't Win

Western OUTLAWS and Sheriffs

CRIMINALS on the Run . . .

Another important feature of a crime comic book is the first page of the first story, which often gives the child the clue to the thrill of violence that is to be its chief attraction. This is a psychological fact that all sorts of children have pointed out to me. *Macbeth* in comic book form is an example. On the first page the statement is made: "Amazing as the tale may seem, the author gathered it from true accounts"—the typical crime comic book formula, of course. The first balloon has the words spoken by a young woman (Lady Macbeth): "Smear the sleeping servants with BLOOD!"

To the child who looks at the first page "to see what's in it," this gives the strongest suggestion. And it gives the whole comic book the appeal of a crime comic book. As for the content of this *Macbeth,* John Mason Brown, the well-known critic, expressed it in the *Saturday Review of Literature:* "To rob a supreme dramatist of the form at which he excelled is mayhem plus murder in the first degree . . . although the tale is murderous and gory, it never rises beyond cheap horror. . . . What is left is not a tragedy. It is trashcan stuff." It is interesting that what adult critics deduce from the whole book, children sense from the first balloon. They know a crime comic when they see one, whatever the disguise.

The educational page, skipped by many children, pointed to with pride by the publishers and approved (but not sufficiently scrutinized) by parents and teachers, could conceivably contain a counterstimulant to the violence of the stories, but often it just gives some historical rationalization of it. For instance, in a jungle comic book what does the educational page show? This one is entitled "The First Americans." A young girl in modern evening dress, her wrists chained to a tall upholstered structure so that she leans backward in a recumbent position revealing the full length of her legs, with a definite erotic suggestion, is being menaced with a big knife held by a gruesome masked figure: "At harvest and planting time they would cut out the heart of a living victim." In other words, the education to sadism permeating this whole book is here fortified in the guise of history.

Other features in the structure of a crime comic book are the first page of or before each individual story, the content of the stories, the type of language used, recurring details of plot or drawing as opposed to the professed ideology, the advertisements and the endorsements in the form of names of endorsers and the prominent institutions with which they are connected.

Endorsements came into fashion after Sterling North, the literary critic, early in the forties, published a number of critical articles based on his reading of comic books. As one boy told me when I asked him what these endorsements by psychiatrists and educators meant to him, "Oh, the more endorsements they need, the more they have." The claim that crime comic books might instill in any adolescent or pre-adolescent of average intelligence the idea or sentiment that prevention of crime or of antisocial activity is their goal, is so farfetched that mere reading of the comic books in question will answer it. . . .

The Superman group of comic books is super-endorsed. A random sample shows on the inside cover the endorsement of two psychiatrists, one educator, one English professor and a child-study consultant. On the page facing this array is depicted a man dressed as a boy shooting a policeman in the mouth (with a toy pistol). This is a prank—"Prankster's second childhood." In the story there is a variant of the comic-book theme of a girl being thrown into the fire: "Her dress will be afire in one split second! She'll need Superman's help!"

In another story a tenement building is set afire—also to be taken care of by Superman after it is afire. Until near the end of the book, attempts to kill people are not looked upon askance, and are not to be prevented apparently by humans but only by a superman. Then the lesson that after all you should not kill is expressed like this: "You conniving unscrupulous cad! Try to murder Carol, will you!" This is scarcely a moral condemnation. The lawyer who does not share in a million-dollar swindle is praised by Superman because he "remained honest." In fact this honesty is rewarded with a million dollars! A gun advertisement with four pictures of guns completes the impression that even if you can't become Superman, at least you can rise above the average by using force. . . .

People neglect the pre-violent manifestations of the trend toward violence. They forget what the philosopher Erwin Edman said: "It does not take long for a society to become brutalized." Comic books are not the disease, they are only a symptom. And they are far more significant as symptoms than as causes. They shed some light on the whole foundation of moral and social behavior. That, I began to feel, was the most positive result of our studies. The same social forces that make crime comic books make other social evils, and the same social forces that keep crime comic books keep the other social evils the way they are. Even the arguments to defend them are the same for both.

Whenever you hear a public discussion of comic books, you will hear sooner or later an advocate of the industry say with a triumphant smile, "Comic books are here to stay." I do not believe it. Someday parents will realize that comic books are not a necessary evil "which, but their children's end, naught can remove." I am convinced that in some way or other the democratic process will assert itself and crime comic books will go, and with them all they stand for and all that sustains them. But before they can tackle Superman, Dr. Payn, and all their myriad incarnations, people will have to learn that it is a distorted idea to think that democracy means giving good and evil an equal chance at expression. We must learn that freedom is not something that one can have, but is something that one must do.

Further Resources

BOOKS

Bongco, Mila. *Reading Comics: Language, Culture, and the Concept of the Superhero in Comic Books.* New York: Garland Pub., 2000.

Gordon, Ian. *Comic Strips and Consumer Culture, 1890-1945.* Washington: Smithsonian Institution, 2002.

Horn, Maurice. *Women in the Comics.* Philadelphia: Chelsea House, 2001 Rev. & updated. 3 vols.

Magnussen, Anne and Hans-Christian Christiansen. *Comics & Culture: Analytical and Theoretical Approaches to Comics.* Copenhagen, Denmark: Museum Tusculanum Press, 2000.

McCloud, Scott. *Reinventing Comics: How Imagination and Technology are Revolutionizing an Art Form.* New York: Perennial, 2001.

Sabin, Roger. *Comics, Comix & Graphic Novels: a History of Graphic Novels.* London: Phaidon Press, 2001.

Varnum, Robin and Christina Gibbons. *The Language of Comics: Word and Image.* Jackson, Miss.: University Press of Mississippi, 2002.

Walker, Brian. *The Comics: Since 1945.* New York: H.N. Abrams, 2002.

WEBSITES

Commentary on the Seduction of the Innocent. Available on-line at http://www.psu.edu/dept/inart10_110/inart10/cmbk4cca .html; website home page: http://www.psu.edu (accessed March 18, 2003).

Davy Crockett

"Wild Frontier Was Never Like This as Cincinnatians Welcome 'Davy'"

Newspaper article

By: *Cincinnati Enquirer*
Date: June 16, 1955
Source: "Wild Frontier Was Never Like This as Cincinnatians Welcome 'Davy.'" *Cincinnati Enquirer,* June 16, 1955, 34.

"Davy Crockett, Pal Git Right Smart Greetin'"

Newspaper article

By: *Cincinnati Times-Star*
Date: June 15, 1955
Source: "Davy Crockett, Pal Git Right Smart Greetin'." *Cincinnati Times-Star,* June 15, 1955.

"Birthplace Battle"

Newspaper article

By: *The New York Times*
Date: May 30, 1955
Source: "Birthplace Battle." *The New York Times,* May 30, 1955, 40.

About the Publication: Founded in 1850 as the *New-York Daily Times, The New York Times* was originally a relatively obscure local paper. By the early twentieth century, however, it had grown into a widely known, well-respected news source. Its banner, "All the News That's Fit to Print," is recognized across the United States and throughout the world.

"Disneyland Davy Crockett"

Magazine article

By: *Newsweek*
Date: April 18, 1955
Source: "Disneyland Davy Crockett." *Newsweek,* April 18, 1955, 40.
About the Publication: *Newsweek* was founded in 1933 by Thomas J.C. Martyn. By 2003, it had a circulation of 4 million. It is owned by the Washington Post company, who bought *Newsweek* in 1961, and headquartered in New York City. *Newsweek* has had a history of mixing text and art to discuss current issues, as its first cover had photographs from that week's news. ∎

Introduction

Davy Crockett (1786–1836) was a frontiersman and politician who served in the Tennessee Legislature in the early nineteenth century. He was born in Hawkings County, Tennessee. After leaving Congress, Crockett went to Texas and died defending the Alamo—along with about 180 others, including Jim Bowie, inventor of the Bowie knife. Crockett was a national folk hero. Part of his iconography was his coonskin cap and his "trusty rifle Betsy." Many stories were told about him, and he passed into the mythology of America, in large part due to his death at the Alamo.

Crockett, though, had become "just another one" of America's heroes by the start of the twentieth century. Newspapers and the radio, the main forms of mass communication, did not particularly emphasize the accomplishments of Davy Crockett. When movies became popular in the 1920s and 1930s, they did not select Crockett for glorification. In the 1940s, America was more focused on World War II (1939–1945), and so did not feel the need to reach back to past heroes to admire. The 1940s did see, though, the advent of television.

The 1950s was the decade when American television truly came into its own. The number of television sets increased from 17,000 in 1946 to 40 million in 1957, an average of nearly one per family. Specific corporations sponsored most shows. For example, Philip Morris sponsored "I Love Lucy." Many of the early shows were taken directly from radio, but new shows were continually developed. One of the prime movie developers, Walt Disney, decided to make Davy Crockett the subject of a television mini-series.

Davy Crockett items, from coonskin caps to lamps, were popular items for children. GETTY IMAGES. REPRODUCED BY PERMISSION.

Significance

"Disneyland's" three-part series on Davy Crockett was tremendously successful. It was released as a film later that summer and played to packed houses. Fess Parker, who played Davy Crockett, made personal appearances all over the country to promote the movie. One fad launched by the movie was wearing a Davy Crockett coonskin cap, the prize offered in the coloring contest. Boys by the millions across the country wanted coonskin caps. This was the most popular product to come out of the series, but not the only one—fringed jackets, moccasins, and even a toy version of Betsy hit the toy stores. The show's theme song, "The Ballad of Davy Crockett," became enormously popular as well. Thus, Davy Crockett coonskin caps were one of the first television-inspired crazes. Davy Crockett has not been as popular since, but he has not faded back to his former relative obscurity either. He is still celebrated at the Alamo in Texas.

TV has since created many additional fads. The 1960s saw the popularity of the hula-hoop and the Nehru jacket. One of the most popular "toys" of the 1970s was the pet rock, where people "adopted" pet rocks—a phenomenon incomprehensible to those not living through the era. The 1980s saw the Cabbage Patch doll craze, where the intentionally homely doll flew off the shelves. Even educational television has occasionally triggered fads, such as "Tickle Me Elmo" dolls, from the Public Broadcasting Services's Sesame Street, incredibly popular in the late 1990s. Hollywood has even cashed in by mocking America's tendency for fads, as Arnold Schwartzenegger's 1996 movie, *Jingle All the Way*. One thing is sure though—there will be a new fad this year.

Primary Source

"Wild Frontier Was Never Like This as Cincinnatians Welcome 'Davy'"

SYNOPSIS: This piece notes that the Davy Crockett mini-series was a great hit, and that Davy Crockett's death at the Alamo brought a national outcry.

Cincinnati's small fry went all out yesterday to welcome Davy Crockett (alias actor Fess Parker) to the Queen City for Davy Crockett Day.

By the thousands, the youngsters, most of them in coonskin caps, stood in line 10-abreast in a parking lot on Shillito Place to shake hands with the Disneyland hero and his pal, Buddy Ebsen, from 2 to 4 p. m.

White-capped police officers by the two-score, and 10 detectives from the Cal Crim agency joined 50 of Shillito's personnel in supervising the crowd at the informal outdoor reception.

One of the busiest spots at the scene was the lost child booth. Every few minutes a message came over the loud speaker for some little Davy pro tem to meet his mother, aunt or some other adult in charge at "lost" headquarters.

There was no doubt as to what the attraction of the day was because records blared forth constantly with the popular Davy Crockett tune.

The "king of the wild frontier," with his hair reaching almost to the shoulders of his fringed chamois outfit, seldom had a chance to straighten himself up to his full six feet five inches as he greeted his many little admirers.

The crowd was not limited to would-be young frontiersmen, either. There were plenty of little girls on hand and one five-year-old told the 30-year-old bachelor star that she would like to marry him if he would wait until she grew up.

The visiting "king" came to Cincinnati late Tuesday in his airborne covered wagon. When he landed at Greater Cincinnati Airport he was welcomed by a tremendous yell from 100 idolizing fans in a "kiddie calvacade" sponsored by Shillito's and the Hudson Motors Division, American Motors Corp.

Mayor Carl W. Rich was on hand, with his proclamation of Davy Crockett Day, as were Jeffrey Lazarus, president of Shillito's, and R. T. Morris, zone merchandising manager of Hudson Motors, all joining in the fun with man-size coonskin caps.

Two personal appearances, one at 1 p. m. and the other at 4 p. m., were on Fess Parker's schedule yesterday at the Palace Theater for the opening of the Disney film starring him as Davy Crockett.

Adding to the downtown commotion for his special day here was a motorcade which formed at 12:30 p. m. at the Netherland Plaza.

Another police escorted motorcade roared out of Lodge Street onto Sixth Street to get Davy and Buddy to the airport after the 4 p. m. bow from the Palace stage.

They are on their way for more personal appearances in their long tour, which ends Saturday at Morganfield, Ky., where the two heroes of the Alamo will begin work on two fictional Crockett movies.

Primary Source

"Davy Crockett, Pal Git Right Smart Greetin'"

SYNOPSIS: This piece is a contest to win a "Davy Crockett Coonskin Cap" in which children had to color a picture of Davy fighting off Native Americans.

"How many bars you grinned down lately, Davy?"

That question, shouted over a sea of bobbing coonskin hats, brought a wide grin to the face of

Children reenact Davy Crockett at the Alamo, 1955. RALPH MORSE/TIME LIFE PICTURES/GETTY IMAGES. REPRODUCED BY PERMISSION.

Fess Parker, the "original Davy" of Disneyland as he stepped from his airborne covered wagon at Greater Cincinnati Airport late Tuesday.

Davy and his pal, Georgie Russell, portrayed by Buddy Ebsen, were in full frontiersman regalia. They are to appear at Shillito's and the Palace Theater. The Disney production, Davy Crockett, opens at the theater Wednesday, proclaimed "Davy Crockett Day."

Fifty children were in a motorcade of 30 vehicles to greet Davy at the airport, sponsored by Shillito's and Hudson Motors Division of the American Motors Corp. The children and many adults, including Mayor Carl W. Rich, wore coonskin caps for the welcoming.

As Parker and Ebsen worked their way past the knot of small-fry and adult admirers, shaking hands, chatting, and posing for snapshots, one woman called out, "Could I touch your hand?" and then added to a friend, "I wish I was 20 years younger."

Five-year-old Sandra Haste, 915 Walnut Street, stopped Davy and pulled him down to her level for a big kiss. A Hooven father, caught wearing his son's coonskin cap, denied being a Davy Crockett fan and claimed Abraham Lincoln as his favorite historical character.

The bar situation was the concern of both Ricky Williams, 9, 4896 Riedlin Avenue, Covington, and Jack Eicher, 6, 62 Summit Avenue, Ft. Thomas.

Pamela Burbank, 7, 11125 Springfield Pike, wanted Davy's "phonograph." She said later that she meant autograph. Another autograph-seeker was 11-year-old Jack Homes, 7536 Beechmont Avenue, who had orders for several signatures for friends.

Mayor Rich and Jeffrey Lazarus, president of Shillito's, drove back to town with Parker.

All along the motorcade route were groups of people waiting for a glimpse of Davy Crockett. In Erlanger, Ky., Davy was greeted with a sign reading, "Yea, Dan'l Boone." A boy in a wheelchair was in one of the roadside groups.

Charles Levy, eastern publicity director for Walt Disney, described the Cincinnati welcoming committee as the best controlled group of 23 cities visited so far on this personal appearance tour.

The tour will continue until Saturday after which Fess and Buddy will go to Morganfield, Ky., to begin work on two fictional Crockett movies.

Primary Source

"Birthplace Battle"

SYNOPSIS: This piece talks about the tourists who flocked to Davy Crockett's boyhood home, and the reaction of the farmer living there.

W.L. Carter, a mountaineer who owns the Tennessee farm where Davy Crockett was supposed to have been born, arrived at the home of Rep. B. Carroll Reece in Johnson City, Tenn., and angrily protested: "Can the sight-seers take over my property? Can they cut a piece of log out of my house? Can they tromp down my garden and knock over my fences? Last Sunday there must have been 2,000 out there." "Why," Reece asked, "don't you charge admission?" "Hadn't thought of that," the mountaineer drawled, and headed happily home.

Primary Source

"Disneyland Davy Crockett" [excerpt]

SYNOPSIS: This article explains the popularity of Davy Crockett after Disneyland releases its three-installment series.

The runaway hit of this year's "Disneyland" series is a three-installment resurrection of an old American folk hero, Davy Crockett. It contains the irresistible Disney mixture of fantasy and fact, corn and authenticity, and it aptly supports an envious rival's remark that "the more Disney changes, the more he stays the same." When, in accordance with history, Crockett was doomed to die at the Battle of the Alamo, the public outcry was the greatest since the late Sid Smith allowed a lovable character named Mary Gold to die in his comic strip, "The Gumps."

Rugged Types

"If you don't get Davy Crockett out of the Alamo unharmed," wrote one outraged household, "the

Bonniwell family will go back to Arthur Godfrey next week." Disney killed off Davy, but that hardly put an end to the Crockett show. An encore begins on the air this week, and the movie made for TV is to be released to the country's picture houses in June. In addition, Disney's 1955–56 television series will include four one-hour folklore segments entitled "The Legend of Davy Crockett."

Further Resources

BOOKS

Davis, William C. *Three Roads to the Alamo: The Lives and Fortunes of David Crockett, James Bowie, and William Barret Travis.* New York: HarperCollins Publishers, 1998.

Derr, Mark. *The Frontiersman: The Real Life and the Many Legends of Davy Crockett.* New York: W. Morrow, 1993.

Johnson, Richard A. *American Fads.* New York: Beech Tree Books, 1985.

Lofaro, Michael A. *Davy Crockett: The Man, the Legend, the Legacy, 1786-1986.* Knoxville, Tenn.: University of Tennessee Press, 1985.

Shackford, James Atkins, and John B. Shackford. *David Crockett: The Man and the Legend.* Chapel Hill, N.C.: University of North Carolina Press, 1986.

PERIODICALS

Crisp, James Ernest. "An Incident in San Antonio: The Contested Iconology of Davy Crockett's Death at the Alamo." *Journal of the West,* Vol. 40, No. 2, Spring, 2001, 67–77.

WEBSITES

American West-Davy Crockett. Available online at http://www.americanwest.com/pages/davycroc.htm; website home page: http://americanwest.com (accessed March 18, 2003).

AUDIO AND VISUAL MEDIA

Parker, Fess, and Buddy Ebsen. *Davy Crockett: The Complete Televised Series.* Burbank, CA: Disney DVD, 2000.

Montgomery Bus Boycott

"The Rise of Negroes in Industry: Problems . . . and Progress"

Magazine article

By: Clem Morgello

Date: September 12, 1955

Source: Morgello, Clem. "The Rise of Negroes in Industry: Problems . . . and Progress." *Newsweek,* September 12, 1955, 86–88.

About the Author: Clemente Frank Morgello (1923–) graduated from City College of New York and the University of Wisconsin. He worked for the *Wall Street Journal* for one year before joining *Newsweek,* where he worked from 1950

to 1975. After leaving *Newsweek,* he joined *Dun's Review* in 1976. Among other honors, he won the Gerald Loeb Award from University of Connecticut in 1972.

"Report on Montgomery a Year After"

Newspaper article

By: Abel Plenn

Date: December 29, 1957.

Source: Plenn, Abel. "Report on Montgomery a Year After." *The New York Times,* December 29, 1957, 11, 36, 38. ∎

Introduction

Segregation and discrimination existed long before the United States was formed. Racial discrimination continued after the founding of America, despite the Declaration of Independence's claim that "all men are created equal." Most African Americans were slaves, and those free were kept in a subjugated class. Most freed blacks had few rights, and some states even required blacks to leave the state immediately after emancipation.

Slavery in the United States ended formally with the Civil War (1861–1865) and the Thirteenth Amendment. However, the attitude of most whites did not change. The Fourteenth and Fifteenth Amendments promised voting rights and equal treatment, but most states of the South codified legal systems of segregation (referred to as "Jim Crow" laws)—promising "separate but equal" systems in education, theaters, and restrooms. The resulting systems were separate, but not close to equal in any respect. Many southern states spent only a small fraction on African American schools relative to schools for whites, resulting in poor educational opportunities for African Americans. African Americans had to overcome racism as a fact of life, especially in the South. African Americans were forced to ride in the back of buses, and they were only hired to perform the most menial jobs. For instance, most blacks in industry were employed as janitors.

During this whole period, African Americans fought this segregation with varying results. Civil Rights leaders staged an effective boycott of the Montgomery (Alabama) bus system in 1955, sparked by Rosa Parks refusing to give up her seat to a white passenger. The bus system, economically damaged by this boycott (and influenced partly by a Supreme Court ruling holding such segregation unconstitutional) desegregated. Around this same time, African Americans were given new opportunities for employment in some industries.

Significance

In Montgomery, one year after the protest ended, individuals were riding the buses in peace, and African Americans had gained a new sense of pride in what they could accomplish. In Alabama, and across the South, the Montgomery Bus Boycott taught African Americans that if they refused to accept segregation, it did not have to exist. The boycott also informed whites as well. By adopting this attitude in the 1960s, great achievements in furthering the civil rights of African Americans were made. The violent reaction of some white Southerners to the boycott, and the lack of prosecutions for the violence, was also a pattern that was to repeat during the next decade.

African Americans moving into higher positions within industry also foreshadowed an impending change. The article points out, though, that many companies still resisted hiring African Americans, providing opportunities for individuals to discriminate. This situation did not change substantively, however, until the passage of the 1964 Civil Rights Act made it illegal to discriminate on the basis of race or sex. The language of both articles reflects the era as well. The article discussing the hiring of African Americans notes that African Americans were not qualified for many positions. (The lack of technical training was the result of exclusion from all-white colleges and the poor funding and quality of African American high schools.) The article, though, blames the African Americans despite the injustices they faced.

The lifestyles reflected in these articles greatly changed across the nation—even in the South—in the 1960s and 1970s. Segregation was banned, education was slowly integrated, and the percentage of African Americans in industry slowly grew. With the changing education, transportation and work patterns, life in general changed. More African Americans became middle and upper class, and they started to adopt middle and upper class lifestyles, vacations and spending habits. While there still are fewer African American CEOs than there should be, the situation continues to improve.

Primary Source

"The Rise of Negroes in Industry: Problems . . . and Progress"

SYNOPSIS: This article notes discrimination that exists in some areas of hiring, and efforts by the Urban League to decrease this discrimination. It also profiles some African Americans who have been hired into upper-level positions.

Negroes have taken some impressive strides toward social and educational equality in recent years. But what kind of progress have they made in industry? *Newsweek* asked businessmen and race-relations experts across the country. Here are their answers, as assembled and analyzed by Associate Editor Clem Morgello.

A few years ago a young Negro mathematician quit his government job at White Sands Proving Grounds, N. M., because his sick wife had been mistreated in a clinic. He migrated to Los Angeles where he answered an aircraft company's ad for a mathematician. Nothing happened. He took his problem to the Urban League, an interracial organization supported by contributions from industry, individuals, and community chests, which put him in touch with the aircraft-company's engineering department. He was advised to file an application and did so. Still nothing happened. The Negro returned to the Urban League which then called the company's employment director. The applicant, it turned out, was well qualified. But someone in the organization had violated the firm's policy of strictly nondiscriminatory hiring and sat on the application. The matter was straightened out; the Negro was hired.

The turnabout did not come out of a feeling of charity. It was purely a business proposition. "We feel it is sound economics to hire Negroes and to take advantage of every person in the labor pool," said the aircraft company's employment director. The company needed good mathematicians, and "if you discriminate you reduce your labor pool."

Good Business

More and more companies these days are finding that it is sound business to hire qualified Negroes. In recent years new and greater opportunities have opened up in banking and retailing, in the telephone and aviation industries, in farm and communications equipment, to mention a few. While well over half the Negro workers are still below the semiskilled level (compared with one sixth for whites), increasing numbers of nonwhites are finding jobs as stenographers and drill-press operators, bank tellers and shop foremen, plant engineers, chemists, and art directors.

Some of these gains have been provided willingly by such companies as Radio Corp. of America, North American Aviation, International Harvester Co., Lockheed Aircraft, Detroit Edison, and Westinghouse Electric. Some important gains have come through collective bargaining. Antidiscrimination laws have helped. On top of that there is constant prodding and coaxing by the National Urban League and the National Association for the Advancement of Colored People.

While it is still difficult to find a Negro in a top executive job in any of the big integrated companies, growing numbers are filling important $10,000 and even $15,000 jobs. Examples:

- *Lloyd Hall,* 61, technical director of laboratories for Griffith Laboratories of Chicago who reportedly made millions from his many patents (including one for a skinless wiener). A Northwestern graduate (1916), Hall joined Griffith as chief chemist and lab director in 1925. Before that, he had worked for the city health laboratories, Army Ordnance, and meatpacking, and chemical firms. He specializes on food and biological chemistry.

- *George Olden,* 35, graphic-arts director for the CBS-TV network. Olden freelanced for a while after he received his fine-arts degree from Virginia State College in 1940. After a hitch in the OSS art department during the war, he was assigned to the United Nations organizing conference in San Francisco in 1945 as a graphic designer. He joined CBS the same year to set up the network's graphic-arts department, was named director in 1946. Among other things, he's responsible for station-break cartoons.

- *Dr. Percy Julian,* 56, grandson of slaves, who as research director for the Glidden Co. helped develop methods for synthetically producing such drugs as cortisone, progesterone, testosterone, and estrone. One of the nation's top organic chemists, Dr. Julian now heads his own research laboratory in Chicago.

These are the success stories. But there is a bleak side of the picture. While opportunities for the Negro are good in the auto industry, there are no Negroes in the 200 tool-and-die shops covered by contracts between the United Auto Workers and the Automotive Tool and Die Association. White-collar jobs for Negroes are rare in steel, still rarer in tobacco and textiles. There are growing numbers of Negro retail clerks, but only about 40 Negro certified public accountants in the whole country.

Lester Granger, executive director of the Urban League, gives this over-all evaluation of Negro job opportunities: "Fair to good in the Middle Atlantic States, Northeast, and Midwest; poor to fair in the Border States, Northwest, Southwest; poor in the Deep South." Julius A. Thomas, the league's industrial-relations director, estimates that only 15 to 20 per cent of the major companies make a sustained effort to hire Negroes. An equal amount are hostile to the idea. The rest, he says, are indifferent.

The fault lies by no means solely with management. Many unions have done little to encourage Negro employment, and some discourage it. There are few if any Negroes in the Big Four railroad brotherhoods, for instance, and in many old-line craft unions like the carpenters, printers, electricians, and masons.

Inadequate—and misdirected—Negro education is partly to blame for the employment lag. Though Negro college enrollment has increased from about 65,000 in 1940 to 100,000 today, the majority of students are in liberal arts, relatively few in technical fields. But most job opportunities are in the technical end.

Improving

The upshot of it all is that the average annual income of Negro workers, though it has climbed 300 per cent since before the war, is still only $1,300, about half white-worker averages.

In the long pull, though, it is the trend that is important for Julius Thomas and his colleagues in the Urban League. They readily admit that the trend is for the better. It is being set by firms like J. L. Hudson Co., Detroit's largest department store; International Harvester; RCA; Ford; Pitney-Bowes; General Electric; CBS; General Cable; and the American Telephone & Telegraph Co.

Once hired, what kind of job experience do Negroes have?

Just the same as white workers, say those who should know. For instance:

• Efficiency: "The good ones are very, very good. The bad ones? We blame ourselves for hiring them in the first place," says a Detroit executive.

• Adjustment: Few problems here. Negroes are sometimes embarrassed, however, by too much attention from well-meaning white coworkers.

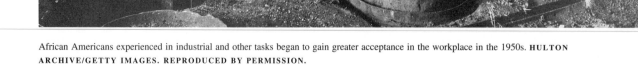

African Americans experienced in industrial and other tasks began to gain greater acceptance in the workplace in the 1950s. HULTON ARCHIVE/GETTY IMAGES. REPRODUCED BY PERMISSION.

Best thing to do, says RCA, is "treat Negroes as people, not as social problems." How do the white workers react? A Detroit firm's experience is typical: "We encountered resistance at first. But when we explained it, integration went smoothly."

• Customers: A common argument against integration is that "it will hurt business." But department stores with Negro retail clerks report they have experienced no adverse effects. RCA has Negro TV servicemen. It has received no complaints.

The steadily improving Negro job picture helps business in another obvious way. It makes for better consumers. Negroes already account for a sizable $15 billion in income. As RCA's president Frank M. Folsom puts it: "Equal job opportunities for Negroes and other minority groups will increase the income of this part of our population and hence widen the market for many products, including our own."

Primary Source

"Report on Montgomery a Year After" [excerpt]

> **SYNOPSIS:** This article discusses the boycott and the reaction of whites and African Americans to the boycott after one year. The article notes the sense of self-discovery by African Americans and the continuing efforts of the Montgomery Improvement Association, which led the boycott.

A year ago, in the first days of bus integration, Montgomery was a city caught in a swelling tide of racial violence. Telephoned and mailed warnings couched in foul language, shootings at buses, dynamitings of homes and churches—these suddenly threatened to become the frightening pattern of everyday life in a proud city once known throughout the South for its quiet and genial ways. The high point in this campaign of terror was reached one night when four Negro churches and the home of a young white Lutheran minister, Robert Graetz, were bombed in the space of a single hour. Thereupon the City Commissioners, avowed members of the militantly segregationist White Citizens Council, ignoring the plea of the bus companies for police protection, ordered the integrated buses off the streets.

For six days and nights the city was without a public transportation system of any kind. A complete breakdown in the economic life of the community, and in law and order itself seemed imminent.

When a Negro taxi stand was bombed and an attempt made to blow up the house where the Rev. Dr. Martin Luther King lived with his wife and baby, public alarm became general. Shortly thereafter, four white workingmen believed to be acting under a Ku Klux Klan directive, were arrested and charged with shooting at buses and dynamiting homes and churches.

Two of the houses had been occupied when dynamited—making the crimes a capital offense in Alabama. No one in Montgomery expected any of the men to be convicted (two of them were acquitted this summer, and the remaining two cases have just been dropped), but the arrests did bring about an immediate and important change in the local situation. Open violence came to an abrupt end.

Integration on the buses since that initial threatening period has proceeded orderly enough. One reason is that many Negro passengers (not the younger people, however) continue to sit in the rear of the buses by themselves. There are occasional minor incidents, but no serious flare-up has occurred.

Although the white people of Montgomery hardly regard the end of segregation on the buses as a gratifying change, an interesting new attitude toward the Negro does seem to be developing. This can best be described, perhaps, as a reflection of the secret admiration aroused by the unexampled display of Negro unity, fortitude and leadership. From an astonishing variety of sources also came symptoms of growing respect for Dr. King's intelligence and leadership and increasing recognition of the vital pacifying role he performed during crucial periods of the boycott.

"Don't let anyone fool you," says a taxi driver, Montgomery-born, who fought in Korea. "That young colored preacher has got more brains in his little finger than the City Commissioners and all the politicians in this town put together." And the local newspapers and TV and radio stations, while quite frankly segregationist in their views, have begun to accept the fact that Dr. King is now a figure of national and international prominence. That acceptance is not without its risks, either. A local television station which recently refused a request from the White Citizens Council not to carry a national network's interview with Dr. King was blacked out during the program by sabotage. The station carried a filmed version of the interview, nevertheless, on the following day. . . .

The year-long protest against bus segregation gave Montgomery's 50,000 Negroes an exciting sense of self-discovery. A 70-year-old charwoman who covered something like 4,000 miles on foot in her daily journeys to and from work during the boycott reminisces, "O child, that was the year we walked!" She says it with a sigh of relief—but there is also a look of honest pride on her aged face. Similarly, but in a more determined vein, a middle-aged janitor (Negroes here are employed mostly in domestic or other service jobs) in one of the local stores says: "We got our heads up now, and we won't ever bow down again—no, sir—except before God!"

Such feelings are seldom expressed openly to white people for fear of being questioned about them later by an employer or by the manager of a credit store, a bank or one of the numerous loan-shark companies on which Montgomery's Negroes depend. But at the public meetings of the M. I. A., which are held in a different Negro church each week, there is an outpouring of such sentiments. . . .

The Negro's growing sense of strength and hope lies, too, in his consciousness of the high caliber of leadership that has emerged among his own people—largely, though not entirely, as a result of the mass bus protest. Among the top command in the M. I. A. today one finds young university graduates like Dr. King (with a Ph.D. degree from Boston University) and the Rev. Ralph D. Abernathy—president and vice president, respectively, of the organization. On the executive board sit college professors, college-trained business men, and professional men like the youthful attorney, Fred Gray, who handled legal cases from the bus controversy.

The prototype and principal spokesman of the new Negro leadership is, of course, the 29-year-old Dr. King—a man with wide-set eyes and a keen vision of what is going on here and in the space-minded world of today—who came to Montgomery three years ago from his native Atlanta, Ga. He is minister of the Dexter Avenue Baptist Church, situated on Montgomery's principal thoroughfare, and his congregation of more than 1,000 members includes many of the most prominent men and women in the Negro community. Dr. King is known mainly, however, as the man most responsible for bringing to the new Negro movement in the South the unifying and revivifying principle of nonviolent resistance—an adaptation of the great Indian leader Gandhi's philosophy and methods—which proved successful in the bus boycott.

The present program of the M. I. A. is concerned principally with the effort to raise moral and social standards within the Negro community itself. The challenging events of the past two years have done much to give a sense of responsibility to the Negro community as a whole. There has been a decline in heavy drinking, once prevalent among the poorest people. The crime rate appears to be on the decrease. The Negro leaders are now stressing the need for a program of health education, youth recreation and adult education and employment aid among their own people. Dr. King and others feel that such a program will serve to indicate that Negroes are seeking, in the main, to lift themselves by their own bootstraps.

There is also an underlying hope that this program will help to ease the racial tensions which are still far from eradicated in this former capital of the Confederacy.

Both the Negro and white populations are sensitively aware that since bus desegregation went into effect the two races have, paradoxically, been drifting farther apart. This seemingly odd development is explained by a white lawyer. "Here is how it was before," he says, placing the palm of one hand about six inches above the other. "We were that close—even though, of course, we white folks were very much on top." Then, shifting the position of his hands until both are on the same level, but at least a yard apart, he declares: "And this is how it is now."
. . .

The spearhead of the movement to delay the coming of racial integration indefinitely is, in Montgomery as elsewhere through the Deep South, the White Citizens Council. Membership in that militant organization here was, not so long ago, the highest anywhere. Over the last twelve months it has suffered a sharp decline but council leaders are still able to exert strong political pressure.

A rash of fresh segregation laws has been unloosed in recent months by both the State Legislature and the Montgomery City Commissioners. Among the brave new measures the city fathers have promulgated is one outlawing the playing of checkers or dominoes between local white and Negro enthusiasts.

Both the M. I. A. and the White Citizens Council, meanwhile, are busy recruiting new members and appealing to potential voters. An intensive campaign is under way, under the M. I. A.'s direction, to increase the number of registered Negro voters here, where less than 5 per cent of the total Negro population is presently able to vote. The current goal is to obtain enough of an increase in Negro voting

Martin Luther King, leader of a boycott against a segregated transit system, rides a Montgomery, Alabama, bus, 1956. Sitting beside him is Rev. Glenn Smiley. © **BETTMANN/CORBIS. REPRODUCED BY PERMISSION.**

strength to help elect at least a more moderate city administration next November.

M. I. A. leaders are keeping a careful record of the all-white registration board's refusals to register Negroes and its grounds for doing so, and some of those actions may be challenged soon, for the first time, under the provisions of the Federal civil rights legislation passed by Congress this year.

A Negro business man comments: "We've got the fatherhood of God, the brotherhood of man, the Bill of Rights, the United States Supreme Court, American democracy and democratic principles and sentiment, Republican and Democratic sympathy, national politics, and world history all on our side. But what good is any of it if we can't vote and help elect officials who will at least be willing to sit down and talk to us about working to make this a better community for everybody to live in?"

The hope for a gradual solution of the racial problem on a local level, across the table of common economic needs and a common desire for peace and tranquility, is shared by an increasing number of levelheaded business men and other civic leaders in the white community. They have not forgotten that several big industrial projects which were pend-

ing a year ago failed to materialize after the outbreak of racial violence and have not been revived since. There is also a growing concern over the possible shrinkage of Federal expenditures here because of the unstable situation. Maxwell Air Force Base, for instance, today provides a large proportion of the city's income. . . .

A victim of such persecution was the reference librarian at the Montgomery Public Library, Miss Juliette Morgan—a sensitive, delicate young woman from a fine old Alabama family. She became the chief target of local extreme segregationists earlier this year because of her openly expressed views in favor of integration. Increasing pressure was brought to have her fired; she was harassed by a constant stream of lewd and threatening telephone calls to the library and to her home where she lived with her mother. Her nerves were weakened and she had to take temporary leave from her job. The suffering was greater than she could bear, and overnight, last summer, her life came to an end.

No one in Montgomery will venture to guess how long the present surface calm is likely to continue. In this respect the local situation is typical of that prevailing throughout the Deep South.

In another and more important sense, however, there is a sharp difference between what is happening in Montgomery and in the rest of the Deep South. Here in this old "Cradle of the Confederacy" a start has been made toward civic integration as part of a way of life in keeping with our basic American heritage of liberty and equality. The road ahead will be a hard one, but there can be no turning back.

Much more is involved than the future of this city alone. Since the bus protest, Montgomery has become—more or less in spite of itself—a symbol, all over the world, of man's heroic determination to end human oppression by peaceful means. Far beyond the immediate issue of segregation, therefore, something else is at stake in the struggle now taking place in this corner of the Deep South. For in a final sense, upon its outcome rest our unity, strength and dignity as a nation, and our vital need to keep faith with the millions of people on every continent who regard us as a unique, democratic world power dedicated to the cause of peace at home as well as abroad.

The question looming larger each day is whether, when the next, inevitable major test involving integration occurs, Montgomery will become another and far more dangerous Little Rock—or a new guiding beacon of hope and progress.

Further Resources

BOOKS

Alderman, Ellen, and Caroline Kennedy. *In Our Defense: The Bill of Rights in Action.* New York: Morrow, 1991.

Branch, Taylor. *Parting the Waters: America in the King Years, 1954-63.* New York: Simon and Schuster, 1988.

Burns, Stewart. *Daybreak of Freedom: The Montgomery Bus Boycott.* Chapel Hill: University of North Carolina Press, 1997.

Hampton, Henry et al. *Voices of Freedom: An Oral History of the Civil Rights Movement From the 1950s Through the 1980s.* New York: Bantam Books, 1990.

Levy, Peter B. *Documentary History of the Modern Civil Rights Movement.* New York: Greenwood Press, 1992.

Robinson, Jo Ann Gibson, and David J. Garrow. *The Montgomery Bus Boycott and the Women Who Started It: The Memoir of Jo Ann Gibson Robinson.* Knoxville: University of Tennessee Press, 1987.

WEBSITES

Montgomery Bus Boycott Page. Available online at http://sobek .colorado.edu/~jonesem/montgomery.html; website home page: http://sobek.colorado.edu (accessed March 18, 2003).

"Situations Wanted"

Newspaper advertisements

By: *The New York Times*

Date: December 4, 1955; November 18, 1956; September 27, 1959

Source: "Situations Wanted" *The New York Times,* December 4, 1955, 18; November 18, 1956, 15. September 27, 1959, 28

About the Publication: *The New York Times,* founded in 1850 as the *Daily Times,* was originally a relatively obscure local paper. However, by the early part of the twentieth century, it had grown into a widely known, well-respected news source. Its banner reading "All the News That's Fit to Print" is recognized across the United States and throughout the world. ■

Introduction

America in the nineteenth and early twentieth century was a very segregated, ordered and regimented society in many ways. Admission to college was largely a

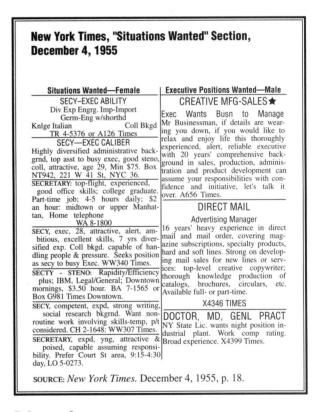

New York Times, "Situations Wanted" Section, December 4, 1955

Situations Wanted—Female	Executive Positions Wanted—Male
SECY–EXEC ABILITY Div Exp Engrg. Imp-Import Germ-Eng w/shorthd Knlge Italian Coll Bkgd TR 4-5376 or A126 Times	**CREATIVE MFG–SALES** ★ Exec Wants Busn to Manage Mr Businessman, if details are wearing you down, if you would like to relax and enjoy life this thoroughly experienced, alert, reliable executive with 20 years' comprehensive background in sales, production, administration and product development can assume your responsibilities with confidence and initiative, let's talk it over. A656 Times.
SECY—EXEC CALIBER Highly diversified administrative backgrnd, top asst to busy exec, good steno, coll, attractive, age 29, Min $75. Box NT942, 221 W 41 St, NYC 36.	
SECRETARY: top-flight, experienced, good office skills; college graduate. Part-time job; 4-5 hours daily; $2 an hour: midtown or upper Manhattan, Home telephone WA 8-1800	**DIRECT MAIL** Advertising Manager 16 years' heavy experience in direct mail and mail order, covering magazine subscriptions, specialty products, hard and soft lines. Strong on developing mail sales for new lines or services: top-level creative copywriter; thorough knowledge production of catalogs, brochures, circulars, etc. Available full- or part-time.
SECY, exec, 28, attractive, alert, ambitious, excellent skills, 7 yrs diversified exp. Coll bkgd. capable of handling people & pressure. Seeks position as secy to busy Exec. WW340 Times.	
SECTY - STENO: Rapidity/Efficiency plus; IBM, Legal/General; Downtown mornings, $3.50 hour. BA 7-1565 or Box G981 Times Downtown.	**X4346 TIMES**
SECY, competent, expd, strong writing, social research bkgrnd. Want nonroutine work involving skills-temp, p/t considered. CH 2-1648; WW307 Times.	**DOCTOR, MD, GENL PRACT** NY State Lic. wants night position industrial plant. Work comp rating. Broad experience. X4399 Times.
SECRETARY, expd, yng, attractive & poised, capable assuming responsibility. Prefer Court St area, 9:15-4:30 day, LO 5-0273.	

SOURCE: *New York Times.* December 4, 1955, p. 18.

Primary Source

"Situations Wanted" **(1 OF 4)**

SYNOPSIS: These ads posted in *The New York Times* sought to catch the attention of established professionals, who, in the 1950s, were overwhelmingly male. The references to "he" and "men" in these ads were mostly correct in describing those who would be qualified or interested in these positions.

Primary Source

"Situations Wanted" (2 OF 4)
An advertisement for an electronic field engineer. "ELECTRONICS FIELD ENGINEERS." REPRINTED FROM *THE NEW YORK TIMES*, NOVEMBER 18, 1956, 15.

function of social status, and it helped to be the child of an alumnus. Most prestigious colleges were single-sex schools, and one had to go to the right school to land the right job. Many jobs were open to only men, and most law schools, bar associations, and medical schools accepted only men. This discrimination was perfectly legal, as the Supreme Court in *Bradwell* v. *Illinois* held that

Primary Source

"Situations Wanted" (3 OF 4)
Advertisement for a management position at a woodworking factory. "GENERAL MANAGER WOODWORKING FACTORY." REPRINTED FROM *THE NEW YORK TIMES*, NOVEMBER 18, 1956, 15.

Illinois could exclude women from the practice of law, even if they had passed the bar exam. Women generally were allowed only into the teaching and nursing professions.

Similar discrimination existed in class and race. If one had not gone to the proper school or had not attended college at all, one was shut out of many jobs. African Americans and Hispanics were excluded from many professional societies, and most companies would not hire minorities—except for the most trivial and low-paying jobs. Many Wall Street law firms would not hire Jewish lawyers, even top graduates of Harvard or other elite law schools. America was very segregated, by law and custom, and this discrimination carried on well into the twentieth century.

In the 1950s, women were still excluded from many colleges and considered only for certain jobs. This is evident in the want ads, which segregated jobs into two columns under each subheading - "male" and "female," as did the ads posted by people seeking positions.

Significance

The jobs advertised under the "female" heading include typist and secretary, whereas the jobs which men were looking for included managers and controllers. Similar disparities existed in the help wanted sections, as is shown for the ad for "engineers," which specifically

Primary Source

"Situations Wanted" (4 OF 4)
Other job listings for women in the paper included bookeeper, secretary, clerk, and organist.

refers to "men." Women could apply for these jobs, but very often their applications would not be read or seriously considered. The qualifications listed in the "situations wanted" section is revealing as well. Very often, the women listed their age and that they were "attractive." This indicated their understanding that these attributes, rather than competence in their field, were of primary importance to employers. In the South, a further qualification was often added—race. Help wanted ads very often indicated the race of the person that the company wished to hire.

Listing of jobs by sex ended when the 1964 Civil Rights Act banned discrimination on the basis of sex. Women very often still faced discrimination, though. It commonly was assumed that women would work until they got married or had children. Employers asked female applicants directly, "When will you start a family?" Today such job questions, as well as discriminating on the basis of sex, race or age, are illegal. Women can no longer be kept out of jobs legally because they are women, and the same is true of minorities. The discrimination is not that distant in our past. Sandra Day O'Connor, a justice on the United States Supreme Court, could not find a legal job despite being an honors graduate of Stanford Law School.

Further Resources

BOOKS

Amott, Teresa L., and Julie A Matthaei. *Race, Gender, and Work: A Multicultural Economic History of Women in the United States.* Boston: South End Press, 1991.

Frankel, Max. *The Times of My Life and My Life with the Times.* New York: Random House, 1999.

Jones, Jacqueline. *American Work: Four Centuries of Black and White Labor.* New York: W.W. Norton, 1998.

Kessler-Harris, Alice. *Out to Work: A History of Wage-Earning Women in the United States.* New York: Oxford University Press, 1982.

Meyerowitz, Joanne J. *Not June Cleaver: Women and Gender in Postwar America, 1945-1960.* Philadelphia: Temple University Press, 1994.

Page One: One Hundred Years of Headlines as Presented in the New York Times. New York: Galahad Books, 2000.

Tifft, Susan E., and Alex S. Jones. *The Trust: The Private and Powerful Family behind the New York Times.* Boston: Little, Brown, 1999.

The Man in the Gray Flannel Suit
Novel

By: Sloan Wilson

Date: 1955

Source: Wilson, Sloan. *The Man in the Gray Flannel Suit.* New York: Simon & Schuster, 1955, 299–304.

About the Author: Sloan Wilson (1920–2003) had his greatest success with *The Man in the Gray Flannel Suit.* He graduated from Harvard University in 1942, and he served in the U.S. Coast Guard during World War II (1939–1945). He also wrote another successful book, *A Summer Place.* Besides writing novels, he was a reporter for the *Providence Journal* and an English professor at the University of Buffalo. From 1980 until his death, he held the post of distinguished writer in residence at Rollins College. ∎

Introduction

America during the nineteenth century was mostly a rural country. More people lived in the country than in the city. While not all rural residents were farmers, most were connected in some fashion to the farm economy. Of those living in cities, most worked in factories. The vast majority of factory workers were lower class. People typically worked six days a week, ten hours a day, with only Sunday off. Many of those in the steel industry worked seven days a week, twelve hours a day.

With the start of the twentieth century, this changed a great deal. America became an urban nation. By 1920, more people lived in cities than in the country. Those in factories worked less hours, fewer children worked, and completing high school became the norm. Life was seemingly better than in the past. This was primarily true, though, only for white America. Many African Americans still were sharecroppers, working long hours each day only to end up each year further in debt. The educational prospects for African Americans remained poor in general. After World War II, America passed the GI Bill, enabling veterans to receive a college education. After graduation, many entered the corporate world. In this world, one generally wore a conservative suit, often of gray flannel, worked in an office, drove a sedan, and shuffled paper. Life was much easier for him than for his ancestors, if not completely fulfilling.

Significance

Tom, a veteran of World War II and a businessman who worked in an office, was a "man in a gray flannel suit"—the main character in the novel. He shows one problem with the whole idea of the 1950s bringing happiness for men in his situation. The veterans like Tom had fought for a way of life and now, being home, were supposed to be enjoying that life. However, that life turned out to be merely working in an office and merely shuffling papers. One was supposed to be happy with this— and having everything regimented—and not getting anywhere. Many were not happy, though; and, over time, this dissatisfaction leaked out. Tom, in the novel, epitomizes this dissatisfaction. The 1950s model also required one to paper over his past, which Tom was not willing to do (but many others did). There were few illegitimate children of ex-GIs in Italy, Germany or Japan who received support or even knew who their fathers were. Most were not as lucky as Tom, however. Many were trapped in the "gray flannel suit" lifestyle for their whole working lives.

There were many people who never had the chance to be the man in the gray flannel suit, though. These included African Americans, who often were not allowed into college or hired by corporate America. Women were expected to remain home with the kids and be happy, but many were not. This, however, was not exposed until the publication of *The Feminine Mystique* in the 1960s, well after *The Man in the Gray Flannel Suit*.

This book demonstrates that despite its more pleasant working conditions, a new kind of discontent developed in the 1950s. An entire subculture grew up in the 1950s with the Beatnik group, including the writer Jack Kerouac. This discontent exploded in the 1960s, combining with the coming of age of the baby boomers and the anti-war movement. Often, for lack of an alternative, many settled into the "gray flannel lifestyle." They were not content with the challenge of the 1960s and 1970s from the counterculture, or the challenge of the corporate downsizing of the 1990s—forcing out many who worked their entire careers for these companies. The discontent of the gray flannel lifestyle, that began in the 1950s, continues today for many of the children and grandchildren of those originally afflicted.

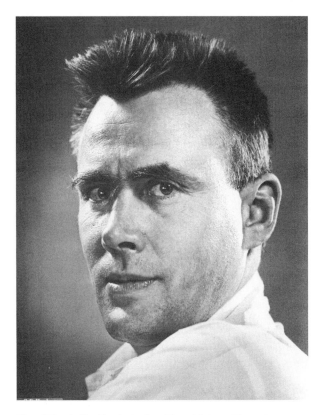

Sloan Wilson's *The Man in the Gray Flannel Suit* was his most successful book. © BETTMANN/CORBIS. REPRODUCED BY PERMISSION.

Primary Source

The Man in the Gray Flannel Suit [excerpt]

SYNOPSIS: *The Man in the Gray Flannel Suit* is the story of Tom, a middle-aged American who like millions of veterans came home from World War II (1939–45) to enter into a working world of boredom and conformity. The selection opens with Tom talking with his wife, and his wife forgiving him. Tom then states that peace was not what he expected it to be. Tom goes to his lawyer and sets up a trust fund for the son that he admits to fathering in Italy during the war. At the end, Tom and Betsy set off for Vermont.

They walked over to the stone wall and sat with their backs against it. He kissed her. "There are some things I have to say," she said. "Don't kiss me again, or I'll never say them."

"Nothing has to be said now."

"This must be said. Tonight while I was driving alone, I realized for the first time what you went through in the war, and what different worlds we've been living in ever since. I'm sorry I acted like a child."

"I love you."

"You're right about helping your boy in Italy. Of course we should do all we can."

"I love you."

"He should have a good education and everything he needs. Do they have trouble getting enough food and medicine and clothes over there? We should find out what he needs and send it. We shouldn't just send money."

"I love you more than I can ever tell."

"I want you to be able to talk to me about the war. It might help us to understand each other. Did you really kill seventeen men?"

"Yes."

"Do you want to talk about it now?"

"No. It's not that I want to and can't—it's just that I'd rather think about the future. About getting a new car and driving up to Vermont with you tomorrow."

"That will be fun. It's not an insane world. At least, our part of it doesn't have to be."

"Of course not."

"We don't have to work and worry all the time. It's been our own fault that we have. What's been the matter with us?"

"I don't know," he said. "I guess I expected peace to be nothing but a time for sitting in the moonlight with you like this, and I was surprised to find that this isn't quite all there is to it."

"I disappointed you."

"Of course you didn't. I was my own disappointment. I really don't know what I was looking for when I got back from the war, but it seemed as though all I could see was a lot of bright young men in gray flannel suits rushing around New York in a frantic parade to nowhere. They seemed to me to be pursuing neither ideals nor happiness—they were pursuing a routine. For a long while I thought I was on the side lines watching that parade, and it was quite a shock to glance down and see that I too was wearing a gray flannel suit. Then I met Caesar, running an elevator. He's the one who knew about Maria—he went through most of the war with me. There was Caesar in his purple uniform, staring at me in my gray flannel suit and reminding me, always reminding me, that I was betraying almost everyone I knew."

"I wish I could have helped you."

"You did help me—you and Caesar. I needed a great deal of assistance in becoming an honest man.

If you hadn't persuaded me to play it straight with Ralph, I would be thinking differently now. By a curious coincidence, Ralph and a good deal of the rest of the world have seemed honest to me ever since I became honest with myself. And if I hadn't met Caesar, I don't think I ever would have had the courage to tell you about Maria. I would have gone on, becoming more and more bitter, more and more cynical, and I don't know where that road would have ended. But now I'm sure things are going to be better. I've become almost an optimist."

"I'm glad we're going to have a week to ourselves. Where are we going in Vermont?"

"I know a place where we can rent a cabin by a lake a thousand miles from nowhere. The foliage on the mountains will be beautiful this time of the year. If we get a few more days of Indian summer, it may not be too late for a swim. The nights will be cold, and we'll sleep by an open fire."

"Do you love me?"

"A little."

"Don't tease me. Do you like the way I look?"

"You're beautiful. You never used to like to have me tell you that."

"I want to hear it now. Often. Tell me again that I am beautiful."

"Every time I look at you, you are a delight to me. Every night when I get off the train and see you, I want to tell you that. I haven't for years, because you told me once that you would rather have other compliments."

"I guess when I decided to be a fool, I had to play it big."

"You've not been as foolish as I," he said, and pulled her down beside him in the fragrant grass and kissed her. A sudden puff of wind set the long ends of the grass shivering all around him. She shuddered. "You're cold," he said. "I'll take you in now."

"No. Hold me tight."

"You're trembling. Why?"

"I don't know. I feel as though we almost died and have just been rescued."

"We're not going to worry any more. No matter what happens, we've got a lot to be grateful for."

"When I think of all you've been through, I'm afraid."

"Don't be. The dead don't have the last laugh. It's the children left by the dead and the survivors who laugh last, and their laughter is not sardonic.

Ever since you came back to me tonight, I've been remembering a line from a poem that used to sound ironic and bitter. It doesn't sound that way any more. Tonight, for a little while at least, I feel it's true."

"What is it?"

"'God's in his heaven,'" he said, "'all's right with the world.'"

41

At eleven-thirty the next morning Judge Saul Bernstein got a telephone call from Tom Rath. "I'm just about to leave town for a week, but I'd like to drop down and see you first," Tom said. "I want your help on a very personal problem."

"Come ahead," Bernstein said. "I'll be expecting you." He hung up and tried to concentrate on the tax form he was completing for a client. Tom's call troubled him. He had had many people telephone to ask immediate help on "a very personal problem," and the approaching trip Tom mentioned was also a bad sign. To Bernstein it all sounded like the usual preliminaries to a divorce case. Divorce cases always saddened Bernstein, and the thought of Betsy and Tom Rath dissolving their marriage especially bothered him. He liked them and he thought that with three young children they had no business splitting up. *I wonder what I might do to talk them out of it,* he thought, and felt a few warning twinges of pain in his stomach.

Ten minutes later when Tom walked into his office, Bernstein was surprised to see that for a man presumably on the verge of divorce, he appeared indecently cheerful. "Good morning!" Tom boomed heartily. "Beautiful day, isn't it?"

"Yes," Bernstein said uneasily. "What can I do for you?"

"Mind if we go into your inner office?" Tom asked, glancing at Bernstein's secretary.

"No," Bernstein said. "Go right ahead." His stomach began to ache quite badly now. People who wanted to go to the inner office even before naming the nature of their business quite often wanted to discuss divorce. He followed Tom into the small book-lined room, and they both sat down.

"I came to you with this because it would be a little embarrassing to discuss with strangers, and I'm sure you'll understand," Tom began.

"I hope so," Bernstein said dubiously.

"The situation is simply this. During the war I had an illegitimate child in Italy. He's been on my mind a lot, but I haven't been absolutely sure of his existence until recently. Now I want to send his mother a hundred dollars a month for his support— they're in real need. When this housing project of ours goes through, I'm going to establish a trust fund, but right now I want to take it out of income. I think it would be less awkward for everyone concerned if we set up some mechanism for having the checks sent regularly by a bank, or perhaps you could do it."

"Are you trying to make this an anonymous gift?" Bernstein asked somewhat guardedly.

"For the sake of propriety I don't want it talked about all over town, and I don't particularly trust the discretion of the local bank, but the person who will get the money will know who it's from. There's no need to keep anything a secret from her."

Bernstein cleared his throat. "You intend this to be a permanent arrangement?" he asked.

"Certainly. At least until the boy has finished his education."

"It might be possible for you to receive considerable tax benefits by having the child legally declared a dependent," Bernstein said. "You ought to look into that if you plan anything permanent."

"I hadn't thought of that," Tom replied. "Fix it up for me if you can, will you? Might as well get all the tax benefits I can."

"It might be necessary for you to admit paternity," Bernstein said. "That might leave you open to further claims by the child's mother, and it might pose certain problems for you in filling out your tax returns."

"I'm not worried about further claims. What would the difficulty be with the tax returns?"

"It might be hard to keep the matter a complete secret here," Bernstein said somewhat embarrassedly. "Especially if you file joint tax returns which your wife has to sign."

"Betsy already knows all about it," Tom said. "She and I are doing this together."

"You are?" Bernstein said, unable to preserve his professional air of detachment any longer.

"I know this must sound a little odd to you," Tom said, "but I met a girl in Italy during the war, and I've told Betsy all about it. The child the girl had needs help, and Betsy and I are going to send it. I suppose that may be a little unconventional, but to us it seems like simple justice."

For a moment Bernstein didn't say anything. Misinterpreting his silence as censure, Tom said a little stiffly, "This is a matter of conscience with me, and I don't intend to try to justify it to anyone. Betsy and I are driving up to Vermont this afternoon, and I would appreciate it if you could arrange to have the checks sent. In this envelope I've brought the money for three months and the name and address I want it sent to. What will you charge me for handling the matter?"

"Nothing," Bernstein said.

"What?"

"No charge."

"Why not?"

Bernstein smiled. "I like what you call 'simple justice,'" he said. "The kind I generally deal with is so complex."

"Thanks," Tom said. Suddenly the air was charged with emotion. Bernstein got up and Tom grabbed his hand. "Thanks!" he said again. "I've got to be running. Betsy's been shopping, but she's probably waiting outside for me now. We're heading up to Vermont!"

He dashed out the door. Bernstein's stomach wasn't aching any more. He walked slowly to the window of his office and stood looking down at the street. Betsy, with her arms full of bundles, was just coming down the sidewalk. Bernstein watched as Tom hurried toward her. He saw them bow gravely toward each other as she transferred the bundles to Tom's arms. Then Tom straightened up and apparently said something to her, for suddenly she smiled radiantly. Bernstein smiled too.

Further Resources

BOOKS

Cheit, Earl Frank. *The Business Establishment.* New York: Wiley, 1964.

Fish, Peter. *Sinclair Lewis's Babbitt.* Woodbury, N.Y.: Barron's Educational Series, 1985.

Fogle, Beverly Diane. *Other-direction, Group-orientation and Conformity Among Businessmen and Academicians.* Master's Thesis, Kansas State University, 1963.

Howard, Robert. *Brave New Workplace.* New York: Viking, 1985.

Kirsch, M. M. *How to Get Off the Fast Track— and Live a Life Money Can't Buy.* Los Angeles: Lowell House, 1991.

Levering, Robert. *A Great Place to Work: What Makes Some Employers So Good, and Most So Bad.* New York: Random House, 1988.

Schmidt, Jeff. *Disciplined Minds: a Critical Look at Salaried Professionals and the Soul-Battering System That Shapes Their Lives.* Lanham, Md.: Rowman & Littlefield, 2000.

Shetty, Y. Krishna, and Vernon M. Buehler. *Productivity and Quality Through People: Practices of Well-Managed Companies.* Westport, Conn.: Quorum Books, 1985.

WEBSITES

Telework and the New Workplace of the 21st Century. Available online at http://www.dol.gov/asp/telework/p3_3.htm; website home page: http://www.dol.gov (accessed March 15, 2003).

"Howl"
Poem

By: Allen Ginsberg

Date: 1956

Source: Ginsberg, Allen. "Howl." In *Howl and Other Poems.* San Francisco: City Lights Books, 1956, 9–11.

About the Author: Allen Ginsberg (1926-1997) was one of the best known writers of the Beat Movement, one of the few who continued to influence culture after the 1960s. His poem, "Howl" and Jack Kerouac's *On the Road*, became leading literary influences on the Beats. He was politically active in the 1960s, leading the anti-war movement. He remained culturally active and continued writing until his death. ∎

Introduction

America has alternated between acceptance and repression of differences and individuality. As late as the end of the eighteenth century, many states still had established organized churches. Anti-Catholic riots broke out in several cities in the 1840s. On an individualized basis, those who believed or acted "different" often have been looked down upon throughout American history. However, in other cities and during other eras, this deviance from the norm has been celebrated—sometimes occurring in the same decade as repression. For instance, in the 1920s, the "flapper" was the rage in many cities; while in the countryside, where religious fundamentalism reigned supreme, the flapper phenomenon was viewed negatively.

However, very little public acceptance of non-traditional sexual behaviors occurred. Most states criminalized homosexual behaviors. Thus, even though homosexuality existed, it was quite repressed and not covered by the mainstream press.

A culture of repression and conformity reigned during the 1950s, and this was reflected in the mainstream press. After World War II (1939–1945), many wanted a return to the "good ol' days." They sought a suburban lifestyle with few disruptions, protests, or challenges to the cultural orthodoxy. The Red Scare and its mindset caused anything new or "radical" to be linked with communism. Into this atmosphere of conformity stepped Allen Ginsberg and his poem, "Howl."

Significance

Ginsberg's "Howl" differed from traditional poems in a number of ways. The poem is seemingly endless; its lengthy first part contains one sentence. The poem then has a section where every line ends with an exclamation point. Also, the poem contains a large amount of repetition. Each of these features is unusual in poetry, especially during that era. Ginsberg, in "Howl," protests icons of 1950s culture—conformity, the relentless pursuit of money, and the repressive sexual mores of America. (Ginsberg publicly acknowledged his homosexuality in an era when very few public figures did so.)

Ginsberg, with this poem and others, moved into the forefront of the "beatnik" (a derogatory label coined by opponents) movement of the 1950s, along with literary figures Jack Kerouac and William Burroughs. In the 1960s, the idea of "New Left"—a blending of the counterculture, youth movement, anti-war movement and other forces—gained wide popularity. Many still opposed Ginsberg and the hippie movement throughout the 1960s. Ginsberg retained his high profile in the counterculture movement. He testified in the "Chicago 7" trial in 1969, the federal government's prosecution of leading figures in the counterculture movement for inciting riots to protest the Vietnam War (1964–1975) during the Democratic National Convention in 1968. Ginsberg remained a celebrity and active in the counterculture movement until his death.

"Howl" and the other protest writings of the 1950s, including Kerouac's *On the Road,* clearly demonstrate that all of America was not happy during the 1950s. This discontent set the foundation for the many protests of the 1960s. The mixed reaction to "Howl," at the time of publication and since, demonstrates that all were not won over to Ginsberg's views. Many made careers out of protesting against protesters like Ginsberg. On the whole, "Howl" demonstrates that Ginsberg and others were howling against the sterility of the 1950s culture.

Primary Source

"Howl" [excerpt]

> **SYNOPSIS:** Ginsberg opens his poem by explaining how the best minds in America were destroyed by American culture.

For Carl Solomon

I

I saw the best minds of my generation destroyed by
    madness, starving hysterical naked,
dragging themselves through the negro streets at
    dawn looking for an angry fix,
angelheaded hipsters burning for the ancient
    heavenly connection to the starry dynamo in the
    machinery of night,

Poet Allen Ginsberg writes in his San Francisco home. © ALLEN GINSBERG/CORBIS. REPRODUCED BY PERMISSION.

who poverty and tatters and hollow-eyed and high sat
    up smoking in the supernatural darkness of cold-
    water flats floating across the tops of cities
    contemplating jazz,
who bared their brains to Heaven under the El and
    saw Mohammedan angels staggering on tenement
    roofs illuminated,
who passed through universities with radiant cool
    eyes hallucinating Arkansas and Blake-light tragedy
    among the scholars of war,
who were expelled from the academies for crazy &
    publishing obscene odes on the windows of the
    skull,
who cowered in unshaven rooms in underwear,
    burning their money in wastebaskets and listening
    to the Terror through the wall,
who got busted in their pubic beards returning
    through Laredo with a belt of marijuana for New
    York,
who ate fire in paint hotels or drank turpentine in
    Paradise Alley, death, or purgatoried their torsos
    night after night
with dreams, with drugs, with waking nightmares,
    alcohol . . .
incomparable blind streets of shuddering cloud and
    lightning in the mind leaping toward poles of
    Canada & Paterson, illuminating all the motionless
    world of Time between,
Peyote solidities of halls, backyard green tree
    cemetery dawns, wine drunkenness over the

rooftops, storefront boroughs of teahead joyride
neon blinking traffic light, sun and moon and tree
vibrations in the roaring winter dusks of Brooklyn,
ashcan rantings and kind king light of mind,
who chained themselves to subways for the endless
ride from Battery to holy Bronx on benzedrine until
the noise of wheels and children brought them down
shuddering mouth-wracked and battered bleak of
brain all drained of brilliance in the drear light of Zoo,
who sank all night in submarine light of Bickford's
floated out and sat through the stale beer
afternoon in desolate Fugazzi's, listening to the
crack of doom on the hydrogen jukebox,
who talked continuously seventy hours from park to
pad to bar to Bellevue to museum to the Brooklyn
Bridge,
a lost battalion of platonic conversationalists jumping
down the stoops off fire escapes off windowsills off
Empire State out of the moon,
yacketayakking screaming vomiting whispering facts
and memories and anecdotes and eyeball kicks and
shocks of hospitals and jails and wars,
whole intellects disgorged in total recall for seven
days and nights with brilliant eyes, meat for the
Synagogue cast on the pavement,
who vanished into nowhere Zen New Jersey leaving a
trail of ambiguous picture postcards of Atlantic City
Hall,
suffering Eastern sweats and Tangerian bone-
grindings and migraines of China under junk-
withdrawal in Newark's bleak furnished room,
who wandered around and around at midnight in the
railroad yard wondering where to go, and went,
leaving no broken hearts,
who lit cigarettes in boxcars boxcars boxcars racketing
through snow toward lonesome farms in grandfather
night,
who studied Plotinus Poe St. John of the Cross
telepathy and bop kaballa because the cosmos
instinctively vibrated at their feet in Kansas,
who loned it through the streets of Idaho seeking
visionary indian angels who were visionary indian
angels,
who thought they were only mad when Baltimore
gleamed in supernatural ecstasy,
who jumped in limousines with the Chinaman of
Oklahoma on the impulse of winter midnight
streetlight smalltown rain,
who lounged hungry and lonesome through Houston
seeking jazz or sex or soup, and followed the
brilliant Spaniard to converse about America and
Eternity, a hopeless task, and so took ship to
Africa,
who disappeared into the volcanoes of Mexico
leaving behind nothing but the shadow of
dungarees and the lava and ash of poetry scattered
in fireplace Chicago,
who reappeared on the West Coast investigating the
F.B.I. in beards and shorts with big pacifist eyes
sexy in their dark skin passing out
incomprehensible leaflets,
who burned cigarette holes in their arms protesting
the narcotic tobacco haze of Capitalism,

who distributed Supercommunist pamphlets in Union
Square weeping and undressing while the sirens of
Los Alamos wailed them down, and wailed down
Wall, and the Staten Island ferry also wailed,
who broke down crying in white gymnasiums naked
and trembling before the machinery of other
skeletons . . .

Further Resources

BOOKS

Burns, Glen. *Great Poets Howl: A Study of Allen Ginsberg's Poetry, 1943-1955* Frankfurt: Peter Lang, 1983.

Cassady, Carolyn. *Off the Road: My Years with Cassady, Kerouac, and Ginsberg*. New York: W. Morrow, 1990.

Coontz, Stephanie. *The Way We Never Were: American Families and the Nostalgia Trap*. New York: BasicBooks, 1992.

Ginsberg, Allen. *Allen Verbatim: Lectures on Poetry, Politics, Consciousness*. New York: McGraw-Hill, 1974.

Halberstam, David. *The Fifties*. New York: Villard Books, 1993.

Schumacher, Michael. *Dharma Lion: A Critical Biography of Allen Ginsberg*. New York: St. Martin's Press, 1992.

Tytell, John. *Naked Angels: The Lives & Literature of the Beat Generation*. New York: McGraw-Hill, 1976.

PERIODICALS

Hass, Robert. "The Howl Heard Round the World: Celebrating 30 Years of a San Francisco Literary Monument." *Image Magazine*. Dec. 21, 1986, 26-39.

WEBSITES

Allen Ginsberg: Shadow Changes Into Bone. Available online at http://www.ginzy.com/ (accessed March 17, 2003).

"Difference Between Victory and Defeat"

Magazine article

By: Willard Bascom

Date: March 18, 1957

Source: Bascom, Willard. "Difference Between Victory and Defeat." *Life,* March 18, 1957, 150, 153–154, 159–160, 162.

About the Author: Willard Bascom (1916–2000) attended Springfield College and the Colorado School of Mines. He was as a research engineer, heading up Seafinders, Inc. and Ocean Science and Engineering. Bascom taught at a number of different institutions, including the Scripps Institute of Oceanography and California State University Long Beach. He authored three filmscripts and at least five books. In the 1950s, he served as a delegate to the International Geophysical Year Conferences on Oceanography. ∎

Introduction

America long considered herself to be protected by two oceans and not directly threatened by anyone. No country in North America was viewed as a threat. By establishing the Monroe Doctrine, America, in the estimation of many, effectively kept the European powers out of the Americas. Also, America adopted a largely isolationist foreign policy during the nineteenth century, staying out of Europe's affairs to a great extent.

This all changed in the twentieth century. America gained more territories as a result of the Spanish-American War (1898) and became more active in foreign affairs. None of the territories gained by the United States posed any real threat of invasion to America either. America next fought World Wars I (1914–1918) and II (1939–1945), but peace did not last long as a "Cold War" began between the United States and Russia (USSR) shortly after the end of World War II. At the time, the United States was the world's only nuclear power. In 1949, the USSR exploded its own atomic bomb. The United States developed a hydrogen bomb, but the USSR matched this technology quickly. With the Soviet atomic arsenal and communism expanding rapidly (with additional expansion possible throughout the world), Americans became fearful of a nuclear attack. Joseph McCarthy and other politicians heightened these fears with accusations of widespread communist infiltration in American institutions. The United States prepared for a possible nuclear attack by building bomb shelters.

Significance

During the 1950s, many people built nuclear bomb shelters, very often in their own backyard. Many schools and public buildings constructed in the 1950s had bomb shelters built under them. Stories appeared in newspapers and magazines of people who did test runs of living in the shelters, including some honeymooners. Unbeknownst to them, the federal government bugged some of these shelters to determine how people reacted while living in cramped conditions. The federal government also built bomb shelters for a government in exile under mountains in Virginia and a command center in the Rocky Mountains.

In the 1960s, the prevalence of bomb shelters lessened, as both the United States and Russia adopted a nuclear policy of Mutually Assured Destruction or "MAD." Under this policy, as both sides had nuclear weapons sufficient to blow up the world many times over, any nuclear war would destroy the entire planet. Given this reality, neither side could "win" a nuclear war. Launching a nuclear attack would begin a chain of events that assured the destruction of the planet. Since any war would mean the end of all life and all vegetation on the planet, bomb shelters seemed pointless. Fears also eased after the Cuban missile crisis, which lessened tensions between the United States and Russia. The bomb shelters already built rusted, and few new ones were built.

At the end of the Cold War in the early 1990s, the threat of nuclear destruction decreased substantially for a time. However, the possession or desire for nuclear arms by rogue states and terrorist organizations—together with the terrorist attacks of September 11, 2001—has sparked a new interest in bomb shelter construction. At least some Americans have built new bomb shelters as a result of the threat of terrorism.

Primary Source

"Difference Between Victory and Defeat" [excerpt]

> **SYNOPSIS:** Bascom argues that civil defenses need to be built as the hydrogen bomb threatens America's very survival. The article states that, although no perfect system exists, the public needs to understand the dangers of nuclear war. Bascom states that shelters need to be built, warning systems put in place, and that the country's assets should be dispersed. He closes with cost estimates, together with a suggestion that Washington, D.C. should be first priority for taking action.

The nuclear bomb poses, for the first time in history, a serious direct threat to the American people. The means to annihilate our unprepared civilian population is already in the hands of our potential enemy and the need for preparation should be obvious. Yet the bulk of our population is totally unprepared today to meet a war emergency.

Our civil defenses are incomplete partly because the public is so little aware of its danger and partly because the few who have investigated the effects of nuclear attack tend to be overwhelmed by the horrors they foresee. There is a temptation to say, "What's the use?"

But there is a use. Civil defense is not a hopeless task. If war should come an adequate program could save millions of people. It could mean the difference between American victory and defeat. And although it cannot guarantee the survival of any specific person, it can guarantee that the U.S. will continue to exist and to work for the things that we believe in.

Civil defense could also be of great value in preventing a war. Our policy in foreign affairs is to take a strong stand against Soviet intimidation of our allies and the neutral nations. But a strong stand, with the threat of war it implies, may be meaningless if the enemy knows that our civilian population is virtually naked before an attack. Protective arrangements for the public would greatly strengthen the hand of our President in a crisis by increasing his

An atomic bomb shelter for the family, designed by Walter Kiddie Nuclear Laboratories, Inc., will sustain a family for 3 to 5 days with a gasoline-powered generator. © BETTMANN/CORBIS. REPRODUCED BY PERMISSION.

bargaining capacity at the international conference table.

The development of adequate civil defenses will be expensive, difficult and time-consuming. Defenses cannot be prepared after a crisis is reached. They must be methodically increased over a period of years as a natural back-up to our military readiness. The most practical way to accomplish this is by emphasizing dual-use projects with peacetime as well as wartime applications. The very fact that all-out nuclear war does not appear to be likely in the near future—one reason for the present indifference—gives us a chance to plan and carry out public defense programs at a pace that will not endanger our economy or cause any raised eyebrows in the world.

Before considering a detailed program of civil defense, we should understand the nature of the threat.

First we must face the fact that there is no complete military defense against atomic attack. Complicated defenses will be invented and improved but they will never be perfect. Nuclear explosives can be carried by planes, or, eventually, by missiles launched from submarines. In a few years intercontinental missiles capable of carrying the H-bomb may become a reality. . . .

A built-in defense

Such are the dangers. A defense must be devised that seems likely to counter them. Its goal should be the best protection we can *actually* provide rather than the best that is *theoretically* possible; it must get public support by being based on more durable motivations than fear or horror; it must offer a promise of better and more secure living; it must be made an effective part of our war deterrent; it must be built into our way of life.

The responsibility for this, as with all forms of national defense rests with the federal government, which must provide the leadership, the over-all planning and much of the financing. A real civil defense requires the following measures:

1. There should be general public understanding of enough of the physical and biological effects of nuclear explosions so that people can take the best possible protective action before, during and after an attack. . . .

2. Stout shelters are required, well equipped and provisioned and easily accessible to all people, especially while they are at home.

Evacuation of the crowded centers of assumed target areas has been ardently proposed as an alternative to shelters. At best it would be an interim measure usable by some if the time between warning and attack is relatively long. Arguments for or against evacuation as a policy have hinged more often on whether it is feasible to move cars out of town rapidly than on whether it is the best thing to do for protection. As one measure that may help reduce casualties from direct bombing by manned aircraft, evacuation is worth consideration so long as it does not block a more permanent defense. Permanent defense means shelters.

It is possible to build shelters which will offer protection anywhere outside of the bomb crater (even within the atomic fireball) either by making them of very thick concrete or by excavating them in solid rock. Perhaps in densely populated areas near obvious targets, or for the protection of valuable facilities or workers, such high-strength shelters will have a place. Outside of this relatively small area, whose location cannot be forecast, shelters of somewhat lesser strength appear to be more economical and offer many other advantages.

Well-protected areas already exist in cities, in the form of deep basements, subways and the like, which could readily be developed into shelters. New shelters can be most efficiently created by the construction of dual-purpose facilities which are kept in constant use in time of peace. For example, most cities seem to be in chronic need of transportation facilities, such as parking garages, bus and railroad terminals, or roadway underpasses. These are designed to bear heavy loads and could be adapted for use as shelters in an emergency. The federal government might subsidize construction of underground parking garage-shelters just as it does that of ocean liners which can be converted to wartime use as troop transports. The cost of such structures would in many cases be self-liquidating.

Most Americans spend about three quarters of their time at home, so the obvious place to have shelters which can be quickly reached at any time is in or near the home. There people will have the security of familiar surroundings and will be able to provide themselves with supplies from the house even when contact with the outside is cut off for several days. Although unattractive by comparison with ordinary living conditions, a family shelter should be incomparably more pleasant than a communal shelter shared with strangers of varying tastes and habits.

How to get shelters built

A federal program is needed to stimulate the construction of such shelters. One or more of the following inducements might be offered: more favorable financing for homes with shelters, making materials or prefab shelter units available at low cost, providing property tax benefits for shelter owners (justifiable because it would be unnecessary to provide public shelter facilities for people who have their own) or offering actual cash of up to two thirds the total cost to shelter builders. As an absolute minimum effort a social atmosphere must be created in which a person can provide a shelter for his family without being regarded as an idiot or an alarmist by his neighbors.

One way of demonstrating government faith in the advisability of having shelters would be to build them for the families of the fighting men on or near military reservations, especially at Strategic Air Command bases and other likely targets.

3. A warning system should be established capable of arousing the attention of everyone in the country within the few minutes that will be available in the era of missiles so that all can quickly receive instructions and take protective measures.

To the present air raid sirens which are effective in densely populated areas must be added a system of warning devices which will be more efficient in suburban and rural areas. One promising means of reaching into each home is via radio receivers which can be modified to monitor continuously for a broadcast warning.

It has been estimated that a system capable of warning 95% of the people in the U.S. could be built and maintained for about 80¢ per person per year. Some of this money would be spent in subsidies to manufacturers of warning devices, some would go into enlarging the public warning system. An effective warning system is absolutely necessary for without it the vastly more expensive shelter program will be of little use.

4. Two major radio communications systems are required, one for the public, the other for the government. The first should be capable of transmitting information to the public continuously from the instant of warning until the emergency has passed. The other should be able to keep government groups at all levels in contact with one another so that central control can be maintained in the emergency. . . .

5. Some of the valuable assets of the country should be dispersed so that neither the bulk of our wealth nor any single irreplaceable element could be lost all at once.

The large nuclear bomb, if used against cities or large groups of civilians, is a cheap weapon. With it, great numbers of people can be killed at relatively small expense. One answer to a cheap weapon is a cheap target, and if people and their facilities can be spread so thinly that few are destroyed by each bomb, then the bomb is no longer cheap. The ideal (but obviously impractical) solution would be to distribute the people, the commerce and industry, the transportation and communications lines and other attractive targets evenly throughout the country. Fortunately, the most flexible and easiest of these to move—the people—is also the most valuable. If the people survive, the physical assets can be rebuilt; if the skilled people are lost it will take generations to replace them. Therefore the principal aim of dispersal must be to keep people spread as thinly as possible and separated from obviously attractive targets while the danger is greatest.

There is already a marked trend away from urban areas toward dispersed living as a result of easy financing and inexpensive subdivision housing and more convenient automotive transportation to the cities and shopping areas.

Continued easy credit and development of highways and other transportation probably will produce as much dispersal as any direct program. The trend could be speeded even more by the construction of broad high-speed roads beyond those now required and by making credit easier in areas of less dense population.

6. A radiological defense plan must be developed so that areas of fallout can be identified and the hazard evaluated. It will be absolutely necessary to make rapid surveys as soon as the onslaught has subsided so that people will not spend unnecessary time in shelters in areas where there is little radioactivity, and will not emerge too soon in dangerous areas. Ground and aerial measurements must be made and passed along to points where they can be plotted and analyzed. The program must also offer instructions about the nature of the danger and means of decontamination.

7. Stockpiles must be accumulated of certain items such as medical supplies, processed foodstuffs, cloth (for tents or window coverings) and the like, as a safeguard against the temporary failure of our production and distribution system.

8. Measures must be taken to redevelop certain urban areas, especially for the purpose of re-

ducing the possibility of great fires in areas which may not otherwise be seriously damaged. Shelters will not afford adequate protection to a populace unless safeguards are also provided against major fires.

A program of replacing slums with garden apartments and of constructing firebreaks in the form of parks and wide boulevards is clearly desirable from the point of view of improving city living as well as of defense. The government could give additional stimulation and impetus to the existing desire for such projects by providing long-term financing at favorable rates.

9. Washington, D.C. must set an example if the U.S. public is to be expected to take a federal program seriously. The government must demonstrate a belief in the measures that are advocated, for it is obvious that our nation's capital is a target of high priority on the enemy list. Government buildings, especially those now planned or under construction, should have built-in shelters.

10. A new department of the federal government should be set up to provide guidance and subsidies to those who require them during the periods of preparation, attack and recovery. . . .

The importance of dual-use projects for improving our defensive capabilities can scarcely be overstated. Many of the things proposed should be done anyway to keep pace with our rapidly expanding population and economy. It is quite clear that the country needs such things as improved educational facilities, especially in the sciences; a greatly expanded network of roads, including access highways to cities and to undeveloped areas; slum clearance; a widespread microwave communications system, and additional parking facilities in cities.

These are all important elements of civil defense. However, they should be undertaken by local governments. They should not be under the centralized control of a civil defense department, nor should an important part of their cost be charged to it. Rather, this agency should 1) harness our protective instincts to furnish an additional motive and help us rationalize the costs; 2) see that the planning for each of these huge programs really does take the possibility of war into account; 3) supply the money for the additional cost of modifying the plans to make them more useful for defense. . . .

How much might such a program cost? Anything that must be provided for 170 million Americans can't help being expensive. But in trying to estimate the price of this insurance against an event that we instinctively feel is unlikely, we must keep two things in mind: defensive facilities cannot be built at the last minute; their cost is necessarily spread over several years. And there can be a considerable contribution to peacetime efficiency and convenience from dual-use projects.

If we set as a goal the provision of 90% of the protective measures outlined here within six years (one year of planning and five of construction), the total cost can be expected to be around $24 billion or an average of $4 billion per year. Not all of this expense, of course, would be borne by the federal government. In any case, it is not beyond our means: $4 billion is about 10% of the present defense department budget.

Most of the sum allotted to civil defense would go into shelters of various kinds. The warning and communications networks, the educational programs, and the stockpiling and radiological defense expenses combined might cost as much as a billion dollars each. The remaining programs as well as some not indicated here, plus the cost of administration for six years, would absorb the balance. After the principal construction period is over, the continuing budget for replacement, maintenance, education, administration and so forth would level off at perhaps $500 million a year.

These are admittedly rough guesses. Only the most rigorous engineering study of each item can be expected to produce accurate figures. However it seems quite probable that they are within a factor of two—that is, the ultimate cost will be between half and twice these sums. For the purpose of making a decision to embark on a real civil defense program that is probably close enough.

■ ■ ■

Most of the foregoing proposals have been offered many times before by others, and some of the needs, long since recognized, have been partly translated into reality. But the bulk of the work is still to be done. Unfortunately, too many people seem to believe that if war comes some magic will intervene to save them and that they are not personally required to make troublesome and expensive preparations on their own behalf. Let us hope that they are right and that evolutionists did not have them in mind when they speculated that war is a eugenic process which eliminates those without a special will to live.

Further Resources

BOOKS

Cable, Carole. *Atomic Bomb Shelters and Blast-Resistant Building: a Selective Bibliography of Periodical Literature.* Monticello, Ill.: Vance Bibliographies, 1985.

Coontz, Stephanie. *The Way We Never Were: American Families and the Nostalgia Trap.* New York: BasicBooks, 1992.

Diggins, John P. *The Proud Decades: America in War and in Peace, 1941-1960.* New York: Norton, 1989.

Keeney, L. Douglas and Stephen I Schwartz. *The Doomsday Scenario.* St. Paul, Minn.: MBI Publishing Co., 2002.

Ormerod, R. N. *Nuclear Shelters: A Guide to Design.* London: Architectural, 1983.

Protection in the Nuclear Age. Washington, D.C.: Defense Civil Preparedness Agency, 1977.

Symposium on Human Problems in the Utilization of Fallout Shelter. Washington, D.C.: National Academy of Sciences, National Research Council, 1960.

WEBSITES

A Growing Business in Bomb Shelters. Available online at http://www.cbsnews.com/stories/2001/12/08/archive/main320577.shtml; website home page: http://www.cbsnews.com (accessed March 13, 2003).

AUDIO AND VISUAL MEDIA

Rafferty, Kevin et. al. *The Atomic Café.* New York: New Video Group, 1982.

"The Colossal Drive-In"

Magazine article

By: Newsweek

Date: July 22, 1957

Source: "The Colossal Drive-In" *Newsweek,* July 22, 1957, 85–87.

About the Publication: *Newsweek* was founded in 1933 by Thomas J.C. Martyn. By 2003, it had a circulation of 4 million. Owned by the *Washington Post,* who bought the magazine in 1961, it is currently headquartered in New York City. *Newsweek* has a history of mixing text and art to discuss current issues, as its first cover had photographs depicting that week's news. ■

Introduction

The movie house started in the late 1800s as a place to meet, visit, and be entertained. The movies grew out of America's experience with the theater, which was quite popular. Many nationalities had their own theaters, where ethnic enclaves could hear ethnic music. The musical comedy and vaudeville, developed for these venues, were enormously popular. After Thomas Edison invented the motion picture in the 1880s, people began seeing movies in amusement parks. By the turn of the century, movie houses were built with their own big screens.

Movies at first were silent. Some of the early long films depicted waterfalls and other nature scenes, mostly to demonstrate what film technology could do. In the 1910s, stories began being told through the movies. In the 1920s, movie popularity boomed, with annual attendance over 100 million by 1930. Movies also began to offer sound, and, later, color.

There was a morals code, the Hays code, placed upon movie content. Censors began to approve movie scripts and review films prior to release to ensure conformity with the strict codes. Movies remained popular in the 1930s and 1940s, despite the Great Depression.

With the end of World War II (1939–1945), movies increased in popularity. However, with the rise of the auto culture and the advent of the baby boom, movie theaters did not fit all lifestyles. Buying tickets for the whole family made attending movies very expensive. To accommodate this market, the drive-in theater was designed.

Significance

Drive-in movies were tremendously popular in the 1950s. By 1958, over 4,000 drive-ins had been built. Drive-ins were marketed as family entertainment. As noted in this story, drive-ins were also very popular with teenagers, providing entertainment and a large amount of privacy. With the per-car admission, going to the drive-in was less expensive than the movie theater. Drive-ins remained popular into the 1970s, and very often, drive-ins showed movies that were not carried anywhere else.

Drive-ins were not the only beneficiaries of developments in the 1950s. With the rise of the automobile and the building of interstate highways, restaurants proliferated, including McDonalds. Drive-in restaurants, which served patrons in their cars, and motels, or motor hotels, also became popular. People began to travel all across the country and experience America as never before. Of course, all of this led to an increase in pollution from the gas that was used.

High gas prices of the 1970s, additional channels (and free movies) available on television—and later cable and the videocassette recorder (VCR)—combined to lessen the popularity of drive-ins. Some drive-ins, with the fall of gas prices, have made a comeback recently. Nostalgia by baby boomers to experience again the events of their youth has led to this resurgence of sorts.

Primary Source

"The Colossal Drive-In"

SYNOPSIS: The article discusses the size of one of the world's largest drive-ins (it held 2,500 cars) and

The River of No Return, directed by Otto Preminger, shows at the Westbury Drive-in in 1954. **THE LIBRARY OF CONGRESS.**

details the activities of the children at the amusement park and food stands. The article notes that many drive-in movie theaters are open year-round and have added attractions, including car washes. The article ends by noting that much of the drive-in's profit resulted from food sales, rather than ticket revenue.

One of the biggest drive-in theaters in the world is the All-Weather Drive-In some 30 miles out of New York City, on the Sunrise Highway where it runs through Copiague, N.Y. The enormous aluminum screen, standing like a great cliff, overlooks a layout with outdoor space for 2,500 automobiles plus an indoor theater seating 1,500 people.

At 6:30 on a pleasant evening recently, about 100 mothers and children were in the indoor theater watching a double bill, which had started at 5, (The outdoor show would not begin until 9.) Outside, two

boys and two girls rode a small Ferris wheel in a miniature amusement park, and twenty others worked the swings, slides, turntables, and a merry-go-round. Ten autos huddled forlornly in the vast lot.

In fifteen minutes, however, as mealtime approached, autos began to arrive every minute or so. A movement of people from the indoor theater to the adjoining cafeteria developed while others headed for the cafeteria from their cars. They were mostly young couples with two or three children in tow (Children under 12, accompanied by adults, get in free.). Most of the women wore slacks and flowered blouses, the boys wore jeans and sneakers, and many of the little girls went in for pony tails and shorts.

"*After* we eat," cried a woman in toreador pants to a very small boy. "First we eat now. Then we ride again. *After.* We'll ride again, understand?"

Food and Trains

Almost nobody stayed in the cafeteria, where there were shelves to eat from but no place to sit down. They took the food back to their cars. Hamburgers were 30 cents, franks 20, pizzas 65, chocolate drink 25. A miniature four-car train packed with children toured among the autos on the lot. There was little to look at but the ride was free.

By 7 p.m. there were 50 or 60 cars standing there. Almost everybody was eating. By 8 o'clock the great lot was almost full. Still people sat eating or just staring at the level outdoors. Many of the children were getting increasingly restless. They raced around, skipped nowhere in particular, threw soda straws, acted a little cranky.

The small amusement park next to the indoor theater was as jammed as a school playground at recess. Fathers in T shirts stood guard.

"I told you *ten times* to pull that zipper up," shouted a mother to a small son. "Now *do* it . . . *do* it . . . *do* it!"

Somebody's little boy was loose in his flannel bathrobe, pajamas, and slippers.

From speakers standing at the side of each car, country music emerged.

It was nearly 9 p.m., a lovely night, with a bright moon in the sky.

The indoor theater, where the performance was continuous, was nearly full by now, but the children were coming out. It was almost time for the outdoor show—the same double bill that had been playing indoors.

Light flooded the great screen and everybody streaked for the cars. By the time the cartoon had materialized they had all got in, slammed the doors, pulled the electronic speaker inside, and settled back for "Johnny Tremain" . . . and "Joe Butterfly."

Year Around

Give or take a few hours, depending upon the time zone and local tastes, this same scene of hushed anticipation was being repeated in some 5,000 drive-ins throughout the country. Ten years ago there were only 500 of them. It seems that the opportunity to go out for the evening without changing one's pants has helped make the drive-in the biggest single development in the movie industry in years. Three times as many people attended these theatrical parking lots last year as went to regular movie houses.

It is a seasonal business to a degree, but not entirely. The drive-ins in the West, where many of the biggest are, do well the year around, as do those in the South. The smallest layout in one chain of California drive-ins takes care of 1,500 autos (the biggest handles 2,300). At last count, Texas had 500 drive-ins. In the North and the East, the season opens in March and runs through October. The peak of the season is at hand right now. Even so, many drive-ins stay open the year around despite the weather, since it is cheaper to keep them open than close and open them every year. Some do a year-around weekend business by providing electric heaters for the customers' cars. (An astute operator in Indiana is now installing an underground pipe system to pump either warm or cool air into the cars, depending on the season.)

Poor Movies

There are drive-ins these days with swimming pools, little amusement parks, playgrounds, and zoos, as well as laundromats, car-washes, and bottle-warmers. Almost all of them, of course, serve refreshments. At regular movie theaters, 10 cents is spent on refreshments for every dollar of admission; at the drive-ins, the average take is 40 cents on the dollar.

As for the movies themselves: When one film executive recently approached a drive-in man with the idea that the movie company should get a percentage of the refreshment sales, since it was the movie that brought in the customers, the drive-in man set him straight. "The worse the pictures are," he reported, "the more stuff we sell."

Further Resources

BOOKS

Coontz, Stephanie. *The Way We Never Were: American Families and the Nostalgia Trap.* New York: BasicBooks, 1992.

Diggins, John P. *The Proud Decades: America in War and in Peace, 1941-1960.* New York: Norton, 1989.

Longstreth, Richard W. *The Drive-in, the Supermarket, and the Transformation of Commercial Space in Los Angeles, 1914-1941.* Cambridge, MA: MIT Press, 1999.

McKeon, Elizabeth, and Linda Everett. *Cinema under the Stars: America's Love Affair With the Drive-in Movie Theater.* Nashville, Tenn.: Cumberland House, 1998.

Segrave, Kerry. *Drive-in Theaters: A History from Their Inception in 1933.* Jefferson, N.C.: McFarland & Co., 1992.

PERIODICALS

Bond, Constance. "Big Screen, Night Sky–Good Times." SmithsonianVol. 25, No. 2, 1994, 109–113.

Butko, Brian, and Shiffer, Rebecca. "Moonbeams and B-Movies: The Rise and Fall of the Drive-In Theater." *Pennsylvania Heritage* Vol. 20, No. 3, 1994, 16–23.

WEBSITES

Drive-In Theater. Available online at http://www.driveintheater .com/index.htm; website home page: http://www.driveintheater .com (accessed March 17, 2003).

The American Teenager

Nonfiction work

By: H.H. Remmers and D.H. Radler

Date: 1957

Source: Remmers, H.H., and D.H. Radler. *The American Teenager.* New York: Charter Books, 1957, 16–17, 40–41, 44–46, 66–67.

About the Authors: H.H. Remmers (1892–1969) received his Ph.D. from Iowa in 1927. He taught psychology at Purdue from 1923 to 1963. He founded the Purdue Opinion Panel in 1940. He served on the advisory committee on research to U.S. Commissioner of Education from 1955 to 1958.

Donald H. Radler (1926–) was educated at Kenyon College and the University of Chicago. He wrote four books and over 100 articles, as well as television and film scripts. ∎

Introduction

Before the twentieth century, working class families and farm families comprised two age groups—those too young to work and workers. Those who went to school were often let out much earlier in the year than today's school children to work in the fields. Urban children were not released from school to work in the factories, but many dropped out at a young age to get factory jobs. There was also a different belief about how much education a child needed. During this period, students commonly dropped out of school after the eighth grade to begin working. High school was not seen as necessary for the working class and farm children. And it was believed that the ability to do the "three Rs"— reading, writing and arithmetic—was sufficient. College was only for the wealthy and a few from the middle class.

All of this began to change after 1900. Child labor laws kept many children out of the factories. The population shift from farms to cities changed the lifestyle of the average American. A rising standard of living also lessened the need for children to work. It began to be expected that one would attend, and possibly finish, high school. This was coupled with a rising standard of living for many in the middle class, and some in the working class, during the 1940s and 1950s. Freed from having to work at a young age, a "teen" culture developed around those aged thirteen to nineteen. These teens had disposable income and a world filled with opportunities.

Significance

The excerpt from Remmers and Radler demonstrates that teens are not necessarily born with radical ideas or a desire to change the world. Many teens, in the early 1950s, were imbued with even more authoritarian ideas than the rest of society. This is not unexpected, however, if one considers the society into which they matured. McCarthyism was rampant during the early 1950s, and before this (and after) the Red Scare pervaded. Growing up fearing an unknown enemy, teens of that generation witnessed loyalty oaths, blacklists, and political witch-hunts. It is not surprising that teens internalized this authoritarian ethos. Teens also reflected the common concerns associated with growing up. The concerns about sex and dating, while discussed more widely today, were still present.

Teens though were not consumed with concern and worry. There was a growth of slang among that generation. With time to "hang out," teenagers developed their own slang in the 1950s, as teens have done in every decade since then.

Teens, part of the Baby Boom, also became a large consumer market in the 1950s. 45-RPM vinyl records, containing one song on each side, were developed along with jukeboxes. They greatly increased music sales. Teen clothes also became a hot market item, with leather jackets and poodle skirts becoming popular. Drive-in movies, although marketed as family venue, also were very popular with teenagers. This trend in marketing has continued until the present, with specialty stores just for teenagers—and teenagers often spending the most of any age group on clothes.

Primary Source

The American Teenager [excerpt]

SYNOPSIS: Remmers and Radler first note that many teenagers are authoritarian, and then note that many teenagers are quite concerned with their bodies. The survey details the connection between this lack of self-confidence and psychological problems. The two authors then discuss difficulties between the sexes and the attitudes of 1950s' teenagers toward sex. The excerpt closes by reporting that most teenagers masturbate, and offers suggestions on safe ways to control teen sexual behavior.

The self-portrait our youngsters paint has (in the view of the authors) some somber tones. Inevitably, so does the larger picture into which this portrait fits—the picture of the United States of tomorrow.

For example, over half the teenagers in America believe that

Most people aren't capable of deciding what's best for themselves.

Politics is over their heads, and besides it's a dirty game run by unscrupulous insiders.

We should help federal and local police maintain obedience by legalizing wiretapping and the third degree.

We should put censorship of books, movies, radio and TV into their hands to protect ourselves against improper thinking.

The proper concern of the people is physical health. By improving our bodies we improve our minds, since physical health leads to mental health. In turn, we grow ever stronger and healthier. After all, lack of will power, not germs, causes disease.

Do you believe these things? The Constitution forbids some. Few thinkers among us accept the others.

The American teenager does. . . .

More than 50 per cent think the large mass of us in these United States simply aren't capable of deciding for ourselves what's right and what's wrong.

Eighty-three per cent of today's teens okay wiretapping.

Sixty per cent go for censorship of books, newspapers, magazines.

Fifty-eight per cent see no harm in the third degree.

In addition . . .

Nearly half of our teenagers are ready to dispense with freedom of the press. One-quarter of them think police should be free to search your home or your person without a warrant. A third of them believe American free speech should be denied certain people if it seems convenient. Another 13 per cent would restrict by law religious belief and worship. . . .

What are the problems of today's teenagers? How common are they? In the several chapters immediately following this one, we'll answer these questions in detail, giving actual statistics where they are available and quoting from the anonymous letters *just as they were written.* At the end of each chapter, detailed tables may be found. But now, let's take a quick and necessarily superficial look at the territory we'll explore more thoroughly later.

In all the surveys, teenagers revealed that the bodies they inhabit trouble them greatly. Fifty-two per cent want to gain weight or lose it. Twenty-four per cent would like to improve their figures. Thirty-seven

per cent are seeking to improve their posture or, in the case of boys, their "body build." Thirteen per cent complain of getting tired very easily. Twelve per cent suffer from frequent headaches. And fully a third have pimples, want to get rid of them and don't know how. Undoubtedly, some of these young people have actual health problems requiring medical attention, but most of their concern for their bodies really stems from their own lack of understanding of the physical changes, the very natural changes, that are a part of growing up. If they knew what to expect in the way of physical growth, the amount of flesh they will naturally put on, and the places where it naturally goes, much of their anxiety might automatically disappear.

There is a direct relationship, too, between these physical phenomena and psychological problems that occur in adolescence. In "Youth," Dr. Arnold Gesell and his co-authors write, "Many of the physical changes of adolescence are so sudden and conspicuous that boys and girls alike become acutely aware of them." Suddenly finding the well-oiled machine that was his body as a child turned into an uncoordinated monster, the boy or girl reacts with fright and nervousness. In turn, these reactions feed back into the physical system, causing more awkwardness and greater physical discomfort. One boy writes, "My legs and arms when I'm nervous want to move real quick-like." An eleventh-grade girl says, "I have had a very small bustline and although I realize that the purpose of them is not to add to your looks but for later when you have children, I still have a complex I can't get rid of." . . .

The process of growing socially, including the tricky and emotionally loaded area of relationships between the sexes, probably constitutes the teenagers' biggest job. That is why the high school has a serious responsibility to serve effectively as a social workshop for its students. Teenagers have unique opportunities to learn to work, play and live together in the classroom, gym and the school social clubs. These are the settings in which our young adults can solve such problems as that of the 54 per cent who want people to like them, the more than 60 per cent who desperately want to make new friends and the 36 per cent who are seeking to develop more self-confidence.

Given the fulfillment of any one wish, most adults would, like Faust, seek fame and fortune. But the common cry of teenagers is, "Oh, to be more popular!" This pervasive need for acceptance, for response from other people, may contribute as much as any other factor to the misdeeds that make the

American teenagers gather at the local diner to sip malts, socialize, and listen to the jukebox. **UPI/CORBIS-BETTMANN. REPRODUCED BY PERMISSION.**

headlines, as we shall see later. They "go along with the gang" even if this means bending or fracturing the edicts of their parents, the regulations of their schools, the proscriptions of their churches and the law of the land. The need just to know what it's all about might lead two teenagers to share the same bed. But the greater need for popularity impels three or four couples in that direction for every one prompted by curiosity.

A senior girl in Philadelphia writes:

Sex is a continual problem. After wavering from the no kiss on first date philosophy to the highly mature (!) one of if you really like him it makes no difference—I'm back to the first.

Another girl's brief letter indicates the urgency of the problem and also shows how little information we give our young adults:

My problem is that I can't say no!!! It seems like I have no resistance at all. Am I becom-

ing a nimpho? Is this the track to becoming a prostitute? I try to refuse but if the boy tries a little harder, I always give way. I don't know what to do. I may lose my reputation at the rate I'm going now.

Poll results reveal that our teenagers know much less about sex than they would like to. Yet what is generally called sex education has become so prevalent that one writer in a woman's magazine recently based an article on this question: "Are we teaching our teenagers too much about sex?" That title printed on the front cover undoubtedly sold a lot of magazines. But it's more than a little unfair to the vast majority of our young adults, who reveal in their answers to polls and in their letters that they still know a great deal less about this all-important topic than they need to know. Take, for example, the statement of an eleventh-grade boy, "I would like to know something about how mating with the opposite sex works." Or the eleventh-grade

"Jelly Tot, Square Bear-Man!" [excerpt]

For the benefit of adults whose command of slang stopped with "Oh you kid!" and "23 Skiddoo!," someone may have to put out a new glossary of teen-age jargon. Parents and other interested parties, who thought they were hep to recent soda-fountain slang, now find that it's corny to say corny, and that solid and icky are "real nothing" words today. Anyone who falls back on such jaded expressions is a simple peasant or a smerk. Square as a bear on current slang, Newsweek conducted a nationwide survey to find what was real squire:

In St. Louis, a reporter munching a ham sandwich in a juke-box joint was startled to overhear a conversation in the next booth. "She's real George all the way," one teen-ager remarked. "Huh, that's close," retorted a second. "I'll give you twenty lashes with a wet noodle," said a third bobbysoxer. With the aid of a high-school journalism class, the reporter translated "real George" into "real squire, flash, excellent." The wet-noodle threat is the current version of a slap on the wrist. St. Louis teen-agers also borrow their father's bug to go to the hecklethon (take his car to go to the movies). If they can't get the car, that's the way the ball bounces (tough luck) or ain't that a bite? (too bad).

Seattle bobbysoxers don't worry about George, but they are great exponents of get on the stick (get on the ball). A dolly is a cute girl, an odd ball is a character, and a dis is a dissipated person. Party pooper has taken the place of wallflower or wet blanket. "You said a foo-fad" means you said a bad word; a passion pit is a drive-in movie, and a squirrel is a reckless driver of a mill (automobile). "That has it!" and "My, how sanitary!" are widely used expressions of approval.

Nerds and Scurves

In Detroit, someone who once would be called a drip or a square is now, regrettably, a nerd, or in a less severe case, a scurve. A Cadillac convertible is real cool or even shafty, and its driver, particularly if he be cat, or well-dressed, is cool Jonah. Cut the gas has replaced shut up. Cream means to bang up an auto fender, and to ramble is to be cooking with gas, or on the beam. When a good-looking girl passes a "big man" on the street, instead of a whistle she gets an approving Motha Higby, especially if she's cool mother.

No one seems certain whether the current slang stems from cleaned-up Army lingo, brought home by big brother, or from musicians' small talk. An Atlanta bobbysoxer said: "I get squishy [have a lapse of memory] when you ask me." But in Atlanta, a pink is a snooty boy or girl, lighter is crew-cut hair, and straighten up and die means go away. A jelly tot is a very young boy who tries to act adult, and a tapper is a boy who tries repeatedly for a date. Joe Roe and Joe Doe are names for blind dates, and a hub cap is a boy who tries to be a big wheel but fails.

SOURCE: "Jelly Tot, Square Bear-Man!" *Newsweek,* October 8, 1951.

---

girl who asks, "Why do parents tell you not to do *this* or *that* on a date, when they are referring to sexual union, when they've never explained it in detail?"

One constantly recurring question is "how far to go" on a date. Another is when to take that important step, the first kiss. (One practical-minded senior boy in Wyoming answers: "I think that if this boy or girl ever intends to kiss each other that they might as well do it on the first than to wait a date or so.") A sixteen-year-old Michigan girl finds the advice we usually give our young people somewhat impractical. She says, "Most of the articles say holding hands, or kissing good-night is *far* enough. This just doesn't work." . . .

Masturbation is almost universal during adolescence. One can't find any figures from polls substantiating this, but doctors and psychiatrists who win the confidence of their adolescent patients can often be heard to say: "Ninety-nine out of a hundred teenage boys and girls masturbate—and the other one's a liar."

Actually, puberty does not bring the first appearance of masturbation. Young infants discover their own bodies at a very early age, and this, too, is masturbation. But because it seems so unlikely to most people and because it has no more importance to the infant than does play with any other part of his body, infant sexuality is usually not recognized for what it is. Again, at age four, five or six, children experiment with autoeroticism. At this point, troubles often arise. Acting on the mistaken notion that the child will harm himself, parents often punish him to stop him from masturbating. When he reaches adolescence and the feverish activity of his awakening sex glands and organs creates strong new stirrings within him, the adolescent naturally begins to masturbate again. If he was punished for masturbating at an early age, he feels guilty and sinful, but he still can't stop.

Sheer curiosity leads little children to investigate their bodies and those of their playmates. When they first discover that Jerry looks different from Susie, they want to find out *how* he is different and *why.*

Preschoolers often play doctor or nurse merely to create a situation in which they can investigate these interesting differences. There is little or no harm that can come from this innocent sexual play—except for the over-excitability of many parents and teachers who punish the children involved and talk accusingly of "sin." What they really should do, according to most child-guidance specialists, is satisfy the youngsters' curiosity with brief, down-to-earth information, then channel their play in other directions.

The same sex experimentation after puberty is another matter. To discourage it completely might prevent teenage boys and girls from ever developing healthy relationships with the other sex. On the other hand, to allow it to go to its logical extreme can cause tragedy, since adolescents are no longer children. Boys can become fathers and girls can become pregnant. The two striking things about sex before marriage are these: (1) it's fun, and (2) it's dangerous. The real solution to the sex problem of the teenage boy or girl is to avoid the dangers but not to miss out on all the fun.

Further Resources

BOOKS

Coles, Robert, and Geoffrey Stokes. *Sex and the American Teenager.* New York: Harper & Row, 1985.

Dalzell, Tom. *Flappers 2 Rappers: American Youth Slang.* Springfield, Mass.: Merriam-Webster, 1996.

Fuller, Shelia, et al. *The No-Nonsense Parents' Guide: What You Can Do About Teens and Alcohol, Drugs, Sex, Eating Disorders and Depression.* Greenwich, Conn.: Parents' Pipeline, 1992.

Heron, Ann. *One Teenager in Ten: Writings by Gay and Lesbian Youth.* Boston: Alyson Publications, 1983.

Kolodny, Robert C. *How to Survive Your Adolescent's Adolescence.* Boston: Little, Brown, 1984.

Ridenour, Fritz. *What Teenagers Wish Their Parents Knew about Kids.* Waco, Tex.: Word Books, 1982.

Thomas, Darwin L. *Family Socialization and the Adolescent; Determinants of Self-Concept, Conformity, Religiosity and Counterculture Values.* Lexington, Mass.: Lexington Books, 1974.

WEBSITES

The Wonder Years as an American Narrative. Available online at http://www-personal.umich.edu/~kpearce/wy.html; website home page: http://www-personal.umich.edu (accessed March 18, 2003).

The Other America

Nonfiction work

By: Michael Harrington

Date: 1962

Source: Harrington, Michael. *The Other America: Poverty in the United States.* New York: The MacMillan Company, 1962, 1–4, xii.

About the Author: Michael Harrington (1928–1989) received a bachelor's degree from Holy Cross (1947) and a master of arts degree from the University of Chicago (1949). As a social worker, he encountered the severe poverty of his clients. He moved to New York City, where he wrote several articles for various publications. In 1962, Harrington published *The Other America.* This book helped to spark President Johnson's War on Poverty. He served as a professor at Queens College from 1972 to 1989. ∎

Introduction

In the nineteenth century, Americans worked long hours, and most Americans were in the working class. People worked six days a week, ten hours a day in many industries. There was no minimum wage, nor was there a maximum number of hours in a workweek. There was little time for leisure, and little money to save or to spend on leisure. If an employee complained or tried to form a union to ensure better working conditions, the employee was typically fired—and often forced to look for a job in a different city. Things slowly changed in the early twentieth century. Wages gradually rose. In the 1920s, a few workers were given pensions and one week of vacation per year. Employment conditions declined markedly during the Great Depression.

During the prolonged economic malaise, the government established limits on the maximum workweek and minimum pay. A forty-hour workweek was established, with a minimum hourly wage of twenty-five cents. Also, people who wanted to form unions were protected, and union membership boomed during this time. After World War II (1939–1945) ended, the public had discretionary income and leisure time. One was assumed to be either working class or part of the "new" middle class. Everyone in America during this time seemed to be doing relatively well. The media reinforced this image of universal prosperity within America. Michael Harrington, in his research, found that some in America still were mired in desperate poverty, and that not everyone had adequate food and shelter.

Significance

Harrington found that poverty still existed in America, even though it was given little attention. Harrington defined poverty not as starving to death, but, rather, as not having enough to survive in a meaningful sense. In

Residents of Baltimore tenement housing use an old Model T as a storage shed. © **BETTMANN/CORBIS. REPRODUCED BY PERMISSION.**

The Other America, Harrington surveyed those hardest hit by poverty—those in the country, inner city, minorities, and the elderly. Harrington brought the plight of America's poor to the nation's attention.

Unlike many crusaders for the poor, Harrington had a substantial impact on the nation's domestic policy. His work encouraged many in Lyndon Johnson's administration to undertake the "War on Poverty." This legislative effort focused on regions Harrington described as forgotten. These included rural areas, especially Appalachia, and the inner city. Medicare and Medicaid helped with medical expenses that made many people poor. The Vietnam War (1964–1975) diverted money earmarked for LBJ's War on Poverty. Although the War on Poverty reduced poverty significantly (poverty decreased 44% during the 1960s), it did not eliminate poverty. That poverty was not eliminated entirely constituted a failure in the eyes of many. This perceived failure, quixotically, caused many to abandon the effort. The conservative political resurgence and economic troubles in America precluded new efforts to expand the War on Poverty.

Between the mid-1970s and 1990, the standard of living among the lowest classes generally declined. The poverty rate, about twelve percent by the end of the 1970s, climbed to eighteen percent by the end of the 1980s. It declined sharply during the 1990s, but only fell to thirteen percent—slightly worse than it had been in the 1970s. "The Other America" still exists in America, unfortunately.

Primary Source

The Other America [excerpt]

> **SYNOPSIS:** Harrington notes that in the 1950s there were 40 to 50 million poor Americans, not starving or dying, but lacking basic necessities of life. Harrington then argues that most people forget about the poor because they are largely invisible to most Americans, and he explains why they are invisible.

There is a familiar America. It is celebrated in speeches and advertised on television and in the magazines. It has the highest mass standard of living the world has ever known.

In the 1950's this America worried about itself, yet even its anxieties were products of abundance. The title of a brilliant book was widely misinterpreted, and the familiar America began to call itself "the affluent society." There was introspection about Madison Avenue and tail fins; there was discussion of the emotional suffering taking place in the suburbs. In all this, there was an implicit assumption that the basic grinding economic problems had been solved in the United States. In this theory the nation's problems were no longer a matter of basic human needs, of food, shelter, and clothing. Now they were seen as qualitative, a question of learning to live decently amid luxury.

While this discussion was carried on, there existed another America. In it dwelt somewhere between 40,000,000 and 50,000,000 citizens of this land. They were poor. They still are.

To be sure, the other America is not impoverished in the same sense as those poor nations where millions cling to hunger as a defense against starvation. This country has escaped such extremes. That does not change the fact that tens of millions of Americans are, at this very moment, maimed in body and spirit, existing at levels beneath those necessary for human decency. If these people are not starving, they are hungry, and sometimes fat with hunger, for that is what cheap foods do. They are without adequate housing and education and medical care.

The Government has documented what this means to the bodies of the poor, and the figures will be cited throughout this book. But even more basic, this poverty twists and deforms the spirit. The American poor are pessimistic and defeated, and they are victimized by mental suffering to a degree unknown in Suburbia.

This book is a description of the world in which these people live; it is about the other America. Here are the unskilled workers, the migrant farm workers, the aged, the minorities, and all the others who live in the economic underworld of American life. In all this, there will be statistics, and that offers the opportunity for disagreement among honest and sincere men. I would ask the reader to respond critically to every assertion, but not to allow statistical quibbling to obscure the huge, enormous, and intolerable fact of poverty in America. For, when all is said and done, that fact is unmistakable, whatever its exact dimensions, and the truly human reaction can only be outrage. As W. H. Auden wrote:

Hunger allows no choice

To the citizen or the police;

We must love one another or die. . . .

There are perennial reasons that make the other America an invisible land.

Poverty is often off the beaten track. It always has been. The ordinary tourist never left the main highway, and today he rides interstate turnpikes. He does not go into the valleys of Pennsylvania where the towns look like movie sets of Wales in the thirties. He does not see the company houses in rows, the rutted roads (the poor always have bad roads whether they live in the city, in towns, or on farms), and everything is black and dirty. And even if he were to pass through such a place by accident, the tourist would not meet the unemployed men in the bar or the women coming home from a runaway sweatshop.

Then, too, beauty and myths are perennial masks of poverty. The traveler comes to the Appalachians in the lovely season. He sees the hills, the streams, the foliage—but not the poor. Or perhaps he looks at a run-down mountain house and, remembering Rousseau rather than seeing with his eyes, decides that "those people" are truly fortunate to be living the way they are and that they are lucky to be exempt from the strains and tensions of the middle class. The only problem is that "those people," the quaint inhabitants of those hills, are undereducated, underprivileged, lack medical care, and are in the process of being forced from the land into a life in the cities, where they are misfits.

These are normal and obvious causes of the invisibility of the poor. They operated a generation ago; they will be functioning a generation hence. It is more important to understand that the very development of American society is creating a new kind of blindness about poverty. The poor are increasingly slipping out of the very experience and consciousness of the nation.

If the middle class never did like ugliness and poverty, it was at least aware of them. "Across the tracks" was not a very long way to go. There were forays into the slums at Christmas time; there were charitable organizations that brought contact with the poor. Occasionally, almost everyone passed through the Negro ghetto or the blocks of tenements, if only to get downtown to work or to entertainment.

Now the American city has been transformed. The poor still inhabit the miserable housing in the central area, but they are increasingly isolated from contact with, or sight of, anybody else. Middle-class women coming in from Suburbia on a rare trip may catch the merest glimpse of the other America on the way to an evening at the theater, but their children are segregated in suburban schools. The business or professional man may drive along the fringes of slums in a car or bus, but it is not an important experience to him. The failures, the unskilled, the disabled, the aged, and the minorities are right there, across the tracks, where they have always been. But hardly anyone else is.

In short, the very development of the American city has removed poverty from the living, emotional experience of millions upon millions of middle-class Americans. Living out in the suburbs, it is easy to assume that ours is, indeed, an affluent society. . . .

Still the very same groups which were poor when this book was written in 1961 and published in 1962 are poor today: the blacks, the Spanish-speaking, the unemployed and the underemployed, the citizens of depressed regions, the aging. And I should add one minority that I quite wrongly omitted from my original analysis: the American Indian, probably the poorest of all.

Further Resources

BOOKS

Ehrenreich, Barbara. *Nickel and Dimed: On (Not) Getting By in America.* New York: Metropolitan Books, 2001.

Goode, Judith, and Jeff Maskovsky. *New Poverty Studies: The Ethnography of Power, Politics, and Impoverished People in the United States.* New York: New York University Press, 2001.

Harrington, Michael. *The Long-Distance Runner: An Autobiography.* New York: Holt, 1998.

Hartman, Chester W. *Challenges to Equality: Poverty and Race in America.* Armonk, N.Y.: M.E. Sharpe, 2001.

Isserman, Maurice. *The Other American: The Life of Michael Harrington.* New York: PublicAffairs, 2000.

O'Connor, Alice. *Poverty Knowledge: Social Science, Social Policy, and the Poor in Twentieth-Century U.S. History.* Princeton: Princeton University Press, 2001.

Okroi, Loren J. *Galbraith, Harrington, Heilbroner: Economics and Dissent in an Age of Optimism.* Princeton: Princeton University Press, 1988.

WEBSITES

Poverty USA. Available online at http://www.usccb.org/cchd/povertyusa/povfacts.htm; website home page: http://www.usccb.org (accessed March 13, 2003).

AUDIO AND VISUAL MEDIA

Harrington, Michael. *Michael Harrington and Today's Other America.* New York: Filmakers Library, 1999.

8

THE MEDIA

SCOTT A. MERRIMAN

Entries are arranged in chronological order by date of primary source. For entries with one primary source, the entry title is the same as the primary source title. Entries with more than one primary source have an overall entry title, followed by the titles of the primary sources.

Important Events in Media, 1950–1959

1950

- A total of 101 television stations are operating.
- Some 4,835,000 television sets are installed.
- In *The Lonely Crowd,* published this year, social scientists David Riesman, Nathan Glazer, and Reuel Denney argue that the mass media is a powerful force in shaping behavior and enforcing conformity.
- On February 21, the Justice Department files a civil antitrust suit charging Lee and Jacob Shubert with monopolizing U.S. theater ownership.
- On April 13, the Federal Communications Commission (FCC) warns radio stations that present editorial opinions on controversial issues that they have a "duty to seek out, aid and encourage the broadcast of opposing views."
- On October 2, Charles Schulz's comic strip *Peanuts* begins appearing in newspapers across the country. This is Schulz's second try at syndicating the cartoon. His strip was previously rejected by several major newspaper syndicates when it was titled *Lil' Folks.*
- On October 11, the FCC votes to allow CBS to begin color television broadcasts starting 20 November.
- On December 12, CBS asks twenty-four hundred employees to sign loyalty oaths.

1951

- Marquette University televises the first course over television.
- Comedian Milton Berle signs a thirty-year, seven-figure contract with NBC.
- In March, the TV networks begin broadcasting Senate hearings investigating organized crime in America. By October, the hearings' TV audience reaches 30 million, equaling the ratings of the World Series that month.
- On May 2, a coast-to-coast cable link is completed, allowing simultaneous bicoastal broadcasting.
- On June 14, a human birth is shown on television for the first time.
- On June 25, CBS begins broadcasting color commercial television programs; conventional black-and-white sets are unable to receive them.
- On August 5, the Ford Foundation allots $1.2 million for cultural and public-service television broadcasts.

- On September 9, the soap operas "Search for Tomorrow" and "Love of Life" premiere on CBS.
- On October 15, "I Love Lucy" premieres on CBS.
- On November 18, the CBS television show "See It Now," starring Edward R. Murrow, premieres.

1952

- The FCC lifts the freeze on television broadcast licenses which had been imposed in 1948. The action reinvigorates the television business.
- The transistor radio is introduced in the United States by Sony Corporation.
- On January 16, "The Today Show" premieres on NBC.
- On August 20, *American Mercury* magazine is sold.
- In November, *Mad* comic books, forerunners of *Mad* magazine, are introduced. They are the first humor comic books to parody nearly every part of American culture—movies, television, and advertising in particular.

1953

- RCA demonstrates videotape recording.
- 55 percent of American families owns a television.
- 311 television stations are in operation.
- *TV Guide* and *Playboy* begin publication.
- On January 20, the inauguration of Dwight D. Eisenhower is the first televised presidential inauguration broadcast coast to coast.
- On November 8, photoengravers go on strike in New York City for eleven days, leaving the city without a daily newspaper for the first time since 1778.
- On November 27, the FCC rules that no person or firm may have a financial interest in more than five television stations.

1954

- Newspaper vending machines first appear.
- General Electric hires actor Ronald Reagan to host its popular TV drama show *The General Electric Theater.* Reagan's contract also requires him to visit GE plants to speak on the virtues of free enterprise and the American way.
- On April 4, Walt Disney signs an agreement with the ABC television network to produce twenty-six television films per year.
- From April to June, the networks broadcast about 190 hours of Senate hearings investigating Senator Joseph McCarthy's charge the U.S. Army has been infiltrated by Communists. As many as 20 million Americans watch at least some of the proceedings.
- On September 11, the Miss America pageant is first televised; Lee Ann Meriweather, Miss California, is the winner.
- On October 25, President Dwight D. Eisenhower holds the first televised cabinet meeting.
- On October 27, twenty-six comic-book publishers announce the adoption of a code restricting violent or vulgar scenes.

- On November 19, the CBS public affairs TV program *Face the Nation* premieres.

1955

- *Gunsmoke* premiers as the first adult western series on television.
- CBS passes NBC to become the number one network with viewers for the first time.
- Eppie Lederer begins writing the "Ask Ann Landers" advice column in the *Chicago Sun-Times.*
- On January 19, President Dwight D. Eisenhower holds the first televised presidential news conference.
- On February 22, the owners of the *Kansas City Star* are convicted in federal court of attempting to monopolize news coverage and advertising in the Kansas City area.
- On April 6, Zenith Radio Corporation denounces CBS for "unwarranted censorship" and withdraws as sponsor of "Omnibus" when CBS refuses to let Zenith air a commercial for Phonevision, a subscription television service opposed by the networks.
- On July 18, Howard Hughes sells RKO Radio Pictures and its pre-1948 movie titles to General Tire for $25 million.

1956

- CBS moves production of several of its shows, including "Playhouse 90," to Television City in California.
- On January 14, Detroit newspaper deliverers end a six-week strike by accepting a two-year contract containing increased pay and benefits.
- On March 27, the communist newspaper, *Daily Worker* is seized by agents of the Internal Revenue Service for non-payment of income taxes. The paper's New York, Chicago, and Detroit offices reopen a week later after its officers post a bond against its tax bill.
- On June 20, Loew's Inc. releases M-G-M's pre-1949 film library, except *Gone With the Wind,* for television broadcast.
- In August, *American* magazine, first published in 1876 as *Frank Leslie's Popular Monthly,* is discontinued by the Crowell-Collier company.
- On September 9, the appearance of gyrating rock and roll music sensation Elvis Presley on the Ed Sullivan Show attracts a record TV audience of 54 million. On his next appearance, in January 1957, TV censors require that cameras show only his face.
- On September 24, the first transatlantic telephone cable system begins operating. It offers triple the capacity of radiotelephone circuits between the United States and Europe.
- On November 30, the first commercial use by television of videotape for "Douglas Edwards with the News" occurrs on CBS.

1957

- Aware that its brown package will not sell well on color TV, cigarette-maker Philip Morris spends $250,000 to develop a new, colorful package.
- On January 4, Alliance of Television Film Producers agrees to adopt the ethical-production code of the National Association of Radio and Television Broadcasters.
- On March 7, the publisher and the distributor of *Confidential* magazine are indicted on charges of mailing obscene or crime-inciting material.
- On May 4, a nightly rock and roll music radio show, hosted by Alan Freed, reaches a national audience.
- On May 25, comedian Sid Caesar quits NBC after the mutual cancellation of the remaining seven years of his $100,000 per year contract.

1958

- On March 3, Richard Mack resigns as FCC member after admitting to the Special House Subcommittee on Legislative Oversight that he received loans and gifts of stock from a friend who is interested in the FCC award of a valuable Miami television channel.
- On May 24, United Press Association and International News Service merge to form United Press International (UPI).
- On September 18, FCC announces that it would consider applications from television stations to test subscription television telecasts experimentally over a three-year period.
- On October 11, in a new guideline interpreting the equal time clause, the FCC says television and radio stations must give equal time to all legally qualified political candidates.
- On October 16, Sponsors drops the NBC quiz show "21," under grand jury investigation for prearrangement of quiz contest results.

1959

- Westerns dominate television entertainment. Among the most popular are *Bonanza* and *Rawhide,* staring Clint Eastwood
- On June 3, using radio signals bounced off the moon, President Eisenhower sends a message to Canada's prime minister.
- On July 28, the Senate passes and sends to the House a bill exempting radio and television news shows from an FCC requirement that all competing political candidates be given equal time if any one of them appeared on a broadcast.
- On October 6, the Special House Subcommittee on Legislative Oversight begins a probe into television quiz programs.
- On October 16, CBS President Frank Stanton bans quiz shows from the network.
- On November 3, Bandleader Xavier Cugat testifies that he received questions and answers on CBS's "$64,000 Question."

Charles Schulz's *Peanuts*

Peanuts

Cartoon

By: Charles M. Schulz

Date: November 16, 1952

Source: Schulz, Charles M. *Peanuts* comic strip. Syndicated by United Features. November 16, 1952. Reprinted in Charles M. Schulz. *Peanuts Revisited: Favorites Old and New.* New York: Holt, Rinehart, and Winston, 1955.

About the Artist: Charles M. Schulz (1922–2000) was born in Minneapolis, Minnesota, and attended art school there. His comic strip *Li'l Folks* first appeared in *The St. Paul Pioneer Press* in the late 1940s and was later picked up by the United Features Syndicate in 1950 and renamed *Peanuts*. Shultz wrote and and drew *Peanuts* for fifty years, and it became the most well-loved comic strip in history. Schulz also developed a musical, "You're a Good Man, Charlie Brown," and numerous books and animated TV specials based on his comic strip characters.

"You're a Good Man, Charlie Schulz"

Magazine article

By: Barnaby Conrad

Date: April 16, 1967

Source: Conrad, Barnaby. "You're a Good Man, Charlie Schulz." *The New York Times Magazine,* April 16, 1967, 33–35, 42–49, 52–53.

About the Author: Barnaby Conrad (1922–), who wrote about Schulz for *The New York Times Magazine,* is a professional writer and painter. He has written books on bullfighting, several novels, an autobiography, and more than eight works of nonfiction, and is the translator of several more books. ∎

Introduction

Newspapers began to develop a mass audience in the late nineteenth and early twentieth centuries. This was due to a number of factors, including a drop in production costs, an increase in advertising revenue, the development of national syndicates, and an increase in leisure time for the middle class. Besides providing news, sports and columns, newspapers also brought comics. Among the best-known early newspaper comic strips were *Bringing Up Father, Mutt and Jeff, Doings of the Duffs,* and *The Katzenjammer Kids.* Many of the early Sunday strips were printed in color and took up a full page.

During the 1920s, 1930s, and 1940s, newspapers were challenged by radio and the movies, and later on by television. Newspapers also had difficulties in the 1950s as labor and paper costs rose but advertising revenues fell. Many newspapers consolidated, and many towns that had three or four newspapers ended up with only one or two by the end of the decade.

Throughout this period, however, comics pages remained popular features in most newspapers. After an earlier run as *Li'l Folks* in *The St. Paul Pioneer Press,* Charles Schulz's *Peanuts* debuted in seven newspapers on October 2, 1950.

Significance

Peanuts became extremely popular, eventually spawning more than a thousand books, a hit Broadway musical, sixty animated television programs, and a variety of merchandise—greeting cards, toys, games, clothing—making it a multimillion dollar industry. It appeared in 2,600 newspapers around the world daily until 2000, reaching some 335 million readers.

This *Peanuts* sequence, first published in the early 1950s, depicts one of the comic strip's most well-known reoccurring situations: Charlie Brown tries to kick a football held in place (and always snatched away at the last minute) by Lucy. It's also a good example of why *Peanuts* was so well-liked. Most people have some experience with failure, so readers identified with Charlie Brown and admired his willingness to try to kick the ball yet another time.

"You're a Good Man, Charlie Schulz," an article that appeared in the April 16, 1967, issue of *The New York Time Magazine* offers additional insights into the strip's longtime popularity. Part of its success was due to the fact that Schulz himself was very likable, and people came to identify with the strip's creator as well as its characters. Schulz always drew the strip himself, so it maintained a consistent "voice" and heart.

As the article points out, Schulz's characters, each with his or her own distinctive personality and charm, became known around the world. Some of the strip's catch phrases, such as "Good grief," and "Happiness is . . . ," have entered the American lexicon; *Peanuts* also inspired the term "security blanket." As the Act of Congress awarding Schulz a Congressional Gold Medal points out, "Charles Schulz's lifetime of work linked generations

Primary Source

Peanuts

SYNOPSIS: Lucy pulls the football away from Charlie Brown for the very first time in an early *Peanuts* strip, November 16, 1952. PEANUTS REPRINTED BY PERMISSION OF UNITED FEATURES SYNDICATE, INC.

of Americans and became part of the fabric of our national culture."

Other comic strips have risen to the No. 1 spot, but the remarkable thing about *Peanuts* is that it stayed popular for fifty years, and reruns of the comics are still enjoyed today. The strips' combination of longevity and sustained quality and popularity remains unmatched. Thus *Peanuts* lays claim to the title "best comic ever."

Primary Source

"You're a Good Man, Charlie Schulz" [excerpt]

> **SYNOPSIS:** This 1967 magazine article gives readers a personal look at the man behind Charlie Brown.

"Cartooning is a *fairly* sort of a proposition," said Charlie Brown's creator recently. "You have to be fairly intelligent—if you were really intelligent you'd be doing something else; you have to draw fairly well—if

you drew really well you'd be a painter; you have to write fairly well—if you wrote really well you'd be writing books. It's great for a fairly person like me."

For an only *fairly* person, Charles (Sparky) Schulz bids fair to becoming the most successful newspaper cartoonist of all time. "Peanuts," which appears in some 900 newspapers in the U.S. and Canada, plus 100 abroad, has endeared the characters of Charlie, Lucy, Linus, Schroeder and Snoopy to an estimated 90 million readers. Records, films, advertisements, sweatshirts, dolls, books, cocktail napkins and other "Peanuts" paraphernalia have capitalized on the craze to make it a $20-million-a-year industry. The statistics of the triumphs of the strip and its various offshoots are so staggering that its millions of fans—and even its creator—are wondering how the original quality and simplicity of the product can be maintained. As I was interviewing him in his studio—an unexpectedly overdecorated and plush office—near Sebastopol, Calif. (an hour north of San Francisco), the telephone interrupted constantly: A Hollywood producer wanted to talk about a big "Peanuts" musical movie; a caller wanted to know something about the London opening of the hit play "You're a Good Man, Charlie Brown," (now running Off Broadway in New York), another wanted information on his new paperback, "The Unsinkable Charlie Brown." And then there were all the calls from people who wanted him to paint posters for charities, make personal appearances or donate money to this or that cause. Each time Schulz—who, with his crew cut and serious boyishness looks like every freshman's senior adviser—hung up the phone with a sigh. It was not a sigh of exasperation, but rather regret—regret that he was not always able to do the many things that people demand of him.

"I usually get between 400 and 500 letters a week and for years I've managed to answer all of them personally, but I don't know." He leafed through some of the letters. "Most of them are so nice and their requests are so polite and worthwhile—a drawing for a crippled kid, a poster for a special high-school dance, 'Just do a quick sketch of Snoopy,' they ask; 'it'll only take five minutes.' And they're right—it *would* only take five minutes. But they think their letter is the only one on my desk. The five minutes have to be multiplied by hundreds." He looked mournfully at the heap of mail. "Thousands. They forget that I not only have to do some drawing. I occasionally have to do some thinking."

He looked out of his studio window and studied a clump of trees beyond an artificial pond. "It's hard to convince people when you're just staring out of the window that you're doing your hardest work of the day. In fact, many times when I'm just sitting here thinking and therefore working like heck I hear the door open and I quickly grab the pen and a piece of paper and start drawing something so that people won't think I'm just goofing off and anxious to have a little chat. But I like visitors when I'm drawing. It gets lonely up here all day, not like an office or a dentist or somebody who has company around him all the time." Schulz has been termed a recluse but he says: "Oh, we go to San Francisco about once a month, see friends, go to a play. But we aren't nightclubbers or cocktail types. Neither of us drink, never have, just isn't part of our life and our friends just have to accept us like that."

He picked up some more letters. "Lots of people write in ideas. Some are good, but I don't seem to be able to use other people's suggestions. Here's a pretty good one—'Why not make Snoopy pretend he's a Grand Prix racing driver?' Now that's not a bad idea, and I guess it would work. But first of all, I didn't think of it, and secondly I'd be imitating myself—sort of copying the Snoopy and the Red Baron business. It's always dangerous to copy yourself. Al Capp had a great success with the Schmoos, so then he had to try to repeat with the Kigmies and it wasn't as good. The Red Baron was a good idea but let's not imitate it. My son says he gave me the idea for that—he was working on a World War I model and claims he suggested the Red Baron business, but I don't remember. People think I'm a World War I nut and send me these"—he gestured at shelves of flying books. . . .

Schulz begins his day at 9:30 by walking the quarter mile from his sprawling one-level house across the lawns of his golf holes, past the big swimming pool to his studio. With a secretary in the outer office and a plush living room before you arrive at the place where he actually draws, it could very well be the office of a successful real-estate broker or a pre-need cemetery-lot salesman.

Clinically neat and organized, Schulz sits at the drawing board and begins by playing around on a scratch pad with a pencil, doodling situations and ideas. He tries to conceive of the week's work as a whole; six separate days' drawings which will somehow make a unity. When he has the ideas fairly well set in his mind he takes a 28-inch illustration board, which has the margins of the four panels printed on it already, and inks in the dialogue. When he has all six days' strips "dialogued in," he begins to draw the figures and the action, preferring to draw directly with the pen with a minimum of penciled guidelines.

One day's strip takes him about an hour to draw. The Sunday page takes the whole day. He is required by the syndicate to be five weeks ahead on the daily and eleven weeks ahead on the Sunday. When I called on him he was just finishing up the strips for the week of May 8 to May 13, the theme being "Be Kind to Animals Week." (In one sequence, Snoopy is holding a sign with that legend on it, and as Lucy goes by he shuts his eyes and puckers up for a kiss. "Not on your life!" bellows the dear girl, bowling the dog and his sign over backward. Another day ends with Snoopy's saying: "This was a good week—I didn't get kicked.")

Right now Schulz is also busy preparing an hour-and-a-half film, plus another TV special. (He writes every word, and supervised the animation of the other three TV specials.)

The books are a further drain on his time. Since the first one, called plain "Peanuts," Holt has published some 4,493,000 copies, and they are all in print. After Holt has had a year or two to sell a "Peanuts" book at $1, the rights are turned over to Fawcett, which takes the Holt volume, splits it in two, and sells each copy for 40 cents. To date Fawcett has sold 12 titles to the tune of 10 million copies. But the publishing doesn't end there. A few years ago an enterprising San Francisco woman named Connie Boucher persuaded Schulz to do a book for her Determined Productions company. It turned out to be "Happiness Is a Warm Puppy," and it was on *The New York Times* best-seller list for 45 weeks in 1962 and 1963. This was followed by more "Happiness Is—" books, plus a Peanuts Date Book, totaling around three million copies in all. In 1965 the John Knox Press published "The Gospel According to Peanuts," being the theological thoughts extracted from the strip, which has been that firm's best seller of all time at more than 635,000 copies.

Which brings one to another consuming interest of Charles Schulz: religion. A member of a Scripture-oriented Protestant nondenominational organization called the Church of God, he keeps 12 Bibles, plus a set of the dozen volumes of the Interpreters' Bible, in his studio. On Sundays he teaches Sunday School in Sebastopol ("to adults only—I could never teach other people's children"). A pushover for charities and organizations designed to help people, he recently consented to accept the chairmanship of the National Aid to the Visually Handicapped and set about organizing a huge golf tourney, to be known as the "Charlie Brown-Lucy Tournament," the proceeds of which will go to the aid of partly blind children. He brooded for weeks over a request to do a poster for Aid for Retarded Children, tried dozens of ideas, and finally had to give up. "There was simply no way to do it without the danger of seeming to mock them."

So this is the hectic world that was created by Charlie Brown/Schulz (he confesses that they are one and the same person). How did it come about and how did it snowball into these proportions?

Charles Monroe Schulz, as every good "Peanuts" aficionado knows, was born 44 years ago in Minneapolis, Minn. When he was two days old, he was nicknamed "Sparky" by his family for Barney Google's horse Sparkplug, and is still called that by his family and friends. From almost the beginning he wanted to become a cartoonist, thinking it among the noblest of the artistic professions.

"It's a great art," he says now. "I'm convinced it's much harder and more important than illustration. Look at that"—he points to a framed original cartoon page of "Krazy Kat" by George Herriman—"that's art. It was done around 1912 and its humor is every bit as fresh today as then."

Sparky's early life was very Charlie Brownish. "People read a lot into the strip, and I guess what people see in it, that's what's in it. But actually the strip is just about all the dumb things I did when I was little."

In fine Charlie Brown fashion he was the goat on the baseball field, once losing a game 40 to nothing, and even his drawings were turned down by the high-school yearbook. . . .

After the war he got a job lettering a comic magazine, then taught in a Minneapolis art school of the "Draw-me-and-win-a-scholarship" mail-order variety. A fellow instructor was named Charlie Brown, and later unwittingly lent his name to posterity. Another had a pretty blue-eyed sister named Joyce Halverson, and Schulz married her. In 1948, he sold his first cartoon, to *The Saturday Evening Post*. Then he did a weekly cartoon for *The St. Paul Pioneer Press* called "Li'l Folks." Within a year it was dropped. After many rejections from other syndicates, it was picked up by United Features in Manhattan. Over Schulz's protests it was renamed "Peanuts." To this day he is still indignant.

"What an ugly word it is," he says disgustedly. "Say it: *Peanuts!* I can't stand to even write it. And it's a terrible title. Now 'Peppermint Patty' is a good title for a strip. I introduced a character named that into the strip to keep someone else from using it. Funny, people don't tell you how to draw or write but EVERYBODY's an expert on titles."

The first month Schulz made $90 with his newly titled strip. A few months later it was up to $1,000 a month. Now, 17 years later, it is close to $1,000 a day.

"Funny," Sparky muses, "I never set out to do a cartoon about kids. I just wanted to be a good cartoonist, like, say, Herriman or my boyhood idol, Roy Crane, who draws 'Buz Sawyer'—a fine cartoonist. I always dreamed of some day coming up with some permanent idea or phrase that would pass into the language, like Snuffy Smith's 'bodacious' or some of Al Capp's gimmicks. I guess maybe 'Good grief'

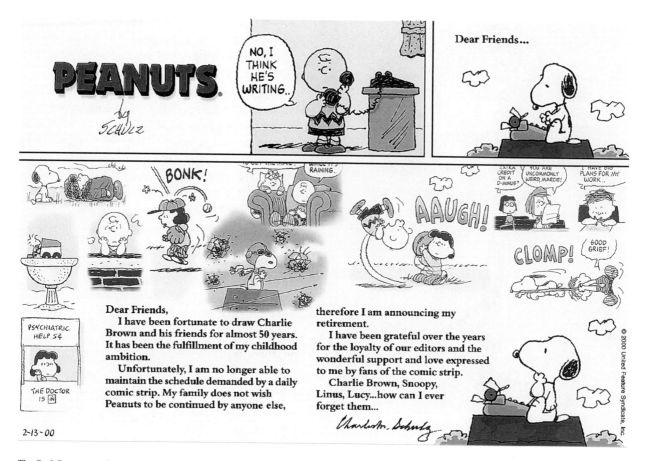

The final *Peanuts* comic strip, which Charles Schulz had drawn for nearly fifty years, February 13, 2000. **PEANUTS REPRINTED BY PERMISSION OF UNITED FEATURES SYNDICATE, INC.**

has made it. And perhaps the Great Pumpkin. And the 'Happiness Is . . . ' title. . . .

When asked about Snoopy, who is my family's favorite character in the strip, he said, "Snoopy's not a real dog, of course—he's an image of what people would like a dog to be. But he has his origins in Spike, my dog that I had when I was a kid. White with black spots. He was the wildest and smartest dog I've ever encountered. Smart? Why, he had a vocabulary of at least 50 words. I mean it. I'd tell him to go down to the basement and bring up a potato and he'd do it. I used to chip tennis balls at him and he'd catch and retrieve 'em." Schulz's sensitive face clouds at the memory. "Had him for years before he died."

Many psychiatrists who charge a good deal more than Lucy van Pelt's 5-cent consultation fee have tried to analyze the special appeal of "Peanuts." My pedestrian conclusion is that Charles Schulz feels the loss of his dog Spike today as deeply as—or more deeply than—he did a quarter of a century ago, just as he feels the loss of his childhood. Happily

for the readers, he is able to translate this long memory and deep feeling into words and pictures. It seems to be universal, either because we had a childhood like that, or wish we had. There's a little Charlie Brown in all of us males and, Lord knows, we've all known, and maybe even married, a Lucy van Pelt, a girl who shouts: "I don't want any downs—I just want ups and ups and ups." Certainly there's been *someone* in each one of our lives ready and eager to pull away the football just as we're about to kick it.

So very often the strip touches chords that remind us of things and homely events we thought we had forgotten. . . .

Another factor in the strip's popularity with all ages is his sublime handling of how far the fantasy should go. For example, Snoopy's dog house is always shown in profile; we never see it three-quarters view or actually go inside it. We just accept the fact when it is said that Snoopy has a Wyeth and a Van Gogh and a pool table in there, but if we actually saw inside and discovered an unbelievable dog house we

Cartoonist Charles Schulz, creator of *Peanuts,* at work on a drawing of Charlie Brown. **THE LIBRARY OF CONGRESS.**

would cease to believe in Snoopy as a dog and his relationship with the children. Another all-important factor in Schulz's astonishingly good batting average is his unfailing sense of what is subtly funny.

"I get letters all the time," he told me, "from optometrists saying, 'How come you're always talking about ophthalmologists'—Linus wore glasses, you know—'why not give us a break?' It's hard to tell them that ophthalmology is somehow funny and the word optometry just isn't. Like Beethoven. My favorite composer is Brahms—I could listen to him all day—but Brahms isn't a funny word. Beethoven is, so I gave him to Schroeder. Like names: Linus is a good name. I borrowed that from a friend, Linus Maurer. Funny, the other night I was trying to think of a good last name for Pigpen—he hasn't got one—and I fell asleep and I dreamed of a new character named José Peterson. That's a good name, isn't it? But I only put him in the strip for a week—he was a baseball player—but he just didn't belong, so out he went, along with some others I've gotten rid of. My strip is not like the kind that depends on variety or new characters. I've got pretty much the same characters and basic idea that I had 17 years ago. I want to keep the strip simple. I like it, for example, when

Charlie Brown watches the first leaf of fall float down and then walks over and just says, 'Did you have a good summer?' That's the kind of strip that gives me pleasure to do.

"I liked one I did that I got from one of my children—the only idea I've ever gotten right from something they did or said. We were at the dinner table and Amy was talking away on a real talking streak and finally I said, 'Can't you *please* be quiet?' and she was silent for a moment and then picked up a slice of bread and began to butter it, saying, 'Am I buttering too loud for you?'

"I gave the line to Charlie Brown after Lucy yelled at him. And I like the violent action ones, kids getting bowled over and such things that cartoons were born to do. Too many of these new strips are not cartoons—they're imitations of films, and the movies can do it so much better, beat them at their own game. But I like the quiet ones too. I like it when Linus says, simply: 'Sucking your thumb without a blanket is like eating a cone without ice cream.' I like it when Charlie Brown gets all excited about a big spelling bee and then goes out on the first word because they say, 'Spell "maze,"' and, being the good baseball fan he is, he spells it 'Mays.' I like to keep it all simple. For instance, it seems to me that Snoopy's been getting pretty fantastical lately. I think I'll simplify him, let him just be a dog for a while.

"Incidentally, Snoopy wasn't in the most popular strip I ever did, the one I've had the most mail on. That was the one where the kids are looking at the clouds and Linus says, 'See that one cloud over there? It sort of looks like the profile of Thomas Eakins, the famous portrait painter. And that other group over there—that looks as though it could be a map of British Honduras. And then do you see that large group of clouds up there? I see the stoning of Stephen. Over to the side I can see the figure of the apostle Paul standing.' Then Lucy says, "That's very good, Linus. It shows you have quite a good imagination. What do you see in the clouds, Charlie Brown?' And Charlie says, 'Well, I was going to say I saw a ducky and a horsey, but I've changed my mind.'"

The phone rang and he talked for a while. When he hung up he said, "That was something about having a helicopter be attacked by the Red Baron. Over Chicago. They've got a real German World War I plane. Publicity stunt of some kind." He shook his head incredulously, and a little sheepishly, at the world he had created. "Where's it all going to end?"

Further Resources

BOOKS

Conrad, Barnaby. *Snoopy's Guide to the Writing Life.* Cincinnati: Writer's Digest Books, 2002.

Johnson, Rheta Grimsley. *Good Grief: The Story of Charles M. Schulz.* New York: Pharos Books, 1989.

Inge, M. Thomas. *Charles M. Schulz: Conversations.* Jackson, Miss.: University Press of Mississippi, 2000.

Schulz, Charles M., and David Larkin. *Peanuts: A Golden Celebration. The Art and the Story of the World's Best-Loved Comic Strip.* New York: HarperCollins, 1999.

Twerski, Abraham J., and Charles M. Schulz. *When Do the Good Things Start?* New York: Topper Books, 1988.

WEBSITES

An Act to Authorize the President to Award Posthumously a Gold Medal on Behalf of the Congress to Charles M. Schulz in Recognition of His Lasting Artistic Contributions to the Nation and the World, and for Other Purposes. Public Law 106-225. 106th Cong., 2nd sess., June 20, 2000. Available online at http://purl.access.gpo.gov/GPO/LPS5781 (accessed March 31, 2003).

The Official Peanuts Website. Available online at http://www.snoopy.com/ (accessed March 20, 2003).

"New York: Nightmare"

Magazine article

By: *Newsweek*

Date: December 14, 1953

Source: "New York: Nightmare." *Newsweek,* December 14, 1953, 29–31.

About the Publication: *Newsweek* was founded in 1933 by Thomas J.C. Martyn. It was purchased by the Washington Post company in 1961. Headquartered in New York City, *Newsweek* had a circulation of four million in 2003. The news magazine mixes text and images in its coverage of the previous week's events. ■

Introduction

The first American newspapers existed even before there was a United States of America. One famous early American newspaper publisher was Benjamin Franklin, who published the *Pennsylvania Gazette* starting in 1729. One of the leading radicals in the colonies was Samuel Adams, who published his *Journal of the Times* in Boston. It, and other newspapers like it, spread the ideology of the American Revolution in colonial cities in the 1770s. During the American Revolution, one advantage that the colonists had over the British was that the colonists destroyed the printing presses of many of the Loyalist newspapers and controlled many of the surviving newspapers.

The city room at the New York *Herald Tribune* is virtually deserted because of the photo engravers union strike in December 1953. © BETTMANN/CORBIS. REPRODUCED BY PERMISSION.

Newspapers remained important sources of ideas and information well into the nineteenth century. During the Sedition Act crisis of 1798–1799, several newspaper editors were arrested for daring to criticize President John Adams. Many abolitionists used newspapers in their fight to abolish slavery in the United States. Abolitionist Elijah Lovejoy was killed in 1837 when he tried to defend his Illinois newspaper, the *Alton Observer,* from a mob attack.

During the late 1800s, newspapers were most people's primary source of news and information. Most sizable cities had at least two newspapers, one published in the morning and one in the afternoon. In most cities where politics were contested, there was at least one Democratic and one Republican newspaper. Ethnic and religious groups also had their own papers. With the rise of radio and television in the mid-1900s, newspapers decreased in importance, and many newspapers merged. Surviving local papers often were bought out by national chains.

Only in the large cities did more than one or two papers survive. In New York, for example, there were still six daily newspapers into the 1950s. Labor and material costs were troublesome, however. In 1953, attempts by New York City newspaper publishers to cut costs and

Men read a scaled-down version of the New York *Herald Tribune* that was printed after the strike began. December 5, 1953. © **BETTMANN/CORBIS. REPRODUCED BY PERMISSION.**

wages provoked an eleven-day strike by newspaper workers.

Significance

The newspaper stike of 1953 did not end daily newspapers in New York City, but it did signal the existence of hard times in the newspaper industry. In the large cities, there was enough competition that newspapers could not raise prices, but there was not enough advertising revenue to make up the difference between the cost of production and the revenue generated. Newspapers also faced increasing competion from television, as

more people turned to the nightly newscast as their primary news source. In the 1960s, many papers in New York and other cities either died off or adopted the smaller, tabloid format. By the end of the 1960s, fully half of the six New York dailies that had existed in 1953 had failed.

Newspapers faced continued challenges during the 1970s, 1980s and 1990s. In many cities which still maintained a morning and an afternoon paper, such as Cincinnati, both papers were owned by the same company. During the 1990s, newspapers were challenged by news sites on the Internet and 24-hour news channels on cable television. Some newspapers responded by creating their own websites and/or by becoming more flashy, with less substance. Newspapers also tried to become more "customer-oriented," conducting polls on what features and comics to run. They also became more aggressive in recruiting subscribers.

Many media observers had predicted that the Internet would be the final death knell of newspapers, but the first decade of competition between the Internet and newspapers actually killed off fewer daily newspapers than the first decade of competition between television and newspapers. As this 1953 article points out, the daily newspaper has long been an important part of the lives of New Yorkers—and Americans in general. What will happen to American newspapers in the future remains to be seen.

Primary Source

"New York: Nightmare"

SYNOPSIS: As this *Newsweek* article attests, most New Yorkers sorely missed their daily paper during the New York newspaper strike of 1953.

To the occasional visitor, New York had changed, but what the change was could not be defined offhand. There was a new here-but-not-here look in the eyes of New Yorkers as they bustled along Manhattan streets intent on pre-Christmas business. In the subways and the commuter trains they gazed at each other with a new curiosity, apparently not having seen the like before. They seemed vaguely conscious, in a night-marish way, of having forgotten something important, of having got on the wrong train, of a slip showing. There was a virus in the smazy, smoky, smoggy air, an epidemic of some kind, and the impulse was to fumble for a newspaper and find the answer there.

Ah, that was the answer! There were no newspapers. There had been no major newspapers since Sunday, and New Yorkers were living in a strange twilight world, partially informed, growing jittery, feeling that something was happening somewhere that they ought to know about.

Nothing at the Door

Habits of years' standing were hard to break, and New Yorkers reacted to the news blackout each according to his class and kind. Typical apartment dwellers in dressing-gowns and slippers, padded to drafty doors and found nothing there that could be propped against the percolator. For a day or two, ra-

dio and TV newscasts were a substitute for Page 1 headlines, but after the first flush these seemed to fill only a small corner of a vast, aching void. One housewife spoke for many New Yorkers when she looked bleakly across the breakfast table and commented: "It sure is queer."

To The *Times* or *Tribune* reader, it was good to know from the radio that stock market averages were at new highs for the recovery. But how could one find out without the tables whether the low-priced shares were keeping pace with the blue chips? (Only limited copies of The Wall Street Journal were available.) For the tabloid addicts there were no pictures of the Florida youth who put his head into the mouth of an absent-minded alligator, no frightening shots of Hollywood's moonbeam killer, no details of the Jack Dempsey-Kirk Douglas battle for the hand of a wealthy widow.

Why Rise and Shine?

For the chronic horseplayer, a breed unusually common in New York, there were no entries for Bowie or Tropical or Fair Grounds, no morning lines for calculating likely winners. (Only the 35-cent Morning Telegraph and the form sheets were available.) For the jobless, there were no classified Help Wanted columns, no incentive to rise and shine. For the average woman there were no big display advertisements, summoning her to the bargain counters.

New Yorkers, metropolitan and suburban, made the best of a bad situation. Some stores reported a drop in mail orders but otherwise the pre-Christmas shoppers were out in force clamoring for "unadvertised bargains." In transit, New Yorkers read magazines, even books, or just sat empty-handed looking with envy on more fortunate neighbors who had acquired copies of scarce out-of-town papers or local items such as *The Wall Street Journal*, The *Brooklyn Eagle, I Progresso Italiano, La Prensa,* and *Novoye Russkoye Slovo* (Russian-language daily). Newsdealers reported increased demand for anything in print.

Artists Unreviewed

All around were human casualties of a strange and unusual type that newspaper readers didn't know about. Among the innocent bystanders who got caught in the machinery and came out severely hurt were Nicanor Zabaleta, a Spanish harpist, and Herman Godes, Latvian pianist. They had invested about $1,500 each in Town Hall recitals, getting not one word of criticism or comment in papers that did not appear the morning after. "Good reviews here can make an artist's whole year profitable; absence of reviews can be disastrous," said one artists' agent.

Another casualty was Georgia Laster, 26-year-old Negro soprano from the West Coast, who had won her Town Hall debut as a Naumburg Foundation Award. She had hoped to follow in the steps of last year's winner, who got rave reviews and was overwhelmed with contract offers. Miss Laster sang beautifully, justifying the West Coast raves, but got no reviews in New York and not one offer. Also left without notices in the papers was Lucine Amara who, without warning, sang Mimi in "La Bohème" at the Metropolitan Opera, substituting for a sick star. "She did an outstanding job, but nobody outside the audience heard about it," said a Met spokesman.

Plugs by Television

A play called "Madam, Will You Walk," starring Jessica Tandy and Hume Cronyn, was launched without benefit of reviews, favorable or otherwise, and only the future will tell how it and the new Phoenix Theater survive the vicissitudes of untimely birth. New Yorkers had been vaguely aware that something important, a costly musical version of the old favorite, "Kismet," was about to open. On Friday, both radio and television informed New York that "Kismet" had opened all right. . . . Producers, performers, critics, and notable first-nighters were paraded before the microphones and TV cameras to hammer the idea home that "Kismet" was indeed showing on Broadway.

Meanwhile, the Associated Press conducted a sort of survey of men and women on the street, asking them if they missed the papers and what in particular. A movie cashier missed the want ads which to her for some reason or other were fascinating. A bank teller (female) bemoaned the dearth of crossword puzzles. A taxi driver liked to read about sports between fares. A traffic policeman needed a paper so he could turn on the television. "How do I know what's on if I can't get a paper with the programs?" he demanded. A man from Ohio hadn't even noticed that there weren't any papers. "Doesn't make a particle of difference to me," he said.

But to 8,000,000 New Yorkers, the lack of newspapers did make a great deal of difference. They wanted desperately to find out what was going on, and they wanted to see the news in print.

Further Resources

BOOKS

Columbia University. *Effects of the New York Newspaper Strike: First Report.* New York: Columbia University, 1963.

Leonard, Thomas C. *News For All: America's Coming-of-Age With the Press.* New York: Oxford University Press, 1995.

Page One: Major Events, 1900–1998, as Presented in the New York Times. New York: Galahad Books, 1998.

Tebbel, John William. *The Compact History of the American Newspaper.* New York: Hawthorn Books, 1963.

Vigilante, Richard. *Strike: The "Daily News" War and the Future of American Labor.* New York: Simon & Schuster, 1994.

PERIODICALS

Sterngold, James. "The Future of Newspapers: James Sterngold Interviews Mark Willes of Times Mirror Co." *The Bulletin of the American Society of Newspaper Editors,* no. 770, September 1, 1995, 16.

WEBSITES

New York State Newspaper Project. Available online at http://www.nysl.nysed.gov/nysnp/index.html (accessed March 27, 2003).

Celebrity Deaths in the 1950s

"James Dean, Film Actor, Killed in Crash of Auto"

Newspaper article

By: *The New York Times*

Date: October 1, 1955

Source: "James Dean, Film Actor, Killed in Crash of Auto." *The New York Times,* October 1, 1955, 10.

"Services for James Dean"

Newspaper article

By: *The New York Times*

Date: October 9, 1955

Source: "Services for James Dean." *The New York Times,* October 9, 1955, 87.

"Iowa Air Crash Kills 3 Singers"

Newspaper article

By: *The New York Times*

Date: February 4, 1959

Source: "Iowa Air Crash Kills 3 Singers." *The New York Times,* February 4, 1959, 66.

The remains of actor James Dean's Porsche 550 Spyder, totaled in the crash that also took the young actor's life, September 30, 1955. © **JOHN SPRINGER COLLECTION/CORBIS**

About the Publication: Founded in 1850 as *The Daily Times, The New York Times* was originally a relatively obscure local paper. However, by the early part of the twentieth century, it had grown into a widely known, well-respected news source, and remained so into the twenty-first century. ■

Introduction

The media in America has often focused more—or at least as much—on the way that someone died as how they lived. For instance, nineteenth-century president James Garfield is much more remembered for being assassinated than for what he did as president or during the rest of his life. In the military realm, Colonel Custer is remembered much more for his last stand than for anything he did leading up to that event. Part of this phenomenon is probably due to a belief that had the person lived, they would have accomplished great things, but when they were struck down, they no longer had that opportunity.

With the rise of radio and television in the 1940s and '50s, singers, movie stars and other popular entertainers became celebrities, teen idols and, in some cases, cultural icons. Success in the music and movies industries was strongly linked creating a public image.

In 1955, James Dean was killed in a car accident. The young actor had only released one film up to that

point, and many people were moved more by his accidental death than by his career. A similar outpouring of grief followed the deaths of three up-and-coming rock and rollers, the Big Bopper (J.P. Richardson), Ritchie Valens, and Buddy Holly, in a 1959 plane crash.

Significance

The premature and accidental deaths of these four young stars of the 1950s gave them a stature that they may or may not have sustained—or even attained—had they lived. Songs, movies, and posters have helped to keep their memories alive long after their deaths.

When James Dean died, he almost immediately became a cultural icon. He is particularly remembered for his prophetic quote: "Live fast, die young and leave a beautiful corpse." His untimely death led to lasting fame, even though he had only appeared in one movie, *East of Eden,* before he died. His other two feature films, *Giant* and *Rebel Without a Cause,* were released after his death. There is no way of knowing whether Dean would have been as famous had he survived the accident. But he was a talented actor who received positive reviews and two acting awards for his role in the Broadway production of *The Immoralist.* Movie posters of Dean, showing him young, handsome, and rebellious, have helped to preserve his mythic image and still sell well some fifty years after his death.

The wreckage of the plane that was transporting musicians Buddy Holly, Ritchie Valens, and J.P. Richardson (the Big Bopper) to the next stop on the "Winter Dance Party" tour, February 3, 1959.
© BETTMANN/CORBIS. REPRODUCED BY PERMISSION.

In 1971, Don MacLean's song "American Pie"—the songwriter's response to the deaths of the Big Bopper, Ritchie Valens, and Buddy Holly—was a huge hit. It is telling, however, that the Big Bopper (whose biggest hit was "Chantilly Lace") is probably best remembered for being one of the three who died, "the day the music died," than for his accomplishments in life. For the most part, Ritchie Valens has been similarly ignored, except during a period in the 1980s when the mainstream "rediscovered" Latino music. In 1987, the group Los Lobos rerecorded his hit "La Bamba." The remake made it to the top of the record charts, something that Valens's version failed to do. That same year, a motion picture, also called *La Bamba*, was made about his life. Valens was a talented musician whose songs were more than just copies of rhythm and blues hits, so he could have played a larger role on the music scene had he lived. As it is, though, he, like the Big Bopper, is mostly remembered for how he died.

Of the three musicians who died in the 1959 plane crash, only Buddy Holly is remembered primarily for his music. Generally considered an important part of the history of American rock and roll, his music has influenced several generations of musicians, from Paul Simon to Wheezer. His records were still regularly played by radio stations in the 2000s.

Primary Source

"James Dean, Film Actor, Killed in Crash of Auto"

> **SYNOPSIS:** This *New York Times* article reports on James Dean's death in a car crash and provides a brief overview of his acting career. The brevity of the article and its location inside the entertainment section indicate that Dean's passing was not considered a major event at the time.

Paso Robles, Calif., Sept. 30 (AP)—James Dean, 24-year-old motion picture actor, was killed tonight in an automobile accident near here.

A spokesman for Warner Brothers, for whom Mr. Dean had just completed "The Giant," said he had no details of the accident except that the actor was en route to a sports car meeting at Salinas. He was driving a small German speedster.

The actor had appeared in "East of Eden," released last April, and in "Rebel Without a Cause," still unreleased.

Mr. Dean was the star of Elia Kazan's film, "East of Eden," taken from John Steinbeck's novel. It was his first starring role in films. The year before he had attracted attention of critics as the young Arab servant in the Broadway production of "The Immoralist." His portrayal won for him the Donaldson and Perry awards.

Primary Source

"Services for James Dean"

> **SYNOPSIS:** Although it's only a small news item, *The New York Times* did feel the need to cover the services for James Dean in Indiana, noting that some 3,000 attended.

Fairmount, Ind., Oct. 8 (AP)—James Dean, the motion-picture actor, was buried today in a quiet country cemetery in the community where only five years ago he had been an outstanding high school athlete. A crowd estimated at 3,000 milled quietly as final services were read. Mr. Dean died a week ago at the age of 24 in the crash of his sports car near Paso Robles, Calif.

Primary Source

"Iowa Air Crash Kills 3 Singers"

> **SYNOPSIS:** The *New York Times* reported on the plane crash that killed the Big Bopper, Ritchie Valens and Buddy Holly. Of interest at the time primarily to the musician's teenage fans, the story did not make the front page.

"American Pie"

A long long time ago
I can still remember how that music used to make me
  smile
And I knew if I had my chance
That I could make those people dance
And maybe they'd be happy for a while.
But February made me shiver
With every paper I'd deliver
Bad news on the doorstep
I couldn't take one more step
I can't remember if I cried
When I read about his widowed bride
But something touched me deep inside
The day the music died

(Refrain)
So bye-bye, Miss American Pie
Drove my chevy to the levee
But the levee was dry
And them good old boys were drinkin' whiskey and
  rye
Singin' this will be the day that I die
This'll be the day that I die

Did you write the Book of Love
And do you have faith in God above
If the Bible tells you so
Do you believe in rock 'n roll
Can music save your mortal soul
And can you teach me how to dance real slow
Well, I know that you're in love with him
'Cause I saw you dancin' in the gym
You both kicked off your shoes
Man, I dig those rhythm and blues
I was a lonely teenage broncin' buck
With a pink carnation and a pickup truck
But I knew I was out of luck
The day the music died

I started singin'
(Refrain)

Now for ten years we've been on our own
And moss grows fat on a rollin' stone
But that's not how it used to be
When the jester sang for the King and Queen
In a coat he borrowed from James Dean
And a voice that came from you and me
Oh, and while the King was looking down
The jester stole his thorny crown
The courtroom was adjourned
No verdict was returned
And while Lenin read a book of Marx
The quartet practiced in the park
And we sang dirges in the dark
The day the music died

We were singing

(Refrain)
Helter Skelter in a summer swelter
The birds flew off with a fallout shelter
Eight miles high and falling fast
It landed foul out on the grass
The players tried for a forward pass
With the jester on the sidelines in a cast
Now the half-time air was sweet perfume
While the Sergeants played a marching tune
We all got up to dance
Oh, but we never got the chance
'Cause the players tried to take the field
The marching band refused to yield
Do you recall what was revealed
The day the music died

We started singing
(Refrain)

Oh, and there we were all in one place
A generation Lost In Space
With no time left to start again
So come on, Jack be nimble, Jack be quick
Jack Flash sat on a candlestick
'Cause fire is the Devil's only friend
Oh, and as I watched him on the stage
My hands were clenched in fists of rage
No angel born in hell
Could break that Satan's spell
And as the flames climbed high into the night
To light the sacrificial rite
I saw Satan laughing with delight
The day the music died

He was singing
(Refrain)

I met a girl who sang the blues
And I asked her for some happy news
But she just smiled and turned away
I went down to the sacred store
Where I'd heard the music years before
But the man there said the music woudn't play
And in the streets the children screamed
The lovers cried, and the poets dreamed
But not a word was spoken
The church bells all were broken
And the three men I admire most
The Father, Son and the Holy Ghost
They caught the last train for the coast
The day the music died

And they were singing
(Refrain)

They were singing bye-bye, Miss American Pie
Drove my chevy to the levee
But the levee was dry
Them good old boys were drinking whiskey and rye
Singin' this'll be the day that I die

SOURCE: McLean, Don. "American Pie." EMI. Audio recording, 1971.

Rock 'n' Roll Stars and Pilot Die as Chartered Craft Falls After its Take-Off

Mason City, Iowa, Feb. 3 (AP)—Three rock 'n' roll singers whose records and appearances have stirred millions of teen-agers were killed early today in a plane crash near here.

The four-place chartered craft carrying the trio and their pilot crashed within minutes after taking off in light snow from the Mason City airport.

The victims were Buddy Holly, 22 years old, of Lubbock, Tex.; Ritchie Valens, 17, of Los Angeles; J. P. (Big Bopper) Richardson, 24, of Beaumont, Tex., and Roger Peterson, 21, of near-by Clear Lake, Iowa, the pilot.

The troupe with which the singers had appeared had played before about 1,100 teen-agers and their parents at the surf ballroom in Clear Lake last night.

The Beachcraft Bonanza, chartered from the Dwyer Flying Service here was to take the three singers to Fargo, N.D., in advance of the troupe's engagement there tonight. The others went by chartered bus.

Bad Weather Blamed

Authorities blamed weather conditions for the crash. Snow was falling, the temperature was 18 degrees and a southerly wind was blowing at 35 miles an hour when the plane took off about 1 A.M.

The plane came down about five miles northwest of the airport on the Albert Juhl farm. No one heard the crash.

The left wingtip apparently struck the ground first and flew off. Pieces of the wreckage ripped off as the plane plowed about two-city-blocks distances across the field and piled up against a fence.

Mrs. Carroll Anderson, whose husband manages the Surf Ballroom, said "everything sounded o.k. when the plane took off."

Hollywood trade sources said the combined record sales of the three singers was in the millions.

Just Finished Movie

Mr. Valens, whose real name was Richard Valenzuela and who left a San Fernando, Calif., high school last year to seek a singing career, recently finished his first motion picture, "Go, Johnny! Go."

His first recording six months ago, was "Donna," which sold more than a million copies, the Del-Fi Record Company said.

Mr. Holly, star of the Crickets, who also appeared at the surf, hit the rock 'n' roll pinnacle with his recordings of "Peggy Sue" and "That'll Be the Day." Both reportedly sold more than a million and a half copies.

Mr. Richardson was on leave as a disc jockey, singer and program director at station KTRM in Beaumont.

His "Chantilly Lace" was rated by Billboard for a time as the third-most-played record and has been released in thirty-seven other countries.

Further Resources

BOOKS

Alexander, Paul. *Boulevard of Broken Dreams: The Life, Times, and Legend of James Dean.* New York: Viking, 1994.

Amburn, Ellis. *Buddy Holly: A Biography.* New York: St. Martin's Press, 1995.

Bankston, John. *Ritchie Valens.* Bear, Del.: Mitchell Lane Publishers, 2003.

Beath, Warren Newton. *The Death of James Dean.* New York: Grove Press, 1986.

Cosgrove, David. *Heaven Can Wait: A Play in Two Acts.* London: Josef Weinberger Plays, 2001.

Lehmer, Larry. *The Day the Music Died: The Last Tour of Buddy Holly, the Big Bopper, and Ritchie Valens.* London: Schirmer Books, 1997.

Norman, Philip. *Rave On: the Biography of Buddy Holly.* New York: Simon & Schuster, 1996.

WEBSITES

JamesDean.com: The Official Web Site. Available online at http://www.JamesDean.com (accessed March 25, 2003).

AUDIO AND VISUAL MEDIA

James Dean: Live Fast, Die Young. York Home Video. Directed by Casper Van Dien. VHS, 1999.

News is a Singular Thing
Memoir

By: Marguerite Higgins

Date: 1955

Source: Higgins, Marguerite. *News is a Singular Thing.* Garden City, N.Y.: Doubleday, 1955.

About the Author: Marguerite Higgins (1920–1966) was one of the most highly publicized news reporters during the 1950s. Although she had also reported on World War II, she gained her fame largely in Korea as a war correspondent for the *New York Herald Tribune.* In 1951, her book *War in Korea* became a best-seller, and she won the Pulitzer Prize for international reporting. She later covered and wrote books about Vietnam and the Soviet Union and reported on the civil war in the Congo. In 1966, she died of a tropical disease she had contracted in Vietnam. In recognition of her war reporting she is buried in Arlington National Cemetery. ■

Introduction

The role of women in public life has long been a controversial issue in the United States. As America began to prosper in the nineteenth century and a middle class developed, women were moved out of the workplace and into the home. According to the "cult of domesticity" that developed, women existed to make the home a safe and moral place, and they possessed special skills for that role. Women were supposed to be kept, for their own protection, out of the realms of media and business.

This whole system was ably countered by women who argued for full participation of their sex in public life, and by women who, turning the cult of domesticity on its side, argued that women were best suited to reform politics and the inner city, and to combat racial injustice and other societal problems by bringing their "special virtues" to those areas. Women often wrote in newspapers about these subjects or edited their own newspapers that advocated societal reforms. Ida B. Wells, Ida Tarbell, and Jane Addams were just three of the most well-known women who gained fame in these areas.

Despite this tradition of women in the media, men dominated newspapers, radio, and television in the 1950s. Most of the early TV anchors and media personalities were men. In the area of radio and TV entertainment, women often designed their own shows, but were not given public credit for them. *I Love Lucy* bore the direct imprint of Lucille Ball, as well as several women who worked behind the scenes, but Lucy was portrayed as a dizzy redhead, and it took decades for the behind-the-scenes women to gain credit. It was little different in the world of print journalism—most reporters were men. Marguerite Higgins was one of the few women war correspondents during both World War II and the Korean conflict.

Significance

Higgins was not fully accepted in Korea as a war correspondent; in fact, women reporters were banned from the front line. It took an order from the American commander General Douglas MacArthur for her and other female reporters to be readmitted. Higgins, unlike some earlier women media figures, did not argue that her sex gave her any special insight or virtues. She decried the attempts of women to write stories about their special status or to produce pieces about themselves. Instead, she fought for equal treatment with her male colleagues. In this excerpt from her memoir, she argues that women war correspondents need to do the same job as men and will succeed if allowed to do so.

Higgins's success, however, did not open many doors for women in the media. Television in the 1950s

Pulitzer Prize winning journalist Marguerite Higgins talks with Brigadier General John Bradley while covering the Korean War for the New York *Herald Tribune*. AP/WIDE WORLD PHOTOS. REPRODUCED BY PERMISSION.

was replacing newspapers as the premier media outlet and most television journalists, particularly in the high-profile positions, were men. The leading TV newscasters and anchors in the decades that followed have also been men. From the 1980s to the present, there has been a proliferation of news outlets, and more women are news desks anchors and TV correspondents. But at the beginning of the twenty-first century, all the major networks still had men anchoring their nightly news. Nearly all sportscasters and commentators are men, and women are relegated, literally, to reporting from the sidelines. Thus, even fifty years after Marguerite Higgins asked only for the chance to be treated equally in Korea, women are still fighting for a chance to report the news. They can point to her example, however, as proof that women can handle even the most difficult aspects of reporting.

Primary Source

News is a Singular Thing [excerpt]

> **SYNOPSIS:** In this excerpt from her memoir, Marguerite Higgins explains that all a reporter needs to be a good war correspondent is lots of physical sta-

mina and the ability to take extreme chances. She describes some of the dangerous events she covered in Korea, including the crucial amphibious attack on Inchon.

First-rate war coverage, it seems to me, requires only two qualities that are not normally demanded of any first-rate reporter on a big story. They are a capacity for unusual physical endurance and the willingness to take unusual personal risk. Other requirements of the good reporter remain the same in peace and war and of course range from such qualities as persistence, strong nerves in the face of crises, and diligent homework on your assigned subject, to the ability to get to the main sources of news.

Now some of us in the Korean war, including myself and Keyes Beech, with whom I sometimes shared a jeep (his), were described as taking risks that were foolhardy. I don't think we were. No more, anyway, than any of the top correspondents who covered the front lines instead of hanging around headquarters. To name just a few old-timers, this category included Tom Lambert of the Associated Press, Homer Bigart of my paper, Robert Vermillion of the United Press, Jim Lucas of Scripps Howard, and Don Whitehead of the Associated Press; and later on in the war such intrepid young men as the Associated Press's young John Randolph. The photographers, like Carl Mydans, Hank Walker, and Dave Duncan, had to expose themselves more than any of us because the process of taking photographs usually precluded the reporter's privilege of at least being able to keep his head down under fire. And then there was the long list of press corps casualties (fourteen killed or captured in the first four weeks of the war alone): among them are the men who will never collect the Pulitzer prizes and who probably deserved them most.

Obviously the war correspondent must spend a large share of his time describing the deeds of fighting men in the thick of battle: the soldier on patrol, the sailor or Marine involved in an amphibious landing, or the airman out on a mission. But before going to the front, any workmanlike war correspondent will brief himself carefully at battalion, regiment, or division headquarters concerning the enemy's estimated strength, the terrain, and our side's chances of success. He then figures out his coverage accordingly. He may elect to go along with the troops if opposition seems light and success seems reasonably assured. If it looks like a rough fight against heavy odds, he may decide to stick around the head-

quarters with which the troops will be in radio contact and interview the men and officers after the engagement is over.

No one who covered the war in Korea would, to my knowledge, quarrel with the view that the duty of the good war correspondent is to obtain the most vivid account possible of the battle and the men in it *without getting himself killed.* As it was frequently remarked around Korea, dead correspondents don't meet deadlines.

In my case it's certain that I never went out on a patrol or participated in any front-line engagement, big or little, without the conviction that I had a much better than even chance of getting back.

On the occasions in Korea when it seemed as if, despite calculations, I might after all end up dead, it was always the result of highly unexpected developments. One time the Communists infiltrated behind our lines at night and staged a surprise attack on the regimental headquarters of the 27th (Wolfhound) Regiment, which they had surrounded. The first machine-gun spurt was aimed from a point only a few yards from where I was eating breakfast—calmly enough, I grant you, but only because of complete ignorance of what was to happen. Courage? This remains extremely hard for me to define precisely, though, like anybody else, I recognize it instantly and with sharp emotion when I encounter it personally.

Some for want of a more comprehensive definition have described courage as self-control or absence of panic in the face of danger. I'd go along with that. Others call courage absence of fear. I would not go along with that. At any rate if absence of fear is a requirement of courage, then that term has been wrongly used on those occasions when it has been applied to my activities.

I can remember innumerable times—times that were later lauded as displays of courage—when I found myself silently muttering, "Why am I here? Why did I ever get myself into this?" And one of the times I felt this reaction most strongly was in the process of getting the story which I think was the best I wrote out of Korea. It was the eyewitness account of the fabulous amphibious assault behind the North Korean enemy lines at Inchon Harbor.

When news of the operation—one of the most technically difficult seaborne attacks in history as well as one of the worst-kept secrets of the war—leaked to the press, I seriously debated whether to go in with the assault troops or seek the compara-

"Pride of the Regiment"

When the hard-fighting 27th (Wolfhound) Infantry Regiment stopped a Communist tank drive on Taegu a month ago, the New York *Herald Tribune's* pert, fearless Correspondent Marguerite Higgins cabled an eyewitness story of the four-hour battle. Last week, in a letter to the *Trib,* the regiment's hard-bitten Colonel J. H. ("Mike") Michaelis complained that she had left out something important. He supplied it:

> Miss Higgins, completely disregarding her own personal safety, voluntarily assisted by administering blood plasma to the many wounded as they were carried into the temporary Aid Station [which] was subjected to small arms fire throughout the attack . . . The Regimental Combat Team considers Miss Higgins' actions on that day as heroic . . . in saving the lives of many grievously wounded men.

Me-&-the-War

Slender, durable Newshen Higgins, who covers Korea in tennis shoes, baggy pants and shirt and a fatigue cap that usually conceals her bobbed blonde hair, has done more than win the admiration of soldiers in her front-line reporting. She has also forced her male competitors, who at first tended to regard her as an impudent upstart in the business of reporting battles, to admit grudgingly that she was their match when it came to bravery and beats. More than once, Maggie Higgins has jeeped or hiked to hot spots while other correspondents hung back, thus forced them to go along, too. Said one colleague ruefully: "She's either brave as hell or stupid. Her energy and recklessness make it tough on all the others." She likes to send back such me-&-the-war stories as: "A reinforced American patrol, accompanied by this correspondent, this afternoon barreled eight miles deep through enemy territory . . . The jeep flew faster than the bullets which knicked just in back of our right rear tire."

Correspondent Higgins travels light, usually carries only a typewriter and a musette bag of toilet gear, eats & sleeps where she can (often on the ground), insists on no billeting favors because of her sex. As an all-round journalist, Newshen Higgins may not be quite up to her *Trib* colleague, Homer Bigart (with whom her feud for beats is already a Korean legend), or with some of the other crack correspondents in Korea. But she tries to make up for it by getting up earlier, and if necessary, working 24 hours a day. Said one colleague: "There's nothing she won't do for a story."

Campus Cub

Daughter of a globetrotting businessman and a French mother, Marguerite Higgins was born in Hong Kong in 1920, got her schooling in France and the University of California ('41). During the summer after graduation, she cubbed for the Vallejo (Calif.) *Times-Herald.* While she worked for her master's degree at Columbia's School of Journalism, she landed her first *Trib* job as a campus correspondent, was taken on full time when she finished Columbia in 1942. She was sent to the London bureau in 1944, got to Germany in time to cover the closing battles of World War II. At the Dachau concentration camp, while some correspondents dodged *SS* bullets, she and another correspondent jeeped blithely past and were the first reporters inside the central enclosure (an *SS* officer tried to surrender to her).

After three years of able postwar reporting in Germany, she became the *Trib's* Tokyo bureau chief in late June, was one of the first reporters to get to Korea when the war started. She flew to Seoul's Kimpo airfield, joined the retreat to Suwon, later covered the heartbreaking retreats of green, outnumbered U.S. troops. ("This is how America lost her first infantryman," she began her story of seeing Private Kenneth Shadrick fall in action.) She fought off attempts by officers, worried about her safety, to ship her out of Korea (Time, July 24, 31), now stays at the front most of the time. She ranges such a wide beat that her New York office seldom knows where she is. This week, after days of suspiciously un-Higgins-like silence, they learned from her first delayed dispatch that Maggie Higgins had landed with the fifth wave of marines at Inchon and stayed with them under mortar and rifle fire and grenades until the beachhead was secured. She was making good an earlier promise: "I walked out of Seoul, and I want to walk back in."

SOURCE: *Time,* September 25, 1950, 63–4.

tive security of a carrier or destroyer. In the period just before the landing Keyes Beech and I had had an unusual number of experiences in which it looked indeed as if we would be permanently looking on life from very far away. Also I'd been in a jeep accident. All that happened to me was a slight brain concussion, a pair of black eyes, and a cracked nose. But the accident plus the strain of the war had left me tired. Physical condition of course has a lot to do with whether your mood is bold or cautious. Beech and I used to refer to the mood that accompanied physical exhaustion as the "I'm-going-to-get-killed-today" feeling. The opposite was the "nothing-can-touch-me" mood. It happened that on many of the occasions when I was having an "I'm-going-to-get-killed" mood Beech was buoyed up in a "nothing-can-touch-me" phase. And vice versa. This probably affords one explanation of why we both managed to spend so much time in the war's hottest spots. If one of us wanted to press on, the other wasn't going to be left behind, no matter what his forebodings.

In the midst of my debate with myself concerning the Inchon coverage, a naval public relations officer announced that no women reporters at all would be permitted on any phase of the Inchon operation. My reflexes to this order were automatic for many reasons, including the fact that my paper's competitive position would be undermined by such a ban. And to make the issue crystal-clear, I asked to go in with the assault troops. It remained touch and go until the very hour of the attack. And until the moment I was en route to the beach I was so consumed with the effort of merely making sure that I could cover the story that I had no time or energy left for hesitation. (In fact I've often wondered how many battles I might have stayed clear of if I had not been propelled by opposition-created energy.)

At Inchon the hesitation came as usual when it was too late. As our steel-sided landing craft (LCVP) wove its way toward the sea wall through bright orange and blue tracer bullets another correspondent, a photographer for a news agency, said (with considerable common sense), "I've had enough! I'm heading back to the ship, are you?"

But when I answered, "No, I'm going ahead," I distinctly recall a start of surprise. For even as the photographer spoke, I had been saying to myself, "I wish there was a way to get out of this." My decision to push ahead was no particular credit to me. For it was not rational. It was instinctive. Instinctive pride perhaps; if I'd turned back then, I would have had a hard time facing not only the Marines who hit the beaches but the other correspondents, and above all the various officials with whom I'd raised such cain in order to be allowed on the landing in the first place.

And do I still think women correspondents should be allowed at the war fronts? Of course, if they are there to do a bona fide reporting job and if they have the common sense not to make nuisances or fools out of themselves.

I have some pet dislikes in journalistic styles and high on the list is the story we used to call the "lookee here, I'm only a girl but look where I am." An example is the young lady who in the waning days of the Korean war went out on a tank patrol and spent two thirds of the story describing the few seconds she

was allowed to guide the steering mechanism. Her story never did mention whether the patrol accomplished its mission or who else was in the tank.

Certainly unusual disadvantages face a woman war correspondent. One is the fact that since her presence is highly unusual anything she does, good or bad, is bound to be exaggerated and talked about. More important are some of the antediluvian regulations, like the one that prevented me from sending an exclusive eyewitness account of a dramatic Marine Corps battle. The story could not be dispatched because females were not allowed on the naval flagship, the *McKinley,* which was our only point of communication at the time with the outside world.

But for a woman war correspondent the rewards are unusual too, especially once you begin to get the breaks. The advantages balance the disadvantages. In Korea the mere fact that for a time I was a unique phenomenon meant that my work attracted unusual attention. So I received far more national acclaim and publicity than many of my male colleagues who did just as fine or better jobs.

Further Resources

BOOKS

Keeshen, Kathleen Kearney. "Marguerite Higgins: Journalist, 1920–1960." Doctoral thesis, University of Maryland, 1983.

Higgins, Marguerite. *War in Korea: The Report of a Woman Combat Correspondent.* N.Y.: Doubleday, 1951.

May, Antoinette. *Witness to War: A Biography of Marguerite Higgins.* New York: Beaufort Books, 1983.

Sebba, Anne. *Battling for News: The Rise of the Woman Reporter.* London: Hodder & Stoughton, 1994.

Soderbergh, Peter A. *Women Marines in the Korean War Era.* Westport, Conn.: Praeger, 1994.

Stueck, William Whitney. *Rethinking the Korean War: A New Diplomatic and Strategic History.* Princeton, N.J.: Princeton University Press, 2002.

West, Philip, and Chi-mun So. *Remembering the "Forgotten War": The Korean War Through Literature and Art.* Armonk, N.Y.: M.E. Sharpe, 2001.

WEBSITES

"Marguerite Higgins." Sparticus Educational. Available online at http://www.spartacus.schoolnet.co.uk/USAhigginsM.htm; website home page http://www.spartacus.schoolnet.co.uk/ (accessed March 25, 2003).

Alan Freed Popularizes Rock 'n' Roll

"Alan Freed"

Magazine article

By: Alan Freed

Date: December 1956

Source: Freed, Alan. "Alan Freed." *Photoplay,* December 1956. Available online at www.alanfreed.com (accessed March 24, 2003).

"What Alan Freed Really Thinks About Rock 'n' Roll"

Interview

By: Alan Freed

Date: 1958

Source: Freed, Alan. "What Alan Freed Really Thinks About Rock 'n' Roll." Interview by Anita Behrman. *People Weekly,* October 1958, 20–26.

About the Author: Alan Freed (1922–1965), a disk jockey from Cleveland, helped to make that city an early center of rock and roll. He was one of the first white DJs to popularize rhythm and blues music, at first in Cleveland and then on a national radio program. In 1954 Freed moved to New York, where he was a disk jockey for a radio station there. Freed lost his job in the 1959 radio payola scandal, in which he was accused of accepting money from record companies in return for playing their records on the air. He slipped into anonymity, dying after an extended illness some six years later. ■

Introduction

Before the end of the nineteenth century, new music was largely disseminated through the theater. Among the songwriters who used the theater, and often the ethnic theater, to spread their music were George M. Cohan and Irving Berlin. These songwriters' efforts remained popular for the next century. As the twentieth century opened, radio brought news, sports and music into American households. Radio gave many people an opportunity to hear many types of music for the first time ever. Much of radio was censored in the 1920s and 1930s, however, as radio executives and national radio networks carefully controlled what went on the air.

Swing music became popular in the 1930s and 1940s, and its audience was greatly increased by the radio. The 1940s also brought the first teen idol, Frank Sinatra. During this period, some people called for censorship of swing, jazz, and Frank Sinatra music, all of which were considered too overtly sexual and a cause of juvenile delinquency.

That controversy was nothing, however, compared to the one that would soon blow up over rock and roll. Rhythm and blues (R&B) were becoming more popular among white teens (and had long been popular among African Americans). However, before R&B would be accepted by the white mainstream, the music needed to be recast and "sanitized" in the eyes of white America. A new music form was created and labeled—a form dubbed "rock and roll." Rock and roll was essentially R&B "cleaned up" and (usually) performed by white artists. The most overt sexual references were removed, but many were still there, and constituted much of the appeal of these records.

Alan Freed played an instrumental role in developing rock and roll into a mainstream musical form. In 1951, he began broadcasting his rhythm and blues radio show on WJW in Cleveland, Ohio. At first the songs he played were mostly by African Americans, such as The Dominoes. Much of his early listening audience was also African American. Soon, more and more white teenagers were tuning in, and Freed was playing songs by new, white, bands. By the mid-1950s his shows were broadcast nationally by CBS radio.

Significance

Freed called the music he played "rock and roll," and the name stuck. Although he is often credited with it, Alan Freed did not actually coin the term himself. It was a common euphemism for sex in the R&B music he played in the early 1950s, such as The Dominoes's "Sixty Minute Man," the first verse of which includes the phrase "rock 'em, roll 'em"

Sixty-minute man, sixty-minute man
Look a here girls I'm telling you now
They call me "Lovin' Dan"
I rock 'em, roll 'em all night long
I'm a sixty-minute man

However, Freed was the first to apply it to the music that came to be known by that name, and his radio shows made the music and the phrase known nationwide. As he points out in his interview and his 1956 article in *Photoplay,* the popularity of rock and roll in the 1950s was actually due to a number of factors. Perhaps the most important one was Elvis Presley, who did much to create a mass audience for rock and roll. Another factor was the increasing affluence of suburban youth, who had more money to spend on jukeboxes and records. A third was the development of the single record, or "45," which had only one song on each side and was very inexpensive. Record sales tripled between 1954 and 1960, and radio stations also began to focus more on recorded music. Television also promoted rock and roll, as programs such as *American Bandstand* brought the music to larger audiences.

Rock and roll was not without its detractors. Many called for radio and TV stations not to play or televise

Disc Jockey Alan Freed, who coined the phrase "rock n' roll," broadcasts from WABC. **FREED, ALAN, PHOTOGRAPH.**

rock and roll, and Presley's appearance on *The Ed Sullivan Show* in 1956 evoked loud public protest. *American Bandstand* walked a fine line as it sold rock and roll, carefully selecting its studio audience to make sure it was clean-cut—and white. Other television music programs did the same. Freed was a vocal defender of rock and roll against those who would say, "They're not writing songs like they used to," as well as those who thought the teenagers who liked it were all hooligans and delinquents.

The part of the article in which Freed explains how the records for his show are chosen is also significant. Freed claims that he and his staff picked out the music to be played. The fact that Freed was later convicted of accepting bribes from record companies to play their records indicates this may have been less than truthful.

Rock and roll stormed onto the scene in the 1950s, with assistance from Alan Freed. It has yet to lose its popularity, even though it is in many ways quite different from the music that Freed first popularized.

Primary Source

"Alan Freed"

SYNOPSIS: In this magazine article, Alan Freed, a radio disk jockey and an early promoter of rock and roll, stresses the importance of "Freedom to play the type of music the public wants to hear." He also maintains that music fans are a powerful force in determining which songs will be hits. This is somewhat ironic, given his involvement in the radio payola scandal, but also true in that rock and roll became enormously popular despite early attempts to stifle it.

I happened to be born with the name of Freed. Maybe that was part of my lucky star—because that's the first four letters of a very important word—FREEDOM. That about sums up my idea of music: Freedom to play the type of music the public wants to hear. What kind of music is that? The way the musical wind blows in my direction, it spells out Rock N' Roll. Who is the mainstay of the recording business, aside from the performers? The listening audience. Who puts the most dimes in the juke box? And who gets up at every record counter across the land, day after day, week after week, month after month? Teenagers, my favorite audience. I love 'em, especially when they give me the lowdown on this wonderful upbeat world we live in. And don't be fooled, Rock n' Roll isn't down beat by intent, just in musical content. It really swings. It not only moves the feet, but the spirit as well. Go to any record hop and bear me out.

As far as I can see through my television show on WNEW-TV, New York, and through my radio show, rock n' roll is firmly established as a musical medium, whether it be the song with a screaming type vocal or the ballad with a beat. Even Rock n' Roll cools off but the beat never dies. I'll tell you why this is. Most of all your recording stars today are teenagers like the listening audience. There's a rapport between record artist and record buyer. They have a common ground to meet upon . . . age . . . This is important because there is representation there.

Contrary to a lot of people I did not make Rock n' Roll what it is today. The world at large helped it a great deal. It was like making a cake, the ingredients were there, they were just waiting to be put together and accepted. The oven was being preheated at a high temperature, meaning, our children had a lot of emotion in them but no way to express it. Thus came "The Big Beat" and a way of letting go. A loud trend was born.. The parade was started . . . Unknown talent flooded the market . . . Young good looking boys and groups established themselves on wax. Then came Elvis and the cycle was complete.. An Idol was born. That's all that any musical trend needs.. an Idol. Now there was no stopping it.. Our young people today had a way of expressing themselves and they liked it. The mothers of today had their musical idol in Sinatra. It wasn't a bad thing.. They swooned every time they saw his face.. Frankie didn't have to sing. All he had to do was stand there . . . Johnny Ray had the same effect. If you want to be literal, Johnny's style was the start of rock n' roll. Johnny today is a great performer.. Elvis has toned down and is on his way to becoming polished . . . I'm sure you all agree on this point.

Let me give you a little information as to how we choose the records for my show.. we get hundreds of records into the studio weekly. We know we can't play them all and yet we have to listen to them all and pick out the best of the lot and the few with the greatest potential of making the best seller list. So with the help of my staff which includes (God Bless him) Johnny Brantly and my right hand man and Manager Jack Hooke, we wade through these records and train our ear to all sounds and voices.. We get the best of the lot and give them the spins needed on our magic turn table.. The rest is up to our listening audience. You send in cards, letters and telegrams (aren't they extravagant?) This tells me how well you liked the records and how often I should play them. You, my audience, have the power to make new hit recording artists and songs. I like it that way because it's as though at an early age you have the power to vote. You made "SHORT SHORTS," "BLUE SUEDE SHOES," "FOR YOUR LOVE," FATS DOMINOE, ELVIS PRESLY, RICKY NELSON, TOMMY SANDS, ED TOWNSEND, GINO & GINA.. I can go on and on.

If you go to the midwest where I started as a D.J. or if you go any place in the U.S.A. you will find that music is the same regardless of what name it goes under.. Pop, Rhythm and Blues, Rock n' Roll.. Cha, Cha, Cha, it all has a beat.. Opera has a beat.. Listen to Bizet's "Carmen"! First they made a modern play of it entitled "Carmen Jones" The music had to have popular appeal or they couldn't do it. Then they took the Habanera and made a popular record out of it. It turned out well and has a strong beat behind it. The original has the same beat.. many operas have this beat.. Music is the same in all mediums.. Time marches on and so does music.. it goes with the future and is remembered in the past.. "They're not writing songs like they used to" is the cry.. I sincerely believe that in ten years you'll hear the same plea.. There are just so many bad songs per era but there are also some very beautiful songs.. We have come up with some beautiful songs.. "Tammy," "Fascination," "Unchained Melody," "And That Reminds Me" . . . There are

countless more, which only goes to prove that they are writing songs the way they used to and will continue to write them.. It isn't a case of what do I think of Rock n' Roll or for that matter what I think of any type of music. It's all a matter of individual taste and desire.

Now that I've given my opinion on music and what I think will happen to it, I think I ought to mention what an interesting job it is to be a disc jockey. The people you meet and the things you do.. Knowing that if you are a name that stands out in the field of platter spinners how much good you can do where people are concerned.. I get letters everyday from teenagers and their parents alike.. Sometimes I feel like a father to all the kids that dance on my TV show. I am asked questions and I give advice.. I try to make it the same advice I would give to my son if he were to ask the same questions. I meet my teenage admirers at my Rock n' Roll shows.. They tell me how much they enjoy the entertainment.. I put on these shows for them and I know in the end that it will all be a great reward . . . I have high hopes that these same teenagers will one day hold the future of our country in their hands and I have no doubt but that it will be very capable hands to be in.

Primary Source

"What Alan Freed Really Thinks About Rock 'n' Roll"

SYNOPSIS: Freed was always very outspoken. In this interview, he defends teenagers as a group. With the rise of rock and roll, youth culture was beginning to take form for the first time. Young people had achieved notoriety because of Freed's riot-inducing concerts. The notion of the "juvenile delinquent" was exacerbated by newspaper coverage of these concerts, as well as, according to Freed, Hollywood films portraying teenagers unfavorably. Here, Freed serves as a spokesperson for what teenagers were listening to at the time, and describes his own musical tastes, which actually tended toward classical.

Give Teenagers a Chance—They May Surprise You!!!

"Is Rock 'n' Roll responsible for juvenile delinquency," I asked Alan Freed, the most controversial figure in the popular music field.

His vehement reply was a loud, clear, "No!"

He continued, "Adults have to find a scapegoat for their own shortcomings and Rock 'n' Roll seems to be it. Kids today are looking for something to dance to and have found the beat they want in Rock 'n' Roll."

We were sitting in Alan's tastefully furnished Manhattan apartment with his wife Jackie and his business manager, Jack Hoek. Mrs. Freed and Alan sat on the modern sectional couch. Mr. Hoek and I were each on one of the four comfortable club chairs. On the wall facing the couch there is a large hi-fi unit and many cabinets filled with records of all kinds.

This was my first meeting with the man who has caused such a sensation among teenagers and I found him charming, soft-spoken and intelligent.

"You gave Rock 'n' Roll its name, didn't you," I asked.

"Yes. In 1951 I first called it Rock 'n' Roll. Actually, Rock 'n' Roll is rhythm and blues and was called "Race Music" because the Negroes originated the blues. Today it's not as pure, but the basis for all Rock 'n' Roll is still blues."

"What do you think of Elvis? "

Alan lit a cigarette, thought a moment, and said, "He's the only white man who can really sing the blues. He's got a real feeling for it. It comes from the contact he had as a child with Negroes in Tennessee. Elvis is truly a phenomenon in the music business. He's a kid loaded with emotion and that shows when he sings. I honestly feel that Elvis' future lies in movies. He's going to be a fine actor some day. He can't miss. Not with his appearance and the depth of feeling he's able to display."

Getting back to delinquency, do you have any ideas for its cause or any for its solution?"

"I very definitely feel that the world situation has a great deal to do with it. The youngsters today are living under the shadow of the atom bomb. This generation is wiser than my generation was. They grow up faster.

"Hollywood has been, in my opinion, no help in the problem. Pictures like "Blackboard Jungle," and "High School Confidential," have painted pictures of teenagers as monsters and beasts. This is unfair. Why should all kids be accused when only a few of them are bad. "

Alan hesitated for a moment and got up. "Just a minute," he said. "I want to show you something."

He returned with a letter in his hand. "This is from a young man who is studying to be a minister."

Alan read the letter to me. It was most complimentary, and beautifully written. The young man congratulated Alan on his good work with young people and asked Alan to please tell his audience to look more to God and to worship in their churches and temples.

Alan does this quite often. He says, "We try to make our show a deterrent to delinquency. We entertain them and give them something to do after school."

Alan spoke with sincerity and conviction. It's apparent that this man has faith in young people, and more important, really cares what happens to them.

An angry look crossed his face. He said, "I'd like to tell you about something that happened about a year ago.

"I was head of the Nephrosis Drive. I told my audience to go to their local headquarters and find what they could do to help.

"13,000 kids showed up at various headquarters and lots of money was collected. Not one word was printed in any newspaper."

"You don't read about the good things, only the bad."

Alan Freed was born on October 15, 1922 in Johnstown, Pennsylvania. At the age of 12 he played the trombone and organized his own band. In his last few months at Ohio State, he was bitten with the radio bug and after graduation got a job paying $17 a week on station WKST in New Castle, Pennsylvania.

"It seems you've always loved music. Do you like all kinds or just Rock 'n' Roll?" I asked.

"All kinds. In fact, my favorite classical composer is Bach. The best composer today, in my opinion, is Jimmy Van Heusen. He wrote 'Imagination' and 'All the Way.'"

"Are your audiences composed mainly of girls?"

"We have a fairly equal division. The girls come to the afternoon, the boys to the evenings.

"The girls like the swooner types like, Ricky Nelson, The Everly Brothers. The boys prefer the frantic singers like Jerry Lee Lewis."

The interview was coming to an end. I asked, "anything you want to add, Alan."

"Just this," he said. "Don't blame the youngsters for everything. There are good and bad in every group, every generation. I work with teenagers and I've found them, loyal, sincere and willing to help. Give the kids a chance, they deserve it. Don't prejudge them."

Further Resources
BOOKS

Jackson, John A. *Big Beat Heat: Alan Freed and the Early Years of Rock & Roll.* New York: Schirmer Books, 1991.

Nite, Norm N. *Rock On Almanac: The First Four Decades of Rock 'n' Roll Chronology.* New York: Harper & Row, 1989.

Stuessy, Joe *Rock and Roll: Its History and Stylistic Development.* 2nd edition. Englewood Cliffs, N.J.: Prentice Hall, 1994.

Talevski, Nick. *The Unofficial Encyclopedia of the Rock and Roll Hall of Fame.* Westport, Conn.: Greenwood Press, 1998.

WEBSITES

The Official Alan Freed Website. Available online at http://www.alanfreed.com (accessed March 24, 2003).

"Top 40 Hits of 1930–1999." Lyrics world. Available online at http://ntl.matrix.com.br/pfilho/html/top40/index.html; website home page: http://ntl.matrix.com.br/pfilho/summer.html (accessed September 30, 2003). *Complete lyrics to "Sixty-Minute Man" can be found on this website.*

VIDEOCASSETTES

Lane, Christy. *Christy Lane's Learn the Dances of the '50s & '60s.* Brentwood Home Video. VHS, 1996.

Mr. Rock 'n' Roll: The Alan Freed Story. Artisan Home Entertainment. Videocassette, 1999.

"What Killed Collier's?"

Magazine article

By: Hollis Alpert

Date: May 11, 1957

Source: Alpert, Hollis. "What Killed Collier's?" *The Saturday Review,* May 11, 1957, 9–11, 42–44.

About the Author: Hollis Alpert (1916–) is best known as a film critic, but he has written and edited a variety of articles and publications. He served in the U.S. Army during World War II (1939–1945) and has written for a number of magazines, including *Woman's Day* and *The Saturday Review.* He is the author or editor of more than a dozen works, including two screenplays, a biography of the Barrymore family, and *The Life and Times of Porgy and Bess.* ∎

Introduction

Mass-market magazines, designed to be sold to the entire country and to have a wide reach, developed in the late 1800s. One of the first was *Ladies' Home Journal,* which aimed to appeal to all women. *The Saturday Evening Post,* founded in 1871, emphasized small-town and traditional values in an attempt to attract readers across the United States. *Collier's,* founded in 1883, covered the news and culture of the day.

Another wave of popular and successful mass market magazines arose in the 1920s, most notably *Time,* which was launched in 1923. During that era, middle-class Americans found that they had more leisure time as work weeks became shorter and some workers were even granted an annual vacation week. Advertising became much more sophisticated in the 1920s; it both pro-

moted and benefitted from consumerism and helped many magazines thrive. During the 1930s and 1940s, magazines fought for survival, due to America's economic difficulties and World War II. In the 1950s, some magazines failed, including *Collier's.*

Significance

The failure of *Collier's* was symbolic of the troubles that many magazines faced in the 1950s. As Hollis Alpert noted in his article about the magazine's demise, a number of new forms of entertainment competed with magazines for people's time and money in the 1950s, as people gained access to automobiles, went on vacations and started to go to the drive-in. An alternative new media, television, also provided some stiff competition. Television brought entertainment and news into people's homes on a daily basis, something general-interest magazines, which covered some of the same topics as TV, could not match.

Many magazines experienced trouble in the post-war period. *Women's Home Companion,* like *Collier's,* ceased publication in December 1957. The only reason *Harper's* was able to continue was that it was supported by a foundation. Alpert noted that the reason some other magazines continued to be successful is that they appealed to niche audiences. He cited *Fortune* and *Sports Illustrated* as successful examples of these specialized publications. Both magazines were still on the newsstands some fifty years later.

While general-interest magazines continue to be published in the twenty-first century, they face continued competition from other media and are constantly updating themselves and adding new features in an effort to retain readers and appear relevant.

Magazines, even those that no longer publish, have made lasting contributions to American society. Many of the most memorable photographs of recent decades were published in magazines and have become part of the country's visual history. Norman Rockwell would not have been anywhere near as beloved had it not been for his *Saturday Evening Post* covers. Magazines are particularly useful to historians. They serve as archives of the ideas that dominate America at any given time. Thus, while *Collier's* may have ceased publishing, it and similar general-interest magazines did not truly fail.

Primary Source

"What Killed Collier's?"

SYNOPSIS: In this article, Hollis Alpert examines the factors that led to the demise of *Collier's* magazine. He notes that its generalized nature created difficulties for the publication and also points out how rumors of *Collier's* imminent demise helped bring about its close, as advertisers no longer wanted to

Princess Grace of Monaco is featured on the final issue of *Collier's* magazine, dated January 4, 1957. **COLLIER'S MAGAZINE, JANUARY 4, 1957.**

spend money for ads in what was perceived as a dying magazine. While he laments the magazine's death, Alpert also observes that the life of each magazine, even a popular and well-respected one such as *Collier's,* must at some point come to an end.

No one claims that either *Collier's* or *Woman's Home Companion,* both of which died this past December, were indispensable to the culture of America. But they were magazines, disseminators of the written word, carriers of opinion, reporting, and entertainment, and they were a part of the corrective apparatus which journalism furnishes to a democratic state. Now there is some professional journalism missing from the scene; skills used to put out the magazines are lying fallow or going to waste; and a cloud of doubt hovers over the profession and business of large magazine publishing.

Which other of the large, established magazines are apt to run into trouble or are faltering under the stress of competition? For an appropriate answer, one must look beneath the surface, disregard the proud boast of multi-million circulations and even vaster readership and find out whether they pay, whether advertising is sufficient, whether readers want the magazines or are handed them at far below cost, whether they are editorially alive (*i.e.,* modern, up to date, geared to today's psychology and living habits, high in prestige, and possessing a clearly defined policy).

Circulation is not the whole story. *Collier's* and *Companion* had reached their all-time highs at the time of their expiration, both over 4,000,000 copies per issue. But advertising was declining, had been on a continual downhill slide from 1947 on. The decline was halted momentarily when *Collier's* turned fortnightly in 1953, but then it started again. The outlook for 1957 was dismal indeed for both magazines.

Ten years ago the Crowell-Collier magazines (which included *American,* suspended earlier in 1956) were healthy by nearly all criteria. *Collier's,* particularly, had made big gains during the Depression years, looked upon *The Saturday Evening Post* as its competition, and went into the years of war and paper shortages with a well-maintained circulation, firm ad rates, and a margin of profit. "The magazine," said *Scribner's* Magazine in 1939, "is an article of commerce more brightly packaged and more efficiently sold than any breakfast cereal; a vehicle of light entertainment as dependable and competently engineered as a V-8 straight from the assembly line; a slick journal with a zip of showmanship in every line, as lively as a swing band."

It is a puzzling phenomenon, this rise and decline of magazines, and the pattern of *Collier's* may be significant. It was the creation, in 1888, of Peter Fenelon Collier, a salesman of books on the instalment plan who used the magazine as a premium. Later it had some influence under Norman Hapgood, an editor who, according to the same article in *Scribner's,* "used facts to expose evil, quoted Browning and Wordsworth at its readers, thundered at corruption and corporations." But the magazine, as we knew it when it died, was largely the creation of Thomas Beck, a super-salesman for Procter and Gamble and popularizer of Crisco, who as advertising manager for *Collier's* went to Joseph Palmer Knapp (head of the Crowell Publishing Corporation) in 1919 and sold him on the idea of adding the magazine to the three monthlies Knapp then published. They were *American, Woman's Home Companion,* and *The Country Home.*

The secret of publishing a successful weekly eluded Beck and Knapp for a time. Knapp had purchased *Collier's* for the price of settling its debts; it began to roll up new ones. It was so sick that in the early Twenties the back cover had to be given away. (The influence of Knapp, by the way, is said to have been felt on the magazine in terms of its occasional puppy-and-kitten covers as well as its later anti-Prohibition stand. Knapp, it is reported, drank a daily bottle of brandy until the day of his death, and mixed martinis in a giant-sized shaker.)

Three editors were hired and fired between 1920 and 1924, a rapid rate for those days. Then William Chenery was made editor. Chenery was a literate Virginian gentleman who, while taking his time about bringing the magazine out of the red, brought in such lively and convivial spirits of the day as Walter Davenport, W. B. Courtney, John T. Flynn, and Kyle Crichton.

Some of their high spirits flowed over into the magazine. The circulation of *Collier's,* when Chenery came along, was 850,000. It went up to 1,500,000 in 1927, and 2,000,000 in 1929, the first year the magazine reached the break-even point. One of Chenery's first acts was to reaffirm a strong stand on Prohibition—against. This stand, though it alienated a few hundred devout Prohibitionist subscribers, brought in a great many more free-drinkers, and *Collier's* was on its way. . . .

During the Forties, *Collier's,* as one editor put it, "tried to find a political area for itself quite a bit to the right of its old position. Since several other weeklies were already in this area there was, unfortunately, not enough room." Contributing to this state of uncertainty is the fact that there was continual interference from the Board with editorial policy. And when Louis Ruppel was made editor of *Collier's* in 1948 a clear-cut ideological split developed between editor and publisher, particularly when Edward Anthony came into the latter spot in 1952.

Ruppel has come in for some criticism. However, during his four-year tenure he brought the semblance of a policy to the magazine, and whether he helped or hurt all the more is still debatable. He was strong on hot journalism, originating a series of exposes that gave *Collier's* a certain sensational tone for a while. He also raised circulation. According to an editor who worked with him he was "a rough, tough-talking newspaperman type, closer to 'The Front Page' than reality. He liked to originate projects himself, often rushed in like a wild bull with hot enthusiasms. Being a newspaper man he avoided literary agents, and alienated some of the best ones." One of his projects was the issue devoted to "The War We Do Not Want." This presupposed a push-button war with Russia, and some well-known writers and authorities were recruited to put forth their views. "No one intended it," said an editor of that time, "but the net effect was one of extreme belligerency. There were protests from all over the world, and it distinctly hurt the magazine." Another editor speaks of an atmosphere of intrigue and fear that permeated the staff at that time.

Under Roger Dakin's editorship (he succeeded Ruppel in 1952) foreign affairs were played down, fiction grew even lighter in tone, and agents were told that stories with foreign characters and locales were out of bounds for *Collier's.* Under all these changes, the magazine was slowly losing the character it had developed under Chenery and Colebaugh. There was editorial floundering and—until shortly before the end—there was a hesitancy to invest in the long-range editorial projects that, when successful, boost circulation.

And there was financial trouble. In 1946 the Crowell-Collier Corporation had racked up the largest earnings in its history. But even then this prosperity was due almost entirely to the very profitable book department, which included the Collier's Encyclopedia, Dr. Eliot's Five-Foot Shelf of Books, and sets of standard authors in fairly garish bindings. (Incidentally, this operation continues, and the spirit of Peter Fenelon Collier can be said to be living on.) As the Forties rolled on the earnings of the book department were used increasingly to keep the magazines alive.

The last big man on the scene was Paul C. Smith, brought in in 1953 by Clarence Stouch, chairman of the board. Smith, who went from vice-president without portfolio to simultaneous president, chairman, and editor-in-chief of the publications at the end, had to cope with the hard facts of magazine publishing under present-day economics. With the cost of paper and manufacturing inexorably rising, he saw little chance for an upturn before 1958. Smith was not a banker, but after assuming his new job he spent far more time raising money than running magazines.

Smith had been general manager of the *San Francisco Chronicle,* resigned after a management row. According to *Time* he was once known as "the wonder-boy of American journalism." From 1954 on he was running Crowell-Collier's, achieved the extraordinary feat of getting banks to loan money for the magazines, managed to meet cost deadlines, but was always running into more cash shortages. A careful examination of the magazines during his tenure shows no startling editorial changes. "I want a magazine with scope, not scoop," was one of his bywords, and near the end he made this observation: "I think we may have going on what may be one of the great publishing turnarounds in history." But this was not to be. On December 11, 1956, about thirty years after the decision of Knapp and Beck, now both dead, to push ahead with the magazines at all costs, the directors met again. This time their decision was different; and the journals closed down. . . .

Both *Collier's* and *Companion,* say some theorists, were bucking today's trend towards specialization—the taking of a dead aim at a particularized audience with clearly defined interests. If an audience exists, then so must advertisers anxious to reach it. Many editors look with envy on the shelter magazine field, led by *Better Homes and Gardens* with its nearly 5,000,000 circulation. These magazines are aimed directly at the home-owner, who is assumed also to be a home-dreamer, one who would like to mortgage a bigger, more modern home than the one he already mortgages. This reader is serviced with the ingredients of his needs and dreams. The concept of escape, once thought essential for attracting the mass audience, has given way to the concept of service. The editors of *Companion* were mulling over the idea of specializing along the lines of a magazine for the working woman. "It was an audience of 20,000,000," said the last managing editor, "but I couldn't sell the idea to the Board."

Collier's had little to offer in the way of service, and according to *Printer's Ink,* "was almost in direct competition with TV in the fiction-entertainment area." But it was also in direct competition with *Life,* the *Post,* and *Look,* all of which had more aggressive editorial policies. . . .

In this realm the intangibles are considered important. But can rumors kill magazines? Consider the following fact: while both *Collier's* and *Companion* were making gains on newsstands in the latter half of 1956, the advance advertising billing for the first half of 1957 fell off 50 per cent below the figure for the previous year. "We started the uphill climb too late," a *Collier's* editor said. "We were still being evaluated on figures for 1955 and early 1956." *Collier's* newsstand sales had dropped, in 1955, to a low of 550,000. To maintain its position, it would have had to compare favorably with *Look,* in the neighborhood of 900,000. Other magazines were down, too, on newsstands, but the *Collier's* curve was a good deal steeper. . . .

Now, what has this inquest arrived at? It tries to make the point that a large combination of factors—rising costs, inability to command the confidence of enough advertisers, lack of any clear line of development in the editorial personality of the magazine, TV competition, a corporate structure that combined a magazine and bookpublishing venture (with the corresponding danger that a losing situation on the former and a profit situation on the latter would create a strong stockholder's incentive to eliminate the loss)—all these factors are involved with varying degrees of importance. In addition to all this there is perhaps something else. A magazine is like a person.

The sad but true fact is that some people are healthier and more successful than other people. It has also been suggested that magazines have a life cycle, like people: a youth, a middle age, and an old age. Old age came relatively early to *Collier's,* and it died.

Further Resources

BOOKS

Abrahamson, David. *Magazine-Made America: The Cultural Transformation of the Postwar Periodical.* Cresskill, N.J.: Hampton Press, 1996.

Baron, Sara B. "Changing Reality: Collier's Crusade, Conspiracy and The Great American Fraud." Master's thesis, Southwest Texas State University, 1994.

Haining, Peter *The Classic Era of the American Pulp Magazine.* Chicago: Chicago Review Press, 2001.

Harle, Kelly McSpadden. "The Influence of Cubism and its Stylistic Descendants, Futurism and Cubo-Futurism, on Advertising and Graphic Arts in *Collier's: The National Weekly Magazine,* 1905–1930." Master's thesis, Michigan State University, 1992.

Mott, Frank Luther. *A History of American Magazines.* Cambridge, Mass.: Harvard University Press, 1968.

Reed, David. *The Popular Magazine in Britain and the United States, 1880–1960.* Toronto: University of Toronto Press, 1997.

Tebbel, John William, and Mary Ellen Zuckerman. *The Magazine in America, 1741–1990.* New York: Oxford University Press, 1991.

WEBSITES

"Magazine Cover Sequences: *Collier's.*" University of Brighton School of Design. Available online at http://www.adh.brighton.ac.uk/schoolofdesign/MA.COURSE/LMC02.html; website home page: http://www.adh.brighton.ac.uk/schoolofdesign (accessed March 31, 2003).

"Common Sense and *Sputnik*"

Magazine article

By: *Life*

Date: October 21, 1957

Source: "Common Sense and *Sputnik.*" *Life* 43, October 21, 1957, 35. Reprinted in *Voices of the American Past: Documents in U.S. History,* vol. 2. Raymond M. Hyser and J. Chris Arndt, eds. New York: Harcourt Brace, 1995, 200–202.

About the Publication: *Life* magazine was launched in 1936 by Henry Luce, the publisher of *Time* magazine. A weekly news and picture magazine, *Life* was popular for several decades and was best known for its photography. The magazine has been credited with inventing the photo essay. The weekly ceased publication in 1972, but semiannual special editions of *Life* were published until it was re-established as a monthly in 1978. ∎

Introduction

The United States long felt safe due to its geographical isolation from the rest of the world. In 1823, the country issued the Monroe Doctrine, which stated that it would oppose any further colonialism in the Americas on the part of any European power. This policy led many Americans to regard all of North and South America as the domain of the United States. The Monroe Doctrine was reinforced with the idea of Manifest Destiny, which held that the United States was destined to sweep across North America, from the Atlantic to the Pacific Oceans. The America media pushed this idea, keeping it in front of the public. By the 1870s, the United States did extend across the continent, and politicians, newspapers, and writers began to trumpet a new version of Manifest Destiny, which held that America's duty was to spread across the Pacific and trade with Asia.

World War I (1914–1918) saw the first significant American military action abroad, but it was far from U.S. borders. Before World War II (1939–1945), many in the United States advocated an "America first" policy, believing that the nation's first concern should be its own security, and only then should it consider helping those fighting overseas. Some in the media backed this opinion, including many columnists. All of this changed after the Japanese attack on Pearl Harbor.

World War II brought a quantitative leap in weaponry in the form of the atomic bomb. At first, the United States was the only country that had the bomb— and the long-range bombers to deliver it. But in 1949, the Soviet Union exploded its first atomic weapon, and it soon followed that up with the more powerful hydrogen bomb. At first, the USSR still did not have a way to deliver these weapons, and Americans remained confident that the U.S. weapons and technology were superior to those of its Cold War enemy. But that changed on October 4, 1957, when the Soviets launched *Sputnik,* the first man-made satellite to orbit the earth. Americans were afraid that if the Soviets could launch satellites, they could also launch ballistic missiles that could carry nuclear weapons from Europe to the United States.

Significance

The early 1950s Red Scare seemed to lessen for a time after the fall of Joseph McCarthy in 1954, but the launching of *Sputnik* brought the fear back. The alarmist tone of this magazine editorial, published just weeks after the launch, is typical of the media's approach to the event at the time. The writer suggested that the United States had fallen far behind the production of nuclear weapons. Political candidates also embraced this idea and followed it up with discussion of a "missile gap" between the United States and the Soviet Union in the 1960 elections. No such gap existed, but this did not deter politicians and members of the media from discussing it at length—even though the exact missile counts on both sides was classified information. The media coverage helped to pressure Congress to pass increased funding for nuclear weapons, which in turn caused the USSR to build more. The media's alarmist coverage also led a sizable number of people to build expensive bomb shelters in their homes.

The biggest effect of the media's coverage of *Sputnik* was that President John F. Kennedy pledged in 1961 to have a man on the moon by the end of the decade. The United States achieved that goal, but at high cost. Space was converted into another place for the U.S. to compete with the Soviet Union. Thus, the media played a large role in creating the space race and modeling the public's view towards it.

By the end of the 1960s, some writers and filmmakers began to mock the alarmist tone of pieces such as this one. A good example of this is the movie *Dr. Strangelove, Or How I Learned to Stop Worrying and Love the Bomb* (1964).

Primary Source

"Common Sense and *Sputnik*"

SYNOPSIS: This 1957 article, published in *Life* shortly after the launch of *Sputnik.* asserts that the Russians had quickly overtaken the United States in the production of atomic bombs and hydrogen bombs, and were now ahead in Intercontinental Ballistic Missiles (ICBMs). It insists that the United States "cannot lag in weapons against Communism," and links the mission of preserving human freedom with the development of new technology to defeat the USSR.

A young rocketeer named G. Harry Stine who was fired last week by the Martin Company for too volubly belittling the U.S. missile program, made a sharp remark about Sputnik. "This is really and truly 'the shot heard round the world,'" said he. "I wonder what the dead veterans of Lexington and of Korea are thinking."

The Korean veteran may be reminded of those Russian MiGs of 1950, the deadliest but not the first notice we had had that the Russians are not a technologically backward people. It had taken them only four years to break our A-bomb monopoly. It took them nine months to overtake our H-bomb. Now they are apparently ahead of us on intercontinental ballistic missiles. For years no knowledgeable U.S. scientist has had any reason to doubt that his Russian opposite number is at least his equal. It had been doubted only by people—some of them in the Pentagon—who confuse scientific progress with freezer and lipstick output. Sputnik should teach them what the Korean veteran learned the hard way.

The dead Korean veteran may be reminded of other hard military realities. One is that the conflict between freedom and Communism is a long, tiresome and seesaw business in which the apparent lead can change many times. Sputnik is not a weapon, but it has immense military meaning. The propulsive thrust that launched it could launch an ICBM. Right now its coded messages are probably telling Russian weaponeers more about the upper atmosphere in which ICBM must travel and more about target-finding than they knew two weeks ago or than we know yet. But Sputnik's monopoly of outer space will be brief. The U.S. moons that will challenge it are likely to be even more informative—and less secretive, as befits our strategy of alliances.

Korea was a military standoff. The balance of caution that kept that war local and nonatomic has since been frozen into a "balance of terror." The insect analogy first tested in Korea is still the key to such peace as we enjoy: two scorpions in a bottle will claw but not sting each other. Our retaliatory sting is as mortal and deterrent as ever, even when carried in the SAC bombers Khrushchev has prematurely declared obsolete. Sputnik has not broken the bottle, just clouded and swollen it.

The clawing may also not be over. The more heat we turn on our own ICBM program, the less we can afford to neglect preparedness for limited and peripheral warfare. If SAC is not obsolete, neither are the U.S. Marines—or the guerrilla and platoon tactics so heroically learned by 16 nations in Korea. Sputnik surveys a dirty planet.

So much for hard military realities. They are only part of the common sense about Sputnik. In the long run, political realities are more important.

Russia's political prestige has been enormously magnified overnight, but not everywhere and not for long. A Swiss paper credits Sputnik's timeliness with having "virtually saved the 40th anniversary of the October revolution," since the rest of the fare for that event "was so sterile and pitiful that they could hardly expect to spark any enthusiasm even in their own Communist ranks." A Paris paper reminded its readers: "The cost of this satellite is 40 years of deprivations by the Russian people." Said another: "It is easier to make a revolution in the sky than on earth."

Perhaps that is what the dead heroes of Lexington would be thinking. The revolution they began is still a tremendous though unfinished *human* success. But Sputnik will not feed Khrushchev's subjects or cement the crumbling walls of his inhuman empire and irrational economic system. Indeed the failures of Communism have made its political defeat not only a necessary but an increasingly visible goal of U.S. policy.

Instead of changing this goal, Sputnik should remind us of what we ourselves have proved many times from Lexington to the Manhattan Project: that any great human accomplishment demands a consecration of will and a concentration of effort. This is as true of the liberation of men and nations as it is of the conquest of space.

It may seem impious to summon the ghost of the "embattled farmers" of Lexington, with their quaint optimism and simple certitudes, into our complex "age of technological imperialism," as Columbia's dean of engineering calls it. What has the assertion about human liberty heard round the world of 1775 to do with Sputnik?

"Technological imperialism," which draws or forces all human knowledge into the service of the state, is a frightening reality as man's knowledge and power increase. So is the "cultural lag" that abets this imperialism. In the next 20 years our environment may be altered more radically than in the last 200. Yet most living men are still poorer, more ignorant and more alien to scientific ways of thinking in our time than those embattled farmers in theirs. Faced with subtler and more plausible tyrannies than George III ever knew, we inherit from them a revolution that has scarcely begun. And our weapons against this new "technological imperialism" are still the weapons of Lexington: courage and reason.

U.S. foreign policy has developed in a straight line from the assertion of human freedom made at Lexington. It has been generally faithful to that assertion as a universal cause. It has been generally ready to combat and limit freedom's perennial foe, which is any form of uncontrolled power. Early in our brief atomic monopoly we began seeking international methods to control the weapons that could interrupt human history. The key feature of all our plans for controlling these weapons is an inspection system that would invite the confidence, if not guarantee the security, of reasonable men. This quest has been repeatedly rebuffed by the Iron Curtain, whose menacing mysteries inspection would undermine. Last week Henry Cabot Lodge presented still another version of this plan to the U.N., proposing immediate discussions for keeping deadly weapons out of the ionosphere, so that this vast new realm will be used for the "exclusively peaceful and scientific purposes" of the human race.

Commander George Hoover, U.S.N., a veteran of Project Vanguard, remarked last week of Sputnik: "I think this is the first step toward the unification of the peoples of the world, whether they know it or not." These words may or may not be good prophecy, for obviously the common cause is yet to be found. But they surely suggest the right vision of policy for any nation which identifies its own cause, as the U.S. identified its liberty, with the cause of all mankind.

The U.S. cannot lag in weapons against Communism, indeed we must recover our lead to strengthen our hand in seeking a reasonable agreement with Russia that free nations can accept. But while doing so we must gain strength also from our older, grander mission, the one Communism can never share. The mission is to make this world more habitable even while we explore others; and to keep the light of freedom and reason accessible to all our fellow men.

Further Resources

BOOKS

Berlin, Peter, and John Rhea. *Roads to Space: An Oral History of the Soviet Space Program.* Washington, D.C.: Aviation Week Group, 1995.

Dickson, Paul. *"Sputnik": The Shock of the Century.* New York: Walker, 2001.

Diggins, John P. *The Proud Decades: America in War and in Peace, 1941–1960.* New York: Norton, 1998.

Green, Constance McLaughlin, and Milton Lomask. *Vanguard: A History.* Washington: Smithsonian Institution Press, 1971.

Portree, David S. F. *NASA's Origins and the Dawn of the Space Age.* Washington: NASA History Division, 1998.

Reconsidering "Sputnik": Forty Years Since the Soviet Satellite. Springfield, Va: National Aeronautics and Space Administration, 1997.

WEBSITES

Sputnik: The Fortieth Anniversary. Available online at http://www.hq.nasa.gov/office/pao/History/sputnik/; website home page: http://www.hg.nasa.gov (accessed March 25, 2003).

Leave It to Beaver

"A Gift From the Children"

Newspaper article

By: *The New York Times*

Date: December 8, 1957

Source: Golbout, Oscar. "A Gift From the Children." *The New York Times,* December 8, 1957, sec. 2, 14.

"Busy 'Beaver' and His Brother"

Newspaper article

By: *The New York Times*

Date: October 30, 1960

Source: Shepard, Richard F. "Busy 'Beaver' and His Brother." *The New York Times,* October 30, 1960, sec. 2, 15.

About the Publication: Founded in 1850 as *The Daily Times, The New York Times* was originally a relatively ob-

scure local paper. By the early part of the twentieth century, it had grown into a widely known, well-respected news source, and has remained such since. ∎

Introduction

Newspapers were the main form of media in the United States during the nineteenth century. However, even the farthest-reaching newspapers did not reach most of America. Newspapers were primarily a local media and were expected to reflect the influence of that area. Radio changed that somewhat, as some broadcasts were heard nationwide and some stations could reach most of the nation. Movies appeared in the early 1900s, but they were not available every day, even for those with some surplus income. Movie chararacters were generally larger than life, and very few movies were based on everyday events.

The influence of the mass media on the way Americans lived their day-to-day lives increased significantly with the advent of television and the arrival of TV sets in the average home. By the 1940s, television programs were broadcast every week, and by the 1950s these programs were widely watched nationwide. Attention to some programs even changed American living habits, as water usage and phone calls dropped during *I Love Lucy* episodes. People also began to look to television as a source of role models and for information on how to live their lives.

October 4, 1957, saw the premiere of a new television program that portrayed the supposedly average American suburban family living the ideal life. The program, *Leave It to Beaver,* depicted the daily live of the Cleaver family: the father, Ward, who went off to the office in a suit each day; the mother, June, a happy stay-at-home mom and homemaker; and two school-age boys, handsome and sensible Wally and cute and mischievous Theodore, better known as "The Beaver." The series was centered around the comic misadventures of "The Beaver." It became very popular and was produced for six years (until September, 1963); it is still seen in syndication.

Significance

These *The New York Times* articles, published three years apart, demonstrate *Leave It to Beaver*'s widespread popularity in the 1950s. The positive nature of the articles and depiction of the two young stars demonstrates the generally uncritical approach that newspapers took towards television in its early years.

Many people, both at the time and since, have viewed *Leave It to Beaver* as a realistic depiction of suburban American life in the 1950s. There is some truth to this. In broad terms, many suburban families did live their lives like the Cleavers. With few child-care centers and few jobs in suburbia, many suburban women had no choice but to stay at home to care for their children, while their husbands served as the sole breadwinners. Women were also kept out of high-paying jobs, and so staying home was often the most economical measure as well. American society encouraged this lifestyle, in part through TV shows like *Leave It to Beaver*.

The perpetual happiness of June Cleaver, however, did not always reflect reality. Many suburban mothers and homemakers were unsatisfied with their lives, although society made them reluctant to admit it. It was not until the publication of such groundbreaking feminist works as Betty Friedan's *The Feminine Mystique* (1963) that suburban women realized that they were not alone in feeling frustrated as housewives.

Many *Leave It to Beaver* viewers in later decades have assumed that the Cleavers represented the typical family of the 1950s dealing with actual situations faced by average Americans during that period. This, however, is not the case. *Leave It to Beaver* was launched the same day as the Soviet *Sputnik I* satellite, but the word "*Sputnik*" never fell from Ward Cleaver's lips. *Leave It to Beaver* also ignored the whole struggle for civil rights. Most suburbs in the 1950s were monocultural and monochromatic, but the civil rights movement was much more in the news and more widely discussed than is evident on the show.

Viewing *Leave It to Beaver* as "reality TV" leads to a distorted view of history. Not only does it promote a false image of the "innocent" 1950s, but it makes the changes of the 1960s and 1970s seem much more radical then they really were. *Leave It to Beaver* was a successful television show in the 1950s and early 1960s, but did not (and does not) realistically portray American life during this time period.

Primary Source

"A Gift From the Children"

SYNOPSIS: In this article, the two producers of *Leave It to Beaver* talk about the source of some of their ideas for the new show—their own children.

Every parent knows—or should know—his children as a source of affection, concern, tax deductions and pride. At least two fathers in Hollywood, Joe Connelly and Bob Mosher, writer-producers of the "Leave It to Beaver" Columbia Broadcasting System film series, get an added bonus: story material.

Both admit to observing their offspring—not deliberately or intensively, mind you—for incidents, behavior patterns and the speech habits of the young.

"The sort of chopped up dialogue we give to Beaver to speak," Mr. Connelly said last week, "is straight from my 8-year-old, Ricky. Things like "most 'got th' 'all' or "ginners yo-yo,' which translated mean 'I almost forgot the ball' and 'beginners yo-yo.'"

The role of Beaver is played by Jerry Mathers, 8 years old. Tony Dow, 12, portrays his brother.

Mr. Connelly is more blessed quantitatively speaking, than Mr. Mosher. He has six children—"even-Steven on the gender"—ranging from 9 months to 14 years. Mr. Mosher is more restrained parentally with two teen-agers, 12 and 14, Patty and Bobby.

Haircut

A recent program had Beaver getting hold of a pair of scissors and embarking on a do-it-yourself haircut.

"That was my Bobby not too many years ago," Mr. Mosher grinned. "It seems funny now, but it didn't then since he did it on the day of his school play in which he was to be an angel. The 'angel' wore a stocking cap for his celestial performance."

It was suggested to the writers that perhaps the time would come when one of the youngsters would watch their fathers' show and suspect more than imaginary connections between screen happenings and home incidents. Both grinned widely.

"It already has," said Mr. Connelly, "and we've only had three shows on the air. In the first one Tony Dow combs his hair very deliberately. Well, my oldest Jay, 14, is just at the point where hair-combing is important. I think that scene embarrassed him. He made the connection, but then he's just old enough to normally resent me anyway."

"In that same sequence," Mr. Mosher contributed, "where Beaver and Tony fake taking a bath? My kids watched it and they were very, very quiet."

Familiar

As the two are no strangers to the shenanigans of kids so too are they quite familiar with the entertainment business. They have been working as a team since leaving the J. Walter Thompson advertising agency fifteen years ago in New York. After stints writing the old Edgar Bergen, Frank Morgan and Phil Harris radio shows, they embarked on their longest single engagement: ten years of writing radio and television versions of "Amos n' Andy." They have credits on some 1,200 scripts of that series. And they still write a radio version. Their last TV se-

Jerry Mathers (left) and Tony Dow play brothers Wally and Theodore "Beaver" Cleaver on the television program "Leave it to Beaver." **THE KOBAL COLLECTION. REPRODUCED BY PERMISSION.**

ries was the Ray Millard anthology program. After that job, the pair agreed to concentrate on writing "things we know about."

"One day while driving one of my boys to his parochial school, we discovered an interesting situation there," Mr. Connelly recalled. "We developed it into an original script titled 'The Private War of Major Benson.'" The theatrical feature earned them an Academy Award nomination last year.

This "things we know about" philosophy led to the "Beaver" series, which Remington Rand is sponsoring. The two own 50 per cent of the program with Gomalco Productions taking the other half. Gomalco is owned by George Gobel, the comedian, and David P. O'Malley. The whole project, with the exception of financing, according to the writing team, was put together by the Music Corporation of America, asserted to be the Mount Everest of talent agencies.

Problem

"Beaver" appears to be one of the least "shaky" shows of this season. In the event that it survives in the jungle warfare of network programming competition, it seems destined to run into the problem of the children outgrowing their parts. What happens then?

"Nothing," Mr. Connelly said. "Kids grow up, and since we are telling stories about kids and a family, they'll grow up, too."

The collaborators report that finding the right child consists mainly of "looking at hundreds of kids, most of whom are wiseguy little professionals with screwy haircuts. You just wait until a 'real' one walks in, and you know he's it. That's just what happened with Jerry. When he walked in with his mother we just looked at each other and we knew he was Beaver. He was so 'real' he fidgeted through the interview and at the end said 'I gotta go now. Got a Cub Scout meeting.'"

Primary Source

"Busy 'Beaver' and His Brother"

> **SYNOPSIS:** This article is an affectionate look at *Leave it to Beaver*'s two young stars, Jerry Mathers and Tony Dow. It reveals the general fondness for the actors in the popular show, which was then in its fourth season.

When "Leave It to Beaver," a sturdy TV vehicle that recounts the havoc wrought on an otherwise normal household by two lively boys, materializes on Channel 7 Saturdays at 8:30 P.M. there are two youngsters who tune out in search of the competition on other stations.

The two are TV fans as well as vested interests in "Beaver." Their names are Jerry Mathers, who plays the 12–year–old mischief maker of the title role and Tony Dow, his 15–year–old brother in the series. The boys stopped over in New York during a promotional swing around the country and explained why they don't bother to see themselves immortalized before the nation by the American Broadcasting Company.

Jerry, with an earnestness matched only by a manifestation of commendable and normal discomfort of a boy being subjected to questions by an adult who should know better, said, "Well, I know what's going to happen. When you've worked on the show, there's no surprise."

Tony, a handsome teen-ager with an athletic physique, commented that he felt about the same as his junior partner. They both like television but, unlike adult performers who unabashedly leap at the chance to see how they come off in tape or film, they are not particularly interested in electronic narcissism.

At the start of their fourth season, the boys see no signs of any slack in "Beaver." They have aged in three years and the scripts have been appropriately advanced in years to keep up with them. Jerry has grown, in his opinion, not so "silly" and Tony is taking an interest in girls.

Tony and Jerry have every intention of keeping on in show business as long as they can. Of course, Jerry has rather mature ideas on what sidelines may be profitably pursued. "Property," he summed it up. "I want to put my money in property, it's the best thing to make you money."

Future

But as far as acting is concerned, the 12–year–old has a feeling for gangster productions. Either side of the law will do; he enjoys watching underworld exploits on TV and film.

The question of the future having been disposed of, the boys discussed their present chores on "Beaver." One installment is made each week. The boys work closely with the writers, Joe Connelly and Bob Mosher, and the various directors.

"I memorize the script," Jerry said, as Tony, the shy one nodded in assent. "But I have to ask them sometimes how they want me to play the part. Sometimes I make little changes in a word or so and nobody minds."

Jerry divulged that he is studying Latin. "With Latin, you can learn almost any other language," he explained with the authority of an academician. With all their secrets thus disclosed, it was announced that the interview was over and that they were free to go on their way. Both made for the exit, Tony with an adult regard for leave-taking civilities, and Jerry with the headlong, undisguised wholesome relief of a kid who is finally let out of school.

Further Resources

BOOKS

Applebaum, Irwyn. *The World According to Beaver.* New York: Bantam Books, 1984.

Bank, Fred, and Gib Twyman. *Call Me Lumpy: My Leave It to Beaver Days and Other Wild Hollywood Life.* Lenexa, Kans.: Addax Publishing Group, 1997.

Jacobs, Will, and Gerard Jones. *The Beaver Papers: The Story of the "Lost Season."* New York: Crown Publishers, 1983.

Mathers, Jerry, and Herb Fagen. *—And Jerry Mathers as "the Beaver."* New York: Berkley Boulevard, 1998.

Staten, Vince. *Golly, Wally: The Story of "Leave It to Beaver."* New York: Crown Publishers, 1983.

PERIODICALS

Fuller, May Lou. "Today's Demographics Don't Leave It to Beaver. We're Not the Cleavers Anymore." *The Education Digest,* vol. 58, no. 6, February 1993, 54.

Woods, John. "'Leave It to Beaver' Was Not a Documentary: What Educators Need to Know About the American Family." *American Secondary Education,* vol. 24, no. 1, 1995, 3.

WEBSITES

LITB.com: The First Leave It to Beaver Website. Available online at http://www.litb.com/ (accessed March 19, 2003).

The Huntley-Brinkley Report

"Mileage in Morality"

Newspaper article

By: Robert Lewis Shayon

Date: December 28, 1957

Source: Shayon, Robert Lewis. "Mileage in Morality." *The Saturday Review,* December 28, 1957, 24.

About the Author: Robert Lewis Shayon was a radio and TV critic for *The Saturday Review* from 1950–1970 and the *Christian Science Monitor* from 1950–1951. He also wrote TV scripts, and was a producer and director for CBS in the 1940s and NBC in the 1950s and 1960s.

"The Evening Duet"

Magazine article

By: *Time*

Date: October 19, 1959

Source: "The Evening Duet." *Time,* October 19, 1959, 92.

About the Publication: *Time* was founded in 1923 by Henry Luce. It quickly became one of America's most widely read news magazines, remaining popular into the twenty-first century. ■

Introduction

Early in American history, if one wanted to get a point across, or if there was news to be spread, one either used the town crier or printed a pamphlet. Following pamphlets, and still well before the American Revolution, came newspapers. Newspapers did not immediately supplant pamphlets, but the two occupied the media arena side by side. Newspapers became, over time, "the" way to get the news. In the early 20th century came the rise of radio, with the added benefit of being "live." Newspapers still had a strong hold on the news, though. In the 1930s and 1940s, papers faced competition from movie theaters, as many films were preceeded by a newsreel.

In the 1950s, television news became another challenge to newspapers. Television had been around during the 1940s, but most people could not afford TV sets before the 1950s. As TVs entered more and more American homes, the national networks added news to their daily lineups in the form of news specials and spot news coverage. The first network to introduce a daily newscast was NBC, which in 1956 introduced the the fifteen-minute *Huntley-Brinkley Report,* featuring Chet Huntley reporting from New York and David Brinkley reporting from Washington, D.C., every evening.

Significance

Both veteran print and broadcast journalists, Huntley and Brinkley brought television news up to the standard of newspaper news and helped to solidify TV as a major news source and a challenger to the print medium.

Part of the appeal of the team is noted in Robert Lewis Shaydon's December 28, 1957, article "Mileage in Morality." Shaydon wrote of the "morality" of Chet Huntley and David Brinkley, pointing out that they presented more than just the facts in their report, revealing their values through their tone of voice, expressions, and selection of news stories. As *Time* magazine noted in 1959, no other major newscast had received more awards or tried the *Huntley-Brinkley Report*'s distinctive "formula:" two professional newsmen from two cities working as equals. Both articles reflect the groundbreaking nature of the *Huntley-Brinkley Report.*

Huntley and Brinkley were the top news team until the middle 1960s, when Walter Cronkite became the nation's favorite newsman. The *Huntley-Brinkley News Report* remained on the air until 1970, when Huntley retired. Brinkley continued to worked with NBC until 1981.

One aspect of television newscasts that has remained virtually unchanged from the debut of the Huntley-Brinkley team until the present is the dominance of men in the newsroom. To this day, almost all national TV news anchors are men. Connie Chung was hired in the 1980s by CBS, but soon was moved out of the news chair. Women have served as replacement anchors, have had their own news specials and news shows, but have not been anchors on a regular basis on the major networks' nightly newscasts.

In addition to nightly newscasts, which have been aired ever since the Huntley-Brinkley show was launched, the major networks have added news-focused "television magazines," such as *60 Minutes,* and have started programs—such as *Dateline NBC, 48 hours,* and *Primetime*—which focus on investigative journalism. All-news cable television channels were started with the Cable News Network (CNN) in 1980 and have proliferated. And through it all, newspapers and radio have continued to play their roles as important news sources. Thus, the news field is more fractured than ever, and Americans have more sources of news and information than ever before.

Primary Source

"Mileage in Morality"

> **SYNOPSIS:** In this 1957 article, noted radio and TV critic Robert Lewis Shayon discusses what makes the *Huntley-Brinkley News Report,* then just a year old, different from any other television news program.

What I like most about the fairly new (one year old) Chet Huntley-David Brinkley NBC-TV team of newscasters is that they are moralists.

Quincy Howe, one of the classic "commentators" of broadcasting, writing in *SR* several weeks ago, puzzled over the absence of newsmen-in-depth in the contemporary generation. The answer should have been obvious to historian Howe: this has been predominantly an amoral generation. All the more surprising that NBC news (traditionally something less than bold in the area of public affairs) should have produced Huntley and Brinkley. The former is the elder of the two, reared in the old CBS news department, and therefore easier to explain as a "moralizer." How Brinkley, much younger, came by his oldtime spirit is a mystery. In any case, five nights a week on NBC-TV Huntley from New York and Brinkley from Washington deliver a fifteen-minute capsule of news which has rapidly become the most attractive regular package of TV journalism on the air.

This is not due to any outstanding departure from the conventional form of the quarter-hour news show. True, Huntley is pushing at the traditional limits for direct, on-camera talk. He has reached a record four-and-a-half minutes without films and hopes to go even farther with unrelieved "analysis." But, otherwise, the newscasts are made up of the familiar short newsreel clips plus unadorned expository thrusts at the many stories which clamor for attention in a day's history. What distinguishes "Chet" and "David" (they address each other thus in their inter-city duet) is their propensity to introduce, every now and then, a revelatory footnote to the mere facts.

Try as they may to present the mask of neutrality (Huntley has been accused of having an over-solemn poker-face and Brinkley of undisguised boredom) the tones of their voices, ironies on their lips, and subtleties in their eyes betray their values—not to speak of the selectivity in their news items. Huntley, one recent wild Sputnik day, encouraged his viewers with a report of the Navy's enthusiasm over an Arctic cruise of its atomic submarine, *Nautilus*. Navy scientists said they'd gained 100 times more information from this trip than in all previous air or surface explorations. Commented Chet: "The Russians may be ahead in space exploration, but apparently we know more about the bottom of the Arctic Ocean than anyone else in the world." Again, reporting on an anniversary Fascist pilgrimage to Mussolini's grave in Predappio, Italy, Huntley concluded: "Despite the fact that it is now twelve years since Mussolini was killed, trains still run on time in Italy. But, as you saw, not many of them run to Predappio." Brinkley enjoys closing his nightly Washington contributions with provocative items. Example: "And, finally: in Charlotte, North Carolina, the Knights of the Ku Klux Klan announced a Saturday night rally and cross-burning . . . and a discussion of the question: 'What shall we do with Ike'?"

Wry commentary is merely the lighter side of this NBC television team's style. Huntley, in "Outlook," his regular week-end half-hour feature news program, is comparable to Murrow for his concern in getting the "non-consensus" views on vital stories in the headlines. Recently he interviewed Trevor Garner, the former Assistant Secretary of the Air Force for research and development who resigned his post, criticizing the Defense Department's handling of our missile and rocket program. Huntley's introduction, choice of questions, and Garner's replies bristled with challenge. "America's mental Maginot line no longer exists," said the newsman. "We will either be led to restore our position—or we will react the way the French did." Then Huntley noted one already significant reaction. "The live creature in the second satellite," he said, "is a female husky dog. The wire services are supplying pictures of the dog, which they call 'appealing pooch shots'."

On the same telecast John Chancellor, an NBC Chicago colleague, interviewed Carl Lindegren, professor of genetics at Southern Illinois University, whose celebrated young "genius" assistant, Ernest Shult, was drafted into the Army as a clerk-typist. Discussing "anti-intellectualism" in this country, Professor Lindegren hit orthodoxy on the head when he said that "utility and science are, generally speaking, more or less conflicting concepts. . . . Scientific achievements involved the development of new concepts—a new way of looking at life. . . . It's the change in concept which is the essence of perfect science." Concluded Editor Huntley: "Whether we are

Chet Huntley (right) and David Brinkley, hosts of *The Huntley-Brinkley Report*, an NBC news program, pose in front of the Capitol Building. ARCHIVE PHOTOS. REPRODUCED BY PERMISSION.

a mature enough people to allow a scientist to search for truth and beauty, and support him in that search . . . is somewhat less than certain. . . . When most Americans agree that there is a connection between Ernest Shult typing Army training reports and the Russian lead in earth satellites, that day the first step will have been taken."

An even happier note is the apparent success of the new NBC news maturity. Mr. Huntley reports that his superiors are "delighted" with the progress and that there is no front-office interference with the department's handling of the news as it sees it. There is even a sponsor, Ronson's Lighters, two nights a week (perhaps soon a third). Ronson is reported to have switched from Perry Como to the NBC news— perhaps the eggheads are getting sex-appeal, after all. The slippery rating situation for Huntley-Brinkley is good, showing that, on certain spotty checks, NBC is running several points ahead of CBS and ABC in evening news programs. Even members of Congress, polled blindly on "Which are your favorite news commentators?" gave the lead by four points to "Chet and David." All of which suggests that maybe there's still some mileage left in morality.

Primary Source

"The Evening Duet"

> **SYNOPSIS:** This *Time* magazine article provides biographical information about Chet Huntley and David Brinkley and examines the novel and successful format of *Huntley-Brinkley News Report,* which by 1959 had become the second-most-watched and the most-honored newscast in America.

Five nights a week, around dinnertime, the TV sets in some 3,916,000 U.S. homes [figure based on the Nielsen rating.] are tuned to a 15-minute news program, NBC's *Huntley-Brinkley Report.* Although CBS's Doug Edwards commands a slightly larger audience, no other television newscast has collected more major awards (seven in all) or has tried *Report's* distinctive formula: two newscasters of equal rank, working from different cities as a team.

The NBC evening duet by Chester Robert Huntley (New York) and David McClure Brinkley (Washington) presents the news with unusual (for TV) restraint: its stars are both unexcitable men who seldom pontificate but project an air of unassuming authority and easy informality. "I'm a newsman using TV as my special medium," says Chet Huntley. The key to their success is the fact that they are pros (both have spent most of their working lives as newsmen of the air, with early stints on newspapers) dedicated to the principle that news is not show business.

With Nobody Watching

As partners, the stars of the *Huntley-Brinkley Report* are complementary rather than competitive—an unusual circumstance in the jealously competitive TV club. Huntley, 47, is the straight man, tall (6 ft. 1 in.), saturninely handsome, serious, inclined to take a panoramic view of the news, more inclined to pundit. This comes out most in his own Sunday show. *Time: Present—Chet Huntley Reporting,* in which he explores predominantly heavy subjects: integration, world trade, public education. A graduate of Western broadcasting (Seattle, Los Angeles), he was brought East by NBC in 1956 to do the Sunday show, is one of TV's best-paid newsmen (total annual income: $100,000).

The other half of the team, David Brinkley, 39, who has never lost all of his North Carolina drawl or his essentially mischievous disposition, provides the show's seasoning. Viewers have learned to rely on frequent injections of his subtle and astringent wit

and to watch for the point of his sharp needle—often delivered with a squirming body English that is as familiar a Brinkley trademark as his lopsided smile. A onetime United Press staffer, he began doing TV newscasts in Washington in 1943, when there were only a few hundred sets in the city ("I had a chance to learn while nobody was watching"), and still claims to be astonished at his own success ("TV grew up, and I happened to be standing there"). He does some specials in addition to the show with Huntley, writes all of his own material, remembers when TV brought him $60 a week, now collects $75,000 a year.

"People Paid Attention"

The Huntley-Brinkley combination is the product of pure chance. In 1956, planning coverage of the national party conventions, NBC decided to send in some fresh faces, dispatched Huntley from New York and Brinkley from Washington, expecting them to spell each other. They made it a team operation, brought off the assignment so handsomely that NBC decided to make them a habit. (Said Brinkley wryly of this sudden prominence: "I did what I'd been doing for years, but people paid attention.") In October 1956, Huntley and Brinkley—who had not even met before their paths crossed at the conventions—went on the air with the two-headed, 15-minute newscast, have been there ever since.

Not until they go on the air does either know what the other will say; their story assignments must be written—and in some cases reported and filmed—in the hours just before show time. The news budget is restricted to five or six items, and which man takes the lead depends entirely on whether the best story is in Huntley's territory or Brinkley's. What they turn out ranks high not only with Nielsen but also with official Washington. Asked by a survey agency last August to name their favorite news program, members of Congress gave *Huntley-Brinkley Report* top rank (32.8% *v.* 16.1% for the second choice, ABC's John Daly). In a personal note, Viewer Dwight Eisenhower told Huntley that his telecasts in advance of the Khrushchev visit were a major factor in determining the official U.S. approach.

Another memorable letter in their heavy fan mail came from a woman whose devotion made them wince. She and her husband were so attached to the show; she said, that when they went to sleep at night, they always used the Huntley-Brinkley sign-off, one of them saying "Good night, Chet," and the other replying, "Good night, David."

Further Resources

BOOKS

Beaubien, Michael P., and John S. Wyeth. *Views on the News: The Media and Public Opinion.* New York: New York University Press, 1994.

Bliss, Edward. *Now the News: The Story of Broadcast Journalism.* New York: Columbia University Press, 1991.

Brinkley, David. *David Brinkley: 11 Presidents, 4 Wars, 22 Political Conventions, 1 Moon Landing, 3 Assassinations, 2,000 Weeks of News and Other Stuff on Television and 18 years of Growing Up in North Carolina.* New York: A. A. Knopf, 1995.

Huntley, Chet. *The Generous Years: Remembrances of a Frontier Boyhood.* New York: Random House, 1968.

WEBSITES

"Brinkley, David. U.S. Broadcast Journalist." The Museum of Broadcast Communications. Available online at http://www.museum.tv/archives/etv/B/htmlB/brinkleydav/brinkleydav.htm; website home page http://www.museum.tv (accessed March 19, 2003).

"Huntley, Chet. U.S. Broadcast Journalist." The Museum of Broadcast Communications. Available online at http://www.museum.tv/archives/etv/H/htmlH/huntleychet/huntleychet.htm; website home page http://www.museum.tv (accessed March 19, 2003).

AUDIO AND VISUAL MEDIA

Chancellor, John, et. al. *Tributes to Chet Huntley on the Occasion of his Death.* University of Montana. Audiotape, 1974.

David Brinkley: A Reporter's Life. Biography. A&E Home Video. VHS, 1996.

Communists in the Media

"9 More in Entertainment World Refuse to Answer on Red Ties"

Newspaper article

By: *The New York Times*

Date: June 20, 1958

Source: Porter, Russell. "9 More in Entertainment World Refuse to Answer on Red Ties" *The New York Times,* June 20, 1958, 1, 12.

"Statements on Dubin Case"

Newspaper article

By: *The New York Times*

Date: June 20, 1958

Source: "Statements on Dubin Case." *The New York Times,* June 20, 1958, 12.

About the Publication: Founded in 1850 as *The Daily Times, The New York Times* was originally a relatively ob-

scure local paper. However, by the early part of the twentieth century, it had grown into a widely known and well-respected news source, and remained so into the twenty-first century. ∎

Introduction

In the late 1940s and into the 1950s, television began to compete with radio and newspapers as America's most popular source of news and entertainment. During that same time period, the United States began to compete with the Soviet Union for world pre-eminence. These two countries had been wary allies during World War II (1939–1945), but difficulties during that war and misunderstandings at the war's end created greater amounts of tension. These stresses mushroomed into what became known as the Cold War, a political, economic, and ideological struggle that would last for decades and involve the United States in several military conflicts, including the Vietnam War, in an attempt to stifle communism.

One aspect of the Cold War was a fear of communists within the United States working to undermine the country or even overthrow the government. Many government investigations were launched to uncover these supposed threats. The fact that hunting for communists was a good way for politicians to get in the news and please conservative voters encouraged their investigations to be lengthy and wide-ranging.

The news and entertainment industry was one of the major targets in the hunt for communists. The nominal concern was that communists in the industry would use its power over what Americans saw and read to subtly influence them towards communism. The concern was not just whether one still had loyalties with communism, however, but whether one had ever had any connection with communism. People called before government committees such as the House Un-American Activities Committee (HUAC) were often asked, "Are you now or have you ever been a member of the Communist Party?"

Some Americans had in fact been communists or openly sympathetic with their views in the past, especially during the 1940s when the Soviet Union was America's ally against Nazi Germany. When asked about their past association with communism, they faced a difficult choice. If they answered yes, then ostracization and possibly deportation or imprisonment might occur. Even if they avoided this, they would certainly be asked to "name names" of other party members and thus ruin other people's lives. If they lied and answered no, they would be in even worse trouble if their lie could later be demonstrated, as they would then face perjury charges. Faced with these options, many made a third choice: to "plead the Fifth" (Amendment) and refuse to answer questions on the grounds it might incriminate themselves.

Even this choice often led to contempt charges, and could have a disastrous effect on one's professional and social life, as few would associate with a known or supposed communist. As the first news article, which appeared in *The New York Times* on June 20, 1958, reports, Joseph Papp, founder of the New York Shakespeare Festival, was fired from his job as a television stage manager for CBS for his refusal to state whether or not he had ever been a Communist Party member. Days earlier, Charles S. Dubin, a freelance television direction who worked for NBC, lost his job with the network for refusing to answer the HUAC's questions.

Significance

It was not just television stations that were affected by the House Un-American Activities Committee. Several famous film directors and stars refused to cooperate with HUAC and were placed on a "blacklist" by Hollywood, which meant that studios were supposed to refuse to hire them. Some worked under aliases, but most had to leave the country or switch professions. The New York Civil Liberties Union statement that appeared in *The New York Times* argued that the only thing that mattered was whether Dubin could perform his job. But during the Cold War all things with any taint of communism were feared. The best reflection of the times is this anonymous statement made by an American citizen: "I'm not quite sure what Communism is, but there had better not be any of it in Washington." There were those in the television and film industries—not to mention the U.S. government—who wanted to take that idea one step further and eliminate any trace of communism, whatever it was, from the nation.

Primary Source

"9 More in Entertainment World Refuse to Answer on Red Ties"

SYNOPSIS: This news story, which appeared on the front page of *The New York Times* on June 20, 1958, reports on the people brought before the House Un-American Activities Committee and their refusals to testify.

Five witnesses from the entertainment world refused to tell Congressional investigators yesterday whether they were members of the Communist party. Four others declined to say whether they formerly had been members.

The latter group included Joseph Papp, founder and producer of the New York Shakespeare Festival and a television stage manager for the Columbia Broadcasting System, and James D. Proctor, press agent for Kermit Bloomgarden, Broadway theatrical producer.

C. B. S. dismissed Mr. Papp after he had testified. "The circumstances surrounding the case of Mr. Papp are such that we have decided to dismiss him from our employment," the company said.

The witnesses appeared at a public hearing of a subcommittee of the House Committee on Un-American Activities at the United States Court House in Foley Square.

Yesterday's hearing brought to a close a two-day session at which seventeen witnesses from the entertainment world and a former Communist official refused to testify about Communist activities.

Mr. Papp was the second television figure to lose his job after testifying. On Wednesday Charles S. Dubin, director of the quiz program "Twenty-One" on the National Broadcasting Company network, refused to say whether he had formerly been a member of the Communist party.

N. B. C. thereupon declared him "unacceptable" on its future programs. Yesterday N. B. C. was criticized for this action by George E. Rundquist, executive director of the New York Civil Liberties Union. He said it was "an indefensible capitulation" to the committee.

The Workers Defense League also protested Mr. Dubin's dismissal by N. B. C.

A third television change as a result of the hearings was announced by Ed Sullivan for his C. B. S. show a week from Sunday night. He said Arthur Lief, American guest conductor for the Moiseyev Russian dance company, who had been booked to conduct, would not be present when the company appeared on the show. Mr. Lief refused to tell the subcommittee on Wednesday whether he was a member of the Communist party.

Mr. Papp denied current membership in the party but refused to say whether he had been a member at any time before February, 1955.

He was one of several witnesses who refused to say whether they had knowingly allowed their names, talents, prestige and glamour to be used to promote Communist fronts and projects.

Mr. Papp said one of the C. B. S. shows he had worked on was "I've Got a Secret." At C. B. S. it was said he had been a "floor manager," relaying the director's instructions to actors, sound technicians and camera men.

The New York Shakespeare Festival is a non-profit, tax-exempt organization with a state educational charter and free use of city property and facilities for free performances in Central Park and elsewhere, Mr. Papp testified.

Mr. Papp said he had made tape recordings for Voice of America overseas broadcasts, but refused to say whether he had told the State Department whether he had ever been a Communist. The United States Information agency, which operates the Voice of America, said it never had employed Mr. Papp, but he had been interviewed about a Shakespeare Festival for tape recordings.

Mr. Proctor denied current party membership, but refused to say whether he had been a member as recently as Tuesday. He was one of several witnesses who invoked the Fifth Amendment against self-incrimination.

Another witness, Richard Sasuly, a writer, refused to say whether he was a propagandist for the Communist party under the name of Alex Furth or whether he had been a Communist propaganda agent for ten years under various names.

Benjamin Steinberg, violinist in "The Music Man" orchestra, refused to say whether he was a member of the Communist party. He said he was also an assistant conductor and "outside contractor," who helped hire musicians for Broadway shows. He refused to say whether the Communist party had given him "recommendations" on persons to hire and not to hire.

Horace Grennell of South Orange, N. J., refused to say whether he was a member of the party or was president of Young People's Records.

Irwin Silber, press agent for Avon Publications, publisher of pocket books, refused to tell the committee whether he was a member of the party, but told reporters he was not.

Paul Villard, musician and singer, and Leon Portnoy, Brooklyn music teacher, also refused to say whether they were party members. Clifford Carpenter, actor in "Sunrise at Campobello," denied present membership, but refused to say whether he had been a member in the last five years.

Mr. Sullivan said Samson Galperin, the Russian conductor of the Moiseyev troupe, would take Mr. Lief's place on the June 29 television show.

A spokesman for Sol Hurok, under whose auspices the Russian dancers are touring the country, declared that "Mr. Lief never had been scheduled to conduct on the television show." Mr. Sullivan, however, insisted that Mr. Lief had been booked. He

CBS stage manager Joseph Papp (right) takes the Fifth Amendment at the House hearings on un-American activities. CBS fired him as a result of his refusal to testify, June 20, 1958. © BETTMANN/CORBIS. REPRODUCED BY PERMISSION.

said he had informed Mr. Hurok of his decision to drop Mr. Lief with the comment, "I don't want him in the theatre."

Mr. Sullivan added that the decision to drop Mr. Lief was his own and that he had received no request for such action from C. B. S. or from the sponsors of the program, the Eastman Kodak Company and Mercury dealers.

Primary Source

"Statements on Dubin Case"

SYNOPSIS: *The New York Times* reprinted two statements on NBC's dismissal of freelance director Charles Dubin. NBC's statement notes that it does not employ any communists and that Dubin's refusal to answer HUAC questions was "unacceptable." A statement by the New York Civil Liberties Union criticizes NBC for kowtowing to HUAC and dismissing Dubin for anything other than his job performance.

N. B. C. Statement

The National Broadcasting Company does not knowingly employ Communists nor permit their employment on programs broadcast over its facilities. Persons who refuse to testify as to their present or past affiliation with the Communist party render themselves unacceptable as regular employes on N. B. C. programs.

The further use on N. B. C. programs of Charles Dubin, who refused to answer certain questions in his appearance before the House Un-American Activities Committee, is therefore unacceptable to N. B. C.

Mr. Dubin is not an employe of N. B. C. but is a freelance director currently employed by several program packagers whose programs are broadcast over N. B. C. facilities. We are notifying these packagers of our decision.

C. L. U. Statement

N. B. C.'s action shows no regard for common sense or fair play and can only help preserve McCarthyism. The summary dismissal of Mr. Dubin as director of the quiz show "Twenty One" and other programs revives the senseless harassment of an individual merely because of his political views.

The biggest money winner on a quiz program would be stumped by the question of how national security could be endangered by Mr. Dubin's continued employment as director of "Twenty One," regardless of his past—or even present—political affiliation.

The most dangerous threat to civil liberties in recent years has been the widespread investigation by Congress into the political lives of private citizens, often including past associations which have no bearing today on national security.

N. B. C. shows no understanding of the United States Supreme Court's decisions upholding the Constitutional protection of the Fifth Amendment, nor the high court's Watkins decision definitely curbing the powers of the House committee to probe a person's political associations.

Rather, it shows total disregard for the importance of maintaining our Constitutional liberties.

N. B. C. should have been guided by one question—Mr. Dubin's competence in his job. His dismissal by N. B. C. is an indefensible capitulation to the House Committee on Un-American Activities.

Further Resources

BOOKS
Fried, Richard M. *Nightmare in Red: The McCarthy Era in Perspective.* New York: Oxford University Press, 1990.

Herman, Arthur. *Joseph McCarthy: Reexamining the Life and Legacy of America's Most Hated Senator.* New York: Free Press, 2000.

Navasky, Victor S. *Naming Names.* New York: Viking Press, 1980.

Rogin, Michael Paul. *The Intellectuals and McCarthy: The Radical Specter.* Cambridge, Mass.: M.I.T. Press, 1967.

Schrecker, Ellen. *Many Are the Crimes: McCarthyism in America.* Boston: Little, Brown, 1998.

PERIODICALS
Robbins, Louise S. "The Overseas Libraries Controversy and the Freedom to Read: U.S. Librarians and Publishers Confront Joseph McCarthy." *Libraries & Culture* 36, no. 1, 2001, 27–39.

Theoharis, Athan. "Chasing Spies: How the FBI Failed in Counterintelligence But Promoted the Politics of McCarthyism in the Cold War Years." *Sage Public Administration Abstracts* 29, no. 2, 2002, 157–304.

WEBSITES
HUAC. *Spartacus Educational.* Available online at http://www.spartacus.schoolnet.co.uk/USAhuac.htm; website home page: http://www.spartacus.schoolnet.co.uk (accessed March 27, 2003).

"Ed Sullivan—Ten Years of TV"

Newspaper article

By: John P. Shanley

Date: June 22, 1958

Source: Shanley, John P. "Ed Sullivan—Ten Years of TV." *The New York Times,* June 22, 1958. sec. 2, 11.

About the Author: John P. Shanley (1950–), popular playwright and screenwriter, grew up in the Bronx where he encountered some of the rough-and-tough types of characters found in his plays. His dramas feature eccentric, working-class characters and explosive dialogue. *Moonstruck,* Shanley's first produced screenplay, was a surprise hit and won an Academy Award for best original screenplay. *Joe versus the Volcano* marked Shanley's film directing debut. He also wrote screenplays based on novels and several televisions scripts. ∎

Introduction

The early entertainment and news in America came from the newspapers, which had existed since colonial times. Newspapers boomed in the late 1800s, as paper costs dropped and readership surged because many in the middle class had much more leisure time. The news and information presented in newspapers was mostly local; even though national news syndicates existed, local editors controlled what went into each paper. The introduction of radio gave Americans a more immediate source of news and entertainment, but in its early years, much of what was heard on the radio was still quite local.

In the late 1940s, national television broadcasts introduced nationwide entertainment to the United States. There were only three national channels: NBC, CBS and ABC. Ed Sullivan's variety show, at first called *Toast of the Town,* went on the air in 1948. As with many early television shows, it drew on radio for its concept and format. Variety shows had long been a staple of radio entertainment.

Sullivan's show became quite successful. Although Ed Sullivan himself was not a very skilled host, he was able to attract a wide variety of first-class performers. In 1955, the name of his show was changed to *The Ed Sullivan Show,* and in 1958, Sullivan celebrated "Ten Years of TV."

Significance

At the time this *New York Times* article was written in 1958, the ten-year-old *The Ed Sullivan Show* was the third most popular show on TV. The variety show was quite influential in the world of entertainment and helped introduce many performers to mainstream America. For example, Elvis Presley was well known before appearing on *Ed Sullivan Show* in 1956, but the show served as a stamp of approval, helping to popularize his music throughout the country.

The article serves as a good overview of the *Ed Sullivan Show*'s first decade. Of particular interest is its coverage of the various controversies the show caused, which provides insight into what was considered acceptable on television—and in American society in general—in the 1950s.

The most well-known controversy was the one that surrounded the appearances of Elvis Presley on the *Ed Sullivan Show* in 1956. Presley appeared on the show three times, to much public outcry. During his third appearance the camera would only shoot him from the waist up because of his suggestive dancing. Compared with what is regularly shown today on MTV, Elvis was quite tame. In the article, Sullivan acknowledged the protests that the Presley appearances caused, but also defended his audience of Elvis fans as "nice kids from good homes" who were "not the Dick Clark rabble." Of course, Dick Clark also screened his audience to make sure that it was presentable.

The article also alludes to a controversy concerning actress Ingrid Bergman. In response to a flood of viewer letters, her scheduled appearance on the show was cancelled. Bergman was considered a controversial figure at the time because she had left her husband some seven years earlier to marry another man. In the 1950s, both television performers and audiences were expected to conform to society's ideas of propriety.

Ed Sullivan went off the air in 1971, having enjoyed one of the longer runs for any performer on one TV show. While the variety show format, which Sullivan exploited so successfully, remained popular into the 1970s, it has since lost favor among U.S. viewers. The closest thing to a TV variety show in the early twenty-first century is late-night television, with shows such as NBC's *The Tonight Show* and CBS's *Late Night with David Letterman.*

Primary Source

"Ed Sullivan—Ten Years of TV"

SYNOPSIS: This article, which appeared in the June 22, 1958, issue of *The New York Times,* discusses the decade-long success of the *Ed Sullivan Show.* As the article points out, Sullivan was far from a polished performer, but his ability to attract outstanding artists—and large TV audiences—was exceptional. The show would air for another thirteen years.

Ten years ago Ed Sullivan presented the first of his weekly variety shows over the Columbia Broadcasting System television network. . . . [H]e will celebrate the anniversary tonight with a one-hour gala including kinescoped highlights of his telecasts of the last decade.

During these ten years Mr. Sullivan has not improved perceptibly as a performer. He continues to give an impression of awkward uneasiness before the cameras. His impromptu remarks are sometimes rambling and inarticulate. He has, at times, antagonized viewers as well as his television competitors.

But his show has been remarkably successful. His ability consistently to attract outstanding artists from every branch of show business to his stage has enabled him to thrive in a medium where the fatality rate is appalling.

The stars who will appear in the kinescoped portions of tonight's show include Desi Arnaz, Fred Astaire, Lucille Ball, Jack Benny, Victor Borge, Yul Brynner, Perry Como, Gary Cooper, Bing Crosby, Jackie Gleason, Helen Hayes, Oscar Hammerstein 2d, Grace Kelly, Charles Laughton, Luise Rainer, Richard Rodgers, Phil Silvers and Margaret Truman. And they represent only a small segment of the celebrities who have visited the program.

Role

During a conversation the other day in his apartment in the Delmonico Hotel on Park Avenue, Mr.

Ed Sullivan on the set of his weekly variety show.
© BETTMANN/CORBIS. REPRODUCED BY PERMISSION.

Sullivan discussed his role in television and other subjects.

Although he had returned only a short time before from a taxing trip to Europe, during which he suffered from a stomach ulcer that has troubled him periodically for years, he answered questions affably. His morale may have been bolstered by the fact that, according to the latest A. C. Nielsen rating, his show was graded the third most popular show on TV.

Mr. Sullivan, who is 56 years old, is looking forward to at least five years more as a television producer-performer. Then he would like to get into the production end of the medium, he said.

Three years ago he began a twenty-year contract with C.B.S. It brings him a gross income of $4,000 a week. After the contract runs for seven years he would draw $100,000 a year. During the last thirteen years of the pact he would not be required to produce for C.B.S. but would be bound not to create entertainment for a competing network.

He maintains that despite these liberal terms he will never become wealthy. But he indicated also that he would want to continue working in television even if he were a rich man.

Career

"I enjoy what I'm doing," he said. "I would have become a water skier if I could have made money honestly and with integrity." Then he paused and added: "I've never been in any sense stage-struck. But back in the days when I was a writer I used to do a regular sports program on radio."

In addition to his radio work, Mr. Sullivan was, and still is, a readily available volunteer for master of ceremonies assignments at many benefit shows. He is known as a man who contributes his services to organizations regardless of their creed.

He was a sports writer for the New York Evening Mail and the Graphic in the Nineteen Twenties. While on The Graphic he became a Broadway columnist. He joined The Daily News in 1932 but because of the demands of his television activities his syndicated column now appears only twice a week. It is prepared with the help of Carmine Santullo, who has been his assistant for many years.

The first Ed Sullivan Show—it was then called "Toast of the Town"—was done on a budget of $500. Its headliners were Dean Martin and Jerry Lewis, who received $200 for their work. Correspondingly frugal payments for other stars on subsequent shows led some observers to conclude that the performers were anticipating publicity in Mr. Sullivan's column that would compensate for their small fees. The producer-host denied that there was any validity to this assertion.

Today the average weekly budget for his program is said to be $100,000. When the Moiseyev Dancers appear as his guests next Sunday night the program will cost $200,000 according to an unofficial estimate.

The most expensive and controversial visitor to the Sullivan show was Elvis Presley, who was paid $50,000 for three appearances.

Because of the suggestive devices used by the singer during his first performance on the Sullivan program on Sept. 9, 1956, there were widespread protests from viewers and critics.

Mr. Sullivan, recalling the incident, said: "The whole thing irritated me. I was the big villain. When the deluge started, I was it. I didn't back away from it. I controlled it. And the kids who came there were not the Dick Clark rabble. They were nice kids from good homes in places like Englewood and Scarsdale."

One month before the Presley issue arose, Mr. Sullivan drew criticism for his handling of a situation involving Ingrid Bergman. Almost two weeks before he had announced to the press that she would ap-

"TV: Report on a Week-End's Viewing" [excerpt]

Elvis Presley made his appearance on the Ed Sullivan Show over Channel 2, and the National Broadcasting Company didn't even bother to compete; it gave Steve Allen the night off and ran an English film. From his extensive repertoire of assaults on the American ear, Mr. Presley included, "Hound Dog." The maidens in the West Coast studio audience squealed appreciatively over their idol's mobility. On the East Coast Charles Laughton, substituting for Mr. Sullivan, patiently waited until it was all over.

SOURCE: *The New York Times*, September 10, 1956, 55.

Elvis Presley performs on the "Ed Sullivan Show" for the first time September 9, 1956. AP/WIDE WORLD PHOTOS. REPRODUCED BY PERMISSION.

pear on his show, he put the question of the propriety of her appearance to his audience. In a statement during his program he described Miss Bergman as a "controversial figure." He said also that she "had seven and a half years of time for penance." Critics of Mr. Sullivan charged that he was being sanctimonious and unfair to Miss Bergman.

Letters

Mr. Sullivan insists that he was completely right in that instance.

"After it was reported that she would be on the show, we got about 2,000 letters and 1,990 of them were against her," he said. "I decided that I had to stop that flood of negative mail. I probably phrased it badly. I wanted mail from those who were in back of her. I had to get some support. Otherwise I knew I was going to be told to get rid of her."

He said that although the mail that arrived subsequently was more favorable to Miss Bergman—there were about 3,200 in favor—the sponsor of the program decided she should not be seen.

"The thing was conceived in good faith," Mr. Sullivan maintained. "The way it turned out, if you were sitting in your own apartment and you were suddenly hit on the head by the roof, it couldn't have been more shocking."

There have been other storms during Mr. Sullivan's ten years on TV. They have included verbal feuds between him and Frank Sinatra, Walter Winchell and Steve Allen. Mr. Sullivan prefers to remember and discuss more rewarding achievements—his presentation of outstanding opera and ballet performers, scenes from Broadway and Holly-

wood hits and that long list of major stars who have joined him on the show.

Mimics

He is accustomed now to left-handed compliments, such as the following from one critic: "Although he may not be the original personality kid, Mr. Sullivan continues to be quite a showman."

His occasional presentation on the program of mimics who impersonate him is a calculated stratagem, he said.

"I've got a wrestler's neck on a small body," he commented. "Apparently when I turn, the whole body turns around. I used to get letters that said I looked as if I took myself too seriously. Unfortunately I have a graver looking kisser than most. I put these comedians on the show to impersonate me. I want to let the people know I have a sense of humor about myself."

Further Resources

BOOKS

Bowles, Jerry G. *A Thousand Sundays: The Story of the Ed Sullivan Show.* New York: Putnam, 1980.

Charters, Samuel Barclay. *Elvis Presley Calls His Mother after the Ed Sullivan Show: A Novel.* Minneapolis: Coffee House Press, 1992.

Diggins, John P. *The Proud Decades: America in War and in Peace, 1941–1960.* New York: Norton, 1998.

Harris, Michael David. *Always on Sunday: Ed Sullivan, an Inside View.* New York: New American Library, 1969.

Leonard, John, Claudia Falkenburg and Andrew Solt. *A Really Big Show: A Visual History of the Ed Sullivan Show.* New York: Viking Studio Books, 1992.

WEBSITES

The Ed Sullivan Show. TV Tome. Available online at http://tv-tome.com/tvtome/servlet/ShowMainServlet/showid-1156; website home page: http://tvtome.com (accessed March 21, 2003).

AUDIO AND VISUAL MEDIA

The Very Best of the Ed Sullivan Show: The Greatest Entertainers. Sofa Entertainment. VHS, 1996.

Dick Clark's *American Bandstand*

Dick Clark Hosting *American Bandstand*; Dick Clark in Record Library

Photographs

By: Associated Press
Date: June 30, 1958; February 3, 1959
Source: Dick Clark Hosting *American Bandstand.* June 30, 1958; Dick Clark in Record Library. February 3, 1959. AP/Wide World Photos. Available online at http://www.ap-wideworld.com (accessed March 24, 2003). ■

Introduction

In the 1950s, television became America's first truly national mass medium. Newspapers were the first major media in the United States, but a single newspaper did not reach all of America. Radio was more of a mass medium, as all of America could hear a broadcast at one time, but it lacked the impact of visual information. Movies combined sound and pictures, but people could not afford to go to the movies every day. Unlike its media predecessors, TV could bring sound and pictures, news and entertainment, right into American homes every day.

In the 1950s, most of America had only three television channels and so programming space was limited. People also were concerned that only "proper" things be shown on television, and censors had to approve scripts. For instance, Lucille Ball's character on the *I Love Lucy Show* was not allowed to say that she was pregnant—CBS censors banned that word, and "expecting" was used instead.

One of the top television shows of the 1950s was the *Ed Sullivan Show,* which presented a variety of entertainment, including live music. Perhaps inspired by that show's success, many local televisions stations created local shows in which a studio audience of teenagers danced to popular music. In Philadelphia, Bob Horn started *Bandstand* and developed a number of key elements of such programs, including "Rate-A-Record," in which a panel judges new songs. However, Horn was accused of statutory rape and fired in 1956.

Dick Clark was soon hired as Horn's replacement. He had worked as a disk jockey at radio stations in New York and Pennsylvania and had served as a replacement on Horn's radio shows when Horn was on vacation. Presenting himself as a squeaky clean, "100-percent American" boy (even though he was 26), Clark managed to raise the show's ratings. He eventually convinced ABC to broadcast the show nationally as *American Bandstand.* The network agreed, in large part because Clark offered the program for free. At this point ABC was in financial straits and the lowest-rated American network, far behind CBS and NBC.

Significance

American Bandstand became very successful, and as a result many new network affiliates signed on with ABC. This success, in turn, guaranteed that the show would be renewed by the network.

By keeping *American Bandstand* "clean," "moral," and sufficiently sanitized to satify both the TV censors and viewers' parents, Dick Clark contributed to the popularity of rock and roll in America. Clark carefully screened his studio audience, keeping it well-groomed, "all American"—and almost exclusively white. African Americans were generally excluded from the audience. By ensuring that the show remained unobjectionable to Middle America, Clark kept *American Bandstand* on the

Primary Source

Dick Clark's *American Bandstand*

SYNOPSIS: The first photo, taken in 1958, depicts a typical *American Bandstand* audience of the 1950s—clean-cut and white. Dick Clark stands at the podium, top-left, by his board of "Top Tunes," a standard feature of the show. In the second photo, from 1959, Dick Clark, in his usual suit and tie, selects records for his show. AP/WIDE WORLD PHOTOS. REPRODUCED BY PERMISSION.

air throughout the 1950s, a time characterized by both strict social codes and serious racial tensions. This, in turn, allowed some version of rock and roll to reach much of America.

Clark made a large amount of money thanks to *American Bandstand*. He acquired several record companies in the late 1950s and managed to buy or otherwise secure copyrights to many songs played on the

show. Clark was also paid fees by some record companies to play their records on the show. That all officially ended in 1960, after the radio "payola" scandal, which revealed that disk jockeys had been accepting money from record companies in return for playing their records on the air. Clark, too divulged his record company connections to a Congressional committee, and although he did not have to pay any fines, he did have to divest

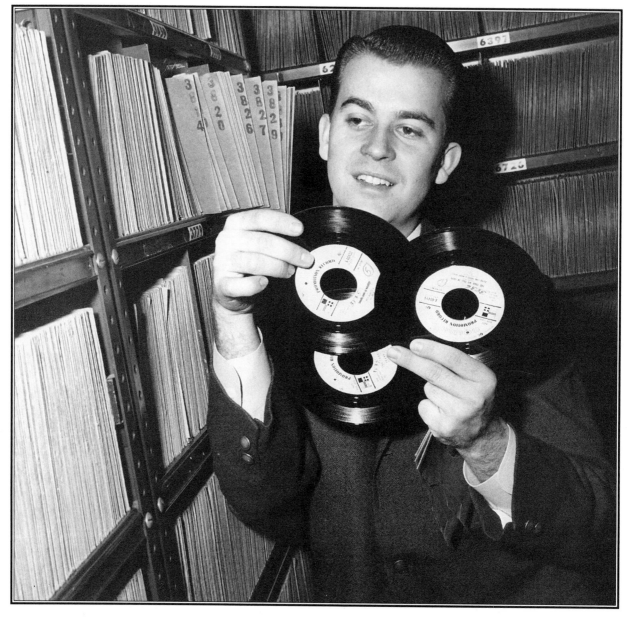

Primary Source

Dick Clark's *American Bandstand*

American Bandstand host Dick Clark searches through the collection of 45s at his station library for songs to play on the popular program in 1959. AP/WIDE WORLD PHOTOS. REPRODUCED BY PERMISSION.

himself of several companies, losing an estimated $8 million. Clark managed to survive the scandal, and continued on *American Bandstand* until 1987, establishing himself as a television icon and amassing a fortune in the process.

Further Resources

BOOKS

Clark, Dick, and Richard Robinson. *Rock, Roll & Remember.* New York: Popular Library, 1978.

Jackson, John A. *American Bandstand: Dick Clark and the Making of a Rock 'n' Roll Empire.* New York: Oxford University Press, 1997.

Nite, Norm N. *Rock On Almanac: The First Four Decades of Rock 'n' Roll Chronology.* New York: Harper & Row, 1989.

Stuessy, Joe. *Rock and Roll: Its History and Stylistic Development.* 2nd ed. Englewood Cliffs, N.J.: Prentice Hall, 1994.

Talevski, Nick. *The Unofficial Encyclopedia of the Rock and Roll Hall of Fame.* Westport, Conn.: Greenwood Press, 1998.

WEBSITES

Rock and Roll Hall of Fame and Museum. Available online at http://www.rockhall.com/ (accessed March 24, 2003).

AUDIO AND VISUAL MEDIA

Christy Lane's Learn the Dances of the '50s & '60s. Brentwood Home Video. Videocassette, 1996.

Charles Van Doren and the Quiz Show Scandal

"Reaction to the Van Doren Reaction"

Magazine article

By: Hans J. Morgenthau

Date: November 22, 1959

Source: Morgenthau, Hans J. "Reaction to the Van Doren Reaction.." *The New York Times Magazine,* November 22, 1959, 17, 106.

About the Author: Hans J. Morgenthau (1904–1980) was a prominent political scientist who studied foreign policy. He was trained at the University of Frankfurt and emigrated to the United States in 1937. He was one of the first to oppose to the Vietnam War and wrote over twenty books, among them being *Politics among Nations* and *The Decline of Democratic Politics*. He taught at a number of universities, including the University of Chicago.

"More Reaction to Van Doren"

Letters

By: *The New York Times Magazine*

Date: December 6, 1959

Source: "More Reaction to the Van Doren." Letters to *The New York Times Magazine,* December 6, 1959, 35. ∎

Introduction

The advent of radio as a mass media in the 1930s and 1940s had a huge impact on American entertainment. Radio required the immediate attention of the listener. Part of the thrill of radio was suspense—the outcome of the sporting event or the Lone Ranger episode was an unknown. Radio program producers used the element of suspense to enthrall listeners and keep them tuned in until the end of the program. Television continued these trends. Many of the early dramas and soap operas on television came straight from the radio. Television also tantalized viewers with new types of programs, including quiz shows. Millions tuned in to see who was the smartest contestant and who would be the champion at the end of each show.

The producers of quiz shows found that repeat winners, particularly if they were appealing to audiences, could raise ratings. When Charles Van Doren, an attractive and charming Columbia University English professor applied to be a contestant on *Twenty-One,* in 1956, its producers saw him as a way of boosting the show's faltering ratings.

After a series of ties with the show's reigning champion, Herb Stempel, Van Doren became the new champion of *Twenty-One,* eventually winning $138,000. The show became wildly popular and Van Doren became a celebrity, appearing on the cover of *Time* magazine. But Van Doren's fame came crashing down when it was discovered that he had been given the answers to the questions. This was divulged by Stempel, who also had been fed answers before he was defeated by Van Doren. The show's producers had been feeding the answers to the contestants whom they wished to win in order to build interest and create a hero. Van Doren confessed before a Congressional committee that had been investigating quiz shows and subsequently resigned from his post at Columbia University.

Significance

America had placed quite a bit of importance on the TV quiz shows, with some people even suggesting that they proved how smart Americans were. Public response to the quiz show scandal, however, was mixed. While people were shocked by the deception, some were sympathetic to Van Doren, who had become a familiar and well-liked public figure.

Hans Morgenthau's article in the November 22, 1959, issue of *The New York Times Magazine,* explores the public reaction to the scandal. Morgenthau asserts that the statements of sympathy and support for Van Doren by members of the congressional committee and by Columbia University students, among others, reflected an overall lack of morality in American society. Interestingly, letters sent to the magazine in response to Morgenthau's article defended Van Doren. Some writers maintained that he should not be stripped of his post or his winnings, and others excused his actions, pointing out that everyone sins occasionally.

Some observers have suggested that America in the 1950s had a stronger streak of morality than the present, but the Van Doren episode, both in terms of the chicanery which created it and the varied public reaction to it, suggests otherwise.

America also received another shock to her media consciousness with the "payola" scandal of 1959. It was revealed that record companies paid Alan Freed and other disk jockeys to play their music on the radio, while the DJs insisted that the music played was selected by listeners. Freed lost his job due to the scandal, and radio stations lost some of the public's confidence in their veracity. Thus the 1950s saw the rise of two new forms of entertainment, radio and television, both of which were found to have abused the public's trust.

Quiz shows were prime-time entertainment before the fall of *Twenty-One,* but after the scandal they were relegated to the early morning for the most part. It was not until the 1990s that quiz shows returned to the prime-time lineup.

Primary Source

"Reaction to the Van Doren Reaction"

SYNOPSIS: In his article, Hans Morgenthau notes that Americans, including members of Congress, were very complacent about Van Doren's fraud. America's acceptance of the deception is an example of how the country has moved away from the truths that it was founded on, he argues.

The willingness of many Americans to condone a professor's lapse from truth, another professor says, reveals not compassion but our society's moral obtuseness.

The facts of the Charles Van Doren case are spread on the record. More important than these facts is the nation's reaction to them. That reaction is reason for the gravest concern and deserves the most careful analysis.

The Van Doren case is a great event in the history of America in a dual sense. It brings to the fore certain qualities of American society, known before but perhaps never disclosed with such poignancy, and it poses a moral issue that goes to the very heart of American society. In what America says about Van Doren, the moral fiber of America itself stands revealed. By judging Van Doren, America bears judgment upon itself.

This is not a case of political or commercial corruption, such as the Tweed, Teapot Dome or Insull scandals. Pecuniary corruption in the political and commercial spheres must be expected. For since the ultimate value of these fields is power, and wealth is a source of power, the possibility of pecuniary corruption is built into these spheres, however great or small the incidence of actual corruption may be in a particular period of history. Many politicians and business men are uncorrupted, and some are uncorruptible, but they are all, by the very nature of their occupations, on familiar terms with corruption, encountering it even if they do not touch it.

Public reaction to political and commercial corruption is as predictable as the incidence of corruption itself. The familiarity of the fact evokes complacency, especially since many an on-looker preserves his virtue only for lack of opportunity to sin. The public rises in indignation only when the magnitude of the outrage exceeds the customary, when corruptive practices run counter to the political and commercial mores—which are indifferent to some offenses, such as implicit bribery, but condemn others, such as open blackmail—or when a prominent member of the other party or of the competition has been caught.

The moral issue that political and commercial corruption raises is but the general issue of human fallibility. The best we can hope and strive for is to restrict its manifestations and mitigate its evil.

The Van Doren case poses a different, more profound issue. It arose in a sphere whose ultimate value is neither power nor wealth but truth. The professor is a man who has devoted his life to "profess," and what he is pledged to profess is the truth as he sees it. Mendacity in a professor is a moral fault which denies the very core of the professor's calling. A mendacious professor is not like a politician who subordinates the public good to private gain, nor like a business man who cheats. Rather, he is like the physician who pledged to heal, maims and kills. He is not so much the corrupter of the code by which he is supposed to live as its destroyer

It is in view of the nature of the deed that the reaction of American society must be judged. The issue must be met head-on. There is no room for a Pontius Pilate washing his hands in skeptical abstention.

That is why the reactions of a considerable segment of the public cause the greatest concern. Of the nine members of the House of Representatives who heard the testimony, five addressed Van Doren in laudatory terms, "commending" and "complimenting" him and expressing their "appreciation."

Two Congressmen expressed the hope that he would not be dismissed from his positions at Columbia University and the National Broadcasting Company, and the chairman of the committee delivered a peroration predicting "a great future" for him. Only one member of the committee openly disagreed with the commendation of his colleagues. But even he did not convey awareness of the real issue, the scholar's special commitment to the truth.

Nor did the comments of most of Van Doren's students, as reported by the press. One expressed "faith in him as a man" and called him "a fine gentleman," another thought that "what he did was not

Charles Van Doren, quiz show contestant on *Twenty One,* grimaces as he tries to come up with an answer. Van Doren and *Twenty One* would later be disgraced when it was revealed that the show was rigged in Van Doren's favor. AP/WIDE WORLD PHOTOS. REPRODUCED BY PERMISSION.

wrong," a third called the acceptance of his resignation "very unfair." A petition bearing the signatures of 650 students demanded that he be rehired. None of the students whose reactions were recorded showed the slightest inkling of the moral issue raised by the case. Nor did many editorials and letters to newspapers

How is this perversion of moral judgment, often praising what deserves to be condemned, and at best remaining indifferent to the real issue, to be explained? The explanation of Congressional reaction is simple. The five members of Congress who approved Van Doren applied the general standards of political behavior to the academic sphere. They saw the Van Doren case as though it were just another instance of political corruption to be dealt with tolerantly, understandingly, even approvingly once the culprit had come clean and returned to the fold of fairly honest politicians.

However, the complacency of the politicians points to a deeper issue, a moral dilemma woven, as it were, into the very fabric of our American democracy. This is the dilemma between objective standards of conduct and majority rule, between compliance in thought and deed with standards

which are true regardless of time and place, and accommodation to the standards prevailing in a particular society in a particular time and place.

America was founded upon the recognition of certain self-evident truths which men do not create but find in the nature of things. Yet American society— and, more particularly, American democracy—has lived increasingly by conforming to whatever values appeared to be accepted by the élite or the majority of the moment. Mr. Justice Holmes' famous dictum, "* * * I have no practical criterion [with regard to laws] except what the crowd wants," is the classic expression of that resolution. It is also expressed in one Congressman's hope that Columbia University would not act "prematurely," but would wait to judge public reaction to Van Doren's statement.

The objective standards which constitute the moral backbone of a civilized society are here dissolved. What a man ought or ought not to do becomes determined not by objective laws immutable, as the stars, but by the results of the latest public opinion poll. A man who gets into trouble because he is temporarily out of step with public opinion needs only to slow down or hurry up, as the case may be, in order to get back into line, and all will

Professor and author Hans J. Morgenthau. **THE LIBRARY OF CONGRESS.**

be right again with him and the world. Moral judgment becomes thus the matter of a daily plebiscite, and what is morally good becomes identical with what the crowd wants and tolerates.

The moral illiteracy of the students is less easily explained. Students, so one would like to think, are apprentices in that noble endeavor of discovering and professing the truth, not yet compelled by the demands of society to compromise their convictions; they must look at a mendacious professor as a student of the priesthood looks at a priest who blasphemes God. How is it possible for a young man of presumably superior intelligence and breeding, predestined to be particularly sensitive to the moral issue of truth, to be so utterly insensitive to it?

These youths were born with a moral sense as they were born with a sense of sight. Who blinded them to the moral standards by which they—at least as students—are supposed to live?

The answer must be sought in the same sphere that produced Van Doren himself: the academic world. There is profound meaning in the solidarity between Van Doren and his students. While public opinion has pinned responsibility on television, advertising, business or teachers' low salaries, nobody

seems to have pointed to the academic system which taught both teacher and students.

A system of higher education, dedicated to the discovery and transmission of the truth, is not a thing apart from the society which has created, maintains and uses it. The academic world partakes of the values prevailing in society and is exposed to social pressures to conform to them. Its very concept of what truth is bears the marks of the relativism dominant in American society and, by teaching that kind of truth, it strengthens its dominance over the American mind.

Yet even commitment to this kind of truth is bound to come into conflict with the values and demands of society. The stronger the trend toward conformity within society and the stronger the commitment of the scholar to values such as wealth and power, the stronger will be his temptation to sacrifice his moral commitment to truth for social advantage. The tension between these contradictory commitments typically results in a compromise.

On the one hand, it keeps the scholar's commitment to the truth within socially acceptable bounds—he exempts, for instance, the taboos of society from investigation. On the other hand, it restrains social ambitions from seriously interfering with the scholar's search for a truth cautiously defined. In the measure that truth is thus limited, the search for it is deflected from its proper goal and thereby corrupted.

At the extreme ends of the academic spectrum, one finds two small groups. One is subversive of the truth by telling society what it wants to hear. The other is subversive of society by telling it what it does not want to hear.

Contemporary America offers enormous temptations to join the first group—that is, not only to corrupt the truth but to betray it. In the process, the academic world tends to transform itself into a duplicate of the business and political worlds. To the temptations of wealth and power held out by government, business and foundations, the scholar has nothing to oppose but his honor committed to a truth which for him, as for society, is but a doubtful thing. The step from corruption to betrayal is big in moral terms but small in execution.

What difference is there between receiving $129,000 under false pretenses from government, business or a foundation, which has become almost standard operating procedure, and receiving the same amount under false pretenses from a television sponsor? The difference lies not in moral relevance but in the technique. Van Doren and his students were formed by a world which condones the betrayal of truth for the sake of wealth and power, provided the academic amenities are preserved.

In the world of Van Doren American society beholds its own world, the world of business and politics, of wealth and power. It cannot condemn him without condemning itself, and since it is unwilling to do the latter it cannot bring itself to do the former. Instead, it tends to absolve him by confusing the virtues of compassion and charity for the actor with the vice of condoning the act. Yet, by refusing to condemn Van Doren, it cannot but condemn itself. For it convicts itself of a moral obtuseness which signifies the beginning of the end of civilized society.

Primary Source

"More Reaction to Van Doren"

SYNOPSIS: The letters in response to Morgenthau's article demonstrate the wide variety of reactions to Van Doren's deception and indicate that not all Americans were outraged by fraud in the "happy days" of the 1950s.

Columbia's Role

The issue at Columbia was never—as Mr. Morgenthau asserts—the condoning of Mr. Van Doren's guilt, a guilt which few, if any, would have bothered to deny. The issue was the moral propriety of Columbia University in so hurriedly blotting a tainted employe from its rolls.

One may safely assume that Mr. Morgenthau has never told, or been forced to live, an embarrassing lie. Other Americans who are not so spotless—college professors among them—have a somewhat different understanding of the complexities of moral living. And does not the story of the casting of the first stone come from a book instrumental in forming that "moral backbone of civilization" to which Mr. Morgenthau refers?

Mr. Van Doren is indeed guilty, but who here is innocent? What was unforgivable in the eyes of the Columbia trustees was not that the man sinned but that he sinned so publicly.

John L. Sechel
New York

Eloquent Essay

Professor Morgenthau's article is a vigorous and eloquent piece of moral indignation which I hope penetrates the thick armor of frivolity with which so many

of our fellow Americans are covered. Also I hope it strikes at the worship of the Golden Calf and at least dents it.

But there is one statement that needs correction: "These youths were born with a moral sense as they were born with a sense of sight." Professor Morgenthau is completely wrong here. Youths are not born with a moral sense, not even with a conscience, nor with knowledge of right and wrong. All these precious qualities must be acquired. That is precisely why there is such reaction to the Van Doren case and to Mr. Morgenthau's essay on the lack of moral indignation among our fellow Americans.

J. M. Martinez
Miami, Fla.

Moral Lesson

When the author compares the "mendacious professor" to the physician who "maims and kills," the nature and gravity of the wrongdoing is strikingly shown. But when he speaks of the ability to discriminate between a right and a wrong action as inborn—as "immutable as the stars"—he is not only unhelpful, but positively harmful, for it tends to remove the entire problem from the scope of human understanding, and consequently, of education.

Might not one say, rather, that moral awareness is a fruit of proper training and environment at home, and effective study at school and college?

Mrs. Tina Stiefel
Englewood, N. J.

Mother's View

The article by Hans J. Morgenthau was like a cool drink to a thirsty traveler.

I am a mother most anxious for my two young children to live in a better world, and I fear the terrible influence of people with "elastic consciences" far more than I fear atomic fallout.

In the daily struggle to maintain one's ideals, self-respect and plain "old-fashioned" honesty, and to pass these on to the next innocent generation, I found Mr. Morgenthau's analysis so thoughtful and touching and helpful that I will keep it to read again and again. My thanks to him and to you for publishing his examination of public morality.

Julia A. Keiser
Williamsport, Pa.

Need Religion

Professor Morgenthau's article tracing the "blind spot" in academic viewpoints on the Van Doren case to the fuzzy morality of the academic world itself, is a resounding alarum indeed.

May I mention one other factor in the development of "bright kids," overlooked in the article but perhaps behind the moral laxity found on so many campuses. I refer to the lack of religious training in childhood.

This is not to say that a grounding in religious principles is a guarantee of righteous, healthful living in adulthood. I hold no brief for the rigid churchmen who say, "Send your child to church and Sunday school, or synagogue and Hebrew school, or else . . ."

But, when I hear young parents, both intelligent and intellectual, say: "I'll let him decide when he grows up," I have one big question on the tip of my tongue: "What will you give your child instead?"

Alma Denny
New York

Further Resources

BOOKS

Boddy, William. *Fifties Television: The Industry and Its Critics.* Urbana, Ill.: University of Illinois Press, 1990.

Schwartz, David, Steve Ryan, and Fred Wostbrock. *The Encyclopedia of TV Game Shows.* 3rd ed. New York: Facts On File, 1999.

Stone, Joseph, and Tim Yohn. *Prime Time and Misdemeanors: Investigating the 1950s TV Quiz Scandal: A D.A.'s Account.* New Brunswick, N.J: Rutgers University Press, 1992.

PERIODICALS

Attanasio, Paul. "Quiz Show: Screenplay." *Scenario* 1, no. 4, Fall 1995, 7–50.

WEBSITES

"Charles Van Doren." *The American Experience: The Quiz Show Scandal.* PBS. Available online at http://www.pbs.org /wgbh/amex/quizshow/peopleevents/pande02.html; website home page: http://www.pbs.org/ (accessed March 30, 2003).

AUDIO AND VISUAL MEDIA

The American Experience: The Quiz Show Scandal. Krainin Productions, Inc., and WGBH Educational Foundation. Directed by Michael R. Lawrence. VHS, 1993.

Quiz Show. 1994. Produced and directed by Robert Redford. Hollywood Pictures Home Video. VHS, 1995.

Love, Alice: My Life As a Honeymooner
Memoir

By: Audrey Meadows

Date: 1994

Source: Meadows, Audrey, with Joe Daley. *Love, Alice: My Life As a Honeymooner.* New York: Crown Publishers, 1994, 25–31.

About the Artist: Actress Audrey Meadows (1925–1996) had her first important role in the Broadway show *Top Banana.* She got her break in television with *The Bob and Ray Show,* for which she was awarded the Emmy for Outstanding Supporting Actress in 1954. She is best known, however, for her role opposite Jackie Gleason in *The Honeymooners.* She later starred in *The Jackie Gleason Show,* appeared in several movies, made guest appearances on TV, and had a regular role in the 1980s sitcom *Too Close for Comfort.* After her success as Alice Kramden, however, she was often typecast as a housewife. ■

Introduction

The early 1950s saw the advent of television sitcoms (situation comedies), many of which were based on radio shows. A number of these shows, such as the *Ozzy and Harriet Show* and *Leave it to Beaver,* reflected an idealized view of what suburban life was like. Other shows had a more blue-collar setting. One of the best-known and most popular of the latter type was *The Honeymooners,* in which Jackie Gleason played a New York City bus driver, Audrey Meadows played his long-suffering wife, and Art Carney and Joyce Randolph played their neighbors. Thirty-nine episodes of the show aired in 1955 and 1956.

Significance

The Honeymooners came to be considered one of the best of the early, live TV sitcoms. As Audrey Meadows's memoir reveals, however, there were many backstage issues that greatly affected the show. For instance, Meadows only got the part when the actress who originally played Gleason's wife became "unavailable." In fact, the actress had been "blacklisted," meaning that due to actual communist connections, or her refusal to answer a congressional committee's questions about her beliefs and associates, she was placed on a list that prevented her from working in the entertainment industry.

The memoir provides other behind-the-scenes insights into the classic show. For instance, Meadows reveals that Jackie Gleason was a greater actor than many people realize. He hardly ever practiced scenes, believing that this would ruin his performances—he simply learned his lines, showed up, and acted on the air. Meadows also describes how she worked with the show's writers to develop her character. Alice, for instance, never attacked Ralph; she only responded to his actions and comments. Unlike other sitcoms of the time, the show was meant to be plausible. The memoir also reveals that, as close as the cast appeared onscreen, they were not that close in real life.

Only thirty-nine episodes of *The Honeymooners* were broadcast in the 1950s, but the show made all four of its stars famous. They and their characters are still well-known nearly half a century after the show went off the air. *The Honeymooners* was a significant part of television history because it was one of the first and most successful attempts to portray working-class life on the TV screen. Although the show had a short run, it continues to live on in reruns, and it influenced several generations of sitcoms that came after it.

Primary Source

Love, Alice: My Life As a Honeymooner [excerpt]

SYNOPSIS: In this excerpt from her memoir, Audrey Meadows describes how she landed the part of Alice Kramden, which would be the role of her lifetime.

So the next afternoon with Val, I went to meet Jackie Gleason at his office, with Bullets blending into the wallpaper following an unnecessary introduction. Actually, I'd met Jackie months before when Eddie Hanley, who was in *Top Banana* with me, had taken me to The Embers after the show to hear Joe Bushkin, the famous piano player. Jackie Gleason came to our table because he knew Eddie and had a drink with us. Wherever there was good music, you could find Jackie, I was to learn.

Jackie was being interviewed and photographed by *Life* magazine when I arrived, so it was certainly an awkward time to visit, but he was cordial and hospitable, breaking away from the magazine group to meet with me. Here are some first impressions of him on the edge of his Big Time debut.

Naturally handsome, he was stylishly barbered and groomed, dressed comfortably and well. This was no overweight slob. He had a pleasantly modulated and unhurried voice, so unlike the husky rasp or side-of-the-mouth slur he used in character. Unlike many actors and most comedians, he was not on when he was offstage. He didn't focus attention on himself but chatted broadly about a range of subjects using a varied vocabulary and often precise words.

I would learn later that he also never used coarse language when women were present. Many comics

Audrey Meadows holds the Emmy Award she won for her performance as Alice Kramden in "The Honeymooners," 1955. **AP/WIDE WORLD PHOTOS. REPRODUCED BY PERMISSION.**

would come to visit Jackie on Saturdays in his dressing room, and if four-letter words started to fly around when Joyce Randolph, who portrayed Trixie Norton in "The Honeymooners," and I were present, Jackie would say, "Watch it, the girls are here!" Like many men of his time and upbringing, he divided women between ladies and hookers and schooled his manners to his perception of the female he was addressing.

As a professional comic, he was known as a great reaction player, whose expressive eyes and mobile face were ideal for television close-ups. ("The test of a real comedian is whether you laugh at him before he opens his mouth," critic George Jean Nathan had said. He had Gleason right.) Because he was big, Jackie featured physical comedy too—lots of flapping limb movements, trips and sprawls, and pratfalls. But even at his heaviest (and that was very heavy), his physical stunts were so smooth and coordinated that they amazed fellow performers. Despite his size, he was agile enough to make a perilous fall funny for the crowd and graceful to appreciative actors.

I was the one who, more or less, ended the meeting, well aware that the *Life* crew was getting

The cast of "The Honeymooners" in a still from the groundbreaking television show. From left to right: Jackie Gleason as Ralph Kramden, Art Carney as Ed Norton, Audrey Meadows as Alice Kramden, and Joyce Randolph as Trixie Norton. **GETTY IMAGES. REPRODUCED BY PERMISSION.**

restless, and while Gleason was being gracious, no performer wants to irritate the press. I exited to my own cue, and he asked Val and Bullets to stay.

I waited outside for Val by the elevators, and when he appeared, he had the look of a friend about to tell you that your dog has died.

"What did he say, Val?"

"He said, 'Why don't you two guys take the needles out of your heads? She's all wrong—she's too young and too pretty! I'll give you she's charming, witty, neat, and smart—everything that Alice Kramden definitely is not.'"

Now I had asked for this interview, more or less, as a lark, but when I realized he'd turned me down, I was very disappointed. I would not have minded a producer saying that, but a man of Jackie's talent should have known I could play the part.

Val walked me back to my apartment, and suddenly an idea came to me. I said, "Val, can you get a photographer to come to my apartment first thing in the morning to photograph me with no makeup? Better get Bill Mark, because he'll have to develop and print the shots by the afternoon so we can get them up to Jackie the same day. They're going to

have to make up their minds pretty quickly, because they only have a little over two weeks before he goes on the air, so we need to work fast. I won't get out of bed till you ring the bell, and we'll get some pictures of me taken looking like his idea of Alice."

Getting Val out of the apartment while ignoring his objections, I began to plot my wardrobe for the character of Alice. I went through my closet looking for an old blouse, a skirt and apron, a hair net, curlers, and some combs to pull my hair up and make it scraggly looking. I figured I was ready for the morning. Of course, this was pretty dreamy stuff, considering the boss had just told me politely, You're a peach, kid. Good luck and good traveling.

Everyone who knows me is aware that not even my reflexes to pain wake up when the alarm goes off. Came the dawn or a reasonable facsimile, and photographer Bill Mark leaned on the bell. I successfully reached the front door without opening my eyes, lit a cigarette while squinting my right eye cautiously, since you get your nose seared if you don't carefully watch your wavering fingers push fire at you, and started to make coffee as the lens of the Speed Graphic whirred noisily for such an early hour.

As phases of consciousness began to stir, I started to do adventurous things like wash a cup or run the carpet sweeper over my bare foot or attempt to apply lipstick while smoking, which may well become an Olympic event. My mother, who was there, was alarmed by what I was doing. She kept saying, "Oh, darling, fix your hair, and you're making terrible faces." Bill was surprised too—he thought he had come to take glamour pictures of me, but soon he was amused and got into the act. I told him these pictures had to get me a job.

I had revved up to a sickly smile and was offering to make him a sandwich by a couple of hours later, when he had shot himself out of film and departed. I collapsed into deep sloth while Bill processed the assembled photos of Meadows aka Alice Kramden and Val got a set over to Bullets by 4:00, after running by the apartment to show them to me.

I looked dreadful.

It was perfect!

No makeup, hair a mess, that ruined blouse hiding a hint of bargain basement skirt. Without a cosmetician and wardrobe mistress, I thought I'd done okay. Now, we'd just see. . . .

We instructed Bullets under no condition to identify the actress.

Bullets told us what happened when he showed the photos to Jackie, identifying the subject just as a "good actress who really wants the part." Jackie glowed as he studied each sorry pose, ending with a shout. "That's our Alice! Who is she? Where is she? Can we get her?"

Bullets said, "That's the girl who was here yesterday, Audrey Meadows, and she arranged the photo shoot to show she could look the part as well as play it." Jackie cheered both the imagination and the stunt. He said, "Any dame with a sense of humor like that deserves the job!"

He was also more than a little relieved. "The Honeymooners" had become one of the hit segments on *Cavalcade of Stars,* and he had to have a new Alice by the opening show. "Hire her" was his simple order to Bullets Durgom.

As a man of legendary thrift with Gleason's budget, Bullets muted Jackie's more admiring adjectives when he reported them to Val and me back at my apartment. In the mind of Bullets, who had been next to weeping about his desperate need to find a talented performer for Alice Kramden and fast, the focus of our discussion had now shifted to fee for services, and he became reserved and reverential when money was spoken of aloud, especially when it was vaguely under his supervision. It became more than personal. Sacred would come close.

Short and sly, Bullets was the most agile dancer outside the Bolshoi when dollars were discussed. My manager, Val, was also adept at all the contractual steps and dips, not to mention the grips and holds of Greco-Roman wrestling, but somehow, when the deal was done, I was hired to work every other week and signed a separate contract for each show.

In a risky business, the risk became all mine. I had bailed out of a surefire, long-running Broadway show to join a one-person-missing comedy quartet which had not yet played to a network audience. If we faltered, CBS surely had ten movies in the can to cover. And, with no annual contract, I would be at liberty to read for the ingenue's fruitcake sister or do crowd noises on radio.

This was not part of my master plan.

So I vowed that I would play the socks off Alice Kramden and prayed that the show would be a blockbuster hit, because the alternative was most depressing.

Being the daughter of missionary parents in China, I was raised to be an optimist, and my mother took on the continent of Asia all by herself. So I guessed I could stand up to Jackie Gleason. After all, Asia is bigger. Isn't it?

Further Resources

BOOKS

Crescenti, Peter, and Bob Columbe. *The Official Honeymooners Treasury: To the Moon and Back with Ralph, Norton, Alice, and Trixie.* New York: Putnam, 1985.

Einstein, Xavier. *Trivia Mania: The Honeymooners.* New York: Kensington, 1985.

Henry, William A. *The Great One: The Life and Legend of Jackie Gleason.* New York: Doubleday, 1992.

McCrohan, Donna. *The Honeymooners' Companion: The Kramdens and the Nortons Revisited.* New York: Workman, 1978.

McCrohan, Donna, and Peter Crescenti. *"The Honeymooners" Lost Episodes.* New York: Workman, 1986.

Starr, Michael. *Art Carney: A Biography.* Milwaukee, Wisc.: Applause Theatre & Cinema Books, 2002.

Weatherby, William J. *Jackie Gleason: An Intimate Portrait of the Great One.* New York: Pharos Books, 1992.

WEBSITES

The Honeymooners. Available online at http://www.honeymooners.net/ (accessed March 25, 2003).

"The Politics of Race: An Interview with Harry Ashmore"

Interview

By: Harry Ashmore

Date: January 15, 1995

Source: Ashmore, Harry. "The Politics of Race: An Interview with Harry Ashmore." Interview by Scott London. *Insight and Outlook* radio program transcript. January 15, 1995. Available online at http://www.scottlondon.com/interviews /ashmore.html; website home page: http://www.scottlondon .com (accessed March 20, 2003).

About the Author: Harry Ashmore (1916–1998) was one of a group of newspaper editors who took pride in speaking for a New South and in pushing for racial tolerance during the 1950s and beyond. Born in Greenville, South Carolina, Ashmore graduated from Clemson College in 1937 and served in the Army infantry during World War II. After working for the *Charlotte News* and other papers, he joined the *Arkansas Gazette* in 1947 and remained there until 1959, eventually becoming editor-in-chief. In 1958, the paper won a Pulitzer Prize for its coverage of the desegregation of Little Rock schools, and Ashmore won a Pulitzer for his editorials. After leaving the *Gazette,* he was editor-in-chief for *Encyclopedia Britannica,* among other posts. ∎

Introduction

The end of slavery and the Civil War did not end the prejudices of white Americans against black Americans. Northern states attempted to rebuild the South and grant the ex-slaves civil rights, but the North soon tired of these efforts and ended Reconstruction in 1877. Once the white Southerners were back in control, they passed discriminatory legislation and imposed segregation. Southern newspapers generally supported this system with their editorials and news stories. The Supreme Court put its stamp of approval upon this system in the 1896 case *Plessy v. Ferguson,* in which the court held that separate systems for the races were legal as long as they were equal. In reality, however, the separate systems were never equal. Segregation persisted throughout the South, with separate drinking fountains, bathrooms, and even separate Bibles for use in the courtroom.

In the early years of the twentieth century, the National Association for the Advancement of Colored People (NAACP) began to protest segregation in the courts and won some victories. The NAACP won its biggest victory in education in 1954, with the case *Brown v. Board of Education,* in which the Supreme Court held that "separate educational facilities are inherently unequal" and struck down segregation in public schools. The response among Southern whites was one of "massive resistance," and most Southern congressmen signed a "Southern Man-

ifesto," which called *Brown* an unconstitutional decision and vowed resistance in every possible way.

In general, Southern newspapers joined in this effort, writing editorials in support of massive resistance and whipping the public up into mobs. One such place of resistance was Little Rock, Arkansas, where President Eisenhower was forced to send in federal troops in 1957 in order to ensure that nine African American students be allowed to attend the formerly all-white public high school. The school board then sought an injunction in federal court to delay any further desegregation.

Ashmore, who wrote for the *Arkansas Gazette* in Little Rock, was one of the few editors in the South with an enlightened view on the subject of race, and one of the very few who argued that the *Brown v. Board of Education* Supreme Court ruling was correct and that segregation was wrong.

Significance

In this radio interview, conducted some forty years after the desegration of the Little Rock schools, Ashmore reflects on the civil rights movement in America. Even though his statements might not strike a modern reader as particularly progressive, he was very liberal when compared to the rest of the South in the 1950s. At the time, Ashmore was widely opposed in the South, and many wanted to run him out of Little Rock. Outside the South, Ashmore's courage was more widely recognized, and he won a Pulitzer Prize for his writings.

Little Rock did not accept integration, even after President Eisenhower sent in troops and the Supreme Court decision upheld the concept of integration. The school district shut down the school board for the 1958–1959 year and even after a federal court declared the closing unconstitutional, the school district did not want to open up the schools. President Eisenhower had to again employ the National Guard in order to force the governor to open the schools. Arkansas Governor Orval Faubus used his defiance of the federal orders to win four more terms, winning reelection in 1958, 1960, 1962 and 1964.

Much of the rest of the South did not accept *Brown v. Board of Education* either and did not follow the policies that Ashmore supports in this interview. In 1964, ten years after the *Brown* ruling, less than two percent of African Americans attended integrated schools in the states of the former Confederacy. It took the Civil Rights Acts of the 1960s to force desegregation, and to some extent, desegregation still was not complete by the beginning of the twenty-first century.

Primary Source

"The Politics of Race: An Interview with Harry Ashmore" [excerpt]

A crowd of students, protesters, sightseers, and press gathers outside of Little Rock, Arkansas' Central High School on the first day of integration in the public schools. September 5, 1957. © BETTMANN/CORBIS. REPRODUCED BY PERMISSION.

SYNOPSIS: In this 1995 radio interview, Harry Ashmore notes that race had always been an important element in American history and discusses how the civil rights movement had its roots in World War II. Ashmore also describes how he came to be aware of the issue of race and the existence of racism in the South.

Ashmore: I think the issue of race is inseparable from American history. If you go back to the founding of the republic, the great issue was slavery. The people in Philadelphia who wrote the Constitution couldn't handle the issue, they didn't know what to do with it, so they swept it under the rug. There is no mention of slavery in the Constitution, (except for the fact that slaves were to be counted as three-fifths of a person for purposes of determining the representation in Congress and so forth). So, roughly half the nation at that time—the seaboard colonies were all there were—were slave states. They had slavery from the time of the first settlement. It was so built into the economy in those plantation states—which were Virginia on down through Georgia. Then the middle part of the country had very few slaves, and the Northeast had practically none.

So all the blacks in the country were slaves and they were all concentrated in the South. That created economic divisions, moral divisions, and questions of political representation which shaped the early history of the country and led finally, of course, to the Civil War. The Civil War was fought not necessarily on the question of whether there should be free slaves or not, although that became one of the issues. But underlying that was the big economic division between the two parts of the country.

After the Civil War, after the Southern states were defeated and became, in effect, a kind of occupied territory, or province, of the North, the great industrial revolution transformed the United States. The South was pretty much left behind. So until World War I a great majority of the blacks were left in the South. They had been slaves and were freed but were treated as second-class citizens. They were denied a lot of their civil rights under dispensations that were approved by the Supreme Court and by the national government.

Harry Ashmore, executive editor of the *Arkansas Gazette*, received the Pulitzer Prize for his editorials on the integration of Central High School in Little Rock. The paper was awarded an unprecedented total of three Pulitzers. © BETTMANN/CORBIS. REPRODUCED BY PERMISSION.

So this goes back and is threaded through all of our history. We haven't settled the problem. I thought we had made a lot of progress beginning in the sixties, and I think in some ways there has been a great deal of progress. At least we have eliminated second-class citizenship as such. But, obviously, race and its offshoot issues are still dominant—as you could see in the last election, for example. The new Congress will be organized around issues that basically go back to the fundamental question of what the role of the central government is toward dealing the disenfranchised and unemancipated poor in this country. . . .

The civil rights movement virtually didn't exist as an important political factor until World War II and the election just preceding it. By the time the war ended, when the GIs all came home . . . the demography of the country had changed. A great number of blacks were removed from the South to the great cities where they became an important factor. The

political balance was changing and the black vote was becoming important enough that it had to be taken into account.

By 1948, when Harry Truman ran for reelection, the black vote provided the margin that won him the election. This was the first time the black vote had become significant enough. There were enough emancipated blacks that were outside the South. And, also, the Supreme Court, in 1944 before the war was over, had ruled out the white primary in the South which had been the primary means of keeping blacks from voting. So blacks were beginning to vote in significant numbers in the South and they were already free to vote outside the South where their numbers had increased and they had become an important factor in the major cities—including some on the West Coast where they had been rather few and of no significance before. But in Chicago, Philadelphia, New York, Washington D.C., the black vote had become an important factor and it has remained that since. . . .

[F]or anybody who was born in South Carolina, as I was, and grew up between the two world wars, [race] was an inescapable issue. I was in college during the first years of the Roosevelt administration and I was a product of the Depression years. Anyone who grew up in that milieu could hardly escape the realization at some point that blacks, who were a very important part of the population numerically, were denied all of their civil rights, even though we professed to believe in democracy and the full participation of all people. Also, we violated all of our religious precepts. We were supposed to be a very religious people and we talked about the "brotherhood of man" and "all men are brothers"—except we wouldn't let blacks worship with whites in the same churches. So I think anybody growing up became conscious that there was a great disparity between what we professed to believe and what we actually practiced. So I suppose that dawned on me, although I was no great crusader. But I became also convinced by seeing the changes that were taking place—enormous changes. And then when I was caught up in the war and out of action for three and a half years, during the time that I was in service, including combat service oversees—when I came back and was stationed in Washington after VE-Day in the Pentagon, I began to realize then what enormous dislocations were taking place demographically. The black population had been redistributed, plus the black vote was going to become a factor that would make an enormous amount of difference in the South itself. So at the end of the war when I went back to North Carolina, as editor of the *Charlotte News,* I was perfectly aware that one of the big changes that was going to take place was accommodating the black voting population into the political system. That, of course, was what the South had to grapple with in the years that followed. . . .

London: [Y]ou had a chance to meet Martin Luther King. What most impressed you about him?

Ashmore: He was an extremely impressive person. He was obviously dedicated. He was a man of faith. And a man of great courage—every time he drew a breath he was exposed to some real danger. And he had faith. He had a great deal of charm. A great deal of commitment. And I think he was one of those people who come along at moments in history when we need someone like that. He had an ability to communicate. Those speeches still have that resonance—the "I have a dream" speech and the last speech in Memphis—"I've been to the mountain top and I've looked over and seen the promised land. I may not get there with you." Well, he had this quality of charisma—I don't like to use the word, but it fits him in the sort of classic sense. I think he had deep conviction, a skill with words and an ability to communicate and project a deeply emotional feeling that got a response from whites, many of whom were hostile to the ideas that he was preaching. That was one of the great qualities of King.

Personally, he was of course very prepossessing. I don't know what else to say about him. About the only time that I had a long conversation with him was toward the end when he was on the wrong side, as far as the public was concerned, on the Vietnam War. The impression I think I mention in the book was one of ineffable sadness. He realized that he had not succeeded in exporting his movement into the great cities. He had tried in Chicago and failed. He also realized that his side was losing out on the Vietnam War, and that he had lost the political influence that he had had in the Johnson administration because he

"Harry S. Ashmore"

Harry Scott Ashmore is an apostle of change for the South. His views have met with a mixed reaction in his own territory, but yesterday they won him a Pulitzer Prize.

The executive editor of the *Arkansas Gazette* was cited for his editorials during the school integration conflict in Little Rock last fall.

Many of his fellow citizens and fellow journalists credited him with a major share in restoring order in the torn community. But his front-page editorials aroused the wrath of White Citizens Councils.

Mr. Ashmore, 41 years old, is a Southerner who preaches that the South must progress to keep pace with history. He said so in a recent book, "An Epitaph for Dixie."

Mr. Ashmore was born in Greenville, S. C. His two grandfathers served in the Confederate Army. He was a lieutenant-colonel of infantry in World War II and later a Nieman fellow at Harvard University. He worked his way through Clemson College.

He was a reporter for The Greenville Piedmont and political writer and editor of The Charlotte, N. C., News before going to Little Rock in 1947.

He was an adviser on civil rights and speech writer for Adlai E. Stevenson during the 1956 Presidential campaign.

Mr. Ashmore helped establish the Southern Regional Reporting Service to give the nation a clearer story of the integration problem. He also edited a book on "The Negro and the Schools," financed by the Fund for the Advancement of Education of the Ford Foundation.

He married the former Barbara Laier of Boston in 1940. They have a daughter, Anne Rogers Ashmore, 12, who attends a Little Rock public school.

SOURCE: *The New York Times,* May 6, 1958, 38.

broke with them on Vietnam. So I think "sadness" would be the word I would use if I had to characterize the impression I had at the last and the only long conversation I've had with him.

Further Resources

BOOKS

Ashmore, Harry S. *Hearts and Minds: The Anatomy of Racism from Roosevelt to Reagan.* New York: McGraw-Hill, 1982.

Bates, Daisy. *The Long Shadow of Little Rock, a Memoir.* New York: David McKay, 1962.

Beals, Melba. *Warriors Don't Cry: A Searing Memoir of the Battle to Integrate Little Rock's Central High.* New York: Pocket Books, 1994.

Edmonds, Bill. "Civil Rights and Southern Editors: Richmond, Little Rock, Tallahassee." Master's thesis, Florida State University, 1996.

Huckaby, Elizabeth. *Crisis at Central High, Little Rock, 1957–58.* Baton Rouge, La.: Louisiana State University Press, 1980.

Waldron, Ann. *Hodding Carter: The Reconstruction of a Racist.* Chapel Hill, N.C.: Algonquin Books of Chapel Hill, 1993.

AUDIO AND VISUAL MEDIA

Will The Circle Be Unbroken?: A Personal History of the Civil Rights Movement in Five Southern Communities and the Music of Those Times. Southern Regional Council. Audiotape, 1997. Available online at http://unbrokencircle.org /scripts14.htm (accessed March 20, 2003).

Love, Lucy

Memoir

By: Lucille Ball

Date: 1996

Source: Ball, Lucille. *Love, Lucy.* With Betty Hannah Hoffman. New York: G.P. Putnam's Sons, 1996, 204–210.

About the Artist: Lucille Ball (1911–1989) began working in films in 1933. She appeared in dozens of movies, with lead roles in a few, but never achieved movie stardom. In 1940 she met and married Desi Arnaz, a Cuban bandleader. She got her break in radio in 1947, with *My Favorite Husband.* In 1951 the radio show was moved to television, with significant changes, as *I Love Lucy.* The show was wildly popular and ran for six years, making Ball a television icon. Ball divorced Arnaz in 1960, and in 1962 she bought out his interest in the couple's joint production company, Desilu Studios. She ran Desilu Studios from 1962 to 1967 and also starred in three other TV sitcoms, all based on a version of the original Lucy character: *The Lucille Ball Show* (1962–1968), *Here's Lucy* (1968–1974), and the short-lived *Life With Lucy* (1986). ■

Introduction

With the rising popularity of television in the 1950s, the national networks needed to create more programs to to put on the air. They turned to radio as a source of programming ideas. Many early television series—*Gunsmoke,* for example—were first radio shows. *I Love Lucy* was based on a radio show called *My Favorite Husband,* which starred Lucille Ball and Richard Denning. Ball had originally suggested that the radio show, or something like it, feature her real-life husband, Desi Arnaz. CBS refused, maintaining that no one would believe that the actress was married to a Cuban bandleader. The couple

subsequently tried to sell CBS on the concept of a TV show starring the two as husband and wife.

CBS eventually bought the idea, and *I Love Lucy* first aired on October 15, 1951. It ran until June 24, 1957, and lives on in syndication.

Significance

I Love Lucy was a groundbreaking television show, one to which subsequent television comedies are often compared. The show enjoyed great popularity, staying at No. 1 for most of its run, therefore proving that sitcoms could be successful. It also revolutionized sitcom production, introducing the three-camera technique, and was one of the first TV shows to be filmed live before a studio audience.

I Love Lucy was responsible for another television landmark as well. It was the first show to feature a pregnant character. (Although CBS censors forbade the term "pregnant"—Lucy was "expecting.") Some 54 million people tuned in on January 19, 1953, to watch the episode in which "Little Ricky" was born. It was the highest-rated television show, in terms of percentages, of the decade, and one of the highest-rated TV shows ever.

I Love Lucy was somewhat paradoxical in terms of its treatment of women. The premise of the show, with its childlike wife and authority-figure husband, was stereotypically 1950s. And the women behind the scenes at the show did not get a great amount of credit for their work. Nonetheless, *I Love Lucy* proved that a woman lead could carry a television show. Lucille Ball was half (or more) of the brains behind the show, and when she took over Desilu Studios, the couple's joint production company, in 1962, she became the first woman president of a major TV studio.

This excerpt from Lucille Ball's memoir provides insights into Ball's acting career and her marriage to Desi Arnaz, as well as a behind-the-scenes view of the creation of *I Love Lucy* and its characters.

Primary Source

Love, Lucy [excerpt]

SYNOPSIS: In this excerpt from her memoir, published after her death, Lucille Ball discusses how she and her husband, Desi Arnez, were given the opportunity to develop the pilot for *I Love Lucy* while she was pregnant with their first child. She also explains how the show came to be filmed in California, rather than New York, and how the now-familiar characters were cast and developed.

When I was going into my fourth month of pregnancy, CBS suddenly gave Desi the green light: they would finance a pilot for a domestic television show featuring the two of us as a married couple. A show that might go on the air that fall.

"What show?" I asked our agent, Don Sharpe. "We don't have a television show."

"You've got a month to put one together," he answered. "They want the pilot by February fifteenth."

For ten years, Desi and I had been trying to become co-stars and parents; now our dearest goals were being realized much too fast. We suddenly felt unprepared for either and began to have second thoughts.

At that time, television was regarded as the enemy by Hollywood. So terrified was Hollywood of this medium, movie people were afraid to make even guest appearances. If I undertook a weekly television show and it flopped, I might never work in movies again.

It would mean each of us would have to give up our respective radio programs, and Desi would have to cancel all his band engagements. It was a tremendous gamble; it had to be an all-or-nothing commitment.

But this was the first real chance Desi and I would have to work together, something we'd both been longing for for years.

We continued to wrestle with the decision, trying to look at things from every angle. Then one night Carole Lombard appeared to me in a dream. She was wearing one of those slinky bias-cut gowns of the thirties, waving a long black cigarette holder in her hand. "Go on, kid," she advised me airily. "Give it a whirl."

The next day I told Don Sharpe, "We'll do it. Desi and I want to work together more than anything else in the world."

We called my radio writers on *My Favorite Husband* and together dreamed up a set of television characters. Originally, we were Lucy and Larry López; it wasn't until we started our first shows that we became the Ricardos. Desi would be a Cuban bandleader who worked in New York City; I would play a housewife with burning stage ambitions.

Because we had so little time, we adapted parts of our vaudeville act for the pilot. I did a baggy-pants clown bit with the cello. For the rest of the show I appeared in bathrobe and pajamas to conceal my obvious condition. Desi sang, played the drums, and exchanged patter with me; he was the perfect partner, capable and funny, and his great charm and vitality came shining through.

The cast of "I Love Lucy," from top left to bottom right: Vivian Vance, Lucille Ball, William Frawley, and Desi Arnaz. The show won two Emmys for Best Situation Comedy. **UPI/BETTMANN ARCHIVE. REPRODUCED WITH PERMISSION.**

A week later our agent phoned to say, "Philip Morris wants to sponsor you!" We were on our way.

However, in the next few weeks the deal twisted and changed and almost blew up. The sponsor had a second demand: they not only wanted a weekly show, they also wanted it done live in New York. In 1951, a show done live on the West Coast appeared on the East Coast in fuzzy kinescope—with the image about as sharp as a piece of cheesecloth.

We refused to move to New York. Desi suggested that we *film* the show, live, in front of an audience. The network people screamed. A filmed show cost twice as much as a live one. The sponsor wouldn't put up more money and neither would CBS. So Desi made a canny offer: In return for a $1,000 weekly salary cut for us, we were given complete ownership of the show; originally, CBS had owned half of it. CBS also agreed to advance the enormous sums of money needed to start film production, with Desi as producer.

All Desi had ever managed was a sixteen-piece Latin band. Now he had to rent a studio and equipment and find actors, cameramen, stagehands, cutters, film editors, writers, and scripts for thirty-nine weekly shows.

When the deal was finally set, it was late March. We had to start filming by August 15 to be on the air by October. We could rehearse and film a half-hour show in a week, but cutting, editing, and scoring would take another five weeks at least.

We began discussing possible writers. First comes the script, and then the interpretation and improvisations. Both of us admired and liked my three radio writers, Madelyn Pugh, Bob Carroll, Jr., and Jess Oppenheimer. As Jess says, "In a show that's destined to be a hit, nothing but happy things happen. God's arm was around us."

As Lucy Ricardo, I played a character very much like Liz Cugat on my radio show. Lucy was impulsive, inquisitive, and completely feminine. She was never acid or vicious. Even with pie on her face she remained an attractive and desirable female, stirred by real emotions.

Lucy Ricardo's nutty predicaments arose from an earnest desire to please. And there was something touching about her stage ambitions. As we were discussing her with our writers, Desi spoke up. "She tries so hard . . . she can't dance and she can't sing . . . she's earnest and pathetic. . . . Oh, I love that Lucy!" And so the title of the show was born.

Desi was cast as the steadying, levelheaded member of the family, a practical man and a good money manager. He tolerated his wife's foibles good-naturedly, but he could only be pushed so far. The audience had to believe that I lived in fear and trembling of my husband's wrath, and with Desi, they could. There was also a chemistry, a strong mutual attraction between us, which always came through.

At the very first story conference, Desi laid down the underlying principles of the show. The humor could never be mean or unkind. Neither Ricky nor Lucy would ever flirt seriously with anyone else. Mothers-in-law would not be held up to ridicule. Most of all, Desi insisted on Ricky's manhood. He refused to ever be a nincompoop husband. "When Lucy's got something up her sleeve that would make Ricky look like a fool, let the audience know that I'm in on the secret," he told our writers.

I had always known that Desi was a great showman, but many were surprised to learn he was a genius with keen instincts for comedy and plot. He has a quick, brilliant mind; he can instantly find the flaw in any story line; and he has inherent good taste

and an intuitive knowledge of what will and will not play. He is a great producer, a great director. He never stays on too long or allows anybody else to.

When we had the characters of Lucy and Ricky clear in our minds, Jess Oppenheimer suggested that we add another man and wife—an older couple in a lower income bracket. The writers could then pit couple against couple, and the men against the women. I had known Bill Frawley since my RKO starlet days as a great natural comic; we all agreed upon him for Fred Mertz. We then started thinking about a TV wife for Bill.

We considered a number of actresses, and then one day Desi heard about a fine actress from the Broadway stage named Vivian Vance. She was appearing that summer in *The Voice of the Turtle* at La Jolla Playhouse. The ride down the coast was too much for my advanced state of pregnancy, so Jess and Desi drove down without me. They liked how Vivian handled herself on the stage and the way she could flip a comedy line. So they hired her on the spot.

As far as I was concerned, it was Kismet. Viv and I were extraordinarily compatible. We both believe whole-heartedly in what we call "an enchanted sense of play," and use it liberally in our show. It's a happy frame of mind, the light touch, skipping into things instead of plodding. It's looking at things from a child's point of view and believing. The only way I can play a funny scene is to believe it. Then I can convincingly eat like a dog under a table, freeze to death beneath burning-hot klieg lights, or bake a loaf of bread ten feet long.

We had no way of knowing how comical she and Bill would be together. Vivian was actually much younger than Bill. Up until then, she'd usually been cast in glamorous "other woman" parts. But she went along gamely with Ethel Mertz's dowdy clothes, no false eyelashes or eye makeup, and hair that looked as if she had washed and set it herself. But she drew the line at padding her body to look fatter.

Time and again she told Jess Oppenheimer, "If my husband in this series makes fun of my weight and I'm actually fat, then the audience won't laugh . . . they'll feel sorry for me. But if he calls me a fat old bag and I'm not too heavy, then it will seem funny."

Vivian was unhappy in her marriage to actor Philip Ober and so she ate; after a while Jess stopped insisting that she pad herself. On summer vacations she'd diet, and once she came back on the set positively svelte. "Well, Vivian," I kidded her, "you've got just two weeks to get fat and sloppy again."

She and Bill scrapped a good deal, and this put a certain amount of real feeling into their stage quarrels. Bill became the hero of all henpecked husbands. He couldn't walk down the street without some man coming up to him and saying, "Boy, Fred, you tell that Ethel off something beautiful!"

So much good luck was involved in the casting. Early in the series, our writers wanted to write a show in which the Mertzes had to sing and dance. We then learned for the first time that both Vivian and Bill had had big musical comedy careers. Vivian had been in *Skylark* with Gertrude Lawrence, and Bill was a well-known vaudeville hoofer.

I had insisted upon having a studio audience; otherwise, I knew, we'd never hit the right tempo. We did the show every Thursday night in front of four hundred people, a cross-section of America. I could visualize our living and working together on the set like a stock company, then filming it like a movie, and at the same time staging it like a Broadway play. "We'll have opening night every week," I chortled.

Further Resources

BOOKS

Arnaz, Desi. *A Book.* Cutchogue, N.Y.: Buccaneer Books, 1977.

Brady, Kathleen. *Lucille: The Life of Lucille Ball.* New York: Hyperion, 1994.

Brochu, Jim. *Lucy in the Afternoon: An Intimate Memoir of Lucille Ball.* New York: William Morrow, 1990.

Fidelman, Geoffrey Mark. *The Lucy Book: A Complete Guide to Her Five Decades on Television.* Los Angeles: Renaissance Books, 1999.

Harris, Warren G. *Lucy & Desi: The Legendary Love Story of Television's Most Famous Couple.* New York: Simon and Schuster, 1991.

Sanders, Coyne Steven, and Thomas W. Gilbert. *Desilu: The Story of Lucille Ball and Desi Arnaz.* New York: Morrow, 1993.

WEBSITES

I Love Lucy. Fifties.Com. Available online at http://www.fiftiesweb.com/lucy.htm; website home page: http://www.fiftiesweb.com (accessed March 19, 2003).

AUDIO AND VISUAL MEDIA

I Love Lucy 50th Anniversary Special. 2001. CBS Special. Paramount. DVD and VHS, 2002.

9

MEDICINE AND HEALTH

CHRISTOPHER CUMO

Entries are arranged in chronological order by date of primary source. For entries with one primary source, the entry title is the same as the primary source title. Entries with more than one primary source have an overall entry title, followed by the titles of the primary sources.

Important Events in Medicine and Health, 1950–1959

1950

- A human aorta transplant is performed, the hepititis A virus is isolated and photographed, and penicillin is synthesized.

- U.S. Department of Agriculture (USDA) microbiologist Robert G. Benedict discovers a new type of streptomycin, the first antibiotic effective against tuberculosis.

- The American Medical Association approves a resolution that white medical schools should admit African American students.

- Americans spent $8.4 billion on medical care.

- On January 1, the U.S. had 134 centers that specialized in the diagnosis and treatment of cancer.

- On January 26, a new antibiotic, Terramycin, is developed.

- On March 7, blood tests for tuberculosis are introduced.

- On April 14, stomach cancers are detected using radioactive pills that a patient swallowed.

- On April 18, heart massage revives a patient pronounced dead during surgery.

1951

- The nausea-inducing drug antabus is marketed as a cure for alcoholism.

- Antibiotics are used to stimulate growth in livestock.

- USDA microbiologist Kenneth B. Raper develops a new technique for producing penicillin.

- On July 25, the full-body X-ray machine is developed.

- On July 30, *Time* reports that neurologists at a median salary of $28,628 earn more money than physicians in any other category. The median U.S. household income is only $3,400.

- From September 3 to September 7, a report suggests that viruses may cause some cancers.

- On October 9, leg veins are transplanted to repair faulty arteries.

- On December 11, Rockefeller University physician Max Theiler receives the Nobel Prize in physiology or medicine for his development of a yellow-fever vaccine.

1952

- A heart-lung machine is developed. Polio strikes a record fifty-five thousand people.

- On January 30, electric shock revives a cardiac-arrest patient.

- On February 10, the 190-million-volt deuteron ray combats cancer without breaking the skin.

- On March 8, a mechanical heart keeps a patient alive for eighty minutes.

- On April 21, holes in a heart wall are repaired surgically.

- On September 19, an artificial heart valve is inserted in a human.

- On November 13, an artificial pacemaker is used to regulate heart rhythm.

- On December 12, Selman Abraham Waksman, a microbiologist at the New Jersey Agricultural Experiment Station of Rutgers University, receives the Nobel Prize in physiology or medicine for his discovery of streptomycin, the first antibiotic effective against tuberculosis.

1953

- On March 28, Dr. Jonas Salk publishes in the *Journal of the American Medical Association* the success of his polio vaccine in trials on monkeys and humans.

- On April 11, Congress creates the Department of Health, Education, and Welfare at the request of President Dwight D. Eisenhower.

- On May 6, Cincinnati, Ohio physician John H. Gibbons, Jr. uses for the first time the heart-lung machine in surgery.

- From October 5 to October 9, a human aorta is repaired using animal tissue.

- On November 4, a two-million-volt anticancer X-ray machine is developed.

- On November 11, the polio virus is photographed.

- On December 8, skin cancer is produced in mice by painting their skins with cigarette tar.

1954

- Full-scale open-heart surgery is introduced.

- Vitamin B-12 deficiency is found to cause pernicious anemia.

- On February 23, mass trials of Jonas Salk's polio vaccine begin.

- On March 6, the Food and Drug Administration approves Chlorpromazine, marketed as Thorazine, as a tranquilizer to suppress symptoms of disturbed behavior.

- On December 11, U.S. scientists John F. Enders, Thomas H. Weller and Frederick C. Robbins share the Nobel Prize in physiology or medicine for their research on the polio virus.

1955

- The antiarthritis steroid drug prednisone is introduced.

- On January 1, less than 5 percent of U.S. medical students are women and less than 3 percent are African American.

- On April 12, University of Michigan physician Thomas Francis announces the success of the Salk polio vaccine.

- On May 12, a surgical procedure for victims of cerebral palsy is developed.

- On September 24, President Dwight D. Eisenhower suffers a heart attack.

- On November 2, the first successful kidney transplant is announced.

1956

- Congress spends $100 million in medical research.

- The kidney dialysis machine is developed.

- In February, Harvard University physician Gregory Pincus begins to test Enovid, a birth-control pill, on fifteen thousand women in Puerto Rico and Haiti.

- On July 15, the U.S. Food and Drug Administration reports that coal-tar dyes may cause some cancers.

- On October 6, American physician Albert Sabin announces the development of a new polio vaccine.

- On October 9, a cancer-immunity mechanism in human cells is discovered through research on prison volunteers.

- On October 15, the development of a live-virus orally administered polio vaccine is announced.

- From October to November, *The Saturday Evening Post* runs a series of articles critical of the substandard care of mental patients at Columbus State Hospital in Ohio.

- On November 22, researchers announce no benefit in the use of citrus-fruit extracts high in vitamin C to fight the common cold.

- On November 25, the American Cancer Society announces that cigarette smoking and lung cancer are related.

- On December 29, Dr. Albert Sabin announces in the *Journal of the American Medical Association* the success of trials of his polio vaccine in monkeys, chimpanzees and humans.

1957

- A one-minute blood test for syphilis is introduced.

- Synthetic arteries of rubberized nylon are used as surgical replacements.

- On January 1, only 14 of 26 southern medical schools admit African American students.

- On March 9, synthetic penicillin is developed.

- On May 17, seven year old Benny Hopper falls into a well. Physician Joseph Kris assists in his rescue and charges Hopper's parents $1,500 for his services.

- In June, the first American contracts a strain of influenza, a viral infection, called Asian flu.

- In June, the Food and Drug Administration approves the pain-killing drug Darvon.

- In July, the Food and Drug Administration approves a vaccine against the Asian flu.

1958

- Ultrasound examination of fetuses is introduced.

- The first catheterization of coronary arteries occurs.

- In March, the first measles vaccine is tested.

- In March, *Science Digest* estimates that 450,000 Americans contract cancer each year.

- In March, Dr. James Watt, head of the National Heart Institute, cautions that no evidence yet links the consumption of fat to heart disease.

- On June 5, athletes' use of stimulating drugs to enhance performance is investigated.

- On October 3, a drug is developed to counteract the side effects of penicillin.

- On October 29, a blind woman reports seeing flashes of light after photocells are implanted in the sight centers of her brain.

- On November 12, Congress ends the ban on the sale of antibiotics to Communist countries.

- From November 18 to November 20, the first National Conference on Air Pollution is held.

1959

- A resuscitator small enough to be used on infants is developed.

- Approximately 123 million Americans have health insurance.

- In March, a combined vaccine for whooping cough, diptheria, and polio is released.

- On September 29, a report estimates that 47 percent of Americans over age 14 smoke.

- On November 25, the pressure test for glaucoma is developed.

Surgeon General, a position he coveted, had he not died of appendicitis in 1902.

Reed's death did not end the story of yellow fever. Control of the disease by reducing the population of mosquitoes is not foolproof. A single viruliferous female is enough to transmit the disease to humans. A vaccine is better protection against disease. A vaccine is a dead or weakened strain of a bacterium or virus of a closely related bacterium or virus injected into a person. That person's immune system develops antibodies against the bacterium or virus that confer immunity against a live strain of the pathogen.

Significance

In his 1951 Nobel Lecture, Max Theiler details his development of the first yellow fever vaccine. Early in his work at Harvard Medical School, he determined that mice infected with the yellow fever flavivirus produced antibodies against the disease. Theiler's colleagues in France used viruses and antibodies extracted from the serum of infected mice in trying to make a vaccine, but Theiler warned against this vaccine because of its potential to damage the central nervous system.

Theiler next grew a strain of the flavivirus in a chick embryo fortified with tissue from the central nervous system of monkeys. This method allowed him to derive several strains of the flavivirus, one of which, through a mutation (a change in the chemistry of the virus), Theiler believed, lost its potency to cause serious infection but which was strong enough to induce infected humans to produce antibodies. Theiler at last had a safe vaccine against yellow fever. He concluded that it, along with depriving the *Aedes aegpyti* mosquito of places to lay her eggs, had reduced yellow fever from an epidemic to a rare disease.

Primary Source

"The Development of Vaccines Against Yellow Fever" [excerpt]

SYNOPSIS: In this excerpt, Max Theiler details his development of the first safe yellow fever vaccine. By growing strains of yellow fever flavivirus in a chick embryo, Theiler extracted a single strain that was less potent than the others but that nonetheless prompted a person's immune system to manufacture antibodies against the flavivirus.

In my early work it was clearly shown that mice could be used for determining the presence of yellow fever antibodies in sera. Standardized tests for antibodies by the use of these animals were soon evolved by Sawyer and Lloyd, and myself. These have

---

"The Development of Vaccines Against Yellow Fever"

Speech

By: Max Theiler

Date: December 11, 1951

Source: Theiler, Max. "The Development of Vaccines Against Yellow Fever." Available online at http://www.nobel.se/medicine/laureates/1951/theiler-lecture.html; website home page: http://www.nobel.se/ (accessed June 9, 2003)

About the Author: Max Theiler (1899–1972) was born in Pretoria, South Africa, and received an M.D. from the London School of Tropical Medicine in 1922. That year he joined Harvard Medical School's Department of Tropical Medicine, rising to the rank of instructor. In 1930, he joined the Rockefeller Foundation, becoming Director of Laboratories in 1951. His development of the first yellow fever vaccine won him the 1951 Nobel Prize in medicine or physiology. ■

Introduction

Before the twentieth century, yellow fever plagued people in warm climates. A flavivirus causes yellow fever, and the flavivirus survives in the *Aedes aegpyti* mosquito without affecting it. When a viruliferous female (one carrying the virus) bites a human, she transmits the flavivirus to that person. After incubation, the flavivirus causes fever, bleeding through the mouth and nose, vomiting, black discharge, liver damage, jaundice, and death within two weeks. Between the 1600s and 1905, yellow fever repeatedly struck the southeastern United States during summer. In densely populated cities, it killed as many as 100,000 people in a summer.

Much attention has focused on the role of the U.S. Army and Walter Reed, a major and physician, in identifying the *Aedes aegpyti* mosquito as the carrier of yellow fever and in eradicating the disease in Cuba and the southeastern United States by 1910 by depriving the female mosquito of places to lay her eggs. This triumph might have won Reed a Nobel Prize in medicine or physiology, promotion in the Army, or appointment as U.S.

proved of great value in the study of the epidemiology and distribution of yellow fever and eventually in testing the efficacy of different vaccines as these became available. . . .

In the development of vaccines for human beings, using my mouse-adapted virus, two paths were followed. In the first, used chiefly by French workers, virus alone was inoculated; and in the second, used by American and English workers, virus and human immune serum were inoculated simultaneously. The first immunizations of humans using mouse-adapted neurotropic virus alone were reported by Sellard and Laigret (1932). Several severe reactions were reported, and the method was modified by Laigret, who introduced the procedure of giving three inoculations at twenty-day intervals of virus which had been exposed for four days, two days, and one day, respectively, to a temperature of 20°C. That this method consisted essentially of the inoculation of three graded doses of fully virulent neurotropic virus and not of attenuated virus, as thought by Laigret, was shown by Whitman and myself. These early vaccines, using the neuroadapted virus alone, though producing a satisfactory immunity, were, nevertheless, not considered entirely safe because of the serious reactions associated in some cases with signs of involvement of the central nervous system. Further investigations by French workers, however, finally led to a safe and efficient method of vaccination, which is at present used on a very large scale in the French territories in Africa. This method introduced by Peltier and his co-workers (1939) consists of applying the mouse-adapted virus to the scarified skin. In retrospect, it seems probable that the early severe reactions were due to the use of a virus which, although it had undergone a considerable degree of modification, was nevertheless not sufficiently attenuated for safe use in man. At the present time this method of vaccination is usually combined with vaccinia virus. A mixture of both viruses is applied to the scarified skin, and the individual is thus immunized to the two agents at the same time. Many millions of people have been immunized thus without any very serious reactions having been reported. . . .

Before these new culture experiments had progressed very far, a very marked change in pathogenicity was observed in the Asibi virus grown in the medium, the tissue component of which was chick embryo containing minimal amounts of nervous tissue. This is called the 17D strain. This attenuation consisted in a partial loss of neurotropism for mice

Dr. Max Theiler. October 17, 1951. Dr. Theiler sits at his desk the night before he would be named winner of the Nobel Prize for his work on the yellow fever virus. © BETTMANN/CORBIS. REPRODUCED BY PERMISSION.

and monkeys, as well as a marked loss of viscerotropism for monkeys. Monkeys inoculated intracerebrally developed a mild encephalitis which as a rule was non-fatal. This was the much hoped-for change, as both the strains then in use for human immunization, namely, the French neurotropic virus and the 17E variant of the Asibi virus, cultivated in mouse embryo tissue, invariably produced a fatal encephalitis when inoculated into the brains of rhesus monkeys.

The marked loss of viscerotropism of the 17D culture virus was clearly shown in experiments in monkeys. As a rule monkeys inoculated with the virus by extraneural routes developed no fever or other signs of illness and in their blood only minimal amounts of virus could be demonstrated. Such monkeys were shown to develop specific antibodies and to be solidly immune to the highly virulent Asibi strain.

After extensive experiments in monkeys by Smith and myself, the 17D strain was used for human vaccination without the simultaneous inoculation of immune serum. It was considered that the

Conquerors of Yellow Fever by Dean Cornwell, N.A., c. 1954. This painting allegorically depicts the first medical breakthrough in the study of yellow fever. Walter Reed and Dr. Carlos Finlay look on as Dr. Jesse Lazear inoculates Dr. James Carroll with an infected mosquito. © BETTMANN/CORBIS. REPRODUCED BY PERMISSION.

loss of both the viscerotropic as well as neurotropic affinities as demonstrated in monkeys made this the virus of choice for human vaccination. In a preliminary study we showed that reactions in man were either absent or minimal and that satisfactory antibody response was obtained. Smith, Penna, and Paoliello, in Brazil, made a more thorough and more extensive study of the reaction in man. The results were eminently satisfactory. The 17D virus has been used as a vaccine in many millions of individuals.

In the two parallel series of cultures with the Asibi virus in which whole-chick tissue and chick embryo brain only were used, no such marked attenu-

ation occurred. Both of these viruses, after several hundred subcultures, produced fatal encephalitis in monkeys when inoculated intracerebrally and both produced a rather severe visceral infection. These results suggested that the amount of nervous tissue was the conditioning factor which produced the change, as loss of neurotropism occurred only in a medium containing minimal amounts of nervous tissue. It was considered at the time that these findings were a confirmation of the hypothesis on which the culture experiments had been planned.

Consequently, in order to obtain more information on the role of nervous tissue, I started three new series of tissue cultures. Virus taken from the culture series that had been maintained in chick brain only and virus that had been cultivated in whole-chick embryo were grown in two new series of cultures, the tissue component of which contained minimal amounts of nervous tissue; and, conversely, the 17D virus, which had been grown in a medium containing minimal amounts of nervous tissue, was transferred to a medium containing chick embryo brain only. At the time of the conclusion of the experiment, more than 200 subcultures in the new series had been made. At intervals, monkeys were inoculated intracerebrally to determine the neurotropism of the cultivated virus. The results showed that no modification had occurred. Thus the 17D strain, cultivated for more than 200 subcultures in chick embryo brain, had not become more neurotropic, and the virus at the beginning and the end of the series was essentially the same in pathogenicity. In like manner, the other two strains, which, it will be recalled, produced fatal encephalitis in monkeys at the beginning of these culture experiments, did not lose their neurotropism even though maintained for more than 200 subcultures in a medium containing minimal amounts of nervous tissue. The conclusion was obvious that the relative amounts of nervous tissue present in the media had not produced any demonstrable change.

The reason for the rapid change noticed in the 17D strain, which occurred between the 89th and 114th subcultures, was and still is completely unknown. However, these experiments indicate that once the mutant had occurred, it was relatively stable.

What was apparently a similar mutant was reported subsequently by Penna and Moussatché (1939). These workers maintained the Asibi virus in series in the developing chick embryo and noted a similar marked attenuation. In their experiments a marked loss of neurotropism occurred in spite of the fact that in the developing chick embryo the virus shows a marked affinity for the brain and multiplies readily there.

Our experiments with the Asibi virus in tissue culture may be summarized as follows. In one of the series of cultures, a sudden modification occurred. The evidence is that this change was not due to the relative absence of nervous tissue in the medium, nor could chick embryo tissue per se be responsible as the change occurred in only one of six series of cultures containing chick embryo tissue.

The results with two other strains of yellow fever, the French and JSS, which were cultivated in media containing varying amounts of nervous tissue are briefly as follows. The French viscerotropic virus was cultured for several hundred subcultures in three different media, the tissue component of which consisted of, respectively, mouse-embryo brain, minced whole-chick embryo, and minced chick-embryo containing minimal amounts of nervous tissue. The results showed that the viscerotropism was rapidly lost, but there was no such extreme attenuation as was observed in the 17D virus. On the contrary, it appeared that an actual increase of neurotropism had taken place in all three parallel cultures, irrespective of the quantity of nervous tissue in the medium.

In the culture experiments with the JSS strain, maintained for over three hundred subcultures in the same media as were used for the French virus, the neurotropism tended to decrease in all three series. However, the least decrease was observed in the virus cultured in the medium containing minimal amounts of nervous tissue. The viscerotropism of the virus grown in the medium containing minced whole-chick tissue became so decreased that on inoculation subcutaneously it failed to produce an infection even when administered in large doses. This is the most extreme case of attenuation so far observed in any yellow fever virus. The loss of infectivity of this highly attenuated strain for monkeys inoculated subcutaneously recalls a somewhat similar, though not so marked, change that occurred in one of the 17D culture series, which became so attenuated for man that it failed in a fair proportion of cases to produce immunity.

In conclusion, we may summarize the culture experiments by stating that any yellow fever virus maintained in tissue culture will become attenuated somewhat in its viscerotropic affinities, irrespective of the tissue used. The neurotropic affinity as a rule does not change. Occasionally, however, for some unknown reason, a mutant appears with marked reduction in both neurotropism as well as viscerotropism. This mutant is comparatively stable, but it too has been observed to undergo change on two occasions. The first time, as reported by Soper and Smith, the cultured virus was found to have become so attenuated that it failed to produce immunity in a fair proportion of persons vaccinated, and the second time, noted by Fox and his co-workers, the virus had regained some neurotropism so that it actually produced encephalitis in a small proportion of persons vaccinated.

In comparing the two vaccines at present in use—viz., the French vaccine and the 17D—it may be stated that both vaccines produce an actual infection and a resulting immunity. The infection produced by the French vaccine is more severe than that produced by the 17D, as manifested both by subjective symptoms as well as by the amount of circulating virus. As a consequence of this relatively severe infection induced by the French vaccine, antibody production is more regular than after the extremely mild infection induced by the 17D vaccine. Only time will tell which of the two is to be preferred.

By the intelligent application of antimosquito measures combined with vaccination, public-health officials have now the means available to render what was once a prevalent epidemic disease to one which is now a comparatively rare infection of man.

Further Resources

BOOKS

Immunization Practices Advisory Committee. *Yellow Fever Vaccine*. Atlanta: Center for Disease Control and Prevention, 1984.

Professional Guide to Diseases, 6th ed. Springhouse, Pa.: Springhouse Corporation, 1998.

Theiler, Max. *The Arthropod-Borne Viruses of Vertebrates*. New Haven, Conn.: Yale University Press, 1973.

PERIODICALS

Cetron, Martin S. "Yellow Fever Vaccine." *Morbidity and Mortality Weekly Report* 8, November 2002, 1–11.

Hussain, Al. "Identification and Characterization of Avian Retroviruses in Chicken Embryo-Derived Yellow Fever Vaccines." *Journal of Virology,* January 2003, 1105–1111.

WEBSITES

The Nobel Prize in Physiology or Medicine 1951. Nobel Foundation. Available online at http://www.nobel.se/medicine/laureates/1951/; website home page: http://www.nobel.se/ (accessed June 9, 2003).

Yellow Fever. World Health Organization. Available online at http://www.who.int/inf-fs/en/fact100.html; website home page: http://www.who.int/ (accessed November 9, 2003).

Yellow Fever—Disease and Vaccine. Centers for Disease Control and Prevention. Available online at http://www.cdc.gov/ncidod/dvbid/yellowfever; website home page: http://www.cdc.gov/ (accessed June 9, 2003).

"The Drugs of Microbial Origin"

Essay

By: Kenneth B. Raper and Robert G. Benedict

Date: 1951

Source: Raper, Kenneth B., and Robert G. Benedict. "The Drugs of Microbial Origin." *Crops in Peace and War: The Yearbook of Agriculture, 1950–1951*. Washington, D.C.: GPO, 1951, 734–741.

About the Author: Kenneth B. Raper holds degrees from the University of North Carolina at Chapel Hill, George Washington University, and a Ph.D. in biology from Harvard University. He was principal microbiologist at the U.S Department of Agriculture's Northern Research Laboratory. His expertise was the culture of fungi, yeasts, and bacteria. Robert G. Benedict holds a Ph.D. in biology from the University of Wisconsin at Madison and is a bacteriologist at the U.S. Department of Agriculture's Northern Regional Research Laboratory. He discovered two antibiotics and improved the culture of penicillin. ∎

Introduction

Bacterial infections long decimated humans. The more frightening—plague, cholera, leprosy, pneumonia, tuberculosis, typhoid, streptococcal gangrene, diphtheria, tetanus, and botulism—have burned their way through populations. Antibiotics have been an imperfect solution to the danger of bacteria.

In 1928, British physician Alexander Fleming tried growing bacteria in a petri dish but failed each time. Something had contaminated his dish, Fleming concluded, and that year he isolated the mold *Penicillium notatum*. Growing the mold in turn, he discovered that it exuded a substance that killed bacteria.

Not until 1939 did British biochemist Ernst Chain and Australian pathologist Howard Florey purify a strain of penicillin suitable for manufacture in large quantities. By 1941, the U.S. Army had quantities large enough to treat soldiers during World War II, and physicians had sufficient supplies for civilian use.

Suitable against a range of bacteria, penicillin had little success against tuberculosis, making plain the need for the discovery of new and more potent antibiotics. In 1943, Selman A. Waksman, a microbiologist at Rutgers University and the New Jersey Agricultural Experiment Station, crowned his search by discovering streptomycin, an antibiotic produced by a soil microbe. Like penicillin, streptomycin killed a range of bacteria; unlike penicillin, it killed the tubercle bacillus. The success of penicillin and streptomycin made the 1940s the beginning of the antibiotic era.

Significance

Kenneth B. Raper and Robert G. Benedict played important roles in the antibiotic revolution. In 1951, Raper announced that he and a colleague had developed a technique for producing penicillin in greater quantities than had hitherto been possible. The technique grew penicillin from *Penicillium chrysogenum,* a species closely related to *Penicillium notatum.*

At the same time, Robert G. Benedict and a colleague developed a nutrient solution in which penicillin grew best. By soaking up a portion of penicillin with filter paper, they could quickly test its purity, adjusting nutrients as the test dictated.

In 1950, Benedict and colleagues discovered a new strain of streptomycin, Selman A. Waksman's antibiotic that was effective against tuberculosis. Benedict also discovered a new antibiotic which other scientists named Polymyxin.

In their closing paragraph, Kenneth B. Raper and Robert G. Benedict hope for a future in which scientists will have found an antibiotic for every bacterial infection. Their hope may be too optimistic, for the nature of antibiotics makes them vulnerable. Inside a human they kill bacteria indiscriminately. They may kill millions of bacteria, yet a few by chance may have genetic resistance to an antibiotic. They will survive and multiply, producing many copies of themselves, each immune to the antibiotic. By the nature of their success, antibiotics catalyze the growth of antibiotic-resistance bacteria.

Resistant bacteria have alarmed physicians and scientists since the 1980s with the rise of antibiotic-resistant strains of tuberculosis and the spread of human immunodeficiency virus (HIV), which destroys the immune system and makes lethal what might otherwise have been a treatable bacterial infection. As HIV spreads through the human population, it undermines the potency of antibiotics, leading some physicians to fear that humans may be nearing the end of the antibiotic era.

Primary Source

"The Drugs of Microbial Origin" [excerpt]

SYNOPSIS: In this excerpt, Kenneth B. Raper and Robert G. Benedict describe their role in growing penicillin in greater quantity and purity. Benedict announced his discovery of a new strain of streptomycin and of a new antibiotic, Polymyxin.

Cultures that can produce substantially greater yields of penicillin were developed by Kenneth B. Raper and Dorothy I. Fennell. All early studies in England and the United States were made in surface cultures with the strain of *Penicillin notatum* originally isolated by Professor Fleming. Other strains were found to be more suitable for submerged production. Extensive search for more productive molds led to the discovery of a strain of the closely related species, *P. chrysogenum,* from which successively better substrains were developed through the selection of natural variants and the production of mutants by exposure of spores to X-ray and ultraviolet

A worker transfers streptomycin medication into bottles in a factory, circa 1950s. AP/WIDE WORLD PHOTOS. REPRODUCED BY PERMISSION.

radiations. The latter steps were carried out at the Carnegie Institution of Washington in Cold Spring Harbor, N. Y., and at the Universities of Minnesota and Wisconsin. The cumulative result of all the studies was the development of a culture capable of yielding 900 to 1,000 units per milliliter of penicillin, in contrast to 75 to 100 units per milliliter obtainable from the unimproved parent. This culture is still universally employed for the manufacture of penicillin in this country and abroad, and additional selections and mutations have undoubtedly been developed in the research laboratories of the penicillin industry to increase productivity further.

Methods of assaying penicillin were much improved by W. H. Schmidt, R. G. Benedict, and others at the Northern Laboratory, by standardizing the composition and thickness of the nutritive agar layer and by controlling the density and uniformity of the test bacterial growth. Discs of filter paper saturated with penicillin-containing samples have been substituted for porcelain, glass, or metal cups, and various devices have been developed for rapid and more accurate measurement of the resulting inhibition zones. Despite the refinements, the method still generally employed rests squarely on the principles which underlie the technique developed by Heatley and his associates. Serial dilution and turbidimetric methods of assay have been perfected and find special applications in industrial practice. Some progress has been made toward developing an assay based upon chemical reactions and analyses. . . .

In 1950, a new form of streptomycin was discovered by Robert G. Benedict, Frank H. Stodola, and co-workers at the Northern Laboratory. The same antibiotic was subsequently reported by W. E. Grundy and co-workers at Abbott Laboratories. The Northern Laboratory workers assigned the name hydroxystreptomycin to the antibiotic since it differs from regular streptomycin in having one more oxygen atom in the molecule. Hydroxystreptomycin is produced by a new actinomycete, *Streptomyces griseocarneus*. At present, the antibiotic is undergoing toxicity and pharmacological tests to determine whether it possesses advantages over streptomycin. . . .

In May 1947, Robert G. Benedict and A. F. Langlykke, of the Northern Laboratory, reported the production by certain strains of *Bacillus polymyxa* of a water-soluble factor that strongly inhibited the gram-negative bacteria. They did not assign a name to the antibiotic, because it had not been purified sufficiently to compare its chemical and physical properties with those of known antibiotics from other members of the genus *Bacillus*. Independently, P. G. Stansly, R. G. Shepherd, and H. J. White, investigators at the American Cyanamid Co., discovered the same antibiotic and designated it polymyxin. In August 1947, G. C. Ainsworth, A. M. Brown, and G. Brownlee, working at the Wellcome Laboratories in England, independently reported the production of an antibiotic, called aerosporin, from *Bacillus aerosporus,* which is synonymous with *Bacillus polymyxa*. . . .

A medium consisting of corn steep liquor, dextrose, and calcium carbonate, developed and recommended by Benedict and Langlykke, was cheaper than Stansly's yeast extract-mineral salts-glucose medium. However, the Stansly medium gave higher yields of polymyxin, and the substitution of soy or peanut meals as protein sources in place of yeast extract lowered its cost. . . .

More than 150 antibiotic substances produced by micro-organisms, higher fungi, and green plants have been reported. Less than one-tenth of them, however, offer promise for the control of human and animal diseases. Some are inactive in the animal body; many are highly toxic. But the search continues, and periodically, from among the many new an-

tibiotics discovered, one is found to combat or forestall some infection against which previously there has been no satisfactory weapon. The list of curative agents is thus constantly enlarged, and in this expanding array of new drugs, those of microbial origin occupy an increasingly prominent position. The vision of a cure for every type of infection gradually assumes reality.

Further Resources

BOOKS

Parascandola, John. ed. *The History of Antibiotics.* Madison, Wisc.: American Institute of the History of Pharmacy, 1980.

Professional Guide to Diseases, 6th ed. Springhouse, Pa.: Springhouse Corporation, 1998.

Waksman, Selman A. *The Antibiotic Era.* Tokyo, Japan: Waksman Foundation of Japan, 1975.

PERIODICALS

"New Antibiotics and New Resistance." *American Scientist,* March/April 2003, 138–150.

WEBSITES

"APUA: Alliance for the Prudent Use of Antibiotics." Available online at http://www.tufts.edu/med/apua; website home page: http://www.tufts.edu (accessed June 12, 2003).

MEDLINEplus: Antibiotics. National Library of Medicine and the National Institutes of Health. Available online at http://www.nlm.nih.gov/medlineplus/antibiotics.html; website home page: http://medlineplus.gov/ (accessed June 12, 2003).

AUDIO AND VISUAL MEDIA

Antibiotics: The Wonder Drugs. New York: A & E Home Video, 1998.

A History of Antibiotics. Princeton, N.J.: Films for the Humanities & Sciences, 2000.

"Studies in Human Subjects on Active Immunization against Poliomyelitis"

Journal article

By: Jonas E. Salk

Date: March 28, 1953

Source: Salk, Jonas E. "Studies in Human Subjects on Active Immunization against Poliomyelitis." *Journal of the American Medical Association.* March 28, 1953, 1081–1098.

About the Author: Jonas Edward Salk (1914–1995) was born in New York City and received his M.D. from New York University College of Medicine in 1939. In 1947, he became head of the Virus Research Laboratory at the University of Pittsburgh. He began the first trial with a polio vaccine in 1952 and released the vaccine for sale in 1955. ∎

Introduction

Poliovirus, a virus that, like influenza, spreads quickly through a population, causes poliomyelitis (polio) or infantile paralysis. The disease first appeared in 1840. Epidemics swept Norway and Sweden in 1905. The virus spread to Europe, the Americas, Australia, and New Zealand, peaking in the 1940s and early 1950s. Stricken as a young man, Franklin Delano Roosevelt, the longest-serving U.S. president, was the most prominent American to suffer from polio, a disease he hid from public view.

Ninety-five percent of all infections cause fever, lethargy, headache, vomiting, and sore throat. A patient recovers in seventy-two hours as though the illness was nothing more than a bout of flu. The remaining five percent of cases afflict the central nervous system. Not all virulent infections paralyze victims, but severe cases leave lesions on the spinal cord, paralyzing victims in varying degrees. The most dangerous cases afflict the brain, stopping its ability to control respiratory muscles, a condition that can be fatal. Poliovirus weakens the immune system, leaving victims vulnerable to other infections.

Cases of paralysis require victims to undergo prolonged physical therapy, wear braces and special shoes, and in the worst cases to undergo orthopedic surgery. Full recovery from paralysis is unknown.

Significance

In his 1953 article, Jonas Salk detailed the precautions he took in preparing a vaccine against polio for human trials. He first tested the vaccine on monkeys to be sure of its safety and weakened the strain of poliovirus in the vaccine by storing it in formaldehyde, a chemical that kills life, for at least twenty-four hours.

A virus displays no sign of life outside a cell, so it cannot be killed when it is outside a cell. It can be weakened by damaging the protein envelope that surrounds the nucleotide bases (the large molecules that build deoxyribonucleic acid) that are the virus. A virus, however, can be destroyed by disintegrating the sequence of nucleotide bases that are the virus.

After testing the vaccine on monkeys, Salk tested it on people whom poliovirus had already paralyzed because he did not want to risk paralyzing healthy humans. His test demonstrated that humans inoculated with the vaccine produced antibodies against poliovirus, evidence of the vaccine's success.

Antibodies protect a person from infection by attacking a pathogen when it enters the body. Because the body of a vaccinated person has antibodies in reserve, they can immediately attack the pathogen, in this case poliovirus. The body of someone without these antibodies would need time to manufacture them by trial and error until it arrived at the correct antibodies. But the body has

Jonas Salk holds bottles of his polio vaccine, c. 1955. Salk developed the vaccine in a laboratory at the University of Pennsylvania.
© BETTMANN/CORBIS. REPRODUCED BY PERMISSION.

no luxury of time. Infection likely will overwhelm the immune system before it can produce the right antibodies.

Salk reported that none of the 161 people inoculated with the vaccine displayed polio symptoms, evidence of the vaccine's safety. Salk thus had developed a vaccine that produced antibodies in an inoculated person and that caused no polio symptoms. These are the prerequisites of a successful vaccine and demonstrate that Jonas Salk developed the first safe and effective polio vaccine.

Primary Source

"Studies in Human Subjects on Active Immunization against Poliomyelitis" [excerpt]

SYNOPSIS: In this excerpt, Jonas Salk reported the results of trials of his polio vaccine in monkeys and humans. The results indicated that his virus was safe and effective against poliovirus.

A Preliminary Report of Experiments in Progress

Investigations have been under way in this laboratory for more than a year, with the objective of establishing conditions for destroying the disease-producing property of the three types of poliomyelitis virus without destroying completely their capacity to induce antibody formation in experimental animals. The success of experiments in monkeys with vaccines prepared from virus produced in tissue culture and referred to briefly elsewhere led to the studies now in progress in human subjects. It is the purpose of this report to present the results obtained thus far in the investigations in man. The voluminous detail of the preliminary and collateral experiments in animals will be elaborated on elsewhere. Before presenting the pertinent experimental data, I would like to review briefly the present state of the problem of immunization against poliomyelitis, and to discuss certain concepts of the nature of the disease as these bear on the studies here reported. . . .

Approaches to Artificial Immunization

Among the earliest reports on immunization of monkeys and then of man were those of Brodie and of Kolmer in the early 1930's. Their studies were conducted before precise knowledge regarding pathogenesis and immunologic complexity were available, and before there had accumulated the vast experience with the many strains that possess different pathogenic characteristics. Moreover, methods had not been developed for adequate purification of virus from suspensions of central nervous system tissue, nor were the dynamics of virus inactivation or modification well enough understood.

More than a decade later, Morgan clearly demonstrated that a formaldehyde-treated suspension of central nervous system tissue from monkeys containing a type 2 strain of poliomyelitis virus did, after a rather rigorous schedule of immunization, induce the formation of appreciable quantities of antibody. She was also able to induce a measurable degree of resistance to intracerebral challenge in monkeys vaccinated repeatedly with similarly prepared type 1 virus.

Other investigators in studies with mice and cotton rats confirmed the fact that preparations of type 2 virus that were noninfectious were still capable of inducing immunity in rodents. Thus, it would appear that materials devoid of demonstrable infectious activity for animals will immunize if given repeatedly in sufficient amount. This approach was extended by Howe, who was able to demonstrate antibody formation in chimpanzees. In parallel experiments in six human subjects, he observed the development of antibody that in most instances persisted over the observation period of six months; each child received 3.5 ml. of human gamma globulin followed by 3 ml. of vaccine.

Another approach that has been suggested for inducing immunity is that of the feeding of attenuated living virus. Koprowski and his associates have recently reported the results of studies in 20 human subjects fed a preparation of type 2 virus, which had been propagated in the central nervous system of rodents. In their studies, an immunologic response was induced and evidence found of virus multiplication in the gastro-intestinal tract. The agent used for feeding was reported to be less pathogenic for the monkey than for rodents, but still caused paralysis when inoculated intracerebrally into the monkey.

It is evident from the foregoing that many observations made both in the laboratory and in the field have for a long time encouraged the expectation that immunization against poliomyelitis should be possible. The greater acceptability now of the idea that invasion of the central nervous system may be primarily via the blood stream rather than primarily along neural pathways has increased the likelihood of such a solution. Moreover, the knowledge now available has reduced to reasonable levels the preliminary requirements expected for the performance of an immunologic method.

Although the objective to be achieved, in terms of serum antibody level, is more clearly defined and more reasonable of attainment, the question that still remains is how antibody formation may be induced in a practicable manner. The basic prerequisites are simple enough. These are first, a rich source of virus reasonably free of extraneous antigenic material and second, a method for destroying pathogenicity without completely destroying antigenic capacity. To these might be added a third, a means for enhancing antigenic activity if the richest source of virus available after treatment for destroying pathogenicity proves to be inadequate or borderline in its effectiveness. It is the purpose of this report to show how these objectives are being approached, and to present data on the degree of antibody response observed in man in the first experiments cautiously undertaken. . . .

Safety Tests

The first problem that had to be resolved before human subjects could be inoculated was the question of safety. It has been the consensus that tests for safety should include the intracerebral inoculation of monkeys. In all of the material employed for human beings, the absence of infectivity for the cynomolgus monkey was established in prior tests by the intracerebral inoculation of 0.5 ml. of fluid in

6 to 10 animals. As an additional safeguard, the only preparations considered satisfactory for use were those that had been exposed to the action of formaldehyde for at least 24 to 48 hours after the test just described indicated that infectivity had been destroyed. The fact that amounts of virus that produce paralysis when given intracerebrally are not paralytogenic when given intramuscularly or intravenously suggests that the intracerebral safety test may provide a more than adequate margin in certifying a given preparation as safe for use in human subjects.

Tissue culture methods have been developed for the detection of residual virus activity in the chemically treated preparations. Studies for correlating the results of tests for residual virus activity as measured in tissue culture and in the monkey are now under way. Until the relative sensitivity of the two has been determined, the number of monkeys used for establishing safety will be at least as great as that employed in the present investigations. . . .

Human Subjects

In extending to man studies on vaccination performed in laboratory animals, tests on more than a few individuals had to be anticipated. The first persons to participate in these studies were patients paralyzed in recent years by a poliomyelitis infection and who were in residence at the D. T. Watson Home for Crippled Children, Leetsdale, Pa. In addition to patients who had recovered from paralytic poliomyelitis, there were others who were in residence at the Watson Home for such diseases as arthritis, spastic paralysis, and a variety of congenital deformities. After the initial investigations were under way at the Watson Home, additional studies were undertaken at the Polk State School, Polk, Pa. . . .

Experimental Procedures and Results

The principal purpose of the experiments to be described was to determine whether or not the experimental vaccines that were made could induce antibody formation in human subjects. In the initial explorations, small doses of aqueous vaccines were inoculated intradermally. From the studies completed thus far, the indications are that only the type 2 preparation then available was effective when administered in this way. Later experiments were performed with experimental vaccines emulsified in mineral oil and inoculated intramuscularly. In these studies it was found that antibody for all three types was induced.

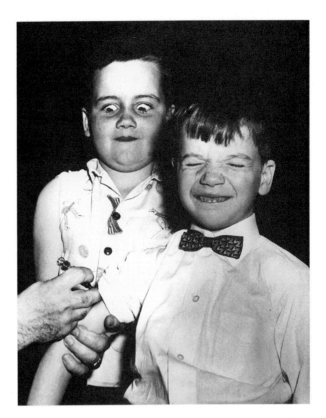

Leo Casey watches as Charles Buzine receives a shot of the Salk polio vaccine, April 29, 1955. Soon after Salk developed his vaccine, school children began receiving inoculations nationwide.
© BETTMANN/CORBIS. REPRODUCED BY PERMISSION.

Since the conditions for destroying infectivity without completely destroying antigenicity were not known in advance, several experimental vaccines were prepared and were tested for antigenic effectiveness in human subjects inoculated with the dose and in the manner indicated. . . . Sufficient time has not elapsed for titrating antibody in all scrums that have already been collected, particularly in the more recent experiments. However, the immunologic results available to date will serve to indicate the trends observed thus far.

Although the primary objective of these studies was to determine whether or not the preparations selected on the basis of their safety for animals still retained antigenic capacity, another purpose was to obtain information in answer to the question of safety for human subjects. It is desired to state at the very outset that in none of the 161 persons involved have there been any signs of illness that could be attributed to the inoculation. Among subjects who received vaccine with mineral oil adjuvant, there have been no untoward local reactions. . . .

Theoretical and Practical Implications

From the theoretical viewpoint, the findings presented are of interest because antibody responses occurred following inoculation with quantities of material that a priori might not have been expected to be effective. It may well be that the quantity of antigenic substance present in the fluids employed is considerably greater than is suggested by the results of titrations for infectious activity. It was this thesis, formulated on the basis of observations made earlier, that influenced the plan for the studies here reported.

Comparative data on the antibody-inducing effect in humans of poliomyelitis virus vaccines with and without emulsification with mineral oil are meager. However, the trend in the observations here reported is in keeping with the results of studies with influenza virus vaccines, in which it has been found that a concentration of virus in sodium chloride solution, just below the threshold necessary to induce antibody formation, can be rendered antigenically effective if prepared in a water-in-oil emulsion. The efficacy of this method for inducing antibody formation with small quantities of antigen has been discussed elsewhere. When a sufficient concentration of influenza virus is emulsified with mineral oil and inoculated into experimental animals, it has been possible to evoke the formation of much greater concentrations of antibody than develop as a result of experimentally induced infection. Similar observations are being accumulated in studies with the poliomyelitis virus. . . .

Summary and Conclusions

Preliminary results of studies in human subjects inoculated with different experimental poliomyelitis vaccines are here reported. For preparation of these vaccines virus of each of the three immunologic types was produced in cultures of monkey testicular tissue or monkey kidney tissue. Before human subjects were inoculated, the virus was rendered noninfectious for the monkey by treatment with formaldehyde.

In one series of experiments it appears that antibody for all three immunologic types was induced by the inoculation of small quantities of such vaccines incorporated in a water-in-oil emulsion. In another series of experiments, antibody formation was induced by the intradermal inoculation of aqueous vaccines containing the type 2 virus. Information at hand indicates that the antibody so induced has persisted without signs of decline for the longest interval studied thus far, i.e., four and a half months after the start of the experiment.

Levels of antibody induced by vaccination are compared with levels that develop after natural infection. The data thus far available suggest that it should be possible with a noninfectious preparation to approximate the immunologic effect induced by the disease process itself.

Although the results obtained in these studies can be regarded as encouraging, they should not be interpreted to indicate that a practical vaccine is now at hand. However, it does appear that at least one course of further investigation is clear. It will now be necessary to establish precisely the limits within which the effects here described can be reproduced with certainty.

Because of the great importance of safety factors in studies of this kind, it must be remembered that considerable time is required for the preparation and study of each new batch of experimental vaccine before human inoculations can be considered. It is this consideration, above all else, that imposes a limitation in the speed with which this work can be extended. Within these intractable limits every effort is being made to acquire the necessary information that will permit the logical progression of these studies into larger numbers of individuals in specially selected groups.

Further Resources

BOOKS

Blakeslee, Alton L. *Polio and the Salk Vaccine.* New York: Grosset and Dunlop, 1956.

Carter, Richard. *Breakthrough: The Saga of Jonas Salk.* New York: Pocket Books, 1967.

Gould, Tony. *A Summer Plague: Polio and Its Survivors.* New Haven, Conn.: Yale University Press, 1995.

Paul, John R. *A History of Poliomyelitis.* New Haven, Conn.: Yale University Press, 1971.

Professional Guide to Diseases, 6th ed. Springhouse, Pa.: Springhouse Corporation, 1998.

Sterling, Dorothy, and Philip Sterling. *Polio Pioneers: The Story of the Fight Against Polio.* Garden City, N.Y.: Doubleday, 1955.

PERIODICALS

"O Pioneers!" *The New Yorker,* May 8, 1954, 24–25.

"Polio: Free Shots." *Newsweek,* November 1, 1954, 62–64.

Vastag, Brian. "At Polio's End Game, Strategies Differ." *JAMA, the Journal of the American Medical Association,* 286, December 12, 2001, 2797–2799.

WEBSITES

The Invention Dimension: Jonas Salk. Lemelson-MIT Program, Massachusetts Institute of Technology. Available online at http://web.mit.edu/invent/iow/salk.html; website home page: http://web.mit.edu (accessed June 17, 2003).

"Polio Vaccine." American Academy of Family Physicians. Available online at http://familydoctor.org/handouts/333 .html; website home page: http://familydoctor.org (accessed June 17, 2003).

Heart-Lung Machine
Illustration

By: John H. Gibbons Jr.

Date: March 26, 1955

Source: Gibbons, John H., Jr. "Heart-Lung Machine." Bettmann/*CORBIS*. Image no. U1279080INP. Available online at http://www.corbis.com (accessed February 20, 2003).

About the Author: John H. Gibbons Jr. (1903–1973) invented the heart-lung machine in 1952 while a surgeon at Jefferson Medical College in Philadelphia, Pennsylvania. He first used the machine on May 6, 1953, while closing a hole in a girl's heart. He deposited his plans for the machine in the archives of the Mayo Clinic in Rochester, Minnesota. ∎

Introduction

In 1956, heart disease was the leading killer of Americans. It killed over a third more men than women and accounted for double the deaths from cancer, the second leading killer of Americans.

Medicine had made little progress against heart disease, whose risk increases with age. As a person ages, the heart shrinks and loses strength, diminishing its capacity to pump blood. Heart valves thicken and lose flexibility, reducing their ability to close completely. Arteries and veins harden, and cholesterol and fat clog arteries and veins, narrowing the area for the flow of blood. This diminution of the heart and vascular system may cause hypertension, stroke, heart attack, and heart failure. All four conditions may be fatal.

Without an ability to correct heart problems through surgery, physicians could do little more than encourage patients to consume less fat and cholesterol and to exercise regularly. Even these measures could not reverse damage in advanced states of cardiovascular disease.

Significance

Surgery on heart patients was possible only if surgeons could stop the heart in order to operate on it. But to stop the heart meant to stop the circulation of blood, a fatal condition unless a machine could substitute for a heart during surgery.

Given the fascination Americans have with technology, a fascination French writer Alexis de Tocqueville

Dr. John Gibbons is the inventor of the Heart Lung machine. **AP/WIDE WORLD PHOTOS. REPRODUCED BY PERMISSION.**

noted in 1835, one may express surprise that a physician or scientist did not invent a heart-lung machine until 1952, when John H. Gibbons Jr. at the Jefferson Medical College in Philadelphia, Pennsylvania, developed the first such machine and used it during surgery on May 6, 1953. The accompanying diagram illustrates the function of the heart-lung machine.

The heart has four chambers, one of which pumps blood to the lungs, which enrich blood with oxygen and remove waste. As blood circulates through the body, it distributes oxygen to the cells, which use it to fuel chemical activity, and collects waste chemicals that accumulate in cells. The blood depleted of oxygen and full of waste returns through the veins to the heart for distribution again to the lungs.

The heart-lung machine takes over this function while the heart has stopped during surgery. Oxygen-depleted and waste-laden blood exits the veins, entering the machine at point 1. Blood then enters a reservoir at point 2, moving to 3 where it receives oxygen and gives off waste. Point 3 thus functions as the lungs. The machine returns the blood, now oxygen rich and without waste, past point 4 to point 5, where it returns to the body. Once in the body, the blood distributes oxygen to and collects waste from cells as it circulates to return to the machine to begin the circuit anew.

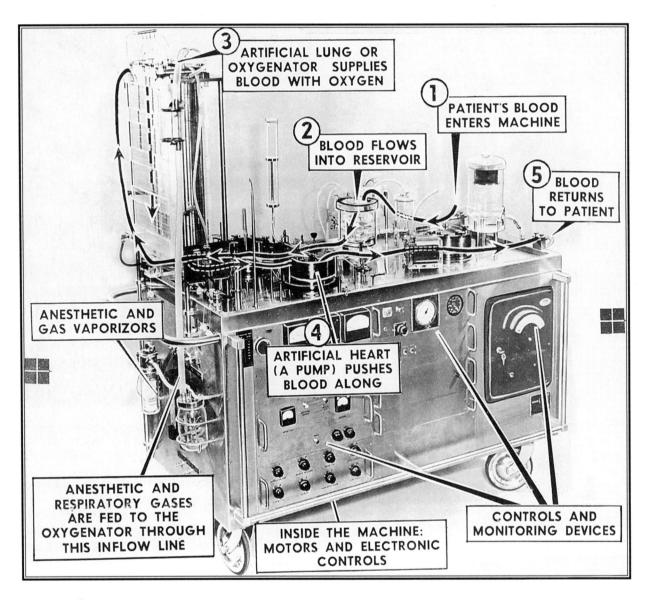

③ ARTIFICIAL LUNG OR OXYGENATOR SUPPLIES BLOOD WITH OXYGEN

① PATIENT'S BLOOD ENTERS MACHINE

② BLOOD FLOWS INTO RESERVOIR

⑤ BLOOD RETURNS TO PATIENT

ANESTHETIC AND GAS VAPORIZORS

④ ARTIFICIAL HEART (A PUMP) PUSHES BLOOD ALONG

ANESTHETIC AND RESPIRATORY GASES ARE FED TO THE OXYGENATOR THROUGH THIS INFLOW LINE

INSIDE THE MACHINE: MOTORS AND ELECTRONIC CONTROLS

CONTROLS AND MONITORING DEVICES

Primary Source

Heart-Lung Machine

SYNOPSIS: The diagram illustrates the heart-lung machine, which functions as a person's heart and lungs while the heart has stopped during surgery. Like the heart and lungs, the machine takes in blood from the veins and enriches it with oxygen and removes waste, returning blood to the body for circulation. © BETTMANN/CORBIS. REPRODUCED BY PERMISSION.

Further Resources

BOOKS

McGoon, Dwight C. *Cardiac Surgery.* Philadelphia: Davis, 1987.

National Heart, Lung, and Blood Institute. *The Heart-Lung Machine: Breakthrough in Cardiac Surgery.* Washington, D.C.: National Institutes of Health, 1987.

Professional Guide to Diseases, 6th ed. Springhouse, Pa.: Springhouse Corporation, 1998.

Rodriguez, Jorge A. *An Atlas of Cardiac Surgery.* Philadelphia: Saunders, 1957.

PERIODICALS

Beltrame, Julian. "Standing in for the Ailing Heart." *Maclean's,* March 25, 2002, 46–48.

"New Smaller Heart-Lung Machine Reduces Risk to Patients." *Heart Disease Weekly,* May 26, 2002, 12–14.

WEBSITES

Levison, Mark M. Learning Center: The Heart-Lung Machine. *The Heart Surgery Forum: A Cardiothoracic Multimedia Journal.* Available online at http://www.hsforum.com/stories /storyReader$1486; website home page: http://www.hsforum .com/ (accessed June 9, 2003)

"Mother! Your Child's Cough at Night May Be the First Sign of Chest Cold or Asian Flu"

Advertisement

By: Schering-Plough Inc.

Date: 1958

Source: *Mother! Your Child's Cough at Night May Be the First Sign of Chest Cold or Asian Flu.* Duke University, Rare Book, Manuscript, and Special Collections Library. Available online at http://scriptorium.lib.duke.edu/mma/ad-images/MM04/MM0439-01-72dpi.html; website home page http://scriptorium.lib.duke.edu (accessed June 12, 2003).

About the Organization: Schering-Plough Inc. manufactured Children's Mild Musterole. Initially a U.S. subsidiary of the German drug manufacturer Schering AG, it incorporated in New York City in 1928 and in New Jersey in 1935. Its role as a drug manufacturer led Congress to nationalize it during World War II, returning it to private investors in 1952. It is

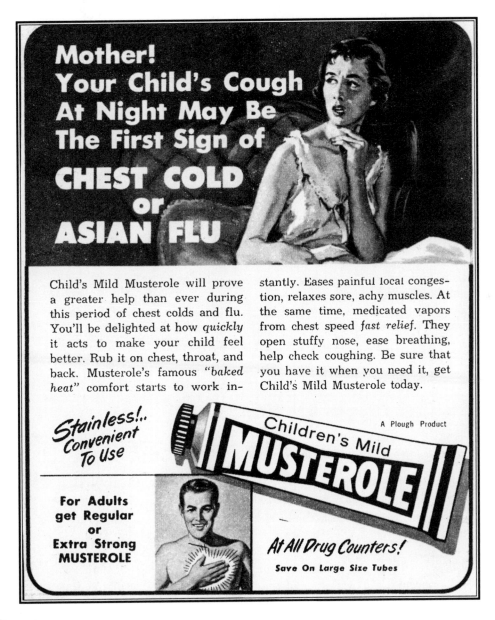

Primary Source

"Mother! Your Child's Cough at Night May Be the First Sign of Chest Cold or Asian Flu"

SYNOPSIS: This advertisement took advantage of the fear Americans had of Asian flu. It advised mothers to rub Children's Mild Mustoerole on the throat, chest, and back of cold and Asian flu sufferers. **SCHERING-PLOUGH HEALTHCARE PRODUCTS, INC. REPRODUCED BY PERMISSION.**

now a number of several health care product brands, including Coppertone® and Dr. Scholl's®. ∎

Introduction

The virus *Myxovirus influenzae* causes influenza, or, more simply, flu. The flu virus is highly contagious. One may inhale it from the air, as is not the case, for example, with the highly lethal viruses of African origin: human immunodeficiency virus (HIV), Marburg, and Ebola. One may also contract the flu virus from a drinking fountain, a cup, a toothbrush or anything else that has the saliva of an infected person.

The virus incubates in the body twenty-four or forty-eight hours, when it causes fever as high as 104 degrees Fahrenheit, chills, headache, fatigue, pain in the muscles and joints, cough, and occasionally laryngitis and hoarseness. Symptoms persist three to five days and are most acute in the young, the old, and those with weak immune systems. In such cases, flu may become viral pneumonia or may weaken the person enough to allow bacteria to settle in the lungs, causing bacterial pneumonia. Thus, the flu virus is able to damage the respiratory system.

The flu virus, like any other virus, is a sequence of nucleotide bases (the large molecules that build deoxyribonucleic acid) covered in a protein coat. The flu virus has a remarkable ability to change the chemistry of its nucleotide bases or its protein coat. These changes account for the fact that the virus may kill few people one year and large numbers the next. These changes also mean that the antibodies a person produces against the flu virus one year will be powerless to defend the body against it the next year. The same is true of flu vaccines.

Significance

Lethal strains of flu virus can sweep across continents. The pandemic of 1918 and 1919 may have killed 20 million people worldwide, a larger number, historians believe, than the Black Death devoured in fourteenth-century Europe. This pandemic led scientists and physicians to become alarmed at reports from the World Health Organization in 1957 that a flu virus was sweeping across China. This Asian flu, they feared, might kill more than 20 million Americans, a number that in the United States alone would exceed the death toll of the 1918–1919 pandemic.

A flu virus vaccine, which did not exist in 1918, saved millions of lives in 1957 and prevented the Asian flu from becoming a pandemic. The Centers for Disease Control and Prevention developed a vaccine in July 1957 and authorized six U.S. drug manufacturers to produce it. By September, they had 8 million doses of vaccine and by year's end, 85 million.

The flu reached San Francisco in June 1957 and infected thirty thousand Americans by September. By then, however, the most vulnerable people—hospital employees, physicians, nurses, and public health officials—had been vaccinated. The flu recurred in 1958, yet the U.S. death toll in 1957 and 1958 underscored the vaccine's effectiveness. In 1957, 35.8 Americans per 100,000 died of flu, and in 1958, 33.2. By comparison, 28.2 Americans per 100,000 died of flu in 1956 and 25.4 in 1959.

Despite the modest death toll, the accompanying advertisements from 1958 exploited the fear Americans had of Asian flu. The advertiser targeted women, the traditional caretakers. One ad advised mothers to rub Children's Mild Musterole on the throat, chest, and back of cold and Asian flu sufferers.

Further Resources

BOOKS

Flu. Bethesda, Md.: National Institutes of Health, 1987.

International Conference on Asian Influenza. Bethesda, Md.: National Institutes of Health, 1960.

Professional Guide to Diseases, 6th ed. Springhouse, Pa.: Springhouse Corporation, 1998.

PERIODICALS

"Asian Flu: The Outlook" *Time,* August 12, 1957, 74.

WEBSITES

Pandemic Influenza. Centers for Disease Control and Prevention, National Vaccine Program Office. Available online at http://www.cdc.gov/od/nvpo/pandemics/default.htm; website home page: http://www.cdc.gov (accessed June 17, 2003).

Schering-Plough: History of Schering-Plough. Schering-Plough Corporation. Available online at http://www.sch-plough.com/about/about02_history.html; website home page: http://www.sch-plough.com (accessed June 17, 2003).

"Recommended Daily Dietary Allowances, Revised 1958"

Table

By: Ruth M. Leverton

Date: 1959

Source: Leverton, Ruth M. "Recommended Allowances."*Food: The Yearbook of Agriculture, 1959.* Washington, D.C.: GPO, 1959, 228–229.

About the Author: Ruth M. Leverton (1908–) received a Ph.D. in nutrition from the University of Nebraska and served as nutritionist at the Nebraska Agricultural Experiment Station before becoming associate director of the U.S. Department of Agriculture's Institute of Home Economics. ∎

Recommended Daily Dietary Allowances, Revised 1958

FOOD AND NUTRITION BOARD, NATIONAL ACADEMY OF SCIENCES-NATIONAL RESEARCH COUNCIL
Designed for the Maintenance of Good Nutrition of Healthy Persons in the United States

[Allowances are intended for persons normally active in a temperate climate]

	Age Years	Weight Pounds	Height Inches	Calories	Protein Gm.	Calcium Gm.	Iron Mg.	Vitamin A I.U.	Thiamine Mg.	Riboflavin Mg.	Niacin equiv. Mg.	Ascorbic acid Mg.	Vitamin D I.U.
Men	25	154	69	3,200	70	0.8	10	5,000	1.6	1.8	21	75	—
	45	154	69	3,000	70	0.8	10	5,000	1.5	1.8	20	75	—
	65	154	69	2,550	70	0.8	10	5,000	1.3	1.8	18	75	—
Women	25	128	64	2,300	58	0.8	12	5,000	1.2	1.5	17	70	—
	45	128	64	2,200	58	0.8	12	5,000	1.1	1.5	17	70	—
	65	128	64	1,800	58	0.8	12	5,000	1.0	1.5	17	70	—
Pregnant (second half)				+300	+20	1.5	15	6,000	1.3	2.0	+3	100	400
Lactating (28 ounces daily)				+1,000	+40	2.0	15	8,000	1.7	2.5	+2	150	400
Infants (age in months)	2–6	13	24	lb. × 54.5	(¹)	0.6	5	1,500	0.4	0.5	6	30	400
	7–12	20	28	lb. × 45.4	(¹)	0.8	7	1,500	0.5	0.8	7	30	400
Children	1–3	27	34	1,300	40	1.0	7	2,000	0.7	1.0	8	35	400
	4–6	40	43	1,700	50	1.0	8	2,500	0.9	1.3	11	50	400
	7–9	60	51	2,100	60	1.0	10	3,500	1.1	1.5	14	60	400
	10–12	79	57	2,500	70	1.2	12	4,500	1.3	1.8	17	75	400
Boys	13–15	108	64	3,100	85	1.4	15	5,000	1.6	2.1	21	90	400
	16–19	139	69	3,600	100	1.4	15	5,000	1.8	2.5	25	90	400
Girls	13–15	108	63	2,600	80	1.3	15	5,000	1.3	2.0	17	80	400
	16–19	120	64	2,400	75	1.3	15	5,000	1.2	1.9	16	80	400

¹Allowances are not given for protein during infancy, but intakes of 1.5 grams of protein for each pound of body weight are ample for healthy infants.

SOURCE: Table from Leverton, Ruth M. "Recommended Allowances." In *Food: The Yearbook of Agriculture, 1959*. Washington, D.C.: U.S. Government Printing Office, 1959, 228–229.

Primary Source

Recommended Daily Dietary Allowances, Revised 1958

SYNOPSIS: The U.S. Department of Agriculture stated of the recommended daily allowances listed in this chart: "The allowances are higher than the least amounts required for health. They are intended to cover the needs of most of the persons who have the highest requirements. The allowances thus provide a margin of safety, more accurately called a margin of sufficiency, above the minimun requirements for protein, minerals, and vitamins but not for calories. The size of this margin above average requirements varies for different nutrients."

Introduction

Before the twentieth century, the study of nutrition focused on protein, calories, and minerals. In 1914, Elmer V. McCollum, a scientist at the Wisconsin Agricultural Experiment Station, discovered the first vitamin, which he named vitamin A. The discovery of other vitamins followed in the 1920s, as did the fortification of milk with vitamins A and D.

Scientists and physicians realized that health requires a diet with sufficient quality and quantity of protein, calories, minerals, and vitamins. Insufficient nutrients cause illness. A deficiency of niacin or the amino acid tryptophan causes pellagra. A deficiency of thiamine causes beriberi; of vitamin C, scurvy; and of vitamin D or sunlight, rickets.

The connection between nutrition and health led the National Academy of Sciences and the U.S. Department of Agriculture in 1941 to issue a recommended daily allowance (RDA) of protein, calories, minerals, and vitamins. The recommendation for calories was as high as 4,500 for men, 3,800 for boys aged 16–20, 3,000 for women, and 2,800 for girls, implying that Americans were more active in 1941 than they are today. The recommendation for protein was 70 grams for men, 60 for women and 100 for lactating women, 100 for boys 16–20 and 80 for girls. The RDA included only a single mineral, iron, which is necessary to form red blood cells. The vitamins included A and D, thiamine, riboflavin, ascorbic acid (vitamin C), and nicotinic acid (niacin).

A woman shops for vegetables, a healthy food choice, in 1956. © BETTMANN/CORBIS. REPRODUCED BY PERMISSION.

Significance

As scientists and physicians learned more about nutrition, they revised the RDA in 1945, 1948, 1953, and 1958. Ruth M. Leverton announced the 1958 RDA. Caloric requirements fell in most categories from the 1941 RDA. The 1958 recommendation for calories was as high as 3,600 for men, 2,300 for women and 3,300 for lactating women, 3,600 for boys aged 16–19, and 2,600 for girls. These numbers imply that Americans were less active then they had been in 1941 but more active than today. Protein requirements remained constant for all categories except for a decrease in 2 grams for women and an increase in 20 grams for pregnant women and 40 grams for lactating women. The 1958 RDA added a mineral, calcium, which is necessary to build and maintain teeth and bones. The number of vitamins held constant, though the 1958 RDA omitted adult recommendations for vitamin D in recognition of the fact that the amount of sunlight one absorbs reduces and can even eliminate the need for dietary vitamin D.

Significant are the RDA list of vitamins. Of the six, four correlate with disease when in deficit: thiamine, niacin, and vitamins C and D. Significant, too, is the 1958 RDA inclusion of only two minerals: iron and calcium. By contrast, the current RDA includes thirteen minerals, underscoring the fuller knowledge today's nutritionists have of the mineral requirements for health, particularly the minerals needed in minute amounts, such as zinc and manganese.

Further Resources

BOOKS

Ashley, Richard, and Heidi Duggal. *Dictionary of Nutrition.* New York: Pocket Books, 1975.

Bender, Arnold E. *A Dictionary of Food and Nutrition.* New York: Oxford University Press, 1995.

Leverton, Ruth M. *Food Becomes You.* Ames, Iowa: Iowa State University Press, 1965.

Professional Guide to Diseases, 6th ed. Springhouse, Pa.: Springhouse Corporation, 1998.

PERIODICALS

Ingram, Leah. "Multivitamin Vitality." *Diabetes Forecast,* February 2003, 87–89.

WEBSITES

Historical Food Guides Background and Development. National Agricultural Library, Food and Nutrition Information Center. Available online at http://www.nal.usda.gov/fnic /history/; website home page: http://www.nal.usda.gov (accessed June 17, 2003).

"Statistics of Health"

Essay, Tables

By: James M. Hundley

Date: 1959

Source: Hundley, James M. "Statistics of Health." *Food: The Yearbook of Agriculture, 1959.* Washington, D.C.: GPO, 1959.

About the Author: James M. Hundley joined the Public Health Service as a physician in 1940, focusing after 1943 on research in human nutrition. In 1953, he became head of the Laboratory of Biochemistry and Nutrition at the National Institutes of Health. ■

Introduction

Infectious diseases have plagued humans since antiquity. Among the most virulent pandemics were the Black Death that carried off as much as half of Europe's population between 1347 and 1351 and the influenza outbreak that killed 20 million people worldwide in 1918 and 1919.

The development of vaccines and antibiotics reduced the spread of diseases. Vaccines predate antibiotics. A vaccine is a dead or weakened strain of a bacterium or virus or of a closely related bacterium or virus injected into a person. The person's immune system produces antibodies against the bacterium or virus, conferring immunity against a potent strain of the pathogen.

In 1796, British physician Edward Jenner developed the first vaccine, one that conferred immunity against smallpox. In 1897, British bacteriologist Almroth Wright developed a typhoid vaccine. Other vaccines followed, including ones against tetanus, diphtheria, and yellow fever in the 1930s, against influenza in 1945, and against polio in 1954.

Vaccines may work against bacteria and viruses. In contrast, antibiotics are a weapon against only bacteria.

Some microbes emit a toxin against bacteria, hence the name antibiotics. In 1928, British physician Alexander Fleming isolated the toxin penicillin that could kill a range of bacteria. In 1939, British biochemist Ernst Chain and Austrian pathologist Howard Florey purified a strain of penicillin suitable for manufacture in large quantities. By 1941, physicians had enough penicillin to treat a range of bacterial infections. In 1943, Selman A. Waksman, a microbiologist at Rutgers University and the New Jersey Agricultural Experiment Station, discovered streptomycin, the first antibiotic toxic against tuberculosis. In 1950, U.S. Department of Agriculture microbiologist Robert G. Benedict discovered a new strain of streptomycin and later that decade discovered polymyxin, a new antibiotic.

Significance

These discoveries have been among the most important in history. Between 1900 and 1955, U.S. deaths from influenza and pneumonia declined to nearly one-tenth of previous levels, wrote James M. Hundley. Deaths from tuberculosis fell to about 4.5 percent of previous levels; from diarrhea and enteritis, to about 3.5 percent; and from bronchitis, to about 1.2 percent. Deaths from typhoid, smallpox, measles, scarlet fever, and whooping cough fell to nearly one-three hundredth of previous levels. Infant deaths fell nearly to 4 percent. Deaths from the diseases of malnutrition, notably pellagra and scurvy, plummeted between 1935 and 1956. For reasons unclear, deaths from cardiovascular disease fell by one-third.

With deaths from viruses, bacteria, malnutrition, and heart disease in retreat, other diseases killed increasing numbers of Americans. Between 1900 and 1955, cancer deaths more than doubled, and deaths from brain hemorrhage increased by one-third.

Given the decline in deaths from infectious diseases, one might expect an increase in longevity, yet Hundley detailed little change in the percentage of Americans who reached ages fifty and seventy between 1900 and 1956. A gain of one-third, however, came in the percentage of Americans who reached age one, a trend borne out by the decline in infant mortality Hundley mentioned earlier.

Particularly ominous was the fact that in the 1950s heart disease and cancer were the first and second leading causes of death in the United States. Nearly half a century later, these diseases remained entrenched as the leading killers of Americans. Government and the private sector have poured money into medical research with little progress against heart disease and cancer. Indeed, Americans at the start of the 21st century feared cancer as a death sentence much as they had feared tuberculosis a century ago.

Leading Causes of Death in 1900 and Deaths From Those Causes in 1955

[Total Population—Rates per 100,000]

	1900	1955[1]
Influenza and pneumonia	203.4	27.1
Tuberculosis	201.9	9.1
Diarrhea and enteritis	133.2	4.7
Diseases of the heart (excluding coronary artery disease)	132.1	108.8
Infectious diseases (typhoid, smallpox, measles, scarlet fever, whooping cough)	115.9	0.4
Congenital malformation and diseases of early infancy	91.9	39.0
Nephritis	89.0	9.6
Cerebral hemorrhage and softening	71.5	106.0
Cancer	63.0	146.0
Bronchitis	45.7	1.7

[1] A few of the figures for 1955 may not be strictly comparable to 1900 data because of a change in the classification of diseases and change in reporting systems.

SOURCE: Table from Hundley, James M. "Statistics of Health." In *Food: The Yearbook of Agriculture, 1959*. Washington, D.C.: U.S. Government Printing Office, 1959, 176.

Primary Source

"Statistics of Health:" Table (1 OF 4)

SYNOPSIS: These four tables accompanied James Hundley's essay. This table shows that advances in medicine and nutrition considerably reduced the cases of diseases of infectious origin.

Moreover, medicine has not quite conquered infectious diseases, as one might infer from Hundley's article. The rise of antibiotic-resistant strains of tuberculosis and the mysterious viruses from Africa—human immunodeficiency virus (HIV), Marburg, and Ebola—have caught medicine off guard. Physicians have had to admit that HIV is an epidemic. If Ebola should penetrate human populations, the carnage may surpass the death toll of the Black Death and the influenza pandemic of 1918 and 1919.

Primary Source

"Statistics of Health" [excerpt]: Essay

SYNOPSIS: In this excerpt, James M. Hundley celebrates medicine's triumph over infectious diseases, a conquest won by vaccines and antibiotics. Yet this victory added little to longevity between 1900 and 1956. Accompanying the text excerpt are the tables that originally appeared in the essay.

Births, deaths, disease rates, longevity, and other aspects of health that can be expressed statistically are used almost universally to assess and follow the status of people's health.

Statistics are simply barren figures, however, and we have to relate or compare them to something else before they have life and meaning. Since no one knows what level of health may be attainable ultimately, vital statistics are most useful in showing trends, detecting changes or problems, and comparing conditions of health. They help us determine what has been accomplished and what remains to be done.

Among the most important vital statistics are those that pertain to the growth of population. The population of the United States was estimated at about 75 million in 1900. It was 130 million in 1940, 150 million in 1950, and 177 million on June 14, 1959. If current trends continue, the population will exceed 220 million in 1970.

This remarkable rate of the growth reflects first of all the numbers of births and deaths. Immigration accounted for considerably less than 10 percent of the increase in recent years.

The birth rate was less than 20 per 1 thousand in the 1930's. It was at a fairly steady level of about 25 during the 1950's. That was not much above the level in 1925; about 1 million more children are now born every year, but that is an increase in number, due to the larger total population, and not in the rate itself. It is interesting to note that the estimated birth rate in 1910 was about 30.

Total Deaths Reported in the United States From Several Nutritional Causes

	1956	1949	1945	1940	1935
Beriberi	25	47	46	63	7
Pellagra	70	321	914	2,123	3,543
Scurvy	7	22	18	26	30
Active rickets	6	65	93	161	261
Other avitaminoses[1]	—	—	108	104	—
Malnutrition: general or multiple deficiencies[1]	588	799	—	—	—

[1] Changes in the system of reporting deaths have altered the reporting of nutritional diseases from time to time.

SOURCE: Table from Hundley, James M. "Statistics of Health." In *Food: The Yearbook of Agriculture, 1959*. Washington, D.C.: U.S. Government Printing Office, 1959, 178.

Primary Source

"Statistics of Health:" Table (2 OF 4)

Diseases like these caused by vitamin deficiencies became more rare in part because food began to be enriched with vitamins.

Relative Life Expectancy of White Males and Females in the United States (in Years)						
	1900			1956		
Year of life	Males	Females	Difference	Males	Females	Difference
1	48.2	51.1	2.9	67.2	73.7	6.5
50	20.8	21.9	1.1	23.1	27.7	4.6
70	9.0	9.6	0.6	10.3	12.2	1.9

SOURCE: Table from Hundley, James, M. "Statistics of Health." In *Food: The Yearbook of Agriculture, 1959*. Washington, D.C.: U.S. Government Printing Office, 1959, 178.

Primary Source

"Statistics of Health:" Table (3 OF 4)

In the early twentieth century, deaths of young children and infants from infectious diseases that have since been conquered considerably lowered the average life expectancy.

Meanwhile the death rate has dropped spectacularly. Except during 1918, when influenza was pandemic, the rate has trended downward, from 17.2 in 1900 to 9.4 in 1956.

Even more striking is the decline in infant mortality (under 1 year of age), which was 162.4 per 1 thousand live births in 1900 and less than 30 in 1955.

Since the birth rate was about 25 in 1959 and the mortality rate about 10, the net population gain was about 15 (per 1 thousand population), a rate of increase of 1.5 percent a year. That is lower than the rates in some of the other countries in the Americas, where increases of 3 percent a year are recorded, but higher than in most of Europe and higher even than in some major Asian countries, such as India.

Some of the reasons for the major drop in the death rate are evident in comparing the 10 leading causes of death in 1900 and the mortality in later years from those diseases. . . . The spectacular decline in disease of infectious origin is the main point to note.

These striking decreases in mortality are reflected in figures of life expectancy. The average life expectancy was about 47 years in 1900. It was 69.3 years in 1957. In a little more than a decade, 5 years have been added to man's expected span.

These gains in health have been shared by most of the economically well-developed countries. In many countries, however, malnutrition and disease continue to exact heavy tolls. Average life expectancies are 35 to 45 years in many of them.

Other types of statistics also have some relationship to nutrition—the incidence of premature babies and maternal mortality, for example. At this point, however, it is pertinent to ask what these statistics mean in terms of nutrition.

Data like those I have given often are used to estimate the probable nutrition situation of a population. In countries where malnutrition is widespread, there is no doubt that nutrition is a major factor in most of the usual vital statistics, but it must be remembered that these statistics are influenced by many factors other than nutrition.

Endemic and epidemic diseases, sanitation, the adequacy of medical care, and the public health

Leading Causes of Death in 1956: Total Population– White Males and Females			
		White	
	Total	Males	Females
Heart diseases	360.5	443.0	296.7
Cancers	147.9	162.5	140.7
Vascular lesions of the central nervous system	106.3	102.3	107.0
Accidents	56.7	76.9	33.5
Certain diseases of early infancy	38.6	40.1	27.1
Influenza and pneumonia	28.2	29.5	21.9
General arteriosclerosis	19.1	19.6	20.4
Diabetes	15.7	12.8	18.6
Congenital malformations	12.6	13.7	11.3
Cirrhosis of liver	10.7	14.7	7.4

SOURCE: Table from Hundley, James M. "Statistics of Health." In *Food: The Yearbook of Agriculture, 1959*. Washington, D.C.: U.S. Government Printing Office, 1959, 178.

Primary Source

"Statistics of Health:" Table (4 OF 4)

By 1956 infectious diseases had been repressed.

facilities exercise major influences. The better medical care that can be given mother and infant in a modern hospital, for instance, unquestionably has been a leading factor in reducing the infant mortality rates in the United States, where 94 percent of all deliveries occur in hospitals.

Deaths among boys and girls 1 to 4 years old in many ways are better indicators of nutritional status than infant mortality is. It is the period when infants change from breast, formula, or other special feeding to the food available to other members of the family. Protein malnutrition then takes a toll in many countries.

That mortality among children 1 to 4 years old is largely preventable is shown by the spectacular decreases in this country. Mortality rates between 1 and 4 were 19.8 per 1 thousand in 1900. The rate in 1955 was 1.1—almost a twentyfold decrease. Mortality in this age group continues high in many countries with major nutrition problems—for example, Mexico, 27.8; Brazil, 16.2; and Egypt, 49.7 (1947 data).

Even in this group, however, many factors besides nutrition influence mortality. The same must be said of tuberculosis mortality, where nutrition is an important factor. Total deaths from tuberculosis in this country exceeded 80 thousand in 1930 and were less than 20 thousand in 1954. The decline has been especially sharp since about 1945—probably due mainly to better therapy.

This decline in tuberculosis mortality has occurred despite the fact that total new cases reported annually have declined only a little since 1930. The illness now tends to be shorter in duration and less severe.

Other types of statistics, such as rates of occurrence of specific nutritional disease, would be more specific indicators of nutritional change. Such disease are not reportable, as are many of the infectious diseases. Only death rates are available, and they have declined to the point where they have little meaning as indicators of changes in nutrition.

. . . The main points to note [about deaths reported from various nutritional diseases] are the decline in deaths from pellagra and rickets and the low incidence of all types of nutritional deaths in 1956.

The decline in pellagra is even more striking because in 1928 more than 7 thousand deaths were reported from this nutritional disease. Niacin, the pellagra-preventing vitamin, was discovered in 1938 and its addition to bread became widespread about 1941. It is not safe to assume, though, that these

were the main causes of the virtual disappearance of pellagra. Foods that could prevent and cure it were known long before the vitamin was discovered. Besides, as I noted, pellagra had been disappearing at a fairly steady pace over three decades or more. It is more likely that continued improvement in general diet was the main factor.

Some statistics are at hand on endemic goiter, which occurs in some regions of the United States because of a lack of iodine. In parts of Michigan before the introduction of iodized salt, the incidence of endemic goiter in schoolchildren was 38.6 percent. In 1928, after people started using iodized salt, the incidence was 9 percent. It was 1.4 percent in 1952. Similar data are available for sections of Ohio.

The data I have reviewed indicate a good nutritional situation today. They support much other evidence that indicates that the average levels of nutrition have improved considerably in the past several decades.

On the other hand, this type of information does not permit measurement of just how great this improvement has been, nor can it be said with certainty just how much improved nutrition has contributed to the spectacular decline of certain diseases and to improved health and longevity generally. The nutritionist can say with certainly, however, that average levels of nutrition must be good and probably have been improving in recent years. Such spectacular gains in health would otherwise have been impossible.

Three facts must be kept in mind.

First, while health has been improving, no one knows what levels of health may ultimately be reached, or how close we are to reaching them.

Second, pressing problems must be met if further gains are to be made. Growing evidence suggests that diet and nutrition may be involved in some of them.

Third, we know that average diets have improved from the standpoint of supporting good growth and preventing deficiency diseases. But we do not know yet how to change diets to promote the best health—partly, because we do not yet know all of the dietary measures that might improve health further.

Health is much more than just the absence of disease. Good health also implies physical and intellectual vigor, vitality, and freedom from emotional, functional, and minor but incapacitating illnesses.

Therefore it is pertinent to look somewhat more deeply at vital statistics to see what they tell about problems ahead.

It is important to realize that most of the gains in longevity have come about through prevention of mortality at young ages. Great progress has been made in this sector. Relatively little has been gained in older age groups. . . .

The infectious diseases that used to take such a heavy toll in infants and young children have been conquered so completely that (except for accidents) cancer—mainly leukemia—is now the leading cause of death among children 5 to 14 years old.

It is significant also that women are living longer than men and are continuing to gain in this respect at all ages. The reasons therefor are not entirely clear. Under age 50, mortality rates for men and women in the United States are among the lowest in the world. During the age periods after 50, mortality in American females is near the average of other similar countries. Mortality in males in the United States after age 50 is among the highest in the world, however. . . .

Little progress has been made thus far in the prevention of atherosclerosis, although a number of quite promising leads are being explored. Current research suggests that diet and nutrition may be important in prevention.

Some progress has been achieved against some diseases in the chronic disease group. Cardiovascular syphilis has been nearly wiped out. It once constituted nearly 25 percent of all cases of heart disease. Now it is well under 1 percent. Rheumatic heart disease—once the most common type of heart disease—is now waning. Whether nutritional improvement had something to do with this is interesting speculation, but we have no proof. Subacute bacterial endocarditis—once almost universally fatal—now can be cured in 75 to 80 percent of cases. Surgical advances have done much to relieve chronic disability in valvular heart disease, chronic constrictive pericarditis, and congenital heart disease. Hypertensive heart disease can now be treated better through drugs, surgery, and diet.

Important advances against certain chronic diseases have been made in other fields, such as cancer, diabetes, and arthritis. As attested by current mortality figures, however, there is still a long way to go.

Nutrition can claim little of the credit for these advances. On the other hand, it may have a key role in preventing or treating many of the still largely unsolved major chronic diseases—atherosclerosis, diabetes, and perhaps even arthritis.

It is important to know not only what kills older people but also what diseases or ailments cause disability and nonfatal illness. Here the situation is somewhat different from the leading causes of death.

In the 45 to 64 age group, the common cold, bronchitis, influenza, arthritis and rheumatism, digestive disturbances, sore throat, diseases of the heart, diarrhea and enteritis, headache, neuritis and neuralgia, hypertension and arteriosclerosis, and genital and breast disturbances in females are, in that order, the most frequent complaints.

In those 65 or over, the list is much the same, except that diseases of the heart, hypertension, and arteriosclerosis are more frequent disabilities, and cerebral "strokes" also come into the picture.

The possibility of further reducing mortality and illness in younger persons must not be overlooked. In children under 5, the leading causes of death are immaturity, postnatal asphyxia, birth injury, pneumonia, congenital malformations, accidents, heart disease, other diseases of early infancy, digestive disease, and hemolytic disease of the newborn. The leading causes of disability are various infectious diseases. The facts suggest that there is still an appreciable amount of mortality that can be prevented in young children.

Vital statistics for the United States depict a rapidly growing, vigorous people whose nutrition is among the best in the world. They tell a story of dramatic, sustained improvements in health and the virtual eradication of recognizable, preventable, nutritional deficiency diseases.

On the other hand, as old problems have been conquered, others have risen in their place. The increasingly large older segment of the population and the chronic diseases that kill or disable so often, are the challenge for the decades ahead.

From the standpoint of nutrition, the challenge is no longer how to prevent the diseases that are due to a lack of vitamins or to some other deficiency. The problem is to maintain the nutritional advantages we now have and at the same time to find the role of diet in the chronic diseases and build better health through feeding for positive health and vigor through a long life.

Much has been accomplished, but there is no reason for complacency. Many new problems in nutrition and health remain to be explored and solved.

Further Resources

BOOKS

Fekete, Irene. *Disease and Medicine.* New York: Facts on File, 1987.

Fry, John. *Common Diseases: Their Nature, Incidence and Care.* Philadelphia: Lippincott, 1974.

Phillips, Jonathon, ed. *The Biology of Disease.* Cambridge, Mass.: Blackwell Science, 1995.

Professional Guide to Diseases, 6th ed. Springhouse, Pa.: Springhouse Corporation, 1998.

PERIODICALS

Eberstadt, Nicholas. "Mortality Rates and Nations in Crisis." *American Enterprise,* September/October 1993, 46–54.

WEBSITES

Disease Trends: State and Local Health Statistics. *Morbidity and Mortality Weekly Report.* Available online at http://www.cdc.gov/mmwr/distrnds.html; website home page: http://www.cdc.gov/mmwr (accessed June 17, 2003).

Infectious Diseases: Current Trends. Stanford Hospital and Clinics. Available online at http://www.stanfordhospital.com/newsEvents/eventsLectures/october2001/ceInfectiousDisease.html; website home page: http://www.stanfordhospital.com (accessed June 17, 2003).

Rubin, Robert H. "General Trends in Infectious Diseases." Presentation given at 2001: The Future of the Pharmaceutical Industry, Cambridge, Mass., December 2001. Available online at http://web.mit.edu/popi/rubin.slides.pdf; website home page: http://web.mit.edu (accessed June 17, 2003).

What Do We Eat?

Study, Graphs

By: Janet Murray and Ennis Blake

Date: 1959

Source: Murray, Janet, and Ennis Blake. *What Do We Eat? Food: The Yearbook of Agriculture, 1959.* Washington, D.C.: GPO, 1959, 609–619.

About the Authors: Janet Murray conducted research on food consumption at Stanford University's Food Research Institute and at the University of Chicago. She served as chief of the Survey Statistics Staff in the Household Economics Research Division of the Agricultural Research Service (ARS), a branch of the U.S. Department of Agriculture.

Ennis Blake was a food economist in the Household Economics Research Division of the Agricultural Research Service (ARS), a branch of the U.S. Department of Agriculture. She conducted food surveys for the ARS, including the 1955 Household Food Consumption Survey. ∎

Introduction

During the twentieth century, American scientists and physicians established a connection between income, diet, and health. Much of their attention focused on the link between poverty and malnutrition. In 1907, for example, physician George H. Searcy linked a diet of milled corn with pellagra. This diet was common among poor southerners, implying a connection between poverty and

pellagra. The Country Life Commission, led by Cornell University Dean of the College of Agriculture Liberty Hyde Bailey, studied the health of rural Americans, linking poverty and malnourishment in its 1911 report. Particularly disturbing was the report's finding that poverty and malnourishment were not confined to a few sections of rural America but instead were endemic to the agrarian masses.

The Depression of the 1930s focused new attention on the connection between poverty and malnourishment. Rural economists, funded by the Bankhead-Jones Act of 1935, conducted that year the first nationwide survey of food-consumption patterns in the United States. The study reaffirmed the findings of the Country Life Commission and led the U.S. Department of Agriculture to mandate additional surveys in 1942, 1948, and 1955.

Significance

The 1955 survey categorized Americans by income as low, medium, and high, though Janet Murray and Ennis Blake omitted what income brackets constituted these categories. The survey's findings nevertheless confirmed the link between income, diet, and health. As income increased, so did consumption of milk, fresh fruit and vegetables, canned and frozen fruit and vegetables, meat, poultry and fish, and baked goods. In contrast, the less people earned, the more flour, cereals, grains, and other starches they ate.

An important point, and one that Murray and Blake omit, is the classification of the potato. The bar graph "Income and Food Consumption" excludes potatoes from the category of "Fresh Fruit and Vegetables" (the potato is often erroneously classified as a vegetable), leaving one to infer that the potato was part of the category "Flour, Cereals, Pastes." This point is important because poor families that subsist on potatoes are healthier than those that subsist on flour and processed white bread. George Searcy understood this fact in 1907 when he switched pellagra sufferers from a diet of milled corn to potatoes, whereupon their symptoms disappeared.

Yet the poor's subsistence on flour and grains meant, as it always had, a diet of corn in the South. Moreover, processed flour and white bread are devoid of nutrients and deserve American writer James Baldwin's scorn in calling white bread "foam rubber." Even whole grains do not supply protein in sufficient quality and quantity.

By contrast, high-income families consumed the most milk, meat, poultry, and fish, ensuring an adequate amount and quality of protein. They also consumed the most fresh fruit and vegetables, sources of vitamins and minerals.

These data imply that high-income families ate a more nutritious and varied diet and were healthier than

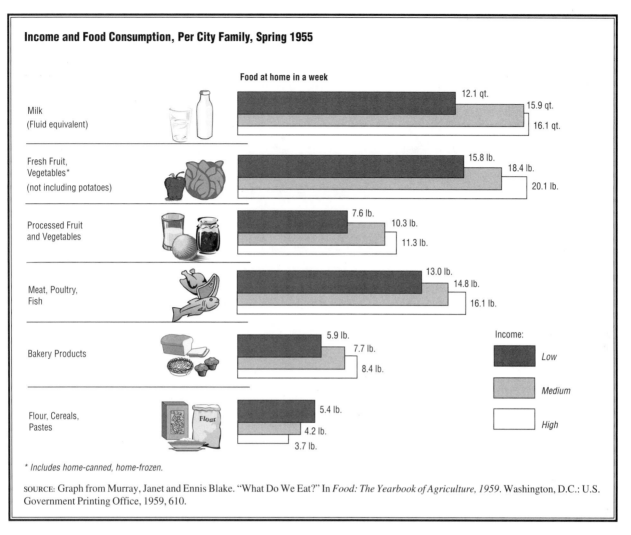

Income and Food Consumption, Per City Family, Spring 1955

Food at home in a week

Milk
(Fluid equivalent)
12.1 qt.
15.9 qt.
16.1 qt.

Fresh Fruit,
Vegetables*
(not including potatoes)
15.8 lb.
18.4 lb.
20.1 lb.

Processed Fruit
and Vegetables
7.6 lb.
10.3 lb.
11.3 lb.

Meat, Poultry,
Fish
13.0 lb.
14.8 lb.
16.1 lb.

Bakery Products
5.9 lb.
7.7 lb.
8.4 lb.

Income:

Low

Medium

High

Flour, Cereals,
Pastes
5.4 lb.
4.2 lb.
3.7 lb.

* *Includes home-canned, home-frozen.*

SOURCE: Graph from Murray, Janet and Ennis Blake. "What Do We Eat?" In *Food: The Yearbook of Agriculture, 1959*. Washington, D.C.: U.S. Government Printing Office, 1959, 610.

Primary Source

What Do We Eat?: Graph (1 OF 2)

SYNOPSIS: These two graphs accompanied the researchers' study of American's diets. This bar graph reveals that as income increased, so did consumption of milk, fresh fruit and vegetables, canned and frozen fruit and vegetables, meat, poultry and fish, and baked goods. In contrast, the less people earned, the more flour, cereals, grains and other starches they ate.

medium and low-income families. The world's wealthiest nation had not banished the evils of poverty and malnutrition.

Primary Source

What Do We Eat? [excerpt]: Study

> **SYNOPSIS:** In 1955 researchers at the U.S. Department of Agriculture studied America's diet. This excerpt from the results of the study describe the process used to collect data and presents results on the distribution of the food dollar among different types of foods for Americans in 1955. The accompanying graphs from the study show the effects of income and region on what Americans ate.

We sometimes get the impression that Americans typically breakfast on a hurried cup of coffee, lunch at a counter, and dine on hotdogs, potato chips, and soft drinks in front of TV sets.

The impression is false.

Most Americans eat a variety of foods in meals served at home. On the average, at least 50 different food items are used at family meals in a week. They include about 10 pounds of vegetables and fruit, 4.5 quarts of milk or corresponding amounts of cheese and ice cream, 4 pounds of meat, 7 eggs, 1 pound of fat, 1.5 pounds of sugar, and 3 pounds of cereal products for each person in the household.

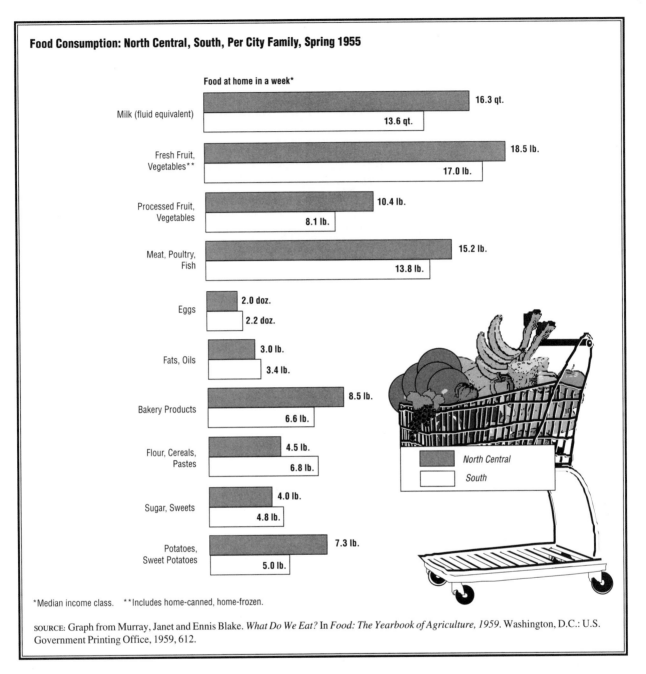

Food Consumption: North Central, South, Per City Family, Spring 1955

Food at home in a week*

	North Central	South
Milk (fluid equivalent)	16.3 qt.	13.6 qt.
Fresh Fruit, Vegetables**	18.5 lb.	17.0 lb.
Processed Fruit, Vegetables	10.4 lb.	8.1 lb.
Meat, Poultry, Fish	15.2 lb.	13.8 lb.
Eggs	2.0 doz.	2.2 doz.
Fats, Oils	3.0 lb.	3.4 lb.
Bakery Products	8.5 lb.	6.6 lb.
Flour, Cereals, Pastes	4.5 lb.	6.8 lb.
Sugar, Sweets	4.0 lb.	4.8 lb.
Potatoes, Sweet Potatoes	7.3 lb.	5.0 lb.

*Median income class. **Includes home-canned, home-frozen.

SOURCE: Graph from Murray, Janet and Ennis Blake. *What Do We Eat?* In *Food: The Yearbook of Agriculture, 1959.* Washington, D.C.: U.S. Government Printing Office, 1959, 612.

Primary Source

What Do We Eat?: Graph (2 OF 2)
Differences in food consumption between city dwellers in the south and north-central United States were slight. Differences in median incomes may have contributed to southern citizens consuming more sweets, starches, eggs, and fats, while northerners ate more meat, fish, and fruits and vegetables.

Put another way, the average American can eat three or four servings of vegetables and fruit, the equivalent of 2 to 3 cups of milk, an egg, and one or two servings of meat, poultry, or fish each day and bread or other grain products at each meal.

These facts are based on information given to trained interviewers by 6,060 American household-ers, who comprised a scientifically designed sample of all households in the United States that do enough cooking to be called housekeeping.

They live in all parts of the country and every type of community. They were so selected that average patterns could be obtained, not State by State—that would require a far larger sample—but for each of four regions (the Northeast, North Central, South, and West) and for three types of communities within each region (rural farm, rural nonfarm, and urban) or for any combination of these 12 basic groups. They were interviewed during April, May, and June of 1955.

Each homemaker spent about 2 hours with the interviewer, giving her information on family members and the meals they had at home and away from home, the money spent, the family income, practices with respect to the use of home-produced food, canning and freezing at home, baking, and other details that help to round out the picture of the household and its food.

Information about the size and composition of the household and the family income was needed for more than merely descriptive purposes.

We can classify the households in the sample by these characteristics—by family size, for example, and then get the average food pattern of each of the family groups. Certainly we can expect the six-person family to spend more for food than the two-person family, although not three times as much.

We may also group families whose incomes are at about the same level and study the differences in use of food and expenditures of families at different positions on the income scale. Again, we will expect the families that earn 10 thousand dollars to spend more for food than those whose income is 2 thousand dollars—but our question will be how much more. Probably not five times as much.

A major purpose of surveys of food consumption, as a matter of fact, is to get the basis for such comparisons. For our overall picture of how much food Americans are getting each year, we can go to statistics of the national food supply. Per capita consumption figures tell us how much food is available for every individual in the country if it were divided evenly among us all—but it is not divided that way. We need to know not just who is eating more or less, the high- or low-income families, large or small, farm or city, but what are their typical selections of food. Only from household surveys can we get the patterns of eating and the dietary levels of different groups.

Since the mid-1930's, a period of depression, war, recovery, and many developments in processing and marketing foods, the Government has made four nationwide surveys of how and what people eat—in 1935–1936, 1942, 1948 (city families only), and 1955.

More frequent large-scale surveys have been neither feasible nor necessary. Food habits and practices change, but they change slowly. Many people must adopt a new practice or use a new food before much of a dent is made on our averages.

Although, strictly speaking, the data we present relate to a particular year, 1955, we can accept them as satisfactory representations for a fairly broad span of time. . . .

The distribution of the food dollar is one way of showing the relative importance of different types of foods. Meat, poultry, fish, or eggs, normally the main dish of our meals, took 35 cents of the food dollar—about 24 cents for beef, pork, veal, and lamb; 5 cents for poultry; 4 cents for eggs; and 2 cents for fish.

Vegetables and fruit, for which 18 cents of the dollar were spent, were next most important as a group. More than half of this was spent for fresh varieties.

Milk and milk products, excluding butter, took 14 cents.

Eleven cents were spent for flour, cereals, bread, and other baked goods.

Beverages took nearly 10 cents—a third of this for alcoholic drinks, which, however, may be underreported by the homemaker.

The remaining 12 cents were divided fairly evenly among fats and oils, sugars and sweets, and a group of such miscellaneous items as soups, nuts, catsup, pickles and olives, fillings, mixtures, and seasonings.

Further Resources

BOOKS

Bailey, Liberty Hyde. *The Country-Life Movement in the United States.* New York: Macmillan, 1911.

Leinwand, Gerald. *Hunger and Malnutrition in America.* New York: Watts, 1985.

Professional Guide to Diseases, 6th ed. Springhouse, Pa.: Springhouse Corporation, 1998.

Shotland, Jeffrey. *Rising Poverty, Declining Health: The Nutritional Status of the Rural Poor.* Washington, D.C.: Public Voice, 1986.

PERIODICALS

Seipel, Michael. "Social Consequences of Malnutrition." *Social Work,* September 1999, 416–426.

WEBSITES

"Malnutrition." *World Resources 1998–99.* World Reource Institute. Available online at http://www.wri.org/wr-98-99 /malnutri.htm; website home page: http://www.wri.org (accessed June 17, 2003).

"Private Expenditures for Medical Care and for Voluntary Health Insurance: 1950 to 1958"

Table

By: U.S. Department of Commerce

Date: 1960

Source: U.S. Department of Commerce. *Statistical Abstract of the United States: 1960.* Washington, D.C.: GPO, 1960, 75.

About the Organization: Congress created the U.S. Department of Commerce and Labor in 1903, separating the Commerce and Labor departments in 1913. Congress authorized the first census in 1790, creating an Office of Census in 1902 and later adding it to the Department of Commerce. Under the direction of the department, the Census Bureau publishes the annual *Statistical Abstract of the United States.* ■

Introduction

Health care costs grew faster than the costs of other goods and services during the 1950s. Between 1950 and 1957, the rise in medical costs outstripped that of food

by 250 percent, of housing by 160 percent, and of total living expenses by 175 percent. One did not need to look far for culprits. Between 1950 and 1960, the cost of a hospital room more than doubled. By 1960, a day's stay in a hospital cost on average $200. The antibiotic revolution also bore costs. Only in 1941 did Americans gain access to large quantities of penicillin. Other antibiotics followed between 1941 and 1950, including two varieties of streptomycin and polymyxin. These drugs saved an incalculable number of lives but cost Americans $344 billion in 1958.

The high cost of medical care elevated physicians to a patrician class. In 1959, the average physician earned $16,000 a year and the average surgeon $25,000 a year, in contrast to the average household income of $6,600.

Two possibilties existed to help individuals pay the cost of medical care: government-sponsored coverage for all Americans or private insurance for Americans who had access to it through their employer. President Harry S. Truman had favored national health care for all Americans. His successor in 1953, Dwight D. Eisenhower, branded it socialized medicine. During the cold war, the phrase "socialized medicine" raised the specter of communism at home. National health care was dead, and pri-

Private Expenditures for Medical Care and for Voluntary Health Insurance: 1950 to 1958

[In millions of dollars. Excludes Alaska and Hawaii. Includes employer contributions to health insurance premiums. Excludes medical care expenditures for the Armed Forces and veterans, those made by public health and other government agencies and under workmen's compensation laws, and those of private philanthropic organizations directly to or by hospitals.]

Expenditure	1950	1952	1953	1954	1955	1956	1957	1958
Total	8,645	10,098	10,991	11,844	12,837	14,288	15,353	16,397
Direct payments	7,351	8,105	8,572	9,088	9,687	10,661	11,209	11,900
Hospital services	1,446	1,528	1,639	1,725	1,833	1,883	1,917	2,170
Physicians' services	2,150	2,172	2,242	2,425	2,385	2,597	2,661	2,725
Medicines and appliances	2,205	2,638	2,741	2,758	3,158	3,083	4,052	4,302
Dentists	901	1,098	1,234	1,406	1,508	1,625	1,658	1,674
Other professional services[1]	482	544	586	634	653	706	741	769
Nursing homes[2]	110	125	130	140	150	170	180	200
Insurance benefits	992	1,605	1,921	2,179	2,536	3,015	3,474	3,877
Hospital services	680	1,074	1,273	1,442	1,679	2,022	2,304	2,591
Physicians' services	312	530	648	737	857	993	1,170	1,286
Expenses for prepayment[3]	299	389	408	577	614	609	670	620
Hospital services	189	232	283	325	339	346	375	341
Physicians' services	110	157	215	252	275	263	294	279

[1] Services of osteopathic physicians, chiropractors, podiatrists, private-duty trained nurses, and miscellaneous curative and healing professions.
[2] Comprises nursing homes with skilled nursing care.
[3] Represents the difference between expenditures for health insurance premiums (earned income) and amounts returned to consumers as benefits.

SOURCE: Table 89 from U.S. Department of Commerce. *Statistical Abstract of the United States: 1960.* Washington, D.C.: GPO, 1960, 75.

Primary Source

Private Expenditures for Medical Care and for Voluntary Health Insurance: 1950 to 1958

SYNOPSIS: The table reveals the growth in medical costs between 1950 and 1958. Private insurers and Americans both paid higher fees to hospitals, nursing homes, physicians and dentists.

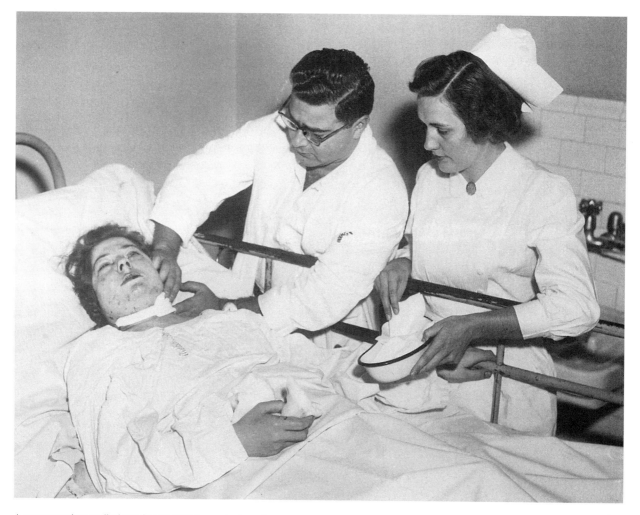

A woman receives medical care in a hospital from a doctor and a nurse. © BETTMANN/CORBIS. REPRODUCED BY PERMISSION.

vate insurers filled the void. In 1950, roughly half of Americans had coverage through their employer. By 1971, the number rose to 71 percent.

Significance

The U.S. Commerce Department reported that medical costs for Americans and private insurers almost doubled between 1950 and 1958. Curiously, out-of-pocket fees for physician services held nearly constant, increasing only 2 percent during those years. Hospital costs, however, increased by one-third, pharmaceutical drugs nearly doubled in price, dentist fees increased 74 percent, and nursing home fees doubled. Expenses that Americans did not pay out-of-pocket shifted to insurers, who paid roughly four times more in hospital and physician fees in 1958 as in 1950.

Perhaps these increases were inevitable. Americans lived on average twenty-two years longer in 1957 than in 1900. Then as now, older Americans needed more care at higher cost than younger Americans. Moreover deaths

from cancer rose during the 1950s as they had since 1900. In 1956, cancer was the second leading killer of Americans, trailing only heart disease. Cancer by then was the leading killer of children ages five to fourteen. By its nature, cancer debilitates its victims, killing them after lengthy and costly hospital and nursing home stays. Cancer consumes money as it does lives. Cancer victims paid $300 million per year by 1958 in hospital fees. The National Cancer Institute estimated that cancer cost Americans $12 billion a year.

Further Resources

BOOKS

Blandon, Robert J., and Jennifer N. Edwards eds. *System in Crisis: The Case for Health Care Reform.* New York: Faulkner and Gray, 1991.

Levitin, Nancy. *America's Health Care Crisis.* New York: F. Watts, 1994.

Sherrow, Victoria. *The U.S. Health Care Crisis.* Brookfield, Conn.: Millbrook, 1994.

WEBSITES

Millenson, Michael. *America's Health Care Challenge: Rising Costs.* American Association of Health Plans. Available online at http://www.aahpechochamber.tv/knowledge/policy/aahp/oth/02_01_22_challenge.pdf; website home page: http://www.aahp.org (accessed June 13, 2003).

PBS—Healthcare Crisis: Healthcare Timeline. Available online at http://www.pbs.org/healthcarecrisis/history.htm; website home page: http://www.pbs.org (accessed June 13, 2003).

"Heart Attack"

| Memoir

By: Dwight D. Eisenhower

Date: 1963

Source: Eisenhower, Dwight D. "Heart Attack" in *Mandate for Change, 1953–1956.* Garden City, N.Y.: Doubleday, 1963.

About the Author: Dwight David Eisenhower (1890–1969) was born in Denison, Texas, and graduated from the Military Academy at West Point in 1915. During World War I, he received the Distinguished Service Medal and in World War II rose to five-star general in command of all U.S. troops in Europe. In 1948, he retired from the Army to become president of Columbia University. From 1953 to 1961, he was president of the United States. ■

Introduction

Despite its advances, medicine had made little headway against heart disease by the 1950s. By then, it was the leading killer of Americans, killing twice the number of people as did cancer, the second leading killer. This is understandable, for aging diminishes the strength and efficiency of the heart and vascular system. The twentieth century's increase in longevity, along with other factors, has made heart disease the fate of millions of Americans.

As a person ages, the heart shrinks and loses strength, diminishing its capacity to pump blood. Heart valves thicken and lose flexibility, reducing their ability to close completely. Arteries and veins harden, and cholesterol and fat clog arteries and veins, narrowing the area for the flow of blood. This diminution of the heart and vascular system may cause hypertension, stroke, heart attack, and heart failure. All four conditions may be fatal. Hypertension, or sustained high blood pressure, may narrow blood vessels, limiting blood flow to organs. As a result, kidneys may fail or victims may suffer stroke or blindness.

Heart failure is the inability of the heart to pump sufficient blood to meet the body's needs. It may result from the heart's declining ability to pump blood as one ages.

Consequently, blood pressure falls in the arteries, which receive blood from the heart, and pressure increases in the veins, where blood pools because the heart is not strong enough to pump blood through a full circuit.

Myocardial infarction (heart attack) results when a portion of the heart receives insufficient blood. The lack of blood and thus oxygen damages that portion of the heart. A person who suffers a heart attack may feel pain through the left arm, jaw, neck, or shoulder, as well as fatigue, nausea, vomiting, and shortness of breath.

People who smoke, are obese, are sedentary or whose close relatives suffer from heart disease are themselves at risk. For years physicians have recommended a diet low in fat and cholesterol and a regime of exercise to limit the risk of heart disease.

Significance

In his memoir, Dwight D. Eisenhower admitted he had always assumed that serious illness occurred to other people, not to him. On September 23, 1955, however, he suffered a heart attack. It might have killed him had his wife not detected the seriousness of his condition and summoned the White House physician.

Eisenhower was not the first president to suffer heart and vascular distress. In 1918, President Woodrow Wilson suffered a stroke, a fact he and his wife hid from the public. Eisenhower was then a young officer and disapproved of Wilson's secrecy. Nearly forty years later, Eisenhower was determined to hide nothing from the media or public.

At the same time, he did not read newspaper accounts of his condition, for he had no desire to wade through reporters' speculations about his health and future. Yet these articles served an important function in bringing heart disease to national attention. Only in 1955 did many Americans reflect on the fact that heart disease was the nation's leading killer and that men were nearly twice as vulnerable as women to the disease.

In this respect, Eisenhower fit the profile of the typical American man who suffers a heart attack. By his own admission, he ate meat high in fat and cholesterol, was more sedentary than he liked to admit, had been a smoker much of his adulthood, and had a stressful job. Men who were honest about their lifestyle and medical history would identify with the president. Eisenhower's heart attack was a more vivid example than any medical report in warning Americans about the danger of heart disease.

Primary Source

"Heart Attack" [excerpt]

SYNOPSIS: In this excerpt from his memoir, Dwight D. Eisenhower describes the symptoms of his heart

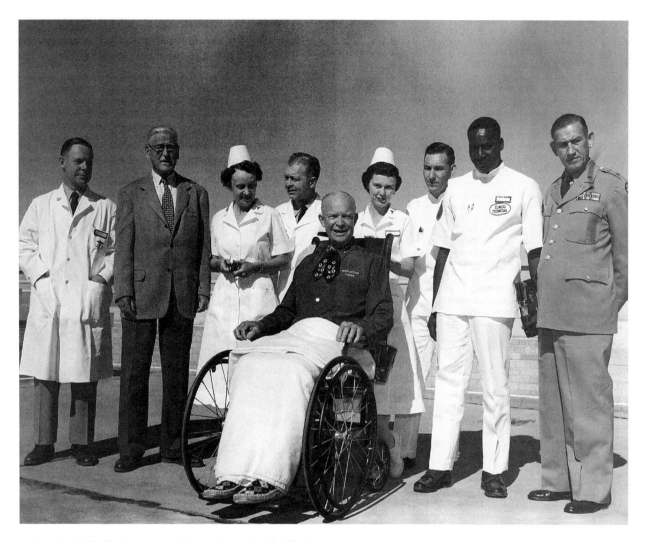

President Dwight D. Eisenhower poses with caregivers and staff of Fitzsimmons Army Hospital in Denver, Colorado, October 25, 1955, one month after he suffered a heart attack. © BETTMANN/CORBIS. REPRODUCED BY PERMISSION.

attack, his hospital treatment, his recovery, and the resumption of his duties as president. He raised public awareness of the dangers of heart disease by hiding nothing about his illness from the public.

Heart Attack

On the night of September 23, 1955, I was struck with a coronary occlusion. Subconsciously, every healthy man thinks of serious illness as something that happens occasionally—but always to other people. But when, after spending a most uncomfortable night under sedation, I awakened to the realization that I was in an oxygen tent, with doctors and nurses in attendance, I had thrust upon me the unpleasant fact that I was, indeed, a sick man. . . .

I went to bed at about 10 P.M. and slept. Some time later—roughly 1:30 A.M., I think—I awakened with a severe chest pain and thought immediately

of my after-luncheon distress the previous noon. My wife heard me stirring about and asked whether I wanted anything. I replied that I was looking for the milk of magnesia again. Apparently she decided from the tone of my voice that something was seriously wrong; she got up at once to turn on the light to have a look at me. Then she urged me to lie down and promptly called the White House physician, General Snyder. She thought I was quite sick.

General Snyder arrived shortly thereafter, and gave me some injections, one of which, I learned later, was morphine. This probably accounts for the hazy memory I had—and still have—of later events in the night. I do remember that one or two doctors came into my room and that later I was helped into a car and taken to a hospital. Then, I think, I slept; but never after that night did I feel any pain or any other symptom connected with the attack.

I followed the doctors' orders exactly, not because I was feeling any differently than the day before but because they said I had a coronary difficulty and should follow a specified routine.

Other doctors arrived on the scene. One was Dr. Paul Dudley White, a noted heart specialist of whom I had heard but had never met. Another was Colonel Tom Mattingly of the Army Medical Corps. I had known him for some time and had the utmost confidence in his skill.

For two or three days I was kept in an oxygen tent, visited only by Mamie and my son, John, who had flown out to Denver on receiving the news. On John's arrival my first thought was to send for my wallet. One of the last things on my mind before the attack was to buy a present for my lovely daughter-in-law, Barbara. Now, as if nothing had happened, I asked John to use the money to take a gift back to her.

During my illness John made two or three trips between Washington and Denver; on one of them he brought me messages from my three grandchildren on a wire recorder. The children were too young, of course, to grasp fully what had happened.

When the oxygen tent was removed, I began to ask about my staff—and whether there was anything important that should come to my attention. There was nothing extraordinary in such a request; I felt fine. I was ready to work. For one thing, I asked Mrs. Whitman to call Acting Attorney General Rogers to ask him about some legal questions I had been examining.

One thing I had already decided. Shortly after my doctors told me that I had suffered a heart attack, they and Jim Hagerty wanted to know my wishes about the kind and amount of information that should be given to the public. I had been one of those who during President Wilson's long illness wondered why the public was kept so much in the dark about his real condition, and thought that the nation had a right to know exactly the status of the President's health. So now I had a quick reply: "Tell the truth, the whole truth; don't try to conceal anything." How well they obeyed this instruction came to my attention some weeks later when I was shown, to my acute embarrassment, an early bulletin describing my health and physiological functions in quite specific terms. When I wryly remarked to Dr. White that I thought he and Jim were carrying "realism" a bit too far, he replied, "That may not mean much to the general public, but to doctors everywhere it will tell a revealing story." I recall thinking,

"Well, in any event it's too late to object now; forget it." . . .

one morning two husky orderlies came to the bed, picked me up, and placed me in a chair. This was for only a short period. After a day or so, a sudden change in the procedure occurred: I was sitting in my chair when a doctor came in and, finding me looking a bit white about the nose and mouth, ordered me back to bed without delay—instantly! He said that the exercise routine was abandoned momentarily because my cardiogram showed that the heart wound, which initially was very small, indicated some enlargement and I needed more complete rest.

Apparently this condition soon stabilized, for a little later I started the exercise program again and from then on progressed steadily until I was sitting at my easel, painting, then at the dining table, and then climbing a few steps each day, increasing the number, until I was making trips, every few hours, to the floor above. My convalescence proceeded smoothly. The doctors advised me from time to time on the nature of the routines I should thereafter pursue in order to minimize the chances of a recurrence of any difficulty with my heart. One morning, for instance, four of them brought up the matter of smoking. They earnestly counseled me to avoid tobacco in all its forms. I listened to them politely and attentively. Then noting that all four of them were smoking, I remarked pointedly that I had used no tobacco for more than six years, and wondered why I should be in bed with a heart attack while they were up and working, apparently hale and hearty.

From the beginning the doctors kept the daily newspapers from me. To this practice I readily agreed because I knew that the papers would probably be filled with stories of my illness, speculation about the outcome, comments about possibilities concerning the government's activities during the coming weeks. I had little interest in reading about myself and most certainly I did not want to worry over speculation about me, my work, and my future.

Of course, I was kept informed of important world events, except during the first few days of my illness. I was taken to the hospital on a Saturday, and just a week later Governor Adams, at my request, came out to devise with me a method for carrying on necessary work without undue strain. . . .

During the entire period of my hospitalization Mamie occupied adjoining quarters; we conversed daily on a wide range of subjects, but on none that might encourage emotional outbursts.

Mamie took on a task which amazed me at the time and has amazed me ever since: Thousands of letters of sympathy and encouragement flowed in—letters and cables and gifts from all over the world; she answered every one individually. With the help of Mrs. Mary Jane McCaffree, who worked at this exhausting task cheerfully and devotedly, Mamie signed every reply with her own rather lengthy signature, a feat which I have seldom seen duplicated. Mamie, above all others, never accepted the assumption that I had incurred a disabling illness. She told John, and I'm sure she told others, too, that she could not reconcile herself to the idea that efforts in behalf of what I believed in had come to an end. While solicitous above all for my health and welfare, she perhaps more than any other retained the conviction that my job as President was not yet finished. . . .

Once at the farm, I settled down to a routine of exercise—primarily walking—and of work. The doctor said that I should resume my favorite exercise before too long. This was good news. Golf had kept my muscles in good shape and this was partly responsible for the good chances of a full recovery. I had a prescribed medical program, but it was far from rigorous. Only one medicine was required, an anticoagulant called Cumadin, taken in pill form. Beyond this a low-cholesterol diet was ordered; I had to give up eggs, fatty and glandular meats, and certain types of seafood. The principal caution was to avoid excessive fatigue, especially if accompanied by overheating. I was also required to keep my weight at 172 pounds instead of my customary 178, no small item for a man with my love of food. One habit that I had to acquire was that of taking a midday rest, before lunch, of thirty to forty-five minutes. This was difficult; to this day I rather resent the inconvenience it causes in planning a day's schedule.

My first post-illness Cabinet meeting took place on November 22, at Camp David. It was a full meeting, largely concerned with the legislative and budgetary program for the next year, although some other subjects were on the agenda. At its conclusion I felt no fatigue or weariness, and concluded that I would soon resume the daily work schedule to which I was accustomed. Now I felt sure my recovery would be complete.

Reviewing the entire period of my first serious illness, I can be grateful for many things, not the least of which was the fact that I could not have selected a better time, so to speak, to have a heart attack, even if I had been able to pick the date. The economy was booming, Congress was not in ses-

sion. I had been able to handle with Foster the major foreign-policy problems, and at the moment there was no new crisis pending in the world. Thus it was not necessary for me to consult daily with members of the Council of Economic Advisers, or to approve or veto bills passed by the Congress, or to send messages recommending courses of action to that body. Probably most important was the fact that I was not required to make any immediate operational decisions involving the use of the armed forces of the United States. Certainly, had there been an emergency such as the detection of incoming enemy bombers, on which I would have had to make a rapid decision regarding the use of United States retaliatory might, there could have been no question, after the first forty-eight hours of my heart attack, of my capacity to act according to my own judgment. However, had a situation arisen such as occurred in 1958 in which I eventually sent troops ashore in Lebanon, the concentration, the weighing of the pros and cons, and the final determination would have represented a burden, during the first week of my illness, which the doctors would likely have found unacceptable for a new cardiac patient to bear. As it was, with a period of rest, I was able to keep my mind clear, to talk to members of the government on matters of long-range interest, and to experience a satisfactory recovery.

Further Resources

BOOKS

Alexander, Charles C. *Holding the Line: The Eisenhower Era, 1951–1961*. Bloomington, Ind.: Indiana University Press, 1975.

Greenstein, Fred I. *The Hidden-Hand Presidency: Eisenhower as Leader*. New York: Basic Books, 1982.

Parmet, Herbert S. *Eisenhower and the American Crusade*. New York: Macmillan, 1972.

PERIODICALS

Atkinson, Rick. "Ike's Dark Days." *U.S. News & World Report*, October 28, 2002, 42–50.

WEBSITES

Biography of Dwight D. Eisenhower. The White House. Available online at http://www.whitehouse.gov/history/presidents /de34.html; website home page: http://www.whitehouse.gov/ (accessed June 12, 2003).

Patty, Mike. "Heart Attack Hit during Eisenhower's Denver Trip." *Rocky Mountain News*. Available online at http:// www.denver-rmn.com/millennium/0810ike.shtml; website home page: http://www.rockymountainnews.com/ (accessed June 12, 2003).

When the President Is the Patient. Health Media Lab. Available online at http://www.healthmedialab.com/presmed/index .html; website home page http://www.healthmedialab.com /index.html (accessed June 12, 2003).

"New Duties, New Faces"

Memoir

By: Dwight D. Eisenhower

Date: 1963

Source: Eisenhower, Dwight D. "New Duties, New Faces" in *Mandate for Change, 1953–1956.* Garden City, N.Y.: Doubleday, 1963.

About the Author: Dwight David Eisenhower (1890–1969) was born in Denison, Texas, and graduated from the Military Academy at West Point in 1915. During World War I, he received the Distinguished Service Medal and in World War II rose to five-star general in command of all U.S. troops in Europe. In 1948, he retired from the Army to become president of Columbia University. From 1953 to 1961, he was president of the United States. ■

Introduction

A thirty-seven-year veteran, Dwight D. Eisenhower was accustomed to the U.S. Army's clear hierarchy and chain of command. As president, he wanted to impose this structure on the federal government. He found, however, that the federal agencies that conducted research in medicine and health were in disparate agencies without centralized control.

Congress had, for example, created the Public Health Service in 1789 as an independent agency. It funded research at public universities and medical schools on the link between nutrition and health. In the nineteenth century, Congress created the Indian Health Service as part of the Bureau of Indian Affairs. In 1946, Congress created the Communicable Disease Center, the precursor of the Centers for Disease Control and Prevention, as yet a third separate agency. The Food and Drug Administration (FDA) and St. Elizabeth's Hospital for the mentally ill were then part of the Federal Security Agency, an agency that Eisenhower believed had become too bloated and unmanageable. The U.S. Department of Agriculture, yet another independent agency, protected public health by ensuring the purity of meat.

Eisenhower did not question the importance of these agencies or their research. Rather, he questioned their organization, which resembled government by feudalism, with each agency an independent fiefdom. Agency chiefs sought to protect and enlarge their turf, competing against one another for power and congressional funding.

Significance

Such a system, Eisenhower believed, encouraged waste and duplication of research and discouraged presidential and congressional oversight. He stressed in this excerpt the importance of bringing agencies with common goals under a single cabinet department. Once Congress had established this order, Eisenhower delegated responsibility to his cabinet secretaries, believing they could best administer their departments with minimal presidential oversight.

This vision of the federal government led Eisenhower on March 12, 1953, to ask Congress to replace the Federal Security Agency with the new Department of Health, Education and Welfare. Congress created the department on April 11, 1953. It subsumed many of the disparate federal agencies that conducted research on improving the health of Americans. The department maintained control of the FDA and St. Elizabeth's Hospital, as had the defunct Federal Security Agency. In addition, the department took charge of the Communicable Disease Center and in 1955 the Indian Health Service.

The department, Eisenhower implied, fulfilled his campaign pledge that the Republican Party was the party that made Americans' health a priority. Yet he never took the next step of proposing government-sponsored medical coverage for all Americans. His predecessor, Harry S. Truman, had wanted national health care, but Eisenhower labeled it socialized medicine. The label killed any impetus toward national health care, for Americans feared any hint of socialism as a step toward communism, an economic system the United States had combated since the 1940s.

Primary Source

"New Duties, New Faces" [excerpt]

> **SYNOPSIS:** In this excerpt from his memoir, Dwight D. Eisenhower stresses the importance of bringing agencies with common goals under a single cabinet department. This vision led Eisenhower to propose the creation of the Department of Health, Education and Welfare.

Constantly in those early months I searched for ways of improving the organization of the entire Executive branch.

Between March 12 and June 1 I sent to the Congress for approval, in accordance with the Reorganization Act of 1949, ten plans for changes in Executive-branch organization.

Reorganization Plan Number One, sent up March 12, established a new department of government, the Department of Health, Education and Welfare. Its principal functions were indicated by its title.

During the campaign, in speeches in Boise, Los Angeles, and other cities, I had hammered home the fact that the Republican party yielded to no one its concern for the human needs of human beings. To implement this promise, we hoped to extend social-security coverage to millions of additional workers.

President Dwight D. Eisenhower introduces the newly appointed Secretary of Health, Education, and Welfare, Oveta Culp Hobby, to the nation in a television broadcast, July 9, 1954. © BETTMANN/CORBIS. REPRODUCED BY PERMISSION.

The new Department of Health, Education and Welfare replaced the old Federal Security Agency, which by 1952 had become a conglomeration of bureaus employing more than thirty-six thousand people, getting its money through sixty-seven active appropriations, spending it at the rate of more than $4 billion a year, and lacking adequate administrative direction and control.

When, on April 11, 1953, Mrs. Hobby, Federal Security Administrator, became Secretary Hobby, the Department of Health, Education and Welfare—the first new Cabinet department established in forty years—was on its way to becoming a far more disciplined and efficient servant of the ever-increasing number of American people.

My interest in organization in those early months of 1953 went to the limits of the federal establishment and beyond them. On March 30 I sent a spe-

cial message to Congress urging that it set up a commission to study the division of responsibilities among federal, state, and local governments, to take a hard look at all programs of financial aid that reached down from Washington into the state and the individual community. This Commission on Intergovernmental Relations, which became a reality when I signed the legislation into law on July 10, had as its first chairman Clarence Manion, and as its second, an unusually astute man, Meyer Kestnbaum.

The same day I signed into law the bill establishing the second Hoover Commission—a commission to scrutinize specifically the functions and organization of the federal government.

Again and again I emphasized the need for efficient decentralization within each agency of the government. My principal assistants, I insisted, in the interests of sanity and efficiency, should save for themselves time for thinking and study. The only way they could get such time was to delegate as much as possible to their subordinates. "The marks of a good executive," I wrote to the heads of agencies on September 29, 1953, "are courage in delegating work to subordinates and his own skill in coordinating and directing their effort." And I should have added, as I so often did in wartime, to take personal responsibility for mistakes and give subordinates credit for success.

Further Resources

BOOKS

Alexander, Charles C. *Holding the Line: The Eisenhower Era, 1951–1961.* Bloomington, Ind.: Indiana University Press, 1975.

Greenstein, Fred I. *The Hidden-Hand Presidency: Eisenhower as Leader.* New York: Basic Books, 1982.

Parmet, Herbert S. *Eisenhower and the American Crusade.* New York: Macmillan, 1972.

PERIODICALS

"Dwight D. Eisenhower." *Kirkus Reviews,* September 1, 2002, 1295.

WEBSITES

FDA—Reorganization Plan of 1953. U.S. Food and Drug Administration. Available online at http://www.fda.gov/opacom/laws/reorg.htm; website home page: http://www.fda.gov (accessed June 17, 2003).

HHS—History. U.S. Department of Health and Human Services. Available online at http://www.hhs.gov/about/hhshist.html; website home page: http://www.hhs.gov (accessed June 17, 2003).

"John F. Nash, Jr.—Autobiography"

Autobiography

By: John F. Nash Jr.

Date: 1994

Source: Nash, John F. "John F. Nash, Jr.—Autobiography." The Nobel Foundation. Available online at http://www.nobel.se/economics/laureates/1994/nash-autobio.html; website home page: http://www.nobel.se/ (accessed June 13, 2003).

About the Author: John Forbes Nash Jr. (1928–) was born in Bluefield, West Virginia, and received a Ph.D. in mathematics from Princeton University in 1950. He joined the faculty at the Massachusetts Institute of Technology, resigning in 1959 when schizophrenia began to impair his judgment. Intermittent stays in asylums punctuated travel in Europe and periods of lucid concentration on mathematics. He seems to have willed his own recovery and won the 1994 Nobel Prize in economics. ■

Introduction

The roots of American mental health care extend back to the eighteenth century. In 1773, the Virginia House of Burgesses created the first American mental hospital in Williamsburg, Virginia. Treatment was primitive. American physician Benjamin Rush believed at the end of the eighteenth century that an excess of blood in the brain caused mental illness, leading physicians to bleed patients. This practice weakened patients, leading Rush to conclude their sedation as evidence of cure.

The Quakers took the first strides toward humane treatment of the mentally ill. In 1796, Quakers founded the York Retreat in New York to give the mentally ill a quiet, religious place where they could rest. In 1817 and 1824, Quakers founded retreats in Pennsylvania and Connecticut.

The Quakers were ahead of their time. By the 1950s, mental health treatment had degenerated from the Quaker ideal. Mental institutions were less places of treatment than of isolation that separated the mentally ill from the rest of society, confining many until their death. In 1956, *The Saturday Evening Post* broke the scandal of abuse and neglect at Columbus State Hospital in Ohio. The hospital housed 2,700 patients of which 117 received electroshock therapy (EST). A medical attendant sent an electric current through a patient's brain, causing convulsions so violent that some patients broke bones. Psychiatrists favored EST as treatment for depression.

On average a patient had a 50 percent chance of release during the first year of confinement. Thereafter, prospects plummeted to 4 percent in the second year and 1 percent in subsequent years. These odds had the effect of sentencing long-term patients to death.

Significance

John Nash entered this dysfunctional system in 1959, when, by his own account in his autobiography, in the midst of a career as a mathematician at the Massachusetts Institute of Technology he resigned his professorship. Schizophrenia had begun to impair his judgment. Against his will, he spent fifty days at the McLean Hospital, undergoing EST. Upon his release, he sought asylum in Europe. After his return to the United States, he spent intermittent periods in New Jersey hospitals. Periods of lucidity punctuated his illness, allowing him to resume work on mathematical problems. These periods gave way to additional bouts with schizophrenia, though symptoms were moderate enough that he avoided hospitalization. He came finally to reject delusional thoughts and appears to have willed his recovery.

Nash's autobiography of his illness and recovery is uplifting. Mental illness need not be a lifelong scourge. Many patients do recover to lead normal lives. At the

After years of suffering from schizophrenia, John Nash willed his way to recovery and was named the winner of the Nobel Peace Prize in Economics in 1994. AP/WIDE WORLD PHOTOS. REPRODUCED BY PERMISSION.

same time, Nash's schizophrenia reveals how much mental illness remains a mystery to medicine. His autobiography implies that he recovered his sanity without the aid of psychiatrists and other mental-health professionals. Indeed Nash's hospitalizations appear to have done nothing to abate his symptoms.

Nash's autobiography leads to the uneasy conclusion that no one is immune from mental illness. For years, psychiatrists have debated whether Isaac Newton suffered from bipolar disorder. Mental illness devoured the brilliance of German philosopher Friedrich Nietzsche and led the German composer Robert Schumann to kill himself. Perhaps greater awareness of mental illness will lead to greater compassion for its victims.

Primary Source

"John F. Nash, Jr.—Autobiography" [excerpt]

SYNOPSIS: In his autobiography, John F. Nash Jr. describes the onset of schizophrenia in 1959, his twenty-five-year battle against it, and his recovery.

Now I must arrive at the time of my change from scientific rationality of thinking into the delusional thinking characteristic of persons who are psychi-

atrically diagnosed as "schizophrenic" or "paranoid schizophrenic." But I will not really attempt to describe this long period of time but rather avoid embarrassment by simply omitting to give the details of truly personal type.

While I was on the academic sabbatical of 1956–1957 I also entered into marriage. Alicia had graduated as a physics major from M.I.T. where we had met and she had a job in the New York City area in 1956–1957. She had been born in El Salvador but came at an early age to the U.S. and she and her parents had long been U.S. citizens, her father being an M.D. and ultimately employed at a hospital operated by the federal government in Maryland.

The mental disturbances originated in the early months of 1959 at a time when Alicia happened to be pregnant. And as a consequence I resigned my position as a faculty member at M.I.T. and, ultimately, after spending 50 days under "observation" at the McLean Hospital, travelled to Europe and attempted to gain status there as a refugee.

I later spent times of the order of five to eight months in hospitals in New Jersey, always on an involuntary basis and always attempting a legal argument for release.

And it did happen that when I had been long enough hospitalized that I would finally renounce my delusional hypotheses and revert to thinking of myself as a human of more conventional circumstances and return to mathematical research. In these interludes of, as it were, enforced rationality, I did succeed in doing some respectable mathematical research. Thus there came about the research for "Le Probleme de Cauchy pour les Équations Differentielles d'un Fluide Generale"; the idea that Prof. Hironaka called "the Nash blowing-up transformation"; and those of "Arc Structure of Singularities" and "Analyticity of Solutions of Implicit Function Problems with Analytic Data."

But after my return to the dream-like delusional hypotheses in the later 60's I became a person of delusionally influenced thinking but of relatively moderate behavior and thus tended to avoid hospitalization and the direct attention of psychiatrists.

Thus further time passed. Then gradually I began to intellectually reject some of the delusionally influenced lines of thinking which had been characteristic of my orientation. This began, most recognizably, with the rejection of politically-oriented thinking as essentially a hopeless waste of intellectual effort.

So at the present time I seem to be thinking rationally again in the style that is characteristic of scientists. However this is not entirely a matter of joy as if someone returned from physical disability to good physical health. One aspect of this is that rationality of thought imposes a limit on a person's concept of his relation to the cosmos. For example, a non-Zoroastrian could think of Zarathustra as simply a madman who led millions of naive followers to adopt a cult of ritual fire worship. But without his "madness" Zarathustra would necessarily have been only another of the millions or billions of human individuals who have lived and then been forgotten.

Statistically, it would seem improbable that any mathematician or scientist, at the age of 66, would be able through continued research efforts, to add much to his or her previous achievements. However I am still making the effort and it is conceivable that with the gap period of about 25 years of partially deluded thinking providing a sort of vacation my situation may be atypical. Thus I have hopes of being able to achieve something of value through my current studies or with any new ideas that come in the future.

Further Resources

BOOKS

Belknap, Ivan. *Human Problems of a State Mental Hospital.* New York: McGraw-Hill, 1956.

Grimes, John M. *When Minds Go Wrong: The Truth about Our Mentally Ill and Their Care in Mental Hospitals.* New York: Devin-Adair, 1954.

Mental Health: A Report of the Surgeon General. Rockville, Md.: U.S. Public Health Service, 1999.

Nasar, Sylvia. *A Beautiful Mind: A Biography of John Forbes Nash, Jr., Winner of the Nobel Prize in Economics, 1994.* New York: Simon and Schuster, 1998.

Professional Guide to Diseases, 6th ed. Springhouse, Pa.: Springhouse Corporation, 1998.

PERIODICALS

"A Beautiful Mind: Movie Misrepresents the Recovery of John F. Nash, Jr." *HealthFacts,* April 2002, 3.

AUDIO AND VISUAL MEDIA

A Beautiful Mind. Directed by Ron Howard. Universal, 2001. Videocassette.

10

RELIGION

PETER J. CAPRIOGLIO

Entries are arranged in chronological order by date of primary source. For entries with one primary source, the entry title is the same as the primary source title. Entries with more than one primary source have an overall entry title, followed by the titles of the primary sources.

Important Events in Religion, 1950–1959

1950

- A House bill that excludes parochial schools from education funding is rejected by the Education and Labor Committee.

- In May, two Southern Baptist seminaries are recognized, one at Berkeley, California, the other at Wake Forest, North Carolina.

- On May 22, the American Baptist Convention extends an invitation to all organized Baptist Conventions (including Southern Baptists and two African-American Conferences) to join the National Baptist Convention.

1951

- The Supreme Court assumes the right to review cases of state interference in religious freedom.

- The Supreme Court agrees to review the constitutional status of released-time programs for religious study in public schools in New York City.

- Because of the fighting in Korea, American missionaries are no longer accepted in China.

- Several Jewish synagogues are bombed in Miami, Florida.

- The United States fails to ratify the UN Genocide Convention.

- California joins other states in granting tax exemption to parochial schools.

1952

- The Methodist church grants the right of African-American churches to transfer to white jurisdictions upon mutual agreement.

- New York State's released-time program for religious studies is upheld by the Supreme Court.

- The Supreme Court holds that states and cities may not ban movies on the grounds of being sacrilegious.

- The Eastern Orthodox church begins training American youths to become priests rather than bringing priests to America from abroad.

- On September 30, the National Council of Churches publishes the New Revised Standard Version Bible.

- On November 23, the dedication of a Buddhist temple for 250 Kalmucks (Russian Buddhists) takes place at Farmington, New Jersey.

1953

- Distribution of Bibles in New Jersey public schools is held unconstitutional by the state supreme court.

- President and Mrs. Dwight D. Eisenhower join the National Presbyterian Church in Washington, D.C.; Eisenhower becomes the first president to join a church while in office.

- The oldest Yiddish newspaper in the United States, the *Jewish Morning Journal,* suspends publication after fifty-two years.

- In July, Dr. J.B.S. Mathews charges the clergy as the "largest single group supporting Communist apparatus in U.S. today," in an *American Mercury* article.

1954

- A Pennsylvania court orders Amish children to attend high school.

- The Revised Standard Version Bible breaks all-time publishing records, selling over three million copies.

1955

- California's attorney general rules that Gideon Bibles cannot be handed out inside public schools.

- Evangelist Billy Graham conducts a successful series of revivals in Great Britain and France.

1956

- During the Methodist General Conference women are granted full clergy rights.

- The Presbyterian Church in the U.S. gives final approval to the ordination of women.

- A court ruling allows the Reverend William Howard Melish to remain as supply pastor to an Episcopal church in Brooklyn in spite of alleged left-wing loyalties.

1957

- A Florida circuit court rules that a Jewish couple can retain custody of the six-year-old daughter of a Catholic woman.

- The New York State Education Commission rules against classroom display of an interdenominational version of the Ten Commandments.

- On June 25, the United Church of Christ is formed by the union of the Congregational Christian church with the Evangelical and Reformed church.

1958

- As a means of curbing juvenile delinquency in Michigan, a constitutional amendment mandating Bible reading in public schools is proposed.

- On May 28, the United Presbyterian Church in the U.S.A. is formed by the merger of the former Presbyterian Church in the U.S. and the United Presbyterian Church.

- On October 12, President Dwight D. Eisenhower participates in the laying of the cornerstone of the Interchurch Center in New York City.

1959

- A New York Supreme Court justice holds that morning prayers in public schools should be allowed if the prayers are nondenominational and non-mandatory.
- The Interchurch Center in New York City increases opportunities for contact between Protestant and Orthodox churches.

- Most Protestant churches speak out in favor of birth-control measures in family planning.

- President Dwight D. Eisenhower says in a press conference that a Roman Catholic can be elected president.

- In summer, the National Student Christian Federation is formed.

Joseph Burstyn, Inc. v. Wilson

Supreme Court decision

By: Thomas Campbell Clark

Date: May 26, 1952

Source: *Joseph Burstyn, Inc. v. Wilson,* 343 U.S. 495 (1952). Available online at FindLaw for Legal Professionals. http://caselaw.findlaw.com/cgi-bin/getcase.pl?court=us&vol=343&invol=495 (accessed February 9, 2003).

About the Author: Thomas Campbell Clark (1899–1977) was born in Dallas, Texas. In 1922, he received a law degree from the University of Texas. He was appointed a special assistant to the U.S. attorney general in 1937 and rose to U.S. attorney general in 1945. In 1949, Clark was appointed to the U.S. Supreme Court, where he served until he retired in 1967. ∎

Introduction

In the 1950s, New York State had a law mandating that films had to be licensed by the state to be publicly shown. The law read, "The director of the [motion picture] division [of the education department] or, when authorized by the regents, the officers of a local office or bureau shall cause to be promptly examined every motion picture film submitted to them as herein required, and unless such film or a part thereof is obscene, indecent, immoral, inhuman, sacrilegious, or is of such a character that its exhibition would tend to corrupt morals or incite to crime, shall issue a license therefore. If such director or, when so authorized, such officer shall not license any film submitted, he shall furnish to the applicant therefor a written report of the reasons for his refusal and a description of each rejected part of a film not rejected in toto."

Joseph Burstyn, Inc., was a corporation that distributed motion pictures in New York, including a movie entitled *The Miracle*. Some groups in the state considered the movie sacrilegious and therefore religiously offensive and called on Commissioner Wilson of the New York State Department of Education, which denied or granted licenses for movies to be shown in theaters, to withdraw the film's license. Wilson agreed, and the film could no longer be shown in public theaters.

The film's distributor sued in the state court to force Commissioner Wilson to grant the license. The New York Appellate Division sustained the revocation of the license, deeming the film "sacrilegious," and the Court of Appeals of New York affirmed the decision. Burstyn then appealed to the U.S. Supreme Court, arguing that the state law violated the First and Fourteenth Amendments to the Constitution. In a unanimous decision delivered by Justice Clark, the Court agreed.

Significance

This landmark decision was a victory for those who opposed the imposition of religious standards by state or federal governments. According to the Court, movies, like books, newspapers, and other printed matter, are important methods for communicating ideas among people. The free exchange of ideas in an open society like the United States had to be protected from the imposition of religious views on public discourse, including films.

The Court's decision reinforced the guarantees of freedom from religious censorship under the First and Fourteenth Amendments. The First Amendment states, "Congress shall make no law respecting an establishment of religion, or prohibiting the free exercise thereof; or abridging the freedom of speech, or of the press. . . ." The Fourteenth Amendment, which extends the federal protections of the First Amendment to the states, says, "No state shall make or enforce any law which shall abridge the privileges or immunities of citizens of the United States; nor shall any state deprive any person of life, liberty, or property, without due process of law; nor deny to any person within its jurisdiction the equal protection of the laws."

Primary Source

Joseph Burstyn, Inc. v. Wilson [excerpt]

SYNOPSIS: In these excerpts, Justice Clark explains why the New York State law banning sacrilegious films was unconstitutional: the standard for deciding what was sacrilegious or not was too vague; the censor had no clear guidelines in making such decisions; and the state should not be in the business of protecting people from views that it may find to be offensive.

Mr. Justice Clark delivered the opinion of the Court.

. . . The issue here is the constitutionality, under the First and Fourteenth Amendments, of a New York statute which permits the banning of motion picture films on the ground that they are "sacrilegious." That statute makes it unlawful "to exhibit, or to sell, lease or lend for exhibition at any place of amusement for pay or in connection with any business in the state of New York, any motion picture film or reel [with specified exceptions not relevant here], unless there is at the time in full force and effect a valid license or permit therefor of the education department . . ." The statute further provides:

"The director of the [motion picture] division [of the education department] of, when authorized by the regents, the officers of a local office or bureau shall cause to be promptly examined every motion picture film submitted to them as herein required, and unless such film or a part thereof is obscene, indecent, immoral, inhuman, sacrilegious, or is of such a character that its exhibition would tend to corrupt morals or incite to crime, shall issue a license therefor. If such director or, when so authorized, such officer shall not license any film submitted, he shall furnish to the applicant therefor a written report of the reasons for his refusal and a description of each rejected part of a film not rejected in toto."

Appellant is a corporation engaged in the business of distributing motion pictures. It owns the exclusive rights to distribute throughout the United States a film produced in Italy entitled "The Miracle." On November 30, 1950, after having examined the picture, the motion picture division of the New York education department, acting under the statute quoted above, issued to appellant a license authorizing exhibition of "The Miracle," with English subtitles, as one part of a trilogy called "Ways of Love." Thereafter, for a period of approximately eight weeks, "Ways of Love" was exhibited publicly in a motion picture theater in New York City under an agreement between appellant and the owner of the theater whereby appellant received a stated percentage of the admission price.

During this period, the New York State Board of Regents, which by statute is made the head of the education department, received "hundreds of letters, telegrams, post cards, affidavits and other communications" both protesting against and defending the public exhibition of "The Miracle." The Chancellor of the Board of Regents requested three members of the Board to view the picture and to make a report to the entire Board. After viewing the film, this committee reported to the Board that in its opinion there was basis for the claim that the picture was "sacrilegious." Thereafter, on January 19, 1951, the Regents directed appellant to show cause, at a hearing to be held on January 30, why

In the case of *Joseph Burstyn, Inc. v. Wilson* (1952), Justice Thomas Clark handed down the decision by which the Supreme Court unanimously ruled that motion picture films were protected as free speech. A New York State law that banned "sacrilegious" films from being shown in public theaters was struck down as unconstitutional. © BETTMANN/CORBIS. REPRODUCED BY PERMISSION.

its license to show "The Miracle" should not be rescinded on that ground. Appellant appeared at this hearing, which was conducted by the same three-member committee of the Regents which had previously viewed the picture, and challenged the jurisdiction of the committee and of the Regents to proceed with the case. With the consent of the committee, various interested persons and organizations submitted to it briefs and exhibits bearing upon the merits of the picture and upon the constitutional and statutory questions involved. On February 16, 1951, the Regents, after viewing "The Miracle," determined that it was "sacrilegious" and for that reason ordered the Commissioner of Education to rescind appellant's license to exhibit the picture. The Commissioner did so.

Appellant brought the present action in the New York courts to review the determination of the Regents. Among the claims advanced by appellant were (1) that the statute violates the Fourteenth Amendment as a prior restraint upon freedom of speech and of the press; (2) that it is invalid under the same

Amendment as a violation of the guaranty of separate church and state and as a prohibition of the free exercise of religion; and, (3) that the term "sacrilegious" is so vague and indefinite as to offend due process. The Appellate Division rejected all of appellant's contentions and upheld the Regents' determination. On appeal the New York Court of Appeals, two judges dissenting, affirmed the order of the Appellate Division. The case is here on appeal.

As we view the case, we need consider only appellant's contention that the New York statute is an unconstitutional abridgment of free speech and a free press. . . .

It cannot be doubted that motion pictures are a significant medium for the communication of ideas. They may affect public attitudes and behavior in a variety of ways, ranging from direct espousal of a political or social doctrine to the subtle shaping of thought which characterizes all artistic expression. The importance of motion pictures as an organ of public opinion is not lessened by the fact that they are designed to entertain as well as to inform. As was said in *Winters v. New York* (1948):

> The line between the informing and the entertaining is too elusive for the protection of that basic right [a free press]. Everyone is familiar with instances of propaganda through fiction. What is one man's amusement, teaches another's doctrine. . . .

We conclude that expression by means of motion pictures is included within the free speech and free press guaranty of the First and Fourteenth Amendments. . . .

The statute involved here does not seek to punish, as a past offense, speech or writing falling within the permissible scope of subsequent punishment. On the contrary, New York requires that permission to communicate ideas be obtained in advance from state officials who judge the content of the words and pictures sought to be communicated. This Court recognized many years ago that such a previous restraint is a form of infringement upon freedom of expression to be especially condemned. . . . The Court there recounted the history which indicates that a major purpose of the First Amendment guaranty of a free press was to prevent prior restraints upon publication, although it was carefully pointed out that the liberty of the press is not limited to that protection. . . .

The most careful and tolerant censor would find it virtually impossible to avoid favoring one religion over another, and he would be subject to an inevitable tendency to ban the expression of unpopular sentiments sacred to a religious minority. Application of the "sacrilegious" test, in these or other respects, might raise substantial questions under the First Amendment's guaranty of separate church and state with freedom of worship for all. However, from the standpoint of freedom of speech and the press, it is enough to point out that the state has no legitimate interest in protecting any or all religions from views distasteful to them which is sufficient to justify prior restraints upon the expression of those views. It is not the business of government in our nation to suppress real or imagined attacks upon a particular religious doctrine, whether they appear in publications, speeches, or motion pictures. . . .

We hold only that under the First and Fourteenth Amendments a state may not ban a film on the basis of a censor's conclusion that it is "sacrilegious."

Reversed.

Further Resources

BOOKS

Censorship: For & Against. New York: Hart, 1971.

Jones, Derek, ed. *Censorship: A World Encyclopedia.* London: Fitzroy Dearborn, 2001.

WEBSITES

Basinger, Jeanaine. "HUAC and Censorship Changes." From *American Cinema: One Hundred Years of Filmmaking,* 1994. Available online at http://www.moderntimes.com /palace/huac.htm; website home page: http://www.modern times.com/palace/index.html (accessed February 9, 2003).

National Council of Teachers of English. "Anti-Censorship." Available online at http://www.ncte.org/censorship; website home page: http://www.ncte.org/index.shtml (accessed February 9, 2003).

The Power of Positive Thinking
Nonfiction work

By: Norman Vincent Peale

Date: 1952

Source: Peale, Norman Vincent. *The Power of Positive Thinking.* New York: Prentice-Hall, 1952. Reprint, Pawling, New York: Foundation for Christian Living, 1978.

About the Author: Norman Vincent Peale (1898–1993) was born in Bowersville, Ohio, and ordained a Methodist Episcopal minister in 1922. He served as pastor at Marble Collegiate Reformed Church in New York City from 1932 to 1984. He helped found the American Foundation of Religion and Psychiatry in 1937. He was a prolific author of books, a noted radio and television personality, and a stimulating lecturer. ■

Introduction

Norman Vincent Peale believed that psychological principles and psychotherapy should be combined with religious beliefs and practices to help people resolve their personal problems. He found that many of these problems resulted from negative feelings and thoughts people had about themselves. They lacked the self-confidence and positive attitude to overcome their psychological difficulties.

More than thirty years earlier, Sigmund Freud, in *Civilization and Its Discontents,* had argued that psychoanalysis unlocked the unconscious mind. Peale argued that religious faith also unlocked the unconscious mind. For many years, psychologists and theologians had believed that psychology and religion should keep their distance from one another. Peale, though, believed that religion and psychotherapy should not be antagonists. After years of study and prayer, he concluded that neither therapy nor religion alone provided the complete answer. Both were necessary in achieving personal change and growth. Armed with a strong belief in God, the troubled individual could be helped through counseling to develop a habit of thinking positively and thus develop a healthy self-concept. Personal problems could be overcome, or at least their impact could be reduced, by merging religion and psychology.

Peale successfully applied this unique combination in his ministry at Marble Collegiate Reformed Church in New York City, helping scores of his parishioners overcome their personal problems by looking at life in a mentally and spiritually healthier manner. He wanted others to benefit from his discovery, so he wrote *The Power of Positive Thinking.* He also spread his message to the American public through other writings and radio and television programs.

Significance

One of the most influential religious works of the time, *The Power of Positive Thinking* sold more than a million copies in the first two years after its publication and has been translated into more than forty languages. The book was successful because of two important factors: Peale's belief that religion could improve people's lives and his faith not just in God but also in the ability of people to help themselves.

The 1950s was a time of economic prosperity for many Americans, but cold war tensions loomed. There was fear of atomic warfare that would kill millions of people and destroy civilization. Some people began to

wonder whether there would be a future for themselves or their children. This negative, pessimistic thinking adversely affected some people's mental state. *The Power of Positive Thinking* was a powerful antidote to help them cope with fearful times and self-destructive ideas. In a clear and readily understandable manner, Peale gave people reasons to abandon pessimism and ways to embrace optimism. Understanding the need for spiritual uplifting and renewal, he presented recommendations to help people achieve these goals, including large doses of prayer.

Primary Source

The Power of Positive Thinking [excerpt]

> **SYNOPSIS:** The following excerpts include the Introduction and portions from the chapter entitled "Believe in Yourself." The Introduction summarizes what the book can do for the reader. "Believe in Yourself" offers ten recommendations for building self-confidence.

Introduction

What This Book Can Do for You

This book is written to suggest techniques and to give examples which demonstrate that you do not need to be defeated by anything, that you can have peace of mind, improved health, and a never-ceasing flow of energy. In short, that your life can be full of joy and satisfaction. Of this I have no doubt at all for I have watched countless persons learn and apply a system of simple procedures that has brought about the foregoing benefits in their lives. These assertions, which may appear extravagant, are based on bona-fide demonstrations in actual human experience.

Altogether too many people are defeated by the everyday problems of life. They go struggling, perhaps even whining, through their days with a sense of dull resentment at what they consider the "bad breaks" life has given them. In a sense there may be such a thing as "the breaks" in this life, but there is also a spirit and method by which we can control and even determine those breaks. It is a pity that people should let themselves be defeated by the problems, cares, and difficulties of human existence, and it is also quite unnecessary.

In saying this I certainly do not ignore or minimize the hardships and tragedies of the world, but neither do I allow them to dominate. You can permit obstacles to control your mind to the point where they are uppermost and thus become the dominating factors in your thought pattern. By learning how

Dr. Norman Vincent Peale holds a copy of his book, *The Power of Positive Thinking.* GETTY IMAGES. REPRODUCED BY PERMISSION.

to cast them from the mind, by refusing to become mentally subservient to them, and by channeling spiritual power through your thoughts you can rise above obstacles which ordinarily might defeat you. By methods I shall outline, obstacles are simply not permitted to destroy your happiness and well-being. You need be defeated only if you are willing to be. This book teaches you how to "will" not to be.

The purpose of this book is a very direct and simple one. It makes no pretense to literary excellence nor does it seek to demonstrate any unusual scholarship on my part. This is simply a practical, direct-action, personal-improvement manual. It is written with the sole objective of helping the reader achieve a happy, satisfying, and worthwhile life. I thoroughly and enthusiastically believe in certain demonstrated and effective principles which, when practiced, produce a victorious life. My aim is to set them forth in this volume in a logical, simple, and understandable manner so that the reader feeling a sense of need, may learn a practical method by which he can build for himself, with God's help, the kind of life he deeply desires.

If you read this book thoughtfully, carefully absorbing its teachings, and if you will sincerely and persistently practice the principles and formulas set forth herein, you can experience an amazing improvement within yourself. By using the techniques outlined here you can modify or change the circumstances in which you now live, assuming control over them rather than continuing to be directed by them. Your relations with other people will improve. You will become a more popular, esteemed, and well-liked individual. By mastering these principles, you will enjoy a delightful new sense of well-being. You may attain a degree of health not hitherto known by you and experience a new and keen pleasure in living. You will become a person of greater usefulness and will wield an expanded influence.

How can I be so certain that the practice of these principles will produce such results? The answer is simply that for many years in the Marble Collegiate Church of New York City we have taught a system of creative living based on spiritual techniques, carefully noting its operation in the lives of hundreds of people. It is no speculative series of extravagant assertions that I make, for these principles have worked so efficiently over so long a period of time that they are now firmly established as documented and demonstrable truth. The system outlined is a perfected and amazing method of successful living.

In my writings, including several books, in my regular weekly newspaper column in nearly one hundred dailies, in my national radio program over seventeen years, in our magazine, *Guideposts,* and in lectures in scores of cities, I have taught these same scientific yet simple principles of achievement, health, and happiness. Hundreds have read, listened, and practiced, and the results are invariably the same: new life, new power, increased efficiency, greater happiness.

Because so many have requested that these principles be put into book form, the better to be studied and practiced, I am publishing this new volume under the title, *The Power of Positive Thinking.* I need not point out that the powerful principles contained herein are not my invention but are given to us by the greatest Teacher who ever lived and who still lives. This book teaches applied Christianity; a simple yet scientific system of practical techniques of successful living that works.

Believe in Yourself

Believe in yourself! Have faith in your abilities! Without a humble but reasonable confidence in your own powers you cannot be successful or happy. But with sound self-confidence you can succeed. A sense of inferiority and inadequacy interferes with the attainment of your hopes, but self-confidence leads to self-realization and successful achievement. Because of the importance of this mental attitude, this book will help you believe in yourself and release your inner powers.

It is appalling to realize the number of pathetic people who are hampered and made miserable by the malady popularly called the inferiority complex. But you need not suffer from this trouble. When proper steps are taken, it can be overcome. You can develop creative faith in yourself—faith that is justified. . . .

We build up the feeling of insecurity or security by how we think. If in our thoughts we constantly fix attention upon sinister expectations of dire events that might happen, the result will be constantly to feel insecure. And what is even more serious is the tendency to create, by the power of thought, the very condition we fear. This salesman actually created positive results by vital thoughts of courage and confidence through the process of placing the cards before him in his car. His powers, curiously inhibited by a defeat psychology, now flowed out of a personality in which creative attitudes had been stimulated.

Lack of self-confidence apparently is one of the great problems besetting people today. In a university a survey was made of six hundred students in psychology courses. The students were asked to state their most difficult personal problem. Seventy-five per cent listed lack of confidence. It can safely be assumed that the same large proportion is true of the population generally. Everywhere you encounter people who are inwardly afraid, who shrink from life, who suffer from a deep sense of inadequacy and insecurity, who doubt their own powers. Deep within themselves they mistrust their ability to meet responsibilities or to grasp opportunities. Always they are beset by the vague and sinister fear that something is not going to be quite right. They do not believe that they have it in them to be what they want to be, and so they try to make themselves content with something less than that of which they are capable. Thousands upon thousands go crawling through life on their hands and knees, defeated and afraid. And in most cases such frustration of power is unnecessary. . . .

So if you feel that you are defeated and have lost confidence in your ability to win, sit down, take a piece of paper and make a list, not of the factors that are against you, but of those that are for you. If you or I or anybody think constantly of the forces that seem to be against us, we will build them up into a power far beyond that which is justified. They will assume a formidable strength which they do not actually possess. But if, on the contrary, you mentally visualize and affirm and reaffirm your assets and keep your thoughts on them, emphasizing them to the fullest extent, you will rise out of any difficulty regardless of what it may be. Your inner powers will reassert themselves and, with the help of God, lift you from defeat to victory.

One of the most powerful concepts, one which is a sure cure for lack of confidence, is the thought that God is actually with you and helping you. This is one of the simplest teachings in religion, namely, that Almighty God will be your companion, will stand by you, help you, and see you through. No other idea is so powerful in developing self-confidence as this simple belief when practiced. To practice it simply affirm "God is with me; God is helping me; God is guiding me." Spend several minutes each day visualizing His presence. Then practice believing that affirmation. Go about your business on the assumption that what you have affirmed and visualized is true. Affirm it, visualize it, believe it, and it will actualize itself. The release of power which this procedure stimulates will astonish you.

Feelings of confidence depend upon the type of thoughts that habitually occupy your mind. Think defeat and you are bound to feel defeated. But practice thinking confident thoughts, make it a dominating habit, and you will develop such a strong sense of capacity that regardless of what difficulties arise you will be able to overcome them. Feelings of confidence actually induce increased strength. Basil King once said, "Be bold, and mighty forces will come to your aid." Experience proves the truth of this. You will feel these mighty forces aiding you as your increasing faith reconditions your attitudes.

Emerson declared a tremendous truth, "They conquer who believe they can." And he added, "Do the thing you fear and the death of fear is certain." Practice confidence and faith and your fears and insecurities will soon have no power over you.

Once when Stonewall Jackson planned a daring attack, one of his generals fearfully objected, saying, "I am afraid of this" or "I fear that . . ." Putting his hand on his timorous subordinate's shoulder, Jackson said, "General, never take counsel of your fears."

The secret is to fill your mind with thoughts of faith, confidence, and security. This will force out or expel all thoughts of doubt, all lack of confidence. To one man who for a long time had been haunted by insecurities and fears I suggested that he read through the Bible underlining in red pencil every statement it contains relative to courage and confidence. He also committed them to memory, in effect cramming his mind full of the healthiest, happiest, most powerful thoughts in the world. These dynamic thoughts changed him from cringing hopelessness to a man of compelling force. The change in him in a few weeks was remarkable. From almost complete defeat he became a confident and inspiring personality. He now radiates courage and magnetism. He regained confidence in himself and his own powers by a simple process of thought conditioning.

To sum up—what can you do *now* to build up your self-confidence? Following are ten simple, workable rules for overcoming inadequacy attitudes and learning to practice faith. Thousands have used these rules, reporting successful results. Undertake this program and you, too, will build up confidence in your powers. You, too, will have a new feeling of power.

1. Formulate and stamp indelibly on your mind a mental picture of yourself as succeeding. Hold this picture tenaciously. Never permit it to fade. Your mind will seek to develop this picture. Never think of yourself as failing; never doubt the reality of the mental image. That is most dangerous, for the mind always tries to complete what it pictures. So *always* picture "success" no matter how badly things seem to be going at the moment.

2. Whenever a negative thought concerning your personal powers comes to mind, deliberately voice a positive thought to cancel it out.

3. Do not build up obstacles in your imagination. Depreciate every so-called obstacle. Minimize them. Difficulties must be studied and efficiently dealt with to be eliminated, but they must be seen for only what they are. They must not be inflated by fear thoughts.

4. Do not be awestruck by other people and try to copy them. Nobody can be you as efficiently as YOU can. Remember also that most people, despite their confident appearance and demeanor, are often as scared as you are and as doubtful of themselves.

5. Ten times a day repeat these dynamic words, "If God be *for* us, who can be *against* us?" (Romans 8:31) (Stop reading and repeat them NOW slowly and confidently.)

6. Get a competent counselor to help you understand why you do what you do. Learn the origin of your inferiority and self-doubt feelings which often begin in childhood. Self-knowledge leads to a cure.

7. Ten times each day practice the following affirmation, repeating it out loud if possible. "I can do all things through Christ which strengtheneth me." (Philippians 4:13) Repeat those words NOW. That magic statement is the most powerful antidote on earth to inferiority thoughts.

8. Make a true estimate of your own ability, then raise it 10 per cent. Do not become egotistical, but develop a wholesome self-respect. Believe in your own God-released powers.

9. Put yourself in God's hands. To do that simply state, "I am in God's hands." Then believe you are NOW receiving all the power you need. "Feel" it flowing into you. Affirm that "the kingdom of God is within you" (Luke 17:21) in the form of adequate power to meet life's demands.

10. Remind yourself that God is with you and nothing can defeat you. Believe that you *now* RECEIVE power from Him.

Further Resources

BOOKS

Peale, Norman Vincent. *A Guide to Confident Living.* New York: Macmillan, 1948.

———. *The True Joy of Positive Living: An Autobiography.* New York: Morrow, 1984.

———. *You Can If You Think You Can.* Greenwich, Conn.: Fawcett, 1974.

WEBSITES

Biblical Discernment Ministries. "Additional *Guideposts* Notes: Norman Vincent Peale." Available online at http://www.rapidnet.com/~jbeard/bdm/Psychology/guidepo/peale.htm; website home page: http://www.rapidnet.com/~jbeard/bdm (accessed February 10, 2003).

Horatio Alger Association of Distinguished Americans. "Norman Vincent Peale." Available online at http://www.horatioalger.com/member/pea52.htm (accessed February 10, 2003).

The Courage to Be

Theological work

By: Paul Tillich

Date: 1952

Source: Tillich, Paul. *The Courage to Be.* New Haven, Conn.: Yale University Press, 1952, 155–156, 157, 158–159, 186–190.

About the Author: Paul Tillich (1886–1965) was born in Starzeddel, Prussia, and taught theology and philosophy at several German universities before coming to the United States in 1933. He was appointed professor of philosophical theology at Union Theological Seminary in New York City, where he remained until 1955. He then completed his career as university professor at Harvard. ■

Introduction

Theologian and philosopher Paul Tillich's classic, *The Courage to Be,* described the dilemma of twentieth-century life and how to conquer the persistent problem of anxiety. Anxiety may take several forms, but usually people experience it as a condition of uneasiness and apprehension concerning the uncertainties of the future.

Anxiety about the future and the meaning of existence and God affected many Americans in the 1950s. They had experienced the hardships and uncertainties of the stock market crash and the economic depression of the 1930s. While they survived World War II in the 1940s, many of their relatives and friends had not. Further, the 1950s was marked by the threat of nuclear war between the United States and the Soviet Union or China. Tillich noted this anxiety and the need to adequately deal with it in a philosophical and religious manner. In his brief existential work *The Courage to Be,* he concentrated on God as the object of ultimate concern in attempting to cope with this anxiety.

The first chapter summarized the philosophical history of being and courage by reviewing some of the major ideas of Aristotle, Plato, Thomas Aquinas, the Stoics, Spinoza, and Friedrich Wilhelm Nietzche. The next focused on the nature of being, nonbeing, and anxiety. Within this context, he discussed the interdependence of fear and anxiety, including the anxiety of fate and death, the anxiety of emptiness and meaninglessness, and the anxiety of guilt and condemnation. Tillich then explored the meaning of despair and periods of anxiety.

The third chapter addressed the nature of pathological anxiety, anxiety and religion, anxiety and medicine, and vitality and courage. The fourth discussed the nature of courage in individualization, collectivist life, and democratic conformism. He then turned to the rise of modern individualism, the courage to be oneself, existential forms of the courage to be, and courage and despair in art, literature, and philosophy. The book's final chapter focused on courage and transcendence, the courage to accept acceptance, the Power of Being as the source of the courage to be, the divine-human encounter, absolute faith and the courage to be, the courage to be as the key to being itself, and finally, the God above God and the courage to be.

Significance

Believed by many to be one of the most important books on religion published in the second half of the twentieth century, *The Courage to Be* was named by the New York Public Library as one of the Books of the Century. *Time* magazine published Tillich's picture on the cover, and academic polls indicated that he was the major figure in contemporary theology.

Because of his search to harmonize Christianity and modern culture in his sermons, lectures and writings, Tillich became known as the apostle to the skeptics. His theology confronted the hopelessness of relativism and encouraged people to seek meaning in their lives through their own search for God. His works had an important impact on twentieth-century theology. Through his presentation of Christian fundamentals in an anxiety-ridden world, he attempted to defeat cultural and spiritual emptiness. His battle against the destructive effects of nonbeing and alienation was met with enthusiasm in both the theological community and the general public. His works had a lasting impact not only on theology and philosophy but also on existential psychology, political theory, and even art criticism.

Primary Source

The Courage to Be [excerpt]

> **SYNOPSIS:** These excerpts are taken from Chapter 6, "Courage and Transcendence." To transcend means to go beyond the usual means of perception (mysticism, for example.) The excerpts illustrate Tillich's theological definitions and interpretations of both courage and transcendence. Basic to his writings is the subject of existentialism, or the search for the meaning of one's existence.

Courage and Transcendence [The Courage to Accept Acceptance]

Courage is the self-affirmation of being in spite of the fact of nonbeing. It is the act of the individual self in taking the anxiety of nonbeing upon itself by affirming itself either as part of an embracing whole or in its individual selfhood. Courage always includes a risk, it is always threatened by nonbeing, whether the risk of losing oneself and becoming a thing within the whole of things or of losing one's world in an empty self-relatedness. Courage needs the power of being, a power transcending the nonbeing which is experienced in the anxiety of fate and death, which is present in the anxiety of emptiness and meaninglessness, which is effective in the anxiety of guilt and condemnation. The courage which takes this threefold anxiety into itself must be rooted in a power of being that is greater than the power

Paul Tillich spoke of courage and transcendence in struggling with issues of being and nonbeing. **GETTY IMAGES. REPRODUCED BY PERMISSION.**

of oneself and the power of one's world. Neither self-affirmation as a part nor self-affirmation as oneself is beyond the manifold threat of nonbeing. Those who are mentioned as representatives of these forms of courage try to transcend themselves and the world in which they participate in order to find the power of being-itself and a courage to be which is beyond the threat of nonbeing. There are no exceptions to this rule; and this means that every courage to be has an open or hidden religious root. For religion is the state of being grasped by the power of being-itself. In some cases the religious root is carefully covered, in others it is passionately denied; in some it is deeply hidden and in others superficially. But it is never completely absent. For everything that is participates in being-itself, and everybody has some awareness of this participation, especially in the moments in which he experiences the threat of nonbeing. . . .

In mysticism the individual self strives for a participation in the ground of being which approaches identification. Our question is not whether this goal can ever be reached by a finite being but whether and how mysticism can be the source of the

courage to be. . . . [A]ll mystics draw their power of self-affirmation from the experience of the power of being-itself with which they are united. But one may ask, can courage be united with mysticism in any way? It seems that in India, for example, courage is considered the virtue of the *kshatriya* (knight), to be found below the levels of the Brahman or the ascetic saint. Mystical identification transcends the aristocratic virtue of courageous self-sacrifice. It is self-surrender in a higher, more complete, and more radical form. It is the perfect form of self-affirmation. . . .

In the strength of this courage the mystic conquers the anxiety of fate and death. Since being in time and space and under the categories of finitude is ultimately unreal, the vicissitudes arising from it and the final nonbeing ending it are equally unreal. Nonbeing is no threat because finite being is, in the last analysis, nonbeing. Death is the negation of that which is negative and the affirmation of that which is positive. In the same way the anxiety of doubt and meaninglessness is taken into the mystical courage to be. . . . Without a consciousness of truth itself doubt of truth would be impossible. The anxiety of meaninglessness is conquered where the ultimate meaning is not something definite but the abyss of every definite meaning. The mystic experiences step after step the lack of meaning in the different levels of reality which he enters, works through, and leaves. As long as he walks ahead on this road the anxieties of guilt and condemnation are also conquered. They are not absent. Guilt can be acquired on every level, partly through a failure to fulfill its intrinsic demands, partly through a failure to proceed beyond the level. But as long as the certainty of final fulfillment is given, the anxiety of guilt does not become anxiety of condemnation. . . .

The mystical courage to be lasts as long as the mystical situation. Its limit is the state of emptiness of being and meaning, with its horror and despair, which the mystics have described. In these moments the courage to be is reduced to the acceptance of even this state as a way to prepare through darkness for light, through emptiness for abundance. As long as the absence of the power of being is felt as despair, it is the power of being which makes itself felt through despair. To experience this and to endure it is the courage to be of the mystic in the state of emptiness. Although mysticism in its extreme positive and extreme negative aspects is a comparatively rare event, the basic attitude, the striving for union with ultimate reality, and the corresponding courage to take the nonbeing which is implied in finitude upon oneself are a way of life which is accepted by and has shaped large sections of mankind. . . .

The God above God and the Courage to Be

The ultimate source of the courage to be is the "God above God"; this is the result of our demand to transcend theism. Only if the God of theism is transcended can the anxiety of doubt and meaninglessness be taken into the courage to be. The God above God is the object of all mystical longing, but mysticism also must be transcended in order to reach him. Mysticism does not take seriously the concrete and the doubt concerning the concrete. It plunges directly into the ground of being and meaning, and leaves the concrete, the world of finite values and meanings, behind. Therefore it does not solve the problem of meaninglessness. In terms of the present religious situation this means that Eastern mysticism is not the solution of the problems of Western Existentialism, although many people attempt this solution. The God above the God of theism is not the devaluation of the meanings which doubt has thrown into the abyss of meaninglessness; he is their potential restitution. Nevertheless absolute faith agrees with the faith implied in mysticism in that both transcend the theistic objectivation of a God who is a being. For mysticism such a God is not more real than any finite being, for the courage to be such a God has disappeared in the abyss of meaninglessness with every other value and meaning.

The God above the God of theism is present, although hidden, in every divine-human encounter. Biblical religion as well as Protestant theology are aware of the paradoxical character of this encounter. They are aware that if God encounters man God is neither object nor subject and is therefore above the scheme into which theism has forced him. They are aware that personalism with respect to God is balanced by a transpersonal presence of the divine. They are aware that forgiveness can be accepted only if the power of acceptance is effective in man—biblically speaking, if the power of grace is effective in man. They are aware of the paradoxical character of every prayer, of speaking to somebody to whom you cannot speak because he is not "somebody," of asking somebody of whom you cannot ask anything because he gives or gives not before you ask, of saying "thou" to somebody who is nearer to the I than the I is to itself. Each of these paradoxes

drives the religious consciousness toward a God above the God of theism.

The courage to be which is rooted in the experience of the God above the God of theism unites and transcends the courage to be as a part and the courage to be as oneself. It avoids both the loss of oneself by participation and the loss of one's world by individualization. The acceptance of the God above the God of theism makes us a part of that which is not also a part but is the ground of the whole. Therefore our self is not lost in a larger whole, which submerges it in the life of a limited group. If the self participates in the power of being-itself it receives itself back. For the power of being acts through the power of the individual selves. It does not swallow them as every limited whole, every collectivism, and every conformism does. This is why the Church, which stands for the power of being-itself or for the God who transcends the God of the religions, claims to be the mediator of the courage to be. A church which is based on the authority of the God of theism cannot make such a claim. It inescapably develops into a collectivist or semicollectivist system itself.

But a church which raises itself in its message and its devotion to the God above the God of theism without sacrificing its concrete symbols can mediate a courage which takes doubt and meaninglessness into itself. It is the Church under the Cross which alone can do this, the Church which preaches the Crucified who cried to God who remained his God after the God of confidence had left him in the darkness of doubt and meaninglessness. To be as a part in such a church is to receive a courage to be in which one cannot lose one's self and in which one receives one's world.

Absolute faith, or the state of being grasped by the God beyond God, is not a state which appears beside other states of the mind. It never is something separated and definite, an event which could be isolated and described. It is always a movement in, with, and under other states of the mind. It is the situation on the boundary of man's possibilities. It *is* this boundary. Therefore it is both the courage of despair and the courage in and above every courage. It is not a place where one can live, it is without the safety of words and concepts, it is without a name, a church, a cult, a theology. But it is moving in the depth of all of them. It is the power of being, in which they participate and of which they are fragmentary expressions.

One can become aware of it in the anxiety of fate and death when the traditional symbols, which enable men to stand the vicissitudes of fate and the horror of death have lost their power. When "providence" has become a superstition and "immortality" something imaginary that which once was the power in these symbols can still be present and create the courage to be in spite of the experience of a chaotic world and a finite existence. The Stoic courage returns but not as the faith in universal reason. It returns as the absolute faith which says Yes to being without seeing anything concrete which could conquer the nonbeing in fate and death.

And one can become aware of the God above the God of theism in the anxiety of guilt and condemnation when the traditional symbols that enable men to withstand the anxiety of guilt and condemnation have lost their power. When "divine judgment" is interpreted as a psychological complex and forgiveness as a remnant of the "father-image," what once was the power in those symbols can still be present and create the courage to be in spite of the experience of an infinite gap between what we are and what we ought to be. The Lutheran courage returns but not supported by the faith in a judging and forgiving God. It returns in terms of the absolute faith which says Yes although there is no special power that conquers guilt. The courage to take the anxiety of meaninglessness upon oneself is the boundary line up to which the courage to be can go. Beyond it is mere non-being. Within it all forms of courage are re-established in the power of the God above the God of theism. *The courage to be is rooted in the God who appears when God has disappeared in the anxiety of doubt.*

Further Resources

BOOKS

Pauck, Wilhelm. *Paul Tillich, His Life and Thought.* New York: Harper & Row, 1976.

Thomson, James Sutherland. *Paul Tillich.* Toronto: CBC Publications Branch, 1955.

Tillich, Paul. *Paul Tillich Comments.* Richmond, Va: Outlook, 1955.

WEBSITES

Irish Theological Association. "Paul Tillich." Available online at http://www.theology.ie/theologians/tillich.htm; website home page: http://www.theology.ie (accessed February 10, 2003). This site contains links to numerous resources about Paul Tillich.

Kimberling, Clark. "Paul Johannes Tillich." Available online at http://www2.evansville.edu/ck6/bstud/tillich.html; website home page: http://faculty.evansville.edu/ck6/ (accessed February 10, 2003).

Resolutions Adopted by the Central Conference of American Rabbis on Religious and Social Freedoms

Statement

By: Central Conference of American Rabbis

Date: 1953–1954

Source: Stevens, Elliot, and Simon Glaser, eds. *Resolutions of the Central Conference, 1889–1974,* rev. ed. New York: Central Conference of American Rabbis, 1975. Available online at http://www.ccarnet.org/reso (accessed February 9, 2003).

About the Organization: The Central Conference of American Rabbis, established in 1889, consists of Reform Judaism rabbis. At a meeting in Columbus, Ohio, in 1937, the group produced a document called "The Guiding Principles of Reform Judaism." The continuing purpose of the Central Conference is to help rabbis and laity in their practice of Reform Judaism. ∎

Introduction

These resolutions issued by the Central Conference of American Rabbis dealt with cherished freedoms in America: to practice the religion of one's choice; to preach from the pulpit about any relevant issues that the rabbi, minister, or priest wishes; and to discuss openly and freely any beliefs that one might have. The resolutions countered a belief held by some Americans at that time that anyone who did not conform to the general religious, political, or social values of the community was "un-American" and possibly a communist or communist sympathizer.

Even some members of Congress held this view. The House Un-American Activities Committee was charged with the responsibility of investigating potential threats of subversion against America, specifically communist threats. The committee investigated the activities of any group that it considered to hold radical or extremist views. The committee's search for communist influences extended widely. People from a number of professions were accused of working against the interests of the nation, including journalists, entertainers, college professors, librarians, and clergy. Some people who held unpopular or controversial views were "blacklisted" and thus prevented from gaining employment in certain jobs.

The Central Conference of American Rabbis wanted to make clear to their congregations and other Americans that they opposed any efforts to stifle freedom of thought, not only among Jews but among all Americans. They were especially disturbed by the growth of what was termed "McCarthyism," named after Wisconsin senator

Joseph R. McCarthy. In response to cold war tensions in the 1950s, McCarthy charged private citizens and public officials, frequently without evidence, with supporting communism. Many of these targets were Jewish. The rabbis were also troubled by the anti-Semitism of organizations such as the Ku Klux Klan, which spread assertions that communism and Judaism were intertwined, lending support to those who believed that some Jews were un-American.

Significance

The resolutions, and the resulting actions taken by the Jewish community and others, contributed to the end of congressional investigations that frivolously charged people with un-American activities. Their efforts were buttressed by those of the American Civil Liberties Union (ACLU), an organization that defends the rights and freedoms of people in the United States, and by the U.S. Supreme Court. Throughout the 1950s and into the 1960s, the Court curbed the activities of the House and Senate in investigating un-American activities. McCarthyism gradually faded after 1954, when Senator McCarthy was condemned by the Senate for conduct unbecoming a senator. The House Committee on Un-American Activities lost much of its power until the House abolished it in 1975.

Primary Source

Resolutions Adopted by the Central Conference of American Rabbis on Religious and Social Freedoms [excerpt]

SYNOPSIS: In the 1950s, the Central Conference of American Rabbis issued a number of resolutions on freedoms of religion and thought. "Freedom of Religion" dealt primarily with the plight of Jews in communist nations. "Freedom of Pulpit" and "Rabbi (Freedom of)" affirmed the right of rabbis to preach and to dissent. "Social Betterment" specifically addressed the activities of the House Un-American Activities Committee. "Freedom of Thought" applauded those who had the courage to dissent in the face of political persecution and defended the American public school system. "Freedom, Political" discussed the need for an "alert and unrepressed citizenry, free to speak its thought."

Freedom of Religion

There is no evidence that the intensity of discrimination directed against Jews and other religions and ethnic groups in the Soviet Union and its satellites has abated. Jewish life is still attacked and its few remaining manifestations religiously and culturally are ruthlessly curtailed. Ludicrous charges are still being flung by Soviet spokesmen in the United Nations and in the Communist press against Jewish

A rabbi reads to a young man from the Torah. In the early 1950s, the Central Conference of American Rabbis adopted several resolutions affirming the freedom of the rabbi to interpret Scripture in the light of contemporary problems, to preach on any and all moral issues, but also affirming the right of the lay people to dissent. **HULTON ARCHIVE/GETTY IMAGES. REPRODUCED BY PERMISSION.**

organizations and their representatives who have sought only to bring a measure of relief to our brethren behind the Iron Curtain. The CCAR calls upon the leadership of all freedom-loving people to help seek an end to the communist denial of religious and cultural freedom of religious and ethnic groups and the communist repudiation of the human rights of individuals. (1953. p. 123)

Freedom of Pulpit

We welcome the resolution on Freedom of the Pulpit passed at the recent Biennial of the Union of American Hebrew Congregations. This resolution said, in part: "Rabbis have the right to interpret the words of Scripture in the light of contemporary problems and the exercise of this right must be zealously guarded Congregations have the right to disagree with the utterances made from the pulpit and to express their dissent in Congregational meetings, Temple gatherings and membership meetings. We would urge rabbis and laymen alike to cherish this precious freedom, and to ensure that no restraints are placed upon it, while at the same time recognizing that it imposes an obligation to respect the rights and opinions of those who disagree." (1953 p. 125)

Rabbi (Freedom of)

The rights of the individual to apply the teachings of his faith to all issues involving moral and ethical implications must be safe-guarded within congregations just as effectively as in the larger arena of public life. This right applies both to the Rabbi and to members of the congregation. Wherever possible, Rabbi and congregation should work unitedly in this regard. Where there are differences of opinion on social, political, or economic matters between pulpit and pew, the Rabbi's right to preach and the layman's right to dissent must both be preserved.

By the demands of prophetic precedent, the Rabbi has the right, duty and obligation to express himself on all matters which he feels involve moral and ethical issues. He is not necessarily the spokesman of his individual congregation, but is a spokesman for Judaism and its principles. His expressed opinions are his own, but must reflect the principles enunciated by Judaism.

The right to dissent is inherent in Judaism. There should exist in every congregation a climate welcoming differences of opinion. The layman, like the Rabbi, has religious duties, obligations and privileges in the spheres of social justice and action. He should be informed about the teachings of Judaism and should endeavor to apply them to specific issues and problems. Every opportunity should be given to laymen to express publicly opinions and beliefs which may not necessarily mirror those of the Rabbi. Both Rabbi and layman have the right to their views, which must be expressed in good faith and consistent with Judaism. (1953, pp. 132–33)

Social Betterment

Since this Conference last went on record in opposition to the then-pending Mundt-Nixon bill and deplored the hysteria against government employees and public figures, there has been a further extension of that hysteria which touches the spokesmen of religion even more intimately. In recent months the House Committee on Un-American Activities has released publicly the names of large numbers of clergymen who are alleged to have signed the Stockholm Peace Petition or otherwise to have cooperated with communist-front organizations. In no case was any effort made to ascertain the real position of these clergymen before publication of their names.

In some instances the names published were those of men who had supported a given organization or cause long before there was any indication that it constituted a communist front or at a time before had been "taken over" for such purposes. No distinction was made between such individuals and those who may have supported the same cause knowing the identity and purpose of its sponsors. Despite a rather perfunctory explanation by the Committee that not all names so publicized were those of communist sympathizers, the fact remains that a stigma is unavoidably attached to all such individuals.

The equation of all criticism and reforms with communist is not only a violation of the individual's right to free thought and free speech, but represents a vicious obstacle to all social progress in a democracy.

There is reason to suspect that this may have been a conscious device to intimidate the spokesmen of liberal religion and to discourage their communicants from following them. Because we believe this is to represent a very real danger to the freedom of American thought, we urgently recommend the following: That Committees of the Congress be enjoined from publicizing the names of any American Citizens who have not been given an opportunity to defend themselves against specific charges.

That provision be made for the protection of an individual against libelous remarks made by Congressmen on the floor of either the Senate or the House. That members of this Conference refuse to abdicate their prophetic responsibility to expose political, social and economic corruption wherever they may be found. Especially in such times as these, when so many other voices have been silenced, is it incumbent upon us not to be intimidated. We reaffirm the sacred duty of religious leaders and teachers to act as the conscience of society. (1951, pp. 105–6)

Teachers and clergymen who are especially concerned with the moral and ethical principles on which our democracy is founded, have a special responsibility for the preservation of those principles. We are enheartened by the number of our own colleagues who have courageously brought the message of prophetic Judaism to bear on the problems of contemporary society, and we urge this Conference as well as the Union of American Hebrew Congregations to uphold and encourage these men. (1954, p. 55)

Freedom of Thought

In these days of fear and hysteria, we are heartened by the example of those courageous clergymen, educators, college presidents and public servants who have affirmed freedom of thought and expression. We condemn McCarthyism. We call upon the President and the Congress to protect the right of dissent. In the words of the late Chief Justice Charles Evans Hughes of the Supreme Court of the United States, "the right to be free is the right to be different." (1952, p. 179)

We believe in the American Public School System as a pillar of our democracy and we oppose growing tendencies in various cities and states to impose thought control and loyalty tests upon authors, teachers and text books. Any threat to the intellectual liberty of the school imperils the whole structure of American freedom. (1952, p. 180)

We applaud those religious leaders of all faiths as well as those university teachers and administrators who have courageously resisted the pressures toward conformity which threaten our freedom. We recommend a convocation of distinguished religious leaders who will apply the ethical insights of Judaism and Christianity to the problems confronting us. We urge the CCAR and the Joint Commission on Social Action to encourage the calling of such a convocation as soon as possible. We also recommend to our colleagues that wherever possible on the local level, they cooperate with liberal religious leaders of all faiths by setting aside one weekend on which all liberal pulpits will be devoted to the flagrant abuse of moral principles on the part of many who presume to be protecting American democracy. (1954, p. 53)

The history of our nation is the best proof that our free system of American education is the most effective guarantee of an intelligent citizenry. This has been largely due to the integrity and loyalty of the great body of American public school teachers, operating in an atmosphere of academic freedom.

It is imperative that our children and American democracy be protected by the heroic defense of loyal teachers from attack by nativist philosophies of conformism and destruction which attempt to utilize the present emergency to advance their vested interests.

Our children must not be deprived of their birthright of education. Their teachers must not be robbed of the academic freedom without which education becomes strangled and all free inquiry per-

ishes. We therefore oppose the effort to suppress liberal ideas in the curricula of our schools. We oppose the imposition of special loyalty oaths for teachers as a measure casting unwarranted doubt on their patriotism and one which is not an effective deterrent to the nearly negligible number of subversives among them.

While recognizing that proven Communists should not be teachers in our public schools, we are convinced that the danger to our democracy from uninhibited witch hunts and spurious investigations is even greater than that of Communist or Fascist teachers. There is no freedom without risk. We believe that the greater risk by far in this instance is that of creating among teachers an hysteria which would stifle creativity in favor of conformity.

We concluded, therefore, that while Boards of Education should not employ teachers proved by legally constituted authority to be Communists, they should neither conduct nor countenance witch hunts among teachers.

We proclaim our continuing support of the American public school in face of attacks by those who would break down the wall of separation between Church and State. (1953, pp. 130–31)

Freedom, Political

We believe that the national security of our country is rooted in the individual freedom of its citizens. We reject the concept that there is any incompatibility between freedom and security, and that individual freedom must be abrogated in the interests of national security. Freedom is not only the moral and spiritual basis of our national life; it is the bulwark of our security. The indissoluble bond between freedom and religion found early expression in the command, "Let My people go that they may serve Me." In this perspective, we have carefully studied the relationship between freedom and security in political and economic life, in education and religion.

Only an alert and unrepressed citizenry, free to speak its thoughts and to develop new ideas, will be able to solve the complex domestic and international problems facing the nation. Yet there is abroad in the land today a wave of repression threatening this development of new ideas in government, in science, in economics, and in education, upon which our very security depends.

An America strong in military resources and in individual freedom can defeat the external threat of Communism. Our counter-intelligence agencies can cope with the internal threat of Communist spies and saboteurs and our national good sense can defeat the false doctrines of totalitarianism before they become a clear and present danger to our way of life. We have no need for the restraints on freedom of speech contained in the Smith Act or the McCarran Internal Security Act. We condemn the undemocratic methods used in the investigations conducted by McCarthy, Jenner and Velde, and their state and local imitators. We endorse the vigorous criticism of these methods voiced by the National Council of Churches, and call upon other religious bodies to join in the defense of our cherished American institutions. (1953, pp. 127–8)

Further Resources

BOOKS

Blau, Joseph L. *Reform Judaism: A Historical Perspective: Essays from the Yearbook of the Central Conference of American Rabbis.* New York: Ktav, 1973.

Gurock, Jeffrey S., ed. *History of Judaism in America: Transplantations, Transformations, and Reconciliations.* New York: Routledge, 1998.

Reform Judaism in America: A Biographical Dictionary and Sourcebook. Westport, Conn.: Greenwood, 1993.

WEBSITES

Central Conference of American Rabbis. "CCAR Platforms." Available online at http://www.ccarnet.org/platforms; website home page: http://www.ccarnet.org/ (accessed February 9, 2003).

Religious Action Center of Reform Judaism. "Who We Are." Available online at http://www.rac.org/aboutrac/aboutrac .html (accessed February 9, 2003).

Union of American Hebrew Congregations. "Reform Judaism." Available online at http://www.rj.org/ (accessed February 9, 2003).

"Loving Your Enemies"

Sermon

By: Martin Luther King, Jr.

Date: November 17, 1957

Source: King, Martin Luther, Jr., Speeches. "Loving Your Enemies," November 17 1957. Available online at http://www.mlkonline.com/ (accessed February 10, 2003).

About the Author: Martin Luther King, Jr. (1929–1968) was born in Atlanta, Georgia. He was ordained a Baptist minister in 1954 and received his doctorate from Boston University in 1955. Instrumental in the founding of the Southern Christian Leadership Conference in 1957, he advocated nonviolence in the Civil Rights movement. He was a major organizer of the

Montgomery, Alabama, bus boycott in 1956 and the March on Washington in 1963. He was awarded the Nobel Peace Prize in 1964, but four years later was assassinated in Memphis, Tennessee. ■

Introduction

In then racially segregated Alabama, the Montgomery bus boycott of 1955 was an effort to change the practice of requiring African American passengers to sit at the back of buses. Martin Luther King, Jr., and his followers reasoned that if African American people walked instead of riding the buses, the loss of revenue to the bus lines would end segregation on the buses. The boycott attracted nationwide, even worldwide, attention, and in 1956, a federal court ordered Montgomery to desegregate its buses.

About a year later, on November 17, 1957, King delivered a sermon at the Dexter Avenue Baptist Church in Montgomery. While the goal of desegregating the city buses had been achieved, much more had to be accomplished in order to achieve equal rights for African Americans. A firm believer in the philosophy of nonviolence and civil disobedience against unjust laws and conditions, King wanted to set the tone for the future, and the Dexter Avenue Baptist Church was the right locale. He wished to make clear to all present, and to the American public, his belief in loving your enemy in the pursuit of civil rights for African Americans. He knew that loving opponents of civil rights would not be easy. King was asking for a Civil Rights movement that would hold to the ideal of loving others in the face of hostility. Violence directed at civil rights workers would not be met with violence but with love.

King urged listeners to follow what Christ had preached almost two thousand years earlier: If your enemy strikes you, do not strike back but turn the other cheek. He modeled his nonviolence and civil disobedience approach upon the practices of pacifist Mahatma Gandhi (1869–1948). Gandhi was a popular nationalist and the spiritual leader of India who urged his followers to practice nonviolent disobedience in their attempt to achieve independence from Great Britain, a goal finally accomplished in 1947.

Significance

King began his involvement in the struggle for civil rights during the 1950s. In this sermon, delivered in 1957 at the Dexter Avenue Baptist Church in Montgomery, he stated the basic principles that would guide his civil rights activity.

The Montgomery protest marked the beginning of a movement that challenged the traditional segregation practices of the South. In later years, Coretta Scott King,

King's wife, noted that "Montgomery was the soil in which the seed of a new theory of social action took root. African Americans found in nonviolent, direct action a militant method that avoided violence but achieved dramatic confrontation which electrified and educated the whole nation." Montgomery, though, was just the beginning for King. Through the Southern Christian Leadership Conference, he continued his civil rights efforts not only in the South but also nationwide—often at the price of being arrested. Under his leadership, the March on Washington in 1963 brought together more than two hundred thousand people, including African Americans, whites, and members of other racial groups.

Although King was assassinated on April 4, 1968, the Southern Christian Leadership Conference and other followers of King preserved his nonviolent model in the quest for racial justice, despite the emergence of more militant groups.

Primary Source

"Loving Your Enemies" [excerpt]

> **SYNOPSIS:** In these excerpts, King preaches why he believed that people should love their enemies. The most basic reason is that Christ commanded people to love their enemies. But there are a number of other reasons as well: Love is creative, not destructive; love produces understanding and goodwill; love breaks the chain of evil; hate distorts the personality of the hater; finally, love has redemptive powers.

Dr. Martin Luther King, Jr., c. 1953. A Baptist minister, Dr. King was one of the most influential leaders in the Civil Rights movement in the 1950s and 1960s. His sermon "Loving Your Enemies" sets forth the principles of nonviolence and love—rooted in Jesus' command "Love your enemy"—which guided his activity in struggle to bring about racial justice. THE NEW YORK TIMES CO./GETTY IMAGES. REPRODUCED BY PERMISSION.

I want to use as a subject from which to preach this morning a very familiar subject, and it is familiar to you because I have preached from this subject twice before to my knowing in this pulpit. I try to make it a, something of a custom or tradition to preach from this passage of Scripture at least once a year, adding new insights that I develop along the way out of new experiences as I give these messages. Although the content is, the basic content is the same, new insights and new experiences naturally make for new illustrations.

So I want to turn your attention to this subject: "Loving Your Enemies." It's so basic to me because it is a part of my basic philosophical and theological orientation—the whole idea of love, the whole philosophy of love. In the fifth chapter of the gospel as recorded by Saint Matthew, we read these very arresting words flowing from the lips of our Lord and Master: "Ye have heard that it has been said, 'Thou shall love thy neighbor, and hate thine enemy.' But I say unto you, Love your enemies, bless them that curse you, do good to them that hate you, and pray for them that despitefully use you; that ye may be the children of your Father which is in heaven." . . .

Now let me hasten to say that Jesus was very serious when he gave this command; he wasn't playing. He realized that it's hard to love your enemies. He realized that it's difficult to love those persons who seek to defeat you, those persons who say evil things about you. He realized that it was painfully hard, pressingly hard. But he wasn't playing. And we cannot dismiss this passage as just another example of Oriental hyperbole, just a sort of exaggeration to get over the point. This is a basic philosophy of all that we hear coming from the lips of our Master. Because Jesus wasn't playing; because he was serious. We have the Christian and moral responsibility to seek to discover the meaning of these words, and to discover how we can live out this command, and why we should live by this command.

Now first let us deal with this question, which is the practical question: How do you go about loving your enemies? I think the first thing is this: In order to love your enemies, you must begin by analyzing self. And I'm sure that seems strange to you, that I start out telling you this morning that you love your enemies by beginning with a look at self. It seems to me that that is the first and foremost way to come to an adequate discovery to the how of this situation.

Now, I'm aware of the fact that some people will not like you, not because of something you have done to them, but they just won't like you. I'm quite aware of that. Some people aren't going to like the way you walk; some people aren't going to like the way you talk. Some people aren't going to like you because you can do your job better than they can do theirs. Some people aren't going to like you because other people like you, and because you're popular, and because you're well-liked, they aren't going to like you.

Some people aren't going to like you because your hair is a little shorter than theirs or your hair is a little longer than theirs. Some people aren't going to like you because your skin is a little brighter than theirs; and others aren't going to like you because your skin is a little darker than theirs. So that some people aren't going to like you. They're going to dislike you, not because of something that you've done to them, but because of various jealous reactions and other reactions that are so prevalent in human nature.

But after looking at these things and admitting these things, we must face the fact that an individual might dislike us because of something that we've done deep down in the past, some personality attribute that we possess, something that we've done deep down in the past and we've forgotten about it; but it was that something that aroused the hate response within the individual. That is why I say, begin with yourself. There might be something within you that arouses the tragic hate response in the other individual. . . .

When the opportunity presents itself for you to defeat your enemy, that is the time which you must not do it. There will come a time, in many instances, when the person who hates you most, the person who has misused you most, the person who has gossiped about you most, the person who has spread false rumors about you most, there will come a time when you will have an opportunity to defeat that person. It might be in terms of a recommendation for a job; it might be in terms of helping that

person to make some move in life. That's the time you must do it. That is the meaning of love.

In the final analysis, love is not this sentimental something that we talk about. It's not merely an emotional something. Love is creative, understanding goodwill for all men. It is the refusal to defeat any individual. When you rise to the level of love, of its great beauty and power, you seek only to defeat evil systems. Individuals who happen to be caught up in that system, you love, but you seek to defeat the system. . . .

[Jesus] says, "Love your enemy." And it's significant that he does not say, "Like your enemy." Like is a sentimental something, an affectionate something. There are a lot of people that I find it difficult to like. I don't like what they do to me. I don't like what they say about me and other people. I don't like their attitudes. I don't like some of the things they're doing. I don't like them. But Jesus says love them. And love is greater than like. Love is understanding, redemptive goodwill for all men, so that you love everybody, because God loves them. You refuse to do anything that will defeat an individual, because you have agape in your soul. And here you come to the point that you love the individual who does the evil deed, while hating the deed that the person does. This is what Jesus means when he says, "Love your enemy." This is the way to do it. When the opportunity presents itself when you can defeat your enemy, you must not do it. . . .

Men must see that force begets force, hate begets hate, toughness begets toughness. And it is all a descending spiral, ultimately ending in destruction for all and everybody. Somebody must have sense enough and morality enough to cut off the chain of hate and the chain of evil in the universe. And you do that by love.

There's another reason why you should love your enemies, and that is because hate distorts the personality of the hater. We usually think of what hate does for the individual hated or the individuals hated or the groups hated. But it is even more tragic, it is even more ruinous and injurious to the individual who hates. You just begin hating somebody, and you will begin to do irrational things. You can't see straight when you hate. You can't walk straight when you hate. You can't stand upright. Your vision is distorted. There is nothing more tragic than to see an individual whose heart is filled with hate. He comes to the point that he becomes a pathological case.

For the person who hates, you can stand up and see a person and that person can be beautiful, and you will call them ugly. For the person who hates, the beautiful becomes ugly and the ugly becomes beautiful. For the person who hates, the good becomes bad and the bad becomes good. For the person who hates, the true becomes false and the false becomes true. That's what hate does. You can't see right. The symbol of objectivity is lost. Hate destroys the very structure of the personality of the hater. . . .

Now there is a final reason I think that Jesus says, "Love your enemies." It is this: that love has within it a redemptive power. And there is a power there that eventually transforms individuals. That's why Jesus says, "Love your enemies." Because if you hate your enemies, you have no way to redeem and to transform your enemies. But if you love your enemies, you will discover that at the very root of love is the power of redemption. You just keep loving people and keep loving them, even though they're mistreating you. Here's the person who is a neighbor, and this person is doing something wrong to you and all of that. Just keep being friendly to that person. Keep loving them. Don't do anything to embarrass them. Just keep loving them, and they can't stand it too long. Oh, they react in many ways in the beginning. They react with bitterness because they're mad because you love them like that. They react with guilt feelings, and sometimes they'll hate you a little more at that transition period, but just keep loving them. And by the power of your love they will break down under the load. That's love, you see. It is redemptive, and this is why Jesus says love. There's something about love that builds up and is creative. There is something about hate that tears down and is destructive. So love your enemies. . . .

History unfortunately leaves some people oppressed and some people oppressors. And there are three ways that individuals who are oppressed can deal with their oppression. One of them is to rise up against their oppressors with physical violence and corroding hatred. But oh this isn't the way. For the danger and the weakness of this method is its futility. Violence creates many more social problems than it solves. And I've said, in so many instances, that as the Negro, in particular, and colored peoples all over the world struggle for freedom, if they succumb to the temptation of using violence in their struggle, unborn generations will be the recipients of a long and desolate night of bitterness, and our chief legacy to the future will be an endless reign of meaningless chaos. Violence isn't the way.

Another way is to acquiesce and to give in, to resign yourself to the oppression. Some people do that. They discover the difficulties of the wilderness moving into the promised land, and they would rather go back to the despots of Egypt because it's difficult to get in the promised land. And so they resign themselves to the fate of oppression; they somehow acquiesce to this thing. But that too isn't the way because non-cooperation with evil is as much a moral obligation as is cooperation with good.

But there is another way. And that is to organize mass non-violent resistance based on the principle of love. It seems to me that this is the only way as our eyes look to the future. As we look out across the years and across the generations, let us develop and move right here. We must discover the power of love, the power, the redemptive power of love. And when we discover that we will be able to make of this old world a new world. We will be able to make men better. Love is the only way. Jesus discovered that. . . .

So this morning, as I look into your eyes, and into the eyes of all of my brothers in Alabama and all over America and over the world, I say to you, "I love you. I would rather die than hate you." And I'm foolish enough to believe that through the power of this love somewhere, men of the most recalcitrant bent will be transformed. And then we will be in God's kingdom. We will be able to matriculate into the university of eternal life because we had the power to love our enemies, to bless those persons that cursed us, to even decide to be good to those persons who hated us, and we even prayed for those persons who despitefully used us.

Further Resources

BOOKS

Garrow, David J. *Bearing the Cross: Martin Luther King, Jr., and the Southern Christian Leadership Conference.* New York: Vintage, 1986.

King, Coretta Scott. *My Life with Martin Luther King, Jr.* New York: Holt, Rinehart, and Winston, 1969.

Washington, James M., ed. *A Testament of Hope: The Essential Writings of Martin Luther King, Jr.* San Francisco, Calif.: Harper & Row, 1986.

PERIODICALS

Hopkins, Dwight N. Review of *I May Not Get There With You: The True Martin Luther King, Jr.,* by Michael Eric Dyson. *African American Review,* Spring 2002, 169.

"King Speaks to the 21st Century." *Ebony,* January 2001, 53.

"The Martin Luther King, Jr. Center for Nonviolent Social Change." *Footsteps,* May 2000, 42.

WEBSITES

Holidays on the Net. "Welcome to Martin Luther King, Jr. Day on the Net." Available online at http://www.holidays.net/mlk (accessed February 2, 2003).

King Center. Website home page. Available online at http://www.thekingcenter.com/ (accessed February 2, 2003).

Stanford University, "Martin Luther King, Jr. Papers Project." Available online at http://www.stanford.edu/group/King (accessed February 2, 2003).

Christian Ethics

Theological work

By: Georgia Elma Harkness

Date: 1957

Source: Harkness, Georgia Elma. *Christian Ethics*. New York: Abingdon Press, 1957. Available online at http://www.religion-online.org/cgi-bin/relsearchd.dll/showchapter?chapter_id=1084 (accessed February 11, 2003).

About the Author: Georgia Elma Harkness (1891–1974) was born in Harkness, New York, and received her Ph.D. from Brown University in 1912. Her academic career took her to Elmira College in New York; Garrett Theological Seminary in Evanston, Illinois; and, during the 1950s, to the Pacific School of Religion in Berkeley, California. Her major focus was applied theology, and she wrote over three dozen books on religion. ■

Introduction

That Sunday was the most racially segregated day of the week during the 1950s was a truism. On the Christian day of worship, it would not be unusual to visit either small-town America or the cities and find services that were either all white or all black. Segregation was as common in the churches as it was in schools and neighborhoods, not only in the South, with its long history of racial problems, but throughout the nation.

In Chapter 9 of *Christian Ethics*, "Christianity and the Race Problem," Georgia Harkness challenged churches in America to make a major transformation in their social structure: from racially segregated local congregations to Christian-focused integrated ones representing the diversity of God's creation. She believed that it was time for the churches to examine the hypocrisy they had tolerated for centuries and recognize that Christ said to love all your neighbors, not just the ones whose skin color was the same. Harkness wanted churches to lead the fight against segregation, not perpetuate it by ignoring it or waiting for other institutions to deal with it.

Church historians have offered two major reasons for this segregation. First, most churches drew their membership from local neighborhoods. For decades, forced segregated housing produced communities that were racially divided, a division reflected in neighborhood churches. This racial divide was often maintained by the white power structure within the white churches themselves. A second reason for church segregation was doctrinal. A number of black churches, such as the African Methodist-Episcopal Church and the National Baptist Convention of America, had religious differences with the corresponding denominations dominated by whites.

Significance

"Christianity and the Race Problem" served as a wake-up call to the churches, especially white congregations, that the time for action was at hand. It was a message to the clergy and laity that they should not only take a position against segregation but also become active in the fight for racial justice. Harkness's writings were especially relevant in light of the ongoing civil rights movement led by Martin Luther King, Jr., and others. Harkness knew that if the movement were to succeed and justice prevail, the involvement of white and black Christians was essential.

Some members of the churches responded positively to Harkness's call and were stirred to action, but others had doubts, believing that it was not the responsibility of the church to take an active role in the Civil Rights movement. In their view, the church should serve only a specific religious and spiritual function and not be involved in advocating community change and social action. In later years, though, a growing number of Christians adopted Harkness's position, and many churches began to examine their practices and achieve racial integration.

Primary Source

Christian Ethics [excerpt]

SYNOPSIS: These excerpts, from Chapter 9 of *Christian Ethics*, addressed a troubling issue facing Americans in the 1950s: how to achieve the equal treatment of all people, regardless of race. Harkness challenged Christians to put into action the command by Christ, that is, to love your neighbor as yourself. The church must become a leader, not just a follower, in the struggle for civil rights, and she suggests several ways churches can achieve this goal.

We come now to one of the most baffling and difficult of all contemporary problems. In the world scene, questions of race and color mingle with those of national status and of economic abundance and poverty to create great restlessness and tension. In our own land, the violent reactions evoked by the Supreme Court's decision of May 17, 1954, that segregation in the public schools is unconstitutional have revealed how deep are the differences that divide us. Though integration in the schools is accepted more readily in northern states, there is scarcely a community anywhere, North or South, that does not show the marks of racial cleavage in segregated housing, employment, and social attitudes.

Even in churches this virus is widely prevalent. It was not a theological, but a racial, issue that split the Methodist Church in 1844 and kept it in sectional units for almost a hundred years, with the breach only partially healed by the formula of union in 1939. The northern and southern Presbyterians and Baptists are still separated with race in the background, though with important theological differences in addition to the racial attitudes that have prevailed in Methodism. Yet it is the existence not of separate denominations, but of segregation within virtually every denomination, that is the most telling evidence of the depth of the problem. This separateness, whether or not required by organizational structures, is everywhere present. One has but to enter almost any church and look around to discover it. . . .

Let us take a look at the biblical foundations of the Christian view. This can be brief, for the directives are unequivocal.

In the first chapter of Genesis it is written,

> Then God said, "Let us make man in our image, after our likeness; and let them have dominion over the fish of the sea, and over the birds of the air, and over the cattle, and over all the earth, and over every creeping thing that creeps upon the earth." So God created man in his own image, in the image of God he created him; male and female he created them.

> *(1:26–27)*

There is no suggestion here of a white God, or even of a Semitic God. Nor is there any intimation that some who are thus to "have dominion" are to constitute a dominant race while others do the menial tasks of mankind. Even though Negroes be assumed to be the descendants of Ham, the Jews of Shem, and the Aryans of Japheth—a view which anthropologists discredit—all are equally the Sons of Adam and made in the divine image. There is not a little religious exclusiveness in the history of the Hebrews as it is recorded in the Old Testament, and this gave rise to a Jewish particularism which the greater prophets had to condemn as they stressed

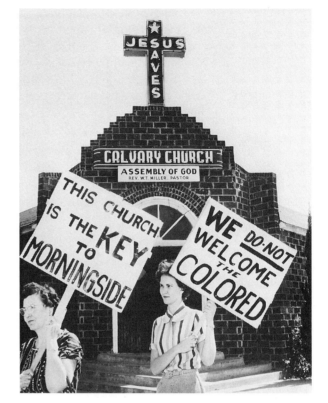

White women picket outside Calvary Assembly of God Church, Fort Worth, Texas, in 1956. They are protesting its sale to an African American congregation. Though Christians believe that all people are equal before God, in the 1950s racial prejudice was still a problem among religious and non-religious alike. © BETTMANN/CORBIS. REPRODUCED BY PERMISSION.

the love of God for all men. Yet the doctrine of creation that is the common heritage of Jewish and Christian faith asserts unequivocally the unity of mankind and leaves no standing ground for racial exclusiveness.

In the New Testament this becomes unmistakable. The equality of all persons before God was basic to the outlook of Jesus. The parable of the good Samaritan is the most dramatic challenge to racial exclusiveness, but it appears again and again in Jesus' own service to human need regardless of racial or national backgrounds and in his portrayal of the conditions of entrance into the Kingdom. In the last judgment scene, it is not one's Jewish ancestry but care for the hungry and thirsty, for the naked, sick, and imprisoned, that will determine one's place (Matt. 25:31–46).

In the great consummation, "men will come from east and west, and from north and south, and sit at table in the kingdom of God" (Luke 13:29). Jesus did not hesitate to condemn the shallow self-confidence of those who trusted in their Jewish prerogatives, or to commend the faith of a Roman centurion as being superior to theirs (Matt. 23; 8:10–13). Had Jesus been willing to be neutral toward Jewish exclusiveness for fear of causing trouble, he might have escaped crucifixion but he would not have been our Lord.

In the early Church, the contest between Jewish exclusiveness and Christian universalism was at first sharp, but the latter won out to become the settled policy. The decision recorded in Acts 15:19–21 thereby becomes a watershed in the history of the Church. Peter's vision (Acts 10) and its bearing on the acceptance of the Roman centurion Cornelius into Christian fellowship bears directly on the issue of segregated churches today, and the truth could hardly be more forcefully put than in Peter's words that clinch the matter, "Truly I perceive that God shows no partiality" (v. 34).

Paul repeatedly declared that "all men, both Jews and Greeks, are under the power of sin" (Rom. 3:9), but that Christ died for the redemption of all, and has reconciled us to God and to one another. "There is neither Jew nor Greek, there is neither slave nor free, there is neither male nor female; for you are all one in Christ Jesus." (Gal. 3:28.) No greater charter of race equality need be cited than that found in Ephesians, "For he is our peace, who has made us both one, and has broken down the dividing wall of hostility" (2:14).

But why multiply citations? The record is so clear that almost any Christian will admit that in principle race prejudice is wrong. But what of our practice? . . .

The Church cannot let these conditions continue without action. The security of the world calls for the mitigation of racial tensions through justice. Yet deeper than the demand for security is the obligation of the Christian gospel to increase love in human relations.

In the first place, the Church must understand and proclaim its gospel. Vague generalities about the fatherhood of God and the brotherhood of man have often been spoken which do not cut down through our crust of convention to where the race problem is. We need to recover the insights of Jesus on this question. And one of the most amazing things about Jesus is how he met the racism of his day. Reared in a Jewish tradition that prided itself on being the chosen people of God, living in occupied territory where Roman superiority and Jewish

superiority were always in uneasy tension, he lived on a plane that made a Roman centurion say of him, "Truly this was a son of God!" (Matt. 27:54). Jew, Roman, Samaritan, Syrophoenician, were to him equally the children of God. In the presence of human need, his healing knew no bounds.

If we examine the democracy of Jesus—a democracy which he never talked about but always practiced—we discover in it both the fountainhead of our democracy and certain radical challenges. We talk much about the dignity of man. This he did not deny; in fact, he assumed it, but always in the framework of man's dependence upon God and the obligation to obey God and love one another. His emphasis was not on the claim of personal rights, as so much of ours is, but on the doing of duties. This may well lead to the claiming of rights for others, but such a demand must first be expressed in the acts and attitudes of daily life. These four—divine dependence, mutual obligation stemming from love, sound judgment of human nature, and the practice of brotherhood in daily experience—are the basis of any true democracy. Not until the Church both preaches and practices such Christian democracy will it touch the fringe of the race question.

Second, the Church must put its own house in order. This means the welcome presence of colored Christians in the membership, the worship services, church schools, discussion groups, and social gatherings of the Church. It means the presence of colored persons in the conferences and policy-making bodies of the Church. It means the refusal to permit segregation in the living arrangements connected with church meetings. It means the sharing of the recreational, educational, and hospital facilities of the Church with all who need them. It means the interchange of pulpits between colored and white ministers, and much further advance in what has already been here and there undertaken, an interracial ministry. As qualified persons can be found or trained, there must be interracial teaching, medical, and administrative staffs in the institutions of the Church. In such arrangements there must be equal and nonsegregated living and working conditions, equal pay, equal opportunities of promotion, regardless of color. Differentiation on grounds of contribution and fitness does not justify differentiation on grounds of race. If such a program arouses opposition, as it is likely to, this calls for the tactful but courageous insistence that the house of God is a place of prayer and service for all peoples and the Church of God cannot sanction discrimination at any point.

I am aware that the relatively mild proposals of the preceding sentences, if acted upon, would be revolutionary. Already I hear someone say, "You couldn't do that in my church!" Have you tried? The ideal of race equality will not arrive all at once. But it will not arrive at all until we stop conforming to prevailing attitudes and practices and give the Church an opportunity to lead in the shaping of community standards. Even conflict, if dealt with in love, can prove a creative experience.

In bringing about such changes, there is particular need to avoid incrimination and self-righteousness and to act upon the basis of true facts and principles, not upon emotional impulse. Race prejudice, we have seen, is basically a matter of emotion, and there can be no effective challenge of it without right counter-emotions. Such depth of concern does not justify unloving attitudes toward or name calling of one's opponents. "Speaking the truth in love" is a supreme need.

It is easy for one to say this who has not personally felt the sting of race discrimination. Yet the need becomes far more eloquent when it comes from the lips of one who bears the brunt of it, yet without hatred. It was put in words that ought to become classic by the Rev. Martin Luther King, Jr., a few hours after his arrest as a leader of passive resistance against segregation in the Montgomery, Alabama, bus lines:

> If we are arrested every day, if we are exploited every day, if we are trampled over every day, don't ever let anyone pull you so low as to hate them. We must use the weapon of love. We must have compassion and understanding for those who hate us. We must realize so many people are taught to hate us that they are not totally responsible for their hate. But we stand in life at midnight; we are always on the threshold of a new dawn.

The race problem must, for the most part, be met by person to person contacts which create understanding. This calls for more intervisitation and social fellowship, both locally and nationally, and as occasion permits, in the world community. It is hard to remain hostile toward a people whose individuals one has come to know and love. Such fellowship has been one of the major contributions of the ecumenical movement.

In cases of racial discrimination by public agencies within the community, the Church must be willing to stand up and be counted on the side of equality. It must act in co-operation with other community forces if possible, but in any case it must act. Not alone prophetic indictment, but patient mediation, is the function of Christian leaders. . . .

Finally, the total problem must be lifted into the realm of prayer and worship. We must pray for those of other races; we must be responsive to the awareness that they are praying for us. When one enters truly into the mood of intercession, bitterness departs and fellowship takes its place. It has been the contention of this chapter that the removal of race prejudice is a duty laid upon us by God, and if it is God's business we are engaged in, we must give God an opening in our souls.

Since it is God's business, let us not despair. The solution will not come tomorrow, but it will come. In the midst of the walls of opposition erected by men stands Christ, who breaks down the "dividing wall of hostility" that separates us. It is the business of Christians to give him a chance to act.

Further Resources

BOOKS

Fredrickson, George M. *Racism: a Short History.* Princeton, N.J.: Princeton University Press, 2002.

Kelsey, George D. *Racism and the Christian Understanding of Man.* New York: Scribner's, 1965.

Okolo, Chukwudum Barnabas. *Racism—a Philosophic Probe.* Jericho, N.Y.: Exposition Press, 1974.

PERIODICALS

Bowman, Jim. "A Conference on Racism." *Commonweal,* February 25, 1994, 63.

Donahue, John R. "What Is True Religion?" *America,* March 18, 2000, 30.

Jones, L. Gregory. "Race and Friendship." *The Christian Century,* October 22, 1997, 950.

WEBSITES

Magenta Foundation. "Crosspoint Anti-Racism." Available online at http://www.magenta.nl/crosspoint (accessed February 11, 2003).

United Nations. "World Conference Against Racism, Racial Discrimination, Xenophobia and Related Intolerance." Available online at http://www.un.org/WCAR; website home page: http://www.un.org (accessed February 11, 2003).

"A Protestant Look at American Catholicism"

Journal article

By: John Coleman Bennett

Date: August 4, 1958

Source: Bennett, John C. "A Protestant Look at American Catholicism." *Christianity and Crisis,* August 4, 1958. Available online at http://www.religion-online.org/cgi-bin /relsearchd.dll/showarticle?item_id=525 (accessed February 11, 2003).

About the Author: John Coleman Bennett (1902–1995) was born in Kingston, Ontario, Canada, and was educated at Williams College, Oxford University, and Union Theological Seminary. In 1943, he joined Union Theological Seminary as a professor of social ethics. In 1964, he was appointed president of the seminary. He was coeditor of the periodical *Christianity and Crisis.* He lectured and wrote about such issues as civil rights, war, and the relationship between church and state. ∎

Introduction

Prior to the 1950s, the numbers of American Catholics had risen significantly. According to the Census Bureau, the number rose from 10 million in 1900 to almost 28 million in 1950, many of them recent European immigrants and their children. Some Protestant Americans viewed this growth with trepidation and wondered if future increases would give Catholics enough political clout to dominate the American government, impose their values on other Christians, and violate constitutional provisions for the separation of church and state. Some also raised questions about the allegiance of Catholics to their church, asking whether it was more powerful than their allegiance to the United States. A small number even believed that Catholics actually received directions from the pope.

These and other issues concerning Catholics in America were discussed among Protestant clergy, theologians, educators, and laity. Sometimes, Catholics were asked for their input into these discussions. They tried to assure Protestants—not always successfully—that Catholics could be loyal to the principles of American society and to their church at the same time.

In this context, John C. Bennett published "A Protestant Look at American Catholicism." In Bennett's view, many of the resentments and fears being expressed by Protestants, while partially justified, were grossly exaggerated. He predicted that Catholics would be absorbed into the mainstream of American life and adopt its values without imposing their way of life or beliefs upon others. Over the long run, he expressed optimism about the religious, social, and political future of the role of Catholics in America.

Significance

By addressing some of these concerns, Bennett gave Protestants guidance in forming their opinions about Catholics in the United States. As a result of his efforts, many Protestants were more willing to accept Catholics as part of mainstream American society. Others, however, were more doubtful. For example, C. Stanley Lowell, who became the associate director of Protestants and Other Americans United for the Separation of Church and State, raised several questions about Bennett's article.

Three years later, John F. Kennedy, a Catholic, became the thirty-fifth president of the United States. During the campaign, the issue of the separation of church and state and a Catholic presidency was hotly debated. During Kennedy's administration, however, it became clear that he respected the principal of separation of church and state.

Primary Source

"A Protestant Look at American Catholicism" [excerpt]

> **SYNOPSIS:** In these excerpts, Bennett cites two major concerns about Catholics in America: the dogmatic intolerance that was characteristic of the faith and the tension between the church's structure and an open, pluralistic, and democratic society. Bennett expressed hope these issues could be resolved and presented a number of reasons for his optimism, particularly the wide diversity of views and traditions among Catholics worldwide.

The attitudes of Americans toward church-state relations depend in considerable measure on their attitude toward Roman Catholicism. The chief concern that lies back of the convictions of non-Catholics is the concern for religious liberty, and the chief threat to religious liberty is seen in the tremendous growth of Roman Catholicism as a cultural and political power in the United States.

There are two deep problems connected with Catholicism that must be emphasized at the outset of any discussion. One is the dogmatic intolerance that is itself a part of the Roman Catholic faith. This dogmatic intolerance need not lead to civil intolerance, but there is a tendency for it to do so just as was the case when it characterized the major Protestant bodies. This dogmatic intolerance becomes all the more difficult for non-Catholics when it is associated not only with distinctly religious dogma, but also with elements of natural law that are not accepted as divinely sanctioned moral demands by most non-Catholics. This is true of birth control, of some matters of medical ethics. It is true even of gambling under limited conditions, though this has to do not with a moral demand but with a moral permission! One symptom of the dogmatic intolerance that is most objectionable to non-Catholics is the strict Catholic regulation concerning the religion of the children of mixed marriages.

The other basic problem is the real tension between an authoritarian, centralized hierarchical church and the spirit of an open, pluralistic, democratic society. There is abundant evidence that Catholics in this country do sincerely believe in democracy and practice this belief, but I do not see how they themselves can deny that their polity poses a problem for democracy that is not posed by churches which make their decisions in regard to public policy by processes of open discussion in which both clergy and laymen share. The polity of the Episcopal Church does give bishops meeting separately a veto over many things, but it also gives the laity voting separately in the dioceses a veto over the choice of bishops. I mention this as an example of one of the more hierarchical forms of polity outside the Roman Catholic Church.

The Roman polity is itself a matter of faith and therefore religious liberty includes the liberty to preserve that type of polity. And if it is said that the papacy creates a problem of peculiar difficulty because it is from the point of view of the nation a "foreign power," the answer that Protestants should be able to accept is that the Church as Church is supranational and the religious liberty of all Christians includes their right to have relationships, suitable to their polity, with the universal Church. . . .

The general thesis of this article is that, while many of these resentments and fears are justified, it is a mistake to project them in indefinitely extended form upon the future and to allow all of our thinking about Catholicism and most of our thinking about church-state relations to be controlled by them in that extended form. After outlining the grounds for some justified resentments and fears in this article, I will deal with other facts about Catholic life that should play a larger part than they do in Protestant attitudes toward Catholicism. . . .

Non-Catholics have grounds for resenting the tendency of Catholics to use their power to impose Catholic ideas of natural law. They see it in the birth control legislation in Massachusetts and Connecticut; they see it in the Catholic pressure to remove welfare agencies that have birth control clinics from local community chests elsewhere; they see it in the Catholic objection to divorce laws that are much more flexible than the law of the Church; they see it in the attempts to have non-Catholic hospitals adopt the Catholic ideas of medical ethics in the field of obstetrics.

Non-Catholics have grounds for resenting and fearing the tendency of Catholics, when they have the power, to seek control of the public school system to bend it to Catholic purposes. Parochial schools could operate as safety valves for the public schools but this is often not the case. When Catholics dominate the public school boards they sometimes discriminate against non-Catholic teachers. In extreme cases that have been much publicized they have operated public schools as though they were parochial schools. Perhaps more serious in the long run is the tendency of Catholics in some places to oppose needed bond issues or appropriations for the public schools. This is not a surprising reaction to the double burden of education costs that they themselves bear, but it is very bad for education.

Non-Catholics have grounds for resenting and fearing Catholic boycotts of communications media, including the publishers of books, and boycotts of local merchants who have some connection with a policy that they oppose. Fear of Catholic boycott often operates as a reason for self-censorship. Newspapers are influenced by this fear and it is very difficult to get news published that may be unfavorable to the Catholic Church. . . .

Having summarized the grounds for Protestant fears and resentments in the face of the growth of Catholic power, I would now like to call attention to four characteristics of Catholicism that are often neglected in American Protestant discussions of this subject.

The first of these characteristics is Roman Catholicism's great variations from culture to culture and from country to country. The vision of many Protestants of a monolithic Catholic Church, built somewhat on the lines of the Stalinist empire, that is controlled from the Vatican is very wide of the mark. Historically it has proved itself capable of adjustment to the greatest variety of cultural conditions instead of being one kind of religious ethos exported from Rome.

The difference between French Catholicism and Spanish Catholicism almost belongs to the study of comparative religion. Catholicism in western Europe

Congregationist minister and educator Reverend John C. Bennett, c. 1960. Bennett sought to reassure American Protestants that the increasing power of Catholics in America did not pose a threat to their way of life. GETTY IMAGES. REPRODUCED BY PERMISSION.

is utterly different from Catholicism in Latin America. In Germany, France, Holland, Belgium, Switzerland, and England we see what Catholicism can be when it is religiously and culturally mature and when it has learned to live with strong Protestant and secularist competition. There is remarkable intellectual ferment in the Catholic Church in those countries. Catholic thinkers take considerable theological freedom and they are especially free in their thinking about political issues. There is a long standing effort to overcome the political and economic conservatism that has been the great handicap of the Church in reaching the working classes.

There is very much more discussion between Protestant and Catholic thinkers on a theological level in Europe than there is in this country. One interesting phenomenon is the fresh study of Luther and the Reformation by Catholic scholars that has shattered the old Catholic stereotypes. American Catholicism differs from western European Catholicism in that it has no rich cultural background. It has a strong feeling of cultural inferiority to American Protestantism as well as to European Catholi-

cism. Intellectual ferment is exactly what it lacks. The reasons for this are obvious as American Catholicism represents the tides of immigration that brought to this country millions of Europeans who had had few opportunities in their own countries.

Protestants as they view the development of Catholicism have good reason to assume that as it becomes more mature culturally and theologically it will have more flexibility of mind and that there will be greater tolerance and breadth in dealing with non-Catholics and with the public issues that concern Protestants most.

I should add here that Catholicism needs not only the kind of maturing that takes time in a new country, but it needs to have two other things. One is the strong competition from non-Catholic sources —Protestant, Jewish, secularist. It has had one or more of these types of competition in every one of the western European countries that I named. The worst thing that can happen to Catholicism is for it to have the religious monopoly to which it feels entitled because of its exclusive claims! Protestants, therefore, have a responsibility to confront Catholicism with a positive Protestant theology, and that is happening today in many countries because of the recent theological revival in Protestantism. . . .

A second characteristic of Roman Catholicism is suggested by the fact that much of the Catholic aggressiveness that is most offensive to Protestants is sociologically conditioned. It is a result of the sheer energy that it has taken for Catholics to improve their position in a new country and in an alien culture, and it also reflects some social resentment for past disabilities on the part of people who have won social power.

We forget today the long and bitter history of nativist anti-Catholicism, but the memories of it do not die so easily among Catholics themselves.

Today changes are coming so rapidly and the economic, social, and cultural opportunities for Americans of many ethnic backgrounds are so much alike that we can expect to see the particular sociological reasons for Catholic aggressiveness become less important. . . .

A third fact about Catholicism that needs to be understood by Protestants is that the Catholic Church is divided from top to bottom, in this country and abroad, on matters of principle in regard to religious liberty. There is a traditional main-line position that favors the confessional Catholic state as the ideal type of relationship between church and state. This view would limit the rights of religious minorities in a nation that has a very large Catholic majority. These limitations would have to do with public propagation of the non-Catholic faith rather than with freedom of worship or freedom of teaching inside the Protestant Church. Under such circumstances there would be a union of state and church and the state as state would profess the Catholic faith.

. . . It is simply not enough for a church that operates in the light of very clear dogmatic principles to make concessions on the issue of religious liberty for non-Catholics on a pragmatic basis alone if its dogmatic principles still point to a confessional Catholic state in which, as the ideal, the religious liberties of minorities are severely restricted.

It is important to realize that a very able and earnest attempt is being made by Catholic scholars in this country, with much support from Catholics in western Europe, to change the principles as well as the practice of the Church in this matter. This attempt is associated chiefly with the work of Father John Courtney Murray, but it is gaining a good deal of support elsewhere too. A careful statement of his position is found chiefly in his many articles in the Jesuit quarterly *Theological Studies.* (See especially March, 1953; June, 1953; December, 1953; March, 1954. Also, "Governmental Repression of Heresy" reprinted from the Proceedings of the Catholic Theological Society of America.)

Here I shall attempt to summarize his main conclusions, but it should be recognized that these are abstracted from very complicated historical expositions and come in large part from Father Murray's analysis of the encyclicals of Pope Leo XIII in order to show what is permanent and what is historically conditioned in those encyclicals. With apologies to Father Murray for oversimplification of the kind that is alien to his own mind, I shall attempt to give the substance of his position in the following propositions:

The idea of a confessional Catholic state belong to an earlier period in European history and it has become an irrelevancy under contemporary conditions.

Anglo-Saxon democracy is fundamentally different from the democracy of the French Revolution which was totalitarian in tendency. The state in this country is, by its very nature, limited, and in principle the Church does not need to defend itself against such a state as it did with the nineteenth century

revolutionary states that formed the immediate background of Leo's political thinking.

There is no anti-clerical or anti-religious motivation behind the American constitutional provision for church-state relations and the Church need not defend herself against this doctrine as such.

The Church in America has, as a matter of fact, enjoyed greater freedom and scope for its witness and activities than it has in the Catholic states of the traditional type.

It is important to emphasize the rights of the state in its own sphere, the freedom of the Church from state control, and the influence of Catholic citizens upon the state.

It is impossible to separate religious freedom from civil freedom, and there can be no democracy if the freedom of the citizen is curtailed in religious matters, for such curtailing can often take place as a means of silencing political dissent.

Error does not have the same rights as truth, but persons in error, consciences in error, do have rights that should be respected by the Church and state.

The Church should not demand that the state as the secular arm enforce the Church's own decisions in regard to heresy.

It does more harm than good to the Church for the state to use its power against non-Catholics.

I think that all of these propositions fit together into a self-consistent social philosophy. They are presented by Father Murray as a substitute for the traditional Catholic thesis concerning the confessional state. They have made considerable headway among both clergy and laity in this country. They correspond to views that are held in Europe and have support in the Vatican itself.

In December, 1953, after this point of view was strongly rebuked by Cardinal Ottaviani in Rome in an address defending the Spanish conception of a confessional Catholic state as the ideal, Pope Pius XII somewhat ambiguously made room for Murray's position in a speech to a convention of Catholic jurists. The fact that he did this in the midst of a transAtlantic controversy within the Church has encouraged American Catholics who hold this view to believe that the Pope was sympathetic to it. That is the most that can be said.

American Protestants should realize, therefore, that the Roman Church is not a vast international machine designed to overturn their liberties, if this were to become politically possible, and that they have many allies in the Catholic Church who share their belief in religious liberty on principle.

The fourth fact about the Catholic Church is that there are many points of disagreement on social policy among Catholics; there is no one Catholic line on most public issues. There is agreement on birth control as a moral issue, but even here there is no agreement as to what the state should do about it. Catholics generally do not today advocate strict laws on the subject except in the two states in which those laws are already in force. On economic issues there is a broad Catholic pattern based upon the organization of producers' groups, but this is far from obligatory and it gives rise to endless differences so far as application is concerned.

Catholics differ as to whether a war with modern weapons can be just. There is a deep difference between Catholics in various nations on forms of government. Catholic doctrine makes room for governments based upon popular sovereignty but does not prescribe this universally. Even on communism there are great differences in temper between European and much American Catholicism.

It is an understatement to say that the Catholic hierarchy did not act helpfully on the issue of McCarthyism, but that was because they were deeply divided. There is no doubt that McCarthy had a strong hold on large groups of Catholics, especially Irish Catholics, but it is also true that some of the most eloquent opposition to McCarthy came from Catholic sources, notably such journals as *The Commonweal* and *America*. American Protestants need not fear that Catholics will usually throw their great weight as a religious community in the same political direction. This will tend to be even less a danger as Catholics move further away from the status of an immigrant bloc. In general we can say that natural law does not guarantee agreement on concrete issues, but we can also say that natural law plus prudence equals flexibility.

I have outlined briefly four aspects of Catholicism of which American Protestants should take account. Though they give no assurance as to the direction that Catholicism may take in the next generation, they may release us from exaggerated fears based on past experience in this country alone. Protestants should put more rather than less emphasis upon positive elements of Protestant faith and doctrine. They should join Catholics in rejecting superficial forms of religious harmony so often urged

in the interests of national unity. But they can live with their Catholic neighbors in the hope that greater mutual understanding and the sharing of moral and political purposes may become possible.

Further Resources
BOOKS
Bennett, John C. *Christian Realism.* New York: Scribner's, 1941.

———. *Christians and the State.* New York: Scribner's, 1958.

———. *The Radical Imperative.* Philadelphia, Pa: Westminster Press, 1975.

Opinions on Catholicism and America
Journal articles

By: C. Stanley Lowell, C. John Bennett, and William Clancy

Date: September 15, 1958

Source: Lowell, C. Stanley. "Salient Facts Overlooked: A Concerned Protestant Suggests Another View of Catholic Religious Liberty." *Christianity and Crisis,* September 15, 1958; Clancy, William. "Complex and Evolving Realities," *Christianity and Crisis,* September 15, 1958. Available online at http://www.religion-online.org/cgi-bin/relsearchd.dll/showarticle?item_id=525 (accessed February 11, 2003).

About the Authors: In 1960, C. Stanley Lowell was the associate director of Protestants and Other Americans United for the Separation of Church and State and editor of the periodical *Church and State.*

William Clancy was an editor of the *Commonweal,* a Catholic weekly. He also edited *Worldview,* a journal of international affairs and religion, and was education director of the interfaith Church Peace Union.

John Coleman Bennett joined Union Theological Seminary as a professor of social ethics in 1943. In 1964, he was appointed president of the seminary. He was coeditor of the periodical *Christianity and Crisis.* He lectured and wrote about such issues as civil rights, war, and the relationship between church and state. ∎

Introduction

In "A Protestant Look at American Catholicism," John C. Bennett expressed optimism that Catholics would assimilate into the mainstream of America and not pose a threat to the freedoms enjoyed by Protestant Americans. He believed this even though he cited two major concerns about Catholics in America: the dogmatic intolerance that was characteristic of the faith and the tension between the church's structure and an open, pluralistic, and democratic society.

C. Stanley Lowell challenged Bennett's position in "Salient Facts Overlooked: A Concerned Protestant Suggests Another View of Catholic Religious Liberty." Lowell's primary concern was his perception that the Catholic Church was not adjusting to the realities of American society in its resistance to the concept of separation of church and state. He believed that Rome still clung to traditional views about church-state relationships and wished to impose its religious values on people, whether they were Catholic or not. In his view, mixed messages were coming from the Vatican: sometimes it supported the more liberal "American view" about the role of the church in society, but more often it espoused a more traditional view. For example, Lowell conceded that the Catholic church had the right to oppose artificial birth control. He opposed, however, the church's attempt to impose that value on non-Catholics and society as a whole.

In "Complex and Evolving Realities," William Clancy challenged Lowell's appraisal of the American Catholic church. Clancy believed that supporters of Protestants and Other Americans United for the Separation of Church and State, of which Lowell was a member, were ignorant of the realities of the modern Catholic church. The church, Clancy asserted, is not static or frozen but capable of adapting to the contemporary world. For decades, Catholic leaders in the United States had tried to convince the hierarchy in Rome that it had to alter its outlook on the relationship between the church and state, especially in America. The church was not monolithic, these leaders had said, and is capable of changing its policies. It was this position that Clancy was reiterating, and supporting, in his article criticizing Lowell's views.

Significance

These articles by Bennett, Lowell, and Clancy illustrate the intellectual and spiritual struggle that was taking place both within American Catholicism and between Catholics and Protestants in the 1950s. By openly debating their views, they helped to bring the issue of separation of church and state before the American public. The debate helped to advance discussions by interested and well-intentioned Catholics and Protestants who were trying to resolve their differences. In the years that followed, both branches of Christianity learned to accommodate each other's religious, social, and political views. The controversy did not vanish, but at least there was better understanding of the issue and compromise by both sides.

Little did these men realize that in just a few years (1960), John F. Kennedy would be elected to the presidency. Not only was he the first Catholic president but he was also perceived by the public and the press as a person of vision and hope for the future.

Primary Source

Opinions on Catholicism and America

SYNOPSIS: Lowell's article is a response to John C. Bennett's defense of Catholicism in "A Protestant Look at American Catholicism." Lowell expressed a less optimistic view than Bennett about the future of Catholicism in America. Bennett was then given a chance to reply to Lowell. Finally, William Clancy, a Catholic, charged Lowell with "outrageous inaccuracies," and defended the role of Catholics in American society.

"Salient Facts Overlooked: A Concerned Protestant Suggests Another View of Catholic Religious Liberty" by C. Stanley Lowell

It impresses me that in his "argument from difference" in regard to Catholic views on religious liberty, John Bennett overlooks some salient facts. He fails to mention that while the "American view" of Father Murray was being advanced against the traditional Catholic view of religious liberty pressed by the Spanish hierarchy, Cardinal Ottaviani's statement settling the issue was approved by the Pope as "unexceptionable." Nor does he mention that Cardinal Ottaviani, as Secretary of the Supreme Congregation of the Holy Office, was perhaps the Pope's closest confidant.

Dr. Bennett does make vague mention of a speech in which the Pope, himself in vague language, seems to lend some approval to "the American view." If any such pronouncement exists, it must appear rather emaciated when contrasted with the overwhelming evidence of pronouncements on the other side.

While it is nice that Father Murray holds "liberal views," the fact is that they have never gained any official recognition at the Vatican. Unfortunately, Father Murray speaks for no one, not even himself. Authoritative teaching of the American hierarchy in regard to religious liberty, a teaching squarely in line with the Church's tradition, has been consistently presented by Father Francis J. Connell.

It seems curious, too, that Dr. Bennett should speak of "the influence of liberal democratic ideas [which] enables Catholics to avoid the civil intolerance that causes most anxiety among Protestants." He apparently wrote this at the very moment that New York was in an uproar over a sectarian medical code that the Roman Catholic Church had for years been imposing on public hospitals of that city.

John Bennett's Reply to C. Stanley Lowell

Mr. Lowell raises an important question. How influential in the Catholic Church is the view of Father Murray that was outlined in my article? I emphasized the fact that it is not the dominant view. It has the tradition of many centuries against it. The most that I can claim is that this issue of the religious liberty of non-Catholics in a nation in which there is a predominance of Catholics is being debated on all levels and in many countries, and that the traditional position is being challenged with great ability. The so-called "dynamic interpreters," to use the name given by Father Gustave Weigel to the Murray position, have strong support among Catholic scholars and laymen in this country and in several other democratic countries.

Professor Kenneth Underwood, in *Protestant and Catholic,* points out that in Holyoke, Mass., 40 per cent of the clergy, and these the younger clergy, are receptive to this position. One difficulty is that, without raising the ultimate question of the theory of religious liberty, Catholics in this country can agree with the practical implications of Father Murray's position on pragmatic grounds. Members of the hierarchy do not want to be put on the spot on a matter that involves revision of basic theory. The discussion is being carried out by scholars and laymen.

The speech by Cardinal Ottaviani actually revealed a division within the Church because he was strongly attacked publicly by Catholic spokesmen in this country even by such a diocesan journal as *The Pilot* in Boston. I have learned by word of mouth about the serious divisions in the Vatican concerning this speech, but this quickly becomes gossip and it is hard to evaluate. Pius XII's address to which I referred (distributed in English translation on December 15, 1953) did not go further than the traditional position allows, but the timing of it suggests that he was in fact rebuking the extreme position advanced by Cardinal Ottaviani. The address itself shows the caution and even studied ambiguity that are common in papal utterances. The most that we can expect of any Pope on such matters is an indication of permissiveness. Remember that we are dealing here with a theoretical challenge of the traditional position; but this challenge has great significance because it fits the experience of Catholics in democratic countries. Elsewhere Pius XII made a very dear place for democracy.

As far as birth control is concerned, I agree with those who fight uncompromisingly for the freedom of non-Catholics on this issue. There are important issues between Protestants and Catholic and I do not want to obscure them. Fortunately there is some disagreement among Catholic as to how far they should press their position on the whole community by law. There is a favorable straw in the wind in the fact that they are not attempting to have laws such as those in Massachusetts and Connecticut enacted in other states. But if this means that they are relying on administrative action, as was the case in New York City hospitals, they need to be resolutely opposed.

"Complex and Evolving Realities," by William Clancy

It is depressing to read the observations of C. Stanley Lowell. They give further evidence of remarkable inability even to glimpse the realities of Catholicism in the modern world. These realities, as John C. Bennett has observed, are complex and, in many areas, evolving. But, whatever may be the evidence to the contrary, Mr. Lowell insists that "the Roman Church" is simple and forever frozen in sonic medieval mold.

I am not hopeful that anything I, or any other Catholic, might say would bring him to a wider vision of Catholicism. Those who see it as authoritarianism pure and simple, a monolithic conspiracy against the "American way of life," are frozen in *their* mold. But for the sake of those Protestants and others who are interested I think some Catholic comment should be made.

The point I would make is general. But I must also point out several of his more outrageous inaccuracies.

Item

Mr. Lowell claims that Cardinal Ottaviani's 1953 defense of the "traditional" Catholic church-state position was "approved" by the Pope as "unexceptionable." He further states that "if" (as Dr. Bennett wrote) the Pope once made a speech which "in vague language seems to approve 'the American view,'" the Pope's pronouncement, "if any such pronouncement exists must appear rather emaciated when contrasted with the overwhelming evidence of pronouncements on the other side."

These are startling observations. The late Pope himself never made *any* comment on Cardinal Ottaviani's address. Someone in "the Vatican," who has never been identified, made a statement that while the Ottaviani position was "neither official nor semi-official" it was, nevertheless, "unexceptionable." And the "vague" papal pronouncement that Mr. Lowell seems to doubt was ever made was, in fact, a major—some think historic—allocution, delivered in 1953 to an audience of Italian jurists, in which Pope Pius XII laid down the principle that "in the interest of a higher and broader good, it is justifiable not to impede error by state laws and coercive measures." It remains true, Pius declared, that error has no rights "objectively," but "the duty to repress religious and moral deviation cannot be an ultimate norm for action. It must be subjected to higher and more general norms." Many Catholics in the West interpreted this principle, clearly stated by the Pope, as "officially" opening the way for the formulation of a new Catholic position on church-state relations.

Item

Mr. Lowell believes that "while it is nice [sic] that Father John Courtney Murray holds 'liberal views,' the fact is that they have never gained any official recognition at the Vatican. Unfortunately, Father Murray speaks for no one, not even himself."

Comment on this seems unnecessary in view of Pius XII's pronouncement to the Italian jurists. One can only observe that it would be "nice" if Mr. Lowell had paid at least as much attention to the official papal address that undercut his view of Catholicism as he did to "the neither official nor semi-official" speech that supported it.

But of course he did not. And here we see the reason why most Catholics despair of any rational discussion with those who hold his views, particularly with supporters of Protestants and Other Americans United. As I observed before, they will insist that the Catholic Church is a simple, forever frozen authoritarian phenomenon, incapable of historic adaptation or self-criticism, no matter how impressive the evidence to the contrary may be. The historic ferment and developments in modern Catholic thought are dismissed (if anything is known about them) as atypical or even hypocritical. For how could it be otherwise in a Church that is "monolithic"? Period.

. . . But though the church has a life that is beyond history, it also moves in history and here it learns, adapts changes. It is not the simple, mechanical "power" that some of its critics fear. The Church is living, not dead.

At the beginning of this century a great Roman pontiff, Leo XIII, wrote:

It is the special property of human institutions and laws that there is nothing in them so holy and salutary but that custom may alter it, or overthrow it, or social habits bring it to naught. So in the Church of God, in which changeableness of discipline is joined with absolute immutability of doctrine, it happens not rarely that things which were once relevant or suitable become in the course of time out of date, or useless, or even harmful.

Here was as "official" an observation as any Mr. Lowell could desire. And, in its spirit, the process of separating out those things that are essential from those that are unessential, of re-evaluating those things which, in the course of time, may have become useless or even harmful, will continue in the Catholic community during the reign of John XXIII. While it proceeds, Catholics will hope for patience and some intelligent understanding from those not of the household of their faith.

Further Resources

BOOKS

Americans United for Separation of Church and State. The Best of Church and State, 1948–1975. Silver Spring, Md.: Americans United for Separation of Church and State, 1975.

Berman, Harold Joseph. *Church and State.* New York: Macmillan, 1987.

Woodruff, Douglas. *Church and State.* New York: Hawthorn, 1961.

WEBSITES

Americans United for Separation of Church and State. Website home page. Available online at http://www.au.org/ (accessed February 11, 2003).

Secular Web. "Library: Modern Documents: Separation of Church and State." Available online at http://www.infidels.org/library /modern/church-state/index.shtml; website home page: http:// www.infidels.org/index.shtml (accessed February 11, 2003).

Separation of Church and State. Website home page. Available online at http://members.tripod.com/~candst/tnppage/tnpidx .htm (accessed February 11, 2003).

"Beat Zen, Square Zen, and Zen"

Journal article

By: Alan Watts

Date: 1958

Source: Watts, Alan. "Beat Zen, Square Zen, and Zen," *Chicago Review*, Spring 1958. Available online at http://www.bluesforpeace.com/beat_zen.htm (accessed February 10, 2003).

About the Author: Alan Wilson Watts (1915–1973) was born in Chislehurst, England, but moved to America in 1939. Watts was ordained in the Episcopal Church in 1944 and served as a chaplain for several years. In 1950, he left the church and took a teaching job at the American Academy of Asia Studies in San Francisco from 1951 to 1957. ∎

Introduction

"Beat Zen, Square Zen, and Zen" was Alan Watts's condensation of the major characteristics of Zen Buddhism, a religion he helped popularize in the West when he wrote *The Way of Zen* (1957). Watts's fascination with Zen Buddhism did not begin in the 1950s, however. Two decades before *The Way of Zen,* Watts had written *The Spirit of Zen* (1936), considered one of the first truly accurate works on this form of Buddhism written by a Westerner.

Buddhism developed from the teachings of Buddha (Siddhartha Gautama), a philosopher from India who lived about five hundred years before Christ. Buddha held that suffering is intrinsic in human life and the problem that all people face is how to overcome it. Buddha believed that a person could be freed from suffering through mental and moral self-purification. Buddhists believe today that when one reaches a state of spiritual enlightenment through self-purification, one becomes like the Buddha. Zen Buddhism, an east Asian form of Buddhism, was originally developed about two thousand years ago as an interpretation of Buddhism in China, where it was called Chan. It was then carried to Japan about nine hundred years ago and is now practiced by many Japanese.

Zen Buddhists believe that meditation, contemplation, and intuition can help the individual attain spiritual enlightenment. They also believe that physical labor and regular reading of the sacred scriptures of Buddhism should be accompanied by periods of meditation and self-contemplation. A teacher or master helps direct the individual's search for this state.

Significance

Since the middle decades of the twentieth century, Zen Buddhism has attracted many followers because it offers an alternative to traditional Western religions. Some Americans who became attracted to Zen Buddhism in the 1950s were members of the "beat generation," or beatniks, particularly some writers and artists. The "beats" tended to reject many of the traditional values of society, behave and dress in unconventional ways, and engage in often radical social criticism. They represented those who were dissatisfied with conformity to the perceived false values advocated by "square" society. To many in this counterculture, what Watts had to say about religion was just what they wanted to hear. He was

viewed as a guru or spiritual teacher for a generation seeking new ways of thinking.

In the 1960s and 1970s, the beatniks diminished in numbers but were succeeded by a new youth-centered counterculture group called the hippies. Many in the "hippie generation," like those in the "beat generation" were attracted to the teachings and writings of Watts and to Zen Buddhism. Hippies, like the beatniks, rejected the customs, traditions, and lifestyles of the larger society and tried to develop their own. Most came from white middle-class families and were drawn into the movement as teenagers or in their twenties. Sometimes referred to as flower children, they viewed the older generation as being overly concerned with making money and obsessing over material things. To many in the hippie generation, Zen Buddhism represented a guiding light to the fulfillment of their hopes for peace and love.

Primary Source

"Beat Zen, Square Zen, and Zen" [excerpt]

SYNOPSIS: In this article, Watts summarizes the meaning and history of Zen Buddhism and its application to modern-day life. In the following excerpts, he demonstrates that for Westerners to truly understand Zen Buddhism, they must restructure their concept of religion.

It is as difficult for Anglo-Saxons as for the Japanese to absorb anything quite so Chinese as Zen. For though the word "Zen" is Japanese and though Japan is now its home, Zen Buddhism is the creation of T'ang dynasty China. I do not say this as a prelude to harping upon the non-communicable subtleties of alien cultures. The point is simply that people who feel a profound need to justify themselves have difficulty in understanding the viewpoints of those who do not, and the Chinese who created Zen were the same kind of people as Lao-tzu, who, centuries before, said, "Those who justify themselves do not convince." For the urge to make or prove oneself right has always jiggled the Chinese sense of the ludicrous, since as both Confucians and Taoists—however different these philosophies in other ways—they have invariably appreciated the man who can "come off it." To Confucius it seemed much better to be human-hearted then righteous, and to the great Taoists, Lao-tzu and Chang-tzu, it was obvious that one could not be right without also being wrong, because the two were as inseparable as back and front. As Chang-tzu said, "Those who would have good government without its correlative misrule, and right without its correlative wrong, do not understand the principles of the universe."

To Western ears such words may sound cynical, and the Confucian admiration of "reasonableness" and compromise may appear to be a weak-kneed lack of commitment to principle. Actually they reflect a marvelous understanding and respect for what we call the balance of nature, human and otherwise—a universal vision of life as the Tao or way of nature in which the good and evil, the creature and the destructive, the wise and the foolish are the insepa-rable polarities of existence. "Tao," said the Chung-yung, "is that from which one cannot depart. That from which one can depart is not the Tao." There-fore wisdom did not consist in trying to wrest the good from the evil but learning to "ride" them as a cork adapts itself to the crests and troughs of the waves. At the roots of Chinese life there is a trust in the good-and-evil of one's own nature which is pe-cularly foreign to those brought up with the chronic uneasy conscience of the Hebrew-Christian cultures. Yet it was always obvious to the Chinese that a man who mistrusts himself cannot even trust his mistrust, and must therefore be hopelessly confused.

For rather different reasons, Japanese people tend to be as uneasy in themselves as Westerners, having a sense of social shame quite as acute as our more metaphysical sense of sin. This was es-pecially true of the class most attracted to Zen, the samurai. Ruth Benedict, in that very uneven work Chrysanthemum and Sword, was, I think, perfectly correct in saying that the attraction of Zen to the samurai class was its power to get rid of an ex-tremely awkward self-consciousness induced in the education of the young.

Part-and-parcel of this self-consciousness is the Japanese compulsion to compete with oneself—a compulsion which turns every craft and skill into a marathon of self-discipline. Although the attraction of Zen lay in the possibility of liberation from self-consciousness, the Japanese version of Zen fought fire with fire, overcoming the "self observing the self" by bringing it to an intensity in which it exploded. How remote from the regimen of the Japanese Zen monastery are the words of the great T'ang master Lin-chi: "In Buddhism there is no place for using ef-fort. Just be ordinary and nothing special. Eat your food, move your bowels, pass water, and when you're tired go and lie down. The ignorant will laugh at me, but the wise will understand." Yet the spirit of these words is just as remote from a kind of West-

Alan Watts is famous for his work in comparative religions and in translating Eastern philosophies for the West. His 1958 article "Beat Zen, Square Zen, and Zen" summarized the knowledge and fallacies Westerners had of the meaning of Zen Buddhism. GETTY IMAGES. REPRODUCED BY PERMISSION.

ern Zen which would employ this philosophy to jus-tify a very self-defensive Bohemianism.

There is no single reason for the extraordinary growth of Western interest in Zen during the last twenty years. The appeal of Zen arts to the "mod-ern" spirit in the West, the words of Suzuki, the war with Japan, the itchy fascination of "Zen-stories," and the attraction of a non-conceptual, ex-periential philosophy in the climate of scientific relativism—all these are involved. One might men-tion, too, the affinities between Zen and such purely Western trends as the philosophy of Wittgenstein, existentialism, General Semantics, the metalinguis-tics of B.L. Whorf, and certain movements in the philosophy of science and in psychotherapy. Always in the "anti-naturalness" of both Christianity, with its politically ordered cosmology, and technology, with its imperialistic mechanization of a natural world from which man himself feels strangely alien. For both reflect a psychology in which man is identified with a conscious intelligence and will standing apart from nature to control it, like the architect—God in whose image this version of man is conceived. This disquiet arises from the suspicion that our attempt to master the world from the outside is a vicious circle in which we shall be condemned to the perpetual insomnia of controlling controls and supervising supervision ad infinitum.

To the Westerner in search of the reintegration of man and nature there is an appeal far beyond the merely sentimental in the naturalism of Zen—in the landscapes of Ma-yuan and Sesshu, in an art which is simultaneously spiritual and secular, which conveys the mystical in terms of the natural, and which, indeed, never even imagined a break between them. Here is a view of the world imparting a profoundly refreshing sense of wholeness to a culture in which the spiritual and the material, the conscious and the unconscious, have been cataclysmically split. For this reason the Chinese humanism and naturalism of Zen intrigue us much more strongly than Indian Buddhism or Vedanta. These, too, have their students in the West, but their followers seem for the most part to be displaced Christians—people in search of a more plausible philosophy than Christian supernaturalism to carry on the essentially Christian search for the miraculous. . . .

But the Westerner who is attracted by Zen and who would understand it deeply must have one indispensable qualification: he must understand his own culture so thoroughly that he is no longer swayed by its premises unconsciously. He must really have come to terms with the Lord God Jehovah and with his Hebrew-Christian conscience so that he can take it or leave it without fear or rebellion. He must be free of the itch to justify himself. Lacking this, his Zen will be either "beat" or "square," either a revolt from the culture and social order or a new form of stuffiness and respectability. For Zen is above all the Liberation of the mind from conventional thought, and this is something utterly different from rebellion against convention, on the one hand, or adopting foreign conventions, on the other.

Conventional thought is, in brief, the confusion of the concrete universe of nature with the conceptual things, events, and values of linguistic and cultural symbolism. For in Taoism and Zen the world is seen as an inseparably interrelated field or continuum, no part of which can actually be separated from the rest or valued above or below the rest. It was in this sense that Hui-neng, the Sixth Patriarch, meant that "fundamentally not one thing exists," for he realized that things are terms, not entities. They exist in the abstract world of thought, but not in the con-

crete world of nature. Thus one who actually perceives or feels this to be so no longer feels that he is an ego, except by definition. He sees that his ego is his persona or social role, a somewhat arbitrary selection of experiences with which he has been taught to identify himself. (Why, for example, do we say "I think" but not "I am beating my heart"?) Having seen this, he continues to play his social role without being taken by it. He does not precipitately adopt a new role or play the role of having no role at all. He plays it cool.

The "beat" mentality as I am thinking of it is something much more extensive and vague that the hipster life of New York and San Francisco. It is a younger generation's nonparticipation in "the American Way of Life," a revolt which does not seek to change the existing order but simply turns away from it to find the significance of life in subjective experience rather then [sic] objective achievement. It contrasts with the "square" and other-directed mentality of beguilement by social convention, unaware of the correlativity of right and wrong, the mutual necessity of capitalism and communism to each other's existence, of the inner identity of Puritanism and lechery, or of, say, the alliance of church lobbies and organized crime to maintain the laws against gambling.

Beat Zen is a complex phenomenon. It ranges from a use of Zen for justifying sheer caprice in art, literature, and life to a very forceful social criticism and "digging of the universe" such as one may find in the poetry of Ginsberg and Snyder, and, rather unevenly, in Kerouac. But, as I know it, it is always a share too self-conscious, too subjective, and too strident to have the flavor of Zen. It is all very well for the philosopher, but when the poet (Ginsberg) says—

    live
in the physical world
  moment to moment
I must write down
      every recurring thought—
  stop every beating second

this is too indirect and didactic for Zen, which would rather hand you the thing itself without comment.

The sea darkens;
  The voices of the wild ducks
    Are faintly white. . . .

Foreign relations can be immensely attractive and highly overrated by those who know little of their own, and especially by those who have not worked through and grown out of their own. This is why the displaced or unconscious Christian can so easily use either beat or square Zen to justify himself. The one wants a philosophy to justify him in doing what he pleases. The other wants a more plausible authoratative [sic] salvation than the Church or the psychiatrists seem to be able to provide. Furthermore the atmosphere of Japanese Zen is free from all one's unpleasant childhood associations with God the Father and Jesus Christ—though I know many young Japanese who feel the same way about their early training in Buddhism. But the true character of Zen remains almost incomprehensible to those who have not surpassed the immaturity of needing to be justified, whether before the Lord God or before a paternalistic society.

The old Chinese Zen masters were steeped in Taoism. They saw nature in its total interrelatedness, and saw that every creature and every experience is in accord with the Tao of nature just as it is. This enabled them to accept themselves as they were, moment by moment, without the least need to justify anything. They didn't do it to defend themselves or to find an excuse for getting away with murder. They didn't brag about it and set themselves apart as rather special. On the contrary, their Zen was wu-shih, which means approximately "nothing special" or "no fuss." But Zen is "fuss" when it is mixed up with Bohemian affectations, and "fuss" when it is imagined that the only proper way to find it is to run off to a monastery in Japan or to do special exercises in the lotus posture five hours a day. And I will admit that the very hullabaloo about Zen, even in such an article as this, is also fuss—but a little less so.

Having said that, I would like to say something for all Zen fussers, beat or square. Fuss is all right, too. If you are hung on Zen, there's no need to try to pretend that you are not. If you really want to spend some years in a Japanese monastery, there is no earthly reason why you shouldn't. Or if you want to spend your time hopping freight cars and digging Charlie Parker, it's a free country.

Further Resources

BOOKS
Watts, Alan W. *The Essential Alan Watts.* Berkeley, Calif.: Celestial Arts, 1977.

———. *The Spirit of Zen.* New York: Grove, 1958.

———. *The Way of Zen.* New York: Pantheon, 1968.

PERIODICALS
Abels, Janet. "How Zen Found Me." (review) *Cross Currents,* Spring–Summer 2000, 7.

"Beginner's Guide to Zen Buddhism." (review) *Publishers Weekly,* January 31, 2000, 100.

Brown, Anna. "The Gifts of Zen Buddhism: An Interview With Robert E. Kennedy." *America,* October 14, 2000, 15.

WEBSITES
Alan Watts.net, "Who Was Alan Watts?" Available online at http://www.alanwatts.net/watts.htm; website home page: http://www.alanwatts.net (accessed February 10, 2003). This site indexes print and sound resources for Alan Watts.

Ciolek, T. Matthew, ed. "Zen Buddhism WWW Virtual Library." Available online at http://www.ciolek.com/WWWVL-Zen.html (accessed February 10, 2003). This site contains links to numerous works about Zen Buddhism.

Zen Guide: The Online Guide to Zen and Buddhism. Website home page. Available online at http://www.zenguide.com/ (accessed February 10, 2003).

"Unity and Diversity in Islam"
Essay

By: Mohammad Rasjidi
Date: 1958
Source: Rasjidi, Mohammad. "Unity and Diversity in Islam." In *Islam: The Straight Path: Islam Interpreted by Muslims,* Kenneth W. Morgan, ed. New York: Ronald Press, 1958. Available online at http://www.religion-online.org/cgi-bin/relsearchd.dll/showchapter?chapter_id=1647 (accessed February 11, 2003).
About the Author: Mohammad Rasjidi, the ambassador to Pakistan from the Republic of Indonesia during the 1950s, was one of the contributors to *Islam: The Straight Path: Islam Interpreted by Muslims.* ∎

Introduction

By the 1950s, a relatively small number of Muslims had immigrated to or been born in the United States. For most Americans who had never met a Muslim or knew little about the faith, Islam was a religion practiced in other parts of the world. But a demographic change was occurring: the Muslim population in the United States was slowly beginning to grow. Because of this trend, Kenneth W. Morgan believed that it was important for non-Muslim Americans to learn more about their Muslim neighbors both at home and around the world. Thus, *Islam: The Straight Path: Islam Interpreted by Muslims* was conceived.

Islam: The Straight Path consists of articles written by Muslims who were experts in their own religion. Taken together, the articles serve as a handy reference to Islam, discussing such topics as the origins of Islam, Muhammad, ideas and movements in Islamic history, beliefs and codes of law, and rational and mystical interpretations of Islam. In addition, Morgan included articles

Elijah Muhammad greets a convert to Islam. Elijah (Poole) Muhammad led a movement known as the Black Muslims, preaching black pride, black separation, and promoting Islam as the religion of African Americans. During the mid-1950s, the Black Muslims began to grow phenomenally under Muhammad's leadership. © HULTON-DEUTSCH COLLECTION/CORBIS. REPRODUCED BY PERMISSION.

about Islamic culture in Arab and African countries, Turkey, Pakistan, India, China, and Indonesia.

According to Anayat Durrani in "Muslims in America," the history of Muslims in the United States can be traced to slavery. Approximately 10 percent of the slaves from Africa were Muslims, but most lost their religious beliefs and cultural attachments with Islam. Durrani also notes that a large number of Arab Muslims from Syria, Lebanon, and Jordan settled in the United States during the nineteenth century. Several hundred thousand eastern European Muslims immigrated to the United States in the early twentieth century. Early mosques were constructed in Maine in 1915, Connecticut in 1919, and New York in 1926.

Significance

Before *Islam: The Straight Path*, little accurate information was available to interested non-Muslim Americans about this growing world religion. While some books written by Westerners who had studied Islam were available, there were few written by Muslims. In the light of the early twenty-first-century tensions between the

Western and Muslim worlds, more non-Muslim Americans than ever before have become interested in furthering their knowledge about the nature and history of Islam. *Islam: The Straight Path* remains a good starting point.

Islam has continued to grow in the United States. As of 2002, there were an estimated two thousand mosques, Islamic centers, and Islamic schools throughout the United States. The U.S. Muslim population is estimated at about six million. According to a study conducted by Fareed H. Numan, the largest percentage of Muslims in the United States—almost half—are African American. The second largest percentage is made up of people from Asia, including Pakistan, India, Bangladesh, Sri Lanka, and Afghanistan. The third largest group are of Arab descent, including nations in the Middle East and North Africa.

Primary Source

"Unity and Diversity in Islam" [excerpt]

> **SYNOPSIS:** This article by Mohammad Rasjidi, the ambassador to Pakistan from the Republic of Indonesia, was included as Chapter 11 of Morgan's *Islam: The Straight Path*. The following excerpts examine the sources of Islam: the Qur'an, the Sunnah and its codification in the Traditions, and human reasoning.

No one can claim to speak with final authority concerning the diversity found among the more than five hundred million Muslims [Note: in 2002, there are over one billion Muslims] who seek to follow the straight path of Islam. One can only record some observations concerning the variations in practices among the Muslims from Morocco and the Balkans to China and Indonesia. It is possible, however, to be much more explicit about the basic unity of Islam, for throughout the Muslim world there is general agreement concerning the sources of Islam, the fundamentals of the faith, and the particular requirements which are the obligations of all believers.

The Sources of Islam

There is general agreement that the sources of Islam are the Qur'an, the Sunnah, and reasoning about them. Of these, the primary source is the Qur'an. Concerning matters not explicitly clear in the Qur'an, the Sunnah is the secondary, supplementary source; and when the answer to questions needs further clarification the third source for Muslims is reasoning about the intent of the Qur'an and Sunnah by those men who are recognized as having the training and experience which qualifies them to reason properly.

The miraculous revelation of the Qur'an has been fully discussed in earlier chapters of this book. It is the final revelation, the Word of God given through His Prophet as a guide to all men everywhere, regardless of race, or color, or nationality. Within two years of the death of the Prophet it was compiled in book form and has been the primary source of Islam for almost fourteen centuries, without question and without variant versions. Since it was revealed in Arabic it has necessitated knowledge of Arabic, and this has been a unifying cultural factor throughout the Muslim world. It was recognized, however, that the people in the various countries often read the Qur'an in Arabic without understanding its meaning. The uneducated people even thought that it was sufficient to pronounce the words correctly, and that such repetition—even without understanding the meaning—would bring them blessings from God and save their souls. Some even used verses of the Qur'an as amulets against dangers and diseases! Half a century ago the orthodox Muslims believed that it was forbidden to translate the Qur'an, fearing that translations would supplant the original Arabic version and that versions in different languages would cause disagreements and misinterpretations of the revelation of God. While it is true that because of its very high literary style it is difficult, if not impossible, to translate the Qur'an into any other language without losing the beauty and vigor of the original, translations in the languages of the people are necessary in order that they may understand the meaning of this book which is the source of Islam. Today the Qur'an is available in translation in most of the languages of the world.

Sometimes people ask why the Qur'an was revealed in Arabic if it is intended to be the Holy Book for all human beings. This question cannot be answered definitely, for if the Qur'an had been revealed in any other language—for example, in English—the question would still remain as to why that one language was chosen. Thus we have to content ourselves with the fact that, regardless of any possible reasons, the Qur'an was revealed in Arabic.

The second source for Islam is the Sunnah. During Muhammad's lifetime, Muslims could ask him to guide them in solving any problem when they did not find a clear answer in the Qur'an. For instance, once a man asked him if it would be proper to perform a pilgrimage on behalf of his deceased mother. The Prophet replied that it would be proper since such an act could be compared to a debt which she owed and the son was obligated to pay. When the

After delivering a speech to dedicate the Islamic Center in Washington, D.C., on June 28, 1957, President and Mrs. Eisenhower view the architectural detail in the mosque. AP/WIDE WORLD PHOTOS. REPRODUCED BY PERMISSION.

Prophet was dying, and knew that he would not be present to give such advice, he told the people that they would not go astray so long as they held to the two guides he was leaving for them—the Qur'an, the Book of God, and the example of his own way of life, the Sunnah. The Qur'an, in Surah XXXIII, verse 21, establishes the Sunnah as the second source of Islam:

> There is a good example in the Apostle of Allah for those who wish to meet God and the Day of Judgment, and to remember God much.

The Sunnah is made up of the deeds, speech, and approbation of the Prophet. His deeds include the way he prayed, or washed his hands, or took a bath, and the like. His words have been preserved for us, as for example when he said, "I am sent to perfect high morality." By approbation is meant that when Muhammad saw something done, or heard words uttered in his presence and did not object, such actions or words are approved. Approbation was applied chiefly to customs of the Arab society which were not in contradiction to the spirit of Islam. For example, when Muhammad saw a man dancing with a sword he smiled and showed his pleasure, so later jurists concluded that dancing with the sword is permitted. Such approval has been applied to customary practices and laws in all Islamic countries where such customs do not contradict the spirit of Islamic laws—for example, in the marriage ceremonies.

The codification of the Sunnah, the Traditions, began a century and a half after the Prophet when Malik Ibn Anas wrote a compilation of the Traditions concerning Islamic laws. The compilation of the Traditions took final form at the hands of Bukhari and Muslim in the third century (ninth century A.D.), and today most Muslims recognize their work as the two correct books on Traditions. Those two compilers established conditions for determining which Traditions would be accepted as authentic, conditions which related only to the persons who narrated the Traditions. Such persons must be of good moral character, pious, honest, of sound discretion, and blessed with a good memory; and the series of such transmitters must be continuous from generation to generation. The first generation was called the Companions, the second was known as the followers, and the third as the followers of the followers. Thus a tradition narrated by the followers only would not be accepted by Bukhari because there would be a gap of a generation from the time of the Prophet.

It must be explained, however, that those conditions for the correctness of a Tradition did not touch the subject matter, for internal criticism was unknown at the time. Consequently we find in the two compilations some Traditions, such as those about the signs of the approaching of the Day of Judgment, which we do not understand even yet. The lapse of two and a half centuries between the death of the Prophet and the compilation of the Sunnah has resulted in many differences between Muslims which continue in our time. In the civil war and struggle for power in the time of Uthman, the third Caliph, irreligious elements among the Muslim people did not refrain from fabricating traditions concerning the merits of some political figures. Accurate judgments concerning the narrators of Traditions became difficult because the political feuds sometimes made the judgments far from objective. A knowledge of the way in which the Traditions were compiled and transmitted facilitates an understanding of the various attitudes toward the Traditions which are found in Muslim countries today.

The Qur'an, which was revealed almost fourteen centuries ago, and the Traditions concerning the Prophet who lived that long ago exclusively in a desert society cannot serve as explicit guides for every situation which might arise centuries later, and especially in the complex societies of the present day. This was recognized by the Prophet himself. Once when he was sending one of his Companions to Yemen to serve as governor, he tested the man by asking him what principles he would follow in his new position. He answered that he would hold to the teachings of the Qur'an. The Prophet asked, "And if you do not find a particular guide in the Qur'an?" He replied, "I shall look for it in the Sunnah." Then the Prophet asked, "Well, what if you do not find it in the Sunnah either?" He replied, "In such a case, I shall make use of my own opinion." The Prophet was very pleased with that answer and said, "Thanks to God who has guided the messenger of the Messenger of Allah."

Thus a third basis for Islam became established, the basis of reasoning. We find in the Qur'an many verses which mention reasoning, or thinking, or knowing—verses which exhort us to make use of our brains instead of following blindly the traditions which our ancestors followed. Concerning the Unbelievers of old, the Qur'an says, "Nay, for they say only: Lo we found our fathers following a religion, and we are guided by their footprints" (Surah XLIII, 22). While exhorting us to contemplate nature, the Qur'an says, "In the creation of skies and the earth, the difference between night and day, the ships which run at sea carrying that which is useful for mankind, the rain water which Allah sends down from the sky to revive the earth after its death, and to spread animals on it, and the arrangement of winds and clouds between sky and earth, in all those things there are evidences (for the existence of God) for those who make use of their brains" (Surah II, 164). There is even a verse which says that once upon a time the people of Hell said to one another, "If we had made use of our ears or our brains we would not have been the inhabitants of this Hell" (Surah LXVII, 10).

Originally the word used for reasoning, qiyas, meant measure, used in the sense of thinking by comparing one thing with another—reasoning by analogy. As the third source of Islamic law it means determining the proper course of action by reasoning from the Qur'an and the Sunnah. Some men, however, speak of a fourth source of the law of Islam—consensus of opinion, or the agreement of capable men in their judgment on a specific question. This concept was introduced by al Shafi'i, the founder of one of the schools of law. Some people have misunderstood consensus to mean simply public opinion, and have asserted that if public opinion approves an action it is therefore acceptable to Islam. For Muslim legislators, consensus is the agreement reached among qualified religious leaders in one place at one time. There has never been a means by which such agreement might be found for all Muslims everywhere. True consensus, ijma, was possible only during the time of the first two Caliphs and part of the rule of the third Caliph. Ijma now only means that some agreement has been found in some places concerning the interpretation of certain verses of the Qur'an. As a basic source for Islam, it is reasoning, not consensus which is the third source. The Qur'an, the Sunnah, and reasoning are the generally accepted sources of Islam.

There are, as has been seen, some exceptions to the position that these are the three sources of Islam, for some people hold that only the Qur'an and Sunnah can give us a solid foundation for Islam. Their attitude, however, is easily refuted for it must be admitted that the problems of the world today are very different from those of the time of Muhammad, and their attitude would make Islam a dead religion. Actually, Islam is a dynamic religion, based on the Qur'an, the Sunnah, and reasoning.

Some people confuse ijtihad with reasoning, but if used in the sense of a personal preference it is obviously not the same thing. In the sense of careful reasoning as to the implications of the Qur'an and the Sunnah, it is the same as reasoning. Unchecked, ijtihad might even lead to disagreement concerning such basic ideas as right and wrong, good and bad!

To understand the unity and diversity in Islam it is necessary to understand these three sources of Islamic law: the Qur'an, the Sunnah, and the proper use of reason.

Further Resources

BOOKS

Azmah, Aziz. *Islams and Modernities.* London and New York: Verso, 1993.

Morgan, Kenneth W. *Asian Religions: An Introduction to the Study of Hinduism, Buddhism, Islam, Confucianism, and Taoism.* New York: Macmillan, 1964.

Numan, Fareed H. *The Muslim Population in the United States: A Brief Statement.* Washington, D.C.: American Muslim Council, 1992.

PERIODICALS

"Christians and Muslims." *Christian History,* May 2002, 46.

"Islam: The Basics." *New Internationalist,* May 2002, 14.

WEBSITES

Ahlul Bayt Digital Islamic Library Project. Website home page. Available online at http://www.al-islam.org/ (accessed February 11, 2003).

Durrani, Anayat. "Muslims in America," June 18, 1999. Available online at http://www.suite101.com/article.cfm/3571/21147 (accessed February 11, 2003).

Ibrahim, I.A. "A Brief Illustrated Guide to Understanding Islam." Avaliable online at http://www.islam-guide.com/ (accessed February 11, 2003).

Ad Petri Cathedram (On Truth, Unity, and Peace)

Papal encyclical

By: Pope John XXIII

Date: June 29, 1959

Source: Papal Encyclicals Online. *Ad Petri Cathedram* Encyclical of Pope John XXIII "On Truth, Unity and Peace, in a Spirit of Charity." Available online at http://www.geocities.com/papalencyclicals/John23/j23petri.htm (accessed February 10, 2003).

About the Author: Pope John XXIII (1881–1963) was born in Sotto il Monte, Italy, as Angelo Giuseppe Roncalli. Ordained a priest in 1904, he was a chaplain during World War I. In 1925, he became an archbishop and served as an apostolic delegate to Bulgaria, Turkey, and Greece. In 1953, he was appointed patriarch of Venice. In 1958, he was elected pope and served to 1963. He summoned the Second Vatican Council to update the church and promote ecumenism. ∎

Introduction

The background of "On Truth, Unity, and Peace" can be found in the moral, religious, and social conditions of the 1950s. Some Catholic leaders noted, first, that mass communication in the forms of television shows, radio broadcasts, and motion pictures had led some people, especially the young, to lose their sense of moral reasoning and to ignore God's truths. Many faithful were also beginning to hold the belief that one religion was just as good as another. Church leaders, including the pope, found this view erroneous. The encyclical was the pope's attempt to recover these strayed souls and to bring them back to Christ.

The church hierarchy also wanted the pope to address the lack of Christian unity. Christianity had endured two major divisions in its almost two-thousand-year history. The first occurred about a thousand years ago when the churches in the East and West split, resulting in the establishment of the Orthodox Church in the East and the Roman Catholic Church in the West. Then in the sixteenth century, the Protestant Reformation in western Europe led to another split from the Roman Catholic Church. Christianity had remained divided ever since those landmark events.

A third immediate problem was the constant threat to peace. Humanity had suffered tremendous losses during World War II, but it still had not learned to accept the brotherhood of Christ and work toward peace. The threat of nuclear confrontation between the superpowers seemed to be unending.

Significance

"On Truth, Unity, and Peace" was met with enthusiasm by some and skepticism by others. Some believed that the pope's words would inspire confidence in the future of humanity. Others believed that not much would change or could be changed. The modification of moral values was a process very difficult to halt. The divisions in Christianity were too long-standing to heal. The cold war seemed to be a fact of modern-day life. Despite such skepticism, the pope's personal charisma inspired hope and enchanted even the roughest skeptics.

Primary Source

Ad Petri Cathedram (On Truth, Unity, and Peace) [excerpt]

> **SYNOPSIS:** On January 25, 1959, Pope John XXIII announced his intention of calling an ecumenical council to consider measures for renewal of the church in the modern world. Almost six months later, he issued "On Truth, Unity and Peace." The encyclical was issued about two years before the opening of the Second Vatican Council in 1962. The following are sections 9 through 35 from the encyclical's 149 sections.

Truth and Error

9. It is clear that We are discussing a serious matter, with which our eternal salvation is very intimately connected. Some men, as the Apostle of the Gentiles warns us, are "ever learning yet never attaining knowledge of the truth." They contend that the human mind can discover no truth that is certain or sure; they reject the truths revealed by God and necessary for our eternal salvation.

10. Such men have strayed pathetically far from the teaching of Christ and the views expressed by the Apostle when he said, "Let us all attain to the unity of the faith and of the deep knowledge of the son of God . . . that we may no longer be children, tossed to and fro and carried about by every wind

of doctrine devised in the wickedness of men, in craftiness, according to the wiles of error. Rather are we to practice the truth in love, and grow up in all things in him who is the head, Christ. For from him the whole body (being closely joined and knit together through every joint of the system according to the functioning in due measure of each single part) derives its increase to the building up of itself in love."

11. Anyone who consciously and wantonly attacks known truth, who arms himself with falsehood in his speech, his writings, or his conduct in order to attract and win over less learned men and to shape the inexperienced and impressionable minds of the young to his own way of thinking, takes advantage of the inexperience and innocence of others and engages in an altogether despicable business.

The Duties of the Press

12. In this connection we must urge to careful, exact, and prudent presentation of the truth those especially who, through the books, magazines, and daily newspapers which are so abundant today, have such a great effect on the instruction and development of the minds of men, and especially of the young, and play such a large part in forming their opinions and shaping their characters. These people have a serious duty to disseminate, not lies, error, and obscenity, but only the truth; they are particularly bound to publicize what is conducive to good and virtuous conduct, not to vice.

13. For we see with deep sorrow what Our predecessor of immortal memory, Leo XIII, lamented: "Lies are boldly insinuated . . . into weighty tomes and slender volumes, into the transient pages of periodicals and the extravagant advertisements of the theater." We see "books and magazines written to mock virtue and exalt depravity."

Modem Media of Communication

14. And in this day of ours, as you well know, Venerable Brethren and beloved sons, we also have radio broadcasts, motion pictures, and television (which can enter easily into the home). All of these can provide inspiration and incentive for morality and goodness, even Christian virtue. Unfortunately, however, they can also entice men, especially the young, to loose morality and ignoble behavior, to treacherous error and perilous vice.

15. The weapons of truth, then, must be used in defense against these weapons of evil. We must strive zealously and relentlessly to ward off the im-

pact of this great evil which every day insinuates itself more deeply.

16. We must fight immoral and false literature with literature that is wholesome and sincere. Radio broadcasts, motion pictures, and television shows which make error and vice attractive must be opposed by shows which defend truth and strive to preserve the integrity and safety of morals. Thus these new arts, which can work much evil, will be turned to the well-being and benefit of men, and at the same time will supply worthwhile recreation. Health will come from a source which has often produced only devastating sickness.

Indifference to Truth

17. Some men, indeed do not attack the truth willfully, but work in heedless disregard of it. They act as though God had given us intellects for some purpose other than the pursuit and attainment of truth. This mistaken sort of action leads directly to that absurd proposition: one religion is just as good as another, for there is no distinction here between truth and falsehood. "This attitude," to quote Pope Leo again, "is directed to the destruction of all religions, but particularly the Catholic faith, which cannot be placed on a level with other religions without serious injustice, since it alone is true." Moreover, to contend that there is nothing to choose between contradictories and among contraries can lead only to this fatal conclusion: a reluctance to accept any religion either in theory or practice.

18. How can God, who is truth, approve or tolerate the indifference, neglect, and sloth of those who attach no importance to matters on which our eternal salvation depends; who attach no importance to pursuit and attainment of necessary truths, or to the offering of that proper worship which is owed to God alone?

19. So much toil and effort is expended today in mastering and advancing human knowledge that our age glories—and rightly—in the amazing progress it has made in the field of scientific research. But why do we not devote as much energy, ingenuity, and enthusiasm to the sure and safe attainment of that learning which concerns not this earthly, mortal life but the life which lies ahead of us in heaven? Our spirit will rest in peace and joy only when we have reached that truth which is taught in the gospels and which should be reduced to action in our lives. This is a joy which surpasses by far any pleasure which can come from the study of things human or from

Soon after Pope John XXIII announced his intention to call an ecumenical council to address the renewal of the Church in the modern world, he issued *Ad Petri Cathedram*, an encyclical on truth, unity, and peace. AP/WIDE WORLD PHOTOS. REPRODUCED BY PERMISSION.

those marvelous inventions which we use today and are constantly praising to the skies.

II

20. Once we have attained the truth in its fullness, integrity, and purity, unity should pervade our minds, hearts, and actions. For there is only one cause of discord, disagreement, and dissension: ignorance of the truth, or what is worse, rejection of the truth once it has been sought and found. It may be that the truth is rejected because of the practical advantages which are expected to result from false views; it may be that it is rejected as a result of that perverted blindness which seeks easy and indulgent excuses for vice and immoral behavior.

Truth, Peace, Prosperity

21. All men, therefore, private citizens as well as government officials, must love the truth sincerely if they are to attain that peace and harmony on which depends all real prosperity, public and private.

22. We especially urge to peace and unity those who hold the reins of government. We who are placed above international controversy have the same affection for the people of all nations. We are led by no earthly advantages, no motives of political dominance, no desires for the things of this life. When we speak of this serious matter Our thoughts can be given a fair hearing and judged impartially by the citizens of every nation.

The Brotherhood of Man

23. God created men as brothers, not foes. He gave them the earth to be cultivated by their toil and labor. Each and every man is to enjoy the fruits of the earth and receive from it his sustenance and the necessities of life. The various nations are simply communities of men, that is, of brothers. They are to work in brotherly cooperation for the common prosperity of human society, not simply for their own particular goals.

A Journey to Immortal Life

24. Besides this, our journey through this mortal life should not be regarded as an end in itself, entered upon merely for pleasure. This journey leads beyond the burial of our human flesh to immortal life, to a fatherland which will endure forever.

25. If this teaching, this consoling hope, were taken away from men, there would be no reason for living. Lusts, dissensions, and disputes would erupt from within us. There would be no reasonable check to restrain them. The olive branch of peace would not shine in our thoughts; the firebrands of war would blaze there. Our lot would be cast with beasts, who do not have the use of reason. Ours would be an even worse lot, for we do have the use of reason and by abusing it (which, unfortunately, often happens) we can sink into a state lower than that of beasts. Like Cain, we would commit a terrible crime and stain the earth with our brother's blood.

26. Before all else, then, we must turn our thoughts to sound principles if we wish, as we should, to guide our actions along the path of justice.

27. We are called brothers. We actually are brothers. We share a common destiny in this life and the next. Why, then, do we act as though we are foes and enemies? Why do we envy one another? Why do we stir up hatred? Why do we ready lethal weapons for use against our brothers?

28. There has already been enough warfare among men! Too many youths in the flower of life have shed their blood already! Legions of the dead, all fallen in battle, dwell within this earth of ours. Their stern voices urge us all to return at once to harmony, unity, and a just peace.

29. All men, then, should turn their attention away from those things that divide and separate us, and should consider how they may be joined in mutual and just regard for one another's opinions and possessions.

Unity Among Nations

30. Only if we desire peace, as we should, instead of war, and only if we all aspire sincerely to fraternal harmony among nations, shall it come to pass that public affairs and public questions are correctly understood and settled to the satisfaction of all. Then shall international conferences seek and reach decisions conducive to the longed-for unity of the whole human family. In the enjoyment of that unity, individual nations will see that their right to liberty is not subject to another's whims but is fully secure.

31. Those who oppress others and strip them of their due liberty can contribute nothing to the attainment of this unity.

32. The mind of Our predecessor, Leo XIII, squares perfectly with this view: "Nothing is better suited than Christian virtue, and especially justice, to check ambition, covetousness, and envy which are the chief causes of war."

33. But if men do not pursue this fraternal unity, based on the precepts of justice and nurtured by charity, then human affairs will remain in serious peril. This is why wise men grieve and lament; they are uncertain whether we are heading for sincere, true, and firm peace, or are rushing in complete blindness into the fires of a new and terrible war.

34. We say "in complete blindness," for if—God forbid!—another war should break out, nothing but devastating destruction and total ruin await both victor and vanquished. The monstrous weapons our age has devised will see to that!

35. We ask all men, but particularly rulers of nations, to weigh these considerations prudently and seriously in the presence of God our protector. May they enter with a will upon those paths which will lead to the unity that is so badly needed. This harmonious unity will be restored when hearts are at peace, when the rights of all are guaranteed, and

when there has dawned that liberty due everywhere to individual citizens, to the state, and to the Church.

Further Resources

BOOKS

Hebblethwaite, Peter. *Pope John XXIII, Shepherd of the Modern World.* Garden City, N.Y.: Doubleday, 1985.

John XXIII, Pope. *Journal of a Soul.* Garden City, N.Y.: Image Books, 1980.

Johnson, Paul. *Pope John XXIII.* Boston: Little, Brown, 1974.

PERIODICALS

Komonchak, Joseph A. "Remembering Good Pope John: He Always Tried To Be a Saint. And He Made It." *Commonweal,* August 11, 2000, 11.

McBrien, Richard P. "Peasant Profundis." *America,* April 8, 2002, 23.

Ruddy, Christopher. "Rediscovering Roncalli." Review of *The Autobiography of Pope John XXIII,* by Pope John XXIII. *Commonweal,* March 10, 2000, 28.

WEBSITES

O'Grady, Desmond. "Almost a Saint: Pope John XXIII." *St. Anthony Messenger.* Available online at http://www.americancatholic.org/Messenger/Nov1996/feature1.asp; website home page: http://www.americancatholic.org/default.asp (accessed February 2, 2003).

Randall, Beth. "Illuminating Lives: Pope John XXIII." Available online at http://www.mcs.drexel.edu/~gbrandal/Illum_html/JohnXXIII.html (accessed February 2, 2003).

11

SCIENCE AND TECHNOLOGY

CHRISTOPHER CUMO

Entries are arranged in chronological order by date of primary source. For entries with one primary source, the entry title is the same as the primary source title. Entries with more than one primary source have an overall entry title, followed by the titles of the primary sources.

Important Events in Science and Technology, 1950–1959

1950

- Commercial color transmission of CBS television "Colorcast," starring Ed Sullivan and Arthur Godfrey.

- The Sulzer weaving machine begins modern commercial production of cloth using an automatic loom.

- In January, inventor George Eastman develops a method to use regular movie cameras to produce color movies. Before this, only Technicolor cameras produced color movies.

- On March 29, RCA demonstrates the first electronic color television tube.

- In November, dairy scientists implant an embryo in the uterus of a cow at the University of Wisconsin.

1951

- The first 3-D movies are produced.

- The first transcontinental television transmission is broadcast from the United States.

- In February, American mathematician Dirk Brouwer uses a computer to predict the orbits of the nine planets in our solar system.

- In February, Du Pont produces Orlon, a synthetic acrylic fiber that can be spun into yarn and knitted. Despite its synthetic origin it feels soft to the touch.

- In April, the Remington Rand Corporation sells the first commercial computer, the UNIVAC I (Universal Automatic Computer).

- In June, the nuclear testing station at Arco, Idaho, produces electricity from nuclear power using molten metal to produce steam, which spins a turbine to generate electricity.

- In October, Chrysler introduces the first production-model car with power steering.

1952

- Former American soldier George Jorgensen undergoes the first sex change operation—and becomes Christine after surgery.

- In August, scientists at the Nebraska Agricultural Experiment Station demonstrated that semen can be frozen without loss of potency, when they thawed frozen bull semen and used it to fertilize an egg and produce a calf.

- In October, Raytheon uses the transistor, produced by Bell Laboratories, to produce a hearing aid.

- On November 1, American physicist Edward Teller leads a team of physicists, mathematicians and engineers in detonating the first hydrogen bomb.

1953

- Indiana University professor Alfred C. Kinsey, an entomologist (a scientist who studies insects) by training, publishes *Sexual Behavior in the Human Female.* Critics profess shock, though the book, a compilation of the frequency and types of sex acts, uses a clinical language that is detached rather than titillating.

- American mathematician Norbert Weiner introduces the new field of "cybernetics," the study of control and communication in animals and machines.

- A Pratt-Whitney J57 engine fitted onto an F-100 propels the plane to a speed of Mach 1.3, or 850 miles per hour (1.3 times the speed of sound).

- Graham and Wydner use tars from cigarette smoke to produce cancers in mice.

- The aerosol valve to deliver liquid by spray is invented.

- On April 25, American chemist James Watson and his British colleague Francis Crick publish the structure of deoxyribonucleic acid (DNA).

- On May 15, University of Chicago chemist Stanley Lloyd Miller simulates Earth's primitive atmosphere, demonstrating the spontaneous formation of amino acids, the building blocks of life. Many scientists accept Miller's finding as evidence that primitive Earth provided the conditions for life's emergence.

- In June, American physicist Charles H. Towns develops the Maser, an acronym for Microwave Amplification by Stimulated Emission of Radiation. The Maser concentrates microwaves, a type of light invisible to humans, to bore through solids.

1954

- Texas Instruments produces transistor chips made out of silicon instead of the rare germanium.

- The commercial transistor radio, the Regency, enters the U.S. market.

- In January, the American geneticists J. H. Tijo and A. Levan determine that each cell in a human has forty-six human chromosomes, not forty-eight as previously thought.

- In March, the U.S. Navy launches *Nautilus,* the first nuclear-powered submarine.

- In May, the U.S. Department of Agriculture and the South Dakota Agricultural Experiment Station plant on a test plot at the experiment station the first hybrid wheat, which tolerates drought and is more resistant to disease than traditional varieties.

- In July, Odeco, Inc., uses the first mobile, submersible oil-drilling unit for offshore drilling in the Gulf of Mexico.

- In December, Bell Laboratories develops the photovoltaic cell, which converts sunlight into electricity.

1955

• Multiple-track recording, in which songs are recorded with voice on one track, music on another, is introduced, leading to the commercialization of stereophonic sound equipment and records.

• A home freezer able to maintain a temperature of −27°F is introduced.

• Radio astronomers Joseph Franklin and Robert Burke detect naturally occurring radio emissions from the planet Jupiter; radio astronomy is improved by development of the interferometer that lets radio telescopes resolve different radio sources accurately.

• Homological algebra, combining abstract algebra and algebraic topology, produces a uniform type of mathematics.

• On January 9, the U.S. Atomic Energy Commission invites private companies to submit proposals for construction of nuclear power plants.

• On April 18, Albert Einstein dies in Princeton, New Jersey. His study reveals a series of equations that Einstein had hoped to unite into the Unified Field Theory.

• In June, biologists Rosalyn Yalow and Solomon Berson develop a sensitive hormone measuring method called Radio Immuno Assay, or RIA, to detect even small traces of a hormone.

• In October, the Field-Ion microscope, the first microscope that can (indirectly) see individual atoms, is developed.

• In October, a New York research firm produces a diamond by putting graphite under high pressure. This synthetic diamond retains the property of being the hardest substance in the world and is used for cutting in such applications as oil-drilling operations.

• In November, American physicist Emilio Segre produces antiprotons, the first antimatter.

1956

• Electrical engineer Alexander Poniatoff develops the "Ampex" system, which produces taped television shows of comparable quality to live shows. CBS first uses this system.

• Bruce Heezen and Maurice Ewing discover the Mid-Oceanic Ridge, a formation of mountains and rifts that circles the world under the oceans.

• FORTRAN, a computer-software language that was developed for scientists and mathematicians, and LISP, the computer language of artificial intelligence, are introduced.

• In February, Harvard University physician Gregory Pincus begins to test Enovid, a birth-control pill, on fifteen thousand women volunteers in Puerto Rico and Haiti.

• In March, Bell Labs produces a transistor computer, "The Leprechaun."

• In July, the B-58 Hustler, an airplane of fiberglass, aluminum, and stainless steel reaches Mach 2, twice the speed of sound.

• In August, the Burroughs Company produces the E-101 desk-size computer for scientists and mathematicians; it has the capabilities of a computer and of an adding machine.

• In August, civil engineers begin building the U.S. interstate highway system Congress had funded earlier that year.

• On September 25, the transatlantic telephone cable from the United States to Europe begins operations.

• In November, American physician Arthur Kornberg synthesizes DNA by using an enzyme to guide the sequence in which nucleotide bases (the large-carbon based molecules that are the building blocks of DNA) bond together. On December 11, 1959, Kornberg will receive the Nobel Prize in physiology and medicine for this work.

• On December 11, Bell Laboratory physicists William B. Shockley, John Bardeen, and Walter H. Brattain share the Nobel Prize in physics for their invention of the transistor.

1957

• Doppler navigation, a device for accurately determining aircraft position and airspeed, makes civil aviation safer.

• The "Airotor," a high-speed dental drill, is introduced; the small cutting blade is rotated by compressed air at a rate of 350,000 revolutions per minute and cooled by a water spray.

• Fifty-six countries participate in the International Geophysical Year, 1957–1958, sponsored by the International Council of Scientific Unions.

• In March, the Hoover Company develops a spin clothes dryer. The heating mechanism in these dryers uses either electricity or natural gas.

• In April, the first U.S. nuclear power generator begins producing electricity in Idaho.

• From April to June, an international team of physical anthropologists, including University of Chicago anthropologist F. Clark Howell, unearth the remains of eleven Neanderthal skeletons in Iraq, the largest Neanderthal find to date. The arrangement of the skeletons, with some in a fetal position, is evidence that Neanderthals (an early man whose relationship to *Homo sapiens* is unclear) were the first people to bury their dead.

• In December, the National Aeronautics and Space Administration develops an intercontinental ballistic missile (or ICBM), the Atlas, two months after the Soviet Union used a similar rocket to launch the first satellite, *Sputnik.*

• In December, the Shippingport, Pennsylvania, nuclear-power plant, a "pressurized water" reactor built by Westinghouse and run by Duquesne Power and Light for the Atomic Energy Commission, opens.

• In December, the Navy attempts to launch *Vanguard,* a satellite to rival the Soviet *Sputnik.* Instead the satellite blows up on the launchpad.

1958

• Bifocal contact lenses are developed.

• In January, the United States launches *Explorer I* from a Jupiter rocket at the Redstone Arsenal, a U.S. Army facility.

• In June, Pan American Airlines flies the first commercial transatlantic route.

- In July, the first U.S. artificial satellite orbits earth.

- In July, the *Explorer IV* satellite verifies that there is a radiation belt around earth. Astronomers name it the Van Allen Radiation Belt after its discoverer, James Van Allen.

- On July 16, Congress creates the National Aeronautics and Space Administration (NASA) to coordinate the U.S. space program.

- In August, the submarine *Nautilus* travels under the ice cap at the North Pole.

- In October, American astronomer Eugene Parker discovers that the Sun produces a stream of particles he calls the solar wind.

1959

- COBOL, a computer software language for business use, is introduced.

- Thermofax (3M) makes large copies from microfilm.

- In January, Bell Laboratories places transistors on a silicon-chip, the workhorse of the modern computer.

- In May, Sony markets the first black-and-white television using transistors in the United States.

- In July, the U.S. Weather Bureau develops the Temperature-Humidity Index.

- In August, President Dwight D. Eisenhower presides over the opening of the Saint Lawrence Seaway, which connects the Saint Lawrence River to the Great Lakes.

- On September 5, Mary Leakey, the wife of British anthropologist Louis S. B. Leakey, discovers the skull of an early man in the rift valley of east Africa. The Leakeys put the skull in its own genus, *Zinjanthropus*.

- In October, Xerox markets the first commercial copier.

- On December 12, Bell Laboratory physicist William Shockley shares the Nobel Prize in physics with two colleagues for the development of the transistor, an electrical device ubiquitous in computers.

The H Bomb

Essay

By: Albert Einstein

Date: 1950

Source: Einstein, Albert. Introduction to *The H Bomb*. New York: Didier, 1950, 13–15.

About the Author: Albert Einstein (1879–1955) was born in Ulm, Germany, and received a Ph.D. in physics from the University of Zurich. In 1905, he published papers on Brownian motion, the photoelectric effect, and the special theory of relativity. In 1916, he announced his general theory of relativity, whose confirmation in 1919 won him worldwide fame. He won the Nobel Prize in physics in 1921. He died in Princeton, New Jersey. ■

Introduction

Albert Einstein played a critical role in the development of the first atomic bomb. As early as 1939, he and a small group of American physicists perceived that Nazi Germany was attempting to build a uranium bomb. In consultation with other physicists, Einstein sent a letter that year to President Franklin D. Roosevelt, warning him of the German threat and asking his help in creating and funding an American project to build a uranium bomb.

Roosevelt responded cautiously, establishing a committee to explore the feasibility of building a uranium bomb and securing for it a $6,000 congressional appropriation. From this modest beginning emerged the Manhattan Project, the American program to build an atomic bomb. In July 1945, physicists and engineers tested a uranium bomb in the New Mexico desert. Then, in August, the United States dropped two atomic bombs on Japan—a uranium bomb on Hiroshima and a plutonium bomb on Nagasaki—effectively ending World War II.

After the war, the United States and the Soviet Union, allies against Nazi Germany, grew suspicious of each other's intentions. Joseph Stalin, the Soviet leader, determined that he needed an atomic bomb, and in 1949 the Soviets stunned Americans by testing one. The Soviet Union was now America's rival in the nuclear arms

race, leading American politicians, scientists, and the public to debate how the United States should respond to the Soviets.

Significance

President Harry S. Truman pledged to surpass the Soviets by building a hydrogen bomb, several orders of magnitude more destructive than either a uranium or plutonium bomb. Although Einstein had endorsed the building of the first atomic bombs, he broke ranks with Truman in 1950. He called Truman's belief that the United States could secure peace by staying a step ahead of the Soviets in the arms race "a disastrous illusion." Einstein believed that if the United States built a hydrogen bomb, its use would poison the atmosphere with radioactive fallout, extinguishing life on Earth.

Einstein's rejection of the hydrogen bomb was courageous but ineffective, and in 1952 the United States tested its first hydrogen bomb. As Einstein foresaw, the hydrogen bomb did not bring security. The following year the Soviet Union tested its first hydrogen bomb, further escalating the nuclear arms race. Each nation now had the power to cause massive destruction. Science, the source of so much good in human history, had fully demonstrated its capacity for destruction, and not even its most reasoned voice could halt the ensuing arms race.

Primary Source

The H Bomb [excerpt]

SYNOPSIS: In the introduction to *The H Bomb*, a collection of essays by various authors, Einstein condemns the belief that the United States can achieve peace by staying a step ahead of the Soviets in the arms race. Trying to do so, he says, would concentrate power in the military and police and create a society in which hysteria replaced rational discourse. Because the hydrogen bomb would give the United States the power to extinguish life on Earth, Einstein rejects its construction as folly.

The idea of achieving security through national armament is, at the present state of military technique, a disastrous illusion. On the part of the United States this illusion has been particularly fostered by the fact that this country succeeded first in producing an atomic bomb. The belief seemed to prevail that in the end it were possible to achieve decisive military superiority.

In this way, any potential opponent would be intimidated, and security, so ardently desired by all of us, would be brought to us and all of humanity. The maxim which we have been following during these

A cartoon by Art Wood reflects the fear of a world-wide nuclear war that developed after the Russians successfully tested an atomic weapon in 1949.
THE LIBRARY OF CONGRESS.

last five years has been, in short: security through superior military power whatever the cost.

This mechanistic, technical-military, psychological attitude had inevitable consequences. Every sin-gle act in foreign policy is governed exclusively by one viewpoint.

How do we have to act in order to achieve ut-most superiority over the opponent in case of war?

Establishing military bases at all possible strategically important points on the globe. Arming and economic strengthening of potential allies.

Within the country—concentration of tremendous financial power in the hands of the military, militarization of the youth, close supervision of the loyalty of the citizens, in particular, of the civil servants by a police force growing more conspicuous every day. Intimidation of people of independent political thinking. Indoctrination of the public by radio, press, school. Growing restriction of the range of public information under the pressure of military secrecy.

The armament race between the USA and the USSR, originally supposed to be a preventive measure, assumes hysterical character. On both sides, the means to mass destruction are perfected with feverish haste—behind the respective walls of secrecy. The H-bomb appears on the public horizon as a probably attainable goal. Its accelerated development has been solemnly proclaimed by the President.

If successful, radioactive poisoning of the atmosphere, and hence annihilation of any life on earth, has been brought within the range of technical possibilities. The ghostlike character of this development lies in its apparently compulsory trend. Every step appears as the unavoidable consequence of the preceding one. In the end there beckons more and more clearly general annihilation.

Is there any way out of this impasse created by man himself? All of us, and particularly those who are responsible for the attitudes of the U. S. and the USSR, should realize that we may have vanquished an external enemy, but have been incapable of getting rid of the mentality created by the war.

It is impossible to achieve peace as long as every single action is taken with a possible future conflict in view. The leading point of view of all political action should therefore be: What can we do to bring about a peaceful co-existence and even loyal cooperation of the nations?

The first problem is to do away with mutual fear and distrust. Solemn renunciation of violence (not only with respect to means of mass destruction) is undoubtedly necessary.

Such renunciation, however, can only be effective if at the same time a supra-national judicial and executive body is set up and empowered to decide questions of immediate concern to the security of the nations. Even a declaration of the nations to col-laborate loyally in the realization of such a "restricted world government" would considerably reduce the imminent danger of war.

In the last analysis, every kind of peaceful cooperation among men is primarily based on mutual trust and only secondly on institutions such as courts of justice and police. This holds for nations as well as for individuals. And the basis of trust is loyal give-and-take.

What about international control? Well, it may be of secondary use as a police measure. But it may be wise not to overestimate its importance. The time of Prohibition comes to mind and gives one pause.

Further Resources

BOOKS

Moss, Norman. *Men Who Play God: The Story of the Hydrogen Bomb.* Harmondsworth, U.K.: Penguin Books, 1972.

Powell, Cecil F. *The Hydrogen Bomb and the Future of Mankind.* London: London Co-Operative Society, 1955.

Rhodes, Richard. *Dark Sun: The Making of the Hydrogen Bomb.* New York: Simon & Schuster, 1995.

Shepley, James R. *The Hydrogen Bomb: The Men, the Menace, the Mechanism.* Westport, Conn.: Greenwood, 1954.

Teller, Edward. *Memoirs: A Twentieth-Century Journey in Science and Politics.* Cambridge, Mass.: Perseus, 2001.

York, Herbert F. *The Advisors: Oppenheimer, Teller, and the Superbomb.* Stanford, Calif.: Stanford University Press, 1976.

PERIODICALS

Flint, Jerry. "Hydrogen Bomb." *Forbes,* March 4, 2002, 100.

WEBSITES

"Developing the Hydrogen Bomb." Nuclearfiles.org. Available online at http://www.nuclearfiles.org/docs/h-bomb.html; website home page: http://www.nuclearfiles.org (accessed December 18, 2002).

"The 'George' Test." *Race for the Superbomb.* American Experience. PBS Online. Available online at http://www.pbs.org/wgbh/amex/bomb/peopleevents/pandeAMEX55.html; website home page: http://www.pbs.org/wgbh/amex (accessed December 18, 2002).

AUDIO AND VISUAL MEDIA

Race for the Superbomb. Directed by Thomas Ott. PBS Home Video, 1999, VHS.

"The Weapon of Choice." Part two of the thirteen-part PBS series *War and Peace in the Nuclear Age.* WGBH, 1988, VHS.

"Should America Build the H Bomb?"

Essay

By: Harold C. Urey

Date: 1950

Source: Urey, Harold C. "Should America Build the H Bomb?" In *The H Bomb*. New York: Didier, 1950, 130–133.

About the Author: Harold Clayton Urey (1893–1981) was born in Walkerton, Indiana, and received his Ph.D. in chemistry from the University of California, Berkeley, in 1923. His discovery of deuterium, a heavy isotope of hydrogen, won him the 1934 Nobel Prize in chemistry. He died in La Jolla, California. ∎

Introduction

The origins of the twentieth-century arms race lay in World War II (1939–1945), when both Germany and the United States worked to develop an atomic bomb. The United States and its allies defeated Germany before Adolf Hitler succeeded in building such a weapon. In July 1945 the United States successfully tested a uranium bomb. Then, in August, it ended the war with Japan by dropping a uranium bomb on Hiroshima and a plutonium bomb on Nagasaki.

These bombs did not bring peace. The Soviet Union, fearful of U.S. power and suspicious of its intentions, tested its first atomic bomb in 1949, initiating the arms race. President Harry S. Truman responded by pledging to build a hydrogen bomb several orders of magnitude more destructive than either the uranium or plutonium bomb. Yet not all scientists supported Truman. In 1950, Albert Einstein, perhaps the most influential dissenter, condemned Truman's belief that the United States could secure peace by staying a step ahead of the Soviets in the arms race.

Significance

Cold War theorists disagreed. They argued that the nation that falls behind in an arms race becomes vulnerable to attack from the stronger rival. At all costs, they felt, one must stay abreast of, and preferably ahead of, one's rival in order to protect national security.

This logic persuaded the majority of American scientists, including Harold Urey, who disagreed with Einstein. He feared that if the United States did not develop the hydrogen bomb, it would lose the arms race to the Soviets. A Soviet Union armed with a hydrogen bomb might be able to impose a communist form of government on the rest of the world. This threat persuaded Urey, though he anguished over the decision and admitted that he was "very unhappy to conclude that the hydrogen bomb should be developed and built." Like Einstein,

Urey understood that building the hydrogen bomb would not secure peace.

He was right. American physicists and engineers developed and tested the first hydrogen bomb in 1952. Only a year later, the Soviets duplicated this feat. Neither nation had found peace—only a heightened sense of anxiety.

Primary Source

"Should America Build the H Bomb?" [excerpt]

> **SYNOPSIS:** In this excerpt from his essay "Should America Build the H Bomb?" Harold Urey concludes that the United States must develop the hydrogen bomb. Otherwise, it will lose the arms race, and a Soviet Union armed with a hydrogen bomb will be emboldened to threaten America and its allies with annihilation. The fear of a future dictated by communism persuades Urey to accept the hydrogen bomb as a necessary evil.

The question before us is this: Should the hydrogen bomb be built? First of all, it has been publicly reported for several years that such bombs would have a capacity of the order of one thousand times the capacity of the atomic bomb which has been developed in the past. It has been reported that if a large enough number of such bombs were dropped off the Pacific Coast of the United States, the prevailing winds would carry the radioactivity over this country and would result in the extinction of all forms of life. I cannot vouch for the accuracy of this statement, but the effects of the radioactivity would certainly be far greater than those so dramatically exhibited at the Bikini Baker Day bomb test. It is unnecessary to emphasize the unpleasantness of such weapons. Many would wish that such weapon developments as these should prove physically impossible; but nature does not always behave in the way we desire. I believe we should assume that the bomb *can* be built.

The Alsop brothers say that the cost of the development of these bombs would be two to four billion dollars. This I doubt seriously. I am not connected with this project in any way, but it is difficult to see how the development itself should cost more than a hundred million dollars, exclusive of the cost of materials. It would, of course, involve a considerable scientific and engineering talent, which I would much prefer to see employed on peace-time developments.

But let us turn to the situation in the world today. We should not be complacent about the inability

This 1950s cartoon shows U.S. Army, Navy, and Air Force saluting a scientist carrying "Nuclear Research." It reflects the feeling at that time that America's safety depended on having technology, especially nuclear technology, superior to that of the Soviet Union. THE LIBRARY OF CONGRESS. CARTOON BY EDWIN MARCUS; REPRODUCED BY PERMISSION OF DONALD E. MARCUS.

of other countries to develop this weapon, as many people were in connection with the development of the ordinary atomic bomb. To be specific, let us assume that the USSR is developing this bomb; and suppose that she should perfect it first. Then it seems to me that there is nothing in the temperament of the present negotiations between East and West that would lead us to believe that the

rulers of the USSR would not reason approximately as follows:

"It is true that the bomb is exceedingly dangerous, and we would not wish to produce so much radioactivity in the world as to endanger ourselves and the people of Russia, but the explosion of a few of these bombs will win us the world. Therefore, we will build these bombs and issue ultimata to the Western countries, and the millenium of communism will be with us immediately. After this the universal government of the USSR will abolish all stocks of bombs, and no more will ever be made in the world."

This is a very good argument. In fact, I doubt if any bombs would need to be exploded. The atomic bomb is a very important weapon of war, but hardly decisive, as everyone has emphasized from the beginning. But I wonder if the hydrogen bomb would not be decisive, so that ultimata would be accepted and it would be unnecessary to deliver the bombs.

Confronted by this possibility, what should the United States do now? Judging from our past decisions, we have apparently decided to lose the armaments race. Suppose instead of deciding this, we decide we will build the hydrogen bomb. And suppose we get it first. What then? It is quite out of character for the democracies to behave as I have suggested that the USSR would behave. Would we wait until the USSR had it, too? In that event, how could we be sure that war would not result from some inflammable incident, or from a calculation that a minor disturbance in a delicate balance of power had brought one of the powers to a decisive advantage?

Suppose that two countries have the hydrogen bomb. Is it not believable that sooner or later an incident may occur which would precipitate the use of bombs? This is a question again which I cannot answer definitely. I would say, however, that the probability that a war will start is increased if two groups each believe that they can win that war. This is true regardless of weapons and their magnitude. An exact balance of power is very difficult to attain. This is what we know in physical science as a situation of unstable equilibrium; one like balancing an egg on its end. The slightest push topples the egg in one direction or another.

I have maintained, and many of my friends have maintained, the only constructive way to solve the present problem is by adopting the Atlantic Union Resolution now in the Senate and House of Representatives of the United States, which would instruct our government to work toward the creation of a Federal Union of the democratic countries. Only in this way will the Western democratic powers be able to maintain an overpowering political, commercial, military, and ideological strength. Only in this way can we have an enormous unbalance of power, so that perhaps one side does not attempt to start a war because it recognizes that it cannot win, and the other side does not need to start a war because it

knows that the weaker side will not dare to attack. If this organization were perfected in the next few years there would be no question about the strength of the West, and this, regardless of the existence of any type of bombs in the world, might lead to a peaceful solution of the problem.

I am very unhappy to conclude that the hydrogen bomb should be developed and built. I do not think we should intentionally lose the armaments race; to do this will be to lose our liberties, and, with Patrick Henry, I value my liberties more than I do my life. It is important that the spirit of independence and liberty should continue to exist in the world. It is much more important that this spirit continue to exist than that I or you or any group should continue this mortal existence for a few years more. Second, there is no constructive solution to the world's problems except eventually a world government capable of establishing law over the entire surface of the earth. It is necessary to take whatever steps we possibly can in that direction, and to take them as rapidly as possible. This, to me, includes *any* step that moves us in the desired direction, including the strengthening of the United Nations, and of all of the international organizations sponsored by the UN, the establishment of an Atlantic Union of the democratic countries of the world, which understand each other from the standpoint of political institutions, general philosophy of life, and religion; and the extension of any such organization to as much of the rest of the world as possible, and in as short a time as possible. May I emphasize: this is the only constructive direction in which to work.

Further Resources

BOOKS

Moss, Norman. *Men Who Play God: The Story of the Hydrogen Bomb.* Harmondsworth, U.K.: Penguin, 1972.

Powell, Cecil F. *The Hydrogen Bomb and the Future of Mankind.* London: London Co-Operative Society, 1955.

Rhodes, Richard. *Dark Sun: The Making of the Hydrogen Bomb.* New York: Simon & Schuster, 1995.

Shepley, James R. *The Hydrogen Bomb: The Men, the Menace, the Mechanism.* Westport, Conn.: Greenwood, 1954.

Teller, Edward. *Memoirs: A Twentieth-Century Journey in Science and Politics.* Cambridge, Mass.: Perseus, 2001.

York, Herbert F. *The Advisors: Oppenheimer, Teller, and the Superbomb.* Stanford, Calif.: Stanford University Press, 1976.

PERIODICALS

Flint, Jerry. "Hydrogen Bomb." *Forbes,* March 4, 2002, 100.

WEBSITES

"Developing the Hydrogen Bomb." Nuclearfiles.org. Available online at http://www.nuclearfiles.org/docs/h-bomb.html;

website home page: http://www.nuclearfiles.org (accessed December 18, 2002).

"The 'George' Test." *Race for the Superbomb.* American Experience. PBS Online. Available online at http://www.pbs .org/wgbh/amex/bomb/peopleevents/pandeAMEX55.html; website home page: http://www.pbs.org/wgbh/amex (accessed December 18, 2002).

AUDIO AND VISUAL MEDIA
Race for the Superbomb. Directed by Thomas Ott. PBS Home Video, 1999, VHS.

"The Weapon of Choice." Part two of the thirteen-part PBS series *War and Peace in the Nuclear Age.* WGBH, 1988, VHS.

"Streptomycin: Background, Isolation, Properties, and Utilization"
Lecture

By: Selman A. Waksman
Date: December 12, 1952
Source: Waksman, Selman A. "Streptomycin: Background, Isolation, Properties, and Utilization." Nobel Lecture, December 12, 1952. Available online at http://www.nobel.se/medicine /laureates/1952/waksman-lecture.html; website home page: http://www.nobel.se (accessed December 18, 2002).
About the Author: Selman Abraham Waksman (1888–1973) was born in Ukraine and became a U.S. citizen in 1916. A microbiologist at Rutgers University's New Jersey Agricultural Experiment Station, he was professor of microbiology at the University and director of the Rutgers Institute of Microbiology from 1949 to 1958. His discovery of the antibiotic streptomycin won him the 1952 Nobel Prize in medicine or physiology. ■

Introduction

In 1928 the British physician Alexander Fleming noticed that a bacterium he was trying to grow in a petri dish failed to grow. He discovered that he had accidentally contaminated the dish with a mold, *Pencillium notatum,* which emitted a substance toxic to the bacterium. Fleming grew the mold and discovered that it killed many bacteria that infect humans. This discovery ushered in a new era in the fight against disease. British chemists Howard Florey and Ernest B. Chain purified penicillin in the late 1930s and in 1941 developed an injectable version effective against bacteria that cause pneumonia, spinal meningitis, gangrene, diphtheria, syphilis, gonorrhea, and strep throat. By 1944 penicillin was in widespread use both in the military, where it was indispensable in the field hospitals of World War II, and in society at large.

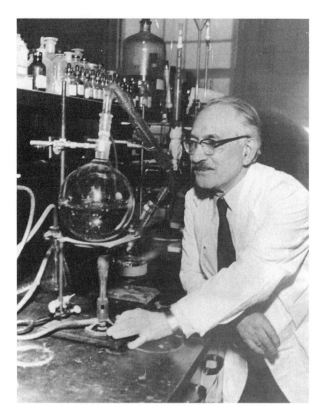

Selman Waksman, microbiologist and discoverer of the antiobiotic streptomycin. **THE LIBRARY OF CONGRESS.**

Antibiotics are of two types: narrow spectrum, which kill only a small range of bacteria; and broad spectrum, which kill a large range of bacteria. Penicillin is broad spectrum, yet its limitations include the inability to kill the bacterium that causes tuberculosis and the tendency of bacteria to develop resistance to it. Resistance occurs in classic Darwinian fashion. The penicillin kills all but a few bacteria in an infected person. These bacteria, which have a natural immunity to penicillin, reproduce and pass their immunity on to their descendents.

Significance

The shortcomings of penicillin led scientists to search for other antibiotics. Selman A. Waksman discovered that a soil microorganism produces the antibiotic streptomycin. In his 1952 Nobel lecture Waksman touted streptomycin's effectiveness against tuberculosis, a disease he called "the 'Great White Plague' of man." In addition Waksman noted streptomycin's effectiveness against the bacteria that cause tularemia, urinary tract infections, klebsiella and hemophilus infections, meningitis, whooping cough, leprosy, typhoid fever, brucellosis, dysentery, cholera, and bubonic plague. Streptomycin also proved effective against bacteria that had developed resistance to penicillin and, in combination with other drugs, against tuberculosis.

Streptomycin's significance goes beyond its therapeutic uses. It demonstrates the close connection between basic science, which seeks knowledge for its own sake, and applied science, which seeks knowledge that will yield a practical gain. The Adams Act (1906) funded Waksman's research at the New Jersey Agricultural Experiment Station. In conducting basic research on soil microorganisms, Waksman discovered streptomycin—demonstrating the close connection between basic and applied science.

Primary Source

"Streptomycin: Background, Isolation, Properties, and Utilization" [excerpt]

SYNOPSIS: In this excerpt Selman Waksman describes streptomycin's effectiveness against tuberculosis and other bacterial infections and emphasizes its use against bacteria that had developed resistance to penicillin.

The highest scientific award and honor presented to me the day before yesterday gives me the opportunity to summarize briefly the discovery and utilization of streptomycin for disease control, notably in the treatment of tuberculosis, the "Great White Plague" of man. . . .

Diseases responding to streptomycin

A variety of human and animal diseases caused by various bacteria respond readily to streptomycin treatment. This was brought out in the first comprehensive study of a group of diseases which could be considered to be definitely controlled by streptomycin or to give promise that they would respond favorably. These included tularemia, urinary track infections, especially those resistant to sulfa drugs and to penicillin, *Klebsiella* and *Hemophilus* infections, bacteremia due to penicillin-resistant organisms, various forms of meningitis, and whooping cough. Streptomycin was also found to be helpful in treatment of a variety of other diseases, such as leprosy, typhoid fever, brucellosis, certain forms of tuberculosis, and probably also bacillary dysentery, cholera, and bubonic plague.

The Committee on Chemotherapy, originally organized by the Committee on Medical Research of the OSRD, undertook the supervision and coordination of the first large-scale series of investigations on the use of streptomycin in the treatment of bacterial infections. The various infectious diseases have been divided, in their relation to streptomycin, as follows:

Diseases definitely indicated for streptomycin treatment

1. All cases of tularemia.

2. All cases of *H. influenza* infections:
   Menningitis
   Endocarditis
   Laryngotracheitis
   Urinary tract infections
   Pulmonary infections

3. All cases of meningitis due to:
   E. coli
   Pr. vulgaris
   K. pneumoniae
   B. lactis-aerogenes
   Ps. aeruginosa
   S. paratyphi

4. All cases of bacteremia due to gram-negative organisms:
   E. coli
   Pr. vulgaris
   A. aerogenes
   Ps. aeruginosa
   K. pneumoniae

5. Urinary tract infections due to:
   E. coli
   Pr. vulgaris
   K. pneumoniae
   B. lactis-aerogenes
   H. influenzae
   Ps. aeruginosa

Streptomycin found to be a helpful agent but position not yet definitely defined

1. Peritonitis due to gram-negative bacteria.
2. B. Friedländer's pneumonia.
3. Liver abscesses due to gram-negative bacteria.
4. Cholangitis due to gram-negative bacteria.
5. Penicillin-resistant but streptomycin-sensitive organisms infecting heart valves.
6. Tuberculosis.
7. Chronic pulmonary infections due to mixed gram-negative flora.
8. Empyema due to gram-negative infections.

Further Resources

BOOKS

Keefer, Chester S., and Donald G. Anderson. *Penicillin and Streptomycin in the Treatment of Infections.* New York: Oxford University Press, 1950.

Laskin, Allen I, and Hubert A. Lechevalier, eds. *Antibiotics.* Boca Raton, Fla.: CRC, 1988.

Mann, John, and M. James Crable. *Bacteria and Antibacterial Agents.* Oxford, England: Spektrum, 1996.

Russell, A. Denver, and Louis B. Quesnel. *Antibiotics: Assessment of Antimicrobial Activity and Resistance.* London, England: Academic Press, 1983.

Waksman, Selman A., ed. *Streptomycin: Nature and Practical Applications.* Baltimore, Md.: Williams & Wilkins, 1949.

Welch, Henry. *The Antibiotic Saga.* New York: Medical Encyclopedia, 1960.

PERIODICALS

Hager, Mary. "Antibiotics." *Newsweek,* Winter 1997/1998, 70–73.

WEBSITES

"The Nobel Prize in Physiology or Medicine 1952." Available online at http://www.nobel.se/medicine/laureates/1952/press .html; website home page: http://www.nobel.se (accessed December 18, 2002).

"Selman Abraham Waksman—Biography." Available online at http://www.nobel.se/medicine/laureates/1952/waksmanbio .html; website home page: http://www.nobel.se (accessed December 18, 2002).

"The Biologic Synthesis of Deoxyribonucleic Acid"

Lecture, Illustrations

By: Arthur Kornberg

Date: December 11, 1959

Source: Kornberg, Arthur. "The Biologic Synthesis of Deoxyribonucleic Acid." Nobel lecture, December 11, 1959. Available online at http://www.nobel.se/medicine/laureates/1959/kornberg-lecture.html; website home page: http://www.nobel.se (accessed December 19, 2002).

About the Author: Arthur Kornberg (1918–) was born and grew up in New York City. He received his M.D. from the University of Rochester. He turned to research, becoming an expert on jaundice and the function of enzymes. He used enzymes to synthesis DNA in the laboratory, an achievement that won him the 1959 Nobel Prize in medicine or physiology. ∎

Introduction

In 1866 Austrian monk Gregor Mendel announced that particles (genes) code for traits in organisms and are passed unaltered from parents to offspring. The re-

---

Diagram of the Structure for Deoxyribose Nucleic Acid (DNA)

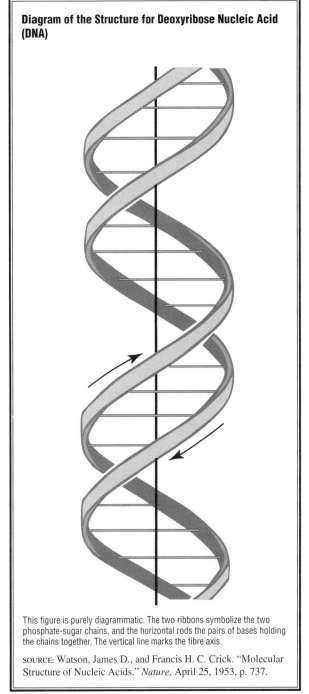

This figure is purely diagrammatic. The two ribbons symbolize the two phosphate-sugar chains, and the horizontal rods the pairs of bases holding the chains together. The vertical line marks the fibre axis.

SOURCE: Watson, James D., and Francis H. C. Crick. "Molecular Structure of Nucleic Acids." *Nature,* April 25, 1953, p. 737.

Primary Source

"Molecular Structure of Nucleic Acids": Diagram

SYNOPSIS: This diagram accompanies Watson and Crick's journal article. It represents their suggested structure for deoxyribose nucleic acid (DNA).

discovery of Mendel's work in 1900 launched the science of genetics. It was obvious to early researchers that genes must code for traits by a chemical pathway. A gene, therefore, must be a molecule, although it took

James Watson and Francis Crick, discoverers of the structure of the DNA model which contains the genetic code. **ARCHIVE PHOTOS, INC. REPRODUCED BY PERMISSION.**

the first half of the twentieth century to identify its size and structure.

By 1910 German chemists Albrecht Kossel and Phoebus A. Levine suspected that DNA was the chemical basis of heredity and had identified its four nucleotide bases: adenine, guanine, cytosine, and thymine. Yet they did not know how these bases bonded, a shortcoming that prevented them from determining DNA's structure. Moreover, confusion arose over the role of ribonucleic

acid (RNA) in heredity, and only during the 1930s did chemists understand that all animal and plant cells contain both DNA and RNA. Both had a role in heredity, although chemists struggled to tease apart these roles. Kossel and Levine focused on DNA, concluding that it was a small molecule of low weight.

This conclusion was wrong, but in the 1930s it led many chemists to discount DNA's role in heredity, for they did not believe that a small molecule could contain enough information to control the behavior of cells. In the 1940s, however, American chemist Theodore Caspersson found DNA to be a thousand times heavier than Kossel and Levine had supposed. In 1949 American chemist Oswald Avery isolated DNA as the basis of heredity. All that remained was to determine its structure.

Significance

American chemist James D. Watson and his British counterpart, Francis Crick, accomplished this goal in 1953, although they borrowed from the work of British biochemist Rosalind Franklin without her consent. They conceived of DNA as a three-dimensional spiral staircase: the famous double helix. The pairing of two nucleotide bases form each rung on the staircase. Adenine always bonds with thymine and cytosine always bonds with guanine. If, then, half a strand of a staircase was adenine, cytosine, guanine, adenine, and thymine, the other half would be thymine, guanine, cytosine, thymine, and adenine in that order.

Independent of Watson and Crick, Arthur Kornberg synthesized DNA in the laboratory by using an enzyme that read half a strand of DNA as a template, directing the correct nucleotide base to pair with its partner in constructing the full strand. Again, in the half strand adenine, cytosine, guanine, adenine, and thymine, the enzyme would direct thymine, guanine, cytosine, thymine, and adenine in that order to bond with its partner.

It would be hard to overstate the importance of the discovery of DNA's structure, as it laid the foundation for a genetics revolution in science and medicine. With this understanding came the ability to study the DNA of different organisms and determine which genes code for which traits. Genetic disorders could now be studied and their likelihood of developing in a given person determined. Understanding the structure of DNA also allowed the study of the unique DNA found in each person. Thus, for example, it became possible to determine if a person had committed a crime by seeing if their DNA matched that left at the scene. Similarly, it allows a mother to determine exactly who her child's father is by matching the child's DNA to its father's. By the early twenty-first century, genetic science held the prospect of being able to control the genes, and thus the development, of plants and animals, even humans

Primary Source

"The Biologic Synthesis of Deoxyribonucleic Acid"
[excerpt]: Lecture

> **SYNOPSIS:** In this excerpt from his Nobel address, Arthur Kornberg announces that he has synthesized DNA in the laboratory by using an enzyme that read

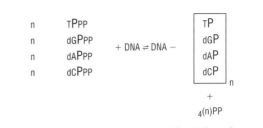

Equation for Enzymatic Synthesis of DNA

SOURCE: Figure 6 from Kornberg, Arthur. *The Biological Synthesis of Deoxyribonucleic Acid.* Lecture presented at Nobel Prize for physiology or medicine awards ceremony, December 11, 1959. Reproduced in "Arthur Kornberg—Nobel Lecture." Available online at http://www.nobel.se/medicine/laureates/1959/kornberg-lecture.html; website home page: http://www.nobel.se (accessed January 3, 2003), p. 671.

Primary Source

"The Biologic Synthesis of Deoxyribonucleic Acid": Illustration (1 OF 2)

SYNOPSIS: These two illustrations accompany Kornberg's nobel lecture. This is an Illustration of the equation for enzymatic synthesis of DNA.

half a strand of DNA as a template, directing the correct nucleotide base to pair with its partner in constructing the full strand. Included with the printed Nobel lecture are two illustrations.

The requirements for net synthesis of DNA with the purified *coli* enzyme are shown [Illustration, "Equation for Enzymatic Synthesis of DNA"]. All four of the deoxynucleotides which form the adenine-thymine and guanine-cytosine couples must be present. The substrates must be the tri- and not the diphosphates and only the deoxy sugar compounds are active. DNA which must be present may be obtained from animal, plant, bacterial or viral sources and the best indications are that all these DNA samples serve equally well in DNA synthesis provided their molecular weight is high. The product, which we will discuss in further detail, accumulates until one of the substrates is exhausted and may be 20 or more times greater in amount than the DNA added and thus is composed to the extent of 95% or more of the substrates added to the reaction mixture. Inorganic pyrophosphate is released in quantities equimolar to the deoxynucleotides converted to DNA.

Should one of these substrates be omitted, the extent of reaction is diminished by a factor of greater than 10^4 and special methods are now required for its detection. It turns out that when one of the de-

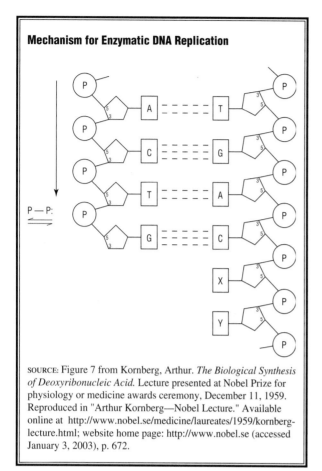

Mechanism for Enzymatic DNA Replication

SOURCE: Figure 7 from Kornberg, Arthur. *The Biological Synthesis of Deoxyribonucleic Acid.* Lecture presented at Nobel Prize for physiology or medicine awards ceremony, December 11, 1959. Reproduced in "Arthur Kornberg—Nobel Lecture." Available online at http://www.nobel.se/medicine/laureates/1959/kornberg-lecture.html; website home page: http://www.nobel.se (accessed January 3, 2003), p. 672.

Primary Source

"The Biologic Synthesis of Deoxyribonucleic Acid": Illustration (2 OF 2)

Illustration of the mechanism for enzymatic DNA replication.

oxynucleotide substrates is lacking, an extremely small but yet significant quantity of nucleotide is linked to the DNA primer. We have described this so-called "limited reaction," and have shown that under these circumstances a few deoxynucleotides are added to the nucleoside ends of some of the DNA chains but that further synthesis is blocked for lack of the missing nucleotide. Current studies suggest to us that this limited reaction represents the repair of the shorter strand of a double helix in which the strands are of unequal length, and that the reaction is governed by the hydrogen bonding of adenine to thymine and of guanine to cytosine.

When all four triphosphates are present, but when DNA is omitted, no reaction at all takes place. What is the basis for this requirement? Does the DNA function as a primer in the manner of glycogen or does it function as a template in directing the synthesis of exact copies of itself? We have good rea-

son to believe that it is the latter and as the central and restricted theme of this lecture I would like to emphasize that it is the capacity for base-pairing by hydrogen bonding between the preexisting DNA and the nucleotides added as substrates that accounts for the requirement for DNA.

The enzyme we are studying is thus unique in present experience in taking directions from a template—it adds the particular purine or pyrimidine substrate which will form a hydrogen-bonded pair with a base on the template [Illustration, "Mechanism for Enzymatic DNA Replication"].

Further Resources

BOOKS

Calladine, Christopher R. *Understanding DNA: The Molecule and How It Works.* San Diego, Calif.: Academic Press, 1997.

Hutchins, Carleen M. *Life's Key—DNA: A Biological Adventure into the Unkown.* New York: Cowand-McCaun, 1961.

Watson, James D. *The Double Helix: A Personal Account of the Discovery of the Structure of DNA.* New York: Atheneum, 1968.

PERIODICALS

Watson, James D., and Francis H. C. Crick. "Genetical Implications of the Structure of Deoxyribonucleic Acid." *Nature,* May 30, 1953, 964–967.

WEBSITES

"Arthur Kornberg-Biography." Available online at http://www.nobel.se/medicine/laureates/1959/kornberg-bio.html; website home page: http://www.nobel.se (accessed December 19, 2002).

Crick, Francis Harry Compton. "On the Genetic Code." Available online at http://www.nobel.se/medicine/laureates/1962/crick-lecture.html; website home page: http://www.nobel.se (accessed December 19, 2002).

"Francis Harry Compton Crick—Biography." Available online at http://www.nobel.se/medicine/laureates/1962/crick-bio.html; website home page: http://www.nobel.se (accessed December 19, 2002).

"James Dewey Watson—Biography." Available online at http://www.nobel.se/medicine/laureates/1962/watson-bio.html; website home page: http://www.nobel.se (accessed December 19, 2002).

"The Nobel Prize in Physiology or Medicine 1959." Available online at http://www.nobel.se/medicine/laureates/1959/press.html; website home page: http://www.nobel.se (accessed December 19, 2002).

"A Production of Amino Acids Under Possible Primitive Earth Conditions"

Journal article, Illustrations

By: Stanley L. Miller

Date: May 15, 1953

Source: Miller, Stanley L. "A Production of Amino Acids Under Possible Primitive Earth Conditions." *Science,* May 15, 1953, 528–529.

About the Author: Stanley Lloyd Miller (1930–) was born in Oakland, California, and received a Ph.D. in chemistry from the University of Chicago in 1954. The previous year he had produced amino acids by simulating the atmosphere of the primitive earth, a finding that may suggest how life on Earth arose. Since 1960 he has taught at the University of California, San Diego, rising to full professor in 1968. ∎

Introduction

The mystery of the origin of life has fascinated people since antiquity. All cultures, including Western Christianity, have mythical accounts of how a divine being created life. But science was at first no more sure of how life arose than was the author of the biblical Book of Genesis. In *The Origin of Species* (1859) Charles Darwin asserted that life arose in the primeval ocean. This idea drew support from the fossil record, whose earliest organisms were marine invertebrates. Yet Darwin did not speculate on how life arose. In the 1870s Swiss physiologist and chemist Friedrich Miescher defined the origin of life as a chemical problem, suggesting that the first life must have been a self-replicating molecule. Then in 1938 Russian chemist Aleksandr I. Oparin suggested that this molecule must have assembled itself on an earth with a different chemistry than today's earth. He believed that the atmosphere of the primitive earth had little oxygen, carbon dioxide, or nitrogen because the earth, containing no life, would have had no plants to produce oxygen when alive and to give off carbon dioxide and nitrogen during decay. Instead, Oparin supposed that the atmosphere of the primitive earth contained methane, ammonia, and hydrogen and that the earth held vast quantities of liquid water as its ocean.

Significance

In 1953 Stanley Miller tested Oparin's assumptions by duplicating the conditions of the primitive earth in the laboratory. He set up a flask with methane, ammonia, and hydrogen gases. He then discharged electricity through these gases to simulate the lightning that must have flashed through the atmosphere of the primitive earth. He allowed these gases to mix with water for a

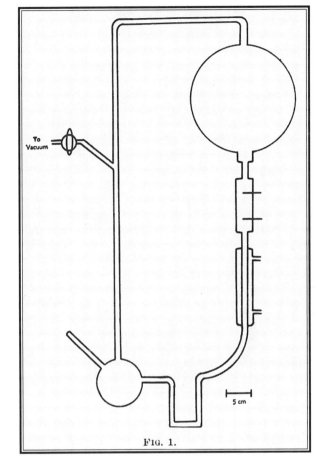

FIG. 1.

Primary Source

Apparatus Used to Produce Amino Acids

Illustration of apparatus used for producing amino acids by simulating primitive Earth's atmospheric conditions (Fig. 1). REPRINTED WITH PERMISSION FROM SCIENCE 117:528–529 (15 MAY 1953), COPYRIGHT 1953 AMERICAN ASSOCIATION FOR THE ADVANCEMENT OF SCIENCE.

week. At week's end he identified three amino acids and the possible presence of two others, possibly more in small amounts. Because amino acids are the building blocks of proteins, Miller believed that he had identified the precursors of life and that life must have arisen from the formation of these amino acids in the primitive ocean.

Miller's experiment remains the classic account of how life may have arisen from inanimate molecules on the primeval earth, but he has not persuaded all scientists. Lehigh University biochemist Michael Behe has led the opposition to Miller's work. Behe maintains that the spontaneous production of amino acids is trivial, for an amino acid is a long way from the complexity of a self-replicating strand of deoxyribonucleic acid (DNA). An amino acid is no more a strand of DNA than a rock is a Gothic cathedral. Behe sees nothing in Miller's experi-

Stanley Miller in his laboratory, where he produced the building blocks of organic life, amino acids, by simulating primitive Earth's atmospheric conditions. May 16, 1953. © BETTMANN/CORBIS. REPRODUCED BY PERMISSION.

ment that would explain how a collection of amino acids assembled into a strand of DNA. Miller's experiment notwithstanding, the origin of life remains an intractable problem of science.

Primary Source

"A Production of Amino Acids Under Possible Primitive Earth Conditions": Journal article

> **SYNOPSIS:** In this article Stanley Miller described an experiment that simulated the chemistry of the primitive earth. The experiment yielded three amino acids, two other possible amino acids, and still others in small amounts. Amino acids like these may have been the precursors of life.

The idea that the organic compounds that serve as the basis of life were formed when the earth had an atmosphere of methane, ammonia, water, and hydrogen instead of carbon dioxide, nitrogen, oxygen, and water was suggested by Oparin and has been given emphasis recently by Urey and Bernal.

In order to test this hypothesis, an apparatus was built to circulate CH_4, NH_3, H_2O, and H_2 past an electric discharge. The resulting mixture has been tested for amino acids by paper chromatography. Electrical discharge was used to form free radicals instead of ultraviolet light, because quartz absorbs wavelengths short enough to cause photo-dissociation of the gases. Electrical discharge may have played a significant role in the formation of compounds in the primitive atmosphere.

The apparatus used is shown in [Illustration, "Apparatus Used to Produce Amino Acids"]. Water is boiled in the flask, mixes with the gases in the 5-1 flask, circulates past the electrodes, condenses and empties back into the boiling flask. The U-tube prevents circulation in the opposite direction. The acids and amino acids formed in the discharge, not being volatile, accumulate in the water phase. The circulation of the gases is quite slow, but this seems to be an asset, because production was less in a different apparatus with an aspirator arrangement to promote circulation. The discharge, a small corona, was provided by an induction coil designed for detection of leaks in vacuum apparatus.

The experimental procedure was to seal off the opening in the boiling flask after adding 200 ml of

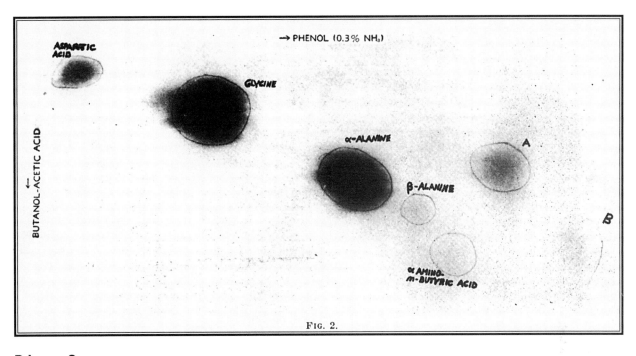

FIG. 2.

Primary Source

Laboratory-created Amino Acids

A paper chromatogram test shows the presence of amino acids created in a laboratory experiment simulating primitive Earth's atmosphereic conditions (Fig. 2). REPRINTED WITH PERMISSION FROM SCIENCE 117:528–529 (15 MAY 1953), COPYRIGHT 1953 AMERICAN ASSOCIATION FOR THE ADVANCEMENT OF SCIENCE.

water, evacuate the air, add 10 cm pressure of H_2, 20 cm of CH_4, and 20 cm of NH_3. The water in the flask was boiled, and the discharge was run continuously for a week.

During the run the water in the flask became noticeably pink after the first day, and by the end of the week the solution was deep red and turbid. Most of the turbidity was due to colloidal silica from the glass. The red color is due to organic compounds adsorbed on the silica. Also present are yellow organic compounds, of which only a small fraction can be extracted with ether, and which form a continuous streak tapering off at the bottom on a one-dimensional chromatogram run in butanol-acetic acid. These substances are being investigated further.

At the end of the run the solution in the boiling flask was removed and 1 ml of saturated $HgCl_2$ was added to prevent the growth of living organisms. The ampholytes were separated from the rest of the constituents by adding $Ba(OH)_2$ and evaporating in vacuo to remove amines, adding H_2SO_4 and evaporating to remove the acids, neutralizing with $Ba(OH)_2$, filtering and concentrating in vacuo.

The amino acids are not due to living organisms because their growth would be prevented by the boiling water during the run, and by the $HgCl_2$, $Ba(OH)_2$, H_2SO_4 during the analysis.

In [Laboratory-created Amino Acids, "A paper chromatogram test shows the presence of amino acids created in a laboratory experiment simulating primitive Earth's atmospheric conditions"] is shown a paper chromatogram run in n-butanol-acetic acid-water mixture followed by water-saturated phenol, and spraying with ninhydrin. Identification of an amino acid was made when the R_f value (the ratio of the distance traveled by the amino acid to the distance traveled by the solvent front), the shape, and the color of the spot were the same on a known, unknown, and mixture of the known and unknown; and when consistent results were obtained with chromatograms using phenol and 77% ethanol.

On this basis glycine, α-alanine and β-alanine are identified. The identification of the aspartic acid and α-amino-n-butyric acid is less certain because the spots are quite weak. The spots marked A and B are unidentified as yet, but may be beta and gamma amino acids. These are the main amino acids present, and others are undoubtedly present but in smaller amounts. It is estimated that the total yield of amino acids was in the milligram range.

In this apparatus an attempt was made to duplicate a primitive atmosphere of the earth, and not to obtain the optimum conditions for the formation of amino acids. Although in this case the total yield was small for the energy expended, it is possible that, with more efficient apparatus (such as mixing of the free radicals in a flow system, use of higher hydrocarbons from natural gas or petroleum, carbon dioxide, etc., and optimum ratios of gases), this type of process would be a way of commercially producing amino acids.

A more complete analysis of the amino acids and other products of the discharge is now being performed and will be reported in detail shortly.

Further Resources

BOOKS

Behe, Michael J. *Darwin's Black Box: The Biochemical Challenge to Evolution.* New York: Free Press, 1996.

Dillon, Lawrence S. *The Genetic Mechanism and the Origin of Life.* New York: Plenum, 1978.

Frank, Louis A. *The Big Splash: A Scientific Discovery That Revolutionizes the Way We View the Origin of Life.* New York: Carol, 1990.

Miller, Stanley L., and L. E. Orgel. *The Origin of Life on Earth.* Englewood Cliffs, N. J.: Prentice-Hall, 1974.

Oparin, Aleksandr I. *The Chemical Origin of Life.* Springfield, Ill.: C. C. Thomas, 1964.

———. *The Origin of Life.* New York: Macmillan, 1938.

Rush, Joseph H. *The Dawn of Life.* Garden City, N.Y.: Hanover House, 1957.

Urey, Harold C. *The Planets.* New Haven, Conn.: Yale University Press, 1952.

PERIODICALS

Dickerson, Robert E. "Chemical Evolution and the Origin of Life." *Scientific American,* September 1978, 70–86.

WEBSITES

"Miller, Stanley Lloyd (1930)." Available online at http://www.xrefer.com/entry/494888 (accessed December 19, 2002).

"The Atom for Progress and Peace"

Speech

By: Dwight D. Eisenhower

Date: December 8, 1953

Source: Einsenhower, Dwight D. "The Atom for Progress and Peace." An address before the General Assembly of the United Nations, December 8, 1953. Department of State Publication 5403. Washington, D.C.: U.S. Government Printing Office, 1954, 3–6.

About the Author: Dwight David Eisenhower (1890–1969) was born in Denison, Texas, and graduated from West Point in 1915. During World War I he received the Distinguished Service Medal and in World War II rose to the rank of five-star general in command of all U.S. troops in Europe. In 1948 he retired from the army to become president of Columbia University. From 1953 to 1961 he was president of the United States. ∎

Introduction

In July 1945 American physicists and engineers unleashed the power of the atom with the development of the atomic bomb. By the 1950s science had harnessed sufficient power from the atom to imperil the world. The hydrogen bomb, built by the United States in 1952 and the Soviet Union in 1953, threatened to cause destruction on a massive scale.

American scientists hardly knew what to make of these developments, for science had accomplished much good during the twentieth century. Agricultural scientists had developed high-yielding varieties of hybrid corn and other grains. Norman Borlaug, who had pioneered the development of high-yielding varieties of wheat, would win the 1970 Nobel Peace Prize, the first for an American scientist. Other scientists had discovered antibiotics and vaccines, cutting the death rate and improving the quality of life for millions of people. Still other scientists had discovered vitamins and developed vitamin-fortified milk and foods. Science had tamed the scourges of disease and famine.

But science had at the same time raised the stakes of warfare. In the 1950s a nuclear-armed United States faced a nuclear-armed Soviet Union. Neither nation could confront the other without fear that nuclear retaliation would cause massive casualties.

Significance

Given this state of affairs, it is no surprise that scientists could not reach consensus. In 1950 Albert Einstein had condemned the building of the hydrogen bomb, but that year Harold Urey spoke for the majority of physicists, who saw no alternative but to build the hydrogen bomb. To do otherwise would be to surrender national security to the Soviets.

President Dwight D. Eisenhower understood both positions and balanced them. He echoed Einstein in fearing that a nuclear arms race between the United States and the Soviet Union could eventually lead to the end civilization. On the other hand, he had spent his career in the army and understood that powerful weapons could deter aggression. He based his international policy on the premise of "massive retaliation": No nation would dare attack the United States for fear that it would be obliterated. In his speech, therefore, Eisenhower tempered the promise of peace with the warning that the United States had no plans to stop stockpiling nuclear weapons. Science, in its ability to devise ever more potent weapons, had become an instrument of American foreign policy.

Primary Source

"The Atom for Progress and Peace" [excerpt]

SYNOPSIS: In this excerpt from his December 8, 1953, address to the United Nations General Assembly, Dwight D. Eisenhower balances an abhorrence of nuclear weapons with the intent to continue stockpiling them. While declaring a nuclear war unwinnable, he warns that the United States is daily increasing its stockpile of nuclear weapons and has no plans to cease this effort.

I feel impelled to speak today in a language that in a sense is new—one which I, who have spent so much of my life in the military profession, would have preferred never to use.

That new language is the language of atomic warfare.

The atomic age has moved forward at such a pace that every citizen of the world should have some comprehension, at least in comparative terms, of the extent of this development, of the utmost significance to every one of us. Clearly, if the peoples of the world are to conduct an intelligent search for peace, they must be armed with the significant facts of today's existence. . . .

Today, the United States' stockpile of atomic weapons, which, of course, increases daily, exceeds by many times the explosive equivalent of the total of all bombs and all shells that came from every plane and every gun in every theatre of war in all of the years of World War II.

A single air group, whether afloat or land-based, can now deliver to any reachable target a destructive cargo exceeding in power all the bombs that fell on Britain in all of World War II.

In size and variety, the development of atomic weapons has been no less remarkable. The development has been such that atomic weapons have virtually achieved conventional status within our armed services. In the United States, the Army, the Navy, the Air Force, and the Marine Corps are all capable of putting this weapon to military use.

But the dread secret, and the fearful engines of atomic might, are not ours alone.

In the first place, the secret is possessed by our friends and allies, Great Britain and Canada, whose

President Dwight Eisenhower and staff walk through a covering by the rose garden on their way to the White House air raid shelter in Washington, D.C. June 14, 1954. AP/WIDE WORLD PHOTOS. REPRODUCED BY PERMISSION.

scientific genius made a tremendous contribution to our original discoveries, and the design of atomic bombs.

The secret is also known by the Soviet Union.

The Soviet Union has informed us that, over recent years, it has devoted extensive resources to atomic weapons. During this period, the Soviet Union has exploded a series of atomic devices, including at least one involving thermo-nuclear reactions.

No Monopoly of Atomic Power

If at one time the United States possessed what might have been called a monopoly of atomic power, that monopoly ceased to exist several years ago. Therefore, although our earlier start has permitted us to accumulate what is today a great quantitative advantage, the atomic realities of today comprehend two facts of even greater significance.

First, the knowledge now possessed by several nations will eventually be shared by others—possibly all others.

Second, even a vast superiority in numbers of weapons, and a consequent capability of devastating retaliation, is no preventive, of itself, against the fearful material damage and toll of human lives that would be inflicted by surprise aggression.

The free world, at least dimly aware of these facts, has naturally embarked on a large program of warning and defense systems. That program will be accelerated and expanded.

But let no one think that the expenditure of vast sums for weapons and systems of defense can guarantee absolute safety for the cities and citizens of any nation. The awful arithmetic of the atomic bomb does not permit of any such easy solution. Even against the most powerful defense, an aggressor in possession of the effective minimum number of atomic bombs for a surprise attack could probably place a sufficient number of his bombs on the chosen targets to cause hideous damage.

Should such an atomic attack be launched against the United States, our reactions would be swift and resolute. But for me to say that the defense capabilities of the United States are such that they could inflict terrible losses upon an aggressor—for me to say that the retaliation capabilities of the United States are so great that such an aggressor's land would be laid waste—all this, while fact, is not the true expression of the purpose and the hope of the United States.

To pause there would be to confirm the hopeless finality of a belief that two atomic colossi are doomed malevolently to eye each other indefinitely across a trembling world. To stop there would be to accept helplessly the probability of civilization destroyed—the annihilation of the irreplaceable heritage of mankind handed down to us from generation to generation—and the condemnation of mankind to begin all over again the age-old struggle upward from savagery toward decency, and right, and justice.

Surely no sane member of the human race could discover victory in such desolation. Could anyone wish his name to be coupled by history with such human degradation and destruction.

Further Resources

BOOKS

The H Bomb. New York: Didier, 1950.

Moss, Norman. *Men Who Play God: The Story of the Hydrogen Bomb.* Harmondsworth, England: Penguin, 1972.

Powell, Cecil F. *The Hydrogen Bomb and the Future of Mankind.* London, England: London Co-Operative Society, 1955.

Rhodes, Richard. *Dark Sun: The Making of the Hydrogen Bomb.* New York: Simon and Schuster, 1995.

Shepley, James R. *The Hydrogen Bomb: The Men, the Menace, the Mechanism.* Westport, Conn.: Greenwood, 1954.

Teller, Edward. *Memoirs: A Twentieth-Century Journey in Science and Politics.* Cambridge, Mass.: Perseus, 2001.

York, Herbert F. *The Advisors: Oppenheimer, Teller, and the Superbomb.* Stanford, Calif.: Stanford University Press, 1976.

PERIODICALS

Flint, Jerry. "Hydrogen Bomb." *Forbes,* March 4, 2002, 100.

WEBSITES

"The 'George' Test." *Race for the Superbomb.* American Experience. Available online at http://www.pbs.org/wgbh/amex/bomb/peopleevents/pandeAMEX55.html; website home page: http://www.pbs.org/wgbh/amex (accessed June 4, 2003).

Nuclearfiles.org: A Project of the Nuclear Age Peace Foundation. "Developing the Hydrogen Bomb." Available online at http://www.nuclearfiles.org/redocuments/h-bomb.html; website home page: http://www.nuclearfiles.org (accessed June 4, 2003).

AUDIO AND VISUAL MEDIA

Race for the Superbomb. Boston: PBS Video, 1999, VHS.

The Weapon of Choice. Boston: WGBH, 1988, VHS.

Sexual Behavior in the Human Female

Study, Graphs

By: Alfred Charles Kinsey

Date: 1953

Source: Kinsey, Alfred Charles. *Sexual Behavior in the Human Female.* Philadelphia: W. B. Saunders Company, 1953, 416–418.

About the Author: Alfred Charles Kinsey (1897–1956) was born in Hoboken, New Jersey. He joined Indiana University's zoology department in 1920, rising to full professor in 1929. An entomologist by training, Kinsey turned to human behavior, founding the Institute for Sexual Research in 1938 and publishing groundbreaking work on male and female sexual behavior in the 1940s and 1950s. ■

Introduction

Kinsey's work followed a century of efforts to understand human sexuality. In *The Descent of Man* (1871) Charles Darwin tied human sexual behavior to his theory of evolution and argued that sexual selection played a role in human evolution. In the early twentieth century, Austrian physician Sigmund Freud built his psychological theories on sexual urges. He argued that these urges, stemming from childhood, are often at odds with prevailing norms and that by repressing them people can undermine their psychological health. The repressiveness of Western society toward sex influenced American anthropologist Margaret Mead. In *Coming of Age in Samoa* (1928) she contrasted the strictures on sex in the West with the sexual freedom of Polynesians, which gave them a healthier attitude toward sex.

Significance

Despite these advances, no one had quantified human sexual behavior. This task fell to Alfred Kinsey and the Institute for Sexual Research at Indiana University. His first report, *Sexual Behavior in the Human Male* (1948), shocked Americans, for Kinsey estimated that 95 percent of American men had masturbated and had engaged in premarital, extramarital, or homosexual intercourse. Princeton University president Harold Dodd dismissed the book as "the work of small boys writing dirty words on fences."

Sexual Behavior in the Human Female (1953) was no less provocative. Kinsey announced that extramarital sex among women was much more common than many people would have liked to believe, that older women had fewer scruples about extramarital sex than did younger women, and that their husbands tended not to object. He

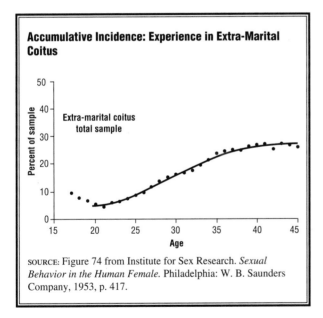

Accumulative Incidence: Experience in Extra-Marital Coitus

SOURCE: Figure 74 from Institute for Sex Research. *Sexual Behavior in the Human Female*. Philadelphia: W. B. Saunders Company, 1953, p. 417.

Primary Source

"Sexual Behavior in the Human Female": Graph

(1 OF 2)

A graph from Alfred Kinsey's *Sexual Behavior in the Human Female* (1953). It shows that the percentage of married women who have ever engaged in extra-marital sex increases with age, leveling off at about twenty six percent at age 40. SOURCE: FIGURE 74 FROM INSTITUTE FOR SEX RESEARCH. *SEXUAL BEHAVIOR IN THE HUMAN FEMAL*. PHILADELPHIA: W. B. SAUNDERS COMPANY, 1953, P. 417.

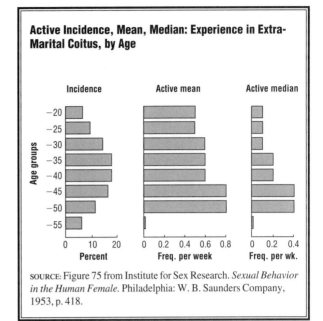

Active Incidence, Mean, Median: Experience in Extra-Marital Coitus, by Age

SOURCE: Figure 75 from Institute for Sex Research. *Sexual Behavior in the Human Female*. Philadelphia: W. B. Saunders Company, 1953, p. 418.

Primary Source

"Sexual Behavior in the Human Female": Graph

(2 OF 2)

This graph shows the percentage of women having sex outside their marriage (incidence), and how frequently these women were having extra-marital sex (mean and median), by age. SOURCE: FIGURE 75 FROM INSTITUTE FOR SEX RESEARCH. *SEXUAL BEHAVIOR IN THE HUMAN FEMAL*. PHILADELPHIA: W. B. SAUNDERS COMPANY, 1953, P. 418.

also asserted that men prefer older women as partners in an extramarital liaison, for they are more experienced and less likely to develop an emotional attachment, allowing the men to enjoy casual sex without complications.

The report sparked renewed criticism of Kinsey. Some Americans condemned it as an attack on motherhood and the family. A New York congressman tried to ban the report from the mail, charging Kinsey with "hurling the insult of the century against our mothers, wives, daughters and sisters." Despite these attacks Kinsey has been credited with elevating the study of human sexual behavior into a science by quantifying it.

Primary Source

Sexual Behavior in the Human Female [excerpt]: Study

SYNOPSIS: In this excerpt Alfred Kinsey announces that 26 percent of the women he surveyed had had extramarital sex by age forty. After age twenty-six women had steadily more extramarital sex, reaching a peak at age forty. He asserts that "middle-aged and older females" had fewer scruples about extramarital sex than did younger women and that

Three women read a review of Alfred Kinsey's provocative 1953 book *The Sexual Behavior of Women.* © BETTMANN/CORBIS. REPRODUCED BY PERMISSION.

their husbands "no longer objected if their wives engaged in such activities."

Relation to Age

Among the married females in the sample, about a quarter (26 per cent) had had extra-marital coitus by age forty [Graph, "Accumulative Incidence: Experience in Extra-Marital Coitus"]. Between the ages of twenty-six and fifty, something between one in six and one in ten was having extra-marital coitus [Graph, "Active Incidence, Mean, Median: Experience in Extra-Marital Coitus, by Age"]. Both the accumulative and active incidences of extra-marital coitus were remarkably uniform for many of the subdivisions of the sample, but they had varied in re-

lation to the ages, the educational levels, the decades of birth, and the religious backgrounds of the various groups. The frequencies had increased somewhat with advancing age.

Since the cover-up on any socially disapproved sexual activity may be greater than the cover-up on more accepted activities, it is possible that the incidences and frequencies of extra-marital coitus in the sample had been higher than our interviewing disclosed.

Accumulative Incidence

In their late teens, 7 per cent of the married females in the sample were having coitus with males other than their husbands. The accumulative incidences did not materially increase in the next five years, but after age twenty-six they gradually and steadily rose until they reached their maximum of 26 per cent by forty years of age [Graph, "Accumulative Incidence: Experience in Extra-Marital Coitus"]. After that age only a few females began for the first time to have extra-marital coitus.

Active Incidence

The number of females in the sample who were having extra-marital coitus in any particular five-year period had been lowest in the youngest and in the oldest age groups [Graph, "Active Incidence, Mean, Median: Experience in Extra-Marital Coitus, by Age"]. The incidences had reached their maxima somewhere in the thirties and early forties. For the total sample the active incidences had begun at about 6 per cent in the late teens, increased to 14 per cent by the late twenties, and reached 17 per cent by the thirties. They began to decrease after the early forties. They had dropped to 6 per cent by the early fifties.

The younger married females had not so often engaged in extra-marital coitus, partly because they were still very much interested in their husbands and partly because the young husbands were particularly jealous of their marital rights. Moreover, at that age both the male and the female were more often concerned over the morality of non-marital sexual relationships. In time, however, many of these factors had seemed less important, and the middle-aged and older females had become more inclined to accept extra-marital coitus, and at least some of the husbands no longer objected if their wives engaged in such activities.

Although it is commonly believed that most males prefer sexual relations with distinctly younger partners, and although most males are attracted by the physical charms of younger females, data which we have on our histories show that many of them actually prefer to have coitus with middle-aged or older females. Many younger females become much disturbed over non-marital irregularities in which they may have engaged, and many males fear the social difficulties that may arise from such disturbances. Older females are not so likely to become disturbed, and often have a better knowledge of sexual techniques. In consequence many males find the older females more effective as sexual partners. All of these factors probably contributed to the fact that the peak of the extra-marital activities of the females in the sample had come in the mid-thirties and early forties.

Further Resources

BOOKS

Gathorne-Hardy, Jonathan. *Sex the Measure of All Things: A Life of Alfred C. Kinsey.* Bloomington, Ind.: Indiana University Press, 2000.

Jones, James H. *Alfred C. Kinsey: A Public/Private Life.* New York: W. W. Norton, 1997.

Pomeroy, Wardell B. *Dr. Kinsey and the Institute for Sex Research.* New York: Harper & Row, 1972.

Robinson, Paul A. *The Modernization of Sex.* New York: Harper & Row, 1976.

Weinberg, Martin S., ed. *Sex Research: Studies from the Kinsey Institute.* New York: Oxford University Press, 1976.

PERIODICALS

Kisseck, Terence, and Leonard Evans. "Alfred Kinsey and Homosexuality in the '50s." *Journal of the History of Sexuality,* October 2000, 474–492.

Money, John. "Once Upon a Time I Met Alfred C. Kinsey." *Archives of Sexual Behavior,* August 2002, 319–323.

WEBSITES

"Alfred C. Kinsey." Available online at http://www.wylde.com /kinsey.html (accessed December 19, 2002).

"The Kinsey Institute for Research in Sex, Gender, and Reproduction." Available online at http://www.indiana.edu /~kinsey (accessed December 19, 2002).

Conquest of the Moon
Nonfiction work

By: Wernher von Braun

Date: 1953

Source: Ryan, Cornelius, ed. "Introduction." In *Conquest of the Moon.* New York: Viking, 1953, 3–5.

About the Author: Wernher von Braun (1912–1977), born in Prussia, shared his mother's interest in astronomy and became fascinated by the idea of space travel. By 1932 he had made eighty-five test flights with rockets, and in 1934 he earned his Ph.D. in physics from the University of Berlin. Von Braun designed the German V-2 rocket in 1938. During World War II he defected to American troops and became a U.S. citizen in 1955. ■

Introduction

While people had long been fascinated by the possibility of traveling to the moon, it was not until the twentieth century that inventors and scientists began the quest for rockets powerful enough for space flight. The American physicist Robert Goddard emerged in the 1920s as a pioneer. In 1926 he launched the first liquid-fuel rocket and later calculated that rockets did not need an atmosphere to push against but could propel themselves through a vacuum. Furthermore, he argued, a rocket that

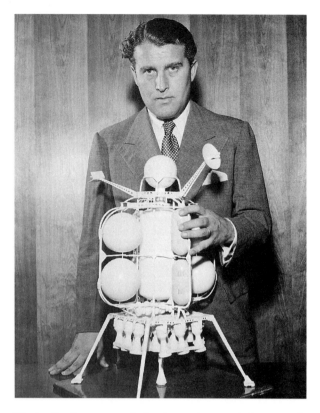

Wernher Von Braun, aeronautical engineer and proponent of space travel, with a model spacecraft intended to travel from a space station orbiting Earth to the Moon. October 11, 1952. © BETTMANN/CORBIS. REPRODUCED BY PERMISSION.

contained sufficient fuel and oxygen could in principle reach the moon. In the 1930s Wernher von Braun emerged as a leader in rocket technology. He designed two rockets that soared more than one and a half miles into space, and in 1938 he developed the German V-2 rocket, which reached an altitude of fifty miles and could travel horizontally more than two hundred miles.

Significance

During World War II von Braun defected to the United States, where he became a spokesperson for space travel. In this excerpt from the introduction to *Conquest of the Moon* he noted that American scientists already had the rocket technology to reach the Moon and predicted that the United States would land a man on the Moon within twenty-five years, or at least by the end of the twentieth century.

Von Braun may have supposed he was being bold in forecasting a Moon landing so soon. But what he did not foresee in 1953 was the space race the United States and the Soviet Union would launch toward decade's end. Both nations had been locked in a cold war (a period of hostilities that did not spark a war) since 1945, each suspicious of the other's intentions. During the Cold War

missile and satellite technology could give one nation military superiority, so the control of space became a matter of national security. In 1957 the Soviets stunned Americans by launching the world's first intercontinental ballistic missile (ICBM) and the first satellite, *Sputnik.* Congress responded the next year by creating the National Aeronautics and Space Administration (NASA). The United States made strides toward regaining superiority by sending Alan Shephard into space in 1961 and John Glenn into orbit around earth in 1962. In answer to President John F. Kennedy's goal of putting a man on the Moon by the end of the 1960s, NASA accelerated project Apollo. In 1969 the United States reached the Moon only sixteen years after von Braun's prediction.

Primary Source

Conquest of the Moon [excerpt]

> **SYNOPSIS:** In this excerpt from the book's introduction, von Braun predicts a Moon landing "within 25 years—certainly by the end of the century." He asserts that American scientists already have the rocket technology to reach the Moon and predicts that space vehicles would have small nuclear reactors for electricity and the decomposition of hydrazine for thrust.

In a previous work entitled *Across the Space Frontier,* the contributors to this book told the story of how man can reach beyond the atmosphere and establish a station in space within ten or fifteen years. Now, from that space station, the reader is taken another step forward—to the moon.

This volume tells how we will make the trip to the moon, what we will do when we get there, and how we will return. How soon could such a pioneer expedition set out? Perhaps within twenty-five years—certainly by the end of this century.

The ships the explorers will use for the long journey through space will bear little resemblance to those depicted by the science-fictionists. In fact, their appearance is even more fantastic. But there is this difference: they work.

The reader may well ask if it isn't rash to attempt a detailed technical description of vehicles that are at least a quarter of a century away. He may also wonder whether, by the time such vehicles are constructed, there may not be better solutions to the technical problems than those presented here. The answer, of course, is yes. The purpose of this book, however, is to show that a lunar voyage is possible even now by applying the basic engineering knowledge and technical ability available to us today. On this account speculations regarding future technical developments have been carefully avoided. . . .

Right now, we can list a number of developments that may be available by the time the first expedition sets out on its voyage to the moon. For example, the problem of generating power for space vehicles to run such utilities as air-conditioning and water-recovery plants, not to mention heating and cooking facilities, is a very difficult one. The only efficient method we know today, apart from using weighty batteries, is to use a solar power plant. This method will probably be replaced by the time lunar vehicles are constructed. We shall probably be able to have a lightweight nuclear reactor for the generation of electric power. The vehicles described in this book are steered by rocket motors mounted on hinges which swivel for maneuvering ability. Within two decades a different method might be developed. The decomposition of hydrogen peroxide for driving the propellant-feeding turbo-pumps may be abandoned in favor of decomposition of hydrazine, which is one of the main propellants used to power the moonships.

In the design of any space vehicle, protective shields surrounding the propellant tanks must be provided to ward off incoming meteors. By the time we are ready to construct a moonship, some type of self-sealing tanks for the propellant, similar to bullet-proof gasoline tanks, might be available. These would permit the designer to do away altogether with the protective meteor shields, provided, of course, that the self-sealing tanks are lighter than normal tanks plus meteor shields.

However, barring entirely new discoveries in the field of nuclear energy, it is not likely that chemical propulsion will be replaced by an atomic power plant. In our proposed lunar trip, the landing on the moon's surface and the subsequent take-off require several hundred tons of thrust, and this involves the transfer of energy on such a scale that chemical propellants will prove to be superior. Nuclear rocket drives may some day be successful for flights between heavenly bodies for surveying and photographing purposes, but not when landings must be made. The weight alone of an atomic plant as we could now conceive it would make the landing and take-off of huge rocket ships not only uneconomical but virtually impossible.

There have been many books written about journeys to the moon, but few of the writers seem to know what to do with their explorers once they get them there. The authors of this book have tried to describe definitely both the types of scientists who will go on the expedition and the experiments and

investigations they will perform. In speculating on these activities, the authors have kept within the boundaries of present-day knowledge of the moon.

We will not go to the moon simply for the sake of getting there. True, man's curiosity and adventurous instincts will play a large part in the enthusiasm for the venture. But the primary reason will be scientific: to increase mankind's knowledge of the universe. Then too the trip may prove to have economic significance: we may find minerals, perhaps such precious ones as uranium ores.

Further Resources

BOOKS

Collins, Martin J. *Space Race: The U.S.–U.S.S.R. Competition to Reach the Moon.* San Francisco: Pomegranate Communications, 1999.

Heppenheimer, T. A. *Countdown: A History of Space Flight.* New York: John Wiley & Sons, 1997.

Schefter, James L. *The Race: The Uncensored Story of How America Beat Russia to the Moon.* New York: Doubleday, 1999.

Siddiqi, Asif A. *Challenge to Apollo: The Soviet Union and the Space Race, 1945–1974.* Washington, D.C.: National Aeronautics and Space Administration, 2000.

Von Braun, Wernher. *History of Rocketry and Space Travel.* New York: Crowell, 1969.

PERIODICALS

McCurdy, Howard. "Forty Years in Space: Human Spaceflight in Perspective." *Ad Astra,* March/April 2001, 12–16.

Petit, Charles W. "Rocket Man Takes a Hit." *U.S. News & World Report,* March 25, 2002, 54–57.

WEBSITES

"Wernher Von Braun." Available online at http://liftoff.msfc .nasa.gov/academy/history/VonBraun/VonBraun.html; website home page: http://liftoff.msfc.nasa.gov (accessed June 9, 2003).

"Wernher von Braun (1912–1977)." Available online at http:// history.nasa.gov/sputnik/braun.html; website home page: http://history.nasa.gov (accessed June 9, 2003).

AUDIO AND VISUAL MEDIA

Heaven and Earth: First Step. Stamford, Conn.: ABC Video, 1999, VHS.

"Polio Vaccine Evaluation Results"

Press release

By: Thomas Francis
Date: April 12, 1955

Source: Francis, Thomas. "Polio Vaccine Evaluation Results." Press Release. University of Michigan, April 12, 1955. Available online at http://www.med.umich.edu/medschool/chm/polioexhibit /press_release.htm; website home page: http://www.med.umich .edu/medschool/chm/index.htm (accessed June 9, 2002)

About the Author: Thomas Francis (1900–1969), the lead researcher on the project described in this press release, was born in Gas City, Indiana, in 1900 and received his M.D. from Yale University in 1925. He isolated two strains of influenza between 1934 and 1940 and developed vaccines against both. In 1954 the University of Michigan appointed him to the National Foundation for Infantile Paralysis, where he tested Jonas Salk's polio vaccine. ■

Introduction

The development of vaccines is one of medicine's triumphs. Edward Jenner, an eighteenth-century British physician, inaugurated the era of vaccination, concentrating on smallpox. He noted that smallpox survivors, including those infected with a mild case, were immune to the disease. Yet to deliberately infect a person with smallpox to confer immunity was dangerous, for the infection could kill the person. So he turned his attention to cowpox, a mild disease contracted from cattle, noting that a person infected with it also became immune to smallpox. He reasoned that if he infected a person with cowpox, he could make that person immune to smallpox. In 1796 he tested this hypothesis by infecting a young boy with cowpox, then, when the boy recovered, injecting him with smallpox. The boy developed no symptoms of the disease. Jenner had developed the first vaccine.

Jenner had no idea, however, why cowpox conferred immunity to smallpox. Modern medicine would discover that a dead or attenuated strain of a virus or bacterium or that of a closely related virus or bacterium causes the body to produce antibodies. Once the body has manufactured these antibodies, it will quickly produce them in large numbers if a person contracts a virulent strain of the bacterium or virus, killing it and thereby preventing it from spreading throughout the body.

Significance

Less lethal than smallpox, polio nonetheless infected some 20,000 Americans a year in the early 1950s. Fortunately vaccination works against polio as it does against smallpox. The American physician Jonas Salk began to study polio when he became head of the Virus Research Laboratory in 1947 at the University of Pittsburgh. He isolated three polio strains, demonstrating that dead cultures conferred polio immunity in monkeys. In 1952 he began testing the cultures on children who had recovered from polio and then on children who had never had the disease. In all cases the inoculations conferred immunity to polio.

In recognition of his work, President Jimmy Carter awarded Salk the Presidential Medal of Freedom in 1977.

In 1954 Thomas Francis Jr. launched a mass field trial of the vaccine, reporting in April 1955 that the vaccine was a success and that it held the potential to eradicate the disease. He proved to be correct, for between 1961 and 1981 only six Americans contracted polio. Like the smallpox vaccine, the polio vaccine tamed a scourge of humanity.

Primary Source

"Polio Vaccine Evaluation Results"

SYNOPSIS: In this press release Thomas Francis Jr. announces that "the [polio] vaccine works. It is safe, effective, and potent." He also announces that medicine now has the means of protecting children from polio, implying that the vaccine could eradicate the disease.

Ann Arbor: The vaccine works. It is safe, effective, and potent.

Dr. Thomas Francis, Jr., U-M Director of the Poliomyelitis Vaccine Evaluation Center, told an anxious world of parents that the Salk vaccine has been proven to be up to 80-90 percent effective in preventing paralytic polio.

At a meeting of over 500 scientists and physicians and before the penetrating eyes of cameras and powerful spotlights, Dr. Francis spoke on the effectiveness of the Salk vaccine. The meeting was held at the Rackham Auditorium in Ann Arbor under the joint sponsorship of the National Foundation for Infantile Paralysis and the University of Michigan.

Dr. Francis declared the vaccine had produced "an extremely successful effect" among bulbar-patients in the areas where vaccine and an inert substance had been tried interchangeably.

Financed by nearly one million dollars worth of dimes which have been donated to the National Foundation, the Francis Report may slow down what has become a double-time march of disease to a snail's pace.

In strong statistical language the historic trial of a vaccine and its subsequent analysis was revealed. Over 113 pages in length, the Report at long last called a halt to speculations and finally reinforced laboratory findings with concrete field evidence. There can be no doubt now that children can be inoculated successfully against polio.

There can be no doubt that humanity can pull itself up from its own bootstraps and protect its children from the insidious invasion of ultramicroscopic disease.

For one thing, what was feared turned out to be unfounded—the vaccine proved incredibly safe. Reactions were nearly negligible. Only 0.4 percent of the vaccinated children suffered minor reactions.

An even smaller percent (0.004-0.006) suffered so-called "major reactions."

And the persistence of protection appears reasonably good. When good antibody responses were obtained from vaccination, the report said "the effect was maintained with but moderate decline after five months."

Distribution of antibody levels among vaccinated persons was much higher than that in the control population from the same areas.

Out of a total population of 1,829,916 children a total of 1013 cases of polio developed during the study period and were reported to the Center.

In placebo control areas, where vaccine was interchanged with an inert substance, 428 out of 749,236 children contracted the disease.

In the observed control areas where only second graders were inoculated, 585 cases out of 1,080,680 children developed the disease.

Percentages in the placebo areas were: 67.5 paralytic, 17.6 non-paralytic, 7.2 doubtful, and 7.6 not polio.

Specifically, 33 inoculated children receiving the complete vaccination series became paralyzed in the placebo areas. This is opposed to 115 uninoculated children. Similarly, in the observed areas there were 38 such children who became paralyzed, as opposed to 330 uninoculated children.

There were four deaths among children who received placebo; none among the vaccinated. In observed areas there were 11 fatalities; none among children receiving the vaccine.

Only one child who had been inoculated with the vaccine died of polio, and this death followed a tonsillectomy two days after the second injection of the vaccine in an area where polio was already prevalent.

The Report also stated that in no area did Type II virus prevail. There was, however, prevalence in certain areas of Types I and III.

Marked sociological differences were noted by the U-M's Survey Research Center among the participating and non-participating children in the study. For example, there was a higher proportion of children participating who had been vaccinated against

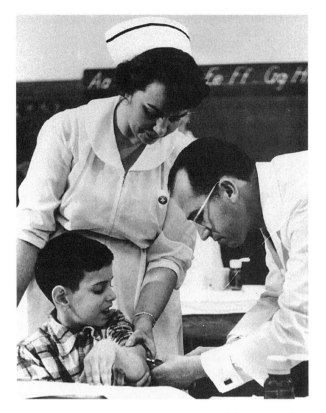

Jonas Salk, inventor of polio vaccine, administers an injection of vaccine to David Rosenbloom. AP/WIDE WORLD PHOTOS.

small-pox, diphtheria, and whooping cough than among the non-participants. Significant auxiliary findings were:

1. The vaccine's effectiveness was more clearly seen when measured against the more severe cases of the disease;

2. Although data were limited, findings in Canada and Finland support the Report in showing a significant effect of the vaccine among cases from whom virus was isolated;

3. Vaccination protected against family exposure. Only 1 out of 233 inoculated children developed the disease, while 8 out of 244 children receiving placebo contracted the disease from family contact. In picking the field trial areas, the National Foundation scored a major victory. Although in placebo areas cases were 27 per cent under the 1949-53 average, and 12 per cent less in the observed control areas, it was found that there had been a 26 per cent greater increase per 100,000 in trial areas as in non-trial areas.

This meant that trial areas were appropriately selected for the best testing conditions for the vaccine. The field trials and the evaluation were made possible by grants totalling $17,500,000 in March of Dimes Funds from the National Foundation for Infantile Paralysis.

Further Resources

BOOKS

Carter, Richard. *Breakthrough: The Saga of Jonas Salk.* New York: Trident, 1965.

Cryz, Stanley J. *Immunotherapy and Vaccines.* New York: VCH, 1991.

Kaufman, Stefan H. E. *Concepts in Vaccine Development.* New York: Walter & Gruyter, 1996.

Plotkin, Stanley A, and Edward A. Mortimer, eds. *Vaccines.* Philadelphia: W. B. Saunders, 1988.

Rowland, John. *The Polio Man: The Story of Dr. Jonas Salk.* New York: Roy Publishers, 1960.

Salk Vaccine. Hearings Before the Committee on Banking and Currency, House of Representatives, Eighty-Fourth Congress. Washington: GPO, 1955.

PERIODICALS

Grady, Denise. "As Polio Fades, Dr. Salk's Vaccine Re-emerges." *The New York Times,* December 14, 1999, D1.

Johnson, Amy. "Jonas Salk." *Ideals,* July 2001, 24–26.

Marks, Marilyn. "Jonas Salk." *Science Teacher,* February 2002, 81–83.

AUDIO AND VISUAL MEDIA

Marching to a Different Drummer: The Life and Career of Jonas Salk. Burlington, N.C.: Carolina Biological Supply Company, 1991, VHS.

Viruses: What They Are and How They Work. Chicago: Encyclopedia Britannica Educational Corporation, 1988, VHS.

War Against Polio. London, England: BBC, 1977, VHS.

"Transistor Technology Evokes New Physics"

Lecture

By: William Shockley

Date: December 11, 1956

Source: Shockley, William. "Transistor Technology Evokes New Physics." Nobel lecture, December 11, 1956, 344–345. Available online at http://www.nobel.se/physics/laureates /1956/shockley-lecture.html; website home page: http://www .nobel.se (accessed December 19, 2002).

About the Author: William Bradford Shockley (1910–1989) was born in London, England, and received a Ph.D. in physics from Harvard University in 1936. That year he joined Bell Laboratories as a research physicist, where he invented the transistor in collaboration with John Bardeen and Walter H. Brattain. All three shared the Nobel Prize in physics in 1956. ∎

Introduction

Vacuum tubes were the workhorse of electronic appliances—radios, televisions, computers—during the first half of the twentieth century. The Electronic Numerical Integrator and Computer (ENIAC) of 1946, the most powerful digital computer of its day, used vacuum tubes, which alter the path, strength, or speed of electrons flowing through a chamber. Vacuum tubes operate well at high temperatures and high voltages, but they are fragile and wear out with use because the stress of repeated heating and cooling fractures them. These deficiencies led physicists at Bell Laboratories to pursue an alternative to the vacuum tube. Conducting applied rather than basic scientific research, Shockley and two colleagues developed the transistor as an alternative to the vacuum tube. Transistors are silicon-based semiconductors. They are smaller and more durable than vacuum tubes and are more efficient because they operate at lower voltages than vacuum tubes.

Significance

In his 1956 Nobel address Shockley acknowledged his preference for applied science over basic science. A scientist conducts applied research with the aim of discovering practical knowledge, for example, to breed a high-yielding variety of wheat; a scientist conducts basic research to discover knowledge for its own sake, for example, to discover the age of the universe. Generally, no immediate practical gain can come from this knowledge.

Shockley claimed that some scientists belittle applied research, an attitude he believed to be shortsighted. He admitted to being uncomfortable with the labels used to characterize research: "pure, applied, unrestricted, fundamental, basic, academic, industrial, practical." In his view these labels hide the fact that all categories of research can lead to practical knowledge. To Shockley one test of the value of "fundamental research" is its potential to yield a practical benefit.

No one can deny the practical benefit of the semiconductor, which led to the development of the microchip and modern computers. By the early 1970s scientists could pack thousands of transistors on a silicon chip of only 3 millimeters to a side. By 2003, a chip of 2 centimeters per side could contain more than 20 million transistors, giving the computer unprecedented speed and memory.

Primary Source

"Transistor Technology Evokes New Physics" [excerpt]

SYNOPSIS: In this excerpt from his 1956 Nobel address, William Shockley acknowledges his prefer-

William Shockley (left), lead scientist on the team that invented the transistor, with Lee de Forest (right), inventor of the "audion," the first vacuum tube at Bell Telephone Laboratories, May 1952. Each is holding the other's invention. Smaller and more efficient than the vaccuum tubes they replaced, transistors made small but powerful electronic devices possible. **AP/WIDE WORLD PHOTOS. REPRODUCED BY PERMISSION**

ence for applied science over basic science. Moreover, he finds the distinction between applied and basic science to be artificial. However scientists classify it, all good science in his judgment has the capacity to yield practical results.

The objective of producing useful devices has strongly influenced the choice of the research projects with which I have been associated. It is frequently said that having a more-or-less specific practical goal in mind will degrade the quality of research. I do not believe that this is necessarily the case and to make my point in this lecture I have chosen my examples of the new physics of semiconductors from research projects which were very definitely motivated by practical considerations.

An important faction of United States industry adheres to the idea that research of a fundamental character is worthwhile from a practical point of view. This is outstandingly the case at Bell Telephone Laboratories where my co-prizewinners and I, together with our many colleagues, carried out the work described in these lectures. The attitude of Bell Telephone Laboratories has undoubtedly resulted to a

substantial degree from the viewpoints of the four men who have been its research directors and subsequently its presidents. Each of these men, H. D. Arnold, F. B. Jewett, O. E. Buckley, and M. J. Kelly, has also been active and effective in governmental or civic affairs. All had obtained a thorough indoctrination in the research viewpoint in the course of their doctorate training in physics. My personal contact with two of these men had a significant influence on my planning of semiconductor research programs as I shall mention below.

My decision to come to Bell Telephone Laboratories immediately after obtaining my Ph.D. in 1936 was strongly influenced by the fact that my supervisor would be C. J. Davisson. Upon my arrival I was assigned by Dr. M. J. Kelly to an indoctrination program in vacuum tubes. In the course of this program Dr. Kelly spoke to me of his ideal of doing all telephone switching electronically instead of with metal contacts. Although I did not choose to continue work on vacuum tubes and was given freedom to pursue basic research problems in solid-state physics, Dr. Kelly's discussion left me continually alert for possible applications of solid-state effects in telephone

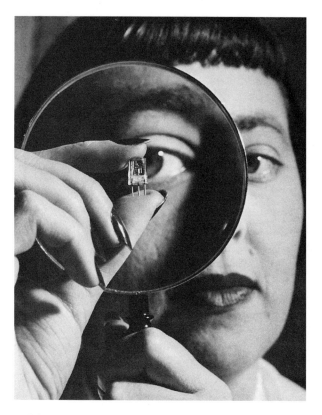

An RCA lab technician uses a magnifying glass to inspect a transistor in May 1952. © BETTMANN/CORBIS. REPRODUCED BY PERMISSION.

switching problems. Insofar as my contribution to transistor electronics has hastened the day of a fully electronic telephone exchange, it was strongly stimulated by the experiences given me during my early years at the Laboratories.

Before leaving the subject of research in industry, I would like to express some viewpoints about words often used to classify types of research in physics; for example, pure, applied, unrestricted, fundamental, basic, academic, industrial, practical, etc. It seems to me that all too frequently some of these words are used in a derogatory sense, on the one hand to belittle the practical objectives of producing something useful and, on the other hand, to brush off the possible long-range value of explorations into new areas where a useful outcome cannot be foreseen. Frequently, I have been asked if an experiment I have planned is pure or applied research; to me it is more important to know if the experiment will yield new and probably enduring knowledge about nature. If it is likely to yield such knowledge, it is, in my opinion, good fundamental research; and this is much more important than whether the motivation is purely esthetic satisfac-

tion on the part of the experimenter on the one hand or the improvement of the stability of a high-power transistor on the other. It will take both types to "confer the greatest benefit on mankind" sought for in Nobel's will.

Further Resources

BOOKS

Kingston, Robert H. *Semiconductor Surface Physics.* Philadelphia: University of Pennsylvania Press, 1957.

Lark-Horovitz, Karl. *Semi-Conducting Materials.* London, England: Butterworth Scientific Publications, 1951.

Riordan, Michael. *Crystal Fire: The Invention of the Transistor and the Birth of the Information Age.* New York: W. W. Norton, 1997.

Shockley, William B. *Electrons and Holes in Semiconductors.* New York: D. Van Nostrand, 1950.

PERIODICALS

Begley, Sharon. "The Transistor." *Newsweek,* Winter 1997/1998, 25–27.

"Dr. Shockley and Mr. Hyde." *U.S. News & World Report,* August 28, 1989, 16–19.

Moore, Gordon. "William Shockley." *Time South Pacific,* March 29, 1999, 106–110.

WEBSITES

Rudberg, E. G. "The Nobel Prize in Physics 1956." Available online at http://www.nobel.se/physics/laureates/1956/press .html; website home page: http://www.nobel.se (accessed December 19, 2002).

"William Bradford Shockley—Biography." Available online at http://www.nobel.se/physics/laureates/1956/shockley-bio .html; website home page: http://www.nobel.se (accessed December 19, 2002).

AUDIO AND VISUAL MEDIA

Rikoski, Richard A. *The Invention of the Transistor.* New York: Institute of Electrical and Electronics Engineers, 1972.

The Transistor. Princeton, N.J.: Films for the Humanities, 1994, VHS.

The Computer and the Brain
Monograph

By: John von Neumann

Date: 1958

Source: Von Neumann, John. *The Computer and the Brain.* New Haven, Conn.: Yale University Press, 1958, 42–44.

About the Author: John Louis von Neumann (1903–1957) was born in Budapest, Hungary, and received a Ph.D. in mathematics from the University of Budapest in 1926. In

1930 he emigrated to the United States, joining the mathematics faculty at Princeton University. After World War II he helped develop the hydrogen bomb and during his career published some 150 articles. He died in Washington, D.C. ∎

Introduction

Scientists have always had difficulty putting the study of human cognition on an empirical basis. The seventeenth-century French mathematician and philosopher René Descartes founded the study of cognition on the dichotomy between mind and body, asserting that because only humans had a mind, humans alone could think. The British cofounder of the theory of evolution by natural selection, Alfred Russell Wallace, substituted the brain for mind as the thinking organ, but he retained Descartes' conviction that only humans can reason and that this ability made humans special. Wallace believed, though, that the human brain was too complex and powerful to have resulted from evolution. He concluded that God rather than evolution had endowed humans with a brain that was, for example, three times the size of a chimpanzee's. Wallace thus preserved Descartes' belief that human cognition was beyond the reach of scientific inquiry.

This belief crumbled in the twentieth century. In the first decade of the century American physician Jacques Loeb rejected the notions of mind, soul, and consciousness. He centered cognition in the brain. To understand human reason was to understand the brain's neurological activity. He thus reduced cognition to the brain's physiology.

Significance

The development of the digital computer provided an analogy for how the brain thinks. In this excerpt John von Neumann examines the action of a neuron as a digital process. By demonstrating the analogy between a brain and a computer in terms of whether the circuitry of either is firing or not, he demonstrates that the brain makes use of the same binary system as a digital computer and thus operates as a type of digital computer.

Von Neumann's position is referred to as reductionism, meaning that complex phenomena, like cognition, can be understood as the sum of simpler physical processes. Reductionism is popular among physicists and computer scientists. An example comes from British computer scientist Alan Turing, who devised the Turing test as a way of equating the computer and the brain. If a person can carry on a conversation with a computer, the computer will have passed the test. That is, it will be indistinguishable from the human brain. Tulane University physicist and mathematician Frank Tipler expects a computer to pass the Turing test by 2030 and equates computers and brains in function: Both process and store information. One may reduce the

John von Neumann, noted mathematician and early proponent of the digital computer and artifical intelligence. **THE GRANGER COLLECTION, NEW YORK. REPRODUCED BY PERMISSION**

human brain to its electrical circuitry, a circuitry analogous to that of a computer.

Primary Source

The Computer and the Brain [excerpt]

SYNOPSIS: In this excerpt John von Neumann characterizes the action of a neuron as a digital process. A neuron that has fired an electric charge is on and may be represented by the digit 1. A neuron that has not fired is off and may be represented by the digit 0. These digits, 0 and 1, are the binary system of a digital computer.

The Process of Stimulation

As I mentioned before, the fully developed nerve impulses are comparable, no matter how induced. Because their character is not an unambiguously defined one (it may be viewed electrically as well as chemically, . . .), its induction, too, can be alternatively attributed to electrical or to chemical causes. Within the nervous system, however, it is mostly due to one or more other nerve impulses. Under such conditions, the process of its induction— the *stimulation* of a nerve impulse—may or may not succeed. If it fails, a passing disturbance arises at first, but after a few milliseconds, this dies out. Then no disturbances propagate along the axon. If it succeeds, the disturbance very soon assumes a (nearly) standard form, and in this form it spreads along the axon. That is to say, as mentioned above, a standard nerve impulse will then move along the axon, and its appearance will be reasonably independent of the details of the process that induced it.

The stimulation of the nerve impulse occurs normally in or near the body of the nerve cell. Its propagation, as discussed above, occurs along the axon.

The Mechanism of Stimulating Pulses by Pulses; Its Digital Character

I can now return to the digital character of this mechanism. The nervous pulses can clearly be viewed as (two-valued) markers, in the sense discussed previously: the absence of a pulse then represents one value (say, the binary digit 0), and the presence of one represents the other (say, the binary digit 1). This must, of course, be interpreted as an occurrence on a specific axon (or, rather, on all the axons of a specific neuron), and possibly in a specific time relation to other events. It is, then, to be interpreted as a marker (a binary digit 0 or 1) in a specific, logical role.

As mentioned above, pulses (which appear on the axons of a given neuron) are usually stimulated by other pulses that are impinging on the body of the neuron. This stimulation is, as a rule, conditional, i.e. only certain combinations and synchronisms of such primary pulses stimulate the secondary pulse in question—all others will fail to so stimulate. That is, the neuron is an organ which accepts and emits definite physical entities, the pulses. Upon receipt of pulses in certain combinations and synchronisms it will be stimulated to emit a pulse of its own, otherwise it will not emit. The rules which describe to which groups of pulses it will so respond are the rules that govern it as an active organ.

This is clearly the description of the functioning of an organ in a digital machine, and of the way in which the role and function of a digital organ has to be characterized. It therefore justifies the original assertion, that the nervous system has a *prima facie* digital character.

Let me add a few words regarding the qualifying "prima facie." The above description contains some idealizations and simplifications, which will be discussed subsequently. Once these are taken into account, the digital character no longer stands out

quite so clearly and unequivocally. Nevertheless, the traits emphasized in the above are the primarily conspicuous ones. It seems proper, therefore, to begin the discussion as I did here, by stressing the digital character of the nervous system.

Further Resources

BOOKS

Boolos, George S., and Richard S. Jeffery. *Computability and Logic*. Cambridge, England: Cambridge University Press, 1974.

Dudai, Yadin. *The Neurobiology of Memory*. Oxford, England: Oxford University Press, 1990.

Eccles, John C. *Evolution of the Brain*. London, England: Routledge, 1989.

Penrose, Roger. *The Emperor's New Mind: Concerning Computers, Minds, and the Laws of Physics*. Oxford, England: Oxford University Press, 1989.

Tipler, Frank J. *The Physics of Immortality*. New York: Doubleday, 1994.

PERIODICALS

Eccles, John C. "A Unitary Hypothesis of Mind-Brain Interaction in the Cerebral Cortex." *Proceedings of the Royal Society of London* 244, 1990, 433–451.

Haarer, David. "Molecular Computer Memory." *Nature*, May 14, 1992, 297–298.

McCarthy, John. "Review of the Emperor's New Mind." *Bulletin of the American Mathematical Society* 85, 1990, 606–616.

Turing, Alan M. "Computing Machinery and Intelligence." *Mind*, March 1950, 433–462.

WEBSITES

"John Louis von Neumann." Available online at http://ei.cs.vt.edu/~history/VonNeumann.html; website home page: http://ei.cs.vt.edu/~history (accessed June 10, 2003).

The Astronomical Universe
Nonfiction work

By: Otto Struve

Date: 1958

Source: Struve, Otto. *The Astronomical Universe*. Eugene, Ore.: Oregon State System of Higher Education, 1958, 9–10.

About the Author: Otto Struve (1897–1963) was born in Ukraine and emigrated to the United States in 1921. He was an astronomer at Yerkes Observatory in Wisconsin and became its director in 1932. That year he organized McDonald Observatory in Texas, becoming its director in 1938. In 1947 he retired from both positions to chair the University of Chicago's astronomy department. During his career he published several books and some seven hundred articles. ∎

Introduction

The alliance between the United States and the Soviet Union during World War II was one of convenience as both cooperated against their common enemy, Nazi Germany. After war's end in 1945, however, the two nations grew suspicious of one another, each viewing the other as expansionistic and as a threat to its security. In this atmosphere each nation sought protection from its military and believed science and technology were the basis of military strength. Americans had felt secure in the superiority of their science and technology. The atomic bomb, after all, was proof of America's leadership in science and engineering.

The Soviet Union shattered this confidence in 1949, when it tested its first atomic bomb and in 1953, when it tested its first hydrogen bomb. Then in 1957 the Soviets launched the world's first intercontinental ballistic missile (ICBM) and launched the first satellite, *Sputnik*. Americans felt uneasy that the Soviets had surpassed them in rocket and satellite technology. The United States, it seemed clear, needed to redouble its efforts in science and technology to recapture leadership.

Significance

Otto Struve shared the belief that *Sputnik* had demonstrated that American science and technology had ceded leadership to the Soviets. In this excerpt he asserted that 1957 had been as momentous a year as 1492, the year in which Christopher Columbus landed in the Americas and Spain seized leadership on the seas from Portugal. Likewise, Struve believed, the United States had thought itself the leading scientific and engineering nation only to discover that the Soviets had surpassed it in 1957.

Struve believed the United States fell behind because it had too few astronomers with expertise in orbit theory and satellite technology. Oregon had but one astronomer and Iowa only two, said Struve. This paucity demanded that the United States double or triple the number of astronomers in "the next ten or fifteen years." Struve warned that the training of astronomers takes more time and money than does the building of new telescopes.

Struve's call for the training of more astronomers was part of a national effort. In 1958 Congress passed the National Defense Education Act, which funded the teaching of science, mathematics, and foreign languages in America's public schools. The act also increased the number of scholarships and loans to college students; the goal was to increase the number of students in colleges and universities, thereby increasing the number of students majoring in science, engineering, and mathematics.

Sputnik spurred the scientific community and Congress into action. By the end of the decade the United States had surpassed the Soviets in the number of long-range bombers,

Sputnik 1, first artificial satellite, launched by the Soviet Union on October 4, 1957. AP/WIDE WORLD PHOTOS. REPRODUCED BY PERMISSION.

submarine-launched ballistic missiles, and ICBMs and recaptured its leadership in science and engineering.

Primary Source

The Astronomical Universe [excerpt]

> **SYNOPSIS:** In this excerpt Otto Struve asserts that 1957 had been as momentous a year as 1492. Just as Portugal lost its maritime lead to Spain that year, the United States lost its superiority in rocket and satellite technology to the Soviet Union in 1957. To recapture its lead, Struve urges that American colleges and universities double or triple the number of astronomers in "the next ten or fifteen years."

The Solar System

When I announced the title of this lecture, several months ago, there was as yet no "sputnik" in the sky, and no one knew whether the efforts of our own engineers or those of the Russians would succeed in launching an artificial satellite. But on October 4 of this year the world of science, and with it the entire world, was suddenly changed by the Soviet announcement of the successful launching of their first "sputnik," now designated by the symbol 1957*a* 1.

Because of this announcement the year 1957 will be remembered in the history of astronomical exploration as the year 1492 is remembered in the history of geographical exploration. There will never again be a lecture on the solar system which does not in some way recognize the great achievement of the Russian scientists in producing the first two artificial satellites and it would be unrealistic on my part not to speak of this development today. As F. L. Whipple and J. A. Hynek have recently stated in the "Scientific American": "In his millenia of looking at the stars, man has never found so exciting a challenge as the year 1957 has suddenly thrust upon him."

I mentioned the year 1492—and it is of some interest to draw a comparison of the discovery of America by Columbus and the conquest of interplanetary space by the Russian rockets. In the second half of the 15th century the leading nation in the field of navigation and geographical exploration was Portugal. Prince Henry the Navigator had assembled at his court the leading astronomers of his time, and had developed astronomical methods of navigation that enabled Vasco da Gama and many others to undertake long voyages along the western coast of Africa and permitted them, ultimately, to reach the shores of India and China by circumnavigating the continent of Africa.

But when Columbus applied to the King of Portugal for aid in organizing an expedition toward the west, across the Atlantic Ocean, he encountered only lack of interest and scepticism. The voyages of Columbus were financed by Queen Isabella of Spain, and from this small investment sprang Spain's great colonial empire which lasted for several centuries and insured Spain's preeminence in the Western world.

Until October 4 we felt secure in our belief that we were the leading nation in science and engineering. But on that date we suffered a humiliating defeat, and one that may go into history as of comparable significance to the defeat which Portugal experienced in 1492 when King John II of Portugal lacked vision and Queen Isabella of Spain possessed it.

It is well for us to recognize clearly two things:

1. The Russian success was not entirely unexpected: last spring several Russian astronomical publications contained an appeal to Soviet astronomers to be prepared for the observation of artificial satellites (but there was no indication that the Russian "sputnik" was nearing completion); there were some vague indications in personal discussions that the Russians were making progress in this field; and in August a distinguished Soviet astronomer mentioned to me in Liège (Belgium) that while a few decades ago many Russian astronomers had thought that they would never overcome the lead of American astronomers, they had already surpassed us in 1957.

2. We are especially ill prepared to meet the Russian competition on the "astro-nautical" front. We are badly understaffed: there are fewer than a dozen astronomers in the United States whose training in celestial mechanics, and experience in orbit theory, qualifies them to derive the scientific information that should come from the observations of the artificial satellites, and we have probably not enough astronomers to secure the vast number of accurate visual, photographic, and radio observations that are now required and that will be required when additional satellites are launched.

The problem of training a sufficient number of competent astronomers is especially serious. I believe that there is only one professional astronomer in the entire state of Oregon, and he (Dr. Edwin Ebbighausen) divides his time between physics and astronomy. To mention only one other case, there are two professional astronomers in Iowa, one at Drake University, the other at the University of Iowa. It seems to me essential that the responsibility for training astronomers and of doubling or tripling their number in the next ten or fifteen years should be shared by the Federal Government, the states, and the private universities: it takes longer and costs more money to train competent scientists than to construct new telescopes!

Further Resources

BOOKS

Dickson, Paul. *Sputnik: The Shock of the Century.* New York: Walker, 2001.

Divine, Robert A. *The Sputnik Challenge: Eisenhower's Response to the Soviet Satellite.* New York: Oxford University Press, 1993.

Krieger, Firmin J. *Behind the Sputniks: A Survey of Soviet Space Science.* Washington, D.C.: Public Affairs Press, 1958.

Launius, Roger D., John M. Logsdon, and Robert W. Smith. *Reconsidering Sputnik: Forty Years Since the Soviet Satellite.* Australia: Harwood Academic, 2000.

PERIODICALS

"Sputnik's Launchpad Is Consigned to History." *Nature,* April 4, 2002, 469–475.

Sturdevant, Rick W. "Reconsidering Sputnik." *Air Power History,* Spring 2002, 64–66.

WEBSITES

"Sputnik and the Dawn of the Space Age." Available online at http://www.hq.nasa.gov/office/pao/History/sputnik; website home page: http://history.nasa.gov (accessed June 10, 2003).

Wright, Michael. "Here Comes Sputnik!" Available online at http://www.batnet.com/mfwright/sputnik.html (accessed December 20, 2002). *This site provides links to numerous books, websites, and other resources about the space race.*

AUDIO AND VISUAL MEDIA

Archival Feature: The Flight of Sputnik. Danbury, Conn.: Grolier Educational Corporation, 1982.

The Control of Fertility

Monograph, Tables

By: Gregory Pincus

Date: 1965

Source: Pincus, Gregory. *The Control of Fertility.* New York: Academic Press, 1965, 226–227.

About the Author: Gregory Goodwin Pincus (1903–1967) was born in Woodbine, New Jersey, and received a Sc.D. from Harvard University in 1927. He taught at Harvard, Clark University, Tufts University Medical School, and Boston University. In 1944 he and a colleague founded the Worcester Foundation for Experimental Biology. Pincus collaborated with Harvard gynecologist John Rock in developing the oral contraceptive Enovid. ∎

Effectiveness of Various Methods of Conception Control

Method	Average pregnancies per 100 woman years
No contraception	115
Douche	31
Safe period (rhythm)	24
Jelly alone	20
Withdrawal	18
Condom	14
Diaphragm (with or without jelly)	12
Norethynodrel + estrogen	1.1

SOURCE: Table 40 from Pincus, Gregory. *The Control of Fertility.* New York and London: Academic Press, 1965, p. 226.

Primary Source

The Control of Fertility: Table

SYNOPSIS: These two tables accompany Pincus's monograph. This table shows how likely a woman is to become pregnant despite the various contraceptive measures available in the 1950s. The method with the lowest pregnancy rate, "norethynodrel + estrogen," is the oral contraceptive Pincus developed, Enovid ("The Pill").

Pregnancies According to Pills Missed (San Juan)

Number of pills missed	Dose (mg/day)	Number of woman years	Number of pregnancies	Pregnancy rate per 100 woman years
0	2.5	411	1[a]	0.2
	5.0	1685	4	0.2
	10.0	686	4	0.6
1–5	2.5	77	0	0.0
	5.0	154	4	2.6
	10.0	95	3	3.2
6–19	2.5	6	4	66.7
	5.0	19	8	42.1
	10.0	31	10	32.3

[a]Patient took ½ tablet (1.25 mg/day).

SOURCE: Table 41 from Pincus, Gregory. *The Control of Fertility.* New York and London: Academic Press, 1965, p. 227.

Primary Source

The Control of Fertility: Table

This table demonstrates that almost all pregnancies among women using Pincus's Enovid birth control pill can be blamed on women missing doses.

Introduction

Oral contraceptives have a long history. Women in antiquity believed that eating various plants, including silphium (a plant related to the herb fennel), Queen Anne's lace, ivy, juniper, hawthorn, willow, poplar, pine, myrrh, rue, the date palm, pomegranate, cabbage, or onion, prevented pregnancy. During the Middle Ages European women drank potions containing lead, arsenic, mercury, and strychnine in the belief these substances were contraceptives—often with fatal effect. During the nineteenth century Canadian women drank brewed beaver testicles and alcohol as a contraceptive.

The study of oral contraceptives did not become a science until the twentieth century. In the 1920s Austrian physiologist Ludwig Haberlandt discovered that ovarian extracts could prevent fertility in animals that ingested them. In 1931 he advocated the use of hormones to prevent conception in women. Following this advice, American chemist Russell Marker began in the 1940s to synthesize progesterone, a steroid, as a contraceptive, and in 1944 he formed the company Syntex to market it. In 1949 Austrian chemist Carl Djerassi joined Syntex and patented the oral contraceptive norethindrone in 1951. Two years later American chemist Frank Colton patented a similar compound, norethynodrel.

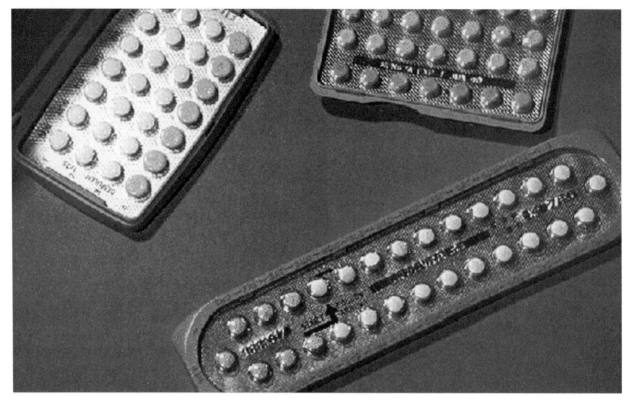

Packages of Enovid 10, the first birth control pill. Developed by George Pincus and John Rock in the 1950s, Enovid 10 went on sale in 1960. **ARCHIVE PHOTOS, INC. REPRODUCED BY PERMISSION**

Significance

In 1950 Margaret Sanger, the founder of Planned Parenthood, persuaded Katherine McCormick, heiress to the International Harvester fortune, to fund the research of Gregory Pincus. In collaboration with John Rock, Pincus developed the oral contraceptive Enovid, better known as "The Pill," in 1952 and began clinical trials outside the United States in 1954. Based on the success of these trials, the FDA approved Enovid in 1957 for women suffering from menstrual irregularities. Only in 1960 would the FDA approve its use as an oral contraceptive. By 1961 some 400,000 American women were using Enovid; by 1965 that number had leapt to 3.8 million, and by 1967, 12.5 million women worldwide were using Enovid.

Enovid's significance would be hard to overstate. It gave women, for the first time, control over their own reproduction. They could now shape their destinies with a drug that was both safe (though some scientists dispute this) and effective. Enovid gave women sexual freedom by reducing their fear of becoming pregnant.

Primary Source

The Control of Fertility [excerpt]: Monograph

SYNOPSIS: In this excerpt Gregory Pincus describes the results of his clinical trials with Enovid. He

boasts that not one woman who used it correctly became pregnant. Only those who failed to take Enovid as directed became pregnant. Also present are tables from the mongraph.

Contraception

The most widespread use of the progestin-estrogen compounds is for preventing conception. For this purpose they have been spectacularly successful. The first preparation to be used in large-scale trial is the combination of norethynodrel and estrogen, known commercially as Enovid. The pregnancy rate in users of this drug even in the initial experimental series with now avoided problems of tablet administration and withdrawal and of general management was remarkably low. This is demonstrated in [Table, "Effectiveness of Various Methods of Conception Control"] which compares pregnancy rates in controlled studies of various contraceptive methods. . . .

That the rate of 1.1 per 100 woman years is due to "patient failure" rather than "method failure" is evident from the data [Table, "Pregnancies According to Pills Missed (San Juan)"] . . . which tabulates, at three doses of Envoid, the pregnancy rates in the cycles during which the women allegedly missed taking no pills, 1–5 pills, and 6–19 pills. It is obvious that the chances of conception increase with the number of pills missed. It is possible, indeed probable, that the pregnancies occurring in cycles when pills were allegedly faithfully taken were due to either unrecalled or unacknowledged error. Indeed, Rice-Wray *et al.* . . . flatly declare that no accidental pregnancies occurred in over 2000 women studied in about 23,000 cycles of use of several estrogen-progestin combinations when these women followed directions for use. Similarly, Cook *et al.* . . . found: "No woman who followed instructions has become pregnant during 518 woman-years of use. Norethynodrel is thus physiologically completely effective." Indeed, these authors found that among their subjects 176 women reporting previous experience with one or more contraceptive methods had a rate of 106 pregnancies per 100 years while the 328 with no such previous experience had a rate of 110. Another fact emerging from the data [Table, "Pregnancies According to Pills Missed (San Juan)"] is that even imperfect use (i.e., tablet missing) affords protection against conception. This experience of the remarkable contraceptive efficiency of the norethynodrel-estrogen combination over the fourfold dosage range indicated [Table, "Pregnancies According to Pills Missed (San Juan)"] has been repeatedly confirmed over the past several years. . . . [Included in these studies are projects in North and South America, Europe, Australia, and Asia.] All who have used the preparation containing 2.5 mg norethynodrel find it to be as effective as preparations containing higher doses. Even the accidental experience in Birmingham . . . remarked on above has failed to inform us of a subeffective dose of norethynodrel since the pregnancies occurring may have been due to a postmedication conception occurring during an amenorrhea consequent on too low a dose of the estrogen.

Further Resources

BOOKS

Briggs, Michael H., and Maxine Briggs. *Oral Contraceptives.* Montreal, Canada: Eden, 1977.

Djerassi, Carl. *This Man's Pill: Reflections in the 50th Birthday of the Pill.* Oxford, England: Oxford University Press, 2001.

FDA Report on the Oral Contraceptives. Washington, D.C.: GPO, 1966.

Gardner, Maureen B. *Facts about Oral Contraceptives.* Bethesda, Md.: National Institutes of Health, 1984.

Marks, Lara V. *Sexual Chemistry: A History of the Contraceptive Pill.* New Haven, Conn.: Yale University Press, 2001.

PERIODICALS

Davidson, Nancy E. "Good News About Oral Contraceptives." *New England Journal of Medicine,* June 27, 2002, 2078–2080.

Seaman, Barbara. "The Pill and I: 40 Years on, the Relationship Remains Wary." *The New York Times,* June 25, 2000, A19.

WEBSITES

The Contraception Report. "Evolution and Revolution: The Past, Present, and Future of Contraception." February 2000. Available online at http://www.contraceptiononline.org/contrareport /article01.cfm?art=93; website home page: http://www .contraceptiononline.org/index.cfm (accessed June 10, 2003).

Junod, Suzanne White. "FDA's Approval of the First Oral Contraceptive—Enovid." *Update,* July–August, 1998. Available online at http://www.fda.gov/oc/history/makinghistory/enovid .html; website home page: http://www.fda.gov (accessed December 20, 2002).

AUDIO AND VISUAL MEDIA

Oral Contraception in the Transition Years. Morris Plains, N.J.: Park, Davis & Company, 1992, VHS.

The Pill. New York: Women Make Movies, 1999, VHS.

"Mutable Loci in Maize"
Essay

By: Barbara McClintock

Date: 1987

Source: McClintock, Barbara. "Mutable Loci in Maize." *Annual Report of the Director of the Department of Genetics, Carnegie Institution of Washington Yearbook,* No. 49, December 15, 1950, 157–167. Reprinted in *The Discovery and Characterization of Transposable Elements: The Collected Papers of Barbara McClintock.* New York: Garland, 1987, 204–205.

About the Author: Barbara McClintock (1902–1992) was born in Hartford, Connecticut, and received a Ph.D. in zoology from Cornell University in 1927. As a graduate student she studied the genetics of corn, a project that absorbed her throughout her career. She received a Guggenheim Fellowship in 1933, served as vice president of the Genetics Society of America in 1939 and president in 1944, and won the Nobel Prize in medicine or physiology in 1983. ∎

Introduction

In 1866 Austrian monk Gregor Mendel announced that particles (genes) code for traits such as eye color and are passed unaltered from parents to offspring. Mendel's contemporaries either dismissed his work as error or ignored it. Only in 1900, when scientists rediscovered

Barbara McClintock, noted zoologist and discoverer of the ability of chromosomes to cause genes to switch on or off and to even switch locations. AP/WIDE WORLD PHOTOS. REPRODUCED BY PERMISSION.

Mendel's work, did they begin to understand its import. American scientists took leadership in the new science of genetics. Columbia University embryologist Thomas Hunt Morgan and his team of researchers united the gene and chromosome theory between 1909 and 1927, discovering that genes are arranged in a line on chromosomes.

Morgan and his associates used drosophila, the fruit fly, for their research, but others chose different organisms or plants. Dutch botanist Hugo de Vries used the evening primrose, and American geneticists George Shull and Edward M. East used corn during the first decade of the twentieth century. Corn was ideal for research because each of its 10 chromosomes look different and is easily identifiable. Moreover, corn occasionally has an extra chromosome, allowing scientists to study the effect of an extra chromosome on the behavior of the rest of the genes in that plant.

Significance

For these reasons Barbara McClintock focused her research on corn beginning in the 1920s. With this 1950 paper she announced that the insertion of an extra chromosome into corn may cause a mutation in one or more

genes in the plant. That is, the new chromosome can turn off genes on other chromosomes, can turn others on, and can even cause genes to switch their location on a chromosome.

These discoveries so astonished geneticists that many rejected her findings, as others had rejected Mendel's. Some historians have asserted that McClintock's critics were males seeking to preserve science as a male sphere. As a woman, McClintock was vulnerable to attack from the men who controlled the scientific agenda at America's research universities. She thus symbolized the difficulty American women face in science. Compared to men they receive fewer Ph.D.'s in biology, chemistry, and physics. On university faculties they cluster in the lower ranks of instructor and assistant professor without tenure, whereas male scientists tend to hold tenure as associate or full professors. Men also outnumber women as chairs of science departments.

Only in the 1970s, when molecular biologists confirmed McClintock's findings, did the scientific establishment begin to acknowledge the legitimacy of her work. This acceptance culminated in her 1983 Nobel Prize in medicine or physiology.

Primary Source

"Mutable Loci in Maize" [excerpt]

> **SYNOPSIS:** In this excerpt, part of a paper entitled "Mutable Loci in Maize," McClintock announces that the insertion of an extra chromosome in corn can cause a mutation in one or more genes in that plant. That is, the new chromosome can turn off genes on another chromosome, turn on others, and even cause genes to switch locations on a chromosome.

Variegation has been described in a wide range of organisms. Some cases of it are known to be associated with the irregular mitotic behavior of ring-shaped chromosomes, or with chromatin deletion produced by the breakage-fusion-bridge cycle. Another class of somatically expressed variegation is known to be related to irreversible changes in self-reproducing cytoplasmic elements, such as the plastids. A third class of somatic variegation is associated with detectable changes in genic action. The terms mosaicism, mutable genes, somatic variegation, mutable loci, and position effect have been used to designate this class. It is on this third type of variegation that the investigations in maize have been focused. It has been described in many organisms. Because the general nature of the phenotypically expressed instability is so similar in these unrelated organisms, it is difficult to avoid the conclusion that a common principle of nuclear and chromosomal organization and functioning is concerned. The evidence obtained during the past year has made it possible to formulate a working hypothesis that incorporates such a principle. The hypothesis is an expansion of the interpretation of the origin and behavior of mutable loci presented in Year Book No. 48. Its salient features may be reviewed here:

A normal, wild-type locus may be totally or partially inhibited in action by the insertion of a foreign piece of chromatin adjacent to it. Total or partial release from inhibition will occur when this foreign chromatin is removed or altered in organization. The insertion, removal, or change in organization of the foreign chromatin occurs because this chromatin becomes adhesive in certain somatic cells at very precise times in the development of a tissue. The adhesiveness causes a rupturing of the chromosome at the adhered positions during the subsequent mitotic cycle, which results in removal, transposition, or alteration in constitution of the chromatin materials involved. The chromatin primarily concerned in these events is heterochromatin. Its behavior as revealed in this study of the origin and expression of mutable loci may reflect one aspect of its normal behavior in the development of an organism.

Mode of Detection of Transpositions of Ds

The first direct evidence with regard to the mode of origin and the operation of mutable loci was obtained from study of the Ac-controlled mutable c^{m-1} locus. The origin of this mutable locus by a transposition of Ds has been reviewed in previous reports. Because transposition of minute bits of chromatin from one location to another in the chromosome complement is basic to the concept of the origin and behavior of mutable loci, extensive investigations of this phenomenon have been undertaken during the past year. Twenty cases of transposition of Ds from its standard location in the short arm of chromosome 9 to another position within this arm have been studied. Several cases of transposition from the new position to still another position have also been investigated. Transpositions of Ds from one location to another within the short arm of chromosome 9 were selected for study because the design of the experiments makes it possible to detect such trans-

positions shortly after they occur, and also because it is possible to locate, readily and accurately, the new positions of Ds activity.

An example may be given of the methods used in detecting and locating new positions of Ds. Pollen of plants that have one or more Ac loci, and carry I, Sh, Bz, Wx, and Ds-standard in one chromosome 9, is placed on silks of tester plants carrying C sh bz wx but having no Ds or Ac loci. The state of the Ds locus in these plants is selected for a high frequency of dicentric-chromatid formation as a consequence of events occurring at Ds. On the resulting ear, kernels that receive an Ac locus and a chromosome 9 carrying the markers I, Sh, Bz, Wx, and Ds-standard should show sectors of tissue with the C sh bz wx phenotype as a consequence of dicentric- and acentric-chromatid-forming events occurring at the Ds-standard location, which result in elimination from the nuclei of the acentric segment of chromatin carrying the markers I, Sh, Bz, and Wx (for details, see previous reports). With very few exceptions, the expected phenotypic characters are present in the sectors of the kernels carrying the stated markers. The few exceptional kernels that have sectors showing unexpected phenotypic characters are important, for from them are derived the strains having new positions of Ds activity.

Further Reources

BOOKS
Fine, Edith H. *Barbara McClintock: Nobel Prize Geneticist.* Springfield, N. J.: Enslow, 1998.

Mayr, Ernest. *The Growth of Biological Thought: Diversity, Evolution, and Inheritance.* Cambridge, Mass.: Harvard University Press, 1982.

Peterson, Peter A., and Angelo Bianchi. *Maize Genetics and Breeding in the 20th Century.* River Edge, N.J.: World Scientific, 1999.

PERIODICALS
McClintock, Barbara. "Chromosome Organization and Gene Expression."*Cold Spring Harbor Symposia on Quantitative Biology,* 1951, 13–47.

WEBSITES
"Barbara McClintock—Autobiography." Available online at http://www.nobel.se/medicine/laureates/1983/mcclintock autobio.html; website home page: http://www.nobel.se (accessed December 20, 2002).

"Barbara McClintock—Nobel Lecture." Available online at http://www.nobel.se/medicine/laureates/1983/mcclintock lecture.html; website home page: http://www.nobel.se (accessed December 20, 2002).

12

SPORTS

COREY SEEMAN

Entries are arranged in chronological order by date of primary source. For entries with one primary source, the entry title is the same as the primary source title. Entries with more than one primary source have an overall entry title, followed by the titles of the primary sources.

Important Events in Sports, 1950–1959

1950

- On February 7, Ted Williams of the Boston Red Sox enters spring training as baseball's highest-paid player, with a $125,000 contract.

- From April to May, American sports continue to desegregate when the Boston Celtics of the NBA draft the league's first African American player, Charles Cooper in the second round, and the American Bowling Congress ends its white-male-only policy.

- On April 23, the Minneapolis Lakers defeat Syracuse Nationals in the first National Basketball Association (NBA) championship.

- On June 11, Ben Hogan completes a courageous comeback from a near-fatal auto accident to win the U.S. Open and earns "golfer of the year" honors.

- On July 11, Red Schoendienst of the St. Louis Cardinals goes five for five and hits the game winning home run in the fourteenth inning in the All-Star baseball game. The National League beats the American League 4-3.

- On August 8, Florence Chadwick swims the English Channel in thirteen hours and twenty minutes, a women's record.

- On August 25, Sugar Ray Robinson is crowned world middleweight champion after knocking out Jose Basora in fifty-two seconds of the first round.

- On August 30, Althea Gibson becomes the first African American woman to compete in a national tennis tournament.

1951

- On January 17, college basketball fans are shocked by a point-shaving scandal that eventually involves seven schools and thirty-two players.

- On March 2, the NBA holds its first All-Star game at the Boston Garden; the East beats the West, 111-94. Boston's Ed McCauley is chosen Most Valuable Player.

- On March 12, Major League Baseball fires its second commissioner A. B. "Happy" Chandler. In 1947, Chandler overrode the baseball owner's vote against signing Jackie Robinson.

- On May 25, future hall of famer Willie Mays goes hitless in his debut with the New York Giants.

- On July 10, world middleweight champion Sugar Ray Robinson loses his title to Randy Turpin of England in fifteen rounds. This is only Robinson's second loss in eleven years.

- On July 18, Jersey Joe Wolcott wins the world heavyweight championship by knocking out Ezzard Charles in the seventh round. Wolcott is, at age thirty-seven, the oldest man ever to hold the title.

- On July 31, Milwaukee Brave Joe Adcock hits four home-runs in a nine-inning game against the Brooklyn Dodgers. Adcock's eighteen total bases in one game remains a baseball record.

- On August 18, one of the greatest stunts in American sports promotion occurs in St. Louis when 3 feet, 7 inches, Eddie Gaedel earns a base on balls for the last place Browns. Gaedel's strike zone measured 1-½ inches. Owner Bill Veeck's ploy results in midgets being banned from participation in Major League Baseball games.

- On August 29, Kid Gavilan defeats Billy Graham in fifteen rounds to win the world welterweight boxing championship.

- On September 12, Sugar Ray Robinson knocks out Randy Turpin in the tenth round to regain the middleweight boxing championship.

- On September 20, Ford C. Frick, president of the National League for eighteen years, is selected Major League Baseball's third commissioner.

- On October 3, Bobby Thomson hits the "shot heard round the world" off Ralph Branca and the New York Giants beat the Brooklyn Dodgers for the National League pennant to complete one of the greatest comebacks in baseball history.

- On October 10, Joe DiMaggio plays in his last game as a New York Yankee, ending one of the greatest careers in American sports.

1952

- *The Natural,* by Bernard Malamud, is published. It is the first serious American novel to employ a sports (baseball) setting, and it is followed in this decade by Mark Harris's *The Southpaw* and *Bang the Drum Slowly,* and Douglas Wallop's *The Year the Yankees Lost the Pennant.*

- In February, at the winter Olympic games in Oslo, Norway, gold medals are won by Andrea Mead (Lawrence) in slalom and giant slalom skiing, and Dick Button in figure skating. Button is the first figure skater to execute a triple jump in competition.

- On April 22, New York Giants relief pitcher Hoyt Wilhelm hits a home run in his first time at the plate. He would not hit another homer for the rest of his career consisting of 1,070 games.

- On May 14, Mexico's Lauro Salas defeats Jimmy Carter for the world lightweight boxing championship.

- On May 30, twenty-two year old Troy Rutman is the youngest winner of the Indy 500 auto race.

- On July 16, the International Olympic Committee (IOC) elects American Avery Brundage its president. Brundage, who has been the USOC president since 1929, will continue as IOC president until 1972.

- On July 19, the summer Olympic games open in Helsinki, Finland. The United States wins forty gold medals, including Bob Mathias in the decathlon and the unofficial title "world's greatest athlete" for the second straight time.

- On September 23, Rocky Marciano knocks out Jersey Joe Walcott in the thirteenth round to earn boxing's heavyweight championship. Marciano defends his title successfully throughout the decade and retires as the only undefeated heavyweight champion.

1953

- On January 11, the National Football League's (NFL) Dallas Texans become the Baltimore Colts.

- On February 15, Tenley Albright becomes the first American to win the World Figure Skating Championship.

- On March 18, the Boston Braves move to Milwaukee and proceed to set a National League attendance record of 1,826,397. At the conclusion of the season, the St. Louis Browns move to Baltimore and become the Orioles.

- On May 6, St. Louis pitcher Bobo Holloman throws a no-hitter against Philadelphia in this first big league start. This was his only complete game of his major league career because later that summer he was sent down to the minor leagues.

- On June 13, Ben Hogan wins the U.S. Open for the fourth time.

- On July 10, Ben Hogan wins the British Open, which along with his wins in the Masters and the U.S. Open make him the first golfer to win all three major championships in the same year.

- On September 7, Maureen Connolly becomes the first woman, and only the second player ever, to win the tennis Grand Slam and the U.S. National Championship. Connolly had previously won the Australian and French Opens, and Wimbeldon.

- On October 5, the New York Yankees become the first team in baseball history to win five consecutive World Series when they defeat the Brooklyn Dodgers in six games.

- On November 9, the U.S. Supreme Court upholds baseball's exemption from antitrust laws by ruling 7-2 against George Toolson, Walter Kowalski, and Jack Corbett. The court rules that baseball is a sport and not a business and any changes in baseball's monopoly would have to be made by Congress.

1954

- On February 13, Furman College's Frank Selvy breaks the NCAA single-game scoring record by scoring 100 points in a basketball game. Furman beat Newberry 149-95.

- On May 6, Roger Bannister of England becomes the first runner to break the four-minute barrier by running 3:59.4 at the Empire Games in Vancouver, B.C.

- On July 12, in response to the Supreme Court's ruling in the Toolson case (1953) the Major League Baseball Players' Association is formed and becomes the first truly effective professional sports union.

- On July 20, nineteen year old Maureen Connoly, America's greatest tennis player, is seriously injured in a truck-horse accident. Connolly's remarkable career is over. She passes away in 1969.

- In September, the All-American Girls Professional Baseball League folds after the 1954 season and dies a quiet death.

- In October, the National Basketball Association introduces the 24-second shot clock, which will revolutionize the game.

1955

- Baseball's Western Expansion begins in full force as the Philadelphia Athletics move to Kansas City.

- On April 12, the Kansas City Athletics beat the Detroit Tigers 6-2 in the first game in Municipal Stadium.

- On April 17, Al Kaline of the Detroit Tigers hits two homeruns in the sixth inning.

- On May 30, Bill Vukovich, winner of the 1953 and 1954 Indianapolis 500s, dies in a four car crash in this year's race. He is one of the first racers to die in a major auto race.

- On September 21, over four hundred thousand fans (at Yankee Stadium and through closed circuit television) see light heavyweight champion Rocky Marciano win for the 49th consecutive time by knocking out the "Old Mongoose" Archie Moore. It is Marciano's last professional fight.

1956

- From January 26 to February 5, American figure skaters Tenley Albright and Hayes Alan Jenkins win gold medals at Cortina d'Ampezzo, Italy.

- On April 27, Rocky Marciano retires as boxing's only undefeated heavyweight champion.

- On June 29, Compton College freshman Charles Dumas becomes the first person to high jump over 7 feet at the Los Angeles Olympic trials.

- On October 8, in only ninety-seven pitches, New York Yankee pitcher Don Larson throws the only perfect game in World Series history. The Brooklyn Dodgers move to Los Angeles following their loss to the Yankees.

- From November 22 to December 8, the first ever Summer Olympics in the autumn are held in Melbourne, Australia. Bobby Morrow becomes the first runner since Jesse Owens (1936, Berlin) to win both the 100- and 200-meter races. Diver Pat McCormick wins both the platform and springboard events for the second consecutive Olympics.

- On November 30, twenty-one year old Floyd Patterson knocks out forty-one year old former champion Archie Moore to win the vacant world heavyweight championship of the world.

1957

- On February 25, the Supreme Court, in *Radovich v National Football League,* rules that the National Football League is not similar to Major League Baseball and must comply with antitrust laws.

- On May 2, for the fourth time Sugar Ray Robinson wins the world middleweight boxing title, knocking out Gene Fullmer in the fifth round.

- On May 4, Iron Leige wins the Kentucky Derby when Willie Shoemaker, riding Gallant Man, misjudges the finish line.

- On June 1, Don Bowden is the first American to break the four-minute mile barrier at 3:58.7.

- On July 6, Althea Gibson becomes the first African American to win a Wimbledon tennis Championship. Gibson also wins the U.S. National in September.

- On July 9, the Major League Baseball All-Star Game is a fiasco when Cincinnati fans stuff the ballot box and seven Reds are voted to the National League team. Commissioner Frick intervenes, and fans lose the voting privilege.

- On August 1, the National Football League Player's Association becomes a recognized labor union.

- On September 3, Boston Brave Warren Spahn pitches his forty-first career shutout against Chicago.

- On September 29, the New York Giants play their last game at the Polo Grounds and move to San Francisco. The Brooklyn Dodgers make their move to Los Angeles official a week later.

- On November 10, Charles Sifford becomes the first African American golfer to win a PGA-sponsored event at the Long Beach Open.

- On November 16, Notre Dame beats Oklahoma 7-0. It is Oklahoma's first loss since 1953, ending a streak of 47 victories.

1958

- The Broadway version of baseball's *Faust* becomes a Hollywood film. *Damn Yankees* stars Tab Hunter as Joe Hardy, who sells his soul to the devil, Ray Walston. Gwen Verdon recreates her Broadway role as the temptress with "Whatever Lola Wants."

- On January 12, NCAA football adopts the two-point conversion. It is the first substantive rule change in forty-five years.

- On January 12, Syracuse's Dolph Schayes breaks the pro basketball record of 11,170 points in a career. He retires with 19,209 points.

- On January 28, Los Angeles Dodger catcher Roy Campanella is paralyzed in an automobile accident. Campanella was baseball's first African American catcher after desegregation and a three-time winner of the Most Valuable Player Award.

- On April 6, Arnold Palmer wins the Masters, his first major golf-tournament victory, and begins a career that will make him sport's first great television hero.

- On April 18, the Los Angles Dodgers defeat the San Francisco Giants before 78,672 fans in the first major league ball game played on the Pacific Coast.

- In April, the Boston Celtics, with Bill Russell injured, lose to the St. Louis Hawks in the National Basketball Association Championships.

- On May 13, St. Louis Cardinal Stan Musial gets his 3,000th hit against Chicago.

- On June 11, Clarence DeMar, winner of the Boston Marathon seven times, dies at the age of 70.

- On September 26, for the first time in twenty years there is a challenge for the America's Cup, yachting's most prized trophy. The United States boat wins again.

- On December 28, in overtime at Yankee Stadium, the Baltimore Colts win the National Football League Championship 23-17 over the New York Giants. It becomes known overnight as the "greatest game ever played" and speaks to the power of television in determining America's sporting spectating habits.

1959

- In January, the National Basketball Association adopts a policy to protect its African American players (the league is now 25% minority) from discrimination at hotels.

- In May the Supreme Court rules that interracial boxing matches are legally protected.

- On April 9, the Boston Celtics sweep the Minneapolis Lakers to win the NBA basketball championship.

- On June 10, Cleveland Indian Rocky Colavito smacks four consecutive home runs in a nine-inning game against the Baltimore Orioles.

- On June 26, Ingemar Johansson becomes the first non-American to win the heavyweight championship of the world in twenty-five years, by knocking out Floyd Patterson in the third round.

- In August the Boston Red Sox become the last Major League Baseball team to sign an African American player.

"Detroit Beats Rangers in 2d Overtime"

Newspaper article

By: Joseph C. Nichols

Date: April 24, 1950

Source: Nichols, Joseph C. "Detroit Beats Rangers in 2d Overtime." *The New York Times,* April 24, 1950, 28. ■

Introduction

When the Hockey Hall of Fame identified the dynasties that have dominated professional hockey, it included the 1949–1950 to 1954–1955 Detroit Red Wings. During those six seasons, the Red Wings finished first each year, won four Stanley Cups (including three in a row, from 1953 to 1955) and solidified Detroit's reputation as "Hockeytown." Thirteen members of those Red Wings teams made it to the Hockey Hall of Fame, including Terry Sawchuk, Sid Abel, Jack Adams, Tommy Ivan, Red Kelly, Ted Lindsay, and Gordie Howe, the most famous of the group. Before the dynasty began, the Red Wings had experienced some success—winning the Stanley Cup in 1943 and back-to-back championships in 1936 and 1937—but they lacked consistency. That would change in 1950.

While the Red Wings had great success in this time period, there were many fundamental differences between the hockey of today and that of the 1950s. In the 1950s, there were only six teams in the NHL: the Montreal Canadians, Toronto Maple Leafs, Boston Bruins, Chicago Black Hawks, New York Rangers, and the Detroit Red Wings. The playoff system used in the 1940s and 1950s saw four teams compete for the Stanley Cup, meaning that the regular season eliminated only two teams. In those days, the semifinals and Stanley Cup were both best-of-seven contests. The Cup was dominated by three franchises: between the 1941–1942 and 1968–1969 seasons, it was won by Montreal, Toronto, or Detroit in all but one year (the Chicago Black Hawks won in 1961).

The game was also far rougher than it is now. Players did not wear helmets, and they suffered more injuries because of this. In the first game of the 1950 playoffs between Detroit and Toronto, Gordie Howe tried to check Toronto's Ted Kennedy and missed, crashing headfirst into the boards. The Red Wings lost their young star for the rest of the playoffs. Sustaining a concussion and multiple fractures to his face, Howe needed to have his skull drilled to relieve pressure on his brain. While he recovered to play the following season, clearly his injuries would have been less severe had he been wearing a helmet. Still, even with these types of incidents, helmets were not popular and were widely viewed as something a "real man" would not wear.

Significance

According to the Hockey Hall of Fame, the 1950 Stanley Cup contest between the Detroit Red Wings and New York Rangers was the beginning of the first Red Wings "dynasty." Though they did not win the Cup the following season, the Red Wings won four out of five Cups between 1949 and 1955. Upsets did happen in hockey, and this series came very close to providing a monumental upset. The Rangers finished fourth overall that year, posting a losing record of 28-31-11. However, they upset the highly favored Montreal Canadians in five games in the first round of the playoffs. In the other first-round matchup, the Red Wings met Toronto, winners of three straight Stanley Cups. After losing Gordie Howe for the rest of the playoffs in the first game, Detroit won a very physical seven-game series on an overtime goal by Leo Reise. The finals featured the team with the best regular-season record (Detroit) against the team with the worst record among playoff teams (New York). Even without the services of Gordie Howe, the Red Wings were expected to have a relatively easy time with the Rangers. Still, the series went a full seven games, with three of the games decided in overtime, including the seventh and deciding game, which the Red Wings won in double overtime on a Pete Babando goal—giving the Detroit capacity crowd reason to rejoice.

Primary Source

"Detroit Beats Rangers in 2d Overtime" [excerpt]

SYNOPSIS: The following excerpt is from *The New York Times* account of the seventh and final game of the 1949–1950 Stanley Cup, won by the Detroit Red Wings over the New York Rangers in double overtime. It was the first Stanley Cup championship decided by sudden-death overtime in game seven.

Tally by Babando Tops New York, 4-3

End of Long Struggle Comes After 28:31 of Overtime Play on Detroit Ice

Rangers and Red Wings players struggle to control the puck behind New York's net in the seventh game of the Stanley Cup finals. The Red Wings won the game in overtime, 4-3, and brought home their fourth Stanley Cup. **AP/WIDE WORLD PHOTOS. REPRODUCED BY PERMISSION.**

Leswick is Ranger Star

Wings Wage an Uphill Battle After Rivals Lead Twice—Rayner Is Injured

Detroit, Monday, April 24—The Detroit Red Wings won the Stanley Cup and the hockey championship of the world this morning.

Coming from behind in the regulation three periods of play and forcing the game into sudden death overtime, the local skaters gained the victory in the seventh and deciding game of the best four-out-of-seven series on a goal by Pete Babando, whose counter at 8:31 of the second overtime session gave the Red Wings the verdict by the score of 4 to 3 over the New York Rangers. The total sudden death play was 28:31.

It was a dramatic denouement to the hockey campaign for the Detroit players, who gained first place in the regular National League campaign and who were favored to romp through the playoffs to bring this city its first ice championship since 1943.

All the favoritism that existed for Detroit was dissipated, though, by the sturdy Rangers, as the series plowed its way down to the very final game and—considering the overtime—beyond.

Given little chance to survive even its first round of play against the Montreal Canadiens, the New York team surprised the hockey world by sweeping that set, 4 to 1, and by forcing the Detroit team to the limit in the final series. . . .

In the game that ended this morning, though, the Red Wings were back in the favored role, but for a good part of the early going it appeared as if the Rangers were on the way to registering an upset. For Lynn Patrick's crew went into a lead of 2 to 0 in the first period, and indications were that, this time, the advantage would stand up. The New Yorkers had the same advantage early in Saturday night's game, but they blew it, and also blew the contest.

The early deficit did not discourage the Red Wings in this seventh battle. They made it up within twenty-one seconds in the middle period when the Rangers' Allan Stanley was sitting out a penalty.

The Rangers pulled ahead again in the same frame, on a goal by Buddy O'Connor, but Jimmy McFadden scored to knot the count before the session ran out, and the teams finished the second period each with three goals.

They battled through a scoreless third period, and through one overtime sudden death chapter. In the second one of these added frames the Detroit team continued the aggressiveness it showed through most of the game, and this aggressiveness bore fruit in 8:31 when Babando beat the Ranger goalie, Charley Rayner, on a straight line shot, after taking a pass from George Gee.

Abel Leads in "Blitz"

For Babando, the goal was his second of the game. He also tallied in the Red Wings' second period blitz while Stanley was out. The other Detroit player to score in the quick sequence was Sid Abel, the Red Wings' captain whose dynamic play in the entire Ranger series was probably the greatest single skater's contribution to the local team's titular achievement.

The New York first-period goals were scored by Stanley and Tony Leswick, each counter occuring while the Blue Shirts were favored through the presence of Detroit men in the penalty box. The second period scores came with each team at full strength.

Although the Rangers went into the lead as early as they did, there was no denying that the Detroit team deserved the victory. Off to a start in which they seemed to stress power rather than skill, the local puck chasers settled down to pure hockey when the score went against them, and for the greater part of the game they had a decided territorial edge.

Although he let one shoddy goal get by him, the drive with which McFadden evened the count, Rayner on the over-all played a sizzling game in the New York net, piling up a total of 39 saves as against only 26 for Harry Lumley in the Detroit cage. In the first overtime, particularly, Rayner was at his best.

His defense slowed down and allowed the Red Wing forwards to "walk in" pretty much as they pleased. The Ranger attack, on the other hand, failed to function smoothly in these late stages, and Lumley had a comparatively soft time of it. Rayner was hurt in the first overtime, but stayed in the game.

In the opening stages of the game the Rangers' slippery passing attack puzzled the Detroiters, and enabled the visitors to acquire a couple of penalty advantages. One of these banishments came when Edgar Laprade and Ted Lindsay roughed it up, Laprade drawing two minutes and Lindsay four, two for fighting and two for slashing.

It was while Lindsay was sitting out his second penalty that the Rangers struck for their initial score.

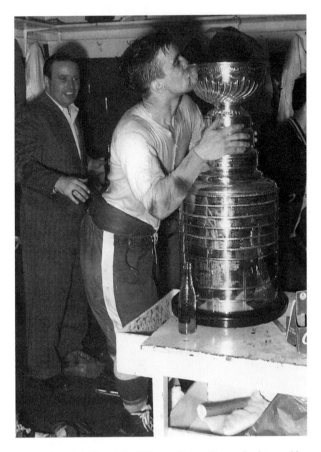

Ted Lindsay of the Detroit Red Wings celebrates his team's victory with the Stanley Cup. AP/WIDE WORLD PHOTOS. REPRODUCED BY PERMISSION.

Before Lindsay returned, he was joined by Marty Pavelich, who was sent out for slashing. This set-up gave the Rangers a 6 to 4 advantage in manpower for 51 seconds, and at the precise expiration of Lindsay's exile the Blue Shirts scored, Leswick caging the disk with the help of Laprade and O'Connor.

Detroiters Move Fast

The Red Wings moved fast in the second period. Stanley, baffled in an attempt to clear the puck, interfered with Jerry Couture and drew a banishment. Detroit capitalized on the setup, and did so beyond the expectations of the most rabid fans in the crowd of 13,095. Red Kelly and Couture set up the disk for Babando, who scored with a sliding shot in 5:09.

Wasting no time at all, Detroit was right back in New York ice and Abel sped in to release a 20-foot drive that eluded Rayner in 5:30. The New Yorkers played a strictly defensive game. A break came when Nick Mickoski broke away to fire at Lumley. The goalie blocked, but O'Connor poked the rebound home in 11:42.

This goal fired the Red Wings to carry the play. Trying to clear quickly, Stanley put the rubber on McFadden's stick and McFadden fired away. The shot looked like an easy one for Rayner, but he lost it in flight, and the puck hit the cords in 15:57.

The third period saw each team draw a penalty, but no harm was done. The Red Wings simply overwhelmed their foes in the first overtime, and only Rayner's dexterity prevented the game from ending much earlier than it did.

Further Resources

BOOKS

Bak, Richard. *Detroit Red Wings: An Illustrated History.* Dallas: Taylor Publishing, 1998.

Fischler, Stan. *Detroit Red Wings: Greatest Moments and Players.* Champaign, Ill.: Sports Publishing LLC, 2002.

McFarlane, Brian. *The Red Wings.* Toronto: Stoddart, 1998.

PERIODICALS

Wigge, Larry. "Where is Hockeytown?" *The Sporting News,* January 7, 2002, 40–42.

WEBSITES

Hockey Hall of Fame. Available online at http://www.hhof.com (accessed April 20, 2003).

"New York Rangers vs. Detroit Red Wings—1950." Sporting News.com. Available online at http://www.sportingnews .com/archives/stanleycup/1950.html; website home page: http://www.sportingnews.com (accessed April 20, 2003).

AUDIO AND VISUAL MEDIA

Moments of Magic: A Celebration of Hockeytown. USA Home Entertainment, 2002, VHS.

"Two Ex-Stars Held in Basketball 'Fix' at $2,000 a Game"

Newspaper article

By: Meyer Berger

Date: January 18, 1951

Source: Berger, Meyer. "Two Ex-Stars Held in Basketball 'Fix' at $2,000 a Game." *The New York Times,* January 18, 1951, 1.

About the Author: Meyer Berger (1898–1959) was a Pulitzer Prize-winning reporter for *The New York Times.* Berger was the author of the "About New York" column in the 1950s, one of the earliest examples of the human interest reporting about the lives of ordinary people and their activities. He was also the author of the book, *The Story of the New York Times, 1851–1951* (1951). He won the Pulitzer Prize in 1950 for local reporting on a mass murder in Camden, N.J. ■

Introduction

In the 1940s and 1950s, college basketball had a growing and dedicated following of fans. While a far cry from the popular sport it is now, college basketball drew a great deal of interest from the sporting pages, and local rivalries became closely followed contests. The allure of college basketball dimmed in the minds of America's sports fans in 1951 with the revelation that two former Manhattan College stars tried to bribe a current player to fix a game. What started with a seemingly inconsequential game between Manhattan and DePaul University grew into a national scandal involving the City College of New York (winners of the previous season's NCAA and NIT tournaments), Long Island University, Bradley University, New York University, the University of Kentucky, and the University of Toledo. In the largest gambling scandal since the "Black Sox" scandal of 1919, this was the first betting scandal to impact amateur sports. Possibly the coverage of the scandal provided a precursor to the growing popularity college basketball would achieve starting in the 1980s.

Significance

In the 1950s, very few college basketball stories warranted a headline on the front page of *The New York Times*—other than the City College of New York (CCNY) NIT and NCAA championships. But on January 18, 1951, the front page was the only place for a story of this magnitude. Star reporter Meyer Berger wrote the article below about the arrest of former Manhattan College stars and co-captains, Henry Poppe and John A. Byrnes, who attempted to bribe a current player, Junius Kellogg, to fix the game between Manhattan and DePaul. They offered Kellogg $1,000 to control the score of the game, telling him before it started that the point spread (not published like it is today) was ten points. The article goes into great detail regarding how Kellogg, who initially refused their offer, accepted and then alerted his coach about the fix. Through contacting the authorities, these men were arrested, along with the gamblers who provided the bribe and reaped the benefits of such fixes.

Also significant is the social station that the former stars (Poppe and Byrnes) had after their fame faded from Manhattan College. Poppe was working as a maintenance man after graduating with a degree in physical education, and Byrnes did not list an occupation and did not graduate. The National Basketball Association was relatively small through the 1950s and did not support many college players. After the fame of playing was over, players moved on to new careers. Through the interrogation after the initial arrests were made in the plot to bribe Kellogg, it became clear that Poppe and Byrnes took money while playing at Manhattan to either pad or shave a lead, depending on the point spread for the game that day. Gamblers had established the points system in the early 1940s to gauge the expected outcome of the game. A betting line determined the number of total points to be scored and the expected margin of victory by the favored team. If teams were evenly matched, the point spread would be small. If one team were clearly the favorite, the points given to the underdog would be large to help make the betting fair. Poppe and Byrnes contended that they were paid to either have their game exceed or come under the betting line established for Manhattan College games.

Possibly since the stakes in collegiate basketball were relatively small in comparison to today, the players played for pride of self and of their school. They were viewed as student athletes, without the money pressures that permeate the sport now. When the allegations were made that Manhattan's games with DePaul, Siena, Bradley and Santa Clara during the 1949–1950 season were fixed, there was complete disbelief. Berger states that these coaches were "unanimous in expressing shock. Almost in chorus they expressed disbelief in the stories." Berger goes on to add the thoughts of Manhattan coach Norton who told him, "I was shocked to hear that gamblers had got to my kids." In many regards, the role of this scandal, while years ahead of the boom of collegiate basketball, was the end of its age of innocence.

Primary Source

"Two Ex-Stars Held in Basketball 'Fix' at $2,000 a Game"

SYNOPSIS: Following is the newspaper account of the initial arrests made in the college basketball betting scandal that rocked the sport in the early 1950s. Initially thought to have been strictly the doing of gamblers and players at Manhattan College, the scandal spread to other schools in the New York area—Long Island University and City College of New York—as well as other schools in the country. The account goes into great detail on how the arrests were carried out and what information was known to date.

Manhattan Co-captains of Last Year and 3 Others Accused of Bribery and Conspiracy

One Admits He Got Cash

Attempt to Induce Player to 'Throw' the DePaul Contest Leads to Call for Police

Henry E. Poppe and John A. Byrnes, co-captains and consistent scorers on Manhattan College's 1949–1950 basketball team, were held in bail yesterday on bribery and conspiracy charges growing out of alleged "fixing" of games for gamblers.

College basketball players Harvey Schaff of New York University (right) and Ed Roman of City College of New York (second from left) are escorted to the police station for booking on charges of bribery, New York, February 18, 1951. © BETTMANN/CORBIS. REPRODUCED BY PERMISSION.

Three other men described by authorities as gamblers, two with long police records, were held on similar charges. They are alleged to have paid Poppe and Byrnes $5,000 each at the rate of $1,000 a game for "fixes" in the 1949–1950 season. The police said Poppe has made a "complete confession."

All five men are to have a hearing on the charges next Wednesday.

The five arrests grew out of alleged attempts by Poppe and the gamblers to persuade Junius Kellogg, center on the Manhattan College team, to "throw" the Manhattan College-DePaul University game played at Madison Square Garden on Tuesday night. Mr. Kellogg said $1,000 was offered to him.

Player Helps to Trap 5

Instead of taking the bribe, Mr. Kellogg pretended to be interested, informed Kenneth Norton, his coach, and helped trap Poppe, Byrnes and the three other men. Manhattan College won the Tuesday night game, 62 to 59. Several hours later the police closed in and made the arrests.

Coach Norton praised Mr. Kellogg for his integrity. So did Brother Bonaventure Thomas, Manhattan College president. Mr. Norton bitterly denounced the gamblers as "termites" and said

Nat Holman, coach of the City College of New York basketball team celebrates on the shoulders of his players after his team won the NCAA title, New York, March 28, 1950. AP/WIDE WORLD PHOTOS. REPRODUCED BY PERMISSION.

that, if the fixers were putting money before his players' faces, men on other teams must have been similarly tempted.

"This racket is not purely local," he said, and indicated he thought that not only players and gamblers were involved, but possibly baseketball court officials, too. He did not amplify this statement.

Edward F. Breslin, chief assistant District Attorney in the Bronx, who conducted the investigation, was up all through Tuesday night and until dawn yesterday questioning Poppe, Byrnes, the alleged gamblers and young Kellogg. Coach Norton sat in with him, obviously dismayed and completely unhappy.

Scandal Third of Kind Here

The scandal was the third of its kind in New York in the last five years. In the two previous cases the

gamblers went to prison for their attempts to corrupt student basketball players.

Mr. Breslin said that Poppe confessed he figured in fixed games against three teams in the 1949–1950 season—on Dec. 3, 1949, when Manhattan College lost to Siena College of Loudonville, N. Y. 48-33; on Dec. 26, 1949, when his team lost to Santa Clara College of California, 73 to 64; and on Jan. 12, 1950, when Manhattan lost to Bradley College of Peona, Ill., 89 to 67.

Poppe is also alleged to have confessed that he and Byrnes agreed for a fee from the gamblers to do all they could to exceed the point spread in their team's victories over St. Francis College of Brooklyn and against New York University in the 1949–1950 season Gamblers do all their betting or points in any given game, rather than on the over-all result. Players in their hire agree to "go under" a fixed score margin, or "go over."

The five men arrested yesterday were brought before Magistrate Vernon Riddick in the Bronx at 7 P.M. after they had been photographed and finger-printed at police headquarters.

Poppe, who is 24 years old, lives at 158-09 Sanford Avenue in Flushing, Queens, and gave his occupation as maintenance man. Byrnes, 22, lives at 31-15 Eighty-second Street in Jackson Heights, Queens. Both are now out of Manhattan College. Poppe was graduated with a B. S. in physical education last year. Byrnes failed of graduation by 3 points last June, but did not return to the campus this year.

The men arraigned with them were described as Irving Schwartzberg, 36, of 44-10 MacNish Place in Elmhurst, Queens; his brother, Benjamin, 35, of 2144 Crown Street, Brooklyn, and Cornelius Kelleher, 35, of 307 East 239th Street, the Bronx.

Poppe, Byrnes and Kelleher had never been arrested before. The brothers Schwartzberg both had been arrested numerous times in the last twenty years, mostly for bookmaking. Irving Schwartzberg's dossier showed fourteen arrests with eight convictions; his brother's eleven arrests with six convictions. Both had served prison terms on felony charges.

Magistrate Riddick fixed Kelleher's bail at $15,000. Poppe's at $4,000, Byrne's at $3,000. All three posted the bonds and were released. The Schwartzberg brothers were held without bail because of their police records.

Joseph Tiger, assistant district attorney, asked that high bail be set for Kelleher, on the ground that "he induced two college boys [Byrnes and Poppe] to enter into a crime which they never would have committed but for his inducement."

Young Kellogg said that Poppe came to him in Jersey City last Thursday night just before Manhattan's game with St. Peter's College of Jersey City and asked him to consider a $1,000 offer to "dump" the Manhattan College-De Paul College game, scheduled or last Tuesday at Madison Square Garden.

Kellogg a War Veteran

Mr. Kellogg said he was not interested, but told the authorities that Poppe begged him to reconsider and announced that he would return on Sunday. Mr. Kellogg, a giant of 6 feet 8 inches, with a good World War II battle record, went immediately to Coach Norton. He did not name Poppe as the man who had

come to him but simply said a former Manhattan College player had preferred the bribe.

On Friday morning Mr. Norton broke the news at an Athletics Advisory Council meeting. It was then that Brother Thomas approved the idea of calling in the police.

Mr. Norton was delegated to the task. He called Inspector Abraham Goldman, assigned to Brooklyn, because he has known him many years. Goldman advised him to get in touch with Deputy Inspector Edward Byrnes, head of the detective force in the Bronx. The coach and the deputy inspector talked the matter over before Mr. Norton left his Stuyvesant Town apartment last Saturday morning for the game with Temple University in Philadelphia that night.

Their talks were resumed on Sunday and the detectives arranged to have Mr. Kellogg lead Poppe on, according to Mr. Breslin. The giant center met Poppe at 9:15 P.M. in a parking lot near the college on Sunday night, and they went together to a bar and grill at Broadway and 242nd Street, Mr. Kellogg indicated, according to Mr. Breslin, that he was willing to "go for the pitch"—the gamblers' term for accepting the offer.

The detectives had told Mr. Kellogg to ask Poppe for instructions on how to "fix" the De Paul-Manhattan College game. When he did, Mr. Breslin said, Poppe merely advised him "Don't stink it up," which the prosecutor interpreted as meaning that Mr. Kellogg was not to make his "fix" plays too obvious.

Arrangements were then completed, Mr. Breslin said, for Mr. Kellogg to meet Poppe just before the game in a hotel lobby in Forty-ninth Street opposite Madison Square Garden, but Poppe did not appear. During these arrangements, the prosecutor said, Poppe confided that he and Byrnes and players on other teams in and outside of New York City had earned money by "fixes for score."

Just before the De Paul game started on Tuesday night. Poppe appeared outside the Madison Square Garden court, Mr. Breslin said, and told Mr. Kellogg that the "book"—the gamblers' group for which he was liaison—had decided that the point spread, or margin, for the game was 10 points. In other words, Mr. Kellogg was to see to it that his team did not come within 10 points of beating De Paul; to lose by a larger margin, if possible.

Though Mr. Kellogg never intended to play along with the gamblers, the whole deal had unnerved him. He was in the game only a little while, scored four points, and then made way for Charles Jennerich, substitute center. Mr. Jennerich made eight baskets in eight tries, an unusual feat, and an upset resulted. De Paul, originally favored to win by more than 6 points, lost by 3. Neither Mr. Jennerich nor any other player on the Manhattan team except Mr. Kellogg knew of the alleged bribe attempt.

Poppe, Mr. Breslin told reporters, had asked Mr. Kellogg to come to the men's room in Gilhuly Brothers Restaurant at 729 Eighth Avenue, after the game, to get the promised $1,000. Detectives followed discreetly behind the big center, but Poppe didn't show up. The police set out in squad cars to round up Poppe and any others involved.

One Talks for Two Hours

Poppe was arrested in his home at 3 A.M. yesterday. For two hours, according to Mr. Breslin, he talked freely and said that Kelleher, acting for "the book" had approached him and Byrnes just before the fall season in 1949 when both were co-captains and high scorers on Manhattan College team. Poppe was one of seven collegians in New York who could show a 1,000-point record for his varsity career and Byrnes was high up too. They were a good team for "making" plays.

Poppe is alleged to have accepted a $40 a week from "the book" before actual inter-college play started, and is reported to have told Mr. Breslin that Byrnes worked under the same arrangement. Byrnes was arrested in his home at 5 A.M. He made no statement to the authorities, though Poppe is alleged to have gone into detail as to what they did to give the gamblers a safe margin in the 1949–50 proves with Siena, Santa Clara and Bradley Colleges and in the "average points" in the St. Francis and New York University games the same season.

Later in the morning the detective brought in Kelicher. It was he, Mr. Breslin said, who paid Byrnes and Poppe their $1,000 after each of the fixed games mentioned. The Schwartzberg brothers were brought in too. Mr. Breslin said the Benjamin Schwartzberg made no statement but that Irving Schwartzberg "admitted participation, up to a point."

The police made it clear that Byrnes was not involved in the alleged attempt by Poppe to fix last Tuesday's match between Manhattan and De Paul.

When the five men involved were arraigned last night all were charged with "conspiring to commit a crime of bribery in violation of section 382 of the Federal Law," which makes it illegal to "attempt to bribe a participant in any sport."

Short affidavits accusing Poppe and Benjamin Schwartzberg of bribery in the Santa Clara, Bradley, Siena and De Paul College games, were presented to the magistrate. Byrnes and Kelleher were accused of bribery in the Santa Clara, Bradley and Siena games. Irving Schwartzberg was accused of bribery only in connection with the De Paul contest.

Coaches of the teams that figured in the allegedly "fixed" games with Manhattan College were unanimous in expressing shock. Almost in chorus they expressed disbelief in the stories.

Mr. Norton was sick over the revelation.

"I loathe the whole stinking business," he told reporters. "I was shocked to hear that gamblers had got to my kids."

Further Resources

BOOKS

Douchant, Mike. *Encyclopedia of College Basketball.* New York: Gale Research, 1995.

Isaacs, Neil David. *All the Moves: A History of College Basketball.* Philadelphia: Lippincott, 1975.

Rosen, Charles. *Scandals of '51: How the Gamblers Almost Killed College Basketball.* New York: Holt, Rinehart and Winston, 1978.

PERIODICALS

Goldstein, Joe. "Explosion: 1951 Scandals Threaten College Hoops." Available online at http://espn.go.com/classic/s/basketball_scandals_explosion.html; website home page http://espn.go.com (accessed on April 20, 2003).

WEBSITES

Naismith Memorial Basketball Hall of Fame. Available at: http://www.hoophall.com (accessed on April 20, 2003).

AUDIO AND VISUAL MEDIA

It Started With a Peach Basket: the History of College Basketball. AdCraft Associates, 1992, VHS.

"New York Giants 5, Brooklyn Dodgers 4"

Newspaper article

By: Red Smith

Date: October 4, 1951

Source: Smith, Red. "New York Giants 5, Brooklyn Dodgers 4." *New York Herald-Telegraph,* October 4, 1951. Reprinted in *Baseball Reader.* New York: McGraw-Hill, 1983, 379–381.

About the Author: Red Smith (1905-1982) was one of the greatest sportswriters in American history. He wrote for newspapers in Milwaukee, St. Louis, and Philadelphia before

New York Giant Bobby Thomson hits his famous home run against the Brooklyn Dodgers on October 3, 1951. The trajectory of the ball is traced to the left field stands. AP/WIDE WORLD PHOTOS. REPRODUCED BY PERMISSION.

settling in New York City in 1945. Ernest Hemingway called Smith "the most important force in American sports writing." Smith won a Pulitzer Prize in journalism for "distinguished commentary," and received the J.G. Taylor Spink Award from the National Baseball Hall of Fame in 1976 "for meritorious contributions to baseball writing." ■

Introduction

In the 1950s, professional baseball was at its peak in holding the attention and admiration of the American sporting fan. And no city held the fans' attention better than New York City. From 1947 through 1958, the New York Yankees won all but two American

League pennants (won by Cleveland in 1948 and 1954). Additionally, the New York Giants and the Brooklyn Dodgers each were perennial pennant contenders and developed a tremendous rivalry for National League fans in New York City. Despite being annual contenders, the Giants and Dodgers would win the World Series only once during this period, before their eventual departures to California (San Francisco and Los Angeles respectively). But in 1951, the Giants and Dodgers staged arguably the most exciting pennant race in baseball history—even far more interesting than the ensuing World Series.

Bobby Thomson kisses the bat he used to belt his pennant winning home run in the Polo Grounds, October 3, 1951. NATIONAL BASEBALL HALL OF FAME LIBRARY, COOPERSTOWN, NY.

In August 1951, the Dodgers had a seemingly insurmountable lead in the National League pennant race. By mid-August, the Dodgers had a commanding 13½;-game lead over the Giants. However, just as the Dodgers started to play poorly, the Giants started to play amazingly well; and the teams ended the season with identical records. Unlike today, there were no playoffs then; only the team with the best record could advance to the World Series. The two teams then played a three-game playoff to determine who would face the Yankees in the World Series. After splitting the first two games—with Brooklyn winning the second game 10-0—the season came down to one game to be played October 3, 1951. Brooklyn broke a 1-1 tie in the eighth inning to go up 4-1. In the bottom of the ninth, the Giants scored four runs—the last three on Bobby Thomson's game-winning home run down the left-field line at the Polo Grounds off Ralph Branca. That moment has remained one of the most memorable moments in baseball history. Russ Hodges, Giants's announcer, described the play, arguably the most

famous announcer call in the history of American sports, as follows: "Branca throws. There's a long fly . . . out to centerfield, I believe . . . THE GIANTS WIN THE PENNANT, THE GIANTS WIN THE PENNANT, THE GIANTS WIN THE PENNANT, THE GIANTS WIN THE PENNANT! Bobby Thomson hits into the lower deck of the left field stands! The Giants win the pennant, and they're going crazy . . . they're going crazy! Oooooo ho!"

Significance

This event is one of the most famous in baseball history and reflects many issues paramount in baseball in the 1950s. First, the dominance of Major League baseball by the New York teams. Teams from New York won all but two World Series in the 1950s, the Yankees winning six and the Dodgers and Giants each winning one. Second, before the playoff system was instituted in Major League baseball, there was a great sense of pride for a team to win the pennant. The pennant was a true accomplishment, a source of great pride rivaling a victory in the World Series. Third, the games were played between the two National League teams from New York that would move to California in six years because of a lack of fan support and growth potential. Fourth, it was the thrilling climax of one of the greatest comebacks in baseball history, with the Giants storming back from 13½; games in the last six weeks of the regular season.

Primary Source

"New York Giants 5, Brooklyn Dodgers 4"

SYNOPSIS: Smith writes an amazing commentary about the third game of the 1951 National League playoff between heated rivals New York Giants and Brooklyn Dodgers. Smith transcends the events on the field, placing them in the context of the great comeback that the Giants orchestrated against the Dodgers at the end of the season. The opening of the article, especially when Smith declares "the art of fiction is dead" and that "reality has strangled invention" symbolizes what the comeback means in the history of baseball.

Now it is done. Now the story ends. And there is no way to tell it. The art of fiction is dead. Reality has strangled invention. Only the utterly impossible, the inexpressibly fantastic, can ever be plausible again.

Down on the green and white and earth-brown geometry of the playing field, a drunk tries to break through the ranks of ushers marshaled along the foul lines to keep profane feet off the diamond. The ushers thrust him back and he lunges at them, struggling in the clutch of two or three men. He breaks free, and four or five tackle him. He shakes them off, bursts through the line, runs head-on into a special park cop, who brings him down with a flying tackle.

Here comes a whole platoon of ushers. They lift the man and haul him, twisting and kicking, back across the first-base line. Again he shakes loose and crashes the line. He is through. He is away, weaving out toward center field, where cheering thousands are jammed beneath the windows of the Giants' clubhouse.

At heart, our man is a Giant, too. He never gave up.

From center field comes burst upon burst of cheering. Pennants are waving, uplifted fists are brandished, hats are flying. Again and again the dark clubhouse windows blaze with the light of photographers' flash bulbs. Here comes that same drunk out of the mob, back across the green turf to the infield. Coattails flying, he runs the bases, slides into third. Nobody bothers him now.

And the story remains to be told, the story of how the Giants won the 1951 pennant in the National League. The tale of their barreling run through August and September and into October. . . . Of the final day of the season, when they won the championship and started home with it from Boston, to hear on the train how the dead, defeated Dodgers had risen from the ashes in the Philadelphia twilight. . . . Of the three-game play-off in which they won, and lost, and were losing again with one out in the ninth inning yesterday when—Oh, why bother?

Maybe this is the way to tell it: Bobby Thomson, a young Scot from Staten Island, delivered a timely hit yesterday in the ninth inning of an enjoyable game of baseball before 34,320 witnesses in the Polo Grounds. . . . Or perhaps this is better:

"Well!" said Whitey Lockman, standing on second base in the second inning of yesterday's play-off game between the Giants and Dodgers.

"Ah, there," said Bobby Thomson, pulling into the same station after hitting a ball to left field. "How've you been?"

"Fancy," Lockman said, "meeting you here!"

"Ooops!" Thomson said. "Sorry."

And the Giants' first chance for a big inning against Don Newcombe disappeared as they tagged Thomson out. Up in the press section, the voice of Willie Goodrich came over the amplifiers announcing a macabre statistic: "Thomson has now hit safely in fifteen consecutive games." Just then the floodlights were turned on, enabling the Giants to see and count their runners on each base.

It wasn't funny, though, because it seemed for so long that the Giants weren't going to get another chance like the one Thomson squandered by trying to take second base with a playmate already there. They couldn't hit Newcombe, and the Dodgers couldn't do anything wrong. Sal Maglie's most splendrous pitching would avail nothing unless New York could match the run Brooklyn had scored in the first inning.

The story was winding up, and it wasn't the happy ending that such a tale demands. Poetic justice was a phrase without meaning.

Now it was the seventh inning and Thomson was up, with runners on first and third base, none out. Pitching a shutout in Philadelphia last Saturday night, pitching again in Philadelphia on Sunday, holding the Giants scoreless this far, Newcombe had now gone twenty-one innings without allowing a run.

He threw four strikes to Thomson. Two were fouled off out of play. Then he threw a fifth. Thomson's fly scored Monte Irvin. The score was tied. It was a new ball game.

Wait a minute, though. Here's Pee Wee Reese hitting safely in the eighth. Here's Duke Snider singling Reese to third. Here's Maglie wild-pitching a run home. Here's Andy Pafko slashing a hit through Thomson for another score. Here's Billy Cox batting still another home. Where does his hit go? Where else? Through Thomson at third.

So it was the Dodgers' ball game, 4 to 1, and the Dodgers' pennant. So all right. Better get started and beat the crowd home. That stuff in the ninth inning? That didn't mean anything.

A single by Al Dark. A single by Don Mueller. Irvin's pop-up, Lockman's one-run double. Now the corniest possible sort of Hollywood schmaltz—stretcher-bearers plodding away with an injured Mueller between them, symbolic of the Giants themselves.

There went Newcombe and here came Ralph Branca. Who's at bat? Thomson again? He beat Branca with a home run the other day. Would Charley Dressen order him walked, putting the winning run on base, to pitch to the dead-end kids at the bottom of the batting order? No, Branca's first pitch was a called strike.

The second pitch—well, when Thomson reached first base he turned and looked toward the left-field stands. Then he started jumping straight up in the air, again and again. Then he trotted around the bases, taking his time.

Ralph Branca turned and started for the clubhouse. The number on his uniform looked huge. Thirteen.

Further Resources

BOOKS

DeLillo, Don. *Pafko at the Wall: The Shot Heard Round the World.* New York: Scribner, 2001.

Goodwin, Doris Kearns. *Wait Till Next Year: Summer Afternoons with My Father and Baseball.* New York: Simon & Schuster, 1998.

Thomson, Bobby, et. al. *The Giants Win the Pennant! The Giants Win the Pennant!* New York: Kensington Publishing, 2001.

PERIODICALS

Lichtenstein, Grace. "The Home Run That Broke a Girl's Heart." *The New York Times* October 1, 2001, D10.

WEBSITES

Ritschel, Rolf D. "Shot Heard Round the World." *Baseball-Almanac,* 2002. Available online at http://www.baseball-almanac.com/poetry/po_tshrtw.shtml; website home page: http://www.baseball-almanac.com (accessed April 20, 2003).

"Shot Heard 'Round the World." Baseball's 25 Greatest Moments. *Sporting News.* Available online at http://www.sportingnews.com/baseball/25moments/1.html; website home page: http://www.sportingnews.com (accessed April 20, 2003).

AUDIO AND VISUAL MEDIA

Baseball: Film By Ken Burns Directed by Ken Burns. PBS Home Video, 1994, VHS.

Baseball's East-West All-Star Game

"East-West Game Faces Death in Chicago Park"

Newspaper article

By: Johnny Johnson

Date: August 21, 1953

Source: Johnson, Johnny. "East-West Game Faces Death in Chicago Park." *Kansas City Call,* August 21, 1953. Reprinted in Lester, Larry. *Black Baseball's National Showcase: The East-West All-Star Game, 1933–1953.* Lincoln, Neb.: University of Nebraska Press, 2001, 387–388.

About the Author: Johnny Johnson was a leading sportswriter for African American newspapers in the 1940s and 1950s. He was listed as the sports editor for the *Call,* the magazine of the Socialist Party, a group sympathetic to the needs of the African American community.

"All-Star Tilt Fails to Impress Scouts from Big Leagues"

Newspaper article

By: Wendell Smith

Date: August 22, 1953

Source: Smith, Wendell. "All-Star Tilt Fails to Impress Scouts from Big Leagues." *Pittsburgh Courier,* August 22, 1953. Reprinted in Lester, Larry. *Black Baseball's National Showcase: The East-West All-Star Game, 1933–1953.* Lincoln, Neb.: University of Nebraska Press, 2001, 388–390.

About the Author: Wendell Smith was a leading sportswriter for African American newspapers in the 1940s and

1950s. He was a prominent sportswriter for the *Pittsburgh Courier* and a leading proponent for the desegregation of baseball with the signing of Jackie Robinson. ∎

Introduction

In 1933, to combat The Great Depression and garner enthusiasm for baseball, *Chicago Tribune* Sports Editor Arch Ward proposed an exhibition game to be played between the best players of the American and National Leagues—an all-star game. The first such game was played in 1933 at Comiskey Park in Chicago. Later that same year, the owners of the Negro Leagues decided that they should do the same thing, so the East-West Game was born. Unlike the Major League Baseball All-Star Game, the East-West Game remained at Comiskey Park throughout its history, bringing the best players of the Negro Leagues to Chicago for their own mid-season classic. The Negro Leagues existed to provide opportunities for African American baseball players prevented from playing in organized baseball because of Jim Crow laws. The Negro Leagues were a vibrant entity—playing a regular schedule, but also encouraging teams to play barnstorming games against town teams to help raise additional revenue. However, that all changed for the 1946 season, when the Brooklyn Dodgers' Branch Rickey signed Jackie Robinson, a standout at UCLA as a baseball and football player, for their top farm team in Montreal. Robinson played the entire season in Montreal and won the International League Rookie of the Year award, while fending off the torments of racist fans across America. In 1947, Robinson would play for the Brooklyn Dodgers, breaking the color barrier that had existed in baseball since the 1880s. With his success, Major League teams quickly signed stars of the Negro Leagues. Many of the great players of the 1950s started in the Negro Leagues, including Willie Mays, Hank Aaron, Jackie Robinson, and Roy Campanella.

While the desegregation of baseball had tremendous positive aspects for the sport and for African Americans everywhere, it provided the death blow to the Negro Leagues. Since relatively few of the Negro League players were signed by Major League organizations, many, especially the older players who had the best years of baseball behind them, were left to play for the Negro Leagues. In the late 1940s and early 1950s, the role and function of the Negro Leagues faded, as more and more African American players were signed after high school with organized baseball. With this decline, the Negro Leagues were forced to be creative to generate interest in their teams. In 1953, the Indianapolis Clowns signed Toni Stone, the first woman to play as a regular on a big-league professional baseball team. Additionally, the East-West game, once a showcase for Hall of Famers such as Satchel Paige, Josh Gibson and Lloyd Warner, now became the showcase for the talent that was not wanted or needed in the Major leagues. With the stars gone from the all-star game, the annual event was bound to fade into history. Though Negro Leagues teams played baseball as late as the early 1960s, their role and purpose deteriorated with the success of African Americans in organized baseball.

Significance

These two accounts of the organizational and fiscal side of the 1953 East-West Game are telling documents about the collapse of the Negro Leagues and its star attraction, the East-West Game. The Jim Crow laws barring African Americans from playing Major League baseball kept the Negro Leagues an important organization both for providing opportunities for players and entertaining the fans. While there was general rejoicing with the breaking of the color line and the signing of players such as Jackie Robinson, Larry Doby, Willie Mays, and others, the negative effect that it had on the Negro Leagues and its institutions were troubling. In these documents, the authors look at the issues that are causing the twenty-first East-West Game to lose the attention of the fans. The decline in attendance (down to between five and ten thousand from a peak of forty thousand plus) was indicative of problems that could be reversed. While Johnson and Smith both saw problems with the current configuration, neither advocated the abolishment of the events.

One of the biggest elements touched upon by Johnson was that the East-West game was not dead, but "sick." In quoting some of his colleagues, he said that the game "is going down hill fast and can't possibly last another two years here in Chicago." While this was referring to the fans at the park, he also directed this towards the management of the game. Johnson felt that moving the game out of Chicago might be necessary to save the game and the league. He proposed primarily southern cities, such as Birmingham and Memphis, as well as Kansas City, in the hopes that their fans would take a greater interest in the game.

But possibly more significant is what both Johnson and Smith say in their articles. With the signing of the best younger players from the Negro Leagues by Major League teams, there was not a great deal of talent left in the Negro Leagues. Many of the younger African American players were playing minor league baseball, bypassing the Negro Leagues altogether. Johnson stated that the East-West game is devoid of "Satchel Paiges, Roy Campanellas, and Larry Dobies," but only offering "unknown and most unarrived youngsters, which excite nobody." Smith, an astute judge of baseball talent, had a more optimistic view of the players on the 1953 all-star squads. While few made it to the Major Leagues, he rightfully pointed out the best prospect in the game as a "22-year-old shortstop owned by the Kansas City Monarchs, Ernie Banks. The flashy youngster failed to hit in four trips to the plate," but nonetheless is the only real prospect in the game. Smith provides a good overview of the game in his article on the contest. Fewer and fewer star African American players signed with the Negro Leagues, and interest at these all-star games waned through the fifties—as the assumption grew that all the good players were taken. The Negro Leagues would hold on for a few more years, but faced its inevitable demise in the years after Jim Crow left baseball.

Primary Source

"East-West Game Faces Death in Chicago Park"

SYNOPSIS: This article discusses both the on-field and off-field activities surrounding the 1953 East-West Game playing in Chicago. Johnson focuses on the problems associated with the promotion and management of the game that has seen its interest and attendance fall in recent years.

Scribes Say Game Needs New Climate and a New Doctor

Consensus of the few scribes who took time out to cover the 21st annual Negro game here in Comiskey Park Sunday afternoon was that the annual classic is sick and needs a change of climate and another doctor.

She's Dying Fast

"She is going down hill fast and can't possibly last another two years here in Chicago," they opinionated in almost unison.

They were referring not only to the crowd which has grown steadily smaller each year, but also to the manner in which the contest is directed and managed.

All expressed reluctance to see the game die, for they are aware of the need for such an annual outing if Negro baseball is to continue.

Many of the scribes shook their heads in disbelief when it was guessed that 10,000 fans were in the park. A few set their own estimation at 7,000; some of the less generous ones declared the total was 5,000.

Less than Last Year

The decline in attendance is shown when the estimation last year was set at 18,000 and there were considerable doubts about that figure.

This year they didn't even bother to open the second balcony. No one was up there except the birds, a quartet of park hanger-ons and a quartet of kids who were being paid to recover baseballs. They did a darned good job.

By Passed Fay Young

Absent from the press box was the dean of Negro sports writers, the somewhat irascible but efficient Frank (Fay) Young.

Although Frank Young has been on the firing line in behalf of Negro baseball in general and the East-West game in particular for many years, he was absent from the game.

The reason! The officials failed to send him a ticket. How ungrateful can people get?

In the past Young has been the major domo of the press box; he has served as the official scorer, the dispenser of press tickets, final decider of hits and errors.

Worked for Game

In other words, Frank Young has done as much as some and more than many to keep alive the East-West game during the past 20 years. But this year they threw him away, discarded him, and forgot him.

As we said, Young has a tendency to speak what he thinks. Sure he is a tyrant but he is a benevolent one in the opinion of many who know him.

No single indication of the need for change in the life of the East-West can be found than this seeming slight to Frank Young.

But others exist and the principle one is falling off in attendance. The management shouldn't be allowed to continue the only Negro league classic in a city where it is starving to death.

Several suggestions have been offered to correct this condition. One of them is a method of rotation. The games, these advocates say, should be moved annually to Birmingham, Kansas City, Memphis or other large cities.

Want Rotation

The advocates of change point out that the game cannot exist permanently in cities like Chicago where major league games with Negro players are present at the same time.

Sunday Milwaukee was playing at Wrigley field with Bill Bruton, and Jim Pendleton with the Brewers [Braves]. Hundreds of fans, it was estimated attended the major league game.

Leroy "Satchel" Paige pitches in the Negro American League's twenty-ninth East-West All Star game in front of a near empty Yankee Stadium, August 17, 1961. **AP/WIDE WORLD PHOTOS. REPRODUCED BY PERMISSION.**

The confusion from this is that the East-West game is not in position to compete with the O.B. clubs. It has no individual stars, no outstanding players to attract with No Satchel Paiges, Roy Campanellas, and Larry Dobies. All it has to offer is unknown and mostly unarrived youngsters, which excite nobody.

Only a Few Sacrifices

Chicago with its hundreds of attractions has shown by the falling attendance that it will no longer support this classic.

The scribes in the press box, only two of which were from out of town, and only seven present in all, pointed out that the local fans had starved the Chicago American Giants to death and they have less love for the East-West game.

So it looks as if they were on the beam when they said the East-West game needs a new climate and a new doctor if death is to be staved off.

Primary Source

"All-Star Tilt Fails to Impress Scouts from Big Leagues"

> **SYNOPSIS:** This article also discusses the activities surrounding the 1953 East-West Game played in Chicago. Wendell Smith focuses on the game itself, but addresses which of the players would be prospects for the Major League teams, including future Hall of Famer Ernie Banks.

Chicago-Negro baseball, once the happy hunting ground for big league scouts, isn't what it used to be, in the East or West. That was the general consensus here Sunday following the Negro-American League's twenty-first All-Star game in which the West defeated the East, 5 to 1, at Comiskey Park.

A disappointing crowd of 10,000, including a caravan of major league scouts, watched the game under perfect weather conditions and during the two-hour demonstration saw very little talent worthy of serious consideration for future employment in the majors.

The forty best players in the Negro American League—twenty from the East and twenty from the West—were on display for the edification of the critics who purchase talent for Major League clubs, and the faithful fans, who have supported the classic down through the years.

No one apparently was overly impressed despite the fact that the players made a sincere and honest effort to give them a skillful, well-played game.

The Best prospect in the contest was a 22-year-old shortstop owned by the Kansas City Monarchs, Ernie Banks. The flashy youngster failed to hit in four trips to the plate but compensated for his futility there by sparkling in the field, handling six chances flawlessly and was on the starting end of the one double-play completed by the West.

The top performer for the East was Ray Neil, a second baseman from the Indianapolis Clowns, currently the best hitter in Negro baseball. He proved it in this game, pounding out three tries, including a triple in the third inning, best extra-base hit of the game.

Unfortunately, Neil, despite his skill at the plate, can't be considered a big league prospect because he has celebrated at least thirty birthdays, which means he is past his peak and in no way attractive to major league scouts.

But he is a good solid ball player. If he were ten years younger, the talent seekers would beat a path to his door and refuse to let him sleep until he signed a contract.

The game itself was only mildly exciting. The West, fortified with good pitching and aided considerably by Eastern infielders, who were stricken with that familiar disease known as "fumble-itis" won the game as early as the third inning.

They broke a 1-1 tie in the third, scoring twice on one hit to take a 3 to 1 lead which was never threatened. The defense of the East cracked wide open in that inning and the West took advantage of three errors.

The East scored its only run in the initial inning, solving starting pitching Sam Woods of the Memphis Red Sox for three hits. Neil got the first hit of the game, a single with two out. The next two hitters, Wesley Dennis and Henry Kimbro, both of Birmingham, also singled and Neil raced home with the East's lone marker.

Woods retired at the end of the third with a record of one run and four hits. Isiah Harris followed and goose-egged the East for the next three stanzas, giving up two hits. Johnny Jackson of Kansas City followed and pitched hitless and scoreless ball through the ninth. Woods, having started, got credit for the win.

Willie Gaines of Indianapolis, started for the East and pitched good ball the first three innings, but errors contributed to his downfall. The West tied it at 1-1 in the second on a double by Willie Patterson, who scored on Ed [Hank] Bayless' [Baylis'] timely single to center.

The West sewed it up in the next inning, scoring twice on one hit: Sherwood Brewer was safe on Hardaway's [Dennis'] error at first base and scooted to third when Eddie Reed singled to right. Successive errors on balls hit by Neil and Gaines enabled Brewer to score and Reed. Those three miscues in one inning set a record for East-West games. They also sealed the East's doom.

The West scored two more in the seventh, after being stopped for three innings by Minski Cartledge of Indianapolis, who succeeded Gaines on the mound.

Dionesio [Dionisio] Amaro, also of Indianapolis, came on to pitch the final three [two] for the East and immediately ran into trouble, Jackson and Brewer singled, and moved up a base when he hit Eddie Reed. Both Jackson and Reed subsequently scored on infield outs. That was the ball game and the thirteenth win of the long series for the West, as against eight for the East. It was also, the second in a row for the West, composed of players from the Kansas City Monarchs and the Memphis Red Sox. The East's roster was made up of players from the Indianapolis Clowns and Birmingham Black Barons.

The pitching for both clubs, incidentally, was acceptable. Each team was held to six hits. The East, however, suffered four miscues and that was fatal.

Further Resources

BOOKS

Clark, Dick, and Larry Lester. *The Negro Leagues Book.* Cleveland, Ohio: Society for American Baseball Research, 1994.

Robinson, Frazier. *Catching Dreams: My Life in the Negro Baseball Leagues.* Syracuse, N.Y.: Syracuse University Press, 1999.

PERIODICALS

Leavy, Walter. "50 Years of Blacks in Baseball." *Ebony,* June 1995, 38–43.

Nathan, Daniel A. "Bearing Witness to Blackball: Buck O'Neil, the Negro Leagues, and the Politics of the Past." *Journal of American Studies,* December 2001, 453–470.

WEBSITES

Blackbaseball.com. Available online at http://www.blackbaseball.com (accessed April 21, 2003).

Negro Leagues Baseball Museum. Available online at http://www.nlbm.com (accessed April 21, 2003).

"Wendell Smith Papers" Available online at http://www.baseballhalloffame.org/library/afas/smith_wendell.htm; website home page: http://www.baseballhalloffame.org (accessed June 4, 2003).

AUDIO AND VISUAL MEDIA

Baseball: Fifth Inning, 1930–1940, Shadow Ball. PBS Home Video, 2000, VHS.

Kings on the Hill: Baseball's Forgotten Men. San Pedro Productions, 1993, VHS.

"Trabert Takes U.S. Tennis Title by Crushing Seixas in Big Upset"

Newspaper article

By: Allison Danzig

Date: September 8, 1953

Source: Danzig, Allison. "Trabert Takes U.S. Tennis Title by Crushing Seixas in Big Upset." *The New York Times,* September 8, 1953, 1, 39

About the Author: Allison Danzig (1898–1987) was a prominent sportswriter for *The New York Times.* She was the author of six books, including the *Fireside Book of Tennis* (1972) and *Winning Gallery: Court Tennis Matches and Memories* (1985). ∎

Introduction

The Grand Slam is one of the greatest accomplishments a tennis player can achieve. To win the Grand Slam, a player (or doubles team) has to win the four major tournaments—Wimbledon, the U.S. Open, the French Open, and the Australian Open—in the same calendar year. This has been accomplished only three times in the history of women's tennis: in 1988 by Steffi Graf, in 1970 by Margaret Smith Court, and in 1953 by Maureen Connolly, nicknamed "Little Mo." In becoming the first woman to win the Grand Slam with her U.S. Open title in 1953, Connolly established a benchmark that is used for players who have dominated tennis. In 1953, Little Mo was only nineteen when she won the Grand Slam by winning her third consecutive U.S. Open championship. Connolly retired from professional tennis shortly after her

Grand Slam because of an injured leg. She won nine titles in nine major tournament events, the last in 1954.

Significance

The U.S. Open championships of 1953 provided tennis fans with two tremendous stories that were covered very differently by *The New York Times.* First, the prominent story of the article presented here is the upset victory by Tony Trabert over Victor Seixas. The secondary part of the story is Maureen Connolly's achievements in winning the women's singles Grand Slam. The coverage of these two stories is significant in reflecting the importance afforded by sports fans to these two events.

The bulk of the article discusses Trabert's surprising victory over Seixas in the men's final. The article emphasized that Trabert had served in the Navy during the Korean War (1950–1953) until just three months before the tournament. Many athletes in this time period were drafted into the military, including baseball Hall of Famer Ted Williams and countless others. When Trabert's term of service ended, he quickly began training for the U.S. Open—and it paid off. His victory in the U.S. Open was the first of ten Grand Slam tournament titles for Trabert. He later covered tennis as a CBS television broadcaster.

Maureen Connolly's accomplishments that day had greater historical impact, yet did not dominate the reporting that day. Only Don Budge, in 1938, previously had won a singles Grand Slam. In the 1953 U.S. Open, Connolly did not lose a set in the five matches she played. Connolly took only forty-three minutes to defeat Doris Hart in the finals, the easy victory perhaps a reason for the lack of coverage. And while Trabert's story was impressive, the general lack of interest in Connolly winning the Grand Slam appears to defy logic. Should a woman get close to winning the Grand Slam today, that possibility would dominate the coverage of the entire tournament. Conversely, it might be that the plot lines for the Trabert match were far more interesting (the returning veteran making a name for himself in tennis through a stunning upset) than Connolly, the favorite, dominating the competition at the U.S. Open for the third consecutive year.

Primary Source

"Trabert Takes U.S. Tennis Title by Crushing Seixas in Big Upset"

SYNOPSIS: The article is the newspaper account of the 1953 U.S. Open championships for men's and women's singles, won by Tony Trabert and Maureen Connolly, respectively. While the victory by Connolly was tremendously significant given that no woman previously won a tennis Grand Slam, much of the article is devoted to Tony Trabert's upset victory over fellow American, Victor Seixas.

Ex-Sailor Victor, 6-3, 6-2, 6-3—Miss Connolly Wins and Completes Grand Slam

An ex-sailor, less than three months out of the Navy, won the amateur tennis championship of the United States yesterday in as stunning a final-round reversal as Forest Hills has seen in many years.

With an onslaught of the leveling fire power of 16-inch rifles, Tony Trabert of Cincinnati silenced the guns of the favored champion of Wimbledon, Victor Seixas of Philadelphia, and in exactly one hour won the match, to the acclaim of 12,000 in the stadium of the West Side Tennis Club. The score was 6-3, 6-2, 6-3.

Preceding the triumph of the 23-year-old six-footer, one of the few to go through a championship without losing a set, Maureen Connolly of San Diego, Calif., carried off the women's crown for the third successive year.

In so doing she completed the first grand slam of the world's four major national tournaments scored by a woman. She, too, went through the ten days of play without yielding a set.

Miss Connolly previously had won the Wimbledon, Australian and French grass-court titles.

The little, blonde Californian, who will shortly attain the age of 19, repeated her victory of last year's final over Doris Hart of Coral Gables, Fla., whom she also defeated in a magnificent final at Wimbledon in July.

In forty-three minutes Miss Connolly, with her devastating speed and length off the ground and showing vast improvement since last year, took the match, 6-2, 6-4.

Miss Hart, a finalist five times and a strong hitter in her own right, resorted to every device, including changes of spin, length and pace, in an effort to slow down her opponent. But Miss Connolly went implacably on to victory in one of her finest performances. She was irresistible except for a momentary wavering when she stood within a stroke of ending matters at 6-2 in the final set and yielded two more games to Miss Hart.

In the final event of the seventy-second annual tournament, Miss Hart paired with Seixas to win the mixed doubles title. They defeated Julia Sampson of San Marino, Calif., and Rex Hartwig of Australia, 6-2, 4-6, 6-4. It was the third time in a row that Miss Hart shared in the crown, which she carried off with Frank Sedgman of Australia in 1951 and 1952.

The victory of Trabert over Seixas, the player with whom he is expected to shoulder the burden of America's challenge for the Davis Cup at Melbourne, Australia, in December, was achieved with the finest tennis to come from his racquet this observer has seen.

Food for Thought

It was disturbing enough for Australia that its two 18-year-old aces, Kenneth Rosewall and Lewis Hoad, failed to win a set in the semi-finals. The performance of Trabert in crushing the Wimbledon champion by almost as decisive a margin as did Sedgman in the 1951 final should be of even more concern Down Under.

On the best day Rosewall and Hoad ever had they could hardly have stood their ground against the all-court attack Trabert turned loose against Seixas.

Two years ago the rugged ex-sailor, who has the proportions of a football player, carried Sedgman to five sets in the championship. In 1952 he laid aside his racquets to serve in the Navy and was out of major competition except for the French championship while his aircraft carrier was in the Mediterranean Sea.

Since leaving the service in June, Trabert has been laboring hours daily in practice and physical conditioning work to bring his game back to where it was in 1951 and to get his weight down and regain his speed of foot.

At the Merion Cricket Club he met Seixas in the final and was crushed after a promising start. He won the Baltimore tournament, lost to Rosewall at South Orange and then met Seixas again at Newport.

The Philadelphian, with his speed and agility and his faultless volleying, won the first two sets, 7-5, 6-0, and then injured his knee early in the third set and lost the match. Trabert got little credit for the victory, under the circumstances.

Yesterday he went on the court again against Seixas. This time the Wimbledon champion was thoroughly fit, with his knee completely healed, and primed with the confidence gained from his earlier victories over Hoad, Kurt Nielsen of Denmark and William Talbert of New York.

Seixas was favored in the final in spite of the excellence of Trabert's tennis against Rosewall. How

Maureen Connolly reaches for a ball during a tournament match, June 28, 1952. Connolly was the first woman to win a Grand Slam in tennis. **HULTON ARCHIVE/GETTY IMAGES. REPRODUCED BY PERMISSION.**

was any one to suspect that Trabert would show the most punishing and solid ground strokes on display at Forest Hills in recent years or that they would wreak such havoc against an opponent who had made a shambles of the highly respected back court game of Talbert?

The explanation of the massacre that was perpetrated in the last two sets yesterday came down to the fact that Trabert on this day suddenly caught fire as he never had before and attained the mastery toward which he has strived over the years. On this day he measured up to a Donald Budge, a Jack Kramer in the fearful toll taken by his forehand and backhand, particularly the latter.

It is premature to rank him with those two former champions, but if he can sustain the form he showed against Seixas, the time may well come when Trabert will receive that recognition. At any rate, Australia has much to worry about as it prepares for the defense of the Davis Cup.

In his powerful serving and deadly play in the forecourt and in his speed in bringing off one amazing recovery after another for spectacular winners, Trabert was a foe for the best to reckon with. But

his ground strokes were what broke Seixas' resistance and turned the match into something of a rout in the second set. The Wimbledon champion was harried at every turn, driven to the far corners and tied in knots as he tried to get his racquet on the ball at the net.

Tactics Fail to Work

In the final analysis, it was Trabert's top-spin backhand that made the match a nightmare for Seixas. The Philadelphian had beaten Hoad by putting his twist service high on the backhand preparatory to rushing in for the finishing volley. Such tactics also had worked successfully against other opponents. They did not succeed against Trabert.

In his overspin backhand Trabert had the antidote, and his return of service from the left side falling low below the level of the tape and usually wide of Seixas' racquet, wrecked the loser's net attack.

In game after game Seixas came rushing in, only to find himself passed or unable to take the ball at his feet with a regularity that finally left him at his wits' end, discouraged and baffled, though he kept going forward to the last.

The Wimbledon champion had little alternative. From the back of the court, with his looping forehand and undercut backhand, he was not sufficiently equipped to stand up to the long, heavy strokes that stemmed from Trabert's racquet. He had to get in.

The inadequacy of his ground strokes was revealed in his inability to return Trabert's powerful service, which was usually directed to the backhand, or to make the passing shot on the run from the forehand as the Cincinnatian angled his following volley across the court. Trabert was using the tactics that his rival had employed so successfully against others.

The play turned into a rout for Seixas beginning with the fourth game of the second set, just before the players donned spikes, with a light rain falling.

In the opening set it had been an even fight until Seixas missed his chance to break through in the 18-point fifth game. Then he lost his service in the seventh as Trabert's returns forced him into volley errors. That was the margin of the difference between them in the set.

Up to this time there had been no inkling of the beating in store for Seixas. Indeed, few of his backers had lost faith in his capacity to win. When he took the opening game of the second set at love and won the third on the strength of his service, he seemed to be strongly in the running.

Then the storm broke and the spectators forgot about the sprinkle of rain as they looked on spellbound at the whirlwind that engulfed the clean-cut and wonderfully, conditioned 30-year-old as Trabert swept through seven games in a row.

Trabert's service, with its length and varying speed and spin, extracted errors or scored outright in the fourth game. In the fifth his return of service had Seixas reeling and diving for the ball, to set up scorching passing shots and volleys. His service won at love in the sixth and Seixas had got just 2 points in the last three games.

Seixas Fights Hard

Then came a magnificently fought seventh game, with Seixas battling might and main and scoring thrice at the net but yielding finally as Trabert scored six outright winners, four with his ground strokes. When Seixas lost the eighth game also, after leading by 40-0, it was seen to be all over.

Trabert continued his string of games to seven by breaking through at love in the first of the final set, making a sensational recovery of a cross-court volley, and taking the second game with a volley and two beautiful backhand drives. Seixas had a brief reprieve as his service picked up to win a love game in the third. Then he pulled out the fifth after being down 0-40.

When the Philadelphian broke through service for the first time in the match to draw even at 3-all, a spark of hope was revived. But Trabert came back like a tiger. The Cincinnati youth broke through in the seventh at love with another of his amazing recoveries and two passing shots down the line, won the eighth with two overhand smashes and then hit two hammering forehand returns of service that Seixas could not volley and finished matters with a tremendous backhand passing shot down the line.

With a cry of joy, Trabert tossed his racquet into the air and then, after shaking hands with his opponent, turned and blew a kiss to his fiancee, Shauna Wood of Salt Lake City, Utah, who was seated in the marquee. Miss Wood, whom Trabert will marry in January, was called on the court to receive the winner's prize from Col. James H. Bishop, president of the United States Lawn Tennis Association.

Further Resources

BOOKS
Condon, Robert J. *Great Women Athletes of the 20th Century.* Jefferson, N.C.: McFarland, 1991.

Frayne, Trent. *Famous Women Tennis Players.* New York: Dodd, Mead, 1979.

PERIODICALS
Deford, Frank. "A Grand Try For the Slam." *Sports Illustrated,* August 29, 1988, 124.

WEBSITES
Maureen Connolly Brinker Tennis Foundation. Available online at: http://www.mcbtennis.org (accessed April 21, 2003).

AUDIO AND VISUAL MEDIA
Sports Heroines: Early Women Sports Stars Heroines, Inc., 1998, VHS.

"On Baseball"

Essay

By: Jacques Barzun

Date: 1954

Source: Barzun, Jacques. "On Baseball." In Barzun, Jacques. *God's Country and Mine: A Declaration of Love Spread with a Few Harsh Words.* Boston: Little, Brown, 1954. Reprinted in *Baseball Reader.* New York: McGraw-Hill, 1983, 35–39.

About the Author: French-born Jacques Barzun (1907–) is a prominent writer, educator, and historian associated with Columbia University since attending there in the 1920s, having served as the provost 1958–1967. He has written a great deal on American culture and life, as well as numerous books on education. ■

Introduction

The 1950s were a critical time for baseball. When the soldiers came home after World War II (1939–1945), professional baseball exploded—with huge attendance increases, unprecedented minor league expansion, and greater interest in the game from the American public. Yet, early in the 1950s, the interest in baseball fell off. Minor league attendance dropped steadily during the 1950s, and Major League attendance would have dropped but for expansion into new markets, including Milwaukee, Baltimore, Kansas City, and the two crown jewels: San Francisco and Los Angeles. By the end of the decade, football, possibly through the interest garnered from the Colts-Giants thrilling, overtime championship game in 1958, took some of the spotlight from baseball, America's recognized national pastime.

Many critics today point to the success of professional football, stock car racing, collegiate football and basketball as indications that baseball is no longer the national pastime. While baseball today clearly does not monopolize the interest of the sporting fans as it did for almost seventy years from the 1890s to the 1950s, no sport has been able to completely replace baseball as the national pastime. It is possible that no sport ever can dominate American sports the way that baseball did through the 1950s. *The Sporting News,* now a newspaper for all sports, devoted over ninety percent of its pages to baseball through the 1950s. While baseball was not the first sport to desegregate, it was the most important in the eyes of African Americans, who could claim a new level of social acceptance after Jackie Robinson signed with the Dodgers. Also, when the soldiers came back from World War II, towns all over the country quickly assembled the capital needed to secure a minor league baseball team; and memorial stadiums designed for baseball sprang up all over the country. With little competition from other sports, baseball was not just the dominant sport, but also practically the only sport.

Significance

Barzun's essay provides one of the greatest descriptions of baseball's role in American culture. Though not written necessarily to become the definitive and most-quoted statement on baseball, the essay, in its simplicity of sentiment, makes the connection between baseball and American culture better than anything written before or since. Near the beginning, Barzun says, "Whoever wants to know the heart and mind of America had better learn baseball, the rules and realities of the game—and do it

by watching first some high-school or small-town teams. The big-league games are too fast for the beginner and the newspapers don't help." This second part of the quote does not often make it in to the quotation books on baseball, but is very important in interpreting what Barzun meant to convey to the reader.

In looking more closely at the second half of this oft-used quote, Barzun talks a great deal about the nuances of the game, the little things that you need to notice to fully appreciate it. His understanding is that these elements would be missed if you were watching a game at Yankee Stadium or Wrigley Field, but would be clearer if viewed in a smaller park somewhere. Barzun writes about the dress of the team, and how the uniform develops a great look of camaraderie and single of purpose. With these examples, he hopes to illustrate not how baseball is cherished because it is the great American game, but how it symbolizes all those aspects of American culture that are great. He comments, "There has never been a good player who was dumb." Though many might argue, it is clear that brawn cannot carry the day with baseball the way that it can in football. He also takes a number of swipes at football, comparing the melee that is a football game against the almost ballet-like nimbleness needed for baseball. In examining baseball, Barzun proposed that the elements that bring together players to form a winning team, no matter at what level, are the same elements that bring together Americans to accomplish greater societal issues and callings.

Primary Source

"On Baseball"

> **SYNOPSIS:** In this essay, Barzun invites people who wish to know more about American society to watch baseball, a sport he acknowledges as one of its greatest cultural accomplishments. From this essay, Barzun offers one of the most quoted sayings on baseball: "Whoever wants to know the heart and mind of America had better learn baseball."

People who care less for gentility manage things better. They don't bother to leave the arid city but spend their surplus there on pastimes they can enjoy without feeling cramped. They follow boxing and wrestling, burlesque and vaudeville (when available), professional football and hockey. Above all, they thrill in unison with their fellow men the country over by watching baseball. The gods decree a heavyweight match only once in a while and a national election only every four years, but there is a World Series with every revolution of the earth around the sun. And in between, what varied pleasure long drawn out!

Youth players participate in the "drama" of a baseball game, May 21, 1954. French-born Jacques Barzun's "On Baseball" (1954) vividly describes baseball's role in American culture. © BETTMANN/CORBIS. REPRODUCED BY PERMISSION.

Whoever wants to know the heart and mind of America had better learn baseball, the rules and realities of the game—and do it by watching first some high-school or small-town teams. The big-league games are too fast for the beginner and the newspapers don't help. To read them with profit you have to know a language that comes easy only after philosophy has taught you to judge practice. Here is scholarship that takes effort on the part of the outsider, but it is so bred into the native that it never becomes a dreary round of technicalities. The wonderful purging of the passions that we all experienced in the fall of '51, the despair groaned out over the fate of the Dodgers, from whom the league pennant was snatched at the last minute, give us some idea of what Greek tragedy was like. Baseball is Greek in being national, heroic, and broken up in the rivalries of city-states.

And that it fitly expresses the powers of the nation's mind and body is a merit separate from the glory of being the most active, agile, varied, articulate, and brainy of all group games. It is of and for our century. Tennis belongs to the individualistic past—a hero, or at most a pair of friends or lovers, against the world. The idea of baseball is a team, an outfit, a section, a gang, a union, a cell, a commando—in short, a twentieth-century setup of opposite numbers.

Baseball takes its mystic nine and scatters them wide. A kind of individualism thereby returns, but it is limited—eternal vigilance is the price of victory. Just because they're far apart the outfield can't dream or play she-loves-me-not with daisies. The infield is like a steel net held in the hands of the catcher. He is the psychologist and historian for the staff—or else his signals will give the opposition hits. The value of his headpiece is shown by the iron-mongery worn to protect it. The pitcher, on the other hand, is the wayward man of genius, whom others will direct. They will expect nothing from him but virtuosity. He is surrounded no doubt by mere talent, unless one excepts that transplanted acrobat, the shortstop. What a brilliant invention is his role despite its exposure to ludicrous lapses! One man to each base and then the free lance, the troubleshooter, the movable feast for the eyes, whose motion animates the whole foreground.

The rules keep pace with this imaginative creation so rich in allusions to real life. How excellent, for instance, that a foul tip muffed by the catcher gives the batter another chance. It is the recognition of Chance that knows no argument. But on the other hand, how just that the third strike must not be dropped. This points to the fact that near the end of any struggle, life asks for more than is needful in order to clinch success. A victory has to be won, not snatched. We find also our American innocence in calling "World Series" the annual games between the winners in each big league. The world doesn't know or care and couldn't compete if it wanted to, but since it's us children having fun, why, the world is our stage. I said baseball was Greek. Is there not a poetic symbol in the new meaning—our meaning—of "Ruth hits Homer"?

Once the crack of the bat has sent the ball skimmering toward second, between the infielder's legs, six men converge or distend their defense to keep the runner from advancing along the prescribed path. The ball is not the center of interest as in those vulgar predatory games like football, basketball, or polo. Man running is the force to be contained. His getting to first or second base starts a capitalization dreadful to think of: every hit pushes him on. Bases full and a homer make four runs, while the defenders, helpless without the magic power of the ball lying over the fence, cry out their anguish and dig up the sod with their spikes.

But fate is controlled by the rules. Opportunity swings from one side to the other because innings alternate quickly, keep up spirit in the players, interest in the beholders. So does the profusion of different acts to be performed—pitching, throwing, catching, batting, running, stealing, sliding, signaling. Hits are similarly varied. Flies, Texas Leaguers, grounders, baseline fouls—praise God the human neck is a universal joint! And there is no set pace. Under the hot sun, the minutes creep as a deliberate pitcher tries his drops and curves for three strikes called, or conversely walks a threatening batter. But the batter is not invariably a tailor's dummy. In a hundredth of a second there may be a hissing rocket down right field, a cloud of dust over first base—the bleachers all a-yell—a double play, and the other side up to bat.

Accuracy and speed, the practiced eye and hefty arm, the mind to take in and readjust to the unexpected, the possession of more than one talent and the willingness to work in harness without special orders—these are the American virtues that shine in baseball. There has never been a good player who was dumb. Beef and bulk and mere endurance count for little, judgment and daring for much. Baseball is among group games played with a ball what fencing is to games of combat. But being spread out, baseball has something sociable and friendly about it that I especially love. It is graphic and choreographic. The ball is not shuttling in a confined space, as in tennis. Nor does baseball go to the other extreme of solitary whanging and counting stopped on the brink of pointlessness, like golf. Baseball is a kind of collective chess with arms and legs in full play under sunlight.

The team is elegance itself in its striped knee breeches and loose shirts, colored stockings and peaked caps. Except for brief moments of sliding, you can see them all in one eyeful, unlike the muddy hecatombs of football. To watch a football game is to be in prolonged neurotic doubt as to what you're seeing. It's more like an emergency happening at a distance than a game. I don't wonder the spectators take to drink. Who has ever seen a baseball fan drinking within the meaning of the act? He wants all his senses sharp and clear, his eyesight above all. He gulps down soda pop, which is a harmless way of replenishing his energy by the ingestion of sugar diluted in water and colored pink.

Happy the man in the bleachers. He is enjoying the spectacle that the gods on Olympus contrived

only with difficulty when they sent Helen to Troy and picked their teams. And the gods missed the fun of doing this by catching a bat near the narrow end and measuring hand over hand for first pick. In Troy, New York, the game scheduled for 2 P.M. will break no bones, yet it will be a real fight between Southpaw Dick and Red Larsen. For those whom civilized play doesn't fully satisfy, there will be provided a scapegoat in a blue suit—the umpire, yell-proof and even-handed as justice, which he demonstrates with outstretched arms when calling "Safe!"

And the next day in the paper: learned comment, statistical summaries, and the verbal imagery of meta-euphoric experts. In the face of so much joy, one can only ask, Were you there when Dogface Joe parked the pellet beyond the pale?

Further Resources

BOOKS
Evans, Christopher Hodge, and William R. Herzog. *The Faith of Fifty Million: Baseball, Religion, and American Culture.* Louisville, Ky.: Westminster John Knox Press, 2002.

National Baseball Hall of Fame and Museum. *Baseball As America: Seeing Ourselves Through Our National Game.* Washington, D.C.: National Geographic, 2002.

PERIODICALS
Messenger, Christian K. "Baseball and the Meaning of America." *Humanities,* July/August 1994, 13–18.

Regan, F. Scott. "The Might Casey: Enduring Folk Hero of Failure." *Journal of Popular Culture,* Summer 1997, 91–110.

WEBSITES
By Popular Demand: Jackie Robinson and Other Baseball Highlights, 1860s–1960s. American Memory digital primary source collection, Library of Congress. Available online at http://memory.loc.gov/ammem/jrhtml/jrhome.html; website home page: http://www.loc.gov (accessed April 22, 2003).

"The National Game: Baseball and American Culture." National Pastime.com. Available online at http://www.national pastime.com/the_national_game.html; website home page: http://www.nationalpastime.com. (accessed April 22, 2003).

AUDIO AND VISUAL MEDIA
Baseball: A Film by Ken Burns. Directed by Ken Burns. Warner Home Video, 1994, VHS.

A Day in the Bleachers
Nonfiction work

By: Arnold Hano

Date: 1955

Source: Hano, Arnold. *A Day in the Bleachers.* New York: Crowell, 1955. Excerpt reprinted in *Baseball Reader.* New York: McGraw-Hill, 1983, 185–193.

About the Author Arnold Hano (1922–) is a New York City writer and educator who held a variety of positions in his career, including junior reporter for the *New York Daily News,* editor for Bantam Books, and instructor of writing in both New York and California. He has written numerous books, including many on baseball. *A Day in the Bleachers,* his first baseball book, was his account of the first game of the 1954 World Series between the New York Giants and the Cleveland Indians. ■

Introduction

The New York Giants and the Cleveland Indians could not have been more dissimilar teams when they took the field on September 29, 1954, at New York's Polo Grounds for the first game of the 1954 World Series. Going 111-43, the Cleveland Indians compiled one of the best season records in Major League history—a .721 winning percentage. The Indians became the first team since 1949 other than the New York Yankees to win an American League pennant. The Yankees had won five consecutive World Series and had last lost the American League pennant to the Cleveland Indians in 1948. Al Lopez managed the Indians, with pitchers Bob Lemon, Bob Feller, and Early Wynn, and a lineup that featured Al Rosen, Larry Doby, and Vic Wertz. Lopez and the Indians won the American League pennant by eight games over the New York Yankees.

Facing the Indians in the World Series were the New York Giants. The Giants had had a losing record in 1953, but rebounded to win the National League pennant with a record of 97-57, finishing five games ahead of the Brooklyn Dodgers. The Giants were a balanced team led by Willie Mays and Monte Irvin, and managed by Leo Durocher. However, given the way that the Indians won the American league pennant, there was little thought, even in New York, that the Giants would have a good chance of winning the World Series.

What would happen in the 1954 World Series would be one of the greatest upsets in baseball history. The Giants, in improbable fashion, swept the Indians in four games. The star of the Giants was not Willie Mays or twenty-one game-winner Johnny Antonelli, but rather journeyman Dusty Rhodes—who, primarily as a pinch hitter, drove in seven runs, with two home runs and four hits in only six at-bats. But he might not have had the chance were it not for one of the greatest catches in Major League history, made by Willie Mays. In the eighth inning of game one, with the score 2-2 and Cleveland runners on first and second, Indians slugger Vic Wertz lined a shot to dead center field. Willie Mays, playing center field for the Giants, turned and ran toward the deepest part of the Polo Grounds. To the amazement of all, Mays made an over-the-shoulder catch, turning a bases-clearing double or triple into a harmless out. The

Indians did not score that inning because of the catch, allowing Rhodes to be the hero in the bottom of the tenth. The Giants won the next three games to take home the series and the improbable title.

Significance

Willie Mays' catch of the long line drive off the bat of Vic Wertz remains one of the greatest catches in Major League Baseball History. Written only one year after the remarkable catch, Arnold Hano's *Day in the Bleachers* does a great job of placing it in the proper historical context. It was clear from the reporting at the time that those in attendance immediately appreciated the significance of the catch. In large part, the document has two elements of significance. First, Hano captures the essence of the catch and is able to provide its significance only months after the occurrence. Second, the catch is a way that the Giants players exploited the unique dimensions of the Polo Grounds, just as they had with Bobby Thomson's "shot heard round the world" in that same stadium in 1951.

Arnold Hano uses a poet's muse to reflect upon Mays' catch. He says that Mays "turned so quickly, and run so fast and truly that he made this impossible catch look—to us in the bleachers—quite ordinary." While this is known simply as "The Catch" even to this day, Hano provides details that help us appreciate the play better. Mays caught a ball with his back to everyone else, some 462 feet from home plate, and made it look simple. After Mays caught the ball, he spun around in one motion and threw it into the infield to keep the runners from advancing. Hano writes, "But the throw! What an astonishing throw, to make all other throws ever before it, even those four Mays himself had made during fielding practice, appear the flings of teenage girls." It was said that the Indians never recovered from that catch, but certainly no one has ever been able to duplicate that feat.

The Polo Grounds, home of the New York Giants through the 1957 season when they then moved to San Francisco, had a very unique shape. Almost a rectangle, the Polo Grounds had very short right and left field lines, but a huge center field that seemed to go on forever. Bobby Thomson's "shot heard round the world," just making the seats down the left field line, would have been an out in virtually any other stadium. In game one of the 1954 series, the Giants got lucky again. Hano points out that he saw Hall of Famers Babe Ruth, Lou Gehrig, Ted Williams and others hit the ball very hard. "None, that I recall, ever hit a ball any harder than this one by Wertz in my presence," he added. The ball that would have been out of any other ball park remained within the vast expanses of center field, allowing Willie Mays to catch it for a harmless out. These two events, so critical to the lore of baseball in the 1950s, were possible because of the odd dimensions of a great old ballpark.

Primary Source

A Day in the Bleachers [excerpt]

SYNOPSIS: In minute detail, based on his observation made during the play, Arnold Hano provides a wonderful account of one of the greatest catches ever made in a baseball game, let alone a World Series game. Hano not only provides an excellent account of the actual catch by Willie Mays off the bat of Vic Wertz, but also places it in its larger historical context.

And like wolves drawn to our fresh play, we had already forgotten him (Maglie), eyes riveted on Liddle, while off to the side of the plate Vic Wertz studied the new Giant pitcher and made whatever estimations he had to make.

Wertz had hit three times already; nobody expected more of him. He had hit one of Maglie's fast balls in the first inning, a pitch that was headed for the outside corner but Wertz's bat was too swift and he had pulled the ball for a triple. Then he hit a little curve, a dinky affair that was either Maglie's slider or a curve that didn't break too well, and drove it into left field for a single. Finally, he had pulled another outside pitch that—by all rights—he shouldn't have been able to pull, so far from the right-field side of the plate was it. But he had pulled it, as great sluggers will pull any ball because that is how home runs are made. Wertz hadn't hit a home run on that waist-high pitch on the outside; he had rifled it to right field for another single.

But that was all off Maglie, forgotten behind a door over five hundred feet from the plate. Now it was Liddle, jerking into motion as Wertz poised at the plate, and then the motion smoothed out and the ball came sweeping in to Wertz, a shoulder-high pitch, a fast ball that probably would have been a fast curve, except that Wertz was coming around and hitting it, hitting it about as hard as I have ever seen a ball hit, on a high line to dead center field.

For whatever it is worth, I have seen such hitters as Babe Ruth, Lou Gehrig, Ted Williams, Jimmy Foxx, Ralph Kiner, Hack Wilson, Johnny Mize, and lesser-known but equally long hitters as Wally Berger and Bob Seeds send the batted ball tremendous distances. None, that I recall, ever hit a ball any harder than this one by Wertz in my presence.

And yet I was not immediately perturbed. I have been a Giant fan for years, twenty-eight years to be exact, and I have seen balls hit with violence to extreme center field which were caught easily by Mays, or Thomson before him, or Lockman or Ripple or Hank Leiber or George Kiddo Davis, that most marvelous fly catcher.

I did not—then—feel alarm, though the crack was loud and clear, and the crowd's roar rumbled behind it like growing thunder. It may be that I did not believe the ball would carry as far as it did, hard hit as it was. I have seen hard-hit balls go a hundred feet into an infielder's waiting glove, and all that one remembers is crack, blur, spank. This ball did not alarm me because it was hit to dead center field—Mays' territory—and not between the fielders, into those dread alleys in left-center and right-center which lead to the bull pens.

And this was not a terribly high drive. It was a long low fly or a high liner, whichever you wish. This ball was hit not nearly so high as the triple Wertz struck earlier in the day, so I may have assumed that it would soon start to break and dip and come down to Mays, not too far from his normal position.

Then I looked at Willie, and alarm raced through me, peril flaring against my heart. To my utter astonishment, the young Giant center fielder—the inimitable Mays, most skilled of outfielders, unique for his ability to scent the length and direction of any drive and then turn and move to the final destination of the ball—Mays was turned full around, head down, running as hard as he could, straight toward the runway between the two bleacher sections.

I knew then that I had underestimated—badly underestimated—the length of Wertz's blow.

I wrenched my eyes from Mays and took another look at the ball, winging its way along, undipping, unbreaking, forty feet higher than Mays' head, rushing along like a locomotive, nearing Mays, and I thought then: it will beat him to the wall.

Through the years I have tried to do what Red Barber has cautioned me and millions of admiring fans to do: take your eye from the ball after it's been hit and look at the outfielder and the runners. This is a terribly difficult thing to learn; for twenty-five years I was unable to do it. Then I started to take stabs at the fielder and the ball, alternately. Now I do it pretty well. Barber's advice pays off a thousand times in appreciation of what is unfolding, of what takes some six or seven seconds—that's all, six or

A view of Willie Mays' game-saving eighth-inning catch of Vic Wertz's 450-foot drive at the Polo Grounds, September 29, 1954. "The Catch," as it became known, preserved a 2-2 score and helped the Giants go on to win the game. **AP/WIDE WORLD PHOTOS.**

seven seconds—and of what I can see in several takes, like a jerking motion picture, until I have enough pieces to make nearly a whole.

There is no perfect whole, of course, to a play in baseball. If there was, it would require a God to take it all in. For instance, on such a play, I would like to know what Manager Durocher is doing—leaping to the outer lip of the sunken dugout, bent forward, frozen in anxious fear? And Lopez—is he also frozen, hope high but too anxious to let it swarm through him? The coaches—have they started to wave their arms in joy, getting the runners moving, or are they half-waiting, in fear of the impossible catch and the mad scramble that might ensue on the base paths?

The players—what have they done? The fans—are they standing, or half-crouched, yelling (I hear them, but since I do not see them, I do not know who makes that noise, which of them yells and which is silent)? Has activity stopped in the Giant bull pen where Grissom still had been toiling? Was he now turned to watch the flight of the ball, the churning dash of Mays?

No man can get the entire picture; I did what I could, and it was painful to rip my sight from one scene frozen forever on my mind, to the next, and then to the next.

I had seen the ball hit; its rise; I had seen Mays' first backward sprint; I had again seen the ball and Mays at the same time, Mays still leading. Now I turned to the diamond—how long does it take the eyes to sweep and focus and telegraph to the brain?—and there was the vacant spot on the hill (how often we see what is not there before we see what is there) where Liddle had been and I saw him at the third base line, between home and third (the wrong place for a pitcher on such a play; he should be behind third to cover a play there, or behind home to back up a play there, but not in between).

I saw Doby, too, hesitating, the only man, I think, on the diamond who now conceded that Mays might catch the ball. Doby is a center fielder and a fine one and very fast himself, so he knows what a center fielder can do. He must have gone nearly halfway to third, now he was coming back to second base a bit. Of course, he may have known that he could jog home if the ball landed over Mays' head, so there was no need to get too far down the line.

Rosen was as near to second as Doby, it seemed. He had come down from first, and for a second—no, not that long, nowhere near that long, for a hundred-thousandth of a second, more likely—I thought Doby and Rosen were Dark and Williams hovering around second, making some foolish double play on this ball that had been hit three hundred and thirty feet past them. Then my mind cleared; they were in Cleveland uniforms, not Giant, they were Doby and Rosen.

And that is all I allowed my eyes on the inner diamond. Back now to Mays—had three seconds elapsed from the first ominous connection of bat and ball?—and I saw Mays do something that he seldom does and that is so often fatal to outfielders. For the briefest piece of time—I cannot shatter and compute fractions of seconds like some atom gun—Mays started to raise his head and turn it to his left, as though he were about to look behind him.

Then he thought better of it, and continued the swift race with the ball that hovered quite close to him now, thirty feet high and coming down (yes, finally coming down) and again—for the second time—I knew Mays would make the catch.

In the Polo Grounds, there are two squarish green screens, flanking the runway between the two bleacher sections, one to the left-field side of the runway, the other to the right. The screens are intended to provide a solid dark background for the pitched ball as it comes in to the batter. Otherwise he would be trying to pick out the ball from the far-off sea of shirts of many colors, jackets, balloons, and banners.

Wertz's drive, I could see now, was not going to end up in the runway on the fly; it was headed for the screen on the right-field side.

The fly, therefore, was not the longest ball ever hit in the Polo Grounds, not by a comfortable margin. Wally Berger had hit a ball over the left-field roof around the four-hundred foot marker. Joe Adcock had hit a ball into the center-field bleachers. A Giant pitcher, Hal Schumacher, had once hit a ball over the left-field roof, about as far out as Berger's. Nor—if Mays caught it—would it be the longest ball ever caught in the Polo Grounds. In either the 1936 or 1937 World Series—I do not recall which—Joe DiMaggio and Hank Leiber traded gigantic smashes to the foot of the stairs within that runway; each man had caught the other's. When DiMaggio caught Leiber's, in fact, it meant the third out of the game. DiMaggio caught the ball and barely broke step to go up the stairs and out of sight before the crowd was fully aware of what had happened.

So Mays' catch—if he made it—would not necessarily be in the realm of the improbable. Others had done feats that bore some resemblance to this.

Yet Mays' catch—if, indeed, he was to make it—would dwarf all the others for the simple reason that he, too, could have caught Leiber's or DiMaggio's fly, whereas neither could have caught Wertz's. Those balls had been towering drives, hit so high the outfielder could run forever before the ball came down. Wertz had hit his ball harder and on a lower trajectory. Leiber—not a fast man—was nearing second base when DiMaggio caught his ball, Wertz—also not fast—was at first when . . .

When Mays simply slowed down to avoid running into the wall, put his hands up in cup-like fashion over his left shoulder, and caught the ball much like a football player catching leading passes in the end zone.

He had turned so quickly, and run so fast and truly that he made this impossible catch look—to us in the bleachers—quite ordinary. To those reporters in the press box, nearly six hundred feet from the bleacher wall, it must have appeared far more astonishing, watching Mays run and run until he had

become the size of a pigmy and then he had to run some more, while the ball diminished to a mote of white dust and finally disappeared in the dark blob that was Mays' mitt.

The play was not finished, with the catch.

Now another pet theory of mine could be put to the test. For years I have criticized base runners who advance from second base while a long fly ball is in the air, then return to the base once the catch has been made and proceed to third after tagging up. I have wondered why these men have not held their base; if the ball is not caught, they can score from second. If it is, surely they will reach third. And—if they are swift—should they not be able to score from second on enormously long flies to dead center field?

Here was such a fly; here was Doby so close to second before the catch that he must have practically been touching the bag when Mays was first touching the drive, his back to the diamond. Now Doby could—if he dared—test the theory.

And immediately I saw how foolish my theory was when the thrower was Mays.

It is here that Mays outshines all others. I do not think the catch made was as sensational as some others I have seen, although no one else could have made it. I recall a catch made by Fred Lindstrom, a converted third baseman who had had legs, against Pittsburgh. Lindstrom ran to the right-center field wall beyond the Giants' bull pen and leaped high to snare the ball with his gloved hand. Then his body smashed into the wall and he fell on his back, his gloved hand held over his body, the speck of white still showing. After a few seconds, he got to his feet, quite groggy, but still holding the ball. That was the finest catch I can recall, and the account of the game in next day's New York *Herald Tribune* indicated it might have been the greatest catch ever made in the Polo Grounds.

Yet Lindstrom could not have reached the ball Mays hit and Mays would have been standing at the wall, ready to leap and catch the ball Lindstrom grabbed.

Mays never left his feet for the ball Wertz hit; all he did was outrun the ball. I do not diminish the feat; no other center fielder that I have ever seen (Joe and Dom DiMaggio, Terry Moore, Sammy West, Eddie Roush, Earle Combs, and Duke Snider are but a few that stand out) could have done it for no one else was as fast in getting to the ball. But I am of the opinion that had not Mays made that slight movement with his head as though he were going to look back in the middle of flight, he would have caught the ball standing still.

The throw to second base was something else again.

Mays caught the ball, and then whirled and threw, like some olden statue of a Greek javelin hurler, his head twisted away to the left as his right arm swept out and around. But Mays is no classic study for the simple reason that at the peak of his activity, his baseball cap flies off. And as he turned, or as he threw—I could not tell which, the two motions were welded into one—off came the cap, and then Mays himself continued to spin around after the gigantic effort of returning the ball whence it came, and he went down flat on his belly, and out of sight.

But the throw! What an astonishing throw, to make all other throws ever before it, even those four Mays himself had made during fielding practice, appear the flings of teenage girls. This was the throw of a giant, the throw of a howitzer made human, arriving at second base—to Williams or Dark, I don't know which, but probably Williams, my memory says Dark was at the edge of the outfield grass, in deep shortstop position—just as Doby was pulling into third, and as Rosen was scampering back to first.

I wonder what will happen to Mays in the next few years. He may gain in finesse and batting wisdom, but he cannot really improve much because his finest talent lies in his reflex action. He is so swift in his reflexes, the way young Joe Louis was with his hands when, cobra-like, they would flash through the thinnest slit in a foe's defense; Louis, lashing Paulino Uzeudun with the first hard punch he threw, drilling into the tiniest opening and crushing the man who had never before been knocked out. That is Mays, too. Making a great catch and whirling and throwing, before another man would have been twenty feet from the ball.

And until those reflexes slow down, Mays must be regarded as off by himself, not merely *a* great ballplayer, but *the* great ballplayer of our time.

(I am not discussing his hitting here; for some strange reason—National League-itis, I guess—when I discuss the native ability of a ballplayer, I invariably narrow my gaze to his defensive ability. DiMaggio was a better hitter in his prime than Mays is now, maybe than Mays ever will be, although no hitter was ever as good as Mays at the same stage

of their respective careers—check Ruth, Wagner, Cobb, Hornsby in their second full year of play and you will see what I mean.)

Still, Willie's 1954 season at the plate may have been some freak occurrence. It happens sometimes that a ballplayer hits all season far above his norm. I am thinking of Ferris Fain who led the league a few years ago, though he had never been an impressive hitter before. My wife inquired about this man Fain, of whom she was suddenly hearing so much. I told her that he was a pretty good ballplayer, an excellent defensive first baseman, and a fair hitter. She said, "Fair? He's leading the league, isn't he?"

I said, "Yes, but that's a fluke. He's hitting way over his head. Watch what happens next year." [The following year Fain led the league again. . . . (Author's note)]

Or take Carl Furillo hitting over .340 in 1953. Furillo is a fine hitter, a solid .300 hitter who can drive in nearly a hundred runs a season, but .340 is not his normal average. Possibly .345 is nowhere near Mays' norm; nothing in the past had indicated he could hit that high.

I do not list Mays among the great hitters, though I concede that one day we all may. As a fielder, he is already supreme.

So much for Mays and the catch.

Further Resources

BOOKS
Einstein, Charles. *Willie's Time*. New York: Lippincott Williams & Wilkins, 1979.

Kahn, Roger. *The Era, 1947–1957: When the Yankees, the Giants and the Dodgers Ruled the World*. Lincoln, Neb.: University of Nebraska Press, 2002

Thornley, Stew. *Land of the Giants: New York's Polo Grounds*. Philadelphia: Temple University Press, 2000.

PERIODICALS
Harper, William T. "The Greatest Catch." *American Heritage*, November 1999, 38–43.

WEBSITES
"The Catch." Baseball's 25 Greatest Moments. *The Sporting News*. Available online at http://www.sportingnews.com /baseball/25moments/9.html; website home page: http://www .sportingnews.com (accessed April 22, 2003).

"Willie Mays." National Baseball Hall of Fame. Available online at http://www.baseballhalloffame.org/hofers_and_hon orees/hofer_bios/mays_willie.htm; website home page: http:// www.baseballhalloffame.org (accessed April 22, 2003).

AUDIO AND VISUAL MEDIA
Baseball's Greatest Memories, Myths and Legends. Greatest Sports Legends, 1994, VHS.

"New York Yankees 2, Brooklyn Dodgers 0"

Newspaper article

By: Shirley Povich

Date: October 9, 1956

Source: Povich, Shirley. "New York Yankees 2, Brooklyn Dodgers 0." *Washington Post,* October 9, 1956. Reprinted in *Baseball Reader.* New York: McGraw-Hill, 1983, 357–361.

About the Author: Shirley Povich (1905–1998) was one of the great sportswriters of the twentieth century. A writer for the *Washington Post* his entire career, it is estimated that he wrote over fifteen hundred columns during a nearly seventy-five year career. *Washington Post* Editor Ben Bradlee repeatedly said that Povich was the sole reason that many people bought that paper. The National Baseball Hall of Fame honored him in 1975 as the recipient of the J.G. Taylor Spink Award for "meritorious contributions to baseball writing." ■

Introduction

The New York Yankees and Brooklyn Dodgers faced off in the 1956 World Series for the second consecutive year, after the Dodgers finally won a Series title in 1955. In 1956, the Yankees once again dominated the American League and were in good position to win yet another World Series title. However, Brooklyn took the first two games of the Series. In games three and four, the Yankees rebounded to even the series at two wins apiece. With the Series tied, the Yankees sent Don Larsen to the mound for game five. If the Yankees were a bit apprehensive about Larsen pitching, they had good reason. Larsen was roughed up in his game two start—giving up six unearned runs in the 13-8 Brooklyn win. Adding to that misery, Don Larsen's wife filed for divorce on the morning of game five.

Don Larsen was a typical pitcher for the New York Yankees during their amazing seasons in the 1940s, 1950s and early 1960s. The Yankees would pick up previously mediocre players and turn them into stars. Don Larsen went 3-21 for the Baltimore Orioles in 1954, only to go 9-2, 11-5, and 10-4 over the next three seasons with the Yankees. Whitey Ford was the dominant pitcher on the Yankees during the 1950s, but the other pitchers all seemed to be a wonderful complement to his Hall of Fame career. So on October 8, 1956, Larsen tried to regroup for game five at Yankee Stadium. All he did was pitch one of the best games ever, under the spotlight of the World Series. On that autumn day, Larsen not only threw a no-hitter against the Dodgers, he pitched a perfect game—retiring all twenty-seven Dodger batters he faced. It was one of only thirteen ever thrown at the Major League level. When the last out was recorded, Hall of Fame Catcher, Yogi Berra, jumped on Larsen's arms

and his teammates mobbed him on the pitchers mound. The Yankees would go on to win the seventh and deciding game of the World Series to capture their seventeenth world title.

Significance

Some of the most amazing performances in baseball history have been by players who never even came close to earning a place in the National Baseball Hall of Fame. Larson put up modest career numbers, posting an 81-91 lifetime record over fourteen seasons. But on that day in October, Larsen's name became forever synonymous with perfection. In over a century and a quarter of play, pitchers have thrown only thirteen perfect Major League games since 1876. Pitchers with perfect games have not always been Hall of Famers, but those who have had great stuff at least for one day, and received all the breaks that they needed. In Shirley Povich's account of the game, he uses the following phrases to emphasize the improbability of a perfect game in the World Series—"The million-to-one shot came in. Hell froze over. A month of Sundays hit the calendar"—before mentioning that Dan Larsen pitched a perfect game. Larson's feat remains the only no-hitter in baseball post-season history.

Also wonderful in Povich's piece is the discussion of the partisan fans rallying around Larsen. In the heated rivalry between Dodger and Yankee fans in New York, Povich noticed that these partisan desires waned in the late innings of the game. Even during the World Series, Larsen converted Dodger fans to his performance so that by the end of the game, Povich could report that the "loyalties to the Dodgers evaporated in sheer enthrallment at the show big Larsen was giving them, for this was a day when the fans could boast that they were there." And boast they did, as it became one of the most famous World Series games of the 1950s, or any decade for that matter.

Primary Source

"New York Yankees 2, Brooklyn Dodgers 0"

SYNOPSIS: Shirley Povich reports on the perfect game thrown by New York Yankee pitcher Don Larsen in game five of the 1956 World Series against the Brooklyn Dodgers. The article goes into great detail on the game and provides a wonderful snapshot of the post-game celebration, especially as Larsen carried catcher, Yogi Berra, off the field. The article also explains several plays in the game—instances where the perfect game could have been lost by a matter of inches, and where balls that were hit sharply went right to Yankee fielders.

The million-to-one shot came in. Hell froze over. A month of Sundays hit the calendar. Don Larsen

New York Yankees pitcher Don Larsen delivers the third strike and final out of his perfect game against the Brooklyn Dodgers, October 8, 1956. Larsen set all twenty-seven Dodgers down—in order—for the 2-0 victory. © BETTMANN/CORBIS. REPRODUCED BY PERMISSION.

today pitched a no-hit, no-run, no-man-reach-first game in a World Series.

On the mound at Yankee Stadium, the same guy who was knocked out in two innings by the Dodgers on Friday came up today with one for the record books, posting it there in solo grandeur as the only Perfect Game in World Series history.

With it, the Yankee right-hander shattered the Dodgers, 2-0, and beat Sal Maglie, while taking 64,519 suspense-limp fans into his act.

First there was mild speculation, then there was hope, then breaths were held in slackened jaws in the late innings as the big mob wondered if the big Yankee right-hander could bring off for them the most fabulous of all World Series games.

He did it, and the Yanks took the Series lead three games to two, to leave the Dodgers as thunderstruck as Larsen himself appeared to be at the finish of his feat.

Larsen whizzed a third strike past pinch hitter Dale Mitchell in the ninth. That was all. It was over. Automatically, the massive 226-pounder from San

Diego started walking from the mound toward the dugout, as pitchers are supposed to do at the finish.

But this time there was a woodenness in his steps and his stride was that of a man in a daze. The spell was broken for Larsen when Yogi Berra ran onto the infield to embrace him.

It was not Larsen jumping for joy. It was the more demonstrative Berra. His battery mate leaped full tilt at the big guy. In self-defense, Larsen caught Berra in mid-air as one would catch a frolicking child, and that's how they made their way toward the Yankee bench, Larsen carrying Berra.

There wasn't a Brooklyn partisan left among the 64,519, it seemed, at the finish. Loyalties to the Dodgers evaporated in sheer enthrallment at the show big Larsen was giving them, for this was a day when the fans could boast that they were there.

So at the finish, Larsen had brought it off, and erected for himself a special throne in baseball's Hall of Fame, with the first Perfect Game pitched in major-league baseball since Charlie Robertson of the White Sox against Detroit 34 years ago.

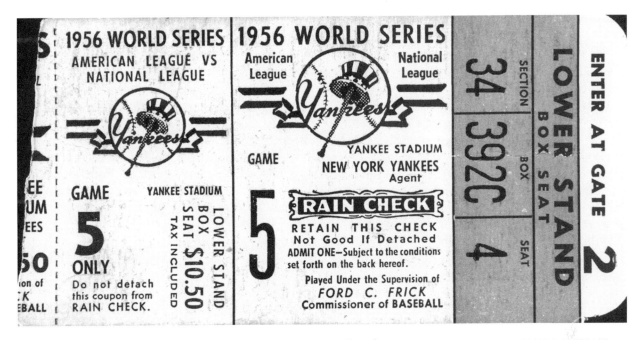

A ticket for game five of the World Series—the game at which Don Larsen threw his perfect game. MILO STEWART JR./NATIONAL BASEBALL HALL OF FAME LIBRARY, COOPERSTOWN, NY.

But this was one more special. This one was in a World Series. Three times, pitchers had almost come through with no-hitters, and there were three one-hitters in the World Series books, but never a no-man-reach-base classic.

The tragic victim of it all, sitting on the Dodger bench, was sad Sal Maglie, himself a five-hit pitcher today in his bid for a second Series victory over the Yankees. He was out of the game, technically, but he was staying to see it out and it must have been in disbelief that he saw himself beaten by another guy's World Series no-hitter.

Mickey Mantle hit a home run today in the fourth inning and that was all the impetus the Yankees needed, but no game-winning home run ever wound up with such emphatic second billing as Mantle's this afternoon.

It was an exciting wallop but in the fourth inning only, because after that Larsen was the story today, and the dumbfounded Dodgers could wonder how this same guy who couldn't last out two innings in the second game could master them so thoroughly today.

He did it with a tremendous assortment of pitches that seemed to have five forward speeds, including a slow one that ought to have been equipped with back-up lights.

Larsen had them in hand all day. He used only 97 pitches, not an abnormally low number because 11 pitches an inning is about normal for a good day's work. But he was the boss from the outset. Only against Peewee Reese in the first inning did he lapse to a three-ball count, and then he struck Reese out. No other Dodger was ever favored with more than two called balls by Umpire Babe Pinelli.

Behind him, his Yankee teammates made three spectacular fielding plays to put Larsen in the Hall of Fame. There was one in the second inning that calls for special description. In the fifth, Mickey Mantle ranged far back into left center to haul in Gil Hodges' long drive with a backhand shoetop grab that was a beaut. In the eighth, the same Hodges made another bid to break it up, but Third Baseman Andy Carey speared his line drive.

Little did Larsen, the Yankees, the Dodgers or anybody among the 64,519 in the stands suspect that when Jackie Robinson was robbed of a line-drive hit in the second inning, the stage was being set for a Perfect Game.

Robinson murdered the ball so hard that Third Baseman Andy Carey barely had time to fling his glove upward in a desperate attempt to get the ball. He could only deflect it. But, luckily, Shortstop Gil McDougald was backing up, and able to grab the ball on one bounce. By a half-step, McDougald got Robinson at first base, and Larsen tonight can be grateful that it was not the younger, fleeter

Robinson of a few years back but a heavy-legged, 40-year-old Jackie.

As the game wore on, Larsen lost the edge that gave him five strikeouts in the first four innings, and added only two in the last five. He had opened up by slipping called third strikes past both Gilliam and Reese in the first inning.

Came the sixth, and he got Furillo and Campanella on pops, fanned Maglie. Gilliam, Reese and Snider were easy in the seventh. Robinson tapped out, Hodges lined out and Amoros flied out in the eighth. And now it was the ninth, and the big Scandinavian-American was going for the works with a calm that was exclusive with him.

Furillo gave him a bit of a battle, fouled off four pitches, then flied mildly to Bauer. He got two quick strikes on Campanella, got him on a slow roller to Martin.

Now it was the left-handed Dale Mitchell, pinch hitting for Maglie.

Ball one came in high. Larsen got a called strike.

On the next pitch, Mitchell swung for strike two.

Then the last pitch of the game. Mitchell started to swing, but didn't go through with it.

But it made no difference because Umpire Pinelli was calling it Strike Number Three, and baseball history was being made.

Maglie himself was a magnificent figure out there all day, pitching hitless ball and leaving the Yankees a perplexed gang, until suddenly with two out in the fourth, Mickey Mantle, with two called strikes against him, lashed the next pitch on a line into the right-field seats to give the Yanks a 1-0 lead.

There was doubt about that Mantle homer because the ball was curving and would it stay fair? It did. In their own half of the inning, the Dodgers had no such luck. Duke Snider's drive into the same seats had curved foul by a few feet. The disgusted Snider eventually took a third strike.

The Dodgers were a luckless gang and Larsen a fortunate fellow in the fifth. Like Mantle, Sandy Amoros lined one into the seats in right, and that one was a near thing for the Yankees. By what seemed only inches, it curved foul, the umpires ruled.

Going into the sixth, Maglie was pitching a one-hitter—Mantle's homer—and being outpitched. The old guy lost some of his stuff in the sixth, though, and the Yankees came up with their other run.

Carey led off with a single to center, and Larsen sacrificed him to second on a daring third-strike bunt.

Hank Bauer got the run in with a single to left. There might have been a close play at the plate had Amoros come up with the ball cleanly, but he didn't and Carey scored unmolested.

Now there were Yanks still on first and third with only one out, but they could get no more. Hodges made a scintillating pickup of Mantle's smash, stepped on first and threw to home for a double play on Bauer, who was trying to score. Bauer was trapped in a rundown and caught despite a low throw by Campanella that caused Robinson to fall into the dirt.

But the Yankees weren't needing any more runs for Larsen today. They didn't even need their second one, because they were getting a pitching job for the books this memorable day in baseball.

Further Resources

BOOKS

Kahn, Roger. *The Boys of Summer*. New York: HarperCollins, 1950.

Larsen, Don, and Mark Shaw. *The Perfect Yankee: The Incredible Story of the Greatest Miracle in Baseball History*. Urbana, Ill.: Sports Publishing LLC, 1996.

PERIODICALS

Kennedy, Kostya. "His Memory Is Perfect." *Sports Illustrated*, October 14, 1996, 13–15.

Kindred, Dave. "The Day Don Larsen Was Perfect." *The Sporting News*, February 24, 1999. Available online at http://www.sportingnews.com/archives/sports2000/moments/143420.html; website home page http://www.sportingnews.com (accessed April 22, 2003).

WEBSITES

Box score of perfect game by Don Larsen. "Boxscores: Historical Games." Baseball Almanac. Available online at http://www.baseball-almanac.com/boxscore/10081956.shtml; website home page: http://www.baseball-almanac.com (accessed April 22, 2003).

"Don Larsen." Baseball Library. Available online at http://www.pubdim.net/baseballlibrary/ballplayers/L/Larsen_Don.stm; website home page: http://www.pubdim.net/baseball library (accessed April 22, 2003).

"Miss Gibson Wins Wimbledon Title"

Newspaper article

By: Fred Tupper

Date: July 7, 1957

Source: Tupper, Fred. "Miss Gibson Wins Wimbledon Title." *The New York Times*, July 7, 1957, sec. 5, 1, 5.

About the Author: Fred Tupper was a reporter for *The New York Times*. He covered tennis and other sports for that newspaper through the 1970s. ∎

Introduction

Aletha Gibson, at twenty-nine, won the 1957 Wimbledon women's singles title, becoming the first African American of either gender to win that tournament and a major tennis championship. Her ascent was difficult, but she persevered to reach the top of the tennis world. Growing up in New York City, Gibson was first pushed toward tennis by a playground superintendent who recognized her talent for the sport. Fred Johnson at the Cosmopolitan Tennis Club in New York City coached her, and Gibson later moved to Wilmington, N.C., where she played on the tennis team at Wilmington Industrial High School. In 1947, she won her first "national Negro championship." In 1950, she joined the major circuit and became the first African American player to compete at the U.S. Open at Forest Hills, nearly winning the tournament that year. From 1951 to 1955, she was ranked in the top thirteen—reaching number seven in 1953—but her game started to falter. In the fall of 1955, she considered retirement; but she stayed on the tour, rejuvenated by a tour of Southeastern Asia sponsored by the U.S. State Department. Gibson had banner years in 1957 and 1958, as she won both Wimbledon and the U.S. Open both years.

Significance

Without question, the most prominent color line broken in sports in the twentieth century was Jackie Robinson entering the Brooklyn Dodger lineup in April 1947. However, there were many other significant color lines that fell in the 1940s and 1950s that had a lessened, but still powerful, impact to American culture and sports. One of these racial barriers existed in tennis, and was broken in 1950 when Althea Gibson participated in the U.S. Open tournament. Gibson had a career of great promise, but it was not until 1957 than that she captured a major singles title with her victory at Wimbledon, the first of her four major titles. Fred Tupper, as well as many of the members of the media, viewed this event as prominently as Jackie Robinson's breaking of the color barrier with the Dodgers. While his article, "Miss Gibson Wins Wimbledon Title," was on the first page of the sports section, the front page of the paper that day had a photo of Gibson accepting a trophy from Queen Elizabeth II, an indication of the importance of her victory.

As a tour member in her eighth year, Gibson was a fixture on the tour. However, her 1957 Wimbledon victory was the crowning moment of her career. She once said, "I encountered no color barriers and none of the

Althea Gibson accepts congratulations from Darlene Hard after winning the singles tennis championship at Wimbledon, July 6, 1957. Gibson was the first African American to win Wimbledon © BETTMANN/CORBIS. REPRODUCED BY PERMISSION.

players have ever been rude to me." And while she gained notoriety as the only African American on the tour, her victory at Wimbledon became something more special to people following her career. Tupper opened the story by noting "Althea Gibson fulfilled her destiny at Wimbledon today and became the first member of her race to rule the world of tennis," when she defeated Darlene Hard, another American. But besides her role as an African American athlete, Gibson clearly was interested in the victory for personal reasons that transcend race or her upbringing. When accepting the trophy from Queen Elizabeth during the queen's first visit to Wimbledon since becoming the monarch in 1952, Gibson said, "At last! At last!"

Primary Source

"Miss Gibson Wins Wimbledon Title"

SYNOPSIS: This newspaper article reports on the Wimbledon women's singles finals match between Althea Gibson and Darlene Hard on July 6, 1957. Highlighting Gibson's win, the article also describes the mixed doubles and women's doubles (won by Gibson and Head) championship matches played on the same day.

Miss Hard Routed

Althea Gibson Becomes First Negro to Take Wimbledon Tennis

Wimbledon, England, July 6—Althea Gibson fulfilled her destiny at Wimbledon today and became the first member of her race to rule the world of tennis. Reaching a high note at the start, the New York Negro routed Darlene Hard, the Montebello (Calif.) waitress, 6-3, 6-2, for the all-England crown.

Later Miss Gibson paired with Miss Hard to swamp Mary Hawton and Thelma Long of Australia, 6-2, 6-1, in the doubles for her second championship.

But the match of the day and the sensation of the year saw Gardnar Mulloy gain the honor of being the oldest man in Wimbledon history to win a title. The 42-year-old Denver executive teamed with 33-year-old Budge Patty, the Californian who lives in Paris, to upset the top-seeded Neale Fraser and Lew Hoad, 8-10, 6-4, 6-4, 6-4, and break an Australian domination in the men's doubles that went back seven years.

The shirt-sleeved crowd jammed in this ivy-covered inferno hailed Mulloy with a roaring ovation that must have echoed wherever he has played. The applause was deafening as Queen Elizabeth went down on the court to present a silver trophy to the American.

With the pressure off, Miss Hard played magnificently with Mervyn Rose to win from Miss Gibson and Fraser, 6-4, 7-5, in the mixed doubles.

U. S. Takes Three Titles

In all, the United States took three titles and divided another of the five contested here. It was the best American showing since 1953. Australia's Hoad won the singles yesterday.

The ladies took the stage amid a sea of waving programs as the temperature touched 96 in the shade. Miss Gibson was in rare form. She had beaten Darlene three times running in the past year and was off in high. Her big service was kicking to Miss Hard's backhand with such speed that Darlene could only lob it back.

Behind her serves and her severe ground shots. Althea moved tigerishly to the net to cut away her volleys. Quickly she had four games running against one of the finest net players in the game. Darlene, white-faced in the heat, kept shaking her head at her failure to find an offensive shot. The set was gone in 25 minutes at 6-3.

Althea was unhurried. Her control was good and she calmly passed Miss Hard every time she tried to storm up to the barrier. The game grew faster as Miss Gibson's service jumped so alarmingly off the fast grass that Darlene nodded miserably as her errors mounted. It was all over in 50 minutes.

Queen Presents Trophy

"At last! At last!" Althea said, grinning widely as the Queen congratulated her and presented the trophy. Althea flies home with her prize Monday evening.

It was Mulloy who was the master strategist in the staggering American victory over Fraser and Hoad. The artful ancient abandoned all pretext of playing the smash-grab Australian game, Cunningly he pitched the ball just over the net, mixing soft floaters with angled chop shots and invariably he was the man who put the ball away at the end of every exchange.

The games went with service in that long first set, but while the Australians were winning their easily, the Americans were struggling to hold service. Mulloy saved a set point at 5-4 as he and Patty tangled racquets, but Budge was finally broken at love as he popped three volleys into the net.

Then Mulloy took command. He hit four shots all of them outright winners, to break Fraser in the first game of the second set. And then he had the crowd in stitches as he chased a Hoad overhead right into the stands and moved a spectator over so he could sit down.

Returning on court, he won the point for the break-through in the first game of the third set. The Americans took both sets at 6-4 as Patty backed Mulloy with his delicate volleying.

Hoad was making errors now, unable to dispatch the tantalizing soft stuff around his ankles. The Americans broke through him again to lead at 4-3 in the fourth. A Patty ace saved the next game and then Mulloy majestically served his game out at love for the match.

Tenth Wimbledon Event

This was Gardnar's tenth appearance at Wimbledon. Patty has played here since the war. He won the singles in 1950. The delighted audience gave a concerted cheer, something reserved for old friends, at the Americans' victory.

After watching Mulloy's performance. Miss Gibson must have regretted discarding him as a partner. Together they reached the final last year in the mixed doubles. Obviously tired after her ordeals in the steaming crater, Miss Gibson was broken four times on service in the mixed doubles as Miss Hard suddenly found her touch overhead. Ecstatically, Darlene bounced about the court and fired Rose to such perfection that they were off court in under an hour.

Miss Gibson and Miss Hard had only to go to the net to command the play against Mrs. Hawton and Mrs. Long.

And to round out a fine American day, the junior champion, Mimi Arnold of Redwood City, Calif., avenged her defeat at the hands of Rosa Reyes of Mexico in the ladies' event by winning, 8-6, 6-2, for the Wimbledon girl's crown.

Further Resources

BOOKS

Condon, Robert J. *Great Women Athletes of the 20th Century.* Jefferson, N.C.: McFarland, 1991.

Phillips, Caryl. *The Right Set: A Tennis Anthology.* New York: Vintage Books, 1999.

PERIODICALS

"10 Greatest Women Athletes." *Ebony,* March 2002, 74–78.

WEBSITES

Official website of Althea Gibson. Available online at http://www.altheagibson.com (accessed April 22, 2003).

Schwartz, Larry. "Althea Gibson Broke Barriers." ESPN.com. Available online at http://espn.go.com/sportscentury/features/00014035.html; website home page http://espn.go.com (accessed April 22, 2003).

AUDIO AND VISUAL MEDIA

Althea Gibson ThunderHead Productions, 1998, VHS.

Sports Heroines: Early Women Sports Stars. Heroines, Inc., 1998, VHS.

"Notre Dame Tops Oklahoma, 7-0"

Newspaper article, Table

By: Associated Press

Date: November 17, 1957

Source: Associated Press. "Notre Dame Tops Oklahoma, 7-0." *The New York Times,* November 17, 1957, sec. 5, 1. ■

Introduction

Many college football programs can stake out claims of greatness. Ohio State, Miami, Nebraska, Michigan, Alabama, Southern California, and even Chicago (if you go

back far enough) have all had their moments of glory. While many college programs are cyclical depending on the strength of an individual recruiting class, some programs have remained consistently strong year after year. However, no program has matched the accomplishments of the Oklahoma Sooners between 1953 and 1957. Over those five seasons, Oklahoma won forty-seven consecutive games and the NCAA National Championship in 1955 and 1956. Although undefeated in 1954, they did not gain a share of the national championship. The Sooners had been practically unstoppable since 1947 after hiring Bud Wilkinson as their coach. He coached the Sooners until 1963 and compiled a record of 139-27-4 over those seventeen seasons.

Ironically, the streak started in 1953, after Oklahoma suffered an opening season loss to Notre Dame, followed by a tie with Pittsburgh. Over the next forty-seven games, they were undefeated and won back-to-back national championships in 1955 and 1956. Playing before a capacity crowd in Norman, Oklahoma, the Sooners were a sixteen-point favorite to make it forty-eight in a row. The Notre Dame Fighting Irish were having a good, but not glorious season—ending with seven victories, five more than in the 1956 season. Notre Dame was also trying to revenge the previous season's 40-0 thrashing by the Sooners. However, the game was extremely close, with the defenses of both teams dominating. After three quarters, the score was tied at 0-0. In the closing minutes of the game, Notre Dame drove the ball down the field and scored the game's only touchdown. While the Sooners threatened, an interception late in the game killed Oklahoma's chance at a victory, its winning streak, and its chance at the national championship in 1957.

Significance

The Notre Dame upset victory over Oklahoma on November 16, 1957, was a very significant game in college football history. While both programs retained their national prominence after the game, the nature of the extended winning streak increased fan interest in college sports and ensured Bud Wilkinson's place in college football history with his teams dominating the era. Although Oklahoma was undefeated coming into the game, they were not the top-ranked team in college football. That honor went to the University of Texas, who was upset that day by Rice University by a somewhat similar score of 7-6. In college football today there are relatively few undefeated Division I teams. It is sometimes difficult to understand how an undefeated team, like the 1954 Sooners, were denied at least a share of the national championship by the AP and UPI polls. In today's environment of greater competition in recruiting student athletes and early entry into the professional draft, few teams would have the ability to remain undefeated over parts of five

Statistics of the Game

	N.D.	Okla.
First downs	17	9
Rushing yardage	169	98
Passing yardage	79	47
Passes attempted	20	11
Passes completed	9	4
Passes intercepted by	1	1
Punts	8	10
Av. dist. of punts, yds.	38.5	36.5
Fumbles lost	1	1
Yards penalized	45	35

Notre Dame (7)

Left Ends—Royer, Prendergast.
Left Tackles—Puntillo, Geremia.
Left Guards—Schaaf, Adamson, Sabal.
Centers—Scholtz, Sullivan, Kuchta.
Right Guards—Ecuyer, Djubasak.
Right Tackles—Lawrence, Nagurski, Dolan.
Right Ends—Stickles, Wetoska, Colosimo.
Quarterbacks—Williams, Izo, White, Hebert.
Left Halfbacks—Reynolds, Doyle.
Right Halfbacks—Lynch, Just.
Fullbacks—Pietrosante, Toth, Lima.

Oklahoma (0)

Left Ends—Stiller, Coyle.
Left Tackles— Searcy, Thompson
Left Guards—Northcutt, Oujesky, Gvinn.
Centers—Harrison, Davis.
Right Guards—Krisher, Corbitt
Right Tackles — D. Jennings, Lawrence, Ladd.
Right Ends—Rector, S. Jennings.
Quarterbacks—Dodd, Baker, Watts, Sherroe.
Left Halfbacks—Sandefer, Boyd, Hobby.
Right Halfbacks—Thomas, Carpenter, Gaut, Pellow.
Fullbacks—Morris, Rolle.

Notre Dame	0	0	0	7—7
Oklahoma	0	0	0	0—0

Touchdown—Lynch (3, run), Conversion—Stickles.

SOURCE: Table from "Notre Dame Tops Oklahoma 7–0." *New York Times*, November 17, 1957.

Primary Source

"Notre Dame Tops Oklahoma, 7-0": Table

SYNOPSIS: This table accompanies the AP newspaper article. It is a summary of the game between Notre Dame and Oklahoma Sooners, November 16, 1957.

consecutive seasons. It is unlikely that Oklahoma's record will be matched by any school in college football.

Fan interest in college football far outweighed that of professional football in the 1950s, especially in the Midwest—where college football, led by the large state universities, was the region's most popular sport. On that November day, the capacity crowd of 62,000 proved to be true fans of the sport, not just partisan boosters. The AP reporter commented that the fans were "stunned into

silence as the Sooners were unable to pull their usual last-quarter winning touchdowns—a Wilkinson team trademark. . . . As the game ended when Oklahoma's desperation passing drive was cut off by an intercepted aerial, the crowd rose as one and suddenly gave the Notre Dame team a rousing cheer." Their ability to acknowledge both Notre Dame's victory and their appreciation of the achievements and effort given by the Sooners over the previous forty-seven games led to the spontaneous celebration of the end of an era unmatched in college football history.

Primary Source

"Notre Dame Tops Oklahoma, 7-0": Text

SYNOPSIS: The newspaper article describes the hard-fought game between Notre Dame and Oklahoma that ended Oklahoma's forty-seven game winning streak. The game featured two dominant defenses; Notre Dame, a sixteen-point underdog, scored late and held off a furious Oklahoma threat to win the game. Both teams ended the season ranked in the top ten in the country.

Skein Ends at 47

Oklahoma Toppled as Lynch Scores From 3 in the Final Quarter

Norman, Okla., Nov. 16—Oklahoma's record streak of forty-seven football victories was ended today by a Notre Dame team that marched 80 yards in the closing minutes for a touchdown and a 7-0 triumph.

Oklahoma, ranked No. 2 in the nation and an 18-point favorite, couldn't move against the rock-wall Notre Dame line and the Sooners saw another of its streaks shattered—scoring in 123 consecutive games.

The defeat was only the ninth for the Oklahoma coach, Bud Wilkinson, since he became head coach at Oklahoma in 1947. It virtually ended any chance for the Sooners of getting a third straight national championship.

Although the partisan, sellout crowd of 62,000 came out for a Roman holiday, they were stunned into silence as the Sooners were unable to pull their usual last-quarter winning touchdowns—a Wilkinson team trademark.

Rousing Cheer for Irish

As the game ended when Oklahoma's desperation passing drive was cut off by an intercepted aerial, the crowd rose as one and suddenly gave the Notre Dame team a rousing cheer.

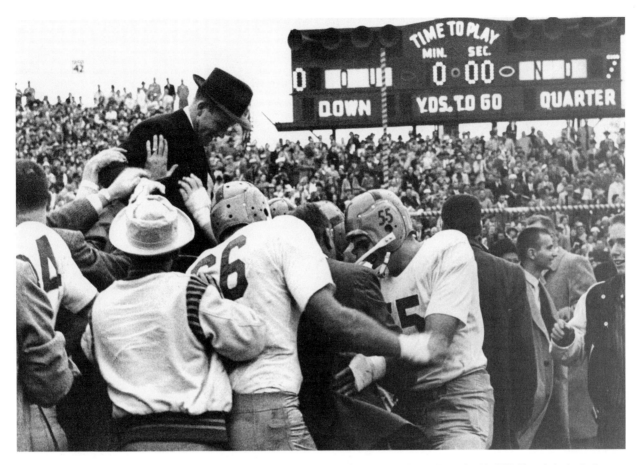

Notre Dame players and coaches celebrate their victory over the Oklahoma Sooners, Norman, Oklahoma, November 20, 1957. The win broke the forty-seven-game winning streak of the Sooners. © BETTMANN/CORBIS. REPRODUCED BY PERMISSION.

It was a far cry from last year when the Sooners ran over Notre Dame, 40-0. The victory gave the Irish a 3-1 edge in the five-year-old series dating back to 1952.

The smashing, rocking Notre Dame line didn't permit the Sooners to get started either on the ground or in the air.

The Sooners were able to make only 98 yards on the ground and in the air just 47. Notre Dame, paced by its brilliant, 210-pound fullback Nick Pietrosante, rolled up 169. In the air, the Irish gained 79 yards by hitting nine of twenty passes. Bob Williams did most of the passing for Notre Dame.

Notre Dame's touchdown drive, biting off short but consistent yardage against the Sooners' alternate team, carried from the 20 after an Oklahoma punt went into the end zone.

Sooners Call First Team

Time after time, Pietrosante picked up the necessary yard he needed as the Irish smashed through the Oklahoma line. Notre Dame moved to the 8 and the Sooner first team came in to try to make the third Sooner goal-line stand of the day.

Pietrosante smashed four yards through center and Dick Lynch was stopped for no gain. On the third down, Williams went a yard through center.

Then Lynch crossed up the Sooners and rolled around his right end to score standing up. Monty Stickles converted to give Notre Dame the upset and end collegiate football's longest winning streak.

The closest Oklahoma could get to Notre Dame's goal was in the first quarter when the Sooners' alternate team moved to the 3 before being held on downs.

In the third period, brilliant punting by Clendon Thomas and David Baker kept Notre Dame back on its goal line but the Sooners couldn't capitalize.

Thomas sent punts down on the Notre Dame 15 and 4 and Baker put them down on the 3 and 7.

This time there were no breaks as Notre Dame shook off last week's jitters that saw the Irish fumble away the ball five times in losing to Michigan State 34-6.

Pietrosante gained almost a third of Notre Dame's rushing yardage as he made 56 yards on seventeen carries. Lynch was just two yards behind with 54 in seventeen carries. The best an Oklahoma player could muster was 36 yards in ten tries. This was made by Thomas.

Williams completed eight of nineteen passes for 70 yards. In Oklahoma's last-minute desperation drive, Quarterback Bennett Watts made two of three aerials for 31 yards.

Notre Dame was the last team to beat Oklahoma, at the start of the 1953 season on the same field that it smothered the Sooners today. Then Coach Frank Leahy's Irish beat Oklahoma, 28-21. The next game, Oklahoma and Pittsburgh tied at 7-7. Then the Sooners set sail through the forty-seven games until Terry Brennan's Irish stopped the string today.

Wilkinson, the nation's winningest, active coach, had amassed 101 victories in his ten years at Oklahoma. There were three ties.

Oklahoma started as if it would stretch its string. It marched the first time it got its hands on the ball from the Sooner 42 down to the Irish 13, but the big Notre Dame line stiffened on the 13.

Oklahoma continued to play in Notre Dame territory the rest of the first quarter. It had another chance when a fumble, with nine minutes gone, was recovered by Guard Dick Corbitt on the Notre Dame 34. However, the Sooners were stopped cold and finally Baker had to punt on fourth down.

In the second quarter another Sooner drive got down to the 23 but on the first play of the second quarter, Carl Dodd fumbled. The ball was punched around in the Sooner backfield and Pietrosante finally smothered it on the Notre Dame 48.

Then Williams started his passing attack to three different receivers and piloted the Irish down to the 3 with first and goal. Pietrosante picked up a yard in each of two plunges, Frank Reynolds went to the one-foot line and then Jim Just was held for no gain.

Later Notre Dame came back with its bruising ground game and moved to the 16. With fourth down Stickles came in for his fake place kick but instead Williams hit Just on the 6 for a first down. It was then on the second play that Reynolds' pass was intercepted by Baker in the end zone.

Further Resources

BOOKS

Dent, Jim. *Undefeated: The Oklahoma Sooners and the Greatest Winning Streak in College Football History.* New York: St. Martin's Press, 2001.

Garner, Joe. *Echoes of Notre Dame Football: Great and Memorable Moments of the Fighting Irish.* Naperville, Ill.: Sourcebooks MediaFusion, 2001.

Wilkinson, Bud. *Oklahoma Split T Football.* New York: Prentice-Hall, 1952.

WEBSITES

"History." CBS Sportsline.com. Available online at http://www.cbs.sportsline.com/collegefootball/history; website home page: http://www.cbs.sportsline.com (accessed April 22, 2003).

Maiorana, Sal. "Forty Years Ago, the Fighting Irish Put an End to Oklahoma's Record 47-game Winning Streak." CBS Sportsline.com. Available online at http://cbs.sportsline.com/u/page/historian/oklahoma.htm; website home page: http://cbs.sportsline.com (accessed June 4, 2003).

AUDIO AND VISUAL MEDIA

Rites of Autumn. Lions Gate Home Entertainment, 2002, VHS.

"Palmer's 284 Beats Ford and Hawkins by a Stroke in Masters Golf"

Newspaper article

By: Lincoln Werden
Date: April 7, 1958
Source: Werden, Lincoln. "Palmer's 284 Beats Ford and Hawkins by a Stroke in Masters Golf." *The New York Times,* April 7, 1958, 29. ■

Introduction

Arnold Palmer was born on September 10, 1929 in Latrobe, Pennsylvania, a few days before the great stock market crash that year. Latrobe is in the green foothills of the Allegheny Mountains, near Pittsburgh. Palmer's childhood house sat just a few feet from the sixth hole of the Latrobe County Golf Course. Caddying and playing golf at an early age, Palmer learned a great deal from his father, the golf professional at the club. Palmer won a number of Western Pennsylvania amateur championships in high school, and he played collegiate golf at Wake Forest College in North Carolina. After serving in the Coast Guard, Palmer returned to the amateur golf circuit and won the U.S. Amateur Championship in 1954. Later that year, Palmer turned professional and made an immediate impact on the tour. From 1958 to 1964, Palmer won seven major championships (the major tournaments being the U.S. Open, the British Open, the Masters, and the PGA Tournament). The majors have greater significance because all of the best golfers participate in these events, whereas other tournaments attract fewer stars. For professional golfers, winning major events remains the critical factor in judging their skills and impact on the professional tour. Despite Tiger Woods's relative ease in wining major championships in the late 1990s and early 2000s, few golfers could match or even approach the seven major titles that Palmer won in the late 1950s and early 1960s, while at the top of his game.

Palmer's skills as a golfer and his amenable personality led to the creation of the largest non-uniformed military organization ever, Arnie's Army. Though golf had its share of national figures such as Ben Hogan, Walter Hagen and Bobby Jones, Palmer was about to reach out to fans that would come to embrace him and his approach to the game. Somewhat reminiscent of Francois Ouimet, the 1913 winner of the U.S. Open, Palmer was a different type of player. Despite that Palmer's father was golf professional and Palmer won the U.S. National Amateur title in 1954, his background was that of a typical working class family. During a Christmas vacation over college, Palmer worked as a bricklayer in a Latrobe steel mill. In fact, his close association with Latrobe, a steel town, prompted Doug Ford, one of his closest competitors in that 1958 Masters to comment, "If I do not win today, Palmer will. He's strong enough for this big course. He'll never tire. He's got a game like steel." Palmer used his wide popularity to launch a tremendous business career that not only focused on golf, but also included automobile dealerships and aviation services across the country. In addition, Palmer designed over two hundred golf courses around the world, providing another association with his name and golf.

Significance

Arnold Palmer is one of the true greats of golf and was responsible for generating a great deal of fan interest in the game. While he was known among those interested in golf, his true rise to prominence in the golf world came on the heels of his 1958 Masters victory at Augusta National Golf Cub. Though Palmer shot a seventy-three in the fourth and final round, he held off defending champion Doug Ford and Fred Hawkins to win by one stroke. While he had won a number of tournaments, including the Canadian Open, prior to the 1958 Masters, the victory in the Majors has been, and remains, the point when a good player becomes great.

While today's sports fans have Tiger Woods, who has frequently rewritten the record books, the path to greatness was much different for players in the 1950s.

Arnold Palmer watches his final putt on the eighteenth hole of the Masters Tournament, Augusta, Georgia, April 8, 1958. The putt went in, giving Palmer a total of 284 strokes—good enough for the victory. © BETTMANN/CORBIS. REPRODUCED BY PERMISSION.

For Woods, golf was his life and occupation from an early age and he was able to join the pro ranks at a young age. On the other hand, Palmer fulfilled his other societal obligations—including military service and regular employment—before embarking on a professional golf career. For Palmer, golf was a lifelong passion that became his occupation only after college, service in the Coast Guard, and a short business career. It is only possible to wonder the numbers of majors Palmer could have won had he been able to focus solely on golf and play professionally in his early 20s.

Palmer won the tournament by one stroke over Ford and Hawkins, but could have easily lost because of the twelfth hole. Because of a storm on the evening before the final round, the course was soggy and U.S. Golf Association regulations for wet conditions were used. On the twelfth hole, Palmer's shot imbedded into the hill and he was entitled to clean and replace his ball without penalty. However, it was not fully clear to him or the spectators what rules applied to the situation; and a score of five was originally posted for Palmer on the hole. While it was not fully clear until he was playing the fifteenth hole, Palmer played aggressively and made an eagle (two strokes less than par) on the thirteenth hole to try to make up the difference. Palmer gained two strokes when his score on twelve was changed from a five to a three, rescuing his chance to win the tournament. Though he ended the round with a bogey five on the last hole, it was enough to win the championship.

Primary Source

"Palmer's 284 Beats Ford and Hawkins by a Stroke in Masters Golf"

SYNOPSIS: The newspaper describes the final round of the 1958 Masters Tournament, won by Arnold Palmer. This was Palmer's first victory in a major tournament as a professional, and it represented his rise to prominence on the professional golf tour. Also of note in the article is a description of the controversy on the twelfth hole that could have changed the outcome of the tournament.

Winner Cards 73 on Soggy Course

Ruling on 12th Green and an Eagle at 13th Help Palmer—Venturi, Leonard at 286

Augusta, Ga., April 6—One of the game's young stars, Arnold Palmer, earned the Masters title today with a closing 73 at the Augusta National Golf Club.

The husky 28-year-old athlete from Latrobe, Pa., who won the National Amateur crown in 1954 two months before he joined the pro ranks, finished with a total of 284. Then he waited two hours for assurance that victory was his.

When Doug Ford, the 1957 winner, and Fred Hawkins, the slim star from El Paso, failed to bag birdies at the home green that would have forced a deadlock, Palmer was safely in.

Ford made an exciting bid with one of the two sub-par rounds recorded on the soggy course. He raced around with a 70 that almost closed the gap, Hawkins had a 71, but he, too, failed to catch Palmer. His birdie putt at the eighteenth hole swerved off the cup and stayed out, sending him into a tie with Ford for second place at 285.

Venturi, Snead Falter

Under sunny skies, and with a crowd estimated at 20,000, Ken Venturi, the leader for two rounds, and Sam Snead, who shared the pace-setter's role with Palmer yesterday, fell back in the competition for top honors.

Venturi three-putted three holes in a row starting at the fourteenth, after going out in 35. The Californian, paired with Palmer, equaled the par of 72, but it proved two strokes too high.

Venturi's 286 tied Stan Leonard, the Canadian Professional Golfers Association champion from Vancouver, B. C., for fourth place. Leonard posted a 71 after a scorching 33 for the first nine.

Snead finished badly. At the first hole, the Slammer's No. 2 iron shot landed on soggy ground and Snead needed three more strokes to move the ball to the green. He holed out with a 6. Snead went to the turn in 38 and was back in 41. He ended with a 290 for the seventy-two holes.

The weather helped set the stage for a dramatic experience by Palmer at the water-hole twelfth. Because of an all-night storm and a cloudy morning, there had been doubts at breakfast time whether the fourth round could be completed today.

Rules Cover Weather

Under United States Golf Association regulations applying to weather conditions, the ball can be cleaned on the greens without penalty. An imbedded ball "through the green" also may be lifted and cleaned without penalty, then dropped as near as possible to the original lie. "Through the green," by definition, is the whole area of the course, except the tee, the putting green or any of the hazards.

After the eleventh hole, Palmer was leading Venturi by one stroke. Palmer knocked his tee shot over the pond to the green and the ball bounded up a slope short of the sandy trap beyond the putting surface. Venturi's tee shot stopped on the back edge of the green.

Spectators are not allowed to cross the newly dedicated Ben Hogan Bridge that spans the creek to the green. Viewers consequently stayed on a bank some 200 yards away to witness the action that then took place. It was almost as if the principals were engaged in pantomime as far as the onlookers were concerned.

They saw Palmer go into a huddle with one official and later with another. He talked to Venturi, too. Then he stroked his ball about two feet into casual water at the base of the mound. He picked it up, dropped it over his shoulder, chipped to the green and two-putted for a 5.

But to the amazement of the crowd, Palmer went back, placed the ball a few inches from where it had been originally on the slope, chipped close to the pin and sank a 3.

Mystery to Spectators

The confusion of the spectators was compounded when a 5 was posted for Palmer on the scoreboards. But as the Pennsylvanian was playing the fifteenth hole, he was advised officially that his score at the twelfth was 3 and not 5.

It was disclosed later that he had had an imbedded ball in the moundside and was entitled to a free lift under today's playing conditions. But Palmer said he had been originally advised by one of the officials that he could not "lift" at that point.

On the thirteenth, even before he knew what his twelfth-hole score would be, Palmer turned in a prodigious 3 for an eagle. He walloped a No. 3 wood to the green at the 475-yard par-5 hole over the meandering creek and sank a twenty-foot putt.

Venturi was still in contention but his putting difficulties beginning at the fourteenth smashed his hopes. He missed two-footers at the fourteenth and fifteenth.

Palmer wavered a bit, too, He was trapped at the short sixteenth and took a 4. He carded a par 4 at the seventeenth, but three-putted from the back of the eighteenth green for a one-over-par 5. He was taken to a committee room and waited eagerly for reports on the progress of Ford and Hawkins.

Art Wall finished with 74 to tie Cary Middlecoff at 287. Middlecoff, twice the United States Open champion and the Masters winner in 1955, tossed away an opportunity after starting at 4, 4. A 6 marred his card at the third where he hooked this second shot and needed three more to get close to the pin. Middlecoff turned in 88, 37 for a 75.

Billy Joe Patton of Morganton, N. C., was the low amateur with 288. Patton had 74 for his fourth round.

Disaster struck Francis (Bo) Winninger, who put two balls into the pond at the eleventh and ran up a 9. This contributed to an inward 43 and a 79 finish for 292. Bill Casper, the leading money-winner before the tourney started, also had a 9. This came at the thirteenth and he took a 74 for 293.

Claude Harmon was the other 70 scorer. He placed at 289, along with Billy Maxwell, Al Mengert and Jay Hebert. Ben Hogan had 291, the same total as Jimmy Demaret and Mike Souchak.

Further Resources

BOOKS

Feinstein, John. *The Majors: In Pursuit of Golf's Holy Grail.* Boston: Little, Brown, 1999.

Palmer, Arnold. *A Golfers Life.* New York: Ballantine Books, 1999.

Sumerall, Pat. *Pat Summerall's Sports in America: 32 Celebrated Sports Personalities Talk About Their Most Memo-* rable Moments In and Out of the Sports Arena. New York: Harper Collins, 1996.

PERIODICALS

Kindred, Dave. "A Master Bids Adieu." *The Sporting News,* April 22, 2002, 64.

LUPICA, MIKE. "THE IMPORTANCE OF BEING ARNIE." *ESQUIRE,* MAY 1991, 38–40.

WEBSITES

Biography of Arnold Palmer. Arnold Palmer Enterprises: The Name Means Golf. Available online at http://www.arnold palmer.com/page.asp?pageid=2; website home page: http://www.arnoldpalmer.com (accessed June 4, 2003).

"History of Golf." Available online at http://www.golfing-scot land.com/history.asp; website home page: http://www.golf ing-scotland.com/default.asp (accessed April 22, 2003).

AUDIO AND VISUAL MEDIA

Golf, Links in Time. A & E Television Networks, 1999, VHS.

Arnold Palmer: Golf's Heart and Soul. The Golf Channel Home Video, 1998, VHS.

"Overtime at the Stadium"

Newspaper article

By: Arthur Daley

Date: December 29, 1958

Source: Daley, Arthur. "Overtime at the Stadium." *The New York Times* December 29, 1958, 25.

About the Author: Arthur Daley (1904–1974) was born in New York City. A baseball player at Fordham University, Daley turned to writing and was sports editor of the college newspaper. After graduation, he joined *The New York Times* in 1926, which became his lifelong job. He took over the "Sports of the *Times*" column in 1942 "until further notice," which lasted nearly thirty years until his death. Daley was a well-prepared interviewer who predicted the rise of professional basketball and football as major spectator sports. He won the Pulitzer Prize in 1956, the first sportswriter to do so, and wrote five books and numerous magazine articles. ■

Introduction

By all accounts, professional football became the game it is now on Sunday, December 28, 1958. It was not when the game incorporated the forward pass, or first witnessed a rising superstar. It was, however, one of the greatest championship games ever played, and the first game ever to go into overtime. But what happened on that cold day in Yankee Stadium was that the fans finally accepted professional football, and turned the sport that had paled in comparison to its college counterpart into a legitimate challenger to baseball's dominance as America's National Pastime.

The Baltimore Colts were favored going into that championship game. Led by Johnny Unitas (called by Daley the best pitcher in Baltimore since Iron Man McGinnity in the late nineteenth century), the Colts were the best team in football and had a loyal fan base to match. The Baltimore football fans were very supportive and made the Colts an institution in the 1950s and 1960s. With the possible exception of the Green Bay Packers, the Colts had the best fans and local support in the country. Many Colts fans made the trip to Yankee Stadium to see the Colts play their game.

In the game, the Giants scored first, but then surrendered two touchdowns to Baltimore that put the Colts up 14-3. In the second half, the Giants scored two touchdowns to go ahead 17-14 with only seconds left to play. However, Johnny Unitas drove Baltimore downfield, and the Colts tied the game on a field goal with seven seconds left. In overtime, a short run by Baltimore's Alan Ameche gave Baltimore a touchdown, the game, and the championship of football. Over the coming months and years, the fame of this game grew. People who did not see the game, but read the newspaper accounts of the tension and drama of the overtime affair, became more and more interested in professional football.

Significance

The sudden-death overtime championship game between the New York Giants and the Baltimore Colts in 1958 put professional football on the map. In the 1950s, the only truly national professional sport was baseball, and it remained the national pastime—despite sagging attendance from the early 1950s through the end of the decade. Baseball was presented with a large number of different challenges for the interest of the sporting fan from younger professional sports including hockey, basketball, and football. While basketball and hockey would not become huge sporting entities until the 1970s and 1980s, football was the first sport to challenge the preeminence of baseball in the minds of American sports fans.

The game was carried on television and radio, but gained greater notoriety in the reporting, as word spread about the fantastic game that many people missed. (The game took in gross receipts, including radio and television, of just under $700,000.) But in Arthur Daley's prose, we see the excitement, transmitted to the readers, which helped boost interest in professional football. Daley wrote, "The enthusiasm shows how completely pro football has arrived. Giant fans were as vociferous as their leather-lunged Baltimore counterparts. There was more partisanship at the Stadium yesterday than at a Yale-Harvard game." He ends the column with a simple interjection, "Wow!" Through this coverage and others like it, people

who did not see the game, heard about it and read about it, and the interest grew. Over the next few years, football became a national sport that could challenge baseball in the minds and hearts of many American sporting fans.

Primary Source

"Overtime at the Stadium"

SYNOPSIS: In this column, Daley writes on the mood and spirit of the Colts-Giants championship game, focusing on the excitement of the game and the role of the fans. In looking at the excitement of the game, Daley recounts primarily the final drive by the Colts in regulation, and the mayhem that erupted when Ameche scored the winning run in overtime. In focusing on the role of the fans, Daley discussed the resignation of the Giants fans in attendance and the elation of the Colts fans. Also, he sent a message to those fans at home that this was a great football game.

It was a lovely day. But if the weather was balmy, the play-off game between the Baltimore Colts and the New York Giants was even balmier. It was a wildly exciting and utterly mad affair that was staged at the Yankee Stadium yesterday. The final touch of insanity came when these massive meatballs couldn't settle supremacy after sixty minutes of bitterly bruising battling. They had to go into overtime.

This sudden-death extra period was the first ever required in formal football warfare. An experimental overtime was tried a few years ago in an exhibition game between the Giants and the Los Angeles Rams. The score then was 17-17, as it was yesterday. But in the exhibition the Giants didn't care. They yielded a touchdown without half-trying.

However, they gave all they had against the Colts. It wasn't enough. The Giants had come within seven fleeting seconds of beating a better team in regulation time. Then a downfield sortie that was engineered by the incomparable Johnny Unitas set up a field goal by Steve Myhra. The overtime touchdown by Alan (The Horse) Ameche was almost an anticlimax. And heart-rending though it was to Giant fans, it was deserved.

Into the Corral

When The Horse burst into the end zone with the winning points, he ran into the arms of deliriously happy Colt fans—a breed that knows no equal. They never let Ameche hit the ground, but hoisted him to their shoulders and carried him down the gridiron.

Baltimore Colts fullback Alan Ameche plunges through a hole for the winning touchdown in the overtime period against the New York Giants, December 28, 1958. Baltimore won, 23-17, for the National Football League title in the first overtime finish in title history. **AP/WIDE WORLD PHOTOS. REPRODUCED BY PERMISSION.**

The fanatics from Baltimore were parading up and down the field long after the combatants had dragged themselves to the clubhouses. The band played, drums boomed and miniature bombs were exploded.

The Colt delegation had the goal-posts leveled as soon as Ameche hit paydirt. There was no attempt to try for the extra point. It was not only unnecessary, but also impossible.

The enthusiasm shows how completely pro football has arrived. Giant fans were as vociferous as their leather-lunged Baltimore counterparts. There was more partisanship at the Stadium yesterday than at a Yale-Harvard game. The play-for-pay rooters have no ivy. The green stuff was money.

The Yankee Stadium press box had been a ghost town of sorts during the newspaper blackout of recent weeks. But no cobwebs had a chance to form, though sports writers, incorrigible fans deep below that hard-boiled crust, filled the shelf in front of the mezzanine deck to overflowing each week.

This made for an odd situation. Instead of the clatter of typewriters and the click of telegraph instruments there was often total silence. But one of the out-of-town brothers was banging away at his machine last week.

"Listen," he said slyly, "if the noise of this typewriter disturbs you, just let me know. I don't want to embarrass you."

With the end of the strike in view, the boys were back on the job in earnest yesterday. It would seem, however, that the Giants play better when there's no one to record their deeds of derring-do.

Always the Unexpected

There were more daffy plays yesterday than one would find in a full season, as well as spectacular long-gainers by both teams. Unitas spun a 60-yard pass to Lenny Moore; Frank Gifford threaded a needle for 43 yards with a brilliant run and, just as the Giants seemed on their way to being routed, a Charley Conerly pass to Kyle Rote, a fumble and Alex Webster's recovery put the ball on the goal-line in a dizzy 87-yard swoop.

But the real dramatics came when the Colts were seemingly beaten, 17-14, only a little more than a minute from the end. That's when Unitas, the best pitcher Baltimore has had since Iron Man McGinnity before the turn of the century, delivered three clutch plays. Clutch is the right word in another sense, too. Ray Berry clutched the ball on three passes that whisked 62 yards and set up the tying field goal.

This was a football game. Wow!

Further Resources

BOOKS

Gildea, William. *When the Colts Belonged to Baltimore: A Father and a Son, a Team and a Time.* Baltimore, Md.: Johns Hopkins University Press, 1996.

Olesker, Michael. *Growing up—and Growing Together—in Baltimore: Journeys to the Heart of a City.* Baltimore, Md.: Johns Hopkins University Press, 2001.

PERIODICALS

Lord, Lewis. "He Brought the NFL into Your Living Room." *US News and World Report,* September 23, 2002, 12.

Maule, Tex. "The Greatest Game of All." *Sports Illustrated,* February, 7, 2001, 22–27.

WEBSITES

Hughes, Bill. "The Greatest Game: Baltimore Colts Vs. New York Giants." Available online at http://www.artbabyart.com /1958_game.htm; website home page: http://www.artbabyart .com (accessed April 22, 2003).

AUDIO AND VISUAL MEDIA

Diner. Directed by Barry Levinson. Warner Home Video, 1982, VHS.

"Beauchamp Wins 500-mile Stock Car Race at 135 M.P.H. Average"

Newspaper article

By: Frank M. Blunk

Date: February 23, 1959

Source: Blunk, Frank M. "Beauchamp Wins 500-mile Stock Car Race at 135 M.P.H. Average." *The New York Times,* February 23, 1959, 30. ∎

Introduction

In 1959, Bill France, the father of NASCAR (National Association of Stock Car Racers), opened the Daytona International Speedway for the inaugural Daytona 500. He had come quite a long way since starting NASCAR in 1949, and his proposal for the asphalt speedway in 1954. Stock car racing was a distant cousin of the far more popular Indy car racing (from the name of the cars that race in the Indianapolis 500). The stock cars were raced primarily in the South and the Midwest, and incorporated standard car bodies with modified engines and safety measures to make them faster and safer. In Daytona, the big stock car race every year was one that was driven half on the beach and half on asphalt. In 1954, Bill France conceived of a giant super speedway that would rival the Indianapolis speedway as the best racetrack in the country. While being ridiculed by the Indianapolis press, France persevered and opened this two-and-one-half-mile high-banked track in the resort town of Daytona Beach. Like the Indianapolis Motor Speedway, the track was two and a half miles. However, instead of being an oval, the track was shaped as a triangle, or "tri-oval" as it was to be known. Like its Indianapolis counterpart, Bill France wanted to open the track with a 500-mile race of international note. The Daytona 500 became the biggest event in the week-long series of races, and has challenged the Indy 500 as the biggest race of the year.

Significance

The initial Daytona 500 race on February 22, 1959 was one of the greatest races ever held at the speedway. The race was significant for a number of reasons: the speeds attained by the cars, the closeness of the race, and the photo finish. The speeds attained by the cars in the race warranted a mention in the article's headline. The average speed of 135 miles per hour was the highest speed ever attained by stock cars, and only one mile per hour less than the previous record set for a 500-mile race at the Indianapolis 500 the year before. While the Indy cars are faster in qualifying laps, the

Johnny Beauchamp (73) and Lee Petty (42) drive neck and neck on the last lap of the 500-mile race at Daytona International Speedway, February 2, 1959. Although Beauchamp was declared the winner at the end of the race, photos at the finish line indicated that Petty had won. AP/WIDE WORLD PHOTOS. REPRODUCED BY PERMISSION.

average speed takes into account all the laps raced under caution flags and less than the full speed of these cars. The stock cars, very boxy in comparison to today's racers, were able to generate great speeds on the high-banked turns at Daytona.

The other aspect of the race is the "photo finish" that lead to a great deal of confusion for hours and days after the race. Johnny Beauchamp and Lee Petty, the defending NASCAR champion, pulled away from the pack and were the only two cars in the lead lap toward the end of the race. Over the last thirty laps, they changed positions frequently, with Lee Petty taking the lead on lap 197 of the 200-lap race. On lap 199, Beauchamp took over first place, but Lee Petty tried to pass him when the checkered flag waved to indicate the end of the race. The NASCAR official posted at the finish line gave the win to Beauchamp, but buy a few inches at best. When the cars came to a stop, Lee Petty challenged that assertion and claimed that he won the race by the same margin of a few inches. There was no photo finish camera setup for that race, so Bill France was in a bit of a predicament. Since it was not clear who won the race, France declared Beauchamp the unofficial winner and wanted to see photographs and film

that were taken at the race to determine the official winner. After three days of examining the information, France declared that Lee Petty passed Beaucamp just before the finish line to become the official winner of the inaugural Daytona 500. In this regard, the photo in "photo finish" was not from an official camera, but a combination of different ones to help clearly determine the winner. Despite getting the finish wrong, the article does a great job of describing the speed, closeness of the race and the enthusiasm of the fans in attendance at the event.

Primary Source

Beauchamp Wins 500-mile Stock Car Race at 135 M.P.H. Average

SYNOPSIS: This newspaper article details the inaugural Daytona 500 on February 22, 1959. While the article declares Beauchamp the winner of the race, the fifth paragraph states that the results were unofficial, pending the full investigation by NASCAR, the sanctioning body of the event. The article includes general information on the race including the winner's share (a record for stock cars), the number of starters, and the dramatic finish of the race.

Johnny Beauchamp poses with the trophy and speed week queen after seemingly winning the first Daytona 500. NASCAR officials studied the race photos for three days before finally declaring Lee Petty the winner. © BETTMANN/CORBIS. REPRODUCED BY PERMISSION.

Thunderbird has Margin of Inches

But Track Chief Says Later That Result Is Unofficial Pending Study of Photos

Daytona Beach, Fla., Feb. 22—Johnny Beauchamp, 35-year-old Harian, Iowa, driver, thrilled a crowd of more than 60,000 with a victory by inches today in the first 500-mile stock race run on the new Daytona International Speedway. He averaged 135.521 miles an hour in a 1959 Thunderbird hard-top sedan.

This fantastic speed, never before achieved by American-built stock cars, came close to beating the world record of 135.601 m.p.h. for continuous 500-mile races established by Sam Hanks of Pacific Palisades, Calif., at Indianapolis in 1957.

The only averages exceeding these were made at Monza, Italy, in 1957 and 1958 by Indianapolis-type cars. But the Monza races were run in three sections with one-hour intermissions.

Beauchamp was less than a foot ahead of the 1959 Oldsmobile driven by Lee Petty of Randleman, N. C., at the finish. The two had been in a bumper-to-bumper duel for the last fifteen laps on the two-and-a-half-mile asphalt course, with the lead changing hands five or six times.

[More than six hours after the race ended, Bill France, president of the speedway and the National Association of Stock Car Racers, said results would be ruled unofficial pending examination of photographs and movies of the finish, the Associated press reported.]

Beauchamp would be in front, buffeting the wind, for a lap or two with Petty riding his slipstream. Then the positions would be reversed. Both were striving to save fuel in this way for the final thrust that both knew would be necessary.

Winner On Inside

Through the last three laps they were running, most of the time, side by side, waiting for that last desperate dash. In the final fifty yards Beauchamp, on the inside, swung his car just enough to produce the burst of speed that meant victory, a lion's share of the $70,000 prize pot and a $5,000 bonus.

Fifty-eight late-model sedans and late-model convertibles moved to the main track for the one parade lap shortly before 1 o'clock this afternoon. Then came a faster pace lap and they were off on their long grind. The terrific speeds set from the start soon took a toll of engines. At the end only thirty-two cars were running.

Beauchamp and Petty were the only two to complete the full 200 laps. Among the early leaders were Cotton Owens of Spartanburg, N. C., in a 1958 Pontiac; Bob Welborn of Greensboro, N. C., in a 1959 Chevrolet; Fireball Roberts of Daytona Beach in a 1959 Pontiac; Joe Weatherly, Norfolk, Va., in a 1959 Chevrolet; Jack Smith of Atlanta in a 1959 Chevrolet Impala and Tom Pistone of Chicago in a 1959 Thunderbird.

Charlie Griffith of Chattanooga, in a 1957 Pontiac, finished third, more than a lap behind the first two. Owens was fourth, Weatherly fifth, Jim Reed of Peekskill, N. Y., sixth in a 1959 Chevrolet; Smith seventh, Pistone eighth, Tim Flock of Atlanta, ninth in a 1959 Thunderbird, and Speedy Thompson of Charlotte, N. C., tenth in a 1957 Chevrolet.

Four Pit Stops Made

The winner made four pit stops, taking fuel each time. The two outside tires were changed on one stop. All cars were equipped with special Firestone and Goodyear tires and there were no failures at high speeds.

This 500-mile event capped three days of racing at the new course. There were two 100-mile races on Friday, and a 200-mile and a twenty-five-mile race on Saturday. Another incredible record for stock-car tracks was set when the whole program was run off without a single serious crack-up or jam.

The track is built so that four cars can run abreast, even on the high, 31-degree banked turns. There is a broad, flat safety apron below each turn.

Beauchamp, an automobile salesman when he isn't racing, stands 6 feet 2 inches and weighs 197 pounds. He was a basketball and baseball player in high school at Irvin, Iowa, and turned to automobile racing when he was 23.

Star in Middle West

He won championships of a Middle West stock car racing group in 1956 and 1957 and finished fourth in that field last year. Two years ago, when all races were run on the beach, he finished second to Owens in the 160-mile Grand National here.

Beauchamp's share of the prize money today was estimated at more than $20,000, a record in the stock car world.

Further Resources

BOOKS

Editors of Life Magazine. *American Speed: From Dirt Tracks to NASCAR.* New York: Time-Life Books, 2002.

Hinton, Ed. *Daytona: From the Birth of Speed to the Death of the Man in Black.* New York: Warner Books, 2001.

Zeller, Bob. *Daytona: An Official History.* Phoenix, Ariz.: David Bull Publishing, 2002.

PERIODICALS

Smith, Stephen Cole. "NASCAR: B.C. and A.D." *Car and Driver,* April 2002, 130–136.

WEBSITES

"NASCAR History." NASCAR-info.net. Available online at http://www.nascar-info.net/nascar_history_1.html; website home page: http://www.nascar-info.net (accessed April 22, 2003).

"Petty's Photo Finish." NASCAR.com. Available online at http://www.nascar.com/2003/kyn/history/daytona/01/03/daytona_1959/index.html; website home page: http://www.nascar.com (accessed April 22, 2003).

AUDIO AND VISUAL MEDIA

NASCAR Story, Vol. 1 ABC Video/Disney, 1995, VHS.

The Chavez Ravine Agreement

Agreement

By: City of Los Angeles and Los Angeles Dodgers

Date: June 3, 1959

Source: The Chavez Ravine Agreement. Reprinted in Sullivan, Neil. *Dodgers Move West.* New York: Oxford University Press, 1987, 220–227. ■

Introduction

In the period after World War II (1939–1945), Major League baseball attendance jumped to unprecedented levels. While only a few teams ever drew over a million fans before the war, fan interest in baseball exploded after soldiers came home; and teams consistently drew near or over one million fans in the late 1940s. However, in the early 1950s, the attendance at Major League games started to drop. Complicating matters was that a number of cities had two baseball teams, one in each league. Cities with two teams included Chicago, Boston, St. Louis, Philadelphia, and New York—home to three teams, the Dodgers, Giants and the Yankees. In Boston, St. Louis, and Philadelphia, there was a clear fan favorite, and a team that did not draw very well. These teams—the Boston Braves, the St. Louis Browns and the Philadelphia Athletics—became the teams that first tested expansion in Major League baseball. The American and National Leagues were primarily in the Northeast, going as far west as Chicago and St. Louis. But when the teams moved west, it changed the map of baseball.

The early moves of Major League teams were the Braves to Milwaukee in 1953, the Browns to Baltimore in 1954, and the Athletics to Kansas City in 1955. While each of these teams generated far more interest in their new cities than they ever did in their old one, the biggest prize for Major League baseball was California. The biggest prizes for California were two teams, secondary in their market, and still in their original location: The Brooklyn Dodgers and the New York Giants. Walter O'Malley was the owner of the Dodgers, and he conceived of a plan to have the Dodgers and Giants move to California's two biggest cities, Los Angeles and San Francisco, and recreate their cross-town rivalry as a cross-state rivalry. It is still, from a business point of view, one of the best propositions ever made. But the critical aspect of the deal for the Dodgers was to get what they could not get in Brooklyn, a new stadium with ample parking. Ebbett's Field in Brooklyn, a typical urban ballpark, had practically no parking and no growth potential. While people could get to the game on New York's mass-transit system, the new generation of suburban families who needed to drive to events did not find the ballpark inviting. Key to any deal for a Major League team to move out west was a government financed or subsidized stadium that would feature both a state of the art facility with plenty of parking for baseball's new fans. Every team would get one, but the Dodgers would be a little different.

Walter O'Malley was a shrewd negotiator and offered to build the stadium himself, as long as the city could provide the land. They settled on a site in Chavez Ravine, and the City of Los Angeles went about acquiring the land. Using Eminent Domain, the city was able to purchase the land for cheap prices and evict people who would not voluntarily sell. They in turn, sold the land to O'Malley and the Dodgers at a low price. The Dodgers then built the first privately financed stadium since Yankee Stadium in 1922, opening in 1962. Despite privately financing the stadium, the team tremendously benefited from the land deal that the city was able to provide. The Dodgers remain one of the most profitable teams in the Major Leagues more than forty years later.

Significance

The Chavez Ravine Agreement is indicative of the measures that cities went to in the 1950s to attract Major League teams. In the 1950s and 1960s, Milwaukee, Baltimore, Kansas City, Atlanta, Oakland, San Francisco, Minneapolis and Los Angeles all had teams move into their market and all dangled incentives—stadiums and other perks to make their city "Major League." This desire continues to this day, as cities such as Portland, Oregon, Washington, D.C., and Charlotte, North Carolina continually solicit Major League teams to move to their city.

Significant in this document is the assumptions made of the value and needs of a baseball team by the fifteen statements beginning with "WHEREAS." One that stands out, the third, states "bringing of major league baseball to Los Angeles would result in direct and indirect benefits to the City." Also of note is the fact that the city would present 185 acres to the Dodgers and acquire 115 acres to be sold to the Dodgers "at a reasonable cost" to create the ball park. While technical in nature, the document provides the justification and process for transferring the land from the city, acquired through eminent domain, to the Dodgers for their new stadium. Nowhere is anything mentioned about the current residents or the changes that would take place in the Chavez Ravine neighborhood.

Also significant is Exhibit B, the original resolution from the County of Los Angeles Board of Supervisors, dated September 17, 1957, executed when the Dodgers were still playing in Brooklyn. The document reveals the core of the Dodgers' request when it called for the con-

struction of a "modern baseball stadium—with parking facilities for 25,000 cars." Despite making overtures to the city of Brooklyn about staying in the New York area, O'Malley was leaving for something that Brooklyn could never give him, space for 25,000 cars.

Primary Source

The Chavez Ravine Agreement

SYNOPSIS: The Chavez Ravine Agreement between the City of Los Angeles and the Los Angeles Dodgers formalizes the land transfer deal that brought the Dodgers to California. The agreement establishes the method by which land acquired by the City of Los Angeles in Chavez Ravine will be transferred to the Dodgers for the construction of Dodger Stadium, and provides them a permanent home in Southern California. They had been playing in the Los Angeles Coliseum, but the permanent stadium in Chavez Ravine was the reason the franchise moved to California.

Agreement

THIS AGREEMENT, made and entered into this 3rd day of June, 1959, by and between THE CITY OF LOS ANGELES, a municipal corporation (hereinafter called City), and the LOS ANGELES DODGERS, INC. (formerly known as the BROOKLYN NATIONAL LEAGUE BASEBALL CLUB. INC.), a New York corporation (hereinafter called the Ball Club).

Witnesseth:

WHEREAS, City is the owner of certain property in an area generally known as Chavez Ravine, and is in the process of acquiring additional property in said area; and

WHEREAS, such property is no longer required for the use of the City; and

WHEREAS, the bringing of major league baseball to Los Angeles would result in direct and indirect benefits to the City, and would be highly beneficial to the City, to the public, and to its inhabitants to have such property the site of a major league baseball stadium; and

WHEREAS, the placing of such property on the tax rolls would produce substantial additional property tax revenues to the City; and

WHEREAS, the City would receive substantial tax revenues from sources, other than the Ball Club, incident to major league baseball in Los Angeles; and

WHEREAS, the Ball Club is willing to acquire such property, and would, at its cost and expense, construct a major league baseball stadium for the purpose of providing facilities for the major league

The Los Angeles Dodgers play their last game in the Coliseum against the Chicago Cubs, September 20, 1961. They opened the 1962 season in their new stadium at Chavez Ravine. AP/WIDE WORLD PHOTOS. REPRODUCED BY PERMISSION.

baseball club known as the LOS ANGELES DODGERS (formerly known as the BROOKLYN DODGERS); and

WHEREAS, such Club has a long-standing policy of admitting juveniles to various games free of charge as a method of combating juvenile delinquency and stimulating interest in healthful recreational activities; and

WHEREAS, as part of this policy said Ball Club will construct recreational facilities costing not to exceed a half million dollars on a 40-acre portion of the property to be conveyed by the City, as herein provided, in Chavez Ravine, such recreational facilities to be mutually agreed upon by the parties hereto before such property is conveyed to said Ball Club, such recreational facilities to be constructed simultaneously with the construction of said stadium; and as a further part of said policy Ball Club will maintain such recreational facilities for a period of 20 years, at an annual cost of $60,000, but shall be under no obligation to furnish personnel for the op-

eration thereof; provided, that in the event such maintenance cost in any one year does not amount to $60,000, then as a further part of said Ball Club policy the difference between such maintenance cost and $60,000 shall be paid to City so that it may be used by City for the providing of or maintaining recreational facilities elsewhere in said city.

In this connection, it is understood that such recreational facilities shall be under the control of City, but City shall not permit the scheduling of any event at any of the recreational facilities on said 40 acres which would involve the concentration of a large number of participants or spectators during any time when Ball Club has scheduled an event at said baseball stadium, and that during any event at said baseball stadium Ball Club shall have the right to use any facilities suitable for parking as may be provided within said 40 acres; and

WHEREAS, such additional recreational facilities are sorely needed by the City and will fill a definite public need and will be of great value to the City; and

WHEREAS, the City is also in need of a suitable place for the holding of various events, including but not limited to amateur baseball games and similar activities; and

WHEREAS, Ball Club is able to have the baseball stadium and grounds known and Wrigley Field conveyed to City; and

WHEREAS, said Wrigley Field would be suitable for such purposes and would be of great value to the City and its inhabitants; and

WHEREAS, Ball Club is willing to cause Wrigley Field to be conveyed to the City for said property now owned and to be acquired as aforesaid by the City in Chavez Ravine; and

WHEREAS, the bringing of said Major League Baseball Club to Los Angeles would result in a large additional payroll in this area; and

WHEREAS, all of the foregoing is useful and convenient in connection with the exercise of the City's rights and powers and is in the public interest.

NOW, THEREFORE IT IS UNDERSTOOD AND AGREED AS FOLLOWS, TO WIT;

1. City will convey the property presently owned by it in Chavez Ravine consisting of 185 acres, more or less, and will use its best efforts to acquire, at a reasonable cost, and convey additional land, to make a total of 300 acres, more or less, all as shown in Exhibit A, to Ball Club, or nominee; provided, however:

(a) City shall reserve all mineral rights which it now owns or may hereafter acquire, and a suitable drill site for the production of oil from said property, the location of such site to be mutually agreed upon by the parties hereto, which location shall not interfere with Ball Club's operations, and not exceed 5 acres in size.

(b) One-half of all monies, payments, royalties, or other consideration received by City from said mineral rights, or any of them, in whole or in part, shall be placed in a special trust fund by City, and such funds shall be expended solely for the purpose of providing and maintaining recreational facilities to promote the youth program of Ball Club, the location and type of such recreational facilities to be mutually agreed upon by the parties hereto, with approval by the City Council by ordinance.

(c) That title to said 40 acres thereof, the location of such 40 acres to be designated by Ball Club,

shall be retained by the City for a period of 20 years to assure performance by Ball Club of its policy of providing and maintaining recreational facilities. In the event such policy, and all of the terms of this agreement pertaining to the recreational facilities on said 40 acres, shall have been fully and faithfully performed for a period of 20 years, title of such 40 acres shall be conveyed to the Ball Club, or nominee, forthwith, without further consideration.

It is understood and agreed that any violation of the terms of the agreement with reference to the recreational facilities shall not invalidate or affect any transfers of land which may therefore have been made pursuant to this agreement.

(d) All property herein agreed to be conveyed by City, including said 40 acres, will be conveyed free and clear of any deed restriction on use, and title policy shall be furnished to Ball Club. In this connection, it is expressly understood and agreed that the portion of property described in paragraph 1 now owned by the City and which was acquired by City from the Los Angeles Housing Authority has a deed restriction reading, in part, as follows:

"To be used for public purpose only; and not to be used directly or indirectly by the City of Los Angeles, or its grantees, successors in interest, assigns, or any other person or persons whatsoever claiming by, through or under the City of Los Angeles, for a period of 20 years from and after the date hereof, for residential development or residential subdivision."

City agrees to use its best efforts to have such deed restrictions eliminated or modified so as to permit the use contemplated by Ball Club; provided that in the event City is unable to have such restriction so eliminated or modified, this contract shall be of no further force or effect.

2. Upon conveyance of such property to Ball Club, the existing public streets therein which would no longer be needed for present or future street purposes will be vacated and the City shall, upon demand of Ball Club, commence proceedings to vacate said streets and deliver any title which may remain in the City without further consideration.

3. Prior to passage of title to any of the acreage described in paragraph 1, City shall spend up to but not to exceed $2,000,000 to place such property in a proper condition to convey to Ball Club or its nominee, the manner in which such money will be spent for such purpose to be designated by Ball Club.

4. City agrees to provide such public streets as may be needed within the periphery of the area to be acquired by Ball Club; provided, however, that the cost thereof, other than the cost of acquiring necessary land, shall be considered a part of the $2,000,000 which the City is to spend to prepare the site for sale.

5. Ball Club shall cause to be conveyed to City the land and improvements now known as Wrigley Field, including all mineral rights; provided, however, that one-half of all monies, payments, royalties, or other consideration received by City from said mineral rights, or any of them, in whole or in part, shall be placed in a special trust fund by City and such funds shall be expanded solely for the purpose of providing and maintaining recreational facilities to promote the youth program of Ball Club, the location and type of such recreational facilities to be mutually agreed upon by the parties hereto, with approval by the City Council by ordinance; further provided, that Ball Club reserves the right to the use of said Wrigley Field until the stadium referred to in paragraph 6 shall be completed and ready for use, conditioned upon payment to City of a rental to be mutually agreed upon.

6. Ball Club shall cause to be constructed on property conveyed by City, at Ball Club's cost and expense, a modern baseball stadium, seating not less than 50,000 people.

7. Ball Club will cause to be moved to the City of Los Angeles the present Brooklyn National League Baseball franchise and ball team known as the "DODGERS."

The City of Los Angeles agrees that it will initiate proceedings for the purpose of rezoning said property to "C-3" and for the granting of a conditional use permitting its use for a baseball stadium as herein provided.

It is recognized that the method or means of carrying out the terms and conditions of this contract in detail have not been provided herein in every instance but that the parties hereto will use their best efforts in arriving at mutually acceptable methods of procedure and modes of operation as to such details. Any such action on the part of the City shall be submitted to the City Council for approval.

IT IS EXPRESSLY UNDERSTOOD AND AGREED that this agreement is made in reliance upon the action taken by the Board of Supervisors of the County of Los Angeles in Resolution of said Board of Supervisors adopted and entered in the minutes of said

Board on Tuesday, September 17, 1957, a copy of which said resolution is attached hereto, marked Exhibit "B," and made a part hereof, providing for the furnishing of funds to construct necessary access roads, including cost of acquiring any required rights of way, and the City agrees that upon the County's making such funds available to City it will diligently proceed with the construction of such access roads, City agrees that it will make demand as required upon the County of Los Angeles to furnish the funds heretofore voted and/or appropriated for said access roads.

IN WITNESS WHEREOF, The City of Los Angeles has caused this instrument to be executed in its behalf by its duly authorized officers, and the Ball Club has executed the same by its duly authorized officers and has caused its corporate seal to be hereunto affixed, all on the day and year first hereinabove written.

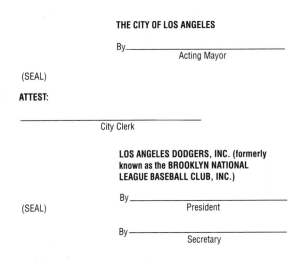

THE CITY OF LOS ANGELES

By_____
Acting Mayor

(SEAL)

ATTEST:

_____
City Clerk

LOS ANGELES DODGERS, INC. (formerly known as the BROOKLYN NATIONAL LEAGUE BASEBALL CLUB, INC.)

By_____
President

(SEAL)

By_____
Secretary

Exhibit "B"

Gordon T. Nesvig, Chief Clerk of the Board.

COUNTY OF LOS ANGELES BOARD OF SUPERVISORS, 501 HALL OF RECORDS, LOS ANGELES 12.

Members of the Board: John Anson Ford, Chairman; Herbert C. Legg, Kenneth Hahn, Burton W. Chace and Warren M. Dorn.

Resolution

Introduced by Supervisors

Tuesday, September 17, 1957

The Board met in regular session. Present: Supervisors John Anson Ford, Chairman presiding, Herbert C. Legg, Kenneth Hahn, Burton W. Chace and

Warren M. Dorn; and Harold J. Ostly, Clerk, by Gordon T. Nesvig, Deputy Clerk.

■■■

IN RE MAJOR LEAGUE BASEBALL IN COUNTY OF LOS ANGELES: RESOLUTION DETERMINING THAT COUNTY OF LOS ANGELES WILL MAKE AVAILABLE 2,740,000.00 TO CITY OF LOS ANGELES FOR PUBLIC APPROACH ROAD IMPROVEMENTS TO THE CHAVEZ RAVINE AREA AND INSTRUCTING CHIEF ADMINISTRATIVE OFFICER AND ROAD COMMISSIONER RELATING TO FUNDS REQUIRED.

On motion of Supervisor Hahn, duly carried by the following vote, to wit: Ayes: Supervisors Legg, Hahn, Chace, Dorn and Ford: Noes, none, it is ordered that the following resolution be and the same is hereby adopted:

WHEREAS, the Board of Supervisors of the County of Los Angeles believes that Major League Baseball would be a recreational and economic asset to this community; and

WHEREAS, both the City and the County have entered into negotiations with the Brooklyn Dodgers, looking toward the transfer of that Club's franchise from New York to Los Angeles; and

WHEREAS, these negotiations contemplate that a site in the Chavez Ravine area will be made available for the construction by the Brooklyn Ball Club of a modern baseball stadium—with parking facilities for 25,000 cars; and

WHEREAS, the Brooklyn Ball Club is also proposing to develop on the site a regional sports center covering approximately 40 acres, these recreational facilities to be available for free public use; and

WHEREAS, if this total development is accomplished, there will be a major increase in vehicular traffic in the Chavez Ravine area because of the public use of the proposed facilities; and

WHEREAS, traffic engineering studies show that present access streets to the Chavez Ravine site are entirely inadequate to accommodate the public use thereof, as contemplated:

NOW, THEREFORE, BE IT RESOLVED that the County of Los Angeles determines that if the proposed improvements are located in the Chavez Ravine area as contemplated the public necessity and convenience will require approach road improvements to the area, and that such improvements will be of general county interest; and

BE IT FURTHER RESOLVED that if a site in the Chavez Ravine area is made available by the City of

Los Angeles for these purposes—and concrete evidence of its contemplated or actual improvement in the manner and for the purposes referred to herein is presented to the County, the County of Los Angeles will make available in the manner provided by law a sum of money not to exceed $2,740,000.00 or as much thereof as is needed, to the City of Los Angeles payable on demand by the City, for public approach road improvements to the Chavez Ravine area; and

BE IT FURTHER RESOLVED that the Board of Supervisors hereby instruct the Chief Administrative Officer and the Road Commissioner to include within the Road Department 1958–59 budget (Motor Vehicle Fund) for the purposes recited herein an appropriation in an amount estimated to be required for expenditure in 1958–59, and in subsequent years as required, appropriations representing the balance required out of the total commitment of $2,740,000.00, provided that such balance be further reduced by any funds which may be advanced during the current fiscal year by action of the Board of Supervisors.

I hereby certify that the foregoing is a full, true and correct copy of a resolution which was adopted by the Board of Supervisors of the County of Los Angeles, State of California, on September 17, 1957, and entered in the minutes of said Board.

HAROLD J. OSTLY, County Clerk of the County of Los Angeles, State of California, and ex officio Clerk of the Board of Supervisors of said County.

Further Resources

BOOKS

McNeil, William. *The Dodgers Encyclopedia.* Champaign, Ill.: Sports Pub, 1977.

Sullivan, Neil. *Dodgers Move West.* New York: Oxford University Press, 1987, 221–227.

PERIODICALS

Hines, Thomas S. "Housing, Baseball, and Creeping Socialism." *Journal of Urban History,* February 1982, 123–144.

WEBSITES

"Dodger Stadium." BasballLibrary.com. Available online at http://www.pubdim.net/baseballlibrary/ballplayers/D/Dodger_Stadium.stm; website home page: http://www.pubdim.net (accessed April 22, 2003).

"The Chavez Ravine Story." Available online at http://www.toonist.com/flash/ravine.html; website home page: http://www.toonist.com (accessed April 22, 2003).

AUDIO AND VISUAL MEDIA

Dodger Stadium: The First 25 Years. Scotch, 1987, VHS.

General Resources

General

Baker, Patricia, and Robert Price. *Fashions of a Decade: The 1950s.* New York: Facts on File, 1991.

Carter, Paul Allen. *Another Part of the Fifties.* New York: Columbia University Press, 1983.

Coontz, Stephanie. *The Way We Never Were: American Families and the Nostalgia Trap.* New York: Basic Books, 1992.

Diggins, John Patrick. *The Proud Decades: America in War and Peace, 1941–1960.* New York: Norton, 1988.

Duden, Jane. *1950s.* New York: Crestwood House, 1989.

Feinstein, Stephen. *The 1950s From the Korean War to Elvis.* Berkeley Heights, N.J.: Enslow, 2000.

Flammang, James M. *Cars of the Fabulous Fifties: A Decade of High Style and Good Times.* Lincolnwood, Ill.: Publications International, 2000.

Foley, Karen Sue. *The Political Blacklist in the Broadcast Industry: The Decade of the 1950s.* New York: Arno Press, 1979.

Halberstam, David. *The Fifties.* New York: Villard Books, 1993.

Hart, Jeffrey Peter. *When the Going Was Good: American Life in the Fifties.* New York: Crown, 1982.

Harvey, Brett. *The Fifties: A Women's Oral History.* New York: HarperCollins, 1993.

Kaledin, Eugenia. *Mothers and More: American Women in the 1950s.* Boston: Twayne Publishers, 1950–1984.

Kallen, Stuart A. *The 1950s.* San Diego: Greenhaven Press, 2000.

Levine, Ellen. *Freedom's Children: Young Civil Rights Activists Tell Their Own Stories.* New York: Putnam, 1993.

Lewis, Peter. *The Fifties.* New York: Lippincott, 1978.

Llamon, W.T. *Deliberate Speed: The Origins of Cultural Style in the American 1950s.* Washington, D.C.: Smithsonian Institution Press, 1990.

Malinoski, Robert R. *A Golden Decade of Trains: The 1950s, in Color.* Edison, N.J.: Morning Sun Books, 1991.

Mickelson, Sig. *The Decade That Shaped Television News: CBS in the 1950s.* Westport, Conn.: Prager, 1998.

Miller, Douglas T. *The Fifties: The Way We Really Were.* Garden City, N.J.: Doubleday, 1977.

Montgomery, John. *The Fifties.* London: George Allen & Unwin, 1966.

Oakley, J. Ronald. *God's Country: America in the Fifties.* New York: Dembner Books, 1986.

Satin, Joseph Henry. *America's Placid Decade.* Boston: Houghton Mifflin, 1960.

Sharman, Margaret. *1950s.* Austin: Raintree Steck-Vaughn, 1933.

Skolnick, Arlene S. *Embattled Paradise: The American Family in an Age of Uncertainty.* New York: Basic Books, 1991.

This Fabulous Century, 1950–1960. Alexandria, Va.: Time-Life Books, 1970.

Wakefield, Dan. *New York in the Fifties.* Boston: Houghton Mifflin/Seymour Lawrence, 1992.

The Arts

Ashton, Dore. *American Art Since 1945.* New York: Oxford University Press, 1982.

Bawden, Liz-Anne. *The Oxford Companion to Film.* New York: Oxford University Press, 1976.

Bell, Bernard. *The Afro-American Novel and Its Tradition.* Amherst: University of Massachusetts Press, 1987.

Belz, Carl. *The Story of Rock,* 2nd ed. New York: Oxford University Press, 1972.

Berkow, Ita G. *Edward Hopper: An American Master.* New York: Smithmark, 1996.

Bordman, Gerald. *The Oxford Companion to the American Theatre.* New York: Oxford University Press, 1984.

Brooks, Elston. *I've Heard Those Songs Before, Vol. II: The Weekly Top Ten Hits of the Last Six Decades.* Fort Worth, Tex.: The Summit Group, 1991.

Charters, Ann, ed. *Dictionary of Literary Biography 16: The Beats: Literary Bohemians in Postwar America.* Detroit: Bruccoli Clark Layman/Gale Research, 1983.

Charters, Samuel, B. *The Bluesmen.* New York: Oak, 1967.

Christgau, Robert. *Grown Up All Wrong: 75 Great Rock and Pop Artists From Vaudeville to Techno.* Cambridge: Harvard University Press, 1998.

Craven, Wayne. *American Art: History and Culture.* New York: Harry N. Abrams, Inc., 1994.

Curtis, Jim. *Rock Eras: Interpretations of Music and Society, 1954–1984.* Bowling Green, Ohio: Bowling Green University Popular Press, 1987.

Davis, Thadious M., and Trudier Harris, eds. *Dictionary of Literary Biography 33: Afro-American Fiction Writers After 1955.* Detroit: Bruccoli Clark Layman/Gale Research, 1984.

Dictionary of Literary Biography 38: Afro-American Writers After 1955: Dramatists and Prose Writers. Detroit: Bruccoli Clark Layman/Gale Research, 1985.

Duberman, Martin. *Black Mountain: An Exploration in Community.* New York: Dutton, 1972.

Ehrlich, J.W., ed. *Howl of the Censor.* San Carlos, Calif.: Nourse Publishing, 1961.

Eliot, Marc. *Rockonomics: The Money Behind the Music.* New York: Franklin Watts, 1989.

Ennis, Philip, H. *The Seventh Stream: The Emergence of Rock-'n'roll in American Popular Music.* Hanover, U.K.: Wesleyan University Press, 1992.

Enser, A.G.S. *Filmed Books and Plays, 1928–1983.* Aldershot, U.K.: Gower, 1985.

Ewen, David. *History of Popular Music.* New York: Barnes & Noble, 1961.

———. *New Complete Book of the American Musical Theater.* New York: Holt Rinehart and Winston, 1970.

Feather, Leonard. *The Book of Jazz: A Guide to the Entire Field.* New York: Horizon, 1965.

Fiedler, Leslie. *An End To Innocence.* Boston: Beacon, 1955.

Fucini, Joseph J., and Susan Fucini. *Entrepreneurs: The Men and Women Behind Famous Brand Names and How They Made It.* Boston: G.K. Hall, 1985.

Gaugh, Harry, F. *Willem de Kooning.* New York: Abbeville Press, 1983.

Gianetti, Louis, D. *Understanding Movies.* Englewood Cliffs, N.J.: Prentice-Hall, 1987.

Gordy, Berry. *To Be Loved: The Music, The Magic, The Memories of Motown.* New York: Warner Books, 1994.

Grant, Barry K., ed. *Film Genre: Theory and Criticism.* Metuchen, N.J.: Scarecrow Press, 1977.

Greiner, Donald J., ed. *Dictionary of Literary Biography 5: American Poets Since World War II,* 2 vols. Detroit: Bruccoli Clark Layman/Gale Research, 1980.

Guilbaut, Serge. *How New York Stole the Idea of Modern Art: Abstract Expressionism, Freedom, and the Cold War,* translated by Arthur Goldhammer. Chicago: University of Chicago Press, 1983.

Guttman, Allen. *From Ritual to Record.* New York: Columbia University Press, 1978.

Harris, Mary Emma. *The Arts at Black Mountain College.* Cambridge, Mass.: MIT Press, 1987.

Harris, Trudier, ed. *Dictionary of Literary Biography 76: Afro-American Writers, 1940–1955.* Detroit: Bruccoli Clark Layman/Gale Research, 1988.

Helterman, Jeffrey, and Richard Layman, eds. *Dictionary of Literary Biography 2: American Novelists Since World War II.* Detroit: Bruccoli Clark Layman/Gale Research, 1978.

Hobbs, Robert Carleton, and Gail Levin. *Abstract Expressionism: The Formative Years.* Ithaca, N.Y. and New York: Herbert F. Johnson Museum of Art and Whitney Museum of American Art, 1978.

Houston, Penelope. *The Emergence of Film Art: The Evolution and Development of the Motion Picture as an Art, From 1900 to the Present.* New York: Norton, 1979.

Hughes, Robert. *American Visions: The Epic History of Art in America.* New York: Alfred A. Knopf, 1997.

Karl, Frederick R. *American Fictions, 1940–1980: A Comprehensive History and Critical Evaluation.* New York: Harper & Row, 1983.

Kazin, Alfred. *Bright Book of Life,.* Boston: Little, Brown, 1973.

Kibler, James E., Jr., ed. *Dictionary of Literary Biography 6: American Novelists Since World War II,* Second Series. Detroit: Bruccoli Clark Layman/Gale Research, 1980.

Koch, Lawrence, O. *Yardbird Suite: A Compendium of the Music and Life of Charlie Parker.* Bowling Green, Ohio: Bowling Green University Popular Press, 1988.

Lane, Mervin, ed. *Black Mountain College: Sprouted Seeds: An Anthology of Personal Accounts.* Knoxville: University of Tennessee Press, 1990.

Leadbitter, Mike, and Neil Slaven. *Blues Records 1943–1966.* New York: Oak, 1968.

Lindgren, Ernest. *The Art of the Film.* New York: Macmillan, 1963.

London, Herbert I. *Closing the Circle: A Cultural History of the Rock Revolution.* Chicago: Nelson-Hall, 1984.

MacNicholas, John, ed. *Dictionary of Literary Biography 7: Twentieth-Century American Dramatists.* Detroit: Bruccoli Clark Layman/Gale Research, 1981.

Myron, Robert, and Abner Sundell. *Modern Art in America.* New York: Crowell-Collier, 1971.

O'Hara, Frank. *Art Chronicles, 1954–1966.* New York: George Braziller, 1975.

Phillips, Lisa. *The American Century: Art and Culture 1950–2000.* New York: W.W. Norton & Co., 1999.

Podhoretz, Norman. *Doings and Undoings: the Fifties and After in American Writing.* New York: Farrar, Straus, 1964.

Poteet, G. Howard. *Published Radio, Television, and Film Scripts.* Troy, N.Y.: Whitston, 1975.

Reisner, Robert George. *Bird: The Legend of Charlie Parker.* New York: Da Capo Press, 1962.

Rosset, Barney, ed. *Evergreen Review Reader, 1957–1967: A Ten-Year Anthology.* New York: Grove, 1968.

Rotha, Paul, with Richard Griffith. *The Film Till Now.* London: Spring Books, 1967.

Sablosky, Irving. *American Music.* Chicago: University of Chicago Press, 1969.

Sandler, Irving. *The New York School: The Painters and Sculptors of the Fifties.* New York: Harper & Row, 1978.

Sanjet, Russell. *From Print to Plastic: Publishing and Promoting America's Popular Music 1900–1980.* Brooklyn, N.Y.: Institute for Studies in American Music, 1983.

Southern, Eileen. *The Music of Black Americans: A History,* 2nd ed. New York: Norton, 1983.

Tanner, Tony. *City of Words: American Fiction, 1950–1970.* New York: Harper & Row, 1971.

Trowbridge, C. Robertson. *Yankee Publishing, Inc.: Fifty Years of Preserving New England's Culture While Extending Its Influence.* New York: Newcomen Society, 1986.

Ward, Brian. *Just My Soul Responding: Rhythm and Blues, Black Consciousness, and Race Relations.* Berkeley: University of California Press, 1998.

Whitburn, Joel. *The Billboard Book of Top 40 Hits,* 5th ed. New York: Billboard Books, 1992.

Business and the Economy

Bernard, John. *Walter Reuther and the Rise of the Auto Workers.* Boston: Little, Brown, 1983.

Biskind, Peter. *Seeing Is Believing: How Hollywood Taught Us to Stop Worrying and Love the Fifties.* N.Y.: Henry Holt, 2000.

Bowles, Samuel, David M. Gordon, and Thomas E. Weisskopf. *Beyond the Waste Land: A Democratic Alternative to Economic Decline.* N.Y.: Anchor Books, 1984.

Brooks, John. *The Autobiography of American Business.* Garden City, N.Y.: Doubleday, 1974.

Bryant, Keith L., Jr., and Henry C. Dethloff. *A History of American Business.* Englewood Cliffs, N.J.: Prentice-Hall, 1983.

———, eds. *Encyclopedia of American Business History and Biography Railroads in the Age of Regulation, 1900–1980.* New York: Facts On File, 1988.

Davis, Mike. *Prisoners of the American Dream: Politics and Economy in the History of the U.S. Working Class.* London: Verso, 1986.

Denison, Edward F. *The Sources of Economic Growth in the United States and the Alternatives Before Us.* New York: Committee for Economic Development, 1962.

Dobson, John M. *A History of American Enterprise.* Englewood Cliffs, N.J.: Prentice-Hall, 1988.

Galbraith, John K. *Economic Development.* Cambridge, Mass.: Harvard University Press, 1964.

Gilder, George. *The Spirit of Enterprise.* New York: Simon & Schuster, 1984.

Gilland, Charles E., Jr., ed. *Readings in Business Responsibility.* Braintree, Mass.: D. H. Mark Publishing, 1969.

Green, James R. *The World of the Worker: Labor in Twentieth-Century America.* New York: Hill & Wang, 1980.

Griffith, Barbara. *The Crisis of American Labor: Operation Dixie and the Defeat of the CIO.* Philadelphia: Temple University Press, 1988.

Leary, William M., ed. *Encyclopedia of American Business History and Biography: The Airline Industry.* Bruccoli Clark Layman / New York: Facts On File, 1992.

Levenstein, Harvey. *Communism, Anti-Communism, and the CIO.* Westport, Conn.: Greenwood Press, 1981.

Markusen, Ann R. *The Rise of the Gunbelt: The Military Remapping of Industrial America.* New York: Oxford University Press, 1991.

May, George S., ed. *Encyclopedia of American Business History and Biography: Banking and Finance, 1913–1989.* Bruccoli Clark Layman / New York: Facts On File, 1990.

Patterson, James T. *America's Struggle Against Poverty, 1900–1980.* Cambridge, Mass.: Harvard University Press, 1986.

Porter, Glenn, ed. *Encyclopedia of American Economic History: Studies of the Principal Movements and Idea.* 3 vols. New York: Scribners, 1980.

Pusateri, Joseph C. *A History of American Business.* Arlington Heights, Ill.: Harlan Davidson, 1984.

Rae, John B. *The American Automobile: A Brief History.* Chicago: University of Chicago Press, 1965.

Ratner, Sidney, James H. Soltow, and Richard Sylla. *The Evolution of the American Economy.* New York: Basic Books, 1979.

Robinson, Archie. *George Meany and His Times: A Biography.* New York: Simon & Schuster, 1981.

Robinson, Graham. *Pictorial History of the Automobile.* New York: W. H. Smith, 1987.

Schweikart, Larry, ed. *Encyclopedia of American Business History and Biography: Banking and Finance, 1913–1989.* Bruccoli Clark Layman / New York: Facts On File, 1990.

Seely, Bruce, ed. *Encyclopedia of American Business History and Biography: Iron and Steel in the Twentieth Century.* Bruccoli Clark Layman / New York: Facts On File, 1993.

Simon, Herbert Alexander. *The New Science of Management Decision.* New York: Harper & Row, 1960.

Theoharis, Athan G. *The Boss.* Philadelphia: Temple University Press, 1988.

Zieger, Robert. *American Workers, American Unions, 1920–1985.* Baltimore: Johns Hopkins University Press, 1986.

Websites

"AFL-CIO." Available online at http://www.aflcio.org.

"Cover of 1955 Disneyland Guide Book." Available online at http://www.perrific.com/disney/guides/55/cover.html.

"Edsel.com." Available online at http://www.edsel.com.

"Ford Thunderbird History—1955–57." Available online at http://www.fordheritage.com/tbird/history/index55.html.

"General Dynamics." Available online at http://www.generaldynamics.com.

"The Reality of Nuclear Power." Available online at http://www.ucsusa.org/clean_energy/nuclear_safety/page.cfm?pageID=187.

Sims, Christopher A. "Stability and Instability in U.S. Monetary Policy Behavior." Available online at http://eco-072399b.princeton.edu/yftp/Stockholm/Reactions.pdf.

"Small Business Administration (SBA)." Available online at http://www.sba.gov.

"The Transistor—Function." Available online at http://www.nobel.se/physics/educational/transistor/function/index.html.

Weingroff, Richard F. "Federal-Aid Highway Act of 1956: Creating the Interstate System." Available online at http://www.fhwa.dot.gov/infrastructure/rw96f.htm.

Education

Aries, Philippe. *Centuries of Childhood.* New York: Knopf, 1962.

Berube, Maurice R. *American School Reform: Progressive, Equality, and Excellence Movements, 1883–1993.* Westport, Conn: Praeger, 1994.

Chisholm, Leslie Lee. *The Work of the Modern High School.* New York: Macmillan, 1953.

Clowse, Barbara B. *Brainpower for the Cold War: The Sputnik Crisis and National Defense Education Act of 1958.* Westport, Conn.: Greenwood Press, 1981.

Columbia University Teachers College. *Are Liberal Arts Colleges Becoming Professional Schools?* New York: Columbia University Teachers College, 1958.

Conant, James, B. *Citadel of Learning.* New Haven, Conn.: Yale University Press, 1956.

———. *The Revolutionary Transformation of the American High School.* Cambridge, Mass.: Harvard University Press, 1959.

De Vane, William Clyde. *The American University in the Twentieth Century.* Baton Rouge: Louisiana State University Press, 1957.

Ehrlander, Mary F. *Equal Educational Opportunity: Brown's Elusive Mandate.* New York.: LFB Scholarly Publishers, 2002.

Hutchins, Robert M. *Conflict in Education in a Democratic Society.* New York: Harper, 1953.

———. *Some Observations on American Education.* Cambridge, Mass.: Cambridge University Press, 1956.

Jacoway, Elizabeth, and C. Fred Williams. *Understanding the Little Rock Crisis: An Exercise in Remembrance and Reconciliation.* Fayetteville: University of Arkansas Press, 1999.

Karier, Clarence J. *Shaping the American Education State, 1900 to the Present.* New York: Free Press, 1975.

Kirk, Russell. *Academic Freedom.* Chicago: Regnery, 1955.

Kluger, Richard. *Simple Justice: The History of Brown v. Board of Education and Black America's Struggle for Equality.* New York: Notable Trials Library, 1994.

Knapp, Mary, and Herbert Knapp. *One Potato, Two Potato . . . The Secret Education of American Children.* New York: Norton, 1976.

Latimer, John Francis. *What's Happened to Our High Schools.* Washington, D.C.: Public Affairs Press, 1958.

Lee, Gordon C. *An Introduction to Education in America.* New York: Holt, 1957.

Machlup, Fritz. *The Production and Distribution of Knowledge in the United States.* Princeton, N.J.: Princeton University Press, 1962.

Opie, Iona Archibald. *The Lore and Language of Schoolchildren.* Oxford: Clarendon Press, 1959.

Perdew, Philip W. *The American Secondary School in Action.* Boston: Allyn & Bacon, 1959.

Piaget, Jean. *Play, Dreams and Imitation in Childhood.* New York: Norton, 1962.

Pride, Richard A. *The Political Use of Racial Narratives: School Desegregation in Mobile, Alabama, 1954–1997.* Urbana: University of Illinois Press, 2002.

Rickover, Hyman G. *Education and Freedom.* New York: Dutton, 1959.

Schramm, Wilbur, ed. *The Eighth Art.* New York: Holt, Rinehart & Winston, 1962.

Schramm, Wilbur, J. Lyle, and I. de Sola Pool. *The People Look at Educational Television.* Stanford, Calif.: Stanford University Press, 1963.

Seller, Maxine Schwartz, ed. *Women Educators in the United States, 1820–1993: A Bio-Bibliographical Sourcebook.* Westport, Conn.: Greenwood Press, 1994.

Turow, Joseph. *Entertainment, Education, and the Hard Sell: Three Decades of Network Children's Television.* New York: Praeger, 1981.

Websites

"1950–1959: Watauga Underwent Educational Revolution in 1950s." Available online at http://www.mountaintimes.com/history/1950s/education.htm.

"1959: John Goddlad Proposes 'Non-Graded' Schools." Available online at http://fcis.oise.utoronto.ca/daniel_schugurensky/assignment/1959goodlad.html.

"Blackboard Jungle." Available online at http://www.destgulch.com/movies/bjungle.

Bybee, Rodger W. "The Sputnik Era: Why Is This Educational Reform Different From All Other Reforms?" Available online at http://www.aps.org/units/fed/apr98/sput.html.

"Department of Health, Education and Welfare." Available online at http://www.umass.edu/research/infcons+441.doc.

"High Court Bans School Segregation; 9-to-0 Decision Grants Time to Comply." Available online at http://www.nytimes.com/learning/general/specials/littlerock/051854ds-upset.html.

"History: The 1950's." Available online at http://www.pueblocc.edu/history/1950.htm.

"The New York Times on AOL: Little Rock 40 Years Later." Available online at http://www.nytimes.com/learning/general/specials/littlerock/little-rock-home.html.

"Summary of Major Provisions of the National Defense Education Act of 1958." Available online at http://ishi.lib.berkeley.edu/cshe/ndea/ndea.html.

"Supreme Court Forbids Evasion or Force to Black Integration; Lower Court Bans Faubus Plan." Available online at http://www.nytimes.com/learning/general/specials/littlerock/093058ds-court.html.

Fashion and Design

Baker, Pat. *Fashions of a Decade: The 1950s.* New York and Oxford: Facts On File, 1991.

Ballard, Bettina. *In My Fashion.* New York: McKay, 1960.

Batterberry, Michael. *Mirror, Mirror: A Social History of Fashion.* New York: Holt, Rinehart & Winston, 1977.

Brown, Curtis F. *Star-Spangled Kitsch.* New York: Universe Books, 1975.

Byrnes, Garrett Davis. *Fashion in Newspapers.* New York: Columbia University Press, 1951.

Dorner, Jane. *Fashion in the Forties and Fifties.* London: Ian Allen, 1975.

The Encyclopedia of Fashion. New York: Abrams, 1986.

Epstein, Beryl William. *Young Faces in Fashion.* Philadelphia: Lippincott, 1956.

Garland, Madge. *The Changing Form of Fashion.* New York: Praeger, 1970.

Horn, Richard. *Fifties Style: Then and Now.* New York: Beech Tree Books, 1985.

Howell, Georgina. *In Vogue: Six Decades of Fashion.* London: Allen Lane, 1975.

Jackson, Lesley. *The New Look: Design in the Fifties.* London: Thames & Hudson, 1991.

Kultermann, Udo. *Architecture in the 20th Century.* New York: Reinhold, 1993.

Mulvagh, Jane. *"Vogue" History of 20th Century Fashion.* New York: Viking, 1988.

Nash, Eric Peter. *Frank Llyod Wright: Force of Nature.* New York: Smithmark Pulishers, 1996.

Peacock, John. *20th Century Fashion: The Complete Sourcebook.* New York: Thames & Hudson, 1993.

Reid, Aileen. *I.M. Pei.* New York: Crescent Books, 1995.

Ryan, Mary Shaw. *Clothing: A Study in Human Behavior.* New York: Holt, Rinehart Winston, 1966.

Stegemeyer, Anne. *Who's Who in Fashion.* New York: Fairchild, 1988.

Trahey, Jane. *Harper's Bazaar: One Hundred Years of the American Female.* New York: Random House, 1967.

Truett, Randle Bond. *The First Ladies in Fashion.* New York: Hastings House, 1954.

Wilson, Elizabeth. *Adorned in Dreams: Fashion and Modernity.* Berkeley: University of California Press, 1987.

Wolfe, Tom. *From Bauhaus to Our House.* New York: Farrar, Straus & Giroux, 1981.

Yarwood, Doreen. *Fashion in the Western World, 1500–1990.* New York: Drama Book Publishing, 1992.

Government and Politics

Ambrose, Stephen E., and Douglas G. Brinkley. *Rise to Globalism: American Foreign Policy Since 1938.* New York: Penguin, 1997.

Barnard, John. *Walter Reuther and the Rise of the Auto Workers.* Boston: Little, Brown, 1983.

Bickel, Alexander M. *Politics and the Warren Court.* New York: Harper & Row, 1965.

Boorstin, Daniel J. *The Genius of American Politics.* Chicago: University of Chicago Press, 1953.

Boyer, Paul. *By the Bomb's Early Light: American Thought and Culture at the Dawn of the Atomic Age.* New York: Pantheon, 1985.

Branch, Taylor. *Parting the Waters: America in the King Years, 1954–1963.* New York: Simon & Schuster, 1988.

Burk, Robert F. *The Eisenhower Administration and Black Civil Rights.* Knoxville: University of Tennessee Press, 1984.

Busch, Noel Fairchild. *Adlai E. Stevenson of Illinois: A Portrait.* New York: Farrar, Straus & Young, 1952.

Coon, Horace. *Triumph of the Eggheads.* New York: Random House, 1955.

Devine, Robert A. *The Sputnik Challenge: Eisenhower's Response to the Soviet Satellite.* New York: Oxford University Press, 1993.

Donovan, Robert J. *Eisenhower: The Inside Story.* New York: Harper, 1956.

Dulles, John Foster. *War or Peace.* New York: Macmillan, 1950.

Ekich, Arthur Alphonse. *The Decline of American Liberalism.* New York: Longmans, Green, 1955.

Foot, Rosemary. *The Wrong War: American Policy and the Dimensions of the Korean Conflict, 1950–1953.* Ithaca, N.Y.: Cornell University Press, 1985.

Frankel, Benjamin. *The Cold War, 1945–1991: Leaders and Other Important Figures in the United States and Western Europe.* Detroit: Gale Research, 1992.

Friedman, Milton, and Rose Friedman. *Capitalism and Freedom.* Chicago: University of Chicago Press, 1962.

Fuchs, Lawrence H. *The Political Behaviour of American Jews.* Glencoe, Ill.: Free Press, 1956.

Griffith, Robert. *The Politics of Fear: Joseph R. McCarthy and the Senate.* Lexington: University Press of Kentucky, 1970.

Gunther, John. *Eisenhower, the Man and the Symbol.* New York: Harper, 1952.

Halberstam, David. *The Fifties.* New York: Villard, 1993.

Harrington, Michael. *The Other America: Poverty in the United States.* New York: MacMillan, 1962.

Harris, Louis. *Is There a Republican Majority? Political Trends, 1952–1956.* New York: Harper, 1954.

Harrison, Gordon A. *The Road to the Right: The Tradition and Hope of American Conservatism.* New York: Morrow, 1954.

Hartz, Louis. *The Liberal Tradition in America.* New York: Harcourt, Brace & World, 1955.

Jackson, Kenneth T. *The Crabgrass Frontier: The Suburbanization of the United States.* New York: Oxford University Press, 1995.

Johnson, Walter. *How We Drafted Stevenson.* New York: Knopf, 1955.

Kaufman, Burton I. *The Korean War: Challenges in Crisis, Credibility and Command.* Philadelphia: University Temple Press, 1986.

Keogh, James. *This Is Nixon.* New York: Putnam, 1956.

Kirk, Russell. *The Conservative Mind.* Chicago: Regnery, 1953.

Low, David. *The Fearful Fifties: A History of the Decade.* New York: Simon & Schuster, 1960.

Martin, John Bartlow. *Adlai Stevenson.* New York: Harper, 1952.

Melanson, Richard A., and David Allan Mayers. *Reevaluating Eisenhower: American Foreign Policy in the 1950s.* Urbana: University of Illinois Press, 1987.

Merson, Martin. *Private Diary of a Public Servant.* New York: Macmillan, 1955.

Nader, Ralph. *Unsafe at Any Speed: The Designed-in Dangers of the American Automobile.* New York: Knightsbridge 1991.

Nadich, Judah. *Eisenhower and the Jews.* New York: Twayne, 1953.

Neal, Steve. *The Eisenhowers: Reluctant Dynasty.* Garden City, N.Y.: Doubleday, 1978.

Olson, Keith W. *The G.I. Bill, the Veterans, and the Colleges.* Lexington: University Press of Kentucky, 1974.

Parmet, Herbert S. *Eisenhower and the American Crusades.* New York: MacMillan, 1972.

Pusey, Merlo John. *Eisenhower the President.* New York: Macmillan, 1956.

Reeves, Thomas C. *The Life and Times of Joe McCarthy.* New York: Stein and Day, 1982.

Schor, Juliet B. *The Overworked American: The Unexpected Decline of Leisure.* New York: Basics, 1991.

Schrecker, Ellen W. *Many Are the Crimes: McCarthyism in America.* Boston: Little, Brown, 1998.

Sharlitt, Joseph H. *Fatal Error: The Miscarriage of Justice That Sealed the Rosenbergs' Fate.* New York: Scribners, 1989.

Snyder, Marty. *My Friend Ike.* New York: F. Fell, 1956.

Stevenson, Adlai E. *The New America.* New York: Harper, 1957.

———. *What I Think.* New York: Harper, 1956.

Theoharis, Athan. *Spying on Americans: Political Surveillance From Hoover to the Huston Plan.* Philadelphia: University of Temple Press, 1978.

de Toledano, Ralph. *Nixon.* New York: Holt, 1956.

Weinstein, Allen. *Perjury: The Hiss-Chambers Case.* New York: Knopf, 1978.

Wilson, Francis Graham. *The Case for Conservatism.* Seattle: University of Washington Press, 1951.

Zieger, Robert. *The CIO, 1935–1955.* Chapel Hill: University of North Carolina Press, 1995.

Zornow, William Frank. *America at Mid-Century: The Truman Administration, the Eisenhower Administration.* Cleveland: H. Allen, 1959.

Law and Justice

Abraham, Henry J. *Justices, Presidents, and Senators: A History of the U.S. Supreme Court Appointments From Washington to Clinton.* Rowman & Littlefield, 1999.

Chafe, William Henry, ed. *Remembering Jim Crow: African Americans Tell About Life in the Segregated South.* New York: New Press, 2001.

Franklin, John Hope, and Alfred A. Moss, Jr. *From Slavery to Freedom: A History of African Americans.* New York: Knopf, 2000.

Hall, Kermit L., ed. *The Oxford Companion to the Supreme Court.* New York: Oxford University Press, 1992.

Harrison, Maureen, and Steve Gilbert, eds. *Landmark Decisions of the United States Supreme Court II.* Beverly Hills: Excellent Books, 1992.

Horwitz, Morton J. *The Warren Court and the Pursuit of Justice.* New York: Hill and Wang, 1999.

Kelly, Alfred H., Winfred A. Harbison, and Herman Belz. *The American Constitution: Its Origins and Development.* Vol. 2. 7th ed. New York: Norton, 1991.

Kluger, Richard. *Simple Justice: The History of Brown V. Board of Education and Black America's Struggle for Equality.* 7th ed. New York: Random House, 1976.

Martin, Waldo E. *Brown v. Board of Education: A Brief History With Documents (The Bedford Series in History and Culture).* 7th ed. New York: Bedford/St. Martin's Press, 1998.

Mikula, Mark F., and L. Mpho Mabunda, eds. *Great American Court Cases.* Farmington Hills, Mich.: Gale Group, 2000.

O'Reilly, Kenneth. *Hoover and the Un-Americans.* Philadelphia: Temple University Press, 1983.

Palmer, Kris E., ed. *Constitutional Amendments: 1789 to the Present.* Farmington Hills, Mich.: Gale Group, 2000.

Radosh, Ronald, and Joyce Milton. *The Rosenberg File: A Search for Truth.* New Haven, Conn.: Yale University Press, 1997.

West's Encyclopedia of American Law, 2nd ed. 12 vols. St. Paul, Minn.: West Publishing Co., 1998

Websites

"The Oyez Project of Northwestern University, a U.S. Supreme Court Multimedia Database." Available online at http://www .oyez.com (accessed April 20, 2003).

"The Presidents of the United States." Available online at http:// www.whitehouse.gov/history/presidents/; website home page: http://www.whitehouse.gov (accessed April 20, 2003).

"The Trial of Ethel and Julius Rosenberg." Available online at http://www.law.umkc.edu/faculty/projects/ftrials/rosenb /ROSENB.HTM; website home page: http://www.law.umkc .edu/faculty/projects/ftrials/ftrials.htm (accessed April 20, 2003).

"U.S. Supreme Court Opinions." Available online at http:// www.findlaw.com/casecode/supreme.html; website home page: http://www.findlaw.com (accessed March 16, 2003).

Lifestyles and Social Trends

Bailey, Beth L. *From Front Porch to Back Seat: Courtship in Twentieth-Century America.* Baltimore: Johns Hopkins University Press, 1988.

Branch, Taylor. *Parting the Waters: America in the King Years, 1954–1963.* New York: Simon and Schuster, 1988.

Breines, Winni. *Young, White, and Miserable: Growing Up Female in the Fifties.* Boston: Beacon, 1992.

Brookeman, Christopher. *American Culture and Society Since the 1930s.* London: Macmillan, 1984.

Carter, Paul A. *Another Part of the Fifties.* New York: Columbia University Press, 1983.

Cervantez, Ernesto E. *Once Upon the 1950s.* Bethel, Conn.: Rutledge Books, 1997.

Donaldson, Gary A. *Abundance and Anxiety: America, 1945–1960.* Westport, Conn.: Praeger, 1997.

Eisler, Benita. *Private Lives: Men and Women of the Fifties.* New York: Franklin Watts, 1986.

Fairclough, Adam. *Better Day Coming: Blacks and Equality, 1890–2000.* New York: Viking, 2001.

Gitter, Michael, and Sylvie Anapol. *Do You Remember?: The Book That Takes You Back.* San Francisco: Chronicle Books, 1996.

Gregory, Ross. *Cold War America, 1946 to 1990.* New York: Facts on File, 2003.

Gross, Michael. *My Generation: Fifty Years of Sex, Drugs, Rock, Revolution, Glamour, Greed, Valor, Faith, and Silicon Chips.* New York: Cliff Street Books, 2000.

Halberstam, David. *The Fifties.* New York: Villard Books, 1993.

Hampton, Henry, and Steven Fayer. *Voices of Freedom: An Oral History of the Civil Rights Movement From the 1950s Through the 1980s.* New York: Bantam Books, 1990.

Hart, Jeffrey. *When the Going Was Good: American Life in the Fifties.* New York: Crown 1982.

Harvey, Brett. *The Fifties: A Women's Oral History.* New York: HarperCollins, 1993.

Issel, William. *Social Change in the United States, 1945–1983.* New York: Macmillan, 1985.

Jezer, Marty. *The Dark Ages: Life in the United States, 1945–1960.* Boston: South End Press, 1982.

Jones, Landon Y. *Great Expectations: America and the Baby Boom Generation.* New York: Coward, McCann & Geoghegan, 1980.

Kaledin, Eugenia. *Daily Life in the United States, 1940–1959: Shifting Worlds.* Westport, Conn.: Greenwood Press, 2000.

Kallen, Stuart A., ed. *The 1950s.* San Diego: Greenhaven Press, 2000.

Kowinski, William. *The Malling of America: An Inside Look at the Great Consumer Paradise.* New York: Morrow, 1985.

Leuchtenburg, William E. *A Troubled Feast: American Society Since 1945.* Boston: Little, Brown, 1983.

Meltzer, Milton, ed. *The American Promise: Voices of a Changing Nation, 1945–Present.* New York: Bantam Books, 1990.

O'Neill, William L. *American High: The Years of Confidence, 1945–1960.* New York: Free Press, 1986.

Oshinsky, David M. *A Conspiracy So Immense: The World of Joe McCarthy.* New York: Free Press, 1983.

Rock & Roll Generation: Teen Life in the 50s. Alexandria, Va.: Time-Life Books, 1998.

Salamone, Frank A. *Popular Culture in the Fifties.* Lanham, Md.: University Press of America, 2001.

Salmond, John A. *"My Mind Set on Freedom": A History of the Civil Rights Movement, 1954–1968.* Chicago: Ivan R. Dee, 1997.

Schrecker, Ellen. *Many Are the Crimes: McCarthyism in America.* Boston: Little, Brown, 1998.

Skolnik, Peter L. *Fads: America's Crazes, Fevers, and Fancies From the 1890s to the 1970s.* New York: Crowell, 1978.

Sommer, Robin. *"I Had One of Those": Toys of Our Generation.* New York: Crescent Books, 1992.

Weiss, Jessica. *To Have and to Hold: Marriage, the Baby Boom, and Social Change.* Chicago: University of Chicago Press, 2000.

Websites

"The 1950s: Primary Sources From American Popular Culture." Available online at http://www.authentichistory.com/1950s .html (accessed April 22, 2003).

"American Cultural History, 1950–1959." Available online at http://kclibrary.nhmccd.edu/decade50.html (accessed April 22, 2003).

"The Civil Rights Era." Available online at http://memory.loc .gov/ammem/aaohtml/exhibit/aopart9.html (accessed April 22, 2003).

"The Fifties Web." Available online at http://www.fiftiesweb .com/fifties.htm (accessed April 22, 2003).

"Levittown: Documents of an Ideal American Suburb." Available online at http://tigger.uic.edu/pbhales/Levittown/index.html (accessed April 22, 2003).

"The Silent Generation." Available online at http://www.csulb.edu/wwwing/Silents/ (accessed April 22, 2003).

"United States Culture and Society in the 1950s." Available online at http://home.earthlink.net/neuhausj/1950s/ (accessed April 22, 2003).

The Media

Altschuler, Glenn C., and David I. Grossvogel. *Changing Channels: America in TV Guide*. Urbana: University of Illinois Press, 1992.

Andrews, Bart. *Lucy & Ricky & Fred & Ethel: The Story of "I Love Lucy"*. New York: Dutton, 1976.

Applebaum, Irwyn. *The World According to Beaver*. New York: Bantam, 1984.

Barnouw, Erik. *Tube of Plenty: The Evolution of American Television*. 2nd ed. New York: Oxford University Press, 1990.

Collins, Jim, ed. *High-Pop: Making Culture into Popular Entertainment*. Malden, Mass.: Blackwell Publishers, 2002.

Cook, Philip S., Douglas Gomery, and Lawrence W. Lichty, eds. *The Future of News: Television-Newspapers-Wire Services-Newsmagazines*. Baltimore: Johns Hopkins University Press, 1992.

Corey, Mary F. *The World Through a Monocle: The New Yorker at Midcentury*. Cambridge, Mass.: Harvard University Press, 1999.

Douglas, Susan J. *Listening In: Radio and the American Imagination: From Amos 'n' Andy and Edward R. Murrow to Wolfman Jack and Howard Stern*. New York: Times Books, 1999.

Erickson, Hal. *Syndicated Television: The First Forty Years, 1947–1987*. Jefferson, N.C.: McFarland, 1989.

Greenfield, Jeff. *Television: The First Fifty Years*. New York: Crescent Books, 1981.

Jones, Gerard. *Honey, I'm Home: Sitcoms, Selling the American Dream*. New York: Grove Weidenfeld, 1992.

Kisseloff, Jeff. *The Box: An Oral History of Television, 1920–1961*. New York: Viking, 1995.

Kozol, Wendy. *Life's America: Family and Nation in Postwar Photojournalism*. Philadelphia: Temple University Press, 1994.

MacDonald, J. Fred. *Don't Touch That Dial: Radio Programming in American Life From 1920 to 1960*. Chicago: Hall, 1979.

———. *One Nation Under Television: The Rise and Decline of Network TV*. New York: Pantheon Books, 1990.

———. *Television and the Red Menace*. New York: Praeger, 1985.

Marling, Karal Ann. *As Seen on TV: The Visual Culture of Everyday Life in the 1950s*. Cambridge, Mass.: Harvard University Press, 1994.

McNeil, Alexander. *Total Television: A Comprehensive Guide to Programming From 1948–1980*. New York: Penguin, 1980.

Stark, Steven D. *Glued to the Set: The 60 Television Shows and Events That Made Us Who We Are Today*. New York: Free Press, 1997.

Trow, George W.S. *My Pilgrim's Progress: Media Studies, 1950–1998*. New York: Pantheon, 1999.

Websites

"Cinema of the Fifties: Great Movies, Great Stars." Available online at http://trurl.npac.syr.edu/alex (accessed April 22, 2003).

"Classic TV." Available online at http://www.fiftiesweb.com/tv50.htm (accessed April 22, 2003).

"Edward R. Murrow." Available online at www.pbs.org/wnet/americanmasters/database/murrow_e.html (accessed April 22, 2003).

"Herblock's History: Political Cartoons From the Crash to the Millennium." Available online at http://www.loc.gov/rr/print/swann/herblock/ (accessed April 22, 2003).

Medicine and Health

Bender, Arnold E. *A Dictionary of Food and Nutrition*. New York: Oxford University Press, 1995.

Berkowitz, Leonard. *Aggression: A Psychological Analysis*. New York: McGraw-Hill, 1962.

Caldwell, Mark. *The Last Crusade: The War on Consumption, 1862–1954*. New York: Antheneum, 1988.

The Cambridge World History of Human Disease. New York: Cambridge University Press, 1993.

Carlson, Rick J. *The End of Medicine*. New York: Wiley, 1975.

Cartwright, Frederic Fox. *Disease and History*. New York: Crowell, 1972.

Cassedy, James H. *Medicine in America: A Short History*. Baltimore: Johns Hopkins University Press, 1991.

Clark, Faith, ed. *Symposium III: The Changing Patterns of Consumption of Food*. International Congress of Food Science and Technology, Proceedings of the Congress Symposia, 1962. 5 vols. New York: Gordon & Breach Science, 1967.

Companion Encyclopedia of the History of Medicine. London: Routledge, 1993.

Curson, Marjorie. *Jonas Salk*. Englewood Cliffs, N.J.: Silver Burdett, 1990.

Dixon, Bernard. *Beyond the Magic Bullet*. New York: Harper & Row, 1978.

Dolan, John Patrick. *Health and Society: A Documentary History of Medicine*. New York: Seabury, 1978.

Duke, Martin. *The Development of Medical Techniques and Treatments: From Leeches to Heart Surgery*. Madison, Conn.: International Universities Press, 1991.

Gould, Tony. *A Summer Plague: Polio—Polio and Its Survivors*. New Haven, Conn.: Yale University Press, 1995.

International Conference on Asian Influenza. Bethesda, Md.: National Institutes of Health, 1960.

Long, Esmond R. *A History of Pathology*. New York: Dover, 1965.

Lyons, Albert S. *Medicine: An Illustrated History.* New York: Abrams, 1978.

Mann, John, and M. James Crable. *Bacteria and Antibacterial Agents.* Oxford, England: Spektrum Press, 1996.

Nolen, William A. *A Surgeon's World.* New York: Random House, 1972.

Nuland, Sherwin B. *Doctors: The Biography of Medicine.* New York: Knopf, 1988.

Paul, John R. *A History of Poliomyelitis.* New Haven, Conn.: Yale University Press, 1971.

Professional Guide to Diseases. 6th ed. Springhouse, Pa.: Springhouse, 1998.

Reiser, Stanley Joel. *Medicine and the Reign of Technology.* New York: Cambridge University Press, 1978.

Stevens, Rosemary. *American Medicine and the Public Interest.* New Haven, Conn.: Yale University Press, 1971.

Valenstein, Elliot S. *Great and Desperate Cures.* New York: Basic, 1986.

Websites

"American Experience: A Brilliant Madness." Available online at http://www.pbs.org/wgbh/amex/nash/sfeatures/sf_nash.html (accessed April 22, 2003).

"CDC NVPO: Pandemic Influenza." Available online at http://www.cdc.gov/od/nvpo/pandemics/flu3.htm (accessed April 22, 2003).

"Department of Health, Education and Welfare." Available online at http://www.umass.edu/research/infcons+441.doc (accessed April 22, 2003).

"Heart Attack Hit during Eisenhower's Denver Trip." Available online at http://www.denver-rmn.com/millennium/0810ike.shtml (accessed April 22, 2003).

"Heart Lung Machine." Available online at http://www.museumofhealthcare.ca/heartlung.htm (accessed April 22, 2003).

"Medicine and Madison Avenue—Timeline." Available online at http://scriptorium.lib.duke.edu/mma/timeline.html (accessed April 22, 2003).

"The Microbial World: Penicillin and Other Antibiotics." Available online at http://www.helios.bto.ed.ac.uk/bto/microbes/penicillin.htm (accessed April 22, 2003).

"Polio History Timeline." Available online at http://www.pbs.org/storyofpolio/polio/timeline/1921.html (accessed April 22, 2003).

"Recommended Daily Allowances for Specific Nutrients." Available online at http://www.nal.usda.gov/fnic/history/8546v.gif (accessed April 22, 2003).

"A Science Odyssey: People and Discoveries: Salk Polio Vaccine." Available online at http://www.pbs.org/wgbh/aso/databank/entries/dm52sa.html (accessed April 22, 2003).

Theiler, Max. "The Development of Vaccines Against Yellow Fever." Available online at http://www.nobel.se/medicine/laureates/1951/theiler-lecture.html (accessed April 22, 2003).

"United States Cancer Mortality From 1900 to 1992." Available online at http://www.healthsentinel.com/Vaccines/DiseaseAndRelatedData_files/she (accessed April 22, 2003).

Waksman, Selman A. "Streptomycin: Background, Isolation, Properties, and Utilization." Available online at http://www.nobel.se/medicine/laureates/1952/waksman-lecture.html (accessed April 22, 2003).

Religion

Ammerman, Nancy T. *Bible Believers: Fundamentalists in the Modern World.* New Brunswick, N.J.: Rutgers University Press, 1987.

Beckwith, Bernham P. *The Decline of U.S. Religious Faith, 1912–1984.* Palo Alto, Calif.: B. P. Beckwith, 1985.

Bellah, Robert N., and Frederick E. Greenspahn, eds. *Uncivil Religion: Irreligious Hostility in America.* New York: Crossroads, 1987.

Brown, Charles C. *Niebuhr and His Age: Reinhold Niebuhr's Prophetic Role in the Twentieth Century.* Philadelphia: Trinity Press International, 1992.

Carroll, Jackson W. *Beyond Establishment: Protestant Identity in a Post-Protestant Age.* Louisville, Ky.: Westminster/John Knox, 1993.

Cavert, Samuel McCrea. *The American Churches in the Ecumenical Movement, 1900–1968.* New York: Association Press, 1968.

Cooney, John. *The American Pope: The Life and Times of Francis Cardinal Spellman.* New York: Times Books, 1984.

Cox, Harvey. *Turning East: The Promise and Peril of the New Orientalism.* New York: Simon & Schuster, 1977.

Eighmy, John L. *Churches in Cultural Captivity: A History of the Social Attitudes of Southern Baptists.* Knoxville: University of Tennessee Press, 1987.

George, Carol V. *God's Salesman: Norman Vincent Peale and the Power of Positive Thinking.* New York: Oxford University, 1992.

Gilkey, Langdon B. *Catholicism Confronts Modernism: A Protestant View.* New York: Seabury, 1975.

———. *Gilkey on Tillich.* New York: Crossroad, 1990.

Jones, Donald G., and Russell E. Richey, eds. *American Civil Religion.* San Francisco: Mellen Research University Press, 1990.

Mahan, Wayne W. *Tillich's System.* San Antonio, Tex.: Trinity University Press, 1974.

Martin, Bernard. *The Existentialist Theology of Paul Tillich.* New York: Bookman Associates, 1963.

Martin, William C. *A Prophet With Honor: The Billy Graham Story.* New York: Morrow, 1991.

Marty, Martin. *Pilgrims in Their Own Land: 500 Years of Religion in America.* Boston: Houghton Mifflin, 1984.

Miller, Robert Moats. *Bishop G. Bromley Oxnam: Paladin of Liberal Protestantism.* Nashville, Tenn.: Abingdon Press, 1990.

Pauck, Wilhelm, and Marion Pauck. *Paul Tillich: His Life and Thought.* New York: Harper & Row, 1976.

Stone, Ronald H. *Reinhold Niebuhr: Prophet to Politicians.* Nashville, Tenn.: Abingdon Press, 1972.

Walker, Brooks R. *Christian Fright Peddlers*. Garden City, N.Y.: Doubleday, 1964.

Wilson, Edmund. *The Dead Sea Scrolls, 1947–1969*. New York: Oxford University Press, 1969.

Science and Technology

Abshire, Gary M., ed. *The Impact of Computers on Society and Ethics: A Bibliography*. Morristown, N.J.: Creative Computing, 1980.

Alperovitz, Gar. *Atomic Diplomacy*. New York: Penguin Books, 1985.

Ball, Howard. *Justice Downwind: America's Atomic Testing Program in the 1950s*. New York: Oxford University Press, 1986.

Belzer, Jack, Albert G. Holzman, and Allen Kent, eds. *Encyclopedia of Computer Science and Technology*. 16 vols. New York: Marcel Dekker, 1975–1981.

Bernstein, Jeremy, and Gerald Feinberg, eds. *Cosmological Constants: Papers in Modern Cosmology*. New York: Columbia University Press, 1986.

Blinderman, Charles. *The Piltdown Inquest*. New York: Prometheus Books, 1986.

Carnegie Library of Pittsburgh, Science and Technology Department. *Science & Technology Desk Reference*. Detroit: Gale Research, 1993.

Goldstein, Herman H. *The Computer From Pascal to von Neumann*. Princeton, N.J.: Princeton University Press, 1972.

Haugelan, J. *Artificial Intelligence: The Very Idea*. Cambridge, Mass.: MIT Press, 1985.

Katz, Leslie, ed. *Fairy Tales for Computers*. Boston: Nonpareil Books, 1969.

Lewis, Anthony O., ed. *Of Men and Machines*. London: Dutton, 1963.

Maeder, Andre, ed. *Observational Tests of the Stellar Evolution Theory*. Boston: Reidel, 1984.

McGraw-Hill Encyclopedia of Science and Technology. 9th ed. 14 vols. New York: McGraw-Hill, 1993.

Mescowitz, Sam, ed. *The Coming of Robots*. New York: Collier, 1963.

Metropolis, N., ed. *A History of Computing in the Twentieth Century*. New York: Academic Press, 1980.

Mumford, Lewis. *The Myth of the Machine: The Pentagon of Power*. New York: Harcourt Brace Jovanovich, 1964.

Schichtle, Cass. *The National Space Program From the Fifties to the Eighties*. Washington, D.C.: GPO, 1983.

Silverberg, Robert, ed. *Men and Machines*. New York: Meredith Press, 1968.

Simon, Herbert Alexander. *Sciences of the Artificial*. Cambridge, Mass.: MIT Press, 1969.

Snow, C.P. *The Two Cultures and the Scientific Revolution*. New York: Cambridge University Press, 1961.

Triggy, George L. *Landmark Experiments in Twentieth Century Physics*. New York: Crane, Russak, 1975.

Watson, James D. *The Double Helix*. New York: New American Library, 1969.

Websites

Crick, Francis Harry Compton. "On the Genetic Code." Available online at http://www.nobel.se/medicine/laureates/1962/crick-lecture.html (accessed April 22, 2003).

"John Louis von Neumann." Available online at http://ei.cs.vt.edu/history/VonNeumann.html (accessed April 22, 2003).

"The Kinsey Institute." Available online at http://www.indiana.edu/kinsey (accessed April 22, 2003).

McClintock, Barbara. "The Significance of Responses of the Genome to Challenge." Available online at http://www.nobel.se/medicine/laureates/1983/mcclintock-lecture.html (accessed April 22, 2003).

Miller, Stanley Lloyd. Available online at http://www.xrefer.com/entry/494888 (accessed April 22, 2003).

"Race for the Superbomb." Available online at http://www.pbs.org/wgbh/amex/bomb/peopleevents/pandeAMEX55.html (accessed April 22, 2003).

"The Reality of Nuclear Power." Available online at http://www.ucsusa.org/clean_energy/nuclear_safety/page.cfm?pageID=187 (accessed April 22, 2003).

Shockley, William B. "Transistor Technology Evokes New Physics." Available online at http://www.nobel.se/physics/laureates/1956/shockley-lecture.html (accessed April 22, 2003).

"Sputnik and the Dawn of the Space Age." Available online at http://www.hq.nasa.gov/office/pao/History/sputnik (accessed April 22, 2003).

"Wernher von Braun (1912–1977)." Available online at http://history.nasa.gov/sputnik/braun.html (accessed April 22, 2003).

Sports

Adelson, Bruce. *Brushing Back Jim Crow: The Integration of Minor-League Baseball in the American South*. Charlottesville: University Press of Virginia, 1999.

Banks, Ernie, and Jim Enright. *"Mr. Cub."* Chicago: Follett, 1971.

Bannister, Roger. *The Four-Minute Mile*. New York: Dodd, Mead, 1981.

Berra, Yogi, and Tom Horton. *Yogi: It Ain't Over*. New York: McGraw-Hill, 1989.

Connolly, Maureen, and Tom Gwynne. *Forehand Drive*. London: Macgibboon and Kee, 1957.

Cramer, Richard Ben. *Joe DiMaggio: The Hero's Life*. New York: Simon and Schuster, 2000.

DeLaet, Dianne Tittle. *Giants & Heroes: A Daughter's Memoreis of Y.A. Tittle*. South Royalton, Vt.: Steerforth Press, 1995.

Eskenazi, Gerald. *Bill Veeck: A Baseball Legend*. New York: McGraw-Hill, 1988.

Gibson, Althea. *I Always Wanted to be Somebody*. New York: Harper, 1958.

Gifford, Frank, and Harry Waters. *The Whole Ten Yards.* New York: Random, 1993.

Goodwin, Doris Kearns. *Wait Till Next Year: A Memoir.* New York: Simon and Schuster, 1997.

Greene, Lee. *The Johnny Unitas Story.* New York: Putnam, 1962.

Gregston, Gene. *Hogan: The Man Who Played for Glory.* Englewood Cliffs, N.J.: Prentice-Hall, 1978.

Guttman, Allen. *The Games Must Go One: Avery Brundage and the Olympic Movement.* New York: Columbia University Press, 1984.

Kahn, Roger. *The Boys of Summer.* New York: Harper & Row, 1972.

———. *Joe and Marilyn: A Memory of Love.* New York: Morrow, 1986.

———. *The Era: 1947–1956, When the Yankees, the Giants, and the Dodgers Ruled the World.* New York: Ticknor & Fields, 1993.

Karras, Alex, and Herb Gluck. *Even Big Guys Cry.* New York: Holt, Rinehart, and Winston, 1977.

Kell, George, and Dan Ewald. *Hello Everybody, I'm George Kell.* Champaign, Ill.: Sports Publishing, 1998.

Larsen, Don, and Mark Shaw. *The Perfect Yankee: The Incredible Story of the Greatest Miracle in Baseball History.* Champaign, Ill.: Sagamore, 1996.

Lynch, Michael T. *American Sports Car Racing in the 1950s.* Osceola, Wis.: MBI Publishing, 1998.

MacSkimming, Roy. *Gordie: A Hockey Legend. An Unauthorized Biography of Gordie Howe.* Vancouver: Greystone Books, 1994.

Malamud, Bernard. *The Natural.* New York: Harcourt, Brace, 1952.

Maraniss, Dave. *When Pride Still Mattered: A Life of Vince Lombardi.* New York: Simon and Schuster, 1999.

Maury, Allen. *Roger Maris: A Man for All Seasons.* New York: Doubleday, 1964.

Mays, Willie, and Lou Sahadi. *Say Hey: The Autobiography of Willie Mays.* New York: Simon and Schuster, 1988.

Mikan, George, and Joseph Oberle. *Unstoppable: The Story of George Mikan, the First NBA Superstar.* Indianapolis: Masters Press, 1997.

Musial, Stan, and Bob Broeg. *Stan Musial: "The Man's" Own Story.* New York: Doubleday, 1964.

Ralbovsky, Martin. *Destiny's Darlings.* New York: Hawthorn Books, 1974.

Rampersad, Arnold. *Jackie Robinson: A Biography.* New York: Knopf, 1997.

Richard, Maurice. *The Flying Frenchmen: Hockey's Greatest Dynasty.* New York: Hawthorne, 1971.

Rosen, Charles. *Scandals of '51.* New York: Holt, Rinehart & Winston, 1978.

Ross, Charles Kenyatta. *Outside the Lines: African Americans and the Integration of the National Football League.* New York: New York University Press, 1999.

Skehan, Everett M. *Rocky Marciano: Biography of a First Son.* Boston: Houghton Mifflin, 1977.

St. John, Bob. *The Heart of a Lion: The Wild and Wooly Life of Bobby Layne.* Dallas: Taylor, 1991.

Thomson, Bobby, et al. *The Giants Win the Pennant! The Giants Win the Pennant!* New York: Kensington Publishers, 1991.

Tygiel, Jules. *Baseball's Great Experiment: Jackie Robinson and His Legacy.* New York: Oxford University Press, 1983.

Williams, Ted, and Jim Underwood. *My Turn at Bat: The Story of My Life.* New York: Simon and Schuster, 1969.

Wolff, Rick. *Ted Williams.* New York: Chelsea House, 1993.

Zeigler, Earle F., ed. *A History of Physical Education and Sport in the United States and Canada.* Champaign, Ill.: Stipes Publishing Company, 1975.

PRIMARY SOURCE TYPE INDEX

Primary source authors appear in parentheses. Page numbers in italics indicate images, and those followed by the letter t *indicate tables.*

Primary source authors appear in parentheses. Page numbers in italics indicate images, and those followed by the letter *t* indicate tables.

Primary source authors appear in parentheses. Page numbers in italics indicate images, and those followed by the letter *t* indicate tables.

Primary source authors appear in parentheses. Page numbers in italics indicate images, and those followed by the letter *t* indicate tables.

GENERAL INDEX

Page numbers in bold indicate primary sources; page numbers in italic indicate images; page numbers in bold italic indicate primary source images; page numbers followed by the letter t *indicate tables. Primary sources are indexed under the entry name with the author's name in parentheses. Primary sources are also indexed by title. All primary sources can be identified by bold page locators.*

A

A line (Dior), 175

Aaron, Cooper v. (1958), 313, 327–331

Abbitt, Watkins M., 316

Abel, Sid, 591

Abernathy, Thomas G., 316

Abstract Expressionism, 12, 22

Academic freedom, William F. Buckley, Jr. on, 110–113

Acheson, Dean, 200, 202, 207

ACLU, Reno v. (1997), 325

ACLU (American Civil Liberties Union), 511

Actor's Studio, 148

Ad Petri Cathedram, 537–541

papal encyclical (John XXIII), **538–541**

Adams Act (1906), 554

Address to the American People on the Situation in Korea (Truman), **216–218**

Address to the American People on the Situation in Little Rock (Eisenhower), **255–257**

Adler, Irving, 102

Adler v. Board of Education (1952), 102, 284–288

Supreme Court decision (Clark), **285–288**

Advertising

automobiles, 188–190

decline in magazines, 417, 419

growth in 1920s, 415

motivation research use in, 84

public's suspicion of, 83

to women, 170, 174, 179

Advisory Committee of the National Citizens Committee for Educational Television, 116

Advocacy of abstract doctrine, 318

Aerosporin, 466

AFL-CIO, 78, 79–81

African American and Women Voters in the 1950s, 248–253

"The Negro Voter: Can He Elect a President?" (White), **249–252**

"Where Men Go Wrong About Women Voters" (Davenport), **252–253**

African Americans

higher education enrollment, 360

poverty in Baltimore, *386*

students at Central High School (Little Rock, AR), *256*

unemployment during 1957–1958 recession, 87

upward mobility of, 358–361

voting, *249,* 249–252, 362–363, 450

wages of, 76

See also Civil Rights movement; Segregation

Agreements between the United States and Japan, 225–230

"Security Treaty Between the United States and Japan, September 8, 1951" (U.S., Japan), **226–227**

"U.S. and Japan Mutual Defense Assistance Agreement" (U.S., Japan), **227–230**

Aiken, George D., 202

Ainsworth, G. C., 466

Airline industry growth, 87–90

Airline safety, 89

Akari light sculptures (Noguchi), 8, *9,* 10

Alan Freed Popularizes Rock 'n' Roll, 411–415

"Alan Freed" (Freed), **412–413**

"What Alan Freed Really Thinks About Rock 'n' Roll" (Freed), **413–414**

Alberoni, Sherry, 192

Alexander, Hugh Q., 316

Alien and Sedition Act (1798), 313

"All-Star Tilt Fails to Impress Scouts from Big Leagues" (Smith), **603–604**

All-Weather Drive-In (NY), 379–380

Allen, Board of Education v. (1968), 293

Allison, John, 213

telegram, **215**

Alpert, Hollis, 415

magazine article, **415, 417–419**

Page numbers in bold indicate primary sources; page numbers in italic indicate images; page numbers in bold italic indicate primary source images; page numbers followed by the letter *t* indicate tables.

Page numbers in bold indicate primary sources; page numbers in italic indicate images; page numbers in bold italic indicate primary source images; page numbers followed by the letter *t* indicate tables.

Page numbers in bold indicate primary sources; page numbers in italic indicate images; page numbers in bold italic indicate primary source images; page numbers followed by the letter *t* indicate tables.

Page numbers in bold indicate primary sources; page numbers in italic indicate images; page numbers in bold italic indicate primary source images; page numbers followed by the letter *t* indicate tables.

Page numbers in bold indicate primary sources; page numbers in italic indicate images; page numbers in bold italic indicate primary source images; page numbers followed by the letter *t* indicate tables.

Page numbers in bold indicate primary sources; page numbers in italic indicate images; page numbers in bold italic indicate primary source images; page numbers followed by the letter *t* indicate tables.

Page numbers in bold indicate primary sources; page numbers in italic indicate images; page numbers in bold italic indicate primary source images; page numbers followed by the letter *t* indicate tables.

Page numbers in bold indicate primary sources; page numbers in italic indicate images;
page numbers in bold italic indicate primary source images; page numbers followed by the letter *t* indicate tables.

Page numbers in bold indicate primary sources; page numbers in italic indicate images; page numbers in bold italic indicate primary source images; page numbers followed by the letter *t* indicate tables.

Page numbers in bold indicate primary sources; page numbers in italic indicate images;
page numbers in bold italic indicate primary source images; page numbers followed by the letter *t* indicate tables.

Page numbers in bold indicate primary sources; page numbers in italic indicate images; page numbers in bold italic indicate primary source images; page numbers followed by the letter *t* indicate tables.

Page numbers in bold indicate primary sources; page numbers in italic indicate images;
page numbers in bold italic indicate primary source images; page numbers followed by the letter *t* indicate tables.

Page numbers in bold indicate primary sources; page numbers in italic indicate images;
page numbers in bold italic indicate primary source images; page numbers followed by the letter *t* indicate tables.

Page numbers in bold indicate primary sources; page numbers in italic indicate images;
page numbers in bold italic indicate primary source images; page numbers followed by the letter *t* indicate tables.

Page numbers in bold indicate primary sources; page numbers in italic indicate images;
page numbers in bold italic indicate primary source images; page numbers followed by the letter *t* indicate tables.

Page numbers in bold indicate primary sources; page numbers in italic indicate images;
page numbers in bold italic indicate primary source images; page numbers followed by the letter *t* indicate tables.

Page numbers in bold indicate primary sources; page numbers in italic indicate images;
page numbers in bold italic indicate primary source images; page numbers followed by the letter *t* indicate tables.

Page numbers in bold indicate primary sources; page numbers in italic indicate images; page numbers in bold italic indicate primary source images; page numbers followed by the letter *t* indicate tables.